Feasting on the Word®

Editorial Board

Feasting on the Word®

Preaching the
Revised Common Lectionary

Year A, Volume 2

DAVID L. BARTLETT and BARBARA BROWN TAYLOR

General Editors

WESTMINSTER
JOHN KNOX PRESS
LOUISVILLE · KENTUCKY

Book design by Drew Stevens
Cover design by Lisa Buckley

First edition
Published by Westminster John Knox Press
Louisville, Kentucky

This book is printed on acid-free paper that meets the American National Standards Institute Z39.48 standard. ♾

PRINTED IN THE UNITED STATES OF AMERICA

11 12 13 14 15 16 17 18 19 —10 9 8 7 6 5 4 3 2

Library of Congress Cataloging-in-Publication Data

Feasting on the Word : preaching the revised common lectionary / David L. Bartlett and Barbara Brown Taylor, general editors.
     p. cm.
  Includes index.
  ISBN 978-0-664-23105-7 (v. 10 alk. paper)
  ISBN 978-0-664-23104-0 (v. 9 alk. paper)
  ISBN 978-0-664-23103-3 (v. 8 alk. paper)
  ISBN 978-0-664-23102-6 (v. 7 alk. paper)
  ISBN 978-0-664-23101-9 (v. 6 alk. paper)
  ISBN 978-0-664-23100-2 (v. 5 alk. paper)
  ISBN 978-0-664-23099-9 (v. 4 alk. paper)
  ISBN 978-0-664-23098-2 (v. 3 alk. paper)
  ISBN 978-0-664-23097-5 (v. 2 alk. paper)
  ISBN 978-0-664-23096-8 (v. 1 alk. paper)
  1. Lectionary preaching.   2. Common lectionary (1992)   I. Bartlett, David Lyon, 1941–
II. Taylor, Barbara Brown.
  BV4235.L43F43 2008
  251'.6—dc22

2007047534

Contents

Publisher's Note

Feasting on the Word: Preaching the Revised Common Lectionary is an ambitious project that is offered to the Christian church as a resource for preaching and teaching.

The uniqueness of this approach in providing four perspectives on each preaching occasion from the Revised Common Lectionary sets this work apart from other lectionary materials. The theological, pastoral, exegetical, and homiletical dimensions of each biblical passage are explored with the hope that preachers will find much to inform and stimulate their preparations for preaching from this rich "feast" of materials.

This work could not have been undertaken without the deep commitments of those who have devoted countless hours to working on these tasks. Westminster John Knox Press would like to acknowledge the magnificent work of our general editors, David L. Bartlett and Barbara Brown Taylor. They are both gifted preachers with passionate concerns for the quality of preaching. They are also wonderful colleagues who embraced this huge task with vigor, excellence, and unfailing good humor. Our debt of gratitude to Barbara and David is great.

The fine support staff, project manager Joan Murchison and compiler Mary Lynn Darden, enabled all the thousands of "pieces" of the project to come together and form this impressive series. Without their strong competence and abiding persistence, these volumes could not have emerged.

The volume editors for this series are to be thanked as well. They used their superb skills as pastors and professors and ministers to work with writers and help craft their valuable insights into the highly useful entries that comprise this work.

The hundreds of writers who shared their expertise and insights to make this series possible are ones who deserve deep thanks indeed. They come from wide varieties of ministries. They have given their labors to provide a gift to benefit the whole church and to enrich preaching in our time.

Westminster John Knox would also like to express our appreciation to Columbia Theological Seminary for strong cooperation in enabling this work to begin and proceed. Dean of Faculty and Executive Vice President D. Cameron Murchison welcomed the project from the start and drew together everything we needed. His continuing efforts have been very valuable. Former President Laura S. Mendenhall provided splendid help as well. She made seminary resources and personnel available and encouraged us in this partnership with enthusiasm and all good grace. We thank her, and look forward to working with Columbia's new president, Stephen Hayner.

It is a joy for Westminster John Knox Press to present *Feasting on the Word: Preaching the Revised Common Lectionary* to the church, its preachers, and its teachers. We believe rich resources can assist the church's ministries as the Word is proclaimed. We believe the varieties of insights found in these pages will nourish preachers who will "feast on the Word" and who will share its blessings with those who hear.

Westminster John Knox Press

Series Introduction

A preacher's work is never done. Teaching, offering pastoral care, leading worship, and administering congregational life are only a few of the responsibilities that can turn preaching into just one more task of pastoral ministry. Yet the Sunday sermon is how the preacher ministers to most of the people most of the time. The majority of those who listen are not in crisis. They live such busy lives that few take part in the church's educational programs. They wish they had more time to reflect on their faith, but they do not. Whether the sermon is five minutes long or forty-five, it is the congregation's one opportunity to hear directly from their pastor about what life in Christ means and why it matters.

Feasting on the Word offers pastors focused resources for sermon preparation, written by companions on the way. With four different essays on each of the four biblical texts assigned by the Revised Common Lectionary, this series offers preachers sixteen different ways into the proclamation of God's Word on any given occasion. For each reading, preachers will find brief essays on the exegetical, theological, homiletical, and pastoral challenges of the text. The page layout is unusual. By setting the biblical passage at the top of the page and placing the essays beneath it, we mean to suggest the interdependence of the four approaches without granting priority to any one of them. Some readers may decide to focus on the Gospel passage, for instance, by reading all four essays provided for that text. Others may decide to look for connections between the Hebrew Bible, Psalm, Gospel, and Epistle texts by reading the theological essays on each one.

Wherever they begin, preachers will find what they need in a single volume produced by writers from a wide variety of disciplines and religious traditions. These authors teach in colleges and seminaries. They lead congregations. They write scholarly books as well as columns for the local newspaper. They oversee denominations. In all of these capacities and more, they serve God's Word, joining the preacher in the ongoing challenge of bringing that Word to life.

We offer this print resource for the mainline church in full recognition that we do so in the digital age of the emerging church. Like our page layout, this decision honors the authority of the biblical text, which thrives on the page as well as in the ear. While the twelve volumes of this series follow the pattern of the Revised Common Lectionary, each volume contains an index of biblical passages so that all preachers may make full use of its contents.

We also recognize that this new series appears in a post-9/11, post-Katrina world. For this reason, we provide no shortcuts for those committed to the proclamation of God's Word. Among preachers, there are books known as "Monday books" because they need to be read thoughtfully at least a week ahead of time. There are also "Saturday books," so called because they supply sermon ideas on short notice. The books in this series are not Saturday books. Our aim is to help preachers go deeper, not faster, in a world that is in need of saving words.

A series of this scope calls forth the gifts of a great many people. We are grateful first of all to the staff of Westminster John Knox Press: Don McKim, Jon Berquist, and Jack Keller, who conceived this project; David Dobson, who worked diligently to bring the project to completion, with publisher Marc Lewis's strong support; and Julie Tonini, who has painstakingly guided each volume through the production process. We thank former President Laura Mendenhall and former Dean Cameron Murchison of Columbia Theological Seminary, who made our participation in this work possible. We thank President Steve Hayner and Dean Deborah Mullen for their continuing encouragement and support. Our editorial board is a hardworking board, without whose patient labor and good humor this series would not exist. From the start, Joan Murchison has been the brains of the operation, managing details of epic proportions with great human kindness. Mary Lynn Darden, Dilu Nicholas, Megan Hackler Denton, and John Shillingburg have supported both her and us with their administrative skills.

We have been honored to work with a multitude of gifted thinkers, writers, and editors. We present these essays as their offering—and ours—to the blessed ministry of preaching.

David L. Bartlett
Barbara Brown Taylor

A Note about the Lectionary

Feasting on the Word follows the Revised Common Lectionary (RCL) as developed by the Consultation on Common Texts, an ecumenical consultation of liturgical scholars and denominational representatives from the United States and Canada. The RCL provides a collection of readings from Scripture to be used during worship in a schedule that follows the seasons of the church year. In addition, it provides for a uniform set of readings to be used across denominations or other church bodies.

The RCL provides a reading from the Old Testament, a Psalm response to that reading, a Gospel, and an Epistle for each preaching occasion of the year. It is presented in a three-year cycle, with each year centered around one of the Synoptic Gospels. Year A is the year of Matthew, Year B is the year of Mark, and Year C is the year of Luke. John is read each year, especially during Advent, Lent, and Easter.

The RCL offers two tracks of Old Testament texts for the Season after Pentecost or Ordinary Time: a semicontinuous track, which moves through stories and characters in the Old Testament, and a complementary track, which ties the Old Testament texts to the theme of the Gospel texts for that day. Some denominational traditions favor one over the other. For instance, Presbyterians and Methodists generally follow the semicontinuous track, while Lutherans and Episcopalians generally follow the complementary track.

The print volumes of *Feasting on the Word* follow the complementary track for Year A, are split between the complementary and semicontinuous tracks for Year B, and cover the semicontinuous stream for Year C. Essays for Pentecost and the Season after Pentecost that are not covered in the print volumes are available on the *Feasting on the Word* Web site, www.feastingontheword.net.

For more information about the Revised Common Lectionary, visit the official RCL Web site at http://lectionary.library.vanderbilt.edu/ or see *The Revised Common Lectionary: The Consultation on Common Texts* (Nashville: Abingdon Press, 1992).

Feasting on the Word

Isaiah 58:1-12

¹Shout out, do not hold back!
  Lift up your voice like a trumpet!
  Announce to my people their rebellion,
  to the house of Jacob their sins.
²Yet day after day they seek me
  and delight to know my ways,
  as if they were a nation that practiced righteousness
  and did not forsake the ordinance of their God;
  they ask of me righteous judgments,
  they delight to draw near to God.
³"Why do we fast, but you do not see?
  Why humble ourselves, but you do not notice?"
  Look, you serve your own interest on your fast day,
  and oppress all your workers.
⁴Look, you fast only to quarrel and to fight
  and to strike with a wicked fist.
  Such fasting as you do today
  will not make your voice heard on high.
⁵Is such the fast that I choose,
  a day to humble oneself?
  Is it to bow down the head like a bulrush,
  and to lie in sackcloth and ashes?
  Will you call this a fast,
  a day acceptable to the LORD?

⁶Is not this the fast that I choose:
  to loose the bonds of injustice,
  to undo the thongs of the yoke,

Theological Perspective

This passage is one of the highlights of Third Isaiah (Isa. 56–66), and it serves as a poetic re-presentation of the redemptive theology that runs throughout the book.[1] Whereas the social location for most of Isaiah has been of a community in exile, in this passage it is of a community in conflict. The passage finds the root of this conflict in a hypocritical gap between the conduct of the community and the community's worship.

The community's fasting is ineffectual, because its purpose is to cloak lives that are selfish, unjust, and violent. "Look, you serve your own interest on your fast day, and oppress all your workers. Look, you fast only to quarrel and to fight and to strike with a wicked fist" (vv. 3b–4a). The true purpose of fasting is to instill the virtue of humility and the commitment to justice: "Is not this the fast that I choose: to loose the bonds of injustice, to undo the thongs of

1. For more on the historical and theological issues present in this passage, see Walter Brueggemann, *Isaiah 40–66* (Louisville, KY: Westminster John Knox Press, 1998), 164–95; Brevard S. Childs, *Isaiah: A Commentary* (Louisville, KY: Westminster John Knox Press, 2001), 440–81; Paul D. Hanson, *Isaiah 40–66* (Louisville, KY: Westminster John Knox Press, 1995), 204–7.

Pastoral Perspective

Ash Wednesday is not merely a time to meditate on our mortality ("Dust you are, and to dust you shall return") or to confess our individual sins and failings. The words of Isaiah 58 save us from wallowing in introspection by forcing us to acknowledge our *social sins*. Especially for those in the North American church, this is not easy.

Because the words of Isaiah are so powerful and applicable to life in our society, the pastor is well advised to stay close to the text itself and let its words sound "like a trumpet" in the ears of the congregation. An "in-your-face" overpreaching of the text will likely result more in resistance than in faithful response. Here is an opportunity to engage the text in a way that invites the congregation to overhear its "word of the Lord" to them.

On Ash Wednesday it is particularly appropriate we be reminded that the Lenten discipline God desires has nothing to do with "giving up" things of little consequence and has everything to do with taking on a more disciplined concern for meeting

> to let the oppressed go free,
> and to break every yoke?
> ⁷Is it not to share your bread with the hungry,
> and bring the homeless poor into your house;
> when you see the naked, to cover them,
> and not to hide yourself from your own kin?
> ⁸Then your light shall break forth like the dawn,
> and your healing shall spring up quickly;
> your vindicator shall go before you,
> the glory of the Lord shall be your rear guard.
> ⁹Then you shall call, and the Lord will answer;
> you shall cry for help, and he will say, Here I am.
>
> If you remove the yoke from among you,
> the pointing of the finger, the speaking of evil,
> ¹⁰if you offer your food to the hungry
> and satisfy the needs of the afflicted,
> then your light shall rise in the darkness
> and your gloom be like the noonday.
> ¹¹The Lord will guide you continually,
> and satisfy your needs in parched places,
> and make your bones strong;
> and you shall be like a watered garden,
> like a spring of water,
> whose waters never fail.
> ¹²Your ancient ruins shall be rebuilt;
> you shall raise up the foundations of many generations;
> you shall be called the repairer of the breach,
> the restorer of streets to live in.

Exegetical Perspective

The postexilic Judean community, living under the rule of the newly empowered Persian Empire, provides the societal context for today's passage and the surrounding chapters of Isaiah 56–66. For this vulnerable, disoriented population, it is a time of political and religious restoration, as both the exiles who are returning from Babylon and the people who never left the region of Judah stake out their claims on the land and important theological issues.

The biggest question, perhaps, is this: What does the future hold after such great destruction and displacement? This inquiry quickly engenders more specific ponderings: How does the nascent Jewish community rethink the status of the Jerusalem temple and Davidic monarchy in light of their recent dissolution? What are the religious priorities to consider when rebuilding and starting afresh? Where is God in this process?

The prophetic literature of this time period testifies to the sustained role of prophetic figures in answering these seminal questions. Third Isaiah, as scholars often call Isaiah 56–66, addresses especially

Homiletical Perspective

This passage from Isaiah's postexilic prophecies begins with a sense of excitement. God commands the prophet to shout without reservation, as if using a battle trumpet to call the people to action; but the call is not a joyous one. The people think that they have been seeking God, but they need to face the reality that they have been chasing other things instead. We mislabel our sins as attempts to reach out to God.

Human Distance from God. Isaiah's audience thinks that they are seeking God (v. 2). They may honestly believe that they want to be in God's paths and presence, but they have deluded themselves. These people think that acts of worship such as fasting and humility will draw God's attention and admiration. God tells them that such fasting will not impress God (v. 4). Instead, God is present in acts of righteousness. To seek God truly means to look where God is—in the midst of work for justice.

The problem with the people's actions is that they are fasting while at the same time engaging in acts of

Isaiah 58:1-12

Theological Perspective

the yoke, to let the oppressed go free, and to break every yoke?" (v. 6). True fasting involves not just solitary abstinence, but the deliberate choice to give to those in need: "Is it not to share your bread with the hungry, and bring the homeless poor into your house; when you see the naked, to cover them, and not to hide yourself from your own kin?" (v. 7). Those who fast in this way will encounter God's abundance, an overflowing of light and life.

Early Christian commentators tended to spiritualize the connection between abstinence and justice. In his commentary, Jerome (ca. 347–420) read the imperative to attend to earthly needs as a typological anticipation of the greater imperative to attend to spiritual needs: "When you see people freezing outside the church in the frigidity of unbelief, without the warmth of faith, impoverished and homeless, lead them home to the church and clothe them with the work of incorruption, so that, wrapped in the mantle of Christ, they will not remain in the grave."

It would be wrong to read Jerome's typological interpretation as counsel to ignore those who suffer from material poverty. Clearly, early commentators also recognized the call for justice in this passage. Augustine of Hippo (354–430) asked, "Will your fast be approved of when you fail to acknowledge your brother?"[2] It is clear, however, that such readings eroded the connection between abstinence and justice in the church's liturgical life, particularly those practices connected to Ash Wednesday.

On Ash Wednesday, in addition to reading this passage, it is customary to impose ashes on the forehead with the words, "Remember that you are dust, and to dust you shall return" (Gen. 3:19) or "Turn away from sin and be faithful to the gospel" (Mark 1:15). This observance signals the beginning of Lent, when many Christians fast or abstain from certain foods in order to focus on the things that need to be set aside, or taken on, in the course of Lent—things that stand in the way of a living, vibrant, and wholehearted relationship with God.

Given this setting, today's reading from Isaiah is particularly appropriate, because it addresses the role fasting and similar penitential practices play in the spiritual life of both individuals and communities. At the root of these practices is a relationship with God from which flow personal piety and social justice. Getting back in touch with that relationship is the

2. Jerome, Commentary on Isaiah 16.8, in *Ancient Christian Commentary on Scripture: Old Testament XI, Isaiah 40–66*, ed. Mark W. Elliott (Downers Grove, IL: InterVarsity Press, 2007), 211. Augustine, Sermon 400.7, in *The Works of Saint Augustine: A Translation for the 21st Century, Sermons III/10*, ed. and trans. Edmund Hill, OP (Hyde Park, NY: New City Press, 1995), 476.

Pastoral Perspective

concretely the "needs of the afflicted." In any good bookstore you will find shelves marked "Self-help." Some may even be labeled, ironically enough, "Christian Self-help." Is it not clear to every thoughtful pastor that our programs of self-help offer precious little help? We vainly seek self-fulfillment through what we think will build up our self-esteem, instead of through the giving of ourselves to concerns larger than ourselves. The words of Isaiah 58 call us to the larger purposes of God's own mission among us.

Before we announce to God's people "their sins," we first must deal honestly with our own complicity in the sins unmasked by Isaiah. To what degree are we more concerned with the aesthetics of worship than with the "fast acceptable to the Lord"—the worship that requires personal participation in God's own passion for the hungry, the poor, and the naked?

If worship in our churches seems tame and boring, could it be that it has too little to do with the worship God desires? Instead of attending to God's agenda, we take matters into our own hands. We seek to jazz up our worship by hiring a band, getting the pastor to take guitar lessons, and projecting the banal words of a "praise chorus" on a big screen. However entertaining it may be, it is not the worship God desires and demands—at least not if we leave worship unchallenged and unchanged in the ways we treat the weak and vulnerable among us.

Isaiah makes it clear that the worship God desires is both inescapably social and compellingly personal. It calls us "to loose the bonds of injustice, to undo the thongs of the yoke, to let the oppressed go free, and to break every yoke. . . . to share [our] bread with the hungry, and bring the homeless poor into [our] house . . . to cover [the naked] and not to hide [ourselves] from [our] own kin" (vv. 6–7). Authentic worship is not a matter of elegant ritual or self-congratulating piety. It is a matter of both social justice and costly personal concern for the bruised and battered of the world.

Seeking to "satisfy the needs of the afflicted" is not merely an obligation that is laid on the covenant community. It is a way of life that makes for the fullness of life, both for the individual and for the whole community. In attending socially and personally to the needs of the afflicted, "[our] light shall break forth like the dawn, and [our] healing shall spring up quickly. . . . Then [we] shall call, and the Lord will answer; [we] shall cry for help, and [God] will say, Here I am" (vv. 8–9). Just as earlier in the presence of the awesome holiness of God in the temple, Isaiah had responded to the call of God, "Here I am, send

relevant topics such as the function of rituals and temple practices, the place of Zion in the restoration, and the role of foreigners within the community, while also maintaining some of the classic themes of the preexilic prophets, for example, judgments against idolatry (Isa. 57) and corrupt leaders (Isa. 56:9–12).

Chapter 58 stands near the beginning of Third Isaiah and comments on one of the common religious tensions found within the prophetic literature: the function of ritual exercises and cultic practices vis-à-vis the obvious need for social justice. The great prophetic figures such as Amos are often perceived as emphasizing the lack of social justice within Israelite society, while downplaying the need for pious, more ritualistic actions such as sacrifice.

This sharp dichotomy between "prophetic justice-oriented thought" and "priestly minutiae-minded thought" probably reflects modern Protestant sentiments more than ancient religious ones, since the need for both streams (along with others!) is clearly maintained throughout the biblical corpus. Isaiah 58 comments on the true nature and purpose of fasting, while maintaining the relevance and significance of the practice.

The somewhat disjointed, rambling passage does not create a clear, linear argument building upon itself point by point, but the general message is not obscured, and a rough outline is discernible. First, a divine command is given to the prophet to announce the people's rebellion. Then, the people voice succinctly their complaint, and three divine answers are given.[1]

Prophetic Call: Announce Rebellion (vv. 1–2). The divine command to the prophet in verse 1 captures one of the quintessential tasks of the biblical prophet: to warn the people about their social wrongdoings. This verse presents two sets of parallel lines, with the first couplet highlighting the loud volume needed by the prophet ("Shout out," "like a trumpet") and the second couplet proclaiming both the addressee ("my people," "house of Jacob") and the problem ("rebellion," "sins").

Complaint: Our Actions Go Unseen (v. 3a). In this section, two brief questions give voice to the people's complaint. They desire to know why their perfectly laudable action of fasting does not receive a response from God. Fasting is, after all, associated with personal, pious activity (along with mourning and penitence). In the context of this passage, it is apparent

unrighteousness. Is God condemning all fasting here— or only the fasting by those who avoid righteousness? Is God critical of their worship because they think that good worship can substitute or make up for the unrighteousness they do? In our context, would God be critical of any of our favorite worship practices?

When Isaiah's audience leave their worship, they oppress workers, and then they quarrel and fight (vv. 3–4). God most pointedly rebukes the people for one thing: they pay more attention to their own interests than to the welfare of others. When people distract themselves with their own affairs, they miss the opportunities for righteousness that could lead them into God's presence. By walking in righteousness, we come to God (Ps. 85:13). Righteousness is not a test, a prerequisite, or a barrier to life with God; righteousness is the day-by-day, step-by-step process of life with God. Right worship correctly diagnoses our problems: we are too distant from God, and we have wandered from God's path.

What would God's righteous judgment be upon our worship practices today? In what ways do we serve ourselves in worship? When we leave worship, do our relationships with the other lead us to where God is, or do our actions increase the distance we keep? How can our worship point us back to God's path?

Social Justice. Isaiah urges us to get back on track, to rejoin God's path. We must undo and break the yoke (vv. 6–7). Isaiah uses the "yoke" as a symbol for the bonds of oppression in the world, or any of the ways that we tie others to ourselves in order to bend their actions to our benefit. The yoke means selfishness, using others to gain for ourselves and to achieve our own purposes. To loose the yoke means to offer freedom and release for people who have been used for someone else's gain; such release is a consistent theme of Isaiah (61:1) and a cornerstone of Jesus' ministry (Luke 4:18).

Here Isaiah goes a step further, by calling for us to *break* the yoke, as in Isaiah 9:4. Not only do we need to cease our own acts of oppression and offer liberty to those whom we have used and abused, but we must also destroy the yoke. This will prevent us and everyone else from using this kind of exploitation in the future. Social justice requires not only actions of liberation, but structural change to remove the possibility of future injustice. We should think of Isaiah 2:4 in this regard: not only do we lay down our weapons of battle, but we turn our swords into plows, so that we lose the capacity for war and transform the weapons into implements of provision for others.

1. Joseph Blenkinsopp. *Isaiah 56–66*, Anchor Bible 19B (New York: Doubleday, 2003), 176.

Isaiah 58:1-12

Theological Perspective

very meaning of repentance, the deliberate work of repairing a relationship that has been broken or thwarted by our own sin and selfishness. So the passage ends with a promise: "you shall be called the repairer of the breach, the restorer of streets to live in" (v. 12b).

What does it mean live into this relationship more deeply? If early Christian commentators tended to emphasize personal piety to the detriment of social justice, contemporary readers have tended to identify the imperative to do justice and their own favored policies for social renewal and change. It would be misleading to draw from this passage specific imperatives to increase international aid or to oppose globalization, as worthy as these may be.

Rather, the connection in the passage between worship, fasting, justice, and reconciliation creates space for the renewal of a faithful imagination that prayerfully tries to develop a way forward. Consequently, the purpose of this passage is to bring the personal and political together and to renew a particular community that seeks to practice God's redemptive politics in its own location. For this reason, T. S. Eliot in his poem "Ash Wednesday" ends with the following prayer that resonates with the imagery in this passage and speaks to the personal and political at once:

> Suffer us not to mock ourselves with falsehood
> Teach us to care and not to care
> Teach us to sit still
> Even among these rocks,
> Our peace in His will
> And even among these rocks
> Sister, mother
> And spirit of the river, spirit of the sea,
> Suffer me not to be separated
>
> And let my cry come unto Thee.[3]

If, as contemporary commentators believe, communal conflict lies behind the text's origin, then the reparative actions promoted in the passage prompt contemporary churches to imagine practices that bear witness to the peaceful politics of the kingdom in their immediate community. Ash Wednesday provides not only the opportunity for individual Christians to mark the beginning of Lent, but for churches to renew their corporate life, in order to learn, as if for the first time, what it means to be a "spring" of "waters" that "never fail" (v. 11b).

WILLIAM JOSEPH DANAHER JR.

Pastoral Perspective

me" (Isa. 6:8), so now the Lord responds and becomes available to our cries: "Here *I* am." I will send you.

The result is more than we might have expected. The "gloom," which pastors know painfully well, "will be like the noonday" (v. 10b), and the Lord, guiding us in ways of life abundant, will make our lives flourish "like a watered garden" (v. 11b). The true fulfillment of self comes through the giving and investing of self in God's own passion for the poor.

Not only will our own lives flourish; so will the life of our whole society: "Your ancient ruins shall be rebuilt" (v. 12a). What a precious promise that would be to a people returning from exile to the ruins of what once had been their homes and temple. "You shall raise up the foundations of many generations; you shall be called the repairer of the breach, the restorer of streets to live in" (v. 12). In the gathering ruins of our society—which for too long has neglected the foundations of common life by allowing its essential infrastructure to collapse in order to continue cutting taxes on the wealthiest of our citizens, by neglecting public education, and turning its back on the neediest and most vulnerable among us—the promise of Isaiah can give hope and energy for the struggles ahead.

Youth and young adults often seem to understand this better then their elders. Youth return from mission trips with a new sense of what it means to experience the presence of God in the faces of the truly poor. College students volunteer their time to tutor children and build Habitat houses, not just to "do good," but to find meaning and purpose for their lives exactly where God promised. People of all ages come to their pastors asking for more of life than they have yet experienced. Do we offer them second-rate entertainment? Do we set before them God's own promise that the fullness of life is to be found in the giving of life to the larger purposes of God's liberating love in the world, and call them to live into that promise?

ALLEN C. MCSWEEN JR.

---

3. T. S. Eliot, *Collected Poems 1909–1962* (London: Faber & Faber Ltd., 1963), 105.

Exegetical Perspective

that God should see this activity; yet it remains unclear exactly how the people wish for God to acknowledge their fasting. Interestingly for the answers that immediately follow, the people do not highlight other religious practices, such as charity to the disadvantaged, only this single ritual.

First Answer: Selfish, Violent Fasting Will Not Be Heard (vv. 3b–4). The textual voice switches back to the prophet in these verses and critiques their fasting by stating that it is accompanied by self-interest, coercion, squabbling, and even physical violence. If a specific situation is intended here by the prophet, it is most likely related to improper business/financial affairs. The text uses the repetition of "look" to divide the section in half. Participation in the fast day does not affect their actions toward other people; therefore, their fasting is in vain.

Second Answer: The Correct Way to Fast (vv. 5–9a). The second divine response constitutes a list of rhetorical questions. Verse 5 presents a satirical triad of questions that mocks the type of fasting described directly above. The bodily manipulations that typically accompany fasting are trivialized. Then verses 6–7 transform the whole notion of fasting into specific actions concerned with liberation and societal welfare. In the end, God's preferred style of fasting has more to do with helping other people than with bowing down or lying in ashes. Verses 8–9a follow with the reward or repercussions of doing this new type of fasting: in summary, God will hear and answer.

Third Answer: The Benefits of Helping Others (vv. 9b–12). The third divine response is an expansion of the theme in the second answer with a reversal of the literary form. Instead of a long section of rhetorical questions resulting in a short set of *then*-clauses, as in verses 5–9a, verses 9b–12 has a short set of *if*-clauses resulting in a long, single *then*-clause. The emphasis here is on the positive consequences of instituting a new type of fasting practice. The promises involve light, as in verse 8, as well as God's guidance and provision. Given the recent desolation of Jerusalem, verse 12 is especially poignant in its promise of rebuilt ruins and raised foundations.

TYLER MAYFIELD

Homiletical Perspective

A passage such as this tempts us to discuss politics, and to ask what the world would be like if our nations gave up the capacity for war and invested instead in feeding the hungry people of the world. We should not forget that Isaiah has a religious agenda in mind as well. We need to ask how our congregations and our church can give up our capacity to defend and to attack, and instead pour all of our energies into helping others.

Isaiah also offers positive direction for us to follow God in the right path. We need to offer food for the hungry (v. 10). This social justice is directed to the most basic of human needs and addresses those who need it most. Moreover, we are called to satisfy the needs of the afflicted. This allows suffering people to identify what they need, so that we can then meet their needs, rather than our perceptions of what might be best for them. Our own perception of God and God's activity begins to clear when we focus on the needs of others.

Here, the preacher has the opportunity to move from Isaiah's world to our own context. Who are the suffering people to whom our church should listen? What acts of social justice would they have us do on their behalf? What are the basic human needs in our own communities? What can we do about those needs? How would those actions sharpen our focus on God's work in the world?

A Vision for the Future. The end of Isaiah's vision gives us hope for the future. When we are following God's path through worship and justice, light breaks forth into the world (v. 8), bringing dawn and healing to us and to all around us. Justice does not bring a mere temporary improvement, but leads to God's abundance that provides enough for everyone. With rebuilt foundations (v. 12) for all society, God's justice lasts forever. The barriers of separation are removed (cf. Eph. 2:14), and God builds a new world, full of streets where we all can live (cf. Zech. 8:1–6). Receiving our heritage from God, we reside with God as we were always meant to live.

JON L. BERQUIST

Psalm 51:1-17

¹Have mercy on me, O God,
　　according to your steadfast love;
　　according to your abundant mercy
　　blot out my transgressions.
²Wash me thoroughly from my iniquity,
　　and cleanse me from my sin.

³For I know my transgressions,
　　and my sin is ever before me.
⁴Against you, you alone, have I sinned,
　　and done what is evil in your sight,
　　so that you are justified in your sentence
　　and blameless when you pass judgment.
⁵Indeed, I was born guilty,
　　a sinner when my mother conceived me.

⁶You desire truth in the inward being;
　　therefore teach me wisdom in my secret heart.
⁷Purge me with hyssop, and I shall be clean;
　　wash me, and I shall be whiter than snow.
⁸Let me hear joy and gladness;
　　let the bones that you have crushed rejoice.

Theological Perspective

As the church enters the Lenten season, we are anointed with ash to signify our finitude and frailty: "Remember, O human, that you are dust, and unto dust you shall return." It is equally a sign of repentance, a messy memorial to our more fundamental problem: not our creaturely state, but our fallen state, our enmeshment in sin's power. It is this reality of which, and from which, the guilt-ridden King David cries so poignantly in this psalm.

Our temptation is to psychologize this psalm, to read it simply as the anguished self-loathing of David—not, as it turns out, immediately after his adultery with Bathsheba nor even his arranged murder of Uriah her husband, but only after the prophet forces the king to acknowledge his transgressions. In this reading, David cries to God from a heart shredded by the guilt of having been found out, wallowing in the depth of a shame that most of us have never plumbed. We might even suspect David of a kind of guilt neurosis that hopes for atonement by way of self-inflicted psychic pain, a catharsis purchased at the heavy price of practically disowning himself. "Indeed, I was born guilty, a sinner when my mother conceived me" (v. 5). We may be tempted to suspect that David got carried away by his guilt feelings, and

Pastoral Perspective

It is no coincidence that Psalm 51 is appointed for Ash Wednesday, the day that marks the beginning of the liturgical season of Lent. The psalmist's words encapsulate the depth of the meaning of the forty days leading up to Easter. Lent is a time of self-reflection and penitence, a time to acknowledge our sinfulness and need for God's mercy.

Psalm 51 is a plea to God, a prayer for forgiveness. The psalmist displays a painful awareness of his sins: "For I know my transgressions, and my sin is ever before me" (v. 3). Not only has he committed evil; he also laments that he has been a sinner since he was born (vv. 4–5).

In addition to lamenting his sins, the psalmist is clear that deliverance from them comes from God alone. He wastes no time getting to his point; he begins, "Have mercy on me, O God" (v. 1). Then the psalmist invokes powerful images of being cleansed. He implores God, using descriptive verbs like "blot out," "wash," and "purge."

This psalm reflects our own reality as Christians. We are sinners. We do things, whether big or small, that draw us away from God, and we do things that hurt others. Christians in many churches regularly say a confession, asking God for forgiveness for the

⁹Hide your face from my sins,
   and blot out all my iniquities.

¹⁰Create in me a clean heart, O God,
   and put a new and right spirit within me.
¹¹Do not cast me away from your presence,
   and do not take your holy spirit from me.
¹²Restore to me the joy of your salvation,
   and sustain in me a willing spirit.

¹³Then I will teach transgressors your ways,
   and sinners will return to you.
¹⁴Deliver me from bloodshed, O God,
   O God of my salvation,
   and my tongue will sing aloud of your deliverance.

¹⁵O Lord, open my lips,
   and my mouth will declare your praise.
¹⁶For you have no delight in sacrifice;
   if I were to give a burnt offering, you would not be pleased.
¹⁷The sacrifice acceptable to God is a broken spirit;
   a broken and contrite heart, O God, you will not despise.

Exegetical Perspective

Theologically rich and poetically powerful, Psalm 51 is an earnest prayer of contrition in the form of an individual lament. As one of the seven Penitential Psalms of the Christian tradition (Pss. 6; 32; 38; 51; 102; 130; 143), it is most appropriate for Ash Wednesday. This elegant poem utilizes expressive imagery and vocabulary for both human sinfulness and divine grace. It portrays sincere penitence for deliberate sin and rebellion against God. Perhaps for this reason the editors of the Psalter attribute its composition to Nathan's confrontation of David over his adultery with Bathsheba (2 Sam. 12). Historically, the text more likely dates to the seventh or sixth century BCE, but the Davidic setting provides a useful context for this cry of a "broken and contrite heart" (v. 17).

The text's structure moves from an appeal to divine mercy (1–2), through confession of sins (3–5) and pleas for cleansing and renewal (6–12), to a vow with thanksgiving and further petitions (13–17).

This confessional psalm applies traditional terms for "transgression" (*pešaʿ*), "iniquity" (*ʿawon*), and "evil" (*raʿ*). The appeal for divine forgiveness is contingent upon God's gracious nature, and the psalmist begs God to "have mercy" or "be gracious" (*ḥnn*, v. 1). The penitent invokes God's "steadfast love"

Homiletical Perspective

In many Catholic and Protestant churches, an Ash Wednesday worship service marks the beginning of the Lenten season. It is a solemn, penitential liturgy that launches worshipers on a reflective journey toward the climactic events of Holy Week. Several traditional rituals frame the meaning of the service; the most visible and widespread of these rituals is the marking of the forehead with ash, in the sign of a cross. Usually applied with some variation of the words "Remember that you are dust, and to dust you shall return," the ashes suggest a posture of penitence, and they remind us of our mortality and our humble place before God.

Perhaps the second most familiar practice of a typical Ash Wednesday service is the communal recitation of Psalm 51. This Penitential Psalm provides the poetic language to accompany the stark visible symbol of a marked forehead. The words of the psalm are heartrending. Expressing clear humility and contrition, the psalmist acknowledges his transgressions and pleads for God's mercy (vv. 1–3). Indeed, the writer's sins seem to haunt him (v. 3), and he allows that he deserves whatever consequences come his way (v. 4). His urgent prayer is for God's forgiveness and salvation, that God might

Psalm 51:1-17

Theological Perspective

that in the interests of psychological health we need not follow him in his prayer of wallowing self-hatred.

The church's traditional reading of this psalm, thankfully, does not encourage us to embrace such a dismissive interpretation of the text. Granted, the text's own heading (not printed above) recalls for us that this is David's plea. The prayer arises from a specific narrative and relational context, but it is more than solely David's anguished prayer, more than hyperbole born of shame-drenched desperation. It is the prayer of us all as we kneel in the name of Jesus Christ, marked by ash, in the presence of the One "before [whom] no creature is hidden," before whose eyes "all are naked and laid bare" and "to whom we must render an account" (Heb. 4:13). Our sin *is* ever before us.

Early in his *Confessions*, Augustine wondered to God about his life in Monica's womb and later at her breast. "I do not like to think of that period as part of the same life I now lead," Augustine confessed, "because it is dim and forgotten."[1] Nevertheless, the bishop of Hippo submitted the self-narrative of his earliest days to this very psalm, adding, "But if *I was born in sin and guilt was with me already when my mother conceived me*, where, I ask you, Lord, where or when was I, your servant, ever innocent?"[2]

Of course, Augustine himself would be instrumental in the development of the Christian teaching on original sin. In the light of this doctrine, the reply to Augustine's own query about his innocence is "Never." If that is indeed the correct reply, it is not because a little child is already personally guilty, nor is it because the act of sexual intercourse is sinful per se (as Augustine unfortunately surmised on occasion). Rather, we are never innocent because the reality and power of sin—alienation from God, from one another, and from the more-than-human world—is pervasively present throughout all the webs of our interconnected lives. Like a corrosive acid, the power of sin eats away at us all in all of our relations—relations that indeed make us who we are becoming— such that none of us is a stranger to abuse, shame, fear, suspicion, and pain. This is our world. Scripture—and this psalm in particular—helps us to name it rightly.

Psalm 51 also leads us to hope in the God of Israel, who acts toward us "according to steadfast love" and "abundant mercy" (v. 1). We can hope because we confess and believe that this God of Israel is indeed the Creator of all things. Only the Creator

Pastoral Perspective

times that they have sinned against God and against others. The season of Lent is, in part, a more deliberate time of reflection and penitence. Like the psalmist who acknowledges his sins, we are called to confess the ways that "we have not loved you with our whole heart; we have not loved our neighbors as ourselves."[1] Part of the process of repentance is recognizing our utter dependence on God. Just as the psalmist pleads to God for deliverance (v. 14), we must realize our own need for God's mercy.

There is a great church camp skit that reflects this Christian reality. Peter is seated at the pearly gates, and a woman approaches. "Tell me why I should let you in," Peter says. "I have gone to church my whole life," the woman says. Then Peter reminds her that she had been unkind to some of the members of the church. "Well," she says defensively, "I brought groceries every week to my elderly neighbor."

Peter points out that she often used the neighbor's money to buy a few things for herself as well. The conversation continues like this, and the woman becomes more and more defensive and distraught, clearly beginning to panic at the thought that she might not be allowed in to heaven. Finally, she falls to her knees in tears and desperation and says, "Forgive me, Lord, for I have sinned." Immediately, the pearly gates swing wide open and Peter says, "Welcome home, my child."

This simple skit illustrates that we are sinners who are utterly dependent upon God for forgiveness and salvation. This is not the end of the story, however. There is a promise inherent in the psalm, one of re-creation and redemption, recognizing that God not only saves us from our sins, but also gives us new life. "Create in me a clean heart, O God, and put a new and right spirit within me," the psalmist prays. "Restore me to the joy of your salvation, and sustain in me a willing spirit" (vv. 10a, 12).

The intentionality of focus on our sins and our dependence on God during Lent allows us to recommit ourselves to living as the people we were created to be. The Christian writer Frederick Buechner writes: "After being baptized by John in the river Jordan, Jesus went off alone into the wilderness where he spent forty days asking himself the question what it meant to be Jesus. During Lent, Christians are supposed to ask one way or another what it means to be themselves."[2]

---

1. Augustine, *Confessions*, trans. R. S. Pine-Coffin (London: Penguin Books, 1961), 28.
2. Ibid.

---

1. All liturgical references are from *The Book of Common Prayer* (New York: Oxford University Press, 1979), 267, 268, 265.
2. Frederick Buechner, *Listening to Your Life*, ed. George Connor (San Francisco: HarperCollins, 1992), 56.

(ḥesed), using an important relational or covenant term, and "abundant mercy" or "compassion" (rḥmyk) (v. 1). Psalm 51 shares much of its vocabulary with God's self-revelation in Exodus 34:6–7, which describes the Lord as "merciful and gracious" (raḥûm weḥannûn), "abounding in steadfast love [ḥesed] and faithfulness ['emet]," and "forgiving iniquity and transgression and sin."

Psalm 51 employs five images for the remission of sin while avoiding the common verb "to forgive" (ns'). The penitent urges God to "blot out [mḥh] my transgressions" (vv. 1, 9), as though they were written in a book of guilt (cf. Isa. 43:25; 44:22; Ps. 109:14; Num. 5:23). The verb kbs in "wash me" (vv. 2, 7) means "to wash by treading," usually applied to stained clothing (Exod. 19:10, 14; 2 Sam. 19:24). Jeremiah (2:22) artfully applies this verb: "Though you wash yourself with lye and use much soap, the stain of your guilt is still before me."

The third verb, "cleanse" (ṭhr, vv. 2, 7, 10), is a priestly term used in the ritual purification of uncleanness (e.g., Lev. 13:13–17; 16:30). Using the hiphil stem of ḥṭ', verse 7 eloquently prays, "Purge me with hyssop, and I shall be clean; wash [kbs] me, and I shall be whiter than snow" (cf. Isa. 1:18). Hyssop ('ezôb) is used in priestly rituals of purification (Lev. 14; Num. 19) and to mark the doorposts with blood during the first Passover (Exod. 12:22). Finally, verse 9 turns the negative image of God's hidden face (e.g., Pss. 88:14; 102:2; 143:7) into a positive metaphor: "Hide [hstr] your face from my sins."

Although extensive exegetical comments are not possible here, a few textual issues should be noted. The NRSV translation of verse 4, "Against you, you alone, have I sinned," correctly reflects the grammatical emphasis in Hebrew. Ethical sins against other humans are also sins against God in the Hebrew Bible, as David confesses in 2 Samuel 12:13 (cf. Gen. 39:9). This rhetoric highlights the importance of the individual's personal relationship with God in this psalm. The author of Romans 3:4 aptly quotes verse 4b to justify the judgments of God against sinful humans. "Indeed I was born guilty" (v. 5) refers not to the Christian concept of original sin but to the impure nature of humanity before God (cf. Gen. 8:21; Jer. 17:9; Job 4:17–19; 15:14–16).

Although the nuance of verse 6b is uncertain, the NJPS rendition, "teach me wisdom about secret things," is better than NRSV's "teach me wisdom in my secret heart." Regardless, the psalmist realizes the need for wisdom as well as piety. The metaphor of crushed bones in verse 8b is odd, but "bones" can

withhold punishment and instead wash him clean and purify his soul (v. 2 and vv. 7–12). For his part, the writer knows that simple platitudes are not sufficient as he petitions for mercy; he offers God the sacrifice of a broken heart (v. 17) and promises to praise God continuously and to teach others the ways of God (vv. 13–15).

In short, the psalmist begs for a new start, a second chance, and he knows that he cannot begin again without God's mercy and grace. In the climactic verse 10, the writer prays: "Create in me a clean heart, O God, and put a new and right spirit within me." This beautiful verse is echoed by the prophet Ezekiel (Ezek. 36:25–27), who envisions God restoring the divine/human covenant by transplanting new hearts into the wayward people of Israel—an image that captures both the corrupting power of sin and the abundance of God's mercy.

The stories of Scripture and the realities of human experience attest to the fact that sin is not a surface wound; rather, it is a penetrating sickness that like a cancer eats away at the core of our being. Overcoming such an invasive disease requires a dramatic, divine intervention—a heart transplant, nothing less. This is the path to healing and wholeness, the psalmist concludes. It is the only way for him to achieve a restored relationship with God, to share again and always in the life of the Holy Spirit and in the joy of God's salvation (vv. 10–12).

Clearly Psalm 51 offers fruitful ground for preaching, particularly in the context of an Ash Wednesday service. Broad themes include the nature of sin, the practice of confession and repentance, and the assurance of God's forgiveness and mercy. Each of these themes connects well with the journey of Lent. Thinking more specifically, a preacher may choose to focus on this image of a transplanted heart, an image that resonates throughout the Old and New Testaments as a way of describing God's faithfulness to the divine/human covenant.

Another avenue for homiletical exploration, however, lies in what the psalmist does not say. Speaking personally, I have forever heard this psalm differently after listening to a friend's sermon during my second year of seminary. My friend, Natalie Wigg Stevenson, began by noting the ascription that precedes the psalm, which identifies David as the author, writing soon after he had slept with Bathsheba and ordered the murder of her husband, Uriah (2 Sam. 11–12). This is the social context for these penitential words, Natalie emphasized, and she then drew our attention to verse 4: "Against you, you alone, have I sinned," the

Psalm 51:1-17

Theological Perspective

of all things, Athanasius and other early theologians insisted, is the Power able to "create in [us] a clean heart," to "put a new and right spirit within [us]" (v. 10). Any lesser power is not sufficient against the destructive acids of sin that are corroding creation.

Our faith further proclaims that the Creator has undertaken our collective healing and restoration not by fiat, nor from a safe distance. Rather, the God to whom David prays has answered this prayer for mercy and healing, ultimately, in and through Jesus Christ. Surely this is already implied in the genealogy of Matthew 1, in which the Messiah's line is traced through David, "the father of Solomon by the wife of Uriah" (v. 6). David's plea for forgiveness of his transgressions, and even deliverance from the very power of sin, finds its reply in the slow, painstaking labor of God from within the course of human history and human blood—and even, in the case of David's complicating sins, human blood*shed*. Divine mercy is mediated through a Messiah who emerges from within the very midst of our sinful world of betrayal and violence, of mistrust and brokenness, and assumes it as his own.

Perhaps it is significant that this same Gospel of Matthew shares with Psalm 51 at least a mild denigration of ritual sacrifice. David offers "a broken and contrite heart" as "the sacrifice acceptable to God" (v. 17). Twice in Matthew (uniquely among the Gospels) Jesus cites the prophet Hosea (Hos. 6:6), "I [God] desire mercy, not sacrifice" (9:13; 12:7). Granted, Christian tradition has not been particularly hesitant to embrace the language of ritual sacrifice to interpret Jesus' own death, and Lenten liturgies and sermons often are laced with sacrificial imagery. While that language surely has a legitimate place, Psalm 51 should warn us against interpreting Jesus' ministry and crucifixion only in that way.

MICHAEL LODAHL

Pastoral Perspective

The basic questions and truths of the Christian experience that are expressed by the psalmist in Psalm 51 are enacted in the Ash Wednesday liturgy. In many traditions, the liturgy includes the recitation of Psalm 51, as well as a Litany of Penitence. The litany leads worshipers through an explicit confession of ways we have separated ourselves from God and one another, including petitions about "our self-indulgent appetites and ways," "our intemperate love of worldly goods and comforts," and "our blindness to human need and suffering."

One of the most moving parts of the Ash Wednesday liturgy is the imposition of ashes when the presiding minister makes the sign of the cross with ashes on worshipers' foreheads, saying, "Remember that you are dust, and to dust you shall return." This ritual is not intended to be morbid. Rather, it is a visible sign of what the psalmist was so aware of: we are wholly dependent on God. The prayer over the ashes says, "Grant that these ashes may be a sign to us . . . that it is only by your gracious gift that we are given everlasting life."

The person who wrote Psalm 51 was, of course, writing long before the life, birth, and death of Jesus Christ, yet his lament of his sins and his awareness of his need for God's deliverance make this psalm so appropriate for Ash Wednesday. As we begin the season of self-examination and repentance, we follow the psalmist's example by focusing on how we are failing to live as God calls us to live and how we are in need of the salvation and redemption that comes from God alone. As Frederick Buechner says, "It can be a pretty depressing business all in all, but if sackcloth and ashes are at the start of it, something like Easter may be at the end."[3]

ANDREA WIGODSKY

3. Ibid., 58.

refer to the whole person (Ps. 35:10) or one's inmost being. A heart is similarly "crushed" (*ndkh*, "contrite" in NRSV) in verse 17. These are spiritual metaphors rather than physical ailments (cf. Ps. 38). Body imagery throughout this psalm, referring to the poet's heart, spirit, bones, lips, tongue, and mouth, contributes to the prayer's intimate character.

The beautiful prayer for God to create (*br'*) a "clean heart" and a "new and right spirit" in verse 10 is related to Ezekiel 36:25–27. Reference to God's "holy spirit" (v. 10) appears only here and Isaiah 63:10–11 in the Hebrew Bible. The psalmist further requests a "willing spirit" (v. 12). Verse 11 begs God not to abandon the sinner, but actively to "restore" (v. 12), "sustain" (v. 12), and "deliver" (v. 14) one who seeks God. Divine initiative is necessary for human salvation in this psalm beloved by Reformation Christianity. In response, the repentant psalmist promises to teach others the ways of God for their renewal (vv. 13–14).

God does not "delight" in cultic sacrifices in verse 16 (cf. Isa. 1:11–17; Amos 5:21–24; Mic. 6:6–8). This apparently antitemple rhetoric is probably not meant as a wholesale rejection of the Jewish sacrificial system. Here a "broken spirit" (*rwḥ nšbrh*) substitutes for formal sacrifices (v. 17) as either poetic hyperbole or perhaps an exilic reference to the absence of temple rites. Compare Psalm 50:14, where thanksgiving constitutes a sacrifice, and Psalm 69:30–31, in which praise is superior to bloody offerings. Sincere repentance is more efficacious than rituals to remove sin in this psalm's poetic vision.

Our passage appropriately ends with the declaration that "a broken and contrite heart [*lb-nšbr wndkh*], O God, you will not despise." While God delivers the broken-hearted (*nšbry-lb*) in Psalm 34:18 and Isaiah 61:1, this description of a repentant sinner turns the usually negative image of a broken heart into a positive spiritual attribute. The lectionary reading excludes the canonical psalm's last two verses (vv. 18–19), a Persian-period addition that offers an intercession for Jerusalem and the rebuilding of Zion's walls. This passage's image of God "delighting" in animal sacrifices upon the temple altar seems inconsistent with verses 16–17.

NEAL H. WALLS

writer cries to God. "Really?!" Natalie asked. "Was God the only victim of that story? How would those words have sounded to Bathsheba or Uriah? How would they sound today to the countless people caught in similar webs of violence and betrayal?"

Natalie's point was that David could not honestly conclude that God was the only victim of his sin. David's sin surely harmed Bathsheba and Uriah as much as or more than it harmed God. In truth, this is almost always the case. Our sins bear real consequences for our relationships with others. Praying for God's mercy is perhaps a good starting point, but it is not enough. Our goal should not be simple repentance, but reconciliation—a restored relationship with God and with our neighbors. Confessing our sins to God is often the easiest part, because we can count on God's promise of unconditional love and mercy. The more difficult step is seeking forgiveness from the people we hurt, and committing ourselves to the hard, often painful work of reconciliation.

Several sermon illustrations come to mind to further highlight this process of reconciliation. For example, a preacher might use the backdrop of David's story to consider the current realities and consequences of domestic violence, infidelity, and other forms of interpersonal conflict. What might reconciliation look like in those contexts? A preacher may choose to focus on reconciliation at the communal level. The work of the Truth and Reconciliation Commission in postapartheid South Africa offers a powerful and well-documented contemporary example. Indeed, many communities around the world have tried to adapt that model to their own struggles with racial and ethnic conflict.

These illustrations give the preacher an opportunity to emphasize that true reconciliation requires not only repentance, but also truth and justice and a commitment to changed behavior. This deeper understanding not only aids in the restoration of human relationships; it also may help us more faithfully to respond to God's love and mercy in our lives.

JOHN D. ROHRS

2 Corinthians 5:20b–6:10

5:20bWe entreat you on behalf of Christ, be reconciled to God. 21For our sake he made him to be sin who knew no sin, so that in him we might become the righteousness of God.
6:1As we work together with him, we urge you also not to accept the grace of God in vain. 2For he says,

"At an acceptable time I have listened to you,
and on a day of salvation I have helped you."

See, now is the acceptable time; see, now is the day of salvation! 3We are putting no obstacle in anyone's way, so that no fault may be found with our ministry, 4but as servants of God we have commended ourselves in every way: through great endurance, in afflictions, hardships, calamities, 5beatings, imprisonments, riots, labors, sleepless nights, hunger; 6by purity, knowledge, patience, kindness, holiness of spirit, genuine love, 7truthful speech, and the power of God; with the weapons of righteousness for the right hand and for the left; 8in honor and dishonor, in ill repute and good repute. We are treated as impostors, and yet are true; 9as unknown, and yet are well known; as dying, and see—we are alive; as punished, and yet not killed; 10as sorrowful, yet always rejoicing; as poor, yet making many rich; as having nothing, and yet possessing everything.

Theological Perspective

This passage from the heart of Paul's second letter to the Corinthians provides a helpful meditation on the goal of the Christian life as the church begins the season of Lent.

Reconciliation with God. Verse 20b gives a basic summary of the gospel that Paul has preached to the various churches: "Be reconciled to God." The gospel of reconciliation is more challenging than we might think (much as it was for the Corinthians), in two respects. First, it shows us that, left to our own devices, we and indeed the whole world are at enmity with God. Each of us, and human society at large, is profoundly incapable of being the people that God has created us to be, despite the goodness with which God has created us and God's generous covenant with Israel (Rom. 3:20; 9:30–31). In the intentions of our hearts and the destructiveness of our actions, we are in dire need of reconciliation with God.

Second, the gospel of reconciliation may be even more shocking because of the unimaginable goodness of God's plans for us. God intends to do nothing short of restoring the most wayward and broken elements of creation—the greatest of which lie in the hearts of people like us. God does not respond to the sin and evil of our lives by throwing out the bad and starting over with something new; God means to

Pastoral Perspective

Most of us can remember (especially if we had children of our own) the process of being taught to speak politely, to know when to say "please" or "thank you." We teach and are taught to speak courteously as part of our growing up and fitting in. However, at a deeper level, the language of respect is meant to usher us into more meaningful relationships. There is more than an artificial relationship between etiquette and ethics.

That is a clue to understanding the importance of Paul's choice of words in our text and thus the rhetoric with which he proffers the gospel. For instance, in verses 6 and 7 he lists some of the "weapons of righteousness": "patience, kindness, holiness of spirit, genuine love, truthful speech, and the power of God." None of these can contradict any of the others. All are called for by the inherent, sovereign patience of God that is at the heart of the gospel and the life of Jesus. So Paul invites, entreats, and urges; he does not demand, threaten, or order. His rhetoric lives and works because he believes in the power of God. This is even more noteworthy given Paul's description of himself prior to his encounter with Christ.

Attending to Paul's rhetoric, we listen to this text from both a time and a culture in which the church must learn again the language of God's sovereign patience. Today's passage is both a continuation of

Exegetical Perspective

This passage concludes a long section in which Paul defends the integrity of his ministry as God's apostle (2 Cor. 5:11–6:13). Critics felt that his failure to exhibit the domineering traits of a "great man" discredited Paul's claim to speak God's saving word. He lacked the skills of a powerful public orator (2 Cor. 10:10), suffered some form of chronic illness (2 Cor. 12:7–10), worked at a trade rather than demand the support of wealthy patrons (1 Cor. 9:3–18), and adopted a posture of humility in the community rather than acting as a strict disciplinarian (2 Cor. 10:1–2; 13:9–10). During a recent visit to Corinth a member of the church had humiliated Paul in public. Assured that the church now regrets the incident, Paul encourages mutual reconciliation, even a warm embrace of the person responsible (2 Cor. 2:5–11; 6:11–13).

Paul reprimands his critics for focusing on outward appearances, not the heart. His apostolic way of life reflects the gospel that he preaches to others, the Christ who sacrificed his life out of love so that humanity would have eternal life (2 Cor. 5:11–15). Paul describes his own activity as "God's ambassador" extending the gospel of reconciliation throughout the world (2 Cor. 5:16–21). Our reading opens with the concluding verses of that treatment of reconciliation (vv. 20b–21). The final section creates dramatic images of Paul's apostleship (6:1–10).

Homiletical Perspective

When many of us turn to Ash Wednesday and the Lenten lectionary themes of repentance and renewal, there are already audio files playing in our heads: thin, tinny voices murmuring mantras of confession and contrition. Many an Ash Wednesday sermon has slipped Paul's second exchange with the Corinthians in alongside the prophet Joel's "Return to me . . . with weeping, and with mourning" (Joel 2:12), giving the impression that when Paul talks about reconciliation, he is pushing for conversion that is primarily about being sorry and professing belief.

There is certainly a sense in which this passage is part of Paul's attempt to have a "come to Jesus" with certain individuals in the Corinthian community, and maybe the church as a whole. Still, for Paul, reconciliation with God is intimately connected with community and vocation. This insight can draw the Ash Wednesday message out of the cramped, dimly lit rooms of our pre-Easter penitence (Matt. 6:6) and onto a path that is so much less about ourselves and more about rejoicing.

If you are preaching in a congregation where Paul is generally accepted as a great hero of the faith, then this passage can be useful in challenging baseline Christians—which probably includes most of us—to take our faith to another level. A useful sermonic twist can be found in the fact that when Paul says,

2 Corinthians 5:20b–6:10

Theological Perspective

heal and transform *us*, and this is perhaps the most arresting thing of all.

Reconciliation through Christ. Because of the mess that we have created for ourselves and each other, only God can reconcile us to himself, which is just what he has done in Jesus Christ. Through Christ's life, death, and resurrection, God has reconciled the world to himself, forgiving all our sins and offences (5:18–19; Rom. 5:10). The New Testament and the early church fathers do not specify the exact nature of Christ's defeat of sin and death on the cross. Paul himself employs several traditional ideas, including at least three different notions of Old Testament sacrifice. Here we read that although Jesus was sinless, he was "made sin" for us so that we might "become the righteousness of God" (v. 21).

Some interpreters, including Cyril of Alexandria, Augustine, and most of the Western medievals, take this to mean that Christ on the cross became an offering for sin, a view that also agrees with the language of sacrifice in the Greek Old Testament. Others, such as Gregory of Nazianzus, John Chrysostom, and the Reformers Martin Luther and John Calvin, believed that Christ was merely treated as a sinner.

However we may understand it, Christ has definitively dealt with sin and death on the cross, which was the chief purpose of his becoming human in the first place. Through Christ God gives us his own life so that we may be truly and completely reconciled with God. As Paul writes to the Romans, "Since we have been made righteous on the basis of faith (*ek pisteōs*), we have peace with God through our Lord Jesus Christ" (Rom. 5:1, my trans.).

Inward and Outward Righteousness. In 2 Corinthians 5, Paul illustrates in detail the righteousness that believers have received from Christ. Like Jesus in the Sermon on the Mount in Matthew's Gospel, Paul exhorts us to an inward righteousness. We are not to boast in external appearances—in the "face" that we present to the world (*en prosōpō*)—but "in the heart" (v. 12). We must view ourselves and all things in a new way, through the purposes of God as revealed in Christ, rather than "in the flesh" (v. 16). In a different metaphor, we have become a "new creation" in Christ; we have been reconciled, renewed, and transformed (v. 17; Gal. 6:15), which involves a complete revolution of the values that we have known. So we must now live, Paul says, not for ourselves but for Christ, who died and was raised for us (v. 15), so that we actually "become the righteousness of God" (v. 21).

Pastoral Perspective

Paul's magisterial expression of the gospel drama in 5:16–21 and a transition to a statement of how the truth of the gospel has formed Paul's behavior as a human and as an "ambassador for Christ" (5:20).

In chapter 5, verses 16–21 have been a primary focus and starting point for theological reflection upon themes such as the atonement and the relation between the identity of Christ and the work of Christ. However, for the purpose of our reflection upon Paul's etiquette and ethics, it is important to note that the theological material serves primarily as an "apology" for the apostle's behavior and motivation. Thus Paul can say, "For the love of Christ urges us on, because we are convinced that one has died for all" (5:14). He immediately goes on to say, "From now on, therefore, we regard no one from a human point of view" (5:16).

Today's text gives us insight into what it means to see people through the new lens of the reconciling action of God in Christ. We are provided with more than a new set of glasses; we are given the "confessions" of Paul's behavior toward his readers and toward all for whom he bears the message of this reconciliation.

This letter is addressed to those who already have made a confession of faith, members of the Corinthian congregation who presumably embody a new way of being and seeing in the world. They are the ones to whom Paul says, "We entreat you, . . . be reconciled to God . . ." and "We urge you also not to accept the grace of God in vain" (5:20; 6:1). As pastors, we recognize with Paul that being reconciled to God is a relationship one grows into through acts that can become habits, which in turn gradually delineate a character that is the touchstone of a life. It is a life that is "urged" on by the "love of Christ," but focused on the gift of the now, "the acceptable time" (6:2).

Rather than pursuing his argument by calling attention to how *his hearers* must change their behavior, Paul talks about how, in response to Christ's love, *his* behavior is being changed. He argues from personal example as an apostle and "ambassador for Christ." Paul sees no distinction between his personal life, on the one hand, and what is required of him in fulfilling his missionary calling, on the other. The latter has priority; the former is rooted in it. That logic is at the heart of what he is pleading with the Corinthians to grasp. Their lives with one another, their relation to Paul, their engagement with the world are always to incarnate and rehearse the invitation to "be reconciled to God."

Despite the humiliations, punishment, and hardships, this ministry extends the salvation God promised in Isaiah 49:8 (v. 2).

Lectors find this passage difficult to present intelligibly. The catalog of hardships used to describe Paul's ministry (vv. 4b–10) can sound like reading a phone book! Tackling the literary construction of each section makes it easier to understand and read aloud.

Verses 20b–21 conclude an earlier section in which the apostle speaks of himself (and his associates) as "ambassadors for Christ" (v. 20a) entrusted with the message of reconciliation. Verse 21 employs a poetic representation of Christ's death as the capstone of that appeal (cf. Rom. 8:3). The "he" and "him" references get confusing. If we supply the referent for those pronouns and move the relative clause forward, the verse reads, "God made Christ, who knew no sin, to be sin, so that in Christ we might become the righteousness of God." Because the lectionary selection shifts the rhetorical function of these verses from concluding a section to introducing one, the personal appeal (v. 20b) and the soteriological formula (v. 21) now point forward to 6:1–2.

Second Corinthians 6:1–2 drops the diplomatic metaphor and opens with a plural participle, "working together with," translated "As we work together with him" (NRSV), where the "him" likely refers back to the last word of 5:21, which is "God" in the translation. However, the Greek text has the phrase "in him," that is "in Christ," at the conclusion of the verse. Paul's participle is delightfully ambiguous. The apostolic ministry could be associated with God, with Christ, or even an unexpressed hope that the "you" of his audience will join in this task. Paul does consider the life of churches a powerful testimony to the gospel (see 1 Thess. 1:5–10).

Verse 5:21 spoke of reconciliation and "becoming the righteousness of God" as something the audience has received because they believe in Christ. Suddenly Paul's words introduce a note of warning. The church could receive God's grace worthlessly, to no effect. Rhetorically Paul uses the words of Isaiah 49:8 as though God were speaking directly to the community. The "now" of that "day of salvation" puts the practical problem of reconciliation within the Corinthian community in a new light. They stand once again at that juncture in which God's offer of salvation can be accepted or lost.

Since we are unaware of the situation in Corinth, the sharply defensive tone of 6:3–4a comes as a shock. Verses 3–4a call the audience back to the business at hand, criticism of Paul's ministry (see 2 Cor.

"We are ambassadors for Christ," he does not actually seem to be talking about the Corinthians—or, by analogy, any of us—yet. He seems to be talking primarily about himself, and maybe the high-commitment leaders who are working with him—people like Titus. These are people who are living for others in radical, often risky ways. If the Corinthians are included, it is only in the implied sense that they may yet become fully engaged in Paul's radical ministry of reconciliation. It may also help to be clear that Paul is not writing primarily about the hardships that come upon us in the course of everyday life. Rather, Paul is primarily talking about hardship that is *chosen* as part of one's daily ministry.

In congregations where many members live in relative comfort and security, the endurance that can come from having survived beatings, imprisonments, and civil disturbances is likely to seem hypothetical and external to daily life. The homiletical challenge in this context is to avoid both the liberal guilt sermon, in which we spend more time feeling bad than actually doing any good, and the loophole sermon, in which we explore high ideals and then hedge by saying that, of course, none of *us* may be called to ministries as extreme as Paul's.

For congregations where many members live with muggings, jail time, and "too much month at the end of the money," as I have heard many preachers say, the hardships Paul lists may be real and present in the life of the community. The challenge in this case may be to help listeners discern how the Spirit may be calling us to move, from a place of un-chosen endurance for the sake of survival, to chosen endurance for the sake of the gospel.

You may be preaching in a congregation that views Paul's theology and his self-proclaimed apostolic status as did the Corinthians themselves—at least as they are characterized in this letter. In this case, beneath the bravado of Paul's soaring rhetoric about his own good works, there is a more poignant story. It is the story of someone who founded a community, who believed unwaveringly in his unconventional calling and the sacrifices he made to get the community started, and who returned later only to find himself treated as a penniless, bedraggled impostor. The homiletical challenge in this case is to arrive at a second naiveté after we have acknowledged the underside of Paul's agenda-driven rhetoric. For example, when Paul uses the language of reconciliation with God, he is speaking just as much about reconciliation with himself and his way of doing things, as if the two are essentially identical. Even so, for Paul reconciliation with God and reconciliation

2 Corinthians 5:20b–6:10

Theological Perspective

It is amazing how deceptively easy God's extreme generosity can seem to be. One of the most common pitfalls of the Christian faith is to imagine that because Christ's grace is a free gift, it does not necessarily affect or change us in any deep way, or that one can be "saved" without being sanctified. How far such thoughts are from the gospel of Christ! Paul warns the Corinthians not to accept the grace of God in vain (see the similar shift from Romans 5 to Romans 6)—which is in fact not to accept it at all, but to fall away. As Paul writes elsewhere, we must make our conduct "worthy of the gospel of Christ" (Phil. 1:27), because "the only thing that counts is faith working through love" (Gal. 5:6).

Paul exhibits this new life in an account of his own ministry among the Corinthians (6:3–10). Opening his heart in great affection (6:11), he speaks of the ardor and love that his ministry has involved, both as a proof of the authenticity of his apostolate and as an example of God's righteousness. Paul speaks of the inward qualities of righteousness: knowledge, patience, kindness, holiness, love, truthful speech, and divine power (vv. 6–7a), which are the gifts of the Holy Spirit (Gal. 5:22–23), and of his outwardly righteous actions in the face of both positive and negative receptions of his ministry (vv. 7b–8a), some of which have caused him extreme social and physical suffering (vv. 4b–5). In a glorious crescendo, Paul describes the life, joy, and fruitfulness of Christ that he has known, despite repeated assaults on his person and ministry (vv. 8b–10). In other words, Paul himself has been *Christlike*, as every successful pastor should aspire to be.

Being reconciled with God is the agenda of the Christian life at all times, especially during Lent, as we undertake a concentrated period of penance and renewal. As in Paul's own case, reconciliation with God always causes us to have "a ministry of reconciliation" (5:18) toward others.

CHRISTOPHER A. BEELEY

Pastoral Perspective

Paul's rehearsal of his own experience and behavior is meant to encourage the Corinthians. It is in keeping with the rhetoric that the grace in the gospel message requires. Paul "entreats" his readers; he "urges" them. He does not order them or demand of them. There is a magisterial passionate quietness to the gospel that Paul honors with his rhetoric. In Romans 5:8 he says that God "proves his love for us." Another translation says that God "commends" his love. That dimension of the gospel leads Paul, again in Romans 12:1, to say, "I appeal to you." What understanding of God's love and grace is reflected in our choice of words?

Without making a claim or taking personal credit, Paul describes his experience and demeanor as an example to encourage and challenge his readers. He rehearses the myriad of adverse situations and conditions he has weathered as an apostle. Because these constituted the "now" of God's grace toward him, they produced endurance, patience, and perseverance, rather than bitterness, cynicism, or hostility to life.

In words that almost echo several of the Beatitudes (and incidentally reconcile the Matthean and Lukan versions), Paul sums up the vital paradox of reconciled living. It is a life of engagement and exchange. It is "sorrowful" but rejoices. It is poor but nonetheless enriches its companions in life—friend, stranger, and even foe. It does not hold back, so it does not hold on. It lives the larger mystery of the "matter of giving and receiving" (Phil. 4:15) that partakes of the security of God's grace.

What does our preaching sound like? What notes do we strike? What do our admonitions sound like? Somewhere Karl Barth says that the note of Christian ethics is not "you must," but, rather, "you may."

DWIGHT M. LUNDGREN

4:2; 5:11). The NRSV treats "great endurance" as part of the catalog but translates the preposition "in" which introduces the rest of the items in the list as "through." Other interpreters think that the phrase belongs with "in every way" so that the colon should come after "endurance." The catalog following (vv. 4b–10) divides into four sections (vv. 4b–5, 6–7a, 7b–8a, and 8b–10).

Verses 4b–5 (cf. 2 Cor. 11:23, 27) list a series of physical hardships and dangers. Some of them are represented in stories about Paul's missionary efforts in Acts (Acts 13:50; 14:19; 17:5; 18:12; 19:29). Others, such as sleeplessness and hunger, could refer to the hardships he endured by laboring to support himself while founding churches. The next series (vv. 6–7a) contains a generic list of virtues. However, these virtues are not Paul's personal achievement. Rather, they represent God's gift of the Spirit working in the apostle (see Gal. 5:22).

Verses 7b–8a open with a military metaphor (cf. 2 Cor. 10:3–5). The apostle stands armed with "weapons of righteousness" in both hands (v. 7b). Though the NRSV uses "with" to introduce the metaphor and "in" for items listed in verse 8a, Paul's Greek uses the same preposition "through" (*dia*) for the series. What are "weapons of righteousness"? Paul encourages Christians to employ their bodily members as "weapons of righteousness," not of injustice or sin, in Romans 6:13. So Paul appears to be referring to his conduct. Knowing that it conforms to God's will makes him indifferent to the "slings and arrows," the "honor and dishonor" he receives from human beings.

The final section (vv. 8b–10) picks up the distinction between the way in which outsiders look at the apostle and the reality of his ministry. The accusation against Paul is a serious one: that he sells a false teaching for personal gain. Notice how Paul disproves that charge. "Charlatans" seek public honor, wealth, and comfort, not the hardships of the apostle. He ends dramatically on the "personal gain" note. Paul has not enriched himself preaching the gospel. He is impoverished. With the eyes of faith, one can see that the apostle "possesses everything." What is the wealth of an apostle? The churches—even the troublesome Corinthians—his ministry has brought to Christ.

PHEME PERKINS

with others have always been intimately connected (Gal. 3:28).

You may end up choosing to preach Paul as a champion who is challenging a low-commitment church, or as a leader who has fallen prey to his own ego. You may end up preaching about the vocation of ambassador for Christ as having more to do with the proclamation of God's saving work in Jesus, or more to do with healing interpersonal conflict. Either way, Paul's invitation to the Corinthians stands as a theological challenge to churches everywhere. After all, this passage pretty much blows the prosperity gospel out of the water. Paul's call to be reconciled to God and serve as Christ's ambassadors flies in the face of the sermon that says, "If you trust in God and walk in your integrity, God will take you from the bottom of the corporate ladder to the top." Instead, it offers an invitation to ministry in which deprivation and disrepute are par for the course, and the fruits of one's labor may be unclear—at least in the short run.

It would seem illogical to accept Paul's invitation. It can seem foolish to speak of God's reconciling love or engage in ministries of reconciliation when the rewards are often mostly ingratitude and unpopularity. How can Paul invite the Corinthians into his mode of ministry with such excitement? How can he claim to have nothing, and yet possess everything? How can he be *always* rejoicing, even in the midst of his sorrow?

Perhaps only when we begin to plumb the depths of Paul's religious experience will it begin to make sense: "I regard everything as loss because of the surpassing value of knowing Christ Jesus my Lord. For his sake I have suffered the loss of all things, and I regard them as rubbish, in order that I may gain Christ and be found in him" (Phil. 3:8–9). Whether we share Paul's Christology or his particular brand of spirituality, a sermon that helps listeners to explore the deeper spiritual reality that buoys him up may be worth the trip to the pulpit.

CHRISTOPHER GRUNDY

Matthew 6:1-6, 16-21

"Beware of practicing your piety before others in order to be seen by them; for then you have no reward from your Father in heaven.

[2]"So whenever you give alms, do not sound a trumpet before you, as the hypocrites do in the synagogues and in the streets, so that they may be praised by others. Truly I tell you, they have received their reward. [3]But when you give alms, do not let your left hand know what your right hand is doing, [4]so that your alms may be done in secret; and your Father who sees in secret will reward you.

[5]"And whenever you pray, do not be like the hypocrites; for they love to stand and pray in the synagogues and at the street corners, so that they may be seen by others. Truly I tell you, they have received their reward. [6]But whenever you

Theological Perspective

It is probably inevitable that sacred texts tend to become for communities of belief so "sacred" (sacrosanct!) that they fail, in the end, to evoke the very qualities that made them sacred. Especially professionals (clergy, theologians, educators) often become inured to the capacity of Scripture profoundly to engage, question, *and shock*. Sometimes, when our guards are down, a passage of Scripture strikes us as being so *radical* that it astonishes the mind and shakes the foundations of religion and of life itself. This, for those with ears to hear, is such a passage.

Just consider what is being said here (1) about "alms" (charity, stewardship, and, by extension, the *practice* of faith in general): let it be modest, undemonstrative, almost anonymous—"done in secret"; (2) about "prayer": let it be quiet, private, brief—as direct as the Lord's Prayer; (3) about "fasting" (religious observance, discipleship): no ostentation please, no display—wash your face, comb your hair, and keep your attempts at piety to yourself!

Religion is such a noisy affair. Apparently it was that in Jesus' time too, but today we have raised the noise to unbelievable levels. This applies to virtually all the religions, not only Christianity, but Christianity, the conventional religion of the technologically advanced and competitive West, has surely outdone all the others. What would stewardship campaigns

Pastoral Perspective

Lent can be a dangerous time. People come to the church looking for discipline and a new way to live; they come to be challenged—prepared for the heartache and joy of the cross to come. The problem with Lent, however, is a direct outgrowth of this urgency: we contain the season to six weeks of doing good, rather than *building a Lent that becomes a life*. This, very simply, is what Jesus asks his disciples to do at this climax in the Sermon on the Mount. Do not be holy because it is what the world expects of you; rather, learn to live holy lives because a closer relationship to the God who sees in secret will be reward enough.

As a child, I toured the cathedrals of England with my parents. I was fascinated by the tin alms boxes built into the narthex walls. Dropping a coin into those boxes was a delight. The coin would drop, ring, and echo throughout the cavernous cathedral. People would look back to see what the noise was about. One day I watched an older woman, who looked to be on her daily visit to the church, stuff a paper bill in the box. The bill had far more value than my coin, but when dropped in the box, there was no great noise. It was a feather falling from the sky, and no one turned around. No one recognized the gift. Only God could hear it, I supposed.

In God's economy, reward has a different equation than the world's logic. The better our homeless

pray, go into your room and shut the door and pray to your Father who is in secret; and your Father who sees in secret will reward you. . . .

¹⁶"And whenever you fast, do not look dismal, like the hypocrites, for they disfigure their faces so as to show others that they are fasting. Truly I tell you, they have received their reward. ¹⁷But when you fast, put oil on your head and wash your face, ¹⁸so that your fasting may be seen not by others but by your Father who is in secret; and your Father who sees in secret will reward you.

¹⁹"Do not store up for yourselves treasures on earth, where moth and rust consume and where thieves break in and steal; ²⁰but store up for yourselves treasures in heaven, where neither moth nor rust consumes and where thieves do not break in and steal. ²¹For where your treasure is, there your heart will be also."

Exegetical Perspective

Today's Gospel lectionary text stands at the center of Jesus' Sermon on the Mount. After establishing the unique nature of the Lord's community (5:2–12), declaring its mission (5:13–16), and emphasizing God's righteousness as its defining character (5:17–20), a righteousness that surpasses even the law of love (5:21–48; Lev. 19:18), Jesus stresses the essence of genuine faith (6:1–34). As Jesus demonstrated in the wilderness (4:1–11), he now teaches others: the "righteousness [that] exceeds that of the scribes and Pharisees" (5:20) and is as "perfect" as that of God (5:48) is the righteousness that stems from trust in God in every facet of life. In this portion of the Sermon, Jesus shows how righteousness (6:1; the NRSV translates *dikaiosynēn* as "piety") relates to worship. There is often a stark difference between the appearance of faith and its reality, between idolatry disguised as religion and the charitable faithfulness that comes from a radical reliance on God. The essential challenge here is this: where or in whom do you place your trust?

Charade or Charity (vv. 1–4). In the first of three examples that draw the distinction between religious practices as disguised selfishness and acts of faith that please God (v. 1), Jesus turns to the topic of alms (vv. 2–4). Almsgiving has deep roots in Israel's life. The

Homiletical Perspective

Who are these people coming to worship on Ash Wednesday, who want ashes imposed on their foreheads, who want to be reminded of their utter mortality: "Remember you are dust, and to dust you shall return"? They are seriously committed. The church relies on their generous giving. When they tell you they pray for the church, they are not being hostile or flaunting piety; that is what they do. They are disciples not in word alone but as exemplars of a real and rigorous discipline. We count on them for leadership. Others may drop by Sunday morning, but these people chair committee meetings on Tuesday, attend Bible study Thursday, build houses with Habitat on Saturday, teach church school on Sunday; and on Ash Wednesday they come to worship.

So much do we count on these people—and so much admire them—that we may forget the particularly religious temptations that may lure particularly religious people away from God.

We do not have trouble imagining the temptations besetting unbelievers, and we certainly have no difficulty recognizing the temptations that appeal to sensualists. Unbelievers may be tempted, well, by unbelief, by the bland vision of life unable to make distinctions between good and bad, beautiful and ugly, wise and foolish, sublime and vulgar. Finally, unbelief is tempted by the final fruit of unbelief, which is despair.

Matthew 6:1-6, 16-21

Theological Perspective

and every-member canvasses be without the hoopla of strategic planning, grand meetings, charts, publicly displayed "thermometers," and the like? How would seminary and college financial drives fare without those well-publicized lists of givers, arranged according to extravagant categories of generosity reminiscent of the medieval practice of indulgences? As for prayer, how many of the most ardent pray-ers could pass the scriptural test of "keep it short" and as straightforward as the example Jesus gives?

While religious broadcasts and much-touted state prayer breakfasts may indeed occur behind closed doors (v. 6), what would they come to without the television cameras that pipe them or the news of them into every corner of the land? In a society that practically functions on the power of skillful and blatant advertising, a society of "display personalities," hype, and preoccupation with communications, the notion that religious observance should be modest, secret, and camouflaged seems ridiculous! In our increasingly pluralistic planetary context, the religions appear to be as much in competition with one another as are the big industries. Where would a religion be in such a world without regularly exhibiting and promoting its wares and accomplishments? "Holier Than Thou" has been raised to new levels of global competition in our religiously pluralistic context!

On the other hand, what have we lost—what, as Christians, are we missing—in this capitulation to display, publicity, and ostentation? According to this text, we are at least in danger of forfeiting the very essence of the faith Jesus advocates. In our desire to be "seen by others," "heard by others," and "praised by others," we lose touch with the very theological foundations of this faith: communion with and the glorification of God.

John Calvin, for all his alleged austerity and lack of humor, understood this danger very well. His motto, *soli Deo Gloria*, has often been taken to extremes, but the principle remains unshakable: in our worship and practice of the faith, any attitude or influence that causes us to think chiefly of ourselves and the impression we are creating detracts absolutely from the "chief end" of faith, which is to know and be known by God.

I have not forgotten the nugget of insight I received from my first university teacher of psychology. "Why," she asked, "do we so frequently 'forget' the names of persons to whom we are newly introduced? Answer: because we did not *hear* the names to begin with. When we were being introduced, we were

Pastoral Perspective

program, the more clients we gain. The more we focus on evangelism, the more people want to leave the church and start new churches. The better our volunteers become, the less the clergy are needed. Every time we give more of ourselves away, every time we do not ask for a reward, we find that a piece of our own broken lives has been mended. In order to build up, we must give out—"so that by his poverty you might become rich" (2 Cor. 8:9).

This kind of gutsy, risky, radical behavior is true of the Lord's Prayer as well. Though the lectionary jumps over the prayer, we will miss Matthew's meaning if we do the same. There are days when we mutter it with the masses in the sanctuary, pray beside our four-year-olds at bedtime, or speed through it as we taxi down a runway. Then there are days when it stops us cold, moments when we have to ask ourselves if we have offered God anything in return for that daily bread, or if, in seeking God's forgiveness in the last forty years, we have yet to forgive our own mother for the last twenty? To paraphrase James Forbes, when we begin to work on forgiving the sins of others, have we considered how many times we have gone to God's well of grace seeking forgiveness of our own?

There will be days when we offer the prayer with a strong voice in church, and days when we can only pray that there is another strong voice able to pray it for us, when we ourselves are unsure of what we believe. This is the great secret of corporate worship.

Much like the economy of giving, this prayer turns our lives inside out. It reminds us that the Christian life is about "we" and "us," not "me" and "I." It teaches that, as much as we ask God to give to us, we must be willing to give to God and one another in return. The hard truth is that the Lord's Prayer is just a starting place.

At the heart of all these caveats to give, fast, pray, and not hoard the things of this life, Jesus offers one universal truth: The world says, prepare for the worst. Secure your borders. Hoard your money and hide it under the bed. Avoid the stranger. Take care of your own and one day he or she will take care of you. Jesus says, prepare for the best. Live expansive lives. Give generously. Engage the stranger. Care for the needy. As country music singer George Strait reminds us, "The hearse doesn't come with a luggage rack." So Lent is not about feeling holy, but about lifelong commitments that help us hold on to the things that will sustain us.

people learned through their own poverty in slavery and thereafter the importance of gifts to the needy (Deut. 24:6–22). They knew that their origin and life were rooted in God's grace (Exod. 19:4; 20:2; Deut. 7:6–8; 26:5–11). Thus everyone who upheld the law made annual provision for the needy (Deut. 24:19–22) and contributed a full tithe (10 percent) of every third year's produce to their community's "food bank" so that no one—not even a sojourner—would go hungry (Deut. 14:28–29; Ruth 2:2). Care for the poor, the homeless, the fatherless, widows, orphans, and strangers in their midst is a hallmark of Israel's faith (Exod. 22:21–27; Isa. 58:7–8). Jesus insists that his followers continue the practice of giving alms, but Jesus warns his listeners of pride's perverting power. Almsgiving is not a competition for a prize of public esteem (v. 2b). Neither can it hide from God a heart's self-centeredness. Rather, the giving of alms ought to be motivated by genuine concern for the need of the "other," not by a longing for prestige and praise. Indeed, the Greek word translated as "alms" means literally "mercy" (*eleēmosynēn*, v. 3), and it is so important to Matthew that God's final judgment will be based on one's care for the needy (25:31–46). It is self-disinterested charity that pleases God (v. 4).

Pretense or Prayer (vv. 5–6). Prayer may also be corrupted into an act of self-promotion. Personal and corporate acts of prayer ought to be honest, humble expressions of faith that reflect both the disparity between God and humankind and God's desire to communicate personally as beneficent father to child. Regrettably, that which ought to be intimate communication with God to hear God's "voice" can be narcissistic orations extolling one's self-worth. Jesus warns his followers against such misuse of prayer and advises the faithful to pray in secret, where the personal dimension is inescapable and they are free of such temptation. The "room" (*tamieion*, v. 6) is literally a place where stewards keep their provisions, a private office or sanctum. The central issue here is not the kind of place but rather the disposition and focus of those who pray, as the next section makes clear (vv. 7–15). Righteous prayer is God- and community-centered, not self-centered, and it opens to God the most valued aspects of one's life (cf. Matt. 6:24).

Flaunting or Fasting (vv. 16–18). While fasts may require restraint from eating, the practice may feed the practitioner's pride and self-interest, a just "reward" (*misthon*, v. 16; also in 6:1) for anyone who

Sensualists are tempted by the very world of the senses they adore. Their temptations are as evanescent as feelings themselves—now here, now there, never staying put. Those who worship at the altar of "How I feel about it" must always be on the move.

If the temptation of unbelief is not believing in much of anything at all, if the temptation of sensuality is being adrift in the world of the senses, the temptation that comes with being religious people is to substitute religion for God. We mistake our road map for our destination. We turn the means into an end. God gives us the good gifts of almsgiving, prayer, and fasting so that we may draw near to God, and we anxiously transform them into performances.

To those who take their religious discipline seriously, Jesus offers an irreverent parody. Christians may not attend worship on Ash Wednesday expecting a comedy, but Jesus nevertheless barges into our solemn proceedings cracking jokes, spinning wild exaggerations, and demonstrating how to preach to people who take their religion seriously.

Here come the almsgivers into the courts of God, and they are accompanied by the brass section of the symphony. They give a few dollars to this cause, and the trumpets fanfare; a few dollars more to another cause, and the trombones blare a salute. Everyone watching says, "My, they are generous!" Jesus says, "Truly I tell you, they have received their reward."

Over there stand people praying. You know they are praying because everyone in the room knows their praying. People blocks away may hear their praying, and the words go on and on and on, always stretching for one more crumb of emotion and another shred of humility. People listening to them may say, "My, my, they certainly pray well." Jesus says, "Truly I tell you, they have received their reward."

Here come people fasting. You know they are fasting by their gaunt faces and eyes crazed from lack of sugar. They have mussed their hair and torn their garments because you have to do something to show people you are fasting. The problem with fasting is that no one can see what you are not doing. What is the good of that? So these folks stagger forward on Ash Wednesday, hoping for a formidable smudge of ashes to let everyone know they have been to worship. Onlookers will declare, "Oh, they certainly are religious!" Jesus declares, "Truly I tell you, they have received their reward."

Jesus parodies our religious behavior and does so in the most hilarious way, in the hope that we may be caught laughing at ourselves. We need to laugh at

Matthew 6:1-6, 16-21

Theological Perspective

too interested in the impression we ourselves were giving to listen to the names of these others."

What Jesus is teaching his disciples here is the same *kind* of lesson. The very purpose of almsgiving, prayer, and religious observance is to deliver us from the debilitating and exorbitant *self*-consciousness that dogs our lives. "Salvation" for self-absorbed creatures like us means finally—or at least intermittently!—to lose our precious selves in the other: the other who is the recipient of our alms, the Other who hears our prayers, the others who wonder what our religion really comes to if not just more public promotion and self-display! In most of the days and hours of our lives, we are burdened with the thought of how we are being perceived: What will *they* think? When faith is true, Jesus affirms, we find ourselves—at least here and there, now and then—graciously liberated *from* the burden of self, liberated *for* the other. That is faith's essence!

Does this mean that our piety, prayer, and religious observance must *never* have the character of public address or notice? Is the life of discipleship so very internalized that there should be no occasion for open witness, no concern to make a statement, no search for words and deeds that can convey to those outside the confines of our "closets" (v. 6, KJV) the consequence of belief for life in this world? Of course not! This is not the only scriptural text that speaks of these matters.

A little later on in this Gospel, Jesus tells his disciples, "What I say to you in the dark, tell in the light; and what you hear whispered, proclaim from the housetops" (Matt. 10:27). However, this text contains a critique of "religion" that is permanently relevant, especially for Christians who consider themselves true and devout believers. For the propensity to self-promotion—and the hypocrisy that usually accompanies it!—is never stronger than when one's "natural" egocentricity is bolstered by the false assurance that one is the very darling of divinity.

That is why, in this scripture, Jesus' dismissal of ostentatious religion is so unrelenting. It is yet another expression of a theme that runs throughout the prophetic traditions of both biblical testaments: human pride (*superbia/hybris*) is always questionable and pathetic, but never so much so as when it is backed by religious presumption. True faith drives to modesty, not self-promotion.

DOUGLAS JOHN HALL

Pastoral Perspective

Self-proclaimed agnostic A. J. Jacobs wrote a book titled *The Year of Living Biblically*.[1] He was determined to live by the Bible's rules and disciplines, literally, in modern-day New York City. Other than his wife's coming close to kicking him out of their little apartment for his occasionally self-righteous behavior, what Jacobs found is that sometimes the life of faith is (or can be) about cognitive dissonance. *Put yourself in a practice in order to learn it.*

At the conclusion of the book, what Jacobs found was not radical conversion but rather genuine openness of faith, a direct result of the practices and disciplines he had introduced into his life. The truth is that Jacobs lived religion very publicly as an experiment, but real change happened in the quiet of his heart as he learned to pray where only God could hear.

The danger in Lent is that we go through the motions of discipline without learning how to live Lent. The danger is that we do everything "right" but never ask ourselves how "right" behavior changes how we live our lives. We act one way, but we never ask ourselves: Do we give to get? Are we raising our children for heaven or Harvard? Do we pray because we are supposed to or because it gives us hope?

It is a dangerous thing, to lead a holy life, to ask the same questions of ourselves that Jesus asks of his disciples. In these moments of utter truth and honesty, we are assured that, like the feather falling or the paper bill in the cathedral, in the humble act of a faceless person or our quiet prayer when no one else can hear, God does in fact hear us. That is good news.

MARYETTA ANSCHUTZ

---

1. A. J. Jacobs, *The Year of Living Biblically* (New York: Simon & Schuster, 2008).

hungers for notice and prestige among the religiously observant. The ancient ritual of fasting always included prayer and was typically associated with mourning and penance (Judg. 20:26; 1 Sam. 7:6; 2 Sam. 12:15–23; Ezra 8:21; Neh. 9:1; Dan. 9:3; Zech. 7:5). It was an act of personal and corporate humbling. Humility and repentance, though, were not always the driving forces behind fasts. Indeed, as in prayer and the giving of alms, the observance of fasting is susceptible to sin's perverting power and may stand under God's judgment (Isa. 58:1–9; Jer. 14:11–12). Thus the prophets call the people to "sanctify" their fasts (Joel 1:14: 2:15), for the pretense of humility and repentance is unbefitting the people of God. This is also Jesus' point.

Ironically, some render their faces unrecognizable (*aphanizousin ta prosōpa autōn*, v. 16; NRSV "they disfigure their faces") in order to be recognized (*hopōs phanōsin tois anthrōpois*, v. 16). Such exaggerated fasting—like ostentatious charity and affected prayer—is a self-interested distortion of an essential religious observance that is common in God's covenant community. The driving value behind such an act is self-centeredness, which seeks to "be praised" (v. 2) and "seen" (1, 5, 16). Righteous fasting, however, is not a show; it is a profound act of worshipful self-control aimed at solidarity with God and neighbor.

Fool's Gold or Lasting Treasure (vv. 19–21). After exposing three ways that self-worship may masquerade as fervent religious piety, Jesus turns more explicitly to the topic of trusts and commitments (vv. 17–34) by focusing on treasures (vv. 19–21). Over against earthly "treasures" that may be seen and praised by people and lost (including the wealth and security that facilitates ostentatious almsgiving or public displays of religious zeal aimed at promoting one's social status), Jesus asserts that there is a true treasure that is immeasurable and endures forever. It is a treasure valued by God, seen and praised in heaven. It is the treasure of trust in God. The contrast could scarcely be stronger: Jesus is challenging his listeners to confront what and whom they worship. Are they worshiping themselves, something else, or the living God? Righteousness—expressed as piety—is more an inner disposition of the heart than any outward religious observance (v. 33; Jer. 31:33–34).

ROBERT A. BRYANT

ourselves. Our selves are the problem. These selves we are—these fragile, tragic, needy selves that can scarcely imagine that we are dust.

We selves, we long for God and longing for God takes time, takes years and decades, and we selves grow weary. It is so easy to back away from that precipitous edge of longing for God and settle into being satisfied with being religious.

We long to speak to God, see God's face, and sometimes in prayer we almost do. Always out of reach. It is sometimes so tempting to give up on the conversation with God and blandly parrot prayers. We know that there is a difference between praying and praying.

We have this hunger for God. Augustine knew about it, praying, "O Lord, you made us for yourself, and our hearts are restless until they rest in you."[1]

That heart hunger, the restlessness, that fasting, point to and symbolize the hunger only God can fill. We can grow so accustomed to the hunger—so enchanted with our own fasting—that we forget there is One who means to fill us. God gladly will give us God's own self.

Jesus invites us to laugh at ourselves, so that we may finally lose ourselves and find God's own self. Of each of these three groups whom Jesus parodies—the almsgivers sounding their horns, the pray-ers piling up words, the fasters in ashen misery—Jesus says, "Truly I tell you, they have received their reward." They have been recognized for their religiosity.

So also, Jesus promises, rewards will come to those who give themselves away in almsgiving, who shed themselves in prayer, and who empty themselves to be filled by God's goodness. Only a few verses before in this Sermon on the Mount, Jesus tells his disciples, "Blessed are those who hunger . . . for they will be filled." Blessed are those who hunger for God; God will indeed fill them. That is what the church of Jesus Christ celebrates in holy Lent.

PATRICK J. WILLSON

---

1. Augustine, *Confessions*, I.1, trans. R. S. Pine-Coffin (New York: Penguin Books, 1961), 21.

Genesis 2:15-17; 3:1-7

2:15The LORD God took the man and put him in the garden of Eden to till it and keep it. 16And the LORD God commanded the man, "You may freely eat of every tree of the garden; 17but of the tree of the knowledge of good and evil you shall not eat, for in the day that you eat of it you shall die." . . .

3:1Now the serpent was more crafty than any other wild animal that the LORD God had made. He said to the woman, "Did God say, 'You shall not eat from any tree in the garden'?" 2The woman said to the serpent, "We may eat of the fruit of the trees in the garden; 3but God said, 'You shall not eat of the fruit of the tree that is in the middle of the garden, nor shall you touch it, or you shall die.'" 4But the serpent said to the woman, "You will not die; 5for God knows that when you eat of it your eyes will be opened, and you will be like God, knowing good and evil." 6So when the woman saw that the tree was good for food, and that it was a delight to the eyes, and that the tree was to be desired to make one wise, she took of its fruit and ate; and she also gave some to her husband, who was with her, and he ate. 7Then the eyes of both were opened, and they knew that they were naked; and they sewed fig leaves together and made loincloths for themselves.

Theological Perspective

Perhaps more than any other part of the Old Testament, this narrative presents an overlap between the biblical text and the layered meanings it has accrued in the history of biblical interpretation. The passages assigned are from two scenes in a fourfold narrative: God's placement of Adam in the garden (Gen. 2:4b–10, 15–17); the formation of a "helper" for Adam (Gen. 2:18–25); the disruption of the garden by the temptation by the serpent (Gen. 3:1–7); and the judgment and expulsion of the man and woman from the garden (Gen. 3:8–24).

The "tree of the knowledge of good and evil" occurs in both placement and temptation scenes, and this connection sharpens the contrast between them. Precisely what the tree signifies is difficult to determine, given that it is not mentioned elsewhere in Scripture and there are few correlates in other ancient literature. However, its significance is incidental to the main point of the narrative, which is to speak to questions concerning human vocation, permission, prohibition, and punishment as these relate to God.

The tree's appearance in the first and third scenes underscores the connection between obedience to God and human flourishing. When God's command is broken, human flourishing is compromised. As a result, the (1) trust, (2) obedience, and (3) intimacy

Pastoral Perspective

The season of Lent in Year A of the lectionary opens with the narrative theological artistry of Genesis 2–3. The story is often interpreted theologically in terms of temptation, "fall," sin, and death. Read from a pastoral perspective, the story serves to narrate aspects of human brokenness that every pastor deals with professionally and all of us deal with personally.

The story begins with a programmatic statement of our human vocation and its limits. Humankind is placed in the garden of God's creation to "till and keep it." The Creator who gives life also gives meaning and purpose to life. We are called to serve as caretakers in God's good creation—stewards of a world we did not make and can receive only as a gift held in trust.

In the exercise of our vocation the Creator gives us remarkable freedom. "You may freely eat of every tree of the garden"—every tree, that is, except one. The freedom God ordains is expansive but not boundless. There are limits to the exercise of our creaturely freedom. "But of the tree of the knowledge of good and evil you shall not eat, for in the day that you eat of it you shall die" (2:17).

What is the "tree of the knowledge of good and evil," and what becomes of the threat that "in the day that you eat of it you shall die"? In the first serious theological conversation in Scripture, the woman is asked by the "crafty" (or "subtle") serpent, "Did God

Exegetical Perspective

In J's creation account (2:15), God creates the man, *ha adam,* and places him in the garden as its care-taker. The garden is named Eden, which means "delight," "luxury," or "dainty," giving rise to the sense of Eden as paradise, a place that contains "every tree that is pleasant to the sight and good for food" (2:9). The man is "placed" in the garden to "till," literally, to serve and to keep it. The word used to describe God's placement of the man is *nuha,* which means "rest, settle down, and remain," suggesting that the garden is a place of repose for God's creation—the man belongs there.

What comes next is a command (2:16–17). It begins with what is permissible and then gives the exception, namely, he may "freely eat of every tree of the garden; but of the tree of the knowledge of good and evil you shall not eat." This is one of the two named trees, the other being the tree of life (2:9). The exception limits the first part of the command. If you may not eat from this tree, then you may not eat freely of "every tree of the garden." This freedom from the very start has limits, and the crossing of these boundaries has consequences: "for in the day that you eat of it you shall die" (2:17). With this command the idea of death enters Eden.

With this same command in mind, we move to Genesis 3:1–7, where the serpent is introduced.

Homiletical Perspective

When we hear the familiar story of Adam and Eve in the garden of Eden, we are tempted to think of this as the story of sin or even of original sin. Hearing the story at the start of Lent makes the connection to sin all the stronger in our minds. A careful reading of this passage, however, reveals a surprise. The word "sin" never appears, and there are no synonyms for sin, either in this passage or elsewhere in Genesis 2–3. The rest of chapter 3 does not talk about either "punishment" or "the fall."

By starting with 2:15, we begin to get a different sense of this story's subject matter. This verse reads "The Lord God took the man and put him in the garden of Eden to till it and keep it." This is not just a statement of location, in which God moves the first human from one place to another. Clearly the verse concentrates on the purpose for the human: to till and keep this garden. Human purpose is the focus of this crucial statement; and human purpose forms the backdrop for the rest of what happens in the story of the garden of Eden.

The Purpose of Creation. The majestic chapter 1 and the intimate beginning to chapter 2 both tell much about creation, showing God's character and God's priorities through divine initiative and action. So far, however, we have not been told what God's purpose

Genesis 2:15-17; 3:1-7

Theological Perspective

surrounding God's relation to humans, described in the first scene, are broken in the third by: (1) temptation, here portrayed as the erosion of trust (Gen. 3:5), (2) disobedience, here portrayed as wayward desire (Gen. 3:6), and (3) estrangement, here portrayed as alienation not only from God but between the humans themselves (Gen. 3:7).

Because of the power emanating from the narrative alone, contemporary biblical scholars often dispense with the doctrines historically associated with this text in favor of the narrative's plain sense, its thematic resonances in the rest of Scripture, and its possible originating context.[1] However, the narrative's mythic structure and the anthropological claims inherent in the unfolding drama also permit the theological readings that have developed in the history of Christian thought. Indeed, the shape of the narrative itself warrants these later theological readings, which have a claim on us as valid as any other reading that might be generated.

For early Christian interpreters, the narrative represented a "prequel" to the "sequel" of Christ's saving incarnation. Emboldened by the connection drawn between Adam and Christ in the Pauline literature (Rom. 5:12–21; 1 Cor. 15:21–22), Irenaeus (c. 202) drew a parallel between the shape of Christ's redemption as depicted in the Gospels and its anticipation in this narrative from Genesis: not only did Christ's "obedience" correct Adam's "disobedience," but there are other thematic connections between the "tree" by which Adam and Eve fall and the "tree" of the cross by which Christ brings life.

The "serpent" in the original narrative not only identifies human sinfulness, but also anticipates Christ's defeat of Satan in the wilderness, as the deviousness of the "serpent" is overcome by "the harmlessness of the dove."[2] Viewed in this way, the narrative in Genesis depicts a state of innocence that humanity lost but has now recovered through an even greater dispensation by God.

Patristic commentators, in particular Augustine (354–430), developed from this narrative a theological anthropology that explored will, desire, sin, the origin of evil, and grace. God forbade eating the tree of the knowledge of good and evil, not because the "tree was itself bad, but for the sake of commending a pure and simple obedience, which is the great

1. Walter Brueggemann, *Genesis* (Atlanta: John Knox Press, 1982), 40–54.
2. Rowan A. Greer, *Broken Lights and Mended Lives: Theology and Common Life in the Early Church* (University Park: Pennsylvania State University Press, 1986), 28–29.

Pastoral Perspective

[really] say, 'You shall not eat from *any* tree in the garden?'" (3:1). Yes, that is part of what God has said, but the way the question is asked is intended to make the command of God appear arbitrary and unreasonable. In her response the woman goes beyond what God has actually said. "We may eat of the fruit of the trees in the garden; but God said, 'You shall not eat of the fruit of the tree that is in the middle of the garden, *nor shall you touch it*, or you shall die'" (3:2–3, emphasis added). With that "harmless" bit of exaggeration the serpent strikes. "You will not die. . . . Your eyes will be opened, and you will be like God, knowing good and evil" (3:4–5).

What does it mean to have our eyes opened so as to be like God in knowing "good and evil"? Some have argued that the knowledge of "good and evil" here is not a matter of ethical discernment. It is the desire to make *ourselves* the arbiters of good and evil, assuming for ourselves the role of God. The serpent subtly insinuates that it is out of jealousy that God seeks to limit our freedom and forbid our enlightenment. Over against such divine tyranny, you owe it to yourself to resist. Think for yourself! Act for yourself! Do not let anyone, even God, define *for you* what is good and evil.

Just as the fruit of the tree in the story appears "good . . . a delight . . . and to be desired to make one wise" (3:6), so the freedom to determine for ourselves "good and evil" appears enlightened and liberating. Pastors know better than most where this self-determined "good and evil" leads. Too often it leads not to wisdom and authentic liberation, but to messy divorces, to shouting matches between parents and children, to willful disregard of the needs and feelings of others, to chaos in the church, and to degradation of the environment. One does not have to look far to find examples of how our life together is undermined by the refusal to accept the gracious limits of God's truly liberating grace.

Read from a pastoral perspective, the story lends itself to an exploration of the role of human freedom within limits set by the wisdom and grace of God. The limits God sets to our freedom are not a matter of enforcing conformity to arbitrary rules. The *torah* of God is intended for the well-being of the "image-bearing creature" to whom God has entrusted the stewardship of creation. The flourishing of human life in a good and bountiful, but limited, creation requires both freedom and appropriate constraints on the exercise of that freedom.

We continually rebel against such constraints. We turn the expansive freedom that is ours in Christ into

Exegetical Perspective

Throughout this familiar passage, the serpent is one of the "wild animals" (3:1) created by God. Like the woman and man, the serpent is a part of God's creation. He is distinguished from the other animals because he is more "crafty" (3:1) than the other animals God made. The word for crafty, 'arum, resembles the word that appears in the previous verse (2:25) that describes the nakedness, 'arumim, of the woman and man. The similarities in sound and spelling connect the nakedness of the woman and man to the craftiness of the serpent.

The text is not surprised by the serpent's ability to speak. Rather, having established the woman and man as naked and the serpent as crafty, it moves right to the dialogue. The serpent initiates the dialogue in verse 1 with a question: "Did God say, 'You shall not eat from any tree in the garden'?" The question of the serpent is directed to the woman and is about one of God's commands. The serpent's question returns us to limits in the narrative, such as those established by God in 2:16–17.

Although the woman was not created at the time of the instructions (she first appears in 2:22), she provides an answer to the serpent (3:2). The woman's response is a revision of the command; it includes additional information: ". . . nor shall you touch it" (3:3). It is not apparent where the additional information comes from. Did Adam add this when he passed along the command to Eve, or did Eve add it herself? Was the addition intentional or accidental?

The serpent's question is intentional. It is an invitation to question the command of God. The serpent responds with authority, first denying the consequences for trespassing the boundaries established by God and then redirecting Eve by offering an intriguing possibility. Eating of the tree will result in their eyes being "opened." Then they will be "like God, knowing good and evil" (3:5). The opening of the eyes connotes a kind of seeing that is beyond the physical ability that they already possess. It connotes perception and understanding, as does the word for knowing, yada'. This word covers a range of possibilities within the realm of experience, including cognitive knowing and sexual experience. Thus the promise of the serpent could mean they will understand the difference between good and bad and/or mean that they will have a broad range of experiences, both good and bad.

In verse 6 the senses dominate. The woman sees, tastes, and touches. In the previous verse she heard. Eve sees and makes three observations about the tree: (1) it is good for food, (2) it is a delight to the eyes,

Homiletical Perspective

was in the creation. Here we learn for the first time. God made humans in order to till and keep the garden, and perhaps even someday the whole earth.

This purpose is amazing. So many other creation stories of the ancient world depict the creation of humanity as a by-product, an accident, or even a mistake of the gods. Genesis makes it clear that God *intended* to create people, not for a whim but for a reason. Herein lies the possibility for human dignity, because we are designed and fashioned with something in God's mind for us to do. The statement of purpose may well surprise us in another way.

In the modern world, we often think of humanity as the apex of creation, as the goal toward which God was working. We emphasize some other part of the story, such as the assertion in Genesis 1:26 that God gives humanity a responsibility for (or dominion over) all the rest of creation or the command in Genesis 1:28 that humans be fruitful and multiply. Sometimes our science or our psychological theories elevate us humans to the highest point of creation, assuring us that we are God's greatest creation. Genesis 2:15 explains things differently. We humans have a God-given purpose. We were not created for ourselves; we were created in order to till and keep the garden.

Tilling and Keeping. The phrase "till and keep" may be familiar (or perhaps we still remember the "to dress it and to keep it" of the KJV), but this is not the best translation of these two Hebrew verbs. The first, usually rendered "to till," is 'abad, more often translated as "to serve" or "to be a slave of." The second, "to keep," is shamar, which means "to preserve" or "to protect."

Clearly, being a servant or slave of the earth moves us from the center of God's creation. God makes us in order to take care of the earth itself, and to look to its interests instead of our own. We work the ground and work with the earth, and already we know that our brows will sweat in this labor. Not only does God give us purpose, but reason for labor—even hard labor. The garden is no small responsibility, and we are not to be lords of leisure over the garden, but to be its servants and slaves. We are responsible for the garden, now and into the future, so we must preserve and protect it.

Mission and Distraction. Care of the garden, God's earth, and all God's creation is more than a purpose. It is our mission. Living as servants of creation fulfills God's intention for us and lives up to the reasons why we were created in the first place. Caring for

Genesis 2:15-17; 3:1-7

Theological Perspective

virtue of the rational creature set under the Creator as his Lord."[3]

When this commandment was broken, sin and death entered the world, warping humanity's original desires for God so that humans exalted the creature over the Creator, which is the present source of all human misery. Although tempted by the serpent, the point of origin for evil in the world was the human will itself, in particular the free decision to transgress God's will. However, on account of this primal sin in the garden, humanity is enslaved to the powers of sin and death, which can be overcome only by the grace of God in Christ Jesus.

Viewed in this way, the Genesis narrative offers a stark depiction of the advent of a sin-sick humanity looking for love in all the wrong places, helplessly yearning for health and wholeness. Augustine uses this perspective to emphasize the utter gratuity of God's forgiveness and grace. Precisely because the decision to disobey God began in the will, it is the will that must be healed, and this healing can happen only through love. The will is not only the seat of all obedience, but the root of all love, and love alone can heal us—first, God's transformative love working conversion in us, and then, our love returning to God, which is the end of all human striving and the source of true fulfillment.

Throughout history, commentators have taken issue with one or more of the doctrines Augustine developed in this interpretation, particularly his negative view of human desires and human potential. However, his vision of a sinful and fractured humanity, its radical need for grace, and its healing through love presents a reading of the Genesis narrative that has had remarkable staying power, not the least because it offers a vision that resonates with the Genesis narrative itself. His emphasis on forgiveness, grace, and love are important counterbalances to the portrayal of mistrust, disobedience, and alienation depicted in the Genesis narrative.

Particularly in a season of repentance like Lent, both the narrative and its interpretation are important to keep in mind. Together they depict the shape of our redemption as it is found in the paschal mystery, a journey that does not bring us back to the garden but from death to life through the power of the resurrection.

WILLIAM JOSEPH DANAHER JR.

Pastoral Perspective

ideologies of freedom that keep self at the center, with predictable results. Teenagers "push the limits" as a way of discovering their own identity, only to find themselves losing their deepest identity in the crowd. In the name of "free-market deregulation" politicians overturn limits intended to restrain inequity in the financial markets, leaving the markets in turmoil. Some of us who grew up in the '60s remember the almost giddy sense of liberation in throwing off limits of social restraint. Sadder and wiser now, we look back and wonder "what were we smoking" that made us think that untrammeled freedom would lead to the Age of Aquarius with none of the unintended consequences that bedevil us today. It clearly did not!

What we conveniently forget, or mightily repress, is the subtlety of sin this passage narrates. Where there is no realistic acknowledgment of our immense capacity for self-centeredness and our ability to rationalize whatever we desire, the gracious limits of God that restrain our sinfulness can be treated as if they did not greatly matter. The result is not human flourishing but the brokenness of life that issues in a flood of sin and death throughout creation.

Despite the brokenness that results from our defiance of the good and gracious limits that make for the flourishing of life in community, there is already in the story a note of gospel that echoes throughout Scripture. As the narrative unfolds, God does not carry out the threatened sentence of death "in the day that you eat of it" (2:17). In God's sovereign freedom, God responds to human disobedience, not with the full weight of judgment, but with unexpected mercy. "Where sin increased, grace abounded all the more" (Rom. 5:20). "If the Son makes you free, you will be free indeed" (John 8:36). "Only do not use your freedom as an opportunity for self-indulgence, but through love become slaves to one another" (Gal. 5:13).

ALLEN C. MCSWEEN JR.

---

3. Augustine, *The City of God*, in *A Select Library of the Nicene and Post-Nicene Fathers of the Christian Church*, ed. Philip Schaff (Grand Rapids: Eerdmans, 1993), 2:256.

and (3) it has the potential to give wisdom. Eve's desire to know fuels her decision to take the fruit and go outside of the boundary established by God. Only after she takes the fruit do we learn of Adam's location—he is with her, and he eats as well.

Now the eyes of the two are opened (v. 7), and their first "knowing" or experience is of their nakedness. With the second occurrence of the word 'arumim, the reader is reminded of their state of nakedness before the appearance of the serpent. Now they "know" (yada') that they are naked. Their physical state does not change, but their awareness and their experience of that state change, and with that knowing comes shame. Now their nakedness is something to be covered.

J's narrative emphasizes relationships—relationships between God and the creation, and relationships among the created order. In this narrative, Eve and Adam both eat the fruit. Similarly, God addresses Adam first in verse 9, but the two humans are treated as a unit, in that they both have to answer to God and they both experience consequences for their decision. The humans are in community, but Eve's desire for knowledge/experience is key in the narrative, as she is the one addressed by the serpent, even though Adam is with her. Why does the serpent address Eve?

One possible answer comes from ancient Near Eastern myths like the epic of Gilgamesh, which suggests that Eve's presence is essential in the narrative. In Gilgamesh, the female character takes Enkidu away from the animals for a sexual liaison. The sexual encounter with the woman forever separates Enkidu from the animals. He is now fully human. With that context, it can be argued that the serpent speaks to the woman because she is culturally associated with the characteristics that separate humans from animals: wisdom and desire. Thus the woman's desire to know is central as well.

JUDY FENTRESS-WILLIAMS

creation means doing God's work in the world. This is no pastime, nor is it a strategy for us to feel good about ourselves. God sends us into the garden because the garden needs service and preservation, and we are God's instrument for caring for creation.

Even though this mission is compelling and should be all-consuming, we share a human propensity for distraction. In the midst of caring for the garden, we will inevitably find fruit, and we will think that the fruit looks good to eat. We will meet interesting animals and strike up conversations with them to pass the time of day. We will use our God-given intellect to rationalize doing things that are not part of our mission, or we will just settle for doing as others tell us, when we need to concentrate on God's mission in the world.

Even our nakedness becomes distracting, and we know full well that wardrobes to cover our nakedness can also distract us. Human excuses for avoiding our mission may start in the garden, but we experience a full range of such excuses today that distract us from our mission. For people of faith, distraction may prove more frequently troublesome than temptation. We think of ourselves for a while, or we focus more on other humans than on God's mission. With just a glance away, we start to wander from God's mission.

Through Lent. This story of mission and distraction begins our journey through Lent. For the church, it is a time of penitence, of recognizing the ways we have let ourselves be distracted from the mission that God intends for us. God's mission has not changed, and in the aftermath of our stumbling, God still calls us back to the right path. God calls us back every day, and every Lent.

JON L. BERQUIST

Psalm 32

¹Happy are those whose transgression is forgiven,
 whose sin is covered.
²Happy are those to whom the Lord imputes no iniquity,
 and in whose spirit there is no deceit.

³While I kept silence, my body wasted away
 through my groaning all day long.
⁴For day and night your hand was heavy upon me;
 my strength was dried up as by the heat of summer. *Selah*

⁵Then I acknowledged my sin to you,
 and I did not hide my iniquity;
 I said, "I will confess my transgressions to the Lord,"
 and you forgave the guilt of my sin. *Selah*

⁶Therefore let all who are faithful
 offer prayer to you;

Theological Perspective

The divine forgiveness of sin was central to the proclamation of the early church (e.g., Acts 10:43), presumably because it was a crucial aspect of Jesus' own ministry (e.g., Luke 7:47). Martin Luther's momentous discovery of the liberating truth of justification by grace through faith arose from his search for a God who would forgive his sins; indeed, he experienced this grace of forgiveness largely through his reading of Paul, who in his Letter to the Romans cited this psalm (Rom. 4:6–8). The 1999 "Joint Declaration on the Doctrine of Justification" by the Roman Catholic and Lutheran communions celebrates and embodies this universal Christian theme.

Beyond these important considerations, perhaps this psalm may serve to remind the church that our song of praise rejoicing in divine forgiveness and restoration is sung first in a Jewish key. The church did not create the language of divine forgiveness. This psalm and its glorious truths are sung in today's synagogues as well as in churches. This is a fact worthy of remembrance and consideration. Indeed, precisely at the point at which Paul cites this psalm in Romans, he proceeds to ask rhetorically, "Is this blessedness [of iniquities forgiven], then, pronounced only on the circumcised, or also on the uncircumcised?" (Rom. 4:9). The surprise is not that God's people Israel are the recipients of forgiveness, but that we who were

Pastoral Perspective

The liturgical season of Lent is typically a time set aside for penitence. On Ash Wednesday, Christians are invited to enter a period of self-examination, repentance, prayer, fasting, and self-denial. We are called to use these forty days as a time of particular reflection on our sins, the ways that we separate ourselves from God and from one another. Thus, it is easy to characterize Lent as the somber, solemn period of the church year.

The fact that Psalm 32 is appointed for the first Sunday of Lent suggests that there seems to be more to this season than solemnity. The title of the psalm in the NRSV is telling: "The Joy of Forgiveness." The psalmist offers a "before and after" picture of his experience of confessing his sins to God. "While I kept silence, my body wasted away through my groaning all day long. For day and night your hand was heavy upon me; my strength was dried up as by the heat of summer," he laments (vv. 3–4). Then he acknowledges his sins to God: "I will confess my transgressions to the Lord," (v. 5). In doing so, he comes to know God's forgiveness, an experience of relief and joy: "Happy are those whose transgression is forgiven, whose sin is covered. Happy are those to whom the Lord imputes no iniquity, and in whose spirit there is no deceit" (vv. 1–2).

What are the implications of this psalm for us as Christians, particularly at the beginning of Lent?

at a time of distress, the rush of mighty waters
  shall not reach them.
⁷You are a hiding place for me;
  you preserve me from trouble;
  you surround me with glad cries of deliverance.   *Selah*

⁸I will instruct you and teach you the way you should go;
  I will counsel you with my eye upon you.
⁹Do not be like a horse or a mule, without understanding,
  whose temper must be curbed with bit and bridle,
  else it will not stay near you.

¹⁰Many are the torments of the wicked,
  but steadfast love surrounds those who trust in the LORD.
¹¹Be glad in the LORD and rejoice, O righteous,
  and shout for joy, all you upright in heart.

Exegetical Perspective

One of the seven Penitential Psalms of the Christian tradition (also Pss. 6; 38; 51; 102; 130; 143), Psalm 32 is actually an individual thanksgiving psalm that celebrates the forgiveness of sins and spiritual renewal. The complex psalm shows characteristics of the wisdom tradition, including beatitudes (vv. 1–2) and proverbial statements (vv. 9–10). Verses 3–7 address God in prayer, while verses 8–9 are either the didactic instructions of a wisdom teacher or a divine oracle that counsels good judgment.

Some commentators hold that Psalm 32 teaches that unacknowledged sin results in physical sickness while righteousness leads to good health. The psalm alludes to illness (vv. 3–4), but its emphasis rests on the debilitating spiritual effects of guilt and the relief offered by repentance. Uneven meter, textual problems, and odd vocabulary complicate the exegesis of this psalm. Nevertheless, Psalm 32 remains an effective poem of thanksgiving for God's forgiveness and graciousness.

The superscript (not included above) identifies the psalm as a *maskil* attributed to David. Scholars do not have a clear understanding of this musical form or the function of the word *selah*, which follows verses 4, 5, and 7 (but not 9). The date of the canonical psalm is most likely postexilic.

Homiletical Perspective

Psalm 32 begins with words of joy and thanksgiving, as the psalmist exclaims the relief of forgiveness granted. God has withheld punishment and has cleared him of all iniquity, the writer declares. Thus his spirit, or his soul, has been renewed (vv. 1–2). Clearly, this is cause for gratitude and celebration.

The psalmist transitions in verse 3, however, and reflects back on the strain of life lived under the sway of sin. This painful recollection gives the psalm a penitential tone, which fits well with the mood of the First Sunday in Lent. Indeed it is here, in the midst of this meditation on the power of sin, that a preacher might find compelling material for homiletical exploration, because these verses foreshadow the long Lenten journey that precedes the joy of redemption.

In verses 3 and 4, the psalmist gives an aching description of the physical and emotional turmoil he endured before finally confessing his sin and seeking God's forgiveness. He tells of his body "wasting away" under the constant weight of sin and its very tangible consequences. Commentaries note that these verses probably describe an illness that was believed to have been a divine punishment for wrongdoing; alternatively, they may simply use a metaphor of physical distress to describe the inner torment of sin.[1]

1. C. S. Rodd, "Psalms," in *The Oxford Bible Commentary*, ed. John Barton and John Muddiman (Oxford: Oxford University Press, 2001), 377.

Psalm 32

Theological Perspective

"aliens from the commonwealth of Israel" are as well, having been included through Jesus Christ (Eph. 2:12–13).

Divine forgiveness of human sin is predicated upon our open and frank confession (v. 5), but even the act of confession is in reality a response to the convicting presence of God: "day and night your hand was heavy upon me" (v. 4). In many Christian traditions, the Wesleyan in particular, this convicting presence is identified by the phrase *prevenient grace*. This grace is none other than the Holy Spirit. Hence, the human being is never the initiator of the forgiveness transaction; rather, God's gracious presence comes before (*pre-veni*) even the first gleamings of our desire for mercy, prompting and luring us to seek the Holy One. Again, we learn all of this first from Jewish teaching and practice.

Indeed, the profoundly communal nature of Jewish life, particularly in the synagogue, ensures that divine forgiveness is no private affair. Rather, God's mercy toward us sinners is the root reality empowering Israel, and the church, to become the faithful people of God. Accordingly, the Lord's Prayer is a deeply Jewish prayer throughout, and certainly no less so when we are instructed to ask God to "forgive us our debts, as we also have forgiven our debtors" (Matt. 6:12). In this Matthean version of the teaching, couched within the Sermon on the Mount, the intertwining of divine and human forgiveness is the only aspect of the prayer upon which Jesus immediately expounds further: "For if you forgive others their trespasses, your heavenly Father will also forgive you; but if you do not forgive others, neither will your Father forgive your trespasses" (6:14). This is a teaching about the initiative of divine grace in the forgiveness of sins, which also underscores the utter necessity that this grace become shared, amplified, reflected in the community of God's people. This, as Dietrich Bonhoeffer would remind us, is no cheap grace.

For all of this common ground shared by Judaism and Christianity regarding the matter of divine forgiveness, the Gospels themselves identify a crucial parting of the ways. Early in his ministry, Jesus announces authoritatively to a paralytic, "Son, your sins are forgiven" (Mark 2:5). The response of some of the scribes, observing nearby, is "Why does this fellow speak in this way? It is blasphemy! Who can forgive sins but God alone?" (2:7). Jesus' healing of the man is then offered as a sign "that the Son of Man has authority on earth to forgive sins" (2:10), with the result that onlookers "were all amazed and

Pastoral Perspective

Psalm 32 emphasizes the power of sin, but also the promise of joy. It lays out the journey of the forty days that are ahead. We are called to acknowledge our sins, to confess them to God, to receive God's forgiveness, and finally to experience the joy and relief that comes from that new life. Each of these steps deserves further reflection.

A deeper look at Psalm 32 raises interesting questions about who is most affected when we acknowledge and confess our sins. The psalmist experiences God's forgiveness only after he has acknowledged his sins. Presumably God knows our sins before we confess them. Jesus says that God knows us so intimately that "Even the hairs of your head are all counted" (Luke 12:7). According to the psalmist, then, the purpose of our confession is in large part for our sake.

So often, our failure to acknowledge our sins to God is a result of our failure to acknowledge them to ourselves. This denial may be rooted in shame, defiance, or perhaps just plain thoughtlessness. The self-reflection that happens during Lent allows us to "come clean" to God *and* to ourselves. As C. S. Lewis noted, "A man who admits no guilt can accept no forgiveness."[1] In other words, while God's forgiveness is not contingent on our confession, it seems that our experience of it is.

The psalmist does not say anything about the actual process of acknowledging his sins to God. One gets the impression that he simply made the decision to "fess up" and then all was well. In reality, the process of coming to terms with the ways that we have not loved God with our whole heart and not loved our neighbors as ourselves can be very difficult. It means admitting things about ourselves that we would rather ignore. Sometimes it also includes the difficult tasks of putting aside our pride, seeking the forgiveness of other individuals, and, in some cases, seeking the forgiveness of our community. As Christian writer Anne Lamott says, "Though theologians insist that grace is freely given, the truth is that sometimes you pay for it through the nose."[2]

Though the psalmist does not describe his process of confession, he does give us insight into his experience of receiving God's forgiveness. Acknowledging his sins before God brings the psalmist great relief. Likewise for us as Christians, the process of "full disclosure" that begins when we share our sins with God has the effect of taking the ownership of them away from us. We release our sins to God; in turn, as we

---

1. C. S. Lewis, *The Problem of Pain* (New York: Macmillan, 1962), 122.
2. Anne Lamott, *Plan B: Further Thoughts on Faith* (New York: Penguin Group, 2005), 81.

Exegetical Perspective

The psalm opens with a proclamation of the happiness of one whom God has pardoned: "Happy is the forgiven-of-transgression, the covered-of-sin" (my trans.). The psalm uses a comprehensive vocabulary for sin—"transgression" (*peša'*) and "iniquity" (*'awon*) in NRSV—with a matching range of verbs for confession (*hiphil* stems of *yd'* and *ydh*) and forgiveness (*ns'*, *ksh*, and *l' ḥšb*) in verses 1–2 and 5. In verses 1–2 there is a rhetorical progression from being the recipient of forgiveness (v. 1), to the Lord not imputing iniquity (v. 2), to being one "in whose spirit there is no deceit" (*remiyyah*) (v. 2). The passive constructions in verses 1–2 emphasize the divine initiative in pardoning sin. Indeed, the psalm suggests that righteousness is achieved by divine forgiveness rather than a lack of human sin. Romans 4:7–8 quotes verses 1–2 to advance the argument of righteousness apart from works. Luther thus identified Psalm 32 as one of the "Pauline" psalms of divine grace (also Pss. 51, 130, and 143).

More positive statements about human moral agency are seen in references to the "faithful" (*ḥsyd*, v. 6), "those who trust in the LORD" (*hbwḥ byhwh*, v. 10), and the "righteous" (*ḥṣdyqym*) and "upright in heart" (*kl-yšry-lb*) at the psalm's conclusion (v. 11).

Verses 3–4 constitute a lament over affliction attributed to the "hand" of the Lord. The NRSV translates verse 3a as "my body wasted away," but a more literal rendering is "my bones were worn out." The aching of bones as a metaphor for the distress of the soul as well as the body is seen in Psalms 6:2; 38:3; and 51:8. The "hand" of the Lord in verse 4 may refer to physical sickness, as in Psalm 38:2 and Mesopotamian sources, in which the oppressive "hand" of a god refers to plague or disease.

The "hand" of God in Psalm 32, however, may refer primarily to the psychological and spiritual effects of unacknowledged sins (cf. Ps. 39:10). By way of contrast, a clear plea for physical healing, with extensive descriptions of bodily ailments and pains, is seen in Psalm 38. The verbal root for "groaning" (*ša'agâ*) or "anguished roaring" (NJPS) in verse 3c also appears in Psalms 22:1 and 38:8 and Job 3:24.

The second half of verse 4 remains obscure, but most translations refer to the loss of vigor or strength as in the withering heat of summer. Most important, the fundamental cause of this suffering is the psalmist's silence (v. 3) or refusal to confess his sins.

The psalmist offers his sincere and repetitious confession in verse 5: "I acknowledged my sin to you," "I did not hide ['cover'] my iniquity," and "I will confess my transgressions to the LORD." The penitent

Homiletical Perspective

Regardless of the psalmist's intent, to modern ears the latter explanation is more palpable. We no longer understand disease as a punishment for sin, but sin nonetheless remains a disabling force in our lives. These two verses offer a stark snapshot of that reality. Unchecked, sin can indeed eat away at our souls, leaving us feeling weak and deformed, less than our true selves. Sin can also confuse our minds and darken our hearts. At times, sin can even have physical consequences; one obvious example is substance abuse, an addiction to drugs or alcohol that poisons the body along with the soul.

In fact, looking at the dynamics of addiction may help us understand the power of sin in our lives. Many forms of addiction represent initially healthy impulses taken to extremes. For example, an addiction to money or success may begin with the honest desire to provide for one's family. An addiction to power or fame may begin with the desire to share one's gifts and talents to make a difference in the world. A natural longing for love and intimacy may mutate into a propensity for unhealthy sexual behavior or inappropriate relationships.

In each of these cases, the addiction results from a lack of temperance and moderation. Too much of a good thing becomes a bad thing, and risks trapping us in patterns of denial and justification from which it is hard to escape. It becomes all too easy to keep silent, as the psalmist says (v. 3), and to learn to live with the consequences. As described above, the imagery of verses 3–4 of this psalm suggests that sin operates in much the same way as addiction, with a similar capacity to enslave us. Indeed, this is echoed throughout the biblical narrative. The classic example comes, of course, in Paul's Letter to the Romans: "I do not understand my own actions. For I do not do what I want, but I do the very thing I hate. . . . In fact it is no longer I that do it, but sin that dwells within me" (Rom. 7:15, 17).

With its harrowing depiction of the power of sin, Psalm 32 offers many homiletical avenues to consider. A preacher may choose to focus on the nature of sin, perhaps exploring the parallels with addictive behavior. A preacher may wish to build a bridge between this psalm and Paul's theology of sin, raising questions about free will, God's grace, and the role of confession. One might also look to the writing of Augustine of Hippo for further illustrations. In books 7 and 8 of his *Confessions*, Augustine offers an unparalleled meditation on the power of sin and the potential of conversion as it relates to his own spiritual journey. Specifically, Augustine describes his

Psalm 32

Theological Perspective

glorified God" (2:12). Divine forgiveness of our sins, then, redounds to the glory of God.

Further, God has shared this authority with the Son of Man (Matt. 28:18), who in turn bestows it upon his community, the *ekklēsia* (Matt. 16:18–19). If it is true that God alone can forgive sins, the flip side is that there is scant evidence that God is interested in doing anything alone. Divine forgiveness offers the possibility and promise of a human community that is grounded in God's mercy, a fellowship in which forgiveness is the rule practiced throughout. The church is that community, built upon the foundation of Jesus Christ (1 Cor. 3:11; cf. Eph. 2:19–22).

One question persists, however. If Psalm 32 rejoices in God's forgiveness of sins for those who "confess [their] transgressions to the LORD" (v. 5), long before and quite apart from the appearing of Jesus Christ, what role, if any, does Jesus actually play in the process of divine forgiveness? Increasingly, Pauline scholarship is moving away from a solely Lutheran-Augustinian notion of divine forgiveness through faith in Jesus Christ, suggesting that one must constantly remember Paul's own self-understanding as the apostle to the Gentiles.[1] In the preaching of Jesus as the crucified and resurrected Christ, God's mercies toward Israel have been extended to the nations. Thus, after his long and tortured wrestling with the question of the people Israel in relation to the increasingly Gentile church of his own time (Rom. 9–11), Paul's conclusion is that "Christ has become a servant of the circumcised on behalf of the truth of God in order that he might confirm the promises given to the patriarchs, and in order that the Gentiles might glorify God for his mercy" (15:8–9).

A dual purpose for Jesus Christ is clearly suggested in this pregnant Pauline claim, and the purpose God has fulfilled among the Gentiles is our experience of divine mercy—an experience known, according to Psalm 32, in the Jewish tradition.

MICHAEL LODAHL

Pastoral Perspective

receive God's forgiveness, we are released from the burden of them.

Furthermore, according to Psalm 32, knowing God's forgiveness brings joy as well as relief. This aspect of Lent is often overlooked. In our Lenten focus on the process of self-examination and repentance, we fail to remember the outcome of that process: the joy of knowing the forgiveness and grace of God that free us from all of our sins.

Last year during Lent, I discovered a Lenten hymn that, like Psalm 32, reminds us of this larger message of the joy that is the gospel in the season of Lent. It is buried in the *1982 Hymnal* of the Episcopal Church in the midst of the Lenten hymns I have heard all my life. Neither I nor our organist had ever heard it. The words and tunes of the other hymns in its section are slow and somber. This tune of this hymn, however, is a French carol, and it is almost cheerful. One verse says:

> To bow the head in sackcloth and in ashes,
> or rend the soul, such grief is not Lent's goal;
> but to be led to where God's glory flashes, his beauty
>   to come near.
> Make clear, make clear, make clear where truth and
>   light appear. [3]

As we begin this season of self-examination and repentance, this is our prayer: that God will "make clear where truth and light appear." In coming to know and confess the ways that we separate ourselves from God and one another, we will also come to know the joy of forgiveness that comes from God alone. Then, as the psalmist says, we will "Be glad in the LORD and rejoice . . . and shout for joy" (v. 11).

ANDREA WIGODSKY

---

1. The classic and generative essay in this regard remains Krister Stendahl's "Paul and the Introspective Conscience of the West," in *Paul among Jews and Gentiles* (Philadelphia: Fortress Press, 1976).

3. Percy Dearmer, "Now Quit Your Care," *The Hymnal 1982* (New York: Church Publishing Inc., 1985), 145.

Exegetical Perspective

conveys the necessity of repentance as well as the mercy of God. The psalmist no longer tries to "cover" his sin (v. 5), but relief came when God "covered" it (v. 1). Proverbs 28:13 similarly attests to the significance of confession: "No one who conceals transgressions will prosper, but one who confesses and forsakes them will obtain mercy."

Verses 6–7 offer assurance of God's help to those who ask. The onset of distress is described poetically as "the rush of mighty waters" (see Pss. 18:16; 69:15; Isa. 8:7; 17:12–13), from which God protects the faithful as a "shelter" or "hiding place" (cf. Pss. 27:5; 31:20; 61:4; 91:1). The prayer concludes, "You surround me with glad cries of deliverance," with vocabulary shared by the psalm's closing (vv. 10–11).

In verses 8–9 the speaker offers instruction to the individual listener in the form of wisdom sayings or by quoting a divine oracle: "I will instruct you and teach you the way you should go" (v. 8). The phrase "with my eye upon you" (v. 8) suggests that the speaker is God, as Psalm 33:18 notes that the "eye of the Lord" is upon those who fear God. The reference to "the way you should go" in verse 8 leads nicely to the simile of a horse or mule requiring a "bit and bridle" in the next verse. The text of verse 9 is difficult, but the meaning that the hearer is not to be like a senseless horse or stubborn mule that is unable to follow instruction without a physical constraint is clear enough. Compare Proverbs 26:3: "A whip for the horse, a bridle for the donkey, and a rod for the back of fools" who will not accept instruction.

Characteristic of wisdom or proverbial literature, the antithetical parallelism of verse 10 contrasts the fate of the righteous and wicked: "Many are the torments of the wicked, but steadfast love [ḥesed] surrounds those who trust in the LORD." Verse 11 concludes the psalm with a joyful call to worship on the part of the "righteous" and the "upright in heart," a poetic pair favored by the psalmist (e.g., Pss. 64:10; 94:15; 97:11).

NEAL H. WALLS

Homiletical Perspective

agonizing struggle to overcome unhealthy sexual desires and to seek the freedom of new life in Christ.[2]

In addition, a preacher may choose to offer some hope and encouragement by exploring how to break free from the bondage of sin. The second half of Psalm 32 provides such encouragement, as the psalmist describes his release from sin's grasp. After seemingly coming to the end of his strength and resources, the psalmist finally confesses his sin to God; he bares his scarred soul, and God forgives him (vv. 4–5). The story does not end there, however. In the verses that follow, the writer implies an ongoing dependence on God. He points to the importance of prayer in the midst of distress, and he describes God as a refuge in times of trouble (vv. 6–7, 10).

This emphasizes that we are never entirely free from sin; we still have moments of weakness, and we are always surrounded by temptations. Overcoming sin is a lifelong effort. To paraphrase Martin Luther, we are at the same time saved by God's grace and still subject to sin; to use the parlance of addiction, we are always recovering sinners. Psalm 32 describes this dual reality with rich language and imagery. The psalmist embraces the joy of forgiveness but remains painfully aware of the power of sin, which had so recently infected his body and soul. This honest admission makes this a wonderful text to guide us as we embark on the journey of Lent, a journey of self-reflection, confession, and, ultimately, joyful redemption.

JOHN D. ROHRS

---

2. Augustine, *Confessions*, trans. Henry Chadwick (Oxford: Oxford University Press, 1991).

Romans 5:12-19

¹²Therefore, just as sin came into the world through one man, and death came through sin, and so death spread to all because all have sinned—¹³sin was indeed in the world before the law, but sin is not reckoned when there is no law. ¹⁴Yet death exercised dominion from Adam to Moses, even over those whose sins were not like the transgression of Adam, who is a type of the one who was to come.

¹⁵But the free gift is not like the trespass. For if the many died through the one man's trespass, much more surely have the grace of God and the free gift in the grace of the one man, Jesus Christ, abounded for the many. ¹⁶And the free gift is not like the effect of the one man's sin. For the judgment following one trespass brought condemnation, but the free gift following many trespasses brings justification. ¹⁷If, because of the one man's trespass, death exercised dominion through that one, much more surely will those who receive the abundance of grace and the free gift of righteousness exercise dominion in life through the one man, Jesus Christ.

¹⁸Therefore just as one man's trespass led to condemnation for all, so one man's act of righteousness leads to justification and life for all. ¹⁹For just as by the one man's disobedience the many were made sinners, so by the one man's obedience the many will be made righteous.

Theological Perspective

In the second half of Romans 5, Paul gives a powerful reflection on the magnitude of sin and death, and on the even greater abundance of God's grace in Christ.

The Kingdom of Sin and Death. In order to communicate the grace and power of Christ, Paul is concerned to identify the nature and the extent of the human dilemma. Human beings are beset with sin and death in a way that runs both deeper and wider than we might expect.

Having already established that "all have sinned and fall short of the glory of God" (3:23; taken up again at 5:12), Paul is now concerned to give an account of the full scope and effects of sin. His main point is that sin was introduced and somehow passed on to the entire human race by Adam, our first parent (v. 12), so that we were all "made sinners" as a result of Adam's disobedience (v. 19). That is, sin is the result of the first sin of Adam, *and* it is committed anew by each person; it is something that we both cause and suffer at the same time. This is Paul's chief statement of what Augustine appropriately called "original sin," the sin that lies at our origins and affects us all. The problem of sin, in other words, is much larger than ourselves and our immediate environment. Although it may threaten certain

Pastoral Perspective

Consideration of this lectionary passage is initially encumbered in two ways that need to be noted. First and foremost, it is an excerpt of the longer argument that begins with 3:21, Paul's presentation of the saving righteousness of God that has been accomplished and offered in the gospel drama of Jesus Christ. Chapter 5 is structured around three "therefores" at verses 1, 12, and 18. All three initiate what we can call arguments of contrast in which Paul's main point is announced by the word "but," verses 11, 15, and 20b. Our passage contains the latter two of these arguments of contrast. It should be noted that in the last of these sections, the apostle's main assertion occurs in the verse that follows the designated end of the lectionary passage, verse 20b, "but where sin increased, grace abounded all the more."

Secondly, keeping this framework in mind is particularly important because of the apparent focus on Adam and Christ (or, as Barth taught us to think, Christ and Adam). Specifically, it is important not to get sidetracked into discussions of how to read the book of Genesis or lost in the nuances of a doctrine and history of the fall. Obviously Paul is working from and utilizing an understanding of this, but it is the background for, not the fundamental assumption for, another point he wishes to make.

Exegetical Perspective

Paul argued that all humanity, even God's people who had the Mosaic law, were trapped by sin (Rom. 3:20, 23). Christ's death reconciled a sinful humanity to its creator (Rom. 3:24–26; 5:8–11). By dying for sinners, Christ exceeded the example of a noble self-sacrifice, the exchanging of one life to save another. It was assumed that the recipient of such a gift had to merit it (5:7), perhaps as a dear friend, a child or spouse, or a person necessary to society.

From that perspective, it seems pointless for the best person to die while sinners live. However, the story of Christ is not that of a human martyr dying for his people. It is the decisive act in the social, ethical, and religious development of the human race.

To make this point, Paul shifts to the figure of Adam in Genesis 2–3. Christ will undo the consequences of Adam's sin (5:12–21). Today's lectionary reading omits the final two verses (vv. 20–21), an explanation of the relationship between the law and grace. That explanation ties the section together by bringing the Christ event forward as God's response to the sins credited against humanity through the law (cf. vv. 13–14 and 20–21). Dropping the final verses creates a theological short circuit. It ends the story with sinful humanity declared righteous. The long history of sinfulness has been canceled. That is not

Homiletical Perspective

This passage about Adam and Jesus is both foundational for centuries of theological reflection on sin and grace and, in some churches at least, a bit difficult to preach. It is at the same time rich, dense, and occasionally convoluted, offering both a significant challenge (unless you are just pulling sound bites) and a wealth of possibilities.

If you are preaching or teaching in a congregation where the story of Eve, Adam, and the fall are generally accepted and intelligible as a means of understanding the human condition, then this passage may provide you with a number of ready themes. There is the exploration of original sin, perhaps recast in contemporary terminology. There is grace as free gift, not able to be earned by repentance or bribe-offering. What might it mean to live a life in which death does not exercise dominion?

More likely, though, your context is one in which the story of Eden is considered quaint at best. More likely, you will be preaching to a room where Paul's assertion that sin and death spread to humanity through a combination of (Eve and) Adam's rebellion and their subsequent procreation is considered to be odd and irrelevant, if it is understood at all. This passage also raises the parallel, though more delicate, question of Paul's claim that "one man's act

Romans 5:12-19

Theological Perspective

optimisms, at a deeper level there is a sober consolation in this realization of the scope of our sin.

If sin is original to our condition and therefore unavoidable, it is also deeper and more insidious than we may think. By turning against God, our neighbor, and ourselves, we bring about the ruin of all that is good in the world: the consequence of sin is death in the fullest sense of the word. Sin and death are not mere annoyances or particular flaws of human life; they are the central and ultimately destructive problem of our existence, in which human society is catastrophically trapped. Sin is not itself a creature or a form of life, a thing that God has made, but it is the disposition of our wills to oppose God and our own well-being, and therefore lies within our very hearts.

For this reason, many theologians—most notably Augustine in his polemic against the Manichees—have understood sin in terms of the so-called classical doctrine of evil as the privation of the good. Contrary to the popular adage (To err is human, to forgive divine), to sin is *not* what it means to be human, because sin is opposed to the goodness of God's creation, and death, its consequence, is the ultimate enemy (1 Cor. 15:26). Sin is not the result of some flaw in God or in creation. Rather, existence as we know it is marred in an unnatural way. Sin is very much *not* what God intends for us; it represents our worst selves and the worst of human society. Sin is dehumanization and antilife.

For all of these reasons, sin and death hold sway over us, dominating and controlling us, like a tyrannical dictator (3:9; 5:13–14, 17, 21; 6:12, 14), enslaving us under their power (6:16f.); yet the domination of sin, which Paul describes in such active language, is that of an opposition to God and creation, not that of a creature, an existing thing (sin is always parasitic). The dominion of sin results, finally, in our condemnation before the holy God, a result that is tragic but not altogether surprising, given the goodness of God and the wickedness of the human condition.

In Romans 5:12–19, Paul is trying to impress on us that Christ did not die and rise again merely to provide a bit of needed improvement, or to fill some gaps in our life. He died to save us from a mortal disease that lies at the core of our being, affecting all of our thoughts, words, and deeds, and corrupting human society as a whole. The truth about sin is a central part of the gospel, because it illuminates our real condition before God and, consequently, the depth of mercy, love, and forgiveness that God offers us in Christ. Paul's message here resembles Jesus' telling the

Pastoral Perspective

Aware of the context of our text, we may turn to the pastorally rich and spiritually astonishing assertion that is the heart of the chapter and flows from the initial announcement in Romans 3:21–31, namely, the saving righteousness of God in Jesus Christ, offered to and appropriated by faith alone. In the first eleven verses of chapter 5, Paul focuses on the magisterial and sovereign love of God. In today's passage, love is envisioned as an act of identity with and responsibility for our humanity that is offered to each one of us.

Many years ago I was caught in a dramatic snowstorm that closed the airport and stranded me for two days. Not only were flights cancelled, but one could not even leave the terminal for comfort and sanctuary in nearby hotels. I watched the monitors as flight after flight was cancelled. As our plight deepened, frustration grew. People wandered the airport and, in some cases, in and out of restaurants and bars. The late afternoon quickly darkened into the evening; the howl of the wind outside deepened and was easily heard inside.

Suddenly the doors of the main concourse seemed to blow open, and several people wearing the white helmets and insignia of the Red Cross entered. They were soon followed by others with cots and blankets. From down the concourse I could see a large banner being unfurled with a giant Red Cross logo and the epigram "Help Found Here." What struck me were not only the resources they had come to provide but also the effort they had made to reach us, to be with us and share our plight.

Beyond empathy, beyond sympathy, there is identification manifested in acts of personal accountability for others' lives. Somehow, even at the human level, we are left feeling that this is too good to be true, too amazing to be believable. Such identification can be dangerously contagious! I do think that as all these strangers and wanderers made their way to the "cross," they became more respectful of each other's plight. What each received became a collective gift.

The English words "ecstasy" and "ecstatic" are derived from the Greek word that roughly means "being outside oneself." Ecstatic experiences are ones in which we are drawn outside ourselves—and that does not mean out of our minds! We tend to limit our use of the term to refer to very emotional experiences; but ecstasy really should be reserved for all those moments when we are carried outside of and beyond ourselves, especially when we are bound to the lives of others in acts of exchange and identification.

"But the free gift is not like the trespass" (5:15). We may or may not be able to envision a collective

where the story of salvation concludes, however. There is yet another movement in the symphony, "eternal life through Jesus Christ our Lord" (v. 21).

The first section (vv. 12–14) describes the domination of sin and death inaugurated by Adam. It opens like a piece of music that introduces the first half of a theme and then breaks off. One would expect the "just as sin through one man" in verse 12 to be followed immediately by a "grace of the one man, Jesus Christ." Instead, a digression on the rule of sin and death since Adam follows in verses 12b–14. Our theme returns in verse 15 with a series of Adam–Christ parallels (vv. 15–19). The comparisons employ a familiar pattern of argument: what is true in a lesser case must be even truer in the greater or more important one. However, when the comparison is between punishment for sin and salvation, "the free gift is not like the trespass" (v. 15). A series of comparisons contrasts the initial trespass with the abundance of grace.

English translation necessarily obscures the formal parallelism between clauses that runs through these verses. Something of the drum beat created by the repetition of the same terms remains in English. One can follow the notes "sin, trespass, death" and "free gift, grace, life" through the passage. Similarly the two representative figures, the two instances of "one man," Adam and Christ, are placed over against "all" or "the many."

Often readers spontaneously drop the article "the" in the NRSV "the many" (vv. 15, 19). That verbal mistake obscures the argument, since numerically "many" is less than "all." So one might assume that the grace and free gift of salvation actually extends to fewer persons than "all" who suffered sin and death. However, Paul's logic is to compare the impact of these two representative figures in the human story, the "one person," namely, Adam, and then Christ, with the rest of humankind. The parallelism between verses 18 and 19 shows that "the many" is equivalent to "all."

By the fourth century CE most readers were not concerned with how the Mosaic law fit into this story of a sinful humanity, Paul's problem (vv. 13–14, 20). They concluded that all humans inherited a sinfulness from Adam, "original sin," based on verse 12. The NRSV translates "because all have sinned," leaving open the question as to whether sin is inherited.

During a children's sermon, the pastor at my church asked the second-graders, "Everybody does things that are wrong or makes mistakes, right?" Most agreed, but there were a few holdouts. Since Paul speaks of those whose "sins were not like the

of righteousness leads to justification and life for all" (v. 18). If it is unclear to your congregation how (Eve and) Adam's "trespass" affects us all, then it may also be unclear how Jesus' "act of righteousness" is passed on to us as well. You could just press on, of course, assuming the validity of Paul's framework and hoping that the gathered saints at your church will go along with you. The sounder route, however, is probably to do the spade work of wrestling with these ancient perspectives yourself before trying to discern with a congregation what the Spirit might be saying to us today. Keep in mind that not everything the preacher needs to write is something the congregation needs to hear.

The "theological perspective" entry on these pages may be a good place to start your preparation, leading you into conversation with historical figures who have wrestled with original sin. That kind of abstract discourse, or even Paul's discussion of Adam and Jesus, probably is *not* the place to begin your sermon, however. You will need to find some real-life situations where this discourse connects with the lives of your listeners if you want them to go slogging through Paul's rhetoric about Adam and Jesus with you. What is your own sense of original sin—even if you would use different language? What in your life, and the lives of your congregants, corresponds to that sense? What might illustrate how we *all* fall short of the glory of God (Rom. 3:23) and are in need of grace far beyond our individual failings? Where do such things as, say, original blessing[1] or total depravity[2] find examples in our lives, if at all?

After you have spent some time exploring Paul's perspective and its connections to our contemporary worldviews, it may be easier to find themes for preaching. How are Jesus and his acts of righteousness connected to our lives as people living into our baptism? What difference do Jesus' acts of righteousness make when we, like Jesus in the lectionary Gospel passage, face the temptation to be God? When we face intractable systems of injustice? Just how *does* the grace of God in Jesus come down to us today? The passage provides an opportunity to explore aspects of our connection to Jesus that are often assumed or ignored.

If this passage by itself still leaves you stumped or uninspired, then the other lectionary readings for the

1. See Matthew Fox, *Original Blessing: A Primer in Creation Spirituality Presented in Four Paths, Twenty-Six Themes, and Two Questions* (New York: Penguin, 2000).

2. See John Calvin, *Institutes of the Christian Religion*, ed. John T. McNeill, trans. Ford Lewis Battles, LCC (Philadelphia: Westminster Press, 1960), book 2, chapter 1.

Romans 5:12-19

Theological Perspective

Pharisees that he did not come to save the righteous, but those who realize that they are sinners in need of God's mercy (Matt. 9:12–13); or the "Jesus prayer," popular in Eastern Christianity: "Lord Jesus Christ, Son of God, Savior, have mercy on me, a sinner!"

The Kingdom of Grace. Paul's deep analysis of sin and death serves to fill out the gospel of Christ crucified and risen. In the same way that our sin and mortality have their determinative origin in "the one man" Adam, so too our life and salvation are uniquely rooted in "the one man" Christ (v. 15). This is the idea that frames the passage structurally (vv. 12, 21). Adam is thus a "type" of Christ, by both similarity and contrast. While Paul urges us to appreciate the gravity of the human condition, he is even more concerned to impress on us that Christ's power and saving grace exceed the separation and destruction of sin and death. Whereas sin and death have dominion over fallen creation, those who are in Christ live instead under the dominion of grace through a life of righteousness (v. 21; see 6:22). Either way, we are under the domination of a force that is greater than we are (see 6:16–22). We must choose whether to serve sin or to serve Christ, who has set us free for life and joy. Although death is the deserved result of our sin, righteousness and eternal life are God's undeserved gift to us through Christ.

Our sin is deep, unavoidable, and devastating, but the grace of Christ far exceeds the power of sin and death. God is on our side against sin and death, and nothing can separate us from his abundant grace and love in Christ Jesus (5:17, 20; 8:38–39).

CHRISTOPHER A. BEELEY

Pastoral Perspective

human guilt or even a collective identity. Nevertheless we do know of our own waywardness, indulgences, and propensity for either moral lassitude or rigidity. We know we are able to spot these traits in others and indict them. That, in and of itself, creates a collective catastrophe.

In contrast, Jesus Christ lives his life in the midst of and as a part of this human story: he identifies with us completely, so that we may identify our true selves in him. It is this enactment of the sovereign, divine love that precedes and undergirds the "Adam." It says, "Help found here." Notice the accent in verse 8 of this chapter. "But God proves his love for us in that while [not because] we still were sinners Christ died for us." Also notice the personal note when Paul comes to record his own confession in Galatians 2:20: "And the life I now live in the flesh I live by faith in the Son of God, who loved *me* and gave himself for *me*" (my emphases).

The free gift is not like the trespass; its goal is not through some act of cosmic acquittal to return us to the status of the "righteous" or "good" person of verse 7. It is to reclaim us for a life as generous as the love that created us and comes to us in Christ. It identifies and gets us outside the boundaries and barriers within which we currently reside. It is not really until we are redeemed—that is, reconnected to the life of God in Christ—that we can with any clarity begin to understand the awesome and awful dimensions of our common existence as the "Adam." God's intention is to do more than save us from our individual trespasses. God's forgiveness is meant to do more than to get us to behave. It is meant to lead us into "ecstatic" lives that "exercise dominion in life through the one man, Jesus Christ" (v. 17b).

DWIGHT M. LUNDGREN

Exegetical Perspective

transgression of Adam" (v. 14), exegetes generally conclude that Paul is not talking about a sin that humans have marked against them from the moment of conception, but the universality of sinfulness already described in Romans 1:18–3:20.

Paul is not developing a theology of sin in Romans 5:12–21. The repetitions of "if through one person, Adam . . . then how much more through one person, Christ" highlight his theology of grace. One might assume that since the law permits sin to be charged against violators (v. 13), the "free gift" of becoming right with God meant that Christ assumed liability and paid off the debt. A rhetorical question in 6:1 voices such a misunderstanding, "Should we continue in sin that grace may abound?" as though the gift were an unrestricted bailout.

The "free gift" does mean that sin is no longer counted against believers, but it includes more than that. It opens up a way of life no longer enslaved by the power of sin (so 6:1–14). Although the law might be said to make the situation worse by keeping account of sins (5:13, 20), Paul is not describing human history as a progression of increasingly evil ages. Until the coming of Christ makes the new life with God possible, the human condition is static. Not even God's people, privileged to have the Torah, escaped the rule of sin (2:17–3:20).

How does Paul understand salvation to be universal? Romans 3:21–26 presents righteousness based on faith. Romans 6:3–5 interprets baptism as participation in the death and resurrection of Christ. Some exegetes conclude that "all" refers to the fact that the gospel is offered to all humanity. Others point to the future, God's universal reign through the Son (Phil. 2:10–11; 1 Cor. 15:20–28). Just as individual human activities reflect participation in the sinfulness of Adam, so the "righteous deed of the Son's death" also calls forth response in a new way of life.

PHEME PERKINS

Homiletical Perspective

week may help to break the Epistle open for you. A playful, imaginative journey into the story of the fall in Genesis might help you to approach Paul's own rhetorical creativity with a little less wooden argument and a little more theopoetic.[3] Similarly, if you are in a context where the devil is considered to be more metaphorical than ontological (while still pointing to the reality of evil), then some exploration of Matthew's development of the devil as a rhetorical device may allow you to go back to Paul with fresh eyes.

Lastly, if you are a preacher or teacher who is mostly or wholly critical of Paul's logic in this passage, or of atonement theories in general, and you would prefer to skip this passage altogether, at least hear out this plea for the Epistle reading. It is not here in the day's lectionary readings primarily for the member of your congregation who has made a misstep and wants to get back up again during Lent: the husband who had a one-night stand, or the junior executive who knows her colleague should have gotten the promotion instead.

Rather, this reading is more for the Christian who knows all too well that sin remains intractable long after our baptism: the council or session member addicted to painkillers, or gambling, or Internet porn; the self-righteous congregational crusader wracked by long-held hatred for the sinners she or he condemns; the survivor of combat or domestic abuse who carries within his or her body the legacy of the sins of others. This reading is more for them. It is also for the listener long enmeshed in the deadening comfort of privilege or the dense web of oppression.

These members or visitors to your church need to hear that although sin remains, it need not have dominion always (Rom. 6:14). Whether you are drawn to the passage or not, some people in your context may need to hear Paul's message that sin, while remaining part of their human condition, does not have to lead to death, but can lead to grace, and life for all (5:18).

CHRISTOPHER GRUNDY

---

3. See Amos Niven Wilder, *Theopoetic: Theology and the Religious Imagination* (Lima, OH: Academic Renewal Press, 2001).

Matthew 4:1-11

[1]Then Jesus was led up by the Spirit into the wilderness to be tempted by the devil. [2]He fasted forty days and forty nights, and afterwards he was famished. [3]The tempter came and said to him, "If you are the Son of God, command these stones to become loaves of bread." [4]But he answered, "It is written,

'One does not live by bread alone,
   but by every word that comes from the mouth of God.'"

[5]Then the devil took him to the holy city and placed him on the pinnacle of the temple, [6]saying to him, "If you are the Son of God, throw yourself down; for it is written,

'He will command his angels concerning you,'
   and 'On their hands they will bear you up,
so that you will not dash your foot against a stone.'"

Theological Perspective

We miss the point, I think, when we consider this text only from the perspective of its characterization of Jesus and his mission. It is also (and therefore) a statement about the church—a statement, moreover, with high theo-critical potential. Jesus, not without difficulty, resisted these temptations; the church, however, has rarely been able to do so. Indeed too often (and perhaps characteristically) the church has succumbed—with alacrity—to the point of acting as though the devil's proposals were entirely compatible with its Founder's divine commission (Matt. 28:19–20).

There are not really three temptations, but three variations on the same basic theme. The devil has a one-track mind. As from the beginning, he tempts his victims to go for *power* ("you will be like God" [Gen. 3:5]). Evidently he knows there is no surer path to internal contradiction and self-destruction.

First Variation: The Temptation to Attempt the Miraculous. The first temptation is about setting aside the laws of nature and experience and, by an open display of divine omnipotence (or rather, *Deus ex machina*), introducing (hey presto!) a new order—one in which stones may with a flourish be turned into bread, and so forth. That is to say, it is an attempt to displace the quintessentially Hebraic commitment to *creation* (which is "very good," limits and all) with a

Pastoral Perspective

"The greatest trick the devil ever played was to make the world believe he doesn't exist."[1] This is the premise of the 1995 neo-noir film *The Usual Suspects*, the story of five men wrongly interrogated for a crime, who punish the police by masterminding a caper. Payback leaves 27 dead, 91 million dollars worth of drug money missing, and two dark questions lurking: Who is the mysterious Keyser Söze who put these crimes in motion, and what kind of unnamed, sinister hold does he have over these five seemingly unconnected men?

The heart of darkness in this film is not the crime or death; darkness comes from the fact that evil is unrecognizable—it has no face. Only at the very end of the film is Keyser Söze revealed to be one of the men who had pretended to fear Söze. Evil was lurking closer than the audience or the players ever knew.

There is something captivating about seeing evil incarnate on the big screen, in the pages of a novel, or in the names of those said by a nation to pose political threats. It is only human to feel the need to see evil anthropomorphized, to name, visualize, vilify, and separate us from "it" in order to engage "it" as an opponent in battle. This is true in sacred texts as

1. Adapted from French poet Charles Baudelaire and used in *The Usual Suspects*, directed by Byron Singer (Polygram Filmed Entertainment, 1995).

⁷Jesus said to him, "Again it is written, 'Do not put the Lord your God to the test.'"

⁸Again, the devil took him to a very high mountain and showed him all the kingdoms of the world and their splendor; ⁹and he said to him, "All these I will give you, if you will fall down and worship me." ¹⁰Jesus said to him, "Away with you, Satan! for it is written,

'Worship the Lord your God,
    and serve only him.'"

¹¹Then the devil left him, and suddenly angels came and waited on him.

Exegetical Perspective

Matthew's account of Jesus' temptation in the wilderness contravenes the feel-good, prosperity, and success "gospels" proclaimed from some pulpits in every age. Immediately after Jesus' baptism (3:13–17), with its disclosure of Jesus' identity and the quality of his relationship with the Father, the Holy Spirit leads Jesus the beloved Son out into the wilderness to be severely tested. Clearly, easy living is not part of sonship. Indeed, closeness to God involves conflict and struggle that will lay bare one's deepest passion and loyalty. Central to each of the challenges that Jesus faces is a single question: To what extent will he trust God to be God and so be himself?

In the Wilderness (vv. 1–2). While many view the wilderness as a place for recreation and renewal, wilderness in the Bible is nearly always a place of struggle. Remarkably, Jesus follows the leading Spirit into wilderness solitude "to be tempted by the devil." This purpose statement, not in Mark or Luke, suggests that Matthew considered Jesus' intentional confrontation with evil to be instructive. Indeed, Jesus will later teach his disciples to pray that God not lead them into temptation (6:13), but that does not mean God should spare them from all testing (cf. 16:24–26; 18:7; 26:39–41).

Homiletical Perspective

The narratives of the temptation of Jesus may be the traditional Gospel lessons, but they are an uncomfortable fit for preaching the First Sunday in Lent. Jesus' forty days have concluded; our forty days have only just begun. Lent is a time for adopting and practicing the disciplines that would prepare us to receive the mystery of Easter, but Matthew's telling of the temptation resists such practical application. The preacher may therefore resonate all too readily with these temptations, yearning for some hermeneutical magic to transform the durable stones of Matthew's story into something chewable, digestible, and nourishing to satisfy the immediate hungers of the congregation—or seeking some homiletical height from which to launch a sermon that would dazzle disbelief and compel faith. Matthew shows not the slightest inclination to be useful; he simply wants to introduce Jesus. If we do not complain too much about Matthew's impracticality we may learn from him how to preach Jesus the Son of God.

Matthew received the temptation story both from Mark and a source he shares with Luke, but he adds his own touch. To their "forty days" (Mark 1:13, Luke 4:2), Matthew adds "and forty nights." "Forty days and forty nights" may summon for us memories of Noah on Mount Ararat (Gen. 7:4, 12), but in the Scriptures they most frequently refer to Moses on

Matthew 4: 1-11

Theological Perspective

redemption theology that gives us "the kingdom" without "the cross." It is a temptation to work miracle, not in the sense in which Jesus allowed himself sometimes to defy fate in the name of divine compassion, but in the sense of seeking the world's salvation by offering *another world*—or seeming to, trying to—and thereby encouraging believers to abandon or despise and maltreat the one we actually have.

Historic Christianity abounds in that attempt—crassly when it parades alleged miracles as proof of ecclesiastical authenticity; more subtly in every theology that accentuates the "already" and neglects the "not yet," in every sermon that gives us Easter without Good Friday, in every evangel that substitutes finality ("closure") for the courage faith inspires for living with life's paradoxes.

Second Variation: The Temptation to Spectacle. Our world is athirst for spectacle and the conspicuously heroic, as was that of the first-century Christians. Today, when most people feel invisible and superfluous, lost among the billions, the clever are able to turn this ancient longing into big business—the "cult of celebrity." *Our* heroes do not have to jump off towers; they have only to appear tantalizingly sexy. With all that media attention, the most blatant exhibitionism can seem irresistible to the voiceless and the plain.

The church has shown itself remarkably adept at exploring the possibilities of this temptation. Whether through cults of the saints, the exploitation of science-defying medical and other miracles, or the staging of huge media triumphs—above all by presenting Jesus himself as the ultimate celebrity—Christians have sought preeminence for themselves and their own religion.

Third Variation: The Temptation to Political Power. Here the true character of all three temptations shows itself without ambiguity or nuance. Variations 1 and 2 contain some semblance of persuasion; the third goes directly for sheer control.

Only the unreflective can consider this temptation today without conjuring up the whole centuries-long Christendom experiment. As the term itself attests, Christendom was (and, where it still pertains, is) nothing more nor less than a quest for the ultimate domination (*dom* = dominion) of the Christian religion—*not of Christ.* There is still a difference! The pre-Constantinian church certainly knew that quest as a perennial *temptation*: the New Testament depicts the apostles themselves as falling into that

Pastoral Perspective

well. Evil tests Eve and Aaron, the great high priest, Job and King David, Jesus and his disciples. Over and over again, in order to live a life that chooses God, a faithful person must face the choice of acting outside of God. It is easier to make that choice if we can put a face on temptation.

At first glance, Jesus' temptation in the wilderness seems out of place, even heretical. It is almost gratuitous that Jesus is tempted, as we know he will not submit. Much like the inevitability of the cross, the defeat of the devil in his encounter with Jesus is inevitable. Jesus will overcome; yet this scene stands in a central place in Matthew between baptism and ministry, naming the reality of evil in the face of holiness.

Jesus is tempted by bread for his hunger. He is tempted to save himself from danger. Finally, he is tempted to take all the power in the world that the devil can offer. Each time he rejects temptation, he sets up for the reader a way to understand the cross to come. Certainly God can save God's self from death on the cross, and certainly God in Jesus can refuse temptation to sin, but in our humanity we need to see God offer sacrifice and refuse temptation in order to learn the lesson ourselves.

In C. S. Lewis's *The Screwtape Letters,* the author writes of a junior tempter-in-training named Wormwood and his mentor Uncle Screwtape. Young Wormwood's task is to darken the heart of his "patient," to train him to love things worldly and reject God, so that Wormwood may finally escort him into what we can only imagine is hell. The young apprentice is to keep his patient navel-gazing and self-involved, clueless about who he is.

Keep him spiritual and not practical, Screwtape advises, as it is the practical that often brings people to God. Encourage him to pray for tangible, desired ends and so direct his prayers to objects and not to God. Allow the patient to be oversensitive until everything, even his mother, grates on his nerves. Keep his prayers formless, as they are easier to manipulate. Turn his gaze away from God toward himself. Create a subtle conflict when he prays for courage; let him find himself turning boastful. In the final letter, the patient dies and goes to heaven, leaving Wormwood a failure and Screwtape in a spiral of anger.[2]

The captivating part of the story is not that Screwtape and Wormwood are trying to create an army of ruthless killers; rather they are trying to create a generation of people who are defined by selfishness and

2. C. S. Lewis, *The Screwtape Letters* (San Francisco: HarperCollins, 2001).

Exegetical Perspective

The temptation Jesus faces in the wilderness comes after fasting "forty days and forty nights" (cf. Mark 1:13; Luke 4:2), a specification that would resonate with Matthew's predominately Jewish Christian community. The rain of the great flood fell upon the earth for forty days and nights while Noah and his family waited for their deliverance from evil and rain, as God promised (Gen. 7:4, 12–16; 9:8–16). Moses fasted alone in the presence of the Lord for forty days and nights atop Mount Sinai as he wrote the Ten Commandments (Exod. 34:27–28). Elijah followed the Lord's urging and fasted for forty days and nights as he fled to Mount Horeb (Sinai), where he encountered God (1 Kgs. 19:7–12). The number forty is further rooted in Israel's struggle to practice faithfulness in the wilderness, day and night (cf. Exod. 13:21–22; 16:2–21; 24:18; Deut. 8:1–20). Now Jesus has endured forty days and nights of fasting and solitude in the wilderness and arrives at a critical junction where his loyalty to God the Father is tested through his confrontation with the "tester" (the NRSV translates *peirazōn* as "tempter"), who is also called the "devil."

Turning Points (vv. 3–10). As in the Old Testament (cf. Exod. 16:4; Deut. 8:3; Job 1:6–12; 2:1–6; Amos 3:5–6), temptation here occurs with God's allowance, and it reveals the essential character of the tested one. Absent is any mythological exaggeration of the devil's background, character, or role. It is enough for Matthew that God's Spirit has brought Jesus into a struggle with the devil in a place and time of God's choosing and allows Jesus' core commitments to be tested. It may also be helpful for us to observe that the word "devil" is a verbal noun drawn from the Greek words *dia* and *ballō*, which together mean essentially "to throw over or across." In its broader usage, the noun comes to mean "one who attacks, misleads, deceives, diverts, discredits, or slanders." In Matthew, the devil seeks to mislead Jesus about the meaning of sonship and the purposes of God.

In the first confrontation, the "tester" encourages Jesus to satisfy his physical hunger by turning stones into bread. The devil's conditional statement does not reflect doubt about Jesus' identity or power. Indeed, it could be translated "Since you are the Son of God." Nevertheless, the deceiver attempts to mislead Jesus into using his power for himself rather than trusting the Father to satisfy his need. Jesus sees through the deception clearly—just as he sees through a deceitful kiss in the garden (26:48–50)— and he refuses. Citing Scripture (Deut. 8:3), Jesus

Homiletical Perspective

Mount Sinai. While "He was there with the LORD forty days and forty nights; he neither ate bread nor drank water" (Exod. 34:28; cf. Exod. 24:18, Deut. 9:9, 11, 18, 25; 10:10).

No sooner does Matthew summon echoes of Moses than Jesus cites Moses, remembering three teachings from Deuteronomy: "'One does not live by bread alone'" (8:3); "'Do not put the LORD your God to the test'" (6:16); and "The LORD your God you shall fear; him you shall serve" (6:13). These three will point to the ways of the Son of God in the world.

Matthew introduces Jesus with a plethora of titles. He is "the Messiah, the son of David, the son of Abraham" (1:1); God announces "This is my Son, the Beloved" (3:17). "Son of David" evokes memories of the Davidic dynasty and invokes hopes for renewal of a sovereign Jewish nation. Though we may hear the title "Son of God" (4:3) in Trinitarian terms or as a reference to Jesus' divinity, Matthew's hearers would have recognized it as another royal title. In Psalm 2:7–8 the Lord addresses the king, "You are my son; today I have begotten you. Ask of me, and I will make the nations your heritage, and the ends of the earth your possession," a promise now echoing eerily in the third temptation. Only those with the shortest memories of the Davidic dynasty and those with the most idealized vision of the monarchy could greet the approach of a new royal Son of God without some mixed feelings. What is the character of this Son of God?

Matthew preaches Jesus as a king like Moses.[1] Although we seldom think of Moses as a royal figure, first-century Jews certainly did consider him as God's own royalty and an antidote for their poisonous history of kings. The kings of the Davidic dynasty were notorious for serving themselves, but this king has learned the humbling lesson of manna in the wilderness (Deut. 8:1–2) and receives in humility whatever God provides. The Davidic kings tested God's patience for years, but this king has learned the lesson of Massah (Deut. 6:14–17), to trust in the Lord your God. The kings of Israel and Judah had no end of imperial hopes and schemes but "all the kingdoms of the world and their splendor" (4:8) have no allure to compete with his trustful obedience. Moses learned this and taught this; the Son of God who strides in from the wilderness has learned this and lives it.

Matthew's story of the temptation is maddeningly unavailable for moral exhortation and spiritual encouragement. It is simply about Jesus: who he is

---

1. My reading of this text is very much indebted to Dale C. Allison Jr., *The New Moses: A Matthean Typology* (Minneapolis: Fortress Press, 1994).

Matthew 4: 1-11

Theological Perspective

assumption frequently. However, with the adoption of Christianity by imperial Rome, or what remained of it, the search for power through proximity to (and pressure upon) political power became the dominant *pattern* of Western Christianity, including (let many of us admit it) most Protestantism.

Human beings—individually and corporately, institutionally—all know the pull of the quest for power. What could be more human? So it is not unusual that this temptation has also colored the history of the church, but at its most faithful and perceptive, the disciple community has never been without its witnesses to the impossibility of combining the gospel of divine love with a bid for power on the part of those who proclaim that gospel. Yes, one may speak of "the power of love"; but lovers know that love is the only *power* that assumes the utter vulnerability of the lover: "whenever I am weak, *then* I am strong" (2 Cor. 12:10).

"We long," wrote Paul Tillich, "for a Christ of power. Yet if *He* were to come and transform us and our world, we should have to pay the one price which we could not pay: we would have to lose our freedom, our humanity, and our spiritual dignity. Perhaps we should be happier, but we should also be lower beings, our present misery, struggle and despair notwithstanding. . . . Those who dream of a better life and try to avoid the Cross as a way, and those who hope for a Christ and attempt to exclude the Crucified have no knowledge of the mystery of God and humanity."[1]

It is no surprise, then, that the Tempter's final attempt to capture the soul of this "second Adam" as he did the first takes the form of a taunt shouted at Jesus as he hung "despised and rejected" on the cross of Golgotha, a taunt voiced by "those who passed by . . . shaking their heads" (a taunt whose author, Matthew knew, is the same eternal Deceiver who whispered to Jesus in these earlier "variations on the theme"): "If you are the Son of God, come down from the cross" (Matt. 27:40).

That one is still whispering his enticing suggestions to Christian people and institutions today. Many, alas, find his ideas attractive.

DOUGLAS JOHN HALL

Pastoral Perspective

insincerity, pettiness and pride, fear and a need to control the things of this world.

This is true of our own temptations. Most of us cannot imagine the devil offering bread after a forty-day fast. We do not know the fear of being held over the ledge at the top of the Empire State Building. We certainly do not know the temptation of being offered all the power in the world. Each one of us, however, understands the temptations Screwtape and Wormwood offer: pride, vanity, selfishness, and apathy. These are just as dark as Jesus' temptations, and perhaps even more so, because most of the time, like the dreaded Keyser Söze, they do not come with a face.

Temptation comes to us in moments when we look at others and feel insecure about not having enough. Temptation comes in judgments we make about strangers or friends who make choices we do not understand. Temptation rules us, making us able to look away from those in need and to live our lives unaffected by poverty, hunger, and disease. Temptation rages in moments when we allow our temper to define our lives or when addiction to wealth, power, influence over others, vanity, or an inordinate need for control defines who we are. Temptation wins when we engage in the justification of little lies, small sins: a racist joke, a questionable business practice for the greater good, a criticism of a spouse or partner when he or she is not around. Temptation wins when we get so caught up in the trappings of life that we lose sight of life itself. These are the faceless moments of evil that, while mundane, lurk in the recesses of our lives and our souls.

Lenten penitence engages the dark places in our lives that we may come face to face with them, name them, understand them, and seek forgiveness for them. It is not about guilt. It is about freedom from the control that our fears and insecurities have over us all, about the amendment of life and new beginnings.

MARYETTA ANSCHUTZ

1. Paul Tillich, *The Shaking of the Foundations* (New York: Scribner's, 1953), 148.

insists that there is more at stake at the moment than food, as essential as food is (e.g., 25:34–40). Jesus will not misuse his power for personal material gain.

The second test focuses on Jesus' vulnerability and need for safety. The devil invites Jesus to make himself secure from injury or even death. Moreover, he quotes Scripture to prove that God agrees. Jesus is not deceived. The devil is using Scripture out of context; it does not endorse testing God's protective grace for the sake of self-assurance. Thus Jesus rebuts the devil with a text of his own (Deut. 6:16) and applies it faithfully in its context. Jesus is, after all, God's Son and full of the Holy Spirit (3:11, 16–17). Jesus will not misuse his power to make himself safe and secure.

The third temptation attempts to seduce Jesus with domination and prestige. The devil offers Jesus control over all of the world's kingdoms, along with their praise and glory, in exchange for his allegiance. Jesus is not led astray. He rejects the deceiver's misdirection and quotes Scripture again (Deut. 6:13) in its context, saying, "Worship the Lord your God, and serve only him." Jesus will not misuse his power to amass clout and esteem.

Deliverance (v. 11). At this, Satan departs and divine messengers arrive to serve Jesus' needs. He has come through each temptation through total reliance on God the Father. Jesus is God's Son, with whom God is well pleased (3:17). Clearly, temptation is not to be avoided at all costs (cf. 18:7; 26:36–46; Heb. 12:6). It is inevitable for God's children. Indeed, temptations of materialism, security, and prestige are not foreign to us. Whatever form temptation may take, it may be passed through by means of trust in God to provide what is needed (cf. Gen. 22:1–14). The "tester's" power is real, but it is limited. Like Jesus, believers can trust in God's Word and saving power. Victory belongs to those who will follow Jesus through temptation (Heb. 2:14–18; 4:15–16).

ROBERT A. BRYANT

and what sort of character he shows. The temptations are about Jesus, not about us. In this respect our frustration replicates the aggravation that the tempter/devil/Satan knew in ever ascending heights: Jesus refuses to be who we want him to be. He will not turn our stones to bread; he will not prove God to us; he will not turn from God to embrace the kinds of success we would recognize and applaud. He remains maddeningly himself. Perhaps it would be more accurate to say that he remains steadfastly God's.

The manner in which Matthew preaches Jesus is so much at odds with our own preaching. Jesus provides no self-advertisement. There is no impulse to be user-friendly. He does not persuade. There is, as Isaiah said, "nothing in his appearance that we should desire him" (Isa. 53:2). Even when, a few verses later, Jesus calls his first disciples, the word is simply "Follow me" (4:19)—or do not follow; you decide.

Beyond the traditional titles Matthew brings into play—Messiah, son of David, Son of God—the temptation story begins a gospel-long process of revealing this person Jesus. Preachers may well wonder if Matthew's strategy of simply preaching Jesus is enough. There is, however, some inchoate hunger in the church to know Jesus. If Marcus Borg's *Meeting Jesus Again for the First Time* can become a bestseller, surely there may be sufficient interest also in this story that amounts to the Gospel of Matthew's introduction to the person of Jesus. Preaching to his Jewish Christian congregation who already called Jesus "Lord" (Matt. 7:21, 25:11, 37, 44), Borg's title could also serve as Matthew's: "Meeting Jesus Again for the First Time."

Matthew's congregation knows Jesus, knows him as Messiah and Son of God, but they do not know Jesus' embrace of humility. They know his mighty works but mistake their meaning. They rejoice in the hope of his kingdom but have yet to put on the character that would allow them to live as citizens of that kingdom (Matt. 25:31–46). Like our congregations, they know Jesus and are learning Jesus.

PATRICK J. WILLSON

Genesis 12:1-4a

¹Now the LORD said to Abram, "Go from your country and your kindred and your father's house to the land that I will show you. ²I will make of you a great nation, and I will bless you, and make your name great, so that you will be a blessing. ³I will bless those who bless you, and the one who curses you I will curse; and in you all the families of the earth shall be blessed."

⁴So Abram went, as the LORD had told him; and Lot went with him.

Theological Perspective

These few verses that form the bridge between the brief "primal history" and the story of Israel's earliest ancestors serve an important literary function. They bear the weight of substantial theological traffic as well. Through the call and promise to Abram and Sarai, they state in a few lines what it means to be God's chosen people. They also help to make a crucial claim concerning the relationship God has determined to maintain with creatures who have both delighted God and broken God's heart.

For ancient Israel as for Jews today, and for those grafted into the chosen family through baptism, the whole point of being God's chosen ones has to do with God's decision to use special agents in order *to bring blessing to the broader human family* that mostly knows trouble and curse. "Blessed to be a blessing," as so many have phrased it, comes close to the full truth God declares at the beginning of Genesis 12. Audacious as it sounds, given the surrounding story, these verses suggest as well that Abram, Sarai, and their offspring actually serve as God's last hope for the world. If blessing fails to work, the alternatives are unthinkable, even for—especially for—God.

The first human being helps with naming the other creatures. This causes no apparent trouble, but once God leaves man and woman to explore Eden on their own, even for a moment, things fall apart.

Pastoral Perspective

"So Abram went, as the LORD had told him." This is how we are introduced to the patriarch of three faith traditions: "so Abram went." Chapters 10 and 11 of Genesis move us through a long genealogy from Noah's son, Shem, to Terah the father of Abram, making only a brief detour through the tower of Babel story. As we approach our text, we discover that Abram has two brothers, one of whom dies in Ur of the Chaldeans, leaving a surviving son named Lot. We know nothing of Lot's mother. Abram "takes a wife," Sarai, who is barren, "for she has no child." Finally, Abram's father, Terah, dies in Haran and is buried there.

We then read that God tells Abram to go to a place he has never been before—go from your country, go from your kin, go from your father's house—go, and I will show you where. So Abram goes. We know so little about this man. We know nothing of his pedigree, his credentials or qualifications. Was Abram a righteous man as was Noah? We are not told. Why would God call him? The text is silent on these matters, so we do not know—yet, we do.

We know the ways of God through our experience of God today. In our churches, in our congregations, in our own callings as ministers, and in the callings of others to both lay and ordained service, we can see God's method at work. We see that God does not

Exegetical Perspective

This passage concerning God's command to Abram (= Abraham; Gen. 17:5) to go to the land of Canaan serves as the hinge between the primeval history (Gen. 1–11) and the narratives concerning the patriarchs and matriarchs that follow (Gen. 12–36).

In contrast to Genesis 1–11, with its panoramic scope concerning the entire earth, the focus narrows dramatically to the life of one man and his family. While the sense of a new beginning is striking, the editors of the Pentateuch have carefully crafted these verses so that they are embedded in what has come before. Thematically, Genesis 10–11 have given an account of the populating of the entire earth (10:32; 11:9). This passage will conclude with Abram as a blessing for all nations. Narratively, the context for 12:1–4a is to be found in 11:27–32, which includes both a genealogy and an interrupted journey. The genealogy introduces characters who will play central roles in the following chapters: Abram, Sarai, and Lot, as well as Nahor and Milcah, the grandparents of Rebecca.

This passage also begins the story of the journey of Abram's family, for it was originally Terah who had intended to go to Canaan. For reasons not explained, he settled the family in Haran in northern Mesopotamia (11:31). This enigmatic information about the background of Abram, followed by the

Homiletical Perspective

Abram is called by God to serve as a mirror. Instead of images, Abram will reflect blessings and curses on the land where he will sojourn. As the world blesses Abram, so will Abram reflect those blessings back to the world. As the world curses Abram, so will the world's curses be returned. That is not all. This mirror has two sides. The other side of Abram's task is to turn his mirror self so that the blessing that God shines on him shines on the nations as well.

A sermon can also function like a mirror. If the exegete is perceptive, a congregation will hear itself in a sermon. If the exegete is faithful and the Spirit is willing, the congregation will hear the Word of God echoing off the surface of the speaker's voice. A mirror is not for hearing but for seeing. Therefore the particular challenge of Genesis 12:1–4a begins with bridging the senses, from aural to visual.

Unlike other doctrinal passages, the message of these verses is visual in form. The author is not presenting an argument of systematic theology. Nor is the author concerned with the mechanics of how and under what conditions blessings and curses will be administered. Because the medium of the message is visual, the preacher might choose to create a structure for the sermon that effectively and intentionally takes on the nature of a mirror.

Genesis 12:1-4a

Theological Perspective

Human beings play God. Within two brief chapters, they toy with God's words, steal the forbidden fruit, and, in anger toward God's perceived unfairness, take life itself into their own hands. In the process they bring shame and a craving for vengeance into the world. God responds, on one hand, with curses and grievous punishment, on the other, with clothing for the naked and a mark of exemption that spares murderers. These latter, palliative measures serve also to reveal God's willingness to make adjustments, to adopt a Plan B.

By the time we reach Genesis 6, human mischief has gone universal. God grieves, repents of having made humankind, and once again responds with curse. This time the punishment wipes out everything. Still God cannot quit altogether on the broken creation. As a sign of hope, God saves one family from the murderous deluge. However, before Noah proceeds to prove God right with a whole new round of shameful nakedness and badly used fruit, God notes that even a universal purge has not changed the nature of human hearts (Gen. 8:21–22).

In short, curse and punishment have solved nothing. Accordingly, God swears never again to use such measures in response to the incessant flow of evil from human hearts.

As we watch the most righteous man God could find to save, literally the seed for starting over, resume the same, old story, and then behold the Babel generation presuming once more to play God, we wonder what else God might do. The answer comes in Genesis 12. God does not abandon humankind, now scattered about and marked by the same curses and ironic benefits of diversity and confusion that we know so well even today. Instead, God decides on *blessing* as the alternative to curse.

Did that plan succeed? The answer depends in large part on how we understand "blessing." In those first generations, Abraham, Sarah, and their offspring sometimes became the occasion for blessing, blessing defined as prosperity and health for those among whom they settled. At other times, as when they pretended to be siblings rather than spouses, they instead brought trouble to the neighborhood.

Ultimately, however, the larger story of Israel seems to suggest that through this chosen people God gives the world *torah*, and in that gift God reveals the way to choose life over death, blessing rather than curse. For Christians, the larger story includes the saving work of Jesus Christ, particularly the reconciliation between creature and Creator accomplished in the crucifixion.

Pastoral Perspective

always call those with the best credentials or the shining pedigrees. We see, again and again, that a faithful response to God's leading results in a blessing of gifts and talents, of learned and acquired skill sets sufficient for the task to which an individual is called. God calls and Abram responds faithfully. The author of Hebrews writes that because Abram considers the maker of the promise to be the keeper of promises, he responds faithfully and receives the power of procreation and the skill set to become a great nation (Heb. 11:8–12).

The city Haran, from which Abram is called, means "highway" or "crossroads." God's call to Abram at this crossroads and Abram's faithful response is the starting point of Israel's history. This text could be used to explore your own crossroads; the needs, callings, and challenges of your congregation as well as the faithful response of its individual members to God's call. Such exploration may lead to naming some of the unique crossroads faced by your congregation and perhaps the demarcation of new starting points in the ministry of your church. Sunday school teachers, ushers, deacons, liturgists, lay preachers, and individuals sensing a call to ordained ministry are at a crossroad. Do I have the time? Do I have the gifts and talents, the skill set for this task? Am I a "good enough" person to fill this role?

Our own experience and the witness of Scripture concur that the one who calls is the one who equips. The one who equips always leads the called to more complete expression of the persons they were created to be. Consequently, if the call is of God, the answer to all the above questions is yes. A faithful response is the embrace of what God has already called into being—a newness of being—and the release from what is known for what is promised. A faithful response is neither forced nor coerced, but a step freely taken toward our true selves.

The notion of embracing newness and relinquishing what has been connects this text with today's Gospel, the story of Nicodemus (John 3:1–17). To be born from above or anew or again may be understood as the embrace of God's calling—of one's true vocation—that necessitates taking leave of one's self-directed course. To leave the comfort of the known for the promise of the unknown realities of God is a form of birth.

So Abram was born into a new reality that God called into being. Every new birth is a blessing, and every blessing holds the possibility of newness. God promises to make Abram a great nation and to bless him so that through Abram all nations will be

Exegetical Perspective

abrupt command of God to Abram to depart and by God's extraordinary blessing of him, gave rise to midrashic speculation. What made Abram worthy of God's interest in him? What prepared him for the summons from God? These midrashic traditions credited Abram with being the first in his culture and even his family to see the falseness of idols and to worship only God (see, e.g., *Jubilees* 11:14–12:24). While one can understand the desire to fill in the gaps in Abram's story, Genesis itself is completely uninterested in Abram's previous character and experiences. The focus of the narrative is not who Abram was, but who he will become.

The literary structure of the passage is simple. It consists of an address (v. 1a), a command (v. 1b), a promise (vv. 2–3), and a notice of Abram's compliance with the command (v. 4a). From length alone it is evident that the emphasis falls on the blessing. Similar passages containing commands about travel and promises of blessing in Genesis 26:1–6 (Isaac) and 46:1–5a (Jacob) serve to unify the stories about the patriarchs (cf. 31:3; 32:10). The language of 12:1–4a is strikingly beautiful and rhythmic. Key words are repeated, terms are linked in chains of descending scope, and clauses balance one another. Indeed, some translations set the blessing as poetry. These features give a sense of solemnity and significance to God's words to Abram.

The Command (v. 1b). The basic structure of the sentence is expressed by a verb and two contrasting prepositional phrases. "Go from your country . . . to the land." Significantly, neither land is identified by a geographical designation (e.g., Haran, Canaan). Rather "your country" is further specified by two kinship terms, "your kindred" and "your father's house." Here is the textual seed of the later midrashic traditions that emphasized Abram's alienation from his family. While Genesis does not speak of alienation, it does emphasize separation. In traditional societies the kin group is the source of identity, economic benefit, security, and protection. To leave such a fundamental social network is to put a great deal at risk. Thus the costliness of the command is stressed. In a similar fashion, the destination is described only as "the land that I will show you." Although in the larger narrative context it is clear that the land is Canaan, the wording emphasizes that the destination will be known to Abram only when God discloses it (see v. 7).

The Blessing (vv. 2–3). If the command underscores what Abram puts at risk, the blessing reassures him

Homiletical Perspective

A church in which audiovisuals are available would be well suited to Genesis 12:1–4a. Photographs of the nations of the world performing acts of blessing, juxtaposed with pictures of those engaging in acts of cursing, could effectively mirror global kindness and cruelty. Drawing the images closer to home, photographs of a church's own saints (and sinners!) could dramatically pose the question to the congregation: How is your life reflected back to you in Abram's mirror? Are you a person who blesses God's servant or one who curses God's servant? Do you let people know how their actions are blessings? Are you brave enough to show others how their words or actions are a curse?

In a strictly verbal presentation, the preacher might create word pictures of blessings and curses, ranging from global to personal. Through story, the congregation could be led to experience its own gut-level response to receiving word of those far away and those nearby who bless or curse the world. The likeness of those stories to one's own stories is bound to bring about self-reflection. Like Abram, the preacher can be very direct. Proclamation of this passage calls hearers to a simple and basic state of honesty: When I look in the mirror, do I see a blessing or a curse? When I allow myself to see my effect on my family, coworkers, and friends, am I proud of myself or ashamed?

My family recently purchased a puppy who went berserk whenever he saw himself in a mirror. He was certain another puppy had come to take over his domain. He postured and barked, sniffed and growled at his own reflection. He hunted behind the mirror for the rogue puppy. He never found his nemesis. Eventually, we learned that if the puppy and we were ever going to get any rest, we would have to hang our mirrors higher, above his line of sight. In Abram, God lowers the mirror into our line of sight. God calls us to see who we are—as blessings, or curses, or both. An unexamined life may be, on the surface, more restful. Looking into Abram's mirror will not be easy. We may see that we have to challenge our self-perceptions. We may see that we need to challenge the perceptions of others.

In Galatians 6:7, Paul reminds us that as we sow, so shall we reap. More colloquially, "What goes around comes around." Abram's mirror gives only as well as it gets. The preacher who artfully presents this passage must resist the temptation to hold up a distorted funhouse mirror, shading or twisting the truth because of fear, grudges, or niceness.

In other words, naming the congregation's sins too explicitly, or overpraising their good works too

Genesis 12:1-4a

Theological Perspective

In one sense, all these views of blessing hang on a single theological premise: God chooses to remain intimately connected to the creation and particularly to the flesh and blood that became human when God mixed dust with God's own breath. God may grieve and even rant over the incessant evil that humankind dreams up in every generation, but given the nature of God's commitment, God will not or perhaps cannot give up the creatures that share the divine breath.

God's enmeshed relationship with Israel proves even more intense than that with humankind in general. Time after time, God cannot quit on the chosen but failed agents of blessing. To do so would be to abandon all hope for the world or to suffer a complete loss of face and reputation. For example, when God threatens to breathe hot, deadly wrath on those who dance around the golden calf in Exodus 32, Moses reminds God that this would make the neighbors talk, and God would not like the conversation. God agrees, and God repents. When God smites Israel with the awful rod named Babylon, Ezekiel prophesies that this has been such a terrible blot on God's reputation that God has no choice but to save the chosen people one more time (Ezek. 36:16–32). "Not for your sake, mind you," God carefully explains, "but for the sake of my holy name" (Ezek. 36:22). If Israel is God's last hope for the world, then God is stuck with Israel, and Israel is nothing without God. They cannot divorce. They must work things out.

Inevitably, such faithfulness on God's part means that God will suffer all the pain and sorrow that this troubled relationship generates. Prophets like Jeremiah and Hosea understand God's pain better than most who speak for God; but the evidence of what it would eventually cost God to pin God's hopes on flesh and blood appears all through the Scriptures. From the vantage point of Golgotha, the question was never whether, but only when, that faithfulness would finally cost God life itself.

FREDERICK NIEDNER

Pastoral Perspective

blessed. An exploration of blessing offers another perspective on this text.

The notion of blessing may be understood in at least three ways. First, a blessing may be understood as a sense of well-being or the presence of peace in the life of the recipient. Such a blessing is especially effectual when it comes from someone of authority or power. An individual known to carry such a blessing is, in a sense, under the protection of its giver.

The gods of the Sumerian myths dispensed blessing through fertility and civilization. Many ancient traditions held that fertility was the activity of the gods. The story of Abram and Sarai certainly contains such elements. But the First Testament of our Scriptures expands the concept of blessing to include a second understanding of created and cocreated blessings.

The God of Abram is the God of all creation. The whole of humanity is blessed by God's creation of the creatures of sky, field, and sea; the grains, vegetables, and fruits for harvest; and the system of sun, rain, soil, and wind that maintains them for our use and consumption. This blessing is expanded further for a third understanding that includes the gifts, talents, and abilities—even biological abilities—that God bestows upon individuals. One of God's blessings to Abram and Sarai is to change the inability to bear children into the ability to be fruitful. In the whole of the First Testament, God blesses people with the drive and vitality to cocreate with God through discovery, invention, and productivity. The blessing of curiosity and creativity bestows upon humanity the power to create and acquire.

The faithful response of those who have gone before us has showered humankind with wealth, prosperity, freedom, creativity, and family beyond the imagination of Abraham the patriarch. God calls us to go; will our response offer blessings to those who follow us? If our history reads, "So she went, as God told her," blessings will flow for generations beyond our faithful response.

DONALD P. OLSEN

Exegetical Perspective

that God will provide abundantly. The key term in this section is "bless/blessing" (five occurrences). In Hebrew, blessing signifies flourishing. It includes physical vigor, fertility, security, and success in one's undertakings (e.g., Ps. 128). Although this is the key term, it is significant that the opening words are not "I will bless you" but, rather, "I will make of you a great nation." The emphasis is not on Abram the individual but on the future Israel. The term "nation" (Heb. *goy*) is not a kinship term but a word that designates a political entity. Thus this passage looks forward to the kingdom of Israel. The nation will be the result of God's blessing Abram, and the nation is the means by which Abram's name will be "made great."

The end of verse 2 shifts the focus from Abram as the recipient of blessing to Abram as the cause of blessing for others, the topic of verse 3. If verse 2 was God's commitment of abundant progeny to Abram, verse 3a is the commitment of security. By leaving his kindred, Abraham has lost the social protection that such a network entails, which extends mutual benefits to those who cooperate with the family and threatens reprisals to any foes. Here God pledges to perform analogous functions. That too is part of Abram's blessing.

The culmination of the blessing of Abram is in verse 3b, which concerns the way in which Abram's blessing affects the entire world. The Hebrew syntax is ambiguous. The verb (a *niphal*) can be translated either as a passive ("will be blessed"; so the Septuagint and most later Christian interpretation) or as a reflexive ("will bless themselves"). The reflexive is more likely the original meaning and suggests that people would invoke Abram's name as a blessing (e.g., "may I be blessed as Abram was blessed"). Likely, there is little substantive difference in the alternative translations. In either interpretation, God's blessing of Abram ultimately has universal significance for spreading that blessing throughout "all the families of the earth" (v. 3). Not surprisingly, early Christians, especially those concerned with the mission to the Gentiles, found the blessing of Abram to be an important text. There are allusions to it in Acts 3:25; Romans 4:13; Galatians 3:8, 16; Hebrews 11:8–16.

CAROL A. NEWSOM

Homiletical Perspective

overtly, will turn Abram (and the preacher) into a judge. Judges come later in the books of the Bible. Here in the Bible's genesis, the tool of God is one of reflection, not refraction. Reflected light returns to its source. Refracted light is light redirected from one medium to another. Lest the exegete jump too quickly from reflection to refraction, from recognition to redemption, she or he must resist the urge to "overpreach" this passage. This is another reason why the presentation of identifiable images and traits, which allow the congregation to draw its own conclusions, may be the most faithful proclamation of this scripture.

The mirror still has its other side. The other facet of Abram's mirror is the side that reflects God to all the nations. From this half of the visual image comes the church's mandate to mission and evangelism. The church must be more than analyst and commentator, more even than encourager or discourager. Beyond its social and personal purposes is the church's divine calling. Abram is a blessing, not because of his own skill, but because he will be used to purely reflect God's light. The church is called to be a blessing to the nations, not because it is faultless, but because it reflects the One who is.

Thus a sermon on Genesis 12:1–4a would initially call a congregation to empathy, but ultimately call it beyond itself, beyond the limits of its senses, beyond its gifts, to simply sharing the message of God with the world. This may be foreign territory for many. As we read in Genesis 12:1, it was foreign to Abram too; yet God was reflected, blessing was cast, and Abram journeyed on.

JAMES MCTYRE

Psalm 121

¹I lift up my eyes to the hills—
   from where will my help come?
²My help comes from the LORD,
   who made heaven and earth.

³He will not let your foot be moved;
   he who keeps you will not slumber.
⁴He who keeps Israel
   will neither slumber nor sleep.

⁵The LORD is your keeper;
   the LORD is your shade at your right hand.
⁶The sun shall not strike you by day,
   nor the moon by night.

⁷The LORD will keep you from all evil;
   he will keep your life.
⁸The LORD will keep
   your going out and your coming in
   from this time on and forevermore.

Theological Perspective

The setting of this psalm is the subject of consider-able conjecture. It has been argued that the author penned it in anticipation of going into battle; that the author composed it as he was about to set out on a journey; that this psalm was chanted by the people as they went up to Jerusalem to the feasts.

Made of four couplets, the structure of this psalm suggests that it may have been sung in a call-and-response fashion. Each couplet addresses in a highly poetic way themes that were critical in Israel's cultic life. Theologically the structure of the psalm seems to fit the possibility that it was employed as the people approached a sacred moment and a sacred space.

Verses 1–2 affirm that as God's people we receive our help from the Lord. We are admonished to look in the appropriate place for the source of our assistance. The hills referred to in this passage could have been the hills upon which the temple was established. This couplet affirms the transcendence of God. God is not to be found always in the immediacy of our situation, but as the One whose face we seek as we elevate our gaze. This couplet implies that as human beings we stand in constant need of divine assistance, but not just any help. The help called for must proceed from the One who created the very hills. Theologically this couplet suggests that only the one who is Creator can finally be relied on to be Redeemer.

Pastoral Perspective

There is a big difference between having and keeping. For instance, I might *have* a favorite sweater. It is my possession. However, I *keep* my puppy dog. He is not merely a possession; he is my beloved dog. He is dear to me. Therefore, I watch over him not for my sake, but for his. I protect him from harm because if he suffers, it hurts me too.

Likewise, God does not merely have us. God keeps us. We are God's beloved, and immeasurably dear to God. We are not merely possessions in the eyes of the Lord, because if we suffer, it hurts God too. Psalm 121 celebrates the fact that Lord is our keeper.

This short psalm uses some form of the word that means to keep (*shamar*) six times in the course of merely eight verses. English language translations vary in their word choice for *shamar*. The NRSV uses the words "keep" and "keeper." The New Jerusalem Bible uses the language of "guarding," and of God being a "guardian." The NIV uses the language of "watching over" as well as of "keeping." The KJV uses the words "keep" and "preserve."

The psalm appears to be set in the context of a pil-grimage. The psalmist looks to the hills, which may be Mount Zion, God's holy mountain and the place of the temple. Presumably it is not an easy journey, and the opening verse cries out a stark question, "From where will my help come?"

Exegetical Perspective

The observance of the season of Lent is often described as a journey. In Psalm 121, the psalmist seems to be on, or about to embark upon, a journey. In fact, the Songs of Ascent (Pss. 120–134) probably originated as a pilgrimage collection. Not coincidentally, it seems, the opening sequence of Psalms 120–122 moves the psalmist from a location outside the land (Ps. 120:5) toward "the hills" (Ps. 121:1) and finally into Jerusalem (Ps. 122:2). By way of an encounter with Psalm 121, perhaps the ancient psalmist and the contemporary worshiper can become, in some sense, fellow travelers.

The exact referent and precise significance of "the hills" in verse 1 are unclear. Given the context of Psalm 121, it is possible that among "the hills" in the distance, the psalmist can see Mount Zion, the destination of the pilgrimage. In this case, the mention of "the hills" alludes to the source of "my help," which the psalmist asks about in the second part of verse 1. On the other hand, for one about to set out on a journey, "the hills" could well conceal a host of difficulties and dangers, thus explaining why the psalmist needed to ask, "From where will my help come?"

Most commentators prefer the former interpretive option, but the latter has much to commend it. Karl Plank suggests that Psalm 121 be read intertextually with a rabbinic midrash in which Abraham recites

Homiletical Perspective

Somewhere along the way an editor named Psalm 121 "A Song of Ascents." As such, it could be a song sung by pilgrims on their way to the sanctuary in Jerusalem—the dwelling place of God—for one particular festival, or another. Perhaps "I lift my eyes to the hills" is similar to saying, "Tomorrow, I leave for Jerusalem." Once again, a psalm that becomes a psalm of the community begins as a psalm of the individual.

It seems safe to say that even if overused, to think of life as a journey is a true and helpful metaphor. One day God's Spirit breathes us into life, and one day we will breathe our last. In between, we meet people, visit places, grow and develop, and have experiences of all kinds. Folks from the Reformed tradition like to talk of life as a journey of sanctification whereby, one day beyond death, we will be fully formed into the image of Christ. This larger journey is made up of an untold number of smaller journeys, each of them contributing to our eventual wholeness.

For the person who is at least trying to heed the call of God, to follow Jesus, and to attend to the Spirit's prompting, each of these smaller journeys, as well as the lifetime journey, is begun in God. It is as if God runs slightly ahead of us on the path of life and waves at us to come and join God.

This presumes that there is always some distance between where we are standing and where God is

Psalm 121

Theological Perspective

Verses 3–4 affirm the constancy of God. God is steadfast, sure, faithful, and dependable. Theologically the constancy of God's nature has normally been affirmed as an attribute over against God's acts of mercy. The problem with this juxtaposition is that the nature of God and the acts of God both must be discerned in the experience of the faithful. John Calvin thus lifted up the notion of the invisible constancy of God. From the human perspective, one can only point to the constancy of God with the invisible evidence of faith and hope. Further, this constancy is demonstrated in the fact that God is the firm ground on which we stand (God will not let our feet be moved under us) and in the fact that God is the one who watches over us. Constancy is not just a feature of God's nature; it is also the reason for God's vigilance. This constancy has both spatial and temporal manifestations. God is not only the ground of our being, to use a phrase from Paul Tillich; God is also the guardian of our hope.

Verses 5–6 affirm that God is also keeper. God's function as keeper highlights the fact that Israel requires protection from nature itself. Without delving into questions of theodicy, the psalmist declares that the very sun that gives light by day can be dangerous, and the moon that gives light by night can be perilous. Humanity cannot rely even upon nature as if nature did not need redemption. The presence of God assures Israel that they shall not be smitten by sun or moon. These words can provide great insight into the being of God for persons whose experience suggests that nature itself has conspired against them. Its theological message is that God's sovereignty extends to the natural realm. Whether one confronts the demons of the day or the nemesis of the night, God's presence is affirmed.

Verses 7–8 affirm that God is also preserver. In God's role as preserver God's protection extends into the realm of the unknowable; that is, the realm of evil. In preserving the psalmist from evil, God also preserves the soul of the psalmist. There is a clear theological connection here between the menace of evil and the endangerment of the soul. Theologically speaking, the protection that God provides is portable. God as preserver attends both to one's going out and one's coming in. Finally, it is important to note theologically that this preservation is not limited temporally. From this point on, declares the psalmist, God's protection will follow him.

In each of the couplets that comprise this psalm, the nature of God is gradually revealed. God is majestic helper, faithful keeper, and preserver. This

Pastoral Perspective

Even if modern readers do not catch that this psalm takes place in the midst of a pilgrimage, nothing is taken away from the power of the psalmist's cry for help. On a gut level, we know what it means to lift our eyes to the hills in search of help. Inevitably we have all made this cry at challenging times in our lives.

Western culture in the twenty-first century promotes individualism and self-sufficiency, but at some point we all have to face the reality that we simply cannot be our own gods. If we try to be our own gods, life will remind us otherwise sooner or later. We will have to look to the hills and ask for help.

Some people feel closest to God in the midst of good times, when everything seems to be going well. These people get discouraged when they hit challenges. Others, however, find a greater closeness to God in the dark and challenging times. This is because their protective guard comes down, and they have no choice but to recognize their place in relationship to the Almighty. They have no choice but to acknowledge the limits to their own power.

There is a blessing given in the moments when we become aware of our powerlessness. In a sense, these are not so much moments in which we are more powerless than usual. Rather, these are moments when we are more informed than usual about how little power we possess. These are moments when our illusion of power is stripped away and we are blessed to suffer the reality that we need help beyond ourselves. Though it is an uncomfortable realization, it is a blessing to be able to live in the truth, after all, and it provides a footing for our sincere cry to the Lord.

Psalm 121 begins at this point, with this realization of need. It opens with the question, "From where will my help come?" The rest of the psalm is a response to this initial question. The first verse is preparation for all that is to follow. Without a moment's hesitation, the psalmist proclaims an answer to the question, saying, "My help comes from the LORD, who made heaven and earth" (v. 2).

The psalmist then dwells on the ways in which the Lord is our keeper and is worthy of our trust.

First of all, the psalmist reminds us that the Lord comes with some credentials, having made heaven and earth. In the next breath, the psalmist goes from the celestial realm to the immediate physical realm, saying "He will not let your foot be moved" (v. 3). God will not sleep on the job, as it were (vv. 3–4). God will protect us both day and night (v. 6). Finally, the Lord keeps both our going out and our coming in (v. 8). In other words, God will watch over all the

Exegetical Perspective

Psalm 121:1 at the very point at which he has raised the knife to kill his son Isaac (see Gen. 22:10; note that the OT Lesson for this Sunday, Gen. 12:1–4, features Abraham, who is about to depart on a journey). As Plank concludes:

> Assurance means little where no anxiety can exist. . . . The psalm places a human being before hills whose liminality may encourage, but which also must include the dismay of Abraham at Moriah. . . . Lifting eyes to *this* horizon brings to one's lips the genuine question of help and bids those who answer it honor the anxiety of the questioning voice. "Help comes from YHWH, who made the heavens and earth," the psalm proclaims. "But who can speak it without pause?" the midrash replies—a cautionary word of which perhaps the psalmist, too, was aware in the silent space between question and answer.[1]

Hearing verse 1b as a "genuine question of help" is especially appropriate for a Lenten reading of Psalm 121. It puts contemporary readers in touch with our own anxieties and our own authentic neediness, making it more likely that our Lenten journeys will be less about ourselves and our own accomplishments (for instance, what we might manage to give up) and more about our fundamental dependence upon God and God's help.

Repetition of "my help" in verse 2 opens the psalmist's response to her or his own question. This instance of step-like repetition is well suited for a poem about a journey, which in the ancient world would have been undertaken one step at a time (see additional step-like repetition involving "keeps" and "slumber" in vv. 3–4 and "keep" in vv. 7–8). That help comes from God is a frequent affirmation in the Psalms (see 22:19; 33:20; 54:4; 63:7; 70:5; 115:9–11; 124:8). The description of God as the one "who made heavens and earth" is characteristic of the Songs of Ascent (see 124:8; 134:3). It is especially reassuring, given that one of the threats to the journeying psalmist involves major creational features, the sun and the moon (v. 6).

A different voice speaks in verses 3–8, offering further assurance to the psalmist. The change of speakers suggests an original liturgical or life setting, perhaps a farewell ritual at the beginning of a journey. Verses 3–4 contain the first two instances of a Hebrew root that occurs six times. It is translated "keeps" in verses 3–4, where the focus is on God's

1. Karl A. Plank, "Ascent to Darker Hills: Psalm 121 and Its Poetic Revision," *Literature and Theology* 11/2 (June 1997): 163.

Homiletical Perspective

beckoning. Frequently the journey between our standpoint along the way and God's is not entirely smooth sailing. The view where God stands may be spectacular, but getting there nearly always calls for more courage, skill, confidence, and gifts than we currently feel we possess.

The journey could be to leave one job for another or to re-create and reimagine the job one already has. It could be to go to school, to pursue some soul yearning, or to risk giving voice to some deeply held belief. It could be to move to another city and country or to give up some addiction that is holding one hostage.

For a community of faith, the journey could be to develop a new ministry; to engage a social issue; to add, subtract, or breathe new life into the liturgy; to expand or reduce the staff; to sell a building; or to take in a homeless family.

Whatever the particulars, the thing that turns these journeys into journeys of ascent is that a church or an individual perceives that to embark upon them is to respond to the God who calls us to leave one place for another. Perhaps the original destination was Jerusalem, Zion, the city of God; but if we let Jerusalem represent the place where God is, then this psalm can be about all our going out and coming in—our births and our deaths, our hellos and good-byes, our expanding and our decreasing, our risky adventures and our safe returns home.

This psalm begins at the point of departure. A destination is in sight, and it looks to the pilgrim as if God is calling for him, or he at least hopes to find God at that destination. The pilgrim sees the hills but is a little intimidated at the challenge. He cannot make this journey alone and wonders where to look for confidence and support. He remembers the stories of his faith, the testimonies of his friends and family, and his own experiences to date. Like Joshua stating whom he is going to serve, the psalmist places all his eggs in one basket: "My help comes from the LORD, who made heaven and earth." Confidence is established because he is heeding the call of the one who made the world and imagined all the possible journeys one might take, along with their dangerous passages and holy stopping places.

Then a wonderful thing happens. A host of voices rises up to affirm his confession. A brave pilgrim embraces the call of God, and her friends rush to surround her with reminders, blessings, and their own statements of faith. It is a good thing to be immersed in a community that encourages those decisions that lead to life.

Psalm 121

Theological Perspective

psalm must have been the source of great encouragement to Israel, and it still carries the potential to bear up those whose journey through life is filled with uncertainty and danger. To know that God is one "who sits high and looks low" celebrates the majesty of God without sacrificing the sense of God's lovingkindness. To know that God is one who is under our feet and over our head celebrates the fact that God's love is evident both from below and from above.

The structure of the psalm hints at a final theological possibility. It has been suggested that the first verse of each couplet was not originally a declaration but a question, to which the second verse was the answer. The possibility that the psalm was originally a series of questions and answers highlights the fact that the reality of God is sought and found amid the challenges of life as well as the wonders of worship. The notion that the psalms may present not only jubilant answers but also troubling questions for the faithful is a key to their theological durability.

Psalms have often provided the content of African American sacred music. More and more, they provide the content of contemporary Christian music. This type of music, often called "praise and worship" music, is focused on creating a sense of joy and even euphoria in the presence of God. This way of construing the message of the psalms often accompanies the preaching of a "prosperity gospel." While the dimension of praise legitimately belongs to the Psalms tradition, what is often overlooked is its interrogatory dimension. A careful reading of this psalm, and others of its ilk, reveals a balance in the life of the believer. This is the balance between the tough questions of life and the deep answers of faith.

JAMES H. EVANS JR.

Pastoral Perspective

motion of our life. The Lord's protection is all-encompassing.

What a shock this must be to those in the pews who think they are keeping their own lives! They balance their own checkbooks; they stay on top of their own medical appointments; they do their own shopping; and they generally take personal responsibility for their own well-being. The idea that they have a keeper who watches over them and protects them may be tough to understand, let alone to accept.

Having a keeper is a two-way street. For all that we gain, we must first give ourselves to the one who offers the protection. We gain protection, but we lose a sense of total independence. In other words, the singular theme of Psalm 121 may not sound like great news to everybody. It may sound like an enormous encroachment on our lives.

Return for a moment to the simple notion of caring for pets. We do not have them, but we keep them. We provide for them. We take care of them. We do this because of the bond we feel for them.

It is as hard to accept that the Lord is my keeper as it is to accept that the Lord loves me, but these two facts are intertwined. That is the key to understanding not merely what the Lord does for us, but why. God's love is the very foundation of God's trustworthiness. God loves us, and therefore God keeps us.

ROBERT W. FISHER

Exegetical Perspective

constant protection. The reference to a "foot" that will not be "moved" fits well with the setting of a literal journey, but the verb occurs elsewhere in the Psalms to describe more generally God's protecting, even life-saving, work (see 16:8; 55:22; 62:2, 6, NRSV "shaken"; 66:9, NRSV "slip"; 112:6; see also 125:1, where Zion "cannot be moved," and 96:10, where "the world . . . shall never be moved").

The key word is again featured in verse 5a, which is at or very close to the center of the psalm. The subject, "the LORD," precedes the verb, giving it additional rhetorical emphasis. A traveler on foot would have needed protection from the sun (see Isa. 49:10). As for the moon, its light was apparently viewed as dangerous (see Matt. 4:24; 17:15 where the Greek underlying "epileptic" is more literally "moon-struck"; note that the English word "lunatic" is derived from the Latin word for moon).

Three more occurrences of the key word are found in the final section. Each occurrence of "keep" in verses 7–8 extends the reach of God's protecting presence, effectively broadening the image of a journey beyond any particular journey. The real journey becomes "your life"; and on this journey, God will "keep you from all evil . . . from this time on and forevermore." The promise is comprehensive. It is appropriate, therefore, as James Limburg points out, that Psalm 121 is used liturgically in the Lutheran tradition in both services of baptism and services of burial. Limburg calls Psalm 121 "a psalm for sojourners," because it ultimately portrays life as a journey and suggests that we people of faith are always on the way.[2]

As Jesus reminded his followers, and as we remind ourselves during the season of Lent, the way of following Jesus leads to a cross (see Mark 8:34). To read Psalm 121 on our Lenten journey is to claim and celebrate the good news that even as we face that evil of all evils, God is and always will be our keeper.

J. CLINTON MCCANN JR.

Homiletical Perspective

You cannot read this psalm without being struck by the repetition of the various forms of the word "keep." A sermon about what it means to be kept might be powerful. As easy as it seems to lose our grip on God, it is nice to know that God does not lose a grip on us. Our security as a community of faith and as individuals is not ultimately resting on "getting everything right."

God has already decided we are not throwaways. Someone has already assumed a certain amount of responsibility for us and stays vigilant even when we sleep and even when we slip. We can release ourselves into rejuvenating rest, partly because we know God's watchful eye and creative hand never cease. This notion also finds expression in John 10:28, when Jesus reminds his disciples that those who belong to him can never be snatched out of his hands.

A recurring theme of Scripture reminds us that, when we are busy following where God leads us, God assumes responsibility for our safety and our shade. Maybe more accurately, God assumes responsibility for our lives. The psalmist makes a general statement in the first measure of verse 7 and then thickens the statement in the second measure: "The LORD will keep you from all evil," and what I mean by that is that "the LORD will keep your life." There may be some pain in this journey—and even death—but it will not be meaningless pain or meaningless death, and you will not experience it alone. There will be resistance and there will be danger, but the Lord will be with you. So, light out. There is good stuff to be found on the way.

DAVID M. BURNS

2. James Limburg, "Psalm 121: A Psalm for Sojourners," *Word and World* 5/2 (Spring 1985): 180, 185–87.

Romans 4:1-5, 13-17

¹What then are we to say was gained by Abraham, our ancestor according to the flesh? ²For if Abraham was justified by works, he has something to boast about, but not before God. ³For what does the scripture say? "Abraham believed God, and it was reckoned to him as righteousness." ⁴Now to one who works, wages are not reckoned as a gift but as something due. ⁵But to one who without works trusts him who justifies the ungodly, such faith is reckoned as righteousness. . . .

¹³For the promise that he would inherit the world did not come to Abraham or to his descendants through the law but through the righteousness of faith. ¹⁴If it is the adherents of the law who are to be the heirs, faith is null and the promise is void. ¹⁵For the law brings wrath; but where there is no law, neither is there violation.

¹⁶For this reason it depends on faith, in order that the promise may rest on grace and be guaranteed to all his descendants, not only to the adherents of the law but also to those who share the faith of Abraham (for he is the father of all of us, ¹⁷as it is written, "I have made you the father of many nations")—in the presence of the God in whom he believed, who gives life to the dead and calls into existence the things that do not exist.

Theological Perspective

As Paul turns to the example of Abraham to present his thesis of the primacy of grace over law, he inadvertently raises the question of the relationship between theology and the religious community. Clearly Abraham is the father of Israel; this accounts for Paul's turning to Abraham to support his theology and his position that Christian Gentiles are full members of the (Jewish) community of faith. But Paul goes on in support of his position to claim Abraham as the spiritual father of all the nations, of all "those who share the faith of Abraham" (4:16, 17). This raises two important theological concerns: (1) Does the Abrahamic tradition in the biblical narrative provide a unifying principle for the biblical message and therefore for the religious traditions that see Abraham as their spiritual father? (2) What is the connection between theology and religious unity?

Since the time of Marcion, the issue of the relationship between the God of Abraham and the God of Jesus has beset the church. How does the message of good news contained in the Old Testament relate to the message of good news contained in the New? Is the Old Testament primarily preparatory for the New? Is the New Testament the basis for interpreting the Old, even to the point of revising certain aspects of the Old Testament? Is the message in both testaments the same, though seen from different times

Pastoral Perspective

One way to frame and begin using the messages of this text would be to address our confusion about the sequencing of two basic dynamics of Christian faith and life: discipleship and the act of doxology that is our response to the unmerited gift of faith. Doxology is our praise of the God who first loved us. It is praise for the creation God called into existence out of "things that do not exist" (Rom. 4:17). It is praise for redemption through Christ who "died for the ungodly" (Rom. 5:6). It is praise for the sustaining work of the Holy Spirit in us interceding "with sighs too deep for words" (Rom. 8:26). One of the highest moments of Christian liturgy is the doxology. In any act of doxology we assume the role of grateful, albeit unworthy creatures who praise our Creator.

The problem is that we create the impression that discipleship has to come before doxology. Often our emphasis in the church is on what we are to do for God, what we need to accomplish for God and provide for God, for God's church, and for God's kingdom. We never explicitly say we are obligated to do all this before we can bask in God's love and favor, but the impression is created. We have to do God's work before we can savor God's love. We have somehow to prove we merit God's love by our good works for God.

Unfortunately, this unspoken, and to some degree unintended, message coincides with a very strong

Exegetical Perspective

"What then are we to say was gained by Abraham, our ancestor according to the flesh?" Paul's rhetorical question at verse 1 calling attention to the "fleshly" (*sarx*) understanding of Abraham is a provocative way to begin his clarifying argument about the distinction between faith and works.

In order to understand these verses from Romans 4, one must first take into consideration the larger context of this material, Romans 3:21–8:39. Romans 3:21–22 establishes what had been summarily introduced in 1:17: it is not through works of the law that God's righteousness is known, but "through faith in Jesus Christ *for all who believe*." This basic point is developed in chapters 4 and 5 and further defended and expanded in chapters 6–8. Paul's elaborate explanation of God's justifying righteousness and unyielding love (Rom. 8:39) provides the theological core for his lengthy communiqué to all God's beloved in Rome.

The symbolic recasting of Abraham in chapter 4 is Paul's rhetorical tool for presenting his core message. Paul introduces Abraham as the paradigmatic figure for demonstrating the inclusive nature of the gospel, which is God's powerful means for salvation for "everyone who has faith, to the Jew [*Ioudaios*] first and also to the Greek [*Hellēn*]" (Rom. 1:16). Paul has to demonstrate that Abraham, who is understood to be the exclusive patriarch of the Jews, is now to be

Homiletical Perspective

Paul turns in this passage to Abraham's faith as a prototype of the trust fundamental to embracing God's embrace. In so doing, Paul transcends any temptation to make Abraham a poster boy for faithful adherence to the law. The irony of such a parochial confinement of Abraham is not lost on Paul, especially since in Abraham's day there was no Torah. Besides, neither Abraham nor anyone else has the innate capacity to live up to the commands of the law. Such adherence is tantamount to pulling ourselves up by our bootstraps, a losing proposition. In releasing Abraham from association with the confines of the law, Paul recovers Abraham as a model of faith for both Gentiles and Jews. God's promise was a gift of grace to all humankind, to be appropriated solely by faith. To Paul, Abraham is the father of us all, an archetype of faithfulness.

How do we translate these profound Pauline abstractions into contemporary flesh and blood? We will need to alert our hearers to the extent to which our psyches have been hijacked by the competitive, achievement-driven values of Western society. No wonder a noticeable segment of our congregations still naively assumes that we must earn God's approval, like "puff-a-billies" grunting, "I think I can, I think I can." In Western culture, whether we wear work jeans or starched collars, we are conditioned

Romans 4:1-5, 13-17

Theological Perspective

and situations and understood in different ways by differing cultures?

The Christian church ultimately resolved that the unity of the Hebrew and Greek Scriptures must be affirmed, because the God of Abraham and the God of Jesus are the same, one God. This has not, however, resolved all the problems. Over the centuries the church has continued to struggle with issues of law and grace, of cultural practices versus eternal principles, and of the relationship between Judaism and Christianity. A related concern today among Christians is the nature of the revelation of Christ: Is Jesus, the incarnate Son of God, unique? Is salvation only through Jesus?

If Jesus is the only way to God, the only truth, the only path to eternal life (see John 14:6), then the revelation of God in the Old Testament must be seen as inferior, misunderstood, unclear, and inadequate. Such a position logically leads to the conclusion that one cannot assume the revelation of God everywhere in Scripture is adequate, that God's people were misled and mistaken. Therefore we cannot trust that our revelation is adequate and cannot be sure that we are not being misled. Of course there is always the alternative of following the example of Thomas Jefferson and editing the Bible to fit our presuppositions.

On the other hand, if the God of Abraham is also the God of Jesus—as the church determined when it excommunicated Marcion and opposed his teaching—then one task of biblical interpretation is to uncover this unity. The God revealed in Jesus, bringing salvation to all who will accept it, is the same God revealed in Abraham, Moses, Isaiah, and Esther. The unique nature of Jesus will be seen as a unique revelation of the one God who is also revealed in many other places and ways. Salvation, then, is through the revelation and work of God (John 14 makes clear that Jesus and the Father are one) and can be known through other religions. How we understand the relationship between the God of Abraham and the God of Jesus has major implications regarding how we enter into religious dialogue with Jews, Muslims, and followers of other world religions.

The second question concerns the relationship between theology and the religious community. If Paul is correct in saying that Jews and Christians share the same faith and are at least spiritual descendants of Abraham, then the first tragedy was the division between the synagogue and the church. Clearly the differences were perceived as greater than any common heritage. One suspects that interpretation followed communal identity, not the other way

Pastoral Perspective

social message: that you have to work for whatever you are going to receive. This is a universal message; it is hardly limited to the United States, but it is certainly strong in our highly individualistic and competitive society. Over and over again we are told we have to work for what we expect to earn or receive. Even allowing for a healthy amount of skepticism about just how fairly rewards are distributed in our society, parents pass on to children a prevailing belief that you have to work for what you expect to receive. Early in our lives it is hardwired into us. As the text puts it, wages are not a gift but what is due because of work.

So an implicit message in the church and an explicit message in our society conspire to lead people to believe they will be entitled to God's love and worthy of God's love only if they earn it.

Addressing this fundamental misconception about our relationship with God is a wonderful challenge for a pastor. It gives him or her the opportunity to draw people into the experience of doxology. It does not excuse the pastor from addressing the matter of discipleship. It simply and wonderfully allows him or her to put discipleship as the sequel of doxology.

Along the way, there are some language problems, especially with the word "righteousness," which appears several times in these verses and is key to what is being said here. "Righteousness" is not exactly on everyone's tongue, and usually when it is spoken, there is a noticeable shading of disdain. Closely related is the problem with the word "law." In our culture, especially among younger Christians, faith is seen as the experience of relationships: relationships with God and with other people in the community of faith and outside of it as well. It is easy to view something like law as a legalistic intrusion.

Fortunately the traditional definition of "righteousness" has been "to live in a right relationship with God and with other people." The warrant for this definition is the pattern laid down in some of our foundational texts: the Ten Commandments and the Great Commandment among others. So if we want to address the issue of the word "righteousness" the emphasis should be on the relationship it points to. The relationship is with God, not God's decrees. Calvin points us in this direction by stressing that our obedience is not to the law but to Christ, the one who knows us, comes to us, redeems us, and is our advocate with God the Father. Likewise, if we address the word "law," it will be helpful to point out that the law is useful in telling us what beliefs and behaviors please God.

The heart and soul of this text is the proclamation of the unmerited grace that comes from God to us.

reimagined in a more universal, eschatological manner. Because Abraham was so central for Jewish identity, Paul utilizes a type of ethnic reasoning that emphasizes language of ancestry, inheritance, and offspring to redefine and expand the assumptions about the social and ethnic composition of the believers in Rome.

By calling attention to "our ancestor according to the flesh" (*ton propatora hēmōn kata sarka*, v. 1), Paul is charging his audience with the task of reviewing their expectations and assumptions regarding the meaning and extent of faith (*pistis*). This phrase "according to the flesh" is used in other places throughout Romans (1:3; 8:4, 5, 12, 13; 9:3, 5), and Paul refers to his own lineage with ethnic terminology that confirms his connection to the seed of Abraham (*ek spermatos Abraam*, Rom. 11:1; cf. Phil. 3:5).

This emphasis on Abraham stems from the imaginary Jewish interlocutor Paul is debating, introduced at 2:17, who understands Jewish identity and faithfulness solely through the law: "But if you call yourself a Jew and rely on the law and boast of your relation to God . . ." Therefore, in Romans 4, Paul intentionally goes to the "law" and analyzes Abraham's faithfulness as narrated in Genesis 15–17.

Specifically, Paul provides a scriptural proof at verse 3 to demonstrate that the faith *of* Abraham is the means through which he was credited with righteousness: "Abraham *believed* God, and it was *reckoned* to him as righteousness" (v. 3, emphasis added, quoting Gen. 15:6b). In verses 4–5, the gift of righteousness is contrasted with the payment of earned wages, which are obligated because of "works" (*erga*). In contrast, Abraham's righteousness was not something he had earned by reason of his good deeds; rather, it was something freely given to him, solely on the basis of his faith (*pistis*).

In verses 6–12, omitted from this lection, Paul continues his argument about faith by calling attention to the issue of circumcision, another explicit example of the ethnic reasoning evident in this chapter. According to the Genesis narrative, Abraham did not receive the commandment to be circumcised (Gen. 17:9–14) until *after* he had already been reckoned as righteous on the basis of his faith (Gen. 15:6). Paul summarizes this point to indicate that Abraham received the "sign of circumcision" (*sēmeion peritomēs*) as a "seal" (*sphragis*) of the righteousness that he had *by faith* while he was still uncircumcised (*akrobystia*, 4:11).

At verse 13, Paul continues his discourse about Abraham, yet he now ups the ante by referring to the

from birth by the supposition that we are "the masters of our fate, the captains of our soul." Paul could only grimace at this surmise that we have the innate capacity and capability for spiritual self-fulfillment.

Given our cultural addiction to bootstrap psychology, we are not surprised that many would find confounding, if not audacious, Paul's claim for salvation by faith alone. Paul's tag line about God creating something from nothing can only sound strange to contemporary folk who have been nurtured from birth on the fiction that we alone have the gumption to make *of ourselves* something from nothing. We shall need, therefore, to spend time in the sermon deconstructing this spiritual self-help fallacy. Otherwise, our people will be tempted to dismiss what we say as the usual religious bromides that pose little challenge to their deeply engrained, works-oriented value system.

We shall want to be sparing with the time we devote to dismantling spiritual pride. We owe it to the text to blow our trumpet where the text does, on the riches in the unmerited gift of righteousness through faith alone. God's gift of grace is the capstone of this passage. We shall, therefore, want to spend at least half of the sermon picturing for our people this grace at work in our lives. Such a goal can be as threatening as it is rewarding. To picture God's grace at work on the soul's inscape, as well as the culture's landscape, calls for a spiritual acuity that is not easy to keep finely tuned. Some weeks we feel less connected to grace than in others, less certain about where in the humdrum of our dailiness grace is doing her dance. When such a vision dims or even disappears from our radar screen, how tempting in the pulpit to compensate for this void, however unconsciously, by haranguing the people for their absence of faith.

Grace abounds! Even our awaking to this imbalance in our preaching can be a gift of grace. In our growing awareness of the ways in which we shut ourselves off from grace, we become more sensitive to the same dynamic in the people we serve. Hence we are more available to help them discover their possibilities in faith.

It is time now to fill that newly gained space with images of grace at work in our lives. Abstract explanations will not do, nor tired commonplaces. The Word became flesh so that we could *see and feel* grace happening: Jesus incarnating grace by opening a blind man's eyes, by stilling the angry sea, by feeding hundreds with a few loaves and fish; Jesus picturing grace-alive with parables about a resourceful bookkeeper, or a forgiving father, or a grateful debtor.

Romans 4:1-5, 13-17

Theological Perspective

around. Orthodox Judaism saw Abraham as keeping the law by anticipation and therefore in accord with the Mosaic tradition; Paul saw Abraham as preceding the law and therefore saved by faith. The common thread is interpreted differently, depending on the community in which it is read.

At least since the groundbreaking work of sociologists like Ernst Troeltsch and H. Richard Niebuhr, we have understood there are many factors that produce the particular theologies of particular Christian denominations. While the proclamation of the gospel may produce the community, the particular theology emerges from the context of the particular community. This explains why the search for a common doctrine has not produced unity for the churches. The contrary seems to be the case, especially as one considers the fractured nature of Protestantism.

As a particular theological emphasis emerges within a particular church, if members come to believe this represents the true faith and other understandings are inferior, they will use the understanding for division. Each group proclaims it holds the true faith, judges the other, and divides the organization. Far from being a force for unity, theology appears to be a cause of division. Just as Jew and Christian could not find unity in a common spiritual ancestor, so too the Christian churches continue to divide over theological differences while claiming to worship the same God.

The relationship between theological doctrine and the community remains complex. People join and leave churches for numerous reasons—the theological emphasis being one among many. Nevertheless, the church needs theology. Ignoring differences or dumbing down belief to avoid conflict does not provide sufficient intellectual support in today's world. What appears to be needed is humility, recognition that "our truth" may not be the ultimate truth about God; a commitment to unity, recognition that love does not depend on uniformity but welcomes a diversity of gifts; and a priority for mission, coming together with all our diversity, sharing gifts to reach out to those who need good news.

WARD B. EWING

Pastoral Perspective

God's grace is evident in God's choice to love us, which sets us in a right relationship with God. This grace is brought to us in Jesus Christ. As Luther discovered to his great joy, after years of trying to be righteous by his good works, it is simply by faith that we enter into a right relationship with God. "Faith" can be another challenging word. Classically it is described as having three dimensions: trust in God, beliefs about God, and the way of life we are led into by faith. In this text the emphasis is on faith as trust. Faith for Abraham was a willingness to trust in God. He did not have to earn it. He did not have to embark on the long pilgrimage and find his way to that distant land in order for God to love him. He did not even have to take the first step. He was loved, deemed worthy, and called to a new life before he had done anything.

The wellspring of doxology is discovered when we realize we stand before God incapable of earning God's grace and are instead worthy of that grace simply by God's blessed choice.

So we are inspired to say that the Christian life does not consist of doing good works to earn God's love; rather, and wonderfully, it consists of doing good works because of God's love. Doxology really does precede discipleship. Discipleship is still important, always important, an integral expression of our faith; yet it follows from, is inspired by, and is sustained by our doxology.

LAIRD J. STUART

promise (*epangelia*) that came to Abraham, a creative strategy for minimizing the significance of the law. Here, as in Galatians 3:15–18, Paul shows the limited nature of the law (connecting it to wrath at v. 15; cf. 1:18) and further highlights the supreme value of God's promises (e.g., Gen. 12:2–3; 15:5; 17:8; 22:17–18). Paul asserts: "The law, which came four hundred thirty years later, does not annul a covenant previously ratified by God, so as to nullify the promise" (Gal. 3:17).

Once again, Genesis 15:4–6 is crucial for interpreting verses 13–17, because of God's promise of an heir to an overage Abraham and his barren wife Sarah. Neither wavered in their confidence in God (Rom. 4:21). At Romans 4:16 the proof is revealed: "For this reason it [righteousness] depends on faith, in order that the promise may rest on grace and be guaranteed to all his descendants (*panti tō spermati*), not only to the keepers of the law but also to those being descended from the faithfulness of Abraham (*tō ek pisteōs Abraam*) because he is the ancestor of all of us" (my trans.).

Abraham's faith superseded the law. In other words, his faithfulness, not the law, guarantees and activates God's promise. The preposition *ek* (out of, from) is central for Paul's ethnic argument. As noted above, Paul refers to his ethnic lineage several times in his writings by using the preposition *ek* as a means for denoting his origins (e.g., Phil. 3:5; Rom. 11:1; Gal. 2:15). Now, in Romans 4:16, Paul demonstrates to his imaginary Jewish interlocutor how Gentiles, who do not adhere to the law and do not have the marks of circumcision or the birthright of Jewish status, are made righteous before God. It is their "kinship" based on lineage that opens the door for God's promise; and it is through Abraham's faithfulness that this lineage is generated. Therefore the quote in 4:17 is an excellent capstone to Paul's argument: "As it is written, 'I have made you the ancestor of many nations' (*ethnōn*)—in the presence of the God in whom he believed, who gives life to the dead and calls into existence the things that do not exist."

Abraham in Paul's ethnic reasoning becomes the archancestor for Jews and Gentiles alike—indeed, all of humanity. Paul's vision of faith is revealed in an inclusive and fluid fellowship, free of ethnic, class, and gender distinctions in which all who "belong to Christ . . . are Abraham's offspring, heirs according to the promise" (Gal. 3:29).

GAY L. BYRON

Preaching that embodies Jesus by definition majors in brushstrokes of particularity. This means not so much expatiating about forgiveness as picturing parents hugging their unwed, pregnant daughter; not so much expounding about peacemaking as depicting Christians, Jews, and Muslims together sorting out their differences; not so much propounding about sacrifice as describing a soldier falling on a grenade to save his buddy.

How then do we give shape to a sermon on this passage that incarnates more than explains the faith that is ours by grace alone? This could mean linking together several stories that dramatize faith: maybe a narrative of a man depressed by job loss, yet whose stability remains intact through faith in Christ; maybe a following narrative about a divorced single mother finding in her trust in Christ the strength to work two jobs while raising three children. In both instances we show personal integrity grounded in a living faith, rather than in achievements geared to the dictates of community norms.

In a more experimental form, let a story *be* the sermon. Take the mother struggling to maintain her sense of self-worth while scrambling as a parent and worker. The narrative could see her through exhaustion and despair to a point where she discovers in her devotional study of Scripture, or in a conversation in her Bible study group, Abraham's dependence for well-being on faith rather than works. The homily could conclude with her finding a new freedom and buoyancy in this awareness. Such a story-shaped sermon can hold the hearers' attention by its detail and dramatic flow. We take much care in the sermon's creation, because the meaning the story bears is mostly dependent upon the sermon's structure, style, and delivery.

DON WARDLAW

John 3:1-17

¹Now there was a Pharisee named Nicodemus, a leader of the Jews. ²He came to Jesus by night and said to him, "Rabbi, we know that you are a teacher who has come from God; for no one can do these signs that you do apart from the presence of God." ³Jesus answered him, "Very truly, I tell you, no one can see the kingdom of God without being born from above." ⁴Nicodemus said to him, "How can anyone be born after having grown old? Can one enter a second time into the mother's womb and be born?" ⁵Jesus answered, "Very truly, I tell you, no one can enter the kingdom of God without being born of water and Spirit. ⁶What is born of the flesh is flesh, and what is born of the Spirit is spirit. ⁷Do not be astonished that I said to you, 'You must be born from above.' ⁸The wind blows where it chooses, and you hear the sound of it, but you do not know where it comes from or where it goes. So it is with everyone who is born of the

Theological Perspective

This text is theologically rich and deeply provocative. Of the many themes that stir the imagination theologically, two are particularly important: the story's setting and what it suggests about discipleship, and its image of rebirth.

John begins the story somewhat abruptly. The reader is not told where the story takes place. We know only that Jesus is in Jerusalem during the Passover feast (2:23). John does little to introduce Nicodemus. We are told only that he is a Pharisee and a ruler, a member of the Sanhedrin. Readers familiar with the whole of John's story know that Nicodemus will reappear briefly, first interceding for Jesus with other Pharisees (7:50) and then in the story's conclusion (19:38–42), with Joseph of Arimathea, bringing spices to bury Jesus. Both in 3:1–21 and in 19:39 Nicodemus is identified as the one who first came to Jesus by night. He is the original night stalker.

Of the many images in John's Gospel, two major ones are light and darkness. Nicodemus emerges out of the night's darkness, seeking light from the teacher he believes to be sent from God. Just as suddenly as he appears, Nicodemus disappears back into the night from whence he came. Before he does so, Jesus tells him one must be born anew in order to see the kingdom of God, and the last we hear from Nicodemus is, "How can this be?" (v. 9). Jesus' last words are,

Pastoral Perspective

If any character from the Bible can be regarded as representative of twenty-first-century church members, it might be Nicodemus. In many ways he is a sympathetic character. A successful and self-confident man, he plays a leadership role in his community. He is spiritually open and curious, yet also rational. He approaches Jesus directly and tries to figure out Jesus' actions and social networks. He is committed and curious enough that he makes an appointment to talk with Jesus face to face. However, Nicodemus is not ready to go public with his interest in Jesus, so he makes the appointment in the middle of the night, when he can keep his faith secret, separated from the rest of his life. His imagination is caught by Jesus, but he wants to compartmentalize whatever faith he has. Nicodemus is not yet ready to declare his faith in the light of day, not prepared to let it change his life.

Like it or not, we look into the eyes of people like Nicodemus every Sunday morning. Being a mainline Protestant is not exactly trendy, and though people may come to church occasionally or even be active members, many believers with whom we interact are Nicodemuses in their wider life. They have faith, sometimes deep faith, and they are spiritually curious, but they keep faith in its own sphere.

Being a Nicodemus-like Christian is understandable in the twenty-first century. Believers, who have

Spirit." ⁹Nicodemus said to him, "How can these things be?" ¹⁰Jesus answered him, "Are you a teacher of Israel, and yet you do not understand these things?

¹¹"Very truly, I tell you, we speak of what we know and testify to what we have seen; yet you do not receive our testimony. ¹²If I have told you about earthly things and you do not believe, how can you believe if I tell you about heavenly things? ¹³No one has ascended into heaven except the one who descended from heaven, the Son of Man. ¹⁴And just as Moses lifted up the serpent in the wilderness, so must the Son of Man be lifted up, ¹⁵that whoever believes in him may have eternal life.

¹⁶"For God so loved the world that he gave his only Son, so that everyone who believes in him may not perish but may have eternal life.

¹⁷"Indeed, God did not send the Son into the world to condemn the world, but in order that the world might be saved through him."

Exegetical Perspective

The story of Nicodemus is the first of four sequential readings from the Gospel of John during Lent in Year A. Unique to John, it epitomizes key themes for this Gospel. An initial concern for exegesis of this passage is whether or not to extend the reading through 3:21. There are several reasons to reconsider the parameters of the text. First, verse 22 marks a distinctive shift in the narrative action: "After this Jesus and his disciples went into the Judean countryside." Second, Jesus does not stop talking after verse 17. If Jesus' words to Nicodemus continue through verse 21, it seems that the reading should extend through Jesus' intended conclusion.

A recurring structural pattern for the Fourth Gospel is sign, dialogue, discourse. Jesus performs a sign that is followed by a dialogue between Jesus and those present and then a discourse by Jesus that interprets the sign. While Jesus does not perform a sign for Nicodemus, Nicodemus's reference to "signs" in verse 2 introduces the conversation with Jesus and sets up Jesus' discourse in verses 10–21. A third reason to include verses 18–21 in the lectionary reading is theological. In verses 19–21 Jesus discloses a major theme for the Gospel of John, light and darkness. Light represents the realm of belief and darkness the realm of unbelief. When Jesus says to Nicodemus, "This is the judgment, that the light has come into

Homiletical Perspective

Some texts are so familiar and so loaded with associations that the thought of preaching them *one more time* is almost exhausting. What, you wonder, can you possibly say that has not already been said? It reminds me of a violinist I know who gets a little depressed every November, as she contemplates another season of *The Nutcracker* performances. It is not that she does not love and appreciate the music. It is just that every year, she plays the same part in the same way for six weeks straight, and there is only so much innovation one can bring to the third violin section. "I know it's an orchestra classic that comes with the territory, and I'm glad for the work," she says, "but I really wish people knew there was more to the repertoire than 'The Dance of the Sugar Plum Fairy.'"

John 3:1–17 is the preacher's equivalent of *The Nutcracker*: a pulpit classic that comes with the territory. Sooner or later we have to deal with its familiar prose, its theological elegance, its pride of place in our historical confessions. We also have a muddle of associations to manage, and that complicates things. The language of being "born again," and verse 16 in particular (instantly recognizable in its abbreviated form: "John 3:16"), is a staple of highway road signs and bumper stickers and football games. It is shorthand for a certain kind of religious fervor, as people everywhere, Christians and non-Christians alike, can tell you.

John 3:1-17

Theological Perspective

"Those who do what is true come to the light, so that it may be clearly seen that their deeds have been done in God" (v. 21). It will take Nicodemus a long time—until 19:38–42—to come once and for all out of the night and into the light.

Nicodemus is the one who comes to Jesus by night. He hovers on the margins and in the shadows of John's story. He is neither the first in the church nor the last to follow Jesus from afar. No doubt it was difficult, perhaps even dangerous, for Nicodemus to follow Jesus publicly, during the bright light of the day. He was, after all, someone who was part of the Jewish establishment, for whom Jesus seemed to be at first only a nuisance but later a political problem and threat. Nicodemus had to be cautious and to exercise discretion. He was the forerunner of many of Jesus' disciples who have had to be careful about when and where they practiced their discipleship.

In his seven letters to the churches in Asia, John of Patmos warned them to beware of the Nicolaitans (Rev. 2:6, 15), Christians who were willing to offer worship to pagan and Roman gods in order to remain unnoticed, if not tolerated, in a non-Christian world.[1] In the sixteenth century John Calvin referred to those who sympathized with the movement for the reform of the church but were reluctant to be publicly identified with it as "Nicodemites." In the midst of National Socialism, Nicodemus's heirs, the German Christians, sought to accommodate the gospel to the racism and anti-Semitism of Nazi ideology. In response, the Confessing Church in May 1934 declared, in the second thesis of the Theological Declaration of Barmen, "As Jesus Christ is God's assurance of the forgiveness of all our sins, so in the same way and with the same seriousness he is also *God's mighty claim upon our whole life*."[2]

Nicodemus admits that Jesus could not have performed his signs (2:23) unless God were with him. Jesus responds by answering a question Nicodemus did not ask. Not only is Jesus the presence of God, but those who are born from above—recreated in the water of baptism by the power of the Spirit—will see in these things Jesus has done the presence of the kingdom of God. Nicodemus does not understand what it means to be "born from above." Jesus tells him that to be born from above is to be born of the Spirit, and to be born of the Spirit is to believe in Jesus and in believing in him to have eternal life.

Pastoral Perspective

mixed marriages or pluralistic work settings, privilege tolerance and mutual respect over witnessing. Cultural norms push religion into the private sphere, positioning faith as appropriate for family and personal morality, but inappropriate for public issues. For two centuries mainline Protestantism has encouraged such behavior and attitudes. Our brand of religion promotes self-restraint, tolerance, and personal morality, and all are worthy virtues. We support public morality and an engagement in social issues, too, of course, but that message has been muffled by the declining size and increasing marginalization of mainline Protestant denominations. If people in our pews are Christians like Nicodemus, it is not necessarily because they have somehow failed as individual believers. In some cases we have pushed our members into their compartmentalized faith.

In and of itself, there is much to praise about a faith that thrives in the dark. It is genuine, heartfelt, personal, and often deep. The point is not that this hidden faith is somehow faulty—as far as it goes; the point is that it is too small. In this text Jesus suggests that Nicodemus's kind of faith is incomplete, even immature. He likens his midnight encounter with Nicodemus to a child still safe in its mother's womb. You are still gestating, Jesus implies. You must be born again, and declare this faith in the light of day.

Jesus seems impatient as he talks with Nicodemus. He is annoyed when Nicodemus does not immediately understand the metaphor of rebirth. He even mocks the Pharisee.

Jesus' impatience leads some people to read this text as a command: you must be born again. Many interpret rebirth as work that gestating Christians need to do. For these interpreters, the urgency of people making a decision to accept Christ as their Lord and Savior is paramount. However legitimate this interpretation might be, reading this text as a command is not the only option. In fact, it may be as legitimate—and certainly as pastoral—to read it as an invitation. When Jesus tells Nicodemus that he needs to be born again by water and Spirit, he is asking Nicodemus to let God work in his life.

In a wonderful sermon on this text, Debbie Blue observes that the metaphor of birth in this text is surprising and provocative.[1] It is surprising because it is so irrational, so beyond what will ever really happen to us physically, and Nicodemus gives voice to

1. Richard Bauckham, *The Theology of the Book of Revelation* (Cambridge: Cambridge University Press, 1993), 123–25.

2. "The Theological Declaration of Barmen," in *Book of Confessions: Study Edition of the Presbyterian Church (U.S.A.)* (Louisville, KY: Geneva Press, 1996), 311 (8.14). Italics added.

1. Debbie Blue, "Laboring God," in *Sensual Orthodoxy* (St. Paul, MN: Cathedral Hill Press, 2004), 31–37.

world, and people loved darkness rather than light" (v. 19), these words send the reader back to the beginning of chapter 3: Nicodemus comes to Jesus *by night*. The moment of judgment for Nicodemus is in this here-and-now encounter with Jesus.

It is because of Jesus' words in 3:18–21 that Nicodemus's meeting with Jesus is equivocal at best. The last words of Nicodemus to Jesus are "How can these things be?" (3:9), and in his conversation with Jesus he does not make much progress. Nicodemus interprets Jesus' words on a literal level, although (typical of Jesus in the Fourth Gospel) Jesus' words to him are deliberately ambiguous. "From above" (*anōthen*) can be translated three different ways— "again," "anew," or "from above" (3:3). Nicodemus hears only the first option. Whereas the Samaritan woman at the well (John 4) will be able to move to the next level of understanding, Nicodemus is not able to recognize what Jesus offers and, more importantly, who Jesus is.

For John's Gospel, an encounter with Jesus is the salvific moment. The dialogue with Nicodemus is not simply explanatory or conversational on Jesus' part. Rather, Jesus as the Word made flesh makes God known to Nicodemus (1:18). The question is whether or not Nicodemus will be able to see the truth about Jesus that Nicodemus himself confesses, that Jesus is the one who has come from God (3:2). So as to move Nicodemus along, Jesus' answer to Nicodemus's misunderstanding introduces the concept of being born of water and Spirit (v. 5).

While many commentators have interpreted these words through the lens of baptism, the whole of the Gospel narrative suggests other interpretive possibilities. In the next chapter, Jesus will offer himself as the source of living water (4:10) and will again connect water and Spirit, both of which he will provide (7:37–39). It is important, therefore, to situate interpretation of Jesus' words to Nicodemus within the context of Jesus' provision of water and this Gospel's unique understanding of the Spirit. The Spirit, the expressed gift from Jesus to the disciples when he reveals himself to them after the resurrection (20:22), is the Paraclete (Advocate, Comforter, Helper), the one who carries on the work and presence of Jesus when he returns to the Father. It should be this working out of water and Spirit that is brought forward to Jesus' words to Nicodemus.

After Nicodemus's incredulous question, "How can these things be?" (v. 9), he seems to disappear from the scene, and the reader is left with Jesus. All of a sudden, Jesus' words are directed specifically to the

This means that before a preacher has any room to do her job, she has to muck out a lot of stalls. She has to name the stereotypes and bad press that this passage evokes, so that there is space for us to hear the images afresh. John 3:1–17 may seem like the exclusive property of one brand of Christian, but the wisdom it offers is for each of us and all of us. On our Lenten journey to the cross, we need it.

Three homiletical tasks in particular present themselves.

Name the Terms. Let us face it: this passage has been used in some pretty awful ways to sort us into groups. "Are you born again?" is code language for, "Are you saved, like us?" or "Are you crazy, like them?" In its insider mode, it functions as a way to determine a person's salvation as a believer in Jesus Christ. In its outsider mode, it serves as a convenient way to label religious fanatics. Neither version of the question is especially accurate or helpful, because both rely on stereotypes of what it means to be a card-carrying Christian.

So the first thing a preacher has to do is to name how the term "born again" functions in his community, for better or worse: Is this a phrase we use to describe ourselves? Is it a phrase we use to differentiate "us" from "them"? What do we mean by the phrase "born again," and how do our understandings play into stereotypes? How do we decide if a person is "born again"? Who has the power to make that decision? Do our practices bind us together and build up the body of Christ, or do they create separation and conflict? The point, here, is to name your terms and debunk the bunk, so the community can start a conversation.

Shed a Little Light in the Neighborhood. Some artists love the challenge of reinterpreting a tried-and-true classic. Think of the choreographer Mark Morris and his adaptation of *The Nutcracker* (entitled, appropriately, "The Hard Nut"), or the painter Jasper Johns's rendition of the American flag, or Jimi Hendrix's Woodstock performance of the "Star Spangled Banner." Classic texts (or symbols or songs or scores) are classic for a reason: they convey to us a truth that begs to be seen and heard in our own context. That is why actresses memorize Shakespeare and bands play Duke Ellington. You do not need to be brilliant and ahead of your time to do this work. The most important thing is to be *in* your time, right where you are; to be part of your community, rooted in your own context, in the season of Lent; to be a theologian in

John 3:1-17

Theological Perspective

What does it mean to be born from above and to believe in Jesus? Unfortunately the lectionary has omitted the last four verses of this pericope (vv. 18–21), perhaps because the language of condemnation is no longer acceptable in churches that have made their peace with the culture that surrounds them. To be born from above by water and the Spirit, to believe in Jesus, is to leave the darkness and to come into the light (v. 19). What does it mean to live either in darkness or in light? Those who live in the darkness and hate the light do so because their evil deeds will be exposed (v. 20). To come into the light—to be born from above—is to do "what is true" (v. 21), to follow the one who is himself "the way, and the truth, and the life" (14:6).

For many Christians, the gospel is summarized by the words in John 3:16. Everyone who believes in Jesus will not perish but will have eternal life. Some Christians, however, understand faith or "believing in Jesus" to be simply what one does with one's mind. In John's Gospel, being born from above and believing in Jesus are clearly not so much about what one does with one's mind as about what one does with one's heart and one's life. "Those who do what is true come to the light, so that it may be clearly seen that their deeds have been done in God" (v. 21). In John's Gospel believing and doing are inseparable. Nicodemus lives in the darkness and the shadows of this story until its conclusion, when he emerges publicly with Joseph of Arimathea, who is also a "secret disciple," to bury Jesus.

GEORGE W. STROUP

Pastoral Perspective

that. This invitation to rebirth is nonsensical; nobody can literally be born again.

The invitation is provocative too, because it invites us to open our imaginations and reconsider our relationship with God, which is the central focus of this text, and, indeed, of this Gospel. Jesus invites Nicodemus, as he invites each of us, to come into the light of day and become mature believers, full participants in the abundant life he offers. Jesus knows that neither Nicodemus nor contemporary believers can do this on their own. It is God who will give birth in water and Spirit. Rebirth is God's gift to give, God's work to accomplish, and it is God who labors to bring us new life.

God works hard for us and our faith. God conceives us as Christians and nurtures us in the wombs of our faith, safe and warm and secret. At some point, like any pregnant woman who is close to full term, God gets impatient with gestation and wants to get on with it; God wants to push that baby through the birth canal into greater maturity, into fullness of life, into a faith lived wholly in the world. That is what Jesus talks about in this text. Jesus thinks it is time Nicodemus came through that spiritual birth canal. Perhaps he thinks it is time for many others to be reborn too. God is ready to give us birth by water and Spirit.

How many of our church members (or preachers) might be Nicodemuses in twenty-first-century garb? How many of our congregations might be organizational versions of him—people and institutions with compartmentalized faiths that flourish behind the scenes, out of sight, away from the fray, essentially in private? How many of us are gestating Christians? Who among us has room to grow in our faith? The good news of this text is that God is prepared—even eager—to do the hard, messy, sweating labor that will bring us to maturity and new life.

DEBORAH J. KAPP

readers of the story. Verse 11 begins in the second person singular: "Very truly I tell you." Then the "you" in "yet you do not receive our testimony" switches to second person plural. This places the reader in the same position as Nicodemus: in an encounter with Jesus. God loves the world, and this Gospel intends to secure and sustain belief in Jesus as the Christ, the Son of God (20:30–31). Because of the death, resurrection, and ascension of Jesus—all of which are implied in "the Son of Man must be lifted up"—eternal life is possible, but the incarnation ensures that eternal life includes life now, abiding in Jesus.

As for Nicodemus, he appears two other times in the Gospel of John. In 7:50–52 he seems to come to Jesus' defense in the midst of the intense conflict between Jesus and the religious authorities that sets off chapters 7 and 8, but his question to the Pharisees gives the impression of lukewarm advocacy for Jesus. Nicodemus's last appearance in the Gospel is to help Joseph of Arimathea, a *secret* disciple of Jesus, with the burial of Jesus' body (19:38–42). The reader is thereby reminded that Nicodemus first came to Jesus by night (19:39).

Moreover, he brings an extraordinary quantity of burial spices for the preparation of the body. Does this last appearance of Nicodemus finally represent his coming to the light? Or is he still in the dark, weighing down Jesus' body with spices so there will be no doubt that Jesus will remain in the tomb? Given this complicated character and his ambiguous status in the Gospel of John, interpreting this passage should highlight these complications and not smooth them out. Nicodemus does not ask for or require his rescue. His encounter with Jesus and his recurring role in the narrative suggest that believing in Jesus is indeed an ambiguous effort. In the Gospel of John, "faith" is never a noun. Believing for the characters in the Fourth Gospel is a verb (3:15–16) and is subject to all of the ambiguity, uncertainty, and indecisiveness of being human. Having an incarnate God necessitates an incarnational faith: believing is just as complicated as being human.

KAROLINE M. LEWIS

residence, someone who talks about God from the vantage point of truly *living* somewhere.

So what does "being born" look like where you live? Why would we want the chance to do it again? More accurately, since we cannot birth ourselves, why would we need someone to *bear* us again? Who bears us and bears with us today, and who has borne us in the past? Is this clean work, or messy work? How are our bodies and spirits involved? There are hundreds of questions and images to hold up to the light, again and again, to see how they grow in *your* neighborhood.

See the Humor. This text gives us a great foil in Nicodemus: he has already asked all the stupid questions. They are actually very funny questions. We can almost hear Jesus' amusement in verse 10: "Are you a teacher of Israel, and yet you do not understand these things?!" We could hear shame in those words—many have—but humor is often a better motivator than shame.

What if Jesus was exercising a little rabbinical irony instead of divine judgment? It changes our place in the story; suddenly, there is room for *our* ignorance too! Nicodemus reminds us that even the best educated and most authoritative among us are still searching. No sense in clucking over what we fail to understand (and will probably never grasp in its fullness until we see God face to face, as Paul says); better to laugh at our own efforts, and then get up and try again. Wisdom such as this passage offers is mysterious and paradoxical. It begs for a little space—both to be and to laugh.

ANNA CARTER FLORENCE

Exodus 17:1-7

¹From the wilderness of Sin the whole congregation of the Israelites journeyed by stages, as the Lord commanded. They camped at Rephidim, but there was no water for the people to drink. ²The people quarreled with Moses, and said, "Give us water to drink." Moses said to them, "Why do you quarrel with me? Why do you test the Lord?" ³But the people thirsted there for water; and the people complained against Moses and said, "Why did you bring us out of Egypt, to kill us and our children and livestock with thirst?" ⁴So Moses cried out to the Lord, "What shall I do with this people? They are almost ready to stone me." ⁵The Lord said to Moses, "Go on ahead of the people, and take some of the elders of Israel with you; take in your hand the staff with which you struck the Nile, and go. ⁶I will be standing there in front of you on the rock at Horeb. Strike the rock, and water will come out of it, so that the people may drink." Moses did so, in the sight of the elders of Israel. ⁷He called the place Massah and Meribah, because the Israelites quarreled and tested the Lord, saying, "Is the Lord among us or not?"

Theological Perspective

Like many other pieces of the long, complex narrative that tells of Israel's wilderness sojourn, this story of thirst and testing has at its center a critical question concerning God's presence. How can we know if God is with us, more literally, "in our midst"? What signs or evidence do we use for discerning the presence and providence of God?

The quarrelsome wilderness generation makes an assumption that seems quite natural and universal. When they have what they need and want, they believe God is with them. In times of hunger, thirst, and affliction, they deem themselves abandoned or betrayed. Worse, they wonder if God has ever traveled with them. Their venture toward freedom might prove a disastrous self-deceit.

Moses himself taught this theology of sufficiency, and God seemed to play along. In the previous chapter, the lack of food prompted complaints against Moses and Aaron. God responded by providing manna and quail, leading Moses and Aaron to assure the people that these things would prove that it was indeed the Lord who brought them out of Egypt (Exod. 16:6).

In addition to provisions, leaders like Moses also serve as surrogates for God or signs of God's presence. Thus, when the thirsty people bring suit against Moses, Moses replies (v. 2), "Why do you quarrel

Pastoral Perspective

Clergy quote Moses quite often. It could well be that next to Jesus, Moses is the most frequently quoted person in Scripture! As a denominational executive I consulted with numerous congregations in the Congregational tradition, as well as several churches in other traditions. During those consultations, Moses was quoted too many times. The spiritual leader (either lay or ordained) was usually the one who murmured, "Lord! What shall I do with this people? They are almost ready to stone me!" The quote was not precise, but the sentiment was the same. "Lord, you called me here to lead this people with a new vision, which we all agreed upon—it went well for a while, but now the murmurings are out of control."

One can imagine the growing excitement as Moses began to call God's people together, gathering their consent to lead them out of the bondage of slavery into the promise of freedom and a land to call their own. Support for his vision must have been overwhelming. While in Egypt, the people followed his directives to preserve themselves through the plagues, hail, storms, and, finally, Passover. When Pharaoh had had enough, the people packed up what was most important and headed in a hurry toward freedom and promise, not even waiting for the yeast to rise. The yoke of the past had been lifted, and a vision of milk and honey drew them forward.

Exegetical Perspective

This passage is one of several "murmuring stories" that occur in Exodus and Numbers in connection with the wilderness wanderings of the people of Israel between their leaving Egypt and their entering the land of Canaan. These stories cluster both before (Exod. 15–17) and after (Num. 11–20) the giving of the law at Sinai. In the stories that occur in Exodus, the emphasis is on God's provision for the anxious Israelites. In the stories that occur in Numbers, the emphasis is on God's anger and punishment of the people. What accounts for the difference? Apparently, it is the fact of the covenant at Sinai (Exod. 19–24). Before the covenant, the people are simply slaves who have been liberated from Egypt but who still bear the psychological marks of their slavery—and thus their lack of trust. God is patient. After entering into the covenant at Sinai, they should be capable of trust in God. So their lack of faith on the far side of Sinai is a sign of a more serious problem.

The parallel text to Exodus 17:1–7 is Numbers 20:1–13. In Numbers, the similar event is used for a quite different purpose: explaining (though somewhat enigmatically) why neither Moses nor Aaron crossed into the promised land. The narrative structure of the murmuring stories in Exodus and Numbers soberly suggests how hard it is to leave behind an oppression that one has internalized. Sometimes

Homiletical Perspective

What preacher has not wanted to identify with Moses in this passage? You have led the people out of the wilderness of sin, you have proclaimed the message of the Lord each and every week, you have moved in stages through a meticulous long-range planning process. By all accounts you have done everything right, and yet they grumble. The sanctuary is too warm, the floor is too cold, the organist only plays Buxtehude. What preacher, what pastor, has not spent a good many days roasting in the parched land of Massah and Meribah? How does this experience translate into preaching?

If homiletics begins at home, Exodus 17:1–7 calls the exegete to begin by wrestling with his or her own frustrations. The person preparing to proclaim this text does so in a mobile place, jostled back and forth somewhere between the curves of the sublime and the potholes of the ridiculous. All leaders of God's people spend days wandering in the desert of personal and corporate complaints, some of which may well date back to Moses. We wonder, "What is the matter with these people?" or, "What is the matter with me?" and, "Where is my staff?"

How profound it is when a preacher departs from attempts at profundity and speaks from the heart about his or her frustrations. While a steady diet of such speech would upset the stomach of even the

Exodus 17:1-7

Theological Perspective

with me? Why do you test the LORD?" Any word hurled at Moses strikes God as well, or so Moses and the narrator assume.

This notion of Moses as the manifestation of God comes with divine authorization in Exodus. God tells Moses, "See, I have made you like God to Pharaoh, and your brother Aaron shall be your prophet" (7:1). Moses speaks for God, and the sight of Moses will prove the closest Pharaoh will come to seeing the God he engages in battle.

All through Exodus, Israel sees God mostly as Pharaoh had, while Moses himself enjoys direct access. Thus, in this story of thirst and testing at Rephidim, God promises that Moses will see God standing on the rock that will yield water when struck. However, the people will not see God, but only Moses, the one through whom God gives to Israel what Israel needs to live.

This theological theme reaches something of a crisis when Moses tarries too long on the mountain in Exodus 32. In response, Israel makes for itself a new sign of God's presence. Aaron fashions a cherub, a pair of which already sit atop the ark of the covenant constructed, as the story now reads, back in Exodus 25. Cherubim serve as signs of God's presence (see Exod. 25:18–22 and 1 Sam. 4:4). God and Moses argue over whether and how God should punish this presumed apostasy. At least one consequence is a new, seemingly permanent uncertainty over whether God will continue to travel with Israel. Exodus 33, a highly complex series of smaller narratives on the subject of discerning God's presence, concludes with even Moses no longer able to see God face to face. At best, Moses can see God's backside. Now Moses and Israel must look behind God, at the places where God has presumably stepped or visited, for signs of where God may dwell and what God might be doing in the world. All who have looked for God in the vagaries of history know the difficulties inherent in reading and understanding the ambiguities of "God's backside."

Besides providence and people, places have also served as signals of God's presence. For Israel, as for many others, tradition designated temples and other assorted holy places where God dwelled more surely than in common, ordinary spaces. Shiloh, where the ark of the covenant resided in the days of the judges, and Solomon's temple, where God promised to make the divine name live in perpetuity, served in this manner. When the temple fell to the Babylonians, Israel asked, "Where is God now?" Priestly writers, among others, responded by fashioning the

Pastoral Perspective

A vision, coupled with the freedom to reach for it, is a powerful motivator. Freedom is also a taskmaster. It bears the yoke of choice—choosing whom you will follow, where, when, and why. Understanding the responsibility of that choice is the issue here, for these sojourners in the desert and for the sojourners in our pews and pulpits. Both suffer from misplaced authority. Both will murmur.

Having just returned to pulpit ministry, I recently met with several new colleagues from various faith traditions. One of them told me that he once tried to introduce my predecessor as the pastor from Plymouth Congregational Church. He was quickly corrected, and instructed to use the title "minister" instead. Asked why it made such a difference, I suggested that we all fulfill the role of pastor and minister, depending on the task at hand. The preference of one title over the other is rooted in our primary leadership style and our relationship with the membership. Pastor comes from the pastoral setting, a vision of idyllic life in the country—shepherds feeding their sheep, exerting control over the flock as the sheep habitually follow the shepherd who leads them merrily into greener pastures. Most Congregationalists know little of this because our members love their freedoms so much. There are few sheep, if any, to be led in a Congregational church. Our work is more analogous to herding cats!

Moreover, a minister by definition is one who acts upon the authority of another. Ministers are servants of another authority. We act on what we perceive to be God's vision, God's direction, and God's means *after* we check our perception against that of the congregation, because each member has equal access to God's vision! As "creeping congregationalism" has made its way into all denominations, even Catholicism, the act of confirming our vision (as pastor, minister, rector, or priest) with the congregation has become increasingly important, if not imperative. So why is Moses's lament so often sung by clergy, even those in Congregational churches? Misplaced authority.

Despite the congregation's affirmation of a new vision, when the going gets tough, memories shorten. Our sojourners in the desert had a legitimate concern. They were out of water, with none in sight. So they began to quarrel with Moses. With Moses! They forgot that it was the living God who wished to bring them out of slavery. They forgot that it was the living God who protected them during the plagues in Egypt. They forgot that it was the living God who opened the sea for them and then closed it on their enslavers. They forgot that the living God led them with a pillar

Exegetical Perspective

only the second generation (Num. 14:20–23, 31–33) can carry to fruition the promise of liberation.

This short narrative has a simple structure: (1) need (v. 1); (2) complaint (vv. 2–3); (3) response by Moses (v. 4); and (4) miraculous intervention by God (vv. 5–6). The final verse (v. 7) provides an etiology (i.e., explanation) of the name of the place where the events occurred.

The first verse is part of the Priestly writer's itinerary list by which the stages of the wilderness journey are organized. The location of Rephidim is uncertain, but it is not germane to the significance of the story, which is primarily about the relationship between Israel and its God. It is not difficult to sympathize with the plight of the anxious Israelites. Although they have experienced miraculous deliverance from Egypt (Exod. 14–15), the trek through the wilderness is a daily struggle for survival. The resources needed for continual support are different from those needed for the defeat of Pharaoh's army. That the people have no water is a dire condition, and so they "quarrel" (Heb. *rib*) with Moses. This is the first of two key thematic words. Moses's response introduces the other, as he interprets their "quarrel" with him as a "test" (Heb. *nasa*) of God.

Previously God has "tested" the people (15:25; 16:4), by giving them ordinances to obey in connection with God's provision of food for the people. God has reason to wonder if the people are ready to enter into covenant partnership, but the people have no rational grounds to wonder about their God, who has acted reliably toward them in bringing them out of slavery. So for the people to "test" God by challenging Moses, after having already experienced the miraculous provision of water (15:22–25) and food (16:1–36), is to sound a warning note about the readiness of this generation for full liberation. The people are weighing their oppressed but viable lives as slaves against the unknown dangers of the wilderness, which may mean death by thirst (v. 3; cf. 16:3).

Moses's honest protest to God is the first of his distressed pleas concerning the burden of his leadership (see Exod. 18:17–18; Num. 11:11–15). Whereas the people and—especially—Moses have construed the issue as one of Moses's inadequate leadership, God ignores the terms of the quarrel as they have been presented and instead addresses the underlying problem, the provision of water.

As is often the course of delicate negotiations between long-estranged parties, God engages in "trust building" with the people by a miraculous action to provide water. The event will not happen

Homiletical Perspective

staunchest churchgoer, this passage, coming as it does during the season of Lent, sets the table for bits of honest confession. What makes this preacher grumble? What makes his or her family grumble? What deeper reasons lurk beneath the grumbling? Could it be that the preacher and the congregation together are thirsting for spiritual waters they have not yet found?

The passage then calls the exegete, after some careful self-examination, to hear the grumblings of the congregation. As every preacher has complaints about a congregation, every congregation has its own gripes, often about the preacher. Perhaps the exegesis for this sermon begins not in the pastor's study, but in the board or session room. While the people of Israel may have been impatient, they were legitimately thirsty. What thirsts are left unquenched in the church? What complaints are bubbling large? Are these issues widespread among the people, or confined to one or two? This is the stuff of church life. To address these complaints with a prophetic voice, one must listen and then prayerfully discern whether the people of God are grumbling from a legitimate thirst, or because their bellies are full yet their mouths are still open. This is dangerous preaching, balancing across the thin edge between honesty and arrogance.

In a sermon, humor is the baptismal bathwater for those who mistake their own complaints for gospel. Surely even the most Moses-like preacher has tripped over his or her own ego when demonstrating how to beat water out of a rock. Surely pastors who endure the grumbling masses must have provided at least some of the grumble fodder. Rather than a rant about the congregation's failings, a sermon on this passage would invite the preacher to confess a few of his or her more embarrassing moments. Unlike Moses, when we cry, "Lord, what am I to do with these people?" the Lord may answer, "That's funny. I wonder the same thing about you." Likewise, a congregation's history is bound to have a few occasions where trivialities appeared to be signs of the apocalypse. Did we really argue about carpet for three years? Are handbells more biblical than electric guitars? Lifting these issues to the light of Scripture will test our quarreling against the true Rock of our salvation.

While trivialities do kidnap our attention, legitimate life-and-death issues may also be facing a congregation. A church might be clinging to life, doing what it can to minister to a declining membership. A church might be facing budget shortfalls that will impact its mission for years to come. The community around a church, or church members themselves,

Exodus 17:1-7

Theological Perspective

tabernacle tradition we now see in the Pentateuch wilderness story. Once again, Israel lived between times, in this case between exile and home, and the people needed assurance that the Lord did not perish in the temple's fall. Rather, God dwells in a moving, fragile home not made with stones.

In John's Gospel, Christian theologians find a link between the tabernacling God and the divine absence humankind knows amid terrible thirst. In its prologue, the Fourth Gospel speaks of the "word made flesh" that dwelled (literally, "tabernacled") among us as a moving, fragile embodiment of God's glory (John 1:14). At the end, this one cries out in the only word of abandonment we find in John's Gospel, "I am thirsty" (19:28).

Between those moments, in the story of this week's Gospel lesson (John 4:5–42), we hear this same Jesus ask for another drink at noonday, then offer "living water" to a Samaritan woman with whom he also discusses the theology of God's presence. Does God dwell only in Jerusalem, or also in Samaria?

For Christians, John's Gospel teaches, God dwells, speaks, and acts in the fragile one who knows completely the absence of God and who abides even now in that absence, so long as the thirst for living water still lingers in this world. God dwells in the tabernacle of the crucified Christ and in the bride with whom he became one flesh on the cross, the same communal body he restored to life with his own breath when the beloved fainted with fear upon seeing his resurrected but ruined flesh (John 20:22).

Few have known the thirst of God's absence more profoundly than Mother Teresa, whose private writings tell of a long, terrible sense of abandonment that bordered on a living hell. Even in such darkness, however, that tiny, wizened woman of God clung to the belief that she bore in her body and soul "the love of an infinite thirsty God," and that her labors on behalf of Calcutta's hopeless ones helped to satiate the burning thirst of Jesus on the cross.[1]

FREDERICK NIEDNER

Pastoral Perspective

of cloud and fire. They remembered idolatry. As surely as they poured molten gold to fashion a calf to worship, they tried to gold-leaf Moses with the paradox of praise and protest—the idolatry of leadership, the habit of misplaced authority.

Many in leadership succumb to being gold-leafed with accolades for a journey of vision well begun. When difficulties arise and those who once offered praise now protest, the gold-leafed self-image becomes tarnished. Too many respond out of their own misplaced sense of authority, forgetting the One they represent and the vision's path, turning aside to the immediacy of adulation.

Unlike many of us, Moses would have nothing to do with the misplaced authority of the people. In each of their three murmurings (Exod. 15:24; 16:2; 17:3), Moses turned toward God. In each, he redirected the people's emotions toward the source and fulfillment of the promise of a land flowing with milk and honey, saying: "Your complaining is not against us but against the LORD" (16:8). In each, he reminded God's people that he was the servant of another authority: "You shall know that it was the LORD who brought you out of the land of Egypt, and . . . you shall see the glory of the LORD. . . . For what are we, that you complain against us?" (16:6–7). In each instance, Moses deflected the people's gold-leafing of him by affirming his place as a follower among many who follow.

Fruitful church leadership requires one to have the ability to follow. First, we follow our best perception of God's leading, understanding that we see only as in a mirror dimly and we hear with imperfect ears. We may hear some truth, but only one thus far has heard the whole truth and nothing but the truth (so, help me, God! Please!). Secondly, we live amid a faith community of followers who also see dimly and hear only in part. As we gather in the presence of Christ, grace must abound: grace that is able to forgive our misplacement of authority and call us anew to journey together toward the vision promised by God.

DONALD P. OLSEN

---

1. Mother Teresa, *Come Be My Light*, ed. Brian Kolodiejchuk, MC (New York: Doubleday, 2007), 154–57.

out of sight. Moses will first publicly "pass before the people" and will take with him "elders" who can attest to the event (v. 5). Moreover, the same staff that Moses had instructed Aaron to use to turn the Nile and the other waters of Egypt undrinkable (7:19–24) is now used to bring drinkable water from dry rock (v. 5). Thus continuity is established between the wonders previously experienced and the provision in the wilderness. Just as God had been present in leading the people by a pillar of cloud and a pillar of fire (13:21), so God will be present (whether visibly or invisibly) at the rock (v. 6).

The place names given to this location, Massah ("place of testing") and Meribah ("place of quarreling"), commemorate the episode as they pick up on the key verbs used in verse 2. The events of Massah and Meribah were often recalled in later tradition (Deut. 6:16; 9:22; 32:51; 33:8; Pss. 78:15–16, 41, 56; 81:7; 95:8; 106:32). Although occasionally it was the divine provision that was remembered (Ps. 78:15–16), mostly the event conjured up Israel's fatal lack of trust. Indeed, that this is the burden of the story is suggested by the concluding line of the passage, quoting the question of the Israelites: "Is the LORD among us or not?"

Although the narrator clearly views the situation from the perspective of God's and Moses's irritation with the people, the people's own anguished expression of anxiety in verse 3, which encompasses not only themselves but the fate of their dependent children and animals, opens up the episode to more complex points of view and ways in which to evaluate the emotional as well as religious anxieties of the people who had undertaken this hopeful but deeply risky undertaking.

CAROL A. NEWSOM

may literally need food and drink. A poignant turn in an artful sermon could juxtapose laughter at our own absurdities with the heartfelt cries of a world in peril. The Israelites had the benefit of journeying out of the Wilderness of Sin; our pastors and our pastorates languish in the wilderness of our own sin. What is God to do with us? What are we to do as those who have heard the voice of Jesus Christ as well as the voice of Moses? Where will we find water in the rocky soil of this troubled life?

In this sermon the homiletical leap may be a leap backward. If the preacher begins by illuminating the proximity of silliness and seriousness in church life, the remaining step may be an investigation of how Moses solved his problems. First, Moses prayed (v. 4). Moses prayed a brief, humble, and frightened prayer in plain words. Rather than contorting in theological or psychological gymnastics, the role of the homiletician ultimately may be prophetically to call the people to prayer.

Second, God reminded Moses that he possessed the tools to solve his own problems. "Take in your hand the staff with which you struck the Nile, and go" (v. 5). It may be that those who grumble in frustration and wail in trembling simply need to shut up and go do what they already know will work. Congregations and their pastors can spend so much time reinventing the wheels of methodology that they fail to accomplish the goals of the gospel.

Third, Moses worked the miracle of producing water from a rock not in the sight of the whole congregation, but in the company of the elders (v. 6). If the exegesis of this sermon begins in the session or board room, its execution concludes in the same place. This is a passage that calls the proclaimer to be a listener, a prophet, and finally a coach. The sermon may be presented from a pulpit, but it is put to life through the leadership of the people, by the people.

JAMES MCTYRE

Psalm 95

¹O come, let us sing to the LORD;
   let us make a joyful noise to the rock of our salvation!
²Let us come into his presence with thanksgiving;
   let us make a joyful noise to him with songs of praise!
³For the LORD is a great God,
   and a great King above all gods.
⁴In his hand are the depths of the earth;
   the heights of the mountains are his also.
⁵The sea is his, for he made it,
   and the dry land, which his hands have formed.

⁶O come, let us worship and bow down,
   let us kneel before the LORD, our Maker!

Theological Perspective

This psalm is the first of six consecutive psalms of praise. It features the basic themes and affirmations that have come to be emblematic of the worshipful strand of this biblical genre. Psalms 95 to 100 constitute an expanding crescendo of adoration of God and God's wondrous ways. Each of the six psalms declares the greatness of God and invites the faithful to give forth praise.

This psalm appears to address the community of the faithful gathered for worship. The power of the opening declarations is intended to clear the horizon of concern so that God may be worshiped in spirit and in truth. This community is one that has experienced war, invasion, destruction, deportation, and more. Therefore the worship in which they are engaged is not frivolous, shallow, or superficial. It is worship the source of which lies deep in the collective hearts of the people. This praise is grounded both in God's act as creator of all that is and in God's act of calling the community of faith into being.

In the former, God's radical freedom is evident; in the latter, God's radical love is manifest. Like other psalms of its ilk, this psalm promotes the praise of God. However, there is a paradox in this praise. This paradox is apparent in the very structure of the psalm itself. Verses 1–2 constitute the invitation to worship and praise. The point here is that God is to

Pastoral Perspective

Have you ever done something against your better judgment and then realized that it was absolutely the wrong thing to do? Usually, just at that moment when you realize what a boneheaded thing it was, someone asks you, "Why on earth did you do that?" Your jaw drops, and you do not know what to say. This psalm delves into the awkward stance we suffer as people of God who have had every reason to follow God's voice, yet for some inexplicable reason have failed to do so. Why have we gone against God's voice? We cannot say. It is an uncomfortable place to have to stand.

Psalm 95 has two dispositions, and it speaks from two different vantage points. The first part of the psalm speaks from the perspective of God's people, who stand in awe and worship before the Lord (vv. 1–7a). The second part of the psalm speaks from the perspective of the Lord, looking in disappointment on people who have had a history of failing to follow as they should (vv. 7b–11).

The psalm begins on a happy note. The opening verses are invitations for us to praise God and to sing joyfully. It evokes a sense of a people who are still connected to the Lord and who, like exuberant children, respond by singing out from their souls without holding back. To praise God in this way is to be utterly happy and satisfied in that place of smallness in front of a parent whom we adore.

^{7}For he is our God,
   and we are the people of his pasture,
   and the sheep of his hand.

O that today you would listen to his voice!
^{8} Do not harden your hearts, as at Meribah,
   as on the day at Massah in the wilderness,
^{9}when your ancestors tested me,
   and put me to the proof, though they had seen my work.
^{10}For forty years I loathed that generation
   and said, "They are a people whose hearts go astray,
   and they do not regard my ways."
^{11}Therefore in my anger I swore,
   "They shall not enter my rest."

Exegetical Perspective

Recent scholarship has concluded that the crisis of exile left its mark on the shape of the book of Psalms. In particular, the final psalm of Book III, Psalm 89, recounts the rejection of the Davidic monarch, reflecting the events of 587 BCE. A response is offered in Book IV (Psalms 90–106); pivotal in this regard is the affirmation that, while the earthly monarchy may have disappeared, God still reigns. This message is lodged in the enthronement collection (Psalms 93 and 95–99) that forms the primary structural feature of Book IV.

The core of the collection is Psalms 96–99, which are noticeably more similar to each other than they are to Psalms 93 and 95. This fact, plus the fact that Psalms 93 and 95 surround a psalm that does not explicitly proclaim God's reign, suggest that perhaps Psalms 93–95 are a prelude to the core of the collection. Given this possibility, one notices an interesting sequence: Psalm 93 deals with resistance to God's reign by cosmic forces (see "floods" three times in v. 3), Psalm 94 deals with resistance to God by the wicked (see vv. 3, 16), and Psalm 95 deals with resistance to God's reign by God's own people!

The resistance to God in Psalm 95 is articulated by verses 7c–11, an unexpected feature of the psalm, given the fact that it begins like a typical song of praise, or more accurately, two short songs of praise

Homiletical Perspective

Preachers should be astonished that, Sunday after Sunday, folks leave the *New York Times*, the Internet, cups of coffee, and cozy beds, to gather to worship God. They do this, we say, because they have been called to worship by God and by one another.

Psalm 95 might work well as a text to talk about the elements of worship. The psalmist tells us how we are to come before God. We are to sing and make joyful noise. We are to come with thanksgiving and praise. We are to express with exuberance how good it is to belong to God. Then the writer tells us why we should come and bow down. He recalls the fundamental Hebrew family story in verse 1, reminding us that God has been the rock of our salvation—the rock of our rescue. While there may be other gods loose in the world, the Lord is over them and greater than they are. God holds the entire world in his hands. Nothing escapes his grasp, because he made the world like a sculptor who calls out of the rock the object of his love.

If that is not enough to warrant our praise, then the psalmist reminds us that God also made us. Without God we would never have had the chance to get it right and get it wrong. We are alive because God allowed that it was a good thing to be. So come, give thanks and praise to the One who has made all these things possible.

Psalm 95

Theological Perspective

be approached in adoration. Verse 3 affirms God as political ruler, "a great King above all gods." Verse 4 reaffirms God's identity as sovereign sustainer. God holds "the depths of the earth" and is "the heights of the mountains." Verse 5 reaffirms God's role as creator. The seas belong to God, and the dry land was formed by God's hand. Verses 6–7 repeat the call to worship in light of God's immanent and transcendent activity in relation to humanity.

At this point, the tone and tenor of the psalm change dramatically. Verses 7b–11 are a stern warning that, even in this moment of worship and adoration, a more sinister side of Israel's experience emerges. Beneath the veneer of praise lies a history of disobedience, strife, defiance, neglect, rebellion, and transgression. The flaws and failings of past generations become the foundation for future faithfulness. Israel's struggle against apostasy, temptation, and idolatry are brought back to remembrance by the psalmist.

Samuel Terrien, in his classic text *The Psalms and Their Meaning for Today*, observes that when Israel worshiped God, they worshiped as a people who had come through many national challenges and difficulties. The reader is left with this fairly startling and stern warning as a tempering element of praise. Regarding the ending of this psalm, Terrien notes that it "reveals how uneasy some of those poets must have felt when confronted by the discrepancy which opposed the promises of faith to [human] obstinacy."[1]

A more recent scholar has argued that the two disparate parts of this psalm are held together by a common theme of creation/re-creation.[2] Peter Enns argues that the first part of the psalm demonstrates and affirms that God is creator. The second half of the psalm, while apparently shifting focus from the first half, actually reappropriates the creation theme under different circumstances. Viewing the psalm in this manner allows the reader to affirm the constancy of God throughout the psalm.

What does it say about the relationship between God and God's people? Theologically, this psalm reveals that the relationship between God and God's people is multilayered and complex. While the themes of confession and contrition are most often seen in those psalms that fall under the category of psalms of lament, in these psalms of praise the past wrongs forgiven become the wellspring of contemporary thanksgiving for God's grace. Even in the

1. Samuel Terrien, *The Psalms and Their Meaning for Today* (Indianapolis: Bobbs-Merrill Co., 1952), 90.
2. Peter Enns, "Creation and Re-Creation: Psalm 95 and Its Interpretation in Hebrews 3:7–4:13," *Westminster Theological Journal* 55 (1993): 255–80.

Pastoral Perspective

The psalmist then goes on to spell out God's greatness, all the while enticing us to worship and praise. However, the very greatness of God poses a tough question to us. If we have seen the grandeur of the sea and of the mountains, the heights and the depths of all things, and we know that these are in the palm of God's hand, why do we not sing out with praise at all times? Why do we not listen to God's voice? Will we listen today, or will we follow in the way of our ancestors?

At the turning point in verse 7, the psalmist remarks, somewhat ominously, "O that today you would listen to his voice!" The addressee changes from "us" to "you." The speaker does not refer to "the Lord" but instead speaks as the Lord in the first person.

Here is where we begin to squirm a bit. Although the psalm goes on to speak of the ancient Hebrews who did not listen to the Lord, we know full well that we are guilty of the very same shortcomings. Whether or not they are blood ancestors to us, we know that they are our spiritual ancestors. The resemblance is unmistakable.

The first part of the psalm calls for eyes to witness and voices to sing; the second part of the psalm calls for ears to listen and feet to follow. All the while, this psalm points to a people who have failed to follow.

The first part of the psalm makes the second part all the more difficult. If God is so good and worthy of praise, and if we have seen God's glory and were nodding our heads during the first verses of this psalm, why is it that we have so often failed to listen or to follow?

It is fitting that we read Psalm 95 in Lent. Like Jesus' entry into Jerusalem on Palm Sunday, this psalm begins with a joyful noise, but then descends into the darkness of our own guilt as we face our failure to follow. Lent is a season of accountability. The practice of holding a Lenten discipline is valuable not only for the results of added prayer (or less sweets) during the forty days of the season. It is also a way for us to assess our own ability to practice our faith against our own impulses. Brian McLaren has pointed out that if we cannot resist donuts, for instance, how much harder will it be for us to love our enemies?

On the positive side, if one learns to resist the impulse to reach toward potato chips and pizza during a time of fasting, one may be able to draw on the same practice of resisting bad impulses in the future when it counts for more. If we practice doing relatively small things in our power right now, we will grow as Christians so that one day we will be able to

Third Sunday in Lent

Exegetical Perspective

(vv. 1–5 and 6–7b). But verses 7c–11 stand out as something like a prophetic exhortation (see also Pss. 50 and 81). Indeed, so noticeable is this final section that Erhard Gerstenberger categorizes Psalm 95 as a "SERMON with a hymnic introduction" and views it as an example of "early Jewish preaching" of the postexilic era.[1]

To be sure, the hymnic introduction connects Psalm 95 clearly with the rest of the enthronement collection. The language of the invitations in verses 1–2, 6 occurs elsewhere in contexts where God's sovereignty is explicitly proclaimed—for instance, "make a joyful noise" (Pss. 47:1; 98:4, 6); "let us sing" (Pss. 96:12; 98:4, 8); "songs of praise" (Pss. 47:6; 98:4, 5); and "bow down" (Pss. 29:2; 96:9; 99:5). The reasons for praise in verses 3–5, 7 assert God's reign. Not only is God described as "a great King above all gods" (v. 3; see Pss. 96:4–5; 97:7), but also God's claim on the entire cosmos is evident in verses 4–5, which are framed by references to God's "hands." In short, God has the whole world in God's hands!

The cosmic sovereign who is "a great God" (v. 3) also claims the people—this God "is our God" (v. 7). The pastoral imagery in verse 7 is congruent with the reference to God as "King," since kings were viewed in the ancient Near East as the shepherds of their people (see Jer. 23:1–6; Ezek. 34:1–16). Verse 7c, which the NRSV includes with verses 8–11, could also be taken as the culmination of the hymnic introduction. It connects especially with the rest of verse 7, since sheep were supposed to listen to the voice of their shepherd (see John 10:3–5).

Perhaps verse 7c is intended to be transitional, connecting both to the preceding hymnic introduction and to the subsequent sermon. Verses 7, 8, and 10 are three-part lines in a poem that consists otherwise of two-part lines. The effect of this irregularity is to highlight verse 7c, contributing further to the likelihood that it is intentionally transitional. The mention of "today" is an effective invitation to the original hearers to attend to the sermon. It recalls the frequent use of "today" in Deuteronomy (see 4:40; 5:1; 7:11; 8:1), which also has a homiletical orientation. It is also a reminder to contemporary hearers that the function of preaching in any generation is to reactualize the ancient text and its witness in new times and places.

In the case of the sermon in verses 8–11, the preacher's text is Exodus 17:1–7, the OT lesson for

1. Erhard S. Gerstenberger, *Psalms, Part 2, and Lamentations*, Forms of the OT Literature 15 (Grand Rapids: Eerdmans, 2001), 185, 184.

Homiletical Perspective

In addition to considering the elements of worship, Psalm 95 invites us to consider the works of God theologically. Science, philosophy, biblical scholarship, and a growing familiarity with other religious worldviews challenge us to think about what we mean when we say God is the maker of heaven and earth. How do we express the psalmist's belief that God made the world and us? That people continue to gather for worship suggests they still believe God has something powerful to do with the world and with those who live in it. How do we talk about God's presence and creative purpose in making the world and giving us life? For what work can people honestly praise God?

Once we have gathered and spent ourselves in praise and thanksgiving, the psalmist invites us to kneel and bow down before God our Maker. For many in the pews, this is next-to-impossible. They have been duped so many times and by so many people that trusting and submitting are next to impossible acts. Somehow, however, honoring the distinction between human beings and God, between creature and Creator, is essential for the life of faith. The question comes down to whether we are going to place our faith in God or in ourselves. If it is God, then we bow down in preparation for hearing his voice.

Then the psalm suddenly shifts voice, and worshipers are directly addressed by God. As is so often the case, God's address is problematic. We prefer that God win us through gentle wooing rather than through warning. Tell us about the joy of trusting God rather than the consequences when we do not. Is there not a more effective way for God to communicate what God is trying to communicate? The strength of God's words triggers a question that has shaken the foundation of many a congregation.

Tucked into the Lord's reference to Meribah and Massah is what may be the most fundamental question of faith: "Is the LORD among us or not?" (Exod. 17:7). The Hebrews struggled with this question at every turn in the wilderness. We would do well to struggle with this question on behalf of the congregation as well. The Old Testament reading for this Sunday tells of the Israelites complaining to Moses in the wilderness because they had come to a place that did not have enough water. They quarreled with Moses, and Moses said that in so doing they were testing God. Moses complained to God, and God told Moses to strike a rock and water would come out of it for the people. He did, and it did.

Still they asked, "Is the LORD among us or not?" What irked the Lord the most was not that they

Psalm 95

Theological Perspective

midst of the sacrifice of praise, we are reminded in this psalm that obedience is preferred over sacrifice. Without obedience it is impossible to please God, no matter how lavish the offerings of adoration.

Dietrich Bonhoeffer called the psalms "the prayer book of the Bible." More than providing a guide to prayer, this collection of material also has deep theological meaning. This psalm has a particularly important and pertinent message in our time. We live in an era of easy and superficial praise. A "feel-good religion" is more popular than a "do-good faith." The emotional turn in many contemporary expressions of religion has resulted in a "soft spirituality" that would have been foreign to the experience of the psalmist. The faith of which the psalmist speaks is funded by a "rugged spirituality" capable of sustaining the connection with God through tough times. This psalm with its concluding warning reminds us of the ethical foundation of authentic worship.

This psalm, like others of its kind, encourages us to approach God through the corridors of celebration, not through the doorway of doctrine. The God of the psalmist is no abstract deity, but the Shepherd-God who cares for the flock. Thus, our encounter with God is fundamentally personal. The psalmist demonstrates, in a powerful way, the "I-Thou" relationship between God and humanity. Perhaps the greatest contribution that this psalm can make to contemporary devotional life is to remind us that it is not only possible but necessary to praise God in tough times. Indeed, as Israel looked back over a past strewn with disappointments and travails and yet praised God, we may be able to look back over our lives and, in spite of their ebbs and flows, declare that our God is worthy to be praised.

JAMES H. EVANS JR.

Pastoral Perspective

do those things that seem impossible to us today.[1] Lent is a time for us to strive to be better.

Unfortunately, no amount of striving will keep us from stumbling and falling again and again. The paradox is that our sin thrusts us back to the psalm's beginning: the greatness and goodness of the God we were made to worship, the greatness and goodness of the God who alone can forgive our sins.

In our Lenten disciplines, we take stock of what causes us to stumble and to lapse away from what we know God wishes from us. Hopefully, this is not a season of discouragement, but a chance to learn how to ask God for help so that we can do better.

Psalm 95 may seem like a deeply unpastoral psalm, as it ends on a very upsetting note. Its final words are a curse against our wayward ancestors: "Therefore in my anger I swore, 'They shall not enter my rest'" (v. 11). To paraphrase Martin Buber, prayer is not in time, but time is in prayer. So too for Scripture, and especially the psalms, which are prayers after all. We come to the end, and we may want to go back to the beginning. We want to return to that place where we were marveling at God's wondrous works, where we knew the one worthy of our praise, and where we could not help but sing out to the "rock of our salvation" (v. 1). Indeed we must return to that place over and over again.

ROBERT W. FISHER

---

1. Brian McLaren shared these ideas at the Lobero Theatre in Santa Barbara, CA, on Feb. 7, 2009.

Exegetical Perspective

the day. Like all effective homileticians, the ancient Jewish preacher is faithful to the text, but not slavishly so. For instance, Exodus 17:1–7 does not say that the wilderness generation hardened their hearts; but the root translated "harden"(v. 8) occurs in the wilderness material to describe the people's lack of faith (see "stiff" in the phrase "stiff-necked" in Exod. 32:9; 33:3, 5; 34:9.). Neither does Exodus 17:1–7 mention God's anger or the consequences of the people's disobedience (v. 11); but again, the preacher draws upon the larger wilderness context (see Num. 14:33–35; see "rest" in Deut. 12:9.).

The effect is that the early Jewish preacher warns his or her generation not to make the same mistake that the wilderness generation made at Massah and Meribah. Having seen God's "work" (v. 9)—that is, the exodus from Egypt, which provided ample evidence of God's reign (see Exod. 15:18)—the wilderness generation should have been inspired to obey. Instead, the people complained, quarreled, and tested God. The early Jewish preacher is challenging the current generation to do better "today"; that is, in response to the proclamation of God's reign and the evidence that supports it (vv. 1–7b), the preacher implores the current generation to hear and obey (v. 7c).

As for us and our "today," we too are reminded that the proclamation of God's reign always calls for a response. In essence, the enthronement collection, including Psalm 95, coheres with Jesus' preaching. Jesus proclaimed God's reign: "The kingdom of God has come near"; and he challenged people to respond: "Repent, and believe in the good news" (Mark 1:15). The effectiveness of the sermon in Psalm 95 is recognized by the author of Hebrews (Heb. 3:7–4:13), who quotes it as part of an appeal for readers to hear and respond with faith and obedience. Along with the preaching of Jesus and the author of Hebrews, Psalm 95 teaches us that the recognition of God's sovereign claim on our lives and world involves praise—praise as a joyful liturgical response (vv. 1–7b) and praise as the offering of our lives in faith and obedience.

J. CLINTON MCCANN JR.

Homiletical Perspective

asked the question, but that they asked it so often. Their faith was fleeting and their memory weak. Even after all that the Lord had done for them, they still fell into a whiny panic when things did not appear to be going as they wished. This is not a shortcoming particular to the Israelites. It is a shortcoming for all of us. How many times must God act on our behalf before we trust God?

God wants us to remember God's graceful acts among us. God want us to trust God today and tomorrow without needing constant verification of God's goodness. How would life be different if we did? There is something life-saving about remembering that God is the one who knows what we need and that we do well not to assume God is here to grant our every want when we want it. God is in charge, not us.

Ironically, the way God expresses the desire for trust in Psalm 95 makes God look like us. Is God really still worked up over the behavior of the Israelites back in the desert so long ago? There must be a hundred sermons about God's steadfast love, but what about this apparent revelation of God's steadfast loathing? How could one take honest note of this before the people of God?

While the story goes that God did not let those hard-hearted Israelites enter the promise land, neither did God abandon them in the wilderness. The relationship continued. Maybe there is something important in noting that not trusting and honoring God might keep us from some of the wonderful things God has in mind for us. This is not to say that God abandons us. God will continue to bring good out of even our faltering and failing. For the beauty and plenty of the promised land, we may need to wait a bit longer.

DAVID M. BURNS

Romans 5:1-11

¹Therefore, since we are justified by faith, we have peace with God through our Lord Jesus Christ, ²through whom we have obtained access to this grace in which we stand; and we boast in our hope of sharing the glory of God. ³And not only that, but we also boast in our sufferings, knowing that suffering produces endurance, ⁴and endurance produces character, and character produces hope, ⁵and hope does not disappoint us, because God's love has been poured into our hearts through the Holy Spirit that has been given to us.

⁶For while we were still weak, at the right time Christ died for the ungodly. ⁷Indeed, rarely will anyone die for a righteous person—though perhaps for a good person someone might actually dare to die. ⁸But God proves his love for us in that while we still were sinners Christ died for us. ⁹Much more surely then, now that we have been justified by his blood, will we be saved through him from the wrath of God. ¹⁰For if while we were enemies, we were reconciled to God through the death of his Son, much more surely, having been reconciled, will we be saved by his life. ¹¹But more than that, we even boast in God through our Lord Jesus Christ, through whom we have now received reconciliation.

Theological Perspective

Paul's theology of justification by faith is about relationships. Presumably from his own experience, Paul developed this theology negatively—law is unable to bring us into a joyful, empowering, free, and full relationship with God. No matter how sincerely we try, we always fall short of fulfilling the requirements of the law. There are always things we have done we should not have done and things we have not done we should have done.

In truth, the very effort to seek perfection leaves us isolated, focused on self, and often torn with feelings of guilt. Therefore we need another way, a way that does not depend on our efforts. Through Christ, God reveals the nature of the divine love—a self-giving love that suffered death on the cross for us, even though we do not deserve this love. Through faith we understand perfection is not necessary for us to be loved by God. We do not need to justify ourselves. We are loved, and that is all the justification we need. We are in relationship with God, not because of our efforts, but because of God's loving action. Through faith we enter into that relationship and discover peace, hope, and perseverance, even in suffering.

While Martin Luther is historically the most important interpreter of Paul's theology of justification by grace through faith, in our day Paul Tillich has articulated the theology powerfully for the

Pastoral Perspective

Pastors sometimes wonder why certain people move through suffering with some measure of triumph and others do not. In this passage, which comes at a hinge in Paul's letter, he reveals a clue. At the beginning of chapter 5, Paul moves from addressing the gift of our justification to addressing the wonder of our sanctification. Echoes of this passage may be found throughout this letter, particularly in Romans 8. Acknowledging and experiencing both aspects of God's work for us is an integral part of Christian faith and life.

Verse 1 reiterates what has come before. We are justified by faith, not works. Justification results in our being at peace with God. Being at peace with God is not a static condition, however. It means God is engaged in our life, not only watching us but also working with us. This has two immediate effects on our always-vulnerable lives. First, we have standing in God's care. Our lives are in God's active custody. Second, we have hope. Our hope is such a great hope that we are inspired to boast not about ourselves but about the power of God at work in us.

Paul then sets before us this inspiring sequence: suffering produces endurance, which produces character, which produces hope. These words are huge and pregnant with meaning. It is immediately helpful to acknowledge that Paul is not being rhetorical or

Exegetical Perspective

This pericope is considered one of the most important sections of Paul's Letter to the Romans. It is a clear continuation of Paul's discourse about justification presented in chapter 4, yet now justification is regarded as a given fact: "We have obtained access to this grace in which we stand" (v. 2). Therefore, Paul discusses the immediate results and benefits of justification, with the chief benefit being a state of peace (*eirēnē*) or harmony with God. It is in this renewed state of peace that one can focus on the "hope of sharing the glory of God" (v. 2).

This peace, similar to what we find in the Psalms (e.g., Pss. 29:11; 85:8; 119:165) is described by Paul in Philippians 4:7 as a peace that "surpasses all understanding." Peace is not the only benefit of justification. Paul goes on to say that believers are now equipped with a new perspective for dealing with the persecution and suffering they encounter. Believers are called to boast or rejoice (*kauchaomai*) in their suffering just as they boast in the hope they have in the glory of God (v. 3). Suffering is necessary for producing endurance (*hypomonē*), a key spiritual discipline for the new life in Christ.

In verses 4–5, Paul further develops his understanding of *hypomonē*. These verses are critical for understanding the justified, grace-filled life in Christ. It is a life that is to be tutored by the Holy Spirit and

Homiletical Perspective

Preaching from Romans can be both invigorating and daunting. On the one hand, we find ourselves transported by Paul to breathtaking climes where we behold awesome theological and spiritual vistas. On the other hand, preachers are faced with the formidable challenge of bringing Paul's revelations back down to earth to make them more accessible to the pew. Paul's density of thought, distinctive vocabulary, and intricate syntax tempt us at the beginning of sermon preparation to turn to a stack of commentaries and sermon helps to see what the experts say about the pericope. Better to make sure we get it right at the outset, goes the habitual thinking, than to waste time and energy trusting our own insights.

For a change, try starting your study from a different angle. For the moment, set aside your homiletical helps. They wait to assist you in due time. Begin, rather, by getting to your feet, moving away from your desk, and reading the text aloud. Record yourself several times in a row reading the passage interpretively. Do not worry about how well informed your oral interpretation should sound: just read feelingly. By your second or third reading you will begin to sense Paul's words taking hold of your psyche. Even your body will almost imperceptibly participate in your expression. You are beginning to incarnate this text, starting to own what of this passage grasps you deeply.

Romans 5:1-11

Theological Perspective

contemporary audience. We are accepted by God although being unacceptable according to the criterion of the law, and all we must do is accept this acceptance.[1]

Paul's focus is on the believer's relationship with God, but it is important to understand that all interpersonal relationships are created and sustained through grace. Just as we are unable to earn God's love, so we cannot earn another's love. The psychology of attraction is very complicated, but the emotional and motivational commitment of love—the willingness to set aside our own needs to respond to the needs of the other—is always a gift. While hurtful actions—be they betrayal of trust, physical violence, emotional neglect, or isolation—can destroy a relationship, what creates the relationship is acceptance of the other with his or her character defects as well as with those aspects of personality that are attractive and represent strengths.

A spirit of judgment or requirement is destructive to the life-giving relationship of love. Paul implicitly affirms this nature of human social relationships in his teaching that the church is the body of Christ with diversity of members and gifts, together with his affirmation that we must bear one another's burdens. All love is a free gift—unearned, undeserved. To receive love, the beloved can only accept it gratefully.

Paul's difficulty is the motivation for doing what is right. If the good is our relationship with God and if works are unnecessary for establishing that relationship, then what is the motivation and importance for right action? Paul addresses this concern in the next two chapters of Romans and elsewhere in his writings. To oversimplify and briefly summarize his teaching, he affirms the importance of works as an outcome of the loving relationship, rather than as a means for that relationship.

Understanding relationship as gift is important on at least three levels: identity, motivation, and unity. Each stage of life from adolescence to retirement presents us with questions regarding purpose and meaning for our life. When we seek to affirm personal worth through works—making money, finding security, being honored and admired, or accomplishing important goals—the result is likely to include isolation, failure, shame, and even despair. Such a basis for personal identity is fraught with risk.

On the other hand, when we discover an identity based on a loving God—that whatever happens, we

1. Paul Tillich, *Systematic Theology*, vol. 2 (Chicago: University of Chicago Press, 1957), 178–79, and *Systematic Theology*, vol. 3 (Chicago: University of Chicago Press, 1963), 224–25.

Pastoral Perspective

theoretical in this passage. Whether he is addressing what can happen when we suffer because of how life works or because of our decision to be actively engaged in discipleship, Paul is clearly talking from personal experience. His sufferings are described repeatedly in Acts and in his own letters. They are summarized powerfully in 2 Corinthians 11:23–33. While people may believe this progression from suffering to hope is credible, they also will know there are alternative routes to take.

One alternative to the progression Paul describes is the abandonment of faith. It can be a shock to realize our faith does not protect us. There is in some of us an unexamined assumption that if we do our best to be faithful to God, God will take care of us, meaning God will protect us. People new to the faith or people who have not been tested by some deep protracted struggle may be prone to question their faith when the going gets tough.

The impetus to abandon faith can also be a result of the discovery that it is precisely our effort to live a faithful life that gets us into trouble. Suffering can come to us as we engage in the struggle for justice, for instance.

Pastorally it is certainly helpful for people to hear the church acknowledge that suffering can create a deep challenge to the very possibility of faith. In fact, the last thing they need to hear is the judgment that such an experience is wrong, bad, or somehow disqualifies them from God's love and care. It is inappropriate simply to confirm the loss of faith, but it is wise and generous to acknowledge that such loss happens.

Similarly, another alternative to the progression Paul describes is anger. Anger in response to suffering is not quite the same as losing faith, although such anger can lead in that direction. Even people who retain their faith in the midst of struggle can very well be angry about it. We may be angry that distress of varying degrees and types happens. We may be angry that some people we believe we can count on will not be available to us. We may be angry at the sheer effort of the struggle. We may certainly be angry at God.

However, it is also possible to acknowledge that anger is one stage along the way as one progresses from suffering to hope in response to a challenging experience. Years ago, Elizabeth Kübler-Ross discerned a similar sequence to Paul's through which many people who were dying might move: denial, anger, bargaining, depression, and acceptance.

It is tempting when working with this text to fall into the trap of assuming the preacher or pastor has to prove that everything Paul says is true. A better

strengthened by the assurance and promise of God's love. With this endurance (*hypomonē*), personal suffering, as well as systemic persecution, can be endured for the purpose of cultivating character, instilling hope, and overcoming injustices in the larger society.

Although most interpreters of Paul view his writings in direct opposition to the teachings found in the book of James, especially the teachings that conclude "faith without works is . . . dead'" (Jas. 2:14–26), upon closer inspection, Paul's understanding of suffering in Romans 5:4–5 is quite similar to the discourse about suffering and persecution in the first chapter of James (vv. 2–12). Though the geographical and historical circumstances are different, both Paul and the author of James appeal to the term *hypomonē* to communicate an important lesson about the value of persevering through suffering, temptations, or trials of any kind.

James says, "whenever you face trials of any kind, consider it nothing but joy, because you know that the testing of your faith produces endurance [*hypomonē*]; and let endurance have its full effect, so that you may be mature and complete, lacking in nothing" (Jas. 1:2–4). *Hypomonē*, generally translated as "patience" or "endurance," has been interpreted quite convincingly as "militant patience" or "nonviolent resistance."[1] Paul, like James, is seeking something more foundational than patience or nonviolence. Paul is connecting suffering to spiritual discipline (*hypomonē*), which will provide strength, support, and a connection to God in the face of various hardships.

The African American mystic, theologian, and pastor Howard Thurman, the grandson of a slave, knew about such spiritual discipline. In his book *Disciplines of the Spirit*, Thurman discusses the ways in which commitment, wisdom, suffering, prayer, and reconciliation can be cultivated as spiritual resources for overcoming trials and for developing strategies for circumventing the ideological and material traps associated with racism in American society. In his explanation about endurance, Thurman says "[t]o learn how to wait is to discover one of the precious ingredients in the spiritual unfolding of life, the foundation for the human attribute of patience."[2] Thurman goes on to say patience is more than mere

Now, listen in the playback for ways your expression catches your ear. In this thoughtful reading you already are interpreting the passage, you already are connecting viscerally with these words. For now, you do not need to know why certain of Paul's words or phrases grasp you as they do, only that you have been energized by them. Later, when you have delved into the text critically, chances are some experiences from your spiritual journey will rise to awareness to reveal why you resonate the way you do with Paul. For instance, maybe the energy you feel in Paul's reference to peace connects you with the peace in Christ that eases your personal struggle with depression, or that reconciles factions in your congregation. Maybe, with God's love bolstering you with hope amid our suffering, your surge of spirit comes from Paul's assurance that God's love will hold you secure amid the conflict of contentious parties in your parish.

Ironically, by standing and speaking interpretively, you are more identified with Paul at this stage of your sermon preparation than you are while seated at your desk, bent over commentaries. Scholars have long since believed that Paul created his letters by dictating them to an amanuensis, or literary assistant. You can see in your mind's eye Paul voicing his letter, gesticulating as he strides back and forth, his voice rising and falling with feeling. Paul was giving full-bodied, intense expression to his convictions. Likewise, when you allow your personal story to connect wholeheartedly and authentically with the text's story, you will preach with power and authority. You will be making appropriate room for affect to fuse with intellect.

Identifying with Paul in this passage, however, is no call for you in your sermon style to buy into Paul's complex rhetoric. Paul was schooled in the intricacies of an abstract, didactic manner of discourse that was a high art in his day. His Letter to the Romans is a good example. People's ears then were tuned to this kind of rhetoric, with its tightly woven logic, spun out in a prolixity of carefully worded supporting evidence, a common currency in public disputations.

We come today to such strategies of presentation with a profoundly different sensibility, one shaped by worldviews and public media unheard of in Paul's time. Language that sticks to the walls of the mind in our day seeks the eye-gate as much as the ear-gate, asking metaphor, image, and narrative to bear the freight of meaning. Our hearers are conditioned by advertising, cinema, and television to think much more *imaginally* than abstractly. The irony, here, is that nearly half

1. For a full discussion, see Gay L. Byron, "James," in *True to Our Native Land: An African American New Testament Commentary*, ed. Brian K. Blount et al. (Minneapolis: Fortress Press, 2007), 464–67.

2. Howard Thurman, *Disciplines of the Spirit* (New York: Harper & Row, 1963), 42.

Romans 5:1-11

Theological Perspective

are beloved by the very Heart of the universe, that nothing can separate us from God, and that nothing is more valuable than being a child of God—then our personal identity is founded on our humanity. Then we do not judge personal worth by comparison with others. Failure and shame become symptoms of misplaced values—idols to be set aside. Motivation becomes directed toward legitimate needs of others and society instead of the quest to establish our personal worth.

Because personal ego is less important, we become free to take risks, to be bold, to dream of God's healed creation and pursue it. Recognizing that our fundamental identity rests in the value of our humanity also means recognizing the worth of every other human being as well. Openness to others becomes easier, empathy toward others is a natural response, and willingness to know and be known binds us together.

Romans 8 is the great expression of the resulting peace and joy that comes from our relationship with God based on God's grace. In the assurance that nothing can separate us from the love of God we know through Christ Jesus, we find strength, hope, and patience. Paul anticipates chapter 8 here in 5:1–5. Having discovered through faith the love that God has for each of us, we have peace and we have hope. We are no longer divided internally with questions of worth or feelings of failure. We are able to accept ourselves as we are because we experience being accepted. We have hope in the certainty that God's love is unfailing. Even though in the present we may face persecution and hardship, knowing God's love is present, we rejoice in that relationship and look forward to enjoying being in God's presence even beyond death.

Grace, not works, is what brings us life. One of the great insights contained in this understanding is the recognition that external conditions are of secondary importance. We may experience being loved and loving in the hospital, in unemployment, and even in emotional pain. This should not reduce the desire to end suffering in this world, especially suffering caused by human action, but it does mean even in hardship we can know the life of grace. That is good news.

WARD B. EWING

Pastoral Perspective

approach is to be a witness, a pastoral and earnest witness. You can then proceed to explicate this sequence, dwelling on the words and building on the way in which they engage each other.

Another trap to avoid is making Paul's progression sound too linear and somehow guaranteed. Each stage is a challenge, and Kübler-Ross's stages and Paul's progression lay a trap for those looking to offer a congregation some sort of spiritual technique or quick fix as they confront suffering. As ministers of the gospel, all we can do is bear witness to the messy, unpredictable, difficult, and daunting experience of tending people who suffer. We know the pilgrimage from suffering to hope is not linear and that suffering, endurance, and character are not bus stops that follow automatically. Each stage is a challenge in which we might dwell as witnesses to God's presence, even in God's apparent absence.

Part of verse 5 helps people dwell in each stage with grace: "God's love has been poured into our hearts through the Holy Spirit that has been given to us." This generosity of God is worth holding up and affirming. God's love is "poured into our hearts." We need to have it poured. We need to drink it in, freely, eagerly, over and over again in order for our lives to move, with God's help, toward the hope that does not disappoint. It is God's power at work in us that makes the progression possible. The passage reminds us that the Christian life is not a do-it-yourself project but a do-it-together project. The exodus was clearly such a project.

So this passage sets us on the pilgrimage of hope. Hope comes from experiencing this progression as God feeds us and leads us through it. Hope also comes because before us is the cross, a sign both of the suffering of Christ and of the triumph over death that God made possible for him and for us. These two sources of hope are intertwined. It is the cross before us, like the north star, that calls us forward through this pilgrimage from suffering into endurance and character on our way to hope.

The closing verses take us back through the case for justification. They reiterate what Karl Barth calls the basic and wonderful paradox of justification: by justification we are what we are not. What God confers upon us makes us children of God, justified by faith and thus able with God's help to move through this wonderful sequence.

LAIRD J. STUART

Third Sunday in Lent

Exegetical Perspective

passive endurance: "One has to take a hard and searching look at the environment, particularly the context in which one is functioning" and respond accordingly.[3] Thurman suggests that "tutoring the human spirit" (*hypomonē*) as a form of self-mastery and social protest leads to an "inward journey" toward freedom.

Such freedom is at the heart of the next section of Paul's message (vv. 6–10), which focuses on the salvific meaning of the death of Christ: "while we were still weak [*asthenēs*], at the right time [*kata kairon*] Christ died for the ungodly [*asebōn*]" (v. 6) and "while we still were sinners [*harmartōloi*] Christ died for us" (v. 8). This state of sinfulness, weakness, or even helplessness is characterized by bondage. These verses mirror the same language used to designate the wickedness of the unredeemed world against which God's wrath is revealed (Rom. 1:18; 4:5). Both 5:6 and 5:8 include the particle "yet" (*eti*) to note that, despite the fallen condition of humanity, God had a plan manifested in the death of Christ—an act that was accomplished in the "fullness of time."

To demonstrate the magnitude of the sacrifice of Christ, Paul uses verse 7, which discusses the plausibility of someone dying for a *good person*, as a foil against which to measure the extremity of God's love, which he presents in verse 8. So now, with proof of God's love exemplified through the sacrificial death of Christ, Paul draws a conclusion for the future: "Much more surely then, now that we have been *justified* [*dikaiōthentes*] by his blood, will we be *saved* [*sōthē-sometha*] through him from the wrath of God" (v. 9). Finally, in verse 10 the same basic argument presented in verses 6–9 is raised again, though the metaphor has changed from sinners to enemies and language of justification has been replaced with language of reconciliation (cf. 2 Cor. 5:18–19): "while we were enemies [*echthroi*] we were *reconciled* [*katallassō*] to God through the death of his Son." As the reconciliation has been effected through the death of the Son, salvation will come about through his life.

This pericope touches upon several key theological teachings of the apostle Paul: justification, reconciliation, suffering, and salvation. Ultimately, this lection teaches us to boast in the hope of sharing in the glory of God while embracing suffering, which leads to spiritual discipline, and to accept the gifts of salvation and reconciliation, which are a reflection of God's eternal love.

GAY L. BYRON

Homiletical Perspective

of Jesus' recorded utterances were in parabolic or metaphorical form, a way of communicating that resonates not only with the Semitic consciousness of his day but with the Western mind-set today.

Even so, Paul aimed the rhetoric in his letter to the Romans at a consciousness more at home in the Gentile than the Semitic world. Consequently, in preaching from Paul's word in Romans, we want to take care, in remaining faithful to his substance, not to be drawn into his style. Most people today simply do not have ears to hear such compressed logic.

These verses offer ready themes for preaching. Take the creative tension between the Christ of the cross and the Christ-to-come that holds us steady when we are confronted with the threats that the world visits upon us (vv. 1–2). What of Christ's peace, which is unlike any of the world's promises? While the world offers peace as an escape from disputes or disorders, Christ's peace assures a stability and serenity, not apart from, but in the midst of "the thousand natural shocks of life." Consider, with all the pain that life visits upon us, the Spirit's transforming our suffering from endurance into character, and from character into certain hope (vv. 3–5). Once more, think of the incredible power of God's love that, in the face of all our foibles, trumps God's own wrath with a reconciling compassion embodied in the crucified and risen Christ (vv. 6–11).

How, then, do we clothe these sermon themes with the kind of images and metaphors that will capture the attention of contemporary hearers? A time-honored way would be to use illustrations to give life to the points we want to make *about* the biblical text. Such an approach still keeps its distance from the text, walking *about* the text, *pointing at* things with an objectifying stance while preaching from the periphery of the text. Consider preaching from the heart of the text rather than from its periphery. To preach *from* the text means to join the life of the text, to draw yourself and your people into the power and drama of the text. Here the story is "the thing to catch the conscience of the king!"

DON WARDLAW

3. Ibid.

John 4:5-42

[5]So he came to a Samaritan city called Sychar, near the plot of ground that Jacob had given to his son Joseph. [6]Jacob's well was there, and Jesus, tired out by his journey, was sitting by the well. It was about noon.

[7]A Samaritan woman came to draw water, and Jesus said to her, "Give me a drink." [8](His disciples had gone to the city to buy food.) [9]The Samaritan woman said to him, "How is it that you, a Jew, ask a drink of me, a woman of Samaria?" (Jews do not share things in common with Samaritans.) [10]Jesus answered her, "If you knew the gift of God, and who it is that is saying to you, 'Give me a drink,' you would have asked him, and he would have given you living water." [11]The woman said to him, "Sir, you have no bucket, and the well is deep. Where do you get that living water? [12]Are you greater than our ancestor Jacob, who gave us the well, and with his sons and his flocks drank from it?" [13]Jesus said to her, "Everyone who drinks of this water will be thirsty again, [14]but those who drink of the water that I will give them will never be thirsty. The water that I will give will become in them a spring of water gushing up to eternal life." [15]The woman said to him, "Sir, give me this water, so that I may never be thirsty or have to keep coming here to draw water."

[16]Jesus said to her, "Go, call your husband, and come back." [17]The woman answered him, "I have no husband." Jesus said to her, "You are right in saying, 'I have no husband'; [18]for you have had five husbands, and the one you have now is not your husband. What you have said is true!" [19]The woman said to him, "Sir, I see that you are a prophet. [20]Our ancestors worshiped on this mountain, but you say that the place where people must worship is in Jerusalem." [21]Jesus said to her, "Woman, believe me, the hour is coming when you will worship the Father neither on this mountain nor in Jerusalem. [22]You worship what you do not know; we worship what we know, for salvation is from the Jews. [23]But the

Theological Perspective

Repeatedly in John's Gospel (and throughout the New Testament) people misunderstand Jesus in their first encounter with him. The unnamed woman at Jacob's well in Sychar and all of Jesus' disciples find themselves initially in this number. Some never come to know who he is. In her conversation with Jesus, the Samaritan woman slowly moves from unbelief to belief, from darkness to light, from blindness to sight, from ignorance to knowledge, from misunderstanding to understanding. Unlike Nicodemus in 3:2–10, she has seen nothing of Jesus' signs previously and has not heard he is a teacher "who has come from God" (3:2). The Jesus she first encounters at Jacob's well is only a thirsty Jewish stranger who dares to ask her for a drink. Jesus' request is daring because by speaking to her he crosses significant social boundaries of religion, ethnicity, and gender. Jesus speaks first to her, however, not only because of social convention, but because "the true light, which enlightens everyone" (1:9), was coming into her world. Light has entered her dark world, even though she is not yet able to see it. Truth is spoken to her, even though she is not yet able to discern it.

Pastoral Perspective

At first glance, the woman whom Jesus meets at the well in Sychar could not be more different from Nicodemus. She is an uneducated woman, a learner; he is an educated man whom Jesus describes as a teacher of Israel. She is a Samaritan; he is a Jew. She has a shameful past; he is a respected moral leader in his community. She meets Jesus at noontime; he comes at midnight. At a literary level the woman stands as a foil to Nicodemus, but in her own right she plays an important role in the Gospel narrative.[1]

One characteristic of the woman is that she is almost totally an outsider. A woman in a man's world, she is a stranger to Judaism, the practices and geography of faith, conventional morality, and the gospel (she remains unnamed to centuries of readers). Is she so much of an outsider that she is considered socially deviant by her community? Is she ostracized by them, stigmatized for her status or behavior? We cannot determine this from the text, and so to go that far is to exaggerate the woman's outsider status.

1. R. Alan Culpepper, *The Anatomy of the Fourth Gospel: A Study in Literary Design* (Philadelphia: Fortress Press, 1983), 91.

hour is coming, and is now here, when the true worshipers will worship the Father in spirit and truth, for the Father seeks such as these to worship him. [24]God is spirit, and those who worship him must worship in spirit and truth." [25]The woman said to him, "I know that Messiah is coming" (who is called Christ). "When he comes, he will proclaim all things to us." [26]Jesus said to her, "I am he, the one who is speaking to you."

[27]Just then his disciples came. They were astonished that he was speaking with a woman, but no one said, "What do you want?" or, "Why are you speaking with her?" [28]Then the woman left her water jar and went back to the city. She said to the people, [29]"Come and see a man who told me everything I have ever done! He cannot be the Messiah, can he?" [30]They left the city and were on their way to him.

[31]Meanwhile the disciples were urging him, "Rabbi, eat something." [32]But he said to them, "I have food to eat that you do not know about." [33]So the disciples said to one another, "Surely no one has brought him something to eat?" [34]Jesus said to them, "My food is to do the will of him who sent me and to complete his work. [35]Do you not say, 'Four months more, then comes the harvest'? But I tell you, look around you, and see how the fields are ripe for harvesting. [36]The reaper is already receiving wages and is gathering fruit for eternal life, so that sower and reaper may rejoice together. [37]For here the saying holds true, 'One sows and another reaps.' [38]I sent you to reap that for which you did not labor. Others have labored, and you have entered into their labor."

[39]Many Samaritans from that city believed in him because of the woman's testimony, "He told me everything I have ever done." [40]So when the Samaritans came to him, they asked him to stay with them; and he stayed there two days. [41]And many more believed because of his word. [42]They said to the woman, "It is no longer because of what you said that we believe, for we have heard for ourselves, and we know that this is truly the Savior of the world."

Exegetical Perspective

The Second and Third Sundays in Lent juxtapose two characters unique to the Gospel of John. Nicodemus comes to Jesus by night and lasts all of nine verses in his conversation with Jesus before fading into the night from whence he came. John 4 narrates the encounter with Jesus of another character, the Samaritan woman at the well. The contrast between Nicodemus and the Samaritan woman is striking. Given the fact that they appear one right after the other in the Gospel, we are meant to notice this contrast in all of its detail.

Nicodemus is a Pharisee—an insider, a leader of the Jews. He is a man, he has a name, but he comes to Jesus *by night*. The character to whom we are introduced in John 4 is a Samaritan—a religious, social, and political outsider. She is a woman, she has no name, but she meets Jesus at noon, in full daylight. The contrast between the conversations these two characters have with Jesus is even more extraordinary. Whereas Nicodemus is unable to move beyond the confines of his religious system, the Samaritan moves outside of her religious expectations to engage Jesus in theological debate (v. 20). Whereas Nicodemus

Homiletical Perspective

If I were asked to pick one story that shows us the most about who Jesus is, it would be this one. Here is a passage for a preaching life and a lifetime of preaching. Here too is a text with its own bucket, ready for the filling. Let it down again and again, and each time it comes up with another sermon of living water, another deep drink from the well that will not go dry.

Thirsty preachers need this text. We need the well and the water in it, and the bucket to draw it up, and the man sitting beside us, telling us everything we have ever done. The story gives us so many places to stand, so many moments of recognition, that maybe the first homiletical task is simply to feel our emptiness, and drink. Feel ourselves coming late to the well, and meeting the stranger—is there not always another stranger?—who asks us for a drink. Feel ourselves muttering about messiahs with no buckets, so that *we* have to do all the work. Feel ourselves dry and empty and sermon-less to boot.

Then, as our buckets go down into the well and the stranger continues to talk, feel ourselves drawn into his words, just as surely as if they were a well of

John 4:5-42

Theological Perspective

Irony abounds in this story, as it does in so many of the stories in John's Gospel. Those who view and understand the world literally do not always fare well with an ironical Jesus and an ironical Gospel. Irony presupposes a distinction between appearance and reality. What appears to be true is indeed true, but it is only a partial truth and not the full truth. Because of this distinction between appearance and reality, irony often takes the form of either humor or tragedy—or both.[1]

The Samaritan woman thinks Jesus is the petitioner and fails to understand that it is not he who needs what only she can provide (water from Jacob's well), but she who needs what only he can give (living water) (vv. 7–15). She tells Jesus the half-truth that she has no husband and Jesus reveals the full truth that she has had five husbands and the man currently living with her is not her husband (vv. 16–18). She then assumes Jesus is a prophet because he knows the truth about her marital situation, but does not realize that he is a very different kind of prophet, one who not only knows the truth about her life but is himself the way, the truth, and the life (vv. 19–24). She believes in a coming Messiah but does not realize that in the person of this Jew from Galilee the Messiah is standing in front of her (vv. 25–26). Only when the woman leaves her water jar, returns to the city, and invites her neighbors to "come and see" Jesus, does she begin to discern a deeper, larger reality beyond the initial appearance. "He cannot be the Messiah, can he?" (vv. 28–29).

No less than the Samaritan woman, Jesus' disciples are caught up in the irony of the moment. They encourage Jesus to eat and are puzzled when he tells them he has food they do not know about. Common sense leads them to ask, "Surely no one has brought him something to eat?" (vv. 31–33). They have no idea what kind of "food" Jesus is talking about. They anticipate a seasonal harvest in four months, but Jesus sees something they do not—fields that are already ripe for the harvesting. Just as the Samaritan woman did not begin to understand until she became a witness to Jesus, so the disciples will not begin to understand that Jesus is the bread of life (6:35) until they too invite others to "come and see" (1:46).

Irony (in this story and in many others from John's Gospel) is a literary device the writer uses to describe how Jesus, the Word become flesh (1:14), was "in the world . . . yet the world did not know

Pastoral Perspective

We may be able to say, however, that in the eyes of the Gospel writer this woman is a nobody. She does not even merit a name, and her gender, religious orientation, social standing, and personal habits distance her from Jesus and her community. We expect that people will try to avoid this woman and ignore her whenever possible.

Being a nobody is not an easy mantle to wear, except maybe for Emily Dickinson, who appeared to relish the role in her poem "I'm Nobody! Who Are You?"[2] For Dickinson the idea of being a public somebody was a gloomy prospect, but she may have been the exception. Most people want to avoid the pain of being nobodies; they want to be recognized and cherished as somebodies who matter.

This text is good news for anyone who has ever felt the humiliation of stigmatization or the pain of being a nobody, because Jesus does not turn away from this woman. On the contrary, he engages her in conversation, takes her seriously, and spends several days in her village. This woman, her community, and their welfare matter to Jesus, whether nobodies or not. That is good news.

It is also challenging news, because it reminds churches and their members that people who are nobodies to them may be somebodies in the eyes of Jesus. Who are those nobodies? They are the people we ignore. Maybe they are a congregation's neighbors, or the strangers who walk through the door, or a potential group to be evangelized and welcomed into the household of faith. This text reminds faithful readers that sometimes our attempts to draw the boundaries of the faith community are too narrow. We often prefer to leave out the nobodies, but Jesus does not do that. He welcomes outsiders, as well as insiders, into discipleship.

He also welcomes people who are just starting the journey of faith. The second characteristic of the woman is that she is a newcomer to faith, and during this conversation with Jesus she takes baby steps. Jesus is so patient with her! His willingness to explain his metaphors and stay with the conversation is in stark contrast to his impatient discussion with Nicodemus. Jesus does not make fun of this woman, as he does of Nicodemus, and he does not chastise her for her left-brain response to his right-brain language. Instead, he nurtures her, nudges her along, like a parent teaching a young child. Though he is hard on Nicodemus, Jesus is kind to this woman.

---

1. For a splendid discussion of irony in John's Gospel, see R. Alan Culpepper, *Anatomy of the Fourth Gospel: A Study in Literary Design* (Philadelphia: Fortress Press, 1983).

2. For the full text of this poem, do an Internet search using its title.

Exegetical Perspective

cannot hear that Jesus is sent by God (3:17), the woman at the well hears the actual name of God, "I AM" (v. 26; "he" in the NRSV is not in the Greek text). While Nicodemus's last questioning words to Jesus expose his disbelief ("How can these things be?" 3:9), the last words of the woman at the well ("He cannot be the Christ, can he?" 4:29) lead her to witness to her whole town.

While the lectionary begins the passage at verse 5, it is essential to extend the reading through the beginning of the chapter. Verse 3 provides the setting for the scene, as Jesus leaves Judea for Galilee. The phrase "but he had to go through Samaria" (v. 4) is geographically true, but more importantly, it sets up the theological necessity of this journey. Jesus' stop in Sychar will result in a new witness to his revelation who becomes the narrative agent in the fulfillment of the claim, "For God so loved the *world*." Indeed, it is necessary for Jesus to pass through Samaria to find this witness to God's revelation in the world.

The Samaritan woman at the well is not a passive recipient of Jesus' offer. She immediately recognizes the societal barriers and boundaries that keep her in her place (v. 9); but at the same time she challenges Jesus' authority over and against the ancestors of the faith (v. 12). Like Nicodemus, she first interprets Jesus' words on a literal level. However, she also recognizes that Jesus has something that she needs and is able to ask for what Jesus has to offer, rather than question the possibility (v. 15).

While many commentators are preoccupied with the woman's "sin" and Jesus' offer of forgiveness as illustrated by verses 16–18, the text itself says nothing of any sin she has committed, nor does Jesus ever forgive her. Jesus' question to her about her husband is not a comment on her marital status, over which she would have had no control anyway. Rather, like Nicodemus, his words are meant to move her to the next level of understanding of who Jesus is, and the conversation is successful. She sees that Jesus is a prophet (4:19). Moreover, sin in this Gospel is not a moral category related to behavior. Sin is unbelief—the inability or unwillingness to acknowledge Jesus as Lord and God.

When the woman successfully moves to a new level of understanding of who Jesus is, she then presses forward in a theological dialogue with Jesus regarding the acceptable place of worship, Mount Gerazim or Jerusalem, over which the Jews and the Samaritans have disagreed for centuries. In essence, her question about the place of worship is also a question about the dwelling of God and represents a

Homiletical Perspective

water themselves, until their coolness splashes over our faces and suddenly, *we know who he is!* Is that not the work of a sermon, pulling until the water comes? Day after day at the well: there is the preacher, waiting. Here is a passage for a preaching life and a lifetime of preaching.

There are so many ways to let down your bucket into this text. Here are some to try.

Notice That Jesus Initiates. There are always good reasons for Jesus *not* to talk with us. This time, it is because the person at the well is a woman and a Samaritan: double jeopardy. We could add a few more reasons to steer clear, based on textual inferences: a shady past, a low-down reputation, a scorching verbal dexterity. Jesus breaks rules to talk with her; his friends are shocked. As preachers and pastors we are conditioned to imagine ourselves in Jesus' role—the ones who break the rules to speak with outsiders. What if we imagine it the other way around?

What rules is Jesus breaking to talk with *us*? What social conventions is he disregarding? What lines is he stepping across, in order to speak about what truly matters, and what may save our life? Human beings are, by definition, rooted in social contexts and ordered by those realities. Sometimes we let "the way it is" determine what we can or are willing to see. Jesus has a distinct fondness for overstepping boundaries. What traditions or customs or conventions might Jesus have to cross in order to speak to you, the preacher? Before we have a word for the folk, we have to feel that word ourselves.

Notice That It Is Jesus Who Is Thirsty. The walk through Samaria is long and tiring. Jesus sits down by the well while his disciples go to buy food in the village; this is where he and the woman meet. It ought to be easy for a thirsty man to get a drink at a well, but notice that Jesus cannot do this by himself. He asks the woman to give him a drink, gives *her* the chance to recognize the face of Christ in a stranger.

There is something beautifully simple in the staging of this scene as well as its premise: Jesus is thirsty at the well, and we are the ones with the bucket. The deeper metaphorical conversation that follows makes no sense until we really take this in. Can a little thing like a cup of cool water, offered in love, be the beginning of a salvation journey? Yes; and we will never know until we meet the stranger, and tend to the human need first.

Notice the Order of Recognition: Prophet, Then Messiah. It is always the flashy bits that get our attention:

John 4:5-42

Theological Perspective

him" (1:10). The world did not know him because it did not understand what it was seeing. When Philip tells Nathaniel that Jesus son of Joseph from Nazareth is the Messiah, Nathaniel responds on behalf of the rest of the world, "Can anything good come out of Nazareth?" (1:46). When Jesus says "I am the bread that came down from heaven," the Jews complain because appearance suggests otherwise. Because they cannot see beyond the apparent, they do not understand. "Is not this Jesus, the son of Joseph, whose father and mother we know?" (6:41–42.) They see only what is apparent, not what the Spirit enables John the Baptist to see, "the Lamb of God who takes away the sin of the world!" (1:29). Only when Nathaniel responds to Philip's invitation, "Come and see" (1:46), does he begin to understand who Jesus truly is (1:49–51).

Irony is not simply a convenient genre for the particular story that John tells. John cannot tell his story about Jesus without using irony, because Jesus is himself an ironical Christ. Irony is not one possibility among others for how John will tell his story. Here content dictates form. Substance determines genre. Jesus is indeed "the "son of Joseph, whose father and mother we know." The appearance is not deceiving, but that is not the full truth about Jesus. He is at the same time "the Word" that "was with God" and "was God" (1:1). It is no accident that John's Gospel dominates the early church's understanding of Jesus and figures prominently in the formula of Chalcedon. Jesus is both "fully human and fully God," but the mystery of his identity is that he cannot be the Word that was God without also being the son of Joseph. From "the beginning" the son of Joseph was the Word made flesh. John tells his Gospel the way he does, not because he is fond of irony. The story that he tells demands irony.

GEORGE W. STROUP

Pastoral Perspective

I had a pastor once who liked to preach about what he called "the toughness and tenderness of Jesus." We see those paradoxical characteristics in Jesus as we put these texts side by side. Jesus can be confrontational, and he can be compassionate. He can be unyielding, and he can be generous.

We see his tenderness as he encourages the woman's growth in faith. Any believer who feels like a newcomer to faith and who is also taking baby steps can take heart in this. Jesus supports us as we move toward him and grow in understanding. He wants us to deepen and extend our faith, to recognize and acknowledge him for who he is.

Jesus can be tough too, and the woman gets a taste of that. In the course of her conversation with him, he uncovers her life story. The exposure comes as Jesus talks with her about her husband and looks beneath her self-presentation. She says of Jesus that he "told me everything I have ever done" (v. 29). There is an honesty in the woman's encounter with Jesus that lays open her past, yet she does not appear to be shamed by this conversation and confession.

Instead, her encounter with Jesus emboldens the woman to go and tell all her friends and neighbors about this man. Like the prophet Isaiah, who is liberated for service when he confesses his sin in the temple (Isa. 6:1–8), the woman is freed for discipleship after Jesus exposes her needs and failings. She becomes his witness.

This story narrates the dramatic transformation of the woman. She begins the story as an outsider and becomes a witness; from her status as a beginner in faith she becomes an apostle sent by Jesus himself to testify on his behalf.[3] As such she is a model for other women, for people who feel like nobodies, for newcomers to the faith, and for people with a past. Jesus encounters and welcomes many into the household of faith—even the least likely and maybe, even, you and me.

DEBORAH J. KAPP

---

3. Culpepper, *Anatomy of the Fourth Gospel*, 137.

Third Sunday in Lent

fundamental issue for this Gospel. In Jesus, the Word made flesh, God has chosen to dwell, to tabernacle among us (1:14). As a result, Jesus reveals that very truth to the woman. "I AM," he says (4:26), the very presence of God before her. This is the first absolute "I AM" statement in the Gospel of John (cf. 6:20; 8:24, 28, 58; 13:19; 18:5, 7). The last absolute "I AM" statements will cause 600 Roman soldiers to fall to the ground (18:5–7).

Jesus makes God known to this woman at the well and, as a result, makes her a cowitness to his work in the world, one whose labor helps bring in the harvest (vv. 34–38). While she is not absolutely certain that Jesus is the Christ (in 4:29 the syntax of the Greek expects a negative answer), she does not let that stop her from leaving behind her water jar, which represents anything that might hold her back. Going into the city, she invites her fellow townspeople to their own encounter with Jesus. She responds to Jesus in a way that leads Jesus to reveal his true identity to her; in doing so, she sees her own identity evolve. We learn from the Samaritan woman that in our own encounters with Jesus, we are not only changed, but what God reveals to us changes as well.

When the woman returns to her village, she invokes the very words that Jesus says to his first disciples, "Come and see" (1:39). Through her invitation and the sharing of her experience, many believe in him (v. 39). The scene that follows replicates Jesus' calling of the first disciples. Jesus "stays" with the Samaritans, as did the first disciples (1:39), which is a fundamental category of relationship for the Fourth Gospel. The verb "stay" is *menō*—"abide" or "remain." It is because of this abiding with Jesus that the Samaritans are able to confess, "We know that this is truly the Savior of the world" (v. 42), the only time that the title "Savior" is ever used in John's Gospel. In this unexpected witness, this Samaritan village is the narrative fulfillment of 3:16, "For God so loved the world that he gave his only Son, so that everyone who believes in him may not perish but may have eternal life."

KAROLINE M. LEWIS

a healing, an exorcism, a reading of someone else's mind. Jesus pulls a few details about the woman's life out of thin air, and she is greatly impressed: "Sir, I see that you are a prophet" (v. 19). Maybe she needed to confront the supernatural power of the man before she could see the messianic truth. Maybe we all do.

The mighty acts of God are wondrous to behold and difficult to ignore; the Lamb of God who takes away the sins of the world is something else entirely. It requires another look before we can begin to get our heads around it. Maybe the prophet is like the cup of cool water: the visible manifestation of a deeper reality. Here is the first step on a journey to provide water for the soul as well as the body.

Notice What Is Said as Well as Not Said. When the woman comes to the startling recognition that she has been talking to the Messiah, she leaves her bucket and runs to the village with the news: "Come and see a man who told me everything I have ever done!" (v. 29) she cries. Notice the unfinished nature of that sentence, especially given what we know about the woman's history: *Come see a man who told me everything I ever did . . . and loved me anyway!* She does not say the last four words, but they are implicit in her action, and in the joy with which she runs.

"Everything she ever did" is a long list of sins, and common knowledge besides; it is always before her, in the judgmental expressions of her neighbors. For Jesus to have intimate knowledge of that list is not as singular as it might be; but for him to *know* her past, and still love and forgive her—well, that is as unbelievably new and fresh as anything she has ever heard! The man who told her everything she ever did *. . . and loved her anyway . . .* is what saves her life.

In that moment, she sees God. She receives Christ—and leaps up to tell.

ANNA CARTER FLORENCE

1 Samuel 16:1-13

¹The Lord said to Samuel, "How long will you grieve over Saul? I have rejected him from being king over Israel. Fill your horn with oil and set out; I will send you to Jesse the Bethlehemite, for I have provided for myself a king among his sons." ²Samuel said, "How can I go? If Saul hears of it, he will kill me." And the Lord said, "Take a heifer with you, and say, 'I have come to sacrifice to the Lord.' ³Invite Jesse to the sacrifice, and I will show you what you shall do; and you shall anoint for me the one whom I name to you." ⁴Samuel did what the Lord commanded, and came to Bethlehem. The elders of the city came to meet him trembling, and said, "Do you come peaceably?" ⁵He said, "Peaceably; I have come to sacrifice to the Lord; sanctify yourselves and come with me to the sacrifice." And he sanctified Jesse and his sons and invited them to the sacrifice.

⁶When they came, he looked on Eliab and thought, "Surely the Lord's anointed is now before the Lord." ⁷But the Lord said to Samuel, "Do not look on his appearance or on the height of his stature, because I have rejected him; for

Theological Perspective

If theology consists of giving God names that adequately describe God's ways, then the first biblical character to practice this art was Hagar, the slave woman who, on the basis of her experience, calls God "El-roi," "the God who sees" (Gen. 16:13). Neither distance nor time imposed limits on God's seeing, Hagar observed. Her own contemptuous looks had rendered her a fugitive, but the Lord had mercifully found her in the wilderness and looked far into the future of the seed growing within her.

Centuries later, the Lord would see the distress and remember the prayers of yet another maidservant, a barren wife named Hannah. As a consequence, she too would bear a son (1 Sam. 1:11, 20). This child, Samuel, would become a judge and prophet, but he would also call himself a seer, one who sees (1 Sam. 9:19). Although he saw what some could not, even Samuel did not see as God sees, and some elements within his story serve as a sobering lesson concerning human limitations, particularly as they apply to the work of theology.

At God's direction, Samuel had anointed Saul as Israel's first king. The story's narrator never states

Pastoral Perspective

What was God thinking? What was Samuel thinking? What do any of us think as we attempt to lead a congregation toward God's will and way? In preceding chapters we learn that Samuel's first attempt at "king making" did not end well.

We read in 1 Samuel 9:1–10:1 that God will send Samuel a man to anoint as Israel's first king. That very day a Benjaminite named Kish lost his herd of donkeys. Kish had a son named Saul who was very handsome (a *GQ* type) and very, very tall. He stood head and shoulders above his peers. Saul was a bit of a Jewish giant! Kish instructed Saul to find the donkeys with the help of a boy. Along the way, Saul ran out of food and money and turned toward home before Kish began to worry about him. The boy produced some coin and persuaded Saul to continue to the village at the top of the hill, where a seer with a pretty good reputation for being right lived. Some young girls near a well directed them to Samuel, and the rest, as they say, is history.

Saul had early victories and did win the approval of his people; but he let the prerogatives of power go to his head. Kingly control emboldened Saul to assume

the Lord does not see as mortals see; they look on the outward appearance, but the Lord looks on the heart." [8]Then Jesse called Abinadab, and made him pass before Samuel. He said, "Neither has the Lord chosen this one." [9]Then Jesse made Shammah pass by. And he said, "Neither has the Lord chosen this one." [10]Jesse made seven of his sons pass before Samuel, and Samuel said to Jesse, "The Lord has not chosen any of these." [11]Samuel said to Jesse, "Are all your sons here?" And he said, "There remains yet the youngest, but he is keeping the sheep." And Samuel said to Jesse, "Send and bring him; for we will not sit down until he comes here." [12]He sent and brought him in. Now he was ruddy, and had beautiful eyes, and was handsome. The Lord said, "Rise and anoint him; for this is the one." [13]Then Samuel took the horn of oil, and anointed him in the presence of his brothers; and the spirit of the Lord came mightily upon David from that day forward. Samuel then set out and went to Ramah.

Exegetical Perspective

This account of the anointing of David by Samuel stands at a critical turning point in the books of Samuel. The preceding chapters have described the failed kingship of Saul and God's rejection of him (15:10–35), though Saul will not die until chapter 31. Now David is privately—even secretly—anointed, and the chapters that follow recount his complex relationship with Saul and his rise to become king over Israel (1 Sam. 16:14–2 Sam. 5:10).

The act of anointing with oil is a ritual that establishes a covenantal relationship between the partners. The one who anoints pledges support to the one who is anointed. Later the men of Judah (2 Sam. 2:4) and the elders of Israel (2 Sam. 5:3) will themselves anoint David, thus obligating themselves to him. God's anointing of David through the prophet Samuel serves as a sign of God's election of and commitment to David. By placing this account at the beginning of the story of David's rise, all that happens is seen through the lens of David's election by God.

The short narrative is a masterful combination of psychological drama, political realism, folkloristic color, and careful intertextual allusion, all designed to

Homiletical Perspective

The Fourth Sunday in Lent provides a liturgical context for the story of David's selection. Laetare Sunday, as the day is also known, is when the church sets aside the mournfulness of Lent, calling the people to *laetare*, to rejoice. Originally the day was intended as encouragement, particularly for children, to persevere through the remaining days of Lent.[1] While Protestant congregations may not be quite so observant of the liturgical calendar, the tradition is noteworthy, especially given the playful way God selects the youngest, ruddiest son to be king. The preacher of this text is thus invited to be equally playful in its proclamation.

In many worship services, children are provided their own children's sermon. After this they are then excused from suffering through the sermon preached to the grownups. How ironic that the church systematically excludes its youngest sons and daughters from the hearing and interpretation of this text. They already have more in common with the absent David

1. George Cyprian Alston, "Laetare Sunday," in *The Catholic Encyclopedia*, vol. 8 (New York: Robert Appleton Co., 1910), http://www.newadvent.org/cathen/08737c.htm.

1 Samuel 16:1-13

Theological Perspective

God's rationale for this choice, but readers do learn that Saul is the tallest, most handsome man in all Israel (1 Sam. 9:2). When Samuel eventually presents Saul to the people as the new ruler whom they have requested, the prophet seems to assume that looks and stature suffice to make one a leader. "Do you see the one whom the LORD has chosen? There is no one like him among all the people," Samuel tells the assembly (1 Sam. 10:24).

When the time comes for Samuel to anoint Saul's successor, God and Samuel see things very differently. For one thing, Samuel cannot fully understand God's rejection of Saul. The tense, heart-wrenching quality of the account that reports this debacle (1 Sam. 15) suggests that the narrator may have attributed to Samuel his own perplexity over this tragedy. In any case, Samuel grieves the rejection of Saul, upon whom the prophet would never again lay his eyes.

For another thing, God tells Samuel, "I have seen me a king" among the sons of Jesse (1 Sam. 16:1, my wording), but Samuel trusts his own eyes and also the visual appeal of beauty and stature as identifying qualities for a new king (v. 6). In rebuke, God contrasts divine and human seeing. "The LORD does not regard appearances, but sees into the heart" (v. 7), God explains to the visually impaired prophet. Indeed, God has seen and chosen one whom Samuel cannot see at all, the shepherding son who remains at some distance in the field.

These observations do not exhaust this reading's optical issues. Another level of theological probing begins when someone fetches the absent but chosen lad so Samuel can anoint him, and the narrator then carefully describes David's appearance. He is ruddy and good-looking, with beautiful eyes (v. 12)—or was it an eye for beauty?

David's eyes too would see, or not see, in ways that led to trouble. From his rooftop, he would look upon Bathsheba. Though he lacked nothing and already had numerous wives, his eyes convinced him that he must have another man's wife (2 Sam. 11). Still later, David would see the same, wanton look in the eyes of his son Amnon, but he would not recognize it. As a consequence, he would send his daughter Tamar, the delectable object of Amnon's hungry eyes, into a terrible trap (2 Sam. 13). All through this story, the sons of David die for the sins of their father, including those that stemmed from the blindness of his beautiful eyes.

If we cannot trust the eyes of prophets or the vision of one like David, "a man after God's own heart," as the Scriptures call him (1 Sam. 13:14), then we must learn to practice a certain wariness of all

Pastoral Perspective

authorities not ascribed to him in his anointing: his call and covenant with God and the people. At Gilgal (13:7–10) he arrogated the priestly role offering sacrifices, an offence to God and and irritation to Samuel. God then spoke to Samuel, lamenting the choice, "I regret that I made Saul king, for he has turned back from following me, and has not carried out my commands" (15:11). Samuel chastised Saul, saying, "Has the LORD as great delight in burnt offerings and sacrifices, as in obedience to the voice of the LORD? Surely, to obey is better than sacrifice, and to heed than the fat of rams. For rebellion is no less a sin than divination, and stubbornness is like iniquity and idolatry. Because you have rejected the word of the LORD, he has also rejected you from being king" (15:22–23).

Boundary issues are almost a given for life in the church. Usurping power and territory with or without malice is commonplace. Such trespasses may cause a member to look for a new church or a church to look for a new minister. It truly is better to ask permission than forgiveness—especially over time.

Still grieving over Saul, Samuel received marching orders. God had identified yet another Benjaminite, whom God saw (now?) from the inside rather than the outside. Despite his grief over the results of his first anointing, his fear of being killed by Saul, the apparent coup being planned, the subterfuge—using sacrifice as cover for meeting with Jesse to anoint a new king—Samuel chose obedience and filled his horn with new oil. With a heifer in hand for cover, Samuel traveled to Bethlehem.

The circle of sacrifice began well. Jesse and his sons were sanctified by Samuel, and a parade of the potentials began. Samuel, however, still saw with his eyes. Eliab, the first presented, was tall and easy on the eye. Samuel began to think his work was done! God rejected Eliab, and the other six, because God was looking for a leader with heart.

Heart was not the center of emotions for the ancients, although it was included. Heart was the center of one's being: emotion, intelligence, discernment, wisdom, commitment, and character were all elements of heart—perhaps what we call soul. The right combination was absent in these seven sons. Samuel asked for more. Surely, he had been obedient to God's command. God had said one was already chosen, so there must have been at least one more. Samuel would not close the circle until even the least likely was presented.

The ruddy youngest was fetched from the flock he was shepherding. The boy with beautiful eyes passed by them all and, even knowing that God was looking

Exegetical Perspective

point to the freedom of the divine choice in the selection of a king. The story divides into four sections: (1) the initial conversation between God and Samuel (vv. 1–4a); (2) Samuel's arrival at Bethlehem (vv. 4b–5); (3) the review of Jesse's seven sons (vv. 6–10); and (4) the anointing of David (vv. 11–13).

Much of the story's *psychological interest* focuses on Samuel. The prophet had been something of a father figure to Saul and yet had been required to tell him that God had rejected him from being king. Poignantly, the preceding chapter closed with the note that Samuel never saw Saul again before his death, but that he grieved for Saul (15:35). Nevertheless Samuel the grieving mentor is required to put aside his own feelings to carry out his duties as God's prophet. God sternly reminds him of this in 16:1. As the story proceeds, God will educate Samuel about the qualities needed in a king who can succeed.

The *political realism* of the narrative is evident in the sense of danger that overshadows events. To anoint a new king while the old one lives would be seen by Saul as treason; consequently Samuel fears for his own life (v. 2). Similarly, when Samuel arrives at Bethlehem, the elders who greet him tremble in alarm (v. 4). As a prophet, Samuel is a figure of uncanny power, and now he is an enemy of the king. No wonder his presence creates anxiety. God, however, has provided Samuel with a cover story: he has come to conduct a sacrifice (vv. 2–3, 5)—though one wonders if it is particularly plausible. The anointing itself (v. 13) is apparently conducted with only David's immediate family present. Saul remains ignorant of what has taken place, though he later draws his own conclusions about God's intention and David's future (23:17; 24:21).

The *folkloristic element* in the story concerns the motif of the overlooked or neglected child who becomes a king or queen. It is, in short, the Cinderella story. The motif is used cleverly in the narrative. Already in verse 1 the reader and Samuel know that God has selected a king from one of the sons of Jesse, but which one is not indicated. When Samuel reviews Jesse's sons, Samuel starts with his own intuitions. He is impressed with Eliab's appearance and height.

The reader who knows the folkloristic convention already knows that none of the favored sons will be the chosen one. The story uses the motif to make a theological point. People tend to judge by outward appearances; but God judges by the "heart," that is, the inner character of a person (v. 7). All of Jesse's sons (or so the reader is led to believe) are brought before Samuel. God, however, has indicated to

Homiletical Perspective

than they know. Whether tending sheep or having snacks in the fellowship hall, the smallest have gone missing.

All children know how it feels to be excluded. Many have experienced the peculiar agony of being picked last for a sports team. The youngest, smallest, least coordinated are forced to watch as one by one the taller, stronger, more athletic specimens are chosen by the captains. A teenage girl knows the pain of being the one who is not asked to a dance. A boy whose birthday falls in the summer watches as each of his friends gets a driver's permit. Drawing on these rich and all-too-common experiences, a preacher can use this text as a guide for speaking directly to the socially *non*-elect, whatever their age.

Instead of segregating the congregation by sermon type—children's or adults'—Laetare Sunday and this text provide an ideal opportunity for the intentional inclusion of all members in participation in the sermon, from the youngest to the oldest. One could forgo the usual grown-up sermon in favor of elevating the children's sermon to *the* proclamation for the day. This liturgical adjustment itself would be an implicit proclamation of the text. With only a little creativity, the Scripture could then be enacted through drama. A hopeful Jesse could call strapping sons one by one before a crusty old Samuel, who inspects them for height, strength, and any number of additional, more humorous traits, some planned and some improvisational. Can this one sing opera? Does this one have good teeth? Can this one disco dance? One by one, each is rejected, perhaps by the children of the congregation playing the part of God, shouting down each one in succession. Finally a young David appears before the jury, and the whole congregation is encouraged to yell and shout approval.

The reason this Scripture passage is inherently funny is because the older, stronger, better sons are passed over. The proud, the vain, the predictable winners are humiliated, while the one child everyone has discounted, or even forgotten, is selected by God. "Do you have *any* other sons, Jesse?" "Well, um, there is one more, I think. I kind of forget about him most days." Hooray for David! Hooray for the little guy! Hooray for the ostracized, the outcast, the dismissed, the forgotten, the missing. At this critical point, a playful sermon turns deadly serious.

The homiletician must remain keenly aware that even in a humorous presentation, this text, like God, sees and speaks to the heart. Anyone who has been the victim of a social pecking order carries scars that

1 Samuel 16:1-13

Theological Perspective

theologians and anybody else who claims to know God's mind or discern God's will. Theology, after all, is made on earth, not in heaven. Accordingly, it suffers from all the flaws and limits that characterize the perceptive capacities of a species whose most stunningly nimble skill is self-deception.

We live in an age in which theologians and prophets, including many of the self-appointed variety, rarely hesitate to make pronouncements about the will of God and the theological messages they discern in current events. Seers on either end of the political spectrum find warrants aplenty for calling down God's judgment on those whose sins they decry, or interpreting the most recent disaster as heaven's blow against evildoers of the sort that they have helped God identify. Others among the prophetic band claim as well to know whom God would have us elect or appoint as leaders.

Theologians, prophets, and Pharisees of all stripes would do well to ponder the story of Samuel and David, in which, ironically, an ancient, anonymous theologian who practiced his art through narrative reminded readers, including peers and colleagues of every age, that God does not see as mortals see. God sees what human observers can never discern, including the hidden depths of their own hearts (1 Sam. 16:7). By making that point, this storyteller also confesses his own blindness and the limitations of his and every other writer's analysis and depiction of human or divine affairs, whether published, perished, scriptural, apocryphal, or otherwise. In so doing, this exemplary narrator also engages in the safest, sanest response to the inevitability and depth of his own blindness. His confession is a form of repentance.

The paradoxical truth implicit in his narrative has obvious echoes in this week's accompanying Gospel lesson. Those who own and confess their blindness can see things to which righteous absolutists who never question their own perceptions remain stubbornly and dangerously blind.

FREDERICK NIEDNER

Pastoral Perspective

internally, Samuel (or the narrator) could not help but comment on the lad's appearance. The beauty of one's heart, the loveliness of one's soul surpasses its physical container and is often seen through its portal to the world: one's eyes. David's name was finally used and he was anointed.

While the story line of our text is the anointing of David, the subtext of this passage, as well as its larger narrative, is about God and Samuel and obedience in leadership. Samuel heard God speak and his first response was protest and inquiry. Samuel wanted to understand the parameters and responsibilities, the realities and consequences, and gain assurance that God understood them too. At times, God responded with more detail or altered plans, giving the impression that it was a cocreative process. At other times, God responded, "We will cross that bridge when we come to it. Go!" Samuel now acted in knowledge and faith, walking where God directed and doing as God instructed. God's call was not to blind obedience, but cocreated purpose, toward which Samuel walked at a steady and healthy pace.

Life in the church may also be a cocreative process, a kind of dance of leadership in which either party may lead from time to time with more detail or an enlarged vision. Perhaps that is why David liked to dance so much; he was dancing out the details with God.

In the life of the church, too often conflicts erupt, opportunities are missed, people are hurt and/or disheartened, and the community takes several steps backward because the boundaries of our covenant and purpose are ignored and broken. Leadership needs to be vigilant about training, informing, and recovenanting with volunteers to make clear the vision and mission of individual and faith community tasks. It really is better to get permission than forgiveness. We know our need for daily forgiveness; that much more do we need permission.

What were God and Samuel thinking? Apparently, they first thought it took a giant to slay giants. The larger story reveals that it really took a faithful, dancing heart. Remember, it was David who slew Goliath. Faithful, dancing hearts are what the church needs too.

DONALD P. OLSEN

Exegetical Perspective

Samuel that none of these is the one. How can that be? Samuel perseveres and asks if there is some other son. That David has not been included is an indication of his status within the family. His father identifies him as "the youngest," a term that could also be translated "the smallest" or even "the least" (v. 11). His job in the family—shepherd—has, however, a strong metaphorical resonance. Shepherd is a common metaphor that ancient Near Eastern kings used to describe their relationship to their peoples. The fact that David is a shepherd is symbolic of his future role in relation to the Israelite people.

The story of the selection of David both echoes and contrasts with that of the selection of Saul. Samuel is initially drawn to Eliab's handsomeness and tall stature, which are similar to Saul's kingly appearance (9:2; 10:23). The "yes/no" word that God gives to Samuel is similar to the lot by which Saul was chosen (10:17–27a). Just as Saul was missing at the crucial moment of his selection (10:21–22), so David is also not on the scene. Of course, it is Samuel who anoints each of them (10:1). Also, just as Saul was seized by the spirit of the Lord (10:6, 10; 11:6), so is David (16:13), though in the case of David, the empowering spirit of the Lord remains with him as a lasting charisma (v. 14).

David's introduction is both climactic and ironic. Although the reader familiar with the history of Israel has known from the beginning—even before Samuel did—that it is David who will be God's choice, David's name is mentioned only in the final verse (v. 13). Though Samuel has been warned not to look on the outward appearance as an indication of kingliness, David is introduced by the narrator in terms of his good looks (v. 12)! Here is someone in whom both the inward and the outward qualities come together. The human and the divine desires for an ideal king seem to intersect, but David will prove to be anything but an ideal king and will receive both divine and human disapproval (2 Sam. 11–12).

CAROL A. NEWSOM

Homiletical Perspective

run deep. Human groups are not as patient as God. Any social organization is by its nature exclusive, but exclusion is particularly painful in the church. Many church people choose to self-exclude before a clique does it for them. So those who do not see well stop attending worship. Those who depend on walkers or wheelchairs sit near the back, arriving late and leaving early, so as not to be an obstacle to the crowd. Those whose skin color or sexuality is different go elsewhere, wherever that may be. After a while, the church forgets these people, not on purpose, not in malice. We just forget.

A congregation's sins of omission may require awakening, prophetic speech. On occasion, the preacher may need to step into the role of Samuel, boldly pointing out the congregation's implicit sin and saying, "No!" to those who unwittingly perpetuate the cycle. On the other hand, the injuries of those who have known exclusion are slow healing and easily reopened. The preacher who steps into the ever-present, serious side of this text need not tread too heavily upon the hearts of those who know rejection. Simple acknowledgment of their pain may well be enough. Rather, this is a time to commend those who have felt the hurt of a church's discrimination for the tremendous courage it takes just to show up on a Sunday morning. This is a chance to applaud the strength of those who wait, and wait, for someone's approval. While it may feel like small consolation to know that God, at least, sees their hearts, it is consolation nonetheless.

Laetare is not the imperative to laugh, but to rejoice. While we might and should laugh at our own vanity, we must also pay close attention to its consequences and, as Christ taught, cry with those who cry. This is not a complicated concept. Even children understand that friends sometimes stop playing with them, although the reason for the change is more difficult to grasp. We laugh at that which scares us. We rejoice when that which we thought was lost is found, whether that lost thing is a person, a relationship, or our own dignity. In proclaiming the gospel of this text, the preacher joins his or her voice in Scripture's central and highest themes of salvation and restoration. That even a child can understand these concepts is cause to rejoice.

JAMES MCTYRE

Psalm 23

¹The LORD is my shepherd, I shall not want.
² He makes me lie down in green pastures;
 he leads me beside still waters;
³ he restores my soul.
 He leads me in right paths
   for his name's sake.

⁴Even though I walk through the darkest valley,
  I fear no evil;
 for you are with me;

Theological Perspective

There is no more well-known psalm in Scripture than Psalm 23. These six short verses have been the source of encouragement for Christians and Jews throughout the centuries. Whether in corporate worship or in personal devotion, this segment of Scripture has a unique place in religious expression. Numerous scholars have attempted to categorize the psalms so that their inner coherence and their interrelationships might be clarified. Psalm 23 is built on a major theme in the psalm literature, the distress and subsequent deliverance of the writer.

In fact, one of the major features of this particular psalm is that it is uttered from the point of view of a deliverance already evident. For this reason it is one of those psalm types called a song of trust and confidence. While the devotional elements of this psalm are prominent, its theological dimensions are often overlooked. Each of the six verses introduces a theological theme or affirmation in which the understanding of the relationship between God and humanity is progressively deepened. While it must be acknowledged that the division of this material into verses may not have been part of its original presentation, they have come to serve an important purpose in understanding its message.

The psalm lifts up the theological themes of *provision, abundance, and restoration*. These themes occur

Pastoral Perspective

When you find yourself in difficult times with darkness drawing near, your close friends may come to you and try to lift your spirits. Some will say, "Cheer up! Your problems are not so bad," or "Why not look on the bright side?" Others will try to solve your problems for you. Out of caring for you, their instinct is to try and abolish the darkness. This view, however, only gives more power to the darkness.

The good shepherd of Psalm 23 takes a different approach. The shepherd walks with you in the midst of your trials. The darkness is not changed, but rather you are changed when you receive the gift of his presence.

In the midst of Lent, here comes Psalm 23. In this season we expect challenging words calling us to penitence and to greater faithfulness, but here we get a psalm of sustenance. Here we find encouragement as we progress along the dark path that leads to Easter. Instead of being called to attend to our sinfulness and our mortality, here we are offered an outstretched hand from one who will walk with us and give us comfort and courage.

The Lord is both shepherd and host in this psalm. These are complementary images—so much so that even people who are very familiar with this psalm may not realize that the metaphor shifts from one to the other. The psalmist speaks in the first person

> your rod and your staff—
> they comfort me.
>
> [5]You prepare a table before me
>   in the presence of my enemies;
> you anoint my head with oil;
>   my cup overflows.
> [6]Surely goodness and mercy shall follow me
>   all the days of my life,
> and I shall dwell in the house of the LORD
>   my whole life long.

Exegetical Perspective

Although there is a long and rich history of using Psalm 23 liturgically (it appears in the lectionary four times), most people are inclined to think of Psalm 23 primarily as a funeral psalm, or at least to associate it almost exclusively with situations of extreme threat or loss. This is not a bad thing; Psalm 23 speaks powerfully in such settings. It probably means, however, that we are missing the potential for Psalm 23 to be a vital resource that speaks to us and guides us in the more ordinary circumstances of daily living.

To assist in the recovery of Psalm 23 for daily living, it is helpful to realize that it is not universally viewed as a funeral psalm. In other parts of the world, Psalm 23 functions quite differently, as Philip Jenkins points out in an essay that invites North Americans to hear the Bible from the perspective of other cultures and contexts:

> Or read Psalm 23 as a political tract, a rejection of unjust secular authority. For Africans and Asians, the psalm offers a stark rebuttal to claims by unjust states that they care lovingly for their subjects—while they exalt themselves to the heavens. Christians reply simply, "The Lord is my shepherd—you aren't!" Adding to the power of the psalm, the evils that it condemns are at once political and spiritual, forces of tyranny and of the devil. Besides its

Homiletical Perspective

One way to approach preaching Psalm 23 is not to preach it. Just read it slowly—preferably in the King James Version—and then sit down. This will not score points among the serious intellects in your congregation, but the middle-school crowd will love you for it. The over-seventy crowd will thank you for not overtalking a text that is so rich in history and meaning that simply the sound of its words and the rhythm of its cadence sing us into the presence of a mystery that cannot be touched by any rhetoric. There are plenty of challenges in preaching Psalm 23, but there are also grand possibilities.

Psalm 23 is so often used in funerals because, in the moment when we reach for our best and truest words about the sum of life, we go here. Paul tells us in Romans 14:7–8, "If we live, we live to the Lord, and if we die, we die to the Lord; so then, whether we live or whether we die, we are the Lord's." The one giving testimony in Psalm 23 says that to belong to God in life and in death, today and tomorrow, is a good thing indeed.

While this psalm early on became a communal psalm of confidence, it began as an individual psalm of confidence. That is, it began as a testimony to what one pilgrim had seen and experienced in his life. Psalms are powerful largely because they are unassailable. This psalmist is not trying to defend his

Psalm 23

Theological Perspective

in the first three verses of the psalm and, after a critical transition, they reoccur in the final verses of the psalm. The first verse, "The LORD is my shepherd, I shall not want," introduces the writer's understanding of God as one who cares and provides. Here God is no distant deity but one who is personified as a shepherd. This designation carries with it no inherent status, but a profound responsibility. Traditionally, ideas about God in Christian theological thought have had to hold in dynamic relationship the affirmation that God is absolutely free and the affirmation that God is essentially love. These affirmations are not, and perhaps cannot be, held in a static balance. Either God's love or God's freedom will be the final word. Here the psalmist has affirmed that God's essential being and God's act of caring cannot be separated. God is one who provides.

The second verse, "He makes me lie down in green pastures, he leads me beside quiet waters" (NIV), takes the provision of God beyond the "wants" of humanity. While verse 1 affirms that under the care of God we shall be free from want, verse 2 declares that a richer, deeper experience is to be had under God's care. Reclining in verdant fields in proximity to placid streams suggests an abundant life. This association of God with a full existence is common in the religious expression of ancient Israel. It also connects the full measure of human happiness with the witness of nature at its best. God is one who provides in abundance.

The third verse, "He restores my soul. He guides me in paths of righteousness for his name's sake" (NIV), points to the care of the inner person. The care of the soul, its restoration is God's concern. To restore the soul means to revive it and to enliven it, but care for the soul is not without an ethical and moral purpose. The restoration of the soul allows for divine guidance in the paths of righteousness. We live not simply to live, but to pursue the appropriate relationship with God. Life with God is a journey with God framed by the holy name. God is one who restores.

The fourth verse introduces the central experiential framework through which the theological affirmations are recast and given social, historical, and political specificity. The writer declares, "Even though I walk through the valley of the shadow of death, I will fear no evil" (NIV). To be noted here is the immediate context of the writer. His life is a journey through some lonesome lowland where death overshadows life's fertile possibilities. Evil is named explicitly as the source of anxiety. Crucial to the understanding of this transitional phrase is "even

Pastoral Perspective

entirely, but it is hard not to feel that we, ourselves, are the subjects of this psalm.

The psalm begins by naming the Lord as our "shepherd" (v. 1). This shepherd leads us, his sheep, to things that are good for us. The psalmist presents vivid images for these things—"green pastures" (v. 2), "still waters" (v. 2), and "right paths" (v. 3). Interestingly, the shepherd does one thing that seems above the job description of a typical Middle Eastern shepherd of sheep: he "restores my soul" (v. 3). Clearly, the psalmist holds the metaphor of a shepherd somewhat loosely. This shepherd provides more than mere protection, rest, and nourishment. The gift that he provides is life itself.

The psalmist then proclaims, "Even though I walk through the darkest valley, I fear no evil; for you are with me" (v. 4). The King James Version translates this phrase as the "valley of the shadow of death." It is the valley of extreme darkness, the place of our deepest troubles and fears, the place where we think no one will ever accompany us. Notice that the shepherd does not lead us away from this place. Instead, we walk right through it. We face the darkness, but it holds no power over us because we are in the presence of the Lord.

Any instance when one person is truly present to another requires a foundation of authenticity. In this case, the darkness has to be acknowledged and not discredited. Anything less would be false. Rather than being an act of healing, it would be an act of pretending. Any comfort brought in that context would be doomed to be hollow and fleeting. It would be like an encouraging slap on the back by the person who cannot look you in the eye. In Psalm 23, however, we get the sense that the shepherd has seen it all. The shepherd is aware of the darkness, but, to paraphrase Psalm 139, the darkness is not dark to him.

This gift of presence is especially meaningful for modern people who find authentic presence with one another an increasingly scarce commodity. More and more, it seems that our busy lives are pulling us away from family meals, from leisurely phone conversations, from long walks with very good friends. We find that human interactions of all sorts, from commerce to courting, are being increasingly facilitated by electronics. All the while, the ability to listen is being corroded, and the experience of being truly heard has become more significant than ever. If we learn from our walk with the shepherd just how healing it is to receive such presence, perhaps we will in turn offer it to others.

The metaphor then shifts as we arrive at the final two verses of the psalm. We are now fully in the realm

Exegetical Perspective

political role, Psalm 23 is much used in services of healing, exorcism and deliverance.[1]

Without major prompting, it would never occur to the huge majority of North American Christians to hear Psalm 23 as "a political tract" that "condemns . . . forces of tyranny." Following Jenkins's lead, this treatment of Psalm 23 will attempt to hear Psalm 23 with new ears that are attuned even to the possibility of its political role.

The first clue to the political dimension of Psalm 23 is its opening metaphor. In the ancient Near East, kings were known as the shepherds of their people. To say, "The LORD is my shepherd," is to affirm that God is our king, and king is a political title. In short, God is for us the absolute authority, to whom we owe our ultimate allegiance.

According to the OT, the foremost responsibility of kings is to provide for their people the resources they need to live, with special attention to those whose lives are most threatened and vulnerable (see Ps. 72:12–14, noticing the repetition of "needy" in conjunction with "poor" and "weak"). Unlike the earthly kings who fail to provide for their people, God does what a king/shepherd is supposed to do (see Jer. 23:1–6; Ezek. 34:1–16). That is to say, God exercises royal authority in such a way that everyone can say, "I shall lack nothing" (v. 1; NRSV "I shall not want"); because God has provided food ("green pastures," v. 2), water ("still waters," v. 2), and protection ("right paths," v. 3). In short, everyone can say, "God keeps me alive" (v. 3; NRSV "restores my soul"). God does this "for his name's sake," which is to say that God is true to character. God wills life, and God provides what people need to live.

The appropriate response to the affirmation that God is sovereign and that God graciously provides us what we need to live is humble gratitude that acknowledges our fundamental dependence upon God. It is at this point that the "political role" of Psalm 23 comes into view. While the democratic capitalism of the United States has been remarkably productive and has much to commend it, it does not foster humility or gratitude, nor does it invite dependence upon God. Rather, it aims at making us perpetually dissatisfied with having enough; it virtually obliterates our ability to distinguish between wants and needs; and it encourages and rewards aggressive self-assertion. The political result is a society characterized by excessive individualism and

1. Philip Jenkins, "Liberating Word: The Power of the Bible in the Global South," *Christian Century* 123/14 (July 11, 2006): 26.

Homiletical Perspective

faith. He is singing of it. He is not waiting for a grade or even your response. It is his testimony. You can do with it what you wish.

This psalm is traditionally understood to be a psalm of David who was obviously old enough to have been through some experiences in which he did not know what the outcome would be. This is the confession of faith of one who has paused to reflect on his life and publicly state what he has come to believe about life under God's care. This is one who has been delivered through some danger. If this is David's psalm, you may find some clues to the nature of the danger he has experienced from Psalm 22.

So often, preachers work hard to keep ourselves out of our sermons. We do not want our preaching to be about us, because our individual lives are not broad or rich enough to remain all that interesting or expressive of the diversity of human experience—or because we do not want to appear to be holding ourselves up for emulation. However, Psalm 23 invites preachers to take a shot at articulating something congregations deeply want to hear. It invites us to pause and find our own language for confessing what we have come to believe about life under God's care. It is an opportunity to speak of our experience of God and how that experience sends us through dark valleys with confidence.

The psalm itself lends structure to the sermon. The fundamental statement is that to be a sheep of the Shepherd Lord is to have everything you need—not because you acquire or earn it, but because God provides it. What language would you use to speak of God's provision in your life? Remember, you are not trying to speak for all. You are trying simply to speak honestly for yourself. What has God's provision looked like? Where has God led you to find rest, refreshment, and restoration?

What does it mean to speak of a right path? The right path is the path that leads to abundant life. God leads God's people to the good things in life because that is who God is and what God does. Theologian and writer Marva Dawn describes the experience of riding her bike one day. She was pedaling down a dirt road and doing her best to deal with a deep rut that had been carved out of the middle of the road by a motorcycle. She kept getting caught in the rut and then tripped up by the rut as she tried to escape it. Finally, it occurred to her simply to ride in the rut. What she discovered was that the rut provided the smoothest ride of her life! As she cruised along she was able to gain her speed and relax and enjoy the beautiful scenery all around her. The rut became a

Psalm 23

Theological Perspective

though." This suggests that the suffering of the present moment is merely conditional and contingent. This acknowledgment of the reality of suffering and the presence of evil allows the writer to revisit the themes of provision, abundance, and restoration in more concrete terms.

The second part of the fourth verse, "for you are with me; your rod and your staff, they comfort me" (NIV), recalls the notion of provision. Not only is the shepherd with the writer, but the shepherd's care is now concretized in the symbols of the rod and the staff. The rod and the staff were not only the tools of the shepherd; they were the concrete manifestations of the defense and protection of the sheep.

The fifth verse, "You prepare a table before me in the presence of my enemies; you anoint my head with oil; my cup overflows," recalls the notion of abundance cited in verse 2. Here, however, the abundance is manifested in the presence of the forces of deprivation. The "enemies" have denied the writer a place at the table, the hospitality due one to another in the hot, desert climate, and the full measure of joy. God has responded with abundance that has political meaning and significance.

The sixth and final verse, "Surely goodness and love will follow me all the days of my life, and I will dwell in the house of the LORD forever" (NIV), declares that the theme of restoration is no longer a goal and righteousness no longer a path. Instead of being guided in the ways of justice, the writer shall always be followed by the defining virtues of goodness and mercy. His restored soul has found a perpetual resting place in the presence of God. Theologically, this psalm brings together the human predicament and divine promise.

JAMES H. EVANS JR.

Pastoral Perspective

of people and not sheep. Suddenly we enter a scene of table fellowship where the Lord sets a table and invites the psalmist to dine in the presence of the psalmist's enemies (v. 5). At this point the Lord anoints the psalmist's head with oil and offers a cup that is over-flowing (v. 5). What the Lord offers is without limit. It is we who are limited in our ability to receive.

The famous last verse is a comfort, but it seems to clash with reality. Experience shows that goodness and mercy follow no people all the days of their lives. There is always a mixture of good and evil that follows us. To say otherwise is almost like saying, "They lived happily ever after." However, the Hebrew word for "follow" may also be translated "pursue," and that changes the picture a little bit. God's goodness and mercy will chase after us, even if we run in the other direction.

When a small child trips and skins her knee, a simple kiss from a loving caregiver brings healing. Does the skinned knee go away? No, of course it does not. The physical pain remains, but the offering of love in the form of a caring kiss makes all the difference. In this same way, Psalm 23 is about finding life in its truest sense, which is union with the Lord, and discovering that it can bring healing to our lives. When we sit at the Lord's table and feel our foreheads anointed, we get a holy kiss that heals our places of hurt. We see the darkness around us lose its power in the midst of the Lord's presence, and we are restored.

ROBERT W. FISHER

Exegetical Perspective

rampant greed, two evil and tyrannical forces that Psalm 23 condemns and invites us to reject.

The shepherd metaphor continues into verse 4. The NRSV is justified in setting off verse 4 to itself, however, since God is now spoken to rather than spoken about. In short, at the point of the greatest threat and vulnerability ("the darkest valley"), the affirmation of trust becomes also a prayer. The exactly central line of the psalm articulates its central theological claim ("you are with me"), bespeaking again a fundamental dependence upon God.

The direct address continues in verse 5. Another shift takes place, however, according to most interpreters, as the shepherd image gives way to the metaphor of the gracious host. The host does for the guest what the good shepherd does for the sheep—provides food ("a table"), drink "(my cup overflows"), and protection ("you anoint my head with oil," which seems to be a gesture of hospitable welcome), even amid threat ("in the presence of my enemies").

The NRSV translation of v. 6a is weak, and I suggest the following: "Surely goodness and steadfast love will pursue me all the days of my life." The NRSV misses the play on words involving "my enemies" and "pursue." Ordinarily in the Psalms, it is the enemies who pursue the psalmist. Here they are present, but the real "threat" is God's goodness and unfailing love! It is crucial that the psalmist ends up in God's "house," a place where others are inevitably present, even the enemies. Thus, the psalmist takes his or her place in the household of God, in communion with God and in solidarity with all God's people. In a society of excessive individualism and rampant greed, the political dimensions of such a location can hardly be overestimated.

As the NRSV note suggests, the psalm's final phrase is literally "for length of days." The word "days" is repeated from the previous line, "all the days of my life." The repetition reinforces the claim that Psalm 23 is a resource not only for situations of threat or loss, but also for our living every day.

J. CLINTON MCCANN JR.

Homiletical Perspective

track—a track of righteousness—a path that led to green pastures and still waters.[1]

Even so, the psalmist does not deny that there will be dark valleys along the way. The journey of life sometimes takes you to sickbeds at which you would rather not be. It presents you with challenges that threaten to overwhelm you. The shedding of tears, the breaking of hearts, the feelings of pain are all found on the path where the Shepherd leads you.

Sometimes the pain comes because you quit trusting the path and the Shepherd. Your imagination and your insatiable appetites get the best of you, and you decide to turn the wheel and bust out of the track into the wild places. You know another reality too. Sometimes pain and suffering come your way, even when you are happily and faithfully pedaling down the middle of the right path.

Sometimes the Shepherd takes you through the woods. The psalmist calls it "the darkest valley" and is not at all surprised that the right path leads through it. This could be an interesting line to explore among folks who assume dark valleys should not accompany faithful living or that dark valleys indicate the absence of God.

In the middle part of this psalm the one who testifies suddenly addresses God directly. I wonder what would happen if a preacher got so carried away telling about the abundance of God's care, and the palpable presence of God, that the preacher slipped into direct praise of God. If you throw yourself into the structure and spirit of this psalm, it may take you there.

DAVID M. BURNS

---

1. Marva Dawn, *My Soul Waits: Solace for the Lonely from the Psalms* (Westmont, IL: InterVarsity Press, 2007), 39.

Ephesians 5:8-14

[8]For once you were darkness, but now in the Lord you are light. Live as children of light—[9]for the fruit of the light is found in all that is good and right and true. [10]Try to find out what is pleasing to the Lord. [11]Take no part in the unfruitful works of darkness, but instead expose them. [12]For it is shameful even to mention what such people do secretly; [13]but everything exposed by the light becomes visible, [14]for everything that becomes visible is light. Therefore it says,

"Sleeper, awake!
  Rise from the dead,
and Christ will shine on you."

Theological Perspective

In the Pauline letters, typically an ethical section follows an opening theological reflection. Ephesians follows this pattern. Today's reading comes from a passage that earlier began, "Therefore be imitators of God, as beloved children, and live in love, as Christ loved us" (5:1–2). Because of our faith, we are to "live as children of light" (5:8). The reading is followed by ethical injunctions that are in tension with contemporary understanding: "Wives, be subject to your husbands" (5:22); "Children, obey your parents" (6:1); "Slaves, obey your earthly masters" (6:5), concluding with a passage on confronting the powers and principalities.

Thus, by its context as well as its content, today's reading raises the questions of how actions relate to belief and how one knows what is right. The relevance of these questions is easily seen in current conflicts in church and society over such issues as human sexuality, abortion, war, the death penalty, the role of government, and the like. It is not easy to know what is right.

Central in this difficulty of knowing is the nature of perception. We perceive through filters that come from our personal history and experience, from our education and social relationships, and from our culture. When we look at the world, the mind is not a passive recipient of data. Since Immanuel Kant we have understood explicitly that the mind is an active

Pastoral Perspective

This passage presents us with the powerful contrast between light and darkness. The contrast is a prevalent dynamic in Scripture, going all the way back to Genesis and moving forward through various psalms, Isaiah, and the New Testament, especially the Gospel of John. The contrast is also found in many religions and cultures as well as in literature and music, to say nothing of films, especially the now somewhat dated *Star Wars* movies.

Since this passage comes to us in Lent and since the contrast between light and darkness is such a significant part of Advent, it is possible and maybe useful to compare these two seasons that are so instrumental in shaping our faith and our trust in what God is willing to do with us and for us. In Advent we celebrate the light of God coming to the world in Jesus Christ. It is God's act. God brings the light to earth and to us. In Lent we witness darkness creeping up to, circling around, and apparently overcoming Jesus. Yet here also God is once again the actor. God brings Jesus to life, taking light into the realm of the dead and raising Christ radiant in light from the grave.

Moving closer to the text, Ephesians 5:1–7 calls on us to be "imitators of God." Given all that can follow, this may not be a major stopping point in the text, but the word "imitator" suggests a number of

Exegetical Perspective

These brief verses are loaded with moral and ethical teachings for the holy ones in Ephesus who are called to walk in the light. The beloved children (*tekna agapēta*), as they are referred to in Ephesians 5:1, are challenged to renounce their former existence and take on a new identity rooted in Christ. This particular passage is part of a larger discourse that outlines the rules for Christian living (Eph. 4:17–5:20).

The author of this material utilizes familiar light/dark imagery to establish the striking contrast between the new life of obedience and faith and the former life of disobedience and debauchery. Such imagery occurs in the undisputed letters of Paul (e.g., 1 Thess. 5:5; 2 Cor. 4:4; Rom. 13:12, 13), in the Johannine literature (e.g., John 1:4, 5, 7–9; 1 John 1:5; 2:8), and throughout many of the writings of the Qumran community (e.g., 1QM 1:1–16, 3:6; 1QS 1:9; 3:13, 19–21). This lection alludes back to Ephesians 2:1–22, which vividly recalls the way they were *then*, dead through trespasses and sins, following the course of this world (2:1–2); and the way they are *now*, reconciled to God in one body through the cross (2:16). This reminder to live (*peripateō*) as children of light (*tekna phōtos*; 5:8) is a necessary help for this community of believers who are constantly facing temptations from the larger secular culture of darkness (*skotos*).

Homiletical Perspective

In this pericope the controlling image of light versus darkness provides a ready focus for a sermon. Given the historical setting of the Letter to the Ephesians, the importance of this particular dualism is understandable. The author of Ephesians, likely a disciple of Paul, knew the centrality of the dualism of light and darkness in the writings of the Essenes, a cloistered, eclectic sect active in the author's day. The Essenes considered themselves the elite heirs of an advanced, esoteric knowledge that could flood our inner darkness with the light of awakened consciousness. The Essenes' way of engaging the forces of darkness consisted mainly of huddling in secluded safety to translate life's mysteries into useful knowledge. They pursued their calling far from the cut and thrust of public life. Such was not the case with the writer to the Ephesians. He calls for his followers to take to the streets in the fight with the minions of darkness. Surely he shares the Essenes' call for separation from the "sons of darkness." More importantly, he charges his readers to storm the ramparts of darkness as moral agents in the world: "Take no part in the unfruitful works of darkness, but instead expose them" (v. 11).

A sermon on this passage will focus on openly taking the fight to the powers of darkness. Such is easier said than done, however. We know from frustrating

Ephesians 5:8-14

Theological Perspective

participant in forming and systematizing our perception of reality. We do not perceive reality simply as it is. Rather, the mind actively shapes the data it receives on the basis of certain presuppositions and interests. Knowledge comes from the dialogue between the reality perceived and the mind's preconceptions. The knowledge and beliefs that emerge from this dialogue then form the preconceptions that filter our perceptions.

At the level of personal values, this process becomes even more complex and more deeply involved in our relationships and history. When we look at ourselves and our actions, objectivity is almost impossible. In the effort to preserve a positive image of self, we rationalize away any actions that seem inappropriate. Out of despair we often see all those actions, thoughts, and desires as assaults on our positive self-evaluation. Thus we begin any reflection on ethics and personal actions with the premise that insights will be filtered to fit our presuppositions and our ego needs.

The use of the metaphor of light points to one way this issue may be addressed. "Everything exposed by the light becomes visible" (v. 13). We are to "live as children of light" (v. 8). Such a spirit of openness can occur only within community. While one could interpret this to imply an inappropriate revelation of personal information, a better understanding would focus on growing and learning within a healthy community. The way to insight and truth is through suitable dialogue and sharing within the community of faith. Openness and transparency, the ability to discuss without demanding conformity, the strength to be influenced as well as to influence—such characteristics allow truth to emerge. The multiplicity of perspectives, honestly shared, instructs the individual perspectives, giving a clearer vision of the issue or concern.

In therapy—individual or group—one shares personal stories to receive responses from other perspectives. This wider vision allows the person to see more clearly and begin to grow personally in new ways. In theology and ethics, the gathering and sharing of a diversity of views through synods and councils is the means for discovering new insights or reaffirming received truths. Inclusion of many different perspectives is critical if the community is to move toward the truth that has come to us in Jesus Christ.

The critical characteristic of the community is that it is led by the Spirit of Christ. "When the Spirit of truth comes, he will guide you into all the truth" (John 16:13). That Spirit above all is a spirit of love. The community led by the Spirit will welcome the

Pastoral Perspective

possibilities. Specifically, we are enjoined to avoid disobedience and to be children of light. There are also indications that this passage and one similar to it in Colossians are taken from an early baptism formula. This too may provide an area to explore and expand.

As we move into the body of the text itself, the subject before us is very clear and prominent. First of all is the affirmation in the text that God has chosen us to be light: "now in the Lord you are light" (v. 8). The line echoes the words of Jesus to his disciples, recorded in John's account of the Last Supper—"You did not choose me but I chose you" (John 15:16)—as well as his words in Matthew's account of the Sermon on the Mount, "You are the light of the world" (Matt. 5:14). God does something for us. God takes the initiative. Here Ephesians makes the same declaration. God has chosen us to be light in this world.

Second comes the call to choose to live into the life God makes possible. The faithful life is programmed for freedom: God's sovereign freedom to choose us and our freedom to choose God in response. We are free to choose to live as children of light. A helpful resource for developing the rest of the text is Reinhold Niebuhr's *The Children of Light and the Children of Darkness*.

The writer of Ephesians describes the basic task of being children of light by calling upon us to bear "the fruit of the light" (v. 9). Here in a few words are two powerful images, both of which recur throughout Scripture: bearing fruit and being light. The images are so different in nature that it may be too much to develop this phrase in one sermon. Still, the option is there and more than just a bit tantalizing. Essentially the text guides us to be the children of light by discerning what is "good and right and true" (v. 9). The major clue to this endeavor is in verse 10: "Try to find out what is pleasing to the Lord."

It is so helpful that the text leads us toward "what is pleasing to the Lord," instead of what simply angers or displeases the Lord. How do we use Christ as the model for a faithful life and a moral life? How do we honor the distinction between being moralistic—that is, focusing upon obedience to laws, rules, and regulations—and being moral, which seeks a blending of rules and regulations with the dynamic requirements of relationships? How can we use the community of faith as a community of moral reflection?

The writer of Ephesians does not stop here, however, but goes on to make two more assertions regarding the choice we are to make in practicing a faithful morality. As a companion to discerning what is "good and right and true" we are called in verse 11

Exegetical Perspective

The language of darkness in this passage should not be viewed as a simple foil to the larger theme of light. In verse 8, the author does not merely claim that the newly converted believers were living *in* darkness (e.g., Jude 6) or children *of* darkness; on the contrary, they were considered to be darkness *itself.* In fact, darkness here calls attention to the Gentiles, mentioned in 4:17, who are alienated from the life of God because of the "futility of their minds" and the greed, licentiousness, and impurity that define their existence. This sharp boundary-marking language calls into focus the chief concern of this passage: *identity matters.*

Although the ethical teachings are of great significance and the call to obedient and righteous living is an undeniable imperative in 5:8–14, the author here is equally concerned with breaking down the barriers that have been a source of division and contention among the many different factions that comprise this community of believers. Ephesians 2:11–12 highlights the identity marker more concretely: "So then, remember that at one time you Gentiles by birth, called 'the uncircumcision' by those who are called 'the circumcision,' . . . were at that time without Christ, being aliens from the commonwealth of Israel, and strangers to the covenants of promise, having no hope and without God in the world." Thus, darkness, understood as an identity in verse 8, is a reflection of hopelessness, death, and despair. It symbolizes hardened hearts, futile minds, and complete alienation from God. It represents the hostility (*echthran*) that undermines unity in the body of Christ (2:14).

Darkness is later used in verse 11 to refer to unfruitful works that should be exposed (*elenchō*; cf. 5:13) or brought to light. The Greek term *elenchō* can mean "correct," "reprove," or "convince" (e.g., Matt. 18:15; 1 Cor. 14:24), and in this case the author is concerned with exhorting the community to confront and avoid any form of "darkened" activity that might deceive the community into shameful behavior. This call to make the invisible visible—to expose—is in essence the true mark of "children of light." They are to make public the life of faith and thus overcome the works of darkness that characterize unbelievers who operate in secrecy and shame. They are to embody the true light of the world that overcomes darkness—Jesus, the living Christ.

Beyond light and darkness, this passage also appeals to imagery of fruit (*karpos*) to further emphasize the manifestation of a Christ-centered life: "For the fruit of the light is found in all that is good and

Homiletical Perspective

personal experience that unmasking evil by dint of guts and gumption alone leads mostly to futility. Who of us by signal willpower has made lasting strides against our destructive compulsions and addictions? Who of us by singular ego-resolve readily slips the shadow of a spouse's dominance, or easily calls out the family demons? Beyond our personal struggles, daily reports on global terrorism, drug wars, poverty, and economic malaise should convince us that we humans, in spite of our professed ethics and ideals, consistently lack the moral muscle to hold back, much less overcome, the forces of evil. Where, then, do we find the mettle and acumen to make inroads against these powers that surround and pervade us?

For our answer we need only note how the passage begins and ends. Call verses 8a and 13–14 the bookends of grace that turn these moral demands into permission. Verse 8a opens the pericope with a triumphal declaration: "For once you were darkness, but now in the Lord you are light." The phrase, "in the Lord," is an early church watchword for "in the risen Christ." The author announces the awesome fact that in our mystic union with the living Christ we *are aglow* with Christ's light. Such a glow is more than inspired intellectual acuity. This light also carries the spiritual energy that can empower us in our struggle with the forces of evil.

If verse 8a serves as a prelude of grace for our passage, verses 13–14 similarly provide a triumphal postlude of God's favor:

> Everything exposed by the light becomes visible,
> for everything that becomes visible is light.
> Therefore it says, "Sleeper, awake!
> Rise from the dead, and Christ will shine on you."

Here the writer trumpets the fact that God's light both reveals and renews, exposing what is in the dark, while also changing into light what it exposes. The unidentified fragment in verse 14b, likely part of a hymn from an early church baptismal ritual, caps the passage with a celebratory declaration that incarnates the light in Christ. This revelatory, renewing light *is* the risen Christ. We awake and rise up from spiritual death, as if emerging from baptismal waters, to stand renewed by and pervaded with Christ's light.

Preaching authentically and effectively on this passage depends on how we connect these imperatives with the grace that introduces and concludes them. We violate the gospel, much less the passage, when we preach either demands without grace, or grace without demands. For instance, we may be tempted to works righteousness by heralding one or

Ephesians 5:8-14

Theological Perspective

stranger and outcast, honor the importance and worth of every member, and provide a culture of acceptance that invites dialogue. Such a community provides the foundation for the pursuit of truth.

At its best, the worshiping fellowship provides Christians with a recentering that begins to bring light to our darkness. As we surrender our lives and wills to God, there is a loss of egoism, a destruction of the core of self-concern. Discovering a community of mutual support where a person not only survives but thrives through serving others, we no longer feel threatened and alone. Secure in the knowledge that nothing can separate us from the love of God known through Christ Jesus, though still afraid, we are no longer controlled by fear of the loss of possessions, position, or even life. We remember the story of Jesus and rediscover our identity as children of God, as people who are worth dying for. True worship results in transformed people who act out of genuine concern for others and for doing the will of God. From within the community that honors the dignity of every human being, we are free to listen carefully to the other, free to express our understanding, and free to find the new understanding that somehow bridges the division and moves toward truth.

Humility is the fundamental personal quality required to be part of such a community of mutual concern and openness to truth. Humility is founded on the premise that our basic value rests on our common humanity. Each person is beloved of God and therefore of ultimate worth. Humility provides the foundation for listening to others. Humility empowers one to speak the truth boldly, but always with the reservation that it is the truth as perceived by the individual, not the ultimately correct insight. Humility provides the motivation for patience; through dialogue, in community, with time, truth will emerge, differences will be resolved, and the community will be healed and empowered to move into God's future. This understanding of humility surely underlies Jesus' statement that the meek will inherit the earth (Matt. 5:5) as well as the Pauline reminder that "once you were darkness" (Eph. 5:8a).

WARD B. EWING

Pastoral Perspective

to resist the works of darkness: "Take no part in the unfruitful works of darkness." A pastor can anticipate a number of responses to this call. There will be people who believe this is basically how they live. After all, a goodly portion of those in the church on a Sunday are there trying to do just this. Yet there are other layers of response to this call. Sometimes we choose darkness without seeing it coming, like the prodigal son. Sometimes we choose darkness even when we try to resist doing so, as Paul explains in Romans 7:15–20. Sometimes we choose darkness hoping somehow the darkness will cover what we have done, as John 3:19 indicates. A pastoral response to these choices will make for an honest sermon and, potentially, a deeply helpful one.

Finally, the writer takes the matter one big step farther and calls on us to expose the works of darkness. Most of us are reluctant to dare this dimension of living as children of light. It suggests being judgmental and moralistic, like so much that passes for Christianity in our society. Yet there is a great tradition in Christian faith and in the lives of people who have challenged and exposed the works of darkness. One obvious example would be the slave trade and segregation. There are people working now to expose current forms of slavery and human trafficking. Yet this is only one in a long list of social ills that warrant attention. Staying neutral contributes to the problem. Choosing innocence over awareness allows injustices to continue. How the preacher guides a congregation to select the works of darkness that need to be exposed is a challenge in itself. For all its risks, exposing darkness is part of the practice of living as children of light.

LAIRD J. STUART

Exegetical Perspective

right and true" (v. 9). Some manuscripts include "fruit of the spirit [*pneumatos*]" in this verse, harmonizing back to one of the undisputed Pauline letters, which describes the fruit of the spirit as a litany of moral attributes that frames the righteous life (Gal. 5:22). Moreover, "bearing fruit in every good work" is considered the ultimate path for pleasing God (Col. 1:10). Thus the Ephesians are summoned to discern or discover (*dokimazō*, NRSV "find out") what is pleasing to God. This is no passive or easy task. It is an ethical call to remain vigilant in actively pursuing a transformed, renewed state of mind that is pure and blameless (Rom. 12:2; Phil. 1:9–10).

The final verse (v. 14) quotes an early Christian hymn, which circulated independently. This hymnic fragment is introduced with the same formulaic language used in Ephesians 4:8. The exact source of the quote is unknown, though it contains allusions to Isaiah 26:19: "Your dead shall live, their corpses shall rise. O dwellers in the dust, awake and sing for joy!" and to Isaiah 60:1: "Arise, shine; for your light has come, and the glory of the LORD has risen upon you." The hymn may have been associated with baptism in that the language of rising from the dead is similar to baptismal language of Romans 6:4–13 and Colossians 2:11–12. Later in the chapter (5:19), language about singing psalms, hymns, and spiritual songs is developed more fully as a liturgical setting for this material is suggested. Regardless of the specific setting, the author is using this quote to close the loop on the light/dark imagery that frames the content of this pericope.

Going back to the theme of identity discussed earlier, the final verse offers a capstone for clarifying how to live (or walk) as children of light. One must rise from the dead and, as in baptism, clothe oneself with Christ. Christ becomes the light who transforms darkness: "Christ will shine on you" (v. 14). Now, those who were darkness actually become like Christ. Their identity is defined by pleasing God, exposing unrighteousness, and producing fruit that overcomes former barriers and distinctions and eliminates the invisible walls erected in their community. *Now,* their lives—illumined by Christ—become living testimonies of the power of God.

GAY L. BYRON

Homiletical Perspective

more of the four imperatives in this pericope while forgetting or shortchanging the surrounding, sustaining grace. Conversely, we may extol Christ's fulfilling and freeing light, but cheapen that grace by offering few or no images of that radiance empowering us to lay bare the works of darkness. The key here is to fuse grace and demand in the crucible of God's love so that the hearers experience God's commands as possibilities. The mystic chemistry of grace serves as the catalyst for this transformation. As preachers we want to show our congregations how grace turns the imperative of what we *ought* to do into the indicative of what we *may* do.

Preaching God's grace calls for more than an obligatory nod at sermon's end toward Christ's transforming light. Rather, offering God's fantastic favor means clearing adequate space in the sermon for picturing the life of the children of light. We shall especially want to avoid the temptation to spend too much time describing the "unfruitful works of darkness." Most of us, whether of pulpit or pew, have already heard plenty about the awesome powers of darkness. What we most need, as bearers of Christ's light, are glimpses of our possibilities for exposing the works of that darkness. This means offering the people brushstrokes of particularity that bring to life Christ aglow in each of us. For some of us, this Christ-driven boldness may find expression in protesting the redlining practices of a local bank. For others, this new Spirit-driven resolve may come to life in joining the battle against the polluting chemical plant north of town. Possibly this newly inspirited courage is voiced in the parish leaders' demand that we as a congregation break out of our insular mentality to address the poverty and crime in the neighborhood. In all, we major in our sermons in *describing* rather than *prescribing* what is "good and right and true." We choose to leave our people with portraits and images of what it looks and feels like to live in the chemistry of God's transforming light.

DON WARDLAW

John 9:1-41

[1]As he walked along, he saw a man blind from birth. [2]His disciples asked him, "Rabbi, who sinned, this man or his parents, that he was born blind?" [3]Jesus answered, "Neither this man nor his parents sinned; he was born blind so that God's works might be revealed in him. [4]We must work the works of him who sent me while it is day; night is coming when no one can work. [5]As long as I am in the world, I am the light of the world." [6]When he had said this, he spat on the ground and made mud with the saliva and spread the mud on the man's eyes, [7]saying to him, "Go, wash in the pool of Siloam" (which means Sent). Then he went and washed and came back able to see. [8]The neighbors and those who had seen him before as a beggar began to ask, "Is this not the man who used to sit and beg?" [9]Some were saying, "It is he." Others were saying, "No, but it is someone like him." He kept saying, "I am the man." [10]But they kept asking him, "Then how were your eyes opened?" [11]He answered, "The man called Jesus made mud, spread it on my eyes, and said to me, 'Go to Siloam and wash.' Then I went and washed and received my sight." [12]They said to him, "Where is he?" He said, "I do not know."

[13]They brought to the Pharisees the man who had formerly been blind. [14]Now it was a sabbath day when Jesus made the mud and opened his eyes. [15]Then the Pharisees also began to ask him how he had received his sight. He said to them, "He put mud on my eyes. Then I washed, and now I see." [16]Some of the Pharisees said, "This man is not from God, for he does not observe the sabbath." But others said, "How can a man who is a sinner perform such signs?" And they were divided. [17]So they said again to the blind man, "What do you say about him? It was your eyes he opened." He said, "He is a prophet."

[18]The Jews did not believe that he had been blind and had received his sight until they called the parents of the man who had received his sight [19]and asked them, "Is this your son, who you say was born blind? How then does he now see?" [20]His parents answered, "We know that this is our son, and that he was

Theological Perspective

Attempts to quantify either sin or evil are difficult, if not impossible. Even more difficult are attempts to assign blame or responsibility. Is one person more sinful than another? How should we measure sinfulness? Has one person suffered more or greater evil than another? Has the twentieth century, for example, been the occasion for more evil than previous centuries? For Jews and Christians the experience of evil, both personally and collectively, has long raised two large theological questions. First, how can God's goodness and sovereignty be defended (or "justified") in light of the reality of evil? Second, does the reality of evil negate human faith in God's covenant faithfulness?

Abraham obeyed God's command and took Isaac, his "only son," the bearer of God's promises to Abraham, to a mountain in Moriah to sacrifice him. An angel intervened and a ram was miraculously provided for the sacrifice. "So Abraham called that place 'The LORD will provide'" (Gen. 22:8, 14). Furthermore, God promised Israel that if it kept God's

Pastoral Perspective

Over the past few decades several cultural observers have voiced concern about the erosion of social capital in the United States: the breakdown of neighborhoods, lower rates of participation in organizations like the PTA and churches, and fewer bowling leagues. People are *Bowling Alone*, as the title of a famous book described it, and that is troubling to many people.[1] Even more troubling to others are reports about the breakdown of a more basic American institution—the family. Many people are understandably concerned about high rates of divorce, the scattering of extended families, and pressures to embrace new family configurations.

This loss of social capital is troubling not just to those who are directly involved in those institutions, but also to social observers, because the latter are aware of the side effects that social isolation can have for communities and individuals. Communities with

1. Robert D. Putnam, *Bowling Alone: The Collapse and Revival of American Community* (New York: Simon & Schuster, 2000).

born blind; ²¹but we do not know how it is that now he sees, nor do we know who opened his eyes. Ask him; he is of age. He will speak for himself." ²²His parents said this because they were afraid of the Jews; for the Jews had already agreed that anyone who confessed Jesus to be the Messiah would be put out of the synagogue. ²³Therefore his parents said, "He is of age; ask him."

²⁴So for the second time they called the man who had been blind, and they said to him, "Give glory to God! We know that this man is a sinner." ²⁵He answered, "I do not know whether he is a sinner. One thing I do know, that though I was blind, now I see." ²⁶They said to him, "What did he do to you? How did he open your eyes?" ²⁷He answered them, "I have told you already, and you would not listen. Why do you want to hear it again? Do you also want to become his disciples?" ²⁸Then they reviled him, saying, "You are his disciple, but we are disciples of Moses. ²⁹We know that God has spoken to Moses, but as for this man, we do not know where he comes from." ³⁰The man answered, "Here is an astonishing thing! You do not know where he comes from, and yet he opened my eyes. ³¹We know that God does not listen to sinners, but he does listen to one who worships him and obeys his will. ³²Never since the world began has it been heard that anyone opened the eyes of a person born blind. ³³If this man were not from God, he could do nothing." ³⁴They answered him, "You were born entirely in sins, and are you trying to teach us?" And they drove him out.

³⁵Jesus heard that they had driven him out, and when he found him, he said, "Do you believe in the Son of Man?" ³⁶He answered, "And who is he, sir? Tell me, so that I may believe in him." ³⁷Jesus said to him, "You have seen him, and the one speaking with you is he." ³⁸He said, "Lord, I believe." And he worshiped him. ³⁹Jesus said, "I came into this world for judgment so that those who do not see may see, and those who do see may become blind." ⁴⁰Some of the Pharisees near him heard this and said to him, "Surely we are not blind, are we?" ⁴¹Jesus said to them, "If you were blind, you would not have sin. But now that you say, 'We see,' your sin remains."

Exegetical Perspective

In the history of scholarship, John 9:1–41 has taken on a life of its own that has effectively detached its content from, and significance for, the Johannine narrative as a whole. Commentaries have neatly divided the chapter into an isolated drama of seven scenes narrating the aftermath of Jesus' healing of the man born blind, who never asked to be healed in the first place. While interpreters have been content to let the meaning of the story reside in the miracle itself, Jesus himself comments on and provides the interpretation of the healing in 10:1–21. Jesus does not stop talking in 9:41, and Jesus' words in 10:1–21 function as the discourse that interprets the meaning of the healing of the blind man. This is a recurring structural pattern in the Gospel of John.

Jesus performs a sign (sēmeion in the Fourth Gospel, not miracle), which is followed by dialogue and then commentary from Jesus that provides the theological framework through which to interpret the meaning of the sign. The actual healing itself is

Homiletical Perspective

A preacher can talk and talk about this story, but it is not a story about talking. It is a story about time: before and after, then and now, years ago and today, always and then suddenly.

In between is what happened, but a preacher cannot really talk about that, either—at least, not in a way that makes sense. There was a moment, you say. There was a thing that happened. There was a man you met. He touched you, with mud and light. The rest is a song.

> Amazing grace, how sweet the sound, that saved a wretch like me!
> I once was lost, but now am found; was blind, but now I see.

The inquisition comes next; you might as well expect it. People notice. Amazing grace does not pass over the body without leaving indelible marks. What happened, they ask? What did *you* do? What did *he* do? How do you explain your new body, your new self, your new life, your new sight? How do you

sign
& miracle

Theological Perspective

commandments, "I will place my dwelling in your midst, and I shall not abhor you. And I will walk among you, and will be your God, and you shall be my people" (Lev. 26:11–12). Not even the devastating experience of exile seemed to shake Israel's belief that in God's own time and way "the Lord will provide." Similarly, Christians have been drawn to Jesus' words, "Are not two sparrows sold for a penny? Yet not one of them will fall to the ground apart from your Father. And even the hairs of your head are all counted. So do not be afraid; you are of more value than many sparrows" (Matt. 10:29–31).

Classical Christian theology sometimes draws a distinction between general and special providence. The former affirms, in the words of John Calvin, that God "watches over the order of nature set by himself." The latter, special providence, affirms that "God so attends to the regulation of individual events, and they all so proceed from his set plan, that nothing takes place by chance."[1] That conviction is reflected in the answer of the Heidelberg Catechism (1563) to the question concerning the meaning of the first line of the Apostles' Creed, "I believe in God the Father Almighty, Maker of heaven and earth." It means that "whatever evil he [God] sends upon me in this troubled life he will turn to my good, for he is able to do it, being almighty God, and is determined to do it, being a faithful Father."[2]

However, the horrors of the twentieth century—the unimaginable slaughter in the trenches of the First World War, the genocide of six million Jews in the Holocaust, the use of the atomic bomb on Hiroshima, the killing fields of Cambodia and Rwanda—have made it difficult, if not impossible, for many to affirm that all events proceed from God's set plan. Do the horrors of the twentieth century mean that Christians must relinquish the Bible's claim that "the Lord will provide"?

The story of Jesus' healing of the man born blind in John 9 may help us think through some of these perplexing questions. It may provide some clues for a contemporary Christian understanding of providence. First, John 9 may suggest that a contemporary doctrine of providence should be chastened, more modest, and less grandiose than its classical predecessors. John 9 does not say that all events reveal God's works, only that in this specific individual, this particular man, God's work—God's providence—is

1. John Calvin, *Institutes of the Christian Religion*, ed. John T. McNeill, trans. Ford Lewis Battles, LCC (Philadelphia: Westminster Press, 1960), 202–3 (1.16.4).
2. The Heidelberg Catechism, in *Book of Confessions: Study Edition* (Louisville. KY: Geneva Press, 1996), 62 (4.026).

Pastoral Perspective

more isolation tend to feel (and maybe are) less safe; people often have less stability when they are isolated from friends and loved ones; and a recent study suggests that they may be less happy too. Happiness, it seems, is contagious, and we are more likely to catch it if we are hooked up with happy family members, friends, or neighbors.

In light of these concerns, some people look nostalgically to the communities of the past, in which people were more connected, attentive to one another, and supportive. That was when people knew how to take care of each other—or did they?

Reading John 9 through the lens of anxiety about collapsing social capital is interesting, because it is so counterintuitive. All our presuppositions about the strength and health of earlier communities and family systems collapse when we read this text, because each of the supports, which we assume are in place, fails to deliver. The text narrates the story of Jesus healing a man who had been blind from birth, and the reactions of his community, the religious authorities, and his family. Nothing plays out the way we might expect it to.

The first surprise is the community's reaction; they do not recognize the man who was born blind. This is so odd. The man has lived in their midst all his life; his neighbors have interacted with him, perhaps helped him cross the street or draw water; they have worshiped with him. Why do they fail to recognize him after he is healed? Is it because the only marker of his identity was his blindness? Has the fact that he was differently abled been the only thing they could ever see in him?

This raises a pastoral issue for any of us who interact with persons who are differently abled. How do we identify and come to know people who are different from us? Do we allow disability to be a defining marker, or are we able to look beyond that and recognize the humanity of people? How limited or keen is our sight when we are with people who are differently abled?

A second pastoral issue surrounds the actions of the religious community, in which leaders seem to want to control the narrative. The Pharisees do not want to hear or believe the man's story, because it opposes the story they want to tell. They want Jesus to be the sinner, not the hero of the story; they want another explanation, one that leaves them in control of all the religious goods and services.

Perhaps it is reassuring to realize that even in the first century religious authorities fought over ecclesiastical authority. The privileges of defining sin or

narrated very succinctly, because it is not the miracle that is the critical point. Rather, as sign, it points to something beyond itself, to what an encounter with Jesus signifies. The narrative weight is given to the dialogue and discourse that follow.

When the discourse on the healing of the blind man is ignored in the interpretation of John 9, the events in chapter 9 are not allowed their full meaning and impact. Unfortunately, the lectionary significantly complicates the issue. Chapter 9 is the lectionary text for Lent 4 in Year A, but the first half of the discourse (10:1–10) is the Gospel reading for Easter 4 in Year A, and the rest of the discourse (10:11–18) is the Gospel for Easter 4 in Year B. Moreover, never included is 10:19–21, where the division among the Jews over whether or not Jesus has a demon, and whether a demon can open the eyes of the blind, directly connects Jesus' words in chapter 10 to the healing of the blind man in chapter 9.

Only after the healing do we learn that the work (9:14) occurred on the Sabbath (cf. 5:9). Much like the Samaritan woman at the well, the blind man grows in his understanding of who Jesus is, yet this time not through direct dialogue with Jesus but through witness to his encounter with Jesus. In his interrogation by the Pharisees, the blind man repeatedly tells his story and comes to know that Jesus is from God (v. 33). This confession is the impetus for the man's expulsion from the synagogue. It is important to note that Jesus has been gone from the narrative since the healing itself and does not reappear until verse 35 when he finds the man who has been cast out of the synagogue (*aposynagōgos*). The truth of who Jesus is, set out immediately in the prologue, is what the blind man is able to see.

Interpreting 9:1–10:21 as a unit yields a number of exegetical insights for the interpretation of the healing of the man blind from birth. While a first interpretation of this story may focus on the importance of seeing, or "spiritual sight," in recognizing who Jesus is, the importance of hearing is revealed in the discourse of the story. In fact, the blind man first responds to Jesus' voice. Jesus tells him, "Go, wash in the pool of Siloam" (v. 7), which the blind man does. He *hears* Jesus before he *sees* Jesus.

Like the woman at the well, the blind man recognizes Jesus gradually. He goes from seeing "the man called Jesus" (v. 11), to calling Jesus a prophet (v. 17), to recognizing that he must be from God (v. 33), to addressing him as "Lord" and worshiping him (v. 38). In fact, in verse 37 Jesus himself reveals the importance of both sight and hearing when it comes

explain what we know cannot be, and what therefore cannot be explained?!

A preacher can talk and talk about this passage, and what happened to the man born blind, but be clear: it is not explanatory talk. Some things, some miracles, can never be explained. We can only describe them, tell what we know, say what happened and what we believe about it. Proof and explanation have their place, but not in this passage. *This* passage is about time: before and after, then and now, who we were for years and years and who we are today. The moment of conversion itself is not as important as the difference it made: *I once was lost, but now am found; was blind, but now I see.* This, a preacher can talk about. This, a preacher can describe.

As we do, here are a few homiletical strategies to keep in mind.

Set the context for blindness as a place to be rather than an ethical shortfall. I have a friend who was born blind. She has taught me the folly of pity: she neither wants nor deserves mine. Her life is rich and full and she lives and moves in that life. To be sure, she has had to learn a measure of adaptation; to be blind in a world structured for sighted people means that she has to find ways to understand and cope with our ways. She also has to teach us, constantly, how to live with (not "help") her, because that is *our* blindness: even if we were to walk around with kerchiefs over our eyes or develop cataracts, we would never know what it is like to be *born blind*.

This is a delicate point, but essential if we are going to enter this passage: we are talking about *different worlds* more than *different ethics*. Many preachers get fascinated by the historical details in this text (for example, the key fact that in Jesus' day, blindness was interpreted as a punishment for human sin) and become preoccupied with how far we have evolved in our theological interpretations of illness; in many cases, thankfully, we have. The text does not ask us to enter its ethical world as much as it asks us to enter the state of blindness itself.

What is it like to be born into one experience of the world that will *never change*? What is it like to live and move among others whose experience of the world is so radically different? What is it like to try to understand their world, and describe yours to them? Blindness is first a state of being, rather than a metaphor for unbelief. Before we can enter this text, we have to try to place ourselves there—in a world that is radically different from the one we know now.

Let the moment of conversion simply be a turning point in the plot, rather than something to explain and

John 9:1-41

Theological Perspective

revealed. Neither this story nor any other story should be used to explain the Holocaust.

Second, just as Jesus never explains why this individual was born blind, so a contemporary doctrine of providence might hew more closely to the language of confession than that of explanation. Jesus' disciples do not know the distinction theologians sometimes draw between natural and moral evil, but they assume that this natural evil—the man's blindness—must in some way be due to (and therefore explainable by) someone's sin, either that of the man himself or that of his parents. Jesus, however, rejects all attempts to explain this man's blindness by means of the category of sin. The man's healing serves a different purpose than that of explanation: "he was born blind so that God's works might be revealed in him" (v. 3). A contemporary doctrine of providence—one that takes its clues from this story—might eschew grand theories that try to explain all events, and focus instead on what particular events reveal about God.

Third, God's presence and activity in the healing of the blind man cannot be explained because it is not publicly accessible. It is not so much perceived as it is revealed, and it is revealed only to those who are given the gift of faith. The irony in John's story, of course, is that the blind man receives his sight, but everyone else in the story loses theirs—not their physical vision, but their capacity to believe and understand what they have witnessed. Without exception, neighbors, Pharisees, and parents are unable to see in this event that "God does provide." Not even the man who has been healed understands what has happened to him. Only after Jesus seeks him out and calls him to faith in the Son of Man, does he truly "see." Only after he first believes does he worship the one who is truly from God (v. 38) and who has healed far more than just his blindness.

Providence is not a Christian explanation of history, nor is it a compelling rational answer to and explanation of the horrors of the twentieth century. Providence is a confession by those who are given the eyes of faith that in particular events God works in, around, through those things that oppose God, to accomplish God's purposes.

GEORGE W. STROUP

Pastoral Perspective

dispensing grace are powerful ones, and it is no surprise that religious authorities covet them. In one form or another we have fought over these privileges, this power, for centuries, and we continue to do so. This text convicts the religious antagonists who battle over definitions of sin or the gifts of grace, and who allow those battles to obscure God's presence in our midst. How do we get caught up in battles like this? What issues or preoccupations divert our attention from God's presence and action and passions?

Almost everybody fails the man born blind. Even his family backs away from him, and his parents put their own safety before his welfare. Maybe we can understand an older couple being reluctant to sacrifice their home, work, and community for their son, but would we not expect them to celebrate with him, to be joyful over his healing? There is nothing of that in this text. The parents' fear overwhelms their joy, and they abandon their son to the authorities.

The community fails. The religious authorities fail. The family fails. The only trustworthy figures in this story are the man born blind and Jesus. The man tells the truth, and even in the face of threats, the abandonment of his community and family, and expulsion, he sticks to his guns. I was blind, but now I see. Again and again and again, the man witnesses to the saving grace he has experienced in Jesus Christ.

Jesus is the only one the man can trust, and he is the only one we can trust in this story. Although the Pharisees lay claim to dispensing grace, it is Jesus who transforms. It is Jesus who heals. It is Jesus who stands with the man in his final isolation. He stands with us too.

Sometimes when the sun is really bright, or when an artificial light is intense, we need to squint or shut our eyes. The brightness seems dangerous to us, and the reflex is automatic. Metaphorically we see this human reaction unfolding in John 9: the light of the world shines bright, and the community, the Pharisees, and the man's family shut their eyes in self-defense. That is the intuitive thing to do, right?

Wrong. In this text, everything is counterintuitive. The light of the world is in our midst, and we need not shut our eyes. In fact, the best thing to do is to open our eyes, wide. We will not be blinded by the light. We will be saved.

DEBORAH J. KAPP

to belief. "You have *seen* him," he says, "and the one *speaking* with you is he."

The importance of hearing and seeing comes into full relief when Jesus' words in 10:1–21 are heard along with the healing of the blind man. In the discourse Jesus integrates seeing and hearing with believing. Jesus reiterates that those who *know* him, his sheep, hear his voice and follow him. In the Gospel of John, such "knowing" articulates relationship. In the figurative language of the sheep and the shepherd, Jesus recasts the importance of seeing and hearing by creating new images for what has already occurred in chapter 9 between the blind man and Jesus.

The blind man is more than one whom Jesus heals; he is one of Jesus' sheep, a member of the fold, a disciple. Like the sheep, the blind man hears Jesus' voice. Like the shepherd, Jesus finds the blind man when he has been cast out (v. 35). Jesus provides for the man born blind much more than sight. He provides for him what he, as the good shepherd, gives all of his sheep: the protection of his fold (10:16; cf. also 21:15–19), the blessing of needed pasture (10:9), and the gift of abundant life (10:10). As a result, hearing and seeing are much more than ways by which one recognizes or believes in Jesus. They are, in fact, expressions of relationship with Jesus, and relationship with Jesus means also relationship with the Father (10:14–15).

Moreover, relationship with Jesus reimagined as the relationship between shepherd and sheep becomes representative of discipleship. Jesus the good shepherd will protect his sheep, his disciples, leaving them safely in the "fold" by coming out of the garden (the Greek verb is *exerchomai*—"came out," not NRSV "came forward") to meet Judas and the soldiers and Jewish police (18:4). In chapter 21, Jesus will ask Peter to take on the role of shepherding the sheep.

Sight and hearing are both critical in this story, as Jesus makes God known in the healing of the blind man. Without both chapters together, one sense is afforded greater significance than the other, and the blind man's "sight" is reduced to mere example or miracle. In fact, he embodies that of which Jesus speaks in 10:1–18.

KAROLINE M. LEWIS

defend. Let us be frank: conversions are messy. They can even be downright revolting, as John 9 illustrates ("He spit in the dirt, made mud with his saliva, and put it on my eyes!"), and most important of all, they never sound convincing. Just because *you* had a holy moment with mud does not mean that the rest of us will stop scraping it off our boots, right?

A preacher has to remember this: one person's ecstatic moment with mud usually looks, to the rest of us, like a classic case of self-delusion. Try to describe it, as the man born blind did, and others will question your sanity, doubt your word, and write you off. The muddy details of John 9 remind us of how carefully we have to tune our ears (and possibly our stomachs) before we can listen to one another's stories. Obsessing about our own discomfort ruins our ability to hear.

Focus on what we can actually describe: the difference between before and after. Notice that the man born blind cannot describe his conversion moment to anyone's satisfaction, but he *can* tell the difference it makes. "All I know," he tells the authorities, "is that I was blind, and now I see!" This is a better tactic, because now he is talking about things others can see and hear for themselves. They knew him before; they can see him now, and clearly, he is no longer blind!

So let description of the before and after be the thing. Once I saw the world like this; now I see it like this. Once I believed this; now I believe this. Once I lived in a place that I now see was blind to certain things. Now my eyes are opened, and here is what I see and know! These are the stories the church needs to hear.

Confess Jesus; do not explain him. In the end, all we can say is that we believe Jesus healed this man. We cannot tell how or why, or offer any proof that will be convincing. Our confession is everything, in the new world of faith. It is everything he asks.

ANNA CARTER FLORENCE

Ezekiel 37:1-14

¹The hand of the LORD came upon me, and he brought me out by the spirit of the LORD and set me down in the middle of a valley; it was full of bones. ²He led me all around them; there were very many lying in the valley, and they were very dry. ³He said to me, "Mortal, can these bones live?" I answered, "O Lord GOD, you know." ⁴Then he said to me, "Prophesy to these bones, and say to them: O dry bones, hear the word of the LORD. ⁵Thus says the Lord GOD to these bones: I will cause breath to enter you, and you shall live. ⁶I will lay sinews on you, and will cause flesh to come upon you, and cover you with skin, and put breath in you, and you shall live; and you shall know that I am the LORD."

⁷So I prophesied as I had been commanded; and as I prophesied, suddenly there was a noise, a rattling, and the bones came together, bone to its bone. ⁸I looked, and there were sinews on them, and flesh had come upon them, and skin had covered them; but there was no breath in them. ⁹Then he said to me,

Theological Perspective

This poignant description of dry bones strewn across a valley is one of the Bible's great gifts to the eschatological imagination of both Jews and Christians. Under Ezekiel's watchful eye, these bones suddenly reassemble themselves in a great clatter, then are strapped with sinew and flesh and skin, and, finally, reanimated with a breath called forth from the four winds. Apart from this passage, the Hebrew Bible is largely silent regarding any blessed afterlife for the dead, and this *Grey's Anatomy* account may be the earliest appearance in the Bible of what became a central belief for both rabbinic Judaism and Christianity: the resurrection of the body.

Most commentaries stress that Ezekiel's intent was more metaphorical than physiological. That is, his vision was about the eventual return to the land of Israel of the descendants of those Jews who had been marched against their will to Babylon. The dry bones represent the dusty sense of hopelessness that the exiles would ever find their way home. "These bones are the whole house of Israel," Ezekiel is told (v. 11), and they will, one day, return to the land of Israel.

John Calvin granted as much. For Calvin, these verses are about arousing the despairing refugees to hope for a return, and it is essential to recognize how this image of the valley of revived dry bones works at this level. It is also worth appreciating the way in

Pastoral Perspective

This passage has captured the imagination of readers of the Hebrew Bible for centuries. Proof of this can be found in visual art, ministerial proclamations, music, literature, and even pop culture. More than 80,000 references to this biblical passage can be found on Google, including drawings, paintings, and illustrations from as early as the third century.

Few parts of the Bible offer richer material for visualization and imagery than Ezekiel and the valley of the dry bones. As you read these Bible verses, it is virtually impossible not to envision a desert scene with bones and skulls lying in disarray as far as the eye can see. Ezekiel stands in the midst of the dry bones listening to the "words of the Lord." In some of the art depicting this passage, God is also present, standing above Ezekiel as a shadow or in a clearer representation. In one book illustration painted in 1372, the Lord is depicted as a young man leaning down from heaven directing Ezekiel's actions. Ezekiel is an old man preaching to bodies rising from wooden coffins and to the bones on the ground.[1]

As we progress through Lent, perhaps it would be valuable for us to consider what dry bones (and dry times) are represented in our own spiritual lives. What

---

1. Description of the illustration of "Ezekiel's Vision of the Valley of Dry Bones" (artist unknown), in Petras Comestor, *Bible Historiale*, France, 1372.

"Prophesy to the breath, prophesy, mortal, and say to the breath: Thus says the Lord God: Come from the four winds, O breath, and breathe upon these slain, that they may live." [10]I prophesied as he commanded me, and the breath came into them, and they lived, and stood on their feet, a vast multitude.

[11]Then he said to me, "Mortal, these bones are the whole house of Israel. They say, 'Our bones are dried up, and our hope is lost; we are cut off completely.' [12]Therefore prophesy, and say to them, Thus says the Lord God: I am going to open your graves, and bring you up from your graves, O my people; and I will bring you back to the land of Israel. [13]And you shall know that I am the Lord, when I open your graves, and bring you up from your graves, O my people. [14]I will put my spirit within you, and you shall live, and I will place you on your own soil; then you shall know that I, the Lord, have spoken and will act, says the Lord."

Exegetical Perspective

Ezekiel 37:1–14 has three sections, an introduction (vv. 1–4), a speech event (vv. 5–10), and an explanation (vv. 11–14). The metaphor "the hand of the Lord" (v. 1; cf. Exod. 9:3) describes divine action for the salvation of the Hebrews. The same phrase also occurs in Isaiah (Isa. 19:16; 25:10; 41:20; 59:1; 66:14) and elsewhere in Ezekiel (Ezek. 1:3; 3:22; and 40:1). As an expression of divine redemption beyond social and political trauma, it appears nearly 190 times in the Hebrew Bible.

The writer builds parallelism between the hand of the Lord and the spirit of the Lord. The parallelism of agency tracks with a parallelism of action. The verbs "brought me out" and "set me down" figure prominently in the recollection of the divine action of the exodus event. However, the current aspiration is not about coming to the promised land. The prophet does not see a land of milk and honey. The valley is a metaphor of opportunity as well as challenge. The writer sends an important descriptive and clarifying note: the valley is full of bones.

When the NRSV says "led me all around them" (v. 2), it has the sense of round and round and time and time again. This is no cursory observation on Ezekiel's part. Here the writer uses nouns to emphasize the capacity of the bones in the second and third measures. The Hebrew term "behold" goes

Homiletical Perspective

As our journey through Lent draws near to Easter, we hear one of the most imaginatively dramatic readings in all Scripture: Ezekiel's vision of the valley of dry bones. This vision reminds every generation that God not only gives life but restores life, that death will not have the last word, even when all signs of life have been taken away. Our God is the Creator God of life, its origin and goal.

The reading opens with Ezekiel, a prophet raised up by God for Israel exiled in Babylon, being brought by the hand and spirit of God to a valley full of dry, human bones. After the prophet walks all around these bones, God asks: "Mortal, can these bones live?" (v. 3a). What could be more lifeless than dry bones?

I remember following a guide through a Franciscan church in Lima, Peru, to an ossuary where the bones of those long dead were stored—piles of skulls, leg and arm bones, in a room whose lighting cast a golden glow on the remains. As impressive as this space was, there was also an impersonal quality to it. These long-deceased persons were nameless to those who looked on them and saw only a room full of dry bones. They were not so once.

A scene in Kenneth Branagh's version of Shakespeare's *Hamlet* takes place in the graveyard just before the burial of Ophelia. While walking, Hamlet and his friend Horatio come upon a gravedigger who

Ezekiel 37:1-14

Theological Perspective

which Ezekiel based this political hope upon a more fundamental hope for the resurrection of the dead that is the source of all hope, "the chief model of all the deliverances that believers experience in this world." More than anything else human beings can hope for, Calvin claimed, the resurrection of the dead is so utterly dependent upon God that there can be no doubt that it lies outside of our powers. There are forms of immortality that one can recognize as intrinsic to existence in the normal course of things—the survival of one's heirs, influence, or reputation, for instance. For a body to be resuscitated long after it has begun to decompose, that is a miracle.[1]

In ways that we find baffling today, Christians of the early church were convinced that life after death required a body. This was a fundamental disagreement between proto-orthodox Christians and gnostic Christians. For the gnostics, nothing was more desirable than the eventual liberation of the soul from its physical encumbrance of a body. Church fathers like Irenaeus and Tertullian, however, were adamant that without flesh, there is no person to overcome death, because a human being, in this life and the next, is an intermingled soul and body. Indeed, for the miracle of resurrection to occur, there must be a corpse. A permanent separation of soul and body, for which the gnostics hoped, would not be immortality, but extinction.

This belief was put to the test in the early centuries when Christian martyrs were hacked to pieces by gladiators, or eaten by lions during waves of persecution. Was there a point at which a body was so mangled, or its parts so widely dispersed, that it could not be reconstituted—even by God? By the mid-second century, according to Eusebius, the Romans in Gaul began decapitating and burning the corpses of Christians executed in the amphitheaters, and then dumping the remains to float down the Rhine, to "rob the dead of their rebirth" and ruin the confidence of surviving Christians that martyrdom would be rewarded with resurrection. Does God have the power to recover and reassemble these particles that have been swept away by the current? To think in even more grisly terms, what becomes of the saintly martyr who is eaten by a lion, which is in turn sacrificed and eaten by pagans? Consumed and digested by two carnivores, whose flesh has the martyr's body become? In response, Tertullian suggested that bones and teeth, as the most enduring particles, even

1. John Calvin, *Institutes of the Christian Religion*, ed. John T. McNeill, trans. Ford Lewis Battles, LCC (Philadelphia: Westminster Press, 1960), 3.25.4.

Pastoral Perspective

can we learn from the lonely and parched periods of our spiritual journeys? The "dark night of the soul" is familiar in literature and the human experience. Most of us can point to periods of time when doubts, hopelessness, depression, fear, and anxiety were prominent in our daily living. Certainly hopelessness and despair were a communal experience for the people of Israel at the time of Ezekiel's vision of dry bones. What could we possibly learn from these "dry" periods of life when we feel as disconnected and brittle as the bones in Ezekiel's vision? The following poem beautifully describes the conditions of these dry periods:

Bone

Bone lay scattered and artifactual
Wind-rowed like dead branches
Whose tree bodies repeat the desiccation
All hope bleached and lost
Living moisture evaporated

Calcified memories of what was
Or seeds of what could be
Wandering shards of vessels
That once thrummed with pure energy
Where honor and dishonor wrestled

Stripped of living water to walk the hills
Needing only gravity to line the valley

It was never about the bones anyway
Rather a glimpse of pure power
A reminder of who's in charge of restoration
Real hope lies in the Source
    Dempsy R. Calhoun (unpublished)

In many interpretations, proclamations, sermons, and other written materials on this passage in Ezekiel, the major theme is renewal, resuscitation, restoration, rest, rejuvenation, and resurrection. There is the temptation to move quickly in our consideration of Ezekiel's vision to the "good" part, the part about the joy of a new, vibrant life. We are drawn away from the lessons buried in the dry, barren landscape. Maybe God's question to us this Lent is, "What can your spiritual dry bones teach you? What can you learn about yourself and your relationship with the world from the painful, difficult paths you are called to walk?"

In a recent issue of *National Geographic*, an article entitled "Lost Tribes of the Green Sahara" describes how archaeologists unearthed some 200 graves near a vanished lake that indicated the Sahara was once a fertile area. The skeletons buried there disclosed amazing information about two groups of people

untranslated in the NRSV before both "very many" and "very dry" (v. 2). The use of the word "dry" makes clear to the reader that death is in fact real, not illusory or temporary.

The use of the metaphor of "desiccated and disarticulated bones" occurs elsewhere in the Hebrew Bible (see Isa. 66:14; Job 21:24).[1] The language of "very dry" indicates that the death and the disarticulated bones are really dead. The "very dry" is also a cue that the bones are absent bone marrow and very white. The NRSV "lying in the valley" (v. 2) can be translated "on the face of the valley." The dry white bones lie strewn on the valley floor. The valley beneath is likely a dry rocky surface.

Imagine the first two verses transpiring in silence, a silence that is broken only in verse 3. The passage begins as a sign event but then quickly becomes a word event. The spirit of the Lord addresses the prophet with the title *ben-adam*, "mortal." The term can be found elsewhere in the Hebrew Bible (see Ps. 80:18; Jer. 49:18, 33; 50:40; 51:43; Dan. 8:17), but the preponderance of use of the term is in the book of Ezekiel. The book of Ezekiel describes one aspect of prophetic vocation as a sentinel (Ezek. 3:16–21; 33:1–9). The confluence of the sentinel language with the "mortal" language in chapter 33 illustrates how the writer fuses these two functions for the job description of the exilic prophet as a sentinel, but also as a representative human being. The representative function includes the intercessory role for the people.

Typically the human reflects a significant amount of deference to the spirit of the Lord (see Isa. 7:10–12). Here the dialogue between the prophet and the spirit of the Lord is appropriately coy. When asked if the bones can live, the prophet retorts with a nod to divine omniscience, "O Lord GOD, you know" (v. 3). The question that frames the passage is embedded in this dialogue: "Can these bones live?" (v. 3).

The instructions coming from the spirit contain two elements. First, "prophesy to these bones" (v. 4). The second part of the instruction lays out for the prophet the message, "Dry bones, hear the word of the LORD" (v. 4). The prophet begins with the formula "thus says . . . " that introduces a prophetic/divine speech (v. 5). The key word in the passage is *ruach*. The term can mean "breath," "wind," or "spirit." Here the writer wants to play on the polyvalence of the term. The verbs of verse 5b build together: "I will cause breath to enter you, and

is preparing her grave. He has just dug up a skull. Hamlet asks whose skull it was; the man answers, "Yorick." Hamlet takes the skull, cradling it tenderly in his hands, and lifts it to his eyes, saying, "Alas, poor Yorick! I knew him, Horatio—a fellow of infinite jest, of most excellent fancy. He hath borne me on his back a thousand times. . . . Here hung those lips that I have kissed I know not how oft. Where be your gibes now? Your gambols? Your songs?"[1] As he ponders what remains of the former court jester, a flashback shows the young Hamlet laughing at Yorick, playfully throwing his arms around him and kissing him. Then, suddenly, we are jolted back to the graveyard and the lifeless skull.

"Can these bones live?" God asks Ezekiel, challenging the prophet and all who have ever looked into the face of death, calling for a response. Ezekiel answers, "O Lord GOD, you know" (v. 3b). God does know. It is the God of Israel, the God who created the world and all that is in it, who brought a people to birth from a childless couple in Haran, who freed their descendants from the living death of slavery in Egypt and entered into covenant with them, who raised up judges and kings and prophets, calling them to life again and again, while they continued to choose death.

Ezekiel's vision is given for a people who have lost heart, who are suffering a death of the spirit, a living death in exile in a foreign land. Their temple has been destroyed, their holy city plundered, their leaders maimed and put in chains, their soldiers put to the sword, their young men and women either killed or dragged off into a foreign land. Ezekiel witnesses the soul of his people gradually wither and die, becoming as lifeless as a valley of dry bones. Can these bones live? That is what God asks.

This vision is held up again today, when so many in the world have had their own experience of dry bones, literally and metaphorically. Our earth has been fashioned into massive graveyards of dry bones, transforming valleys into vales of desolation—from Darfur and the Congo and Zimbabwe to Myanmar and Pakistan and Iraq, from the gang slayings and the drug wars in our cities to all those places lacking food or drink or clothing or shelter or any respect for life. Not only is there the physical toll people continue to pay, but also the spiritual death that poverty, natural disasters, and genocide exact from people to reduce them to a state of dry bones. Can these bones live?

Today we hear a promise only God can give. God tells the prophet to speak to these bones, saying:

---

1. Joseph Blenkinsopp, *Ezekiel*, Interpretation series (Louisville, KY: John Knox Press, 1990), 171.

1. William Shakespeare, *Hamlet*, 5.1.201–9.

Ezekiel 37:1-14

Theological Perspective

though crushed will sprout like blastulas. The view developed among the Fathers that just as God made Adam from dust, God can reconstitute a body from its smallest material bits, and thereby recover the person with identity intact, complete with her peculiar memories and even the precious scars of her martyrdom etched upon her resurrected body.[2] In the Talmud, one of the rabbis suggests that our iniquities are engraved into our bones, an indelible, telltale moral record of how we conducted ourselves through the lives that were given to us.

The Talmud contains a curious mechanism for Ezekiel's vision of the opening of the graves that will enable the Jews to return to the land of Israel. For the righteous who die in exile, God will excavate underground chutes through which their bones will roll until they reach the promised land. As they arrive, God will restore to them their breath, and they will stand and live again.

This brings into the foreground a theme of Ezekiel's vision that is so deeply engrained in Jewish and Christian thought that it can be missed. At the core of biblical narrative is the story of displacement—of having wandered a long way from home, and longing to return. This is the underlying plot of being cast out of Eden, of being foreigners in Egypt, of the journey to the promised land, of the longing of exiles in Babylon to return to the land of their fathers.

While there are additional, and equally biblical, ways to understand the story of salvation—for example, vanquishing the forces of evil or being cleansed of sin and filled with divine purpose—this plot of exile and return is part of the deep structure of the Bible. According to it, we are separated from God and are seeking a way to return, though we may not know it. This is Augustine's confession of the restless heart that will find rest only when it returns to God. It is certainly the unrequited longing that is expressed in Ezekiel's vision of the valley of dry bones.

KELTON COBB

Pastoral Perspective

who had lived at least a thousand years apart. The bones and teeth unearthed from the graves revealed the sex, age, general health, diet, diseases, injuries, and habits of the deceased. The size and condition of the bones gave clues to lifestyles, work, and living conditions of the inhabitants.

Based on the teeth of the Kiffian people, investigators could tell that their diet included coarse grain; they drank from a local water source and probably did not travel far from Gobero, where they lived. The bones of the Ternerian people disclosed that they were more lightly built and may have been herders, but they also likely depended on hunting and fishing.[2]

What would an analysis of our spiritual bones indicate this Lenten season? What would we find out about our spiritual maturity if we examined our spiritual bones? Would we show a deficiency of a substantial diet of study, reflection, prayer, and a meaningful relationship with God? What would this examination tell us about the richness of our spiritual practices? How sincerely do we long and pray for the gifts of the Spirit: love, joy, peace, patience, kindness, goodness, faithfulness, gentleness, and self-control? What would be our answer if the Lord spoke directly to us and questioned, "Can these bones live?"

Can we honestly give the humble Ezekiel's response, "O Lord GOD, you know" (v. 3), to God's great offer of love and mercy? Who is God telling to preach to our bones? What words do we need to hear for our life today? How do we open ourselves up to that living breath of the Spirit? God is so willing to breathe into us and fill us once more with the transformation that allows us to be a part of the kingdom of God. Can we envision our spiritual bones with new flesh and blood? Can we work with the Spirit to prepare ourselves for the resurrection of Jesus and our own resurrection?

The African American spiritual entitled "Dese Bones Gwine Rise Again" has the refrain "I know it, deed I know it, Dese bones gwine rise again."[3] This assurance can underlie all of our living. With the difficulty and joy of living, God continually challenges us to read the bones and then offer them up to God for the breath of restoration and resurrection.

KATHERINE E. AMOS

---

2. Caroline Walker Bynum, *The Resurrection of the Body in Western Christianity, 200–1336* (New York: Columbia University Press, 1995).

2. Peter Gwin, "Lost Tribes of the Green Sahara," *National Geographic* (Sept. 2008), 136, 137, 142.
3. Leonidas A. Johnson, *Go Down, Moses! Daily Devotions Inspired by Old Negro Spirituals* (Valley Forge, PA: Judson Press, 2000), xx.

Exegetical Perspective

you shall live." The resuscitation accompanies any new life. Verse 6 expands on the promise of verse 5. Still the breath/wind/spirit plays a central role. While life would have been enough for the bones, it is not enough for the Deity. The passage grafts life to the knowledge of God (v. 6b). The new creatures will know that YHWH is God.

The next section (vv. 7–8) describes the result of Ezekiel's compliance. The prophet prophesies as instructed. The bones come together; flesh and skin cover the package. However, the narrative tension continues. There is still no breath/spirit. So another command comes to the prophet to prophesy to the wind/spirit. The writer of Ezekiel 37 gives us one of the earliest examples in the Bible of the idea of the four winds (v. 9b) (see 1 Chr. 9:24; Jer. 49:36; Ezek. 42:20; Dan. 8:8; 11:4; Zech. 2:6). The language that describes the bones shifts slightly. At first, they are dry and dead, but in verse 9 they are the "murdered" or "killed" (NRSV "slain"). Verse 10 once again describes the prophet's compliance and its aftermath.

The final section (vv. 11–14) contains the interpretative summary. The bones are the "whole house of Israel." The phrase occurs in the Old Testament some twelve times, with half of the occurrences in the book of Ezekiel (Ezek. 3:7; 5:4; 20:40; 36:10; 39:25; see also Exod. 40:38; Lev. 10:6; Num. 20:29; 1 Sam. 7:2, 3; Jer. 13:11). This marks a return to the pan-Israelite sense of identity after the fall of Samaria (722 BCE) and especially after the fall of Jerusalem (587 BCE). God broke into the cemetery of the dead pan-Israelite community to inspire, bringing the Spirit in order to prompt a new life.

STEPHEN BRECK REID

Homiletical Perspective

"Thus says the Lord GOD: I will cause breath to enter you and you shall live" (v. 5). God promises not only sinews and flesh and skin, but, most importantly, God calls the breath to come from the four winds and breathe upon the slain. So it happens. This breath is the spirit of God, the life-giving *ruach* God breathed into the first human creature in the garden.

This breath moves forth in the Lazarus story. This same breath was breathed into Jesus crucified, lifting him up to resurrection life, and touched us when the Spirit came upon us in baptism. This breath moves through the world, raising people into new life when all the odds are against it. We need to hear the vision of Ezekiel in the valley of dry bones. It is a scene meant to live in the imagination and the heart, when we find ourselves gasping for breath, struggling to stay alive. Preachers can ask themselves, where are the dry bones today, where is the valley of death that needs to hear the promise of the living God?

Lent will move quickly to the three great days of Holy Week. Can the bones of a crucified man live? Yes, just as we live in him, with him, through him, and for him. We live now in the power of that same Spirit given by Jesus and poured into our hearts. We are only two weeks away from that moment on Easter when we renew our baptismal promises: Do you believe in the God of life who created all that is? Do you believe in Jesus, the crucified and risen Lord, who died and rose for us that we might have abundant life? Do you believe in the Spirit of God, the divine breath that brings new life wherever it blows? "Mortal, can these bones live?" Yes, Lord, most definitely yes.

JAMES A. WALLACE

Psalm 130

[1]Out of the depths I cry to you, O Lord.
[2] Lord, hear my voice!
Let your ears be attentive
to the voice of my supplications!

[3]If you, O Lord, should mark iniquities,
Lord, who could stand?
[4]But there is forgiveness with you,
so that you may be revered.

Theological Perspective

Theology, meaning thought and words about God, witnesses to God as being eternal. Talk about the eternal, however, throws us into an abyss, and theologians would have nothing to talk about, or psalmists to pray about, if "being eternal" were the only thing to say about God. They could stand in awe and gasp something about divine mystery, but we who gather to pray and to worship with the psalmist would soon tire of merely standing and gasping. Such a response—to use a word that theologians and people who pray should not shun—is not very *useful*. The poets come to the rescue when they write about how the eternal God is *usefully* in love with the creatures of time.

Time, yes: mention it and there is then something to prompt theological talk. Again, however, mentioning time is not much more useful than is mentioning eternity. Augustine spoke for most of us when he said, "I always know what time is, until someone asks me."[1] So I ask you: what is time? The dictionary offers a bit of help, but not in any interesting ways. In the biblical and Christian mind-set and vocabularies, time is of interest when it has a bearing on our relation to God. In the light of God's acting, we can ponder "in the beginning" and "the end of time," but

Pastoral Perspective

Every Sunday celebrates the resurrection! On this Lord's Day, however, what is implicitly true every Sunday becomes explosively explicit. Ezekiel 37 confounds Israel's despair: dry bones shall live! Romans 8 contrasts the mortality of the flesh with the life of the Spirit: the God who raised Christ Jesus will give you life. John 11 reveals a promise so potent that its early arrival cannot be postponed: Lazarus, come forth! Even this far into the solemn season—so far, in fact, that we can almost hear Palm Sunday hosannas cascading down the slopes of Olivet—even this near the cross, God's people are called to hear the promise of life.

In view of the magnificent texts available for this Sunday, the preacher may be tempted to bench Psalm 130 for a later engagement. Resist the temptation. Psalm 130 cradles the promise of life in a motif powerfully suggestive for pastoral preaching: "Out of the depths I cry to you, O Lord" (v. 1).

As a generic metaphor for trouble, "the depths" is ubiquitous. Economists write of a "deepening" recession; diplomats warn of a "deepening" crisis; therapists see patients who are "deeply" depressed. In ministry with congregants who have lost a loved one, the pastor will encounter persons *over*whelmed by sorrow or *over*come with grief. A colleague may "come down" with the flu. A friend may quietly

---

1. Cf. Augustine, *The Confessions,*, trans. R. S. Pine-Coffin (London: Penguin Group, 1961), book 11, p. 264.

⁵I wait for the LORD, my soul waits,
    and in his word I hope;
⁶my soul waits for the Lord
    more than those who watch for the morning,
    more than those who watch for the morning.

⁷O Israel, hope in the LORD!
    For with the LORD there is steadfast love,
    and with him is great power to redeem.
⁸It is he who will redeem Israel
    from all its iniquities.

Exegetical Perspective

Psalm 130 is famous for its first line: "Out of the depths I cry to you, O LORD." In fact, the poem is often called by the Latin version of the first phrase: *De profundis*. The profound depths out of which the psalmist cries (and writes) may be contrasted with the psalm's superscription (not included above), which designates it as a song of ascents, literally, a song of "going up." The ascent songs comprise a discrete unit in the Psalter (Pss. 120–134) and were likely sung by pilgrims marching to "beautiful, beautiful Zion." Since Jerusalem is set on a hill, one does, quite literally, *go up* to it. All pilgrimages start, that is to say, in the depths—at least relative to Zion.

In the case of Psalm 130, however, that depth is not simply *geographical*, it is much more profoundly psychological and theological, though not necessarily in that order, because both are at issue in the psalm. Regardless, the tension between the *superscription* and *the first line* affords some purchase on the psalm's content: while the psalmist might cry out from the depths, she will not stay there. She is *on the way up*! She is marching to Zion! That is a promise of good news, but it is not to be taken lightly. The tension between title and first line also indicates that *the way up* may be accessed only by the full reality of crying out *from the depths*.

Homiletical Perspective

There may be no need in preaching Psalm 130 to seek any structure or flow for the sermon other than flow of the text itself. We begin with the psalmist, speaking from "the depths." It may be that preachers gravitate as default option to those texts that "accentuate the positive." It is as if cheerfulness has replaced goodness or mercy among those attributes a Christian should desire and practice; but pain lurks in the background of even the happiest life, and in many lives, it all but overwhelms. During Lent and in preaching this psalm, surely we can escape the relentless but superficial good humor of so much of our society and, sadly, of our church life. "Out of the depths" the psalmist cries.

In a first move in a sermon on this psalm, the preacher might devote just enough time for listeners honestly to acknowledge those depths. The preacher ought not dwell in those depths too long, however, for both homiletical and exegetical reasons. The homiletical reason is that it is too easy to image misery and so to immerse listeners in that misery as to obscure the possibility of escape from it. The exegetical reason is that the psalmist does not name those depths extensively. This psalm is not a classic lament, like Psalm 22, which describes the depths at length. Neither should the preacher. This is not to minimize the pain. Sometimes, when trouble is at its worst, we cannot name it; we can only cry out.

Psalm 130

Theological Perspective

these come to focus and carry weight when we experience "God's time" and "our time" as a match or, as in the outset of this psalm, as occasional mismatches.

"I wait for the LORD, my soul waits" (v. 5). The psalmist has checked something in his calendar, punched the time clock, set the watch, looked out to see the Lord—but the Lord does not seem to be easily available. Perhaps it is not only mis-timing that troubles him. The psalm begins (v. 1) with a horrifying special reference: this is a song from the depths, a cry from the pits, a sound muffled because the one who shouts is buried too deep for him assuredly to be heard.

Talking about a cry from the depths does not fit into a theology that markets well, as theology is supposed to do today. When we worship, we prefer to be on the heights, with Moses looking on the promised land, with three followers of Jesus on a mount of transfiguration, with the disciples on the mount of ascension. Worshipers have been beaten down all week: "My spouse does not understand me. My boss never gives me any strokes. Disappointment strangles me when I try to have successes. So I come to the house of God, and am dashed to hear a lector read, a choir chant, a congregation offer responses, about having to wait for the One who is supposed to be present in God's house and who forces me to wait, even though I am here at the scheduled time for God to be present?" If the psalm ended in the depths, as it began, worshipers would all have been better off turning over in bed or turning on television.

The psalm does *not* end as it began, nor does it carry on very long in the depths. Yes, the one who prays it has to "wait for the LORD" (v. 5), but the theology of "waiting" in Christian language is not a trigger for frustration. Here, as so often, it is linked with hope and promise. Never do the psalms gloss over the difficulties and frustrations of life; this psalm is no exception. Before the promise is fulfilled and hope is realized, we hear language that rings true to anyone who has suffered loneliness in the dark of night and in the midst of doubt or guilt. "My soul waits for the Lord, more than those who watch for the morning" is a line so appropriate that the psalmist repeats it, "more than those who watch for the morning" (v. 6).

Just turning and tossing and lying there, watching the digital clock as the minutes pass too slowly, is uncreative. It only prolongs the loneliness, confusion, and agony of night. The person who prays has to have something to do. This psalm is very much about what to do "in the depths" and while "the soul waits." One is to hope. Fine. However, more than hoping is

Pastoral Perspective

mention she is having a hard time getting up for the holidays.

What each of these common expressions share is an intimation of the gravity of mortality. Even the "little deaths" of disappointment, the temporary inconveniences of sickness, or the strain of difficult relationships can steal the life from life. "Out of the depths I cry to you, O LORD. Lord, hear my voice."

To explore further this depths/deep/down motif, the preacher may want to revisit an older study by Robert C. Leslie, an interpreter of Holocaust survivor Viktor Frankl's psychotherapeutic practice. In his *Jesus and Logotherapy*, Leslie credits "depth psychology" with illuminating the role that early formative experience and unconscious forces play in shaping behavior, attitude, and values.[1] He goes on to propose a complement: Frankl's "height psychology." For our purposes, we may think of "height psychology" as "how-we-get-out-of-the-depths psychology." Leslie's development of this theme is suggestive for preaching. His chapters include "Mobilizing the Defiant Spirit," "Filling the Existential Vacuum," and "Restoring Man's Dignity."

The interpreter of Psalm 130 will of course be careful not to reduce the psalm's theology to a psychological exercise, even a highly therapeutic exercise. The purpose in incorporating insight such as Frankl's into the sermon is to demonstrate that the psalm's truth has real consequence in the concrete world. As a Holocaust survivor, Frankl is one whose voice speaks from the depths, not metaphorically but actually. His faith, like that of the psalmist, enables survival. What he learned in the depths he shares, not simply as testimony but as a weathered navigator's sea chart. "When you are in the depths, and when you begin to see, however dimly, the light of morning, here is a foothold, there is another." Let the preacher guide us as we climb.

If verses 1 and 2 are an invocation, verses 3 and 4 may be read as a prayer of confession and assurance of pardon. The deepest depths are those we ourselves help to dig with our own iniquities. "He is digging his own grave," we commonly say. The pastorally sensitive preacher will understand that her congregation includes souls whose depths are deeper because they blame themselves, and not always undeservedly. When through neglect or outright betrayal I have broken promises or hearts, the depths are darkened by regret.

---

1. Robert C. Leslie, *Jesus and Logotherapy* (Nashville: Abingdon Press, 1965), 13–15.

Exegetical Perspective

The psalm can be divided into four parts: (1) verses 1–2 introduce the psalmist's situation and plea; (2) verses 3–4 discuss the Lord's forgiveness; (3) verses 5–6 recount the psalmist's patient waiting on God; and (4) verses 7–8 enjoin all of Israel to similar waiting (cf. vv. 5–6) which will eventuate in forgiveness (cf. v. 4), thus uniting the second and third parts of the psalm in this final section. In this light, the psalm is readily seen to be one about *forgiveness* and *waiting*—though the precise content of the latter is not specified. Is the psalmist waiting for God's forgiveness (v. 4a)? God's word (v. 5b)? God's blessing that comes in the morning, after a long night of trouble, struggle, and prayer (v. 6b; cf. 30:5b)? We are not told, but the poetic structure nevertheless witnesses a movement from the *individual voice of a psalmist* in trouble (vv. 1–2) to the confident voice of a psalmist exhorting *the entire community* to a similar ethic and similar results (vv. 7–8).

Psalm 130 redounds in key repetitions that underscore this structure and provide important clues for interpretation. These repetitions, which cluster around *three nodes*, may be discussed in terms relating to *humans* (theological anthropology and ethics) and *God* (theology properly so-called). It is not surprising to observe that there are close connections between the three nodes and the two subjects.

The psalm is, first, about *watching* and *iniquity*. God's "marking" of iniquities (so NRSV, v. 3) is literally God's "watching" (root: *šmr*) of the same. Verse 8 returns to these iniquities by promising that the Lord will redeem Israel from them. Of course, verse 4 already indicates as much, by stating that forgiveness is "with you [YHWH]" (see below). The verb *šmr* recurs again in verse 6, which twice repeats the exact same line (a rarity in the Psalter)—namely, that the psalmist waits for God "more than those who *watch* for the morning." The repetition and distribution of *šmr* suggests that the waiting in verses 5a, 6a (root: *qwh*) and the hoping in verses 5b and 7a (root: *yḥl*) are also connected to iniquity—or, rather, to the *forgiveness* of iniquity. Those who need such forgiveness long for it, hope for it, and will wait for it—as long as it takes.

Second, three times the psalmist asserts that there is something crucial that resides "with" YHWH. These are "forgiveness" (v. 4a), "steadfast love" (v. 7a), and "great power to redeem" (v. 7b). The three "with him/YHWH" clauses are thus mighty predications about God and God's nature. They are also indications that the psalmist's (and Israel's) waiting, watching, and hoping are well placed. With this kind of

Homiletical Perspective

The preacher might, however, soon move to a vital insight: the psalmist does not simply cry out from the depths; the psalmist cries out *to God*. What makes the psalm remarkable is that in the midst of the pain the psalmist addresses God. In complaint, one grumbles about God. In lament, one cries to God. That kind of cry is actually an expression of a profound faith: a faith that God is present, that God hears, and that God is able and willing to act. The word for depths in the Latin version of the psalm, *profundis*, is, in fact, the source of our word "profound." Some wordplay may be possible here or even with the English words "depths" and "deep."

The psalmist cries out not so much for help as for a hearing—as if, once heard, help is certain. Note the repetition of the word "voice." As long as we can cry out, hope remains. Perhaps shame or hopelessness can silence the sufferer. The preacher's task here may first be simply to say, "Keep shouting!"

The preacher may then turn with the psalmist to the nature of the God who hears. God is the one who does not keep a watcher's eye out for our sins. (The word "mark" in verse 3 comes from the same Hebrew root as the "watchers for the morning" of verse 6. Once again some wordplay may be possible here.) Rather, the characteristic of God is always to forgive. One thinks of *The Book of Common Prayer*: "It is thy nature always to have mercy."

Preachers ought to keep a watcher's eye out for a potential misunderstanding. Listeners may assume here that there is a simple cause-and-effect relationship between our sins and our suffering. If we suffer, it must be because we are paying for our sins. The psalmist may have believed that, but, in light of Scripture as a whole, we must reject that understanding. We can say, however, that the first need of the psalmist is not rescue but forgiveness, the restoration of a right relationship with God, an appropriate Lenten subject. Forgiveness, however, is not about us; it is about God. It takes place so that God may be revered.

The psalmist then turns back from God to himself or herself. If the first human task in the depths is to cry out, the second is to wait. We are not to wait passively but to wait with hope. Hope is an intensive form of waiting, a statement that almost exactly describes the grammar of the Hebrew verb used here. Note that the psalm does not declare, "The Lord helps them that help themselves." This may be a hard word to hear in a society devoted to self-help, confident that with enough effort and the right mental attitudes we can fix our problems. The best definition

Psalm 130

Theological Perspective

in order. That the psalmist and any believer is out of place and not in the right time—in the depths and still waiting—is the root of the problem. The biblical prescription for change, read and heard especially in the Psalms, is for one to repent, to turn around to the right place, and to be ready for the right time.

Interestingly, there is here no command to repent, to turn. Instead we get a question and some witness. Much of the best theology begins with a question, whether it sounds rhetorical or is immediately open to a precise answer. "If you, O LORD, should mark iniquities, Lord, who could stand?" (v. 3) This psalmist knows that the Lord can and does mark iniquities. Here is a prayer that Israel (v. 8) and the one who prays can stand together on high ground and in synch with God's actions for him or her. Then comes the affirmation that is at the heart of Christian theology and witness to God: "But there is forgiveness with you, so that you may be revered" (v. 4).

"There is forgiveness with you" or "with you there is forgiveness," as the other translations have it, sounds strange. It combines the witness to the fact that being a forgiver, a redeemer (v. 8), is central to the way God is known, with the language of relation. "Forgiveness with God" is not by itself very useful or helpful to anyone in the long night watches, in the pits, or left waiting. Implied instead is a movement of the believer, namely, the act of repenting. Repentance means saying good-bye to the old self and leaving an entrance for God to act, to bring morning to the soul.

MARTIN E. MARTY

Pastoral Perspective

There is also a corporate dimension to such confession. Congregations, communities, families, even nations may sin in concert, cooperatively digging deeper and deeper places of confinement from which we will eventually long for deliverance. Let the preacher's social conscience engage here. If you, Lord, should call in the markers on our iniquities, who could stand?

"I wait for the LORD" (v. 5). Here is an opportunity to explore the Christian practice of waiting. Explore it, do not advocate for it—at least not yet. The psalmist does not say, "Be patient." What is Christian waiting? What does it mean to wait, if the waiting is unmodified by adjective or adverb? Wait. Perhaps the particular circumstances make it possible to wait hopefully. That is fine. Perhaps one's temperament makes it possible to wait patiently. That is fine too. What of those occasions when we must—or are able only to—wait?

In my experience the hospital's family waiting room outside the surgery suite is one of the loneliest places on earth—even when it is full of people. "Wait here. The doctor will call you when it is over." Surely here is a priority for pastoral attention. Make time to wait with those who wait.

In preaching, the pastor extends care to those who wait by sensitively acknowledging, naming, and calling the community of faith to attend to particular occasions of waiting. Here is a family separated by the obligations of military service, waiting for a beloved daughter to return. Here is a widow waiting for her home to sell, so she can move closer to her son and grandchildren. Here is a patient waiting for a lab report. Here is a man who has betrayed his wife, asking, praying, waiting to be forgiven. The preacher lifts up such waiting, not in order to tell people *how* they should wait, but to assure them that the pastor, the church, the psalmist, and the resurrected Lord all wait with them!

Five Sundays spent now. We wait—and watch. The morning must be near now. More . . . than the sentries "watch for the morning," we watch (v. 6). More confidently? More expectantly? More impatiently? Perched in hope's highest rampart, peering into the darkness, measuring the horizon lumen by lumen, we watch.

God's people are not merely waiting. We are watching. We watch and hope. What difference does this make? It is the difference between resignation and resurrection!

THOMAS EDWARD MCGRATH

Exegetical Perspective

God, the psalmist can be sure that his voice and his supplication will be heard—even from the depths (vv. 1–2). Moreover, the repetition of the root *pdh* ("redeem") in verses 7 and 8, the final verses of the psalm, places special and insistent emphasis on this aspect and intention of God.

Finally, two human ethics are commended in the psalm before this God of forgiveness, steadfast love, and redemption power. The first is the ethic of *fear* or *reverence* (v. 4)—that is, proper worship, respect, and positioning vis-à-vis Israel's great God, who is clearly worthy of such if for no other reason (and this is a primary point of the psalm) than because YHWH forgives sin (vv. 3–4, 7b, 8). The second is the ethic of *hope/waiting*, which is repeated four different times with two different verbs (see above). The last line of the psalm asserts that such waiting pays off. Invariably and inevitably.

How do these repetitions relate to the opening two verses? Some connections are mentioned above. Additionally, verses 1–2 suggest that the psalmist feels as if the presently experienced depths are because of her sin, which must be forgiven. Such act-consequence theology was common in antiquity and in ancient Israel, and it is common now. Even if we no longer agree with it, we must admit that that is how things feel sometimes. The superscription continues to assert that this is a psalm (and psalmist) on its way up. The way up, evidently, not only begins in the *psychological* depths where one cries out hoping to be heard; evidently it also begins in *theological* depths, where one is attuned to the realities of sin that must also be attended to no less than the voice of grief or despair. That the poem ends with the psalmist's proclamation to the community and confidence in God's inevitable redemption shows that the superscription was well chosen. *Out of* the depths indeed!

BRENT A. STRAWN

Homiletical Perspective

of "depths" in this psalm may be "the state we cannot get out of by our own efforts." Self-help may be the true god of our society, and Oprah is its prophet. In such a society it may not be easy to hear that help comes only from the Lord, so wait eagerly for the Lord, more eagerly than the watchers on a city wall wait for the morning—but who said that biblical preaching is always easy?

The psalm concludes with two remarkable shifts that must not be overlooked: from the individual to the corporate and from addressing God to addressing Israel. Though crying out to God for help is in itself a confession of faith, that confession cannot remain merely personal but must be directed to others. The temporal frame of reference of the psalm is remarkable. It does not look back on the depths from a vantage point of safety; rather, it is written from within those depths. All parts of the psalm—the cry, the hope, and the counsel to Israel—should be understood as emanating from the depths. The help has not come as the psalm ends, only the promise of help. That, surely, is where many of us stand. Help may not yet have come, but we have cried out and have heard and even said that with God there is steadfast love. There is a word for that place where we cry out to God and where we speak and hear the promises of redemption. It is called "church."

STEPHEN FARRIS

Romans 8:6-11

⁶To set the mind on the flesh is death, but to set the mind on the Spirit is life and peace. ⁷For this reason the mind that is set on the flesh is hostile to God; it does not submit to God's law—indeed it cannot, ⁸and those who are in the flesh cannot please God.

⁹But you are not in the flesh; you are in the Spirit, since the Spirit of God dwells in you. Anyone who does not have the Spirit of Christ does not belong to him. ¹⁰But if Christ is in you, though the body is dead because of sin, the Spirit is life because of righteousness. ¹¹If the Spirit of him who raised Jesus from the dead dwells in you, he who raised Christ from the dead will give life to your mortal bodies also through his Spirit that dwells in you.

Theological Perspective

The Christian life is a material life. "Setting our mind on the Spirit" (v. 6) is not about an attempt to put our bodies to the side somehow and concentrate on the inner life of faith. Paul's contrast between Spirit and flesh in this passage is not to be understood as a contrast between soul and body or between spirituality and sensuality. Life "in the Spirit" refers, among other things, to a way of conducting a bodily life: it is manifested in how we use our physical energies and our material resources, how we care for our neighbors and for our planet. When "the Spirit of God dwells in [us]" (v. 9), our corporeal lives, in all their concreteness and messiness, become expressions and instruments of God's grace and peace.

"The mind that is set on the flesh is hostile to God" (v. 7). For Paul, "the mind that is set on the flesh" is synonymous with sin, the basic disposition to turn away from grateful dependence on God. The fleshly mind-set attempts to live in denial of God's creating and sustaining grace, instead seeking life and meaning in our own desires and accomplishments. It is a form of idolatry, setting ourselves up as lords of our own lives. Ironically, "the mind that is set on the flesh" can sometimes produce a life of upstanding morality and outward virtue. As David Kelsey has argued, "living in trust that our lives are justified by what we do in accord with standards of excellence

Pastoral Perspective

Typical Pauline juxtapositions or antitheses—death versus life, flesh versus spirit—are found in this text. These juxtapositions are contextualized by Paul's opening statement in Romans 8:1–2: "There is . . . no condemnation for those who are in Christ Jesus. For the law of the Spirit of life in Christ Jesus has set you free from the law of sin and of death." The flesh, in a corporeal sense, is not understood as evil but as a metaphor for the means through which sin is enacted, a reference to "those whose flesh has been taken captive by the diabolical force in the world."[1] Paul clarifies here what Jesus stated in the Sermon on the Mount: "No one can serve two masters; for a slave will either hate the one and love the other, or be devoted to the one and despise the other" (Matt. 6:24).

Jesus in that instance is addressing whether one will serve God or wealth, a message that challenges the biblical and theological assumptions of today's postmodern preacher/peddlers of the prosperity gospel. Yet the connection between the Matthean and Romans texts is established, as Matthew implicates what Romans makes explicit: the battle between flesh and spirit and the admonition to set one's mind on the life-giving spirit, not the spiritually deadening

1. Calvin J. Roetzel, *The Letters of Paul: Conversations in Context*, 2nd ed. (Atlanta: John Knox Press, 1982), 73.

Exegetical Perspective

Lent is traditionally a time for Christians to focus on the problem of sin and to engage in fasting and repentance in preparation for Easter. That is why the Gospel stories of the temptation of Jesus are lectionary readings for the First Sunday in Lent: there we see how Jesus faced temptation and persevered, and ask how we might persevere in our own times of trial. This Epistle lesson for the Fifth Sunday in Lent focuses on the obstacles to our doing God's will and the way that the Holy Spirit gracefully empowers us to please God.

Romans 8:6–11 is from the second half of an argument that begins back in 7:5–6, where Paul describes two alternative ways of living: "While we were living in the flesh, our sinful passions, aroused by the law, were at work in our members to bear fruit for death. But now we are discharged from the law, dead to that which held us captive, so that we are slaves not under the old written code but in the new life of the Spirit." The remainder of Romans 7 elaborates on 7:5 to show what a life lived "in the flesh" looks like. "Flesh" here refers to the corruptible matter of which human bodies are composed, but because in Paul's view flesh is ruled by passions, the word also stands as a shorthand for life lived in service of one's own selfish interests and desires.

While Paul is familiar with the teaching that Torah can counter the grip of the passions on the human

Homiletical Perspective

Lent is a time of penance and preparation. During Lent, in recognition of our idolizing love of that which is not God, we often give something up (let it be more than chocolate!). We also use these forty days to prepare ourselves for the coming celebration of the resurrection of our Lord. All of this is good; but perhaps there is a way of reframing and expanding how we see Lent. What if, rather than being a time of either self-abnegation or preparation for a future event (though both elements should remain), Lent were seen as a time of self-discovery, a period specifically devoted to discerning who we are and whose we are?

Paul writes, "You are not in the flesh; you are in the Spirit, since the Spirit of God dwells in you" (v. 9). For Paul, it was simply a given: to be a Christian is to be filled with the Holy Spirit. The true question is not, has the Christian received the Spirit, but rather, does the Christian seek to live her life consciously cooperating with the Spirit who already indwells her?

Who is the Spirit? The obvious answer is, the third person of the Trinity. Though the doctrine of the Trinity had yet to be articulated at the time of Paul's writing, Paul clearly thought of the Spirit as divine—indeed, as Lord. "Now *the* Lord is the Spirit. . . . And all of us . . . seeing the glory of the Lord . . . are being

Romans 8:6-11

Theological Perspective

lies at the very heart of sin. What we do sinfully need not even be immoral; even if what we do is morally good, it is sin if we trust the doing of it to show that our lives are worth living."[1] Boasting about our virtue is likewise a sign of our failure to submit to "the law of the Spirit" (8:2, 7). The person who prides herself on giving up all the delights of the flesh for Lent is exhibiting the fleshly mind-set, living in hostility to God's free grace.

We enjoy "the new life of the Spirit" (7:6) only because of our union with the crucified and risen Christ. Paul's programmatic appeal to Habakkuk 2:4, "The one who is righteous will live by faith" (1:17), applies first of all to Jesus Christ. On the cross, Christ was faithful to the end, giving up any claim to life and righteousness apart from God's gift. In the resurrection, God raised him to new life, vindicating his obedience and breaking the hold that death had on him, so that "the life [Christ] lives, he lives to God" (6:10). Now, by grace, "the Spirit of [the same God] who raised Jesus from the dead dwells in [us]" (8:11), uniting us with Christ and bestowing on us the righteousness and hope that come from faith. Because we are in Christ, we have been transferred from the fleshly domain of death and sin to the Spirit's domain of "life and peace" (v. 6).

Life in the Spirit is communal life. This passage does not teach a "this little light of mine" spirituality. The Spirit mediates the character of Christ, so that the hallmark of the Spirit's presence in our lives is love: "God's love has been poured into our hearts through the Holy Spirit that has been given to us" (5:5). The Spirit dwelling in the community binds believers to God and to each other in loving union. In Western Trinitarianism this work of the Spirit is seen as consonant with the Spirit's eternal role in the Godhead as the bond of love between the Father and Son. We "walk according to the Spirit" (8:4) when we live together in mutual affection as members of Christ's body, receiving from each other's hands the gifts that God intends for us (12:4–12). Grateful acknowledgment of our dependence on each other is a mirror of our identity as children of God and joint heirs with Christ (8:17).

Through the Spirit, we already participate in the power of Christ's resurrection—our bodies, which were "dead because of sin" (v. 10) have become means of grace, connection, and joy. God's promise to "give life to [our] mortal bodies" (v. 11) will be

Pastoral Perspective

pursuits of the flesh. This is a conflict with which parishioners and pastors—from those in embryonic stages of faith and leadership to seasoned spiritual veterans—are well familiar, having known victory, defeat, and struggle, whether in the past or the present. Paul offers an orientation to life—a spirituality—that points to an eternal power available to the believer in his or her temporal reality.

It is no coincidence that Paul addresses the manner in which "mind-set" impacts spiritual orientation. The "mind" that is "set" on the flesh is hostile to God, cannot submit to God's law, and cannot please God. Conversely, one whose "mind" is "set" on the Spirit *is* life and peace and *is in the Spirit*. Throughout Romans, the most comprehensive statement of Pauline theology, "the Christian *mind* . . . must become the initial, and transformative, locus of renewal (12:2, contrasting with 1:22, 28)." The mind is central to human activity in terms of "settled and focused activity and concentration."[2]

In the cauldron of American slavery, the African American abolitionist Frederick Douglass realized as a young boy that when he learned the rudimentary alphabet, his freedom, whether by purchase or escape, was inevitable. In light of this discovery, he wrote, "I set out with high hope, and a fixed purpose, at whatever cost of trouble, to learn how to read."[3] Douglass concluded in effect that knowledge is power, recognizing how the mind could be transformed and energy could be redirected and concentrated toward a particular goal.

In his 2005 book *Frederick Douglass: A Precursor of Liberation Theology*, Reginald F. Davis notes that Douglass's yearning for physical freedom was eventually linked with a liberating reconceptualization—again, note the role of mind-set—of his Christian faith: that human beings worked with God to determine the course of history as a result of their *God-given* freedom, a freedom at variance with physical bondage, racism, and its close connection with capitalist exploitation. In Douglass one witnesses the antecedents of contemporary black liberation theology and its prophetic call for personal and social transformation, the embodiment of a faith that engages spirit and intellect as part of the renewal of individual and collective minds.

The Lenten season is a time for reflection upon the things on which our minds are set. How does our

---

1. David H. Kelsey, *Imagining Redemption* (Louisville, KY: Westminster John Knox Press, 2005), 57.

2. N. T. Wright, "Romans," in Leander Keck, ed., *The New Interpreter's Bible* (Nashville: Abingdon Press, 1996), 10:582.
3. Frederick Douglass, *Narrative of the Life of Frederick Douglass, An American Slave, Written by Himself*, ed. Benjamin Quarles (Cambridge, MA: Belknap Press of Harvard University Press, 1980), 59.

Fifth Sunday in Lent

will, he argues that the power of sin perversely uses Torah against God's good purposes to further sin's own aims (7:9–13). Thus it comes about that even humans who try their best to obey Torah are unable to do so (7:14–25). The second half of the argument, elaborating on 7:6, begins in 8:1. Here Paul delivers the good news that Jesus Christ has set us free from our bondage to sin (8:1–2). Liberated, we no longer compulsively set our minds on the passions and desires of the flesh. Rather, we live according to the Spirit and set our minds on the things of the Spirit (8:5; cf. 7:6).

In 8:6–11, Paul sketches out the consequences of these two ways of living. "To set the mind on the flesh is death, but to set the mind on the Spirit is life and peace" (v. 6). To "set the mind on the flesh" does not mean to focus obsessively on sex, as some suppose, but to live a life in which one routinely succumbs to the push and pull of *any* of the sinful passions and desires. These include, for example, anger and hatred, and a lust for wealth, prestige, power, or approval (see also Gal. 5:19–21). Life governed by such passions is life lived in obedience to sin, and it issues in death (see Rom. 6:23). In verses 7–8 Paul elaborates on this bondage suffered by all who live in the flesh. Such persons cannot possibly please God, because their first allegiance is to their own passions and desires, which never incline to the purposes of God.

On the other hand, "to set the mind on the Spirit is life and peace" (v. 6). The presence of the Spirit signifies the Christian's participation in Christ's victory over the powers of sin and death (vv. 2–4). This victory is not a simple and straightforward one, as Paul's comment in verse 10 suggests. Yes, we are freed from sin and no longer obliged to obey its dictates, and yes, we enjoy a new way of life governed not by the works of the flesh but by the marvelous fecundity of the Spirit (see Gal. 5:22–23). Still, "the body is dead because of sin" (v. 10). The body, being of corruptible flesh, will go the way of all flesh. Though Christ has already triumphed over death, we will not enjoy the effects of that triumph in our own bodies until after the end of what Paul elsewhere calls "the present evil age" (Gal. 1:4).

We who are believers participate in two ages at once: the present age, in which our bodies are still subject to suffering, death, and decay, and the age to come, ruled by the Spirit of life. Though we still suffer and die, the full transition to the coming age is imminent (vv. 22–23), and those in whom the Spirit dwells wait for it with confidence. God who raised

transformed into the same image from one degree of glory to another; for this comes from *the Lord, the Spirit*" (2 Cor. 3:17–18).

The Spirit is also the source of eternal life. In his famous exchange with Nicodemus, Jesus says, "No one can enter the kingdom of God without being born of water and Spirit. What is born of the flesh is flesh, and what is born of the Spirit is spirit. . . . The wind blows where it chooses, and you hear the sound of it, but you do not know where it comes from or where it goes. So it is with everyone who is born of the Spirit" (John 3:5–6, 8). In this passage the Greek word translated as "spirit" is exactly the same word later translated as "wind." Much as in English one who is "winded" is out of breath, in Greek the word translated as "spirit" and "wind" can likewise be translated as "breath." Indeed, in the Gospel of John, the risen Lord gives the Holy Spirit to his disciples precisely by breathing on them (John 20:22).

Having received the Spirit, Christians are challenged to decide whether we choose life or death (cf., v. 6). One chooses death by preferring the "flesh" to the Spirit. In bringing this point home, the preacher must hasten to underscore what flesh is and (perhaps more to the point) is not for the apostle Paul.

Flesh is not simply material existence. Paul did not believe, nor does the Christian faith declare, that the material world is evil and the spiritual world is good. God created all that is, the material as well as the spiritual, and all that God created is good in its essence. "God saw everything that he had made, and indeed, it was very good" (Gen. 1:31). The wisdom of the church has always known this. "What Paul means by the flesh in this passage is not the essence of the body but a life which is carnal and worldly, serving self-indulgence and extravagance to the full."[1]

In short, the problem is not flesh but the misuse of flesh, of our creaturely existence. Such misuse of the flesh is a function of one putting oneself, rather than God, in the center of the universe. In light of this, probably the best term to convey what Paul means when he uses the word "flesh" is "ego," defined in a pejorative sense to mean self-centered, self-focused. Hence we could understand verse 9 to say, "You are not in the ego; you are in the Spirit, since the Spirit of God dwells in you."

For postmodern Americans enmeshed in a consumerist culture that encourages the satisfaction of every desire—a culture in which the highest good is

---

1. John Chrysostom, as quoted in Gerald L. Bray, ed., *Ancient Commentary on Scripture, New Testament*, vol. 6 (Downers Grove, IL: InterVarsity Press, 1998), 209.

Romans 8:6-11

Theological Perspective

consummated when our bodies too are raised to be with Christ. Our existence now is in the in-between time: the Lenten season before the final Easter. In this season our new identity through the Spirit is both a gift and a task. It is a gift because Christ is indeed risen, and his resurrection power is already made manifold through the Spirit's life-giving presence in our midst. However, our new identity is also a task, in that we are still subject to suffering and frustration as we wait in hope for our final redemption (8:18–24). Lent then is a time of affirming that our life according to the flesh is dead, and that new life and peace are available even now through the Spirit of Christ.

In Lent, to use T. S. Eliot's poetic words, we proclaim "the vanished power of the usual reign."[2] The ashes of Lent symbolize the death of the usual reign, the death of "living according to the flesh" (v. 5). It is never quite that simple, of course. The old that has passed away still seeks corners of refuge in us. We sometimes find ourselves torn between the old and the new. Eliot asks prayers for himself and people like him, for

> Those who walk in darkness, who chose thee and
> oppose thee,
> Those who are torn on the horn between season and
> season, time and time, between
> Hour and hour, word and word, power and
> power . . .

We live through Lent as those who know they are headed for glory, not because of our own spiritual accomplishments, but because the Spirit has bound us up with the glorified Christ, who is "the firstborn within a large family" (8:29).

AMY PLANTINGA PAUW

Pastoral Perspective

"settled and focused activity and concentration" embody the Spirit of God dwelling in us? Paul highlights the trajectory for the Christian mind in v. 10: "If Christ is in you, though the body is dead because of sin, the Spirit is life because of righteousness." Life in this instance is more than the coursing of oxygen through the body: it is resurrection power, indicative of a transformed reality. There is a transcendent quality immanent in the person who has Christ in her or him that should characterize a life oppositional to the life of the flesh. Though a Christian as a fallible human being will indeed commit *sins*, *sin*—resulting from the life of the flesh—is not the preeminent problem. If one has been justified by faith, one has peace with God through Jesus Christ (Rom. 5:1), addressing the fundamental sin issue.

Does justification by faith preclude Christians from struggles with sins that can gradually become a struggle with sin? No. There are in our faith communities sincere Christians for whom this struggle is real. One's status in Christ does not protect one from "the laws of decay and death," as one still lives in "the body of our humiliation" (Phil. 3:21). As Wright notes, Romans 5:21 reminds us that grace reigns through righteousness unto eternal life, assuring the Christian of life beyond death and promising a future resurrection reflected in 8:11b. The promise, the deposit of the *not yet* fully realized reality of God's kingdom/commonwealth/realm, is operative in us *now* through the presence of what Paul calls interchangeably in this chapter "the Spirit of life in Christ Jesus," "the Spirit," "Spirit of God."

Hence there is accessible to the Christian a force beyond the self available to help one face squarely sin, sins, decay, and death; to grant wisdom to discern if God will work directly, and sometimes miraculously, in one's individual life to address these issues in their various manifestations or through a human-made process (e.g., medicine, counseling, or addiction-relief programs); and to equip one to serve the present age as an agent of God's transformative work in the world.

KENNETH I. CLARKE SR.

---

2. This phrase and the lines below it are from T. S. Eliot, *Ash Wednesday*, available at http://www.msgr.ca/msgr-7/ash_wednesday_t_s_eliot.htm.

Exegetical Perspective

Christ from the dead will give life to our bodies through the Spirit, which dwells in us (v. 11). Soon our mortal bodies—and indeed, all of creation—will be fully liberated from captivity to death and decay (vv. 19–23).

The news for Christians, as Paul sees it, is unequivocally good. Once we were slaves to sin and death, but now we are free and living in the Spirit of Life! Paul thinks that there are practical, visible consequences of our liberated status: we are able to live in ways that please God. Paul really does believe, in other words, that Christians are empowered by the Spirit to resist temptation. This message is sometimes lost, in part because for centuries Protestants have read the portrayal of bondage to sin in Romans 7 as if it described the lives of the converted (rather than the lives of those who try to escape the rule of the passions through obedience to Law, as argued above). Thus Protestants have often been plagued with an introspective and guilty conscience, convinced that they are bound to do the very thing they hate (7:15). Paul, however, regards the Spirit-guided life as the norm for Christian existence, and a falling back into sin as the occasional but startling exception (see, e.g., Gal. 6:1). The preacher must walk a fine line, taking care not to discourage those who might hear a message of our God-given power to persevere in the face of temptation as an indictment of their past failures to do so—but also encouraging those who might be strengthened by such a message to live a Spirit-guided life.

SUSAN R. GARRETT

Homiletical Perspective

often deemed to be self-esteem—this can seem a harsh message indeed. In truth, it is a message of great hope. The "self" matters! After all, Jesus died for all people, and all people are individuals. However, Jesus died that his followers might become who they truly are, who God created them to be. One does not become one's true self by limiting the focus of his universe to what the ego—the "I"—can create, determine, and control. Rather one becomes one's true self by turning her will and life over to the care of God (to use the felicitous language of Step Three of Alcoholics Anonymous Twelve Steps). This action is the absolutely necessary prerequisite for the conscious reception of God's grace.

For Paul—and for generations of Christians—the reception of God's grace is identical to the reception of God's Holy Spirit. God's Holy Breath gives hope for eternal life: "If the Spirit of him who raised Jesus from the dead dwells in you, he who raised Christ from the dead will give life to your mortal bodies also through his Spirit that dwells in you" (v. 11). In addition, recognizing that one has received the Holy Spirit grants the Christian hope for true and satisfying life *now*. "To set the mind on the flesh is death, but to set the mind on the Spirit is *life and peace*" (v. 6).

Might we not see Lent in a different light if we conceived this season as a time of setting the mind on the Spirit in a disciplined fashion so that we might know peace—true peace, the peace that passes all understanding?

DOUGLAS TRAVIS

John 11:1-45

¹Now a certain man was ill, Lazarus of Bethany, the village of Mary and her sister Martha. ²Mary was the one who anointed the Lord with perfume and wiped his feet with her hair; her brother Lazarus was ill. ³So the sisters sent a message to Jesus, "Lord, he whom you love is ill." ⁴But when Jesus heard it, he said, "This illness does not lead to death; rather it is for God's glory, so that the Son of God may be glorified through it." ⁵Accordingly, though Jesus loved Martha and her sister and Lazarus, ⁶after having heard that Lazarus was ill, he stayed two days longer in the place where he was.

⁷Then after this he said to the disciples, "Let us go to Judea again." ⁸The disciples said to him, "Rabbi, the Jews were just now trying to stone you, and are you going there again?" ⁹Jesus answered, "Are there not twelve hours of daylight? Those who walk during the day do not stumble, because they see the light of this world. ¹⁰But those who walk at night stumble, because the light is not in them." ¹¹After saying this, he told them, "Our friend Lazarus has fallen asleep, but I am going there to awaken him." ¹²The disciples said to him, "Lord, if he has fallen asleep, he will be all right." ¹³Jesus, however, had been speaking about his death, but they thought that he was referring merely to sleep. ¹⁴Then Jesus told them plainly, "Lazarus is dead. ¹⁵For your sake I am glad I was not there, so that you may believe. But let us go to him." ¹⁶Thomas, who was called the Twin, said to his fellow disciples, "Let us also go, that we may die with him."

¹⁷When Jesus arrived, he found that Lazarus had already been in the tomb four days. ¹⁸Now Bethany was near Jerusalem, some two miles away, ¹⁹and many of the Jews had come to Martha and Mary to console them about their brother. ²⁰When Martha heard that Jesus was coming, she went and met him, while Mary stayed at home. ²¹Martha said to Jesus, "Lord, if you had been here, my brother would not have died. ²²But even now I know that God will give you whatever you ask of him." ²³Jesus said to her, "Your brother will rise again." ²⁴Martha said to him, "I know that he will rise again in the resurrection on the last day." ²⁵Jesus

Theological Perspective

This reading is commonly referred to as "the raising of Lazarus." The shorthand designation is by no means inappropriate. It is a story about Lazarus, whom Jesus loved—his illness, death, burial and decay, and emergence from his tomb, upon being recalled from death to life, with burial wrappings still dangling around him. Even so, its focus is not so much Lazarus the individual as it is wondrous deliverance from death to life itself (viz., the *sign*, in John's Gospel), the one who brings it about, and responses of others to it. These occasion the most lengthy, searching theological reflection within the narrative itself and among its commentators.

All three foci are bound up with striking, in certain respects singular, theological emphases of the Fourth Gospel. Although all four canonical Gospels are written from a vantage point of a post-Easter faith, John's surfaces that faith notably often and in high relief within his account of the ministry of Jesus itself. In so doing, the discourses of Jesus himself, as

Pastoral Perspective

The tension between the hope of resurrection and the finality of death is palpable during this season of intense personal and communal reflection. Amid painful circumstance and death-dealing social realities, we yearn for resurrection and the *unbinding* that releases us to dream beyond the boundaries and experience life anew. To dream beyond the boundaries is to imagine a world in which wholeness, well-being, health, and prosperity are normative expressions of human existence and to partner with the God of life in making that dream a reality. It is to recognize that our world is not as it should be, while rejecting assertions that the socioreligious strictures that prevent persons from experiencing God's presence in their lives are impervious to change. Our narrative, on this Fifth Sunday in Lent, invites us to consider the possibility of resurrection in the lives of the many persons and communities who deeply need God's presence in the nowness of our existence.

said to her, "I am the resurrection and the life. Those who believe in me, even though they die, will live, ²⁶and everyone who lives and believes in me will never die. Do you believe this?" ²⁷She said to him, "Yes, Lord, I believe that you are the Messiah, the Son of God, the one coming into the world."

²⁸When she had said this, she went back and called her sister Mary, and told her privately, "The Teacher is here and is calling for you." ²⁹And when she heard it, she got up quickly and went to him. ³⁰Now Jesus had not yet come to the village, but was still at the place where Martha had met him. ³¹The Jews who were with her in the house, consoling her, saw Mary get up quickly and go out. They followed her because they thought that she was going to the tomb to weep there. ³²When Mary came where Jesus was and saw him, she knelt at his feet and said to him, "Lord, if you had been here, my brother would not have died." ³³When Jesus saw her weeping, and the Jews who came with her also weeping, he was greatly disturbed in spirit and deeply moved. ³⁴He said, "Where have you laid him?" They said to him, "Lord, come and see." ³⁵Jesus began to weep. ³⁶So the Jews said, "See how he loved him!" ³⁷But some of them said, "Could not he who opened the eyes of the blind man have kept this man from dying?"

³⁸Then Jesus, again greatly disturbed, came to the tomb. It was a cave, and a stone was lying against it. ³⁹Jesus said, "Take away the stone." Martha, the sister of the dead man, said to him, "Lord, already there is a stench because he has been dead four days." ⁴⁰Jesus said to her, "Did I not tell you that if you believed, you would see the glory of God?" ⁴¹So they took away the stone. And Jesus looked upward and said, "Father, I thank you for having heard me. ⁴²I knew that you always hear me, but I have said this for the sake of the crowd standing here, so that they may believe that you sent me." ⁴³When he had said this, he cried with a loud voice, "Lazarus, come out!" ⁴⁴The dead man came out, his hands and feet bound with strips of cloth, and his face wrapped in a cloth. Jesus said to them, "Unbind him, and let him go."

⁴⁵Many of the Jews therefore, who had come with Mary and had seen what Jesus did, believed in him.

Exegetical Perspective

As the last in a series of seven narrated "signs" (see John 12:18), the raising of Lazarus marks a turning point in the narrative concerning the one who is the resurrection and the life (v. 25). Appearing only in John, the episode functions as a narrative bridge connecting Jesus' public ministry with the events (and extended discourse) related to the final Passover and Jesus' death and resurrection. Like much of the rest of this Gospel, the passage points repeatedly to the importance of the act of believing (always a verb in John, never the noun "belief") in the identity of Jesus and in his power to bring life out of death. At the level of the story, the result of this seventh sign is twofold: it leads people to "believe in him" (v. 45), and it accelerates the conflict between Jesus and the religious authorities (vv. 47–53).

Although the episode could stand on its own as a narrative depiction of the one who brings life out of death, a number of verbal threads tie the passage to the prologue of John: the glory of God/Jesus (v. 4; cf.

Homiletical Perspective

An immediate entrée into this last of Year A's successively longer Lenten readings from John's Gospel is provided by what some of us memorized as the shortest verse in the Bible: "Jesus wept" (v. 35). The terseness of the older RSV and AV translations is certainly not improved upon rhetorically in the NRSV's wooden and unnecessary doubling of the word count to "Jesus began to weep."

This verse serves as a truly authenticating mark of Jesus' humanity in John's Gospel, which, despite its unrivalled witness to the Word become flesh, in contrast to the Synoptics tends to picture Jesus as being not quite "grounded" in this world. Helping to counter this is the scene of Jesus' weeping at the sight of his friend Lazarus's corpse. This is an emotionally profound testimony to the truth of the incarnation itself, of Jesus being truly one of us to the point of sharing our human need for friendship and our grief at the loss of a friend.

The Gospel writer informs us that those observing Jesus' weeping remarked: "See how he loved him!"

John 11:1-45

Theological Perspective

well as his exhibition of certain divine attributes, reinforce the Gospel's faith claim that Christ is "one" with God. Such traits lead some later theologians to praise (or fault) John for depicting the least truly human Christ and many others to rely on Johannine Christology as the most truly incarnational. Likewise, while in the Synoptics a fuller understanding of Christ's person and work emerges, despite initial misunderstandings, as later events unfold over time, in John's work the whole truth of the matter is revealed immediately, although in paradoxes, word-plays, and category confusions calling forth explanatory words by Christ the Word.

The wonder, marvel, or miracle of the raising of Lazarus is a case in point. "Did it really happen?" is one nearly irrepressible question. Debates over miracles raged in biblical and theological studies during the Enlightenment era and its aftermath. They have by no means disappeared. In certain respects John's account complicates the discussion. His is the only report of the raising of Lazarus. Given its narrative placement, it is manifestly a prefiguration of the death and resurrection of Jesus. How factual it is may be inconsequential. Even so, in all the Gospels, extraordinary events are associated with the ministry of Jesus and understood as indicative of workings of God's power. The question of whether or not to "believe in miracles" (in general, as it were) in light of what is subject to critical scientific investigation and confirmable by the physical sciences is a far cry from concerns of early Christians.

The Johannine contribution to the discussion is the view of wonders as "signs." The raising of Lazarus is in John's reckoning the climax of the series of signs Jesus performs. It extends the manifestations of the presence and power of God he exhibits to that of supremacy over death itself. Such signs are marvels indeed, displayed for eyewitness viewing, and as such are mighty attestations of God's glory, evoking in some the faith in the glorification of Jesus as well. For John, however, the terms "glory" and "glorification" ultimately have to do with being exalted, "lifted up" on the cross and from death to life, in oneness with God.

The raising of Lazarus, then, *signifies* that God's eschatological promises are here and now, already, being realized amid and despite the ordinariness of the course of life, which includes illnesses, deaths, and burials like those of Lazarus. This and the other such signs point to Jesus, the sign-maker, who in turn by his attitude of prayer points to God. His "oneness" with God is transparent. His life-giving action is not dependent on human faith, whether that of Mary,

Pastoral Perspective

One of the greatest hindrances to imagining possibilities is perceptual distortion. Obstacles appear larger and more ominous than they are, keeping us preoccupied with trying to avoid danger rather than discerning alternatives. This is evident in today's lesson. The disciples have been Jesus' constant companions throughout his ministry, traveling with him from one village, town, and mountainous region to the next, yet they often appear more concerned with situational limitation than with the restorative possibility of resurrection and life. Their interests are often at cross-purposes with Jesus' ministerial focus, as in their concern in last week's lection for the origin of the blind man's condition, rather than in the curative potential of Jesus' encounter with the man.

Having received the news of Lazarus's illness and subsequent death, the disciples again struggle to come to terms with Jesus' decision to make the treacherous journey to Judea after a two-day delay. They question the wisdom of returning to Judea at all, recalling their narrow escape from stoning just a few days earlier. What is more, by Jesus' own admission, Lazarus is already dead. Nonetheless, Jesus insists that they make the journey, emphasizing the revelatory possibility that Lazarus's illness and subsequent death have occasioned and assuring the disciples that the journey will be stumble-free. Although Thomas and the others are not completely convinced—"Let us also go, that we may die with him" (v. 16)—these friends and companions make the journey with him, intrigued by the possibility of resurrection.

As Jesus and the disciples approach Mary and Martha's home, the tension between life and death intensifies and the immediacy of grief is overwhelming. Weeping and lament fill the air as family and friends gather to mourn Lazarus's demise and final sleep. It has been four days since Lazarus's death, marking the completion of the soul's journey from life to death. His soul no longer lingers near the body, indicating that Lazarus is truly dead.

The finality of death deepens the grief of Mary and Martha and their disappointment that Jesus has not arrived until now—"Lord, if you had been here, my brother would not have died" (v. 21). Martha and Mary consider Jesus a friend and believe that God would have honored his requests—if Jesus had arrived sooner. They trust him as a teacher, healer, miracle worker, and believe him to be the Messiah come from God. They unquestionably anticipate the resurrection of the dead *on the last day* and look forward to uniting with their brother Lazarus again. However, they have no experiential referent to support Jesus'

Exegetical Perspective

1:14;); light (v. 9; cf. 1:4–9); life (v. 25; cf. 1:4); believing (vv. 15, 26–27, 40, 42, 45; cf. 1:12); Jesus as "the one coming into the world" (v. 27; cf. 1:9). Several additional words and phrases are similarly Johannine: "I am . . . " (v. 25); love (*agapē; phileō*, vv. 3, 5); resurrection on "the last day" (v. 24); came . . . saw . . . believed (v. 45). In addition, the events taking place at Lazarus's tomb mirror many of those that will occur at the tomb of Jesus. By pointing simultaneously forward and back in the narrative, the raising of Lazarus embodies many of the fundamental themes of the Gospel.

Two distinct reactions to Jesus—belief and conflict—appear together in an inclusio that frames the story. In the first part of the frame, before receiving the news about Lazarus's illness, Jesus is in Jerusalem for the feast of the Dedication, where the Judeans (NRSV "the Jews") push him to reveal whether he is the Christ. Offended by his response, they take up stones to kill him, charging that "you, though only a human being, are making yourself God" (10:22–33). Jesus and his disciples escape, retreating across the Jordan, where "many believed in him there" (10:42). The same two responses—believing Jesus and threatening him—occur again, at the end of our pericope in the other part of the frame, after Jesus calls Lazarus out of the tomb. "Many of the Jews . . . believed in him," but others of them go to the Pharisees, who worry that Jesus is a threat to the nation. They confer to determine how they might put him to death (11:45–53).

Lazarus, for his part, ends up the target of threats as well, even though he had nothing to do with his own resurrection. His return to life adds fuel to the fire of Jesus' enormous popularity, so that a short while later, at a dinner party held in Bethany, a crowd has gathered to see this one whom Jesus had raised from the dead (12:1–9). This crowd, as well as those who continue to talk about Lazarus and Jesus at the time of Jesus' entry into Jerusalem, cause considerable concern to the chief priests and the Pharisees, respectively, who seem to be getting increasingly nervous about the number of people flocking after the doer of signs. The religious authorities, determined to undo the life-giving nature of Jesus' miraculous work, conspire to kill Lazarus as well, since it was on his account that people believed in Jesus (12:10–11, 17). Apparently, being brought to life by the one who is the resurrection and the life can get a person killed.

A good deal of ink is given over to the identity of the people involved in Lazarus's return to life, with emphasis on the two sisters. Could it be that they are

Homiletical Perspective

This is a telling choice of vocabulary, inasmuch as the Greek word for "love" used here is not the verb form of the expected *agapē*—selfless, self-giving love of which the Johannine corpus is so fond. Rather, Jesus' love for his friend Lazarus is *philia*, the common, everyday Greek word for "friendship," "human affection," or "deep feeling," that ordinary human love we have for our friends. It is to this status as friends that Jesus elevates his own disciples from that of servants a few chapters later in 15:13–15. The early American composer William Billings's "When Jesus Wept" is an especially effective setting of this text to music whether sung by a choir or as a congregational round.[1]

Though Jesus' weeping over the death of his friend Lazarus is the emotional heart of today's Gospel story, its salient homiletical point, especially seen in the context of Palm/Passion Sunday and the beginning of Holy Week looming just a week hence, actually occurs in the verses immediately following today's reading. Strangely, these verses, crucial to the plot of John's passion narrative, will never be heard read by those relying exclusively on our three-year Revised Common Lectionary! For Jesus' resuscitation of his dead friend, as much as a flash-forward to Jesus' own resurrection as it may be, serves more instrumentally as the final (if figurative) nail in Jesus' coffin.

Beyond today's assigned reading, the text goes on almost immediately to report: "But some of them went to the Pharisees and told them what he had done. So the chief priests and the Pharisees called a meeting of the council and said, 'What are we to do? This man is performing many signs. If we let him go on like this, everyone will believe in him, and the Romans will come and destroy both our holy place and our nation.' But one of them, Caiaphas, who was high priest that year, said to them, 'You know nothing at all! You do not understand that it is better for you to have one man die for the people than to have the whole nation destroyed.' . . . So from that day on they planned to put him to death" (11:46–50, 53).

Here again, to the NRSV's translation of Caiaphas's words of advice, "it is better," I prefer the older RSV's more politically ominous "it is expedient." The text reveals that it is political expediency, perhaps even a misplaced patriotic, ethnoreligious solidarity, that prompts Caiaphas to recommend Jesus' death, lest the Roman overlords violently intervene in the life of his—and his God's—people. So the plot leading to Jesus' execution is set in motion as an

---

1. William Billings, "When Jesus Wept," in *The New Century Hymnal* (Cleveland: Pilgrim Press, 1995), #192.

John 11:1-45

Theological Perspective

Martha, Lazarus, or the onlookers, but calls it forth. The incident thereby presents yet another of John's leitmotifs: the sheep recognize their shepherd's voice. Lazarus comes out of the tomb at Jesus' word, and "many" of those who see believe.

Preceding this climactic sign is a discourse by Jesus, the climax of the series of "I-sayings" in John's Gospel: "I am the resurrection and the life" (v. 25). Its context is a dialogue regarding the character of Martha's faith, and Mary's. Each is already a believer, and yet each, independent of the other, tells Jesus that had he been there, Lazarus would not have died. The others at the scene say the same thing shortly afterward. The record, earlier on, that Jesus deliberately delayed his response to the sisters' call gives such comments bite. Hence the stage is ready for a Johannine theological clarification. Those who live and believe in the one who is the resurrection and the life shall never die. This life is not a matter of belief in a "general resurrection" to come, but, as Martha's confession tells, a personalized faith: "You are the Christ, the Son of God" (v. 27). Then the raising of Lazarus comes about, in the end time that is already present.

The episode raises theological questions even as it seeks to clarify them. Consider, for example, whether metaphors or metaphysics could offer the most adequate account of "the resurrection and the life" of which Jesus speaks, and in any case what they might be. Consider as well the thrust of Martha's confession, which has as its object of belief not an object at all, but the person of Jesus. It is one of a series of differently worded Johannine confessions of faith, the climactic one that of Thomas, who confesses (20:28) the still-wounded but resurrected Christ as "my Lord and my God."

The confession of Thomas at the conclusion of the Gospel is a reminder that, as a sign, the raising of Lazarus calls for theological consideration of the Johannine signature theme of "seeing and believing." Having *seen* what Jesus has done, many of those who come with Mary believe, and the faith of Martha and Mary themselves becomes, shall we say, enlightened. For Thomas also, *seeing* Christ, crucified yet risen, evokes faith. The Gospel's summary word with regard to the seeing of all such signs, however, is another Jesus saying (20:29): "Blessed are those who have not seen and yet have come to believe." Faith, then, is not based on *seeing*. It is a provocative point for theologians and preachers to address.

JAMES O. DUKE

Pastoral Perspective

self-identification as "the resurrection and life." Jesus is speaking of resurrection as a present reality—"I am"—leaving Martha, Mary, and their community skeptical, yet fascinated with the possibility of new life.

As we observe Mary, Martha, and their community from a distance, we too are intrigued by the possibility of resurrection and feel compelled to join them at the tomb. We listen as they wonder out loud if Jesus' tears are indicative of love or regret; we hear the strain in Jesus' voice as he instructs them to remove the stone that covers the tomb; we sense the anticipatory tension as profound faith and debilitating doubt converge in this single event. We know the conclusion, yet breathlessly awaiting Lazarus's emergence from the tomb. "Lazarus, come out!" (v. 43) reverberates throughout the tomb, awakening Lazarus's lifeless body to the revivifying call of life.

As Christians, we believe in the power of resurrection, having been formed in a liturgical tradition in which birth, life, death, and resurrection are cyclical occurrences. Resurrection and life are central to the meaning that we make for our lives, informing our sense of Christian vocation. In this respect, resurrection confronts us as an urgent call, beckoning us to consider the possibility that those whom our world deems socially, physically, spiritually, and emotionally dead might live into a new reality. We pray for the power of resurrection in the lives of persons and communities bound by the graveclothes of war, genocide, poverty, disease, dis-ease, systematic abuse, and systemic oppression.

Releasing persons and communities from the clutches of death also demands something of us, as did Lazarus's resurrection of his community. Though Jesus called Lazarus from the tomb, he urged those who were alive and well, "Unbind him, and let him go." Resurrected women, men, and children today also require caring communities that are willing to nurture and strengthen them until they are able to walk alone; to remove the graveclothes of self-doubt, social isolation, marginalization, and oppression; to tear away the wrappings of fear, anxiety, loss, and grief, so that unbound women, men, and children might walk in dignity and become creative agents in the world.

A few years ago, a friend gave me a poster with the slogan, "Consider the possibilities . . ."—ellipsis marks indicating that there is more to be said, this slogan provocatively reminds us to dream beyond the boundaries, to consider the possibility of resurrection, anticipating it so profoundly that we stand at the tomb of suffering and pain, listening for the voice of Jesus, ready to unbind those whom God delivers, even now.

VERONICE MILES

Exegetical Perspective

known to the original community for which this Gospel was written? Lazarus is introduced by way of his relationship to these women, and not, as we might expect, the other way around; he is a man from Bethany, "the village of Mary and her sister Martha" (11:1). Fine tuning the identity of the characters, the writer says that Lazarus is the brother of Mary (v. 2) and that Jesus "loved Martha and her sister and Lazarus" (v. 5). Perhaps reflecting later redaction, Mary receives special attention with reference to her act of anointing Jesus and wiping his feet with her hair (v. 2). That event has not yet happened at the level of the narrative, but its occurrence will reemphasize the importance of Jesus' seventh sign as an opportunity to believe in him or not (12:1–11).

Mary and Martha interact with Jesus individually, but they say the same thing: "Lord, if you had been here, my brother would not have died" (vv. 21, 32). Whether their statement is a confession of faith or an accusation is difficult to determine, but their charge echoes repeated assertions that Jesus is the one who brings life (e.g., 1:4; 5:24; 8:12; 10:10). Moved by Mary's weeping, Jesus asks, "Where have you laid him"? (v. 34). Ordering the stone to be taken away from the tomb (v. 39), he cries out in a loud voice, "Lazarus, come out!" (v. 43), and the man who has been dead for four days comes forth from the darkness. In a sign of God's glory (v. 40), death is overcome. However, the burial cloths that bind Lazarus's hands and feet and cover his face are a vivid reminder that death still clings to him.

On another day, another Mary, weeping at another tomb, asks the same question: "Tell me where have you laid him" (20:15). On that day, the burial cloths will be left behind in the tomb—the face cloth rolled up in a place by itself—no longer required for the one whom God has raised. On that day, the disciples will see a sign even greater than the raising of Lazarus. Here, at the tomb of Lazarus, death is denied for a time. There, at the tomb of Jesus, death is overcome for good.

AUDREY WEST

Homiletical Perspective

expedient—meaning, convenient and useful—way of forestalling any threat to the security of the status quo. Church and state connive in the death of yet another innocent, neither the first nor the last scapegoat, neither the most cruel nor the most humane of expedient deaths in that age or any other. The charge against Jesus in bringing him to Pilate according to Luke's Gospel sums it up nicely: "We found this man perverting our nation and forbidding us to give tribute to Caesar, and saying that he himself is Christ a king" (Luke 23:2 RSV).

Caiaphas spoke more than he knew in advising that "it is expedient" for one man to die for the people. The high priest was speaking an ironic truth reverberant with gospel resonances beyond his knowing. In fact, John goes so far as to say that the conniving Caiaphas was unconsciously prophesying (v. 51), both foretelling and forth-telling God's intentions that Jesus should die for the nation. That is just what Jesus' death will turn out to be in what will become the church's theology of atonement (not restricted here to certain "substitutionary" theories)[2]: The self-sacrifice of one by whom not only the nation or the Jewish people or even all believers, but the whole cosmos, the whole created order, will be saved. Caiaphas may not have known what he was doing in setting in motion Jesus' expeditious death, but God is sufficiently creative to transfigure even the evil of this innocent's death into the gospel itself.[3] The beginning of the plot against Jesus that its perpetrators think will find its conclusion on Good Friday begins with Jesus weeping at the death of a friend. Easter will prove to be the real, absolutely unexpected conclusion, in which we will discover what a friend we have not only in Jesus—but in the God who raised him from the dead!

JOHN ROLLEFSON

2. See Colin E. Gunton, *The Actuality of Atonement: A Study of Metaphor, Rationality and the Christian Tradition* (London: T.&T. Clark, 1988). On Jesus as scapegoat/sacrifice, see René Girard, *Things Hidden since the Foundation of the World* (Palo Alto, CA: Stanford University Press, 1987).
3. See Gen. 50:20.

Psalm 118:1-2, 19-29

> [1]O give thanks to the LORD, for he is good;
>   his steadfast love endures forever!
>
> [2]Let Israel say,
>   "His steadfast love endures forever."
> . . . .
> [19]Open to me the gates of righteousness,
>   that I may enter through them
>   and give thanks to the LORD.
>
> [20]This is the gate of the LORD;
>   the righteous shall enter through it.
> [21]I thank you that you have answered me
>   and have become my salvation.
> [22]The stone that the builders rejected
>   has become the chief cornerstone.
> [23]This is the LORD's doing;
>   it is marvelous in our eyes.

Theological Perspective

Theology, meaning thought and words about God, has to be open to the many faces and acts of God as revealed, and ready to address the full range of human emotions and responses. Often, therefore, those who speak and write as theologians have to be open to surprise and ready to surprise others. Keeping that in mind is especially appropriate during Lent and more especially at the end of Lent, at this entrance to the week we call Holy. The reason for that is clear: we have been told and trained to know that Lent's forty days and its Sundays are times for seriousness. They include calls for self-evaluation, and in these activities believers have learned that the self who is exposed in evaluation is not altogether lovely. In fact, to all honest people, it becomes clear that they fall short of what God expects them to be and has made them capable of being as redeemed creatures.

The awareness that comes with self-evaluation in the light of such an expectation, enhanced as it often is with hymns and postures that seem designed to make worshipers glum and force them to be sullen, does not prepare us for psalms like this wonderful intrusion into the world of glumness and sullenness. There we were, repenting, and now comes this bright psalm. What goes on here? Part of what occasions confusion, the biblical theologian will say, is a

Pastoral Perspective

"Blessed is the one who comes in the name of the LORD. We bless you from the house of the LORD" (v. 26).

Imagine that your sermon for the Liturgy of the Palms is a house. Your exegetical work becomes a strong foundation anchoring the whole structure to the ground of biblical truth. Your theological perspective provides the beams and trusses that give the house structural integrity. Beams and trusses are not usually visible in the finished product, but if you want your house to stand, do not cut corners here.

The homiletical perspective helps you imagine how most visitors will enter your house. Will you incorporate a simple design that brings people up the front walk and right through the front door? Perhaps a long driveway will bring friends around to the back door, less obvious but more intimate. The more creative homiletical architects among us may design an unconventional or unexpected entrance—perhaps through the roof! As you consider the homiletical design that will best enable people to enter the Palm Sunday message, what will you make of the theme of entrance, so central to the day? Open the gates; the righteous will enter (v. 19, 20). And do not neglect to consider how folks will depart. Will there be a doorway onto Main Street? Into the garden?

²⁴This is the day that the Lord has made;
　　let us rejoice and be glad in it.
²⁵Save us, we beseech you, O Lord!
　　O Lord, we beseech you, give us success!

²⁶Blessed is the one who comes in the name of the Lord.
　　We bless you from the house of the Lord.
²⁷The Lord is God,
　　and he has given us light.
　　Bind the festal procession with branches,
　　up to the horns of the altar.

²⁸You are my God, and I will give thanks to you;
　　you are my God, I will extol you.

²⁹O give thanks to the Lord, for he is good,
　　for his steadfast love endures forever.

Exegetical Perspective

Psalm 118 contains a number of famous lines, perhaps because it is frequently quoted in the New Testament. The psalm itself may quote from other texts in the Old Testament. Verse 14, for example, is closely paralleled in Exodus 15:2 and Isaiah 12:2. The opening lines' repetition of the endurance of the Lord's steadfast love (ḥesed) is familiar from Psalms 106:1; 107:1; and 136. The lectionary's focus on verses 1–2 and 19–29 may reinforce a piecemeal-like approach to the poem, but preachers should remember that the psalm has a larger integrity that is crucial for the proper interpretation of its constituent parts.

Generically, the psalm is typically classified as an individual song of thanksgiving. Insofar as verses 10–14 evoke images of battle, it is possible that the speaker is the king. Other parts can be read in more democratized fashion, however; even if the king is the speaker, he may well be merely representative.

Scholars have seen in the psalm hints of a liturgical procession ending in the temple. If correct, the procession may have begun subsequent to the battle mentioned in verses 10–14, indicating that the victory God provides must lead, ultimately, to the praise of God in the sanctuary. So, even if the lectionary excises mention of the battleground, the psalmist nevertheless praises God *for specific reasons*—in this

Homiletical Perspective

A preacher is always well advised to look for movement in a text. That movement ought to be capable of being described briefly as *from* one thing *to* another. If the movement is from one state to another it might equally be called a transformation. Sometimes the transformation is so extreme that it can even be called a reversal: one's whole world is turned upside down. This mode of thinking is homiletically useful, because a transformation or transformations identified in the text may serve as the framework for the sermon. That is to say, the sermon in its flow may repeat the transformation identified in the text.

The point is more than a structural or organizational one, however. The preacher can look for a transformation in the text that might be repeated in the lives of the listeners. There may then be a parallelism among the following: transformation that is identified in the text, transformation that shapes the sermon, and transformation that may occur in the listeners. Composing such a sermon requires analogical thinking. It should be noted, however, that analogical thinking is precisely what allowed the writers of various New Testament books to link this psalm to the life of Jesus and the foundation of the Christian church. The preacher may employ that kind of

Psalm 118:1-2, 19-29

Theological Perspective

misreading of biblical descriptions of how repentance is to look and how one is to be in the presence of God and the company of Christ. Repenting, we need to remember, is a serious but joyous act. Jesus once asked why people were grumpy and crabby at his wedding party: he was and is the groom at a festive table, and his disciples wore, and we wear, long faces. In sum of Theological Point One: in many contexts, repenting, turning or being turned from one's old self to God, is a joyful act, a saying good-bye to the old self, and doing so without mourning.

This psalm has a wonderful metaphor or picture of how God, who has started the changing to the new, advances it: by being open. The psalmist responds to this activity by praying, in the form of a command of the sort that only the bidden children of God have a right to utter: "Open to me the gates of righteousness, that I may enter through them and give thanks to the LORD" (v. 19). Then the psalmist acts as a tour guide with a pointer: "This is the gate of the LORD; the righteous shall enter through it" (v. 20).

This psalm has all kinds of references on which the Gospel writers picked up: Jesus passes through the gates of Jerusalem on the way to the cross, where his acts make possible the naming as "the righteous" those who believe in him. Later, the psalmist pleads, "Save us" (v. 25), which in Hebrew was *hoshianna* or "hosanna," the song of Jerusalemites. "Bind the festal procession with branches" (v. 27) anticipates the psalms of Palm Sunday. Those are all details for the biblical commentators. Theological comment turns to what is going on here. Now the key word is eucharistic: "I will give thanks to you" and "O give thanks to the LORD" (vv. 28–29). That is how the psalm also began: "O give thanks to the LORD"—for one reason, a reason rich in theological nuance.

One is to give thanks, not because one has been victorious in battle, as this psalmist may have been, or for good things God gives. No, one gives thanks because God is good. God merits thanks intrinsically, in the nature of the case, because the chief feature in the experience of God and the witness to God is that "he is good; *his love endures forever*" (vv. 1, 29). That phrase is important enough and poetically rich enough to merit being cited at the beginning and the end of this excerpt. God's steadfast love provides the frame that gets filled in by stories of the life and death of Jesus Christ and of the people who greet him with palms and thanks and *hoshianna*.

One other allusion picked up in the New Testament is partly obscure. Almost without context there is a burst: "The stone that the builders rejected has become

Pastoral Perspective

When guests arrive and enter your house, where on this Palm Sunday do you expect the congregation to spend most of their time? In the congregation that you serve, is the Liturgy of the Palms more of a "living room" event or more of a "family room" event? The living room suggests a somewhat formal setting: everything in its proper place, intentional in its order, with no toys under the coffee table. Many of our guests will have been here on Palm Sunday many times before. (My parents have each celebrated Palm Sunday more than eighty times—thanks be to God!) Your experienced guests will know if the furniture is out of place. Perhaps our pastoral experience will lead us to honor their expectations for a comfortably predictable observance and message. There is no need to break new ground on Palm Sunday. Wave the palms. Tell the story. Sit down. Let the grace-filled rhythm of the Lenten calendar hold sway.

On the other hand, in almost every worshiping community, the Palm Sunday crowd will include children. Given the earnest desire of most churches to add and incorporate young families in a visible way, children are likely to be front and center in the palms processional. Perhaps the easy informality suggested by the family room is better suited to the day. Move the furniture. Throw some pillows on the floor. Move the antiques into temporary storage, and make space for some spontaneous Hosannas. Have a party worthy of the unconventional reality of the moment: a grown man riding a donkey down a hill while children frolic and grown-ups fling their clothes to the ground. "This is the day that the LORD has made; let us rejoice and be glad in it" (v. 24). Save the living room for Easter's larger crowd; the family room's casual and unpretentious welcome feels right. Stack slightly used palm branches over there by the dog's bed; sit down in the middle of the floor—it is story time.

Before we retire our extended liturgy-as-a-house simile, there is at least one more room to prompt our consideration of Palm Sunday's pastoral opportunities. While our Last Supper observances are still four days away, the psalm's repeated expressions of thanksgiving are perhaps suggestive of the dining room. "O give thanks to the LORD, for he is good; his steadfast love endures forever" (v. 1; see also vv. 19, 21, 28, 29). In the same spirit in which families gather around the table and give thanks for a meal about to be received, on Palm Sunday God's people gather to give thanks for the salvation about to be accomplished. Palm Sunday is the church's true Thanksgiving Day.

Perhaps our house simile has now run its useful course. If it is to encompass the whole of our experi-

case, the Lord's delivering acts (vv. 5b, 17), support (v. 7), help (v. 13), mighty hand (vv. 15–16), even forbearance (v. 18). These are, in a word, *the necessary prerequisites* for any song of thanksgiving. Trouble resolved, now part of the psalmist's past, is what eventuates in thanks and praise (vv. 21, 28). Thanksgiving devoid of its specific reasons is not psalmic thanksgiving. This is no small matter for the genre and structure of the psalm, but it is also important in the use of Psalm 118 (and the lectionary's selections) in the Liturgy of the Palms. This point is underscored by the fact that Psalm 118 belongs to the Egyptian Hallel (Pss. 113–118), which are sung before and after the Passover meal commemorating the exodus—the delivering act par excellence.

The poet begins by summoning the community to give thanks and to do so for good reasons: because (*kî*) God is good and because (*kî*) "his steadfast love endures forever" (v. 1). This leads to a litany inviting Israel to say the same. An antiphonal or call-and-response format results. As elsewhere in the Psalter, the deliverance of the one (individual) impinges on the many (community). The delivered cannot but tell—even preach!—of the goodness and faithfulness of their Deliverer. One is never saved all by or for oneself, but with reference to, and with impact on, many others.

Though left out of the lectionary, verses 3–18 are integral to the psalm's structure and message. The call-and-response begun in verse 2 continues in verses 3–4 with a move from Israel (v. 2) to the priestly house of Aaron (v. 3) to "those who fear the LORD" (v. 4). Some have thought that these three terms reflect distinct groups: Israelite laity, Israelite priests, and proselytes ("God-fearers"). This is uncertain but intriguing. If correct, it would indicate that everyone—lay and professional, "Israelite" by birth and by faith—is included in the psalmist's address. *All* are invited to hear of the poet's salvation and to participate in it by giving thanks for God's *ḥesed* as well.

The poet's thanks are variously articulated, but boil down to God's deliverance from "distress" (v. 5a), which in Hebrew is derived from the root meaning "to be narrow, restricted." Once one has moved from that kind of place to a "broad place" (v. 5b), one can hardly but have boundless confidence in the Lord and what God can accomplish. Correlatively, there is no need to fear anyone or anything (v. 6). God's support can mean only victory (v. 7), and thus the Lord is the only one who deserves confidence, because God is the only sure refuge from trouble (vv. 8–9). This confidence in God makes the

analogical thinking to take the further step of linking the biblical text to the experiences of the listeners.

This may be the ultimate "transformation text" in the Psalter. It is an entrance liturgy and thus reflects physical movement. It describes a festal procession approaching and entering the temple. An existential analog to this movement might be from distance from God to experience of the divine presence. There is also a transformation from all but certain defeat to victory by the hand of the Lord. That reversal is paralleled by the transformation from the call for help of verse 5 to the call to praise of the final verse of the psalm. One could preach on such transformations from the psalm itself without reference to any New Testament text. Surely Christians might hope that, like the psalmist, they may experience transformation from defeat to victory. Like the psalmist they may say, "I thank you that you have answered me and have become my salvation" (v. 21). Any day is potentially "the day that the LORD has made" (v. 24). The psalm, as it is, represents a classic statement of the experience of rescue from trouble by a merciful God that is very near the heart of biblical faith.

On Palm Sunday, however, with the familiar hosannas of Jesus' entry into Jerusalem echoing through the church, such a choice might be experienced as a violation of the liturgical context of the day. The assumption in this essay is that a preacher will preach the psalm on this day not as a stand-alone text, but in connection with the Gospel reading for the day. When read in that context, the psalm becomes a metaphor for the magnificent reversal that takes place in the passion of Jesus Christ. By extension, it becomes a metaphor for the experience of all those who trust in him.

The transformations in the psalm, then, mirror the transformations that mark the story of the passion of the Lord. Think of the multiple transformations in the Gospels, from "Hosanna" to "Crucify him"; from welcome to rejection; and, of course, the ultimate transformation, from rejected to risen or, phrased more simply, from death to resurrection. That transformation is pictured and, in the view of the early church, anticipated in this psalm. Most particularly it is pictured in the image that is repeatedly quoted in the New Testament: "The stone that the builders rejected has become the chief cornerstone" (v. 22). That verse is used in the New Testament as a metaphor both for the resurrection of Jesus and for the establishment of a church founded on the life of one who is both rejected and raised. One useful homiletical possibility is to use the psalm to identify

Psalm 118:1-2, 19-29

Theological Perspective

the chief cornerstone" (v. 22). Whatever it meant to the psalmist and in Israel of old, to New Testament writers it pointed to another surprise: that the easy-to-reject Jesus, who did not seem important and did not seem respectable to the authorities of his day, became and remains central in the plan and action of God.

Theologians who want to keep their concepts clear often say that it is proper to say, "God is love," but not, "Love is God." So central to the revelation of God is God's initiative in taking action to redeem Israel and the people on the roadsides in Jerusalem and in every gathering of believers, that we would need to say almost nothing else about God, *if* we could grasp that God is love and that God's love endures forever. Since we cannot, psychologists, preachers, historians, and theologians remind us that all the stories, all the sermons, all the doctrinal statements, are correlated with this central assertion: God's love endures forever.

All those assertions have their corollaries in the experience of believers, whose love may be compromised and not always enduring. They are enabled, however, to express this love, the spontaneous, unmotivated outpouring of good on others who do not deserve it any more than they do or did. One way to see this love clarified and enlarged is to gather where the psalms are voiced, the light of that love shines, in special places—the churches are among them—and a special time that elicits a special response: "This is the day the LORD has made; let us rejoice and be glad in it" (v. 24).

MARTIN E. MARTY

Pastoral Perspective

ence, our imagined "Liturgy of the Palms as a house" must include not only living room, family room, and dining room; it must also provide an auditorium adequate for a coronation. Not many houses are so spaciously designed!

To say it more plainly, the day of the palms is our Lord's last public appeal to join the kingdom. Here, Christ confronts Jerusalem. With so much else going on thematically on Palm Sunday, it is easy to lose sight of—and hard to make room for—his claim to our allegiance. Especially for his followers today in North America and Europe, perched so near the top of the world's pyramid of privilege, the invitation to crown him Lord of all can be problematic.

How can we do justice to the unmistakable claim Christ lays upon our hearts? On Palm Sunday, a kingship is claimed. What say you? In our contemporary idiom, Palm Sunday is "edgy," provocative, disruptive of our ordinary loyalties.

The psalm announces the coronation in a most unusual way: "The stone that the builders rejected has become the chief cornerstone" (v. 22). Reading backward from our New Testament point of view, we have a narrative context in which to understand the rejected stone. What did it mean to the psalmist's original readers or, for that matter, to the psalmist? In choosing the stone the builders rejected, is God not teaching us that our salvation is always of God's design and not of our own (v. 23)? As a Palm Sunday text, the psalm disestablishes every human scheme and structure.

So now at the end of our essay, our whole "house" endures a shaking of the foundation! A new cornerstone must be placed, and everything else built around it and upon it. The Liturgy of the Palms is subversive; all pretenders to the throne must yield. Preacher, muster your courage, creativity, and gentleness. Bind yourself to the altar—and preach!

THOMAS EDWARD MCGRATH

Exegetical Perspective

psalmist confident that she will live and retell the Lord's deeds (vv. 17–18).

The procession implied in verses 19–29 begins at the "gates of righteousness" (v. 19) and "the gate of the LORD" (v. 20)—that is, the temple entrance. Verse 20 is widely thought to be the sentiment of a priest, clarifying who can enter (cf. Pss. 15, 24); verse 21 thanks the Lord for answering and for salvation (cf. vv. 5b, 14). Verse 22 may be the voice of the individual psalmist or the voice of the congregation that speaks in verses 23–27 (note the "our," "us," and "we" language). The precise import of verse 22 is unclear, though it seems to be a proverb of some sort, probably testifying once more to the Lord's power to overturn circumstances and expectations (cf. vv. 10–13, 18). What was once worthless is now honored; God has the power to change fortunes! The proverb thus leads directly to praise by the unidentified "us," who recognize "this" as the "LORD's doing" (v. 23). The testimony of the psalmist has paid off: the larger body now joins in praise, prayer, and petition (vv. 24–27).

The "one who comes in the name of the LORD" (v. 26a) is probably the psalmist, who has now entered the sanctuary. He is blessed by the congregation (v. 26b), but the datum that is this delivered person is not to be misconstrued as anything other than the Lord's act of giving light and thus proof of God's goodness, blessing, and protection (v. 27a; cf. Num. 6:25). The procession therefore culminates at the *altar*, where sacrifices are made, and the *horns of the altar*, in particular, where God's protection is physically manifested (1 Kgs. 1:50–51). The procession also culminates with a return to the thanks and praise of the psalmist (v. 28). The psalmist, in turn, returns to the beginning: repeating in verse 29 what was said in verse 1. The psalm is now complete, but (re)turns in on itself. It must be reread amid a never-ending cycle of deliverance, thanksgiving, and praise.

BRENT A. STRAWN

Homiletical Perspective

the lens of reversal through which the passion story as a whole is understood.

Another potential transformation might be summarized as from "Hurray" to "Hosanna." The shouts of welcome to Jesus are akin to the shouts of applause that greet, for example, a president of the United States on inauguration day. Whatever the political fate of a new president, we already know that with Jesus things will not work out the way the crowds hope. They will shout, "Hurray," but those shouts will dwindle and fade. Even the disciples themselves will abandon him. They will fail him in his hour of need. But "Hosanna" does not actually mean "Hurray." It is, rather, a short but urgent prayer, rendered in verse 25, "Save us, we beseech you!" (In Hebrew those words are, roughly, "Hosanna.") We remember how soon the triumphal entry becomes trial before Pilate. We remember how "Hosanna" becomes "Crucify." We remember how thoroughly the disciples fail him, and we consider how we too fail genuinely to welcome him. At that point surely any "Hurray" must also fade from our lips. Surely a sober prayer, "Save us," is more fitting. Save us from our own failures to follow you. Turn our worlds upside down and, this year, help us to welcome you into our lives a little more completely.

In the end the preacher is well advised to return to the possibility that would be taken up if the psalm were to be preached on its own, that the transformations that are named in the text can be experienced in the life of the believer. Anyone who in heart and mind accompanies Jesus through the week to come will find a world turned upside down. That person will see the hand of God in all that follows in the story and be enabled to say, "O give thanks to the LORD, for he is good, for his steadfast love endures forever" (v. 1, 29). In the end, the only appropriate response to reversal is praise.

STEPHEN FARRIS

Matthew 21:1-11

¹When they had come near Jerusalem and had reached Bethphage, at the Mount of Olives, Jesus sent two disciples, ²saying to them, "Go into the village ahead of you, and immediately you will find a donkey tied, and a colt with her; untie them and bring them to me. ³If anyone says anything to you, just say this, 'The Lord needs them.' And he will send them immediately." ⁴This took place to fulfill what had been spoken through the prophet, saying,

⁵"Tell the daughter of Zion,
  Look, your king is coming to you,
    humble, and mounted on a donkey,
    and on a colt, the foal of a donkey."

Theological Perspective

This account of Jesus' entry into Jerusalem, long celebrated by Christians on Palm Sunday, mentions no palm branches. It begins the passion narrative, thematically considered, tracing the events through the crucifixion of Jesus. Details of the account have elicited much interest and many varying opinions among theological commentators. Yet it is not, all told, especially controversial in the history of Christian doctrine overall, neither sparking nor legitimating major church-dividing disputes.

There is a considerable cause for theological reflection on several of the text's interwoven themes. Its "politics" in particular is a provocative matter in which Christology, soteriology, and eschatology are bundled together. The story of Jesus riding into the city to cheering crowds, common to all four Gospels, takes place amid the swirl of messianic expectations during the age of Second Temple Judaism. These expectations, like the traditions to which they appealed and the hopes they raised, were many and diverse, embracing in some cases the violent overthrow of Rome's occupation forces and its collaborators. Critical life-of-Jesus research, as well as Christian Scripture and tradition, generally attests to the import of such expectations in the shaping of understandings of the person and work of Jesus of Nazareth.

Pastoral Perspective

On this Sixth Sunday in Lent the momentum of the season draws us closer to the cross as we experience the synergistic effect of two seemingly divergent events. The Liturgy of the Palms and the Liturgy of the Passion occupy the same stage, their dramas unfolding so close in proximity that we can scarcely make the emotional shift. Celebration and praise converge with loss and grief; strength and vulnerability share one liturgical moment, inviting us to shout "Hosanna!" while also bracing ourselves for the poignancy of the crucifixion and the mourning that follows. The Liturgy of the Palms punctuates the moment with a call to communal faith, courageous proclamation, and conspicuous action as we consider again our shared identity as the church and community of faith.

The communal emphasis is unmistakable. It reveals the uncommon courage of common folk who have experienced a presence so powerful, a message so compelling, and a love so complete that they transgress the boundaries of religious and civil acceptability to make the journey to Jerusalem with Jesus. Many of them live in the villages and towns outside of Jerusalem. Others have traveled from as far away as Jericho, sorely needing the life-sustaining sustenance that Jesus so freely gave. His ministry has captured their imagination and nourished their souls as they

⁶The disciples went and did as Jesus had directed them; ⁷they brought the donkey and the colt, and put their cloaks on them, and he sat on them. ⁸A very large crowd spread their cloaks on the road, and others cut branches from the trees and spread them on the road. ⁹The crowds that went ahead of him and that followed were shouting,

"Hosanna to the Son of David!
 Blessed is the one who comes in the name of the Lord!
 Hosanna in the highest heaven!"

¹⁰When he entered Jerusalem, the whole city was in turmoil, asking, "Who is this?" ¹¹The crowds were saying, "This is the prophet Jesus from Nazareth in Galilee."

Exegetical Perspective

The triumphal entry into Jerusalem is to the crowds what Caesarea Philippi is to Peter: their confession that Jesus is the Messiah. Calling him a "prophet" (Matt. 21:11; cf. 16:13–14), their shouts suggest that they recognize in Jesus the fulfillment of Jewish messianic expectations. This affirmation sets the stage for the escalating conflict between Jesus and the Jerusalem authorities.

"The crowds" function as a character in Matthew, as disciples en masse. They appear at the beginning of Jesus' ministry, coming to him from all around the region (4:25). By the end of the Sermon on the Mount, they are listening to his teaching (7:28–29; cf. 13:2). They are repeatedly astounded at his authority (7:28–29; 9:8; 22:33) as they see his capacity to heal the sick (12:15; 14:14; 15:30; 19:2), and they are amazed when he casts out demons, noting that "never has anything like this been seen in Israel" (9:33). They begin to wonder whether Jesus might be the Son of David (12:23). Before the triumphal entry, the crowds have had their bellies filled—twice!—with just a few loaves of bread and a couple of fish (14:13–21 and 15:32–39). Perhaps it is not surprising, then, that they show such enthusiasm when Jesus rides into the city. Heightening the significance of the procession is the fact that it begins at the Mount of Olives (21:1), the traditional

Homiletical Perspective

"Two processions entered Jerusalem on a spring day in the year 30," write biblical scholars Marcus Borg and John Dominic Crossan in their book titled *The Last Week*: *What the Gospels Really Teach about Jesus' Final Days in Jerusalem*. They continue by contrasting the two processions, one from the east largely composed of peasants, following a certain Jesus from Galilee riding a donkey down the Mount of Olives. On the opposite side of the city, from the west approaches the Roman governor, Pontius Pilate, entering the city on a war horse at the head of a column of imperial cavalry and soldiers. He has come from Caesarea Maritima for the purpose of maintaining law and order during the potentially tumultuous days of the Jewish festival of Passover. "Jesus' procession proclaimed the kingdom of God," the authors note, while Pilate's proclaimed the "power of empire," thereby embodying the "central conflict of the week that led to Jesus' crucifixion."

The Roman procession is Borg's and Crossan's imaginary historical reconstruction based on nonbiblical sources. However, it serves well, as they intended, the purpose of accentuating the political dimensions of what they go so far as to call the "prearranged 'counter procession'" of Jesus and his followers into a city made tense by the heightened sensitivities of what they claim may have been as

Matthew 21:1-11

Theological Perspective

Matthew's Gospel reflects early Christian identification of Jesus as Messiah. This evangelist magnifies the continuities of God's work of salvation in the history and Scriptures of Israel and in Jesus and the community of believers in him. Viewing events associated with Jesus through the lens of the law and the prophets and, vice versa, viewing Scriptures in light of the "career" of Jesus and its aftermath are evident throughout the Gospel. Selective by necessity and design, this process leads to an account involving theological decisions about what sort of messiah is meant; which of the numerous, diverse, even conflicting, messianic expectations are apt; and how the Messiah's coming is made manifest.

Jesus' entry to Jerusalem is recounted in Matthew as messianic and triumphal. Its details are formed by allusions and quotations to Scriptures bearing on messianic hopes and important pilgrimage festivals. In scenes before, the city was to bring death, the Messiah was to die, that the hour had come. Jesus made preparation to enter on an ass and a foal, in fulfillment of chapter 20. The incident itself is an explicit, bold messianic claim. The narrative leaves no doubt of the situation: Jesus plans and carries out a messianic entry, the crowd rejoices and acclaims his arrival, those threatened by the rule of God's Messiah, including hegemonic Rome, ratchet up their security measures.

Bold and explicit are contrasts with expectancies of messianic lordship—chief among them pomp, ceremony, splendor, and the shock and awe of destructive power. In contrast with the reception given kings, Zechariah 9:9 specifies humble or gentle, a donkey and a colt. If *this* Jesus is the Messiah, many of the most popular and uplifting messianic expectations fall by the wayside. This is played out further as predictions of suffering and death told of beforehand follow thereafter.

Recalling scriptural images of great lords and the experience of Rome's triumphal marches, these contrasts represent a form of theological parody. The text encourages such a thought. Considering how Jesus arranged for his mount(s) and the cry "This is the prophet of Nazareth," the precedents of exaggerated, even bizarre, symbolic actions akin to street theatre associated with prophets like Isaiah and Jeremiah come to mind. Theological commentators today have good cause to think of how this passage is a reminder that God's ways are not those of "this world." Lordship, indeed even messianic lordship, is here defined in terms of servanthood. Gentleness, humility, peaceableness, mercy, and self-giving acts of

Pastoral Perspective

have followed him to open-plain revivals, supped at banquets in the fields, experienced his touch, witnessed his miracles, and listened for the gospel that he proclaimed. This moment, however, is different. Jesus' voice gives way to that of the community, an unremarkable company of friends and strangers who announce with unambiguous resolve that Jesus is the one for whom they have been waiting.

The sense of anticipation and excitement must be palpable as they begin this journey, flanking Jesus on all sides with no discernable concern for the potential danger. Surely they are aware that the religious leaders consider him an antagonist and the chief nemesis to their survival, yet the marchers' testimonial proclamation intensifies as they approach the city gates. Their hosannas echo throughout the mountainous region, for Jesus has become the undeniable expression of God's presence in the world. So emphatic is their cry that Matthew likens them to oracles announcing Zechariah's divine warrior who would ride into the city gates, not on a stallion as a messianic military leader, but on the back of a donkey and with peace and reconciliation for all nations in his mouth.

"Save us!" they cry out, creating a royal carpet of coats, cloaks, and tree branches for this proclaimer of good news. "Save us!" they shout, reminding us that the stain of division still permeates the fabric of our existence, thwarting our ability to live in peace and threatening our collective well-being. Almost instinctively, shouts of "Hosanna!" escape our lips, and we join this triumphal march, augmenting our Lenten commitment to self-examination with reflection upon the quality of our lives together. For peace and reconciliation become possible when common folk with uncommon courage oppose exclusionary practices and policies and together stand with "the one who comes in the name of the Lord" (v. 9).

History is replete with the stories of common folk who have recognized that we are able to accomplish more together than we can alone; stories that we might reclaim and rehearse as we continue our Lenten journey. They include the women and men who provided safe passage on the Underground Railroad for persons seeking freedom from chattel slavery in the United States in the mid-nineteenth century. Remember also Dietrich Bonhoeffer and others in the Confessing Church in the 1930s, who took a definitive stance that their loyalty was to Jesus as Lord, not to Hitler and the Nazis. Youths in South Africa stood against apartheid and formed the African National Congress Youth League in 1944 under the leadership

Exegetical Perspective

location whence the Messiah is expected to appear (see Zech. 14:1–11).

The question "Who is this?" and the crowds' response constitute an important modification that Matthew makes to Mark's account. Additional changes include (1) the insertion of a fulfillment prophecy, which highlights Jesus' kingship and places him in continuity with Jewish traditions; (2) the crowds' affirmation of Jesus as Son of David, echoing the opening verse of Matthew and further strengthening the messianic claim; and (3) the "turmoil" in the city at Jesus' arrival, which previews the earthquake at his crucifixion and heightens the cosmic import of the event.

Matthew's narrative includes a number of formula quotations from Israel's Scriptures, marked by the phrase "This took place to fulfill [or This was to fulfill] what had been spoken through the prophet" (e.g., 1:22; 2:15; 8:17). The quotations emphasize Jesus' continuity with and fulfillment of Jewish messianic expectations. In our passage, the formula quotation (v. 5) is a composite from Isaiah and Zechariah, proclaiming the salvation that attends the arrival of the king. In its original context, the first part of the quotation—"Tell the daughter of Zion"—continues with the phrase "See, your salvation comes" (Isa. 62:11b). The original prophecy looks ahead to God's vindication of the holy city, Jerusalem, and to the promise of redemption, expectations that are carried forward by Matthew's quotation.

The latter part of the quotation comes from Zechariah 9:9. Its original context is an oracle concerning the Lord's defeat of enemies and the restoration of Israel, and it portrays God in the image of the victorious, peaceful king entering the city. Matthew renders a literal interpretation of the oracle by suggesting the odd picture of Jesus riding on the backs of the donkey *and* the colt ("he sat on them," v. 7). In any case, the mundane act of borrowing a "ride" from a local villager takes on heightened significance by its connection to these OT prophecies of salvation and restoration. Not only does Jesus enter Jerusalem like a victorious king; he does so under the banner of God in order to bring about the redemption of God's people. There will be a cost, of course—he has already told the disciples about his impending death (20:17–29)—but, for now, that horrifying reality is pushed into the background as the crowds wave branches and spread garments on the road in a first-century version of the ticker-tape parade.

Matthew's opening line identifies Jesus as "the Messiah, the son of David, the son of Abraham" (1:1).

Homiletical Perspective

many as 200,000 pilgrims crowding into the holy city of maybe just 40,000 regular inhabitants.[1]

Their portrait stands in resistance to the temptation to allow the church's liturgical entrance upon the awful events of Holy Week to become merely a frivolous Fourth of July parade with palms instead of flags. "All Glory, Laud, and Honor" simply sings more authentically, if pointedly, as the church's marching song as we remember that it is sung to Jesus and not the emperor as our "redeemer king." It is far more akin to "We Shall Overcome" or "Lift Every Voice and Sing," the church's songs of protest and resistance, than it is to "My Country, 'Tis of Thee" or "God Bless America." Enlivening the political context of the church's procession of palms is authorized by the words following last week's text, which spoke so ominously of Jesus' opponents' felt need to appease their Roman overlords by plotting his "expedient" death (John 11:50 RSV).

Matthew himself attests that when Jesus entered Jerusalem, the whole city "was in turmoil" (v. 10), using a strong Greek word that literally means "was shaken" or "trembled" (a word most Californians know all too well, as it is the root of "seismic"). Further, in answer to the tumultuous question "Who is this?" Matthew reports that the crowds' answer was, "This is the prophet Jesus from Nazareth in Galilee" (v. 11). This answer is underlined by Matthew's citation of the prophecy of Zechariah 9:9–10, in which the triumphant king's advent is portrayed as that of a peaceful monarch "humble and riding on a donkey, on a colt, the foal of a donkey" who will "cut off the chariot from Ephraim and the war-horse from Jerusalem."

This prophetic contrast between donkey and war horse only serves to heighten the irony of Jesus' nonviolent procession into the city. The welcoming crowd had access only to their own cloaks and branches cut from trees to carpet his way as they marked his progress with shouts of "Hosanna to the Son of David." "Hosanna" is one of those rare Aramaic words we find in the Gospels (Matthew, Mark, and John, but not Luke) and only in connection with Jesus' procession into Jerusalem. "Hosanna" is an exclamation of praise that literally means "save (or help), I pray," an appeal that became a liturgical exclamation for the church, after having long been familiar to Jews as a part of the Hallel liturgy (see

---

1. Marcus J. Borg and John Dominic Crossan, *The Last Week: What the Gospels Really Teach about Jesus' Final Days in Jerusalem* (San Francisco: HarperSanFrancisco, 2006), 2–4. Robert H. Smith anticipates Borg's and Crossan's imagining of a double procession from the east and the west in *Proclamation 5, Series A: Holy Week* (Minneapolis: Fortress Press, 1992), 7.

Matthew 21:1-11

Theological Perspective

generosity and compassion are marks of God's domain.

Along with this cycle of reflection, a more or less customary part of Christian thinking about this text, there is a second stroke. It is less often pursued, not always very vigorously, but it is too near at hand and too important to be ignored. It arises within Christian theology when Christians seek to take seriously whether and how reflection on the *otherness* of God's ways, as dramatized in this contra-triumphalist triumphal march of Jesus the gentle king, applies to the many, diverse, and even conflicting messianic expectations of *Christians* themselves.

The line of inquiry might begin by recalling that the Jesus who enters Jerusalem *was* and always *is* a challenge to this world's powers and principalities— not merely a spiritual challenge but a political challenge as well. His cause is not the same as that of the Zealots or any violent insurrectionists, that of some aspiring political party, or that of a legislative or executive agenda. Nevertheless, this "king Jesus" is a threat, both to the power elite and the fickle multitude. Jesus did not come "in triumph," was not crucified and raised, and communities of believers in him did not emerge, in order to leave the ways of the world as they were. However, some theologies have interpreted the domain of his messianic rule as the individual soul alone, not this world but "the next."

The text calls alternative thoughts to mind. This has often been so in theology's history. Some Christians, in writings ranging from martyrologies before Constantine to today's varied social, political, liberation, and postcolonial theologies, have undertaken to consider that the spontaneous people's protest celebrating the arrival of this Jesus, prophet of Nazareth, as the gentle king was altogether justified.

His messianic cause is *not* like that of imperial Rome, its puppet-government cronies, compliant court prophets, propagandists, and hangers-on. Hence his cause is not well served when power politics runs its course and the world's business continues as usual, even if baptized Christians replace Matthew's cast of characters. Visioning and promoting a social world, here and now, in keeping with the character and way of the one called "God with us" is a continuing theological task.

JAMES O. DUKE

Pastoral Perspective

of Nelson Mandela, envisioning a world in which racial domination would no longer exist.

Many others join these exemplars of uncommon courage, including the 250,000 women, men, and children from diverse racial, ethnic, social, and religious backgrounds who gathered in the U.S. capital on August 28, 1963, anchored in an abiding faith in God's gift of justice and human dignity. Like those who walked the dusty road to Jerusalem with Jesus, many of them made the pilgrimage at great personal risk, yet they marched to condemn the systemically oppressive laws that divided the nation.

At the conclusion of his now-famous "I Have a Dream" speech, the Rev. Dr. Martin Luther King Jr. articulated his dream of a people united and a world in which justice would become the normative expression of human relationship. With him, the crowd and numerous others who watched from living rooms and gathering places throughout the nation refused to "wallow in the valley of despair" but, rather, dreamed in the face of insurmountable odds and stood as prophets of a new creation.[1]

We remember these stories and others so that we may find the courage to march with Jesus and proclaim a word of peace and reconciliation, despite our location among the common folk. After all, Jesus' followers possessed no formal authority to change their world, but neighbor and friend, stranger and distant traveler, children and adults marched into the city gates with Jesus to contest the exclusionary practices that had so long defined their existence. When asked "Who is this?" they replied, "This is the prophet Jesus from Nazareth in Galilee" (v. 11).

This disturbed the religious leaders, as verse 46 reveals, but Matthew does not tell us why. Perhaps the fervor of the moment forecast a time when common folk standing on the side of justice would become a recurrent theme in the world. Maybe they were concerned that people would begin to sense their own deep yearning for a just and life-affirming existence. Perhaps the image of Jesus as prophet invites us in this liturgical moment to embody peace and reconciliation as an ongoing practice and stand boldly with "the one who comes in the name of the Lord" (v. 9).

VERONICE MILES

---

1. Martin Luther King Jr., "I Have a Dream," in *The Norton Anthology of African American Literature,* ed. Henry Louis Gates Jr. and Nellie Y. McKay (New York: W. W. Norton & Co., 1997), 80.

Exegetical Perspective

Characters within the narrative make a similar claim, addressing Jesus as "Son of David," particularly in conjunction with his acts of healing (e.g., 9:27; 15:22; 20:30).[1] On one occasion, after he casts out a demon from a man who is blind and mute, the crowds are amazed and ask, "Can this be the son of David?" (12:22–23). Their question is not simply a round-about way of suggesting that Jesus has a good Jewish pedigree (which he does), nor does it imply only that he is a king as important as David (which he is).

In Matthew's narrative, the acclamation of Jesus as son of David is a messianic assertion; even the Pharisees affirm that the Messiah is David's son (22:41–42). So when the crowds shout, "Hosanna! [literally, "Save us"] to the Son of David!" they are celebrating the arrival of their messianic savior, "the one who comes in the name of the Lord" (21:9; cf. Ps. 118:25–26). Their response does not escape the notice of the chief priests and the scribes, whose anger is roused when the children in the temple add their own "Hosannas" to those of the cheering crowds (21:15–16).

By the time Jesus and his entourage enter Jerusalem, the whole city is "in turmoil" (*seiō*, tremble). The verb and its cognate noun refer to the earthquakes at Jesus' final breath upon the cross (27:51; cf. 27:54) and at the appearance of the angel at the empty tomb (28:2). The shaking of the earth is associated with the "day of the Lord" (Joel 2:10–11) and with the presence of God (Ps. 67:8; cf. Job 9:6; Isa. 13:13; Ezek. 38:20; etc.). Although the people of Jerusalem do not fully comprehend the significance of Jesus' arrival (they are asking who he is, Matt. 21:10), their reaction to him is fitting; when the Messiah comes, it is an earthshaking event. Although the crowds will change their tune at the trial, calling for Pilate to crucify Jesus, for now, at his entry into the city, they seem to recognize that Jesus is the one for whom they have been waiting.

AUDREY WEST

Homiletical Perspective

Ps. 118:25), accompanied by the waving of branches at the feast of Tabernacles.

Delores Dufner, OSB, has written a hymn that is becoming widely sung at the end of the liturgical year on Reign of Christ Sunday but that is equally appropriate for today:

> O Christ, what can it mean for us to claim you as
>   our king?
> What royal face have you revealed whose praise the
>   church would sing?
> Aspiring not to glory's height, to power, wealth and
>   fame,
> You walked a diff'rent, lowly way, another's will your
>   aim.[2]

The hymn's opening question simmers at the heart of today's Palm Sunday text: just who is this Jesus—this latter-day prophet from Nazareth in Galilee? It will take the events of the succeeding week fully to answer this question, but a good start toward an answer is implicit in the crowd's shouts of "Hosanna!" which we the church echo in today's recital of Psalm 118 to the waving of our own palm branches. Here our singing, as well our body language, can best be understood in the context of the Jewish Passover liturgy called the haggadah, which reminds its participants:

> It was not only our fathers whom the Holy One, Blessed is He, redeemed from slavery; we, too, were redeemed from slavery; . . . Therefore it is our duty to thank, praise, pay tribute, glorify, exalt, honor, bless, extol and acclaim Him Who performed all these miracles for our fathers and for us.[3]

Our Holy Week liturgies are rooted in this strong Jewish sense of the present faith community's being re-membererd ritually into God's ongoing, liberating action. So begins the church's annual reentry onto the events of Holy Week by marking how the empire of God, whose nearness Jesus came to proclaim and embody, looks to welcome quite "a diff'rent kind of king" indeed.

JOHN ROLLEFSON

---

1. The phrase "son of David" occurs more frequently in Matthew than in Mark and Luke combined.

2. Delores Dufner, "O Christ, What Can It Mean for Us," in *Evangelical Lutheran Worship* (Minneapolis: Augsburg Fortress, 2006), #431.
3. See The *Family Haggadah* (New York: Artscroll/Mesorah, 2008), 45, 47.

Isaiah 50:4-9a

> ⁴The Lord God has given me
>   the tongue of a teacher,
> that I may know how to sustain
>   the weary with a word.
> Morning by morning he wakens—
>   wakens my ear
>   to listen as those who are taught.
> ⁵The Lord God has opened my ear,
>   and I was not rebellious,
>   I did not turn backward.
> ⁶I gave my back to those who struck me,
>   and my cheeks to those who pulled out the beard;

Theological Perspective

In this passage we read Second Isaiah's attempt to describe the prophetic experience. Unlike Jeremiah, who lamented that God smoldered like a fire in his bones whenever he resisted bearing the prophetic message, Isaiah is a seasoned journeyman who knows the routine and trusts it. He understands that his power of speech is a gift from God. When he exercises it, he can console or he can agitate his listeners. He is not an automaton; while he acknowledges that his incisive tongue is a gift from God, he also gives himself credit for knowing when and how to use it.

Those who receive divine instruction, according to Isaiah, have their ears awakened by God each morning. Revelation requires more than evocative words; one must also have ears to hear, and this too depends upon God's initiative. In his commentary on this passage, Martin Luther suggests that this accounts for why the words of Scripture, which have inherent power, do not always entice those who hear them to believe. For the Word of God to be effective, for revelation to occur, there must be "a most harmonious relationship between the learned tongue, the ready ear, and the heart prepared for learning." If any of these three things is missing, the circuit will not be complete. Worse, as Luther concludes: "The Enthusiasts indeed have stirred up ears but exceedingly unlearned tongues. They are quite ready even to hear

Pastoral Perspective

This powerful passage in Isaiah describes an intimate relationship between God and the writer. God personally whispers in the listener's ear what God needs for the listener to learn. This instruction is a revelation from God that provides not only divine wisdom but also the ability to use this wisdom to teach and care for the "weary." The instruction occurs not just once but continues "morning by morning." God "wakens [the] ear to listen" and teaches wisdom and compassion.

We might ask ourselves, Have our ears ever been wakened by God? Are there occasions when God has felt this available and personal in our lives? Are we open to such experiences with God? There are many occasions in both the Hebrew Bible and the New Testament where God speaks directly or indirectly (through another or visions and dreams) to individuals and communities. God spoke to Moses, David, Jonah, the prophets, Mary, the magi, and Paul, among others. Certainly over the several centuries since Jesus was incarnate among us, many have experienced a personal relationship with the Spirit of God.

Two spiritual themes of this passage in Isaiah are "listening for God" and "listening to God." Generally we first listen *for* God and then listen *to* God. In other words, first, we become aware of God's presence and experience openness to God's love and

I did not hide my face
  from insult and spitting.

⁷The Lord GOD helps me;
  therefore I have not been disgraced;
  therefore I have set my face like flint,
    and I know that I shall not be put to shame;
⁸ he who vindicates me is near.
  Who will contend with me?
    Let us stand up together.
  Who are my adversaries?
    Let them confront me.
⁹It is the Lord GOD who helps me;
  who will declare me guilty?

Exegetical Perspective

The third of the Suffering Poems, sometimes called Songs (Isa. 42:1–9; 49:1–7; 50:4–11; 52:13–53:12), inspires no clear consensus on the identity of the Servant. Further, there is no scholarly consensus regarding the historical context of the passages. The major structural strategy in the passage is to move between the description of Lord God (vv. 4, 5a, 7a, 9a) and the self-description of the actions of the Servant (vv. 4b, 5b–6, 7b–8).

The English word "disciple" comes from the Old English word *discipul* from the Latin *discupulus,* from the verb *discere,* to learn. The speaker self-designates the role of "teacher" according to the NRSV. An alternative reading is "one who is taught." On one level this is about socialization. The range of meaning indicates the writer's implicit assertion that the teacher must first be taught. The word occurs in four other places in the Hebrew Bible (Jer. 2:24; 13:23; Isa. 8:16; 54:13). The term in the book of Jeremiah is emphasized as a metaphor for socialization. The book of Jeremiah seems to accent the socialization function more than the teacher/disciple model. Thirdly, the term is used to describe an undomesticated equine, "a wild ass at home in the wilderness" (Jer. 2:24). Finally, the most famous parallel use of this term is found in Jeremiah 13. Here we find the famous saying "Can Ethiopians change their skin or

Homiletical Perspective

Anonymity characterizes the first reading of Holy Week. This day of Palm and Passion begins with the words of the nameless prophet of the Babylonian exile, Second Isaiah, who in turn puts these verses on the lips of an equally nameless figure known as "God's Servant." Our reading is the third of a four-part "song" cycle. Here the Servant sings of suffering and solace, while confessing courage and confidence in the Lord. This song captures both the warm, supportive relationship between the Servant and the Lord, and the threatening, violent relationship between the Servant and an anonymous "those."

It also records the Servant's awareness of what God *has* done, *is* doing, and *will* do for the Servant. At the outset the setting is quite peaceful and congenial, noting the Servant's awareness of the gift of "the tongue of a teacher," given by the Lord "to sustain the weary with a word" (v. 4). In speaking of what God *is* doing, the Servant refers to how the Lord rouses the Servant "morning by morning," a gentle awakening, so that the Servant begins each day as a learner. The Lord God is constant, giving instruction. It all sounds like having residence on a serene campus with a benign, if overeager, instructor. The Servant is appropriately obedient and open, no rebel here, no turning away.

This is followed by a sudden change of scene and mood: "I gave my back to those who struck me, and

Isaiah 50:4-9a

Theological Perspective

lies, but they cannot keep their tongues from fighting against the Word."[1]

The image of the ear that must be wakened to hear what God has to teach it appears to corroborate the theological doctrine of prevenient grace. Prevenient grace is grace by which God initiates the turning of a person's will toward Godself. Augustine insisted that even though one may hear a divine word from the most golden-tongued preacher or even from an angel, in order for this word to be received as life-changing truth, the hearer's mind must be "internally besprinkled with that light . . . which shines even in darkness." At the deepest level, in other words, the rebellious human will must be made pliant *by* God. Augustine writes, "Our turning to God is not possible except God rouses and helps us . . . what have we that we have not received?"[2]

That this wakening must be initiated by God "morning by morning" adds emphasis, and one can find here a view consistent with Karl Barth's insistence in *Church Dogmatics*, I/1 that the Bible becomes the Word of God only in the moment that God speaks to one through it. Words that have proven trustworthy as bearers of revelation in the past can be so only in those moments when our ears are attuned by God. Barth compares the Bible to the pool of Bethesda, which becomes a means of healing only in those passing instants when its waters are divinely stirred.

Something striking about Second Isaiah's yeomanly understanding of revelation (God trains the tongue and attunes the ears of the prophet, who then proclaims the word of God to others—whose ears must also be awakened, we can presume, if this is to be a Word of God to them) is how far it is from the spectacular way God conveyed divine words in earlier times. True, First Isaiah once notoriously dramatized the coming Assyrian conquest of Egypt and Ethiopia by walking naked in Jerusalem for three years. That was nothing compared to the great, numinous spectacles of the burning bush, Mount Sinai, the pillar of fire in the wilderness, or the cloud that descended upon the Holy of Holies.

With Second Isaiah's more mundane understanding of how God reaches out to us, we are taught to value our capacity to hear above our capacity to see. Isaiah invites us not to look (spectate) for God in the

1. Martin Luther, *Luther's Works*, vol. 17: *Lectures on Isaiah*, ed. J. J. Pelikan (St. Louis: Concordia Publishing House, 1972), 194.
2. Augustine, "A Treatise on the Merits and Forgiveness of Sins, and on the Baptism of Infants," in *Nicene and Post-Nicene Fathers*, vol. 5, first series, ed. Philip Schaff (Edinburgh: T.&T. Clark, 1887, 1987), 1.37 and 2.31.

Pastoral Perspective

guidance, and then we can hear and act on a divine revelation. Think of the many ways that God can be present to us, including worship, meditation, in our personal relationships with family and friends, in our vocations and avocations, in nature, in science, in the arts. God comes to us personally in unexpected and surprising ways.

Listening for God. Listening for God is a spiritual practice. Part of this spiritual practice is learning to wait for God. Waiting for God's presence may help us learn the practice of patience. Today's world does not abound in patience. We have little incentive or practice to wait for anything. So how do we learn to wait for God? The traditional Quaker worship service of sitting in silence and waiting for the Spirit to speak is an excellent model for learning to listen for God. An important part of this experience is not only to gain patience in waiting for the Spirit, but also to develop a discerning ear when we experience the Spirit's presence. J. Brent Bill, in his book *Holy Silence: The Gift of Quaker Spirituality*, says, "This holy hush [silence] is about meeting Jesus in an intimate way. Quaker silence encourages us to relax into the love of God until we hear the Spirit's voice whispering softly in our soul's ear."[1]

There are certainly times when we do not have to listen for God because God makes the presence of the divine quite obvious to us without any effort on our part. Paul's journey to Damascus is an example of the sudden, explosive presence of God. Saul thought he was doing the will of God by persecuting Christians, but in an unexpected and forceful way Saul's life was turned around. Saul's transformation included waiting, blindness, dependence on others, and a messenger from God who assisted in bringing forth a new man. God's great love for Saul/Paul made his presence and message available in a way that allowed Paul to live a completely different life.

God's presence may come to us in an awareness of holy company, an awareness that brings fear, confusion, and transformation, as it did for Paul, or the feelings of peace and comfort for daily living. The spiritual practice of listening for God teaches us to develop a willingness to wait for an awareness of the Spirit's presence and to be open to being surprised by God in new, exciting ways.

Listening to God. Listening to God is also a spiritual practice. Once we are open and aware of God's

1. J. Brent Bill, *Holy Silence: The Gift of Quaker Spirituality* (Brewster, MA: Paraclete Press, 2006), 6–7.

leopards their spots?" (Jer.13:23). "Then also you can do good who are accustomed to evil" (Jer. 13:23). However, the use of the term as a cipher for socialization pays no attention to the role of choice.

In contrast, the book of Isaiah emphasizes discipleship as a choice. The book functions as a persuasive document. A human disciple usually chooses whom to follow. Nevertheless, the tongue of the teacher is at the same time the tongue of the instructed one. The use of the term in parallel text undergirds such an observation. The same Hebrew term is translated as "disciple" elsewhere (see Isa. 8:16). The term occurs also in Isaiah 54:13. There as well it may be translated as disciple, for instance "All your children shall be disciples of the LORD." However, the term connotes more than a bucolic teacher and disciples; it point to the varieties of learning situations.

An overarching theme of Isaiah 40–66 is the restoration of the people. The "disciple's tongue" is to support this mission. The Servant must know how to sustain the object of the divine mission. The mission includes the relief of the weary. The term "weary" occurs often in the restoration period. It figures prominently in Isaiah 40 (vv. 28, 29, 30, 31).

The counterpoint to "weary" is the verb "awaken." The same verb is used to describe an eagle (Deut. 32:11). God is the subject of the verb as well (see Job 8:6). However, sometimes "rouse" can have a negative connotation. But the Deity does not rouse divine anger (Ps. 78:38). It is human arrogance that provides a context for divine arousal to anger (Isa. 42:13). The verb "arouse" is like the use of smelling salts. The ammonia carbonate wakes up a person who has been edging into unconsciousness. So God startles the exiles to new consciousness.

The tongue of the disciple is paralleled to divine opening of the ear. Not only does the phrase "opening the ear" hark back to the reference earlier in the poem; it introduces the profession of innocence in the second half of verse 5. The profession of innocence builds through the use of synonymous parallelism with, "I was not rebellious, and I did not turn backward." The verb "rebel" dominates the narratives of the wilderness wandering. The profession of innocence in Isaiah 50:5 stands in stark contrast to the confession of rebellion in Lamentations (1:18, 20).

Verse 6 expands on the profession of devotion started in verse 5. The writer provides three expressions of access: "opened my ear," "I was not rebellious," "I did not turn backward." The Servant manifests the counterintuitive move in the light of attack. The Servant understands this counterintuitive

my cheeks to those who pulled out the beard: I did not hide my face from insult and spitting" (v. 6). What has happened? Where did "they" come from? We do not know. Even so, the Lord is there with the Servant, supporting, so that the Servant has not been disgraced, but instead has the courage to bear what is happening. Finally, referring to the future, the Servant knows that "I shall not be put to shame; [the One] who vindicates me is near" (v. 7). God will stand in solidarity with this faithful Servant.

Scholars do not know with any certainty who this figure of the Servant is, whether a particular prophetic individual or an idealized Israel. However, we can easily see why the church finds it applicable to Jesus and particularly appropriate for entering Holy Week. First of all, it highlights Jesus the teacher, who first listens, ever attentive to the voice and will of the Father, who came preaching and teaching with a special concern for the weary and the poor, "proclaiming the good news of the kingdom and curing every disease and every sickness among the people" (Matt. 4:23), calling out to all who were weary and carrying heavy burdens, "Take my yoke upon you, and learn from me; for I am gentle and humble in heart, and you will find rest for your souls. For my yoke is easy, and my burden is light" (Matt. 11:29–30).

Again and again in Matthew's Gospel, Jesus is presented as the teacher, going up the mountain with his disciples and teaching them about the kingdom of heaven (Matt. 5–7), instructing the Twelve about the mission (Matt. 10:5–42), teaching and proclaiming his message in the cities (Matt. 11:1), teaching in parables (Matt. 13:3–53), and so on. Throughout the Gospel, Jesus teaches through his discourses, his parables, and his deeds.

Even as we listen to Matthew's passion being read, we hear during his last hours the voice of the teacher, instructing the apostles at the Last Supper on the suffering that lies ahead that will shake their faith (Matt. 26:31), on the importance of praying so that they "may not come into the time of trial," (Matt. 26:41), and, as he faces the violence of his enemies, urging them not to yield to violence, "for all who take the sword will perish by the sword," and teaching that all is being done so the Scriptures are fulfilled (Matt. 26:52, 54). Most striking of all, Jesus instructs both the high priest as to who he is in relation to God and how he will be seen as the "Son of Man seated at the right hand of Power and coming on the clouds of heaven" (Matt. 26:64) and, in a most succinct fashion, the Roman governor as to his status among his own people: the "King of the Jews" (Matt. 27:11).

Isaiah 50:4–9a

Isaiah 50:4-9a

Theological Perspective

spectacular, but to elevate the sense of hearing as the premier means of receiving divine guidance and wisdom. The majesty of God has now settled upon this very unremarkable but faithful servant—whether as the individual Isaiah or as Israel itself ("You are my servant, Israel, in whom I will be glorified"; Isa. 49:3).

John Calvin's reading of this passage is interesting. He first acknowledges that as a piece of the Suffering Servant material in Isaiah, these verses are typically related to Christ, but he prefers to zoom out and see them as a template for what characterizes the experience of *all* faithful servants of God. He frames these verses as queries for those who believe they are called to be ministers of the word, and thereby offers the following counsel: they must balance diligent study with supplication to the Spirit of God "so as not to ascend the pulpit until they have been fully prepared." They must be clear that their first duty is to console the afflicted, "to point out what is true rest and serenity of mind," to "soothe wretched men by appropriate consolation, that by means of it their dejected hearts may be encouraged by feeling the mercy of God."

Calvin interprets the "opening of the ear" to consist both in the reception of true understanding and in a movement of the heart (will). This is the import of the confession "I was not rebellious" following immediately after "the Lord GOD has opened my ear" (v. 5). He continues, one ought not be surprised that if God's word is conveyed faithfully, its bearer will be "exposed to a contest with the world." Finally, he advises that those who present themselves as ministers of the word confirm in the inner chambers of their consciences that their calling is genuine, or else they will not be vindicated by God when their adversaries confront them.[3]

KELTON COBB

Pastoral Perspective

presence, we gain experience in the many ways that God communicates with us and opens abundant space for a rich and loving relationship. God teaches us and gives us the ability to hear, understand, and use divine messages.

A popular form of art both nationally and internationally is the art of the contemporary folk artist. Some of these artists are also known as "visionary artists," because they have had a message or vision from God telling them to make religious art.

The Reverend Howard Finster, perhaps the best-known contemporary visionary artist, received a direct message from God to "paint God's pictures." Finster had for years been a bivocational preacher and fixed small machines such as bicycles and lawn mowers. When Finster was sixty, God told him to stop fixing bicycles and lawn mowers and to "paint my pictures." He listened to God's message and became a prolific artist. During the next thirty years of his life he painted many pictures depicting Bible stories, and through these paintings he taught of God's love, care, and saving grace.

The spiritual practice of listening to God goes beyond just intellectually hearing God's words. We must hear God's message with our hearts, so that we will be able to respond to the needs of others. It is important not just to understand God's message but to use our new wisdom for personal and community spiritual growth.

The writer of this passage from Isaiah experienced the joy of a direct revelation and teaching from God and learned through God's teaching to care for others. This faithful response endangered the writer physically, emotionally, and spiritually. However, there was such a strong connection and relationship with God that the abusive treatment received from others could not persuade the writer to abandon this faithful response. As we listen for God and listen to God, we must remember that God does not just teach and ask for a response to the gift of new wisdom. God also promises to remain faithful and supportive as we act on this new wisdom by caring for the weary.

KATHERINE E. AMOS

---

3. John Calvin, *Commentary on the Book of the Prophet Isaiah*, trans. William Pringle (Edinburgh: Calvin Translation Society, 1850), 333–39.

behavior as an expression of devotion and trust in God. These expressions of voluntary vulnerability are not just painful; they also reflect a willingness to be humiliated. The ritual act of shaming and spitting (v. 6) conveys the debasement of the servant. Verse 7 outlines why this counterintuitive behavior is reasonable. The divine election contradicts any expression of humiliation as described in verse 6.

When the NRSV has the Servant say "He who vindicates me is near" (v. 8a), the reader is invited to ponder the function of a vindicator. The Hebrew behind this translation is the participle form from the verb "to make righteous." The vindicator proves to the wider public that the Servant is in the right. Peterson renders this as "champion" (*The Message*). The statement of the proximity frames the statement of trust. The statement of trust contains two rhetorical questions and their cohortative taunts. The first rhetorical question (who will contend with me? v. 8b) uses the verb "bring a covenant lawsuit." The lawsuit makes the metaphor of standing as a plaintiff quite reasonable in this depiction of a juridical proceeding. The taunting cohortative, "let us stand together," acts as a rebuke. The Hebrew "who is ruler of my judgment?" is rendered by the NRSV as "who are my adversaries?" (v. 8d). The NRSV decision to render the Hebrew as "let them confront me" (v. 8e) allows the reader to perceive how the text is using space to accent the conflict. The verbs "stand" and "draw near/ confront" describe a context of intense, close-at-hand conflict.

The final section of the passage concludes this self-disclosure of prophetic authority. None of the ideas in verse 9 is new to the unit. Rather, they reinforce the previous moves in the passage. For instance, the Servant's disclosure that the Lord God is the Servant's indispensible help echoes verse 7. The next section of verse 9 returns to the question as a rhetorical device, as in verse 8. The structure of the passage allows the careful reader to know the answer to the final rhetorical question, "who can declare me guilty?" (v. 9b). Nobody!

STEPHEN BRECK REID

In Matthew's Gospel, Jesus of Nazareth is the teacher—and student—of the way and will of the Father, and the Father, in turn, acknowledges him as such in the transfiguration event: "This is my Son, the Beloved; . . . listen to him" (Matt. 17:5). This Holy Week we remember how fully Jesus lived out the song of the Servant who listened to the Father, who taught a word to sustain the weary, whose words brought down upon him the wrath of those who were his adversaries, who gave his back and cheeks to those who struck him, allowed them to pull his beard, not hiding his face from insult or spitting, but who set his face like flint, knowing he would not be put to shame, and was finally vindicated by the Lord God of Israel, the Father of our redeemer Jesus Christ.

In his poem "Veni Creator" Czeslaw Milosz calls on the Holy Spirit to set before him one man, anywhere on earth, "and allow me when I look at him, to marvel at you."[1] Today's Scripture readings present that one man before us, God's Servant and Son, Jesus Christ. The song in which it sees his saving work mirrored is now the song of God's pilgrim people and all who continue to listen for God's instruction day by day and to engage in God's mission: to speak a word to sustain the weary and the brokenhearted, to work to protect the dignity of the immigrants and the homeless, and to care for the abused and the ignored. The world needs servants willing to carry out God's mission of justice, peace, and reconciliation, and to set their faces like flint, trusting in the God who vindicates and who will bring about the full coming of the kingdom of God.

JAMES A. WALLACE

1. Czeslaw Milosz, *The Collected Poems: 1931–1987* (Hopewell, NJ: Ecco Press, 1988), 194.

Psalm 31:9-16

9Be gracious to me, O LORD, for I am in distress;
  my eye wastes away from grief,
  my soul and body also.
10For my life is spent with sorrow,
  and my years with sighing;
  my strength fails because of my misery,
  and my bones waste away.

11I am the scorn of all my adversaries,
  a horror to my neighbors,
  an object of dread to my acquaintances;
  those who see me in the street flee from me.

Theological Perspective

Theology, meaning thought and words about God, is first, foremost, and finally a witness to the character of God. Of course, theologians and preachers have to and get to talk about many subjects, most of them having to do with the human situation. These are of interest, however, only if they hook up with and reflect on the character of God, as revealed and experienced.

Trustworthiness is the feature of the character of God which Psalm 31:9–16, appointed for the Liturgy of the Passion, stresses. Read and prayed on the Sunday whose Gospel story tells of Jesus' coming to Jerusalem in full knowledge, say the Gospels, that he will soon die there, sets up believers with a problem. If God is trustworthy, why should Jesus, who has bidden for trust in the one he called Father and in whom he placed trust, figure in our lives? Even in his case, that trust certainly seems to be broken, as evidenced near the story's end, when, again according to honest Gospel writers, he is heard to shout in agony, "My God, my God, why have you forsaken me?" Our problem, then, is this: if Jesus' trust was not rewarded with a long life of security and comfort, why should we, who must rank lower than he in God's reckoning, risk so much by placing trust in God?

We leave to the commentators on the Good Friday and other Holy Week Gospels the deeper reflections on the trust of Jesus in the plan of God. There

Pastoral Perspective

A number of us who are preachers today were raised in a time and in churches where the observance of Lent was vaguely suspect. A vigorous engagement with Lenten practices was thought to be too "Catholic." What we lost with this narrow understanding of our liturgical heritage was an opportunity to ground Palm Sunday in a meaningful pastoral context. Those of us raised in such an environment experienced Palm Sunday as a "pop-up." A dozen or so Sundays after Christmas, Palm Sunday arrived as something of a surprise, like the first daffodil through the dead leaves in a field otherwise still in winter slumber. To be sure, it was a welcome surprise—a sure sign of spring, a promise that baseball games and summer vacations were no longer unimaginably distant. Within this limited view, Palm Sunday's cheering crowds and happy disciples were perfect accessories for the occasion. Passion Sunday was nowhere on the radar screen.

"Be gracious to me, O LORD; for I am in distress; my eye wastes away from grief, my soul and my body also" (v. 9). The reading from Psalm 31 reconnects the Palms and the Passion. The reconnection is pastorally imperative. Without the Passion, the day runs the risk of imitating Jesus' parable of the Sower in Matthew 13, where some seeds immediately sprang up because they had no depth of soil, but when the

¹²I have passed out of mind like one who is dead;
   I have become like a broken vessel.
¹³For I hear the whispering of many—
      terror all around!—
   as they scheme together against me,
      as they plot to take my life.

¹⁴But I trust in you, O LORD;
   I say, "You are my God."
¹⁵My times are in your hand;
      deliver me from the hand of my enemies and persecutors.
¹⁶Let your face shine upon your servant;
      save me in your steadfast love.

Exegetical Perspective

Psalm 31 is an individual lament that moves, as the laments typically do, to thanksgiving and praise. The lectionary focuses on verses 9–16, given the liturgical context, but the most obvious resonance with Christ's passion (v. 5a, quoted in Luke 23:46), is not included in the reading. This suggests that preachers should not move to Christ or his death, at least not too quickly, and indicates that other aspects of the psalm (as well as the specific subunit, vv. 9–16) should also be considered.

Psalm 31 includes all the standard elements of lament psalmody: introduction/address (vv. 1–8), complaint (vv. 9b–13), petition (v. 9a), confession of trust (vv. 14–18), and vow to praise (vv. 19–24). However, the psalm intermixes these elements in important and artful ways. An obvious example is the reordering of the typical sequence of complaint-petition to petition (v. 9a), followed then by complaint (vv. 9b–13). In fact, close inspection reveals that several of the psalm's structural elements are not discretely delineated but blend into one another. So, for example, *petition* is found in verses 1b–2, 4a, 15b–18, as well as verse 9a; *confession of trust* is found in verses 3, 4b–5, 6b, in addition to verses 14–15a; and *the vow to praise* is present already in verses 7–8, anticipating verses 21–24. Such "mixings" do not necessarily undercut the significance of the structural

Homiletical Perspective

It is hard to imagine preaching this psalm as a stand-alone text on Passion Sunday. The eight verses selected to be read aloud are but a small sample of the psalm as a whole, and what is excluded is as interesting as what is included. Even a preacher who studiously avoids any passages that do not make it into the lectionary might mention that Jesus includes what the lectionary excludes: "Into your hand I commit my spirit" (Ps. 31:5; Luke 23:46). Our verses are but an episode in the longer story that is the psalm itself. It is, however, an episode that matches in tone the episode from the Gospel for the day. The chief reason not to preach the psalm alone, however, is this: the liturgy for Passion Sunday is designed specifically to center our attention on one thing, the story of the suffering and death of Jesus. Nothing should detract from the Gospel. Those who preach from the psalm on Passion Sunday would be well advised to observe the liturgical context carefully. In that light, the psalm may be treated as a poetic equivalent to the prose of the Gospel story.

Psalms speak with an enduring voice because it is possible imaginatively to identify with the "I" of the psalm. Here it is also possible to see Jesus as the "I" of the psalm. One homiletical strategy would be to interweave the words of the psalm with equivalents in the Gospel. It would be possible to do this

Psalm 31:9-16

Theological Perspective

are answers to the questions we just asked, but our own agenda is to turn to what we have called the human situation. Why did Jesus trust and commend trust? Why does a psalmist trust when nothing seems to be going right? We are back to that fundamental word about risking all on the witness to the character of God.

Most of us may take comfort by finding that Jesus' march to the cross calls forth more agonizing than any of us might encounter in the week ahead. One can almost hear a voice, "And you think you have got problems!" Muffle such a voice: comparing degrees of misery is worthless to someone who has just been diagnosed with a malignant tumor, said good-bye in memorial rites to a young wife, or felt the alienation of children or parents. Such a voice should discourage anyone from praying psalms like this one. Recall that nothing that was on the minds of hearers was too trivial in the eyes and ears of the one who bade, "Ask, and it will be given you" (Matt. 7:7). And they are to be disappointed?

Note well: if one wants to deal with the issues that nag, threaten, or have begun to devastate, turning to psalms like this one represents a good first step. For centuries, even millennia, people in the midst of suffering, doubt, or despair have uttered lines like these that describe the plight of the one who prays. They prayed it again and again and passed the prayer on to the succeeding generations. Something about it must be of help, since it is hard to conceive of those who confide in God all feeling abandoned or being fools. How did they get started?

Answer: exactly as this psalm begins. Those of us who have the sign "No Whining" on our desks or walls have to notice that this lament goes deeper than whining. Lamenting, in Christian theology, is designed to lay bare problems deeper than those whiners whine about. The yield from prayers like this psalm has to be much richer than the silence one gets when a positive thinker shushes with "Get over it!" Notice that in the depths, the fundamental tie is not broken. Verse 9 is hardly the voice of a mere whiner: "Be gracious to me, O LORD"; nor is the closing word in this text, verse 16: "Let your face shine upon your servant; save me in your steadfast love."

It is pointless to ask for grace from a graceless one, for the shining of a face from one who comes in scowling darkness, or for salvation from someone who is not loving "steadfastly," through thick or thin. This asking is most effective when it comes from someone who has long practiced what we might call "the conversation with God." We read and say and

Pastoral Perspective

sun had risen they were scorched (vv. 5–6). The Gospel narratives surely confirm this concern as they trace the disciples' movements from Palm Sunday through Good Friday on a trajectory from celebration to discouragement and desertion. Not only the disciples, but also Jesus himself is subject to this "distress"; more perceptive, perhaps, than his followers on Olivet, he is weeping even before the echo of the last "Hosanna" has faded from the hillside (see Luke 19:41–44). The Palms and the Passion are inseparable.

The reading from Psalm 31 reconnects the Palms and the Passion, first, by letting us hear the psalmist's deepening despair. Members of our congregation may be surprised—but also heartened—to hear a Palm Sunday text speak so plainly of the sorrow, sighing, and failing strength that they also endure (v. 10). By confessing his own misery, the psalmist gives us warrant to search within, to explore what the scholars might call the "interiority" of suffering. Ordinary folks do not need our erudition here. They know what it means when a smile hides a tear. Perhaps there is your theme for the day.

The connection of Palms and Passion is further strengthened as the psalmist describes his isolation and rejection. "I am a horror to my neighbors, an object of dread to my acquaintances" (vv. 11–12). Forgotten. Invisible. Untouchable. Unlovable. In a broken and sinful world, rejection is often hidden within adulation as an inherent possibility. From our vantage point beyond Easter, we know in hindsight how short the distance from "Hosanna" to "Crucify him." How short the distance from "I will love you forever" to "I want a divorce." How near "I trust you" can be to "You betrayed me." Perhaps here is your theme for Palms and Passion.

It gets worse, though. It is one thing to be rejected, excluded, or even betrayed. In verse 13, the psalmist hears the whispering of those who are actively scheming against him, plotting his death. Be careful about interpreting the threats only in psychological terms. Here, perhaps, interiority must yield to actual, not virtual, reality. Countless multitudes of God's people still worship at risk. Persecution is present in many places, and not only for Christians. If the preacher is well prepared by study, and if the Spirit's work of preparation seems evident among the people, this Palm/Passion Sunday may be just the moment to lift up for blessing our threatened sisters and brothers in many lands, including our own.

The final verses of the reading bring us back to the psalmist's original prayer, "Be gracious to me, O LORD" (v. 9). The Lord's answer to his prayer is not,

Exegetical Perspective

elements, but instead suggest that they are all of one piece—part and parcel of prayer to God.

Even so, the mixtures lead to two important observations. First, the complaint has been subsumed under (and after) petition such that it functions as the motivation for God to answer the psalmist's prayer in v. 9a: "Be gracious . . . for I am in distress." Second, the structure of the lament psalm in general, and the complex amalgam of Psalm 31 specifically, suggest that preachers should use caution in treating verses 9–16 in isolation from the larger context. One ignores the larger, integrated psalm at one's own peril!

As a subunit, verses 9–16 include *portions* of the petition, complaint, and the confession of trust—though, again, their intermixture must be recalled. As already noted, verses 9–16 focus on the psalmist's imperative to God, that the Lord be gracious to her in her distress (v. 9a), and then move to a lengthy complaint that functions to motivate God to do precisely that (vv. 9b–13). The complaint states that the psalmist's eye, soul, body, life, years, strength, and bones are all imperiled (vv. 9b–10). The repetition of the verb "to waste" unites this section, and the cause of this pain is clearly stated: it is because of "grief" (v. 9b), "sorrow," "sighing," and "misery" (v. 10).

The psalmist's *physical self* is not the only thing in trouble: his *social self* is equally endangered. Whether enemy, neighbor, or acquaintance—all who see him are horrified and flee (v. 11). The psalmist is as good as dead: forgotten and as worthless as a broken dish (v. 12). In verse 13, the psalmist can no longer discriminate between enemies and friends; they are now just an ominous and nondescript "many" who plot to kill him. The meaning of their whispering (v. 13a) is not clear; perhaps they are simply trying to scare him. "Terror all around" is a favorite phrase in Jeremiah, however (see Jer. 6:25; 46:5; 49:29), and it is even possible that some people used the phrase as Jeremiah's nickname (see esp. 20:10)—not unlike the way the prophet himself applied it to Pashhur (20:3–4). Perhaps the "many" around the psalmist use a similar nickname for him; after all, after verses 9b–12 it is hard to imagine a person in more dire, terrifying straits. (The intertextual connections to Jeremiah, especially his lament in 20:7–18, suggest another possible context—one also marked by passion/suffering—with which to read Psalm 31.)

Suddenly, inexplicably, the psalmist shifts to trust. The move from verse 13 to verse 14 is remarkable. Where before she insisted on God's graciousness (see vv. 3, 4b–5, 6b), she now reiterates her confidence in *"my* God" (v. 14b) and God's ability to deliver, to

Homiletical Perspective

with two threads, the story of the psalm and the story of the Gospel, or we could weave in a third thread, stories from our contemporary world. The possible advantage of that option is apparent relevance. The possible problem is that the contemporary stories may appear trivial in comparison to the biblical story.

The third thread is by no means necessary, however. It is sometimes best to let the psalm (and the Gospel) speak without homiletical interference. We might simply pray through the psalm, linking it to the Gospel story. Another possibility would be to use two good readers, one for the psalm, the other to read the excerpts from the Gospel. Some elements of the interweaving that could be expanded into a sermon might include:

Be gracious to me, O Lord, for I am in distress; my eye wastes away from grief, my soul and body also. (v. 9a)

Then Jesus went with them to a place called Gethsemane; and he said to his disciples, "Sit here while I go over there and pray." He took with him Peter and the two sons of Zebedee, and began to be grieved and agitated. Then he said to them, "I am deeply grieved, even to death; remain here, and stay awake with me." (Matt. 26:36–38)

For my life is spent with sorrow, and my years with sighing; my strength fails because of my misery, and my bones waste away. (v. 10)

And going a little farther, he threw himself on the ground and prayed, "My Father, if it is possible, let this cup pass from me; yet not what I want but what you want." (Matt. 26:39)

I am the scorn of all my adversaries. (v. 11a)

Then they spat in his face and struck him; and some slapped him, saying, "Prophesy to us, you Messiah! Who is it that struck you?" (Matt. 26:67–68)

A horror to my neighbors. (v. 11b)

Now Peter was sitting outside in the courtyard. A servant-girl came to him and said, "You also were with Jesus the Galilean." But he denied it . . . saying, "I do not know what you are talking about." (Matt. 26:69–70)

An object of dread to my acquaintances. (v. 11c)

Another servant-girl saw him, and she said to the bystanders, "This man was with Jesus of Nazareth." Again he denied it with an oath, "I do not know the man." (Matt. 26:71–72)

Those who see me in the street flee from me. (v. 11d)

Psalm 31:9-16

Theological Perspective

sing and chant psalms to further that conversation and the confidence that comes with hearing the Thou to whom these words are addressed.

The psalm passage breaks down into three sections. In the first, we find the isolated and lonely self, who seeks to deepen the experience of trust in a God who cares. The second section deals with the temptation to blame other humans, who, by turning their backs or being out of range, tempt the one who laments to sound paranoid. Enemies scorn him, neighbors shrink in horror from her, acquaintances dread you. Here is the worst: "I have passed out of mind like one who is dead" and have "become like a broken vessel" (v. 12). Watch archaeologists of biblical lands on television, and hear them complain that ubiquitous unearthed chunks of broken pots are hard to locate with a date in history. They and those who made them have "passed out of mind."

They have not passed out of God's mind, however. In the third move of the passage, in the depths of the lament, the lamenter draws upon what he has earlier experienced, or upon the record of witness by others. Almost startlingly, given the mood of what was just uttered, the psalmist does an about-face with the short, dramatic word that has such a huge place in the language of faith: *But.* "But I trust in you, O LORD; I say 'You are my God'" (v. 14), no matter what or when, as is clear from the next line, "My times are in your hand" (v. 15). This is the ultimate word of confidence in a God who beckons for trust. "My times" includes all those negative references about the abandoned one who is praying this psalm. We are where we began: placing all confidence where it belongs, in the relation to a God who is worthy of trust and who acts on the basis of the divine character as the Trustworthy One.

MARTIN E. MARTY

Pastoral Perspective

apparently, in changing the psalmist's outward circumstances. Life may still bring a betraying kiss, a lonely Gethsemane, a cross. The Lord answers his prayer with a gift—the gift of trust. "I trust in you, O LORD; I say, 'You are my God.' My times are in your hand" (vv. 14–15). This is more than confidence that "things will all work out for the best." Sometimes they simply do not. The psalmist is not offering advice here for you to pass along to your Palm Sunday crowd. He is confessing a new reality that has broken in upon his suffering: "I trust in God!"

On the Sixth Sunday in Lent, the pastoral challenge and the liturgical challenge are very nearly one and the same. What we hope and intend is to enable our congregations to experience the day in its fullness, to integrate celebration and anticipated blessing on the one hand with solitude and even suffering on the other.

I have seen it done at least once with astonishingly elegant simplicity. Palm/Passion Sunday of 1969, I was a visitor at the Presbyterian Church in Abingdon, Pennsylvania. The pastor, Dr. William J. Evans, delivered the message entitled "V-E Day." (Both the historical and the emotional impact of "Victory in Europe Day" were more accessible then than now.) The simple outline began with consideration of the *vibrant enthusiasm* of the crowd and moved toward our Lord's *valiant entry* through the gates of Jerusalem. Along the way we were invited also to consider the *virulent emotions* of Jesus' enemies. We were reminded that the road led on to *violent execution.* Each "v-e" provided a window into the complexity of the Palms/Passion story while honoring its narrative integrity.

It was good preaching, to be sure. Innocently clever, perhaps just a bit too contrived for the modern ear. Yet how many sermons have you heard which, after forty years, you expect precisely to remember the last two words? What, the preacher asked, will we find if we follow this path of palms and tears? *Victory eternal!*

THOMAS EDWARD MCGRATH

Exegetical Perspective

make God's face shine (cf. Num. 6:25), and to save (vv. 15–16). Perhaps this confession of trust too is part of the prayer arsenal that motivates God to act (cf. above). What is clear, regardless, is that the psalmist's confidence in verse 5 is reiterated and made emphatic in verses 14–16. These latter verses, in turn, help to define what committing one's spirit into God's hand (v. 5) means, as well as what God's "redemption" (v. 5) might look like.

The silence between verse 13 and verse 14 is not the only place where an important shift takes place. Many Psalms scholars find the same shift between verse 18 and verse 19, which finds the psalmist moving—again inexplicably—from the confession of trust to unrestrained praise. All that had been begged for earlier in the psalm—refuge and help—is now delivered in abundance (cf. vv. 1a, 2b with vv. 19b–20). The psalmist can do nothing but praise and bless the Lord, who has heard (v. 22) and acted with steadfast love (ḥesed, v. 21; also in vv. 7, 16). Moreover, as is so often the case in the Psalms, God's deliverance of an individual leads to the praise of many, who are here designated as God's "saints" (v. 23) and those "who wait for the LORD" (v. 24). Those who experience God's deliverance from massive distress cannot but preach to others about God's goodness (cf. v. 19) and the praise due God. To be precise, however, Psalm 31 commends not praise, but *love* (v. 23). What other emotion does one feel after being so delivered?

Preachers should work hard so that the lectionary's focus on verses 9–16 does not result in a neglect of the psalm as a whole. Preachers might also suspect that the lectionary's focus is a kind of censorship: removing any mention of the enemies and wicked and their demise (vv. 6a, 7b, 17b–18, 23b) from a liturgical context connected to Jesus Christ. Good preachers know that these subjects too are part of Scripture's claims about God and the gospel (cf., e.g., Ps. 31:18 with 1 Pet. 3:10, a citation from Ps. 34:12–13).

BRENT A. STRAWN

Homiletical Perspective

After a little while the bystanders came up and said to Peter, "Certainly you are also one of them, for your accent betrays you." Then he began to curse, and he swore an oath, "I do not know the man!" At that moment the cock crowed. (Matt. 26:73–74)

For I hear the whispering of many—terror all around!—as they scheme together against me, as they plot to take my life. (v. 13)

Then one of the twelve, who was called Judas Iscariot, went to the chief priests and said, "What will you give me if I betray him to you?" They paid him thirty pieces of silver. And from that moment he began to look for an opportunity to betray him. (Matt. 26:14–16)

or

Now the chief priests and the whole council were looking for false testimony against Jesus so that they might put him to death, but they found none, though many false witnesses came forward. (Matt. 26:59–60)

Note that here we are following the order of the psalm rather than of the Gospel. If we want to observe more closely the order of the Gospel story, we might substitute the Barabbas story: "Now the chief priests and the elders persuaded the crowds to ask for Barabbas and to have Jesus killed . . ." (Matt. 27:20–23). Similarly, if following the order of the Gospel, we might reach the mockery of Jesus on the cross (Matt. 27:39–44) and only then bring in the psalmist's words, "the scorn of all my adversaries."

At some point in the meditation parallellism between psalm and Gospel should become contrast:

But I trust in you, O LORD; I say, "You are my God." (v. 14)

"He trusts in God; let God deliver him now, if he wants to; for he said, 'I am God's Son.'" (Matt. 27:43) . . . But God did not deliver him . . . and he died.

The final prayer of the psalm might become, with a few minor changes, the final prayer of the preacher: "Let your face shine upon your servant" (v. 16). The specific pairings laid out here are only indications of how such a meditation might be composed. Preachers need be limited only by the words of the texts and the extent of their imagination.

STEPHEN FARRIS

Philippians 2:5-11

⁵Let the same mind be in you that was in Christ Jesus,

⁶who, though he was in the form of God,
  did not regard equality with God
  as something to be exploited,
⁷but emptied himself,
  taking the form of a slave,
  being born in human likeness.
 And being found in human form,
⁸ he humbled himself
  and became obedient to the point of death—
  even death on a cross.

Theological Perspective

Triumphant processions are familiar to us. There are motorcades for Super Bowl champions, parades for returning war heroes, the inaugural walk down Pennsylvania Avenue for new presidents. Processions are how we honor human victory and achievement. Palm Sunday may look and feel like more of the same—the church's annual pomp and circumstance to honor Jesus. This passage from Philippians upends our customary notion of a triumphant procession, reminding us that Jesus' entry into Jerusalem is part of his passion.

The church at Philippi was not exempt from the chronic human vices of rivalry and envy, selfish ambition and conceit (Phil. 1:15; 2:3). Following his usual pattern, Paul takes the story of the cross and resurrection and transforms it into an exhortation to Christian discipleship: "Let the same mind be in you that was in Christ Jesus" (v. 5). From his prison cell, Paul urges them to let Christ's way of thinking and acting serve as the template for their own lives. Then Paul leads the Philippians into a poetic reflection on Christ's humiliation and exaltation, a reflection that challenges conventional understandings of both divine and human power. Known as the "*kenōsis* hymn" (from the Greek word for *emptying*), verses 6–11 have challenged and captivated theologians for centuries.

Pastoral Perspective

In this celebrated christological hymn highlighting both the humility and exaltation of Jesus, Paul encourages his readers in Philippi to let the "mind" of Christ (v. 5) be operative in them. In the chapter's first four verses Paul highlights character traits that would emanate from a Christlike mind: selflessness and humble regard for others and their interests. Paul goes further in impressing the nature of a Christlike mind on his correspondents in verse 6, citing how Jesus, in the very form of God or equal with God, did not exploit such status but emptied himself in the manner in which Paul, in verses 1–4, sought to persuade the Philippians to live.

Paul places emphasis on the state of the mind as central to faithfulness, not just in the Philippian correspondence, but elsewhere in his corpus. Thirty-nine times in four of the seven letters indisputably authored by Paul (Romans, 1 and 2 Corinthians, Philippians) Paul refers to the mind in singular, plural, or adjective forms. He specifically writes of "the mind of Christ" twice, once in Philippians and again in 1 Corinthians 2:16. In Philippians Paul's appeal is "*both* to the attitude shown by Christ Jesus and to the attitude that is therefore appropriate to those who are 'in him.'"[1]

1. N. T. Wright, "Romans," in Leander Keck, ed., *The New Interpreter's Bible* (Nashville: Abingdon Press, 1996), 10:507.

> ⁹Therefore God also highly exalted him
>   and gave him the name
>   that is above every name,
> ¹⁰so that at the name of Jesus
>   every knee should bend,
>   in heaven and on earth and under the earth,
> ¹¹and every tongue should confess
>   that Jesus Christ is Lord,
>   to the glory of God the Father.

Exegetical Perspective

The Sixth Sunday in Lent may be observed as either Palm Sunday or the Liturgy of the Passion. The lectionary allows for two homilies at services on the Sixth Sunday in Lent (Palm Sunday): one at the beginning (often in the yard of the church) before the procession with palms, and one after the Gospel reading (after the procession has arrived in the church). Accordingly, two Gospel lections are offered for this Sunday (in Year A: Matt. 21:1–11; Matt. 26:14–27:66 or 27:11–54). Whether offering one homily or two, the preacher will find Philippians 2:5–11 an apt reading for this day. The theme in this passage, Christ's voluntary self-humbling, correlates with the self-lowering of the Messiah who rode into Jerusalem "humble, and mounted on a donkey" (Matt. 21:5). The theme of Christ's suffering and death, which emerges in verse 8, correlates with the account of the crucifixion in Matthew 27:11–54.

Philippians 2:5–11 has long impressed readers as remarkable for its lyric quality, and some have speculated that the passage was originally a Christian hymn adapted by Paul (the passage is sometimes called "the Christ hymn"). Non-Pauline origin of the material may also be indicated by its high Christology (cf. John 1:1–14, Heb. 1:1–4, and Col. 1:15–20) and its use of vocabulary that Paul employs nowhere else ("form" [*morphē*, v. 6], "something to be

Homiletical Perspective

Philippians 2:5–11 is read on the Sunday of the Passion in conjunction with Matthew's account of our Lord's crucifixion and death. Combined, these two passages focus attention on the horror of this necessary but utterly tragic execution. Why did this man have to die? Who was he that, 2,000 years later, millions annually commemorate his gruesome demise?

There is no ultimately satisfying answer to the first question. Theories abound, but the only thing we know for certain is that Jesus himself thought such a death necessary and, however reluctantly, obediently accepted the divine will: "My Father, if it is possible, let this cup pass from me; yet not what I want but what you want" (Matt. 26:39).

The answer to the second question likewise brings us to the heart of mystery, for here we encounter something of the true nature of the living God. People have willingly died for each other countless times throughout history. We call such people heroes, and we honor their sacrifice. Their deaths are reckoned the ultimate gift, the truest measure of friendship (cf. John 15:13). However, we do not commemorate these deaths as *the* pivotal moment in history, nor do we make the peculiar argument that these deaths give rise to hope of eternal life.

Jesus is much more than a hero. His death is remembered not simply as an instance of heroic

Philippians 2:5-11

Theological Perspective

To human beings caught up in envy and selfish ambition, equality with God (v. 6) seems like a great prize, something that could be gloried in and exploited for their own purposes. But this attitude betrays a misunderstanding of God's power. The doctrine of the Trinity teaches that the divine life is found in dispossession, in an eternal circle of unrestricted giving to the other. Likewise, God's power in the creaturely world is found in utter self-giving to what is not God. God is not in a rivalry with human agents for glory or majesty. God, the creator of all, is not in competition with creatures for power or resources. Unlike us, God has no position to defend, no personal interests to protect. There is no envy or selfish ambition in the Godhead. Accordingly, to be in the form of God is not to exploit one's superior power but to manifest God's free, dispossessing love.

This is of course exactly what we see in Jesus Christ, whose life is transparent to God, the perfect incarnation of God's love and power. Rather than considering equality with God something to be exploited, Jesus Christ mirrors divine reality by emptying himself, taking on the form of the slave, following a way of life that leads finally to death on a cross (vv. 6–8). In the incarnation Christ does not give up the perquisites of deity, but displays God's own power and wisdom in what looks to the world like weakness and foolishness (1 Cor. 1:24–25). As Gregory of Nyssa notes, God's transcendent power is more conspicuously displayed in the lowliness of Christ's incarnation than in all the natural wonders of the universe.[1]

In the resurrection, God vindicates Jesus' self-giving life and death, exalting him above every human authority (vv. 9–11). The self-serving, violent forces that did their worst toward Jesus are emptied of their power and declared null and void. Paying highest homage to the risen Christ calls forth our allegiance to the generous, equitable, and peaceful order of God's realm. We have the same mind that was in Christ Jesus when we resist ambitious, self-seeking models of power, when we renounce exploitation and loveless indifference. Jesus' resurrection and exaltation have nullified this way of life. In confessing Jesus Christ as Lord (v. 11), we subvert the authority of the lords of privilege and violence.

Christ's triumphant entry into Jerusalem points ahead of itself to his death, when the subversive character of his kingship is definitively revealed. The

Pastoral Perspective

Paul in effect argues that such an attitude leads to action reflective of the reality of a renewed mind (Rom. 12:2); an interpretation of verse 5 could read, "Show among yourselves the attitude that arises from the fact that you are in Christ."

Contemporarily, matters of debate and contention among Christians in congregations can try the capacity to demonstrate such an attitude. At stake could be the interpretation of doctrine; the effort to inject into the veins of ancient church traditions the life-renewing fluids of innovation; the attempt to create greater inclusion—pluralism, beyond mere numeric representation of diversity—in the faith community while traversing the tension-filled fault lines of race, gender, sexual orientation, class, ability, and, sometimes, even age. For these reasons it is no light matter that Paul placed such great emphasis on the mind in his writings in general and the mind of Christ in particular in this text. The relevant question for twenty-first-century Christians, as was the case in the first century, relates to how we exemplify selflessness and humble regard for others, particularly in times of contention and controversy.

Implicit in Paul's hymn is the correlation between the mind and action, hence Paul's emphasis (cited above) that the Philippians *show* among themselves the *attitude* of those who are in Christ. The late Dr. R. Maurice Boyd once said, "We can think ourselves into a new way of acting, or we can act ourselves into a new way of thinking."[2] To be in Christ is to know that the effort to link thought and action is not generated solely by one's own power. It is also to know that the mind of Christ cannot be operational in our personal lives or in the body of the church apart from the exercise of personal agency: our faithful response to God's initiating work, the work of God in Christ reconciling the world unto himself (2 Cor. 5:19).

Our faithful response to divine initiative—an ongoing work—lends itself to the cultivation of habits, what Boyd called "Habits of Being." Habits, he said, gain depth and power through their repetition, expressing who we are. The habit of being is more than rote repetition, more than, say, the technique employed by an artist. The great artists—whether in the graphic, performing, or visual categories, writers or, say, preachers (preaching is an art of sorts)—convey, says Boyd, their own distinctive style symbolic of their being: "the quality of their person." Who we are—our being—infuses what we do.

---

1. Gregory of Nyssa, *The Great Catechism*, chap. 24, in *The Nicene and Post-Nicene Fathers*, 2nd series, ed. Philip Schaff and Henry Wace (Grand Rapids: Eerdmans, 1954), 5:494.

2. R. Maurice Boyd, "A Habit of Being," http://www.citychurchny.org/church/worship/printed/PS-A%20Habit%20Of%20Being.pdf [accessed April 15, 2009].

exploited" [*harpagmos*, v. 6], "highly exalt" [*hyperypsoun*, v. 9]). Such observations have prompted much scholarly speculation about the possible scriptural or mythic background of the ideas expressed. Does the hymn have its roots in the Suffering Servant passages of Second Isaiah? In Jewish wisdom teaching? In gnostic speculation? For purposes of preaching, focusing on the way Paul applies the material to the Philippians' communal life will be more fruitful than pursuing the question of its antecedents.

In verse 5, Paul introduces the hymn with an exhortation to imitate Christ: "Let the same mind be in you that was in Christ Jesus." He has already sounded this theme in 1:27, where he instructed the Philippians to "live your [plural] life in a manner worthy of the gospel of Christ, so that, whether I come and see you or am absent and hear about you, I will know that you are standing firm in one spirit, striving side by side with one mind for the faith of the gospel." Though Paul views the Philippians as devoted servants and full partners with him in his work for Christ, he urges them to work even harder to develop a true team spirit. Indeed, the word *synathlein* in 1:27 means something like "being athletes together" or "contending side by side for a prize." The church is doing well, but can become still stronger and more unified.

Perhaps one motivation for Paul's writing of Philippians was worry that disagreements among certain members would undermine their service of Christ: in 4:2–3, he urges reconciliation between the women Euodia and Syntyche. These women have "struggled beside" Paul (*synathlein* again) in work for the gospel, but now their disagreement threatens to undermine the single-mindedness of the congregation as a whole. Paul will use the Christ hymn to address the need for the Philippians to live and work cooperatively and to aim for the flourishing of the whole body.

The theme of the importance of a unified spirit is carried over from the end of chapter 1 into the immediate preface to the hymn. Paul instructs the Philippians to complete his joy by living in perfect accord (2:2). Each member of the community must eschew rivalry or ambition and desire for personal glory, and cultivate instead an attitude of humility; each must regard others as better than himself or herself and look to serve others' interests (vv. 3–4). Now Paul brings in the hymn to illustrate the point that those who behave in this self-sacrificial way will be imitating Christ himself.

Note that he does not recount stories of how the earthly Christ served the interests of God and God's

sacrifice but as the event that ushers in new life and a new way of life. The hymn to Christ in Philippians 2 is nearly universally conceived to be of earlier composition than any of our Gospels. The Christ it presents is clearly divine, but the Divinity encountered here is not what one would have anticipated in the ancient world (or in ours!). This is a Deity who, "though he was in the form of God, did not regard equality with God as something to be exploited" (v. 6). The Greek word translated "exploited" is equally well translated as "robbed." In contrast with Adam, who wanted to rob that which was manifestly not his—namely, equality with God (see Gen. 3)— this one who is in the form of God precisely does not grasp divinity, but instead relinquishes it. He "empties" himself and takes the form of the human person with the least stature—a slave.

So the heart of God is revealed. The divinity of our Lord is somehow inextricably linked with his willingness to empty himself, with his radical humility, with his ready willingness to identify with "the least of these" (cf. Matt. 25:40, 45).

The pericope most commonly referenced for describing the divinity of our Lord is the prologue to the Gospel of John, but as moving and definitive as this passage is, it makes no explicit mention of the sacrifice entailed in the Word's becoming flesh. In contrast, in Philippians, Paul underscores that it is not divinity as such but self-emptying obedience that leads God to exalt the Christ so that "at the name of Jesus every knee should bend, in heaven and on earth and under the earth" (v. 10). We know the divinity of the risen Lord precisely in Christ's willingness to empty himself and obey.

Two thousand years later we commemorate this one's death, not because he was a hero, nor simply because he was divine, but because in his crucifixion and resurrection the truth is revealed that self-emptying, sacrifice, and obedience are of the essence of divinity. Christ's death and resurrection are likewise of the essence to and for humanity. The followers of Jesus are called to be of the same mind as Christ (v. 5). As our Lord "emptied himself" and "became obedient to the point of death—even death on a cross" (v. 8), so Jesus tells his disciples: "If any want to become my followers, let them deny themselves and take up their cross and follow me" (Matt. 16:24). On the Sunday of the Passion it is important for the preacher to remind her congregation that the call to take up one's cross lies at the heart of the gospel. A contemporary congregation will need to hear that this is good news, not bad! Bearing one's own cross does not sound fun!

Philippians 2:5-11

Theological Perspective

crowd's joyful cries of "Hosanna!" soon turn to angry shouts of "Crucify him!" The procession of Palm Sunday also points ahead of itself to that ultimate triumphant procession, in which every knee shall bow and every tongue shall confess Jesus Christ as Lord (vv. 10–11). This procession will not be like the uncomprehending clamor of the crowd at Jerusalem; nor will it be an exclusive, winners-only celebration like the Super Bowl motorcade.

Flannery O'Connor imaginatively portrays it at the end of her short story "Revelation," when the protagonist Mrs. Turpin sees an enormous procession of "souls climbing upward into the starry field and shouting hallelujah." Her wonder turns to shock as Mrs. Turpin discovers that all the people she considered inferior to herself are leading the procession, and that reputable people like her are pulling up the rear. The respectable types "were marching behind the others with great dignity, accountable as they had always been for good order and common sense and respectable behavior. They alone were on key. Yet she could see by their shocked and altered faces that even their virtues were being burned away."[2] Joining the triumphant procession to honor the crucified and risen Christ requires the humility to join the back of the line, to give up our conceited and envious ways.

As we wait for that ultimate triumphant procession, we honor Jesus best by exercising care in the human processions we join. As those who seek the same mind that was in Christ Jesus, we should beware of processions that exalt rivalry and selfish ambition, knowing that Christ has emptied those human spectacles of their power. We should rejoice in processions that exhibit humility, compassion, and a thirst for God's reign—participants in the Montgomery bus boycott walking and carpooling to work, South Africans moving in long, swaying lines to vote for the first time. There we catch a glimpse of the creaturely glory God has promised us in Christ Jesus.

AMY PLANTINGA PAUW

Pastoral Perspective

Since the life of faith is about a habit of being, our text highlights the state of mind central to what it means to be in Christ. The connection between the habit of being and the mind of Christ in us implicates the priorities of our lives. What issues forth from us as a result of our habit of being? If the mind of Christ is in us, how is this manifest in our character? In our grappling with the internal conflicts and contradictions in our lives? In our receptivity to the new thing God may be attempting to evoke in our lives? In our approach to conflict? In our capacity to sacrifice on behalf of others and to forgive?

The Gospels and the Epistles testify to the manner in which Jesus addressed most of these questions in his own life. Our text grasps how Christ's self-emptying humility in particular led to his exaltation: the universal recognition of Jesus as Lord. To write this to first-century Philippians in the heart of the Roman Empire, where emperor deification was prevalent, was no small thing. The "pattern of behavior Paul had placed before the Corinthians would have been as much of a challenge to the whole Roman social ethos."[3]

As Paul does so often in his letters, he layers—reinforces—a fundamental premise such as Christ's self-emptying humility to hammer home a point: in this case, Christ's exaltation, the implications of which are countercultural. The countercultural dimension of his thought is already implicit in his admonition to his readers, echoing Romans 12:2, to let the mind of Christ be operative in their lives. Now, at the end of the text, Paul declares that the whole creation will acknowledge the lordship of Christ, when the dominant contemporary cultural ethos of Philippi tended toward the cult of the emperor. There is a consistency in what Paul exhorts at the beginning of the pericope and at its end: the mind of Christ, the Lord of all creation, is a habit of being that makes one—and by extension the church—different. This difference is, in effect, what it means in a biblical sense to be holy, a habit of being that the faithful are called to make manifest to the whole creation.

KENNETH I. CLARKE SR.

---

2. Flannery O'Connor, "Revelation," in *The Complete Stories* (New York: Farrar, Straus & Giroux, 1971), 508–9.

3. Wright, "Romans," 510.

Exegetical Perspective

people, such as are told in the Gospel passion accounts (e.g., Matt. 20:28; 26:28, 39). Rather, Paul places the crucifixion in the context of a *cosmic* drama about Christ's self-giving. In the incarnation, we see Christ enacting the perfect generosity and love of God for the created world. Rather than asserting his rightful claim to equality with God, Christ humbled himself by taking human form and being obedient unto death. The Philippians must likewise act humbly and look to the interests of others.

Christ gave himself, but because of his obedience "God also highly exalted him and gave him the name that is above every name" (v. 9). Likewise, those who humble themselves in imitation and service of Christ will share in the resurrection. We know that the pain we suffer when we obey God's call to self-giving will have its reward, because our God is one who turns suffering to joy. Our God is one who raises the dead! Paul anticipates this outcome for himself (3:10–11), and he anticipates it for the Philippians as well (3:20–21). In dealing with this passage in the context of Holy Week, however, the preacher must not rush through the pain to get to the promise. Paul is calling the Philippians to lay aside any personal interest or aim that will not help the body of the church to flourish. He is calling them to suffer on Christ's behalf (see 1:29–30).

After concluding the hymn, Paul exhorts the Philippians to "work out [among yourselves] your own salvation" (v. 12). The plural is crucial: Paul is not telling each individual to figure out a private spirituality, but is (yet again) urging the *community* to unite behind the cause of serving Christ. The Philippians' unity and harmony will be a witness to the world (vv. 14–15) and a sacrificial offering to God on Paul's behalf (vv. 16–17). Today also, a church community united and harmonious in its work for Christ testifies to the world about what it means to be conformed to Christ in his passion and empowered by God to will and to work for God's good pleasure.

SUSAN R. GARRETT

Homiletical Perspective

Jesus bore his cross, not in fulfillment of this or that commandment, but in response to God's call to accept a specific fate and perform a specific task. Likewise each Christian must take up his or her cross, accept a specific fate, and perform a specific task! The cross comes to each of us.

In each Christian life that time will come when we are driven to our knees. Our child dies. We lose a job. A routine doctor's visit reveals we have a terminal disease. We can finally no longer deny that we have an addiction. Through no will of our own we are divorced. The question at such times is not, are we strong enough to bear the pain? We are not! The question is, are we pliant enough to accept the circumstance and give our lives and our will to God? Our own resources are inadequate. We are utterly defeated. This is the moment of grace and likewise the moment of decision. Do we determinedly refuse to acknowledge the reality of our circumstance and continue our feeble attempt to retain the illusion of control, or do we accept our fate and the decision required? Abraham Lincoln famously said, "I have been driven many times to my knees by the overwhelming conviction that I had absolutely no other place to go."[1]

The cross points to the resurrection, but just as surely, the resurrection points to the cross. Without the cross there is no resurrection. "For those who want to save their life will lose it, and those who lose their life for my sake will find it" (Matt. 16:25). Faith is demonstrated in relying upon God in these, the lowest moments of our lives. Hope is born is discovering that indeed God is with us. Love flows from the grateful heart. So the cross proves to be good news.

DOUGLAS TRAVIS

1. Abraham Lincoln, in *The New Encyclopedia of Christian Quotations*, comp. Mark Water (Grand Rapids: Baker Books, 2000), 764.

Matthew 27:11-54

[11]Now Jesus stood before the governor; and the governor asked him, "Are you the King of the Jews?" Jesus said, "You say so." [12]But when he was accused by the chief priests and elders, he did not answer. [13]Then Pilate said to him, "Do you not hear how many accusations they make against you?" [14]But he gave him no answer, not even to a single charge, so that the governor was greatly amazed.

[15]Now at the festival the governor was accustomed to release a prisoner for the crowd, anyone whom they wanted. [16]At that time they had a notorious prisoner, called Jesus Barabbas. [17]So after they had gathered, Pilate said to them, "Whom do you want me to release for you, Jesus Barabbas or Jesus who is called the Messiah?" [18]For he realized that it was out of jealousy that they had handed him over. [19]While he was sitting on the judgment seat, his wife sent word to him, "Have nothing to do with that innocent man, for today I have suffered a great deal because of a dream about him." [20]Now the chief priests and the elders persuaded the crowds to ask for Barabbas and to have Jesus killed. [21]The governor again said to them, "Which of the two do you want me to release for you?" And they said, "Barabbas." [22]Pilate said to them, "Then what should I do with Jesus who is called the Messiah?" All of them said, "Let him be crucified!" [23]Then he asked, "Why, what evil has he done?" But they shouted all the more, "Let him be crucified!"

[24]So when Pilate saw that he could do nothing, but rather that a riot was beginning, he took some water and washed his hands before the crowd, saying, "I am innocent of this man's blood; see to it yourselves." [25]Then the people as a whole answered, "His blood be on us and on our children!" [26]So he released Barabbas for them; and after flogging Jesus, he handed him over to be crucified.

[27]Then the soldiers of the governor took Jesus into the governor's headquarters, and they gathered the whole cohort around him. [28]They stripped him and put a scarlet robe on him, [29]and after twisting some thorns into a crown, they put it on his head. They put a reed in his right hand and knelt before him and mocked him, saying, "Hail, King of the Jews!" [30]They spat on him, and took the reed and struck him on the head. [31]After mocking him, they stripped him of

Theological Perspective

This reading narrates events after the arrest of Jesus, from his "trial" before Pilate to his death, cosmic disturbances thereafter, and the testimony of Roman guards on watch. It includes traditions common to the other canonical Gospels, crafted in light of Matthean theological concerns. Incidents and scripturally based allusions are so tightly interwoven that critical analysis of the narrative struggles to pinpoint whether historical details have generated biblical-theological interpretations or vice versa. One key point nonetheless is certain: here Christian conviction insists that the death of Jesus is *integral* to God's good news in Christ Jesus.

This conviction, prominent in New Testament writings and later creeds, confessions, and catechisms, is so widespread and familiar that Christians are perhaps at risk of taking it for granted and overlooking its theological import. Including the "passion liturgy" in this book and in subsequent proclamations of Christianity's

Pastoral Perspective

In the Liturgy of the Passion we meet Jesus, not as the charismatic teacher who triumphantly rode through the gates of Jerusalem, but as the one betrayed, abandoned, and facing the inevitability of death. Shouts of adulation give way to "Let him be crucified," words of consolation to anguish and uncertainty, and Gospel proclamation to silence. Jesus' voice fades into the background, overshadowed by a cacophony of unsubstantiated claims and misguided assertion as the religious leaders accuse him of treason and convince the people to demand his execution.

The events that unfold are troubling because of the dearth of words from Jesus and the malevolent response from those who contrive to kill him. Discerning the crucifixion's meaning for our lives is similarly difficult, because Matthew will not permit us to engage it as an isolated event, but reveals an

the robe and put his own clothes on him. Then they led him away to crucify him.

³²As they went out, they came upon a man from Cyrene named Simon; they compelled this man to carry his cross. ³³And when they came to a place called Golgotha (which means Place of a Skull), ³⁴they offered him wine to drink, mixed with gall; but when he tasted it, he would not drink it. ³⁵And when they had crucified him, they divided his clothes among themselves by casting lots; ³⁶then they sat down there and kept watch over him. ³⁷Over his head they put the charge against him, which read, "This is Jesus, the King of the Jews."

³⁸Then two bandits were crucified with him, one on his right and one on his left. ³⁹Those who passed by derided him, shaking their heads ⁴⁰and saying, "You who would destroy the temple and build it in three days, save yourself! If you are the Son of God, come down from the cross." ⁴¹In the same way the chief priests also, along with the scribes and elders, were mocking him, saying, ⁴²"He saved others; he cannot save himself. He is the King of Israel; let him come down from the cross now, and we will believe in him. ⁴³He trusts in God; let God deliver him now, if he wants to; for he said, 'I am God's Son.'" ⁴⁴The bandits who were crucified with him also taunted him in the same way.

⁴⁵From noon on, darkness came over the whole land until three in the afternoon. ⁴⁶And about three o'clock Jesus cried with a loud voice, "Eli, Eli, lema sabachthani?" that is, "My God, my God, why have you forsaken me?" ⁴⁷When some of the bystanders heard it, they said, "This man is calling for Elijah." ⁴⁸At once one of them ran and got a sponge, filled it with sour wine, put it on a stick, and gave it to him to drink. ⁴⁹But the others said, "Wait, let us see whether Elijah will come to save him." ⁵⁰Then Jesus cried again with a loud voice and breathed his last. ⁵¹At that moment the curtain of the temple was torn in two, from top to bottom. The earth shook, and the rocks were split. ⁵²The tombs also were opened, and many bodies of the saints who had fallen asleep were raised. ⁵³After his resurrection they came out of the tombs and entered the holy city and appeared to many. ⁵⁴Now when the centurion and those with him, who were keeping watch over Jesus, saw the earthquake and what took place, they were terrified and said, "Truly this man was God's Son!"

Exegetical Perspective

Matthew follows Mark's general account, in which there is a trial before Pilate, Jesus refuses to challenge the accusations, the crowds call for execution, the soldiers mock him, he is crucified between two bandits, he cries out to God at his death, the temple curtain is ripped apart, and a centurion confesses the truth about him from the foot of the cross. There are three scenes: the trial (vv. 11–26); the crucifixion (vv. 27–44); and the death (vv. 45–54).

Notable in the trial scene (vv. 11–26) is the repeated use of the word "governor" (*hēgemōn*) for Pilate, emphasizing that Pilate's authority derives from the earthly, political realm. Jesus, in contrast, receives his authority from God—a truth affirmed in the infancy narrative, when the sages from the East seek the one who was "born king of the Jews" (2:2), and the religious leaders inform King Herod that the Messiah will be a "ruler" (*hēgemōn*, 2:6) to shepherd

Homiletical Perspective

> They crucified my Lord, and he never said a
>   mumbalin' word;
> They crucified my Lord, and he never said a
>   mumbalin' word;
> Not a word, not a word, not a word.

The old African American spiritual may not be literally correct in its claim regarding Jesus' behavior throughout his passion and death, but if one surveys the red-lettered words of Jesus throughout Matthew's account, one cannot help but be struck by his near silence in the face of his accusers and tormentors. In today's reading we hear only his terse two-word (in Greek) response, "You say so," to Pilate's question, "Are you the king of the Jews?" (v. 11) and his cry of dereliction in Aramaic, "Eli, Eli, lema sabachthani?" Even this is misheard by the bystanders, who think that "Eli" is an invocation not of God but of the prophet Elijah. Betrayal, denial, accusation,

Matthew 27:11-54

Theological Perspective

gospel is neither a matter of course nor an unavoidable necessity but a theological *decision*. This decision accepts as facts that "the historical" Jesus died and that his death was by crucifixion, one type of capital punishment that imperial Rome meted out to non-compliant subjects, insurgents particularly. However, these facts alone do not account for the conviction of faith that this dying is an indispensable element of the gospel itself.

Preaching "Christ crucified," as Paul first indicated (1 Cor. 1:23), was not a message with slick, surefire evangelistic appeal. Indeed, some believers who preached Christ and followed him considered his death on the cross theologically irrelevant. For them, his death plays no key role in God's good news or in the unique status and work of Jesus, Christ and Savior. If words and deeds of Jesus during his ministry, or his presence as the spirit and spark of life abiding within the believer, brought about saving wisdom, illumination, healing, hope, and more, what does it matter whether and how he once died, or appeared to do so?

Matthew's Gospel, then, directs us to reflect on the theological *difference* it makes to proclaim that Jesus was, and is, Christ crucified. Of many themes characteristic of Matthew's theology used to unfold the significance of Jesus' suffering and death, several of the most prominent deserve mention here.

One is Matthew's emphasis on the continuities of God's saving acts throughout Israel's history and that of Jesus and his followers. This is evident in the large number and variety of quotations, allusions, and carryovers from the Law, Prophets, and other Scriptures, as it is in the risen Christ's commission to his disciples, issued with "all authority in heaven and on earth" (28:18), to teach obedience to what has been commanded. In this respect this Gospel's placement at the canonical turn of the two testaments is strikingly apt.

A second theme addresses the question of who is authorized to declare God's saving will and way on earth, as in heaven. The evangelist's answer, Jesus of Nazareth, is a messianic claim drawing upon various references to Moses, monarchs, prophets, and others God chose as agents of salvation. Matthew's telling of Jesus in Jerusalem brings to the fore the Messiah as ruler—king! This point recurs from Jesus' entry into the city to the *titulus* on his cross and the guard's word. Pilate's questioning, Jesus' nonanswer answer, the scarlet robe, crown of thorns, reed scepter, and mockery pose the same question over and again. Who speaks and acts with God's authority: Pilate, Rome's soldiers, chief priests and elders, the crowd, or this Jesus who now says next to nothing and

Pastoral Perspective

unequivocal connection between Jesus' crucifixion and his overall life and ministry, especially those events preceding his arrest. In other words, this narrative invites us to engage in the practice of remembering, to hear Jesus' anguished cry from the cross in dialogue with the gospel he proclaimed, so that we might discern the efficacy of the crucifixion for our lives and permit it to create us anew.

Jesus' cry from the cross is daunting: "My God, my God, why have you forsaken me?" These words are indelibly etched upon our hearts, reminding us that we follow the crucified One, who identifies so completely with the message he proclaims that he refuses to relent or acquiesce to the will of those who threaten his well-being. Jesus' resolve is unmistakable as we observe him returning to the Jerusalem temple on the day following his triumphal entry, expelling the money changers and those who bought and sold animals for the sacrifice, while proclaiming words reminiscent of the prophet Isaiah, "My house shall be called a house of prayer; but you are making it a den of robbers" (21:13). In the spirit of Isaiah he also welcomes the "outcasts of Israel" (Isa. 56:8) as they crowd into the temple, sorely needing Jesus' healing touch. Everyone is astounded, including the children whose cries fill the temple, asserting again that Jesus is the anticipated one: "Hosanna to the Son of David!"

On the next day Jesus returns to the temple to teach, intensifying his conflict with the chief priests, elders, and other religious leaders by critiquing their practices and suggesting that social and moral outcasts such as tax collectors and prostitutes are better suited for the kingdom of heaven than they. In effect, he opens the borders of God's domain to all who are willing to "produce the fruits of the kingdom" (Matt. 21:43) and that does not sit well with the religious leaders. Even more, when they try to discredit him as a false prophet by debating him about the Law, Jesus seizes the opportunity and expounds upon the necessity of love and compassion as an expression of God's presence in the world. In other words, Jesus is all *but* silent in the days preceding his crucifixion, hoping to revolutionize their patterns of relationship by suggesting that right relationship with God is inextricably tied to our willingness to love each other and give to the least as unto God.

Perhaps Jesus has said enough and now we must remember. What if his prolonged silence and painful cry from the cross is really intended to call us toward a life of vocation and embolden us to stand in solidarity with those who suffer, so that anguished cries might cease? Maybe Jesus' cry is not his alone, but a

Exegetical Perspective

the people Israel. The question of authority follows Jesus throughout his ministry (e.g., 7:29; 9:6–8), especially in conflicts with religious leaders (21:23–27). In addition, one of the devil's temptations is an offer of "all the kingdoms of the world" (4:8), an offer that Jesus refuses. Thus, the trial before Pilate is a confrontation between an earthly ruler (the "governor") and a heavenly one ("King of the Jews," 27:11; "Messiah," 27:17, 22). Although readers from the other side of the cross know the ultimate outcome, at this point in the passion it appears that earthly power defeats God's anointed one.

Two details in the trial, noteworthy by their presence only in Matthew, stress Jesus' innocence: (1) the dream of Pilate's wife (v. 19); and (2) Pilate's symbolic act of washing his hands (v. 24). The crowds, which days before had cheered for Jesus as a messianic savior, are now bent on his destruction. Whipped up by the chief priests and elders, they repeat the calls for crucifixion, and despite Pilate's recognition that the charges against Jesus arise out of jealousy, he is unable or unwilling to stop them. Pilate's claim that he is "innocent [*athōos*] of the blood [*haima*] of this man" (v. 24) shares verbal threads to Judas, who "sinned by handing over innocent blood" (*haima athōos*, 27:4). Both men add, "see to it yourselves/yourself" (*sy oraō*). While Pilate denies his role in Jesus' death, Judas repents of his; for their part, the people in the crowd claim full responsibility: "His blood be on us and on our children" (v. 25; cf. 23:30–36).[1] Ultimately, all are guilty, heightening both the irony and the power of Jesus' own words of pardon, spoken shortly before his arrest: "this is my blood of the covenant, which is poured out for many for the forgiveness of sins" (26:28).

In the crucifixion scene (vv. 27–44), the "soldiers of the governor" (implying Pilate's continuing culpability) dress Jesus in a scarlet robe and thorny crown, and place a reed (as scepter) in his hand, mocking him as "King of the Jews" (v. 29). Everyone else adds to the jeering taunts: the people, the chief priests, the scribes, the elders, even the bandits who are crucified with him. They deride Jesus as "Son of God," "King of Israel," the one who "saved others" (vv. 40–43), without recognizing the truth behind their sneers, for so he has been identified from the opening chapters (e.g., 1:21; 2:2; 2:15; 3:17). Repeated echoes of Psalms 22 and 69 throughout the crucifixion scene suggest that Jesus also is the Suffering Servant who will be

---

1. Cf. Lev. 20:9–16; 2 Sam. 1:16; Jer. 26:15. It should go without saying that these words must not be viewed (as they have been by many Christians through the centuries) as a condemnation of Jews and/or Judaism in general.

Homiletical Perspective

condemnation, torture, taunting, and even the last temptation, to "come down from the cross now, and we will believe in him" (v. 42) elicit not a "mumblin'" word from the noted storytelling man from Nazareth. Why?

Matthew's decision to tell the passion story as that of a nearly silent Jesus is making room for the resonances from the Suffering Servant songs of Isaiah (one of which we hear as today's first reading and another on Good Friday) and the psalms of lament (like Psalm 22, whose opening strophe Jesus recites with his last breath) to become Jesus' own voice, allowing the Word of God to interpret what Jesus seems to be enduring so passively. It as if this Word of God of old, in which Jesus was so steeped, becomes the *basso continuo* sustaining us hearers through Jesus' silence as the events of his passion and death unfold before us in all their horror.

Many of our churches have moved to making the reading of the entire passion story (26:14–27:66) a congregationally participatory affair, with various voices speaking the individual parts and the congregation serving as the crowd and other plural voices. I find this to be a highly effective liturgical experience but one that, of course, then places severe time limits on the sermon. In recent years I have turned to calling my five-minute reflection "Prelude to the Passion" and moving it up in the liturgy to precede the congregational reading of the passion story. In this way the sermon becomes a kind of propaedeutic for the hearing of the passion story, akin to a preconcert talk given by a musicologist to help the audience better understand and thus become more acute listeners and appreciators of what they are about to hear.

Maybe an even apter image, since the congregation is itself a part of the performance of the Word, is that of a conductor carefully introducing his orchestral players to the piece they are about to play. Here the authorizing key is found in our first reading, from Isaiah, where the Servant observes how "The Lord God has given me the tongue of a teacher, that I may know how to sustain the weary with a word. Morning by morning he wakens—wakens my ear to listen as those who are taught" (Isa. 50:4). Today the preacher's role may well become that of a teacher devoted to helping her or his congregation "to listen as those who are taught," even as "The Lord God has opened my ear" (Isa. 50:5a), as the Servant suggests.

With this preparation for a more attentive, participatory hearing of the passion story, the congregational reading itself then becomes a sort of dress rehearsal for the parts the congregation itself will

Matthew 27:11–54

Theological Perspective

endures merciless treatment at enemy hands? A "suffering Messiah" is here no mere wordplay; its meaning now becomes dramatically clear. Confessing "Jesus is Lord" under such circumstances is a Christian faith of a peculiar, troubling sort indeed, the opposite of one that reckons on self-beneficial gain.

Also troubling, though in a different sense, is another theme. The retrieval of scriptural traditions of prophetic denunciation when the covenant people stray from God, neglect God's ways, and reject God's messengers is a striking feature of Matthew's Gospel. It directs such righteous indignation toward those who rejected Jesus. Indeed, it intensifies the polemic by minimizing Pilate's responsibility for Jesus' death and widening the circle of fellow Jews hostile to Jesus, from some, or an unruly mob, to all the people. One baleful consequence of this form of invective is the emergence of Christian accusations against Jewish people themselves as "Christ-killers" and, with it, a long, tragic history of prejudice and persecution.

This history of interpretation makes it all the more imperative that Christians reflect anew on Matthew's convictions (20:20–28) of the meaning of the events unfolded in the passion narrative. The suffering and death of Jesus are in some profound sense prepared by God and accepted by Jesus, and "according to scripture." They are affirmed to hold salvific significance. The terminology used, "ransom for many" (20:28), is metaphorical, drawn from the redemption of slaves, and unelaborated. Later theologians have found it one source for ongoing discussions and various explanations of the cross as atonement for sin. The phrase "for many," sometimes construed as "not everyone," has figured in disputes about "limited" versus "universal" atonement.

Finally, the stark realism of Matthew's passion narrative prompts theological attention. Isolated and helpless at the end, does Jesus succumb to despair and cry out in God-forsakenness? His cry (27:46) quotes Psalm 22. Is the theological conclusion, then, that he dies, despite physical pain, in spiritual peace, a psalm with a confident ending on his lips? A more kenotic view has also been advanced: fixed on one line of the psalm alone, his is a loud cry of utter desolation. The Matthean theological message, then, would be that in extremis, after Jesus has done everything in his power and his enemies everything in theirs, one power alone remains to act. God declares the final judgment, reversing the status quo, raising Jesus from death, and vindicating the crucified one and his way of loving God and neighbor.

JAMES O. DUKE

Pastoral Perspective

timeless cry on the behalf of millions of suffering people who have felt and will feel forsaken by God and humanity, lest someone answer their call. Perhaps his anguished cry is intended to touch us at the core of our being so that we, his present-day disciples, may remember his teachings and endeavor to live therein.

Remembering Jesus' teachings amplifies the voices of those who suffer in distant lands and within our own national borders, neighborhoods, households, and worship communities, because remembering diminishes distortion. It helps us resist becoming preoccupied with money, position, power, and ceremonialism and invites us truly to notice those who cry out as though with Jesus, "My God, my God, why have you forsaken me." Brian Mahan reminds us, in *Forgetting Ourselves on Purpose,* that "attending to suffering is simply seeing what we see when our eyes are not closed, averted, or glazed over. . . . It is a gentle practice, not a harsh ideal, and just the kind of thing we do when we aren't so busy, so fearful, so preoccupied."[1]

In today's Lenten narrative, those who orchestrated Jesus' death were so preoccupied with power and fearful of change that they missed the possibility of a world in which love and compassion could become a reality. As a result, they and their followers crucified God's Son, mocking and deriding him, lest they believe and be changed. Their actions are both distressing and instructive, affording us an opportunity to reflect upon the mistakes of the past and avoid repeating them in the present. In response, we must remain vigilant in the work of the ministry, engaging in ethical praxes that embody love of God, self, and neighbor as a testament to the crucified One. For the crucifixion is not simply an event to be mourned or an entrée to the resurrection, but a reminder of the malevolence that ensues when faithful persons forget to remember that we stand with the One who has come in the name of the Lord.

"Truly this man was God's Son," the soldiers realize, standing in the midday darkness, feeling the earth shake beneath their feet, witnessing the graves release their dead, and peering into the Most Holy Place. "Truly this man [is] God's Son!"

VERONICE MILES

---

1. Brian J. Mahan, *Forgetting Ourselves on Purpose: Vocation and the Ethics of Ambition* (San Francisco: Jossey-Bass, 2002), 184.

Exegetical Perspective

vindicated by God (e.g., Pss. 22:7, 18; 69:19–21), a suggestion that is strengthened by his words from the cross: "My God, my God, why have you forsaken me?" (v. 46; Ps. 22:1).

In the death scene (vv. 45–54), there is a recounting of Jesus' death. Matthew follows Mark nearly verbatim, up to and including Jesus' cry of dereliction. Unlike some modern retellings of the crucifixion, the canonical Gospels pay little attention to the gruesome details of the death, pointing instead to its import and effects. Matthew offers a vivid display of the crucifixion's cosmic significance: the earth shakes, rocks split, tombs open, and the dead are raised. Just as a rising star brought Gentile sages from the East (2:2–10), the shaking earth proves to a Gentile centurion and all those with him (including later readers of the report) that "truly this man was God's Son!" (v. 54).

In one of the great mysteries of the Gospel, the forsaken one cries out to "*my* God," asserting relationship even at this most desolate hour. Rejected, on the cross, Jesus lives fully into the human experience of bearing the worst that people can inflict on one another. Betrayal, cruelty, suffering: all of it has happened to him. Indeed, earlier in his ministry, before sending the disciples out "like sheep into the midst of wolves" (10:16), Jesus had foretold a hard truth:

> "They will hand you over to councils and flog you in their synagogues; and you will be dragged before governors and kings because of me, as a testimony to them and the Gentiles. . . . Brother will betray brother to death . . . and you will be hated by all because of my name. But the one who endures to the end will be saved." (10:17, 18, 21, 22; cf. 24:9–13)

Matthew's narrative affirms that whatever lies ahead for Jesus' followers has already happened to Jesus. Whatever they might suffer, he has suffered already; the death they face is a death he has already endured. The essential christological claim in this Gospel is that Jesus—even at the most isolated and isolating moment on the cross—is Immanuel, God with us (1:23; cf. 28:20).

AUDREY WEST

Homiletical Perspective

play in the ensuing Holy Week's liturgies, as we assume our roles in the passion drama that will lead us through successive scenes accompanying Jesus from his Last Supper with his disciples on Thursday evening to his burial in a borrowed tomb on Friday. The fact of the matter is that few of our parishoners will end up being present at all of our liturgies of the Three Days. This only heightens the importance of their hearing by participating in the reading of Jesus' entire passion story at least once this week! I have come to depend upon the beautiful six-verse hymn of Samuel Crossman, "My Song Is Love Unknown," to bracket the reading of the passion story, sometimes using the last verse as a fitting "sending" hymn:

> Here might I stay and sing—
> No story so divine!
> Never was love, dear King,
> Never was grief like thine.
> This is my friend, in whose sweet praise
> I all my days could gladly spend![1]

Raymond Brown's massive and magisterial two-volume *The Death of the Messiah* provides a rich resource for reflection on the passion narratives in all four Gospels; his insights are stimulating to dip into, in preparation for preaching each Holy Week. Brown wonders whether a tradition of Jesus' silence during his passion may not have existed prior to its being compared to the Second Isaiah and Psalm passages, and judges it a certainty that the silence of Jesus in time became a model for others (see 1 Pet. 2:21, 23, e.g.).[2]

Much briefer and even more pastorally suggestive is *Christ on Trial*, by Rowan Williams, the currrent archbishop of Canterbury. He cannily suggests that Jesus' "*sy eipas*," or "so you say" (26:64) serves to turn Caiaphas's question, "Tell us if you are the Christ, the Son of God," back upon the questioner. In effect, his judges are made by Jesus' silence to testify to the untruth of their own positions, becoming thereby judges of their own unjust actions.[3] In the face of Jesus' tortured sense of his Abba's having left the scene of the crime on Friday, the only final answer will be God's definitive if astonishing "YES!" encountered on Easter morn.

JOHN ROLLEFSON

1. *Evangelical Lutheran Worship* (Minneapolis: Augsburg Fortress, 2006), #343. My strong preference is for the hymn to be sung to the old Welsh tune "Rhosymedre," with Ralph Vaughan Williams's gorgeous "Fantasy on Rhosymedre" played as an offertory or postlude. The spiritual quoted earlier is #350 in *Evangelical Lutheran Worship*.
2. Raymond Brown, *The Death of the Messiah*, 2 vols. (New York: Doubleday, 1994), 1:464–65.
3. Rowan Williams, *Christ on Trial* (Grand Rapids: Eerdmans, 2003), 30–31.

Isaiah 42:1-9

¹Here is my servant, whom I uphold,
　　my chosen, in whom my soul delights;
　I have put my spirit upon him;
　　he will bring forth justice to the nations.
²He will not cry or lift up his voice,
　　or make it heard in the street;
³a bruised reed he will not break,
　　and a dimly burning wick he will not quench;
　he will faithfully bring forth justice.
⁴He will not grow faint or be crushed
　　until he has established justice in the earth;
　　and the coastlands wait for his teaching.

⁵Thus says God, the LORD,
　　who created the heavens and stretched them out,
　　who spread out the earth and what comes from it,

Theological Perspective

We will never be sure what or who was the original reference of this and other Servant passages. What we do know is that these passages were quickly applied to Jesus by his followers. We know also that from that day to this, the understanding of these passages has been affected by what we know of Jesus, and our understanding of Jesus has been affected by these passages. We continue to make the application today. For us, the writer, whoever he was, and whatever his intention may have been, prophesied about Jesus. He did so in a way that was more perceptive and profound than any of the other passages in the Hebrew Bible that Christians have applied to Jesus.

First, we are told that Jesus is the Servant of God, who has chosen him and placed the divine spirit upon him. His role is to "bring forth justice to the nations" (v. 1). Of special note here is the universality of the Servant's calling. Very often in the Hebrew Bible the focus is on restoring the house of Israel and bringing justice to its people. In this passage, the Servant is called to bring forth justice throughout the world. "The nations" is a phrase that usually does not include Israel. This may be because the original author had in mind that the one called is Israel or one who represents Israel. When applied to Jesus, the focus is on the universal relevance of Jesus' mission.

Pastoral Perspective

He was so gentle that he would not break a reed that was already bent and weakened, so gentle that his breath would not blow out a candle that was dying anyway. He does not meet violence with more violence. This is the gentleness of the Almighty in Old Testament expectation. It makes me think of Gandhi and his march to the sea, of the waves of humanity who simply would not stop coming, no matter what. Each one was quiet and all but powerless on his or her own, but unstoppable together.

I am also thinking of Dr. King, of the people walking to work and to school, of the fathers with one child on the handlebars of a bicycle and another on the back, of the people in Montgomery who simply would not take the bus for a solid year and a little more, no matter what. I am thinking of a tiny woman in Myanmar—or are we calling it Burma again now? Too small to be seen over the high wall of her garden, she stands on an old desk and speaks to the people who are brave enough to come and hear her talk about freedom and community. She invites the military authorities into her house for tea, the house she is forbidden by them to leave, and she tells them that she has a soft spot in her heart for the military, as her father was a military man. The military authorities executed her father.

who gives breath to the people upon it
 and spirit to those who walk in it:
⁶I am the LORD, I have called you in righteousness,
 I have taken you by the hand and kept you;
I have given you as a covenant to the people,
 a light to the nations,
⁷ to open the eyes that are blind,
 to bring out the prisoners from the dungeon,
 from the prison those who sit in darkness.
⁸I am the LORD, that is my name;
 my glory I give to no other,
 nor my praise to idols.
⁹See, the former things have come to pass,
 and new things I now declare;
 before they spring forth,
 I tell you of them.

Exegetical Perspective

The Isaiah passages of Holy Week all come from the part of the book of Isaiah (chapters 40–66) identified with the time of the people of Judah in Babylonian exile. Exile is not just a historical experience, but a concept, a way of seeing the world. It means feeling like a stranger, feeling alienated, carrying a sense of betrayal. Read from the perspective of exile, the Bible is a response to a sense of massive betrayal in the face of history. The temple is destroyed; the people are either in exile in Babylon, have fled to Egypt, or belong to the poorest of the poor remaining in their occupied land. So inevitably questions of faith arise: Why has our God allowed this to happen? Why do we suffer? Where is our salvation?

We are looking here at something unthinkable. Before, there was the covenant with David that was to last forever and ever (2 Sam. 7; cf. Pss. 89 and 132). The current reality is so different (Ps. 44:9–16). In the exile, the Jewish people settled down after a while, chiefly in the city of Babylon, where they were used as laborers in Nebuchadnezzar's building programs. They were allowed to stay together as communities. There is no indication that they were subject to harsh treatment. They were allowed to worship. They were allowed to live in peace as long as they respected the Babylonian law. They corresponded with the remnant

Homiletical Perspective

The Old Testament texts for the Monday, Tuesday, and Wednesday of Holy Week offer parallels to the second, third, and fourth days of the first creation story in Genesis. To recall what each of those days brought forth, and then to play that against the content of Isaiah, gives an intriguing framework out of which sermons may come.

Separation occurred on the second day of creation. We now see the sky, the shape of things, how they stand. There is clarity emerging out of blazing light or deep darkness. Isaiah 42 presents us with the stark and unmistakable presence of the Servant. Here is the one whom we have both feared and hoped for. There is no longer mist or gloom. We see the Servant, and the mission, and the implications with utter clarity. The question is, do we really want to see them?

The Servant is the perfect instrument of the Holy. He possesses the right qualities and has been superbly trained to exercise them. He acts out of a sense of profound belonging. His presence and work bring about global justice. He carries and employs the power of God. The Servant is evenhanded and soft-spoken. His touch is gentle, and the pace of his work is perfect. His energy remains high until the work is done, and he himself will be held in the shadow of God's hand. He is that presence that will

Isaiah 42:1-9

Theological Perspective

A second point of great theological importance is what Jesus will do in the nations. There is nothing here about drawing them into the old or new Israel. Jesus is not expected to turn people everywhere into believers in him. The task is not a matter of the forgiveness of sins or of saving individual souls. He will "bring forth justice" in every land (v. 1).

Verses 2–3 speak of Jesus' methods. Negatively, the emphasis is that he will be quiet and physically harmless. There are no images of political or military might or even of powerful preaching or teaching. Nevertheless, "he will faithfully bring forth justice." Apparently Jesus' power will be very different from worldly power, and verse 4 assures us that Jesus will persevere until this task is accomplished.

The following verses refocus from the task and method of Jesus to the God who has called him. Here the emphasis is on the great works of God in creation and the way that God has chosen and protected and directed Jesus. All of this leads up to the assertion that Jesus is God's covenant with the people and a light to the nations (v. 6). He will give sight to the blind and free the prisoners (v. 7). Presumably this gives specific content to the justice spoken of previously.

The passage concludes with the contrast between what has been and what will be. Apparently the former things are dominated by violence and injustice. What is now coming into being nonviolently is a new order of justice. This will happen through Jesus.

The question for us is whether the application of this passage to Jesus is now justified by history. In general it is correct to think of Jesus as working for change nonviolently. That he aimed at justice, the healing of the blind, and the freeing of prisoners is made clear by his own selection of texts from the Hebrew Bible to apply to his work. Jesus himself, however, worked almost exclusively within Israel, whereas this passage speaks almost exclusively of work beyond Israel.

His followers rightly recognized that his message and his life work had universal meaning, and they spread out far beyond Israel. Passages such as this one no doubt influenced their decision to do so. Visions or prophecies often inspire their own fulfillment.

We know most about the new communities established by Paul in Jesus' name. They can certainly be described as communities seeking to live by a justice not characteristic of the Roman Empire in which they found themselves. Was this the vision of the prophet?

If the prophet meant that all the nations of the earth would in fact become just, then we can hardly claim that there has been any approximation to

Pastoral Perspective

These are the truly powerful. They are not silent—they *speak* but do not shout or injure. So gentle are they that they could lean on a reed that was already bent and not break it; so gentle are they that their breath would not extinguish a flame that was almost out already. Yet they are powerful—more powerful, in the end, than the impressive forces arrayed against them. Their quiet strength comes from within. It also comes from their people. Leaders are not alone. They have people behind them.

What about the rest of us, who are ordinary people who do not walk at the head of a long line of adoring followers, whose oppression is a misery much more solitary? What about people who dare not even speak of what hurts, afraid that they might make it even worse?

> I cannot tell her. She wouldn't understand, and it
> would make her even angrier.
> I might get fired.
> It would just hurt her feelings.
> Better not rock the boat. It might make things even
> harder.

Some pain sees the light of day and begins to heal. Some pain goes to its grave in lonely silence. Is that what nonviolence looks like in a person's life? Nonviolence is not the same thing as nonresistance. It has nothing at all to do with being a doormat. It is not silent. It *speaks*. The private courage it takes for it to speak is tremendous—of a piece with that of Dr. King or Aung San Suu Kyi. At the head of a great movement or in an ordinary home, nonviolent resistance relies on quiet truth for its power. All violence is based on a lie: that some human beings are fit objects of the wrath of other human being, that some people's needs are more important than others, that some people's dignity does not matter. This is not true. Everyone's dignity matters.

Here is Jesus. Everything that can be done to humiliate him *is* done, every torture and every taunt. In his silence, self-contained and still, broken by an occasional word of truth, as a prisoner, he does not and cannot resist physically. Others have dominion over him, but they cannot make him part of their lie.

We know how the story continues. Look at what happened. The dignity of nonviolence did *not* win the day. Jesus was *killed,* for heaven's sake. Power trumped truth. See, I told you so. It is better not to rock the boat.

Ah, but only in the moment. You can purchase a precarious peace from a bully with the coin of your compliance, but you can never buy a permanent one.

back in Jerusalem, back in "the land." They were free to travel. They had their religious meetings. There was limited freedom for the exiled people of Judah as long as they were obedient to Babylon; indeed they were even allowed to engage in agricultural pursuits, business and commercial endeavors. Thus, one did not see extreme external suffering. Nevertheless, it was a time of deep search of the meaning of faith.

Near the end of the exilic period, some time between 550 and 540 BCE, a poet-prophet, who does not give us any information about who he or she is, provides words of comfort and vision, hope, and reassurance ("Comfort, O comfort my people . . ."; 40:1).

Isaiah 42:1–9 introduces the figure of the Servant (*'ebed*), whom God calls to bring justice to everyone. Endowed with the gift of the spirit (v. 1), the chosen one is to persist "until he has established justice in the earth" (v. 4). YHWH God the Creator reminds the Servant of the covenant made with the people at Sinai (vv. 6–7; cf. Exod. 19:1–6). God the Liberator calls the Servant to lead a new exodus (cf. 43:14–19), namely "to open the eyes that are blind, to bring out the prisoners from the dungeon, from the prison those who sit in darkness" (42:7).

In an exilic movement toward universalism ("to the nations," "and the coastlands wait . . .", "in the earth" [vv. 1, 4], etc.), YHWH, the God of the exodus, who required exclusive attention ("you shall have no other gods before me," Exod. 20:3), identifies Godself as the only one who deserves to be God ("my glory I give to no other, nor my praise to idols," v. 8; cf. 44:6–8; 45:5–7, et al.). Thus the realities of monolatry, the worship of one god YHWH, have given way to the claim to monotheism, the existence of only one god, that is, YHWH. As a result, "the former things have come to pass" (v. 9), and God declares a new reality and promises a new creation (v. 9; cf. 43:16–21). There is hope in this claim of another liberation; there is hope in the claim to new realities. The fear of change and the discomfort of unfamiliarity, the prophet does not allow. Indeed, the figure of the Servant is to be YHWH's mediator who will both bring forth justice in the earth and teach the coastlands.

Through the ages interpreters have surmised the identity of the Servant in the book of Isaiah. Two trajectories of interpretation have emerged, one identifying the Servant with a heroic individual, and the other identifying the Servant as the collective Israel (so the Septuagint and Rashi). The individuals identified include Cyrus, the king of Persia, who officially ends the Babylonian exile (see 45:1–8); the prophet himself or herself (so Ibn Ezra); and the Messiah (so Targum).

stir the long-repressed yearning of the wide world. This is how life was meant to be. This is how humanity was meant to rise and follow.

When this Servant has fulfilled his mandate, holy light will abound, eyes will be open, and prisoners will be released. Freedom, insight, zeal, and strength of spirit will stalk the land. It will be a new time for everyone. All walls are down and all bets off.

We can hide the news and the power of this Servant by keeping it inside the text, within the Holy Book, chained to the holy desk and in the hands of the holy few; or we can set it free. The question for preaching is, who dares tell, and who dares hear?

Every new thing is met with resistance. Every life-saving insight risks being labeled heretical. Communities like what they know and tend to measure their progress by holding fast to what came before. To allow Second Isaiah, the folksinger, with his long hair, loose life, and wild vision, into the sanctuary is a big risk.

This brings us to the heart of the matter. Holy Week itself is about the conflict that arises when new meets old; when the light of persistent freedom exposes entrenched resistance. Holy Week demands the clarity of the second day of creation. Contenting ourselves to see through mist and gloom is an abrogation of our deepest human nature. There are clear choices to make in how we shall establish our lives and customs. When light is commanded on day one, we know that implications of that light will follow and divide the players into armed camps.

Push the examples. Apply this to the destiny of the churched and nonchurched, to questions around class and race. Press the edges of courage and flexibility in life's hard places. Ask about war and peace, armaments and manifest destiny. Explore the qualities named as signs of God's hands at work. Cite examples of blindness and imprisonment around you and within.

This is hard going, but then Holy Week is hard going. It is the place where the best of us meets the worst. It hurts and kills. Yet we are deadened already if we refuse to hear the brilliance of this text and the radical freedom it contains. It is about rebirth with all its terrors and gifts.

The Servant here portrayed is both most feared and most sought. He is most *sought* because we know that we need the out-of-body, out-of-routine experience of God's creative touch to become who we were meant to be. Our society needs freshly sighted, newly released lives to tell broader stories, paint brighter pictures, and sing more haunting songs. He is most *feared* because to follow him is step beyond the safety

Isaiah 42:1-9

Theological Perspective

realization of the vision; but it is possible to read the text as establishing more modest goals. According to the NRSV, Jesus is to bring forth justice "*to the* nations" (v. 1) and establish justice "*in the earth*" (v. 4). Perhaps the presence in all countries of communities that embody the justice he proclaimed, the *basileia theou* (I prefer "divine commonwealth" to the usual "kingdom of God") that Jesus assured us was at hand, can count as fulfillment of this prophecy.

If we allow ourselves such an interpretation, then there is at least the possibility of a positive answer. The issue becomes one of the actual nature of the church. Do our congregations embody the justice proclaimed by Jesus? Have they been so swallowed up into a pagan and imperial culture that surrounds them, that it is the pursuit of wealth and power that actually controls our churches?

That is the question with which this passage confronts us at the beginning of Holy Week. Are our congregations shaped in their behavior and attitudes more by the "former things," the values of the great ancient empires and of the contemporary economic and political order, or are they shaped by the new things, the justice of the divine commonwealth, which was the center of Jesus' message?

Each of us can do her or his part in shaping the answer to that question in the congregation in which we participate. It is an immensely important question. If our congregations live by the sort of justice Jesus proclaimed, we can bring forth justice *to* our nations. If we have come to live by the values of the nations, then we will only reflect back to them what they already are.

JOHN B. COBB JR.

Pastoral Perspective

The road to all the righteous victories we remember is littered with the suffering of those who walked it: Gandhi in jail, killed finally. Dr. King first jailed, then killed as well. Thousands of quiet, brave men and women brutally stopped from pursuing their rights. Killed, many of them.

Power does not trump truth forever. Whose names do we remember? Who were the people who turned fire hoses on the marchers in Selma? Who are the generals in Burma? Who were the men pounding in the nails? We do not remember a single one of them. They are nameless. Pontius Pilate and Annas and Caiaphas? We remember them vaguely, and only as names in a story that is not primarily about them. They won, but only in the moment. The story continued without them. This Holy Week will have an end, and its end will be nothing like its beginning. It will be nothing like anything we know. It will be so new that we will have a hard time describing it, but before it springs forth, we tell each other of it.

Sit in your office with a woman whose life with an addict has become unbearable; or with a man whose gambling has ruined him, only nobody knows yet, as he tap dances desperately from one crisis to another; or with a person caught in the increasingly irrational web of an illicit love affair. "I can't tell her," he says. "He must never know," she whispers. "It would ruin everything." "Oh, child, child," you think as you sit in your chair and listen. "Everything is *already* ruined. The damage is already done. You have nowhere to go but up."

Sometimes it is only from the ashes of defeat and even death that new life can emerge. Some people never do get to see the promised land. Sometimes it is only those who follow the ones who have the guts to name it who get to set foot there. Somebody must make a beginning.

BARBARA CAWTHORNE CRAFTON

Exegetical Perspective

If one goes with the collective identification, contemporary readers may replace the exilic Israel with the marginalized communities of our respective contexts. How then do we understand ourselves as chosen by God, as delight to God's being (the Hebrew *nephesh* has a more wholistic meaning than the translation "soul" suggests), as endowed with God's spirit?

Further, the passage suggests that there is joy to be found in the struggle. A gender-fluid God (who has a womb and gives birth) takes a female "you" by the hand. Boundaries, both physical and metaphysical, have become fluid; the goal of the struggle, namely, to "establish justice on the earth," is all that counts— justice for all everywhere. Such a universal promise offers hope, even though some might find God's impartiality hard to bear, because it means God being impartial to ourselves as well. While there clearly remains a tension between God's universal promise and God's choosing of a particular people, the passage suggests an opening up to a global context, as understood at the time.

On a more theological note, chosenness has long been understood as entitlement, which has resulted in violence and terror for many. What would it mean to understand chosenness as belovedness? While such theology offers rich possibilities, it also raises serious questions as to who is left out of choice and left out of love. The Isaiah passage adds an important criterion: the bringing of justice, leading us to claim that if we love, we make justice. Feeling loved leads to more self-esteem and consequently a better ability to act justly and become participants in God's project of liberation.

ANGELA BAUER-LEVESQUE

Homiletical Perspective

of the familiar, beyond approval, beyond belonging. It begins to sever ties with that which is easy and supportive. The sight of the Servant stirs curiosity and general unease. To feel that such servanthood is part of our call to faithfulness either sends us running headlong toward the opportunity, or pedaling backward away from it as fast as we can.

Two other things seem remarkable. One is that someone actually envisioned this portrait. It must have been costly in his day to name all the great things in it. The style of leadership captured here is a judgment against the state, the rule of law, and the political players of the day. The writer is saying that the nation is, above all else, the servant of the Holy One, living out an empowered relationship within an established covenant. Anything narrower, smaller, tighter, or meaner betrays this ancient high calling. Such portrait painters become lightning rods for all the discontented lives struggling unseen and unheard in the land.

The other remarkable thing is that editors over the centuries made certain to include this portrait in the canon of Scripture. In times of trouble, when the people needed to keep their best lives above water, the editors aimed high. To do this, they themselves would need to possess the imagination, intelligence, and faithfulness to recognize a treasure when they saw it. The routine and high daily demands of congregational life may send the preacher scurrying after small themes and immediate fixes to patch and cover the cracks. Our people know inside that after a while small things do not touch the deep places. We starve together consuming starchy offerings week by week. To tackle the big themes at a price opens the variety of rich fare by which the Holy One is known.

G. MALCOLM SINCLAIR

Psalm 36:5-11

⁵Your steadfast love, O LORD, extends to the heavens,
    your faithfulness to the clouds.
⁶Your righteousness is like the mighty mountains,
    your judgments are like the great deep;
    you save humans and animals alike, O LORD.

⁷How precious is your steadfast love, O God!
    All people may take refuge in the shadow of your wings.
⁸They feast on the abundance of your house,
    and you give them drink from the river of your delights.
⁹For with you is the fountain of life;
    in your light we see light.

¹⁰O continue your steadfast love to those who know you,
    and your salvation to the upright of heart!
¹¹Do not let the foot of the arrogant tread on me,
    or the hand of the wicked drive me away.

Theological Perspective

As the Christian community begins its journey through Holy Week, this lection provides a crucial starting point for that journey. It is a reminder of who God is and of God's relationship not only to humans, but to all of creation. In these verses from Psalm 36, the psalmist takes a positive and praising tone, explicating the nature and character of God in poetic imagery and metaphors. At the close of the passage, the psalmist offers up a brief prayer for God's love and protection based on the preceding understanding of who and what God is.

In verses 5–6, God's creation provides the metaphors for God's nature and character. The lection begins with the recognition that God's steadfast love and faithfulness extend "to the heavens" and "to the clouds," respectively, capturing a sense of the broad and boundless nature of God's love and fidelity. The psalmist then likens God's righteousness to the "mighty mountains" (strong, solid, and unwavering) and God's good judgment to the "great deep" (bottomless, profound, and unfathomable). Continuing in this vein of creation language, verse 6 ends with the declaration that not only humans, the "pinnacle" of creation, but animals—and by extension *all* aspects of creation—are saved by God's redeeming love and faithfulness.

The reader is reminded of Paul's corroboration with this theological concept in Romans 8:21–22,

Pastoral Perspective

In all three years of the lectionary cycle, the lection for Holy Monday is sliced out of a larger psalm that describes human wickedness in detail. "Transgression speaks to the wicked deep in their hearts; there is no fear of God before their eyes. For they flatter themselves in their own eyes that their iniquity cannot be found out and hated. The words of their mouths are mischief and deceit; they have ceased to act wisely and do good. They plot mischief while on their beds; they are set on a way that is not good; they do not reject evil" (vv. 1–4). The whole psalm contrasts God's faithfulness with human wickedness. The tension of righteousness and corruption is pulled taut. Who is God: the righteous one of verses 5–11, or the god of rebellion of verses 1–4, 12? While the lectionary resolves the tension by focusing solely on God's faithfulness (except for the last allusions of v. 11), congregants arrive at church knowing the frayed realities of righteousness and wickedness that stretch them to the breaking point.

While scholars and lectionary editors may separate Psalm 36 into two pieces, the pew Bible in the rack does not. The liturgy could highlight this separation of the righteousness of God from the degeneracy of life. Congregants are not unaware or naive about verses 1–4, 12. They know too well the threats. They read other people's Facebook pages, they watch the

Exegetical Perspective

YHWH has the power to protect, order, and nourish all living things. This confession lies at the core of the song of praise (vv. 5–9) that begins this lection. The claims come at an important point within the psalm's larger structure. Indeed, v. 5 is the turning point in the psalm. In the foregoing verses, the psalmist focuses on the utter depravity of the wicked and the real threats such people pose for the psalmist (vv. 1–4). The psalmist paints a picture of the archetypal wicked one and explores the psychological makeup of such persons, going so far as to describe their inner dialogue (vv. 1–2). Lacking the fear of God, these wicked ones arrogantly believe that they can conspire (v. 4), speak, and act (v. 3) with impunity.

The sudden shift to the praise in verse 5 reminds the psalmist—and whoever is listening—what the wicked have failed to recognize to their own detriment (see v. 12!), namely, that YHWH is real and powerful, a force not to be ignored. Verses 5–6 portray YHWH through expansive terms, evoking YHWH's characteristics by coupling them with powerful forces of nature (vv. 7–9a): YHWH's steadfast love with the heavens; his faithfulness with the clouds; his righteousness with the mountains; and his justice (*mishpat*; NRSV, "judgments") with the deep waters. Here the psalmist concretizes otherwise intangible aspects of the divine personality by

Homiletical Perspective

The art of preaching in the early days of Holy Week centers on the ability to rest easily between two sets of profound tensions. The Holy Week preacher stands, on Monday, just after Palm Sunday and looking far ahead to the three great days and especially Easter. So the first tension the preacher must negotiate is the tension between what has come and what awaits. We have already experienced the passion in full, and yet we will reprise that experience as the week unfolds. The Holy Week preacher thus finds herself at the beginning of a process of which we already know the outcome.

There is a second profound tension as well. Holy Week is always most centrally about Jesus and his experience in Jerusalem from the triumphal entry through the critique of established systems to the betrayal, arrest, trial, crucifixion, and empty tomb. Holy Week is about Jesus. However, if I am going to preach about it, it also has to be about me. The task of the Holy Week preacher is therefore to help the listener make the connection between the story of Jesus of Nazareth and the story of the person in the pew. As always in preaching, the art of it has less to do with coming up with ingenious observations about the texts than it does with finding a way into the heart and mind of the hearer that opens the texts up in life-giving and transformative ways.

Psalm 36:5-11

Theological Perspective

where he states "that the creation itself will be set free from its bondage to decay and will obtain the freedom of the glory of the children of God. We know that the whole creation has been groaning in labor pains until now." The redemption made possible through the events of the coming week is something offered to the entire world. We are invited to consider the far-reaching ethical implications of such a theology of creation, especially at a time when all of God's good creation seems to be threatened on so many fronts.

In verses 7–9, the psalmist draws from these statements about God's nature to explicate the ways in which God's children are blessed by this unending love and fidelity to all of creation. God is refuge, which people find "in the shadow of your wings." God is sustainer, through which people "feast on the abundance of your house" and "drink from the river of your delights." God is life and light in a world of death and darkness. In each of these metaphors, the imagery indicates a notion of the profound *nearness* of God: protection beneath God's wings, feasting and drinking in the house of God, life being "with" God and light being "in" God. The psalmist here reveals a side of God's character that invites us into close—even personal—relationship with the Creator of all that was, is, and will be.

Moreover, the notions of God as refuge and sustainer give evidence of God's love as an *active* love. There is little abstraction in the psalmist's understanding of how God's love is enacted. Perhaps the best analogy for God's steadfast love that humans can surmise is that of a parent to a child. What image conjures the concepts of loving protection and sustenance better than that of a mother gazing upon her infant's face as he nurses at her breast, or of a father holding his young child in a strong, protective embrace following a bad dream?

In the concluding prayer (vv. 10–11) as well, the psalmist reinforces the theological position that God gives humans the capacity for nearness to God and invites them into relationship. The psalmist asks for God's continued love for "those who *know*" God (my emphasis). As one commentator has stated, to "'know' indicates more than merely intellectual knowledge. In the Hebrew Bible, there is no division between cognition and action (see Hos. 4:1–3). To know is to act and to act is to know."[1] In other words, it is not enough to know of or about God intellectually; truly to "know" God means that one loves and

Pastoral Perspective

news, and they know their own desires and aspirations as they toss and turn at night. People have come to the sanctuary on a Monday. Do you know how odd that is? The world thinks coming once each week on Sunday is strange. How much more so is coming on a workday? The emptiness in the pews indicates that the church considers it inconvenient too. The folks coming to the assembly on Monday are pulling themselves out of the mire of their everyday affairs in order to see God. While aware of the truthfulness of their own reality, they come on Monday to see a more profound reality, that is, steadfast love and dependable righteousness. They come to profess with their lips their conviction that God can set things right.

During the hours of Holy Week, it is surprising that the church has excised the enemies from the lectionary (vv. 1–4, 12). Including the verses about the wicked scheming of the enemies generates a fitting correlation with John 12:9–11. John's narrative describing Holy Week brings Jesus' enemies to prominence. John characterizes their wickedness in ways that resemble the deleted words of the psalm, for example, "The words of their mouths are mischief and deceit; they have ceased to act wisely and do good. They plot mischief while on their beds; they are set on a way that is not good" (vv. 3–4). The narrative of John in the larger liturgy brings the whole psalm into view.

Domestically, we rely on the Department of Homeland Security to protect us from the outsiders. Like other nations, we build fences lined with barbed wire on our borders in order to safeguard real estate, jobs, and family. Just in case, we also ship our defenses abroad to maintain our national security and protect our interests. We fret over cyber crimes that might rob us of our identities and grasp at all that we are entitled to. Security issues press people from every stratum of society. From well-to-do business persons managing their stock portfolios to young graduates seeking employment and first mortgages, from parents agonizing over life decisions of teenagers to children living on the streets wondering if a worn blanket will be sufficient for the changing seasons, people across the nation work diligently to protect their current state of life and secure their emerging future. Our enemies crouch close by. Sometimes, the enemies are so close that we swear they are looking back at us in the mirror. "They plot mischief while on their beds." We flinch at our vulnerability.

Especially frightening, shaking us to the core of our being, are the times when that which we trusted most is lost. On the Monday of Holy Week, the pastor turns the heads of the congregation toward the cross. The

---

1. Rolf A. Jacobson, "Psalm 36:5–11," *Interpretation* 61, no. 1 (Jan. 2007): 66. http://find.galegroup.com/itx/start.do?prodId=AONE.

Exegetical Perspective

binding them to readily observable aspects of the universe. In the mind of this faithful poet, the elements of nature bear witness to the very nature of YHWH. Indeed, the structure of the universe itself attests YHWH's righteousness and justice.

After extolling YHWH's characteristics, which are completely contrary to those of the wicked (vv. 1–4), the psalmist depicts YHWH's acts of protection (v. 7), sustenance (v. 8), and blessing (v. 9) that are available to the community of the faithful. This community, like YHWH, stands in sharp contrast to the wicked. This community is remarkably inclusive, containing people throughout the world—and even animals (v. 6)! All of these creatures find refuge in YHWH's wings, an image that appears several times in the Psalter to describe the protection afforded by the divine presence (Pss. 17:8; 57:1; 61:4; 63:7; 91:4).

Those who enjoy YHWH's protecting presence also find nourishment through God. Another, more literal, translation of verse 8a is "They will drink from the fatness of your house" (cf. NRSV "They feast on the abundance of your house"). As odd as it may sound to modern health-conscious readers, the psalmist may well be referring here to enjoying the taste of liquefied fat from sacrificial meals in the temple. Further reference to God's protection and provision comes through the images of YHWH's "river" and "fountain" (vv. 8b–9). Elsewhere in the Old Testament, these images are closely associated with the temple (cf. Pss. 46:4; Ezek. 47:1; Joel 3:18; Zech. 13:1; 14:8). The psalmist maintains that in the presence of God, chaotic waters (cf. Gen. 1:1; Ps. 46:3) become orderly, life-giving sources of sustenance. Verse 9 concludes with the striking and evocative phrase "in your light we see light," possibly a reference to a divine solar theophany at the temple (cf. Pss. 4:6; 44:3; 89:15).

Verses 7–9 present a unique constellation of literary imagery for YHWH. If one reads the text rather simply and concretely, a composite picture emerges: a winged god (v. 7) from whom life-giving liquid flows (vv. 8–9b) and from whom—like the sun—light emanates (v. 9b). Remarkably congruent imagery can be found in the art of the ancient Near East, where winged disks representing solar deities appear with streams of water flowing from beneath their wings. Indeed, the picture in Psalm 36:7–9 is remarkably similar. The psalm describes individuals being refreshed and delighted by a winged deity who provides both liquid nourishment and light. No doubt the psalmist drew on contemporary pictorial imagery of other gods and appropriated these images to YHWH. By recasting the religious

Homiletical Perspective

The first stanza (vv. 5 and 6) introduces us to the overarching affirmation of this psalm, the persistence of God's "steadfast love." Whatever else may be going on in Holy Week, whatever Jesus might experience, whatever that experience may dredge up out of the dregs of my own pain or fear, the assertion we begin with is that this week is somehow an enactment of God's steadfast love. This love presides over the events of the week, and when all is said and done at the end of it, God will have stood with Jesus and with us.

The way Psalm 36 gives shape and weight to the hymnic praise of that steadfast love is through a series of natural metaphors that modulate into one another in an ongoing process of transformative comparison. So the speaker of Psalm 36 first characterizes steadfast love as a kind of large abstraction: it extends to the heavens, to the clouds. Though we do not have an image of it in the first stanza, we know what some subsets of it look and feel like: God's righteousness "is like the mighty mountains"; God's judgments "are like the great deep." Whatever God's steadfast love may be, we know that it is big, it is high, it is deep, and that the first way to describe it involves comparison with the natural phenomena at the limits of human consciousness and imagination.

The second stanza (vv. 7–9) both elaborates and clarifies that comparison. What was vaguely abstracted as a kind of celestial penumbra now takes shape as "the shadow of [God's] wings." The human community takes refuge in that shadow; then, in a new comparison, they feast on the abundance of God's house. In yet another metaphor, they "drink from the river of [God's] delights." So in a brisk but subtle way we have moved from cosmic, extensive metaphors (space, sky, mountains, oceans) to personal comparisons—food and water, the essentials of human life. This stanza concludes with two divergent but complementary comparisons. With God is "the fountain of life," and in God's light "we see light." God is at once a presiding cosmic presence and the source of the concrete necessaries of life in the here and now. More than that, God is the source both of "life" figured as a fountain and of "light" (knowledge, goodness, hope) that illuminates us.

The third stanza (vv. 10–11) completes the hymn to God's steadfast love with a prayer that it continue to those who know God and are "upright of heart" and then introduces the lament theme that will come to dominate the remainder of Holy Week: "Do not let the foot of the arrogant tread on me, or the hand of the wicked drive me away." Everything that the speaker has said extolling God's steadfast love now

Psalm 36:5-11

Theological Perspective

serves God by aligning one's life with God's law and keeping the commandments.

The psalmist also prays that God will not let "the hand of the wicked drive me away." The word "away" implies distance from God, movement in a direction other than where God is. The reader is reminded of the wise adage, "If it feels as if God is far away from you, guess who moved?" The psalmist recognizes that despite the boundlessness of God's love and faithfulness and God's invitation to humans to find refuge, sustenance, and life in God's protective arms, the potential to be dragged or lured away from such blessedness is always present.

On this Monday of Holy Week, the looming shadow of Friday and Saturday is not far from us. In the very first Holy Week, Jesus' followers did not have the benefit of hindsight. To them, the profound and inescapable darkness they experienced following Jesus' crucifixion was all-consuming and, in their minds, was to last. This side of the resurrection, the Christian community too enters the darkness, braced to experience the betrayal, loneliness, suffering, and death of its Savior. However, the community enters this darkness already knowing that death and despair will give way to the life and light of Easter. As the community begins a sad and difficult—but ultimately death-defying and joyful—journey this week, it is fortified *from the very start* by the psalmist's reminder that our God is near to us, as savior, refuge, "fountain of life" (v. 9). That Savior will rise again, offering hope and redemption to "the upright of heart" (v. 10) and indeed to all of creation. Even in deepest despair, God offers consolation, rest, and refuge out of God's boundless and steadfast love.

NICOLE L. JOHNSON

Pastoral Perspective

triumph of yesterday's grand entrance into Jerusalem fades into the background of the story. Friday looms. Most people in the congregation have heard the requiem of Monday through Thursday before. The cadence slows on Monday. The psalm text, although full of delight in God's goodness, is read during somber hours. As in no other week, the church needs to turn toward God. It is on Monday that the psalm sings a countermelody to the church that reestablishes faith in the vastness of God's goodness.

Psalm 36 is image-driven with a host of options. Images in the text include the height of God's love, faithfulness, and righteousness, correlated with the depth of God's justice. Other scenes picture refuge in the shadow of God's wings, feasting at a house, drinking from a river, a fountain of life, light in light, and the foot and hand of the enemy. In an image-driven world, where the Internet overloads our imagination like a strobe light, the preacher has the option of imitating the psalmist by multiplying image on top of image, or choosing to concentrate on one scene in order to encapsulate the whole.

The rich imagery of Psalm 36 cascades over us with hope. Imagine sitting in the sanctuary and seeing the stained-glass mural on the east wall. The sun rises just over the mountain to draw attention to a house that invites you in with open arms. The fountain outside provides refreshing water to drink. With the river on one side and the mountain on the other, the home is protected from the elements of nature and the thief who would come at night. The light of the psalmist shining through the stained glass highlights God's steadfast love, faithfulness, righteousness, judgments, and salvation. The vision cast by this scene calls us to rest securely in the shadow of God's wing. Even though Friday is unavoidable, God's wing of refuge still gathers us together.

TIMOTHY R. SENSING

Exegetical Perspective

iconography of the period, the psalmist implicitly argues that it is not any other heavenly god but YHWH who sustains and protects the lives of the faithful ones and, indeed, all of creation (vv. 6b–7). Such power belongs to YHWH alone.

Having painted such a vivid picture of YHWH as a heavenly deity, the psalmist then utters the only direct petition of the psalm (vv. 10–11). Usually such petitions come much earlier in psalms of lament (e.g., Pss. 6; 17; 31). Up to this point in the psalm, however, the psalmist has been concerned primarily to describe two main actors, the enemies (seen as an archetypal wicked one, vv. 1–4) and God. Both of these actors are named in verses 10–11, and the psalmist introduces a third character, namely, the psalmist herself or himself. This psalmist is susceptible to the evil actions of the wicked (v. 11). More importantly, the psalmist is also a potential beneficiary of God's protecting power. This relationship among the wicked, the psalmist, and God has been implicit in the psalm up until this point, but here at the end the psalmist makes an explicit plea for YHWH's protection from the wicked ones.

In this final plea, the psalmist describes himself or herself as among a righteous community. Such people "know" God and are "upright of heart" (v. 10). The description of this community is meant to contrast clearly with the characterization of the wicked in verses 1–4. Rather than living righteously, the wicked live by a lie that resides "deep in their hearts," namely, that God is powerless, even nonexistent; these people have "no fear of God" (v. 1). The threat from them is palpable (vv. 1–4, 11), but the psalmist is utterly convinced of their error and of God's power. The God of the heavens, who protects, orders, and nourishes all life, will in the end bring about justice and salvation (v. 12).

JOEL MARCUS LEMON

Homiletical Perspective

can be seen in a new way. That steadfast love is awesome in its cosmic dimensions, intimately sustaining in its personal manifestations; but the speaker knows how perilous life can be, and we are given the real point of this exultant celebration: given the fragility of life and the contingency of its outcome, the speaker cries out in fear and hope that God will prove faithful now, as God has done in the past.

Therefore, Psalm 36:5–11 provides a preacher with two strong possibilities, one rooted in the hymn, the other in the lament. Bearing in mind the twofold challenge to orient the sermon in the context of the whole week and to connect the Jesus story to the hearer's life, one can take on the larger issue of the psalm as a hymn to God's "steadfast love" and use Monday in Holy Week to outline an approach to the whole week going forward under the protective shadow of God's wings. The focus of the first homily is this: Jesus and we are in for a rough ride this week, but God's steadfast love is overshadowing the whole process. This entails a willingness to engage why bad things happen to good people, but it has the virtue of addressing suffering by putting it in a larger context.

The second option is to take one's cue from verse 11, which introduces the lament motif that will come forward strongly over the next days. Trust as I may in God's steadfast love, when I am up against it, I still ask for specific, personal protection. Even as we gather as a Christian community in Holy Week to focus on Jesus and his suffering, it is OK to offer up prayers for what is on our minds and hearts. Giving the congregation permission to see themselves in the story of Jesus, and Jesus in their stories, is an excellent way to celebrate this Monday in Holy Week.

GARY R. HALL

Hebrews 9:11-15

¹¹But when Christ came as a high priest of the good things that have come, then through the greater and perfect tent (not made with hands, that is, not of this creation), ¹²he entered once for all into the Holy Place, not with the blood of goats and calves, but with his own blood, thus obtaining eternal redemption. ¹³For if the blood of goats and bulls, with the sprinkling of the ashes of a heifer, sanctifies those who have been defiled so that their flesh is purified, ¹⁴how much more will the blood of Christ, who through the eternal Spirit offered himself without blemish to God, purify our conscience from dead works to worship the living God!

¹⁵For this reason he is the mediator of a new covenant, so that those who are called may receive the promised eternal inheritance, because a death has occurred that redeems them from the transgressions under the first covenant.

Theological Perspective

Throughout Hebrews, the theological themes of Christology and atonement intertwine. While both are consonant with theological directives found in Paul's epistles, the themes here express distinct perspectives that enrich the understanding of the nature and work of Christ. Both issues prompt exhortations about exercising moral action or admonitions against allowing faith to atrophy or erode. As throughout Hebrews, here we observe the continuity and discontinuity between the old and new covenants.

The christological theme addresses aspects related to the identity of Christ as high priest, the efficacy of Christ's sacrifice in his redemptive work, and his continuity with and transformation of God's covenant with the readers of Hebrews. This presents a christological paradox, namely, that Christ is simultaneously both high priest and the object of sacrifice. Not only did Christ come "as a high priest of the good things that have come" (v. 11), but in serving in that office "he entered once for all into the Holy Place," wherein "with his own blood" he obtained "eternal redemption" (v. 12). At this point, the author of Hebrews identifies the role of Christ with that of Melchizedek, the "priest of God Most High" who blessed Abraham when he returned victorious from battle (Gen. 14:17–20). As the "king of righteousness," Melchizedek had foreshadowed Christ to such an extent that "the

Pastoral Perspective

The pastor looks out over an interesting congregation on the Monday of Holy Week. One of the saints of the church who finds her way into the sanctuary every time the doors are open and the lights are on is probably there. A newcomer to the congregation's life may be there. His fresh journey of faith includes soaking up every opportunity he can to be in worship. There may be a stranger who happens to be in town for business. She saw the sign announcing Holy Week worship services earlier in the day when she was on her way to a meeting. The pastor could see the very familiar face of a regular Sunday morning worshiper. His life has been turned upside down at work lately and he craves any chance to regroup, reframe, recenter his life. A Monday congregation is going to be different for the preacher, not just smaller, and maybe more attentive.

In the quiet of Monday evening worship, the sanctuary walls still echo the shouts of "Hosanna in the highest!" The threads of palm branches are all over the floor. The memories of a Palm Sunday parade are so fresh that some folks are still humming the melody of "All Glory, Laud, and Honor." Even if the worship planners were successful in beginning to shift the congregation's gaze toward the cross, even if there was a bit of Passion Sunday in the liturgy, Monday worship still happens in the aftermath of Palm Sunday. The

194   *Monday of Holy Week*

Exegetical Perspective

The reading comes in the midst of a complex comparison between the death of Christ and the ritual of the Day of Atonement (Yom Kippur), as described in Leviticus 16. Occupying much of chapters 9 and 10, that comparison is in turn is framed by a reference to the prophecy of Jeremiah 31:31–34, cited in Hebrews 8:1–12 and 10:16–17, which promises the establishment of a new covenant. The prophecy and the comparison work together in an intricate exegetical tapestry that ultimately paints a picture of Christ as the one who makes possible the new covenantal relationship. He does so by his status, as exalted yet merciful heavenly intercessor, and by his example, as the Son whose faith, hope, and love are models for his covenantal brothers and sisters.

The opening verse assumes that Christ is a "high priest," which the author had demonstrated in chapter 7. There he had worked with Psalm 110:1, which had often been applied to Christ by early Christians. Verse 4 of the psalm had named the royal figure addressed in the psalm a "priest forever according to the order of Melchizedek." The author interpreted that verse to apply to Christ as an eternal, and therefore heavenly, high priest. As such, although from the nonpriestly tribe of Judah, he was qualified to perform the perfect Day of Atonement ritual, in the ideal space for it, not an edifice of human origin, but

Homiletical Perspective

"Whatever happened to the Jebusites?" This is not the question with which our parishioners are coming to church this Sunday, wrote Harry Emerson Fosdick some eighty plus years ago.[1] Neither are they coming with questions about how Jesus' blood is superior to that of goats, calves, bulls, and heifer ashes. This is not just Karl Barth's "strange new world within the Bible";[2] it is a world of images and ideas that are so far from twenty-first-century consciousness that they can hardly be imagined.

The preacher could focus on how ideas from this text correlate with the liturgical calendar and the march that God's people are on during Holy Week. The preacher could engage in teaching as a bridge to a message about the significance of Jesus' sacrifice, especially in comparison with Old Testament sacrifice. Another strategy would be to focus on the ultimate result toward which the Hebrews writer is focused. Each argument throughout the letter has a goal. In this context that goal is stated in verse 15: Jesus "is the mediator of a new covenant, so that those who are called may receive the promised eternal inheritance."

1. Harry Emerson Fosdick, quoted in Mike Graves, ed., *What's the Matter with Preaching Today?* (Louisville, KY: Westminster John Knox Press, 2004), 10.
2. Karl Barth, *The Word of God and the Word of Man*, trans. Douglas Horton (New York: Harper & Row, 1957), 28–50.

Theological Perspective

author of Hebrews presents Christ as the completion or fulfillment of the Jewish sacrificial order."[1]

The efficacy of Christ as the object of sacrifice, which establishes the new covenant, is compared with the purification effected by the sacrifice of goats and bulls, which had proved sufficient for the old covenant. The author of Hebrews dramatically contrasts the sacrifices: Even as the offering of the blood and ashes of these animals "sanctifies those who have been defiled" (v. 13), how much more does the blood of Christ, who is without blemish, "purify our conscience from dead works to worship the living God!" (v. 14).

At various points throughout the history of Christian theology, the understanding of the atonement or redemptive work of Christ has focused on the idea that his sacrifice in the crucifixion can be explained in terms of satisfaction or substitution. In the biblical world, atonement for transgression involved a blood sacrifice as compensation for the right of retaliation. Thus the blood of Christ crucified could satisfy the expectation of this practice, or it could substitute adequately for one who might be vulnerable to judgment. Either interpretation essentially considers the sacrifice itself as harmful—as a relinquishing of messianic selfhood, which suggests an emptying of the unblemished nature of Christ. Recently, however, theologians have started to think about Christ's atoning act in terms that shift the focus from featuring the substitution of Christ's purity to celebrating his sharing from the abundance of divine grace. In this regard, the new focus reflects a form of giving that does not feature Christ's divestment of an untainted nature, but identifies the way that his sacrifice fulfills our need for spiritual health with the inexhaustible gift of divine grace. This new perspective on sacrifice suggests that the sacrificial offering "does not result in loss but rather nurtures communion, mutuality, and interdependence."[2] A salient implication of this point is that in the sacrificial giving of self, one does not diminish oneself; rather, one strengthens oneself and others.

As the one who is both the officiant and object of this consummating sacrifice, Christ is also "the mediator of a new covenant" for those who are called beyond "the transgressions under the first covenant" (v. 15). In contrast to the sacrifice offered under the first covenant, the sacrifice effected by Christ as the

1. Daniel M. Bell Jr., "Sacrifice," in *New and Enlarged Handbook of Christian Theology*, ed. Donald W. Musser and Joseph L. Price (Nashville: Abingdon Press, 2003), 447.
2. Ibid., 448.

Pastoral Perspective

unique congregation that gathers on the Monday of Holy Week is ready to complete the shift, to make the turn, to head for Gethsemane and Calvary.

The transition away from Palm Sunday that comes when pastor and congregation encounter the ninth chapter of the book of Hebrews is far from subtle. Biblical scholars often describe the book of Hebrews as one long sermon. The author is often described as the preacher. With this text, the preacher of the book of Hebrews shifts the images, the theological metaphors, even the movement of the plot that lingers after Sunday. Christ is no humble servant who arrives to acclamations of praise. He is the great high priest moving toward the greater and perfect tent of heaven where God will receive his perfect sacrifice. The Messiah who rides on in majesty is now the mediator of a new covenant who offers his own blood. Readers of Scripture in Holy Week may want to rush to a betrayal and a trial, but the preacher of the book of Hebrews invokes a pause when it comes to the plot's inevitable march. Monday's pause is in order to ponder Christ's sacrifice and the cleansing that comes, not of the flesh, but of the heart and of the soul. The songs of "save us, save us" from Sunday morning have been replaced by a reflective whisper that moves through the congregation: "He has saved us! By his blood we are saved."

In the shared preaching life of preacher and listener, the Hebrews text may function in a variety of ways. The text can serve as a sudden immersion into the strange world of the Bible and the language of sacrifice. Terms like "Holy Place," "new covenant," and "first covenant," accompanied with imagery like that of the blood of goats and bulls, can push the listener beyond a comfort zone. So much of the Holy Week journey can be familiar, even safe, for those who gather for weeknight worship, but this language can be a bit jarring, even disconcerting. When the church stands again on the threshold of Christ's passion, a bit of jostling may not be all bad. Few who lead worship during Holy Week would deny that routines and expectations and traditions can be numbing. Many who gather for worship would be hard pressed to describe an expectation of anything fresh in a sermon or in the liturgy. Treading into some unfamiliar territory on Monday can stir up some possibilities. Just when the listeners are prepared to encounter Jesus as the Suffering Servant and the humble king, the preacher in the book of Hebrews directs attention to Christ as the great high priest who enters "the greater and perfect tent" (v. 11) offering his blood for the sins of the world. Just when

Exegetical Perspective

heaven itself. The language of "perfection," as well as other moves in the comparison throughout these chapters, evokes philosophical notions with a Platonic flavor, notions of an ideal or heavenly realm of perfection.

The note that Christ is the high priest of the good things that "have come" (v. 11; for which some manuscripts read "things to come," influenced perhaps by the wording of 10:1) hints that an eschatological event has already taken place in Christ's exaltation. The ideal has been made real, on which the author will insist in 10:1–10.

Earlier in the chapter the homilist describes the cultic action in the ancient tabernacle, as described in Leviticus. He alludes to that action again in verse 12. The tabernacle contained two sections, the outer space, the locus of ordinary ritual, and the inner sanctum (Holy Place, v. 12), into which the high priest entered only one day a year, bringing the blood of the required sacrificial offerings with which to cleanse the ark of the covenant. The reference to the "blood of goats and calves" (v. 12) or "bulls and goats" and "ashes of a heifer" (v. 13) is imprecise as a reference to the Day of Atonement ritual. The language appears designed to include all kinds of atoning and cleansing rituals, including ordinary sacrifices for sin (Lev. 4–5) and the special rite of purification associated with the heifer's ashes (Num. 19).

The analogy to Christ works on the assumption that the tabernacle is a copy of the cosmic temple, in which the lower reaches correspond to the outer court and heaven corresponds to the inner sanctum. By his resurrection and exaltation to the right hand of God, an event which is the focus of the first chapter of Hebrews, Christ, like the high priest, has entered the most holy presence of God. That entry, effected by means of his own blood shed on the cross, provides expiation for sin, but enthroned within that heavenly sanctuary, Christ serves as a constant intercessor for his covenantal fellows (7:23–25).

The author does not spend time on the process by which shedding blood effects atonement. Later Christian theologians would offer abundant speculation on the subject. He does make one crucial point in verse 14, that the offering of blood took place through "the eternal spirit." While the language will contribute to later Trinitarian theology, it is unlikely that the author has a Trinitarian model in view, and we should probably not treat "eternal spirit" here as a personal name. Instead, this verse is best understood as the author's explanation of how "blood" gets into the "heavenly" realm. It is the entry of Christ's spirit

Homiletical Perspective

Preaching the gospel means naming what God has done redemptively to change a situation in the world. It names the bad news and proclaims the good news of God's "over against" actions. These are actions God takes to overcome that which violates what God wishes to be. In this text, the good news of Jesus' eternally sufficient sacrifice is set against the bad news of merely temporally sufficient animal sacrifices. Jesus' sacrifice secures a purification of our consciences so that we are able to worship God without guilt. The new covenant that Jesus' death established is the good news over against the bad news of an old covenant from which those who transgressed could not be ultimately freed. Jesus' once-for-all death is the last sacrifice necessary for true and ultimate forgiveness from all transgressions. That fact establishes the new covenant and provides the possibility for the promised eternal inheritance to be realized. It is only in Christ that the promises of God can have fulfillment; thus Jesus becomes the fulfiller of what formally had become a futile string of insufficient religious observances.

Note the focus on the actions assigned to Jesus' work in verses 11–15: Christ came as a high priest; he was the greater and perfect tent; he entered once for all the Holy Place, with his own blood; he obtained eternal redemption; he offered himself to God; he purified our consciences from dead works; he is the mediator of a new covenant; he gives the promised eternal inheritance; his death redeems from transgressions under the first covenant.

The preacher attends to the reasons for the actions of God in the text. According to the theological worldview of the Hebrews writer, the insufficiency of the earthly high priesthood necessitated that God take this office of bridge-building (i.e., priesthood) into God's own hands. God does so by becoming the high priest. The temporal and insufficient character of animal sacrifice necessitated that God provide one ultimate and incontrovertible sacrifice that would prove eternally sufficient and unrepeatable. God did this in the sacrifice of Jesus on the cross. Jesus' mediation of the new covenant does not negate the old; it fulfills its ultimate intentions. The loose ends of all previous arrangements between God and humanity have been tied up in what God has established in Christ. The temporal has become eternal. The promise has become fulfillment. Insufficiency has been swallowed up by perfection, death by life, sin by forgiveness, shadows by substance.

Preachers of the gospel must answer why the good news they proclaim is truly good news for their

Hebrews 9:11-15

Theological Perspective

foundation of the new covenant is distinct in its duration, degree, and depth. Under the first covenant, the sprinkling of the penitent with sacrificial blood was required to fulfill its demands for the cleansing of the flesh. Through Christ's sacrifice of himself, purification is extended to all. His sacrifice cleanses the spirit, not merely the body; and it is eternal, not merely temporal.

Under the first covenant, the ritual cleansing facilitated by sacrificial blood was subject to repetition, but the sacrifice of Christ is complete and permanent, as confirmed by the author in the following chapter: Christ "offered for all time a single sacrifice for sins" (10:12). Under the first covenant, the cleansing accomplished by the sacrifice applied to the priests themselves and vicariously to the Jews as the covenanted people. With the sacrifice of Christ, however, the purification extends to all—Jews and Gentiles alike. Finally, under the first covenant, sacrifice compensated for the transgressions of the chosen people, signified by material or physical cleansing. By contrast, under the new convenant not only is the sacrifice permanent and for all; it is also complete, cleansing the spirit as well as the body, by removing the sins rather than merely making amends for them.

Thus the Epistle to the Hebrews provides three trenchant points about the work of God in Christ. First of all, as the unique, comprehensive, and permanent act of atonement, the sacrificial death of Christ suffices for all times and all ages. Second, because God's forgiving grace now applies to all people—regardless of their ethnicity, class, or gender—no one is left out; instead, all are included as beneficiaries of Christ's atoning sacrifice. Third, because Christ's atoning death affects every dimension of a person's life—spiritual, emotional, mental, and physical—a veritable new life emerges in the walk of transforming faith (see Heb. 11).

Although the language of this passage in Hebrews may initially sound arcane and esoteric, its understanding of atonement inseparably links the historic and singular significance of Christ's sacrificial work to the lives of believers in any age, who, as Paul emphasizes, are thereby called to be "living sacrifices" unto God (Rom. 12:1).

JOSEPH L. PRICE

Pastoral Perspective

someone in the pew is settling in to sing the same hymns and hear the same readings, the reading from Hebrews announces that they are going to have to work a bit harder to comprehend and to imagine Christ's sacrificial death and how in God's name it may relate to the ordinary pathway of life.

For some, the language of sacrifice challenges the mind; for others, it may be an invitation for the heart. At its best, the spiritual pilgrimage of Holy Week offers the possibility of a fresh encounter with the suffering and death of Jesus. As always, the Gospel narratives through the week will invite the listener into Christ's journey. The faithful find a quiet spot along the way, discovering yet again that our lives are wrapped into his as he experiences betrayal and desertion at the hands of those who loved him. However, here in Hebrews, right at the start of the week, the image is of Christ, the high priest who shed his blood in perfect sacrifice for each one of us. His priestly role allows the individual to ponder anew what his death means "for me."

The Gospel narrative draws us in. With his sacrifice, Christ the great high priest reaches out to us. We are sanctified. We are made pure. Our consciences are purified from dead works so that we may then worship the living God! In the days ahead, the church will trace the familiar steps of Jesus that will lead again to the empty tomb of Easter morning. The preacher of the book of Hebrews invites the faithful to make this journey with Jesus knowing from the beginning that he travels the way of the cross for us. As the week progresses, of course all focus in the unfolding narrative is on him, but do not ever forget that his focus, the focus of the high priest and his perfect sacrifice, is always on us.

DAVID A. DAVIS

Exegetical Perspective

in the realm of God through which atonement is achieved; it is that spirit, embodied in adherents to the new covenant, that makes the faithful life possible. Although his imagery is strikingly realistic, its metaphorical quality is clear. It is by participating in that spirit, through our own spiritual lives of faith, hope, and love (10:19–25), that our consciences become clean of dead works and we serve the living God (9:14). Those "dead works," therefore, are the works of sin.

The final verse in the passage (v. 15) rounds out the discussion of the death of Jesus while introducing the notion of covenant, which will occupy the following verses, which are not part of today's reading. The introduction of the theme ties the exposition of the Day of Atonement typology to the framing prophecy from Jeremiah. The crucial Greek term here, *diathēkē*, can mean either a "treaty" or "pact," the sort of thing that Jeremiah apparently had in mind, or a "testament," the legal device through which an "inheritance" is bestowed. Our author exploits that ambiguity to suggest that Jeremiah's promise is fulfilled through the inheritance that Christians have received from Christ's death. The designation of Christ as a "mediator" suggests the framework of a legal agreement that Christ negotiates. The author had used such a legal image before in calling Christ the "guarantee" of the covenant (7:22).

The result of the transaction in this case is a "promised eternal inheritance." That inheritance consists of access to the heavenly realm through participation in Christ's spirit, "promised" as was the promise of heavenly rest for the faithful (4:1–10). While making this play on the senses of *diathēkē*, the author deploys one more image to describe the saving efficacy of Christ's death, now described as an act that "redeems," that is, a ransom or a purchase price has been paid to release those who were sin's captives.

HAROLD W. ATTRIDGE

Homiletical Perspective

hearers. The good news they proclaim must meet the bad news of the hearers in a real and significant way. The challenge of preaching the gospel in conversation with this text is in identifying how the good news that the Hebrews writer asserts meets the real bad news of our contemporary hearers. The preacher cannot resolve the debate about whether the hearers must recognize the bad news as real or whether the word proclaimed becomes the point of revelation to make the bad news known. To trust the good news that the text reveals as good news is to name the bad news counterpoint to it. In the case of this text, that means that the preacher must name the separation from God that human sin and rebellion creates.

I have a friend who, frustrated with "soft-serve" mainline preaching, likes to ask me, his preacher friend, "What ever happened to sin?" Karl Menninger asked it long ago, and Cornelius Plantinga Jr. echoes the concern.[3] This text absolutely assumes its importance. The preacher of this text has some work to do, then, if its message is to be meaningful to typical sermon receivers in our time.

For what difference does the good news of atonement make, if there is no sense of separation? What difference does a message of forgiveness make, if there is no palpable sense of sin? What difference does a message of purification make, if there are no true feelings of being filthy and impure, and thus unable to worship God rightly? What difference does a new covenant make, if there is no weariness with the old? Awakening a sense of need in the hearers, based on the assumed bad news behind the good news in the text, requires preachers to do the imaginative and creative work of knowing where the good news witnessed to in the text crosses into the real bad news experience of their hearers.

ANDRÉ RESNER

---

3. Karl Menninger, *Whatever Became of Sin?* (New York: Hawthorn Books, 1973); Cornelius Plantinga Jr., *Not the Way It's Supposed to Be: A Breviary of Sin* (Grand Rapids: Eerdmans, 1995).

John 12:1-11

¹Six days before the Passover Jesus came to Bethany, the home of Lazarus, whom he had raised from the dead. ²There they gave a dinner for him. Martha served, and Lazarus was one of those at the table with him. ³Mary took a pound of costly perfume made of pure nard, anointed Jesus' feet, and wiped them with her hair. The house was filled with the fragrance of the perfume. ⁴But Judas Iscariot, one of his disciples (the one who was about to betray him), said, ⁵"Why was this perfume not sold for three hundred denarii and the money given to the poor?" ⁶(He said this not because he cared about the poor, but because he was a thief; he kept the common purse and used to steal what was put into it.) ⁷Jesus said, "Leave her alone. She bought it so that she might keep it for the day of my burial. ⁸You always have the poor with you, but you do not always have me."

⁹When the great crowd of the Jews learned that he was there, they came not only because of Jesus but also to see Lazarus, whom he had raised from the dead. ¹⁰So the chief priests planned to put Lazarus to death as well, ¹¹since it was on account of him that many of the Jews were deserting and were believing in Jesus.

Theological Perspective

This reading is thick with references that illuminate key elements of John's theology of Christ and the church. It begins by noting a time and place. It was shortly before Passover, the celebration of the time when the plague visited Pharaoh's Egypt but passed over the children of Israel. Remembering this reminds us of the theme of salvation in the face of death. The place was Bethany, where, as told in chapter 11, Lazarus was raised from the dead at the behest of his sisters, Mary and Martha, early followers and friends of Jesus. The reunion of Jesus and the disciples with them reflects not only the inclusion of women in the circle of believers, but the turn of Jesus from his ministry to the people of Israel to his ministry as founder of the ongoing church as he faced the trial, crucifixion, and resurrection in Jerusalem.

Jesus and his beloved friends gathered at the table to feast together; for it was a time of transition. The public ministry had been, in some senses, a failure. His own people, especially their religious leaders, to whom he and his disciples have preached his message of truth, light, and life, has largely rejected him. They did not believe that he was the Son of God. Most were too preoccupied with their own world of darkness, and some plotted his death. However, those who believed and followed him gathered to form a loving community of the committed. In addition, as

Pastoral Perspective

The story begins in an idyllic way. Lazarus and his sisters Mary and Martha host an intimate party among friends. Jesus is the honored guest, and the event promises to be one of great joy. The Gospel writer does not say explicitly why this is no ordinary dinner party. Though Jesus has likely dined in this home, with these dear friends, on many occasions, this party is special. The difference is not because of the time of year, just before Passover, or because of Jesus' presence. The presence of Lazarus, recently raised from the dead, makes this dinner a special celebration. The recently empty place at the table has again been filled by Mary and Martha's brother. Healthy and alive, Lazarus hosts a party to honor the miracle worker Jesus and to give thanks to him for the gift of new life.

What a beautiful scene: fellowship, good food, time to linger at the table, and opportunities to express gratitude with words and with actions. Here we see an idyllic portrait of church fellowship. We yearn for the church to be a warm and inviting place. We long for a church where we gather around the table to be fed, not only by the bread and the cup, but by the presence of family and friends and, most of all, by the presence of Jesus. This is a place where Jesus is honored and those who gather are filled with gratitude and love for the gift of new life in Jesus. This is heaven on earth.

Exegetical Perspective

In the week before Passover, according to John's Gospel, Jesus engages in only three public events: (1) Mary's anointing of Jesus at Bethany, (2) the triumphal entry into Jerusalem, and (3) the visit by some Greeks who wished to see Jesus during the festival. Prior to these events, Jesus has gone into seclusion after the raising of Lazarus and subsequent mounting acclaim (11:54); after these events Jesus returns to seclusion (12:36b).

The first event, Mary's anointing of Jesus (12:1–11), follows the raising of Lazarus (11:1–44), which is why the KJV locates Bethany "where Lazarus was" (v. 1). Lazarus joins the meal, reclining at table. In the context of the recent events, Mary's action of anointing Jesus' feet and wiping them with her hair might well be seen as motivated by gratitude. John situates the anointing just before Jesus' entrance into Jerusalem (12:12–19), where the crowd hails Jesus as "King of Israel" (vv. 13, 15). The location of the anointing passage has led to some interpreting this as the anointing of a king—although kings were anointed on their heads, not their feet.

The NRSV translation identifies the setting: "the home of Lazarus." Many modern translations insert the word "home" into the text or use it to render the Greek words, *oikos, oikia* (house, household), but the house of Jesus' time was not the home of our time.

Homiletical Perspective

Kudos to the lectionary divines for inviting preachers to visit this Johannine text at the doorstep of Holy Week. Just as this text serves as a bridge in John's Gospel between the time before and the time of Jesus' glorification, so this text serves as a bridge for the church moving from Lent into Holy Week.

On Monday of Holy Week, at least as John tells the story, Jesus is near Jerusalem, but not in it. He reclines at table for a feast in his honor. Among a company of friends and fresh from wearing his graveclothes, Lazarus lives to enjoy another meal. John does not offer a guest list for this banquet, but he does tell us that it was Martha who served the guests. This may be nothing more than what custom would expect, but it may well anticipate what Jesus will soon tell his disciples, "Whoever serves me must follow me, and where I am, there will my servant be also. Whoever serves me, the Father will honor" (12:26). Gail O'Day and Susan Hylen observe, "While Mary's response forms the center of this passage, Martha's should not be passed over too quickly. . . . Read in conjunction with Jesus' words, Martha's service becomes another model act of discipleship, also enacted before Jesus speaks on the subject."[1]

---

1. Gail R. O'Day and Susan E. Hylen, *John*, Westminster Bible Companion (Louisville, KY: John Knox Press, 2006), 123.

John 12:1-11

the next chapter describes, he humbled himself and washed their feet.

The attention to feet may seem strange today; but it was laden with significance then. People traveled on foot on dusty, rocky roads, where animals also left their droppings. Foot washing was often done by a servant, and signaled a gracious amenity for a guest, as well as good housekeeping. Also, a person of high status was shown respect by a social inferior who falls at the feet of the "better," to show honor and humility, or to plead a petition. When Jesus came to raise Lazarus in chapter 11, Mary "fell at his feet" (11:32 NIV; NRSV "knelt at his feet").

Furthermore, feet carried what was in the head and heart if there was a message to be delivered, as wandering philosophers and religious charismatics also knew. The feet became soiled, calloused, or blistered, if not raw, wounded, and bruised. Thus, care for the feet was necessary in missionary endeavors. From Isaiah (52:7) to Paul (Rom. 10:15) the tradition stated the irony that the feet that carried good tidings are "beautiful" (Heb.: "radiant" or "glorious").

In this passage, however, the washing of feet also had other layers of meaning. When Jesus washed the feet of his disciples, he may have been saying that his own peripatetic days were over, and he was commissioning them to become bearers of the word of truth, light, and life, as well as instructing the new leadership to care for each other as he cared for them; as the Synoptics say: "whoever wishes to be great among you must be your servant" (Matt. 20:26).

John's report of Mary's actions implies still more. She *anointed* the feet of Jesus with a "costly" ointment (v. 3); she did not simply wash his feet. Was this an echo of the anointing of the prophets, priests, and kings of old? Did it anticipate what the Catholic tradition sees as the sacrament of extreme unction? While her sister Martha served Jesus and the disciples in her characteristic way, Mary served Jesus by reminding him of the offices he had to bear and fundamentally to redefine as he faced the crowds of the triumphal entry and then the crowds that wanted to crucify him in Jerusalem.

Her action, however, not only conveyed the echoes of a theological message about his role in life, it was also very personal and intimate. She wiped his feet with her hair in a culture that did not approve of women letting down their hair in the company of men who were not in their family. She ritually and lovingly prepared him for his burial, for he was under threat (as, indeed, was Lazarus, who was living evidence to many that resurrection was a possibility).

There is just one problem. The Gospel writer continues the story in a way that disrupts this happy scene. Conflict arises. Offering the very best she has, Mary anoints Jesus' feet with costly perfume made of pure nard. The perfume and her devotion captivate everyone in the room. Judas Iscariot takes offense at this—not because a woman touches a man in public, but because he thinks this is a tremendous waste of money. In his view, Mary should have used the money spent on perfume for something more important, like caring for the poor. The Gospel writer whispers to us what we cannot be sure the dinner party guests know: Judas is actually more interested in dipping his hand into the treasury for his own purposes than in caring for the poor.

There we have it: trouble in paradise. Both Mary and Judas are followers of Jesus. Among Jesus' chosen band are Simon, a Zealot, and Matthew, a tax collector. These two men represented groups that fought bitterly.[1] The first community of believers did not always live in harmony, and Christians do not always live peacefully today. Conflict exists in congregations. Jesus Christ calls diverse people into the church. With diversity come differences of opinions, split votes, competing priorities, and different ways of expressing devotion to Jesus.

Some have seen in this passage the ongoing tension in some Christian communities between acts of piety and acts of social justice. It often comes to the surface when the church budget is being discussed. Jesus cared for the poor and the marginalized. Should we then give all we have to ministries of justice and compassion? Are there legitimate times to pour our resources into renovating the sanctuary, purchasing a new organ, or expanding our Christian education facilities? How do churches work through the values that lie behind such struggles?

Clearly, Mary's pious act of devotion is lauded by Jesus. The church of Jesus Christ today must give time, attention, and dollars to the programs that help people connect to Jesus in personal ways, so that, like Mary, they may worship and adore him. Mary's love and devotion, enacted in the anointing of Jesus' feet, developed over time and through a personal relationship with Jesus. Worship and education are often primary places where this relationship is developed.

Encountering Jesus in the proclamation of the Word and in the celebration of the sacraments

---

1. Hans Weder, "Disciple, discipleship," in *The Anchor Dictionary of the Bible*, ed. David Noel Freedman et al. (New York: Doubleday, 1992), 2:208.

Exegetical Perspective

Evoking associations of "home" as private and secluded does not convey the public nature of this dining event at which Martha, Mary, Lazarus, disciples, and a "great crowd of the Jews" (v. 9) are present. Dining together was a semipublic social ritual in the Hellenistic and Roman world, intended to enhance the experience for all present. A sentiment we might consider prescriptive for general behavior, "Judge your neighbor's feelings by your own, and in every matter be thoughtful" (Sir. 31:15), actually appears specifically as the ethical basis for table etiquette in Sirach's section on meal ethics (31:12–32:13). The public nature of meals is evidenced by criticisms levied against Jesus: "Look, a glutton and a drunkard, a friend of tax collectors and sinners!" (Luke 7:34).

The Greek word *anakeimai*, for "lie (or recline) at table," that is, dine (v. 2), is also used of those at the meal in the Upper Room (13:23, NRSV "reclining," and 13:28, NRSV "at the table") and at the feeding of the 5,000 (6:11, NRSV "seated"). This reclining posture makes it feasible for Mary to anoint Jesus' feet, which were accessible on his couch, not under the table as would be typical of our usual eating posture. The word for "wipe" or "wipe dry," *ekmassō*, is used by John in the Upper Room narrative also, where it is Jesus who washes feet and "wipes them dry" with a towel (13:5).

There may be two separate incidents behind this scene: One is an incident in Galilee at the house of a Pharisee where a penitent sinner enters and weeps in Jesus' presence. Her tears fall on his feet, and she hastily wipes them away with her hair. The scandalous action of loosening the hair in public (note again the public nature of the house) fits the character of the woman and helps to explain the Pharisee's indignation. This is the backbone of Luke's narrative (7:36–50). Another is an incident at Bethany at the house of Simon the leper, where a woman, as an expression of her love for Jesus, uses her expensive perfume to anoint Jesus' head. Mark (and Matthew, following Mark) relates this incident. John bases his narrative on the second incident, but incorporates details from the first and adds some of his own—the presence of Lazarus, Martha, and Mary, and the comments about Judas.

The observation that the house was filled with the fragrance of the ointment (v. 3) may be presented in contrast to the four-day stench of Lazarus's tomb (11:39). Midrash Rabbah on Ecclesiastes 7:1 comments: "The fragrance of a good perfume spreads from the bedroom to the dining room; so does a

Homiletical Perspective

While Martha serves the food and drink, Mary serves Jesus in another way. The evangelist goes to considerable length in the Greek to describe the contents of what Mary holds. It is a large quantity of very expensive and exquisite perfume. She lavishes this precious ointment on the feet of Jesus, foreshadowing the lavish love that will soon lead him to wash his disciples' feet. In so doing, Mary anticipates the command that Jesus will issue in 13:14 to wash one another's feet.

One homiletical trail then leading from this text is to follow John's concept of discipleship. For John, a disciple is one who does not miss the chance to respond to Jesus and the people of God with extravagant acts of generosity and love. Just look at Martha and, especially, Mary, says the Fourth Evangelist. When you look, notice that the disciple who receives the most praise from Jesus in this text is a woman who by conventional and religious standards of the day had no business even being at the feast.

By harsh contrast to Mary's modeling of faithful discipleship, John spends extended rhetoric discussing Judas. In this Gospel, readers will find no romantic notion about Judas or any suggestion that Judas was a noble, but misguided revolutionary Zealot. For John, Judas is a living example of what a disciple is not. Unlike Mary, Judas finds reasons why *not* to act with extravagant generosity and love. For John, Judas is a thief who steals from the community chest. Far worse, though, John uses the Greek term *kleptēs* to describe Judas, the same word he uses in chapter 10 to describe the one who threatens the flock. For John, not only is Judas not a true disciple of Jesus; he is the essence of the "anti-disciple."

One of the preaching dangers in following this Johannine trail is to miss the nuances of how Jesus perceives the action of Mary and the response by Judas. The church has long been populated by those who, while not thieves like Judas, respond to extravagance and generosity in a similar way. Antidisciples always have a seemingly reasonable explanation for reserving extravagant love and withholding generosity, and they have considerable sympathy for the fiscal concern expressed by Judas. Anyone who has lived through Christmas and Easter in the church will be painfully familiar with how often decorative excess is blithely excused as responding just like Mary. Lamar Williamson captures the essential nuances about discipleship in this text when he writes, "What the evangelist wishes readers to hear

John 12:1-11

Theological Perspective

Not only did the established religious leaders seek to arrest Jesus; some were plotting to kill him, lest the people who believed in him and his power of resurrection undercut the authority of both their temple and their nationhood, which the Romans would love to see (11:48).

The threat was not only external. Judas Iscariot was at the dinner also. Judas questioned the wasting of this costly ointment in a gesture that, even if theologically and emotionally laden, was fleeting. He said it should have been sold and the money given to the poor. John did not think that this was the real reason for Judas's complaint. John thought Judas was a thief who would like to get his hands deeper into the resources of the movement. Setting aside for the moment the assessment of Judas's motive, this part of the text raises a critical issue that every Christian movement has to face. Jesus tells Judas to leave Mary alone, for she has done a beautiful thing. The choice between aesthetically magnificent purchases that glorify the Lord and ethically driven magnanimity for those in need is seldom an easy decision. Do piety and theologically symbolic richness trump ethics and the meeting of human need? John evidently thinks they do, at least when the advocate for "the poor" is tainted with self-serving interests.

Jesus is portrayed as giving another reason: "You always have the poor with you"—a verse that has done much damage to justice when taken out of context. The proper context is this: "but you do not always have me." Living, working, evangelizing, forming the church, and celebrating in the presence of the Lord do take priority, for if that is rightly done, the poor will also be served, as the Pentecostal/evangelical movements in the global South seem to have recently demonstrated.

MAX L. STACKHOUSE

Pastoral Perspective

nurtures faith. Our connection to Christ grows stronger as we listen attentively to Jesus in prayer and in Bible study. The life of discipleship entails bringing our joys and our sorrows to the feet of our Lord. Mary's anxiety, anger, and sorrow over the death of Lazarus are important parts of her growing relationship with Jesus. All that she has learned from Jesus and all that she has experienced in her life, bring Mary to her knees in that amazing act of love and devotion. She anoints Jesus' feet and wipes them with her tresses. There is nothing wasteful about that.

What about the poor? Should this not be considered, even if the concern is raised by one whose integrity is questionable? Jesus intervenes on Mary's behalf as Judas challenges Mary's act of love. He does not, however, dismiss the value of helping the poor. Judas is not wrong for advocating for the needs of the most vulnerable members of our communities. He is wrong for creating a competition between acts of justice and compassion, born from a love of Jesus Christ, with other forms of devotion and discipleship. It must also be noted that Judas is in the wrong because of the deceit of his heart, though Jesus does not confront him about this.

Before us, then, is a first-century dinner party seen as a microcosm of the modern church. The threat of death and the joy of life sit side by side. The richness of worship and the poverty of the world rub shoulders. The quiet and contemplative disciples sit at table with social activists. Sometimes the table feels a bit crowded, and the mood slips from gratitude to pious judgmentalism. So long as Jesus is the honored guest and the focus of the party, the church will live out its life as those called to follow him.

NANCY A. MIKOSKI

good name spread from one end of the world to the other." Raymond Brown suggests that John, if he shared this understanding of perfume, may be symbolically saying the same thing as Mark 14:9, that the woman's deed will be proclaimed in the whole world in remembrance of her. The "fragrance" of her good deed will spread throughout the world.[1]

Mary is the model disciple. She "follows" Jesus' example—albeit prior to the example. She does what Jesus will do—washing and drying feet. Note that this word for "anoint" (*aleiphō*) is sometimes combined with washing (see Matt. 6:17; also Ruth 3:3). Mary's anointing points to an additional meaning in the action; as Brown points out, the feet of the living are not anointed, only those of the dead in preparation for burial. Jesus' words in verse 7 reflect this.[2]

Translation and interpretation difficulties inherent in the text of verse 7 are further obscured by the NRSV insertion of "she bought it." Leave that phrase out, and Jesus is saying that Mary should keep the ointment for his burial. The problem with this, narratively speaking, is that not Mary with her small jar of ointment but Nicodemus with his hundred pounds of myrrh and aloes appears in 19:39. A better interpretation may come if we look at the "dangling" elliptical purpose clause, "in order that [*hina*] she might keep it," in light of two other such constructions in John. In 9:3 and 11:4 a *hina* clause indicates the revelatory purpose of Jesus' speech. In verse 7, Jesus' proleptic injunction reveals the prophetic nature of Mary's action. That Mary of Bethany does not narratively appear at the final anointing of Jesus' dead body is immaterial; with this prevenient anointing, Mary of Bethany, like Mary Magdalene in the garden of the resurrection, gets there first—and gets the point, before the male disciples.

DEIRDRE J. GOOD

in Jesus' words is the beauty of uncalculating love and its importance as a mark of true discipleship."[2]

Another preaching trail, as well as homiletical danger, in this text is found in the final three verses. Readers learn that Jesus is not the sole attraction in Bethany. Word has spread about Lazarus, and curiosity is drawing great crowds to see what the walking dead one looks like. Ironically, what attracts the crowds is precisely what threatens Lazarus with a short-lived resurrection. Not only are the crowds curious about Lazarus, but his new life is prompting new faith in Jesus among the circumcised.

Here is where another homiletical danger awaits the careless preacher. In John, "the Jews" is often a collective statement of all that is in opposition to Jesus. Here "a great crowd of the Jews" (v. 9) is not used in such a caustic way, but it is still far too easy for Christians to hear references to Jews in John as a consistently negative refrain to justify continuing anti-Semitism. That would be a particularly unfortunate interpretation in this text in which the phrase "a great crowd of the Jews" is used to describe people who are embracing the discipleship of Jesus.

Just when Lazarus has been raised from the dead and the crowds arrive, not only in curiosity but with newfound adoration, John reminds the readers that those who follow Jesus never veer far from the haunting smell of death. Lazarus is a public reminder of what Jesus has done; therefore, Lazarus must die—again!

Walk into Holy Week with all the confidence of Easter, but never with the naive notion that Easter will arrive before the shadow of death has had its awful, brutal, and crucifying way with Jesus. John tells us that much on Holy Monday, while several miles away from Jerusalem, at a feast that we remember in part every time the bread is broken and the cup is served.

GARY W. CHARLES

1. Raymond Brown, *The Gospel according to John I–XII*, Anchor Bible Series (Garden City, NY: Doubleday, 1966), 453.
2. Ibid., 454.

2. Lamar Williamson, *Preaching the Gospel of John* (Louisville, KY: Westminster John Knox Press, 2004), 144.

Isaiah 49:1-7

¹Listen to me, O coastlands,
    pay attention, you peoples from far away!
The Lord called me before I was born,
    while I was in my mother's womb he named me.
²He made my mouth like a sharp sword,
    in the shadow of his hand he hid me;
he made me a polished arrow,
    in his quiver he hid me away.
³And he said to me, "You are my servant,
    Israel, in whom I will be glorified."
⁴But I said, "I have labored in vain,
    I have spent my strength for nothing and vanity;
yet surely my cause is with the Lord,
    and my reward with my God."

⁵And now the Lord says,
    who formed me in the womb to be his servant,
to bring Jacob back to him,
    and that Israel might be gathered to him,
for I am honored in the sight of the Lord,

Theological Perspective

Today's passage is more complex than yesterday's (Isa. 42:1–9). There the speaker was God, talking about the Servant. Here there is dialogue between the Servant and God. Twice the text emphasizes that it is God who does the choosing, not the Servant, by saying the choice was made while the Servant was still in the womb.

Although the writer no doubt envisioned the Servant in masculine terms, we can re-vision this. The Servant then begins by emphasizing a two-sided preparation. On the one hand, she uses images of weapons to indicate how she was readied for her mission. On the other hand, she couples this with affirming God's protective concealment. God is to be glorified in her, but she complains that she has already labored in vain. Nevertheless, she is confident that God is on her side.[1]

From a Christian perspective, the next part of the passage does fit Jesus well. Here it is clear that the initial mission of the Servant is to Israel. This was certainly Jesus' self-understanding. God goes on to renew the message of yesterday's passage: "It is too light a thing that you should be my servant to raise up the tribes of Jacob and to restore the survivors of

---

1. I have avoided replacing the "Servant" with "Jesus" in this summary of the first part of our passage. That connection seems a bit forced. Applying these ideas to Jesus does little to illumine his work.

Pastoral Perspective

Does God ordain a life plan for us? Choose our careers? I know a man who says with complete assurance that he was *born* to preach. He has always known this about himself, from the time he was a very young boy. I also know a young woman who came to me in distress when she was halfway through college. As she talked and I listened, an arresting admission poured out of her: "I don't seem to have a *passion* for anything. I don't know what I'm supposed to be doing." It was dispiriting for her because everyone she knew was on fire about *something.* They were certain of a calling in their lives, and she seemed not to be. Now, a decade later, she *is* on fire about her career as a dedicated teacher of mentally disabled children. Was she born to teach? Maybe so. Certainly it seems so now, but it took her a while to know it and then live it.

Not everyone who is certain of a calling is correct about *the nature of it.* It takes more than just your conviction or mine to make a call. It takes the presence of certain gifts. It takes the hard work of marshaling those gifts to become the absolute best they can be. It takes some recognition of the calling by the community in which it will be exercised; the people among whom you will answer your call need *also* to think that you have one. Your own sense of rightness is important, but it is not the whole story. Nobody is

and my God has become my strength—
⁶he says,
"It is too light a thing that you should be my servant
     to raise up the tribes of Jacob
     and to restore the survivors of Israel;
I will give you as a light to the nations,
     that my salvation may reach to the end of the earth."

⁷Thus says the LORD,
     the Redeemer of Israel and his Holy One,
to one deeply despised, abhorred by the nations,
     the slave of rulers,
"Kings shall see and stand up,
     princes, and they shall prostrate themselves,
because of the LORD, who is faithful,
     the Holy One of Israel, who has chosen you."

Exegetical Perspective

Today's passage comes from the same part of the book of Isaiah (chaps. 40–66) as yesterday's. It also speaks from the time of the people of Judah in Babylonian exile, that same historical experience and mind-set of dislocation, distress, and disconnection from their faith of old. As you may remember, exile is not just a historical experience, but also a concept, a way of seeing the world. It means feeling like a stranger, feeling alienated, carrying a sense of betrayal. Read from the perspective of exile, the Bible is a response to a sense of massive betrayal in the face of history. The temple is destroyed; the people are either in exile in Babylon, have fled to Egypt, or belong to the poorest of the poor remaining in their occupied land.

So inevitably questions of faith arise: Why has our God allowed this to happen? Why do we suffer? Where is our salvation? We are looking here at something unthinkable. There was this covenant with David that was to last forever and ever (2 Sam. 7; cf. Ps. 48:13–15). The current reality is so different (Ps. 44:9–16). In the exile, the Jewish people after a while settled down, chiefly in the city of Babylon, where they were used as laborers in Nebuchadnezzar's building programs. They were allowed to stay together as communities. There is no indication that they were subject to harsh treatment. They were

Homiletical Perspective

If the first creation story in Genesis presents a springboard for preaching this text, the third day of creation is the one in play in this text. It speaks of the separation of land from water, the sowing of seeds, and the bounty that follows. The mission envisioned by the Isaiah poet is also one of broad bounty. Its growth bursts traditional borders and flourishes in the wide world. This passage seems to contain the poet's credentials, presented before he offers his message. We can almost see him making notes as to how he will set forth his sense of call and mission:

I became aware of my true status in a time of self-doubt and disillusionment. All the while my cause was with God, our only source of work and hope.

Our work as holy servants involves more than the restoration of our own clans and lands. It is to be a light to the nations, modeling the awaking of lives through human purity, courage and insight.

Our fortunes, so long linked to our caricature as ridiculed underlings, shall change. Our true nature and worth will become known.

I am fulfilling my sacred destiny in this time and place. God fashioned me and held me ready for use. My times are in God's hands.

The author is responding to a revelation. His experience places the following things before us for

Isaiah 49:1-7

Theological Perspective

Israel. I will give you as a light to the nations, that my salvation may reach to the end of the earth" (v. 6). Here the sequence that is prominent in the New Testament account of Jesus and his followers is very clear. Both the primacy of Jesus' mission to Israel and the universality of Jesus' work are rightly prophesied.

The final verses present a contrast of a familiar type. First, the Servant experiences contempt and humiliation, but, later, kings prostrate themselves before him. One may apply this on the one hand, to the passion of Jesus and, on the other, to the Christianization of the Mediterranean world and its rulers by his followers. Theologically it may be this last section of the passage that calls for the most attention. Does it illumine Jesus, or do we need to rethink its meaning in light of Jesus?

In Holy Week we read the story of Jesus in anticipation of Easter. There is little doubt that we receive great satisfaction from the fact that the humiliation and physical suffering during this week turn out not to be the end. He reappears, and his followers spread the word with considerable success. We would probably like the story even better, if the resurrected Jesus appeared to Pilate and to the high priest, and they prostrated themselves before him.

We like the assurance of this kind of justice through the reversal of roles. By stretching the story to cover centuries, we can obtain something like what is prophesied here. We must ask, however, whether this is what the gospel teaches us. Is the good news the reversal of fortunes in which the rich are abased and the poor are lifted up?

This note is certainly struck in the New Testament as well as in the Hebrew Scriptures; but in the actual course of events, including the events of Jesus' life and death, it is rarely played out. Those who had condemned Jesus to death do not come to believe that there has been a resurrection. They go on being who they were, living with the same values as before.

Certainly, the resurrection did involve a profound reversal, but this was not the assurance of believers that kings would bow to them. Quite the contrary, believers were called to risk their lives as Jesus had risked his and, in some cases, to die for acting on their beliefs, as Jesus had died.

The reversal occurred in the community of believers. They heard a different drummer. They were no longer controlled by the values of the dominant community, even the primacy of survival. They served a different Lord, one who had been crucified. The resurrection appearances did not make Jesus' followers powerful or prosperous. They led instead to

Pastoral Perspective

called to anything in a vacuum. We are called in and into a community.

Sometimes the people you hope to serve do not feel called to respond to your call. You feel a call very strongly, but it is not answered by the community's response for which you long—you do not get the job, and then you do not get another one, and still another. This breaks your heart, filling you either with doubt about your own judgment or with anger at the people who did not respond to that of which you were so certain—or with both of these things at the very same time. I was so sure. How could I have been so wrong? Where is God in all this?

Think about it. God has many ways of doing things. The plan of God is not just located in one-thing-after-another time, a blueprint of what is going to happen and what will not. The plan of God is *responsive* as much as it is predictive. Does God *will* everything that happens—the Holocaust, the Rwandan genocide, your cancer, his auto accident? No. Can God bring life from everything that happens? Absolutely. Do you want to see God? Just go where something terrible has happened, and look around. Look carefully, and be sure to look with some creativity. God has many ways of doing things, ways we cannot begin to imagine before they appear. Sometimes our disappointments are signs of God at work in our lives.

Some people will walk through Holy Week this year tasting the bitter ashes of their own disappointed hopes. Something for which they longed is not to be. Something to which they have devoted much time, money, love, and sacrifice has borne no fruit. It feels, as they trudge along, that there is nothing in the future. Why am I even here? they ask themselves. Why do I even try to go on?

I knew a man who was sure beyond a doubt from early boyhood that he was called to priesthood. He went to seminary as a young man, full of passionate resolve to be the best priest he could be. Nobody there studied or fasted or prayed as much as he did, or with greater zeal. Fearing for his health, his superiors forbade him to take on any extra fasts or acts of penance, and this was hard for him. What could possibly be wrong with more and more excellence and fervor? After a time, though, his superiors asked him to leave. They did not see a vocation to priesthood. In fact, they said, it would be a disaster to him personally and to the church if he were to be ordained.

My friend was crushed. He wandered for a while, full of a combination of self-loathing and anger at the church that had rejected his gift of himself. It was years before he began to realize that he had a call to

Exegetical Perspective

allowed to worship. They were allowed to live in peace as long as they respected the Babylonian law. They corresponded with the remnant back in Jerusalem, back in "the land." They were free to travel. They had their religious meetings. Yes, there was limited freedom for the exiled people of Judah as long as they were obedient to Babylon; indeed they were even allowed to engage in agricultural pursuits, business and commercial endeavors. Thus, one did not see extreme external suffering. Nevertheless, it was a time of deep search of the meaning of faith.

Near the end of the exilic period, some time between 550 and 540 BCE, a poet-prophet, who does not give us any information about who he or she is, provides words of comfort and vision, hope and reassurance ("Comfort, O comfort my people . . ."; 40:1).

This same Servant/prophet introduced yesterday is the speaker in today's passage. She or he is addressing the world at large ("listen, . . . O coastlands, pay attention, you peoples from far away," v. 1). Echoing the prophet Jeremiah (Jer. 1:5), she recalls being created from the womb, appointed before birth, brought forth by YHWH the midwife (v. 1; cf. v. 5). Protected by God and steeled for the tasks ahead (v. 2), the Servant/prophet reports YHWH's words: "You are my servant, Israel, in whom I will be glorified" (v. 3). Addressed as Israel, the people collectively, the Servant (*'ebed*) is to restore the remnant of the people, those who have survived, those who have remained faithful. The Servant is also to become a light to the nations for YHWH's liberation to become tangible to the entire world ("the end of the earth," v. 6), thereby contributing to the glory of YHWH, an exilic theme first introduced by the prophet Ezekiel.

Interpreters have argued from of old about whether Israel here refers to the entire nation at its exilic state, or whether the reference is to an ideal Israel, a faithful remnant. Either of these interpretive options can be justified by the text as well as the use of "Israel" and "remnant" in the context of the book of Isaiah.

This group of people is to lead the world to Zion/Jerusalem, to make YHWH known to all. Indeed, YHWH promises a restoration of the nation, so that the respect of other countries lost during the Babylonian exile will be regained (v. 7). YHWH reiterates God's choice of Israel as God's people. So this announcement that the Servant Israel will return to the land rings out as a signal of hope and a memory of liberation.

The reality—that once the Babylonian exile is ended by Cyrus of Persia, only a small number of

Homiletical Perspective

our consideration. We too may become aware that we have been rescued by a Messiah moment. To be aware of this is to become messianic ourselves. We may feel compelled to do something in response to this great thing. Our route may be slow and painful. It may be dotted with obscure and patchy sections. It will also contain moments of supreme inspiration. This process of being honed and hidden is the recurring pattern of our growth in faith and service.

This confession raises the question as to why our experience of spiritual awakening makes us believe it is for some higher purpose. Why do we feel the need to share with others those things that make us sit up and take notice? It has always been so. Great tellers have first been those who realized great things. When the church speaks today, is it telling of great things, or simply relaying small things in old and predictable ways?

This text also leads us to ask, who is the Servant? Is he or she a power broker from outside, or a local person rising to prominence? Is the Servant the moment itself, the time in life and culture for something big to break through? Is it one person or a whole community? Is it a conviction that plays upon us until it takes us deeper than contemporary cultural practices and anchors us in one of the founding rivers out of which our sense of self and destiny have flowed? Who is the Servant today in our situation? What is our range of expectation? Will we permit ourselves to hear a voice from outside? Are our troubling times full of transformative messages? The possibility for creative engagement with our destiny stops dead at the door when met by fear, predictability, or intentional deafness.

George MacLeod of the Iona Community wrote: "Our basic trouble, which is the reason why the impact of the church on our country today is so pallid, is that most of our members do not realize how acute is the angle of the turning we must make."[1] There is value in the preacher spending time in conversation with the poetic Isaiah before attempting to lift the text for preaching. The issues of call and preparation are vital for every faith leader. The process is never finished; so this text can be a teacher, an inspiration, and a corrective through the years. By sitting with this poet, preachers can face the temptation to stop building when the church is strong, equating harmony with faithful service, as if a strong faith community were the goal. We can also share our

---

1. Ron Ferguson, ed., *Daily Readings with George MacLeod* (Glasgow: Wild Goose Publications, 2004), 95.

Isaiah 49:1-7

Theological Perspective

the commitment to the justice of the *basileia theou*, the commonwealth of God. Sometimes we may be called to suffer with no thought of gain. We can apply to our discipleship the famous words of Habakkuk (3:17–18), who trusts God despite the absence of any signs of support.

However, to the Jesus who was resurrected, discipleship is not as bleak as that. Although it is a call to follow Jesus wherever that leads, understanding that such discipleship may include sacrifice and suffering, the idea of reversal of fortunes is also central to the gospel. Part of this reversal is found in the joy that such discipleship entails, regardless of whether, in ordinary human terms, one "is abased" or "abounds." Today's passage speaks of this when, after expressing a sense of failure and futility, the Servant says, "Yet surely my cause is with the LORD, and my reward with my God." Even when she fails, if the cause is God's, the failure is not ultimate or empty.

Nor is the follower of Jesus forbidden to take pleasure when those who have cursed and mocked repent. The pleasure is not, or should not be, the exaltation of those who can now say, "We told you so." Instead, believers share in the joy now experienced by those who have previously lived by the world's norms. Believers find joy in that others join them in Jesus' mission, which in this passage is that God's "salvation [will] reach to the end of the earth" (v. 6). If those who now share our goals recognize that they do so in discipleship to Jesus, that draws us even closer together. Service in God's work of bringing justice or salvation or the divine commonwealth to the world: that is our mission.

JOHN B. COBB JR.

Pastoral Perspective

leadership in the church as a layperson, and that ordained ministry would most likely have confirmed rigidities in him that he was far better off without. "They were right: I *would* have been a disaster," he used to say, "I would have been full of my own righteousness, and I would have spent my life finding fault with everyone else. I would have been a walking commercial for what was wrong with the church." He spoke frequently in public about discernment, and told this story each time he did. People listened with compassion to his youthful disappointment and tasted with gratitude the fruit of his mature self-knowledge. He was everyone's favorite uncle. When he died, the church was filled with people who had been touched by his witness.

Disappointment in vocation is not a sign that God has not called. It is just a sign that discernment is hard work and engages the whole of a person's history—past, present, and mysterious future. Things we could not know at the time become gracefully clear as the years pass. God calls everyone to something, and God can call us again and again, to different things at different times. We respond to life, and within our careful and prayerful response is the mysterious call of God.

BARBARA CAWTHORNE CRAFTON

Exegetical Perspective

Judean exiles return to the land (cf. Ezra 1–3)—does not play into the glorious portrayal of a day of liberation. It is attested elsewhere when Zechariah talks about the rededication of the rebuilt temple as "a day of small things" (Zech. 4:10). At this point, as the people are still captive in Babylon, longing to go "home"; the message is one of comfort and hope.

Endurance, strength, and the ability to stay hidden in the face of the enemy are the images evoked in the passage. The Servant, Israel, confesses his or her identity as born and called by God, endowed with gifts, hidden by God for protection, and then sent to show strength and enlightenment to others. Images of sword and arrow, combined with mouth and body, allow the audience to move beyond the immediate war memories and imagine more tender realities. In the midst of experiences of deprivation, with memories of war and destruction still fresh, restoration is the underlying theme, restoration of those who have been despised. Especially those who experience marginalization in their present contexts can identify with the longing.

In Christian traditions, the Isaiah readings appearing during Holy Week have been read, heard, and reinterpreted in light of the passion narratives in the Gospels of the Second Testament (especially Matthew and John). Jesus in Jerusalem on the way to the cross has been identified with the Suffering Servant. While the analogies are tangible, the challenge remains to hold on to the tensions of the historical realities and avoid conflating Jesus, the Jew at the hands of the Roman Empire, with the people Israel at the hands of the Babylonian Empire almost six hundred years earlier.

ANGELA BAUER-LEVESQUE

Homiletical Perspective

feelings of inadequacy when facing the task of participating in the big picture as "a light to the nations."

According to this text, the faith community is not an end but a means to an end. Churches not only look inward to find a sense of unity, but outward to engage an open-ended mission. The Servant works in the public arena, facing the potential of resistance, ridicule, and misunderstanding. We risk losing identity, particularity, and status as we join with other servant-strangers responding to the same deep awakening.

There is great value found in the poet's conviction that one day the truth shall be told and its Servant known and honored. There is an unhelpful way of employing this insight. It is to do so just to make ourselves feel good, to make us say that we are right and others are wrong, no matter what. A more helpful way is to bear witness to the ribbon of light at the horizon of every working day. We may not all see it together or in the same moments, but members of a faith community do have ribbon-of-light experiences happening to them all the time. A close and trusting group can buoy up its members by sharing the news of light in dark places. It is rarely about one vast dawn rising. It is more often about moments of illumination, clarity, and quiet joy.

In Holy Week it is difficult to keep this Isaiah text from becoming a mere building block in the story of Jesus. This text was never a prediction of Jesus' passion but, rather, a model in which those telling Jesus' story found a framework and meaning. The Isaiah piece stands on its own and challenges every person and nation to consider its life, its inspirations, its revelations and surprises, and to honor the deep convictions that arise and call us to remarkable work beyond boundaries, expectations, and current patterns.

G. MALCOLM SINCLAIR

Psalm 71:1-14

¹In you, O LORD, I take refuge;
　let me never be put to shame.
²In your righteousness deliver me and rescue me;
　incline your ear to me and save me.
³Be to me a rock of refuge,
　a strong fortress, to save me,
　for you are my rock and my fortress.

⁴Rescue me, O my God, from the hand of the wicked,
　from the grasp of the unjust and cruel.
⁵For you, O Lord, are my hope,
　my trust, O LORD, from my youth.
⁶Upon you I have leaned from my birth;
　it was you who took me from my mother's womb.
My praise is continually of you.

⁷I have been like a portent to many,
　but you are my strong refuge.

Theological Perspective

In an initial reading, this psalm is much like other psalms of lament such as Psalm 22, Psalm 42, and Psalm 88. It is a prayer for deliverance and protection from enemies, punctuated by intermittent verses of trusting praise. Closer reading of the lection propels the Christian community toward deeper understanding of God and of human relationship with God, greater trust in God's love and protection, and the importance of remembering God's fidelity in the past for trusting God's fidelity in the future. These are all important lessons to bear in mind as the community continues its journey forward toward the crucifixion of Jesus later in this Holy Week.

The psalmist writes out of the particular circumstances of advanced age, asking that God not "cast me off" at this stage of life (v. 9) and decrying the threats from enemies and those who would do harm (vv. 10–11). These are important words in our contemporary culture, which has often forgotten how to value its aging and elderly and prefers instead to tuck this population away in nursing homes or healthcare centers. In the preceding verses, the psalmist hearkens back to his youth and even to his birth, recalling that even from the moment he was taken from his mother's womb, God has been his "hope" and "trust" and the One on whom he has "leaned" (vv. 5–6) all the days of his life.

Pastoral Perspective

Discourse analysis of any text requires the researcher to look for patterns, slippages, and silences. Often the silences are difficult to locate because the researcher is blinded by hidden presuppositions and personal agendas. The slippages and contradictions found in the results also make interpretation almost impossible. Because of this, it often takes the vantage point of an outside observer to expose the hidden meanings and provide accurate interpretations. Researchers are tempted to press the delete button and begin again the next day. For the researchers who persevere, the themes and the patterns that recur in the data thankfully reassure the investigators that they are on the verge of an exciting and refreshing discovery.

The psalmist spotlights the unsettling silences of our relationship with God. God created humanity for the purpose of fellowship. God desires a communal relationship with us. God promises that God's own presence will abide with us; yet God's absence can be a deafening silence. We long for intimacy but often know only the long days and months of loneliness. Although not as prominent as, for example, Psalm 13, Psalm 71 is a plea for God to come and to deliver us. "O God, do not be far from me; O my God, make haste to help me!" (v. 12).

The slippages in the Psalms are also evident. The most common incongruity clashes against the

⁸My mouth is filled with your praise,
  and with your glory all day long.
⁹Do not cast me off in the time of old age;
  do not forsake me when my strength is spent.
¹⁰For my enemies speak concerning me,
  and those who watch for my life consult together.
¹¹They say, "Pursue and seize that person
  whom God has forsaken,
  for there is no one to deliver."

¹²O God, do not be far from me;
  O my God, make haste to help me!
¹³Let my accusers be put to shame and consumed;
  let those who seek to hurt me
  be covered with scorn and disgrace.
¹⁴But I will hope continually,
  and will praise you yet more and more.

Exegetical Perspective

Psalm 71 presents the voice of an alienated, elderly person who clings to the memory of God's past action and trusts God to act in the future. These two integrally related activities—remembering and hoping—provide an overarching order to the psalm. The first half of the psalm (vv. 1–13) recounts the psalmist's desperate cries of distress alongside confessions of trust. A variegated vow of praise for God's imminent salvation constitutes the second half of the psalm (vv. 14–24), of which the lection includes only the first verse.

The first four verses present two aspects of God's care: God's hiding the psalmist (vv. 1, 3) and God's deliverance (vv. 2, 4). The psalm employs the classic "rock of refuge" metaphor to describe YHWH's solid, steadfast protection (v. 3; cf. 2 Sam. 22:3; Pss. 18:2; 31:2; 94:22). As one wedges oneself into a shady crag (cf. Isa. 32:2), the psalmist imagines herself tightly pressing against YHWH for protection. Overall, these images of hiding (vv. 1, 3) clearly convey the sense that YHWH is close and that YHWH's very nearness shields the psalmist from the enemy's threat.

It is somewhat surprising then that the opening pleas for deliverance suggest that YHWH is indeed very far off, for the psalmist prays that YHWH would hear, come near, and extricate her from the enemy's grip (vv. 2, 4; cf. vv. 11–12). Thus, in light of the

Homiletical Perspective

On a trip to England several years ago, I went for a long walk and got hopelessly lost. As I had been staying in a town that boasted both a cathedral and a castle, I looked in vain for a sign of either one of them as an orienting landmark. At the height of my anxiety and disorientation, the third verse of this psalm sprang involuntarily to mind: "Be my strong rock, a castle to keep me safe; you are my crag and my stronghold" (*Book of Common Prayer* [1979]). While I will not go so far as to suggest that uttering that phrase resulted in my deliverance, about five minutes after I did so, a sympathetic commuter stopped and gave me a lift back into town.

Such is the power of a lament like Psalm 71 that its central image—a figure of God compared to a castle or fortress—suggests itself in a time of danger and confusion. As we move more deliberately into Holy Week, and as the sights and sounds of Jesus' triumphal entry now fade, the senses of disorientation and danger move more emphatically to the foreground. We are not at the central events of the passion yet, but the lectionary builds within us a deepening sense of alarm. Jesus' critique of religious and political systems is beginning to suggest some consequences. Those of us who follow Jesus view that encounter with increasing anxiety and confusion.

Psalm 71:1-14

Theological Perspective

In this psalm, the metaphors used by the psalmist for such lifelong hope and trust are "rock" and "fortress" (v. 3) and, most predominantly, "refuge" (vv. 1, 3, 7). This metaphor of refuge not only dominates this particular psalm, but has been shown to be a key metaphor throughout the Psalter and provides some of the theological "glue" that holds the highly diverse Psalter together.[1] The psalmist's recognition of God's presence, love, and protection throughout his life is further concretized by the personal pronouns used in describing God as his refuge: "my rock" and "my fortress" (v. 3), and "my strong refuge" (v. 7).[2] Similar to a central theme from yesterday's reading from the Psalms, this lection continues a theological view on the nature of God. God is the One who provides unceasing sanctuary to those who seek God. For the psalmist, this is born from love and fidelity, and the psalmist couches this in the repetitive language of God as one's refuge.

This recognition of God's protecting love and fidelity reminds the aging psalmist—and us—that God has the power to provide safety, even in the face of enemies and accusers, and will not "forsake" the psalmist when his "strength is spent" (v. 9), nor when people "pursue and seize that person whom God has forsaken" (v. 11). Of course, read in the context of Holy Week, this lection leaves us feeling rather haunted by the word "forsake," as it reminds us of the words Jesus will cry out to God from the cross just three days from now: "My God, my God, why have you forsaken me?" (Matt. 27:46; Mark 15:34; Ps. 22:1).

More broadly, this present trust in God's protecting love and fidelity is made possible by the activity of *remembering*; the psalmist seems to be able to put hope and trust in God's protection in the present precisely because he is able to recall quite clearly God's protection in times past. "For you, O Lord, are my hope, my trust, O LORD, from my youth. Upon you I have leaned from my birth" (vv. 5–6a).

The concept of remembrance is a theological category throughout Scripture. In the Decalogue, God's people are to "remember the sabbath day" so that they may "keep it holy" (Exod. 20:8). The author of Ecclesiastes reminds one, "Remember your creator in the days of your youth, before the days of trouble come, and the years draw near when you will say, 'I have no pleasure in them'" (Eccl. 12:1). Jesus tells his

Pastoral Perspective

psalmist's understanding of God's protection and the attacks by enemies (vv. 4, 10–11, 13). Throughout Psalm 71, the appeals echo: "rescue me," "help me," "save me," "deliver me," "incline your ear to me." We expect God to intervene eagerly and immediately. We believe that our alliance with God will not only achieve all victories but also preempt all wars. When our experience does not correspond with the God we create and place our faith and hopes in, we are disoriented, confused, and desperate. Our souls are in danger of being crushed between the gears of broken promises. "Rescue me, O my God, from the hand of the wicked, from the grasp of the unjust and cruel" (v. 4).

One of the most prominent themes in the book of Psalms is refuge. The metaphors of "rock" and "fortress" occur repeatedly to signify God's protection and strength. We rest at night knowing that God is our foundation that does not crack during the strongest quakes. We wake up safe, trusting that God is our wall that protects us from the fiercest of winds. "Be to me a rock of refuge, a strong fortress, to save me, for you are my rock and my fortress" (v. 3). In the midst of silence and slippage, Psalm 71 relies upon the primary theme of the Psalter, "God is our refuge." Through petition and praise, the psalmist turns to God for help.

Churches know all too well the silences and the slippages of faith. Psalm 71 reminds us that at birth, through our youth, and in our old age (vv. 5–6, 9), God has cared for us. This remains true, even during times when our lives have been like a "portent" (v. 7), an omen signifying to others that God has forsaken us; we know God is still a "strong refuge." That is why, even during the darkest hours, we can praise God and glorify God's name with our lives "all day long" (v. 8). Further, with this our faith compels us to "hope continually" (v. 14) all the days of our lives.

The lection for Holy Tuesday also weaves praise throughout the fabric of the plea for help (vv. 8, 14). Verses 15–24, the remainder of the text, builds on the praise theme as an element of renewal for those who have advanced in years. With this slippage, it is important to remember that the images of age often make this psalm popular for older congregants. However, the psalm can also function as a reminder to young people to appreciate God's present activity.

To guard against this slippage, the preacher must remind the congregation that it is too soon to see Easter Sunday on Holy Tuesday. True, the storm clouds are gathering, the canary in the mine shaft has died, and Doppler has issued its warning. In such a context, the young often do not have the experience

---

1. William P. Brown, *Seeing the Psalms: A Theology of Metaphor* (Louisville, KY: Westminster John Knox Press, 2002), 18. Brown makes use of a study by Jerome F. D. Creach, *Yahweh as Refuge and the Editing of the Hebrew Psalter* (Sheffield: Sheffield Academic Press, 1996).

2. Brown, *Seeing the Psalms*, 19.

interwoven images of protection and deliverance in the verses, the modern reader is left wondering, where exactly is YHWH in relation to the psalmist? Is God *near*, as v. 1 suggests ("In you, O LORD, I take refuge"), or *far off*, as verse 4 indicates, with the psalmist in "the hand of the wicked . . . the grasp of the unjust and cruel"? The ambiguity of the divine presence in the psalm resonates deeply with modern readers who, in the midst of difficult situations, also struggle with the question, where is God? The psalm presents a scenario where a faithful one suffers and yet, somehow, hopes for God's salvation.

The psalmist knows that she can and should cry out to God because of their long personal history. They *go way back*—all the way back to the womb. Like a midwife, YHWH assisted with this petitioner's birth; YHWH literally "brought to life" the psalmist, after which the psalmist "leaned" (*nismak*) on God (v. 6, cf. Ps. 22:9). The Hebrew here could also be translated "brace oneself for support," evoking images of a child resting on a mother's breast or grasping a father's hand to steady herself during the first steps. The imagery of infancy and childhood in verses 5–6 (also v. 17) provides a fitting counterpoint for the psalm's further characterizations of the psalmist as elderly, frail, and gray (vv. 9, 18). By juxtaposing these images, the psalmist establishes the scope of her relationship with God—a long history of faithfulness to which the psalmist now clings.

The psalmist hopes that recounting this history will motivate YHWH to act once again. The situation now is exceedingly dire. In spite of the psalmist's piety (v. 8), the community considers her a pariah (v. 9). The psalmist's affliction is a force of disorder within the community, the members of which are deeply unsettled because they fear that the same fate may befall them (v. 7). Indeed, the community interprets the misery of the psalmist as a clear sign of God-forsakenness (v. 11), for no one whom God loves could suffer this way—or so they think.

The psalmist, however, maintains that YHWH has *not* forsaken her. Their long relationship convinces the psalmist that her final words will not be pleas for help to an absent God. Rather, the psalmist will praise God once more. As if to usher in the reality of YHWH's deliverance, the psalm abruptly changes mood: from petition to praise and promise. Though only the first verse of the vow of praise (v. 14) is included in the lection, preachers should keep the entire song in view, for it provides keys to understanding the whole.

This vow of praise often returns to descriptions of the passage of time. For example, the word *tamid*,

Before we turn to preaching strategies, there are two critical issues that the preacher should think about before taking on this text. The first has to do with that strong central image, from verse 3, of the "strong rock, a castle to keep me safe" (*BCP*). The second concerns what the psalm's speaker means when self-describing as a "portent to many" (v. 7).

Concerning the first issue, as in many of the psalms, the central image in Psalm 71 pictures God in visual terms that are for us somewhat archaic but for the psalmist's Israelite community were dynamically relevant. Psalm 71 pictures God as a fortress (NRSV; *BCP* "castle"). For us in the twenty-first century "fortress" suggests a castle, a picturesque mansion in which constitutional monarchs live. However, for generations before us, a castle was more like a fortress or, even better, a fort. To be sure, royalty lived there, but the primary purpose of a castle was as a fortification. A castle was less a home than a military encampment. It was the place where you could be secure from the assaults of your enemies.

Psalm 71 pictures God, then, as a fortress, a crag, a stronghold. This is archaic and picturesque language, but it is also very concrete. So all of the connotations a premodern person would have with a fortress—safety from adversaries, something certain in uncertain times—are available to the preacher, if you root around in all the movies and books (and maybe video games) in which castles prominently figure. Think at least of *The Lord of the Rings* books and films and all the times castles are assaulted in them. This fortress image is so romantic and archaic that we are tempted to pass it by. With a bit of connective work, it can serve as an evocative image, both in the story of Jesus and in the story of you and me.

The second issue concerns the situation of Psalm 71's speaker. This is a person who self-describes as a "portent to many." The speaker of this psalm is suffering, from "the clutches of the evildoer and the oppressor" (v. 4; *BCP*), from worries about being "cast off" in old age (v. 9). Whatever the situation this psalm addresses, the speaker is experiencing adversity from human and natural sources.

The speaker's underlying appeal to God here lies in an expression of concern for God's reputation. By self-describing as a "portent to many," and by quoting those who say, in verse 11, "God has forsaken him" (*BCP*), the speaker might be accused of appealing to God's baser instincts: if I as one of your well-known followers go down to defeat, people will say you are not very much of a God. Like the fortress image, this at first glance seems an archaic way to talk

Psalm 71:1-14

Theological Perspective

disciples to share a meal with him, doing so "in remembrance of me" (Luke 22:19). Even God remembers, promising Noah after the flood: "I will remember my covenant that is between me and you and every living creature of all flesh; and the waters shall never again become a flood to destroy all flesh" (Gen. 9:15).

The act of remembering sustains the community, keeps us obedient to God's law, maintains our faith in God through troubled times, and even holds God accountable to God's promises. In Psalm 71, remembering sustains the faith and trust of the aging and afflicted psalmist, allowing him to call God his rock and refuge in the face of his enemies and accusers. The psalmist's circumstances, concerns, and even the metaphor he uses for God's fidelity bring to mind the words from the familiar 1763 hymn by Augustus Toplady, "Rock of Ages":

> While I draw this fleeting breath,
> When mine eyes shall close in death,
> When I soar to worlds unknown,
> See thee on thy judgment throne,
> Rock of Ages, cleft for me,
> Let me hide myself in thee.

On this Tuesday of Holy Week, as the community continues its walk to the crucifixion of its Savior, it too remembers God's love, faithfulness, and provision of refuge and safe haven. Remembering God's faithfulness in the past allows the community to trust in God's faithfulness through the dark days ahead and to join the psalmist's hymn of praise: "But I will hope continually, and will praise you yet more and more" (v. 14).

NICOLE L. JOHNSON

Pastoral Perspective

to interpret the signs and can only interpret the journey of betrayal, arrest, trial, and conviction as the end of all hope. The older saints have traveled this road before. They can help the young begin to understand a longer view as they are the ones in a church who can pray with confidence, "Do not cast me off in the time of old age; do not forsake me when my strength is spent" (v. 9).

Nowhere is the faith of Psalm 71 modeled by Jesus more completely than during Holy Week. Every circumstance and event of the week yells, "Pursue and seize that person whom God has forsaken, for there is no one to deliver" (v. 11). Nevertheless, Jesus, as a psalmist, asserts his hope and trust in God. The Gospel text, John 12:20–36, speaks about the climax of "the hour" that has come when the "Son of Man" will be glorified (vv. 23, 27). In both sections, Jesus encourages others to follow him on this path (vv. 24–26, 35–36). Although the crowd recognizes the slippage between what they had heard about the Messiah living forever and Jesus' talk of being "lifted up" (v. 34), God is not silent here. Psalm 71 blends well with the Gospel lesson and the other readings for today at this point, as they each point to hope and trust in God and do so with the confidence of the long view of faith and hope.

TIMOTHY R. SENSING

Exegetical Perspective

translated "continually" or "every day," occurs frequently (e.g., "but I will hope continually," v. 14; see also vv. 3, 6). Likewise, "all/every day" (*kol hayyom*) appears regularly (e.g., "all day long my tongue will talk of your righteous help," v. 24; see also vv. 8, 15). Finally, in verses 20–21, the word "again," is repeated three times, portraying the continuity of YHWH's actions through time. The psalm's central theme emerges through each of these examples. From youth (vv. 5–6, 17) to old age (vv. 9, 18), the psalmist has trusted and praised YHWH, who has proven faithful again and again. It seems that this passage of time has taught the psalmist that the best way to realize YHWH's deliverance is to wait—that is, hope—for it.

The overall structure of the psalm reveals how one should wait for deliverance, namely, by constantly keeping open the dialogue with God. Whether through bitter complaint, urgent petition, or full-throated praise, the aged psalmist never ceases calling out to God. The psalm begins with a series of petitions intermingled with justifications for hope (vv. 1–6). Confessions of trust (vv. 7–8) stand before a frightening description of the enemies (vv. 9–11), followed by pleas for salvation (vv. 12–13). Next, confident vows of praise appear again, mottled, however, with further petitions for help (vv. 14–18). The psalm finally concludes with an extended, exuberant vow of praise (vv. 20–24).

The tangled form of this psalm is not the mark of elderly dementia. Rather, it shows a mature understanding of the nature of prayer. This aged psalmist has learned how to hold at once the frightening reality of a desperate situation and a firm conviction that YHWH will indeed deliver. In alternating lines, this prayer expresses sure trust, profound anxiety, and, in the end, overarching praise, whereby the psalmist—herself a skilled instrumentalist (v. 22)—becomes an instrument of worship (vv. 23–24)! Providing a model for honest and integrated prayer, this psalm of the aged is a song for the ages—a liturgy of petition, hope, and praise.

JOEL MARCUS LEMON

Homiletical Perspective

about God. Who in the postmodern world believes that God cares about reputation? Nevertheless, this appeal to what may look like God's vanity opens the homily up to some larger questions. What the lament form suggests is that something is going on with me that has cosmic implications. In all suffering, God (and the mystery of God's purposes) is involved.

With the discussion of those two critical issues as prologue, the homilist has two strategic options for preaching on Psalm 71. Remembering that the homily should focus both on the Holy Week experience of Jesus and on the ways it connects with the lives of the congregation, the preacher could adopt the ancient Christian strategy of imagining this psalm as being spoken by Jesus himself. This is certainly one strong intention in the minds of the lectionary's framers. So one strategy for the preacher would be to imagine this lament put into the mouth of Jesus and to expound those two critical issues—the image of the castle, the concern for God's reputation—in a way that connects the hearer with the story of Jesus. Who among us has not wished for a safe place? Who among us has not wondered if our suffering has a point?

The other option would be to engage these two issues on their own terms and to find life or cultural examples that reinforce or exemplify what you are talking about—as I did at the beginning with a true story of being lost and looking hopelessly for a castle. What experiences of vulnerability or disorientation do you have that can give you a connection with the psalm's imagery, the story of Jesus, and the lives of your hearers? What events in your life have sparked your interior speculation about the meaning of it all? Like all of us, Jesus worried about whether anyone was listening. A sermon that takes that question seriously would get the attention of anyone on Tuesday in Holy Week.

GARY R. HALL

1 Corinthians 1:18-31

¹⁸For the message about the cross is foolishness to those who are perishing, but to us who are being saved it is the power of God. ¹⁹For it is written,

"I will destroy the wisdom of the wise,
  and the discernment of the discerning I will thwart."

²⁰Where is the one who is wise? Where is the scribe? Where is the debater of this age? Has not God made foolish the wisdom of the world? ²¹For since, in the wisdom of God, the world did not know God through wisdom, God decided, through the foolishness of our proclamation, to save those who believe. ²²For Jews demand signs and Greeks desire wisdom, ²³but we proclaim Christ crucified, a stumbling block to Jews and foolishness to Gentiles, ²⁴but to those

Theological Perspective

In today's passage Paul applies the language of foolishness in multiple ways to the attitude of nonbelievers, the focus of the Christian message on the cross, and even the character of God. The selection begins with the provocative assessment that "the message about the cross is foolishness to those who are perishing" (v. 18), and it concludes with the charge for Christians to avoid prideful boasting, which is a primary expression of foolishness, by transforming their expressions of glory to boasting "in the Lord" (v. 31). Later in this epistle Paul also applies the foolish label to followers of Christ, calling them "fools for Christ" (4:10). The motif of foolishness provides a counterpoint to Paul's reflections on the inadequacy of human wisdom and his thinking about the wisdom of God.

Within this foolish context Paul introduces several theological themes that are prominent throughout his letters: the greatness of God, the meaning of the cross, and the recognition of the human condition, especially the illusion of human self-sufficiency. Here Paul contrasts the inept attitudes of persons with the unexpected actions of God, which annul prideful, human expressions. He correlates the human aspirations for recognition and accomplishment with a Jewish predilection for signs (that humans are worthy of divine signification) and a Greek respect for wisdom (that persons can attain sufficient levels of

Pastoral Perspective

Some settings influence the reading and the hearing of Scripture more than others. When 1 Corinthians 13 is read at wedding after wedding, it is far from fresh and may be way past overdone. However, Psalm 23 read at every cemetery gathering still has meaning and strikes deep to the heart. You may hear Psalm 121 in a new way and remember it for a lot longer after hearing it read in worship on a mountaintop retreat. Scripture read while traveling in Israel and the Palestinian territories will never be read the same way again. As Psalm 46 is read in worship on a Lord's Day when the economy is in crisis, the listeners have a whole new understanding of what it means that "kingdoms totter" (v. 6). Time and place have an impact when pastor and congregation go to a biblical text.

The second half of the first chapter of 1 Corinthians can be experienced in a variety of ways in the life of the church. A preacher who commits to preaching her way through Paul's epistle *lectio continua* will come upon this teaching about the cross of Christ in light of the divisions and the disagreements within the Corinthian church mentioned in earlier paragraphs (vv. 10–17). A professor of preaching will engage the text in a lecture for an introduction to preaching class and encourage students with Paul's affirmations of the "foolishness of our proclamation" (v. 21). A pastor teaching a course in church officer

Tuesday of Holy Week

who are the called, both Jews and Greeks, Christ the power of God and the wisdom of God. ^{25}For God's foolishness is wiser than human wisdom, and God's weakness is stronger than human strength.

^{26}Consider your own call, brothers and sisters: not many of you were wise by human standards, not many were powerful, not many were of noble birth. ^{27}But God chose what is foolish in the world to shame the wise; God chose what is weak in the world to shame the strong; ^{28}God chose what is low and despised in the world, things that are not, to reduce to nothing things that are, ^{29}so that no one might boast in the presence of God. ^{30}He is the source of your life in Christ Jesus, who became for us wisdom from God, and righteousness and sanctification and redemption, ^{31}in order that, as it is written, "Let the one who boasts, boast in the Lord."

Exegetical Perspective

The stirring description of the Gospel's foolish wisdom opens Paul's letter to Corinth, in which he strives to focus the attention of a divided congregation on what is essential in their lives as followers of Christ, the beliefs and values that they share that should enable them to resolve the issues that divide them. The specific problems are clear enough. Some people are behaving in ways that shock their neighbors, engaging in sexual activity that some find problematic or consorting too freely with pagan culture. Some offend other members of the community by their behavior at worship. These include women who pray and prophesy with head uncovered and those who engage in a mysterious "speaking in tongues" (*glōssalalia*) that mystifies others. Others deny the resurrection.

Lying behind these presenting issues may be some fundamental attitudes. Some of Paul's converts may have thought that the movement they have embraced is a form of "wisdom" that frees and empowers them. They might have derived this notion from Paul himself, or from another evangelist who had visited them, a teacher such as Apollos, a learned Alexandrian (Acts 18:24), whom Paul mentions in 1 Corinthians 1:12; 3:3–4, 22; and 16:12. The learned tradition that valued a wisdom based in God's revealed Scripture is exemplified in the Wisdom of

Homiletical Perspective

"God decided, through the foolishness of our proclamation, to save those who believe" (v. 21b). Maybe Søren Kierkegaard was right. The best image for the preacher may be the clown. The clown hurries out onto the stage before a performance, yelling "Fire!" to all those settling in for a night out at the theatre. The people are impressed by the performance. They are in awe at the authentic-looking pleas—but it is absurd. Clowns just cannot be believed. It is all an entertaining act, for which we can settle comfortably into our seats for the rest of the show.

Perhaps the clown is not the preacher, but the word of preaching. A clownish word is what we have been given to say, to speak, to tell. Why? Because God thought that having you and me get up and tell people outrageous things was a good idea. In fact, God decided and was pleased by the whole notion that if we tell the people the absurd, God will work nothing less than salvation for the hearers.

It gets worse. Our moronic message is stupid only to those who are going down the tubes anyway. Only those who are being saved recognize the absurd as, in fact, potent. Evangelism in Paul's bizarro world sounds like an invitation to get on the inside and see what it looks like from there, because if you wait to enter until it makes sense somehow, you will be waiting forever, maybe even literally.

1 Corinthians 1:18-31

Theological Perspective

understanding). In contrast to these expectations, God's identification with the crucified Christ appears outrageous to those who "demand signs" and to those who "desire wisdom" (v. 22).

The criticism that Paul levies against human wisdom is certainly not an indictment of the Wisdom literature of Hebrew Scriptures. Instead, it is a charge against Greek forms of philosophy that use reason to seek God and against, perhaps, the emerging gnostic tendencies in some Christian communities. Nevertheless, Paul does not condemn human reason in and of itself. Instead, he identifies its inadequacy in being able to reach God; for it is God who, with ways and wisdom befuddling human expectations, establishes reconciliation with persons. The distinctive character of God's wisdom is that it does not conform to sophisticated reasoning but identifies with the one who acted unreasonably, sacrificing even life itself. Consequently, Christian faith is not a special form of knowledge, nor does it emerge from miracle; instead, as Paul attests again and again, it is manifest in discipleship to the way of the cross.

Focusing on the cross as the foolish act of God, Paul contrasts the inability of human wisdom to know God by its own exercise. He also determines that God's foolishness paradoxically evinces the wisdom of God. Still, for all of its wary ways, God's wisdom is not comparable to human wisdom, for God's wisdom so far exceeds the best of human wisdom that God can use foolishness "in the world to shame the wise" (v. 27). At the very least, God's foolishness—an eccentric divine attribute introduced by Paul—certainly surpasses the highest level of human wisdom, which, on its own, fails to know God (v. 21).

As he relates human wisdom to God's foolishness, Paul also contrasts the potential of human power to the vulnerability and weakness of God. Because death is the ultimate human limitation, God's weakness is revealed in the apparent victory of death over Christ. To vanquish death required full submission to and experience of death, a weakness that God manifested in the suffering and crucifixion of Christ. However, Paul affirms that through this weakness God accomplished that which the greatest human strength has been unable to do—defeat death itself. Thus in both wisdom and power, Paul concludes, God is not superlative; rather, God is incomparable.

Among twentieth-century theologians Paul Tillich articulated the incomparable character of God most clearly by insisting that God is not a being, even the grandest being in contrast to other beings. God exceeds the limitations posed by human existence.

Pastoral Perspective

training will draw attention to the close of chapter 1 and Paul's teaching about vocation and considering one's own call. When read on an early Sunday in Lent, the text may point the preacher's eye toward the frailty of human wisdom and strength and the importance of spiritual discipline for the journey that lies ahead. When you stop on a Tuesday of Holy Week and read 1 Corinthians 1:18–31 together in worship, it is the cross of Christ that looms so very large.

The shadow of the cross falls upon every verse. With the cross of Good Friday standing tall on the horizon, Paul's "message about the cross" (v. 18) leaps from the page. It does not matter whether the congregation is gathered in a room around a cross that will be draped in black in a few days, a wooden cross has been built for the week and is lying on the floor, or there is no cross at all in worship space; the epistle lesson places the cross right at the center. On this night in worship, the congregation does not really have to sing beneath it or kneel in prayer at the foot of it, because the apostle Paul, with his most powerful rhetoric, takes you right to the cross and holds you so close to it that you cannot turn away. For pastor and congregation, according to Paul, the cross overwhelms the room and our hearts and our lives.

It is not difficult to make the argument that life in the community of faith is rather countercultural in the post-Christian, postdenominational, postmodern world. If we are honest, even with the church, the liturgy of Holy Week itself is rather countercultural. A huge majority of those who were in worship on Palm Sunday will not be back until Easter morning. Every pastor knows that. Every pastor has lamented it. Most pastors have tried to exhort the community to new levels of spiritual practice when it comes to the Holy Week journey. Many have probably tried a bit of guilt along the way, pointing out to the congregation on Palm Sunday how they really ought to come back sometime before next week. The danger early in the week, of course, is that all who gather for worship could be feeling a bit self-righteous, patting themselves on the back for bucking the trend and basking in the countercultural, odd churchgoing notion of Holy Week worship.

The looming cross casts a shadow upon our own self-righteousness and our own well-intended attempts at religious piety. If there is anything countercultural, anything over and against the world, anything that turns the kingdoms of the earth upside down, anything that challenges the powers and principalities, it has nothing to with us and everything to do with Jesus Christ and his cross. Our best

Exegetical Perspective

Solomon, part of the Apocrypha of the Old Testament, which may have been in circulation in Corinth.

If such teaching did indeed influence the situation in Corinth, Paul's initial strategy in the letter becomes clear. He wants to reorient the Corinthians toward a central element of the gospel he preached that is difficult to square with any system of rational wisdom, namely, the claim that God had done something for humankind through the shameful death of Christ on the cross.

Paul begins (v. 18) with the cross, a sign of shame and instrument of degradation, "foolishness" to ordinary mortals, but to him and his followers, the "power of God." Paul reinforces the paradoxical character of his claim by citing (v. 19) a scriptural verse, Isaiah 29:14, that evokes the image of a God whose ways are not the ways of humankind and who confounds human wisdom. He continues with a series of rhetorical questions (v. 20) and a claim framed as a question: God has in fact, as the Scripture suggests "made foolish the wisdom of the world." Paul asks, in effect, who in his right mind would have thought that God could open up new possibilities of human existence through the miserable death of a condemned criminal? God did do so, and has made salvation available to believers (v. 21).

Paul then evokes the situation of his preaching, in which he has presented his gospel message to people of different backgrounds. Exactly what "signs" his Jewish interlocutors sought is unclear—perhaps proof from prophecy or miracles that would support the truth of his claims about Jesus. The Gospel of John wrestles with a similar concern in its description of the miraculous deeds of Jesus as "signs," and always tries to suggest that the miracles have a deeper meaning. Acts 17:22–34, in describing Paul in Athens addressing the philosophers on the Areopagus, depicts what Paul may be hinting at in his remark about Greeks seeking wisdom.

Paul does not explain how the crucified Christ at the center of his preaching (v. 23) is the "power" and "wisdom of God" (v. 24). Passages in other epistles suggest what he means. The Christ hymn of Philippians 2, for example, portrays Christ's death as a self-emptying (*kenōsis*), vindicated by his resurrection and exaltation, that serves as a model of the "mind" that his followers are to have. Again, 2 Corinthians 5:16–21 describes the death of Christ as an act whereby God effected reconciliation with the world and by which he appointed ambassadors of reconciliation like Paul. Later in 1 Corinthians, Paul will try to

Homiletical Perspective

Ours is a Monty Python–like ministry of silly walks and silly talks. Time and space have removed from us the extreme silliness of which Paul spoke, a fact that raises new issues for those who would continue in the apostolic line of verbal ridiculousness—because the live metaphors have all died and gone to orthodoxy hell. The *cross*, the *power of God*, *signs*, *wisdom*, *Christ crucified*, *stumbling blocks*, the *wisdom of God, redemption, sanctification*—yada, yada, yada. The biblical lexicon is the cemetery of dead metaphors. The words just do not mean much, if anything, anymore—not as they did when Paul was trying to speak them to people for whom these ideas were polarizing ideas.

Reading Paul, I am more and more struck by the idea that ministers of the gospel should probably be asking every week, "How can I speak and embody an appropriately offensive, scandalous, conflict- and anxiety-producing word this Sunday in order to be faithful to God and to the word that God enfleshed in Jesus and wishes to enflesh again in and through me?" However, most ministry in twenty-first-century North American churches seems designed to lessen conflict and anxiety among those with whom we minister. The gospel as Paul understands it seems to require a certain kind of conflict and anxiety in order to be gospel; without this, gospel is lacking.

What would the church do if we told them, "Now do not forget that you people were no prize when God called you! God was picking the low-hanging fruit when this church got formed! You are the shallow end of the human gene pool; don't you forget it! Anything that happens here is God's work, because it could not possibly be traced back to our ingenuity or ability!"

From what you and I know about preaching in most twenty-first-century North American contexts, this definitely will not preach. It will not play to the way the reward system is set up. Sorry. In a guide that is supposed to help preachers, it is ironic that we have a text in which we are told to preach the unpreachably offensive.

Maybe that was Paul's problem: he was not trying to save his job. He was not worried about denominational authorities calling his ordination into question. He was not on a career path, looking for a bigger church in a bigger city. He would get a church barely crawling, then be off to one on life support, or to a city where no church yet existed, there to preach his absurdity and then act quite surprised when anyone believed.

Paul cut a different swath through congregations and their theological consciousness. If they were a

1 Corinthians 1:18-31

Theological Perspective

Underscoring the incomparable nature of God, Tillich believed that the application of superlatives to God (such as greatest, most merciful, and most powerful) reduces the "majesty and power of God because they bring the concept of God into a spectrum of comparison with others."[1] Simply, God is beyond superlatives, which is the point Paul makes by indicating that the weakness of God far exceeds the greatest human power (v. 25).

Paul also describes the message of Christians as foolish, since they proclaim that victory is obtained through Christ's sacrifice. The foolishness of Christian preaching is that reasoning does not lead to the understanding of God; this comes, instead, through the cross, an act in which and through which God establishes solidarity with persons suffering. In so doing, God expresses a preferential priority for the poor and oppressed, the dispossessed and neglected. This marginal social position probably characterized many Corinthian Christians; Paul reminds them that they were not "powerful" or "of noble birth" (v. 26). Their salvation does not depend on their economic privilege or political achievement, and so it cannot be the basis for personal boasting. Paul's assertion about God's choosing the "low and despised" (v. 28) or those who are weak, in order "to shame the strong" (v. 27), resonates with the theme of liberation theology that God prioritizes the poor and marginalized.

Throughout the centuries a number of exemplary Christians have expressed their faith in such radical ways that their faith can be called foolish, especially when they have identified with the broken, the distressed, and the defeated. "By sacrificing themselves to the service of God and subordinating their values to the lordship of Christ," Jaroslav Pelikan avers, "they evidence the madness of the Holy, an insanity that saw what sanity refused to admit, the madness of which Paul was accused and to which he freely confessed when he labeled himself and his followers ever since 'fools for Christ' (1 Cor. 4:10)."[2]

JOSEPH L. PRICE

Pastoral Perspective

faithfulness will not be the sign. Our finest experience of worship is not the world's stumbling block (v. 23). Our strongest effort in advocating for justice and caring for the poor may be startling to the world, but it will never, on its own, rise to the level of foolishness. No, God's foolishness is wiser and God's weakness is stronger than the church at its best. What completely turns the world on end is the message about the cross, the action of Christ and him crucified. All that we can do, in word and action, is to proclaim Christ crucified. The foolishness and the sign and the transformation and the kingdom coming on earth as it is in heaven—that all comes from God.

Preachers should take comfort, and pastors and congregations should take note. According to Paul, this message about the cross not only looms over the night, over the week, and over our lives. The message about the cross rests at the heart of our corporate proclamation. When all is said, the church's witness to Christ and his cross is something we do together. We proclaim Christ crucified. When sharing the Lord's Supper in Holy Week, the liturgy itself affirms that we "proclaim the Lord's death until he comes" (1 Cor. 11:26). The emphasis throughout is on "we." As the cross casts such a striking shadow, the church has the chance to affirm once again that the best sermon, the best preaching of Christ and his crucifixion, comes in the faithfulness of our life together and our witness to the world.

DAVID A. DAVIS

---

1. Donald W. Musser and Joseph L. Price, *Tillich* (Nashville: Abingdon Press, 2010), 24.
2. Jaroslav Pelikan, *Fools for Christ: Essays on the True, the Good, the Beautiful* (Philadelphia: Muhlenberg Press, 1955), ix.

Exegetical Perspective

explain the implications of his being caught up in the mystery of Christ's death and resurrection in both practical and theoretical terms. Following the crucified Christ means not putting oneself first (chap. 9); above all, it means love (chap. 13). In the "foolish" (v. 25) message of such self-emptying love, God manifests a wisdom wiser than the calculating, self-interested wisdom of the world.

Paul shifts his rhetoric (v. 26) and addresses the social situation of the Corinthian community. He remarks that "not many" of the called at Corinth were by human standards "wise," "powerful," or "noble." Paul may, by the way, implicitly recognize that there were some in the community to whom those characteristics would apply, and that may have been a factor leading to the tensions in the community. The argumentative point that he wants to make, however, is a reminder of the community's experience. This is a move that Paul often makes, as in Galatians 3:23–29 and 4:1–7, where, by recalling that community's baptismal experience and life of prayer, he tries to persuade them that they do not need circumcision. Here Paul reminds his addressees who they were: people of all ranks and levels of sophistication, some "foolish" and "weak" by conventional standards (v. 27). God's choice of precisely such people to spread the gospel demonstrates again Paul's basic point: God's wisdom, which may look foolish in human eyes, trumps the wisdom of the world.

Paul concludes by invoking one of his common themes, boasting (v. 29). In a culture that emphasized social standing and claims based on honor, "boasting" does not have quite the negative connotations that it does in the modern West. Paul's "boasting," however, cuts across the grain of that culture. He will boast in things that the culture does not value, as he does, for instance, in 2 Corinthians 11:21b–33. His "boasting" is in the one who has overturned conventional wisdom. He concludes the passage (v. 31) with another scriptural quotation, from Jeremiah 9:24, that summarizes the point.

HAROLD W. ATTRIDGE

Homiletical Perspective

divided and arrogant group of people who thought they could keep living, acting, and thinking exactly the same way that they had always lived, acted, and thought before being folded into this new thing called "the church of God," Paul had another idea. Quite preposterously, he was sure it was not just his idea but was God's idea; and he would plop it down in their laps without sanding off the rough edges. "There, that is who you are, that is who God is, that is what our message is. If you are baptized, you are stuck with it! I hope I did not baptize you because I do not like groupies or whiners!"

So what is the good news here to proclaim? The preacher of the gospel looks for where the text points to God's actions, and this text offers plenty: "The message of the cross is the power of God." "God decided, through the foolishness of our proclamation, to save those who believe." "To all who are called, the proclamation of Christ crucified is the power and wisdom of God." "God chose what is foolish and weak, God chose what is low and despised, God chose what is nothing." "God is our source of life in Christ Jesus." "Jesus Christ became for us the wisdom of God." "God is our source of righteousness, sanctification, and redemption."

There is a lot of good news in this text, but the good news always comes over against bad news—in this case, the bad news of our own arrogance and divisiveness, our own delusions of self-sufficiency and wisdom. The demons that must be exorcised here are very close to home and very dear to our self-esteem. The idols of our own fragile egos must be crucified and buried to experience the resurrection of God's freeing and radically reorienting grace. Good luck with that word this Sunday, preachers.

ANDRÉ RESNER

John 12:20‑36

²⁰Now among those who went up to worship at the festival were some Greeks. ²¹They came to Philip, who was from Bethsaida in Galilee, and said to him, "Sir, we wish to see Jesus." ²²Philip went and told Andrew; then Andrew and Philip went and told Jesus. ²³Jesus answered them, "The hour has come for the Son of Man to be glorified. ²⁴Very truly, I tell you, unless a grain of wheat falls into the earth and dies, it remains just a single grain; but if it dies, it bears much fruit. ²⁵Those who love their life lose it, and those who hate their life in this world will keep it for eternal life. ²⁶Whoever serves me must follow me, and where I am, there will my servant be also. Whoever serves me, the Father will honor.

²⁷"Now my soul is troubled. And what should I say—'Father, save me from this hour'? No, it is for this reason that I have come to this hour. ²⁸Father, glorify your name." Then a voice came from heaven, "I have glorified it, and I will glorify it

Theological Perspective

Jesus went into Jerusalem to celebrate the Passover in spite of the threats against him. As he entered the city, the crowds celebrated him, especially for the sign he had given them by raising Lazarus. Besides being spectacular, that sign seemed to support the Pharisees' belief in resurrection, but when it actually happened at Jesus' command, the Pharisees worried that the "whole world" was beginning to follow him. The crowds' reaction also challenged the Sadducees, who denied the possibility of resurrection and feared that their dominant role among the temple priesthood was threatened (see Acts 23:8).

Greeks who may have been "God-fearers" were also in Jerusalem They were potential converts to Judaism, serious seekers after Christ, or spiritual tourists like those philosophers Paul met in Athens who were always chasing after the latest intellectual or spiritual opinions. For whatever reason, they told those disciples who had Greek names that they wanted to see Jesus, and the disciples told Jesus. Jesus made no response to the visitors, but the mention of them suggests that Jesus had evidence that his message was going out to the world beyond Israel. His comments can be understood as an explanation to the disciples and the crowds of what this situation meant. Since the spreading of the word to the wider world had begun without his direct involvement, it

Pastoral Perspective

The Greeks came to Philip, who was from Bethsaida in Galilee, and said to him, "Sir, we wish to see Jesus." After sharing this request with Andrew, Philip finally approached Jesus with the request. Jesus offered an answer, but it is not entirely clear that he was answering the question from the Greeks. I imagine the disciples listening politely and then, like little children tugging at their father's sleeve, asking, "So can the Greeks see you or not?"

They must have heard about this unique rabbi who taught and healed in ways that set him apart. Maybe among the group were some who were suffering with incurable diseases. Perhaps they brought with them a list of questions for Jesus, questions that were never satisfactorily answered by their hometown religious leaders. In any case, they wanted time with Jesus, time to look him in the eye, time to be in his company.

There are many people in our communities today who long to see Jesus. They may be in our pews week after week, waiting and wondering if they will ever encounter this Jesus of whom we preach. Some of them may never have entered the doors of a church, but their spiritual quest has led them to the place where they "wish to see Jesus." It is not enough to say to them, "He is not here. . . . He has been raised" (Matt. 28:6). We cannot simply dismiss this desire

again." [29]The crowd standing there heard it and said that it was thunder. Others said, "An angel has spoken to him." [30]Jesus answered, "This voice has come for your sake, not for mine. [31]Now is the judgment of this world; now the ruler of this world will be driven out. [32]And I, when I am lifted up from the earth, will draw all people to myself." [33]He said this to indicate the kind of death he was to die. [34]The crowd answered him, "We have heard from the law that the Messiah remains forever. How can you say that the Son of Man must be lifted up? Who is this Son of Man?" [35]Jesus said to them, "The light is with you for a little longer. Walk while you have the light, so that the darkness may not overtake you. If you walk in the darkness, you do not know where you are going. [36]While you have the light, believe in the light, so that you may become children of light."

After Jesus had said this, he departed and hid from them.

Exegetical Perspective

This passage presents the meaning and implications of Jesus' imminent death. It includes both transfiguration and agony. All we need to understand John's account of the crucifixion is here. Here human destiny is identified as "being with Jesus."

John's Gospel presents a battle between God and Satan acted out in the sphere of human history. From the outset, the Gospel describes a conflict between forces of darkness that reject the Word and forces of light that accept the Word and become children of God. Introducing the passion narrative, chapter 12 is a turning point in the conflict, where "the hour has come" (v. 23) and "now is the judgment" (v. 31); the crucifixion is about to occur. The death and resurrection of Jesus are the victory over Satan, "the ruler of this world" (v. 31). Using the language of irony, the cross is the means of Jesus' enthronement as victorious sovereign and the place where Jesus' victory over Satan is made plain. In describing the cross as "glorification," the author uses a mythic pattern to make sense of the shock of Jesus' violent departure. In this pattern the resurrection appearances and the promise of the Paraclete demonstrate the greater power Jesus now has as enthroned sovereign. John's notion of the cross as salvation includes Jesus' present (not deferred) vindication, judgment, and exaltation.

Homiletical Perspective

Holy Week is not a new liturgical notion in Christianity. Faithful Christians have observed this week for centuries. However, in contemporary American religious practice, if Holy Week is observed at all, it is most frequently observed toward the end of the week on Maundy Thursday or Good Friday or for the Easter Vigil. For many Christians, Holy Week is just another week framed by the grand parade of Palm Sunday and the lively festivities of Easter.

This should come as no surprise to preachers in contemporary Western society. Ours is a society that has a visceral aversion to dealing with dying and death. Consumers, including Christians, expend considerable money to deny the realities of aging and, most particularly, to deny death. "Forever Young" is not just an advertising slogan for cosmetics and a memorable pop tune; it is the unspoken slogan for all Palm Sunday/Easter Sunday, death-denying, fantasy-enamored Christianity.

So how is the preacher supposed to proclaim the gospel on a day that most Christians do not observe, in a week that they pretend does not exist? The challenge does not end there. The Gospel for Holy Tuesday is a text from John with the theme of death weaving through it like a coiled snake, ready to strike. After repeated refusals to reveal his glory, saying, "It is not yet time," here Jesus announces,

John 12:20-36

Theological Perspective

was time to finish his messianic mission for all humanity. "The hour has come for the Son of Man to be glorified."

His arguments for this are several. Can a single living unit, a seed or a person, make any difference unless it is destroyed in its old form and enabled to bear much fruit? Can someone who loves temporal life as it is accomplish what one who is willing to sacrifice for the possibility of eternal life for all humanity can? Jesus spells out the implications for any who would serve him in this mission: they must follow his lead, and they will be honored by God as he will be glorified. It is another way of saying what we find also in the Synoptics: "If any want to become my followers, let them deny themselves and take up their cross and follow me" (Matt. 16:24; Mark 8:34; Luke 9:23).

Such teachings disturb one to the very core of one's being; but should one try to get out of it, if one has been called to serve God's purpose of salvation for the world? This is not a gnostic theme—that it is good to get out of this life, this world, and this history—as some have argued. No! It is the reverse of that; it is closer to a wisdom theme: an action in time for the sake of true life. More, it signals a kairotic moment: history is now ripe for the radiance of God's sacrificial love to be revealed in the crucifixion, resurrection, and ascension, much as the "I AM" and laws of God were revealed to Moses as the glory shown all around.

Facing the challenge of this monumental moment brings anxiety to the point of agony. John conveys the true humanity of Jesus when he recognizes that Jesus struggles with his resolve—at least until he comes to the moment of submission: "Father, glorify your name" (v. 28). At that moment, words of divine assurance are heard by the disciples and some of the crowd standing by. Not by all. The voice of God is rarely unambiguously audible. Some account for revelatory moments by identifying them with natural causes, in this case with threatening thunder. Others attribute them to semidivine creatures, such as angels bearing a sacred message. However, to any of the crowd who believe, this is an inward confirmation that, as God's name was once revealed in glory, so in Jesus Christ's obedience it will be revealed in glory again. That will be the beginning of the defeat of the powers of darkness that still rule much of life.

Jesus himself needs no further assurance, but he instructs the listeners that all this is meant for them. He knows what kind of death he has to face; and he is confident that when all is finished, and he is lifted up, believing humanity will be enlightened and enabled

Pastoral Perspective

with our theologies of the resurrection and eschatology. While many in our communities are leaving the church and organized religion, their interest in Jesus may continue. Some of these are the people who tell pollsters that they are "spiritual, but not religious."

The church finds itself in the place of Philip and Andrew, as those who know and love Jesus and are asked to help others see Jesus for themselves. Day by day, "Greeks" of all shapes and sizes, languages and backgrounds are looking to Christians and to the church for answers about Jesus. What are we to say? What are we to do?

The task of evangelism is new for each generation of the church. The gospel message remains constant, but the vehicles for sharing the good news of Jesus have changed over time. Few today would favor the nineteenth-century revival practice of the anxious bench, where individuals who were anxious about their spiritual lives sat in the front row of the church, in order to receive stern warnings and fervent prayers about the condition of their souls. Today many pastors are wrestling with modern forms of electronic communication and the role they may play in sharing the gospel with an e-savvy generation. Can people encounter Jesus on the Internet? Are social networks appropriate places to do evangelism? Does Twittering belong in worship? However we might answer these questions, it appears that God still chooses most often for Christ to be made known through human beings, through Philip and Andrew, through you and me.

Jesus offers sound advice for would-be evangelists of every generation: "Whoever serves me must follow me, and where I am, there will my servant be also" (v. 26). We cannot share Jesus with others if we are not with Jesus ourselves. The challenge then is to serve the Jesus whom we cannot see with our eyes but can follow with our lives. Christ has been made known to new generations of "Greeks" who hunger to see Jesus, by the mysterious and gracious working of the Holy Spirit in the lives of ordinary Christians. If we are to be ready to show people Jesus, we must be serving and following the one whom we call Lord.

The second section of this passage opens a window of insight into what it was like for Jesus to face his own death. His soul, we are told, was "troubled" (v. 27). Some have imagined that Jesus was immune from such ordinary—and, dare I say human—feelings. Surely Jesus could not have felt what we feel. On the contrary, the very soul of Jesus was troubled as he walked through the valley of the shadow of death. These few words are a comfort to us as we are faced

Exegetical Perspective

Some Greeks present the disciples with a request to see Jesus. Jesus answers them, "The hour has come for the Son of Man to be glorified" (v. 23). Since on earlier occasions in the Gospel Jesus declares that his hour was not yet come (2:4; 7:6, 8, 30; 8:20), the realization of "the hour" here is significant. The hour refers to the death and resurrection of Jesus. By offering it to Greeks, Jesus suggests its universal significance. It also anticipates 13:1, "Now before the festival of the Passover, Jesus knew that his hour had come to depart from this world and go to the Father."

The derivation and use of the term "Son of Man" is debated. In this passage the term appears connected to Jesus' teaching that the Son of Man must be lifted up (vv. 32–34). In John's Gospel, the Son of Man is judge and revealer. "To be glorified" refers to Jesus' death; it is John's way of reversing the shame and ignominy of the crucifixion by using imagery of death as a glorious enthronement. In Johannine circles, Revelation also portrays victory leading to enthronement (Rev. 3:21). The imagery of a grain of wheat that falls into the earth and dies (v. 24), whereupon it bears much fruit, uses the language of harvest to interpret a beneficent death.

"Whoever serves me must follow me" (v. 26) not only encourages imitating Christ but also anticipates Jesus' action of washing the disciples' feet (13:3–20) and what happens on the cross. Given the dishonor of the cross, followers can expect honor from the Father (v. 26); this involves being with Jesus and anticipates the narrative of 14:3, in which Jesus explains his departure, "where I am, there you may be also." Perhaps this instills hope in Jesus' followers.

"Now my soul is troubled" (v. 27) alludes to Synoptic accounts of Gethsemane. As is well known, John's Gospel lacks a reference to Gethsemane. Jesus' agony is not absent in the Johannine narrative but is located instead before the last meal with the disciples. The words allude to Psalm 42:5, 11 (Ps. 41 LXX). Using this psalm to convey Jesus' words of agony is ironic, because Psalm 42 affirms the psalmist's trust in God. Here John communicates that Jesus trusts in God at his hour. Another example of the evangelist's ironic handling of the agony tradition is the parallel prayers of verses 27b and 28a. The first "prayer," framed as a question ("And what should I say?"), is never prayed by Jesus and stands as a parody of the prayer associated with Jesus' agony in the garden (Mark 14:36). The second prayer, "Father, glorify your name," is the true prayer for the hour. Jesus lays down his life of his own free will (10:18); he embraces his hour to focus on God and the moment of God's glorification.

Homiletical Perspective

"The hour has come for the Son of Man to be glorified" (v. 23).

To the unseasoned reader of the Fourth Gospel, this announcement from Jesus sounds like the glad tidings of a resurrection prediction—and it is. It is also an unmistakable declaration that the glorification of God involves death, Jesus' death. As this text opens, Greeks come seeking Jesus, because they have heard about the new life Jesus brought forth from Lazarus; but they find a Jesus who wants to talk about death, his own.

Welcome to Holy Tuesday, preachers! The task of preaching the gospel on Holy Tuesday, though, gets easier when you realize that Jesus talks about his impending death as a way to point to the new life that God will accomplish in his resurrection. Clinging to life, then, is the sure route to death, observes Jesus in this text, while giving up life, in the service of God and God's people, is a manifestation of the risen life. Readers need only to return to the first verses of this chapter to see the risen life made manifest in the actions of Martha and then Mary.

Another key homiletical theme in this text surfaces in the opening verses. By highlighting a visit to Jesus from non-Jews, John communicates that the fear expressed by the Pharisees in 12:19, "Look how the whole world has gone after him!" (NIV), has been realized. The glorification of God through the death and resurrection of Jesus will be "good news" for Jew and Greek.

Fred Craddock puts it this way:

> Glorified, Christ is present to his people in all nations, in all generations. The Johannine church, being of another time and place, needed very much to hear this. And so do we, for without some clear doctrine of the continuing and unlimited presence of Christ, the church cannot live. No community of faith can long survive on the thin diet of fond memories of a Camelot, that marvelous time and place when he was here, a time and place that is no more. In such a case, faith would give way to resentment toward a God who was quite active long ago but who has done nothing within our lifetime.[1]

The God we meet in John's Gospel will not be marginalized by modernity or limited to what humanity considers reasonable.

Another preaching portal into this text is through our society's terrified notions of dying and death. This

---

1. Fred Craddock, *John*, Knox Preaching Guides (Atlanta: John Knox Press, 1982), 94.

John 12:20-36

Theological Perspective

to come to him. They will recognize that he is right when he says, "I am the way, and the truth, and the life" (John 14:6). It was, it is, an inbreaking eschatological enlightenment that overcomes the darkness that shadows over all of life in the world as it is.

Indeed, we can say now, in a global context where believers live face to face with other faiths, that this enlightenment differs from that of any other world religion of salvation. It is simply not the same as the moksha of the Hindus, the nirvana of the Buddhists, the paradise of the Muslims, or hope for a messiah who will restore a permanent Israel in history for the Jews (which the crowd expects). It also differs from the humanist enlightenment of modernity, the perfect classless society of the Marxist, and any other human-induced self-fulfillment. Whatever Christianity shares with the great religions and philosophies of the world, its vision of the ultimate future transforms the trajectory of life and thus its purposes and practices.

The passage ends with Jesus' advice to the crowd and to all who expect a final resolution of life's ills immediately. We are to live in the time between the beginning of the end of the moral, intellectual, and spiritual darkness that shadows the world and the final defeat of that darkness. It is but an interim when we have the Messiah with us—then as Jesus in the flesh, now as the resurrected Son of Man, eventually when he comes again. Therefore we must walk in his light, so that we do not lose our way in the darkness or let the darkness of demonic powers dominate the world. We are to bask in the light ethically, believe in it cognitively, and become children of it spiritually, even if Christ seems sometimes to have hidden himself from our view.

MAX L. STACKHOUSE

Pastoral Perspective

with our own mortality or the death of a loved one. The struggle is real, and the questions are undeniable. Death was troubling even to Jesus.

In the end, Jesus came to a place of peace about his death. He gathered strength and courage from knowing that his death was for a divine purpose, for the salvation of our souls. When we are in the position of walking with a parishioner or family member through illness and death, our own anxiety can shape the ways in which we minister. The anxiety and fear of someone who is dying may make us uncomfortable. In this situation, it is not uncommon to try to hurry a person beyond their fear to a place of peace. A troubled soul cannot be hurried along. Listening to another express anxiety or fear about death is to be honored. We must prayerfully trust that the God whose reassuring voice came down from heaven will be with each and every one who is facing death.

A final note of caution is in order as we look at this text. Jesus, though troubled by the torture, suffering, and death he would experience, came to a place of acceptance. He did not ask God to save him from that hour. This text must not be used to encourage victims of violence to remain in dangerous relationships or circumstances. The cruelty and abuse endured by the second person of the Trinity is not meant to be emulated by his followers. All forms of violence must be condemned, and God's desire for wholeness and wellness for all humanity must be proclaimed.

NANCY A. MIKOSKI

Exegetical Perspective

Verses 27–28 are an excellent example of the way the Fourth Evangelist takes traditional material and reshapes it to fit the theological vision that drives the Gospel. An "agony" scene like that in Mark would make no sense in this Gospel, because here God's will and Jesus' will have always been the same. There is no internal struggle in the face of his death, because Jesus recognizes the hour as the purpose of his mission. It is the final revelation of his relationship with God. Jesus' hour results in a glorification of God's name.

The words "casting out," "judgment," and "ruler of this world" indicate that this verse marks a crucial point in the conflict between God and Satan, the "ruler of this world" (v. 31). Thus the term "world" (*kosmos*) here is not used in a neutral sense (as in John 17:5, 6 for example) but in a negative sense, referring to the sphere opposed to Jesus and his followers. In this passage and chapters that follow, the world opposes Jesus, the Paraclete, and Jesus' followers. Jesus' own have been chosen "out of the world" (15:19). The motif of driving out Satan from heaven is found in apocalyptic texts and other NT texts such as Luke 10:18 and Revelation 12:7–9. Note that the specific wording of judgment anticipates 14:30, where the betrayal, arrest, and crucifixion of Jesus are prefaced by the phrase "the ruler of the world is coming." Ironically, the human actions leading to Jesus' death, driven by Satanic powers, are undone by the glorification of the Father and simultaneous judgment and casting out of them at crucifixion. The notion of judgment is a major theme of John's Gospel. In 12:31 forensic judgment is combined with warfare in which the "ruler of this world" is expelled.

At the end of the passage, Jesus' teaching recalls and clarifies the enigmatic 3:14, "And just as Moses lifted up the serpent in the wilderness, so must the Son of Man be lifted up," which is now explained as the exaltation and glorification of the crucifixion. Followers are honorably numbered among the "children of light."

DEIRDRE J. GOOD

Homiletical Perspective

Holy Tuesday text provides a contrast, not only to contemporary notions of dying and death, but a counterview to the death of Jesus presented in the Synoptic tradition. In this text from John, Jesus is not sweating blood in the garden, as in Luke's portrayal. Jesus here confronts glory—his death and resurrection—with the confidence of the One who has sent him into the world. He does not welcome death like some deranged madman, but neither does he fear that death will destroy him and God's purpose. Just the opposite. The all-too-human Jesus is troubled by the thought of his death, yet at the same time is comforted that the name of God will be glorified through it.

For Christians weary of traditional theories of Jesus' atoning death, John provides another biblical perspective. For John, Jesus does not die as a sacrifice to appease an angry God or as ransom for humanity's enslavement to sin. "The world that lives in opposition to Jesus ('this world') is judged by Jesus' death, and its power overcome (vv. 25, 31). Jesus' death has this effect, not because it is a sacrifice that atones for human sin, but because it reveals the power and promise of God and God's love decisively to the world."[2]

A powerful Johannine motif recurs at the conclusion of this text as Jesus urges his followers to walk in the light and not in the darkness. On Holy Tuesday, with the black night of Maundy Thursday and the cosmic darkness of Good Friday just hours away, what better time to invite people of faith to walk in the light. Jesus does not suggest walking in the light as an option to following him, but as essential, "so that you may become children of light" (v. 36).

As John's Gospel opens, we hear "The light shines in the darkness, and the darkness did not overcome it" (1:5). Maybe contemporary "children of light" do not walk through Holy Week, or walk through only a small part of it, because they fear that this Gospel is too optimistic. Maybe a regular preaching diet of God's grace and glory will supply the necessary nutrition to feast on the promises of God in Jesus, even on Holy Tuesday.

GARY W. CHARLES

---

2. Gail O'Day, in *New Interpreter's Bible* (Nashville: Abingdon Press, 1995), 9:714.

Isaiah 50:4-9a

⁴The Lord GOD has given me
   the tongue of a teacher,
 that I may know how to sustain
   the weary with a word.
 Morning by morning he wakens—
   wakens my ear
   to listen as those who are taught.
⁵The Lord GOD has opened my ear,
   and I was not rebellious,
   I did not turn backward.
⁶I gave my back to those who struck me,
   and my cheeks to those who pulled out the beard;
 I did not hide my face
   from insult and spitting.

Theological Perspective

In Monday's lesson, God spoke about and to the Servant. In Tuesday's lesson, there was dialogue between God and the Servant. Today, we hear the Servant only. The Servant speaks of personal experience and conviction. On Monday I proposed that we could usefully appropriate the passage as Christians, seeing Jesus as the Servant who was foretold. With Tuesday's passage, that strategy seemed less useful; but today I return to it. Let us think first of Jesus as God's Servant who is speaking here.

He begins by asserting, certainly truly, that God has given him the gift of teaching, and doing so in a way that "sustains the weary" (v. 4). He goes on to tell us how God enables him to be a student who listens to the divine message and does not refuse it. This leads him to endure suffering and humiliation at the hands of other people. This account fits our understanding of who Jesus was and what he experienced, with special attention to the last days of his life.

Here the tone of the passage changes. God not only directs Jesus' action into channels that lead to suffering and humiliation; God also helps him and vindicates him. Because of God's help, what would otherwise be disgrace is not. This has enabled Jesus to be steadfast.

In applying this passage thus to Jesus, we could interpret the vindication as the resurrection.

Pastoral Perspective

Do you have homework? Each evening, everyone in my household knew that I would have to ask my girls this question eventually. The homework took them hours sometimes, and sometimes they would have to wake up early in the morning to finish it all. Often, I could not help with the math, having forgotten everything I had ever learned about it, and I felt more than a little useless. Why do they give these kids so much homework? I sometimes wondered resentfully, feeling a little as if the heavy assignments were mine, as if I were the one in school.

A teacher can be a hard taskmaster, but Isaiah 50:4 gives us a different view of a teacher. A teacher is not someone who loads us with more than we can carry, but someone who actually helps us lighten our load. A teacher is someone who "sustains the weary with a word."

There are few jobs more important than that of a teacher. I remember every one of mine in school, but I also remember many others: scout leaders, choir directors, older children, more experienced clergy. There is so much to know, so many ways in which to be wise, and none of us can really say we are "self taught." We have all had many teachers, and we are the product of all of them.

Jesus' followers called him Teacher. So did everybody else, in fact, because that is what he was, an

^{7}The Lord God helps me;
  therefore I have not been disgraced;
therefore I have set my face like flint,
  and I know that I shall not be put to shame;
^{8} he who vindicates me is near.
Who will contend with me?
  Let us stand up together.
Who are my adversaries?
  Let them confront me.
^{9}It is the Lord God who helps me;
  who will declare me guilty?

Exegetical Perspective

Today's passage comes from the same part of the book of Isaiah (chaps. 40–66) as Monday's and Tuesday's. Like our passages for Monday and Tuesday, this chapter dates from the Babylonian exile of the Judean people in the sixth century BCE. The passage shows forth poetically what every believer knows existentially. Exile is not just a matter of time and place. Exile represents a nation's (and an individual's) sense of radical dislocation, separation from all that is familiar and beloved. At the deepest level it does not matter entirely whether the land of exile is a land of deprivation or of relative well-being. To be exiled is to be far from home. For the people of Judah, exile meant being cut off from the land that was thoroughly associated with the blessing of God. Exile felt not just like loss but like betrayal— perhaps betrayal by the very God who had promised Judah so much. Much of biblical literature is a response, a lament, a plea, in the light of this sense of betrayal. In the fifth century BCE, even those who remain in the land are separated from their compatriots, from their history, probably from economic benefit.

This is a covenant people, as we remember when we read 2 Samuel 7 or Psalm 48. Now it seems as if the covenant has been broken—by God! The people cry out: Why has our God allowed this to happen?

Homiletical Perspective

Wednesday is the fourth day of creation according to the first Genesis story. It presents a more detailed arrangement of light. On day one, at God's first word, light arrived. Now, on the fourth day, that light is ordered in ways familiar to us all. God creates the sun, the main power source, and the moon that reflects it. Both separate the light from the darkness. So "stimulus and response" is the pattern set up against the overwhelming dark. The sun is the revelation, and the moon is our liturgy by which we meet it.

In this passage from Isaiah we see how deeply the light penetrates the Servant and how costly is the liturgical response of his life. The light intensifies, sharpens, and defines. The response brings rejection, punishment, and pain. To read this might lead us to fear the power of the light and to remain hiding in the darkness. To preach it takes us beyond the safety of tribe, cult, and tradition. The one who listens becomes the enemy. The one being prepared becomes a teacher ripe for rejection.

One way to approach this text is to see its poetry as a running supertitle over a great religious drama. The events of the Christian Holy Week present a passion play in which theology, the history of salvation, and Jewish hopes and aspirations become costumes worn by Jesus, the first-century rabbi, and his fellow players. As stations of the cross, archetypal moments of

Isaiah 50:4-9a

Theological Perspective

However, the more natural understanding is that the vindication accompanies the teaching itself. That means that it is not a publicly visible vindication, but it is Jesus' confidence that he speaks for God, so that no one can overthrow his message. This does not prevent people from slapping him, pulling out his hair, and spitting on him. It does prevent Jesus from understanding himself as put in the wrong by any of these actions. He speaks God's word, and, accordingly, nothing that others do to him actually disgraces him. Indeed, his adversaries do not dare to challenge what he says directly, however cruel their treatment. They know that they cannot succeed in open confrontation.

This assurance that, because the Servant is on God's side, God is on her side, was also the heart of the positive assurance of Tuesday's Scripture. Its application to Jesus seems fully true to our understanding of him. Furthermore, the passage of two millennia has not rendered the words of Jesus erroneous or irrelevant. They address our generation with the same shocking force with which they addressed the generation of Jesus.

Some of the categories through which Jesus has been understood separate him sharply from his disciples. But this is not true of "Servant." We understand ourselves as also called to service. The challenge of this passage to us is the extent to which we can apply it to ourselves.

Not all of us, perhaps, have "the tongue of the teacher." Yet this is a widely shared gift. All parents are teachers of their children, and most of us take part in teaching others in myriad ways. Many who do not speak fluently still "sustain the weary with a word."

In any case, the emphasis here is on the Servant as one who is taught. This certainly applies to all. Disciples of Jesus are those who are taught by him, but the role of learner is not limited to that. The Servant in this passage listens directly to God. Jesus led us to expect to learn from the Holy Spirit. God awakens us each morning to hear the divine word. This too can be meaningful to all of us in our discipleship.

Perhaps the greatest difficulty in appropriating to ourselves this passage about the Servant is that the Servant who speaks here is so sure of the divine accuracy of the message. The Servant knows this message to be truly God's word. Many of us suffer from too great an uncertainty. There is more that we could say in confidence than we do in fact say, but it is healthy for us to know our limits. We will not seek the authority that so impressed the hearers of Jesus.

Pastoral Perspective

itinerant rabbi. He was executed for his teaching, although it is not clear whether that was because of its content or because of its effect on people. Did the Romans really care whether or not Jesus claimed to be the Son of God? Probably not; they were not particularly interested in the Jewish religion. However, they would have cared mightily if enough people *thought* he was, and if they drew revolutionary inspiration from that belief.

One thing about good teaching is that it is indelible. You can never will yourself *not to know* what you know. We may forget—and we hate how forgetful we become as we age—but we cannot "un-know" things. It may take a while to sink in, but good teaching becomes part of the learner. We grow because of it, and we build on it. We see this process in the unfolding story of the disciples of Jesus: frightened, puzzled, and confused, they are not an impressive bunch at first. However, what Jesus has given them endures in them. Long after the events we remember this week, they go on, from strength to strength, becoming the courageous leaders whose memory we revere still. They little resemble the students they once were. Specifically, they develop the courage to live their lives and even *give* their lives for the survival of the Way, and inspire others to do as well.

This kind of growth can happen only when the teacher brings herself or himself into the encounter. I have said that I remember all my teachers, and that is true; but I also remember that not all of them brought themselves to their encounter with us, and—young as we were—we knew it when they did not. We know that the story of the events of this week was the first story taught by Christians to newer Christians and to would-be Christians, and this must be the reason: the awe with which they greeted the lengths of love to which Jesus would go for his people. He held nothing back from his encounter with us, and every last thing he had was taken—up to and including his life.

Holy Week itself is a teacher. Like any good teacher, it embodies what it teaches. It enables us to enter the story ourselves. We may know a lot about the story. We can probably tell it ourselves. We may even be able to recite parts of it from memory, we have heard it so many times. However, knowing about something is not the same thing as living it, and Holy Week gives us the chance to live it. We walk the story again, its sorrow and pain. We even walk its tedium. We fail to walk it well, often: our minds wander, our spirits fail, we fall asleep instead of remaining present to its demand. We are just like Jesus' disciples.

Exegetical Perspective

Why do we suffer? Where is our salvation? Psalm 44 richly portrays this sense of desertion. While the exiles may not have been subject to harsh treatment or even to religious oppression, from their perspective the promise had been broken: "You [YHWH] have made us like sheep for slaughter, and have scattered us among the nations. You have sold your people for a trifle, demanding no high price for them" (Ps. 44:11–12).

Near the end of the exilic period, some time between 550 and 540 BCE, an anonymous poet-prophet provides words of comfort and vision, hope and reassurance ("Comfort, O comfort my people"; Isa. 40:1). So just as today's passage has the same historical location as the Isaiah passages of the previous two days, it also upholds the figure of the Servant ('ebed) who as God's chosen is called to be a leader of their people in an international arena.

As in Isaiah 49:1–7, the prophet/Servant in today's reading speaks in the first person. Understanding himself or herself as a teacher with rhetorical ability, the prophet/Servant functions as a counselor ("I may know how to sustain the weary with a word," v. 4). Reporting persecution for being faithful, the speaker reiterates trust in YHWH God as vindicator (vv. 6–8), and concludes with three rhetorical questions about steadfastness and resistance (vv. 8–9a). In a community where the memories of destruction and deportation are still quite fresh, the acknowledgment of the emotional state of the people, weariness, allows for the recognition of the necessity of growth and thus healing.

Like the readings of the two previous days, today's reading from the book of Isaiah is considered one of the so-called Servant Songs (the fourth one, 52:13–53:12, to be read on Good Friday). Called such by Bernhard Duhm in his commentary on the book of Isaiah in 1892, these four passages in Second Isaiah have long been considered special by Christian interpreters, because they lent themselves to identify the Servant with Jesus of Nazareth—clearly a later Christian reinterpretation, though one going back to the time of the early churches, and one still alive and well in most contemporary ones.

More recent scholarship on the book of Isaiah has disagreed with the limitations of singling out these four passages from the others that involve the Servant figure. Considering all the other mentions of 'ebed/Servant in Isaiah 40–55, Patricia Tull Wiley observes that, in the majority of the other passages, the Servant is identified as Israel/Jacob collectively

Homiletical Perspective

prayer, support, rejection, betrayal, raging violence, desolation, death, grief, and a hope beyond loss stop us along the way. As we place ourselves within them, we begin to feel the power of this sacred season.

The broad range of our potential as learners in God is displayed. This is no surface thing or a disinterested tasting of a banquet of savory delights. We were not created to employ God as our house servant, but rather to awaken to our true place in history and to demanding work amid the grit and grind of human complexity.

The horrors of human rejection also rise before us. We are social animals. To belong, to be loved, to know our place in the dance and to keep it, are such strong themes within us. Yet here the Servant has brought out the worst in his fellow citizens. Not only do they disagree with him and stand against his work. They take time to torture and humiliate him in the most injurious and disheartening ways.

We also catch a glimpse of the resilience of this Servant. His conviction of God's present help deepens. He finds flintlike reserves to help hold his place and do his work. Those who have not dug this deeply or been pushed this far may not readily recognize what is being conveyed here. Those who have dug deeply or been pushed in this manner will be greatly supported by this fellow sufferer's news.

The model of the two lights illustrates the two ways God teaches us. The first is as sunlight, suddenly rising and being present. We cannot but see and feel the illumination. Life is warmed and stimulated to grow. There is clarity. The second light, the reflective moon, illustrates the power of our response. The darker things become, the clearer is our light. We move across the firmament of human affairs in a changing orbit, sometimes fully visible, sometimes only partially recognized, but always reflecting a light greater than ourselves, without which we would have no illumination at all.

This text also pushes us to consider the nature of our message. What is the source of our preaching? Is it the sum total of study and imagination? Is it a selecting and parroting of common law and wisdom? Is it self-preservation dressed in ecclesiastical finery? The poet here describes something far deeper. All of life seems to be churning through a vulnerable and open heart. The Servant is seeing dangerous things and hearing the anguish of souls beneath the social veneer. He is forming a sentiment of root honesty and the compulsion to step out of the masses and speak.

The challenge for preaching is seen in the distance between the heart of this clean word and the ways the

Isaiah 50:4-9a

Theological Perspective

The emphasis in this passage is on the high cost of discipleship to the Servant. Few of us have had dramatic instances of comparable suffering for our faithfulness. Sometimes our lack of suffering may make us unsure that we are true servants of God. That uncertainty is often justified. Many of us who from time to time wish to be disciples are still, much of the time, informed more by our desire for status, power, and prosperity, as these are understood in the world. We continue to care more for how those around us view us than for the inner truth of our faithfulness to God. We have good reason to doubt the authenticity of our servanthood.

However, this does not mean that, in general and overall, those who are most faithful are those who are most persecuted or humiliated. God does not call us to suffering or to sacrifices that truly make us unhappy. Most of those who are most faithful lead happy and fulfilled lives, and many are appreciated and admired even by those who do not seek to be disciples of Jesus. Most of them find the cost of saying no to the world's values, even in the extreme case when it leads to the sacrifice of life, trivial in relation to the joy that is gained in living in faithfulness to God. The call to be a servant of God is not a call to live miserably; it is a call to an abundant life.

Who, then, is the Servant who speaks in this passage? Who or what was intended by the initial writer we will never know, but his vision of the nature of a servant of God has meaning far beyond whatever that intention may have been. The church has long seen Jesus as the purest exemplar of servanthood to God. We too can put on the mantle of this servanthood.

JOHN B. COBB JR.

Pastoral Perspective

"Let's do the passion in real time," somebody said, and we did so. Groups of people studied the texts that the earliest Christians told, the story of the execution of Jesus, and together they built a liturgy that would take the same number of hours, from Maundy Thursday to the afternoon of Good Friday. We would leave the church for a garden we would call Gethsemane. There Jesus would be arrested. We would journey through the dark streets to another place; it would be the courtyard of the home of the high priests. Peter would deny Jesus there. In and out of the roles we came and went; sometimes Jesus was a man, sometimes a woman. Different people would play different parts. There would be poetry and song. We would carry a heavy cross up Ninth Avenue, stopping at places that would call to mind the varieties of human experience and human need: a homeless shelter, a soup kitchen, the Port Authority, the police station.

Up all night, after a Holy Week already long and hard. What were we thinking? We realized, as the hours passed, that this was exactly right. The weariness of it was the most important part. It was important to know how just how long and hard it was.

A hard taskmaster? An exacting teacher? Certainly Holy Week is challenging, even exhausting: extra worship services, extra study, extra preparation, extra self-examination and self-denial. Does it not sustain? Does it not teach us with a word? Is not that word "love"?

BARBARA CAWTHORNE CRAFTON

Exegetical Perspective

(41:8–10; 43:10; 44:1–2, 21).[1] She further notes a correspondence between the mentions of Zion/Jerusalem and Israel/Jacob. Both are introduced as complaining about their treatment at YHWH's hand; both are described as suffering and being promised redemption and vindication; they also share characteristics of language, themes, and motifs. Further, the Servant figure exhibits parallels with descriptions of the prophet in the book of Jeremiah (cf., for example, Jer.1:4–5 and Isa. 49:5; Jer. 1:9 and Isa. 49:2; Jer. 3:1 and Isa. 50:1; Jer. 31:10 and Isa. 49:1).

These observations point to shared experiences of exile, where the people as well as the prophet(s) suffered and longed for liberation. They suggest that the fluidity in identification and self-identification of the prophet and the Servant, whether one or two figures, is born of the circumstance of life and relationships under duress. The prophet/Servant struggles, yet persists; suffers, yet holds on to hope. By speaking in the first person, the prophet/Servant invites the audience to follow the prophetic model in ultimately trusting in God and eventually experiencing deliverance from their current condition (Isa. 51:6).

Sufficient in and of itself, such a message invokes analogies to situations of exiled communities throughout the ages; the images of persistence during experiences of violation and pain invite identifications on the communal as well as the individual level. With such a long history of Christian interpretation of reading the passion of Jesus of Nazareth into the figure of the Isaianic Servant/prophet, contemporary Christians who choose to be conscious of the tendencies of Christian anti-Judaism (closely followed by Christian anti-Semitism in reading the Second Testament as superior) face the challenge of changing their listening habits during Holy Week to be able hear the readings from Second Isaiah afresh on their own terms.

ANGELA BAUER-LEVESQUE

Homiletical Perspective

church and its leaders change it to soften its impact. The poet is not championing institutional survival or personal success. He may well be the kind of person you would never invite into your fellowship. There is a fine line here between a vision that breaks down and then builds up the community, and the ranting of someone raging with pain and scarred by personal need. In hearing the text and the voices of our time, suspicion walks hand in hand with our desire for truth and light. Both to beware of the text and to brave the text is the challenge of the pulpit.

Linking the Holy Week texts to the first creation story might spawn a sermon series called "Rescue." Monday, the second day of creation, presents the "Nature of Things." Tuesday, the third day, gives us "Formation" (seeds, plants, bounty). Wednesday is about the "Cost." Thursday offers the "Model." Good Friday, the sixth day, shows the "Moment." Saturday, the seventh day, is the "Letting Go." Easter Day, the first day of creation, brings "The News of Light."

The poems of Second Isaiah are not Christian, nor do they refer specifically to Jesus. Their themes are human themes touching faithfulness, vision, the strength of community, and the courage to seek justice, love, and truth. The insights are so deep that we see revealed that vast chasm between what we might be in God, and what we are with each other day by day. To rush to place all the pain, sacrifice, and victory on Jesus blunts the fact that we still live in the midst of such horrors. It is we who are called to brave the poetry and costly transformation named in it. The poet is speaking to us. He calls us to hear him beyond the safe haven of the church.

G. MALCOLM SINCLAIR

---

1. Patricia Tull Wiley, *Remember the Former Things: The Recollection of Previous Texts in Second Isaiah* (Atlanta: Scholars Press, 1997), 175–208.

Psalm 70

¹Be pleased, O God, to deliver me.
  O LORD, make haste to help me!
²Let those be put to shame and confusion
  who seek my life.
 Let those be turned back and brought to dishonor
  who desire to hurt me.
³Let those who say, "Aha, Aha!"
  turn back because of their shame.

⁴Let all who seek you
  rejoice and be glad in you.
 Let those who love your salvation
  say evermore, "God is great!"
⁵But I am poor and needy;
  hasten to me, O God!
 You are my help and my deliverer;
  O LORD, do not delay!

Theological Perspective

Perhaps the most immediately striking thing about the lectionary reading for this Wednesday of Holy Week is the utter urgency with which the psalmist speaks, evidenced in the phrases "make haste to help me" (v. 1), "hasten to me, O God" (v. 5), and "O LORD, do not delay!" (v. 5). In this brief individual lament, the reader is caught up in the psalmist's pleas, which evoke a sense of emergency and lead one to surmise that there is some dire circumstance, problem, or other immediate danger facing the psalmist. One can almost see this individual, perhaps pacing back and forth in prayer, perhaps kneeling with arms outstretched in emotionally charged supplication—perhaps even crying out to God from a place of hiding from those "who seek my life" and "who desire to hurt me" (v. 2). It might be said that any person reading this psalm can identify with the urgent pleas of the psalmist. After all, like the psalmist, we have all "been there"—we have, all of us, cried out to God at some point in our lives (and certainly on more than one occasion!) from the depths of our fears, our failures, and our need for God's saving grace in the midst of turmoil and difficulty.

Although brief, there is much in this psalm in terms of the theological insights and lessons it offers to the Christian community. Taken as a whole, it is a

Pastoral Perspective

The Psalms arrive at church without a narrative context. The canon gives a literary arrangement. An editor supplies superscriptions that point to the wisdom of some early interpreters. The lectionary places the church year beside these texts to enhance the conversation. However, most readers of the Psalms rely on their impressions and experiences. Psalm 70 (like many psalms) is interpreted in various and sometimes exclusive ways.

Our need for God's rescuing presence is not always experienced in the same way. Sometimes we drift into a mild yet real depression. We feel melancholy and gloomy. We sense the dark cloud over our heads. Nevertheless, we still do the laundry, pay the bills, and eat lunch with our friends. We cannot isolate what is causing that pasty taste, and nothing seems to wash it away. In such a state, we wander through life, make ends meet, and survive. At other times, the story is more dreadful, for we fall off the ledge of gloom into the pit of despair. Isolation is our closest companion. We need God's presence but lack the gumption either to acknowledge our need or to seek God. Without intervention, we will not survive.

However, the psalmist describes a different experience of desperation. The attack appears imminent. Suddenly, danger assaults us. These threats deafen

Exegetical Perspective

A sense of urgency pervades Psalm 70. In this short prayer, through uncommonly strong rhythm and repetition, the psalmist pleads that God would act quickly to save the psalmist, as enemies are even now seeking his life (v. 2). The psalmist's desperation manifests itself in a number of ways. First, the psalm is quite short, containing just five verses. Such economy of speech is characteristic of those in extreme need. When trouble is bearing down, there is no time to waste on lofty rhetoric or complex, highly metaphorical language. Second, the psalmist frames the prayer with repeated invocations of the divine name: "O God.... O LORD" (vv. 1, 5). This repetition conveys the psalmist's sense that multiple invocations of the name of God might indeed prompt God to hear and respond. Third, the prayer is framed with pleas that describe the limited time God has to act. The introductory strain, "make haste to help me!" (v. 1), reappears in slightly altered form in the very last line of the psalm, "do not delay!" (v. 5). These first and last words of the psalm underscore the desperate need for God's *immediate* action. Fourth, the psalm exhibits a remarkably consistent grammatical pattern in verses 2–4, where five successive lines begin with jussive verbs, that is, verbs that express the will of the speaker: "Let those..." This repetition

Homiletical Perspective

One of the great advantages of preaching from the Psalter comes from the way the psalms allow us to express negative emotions. Because First-World Christians can tend toward the sentimental in our piety, our lectionary tends not to use "'problematic" readings from the Old and New Testaments. On Sundays and major feast days we do not normally hear about massacres, rapes, and other atrocities. Then, of course, we get to Holy Week and do not know precisely how to handle all the enmity and violence directed toward Jesus. (Mel Gibson's film *The Passion of the Christ* is a good example of what happens when sentimental piety meets the dangerous events of Good Friday.) For some unexplained reason, though, the psalms of lament have been an exception to this policy of excluding the painful aspects of life from public reading.

For the first time this week, the appointed psalm speaks plainly about enemies. Humans are limited and fragile creatures, and the psalms give timeless expression to the anxieties that contingency visits on us: we are mortal and subject to all kinds of loss. The forces of nature that nourish us can also annihilate us. This natural vulnerability, however, so prevalent elsewhere in the Psalter, is absent from Psalm 70. The speaker of this psalm knows what

Psalm 70

Theological Perspective

reminder (as are so many other prayers of lament throughout the Psalter) of God's approachability as our loving and concerned Creator. There is no beating around the bush by the psalmist in this passage; he demands God's attention to his predicament and in no uncertain terms. Based in a covenantal understanding of the relationship between humans and the Divine, the psalmist seems to express a certain trust that God will not only hear his pleas but *will* in fact "deliver" and "help" (v. 1) in his time of urgent need.

However, the psalmist's demands are couched in the language of praise for his God. Unlike a petulant and spoiled child with impatient demands, the psalmist strikes a balance between his demands for help and the recognition of his relationship to his Creator. The fundamental differences between humans and God are clearly spelled out in this psalm. The exclamation "God is great!" (v. 4) is juxtaposed against the psalmist's own humble sense of self as a "poor and needy" individual who is utterly dependent on God's love and protection.

In the contemporary American worldview, which prizes ambition, wealth, and independence, to describe a person as poor, needy, and dependent is to speak rather negatively of that person. However, as the psalmist reminds us, in the biblical worldview, the poor and needy are to be identified with those "who seek [God]" and "who love [God's] salvation" (v. 4), who rightfully recognize their need for God's deliverance and help. Here, it seems, to be poor and needy is to understand our dependence upon God's provision and faithfulness in both good and bad times. It is, perhaps somewhat ironically, his very poverty and neediness, along with his understanding of the covenantal relationship, that allows the psalmist to approach God in such a direct manner.

Read in the liturgical context of Wednesday of Holy Week—just one day before Jesus' Last Supper with his disciples and subsequent arrest, and just two days prior to his crucifixion the next day at the hands of the Romans—the passage takes on some significant theological meanings that are connected to the crucifixion and the events just prior to it. The emotionally charged urgency, noted earlier, out of which the psalmist speaks foreshadows the inner battle that Christ will endure, beginning most poignantly in the Garden of Gethsemane. Matthew's account provides a vivid and moving picture, telling us that Jesus was "grieved and agitated" (Matt. 26:37) to the extent that "he threw himself on the ground and prayed, 'My Father, if it is possible, let this cup pass from me'" (Matt. 26:39). Like the psalmist's prayer, the

Pastoral Perspective

our perception of God's protection. Our "flight or fight" mechanisms kick in. We may immediately stand up to defend our rights, our faith, and our way of living. We may grab our resources from within that will enable us to win. We may look to our hands for weapons. On the other hand, we may shrink behind a rock, hoping to go unnoticed while the storm passes. We may flee, knowing our hands are empty. We may run, convinced that we do not have a prayer to survive.

From an experiential angle, Psalm 70 provides fitting words for pastoral care. When threatened, we do have a prayer. We cry out, "Deliver me. O LORD, make haste to help me!" (v. 1) When psychology says that there are only two choices, flight or fight, God gives us an alternative. Our hands are empty, and we do not have the capacity to fight. We are "poor and needy." We cannot stand by our power, gifts, or ingenuity. Therefore, we need an alternative for our rescue. The third path is not one *we* take, but the one that *God* takes. God arrives in the third path to help and deliver. Therefore, we wait with our prayer, "O LORD, do not delay!" (v. 5).

Spoken in the sanctuary during the liturgy, such words speak to congregations that have experienced threat. On any given Sunday, even the doxology may be played in a minor key. The hazards that put churches into peril include the death, retirement, or misconduct of religious leaders; a downturn in the local economy; changing demographics that force school closures or alter the neighborhood's complexion; denominational battles that trickle down to the local constituency; personal conflicts that spill over into the pews; and a host of other issues that stain the bulletin's prayer list. Consequently, the individual plea of the psalmist becomes a communal petition of the saints.

Additionally, some threats against churches can even be more alarming. The voices of nationalism, consumerism, and exclusivism are echoed in prayers and sermons. A flag takes the place of a cross. The expenses of new technologies replace line items in budgets once reserved for the single mothers and the thirsty refugees. New groups of second-class citizens are marginalized based on economic, educational, or ideological criteria. Betrayals come in various shapes and colors. The systemic betrayals perpetrated by ecclesial bodies affect not only congregants, but also society; not only individuals, but also God. Psalm 70 gives the church a prayer during the darkest hours of threat and despair. The church needs a prayer that beseeches God to come immediately and liberate us all.

Exegetical Perspective

embodies grammatically the psalmist's relentless insistence that YHWH would answer the pleas. Again and again and (yet) again, the psalmist implores God to help.

These central verses of this psalm (vv. 2–4) briefly describe two communities and reveal sharp contrasts between them. The first community (vv. 2–3) is one which is set against the psalmist. The psalmist does not indicate why they are so inclined, for again the urgency of the situation does not allow time for much explanation. Instead, the psalmist indicates that this community simply seeks his life and desires to do him harm (v. 2).

This community's voice is characterized by taunts and shaming. The English exclamation "Aha!" (v. 3) usually conveys a sense of surprise at discovery, a connotation that is not quite accurate in this passage. Rendering the Hebrew this way attempts to convey the actual sound of the taunt that is put on the lips of the enemies: *he'akh, he'akh*. However, this sequence of repeated gutturals most often represents an expression of delight in Hebrew, particularly a mocking laugh (e.g., Pss. 35:21, 25; 40:15). Thus, a better translation would simply be "Ha! Ha!" As the plight of the psalmist brings deranged delight to the enemies, the psalmist prays that this laughter will end soon enough. In verses 2–3, the psalmist pleads repeatedly for God to reverse the fortunes of those who ridicule him. Indeed, God's salvation would radically change the status of this community of enemies. The mockers will become the mocked, once they see how powerfully and quickly God can act.

While one community *seeks the life* of the psalmist (vv. 2–3), another contrasting community *seeks God* (v. 4). This community delights in God's nature and activity, not in the psalmist's suffering. The two communities also speak in radically different ways. The enemies look at the psalmist and say "Ha! Ha!" (v. 3). Yet the faithful ones continually say "God is great!" (v. 4). Indeed, for this community, God's saving acts display God's greatness.

In verse 5, the psalmist moves suddenly from a discussion of the two communities to a focus on the individual. This thematic and topical break mirrors a structural break in the psalm. The rhythm that is generated by the grammatical patterning ("Let those. . .") halts as verse 5 begins, "But I am poor and needy." The sudden break in the pattern serves the rhetorical function of highlighting the plight of the psalmist. Having uttered both curses and blessings on the two communities, the psalmist turns to his own lowly status, which appears in particularly vivid relief in that it

Homiletical Perspective

the problem is. As Jean-Paul Sartre said, "Hell is other people."[1]

The first stanza begins with a plea for deliverance from human enemies: "Let those be put to shame and confusion who seek my life. Let those be turned back and brought to dishonor who desire to hurt me" (v. 2). The speaker experiences the human community as a place fraught with danger, and his adversaries add insult to injury by saying, "Aha, Aha!" (v. 3). There is no explanation asked or offered for the motivation of those who torment the speaker. What we have here is an expression of what Samuel Taylor Coleridge called Iago's "motiveless malignity" toward Othello.[2]

The idea of such motiveless malignity provides a way into talking about a couple of large issues that will grow in importance as Holy Week progresses. One is human sin. Another is the particular way in which sin focuses its aggression on innocence. Many of the sermons I have heard and preached try to explain the motives of those who bring Jesus to the cross. He is an affront to religious and political systems and authority. He is either too radical or not radical enough—and so on. As interesting as all those explanations are, they do not finally help us cope with the reality of suffering, and that is as true for Jesus as it is for me. When I am up against it, I want not so much to be explained to as to be heard. The speaker cries out for deliverance from human aggression, not for a policy statement.

Psalm 70 helps anchor the preacher for today in a concrete experience of human sin as seen from the victim's point of view. To the extent that we talk about sin at all in our liturgies, we usually do so in the confession, and so from the viewpoint of what cop shows would call "the perpetrator." Psalm 70 helps us experience sin the other way around, from the perspective of one who knows what it costs. As any person in leadership knows, there are always some people who just cannot stand you. As any person who follows current events knows, we live in a world where human beings are capable, in groups, of doing horrible things to one another—for example, the American treatment of Native Americans and African Americans, the Holocaust, Bosnia, Rwanda, Darfur, the Congo.

Thinking back to Othello, it is also often the case that motiveless malignity directs itself at the

1. Jean-Paul Sartre, *No Exit and Three Other Plays* (New York: Vintage Books, 1989), 45.
2. Samuel Taylor Coleridge, *Lectures 1808–1819 on Literature*, ed. R. A. Foakes (Princeton, NJ: Princeton University Press, 1987), 2:315.

Psalm 70

Theological Perspective

prayers of Jesus in Gethsemane arise out of an urgent need—if not for deliverance, then certainly for the strength to endure the trials ahead.

The theological connection between Psalm 70 and the passion narrative is further made evident in noting the psalmist's request of God to "Let those who say, 'Aha, Aha!' turn back because of their shame" (v. 3). This verse brings to mind the people mocking Jesus as they pass beneath his cross, as described in Mark 15:29–30: "Those who passed by derided him, shaking their heads and saying, 'Aha! You who would destroy the temple and build it in three days, save yourself, and come down from the cross!'"[1] The jeering and mockery by others of our pain and suffering brings our need for God's deliverance and saving grace into even clearer focus.

Finally, a return to the connection in Psalm 70 between praise and lament, noted briefly above, is essential to a theological understanding of and approach to this particular lectionary reading. As Jerome Creach so nicely puts it: "For Christians, the association of Jesus' suffering [with Psalm 70] is instructive. Read in its context in the Psalter and as the prayer of Jesus, Psalm 70 reminds us that praise, when properly framed, emerges from the depths of life."[2] It is from the depths of our fear, anxiety, and even outright danger that humans are most able to recognize that they are "poor and needy" and are therefore in need of God's faithful love and deliverance. It is from such depths of suffering that we are able to shout with genuine praise along with the psalmist, "God is great!"

NICOLE L. JOHNSON

Pastoral Perspective

The liturgy on Holy Wednesday narrates the betrayal of Jesus by Judas. No other betrayal in history receives the same press. From Marcus Brutus to Benedict Arnold, betrayers have received universal condemnation. Dante's *Inferno* reserves the ninth and lowest circle of hell for traitors. Adultery, embezzlement, fraud, and other acts of disloyalty remain despicable and loathsome in all societies and cultures. No one chooses as a confidant someone he or she does not trust.

When Judas's story is read in church, we are reminded that it was one who sat at the table who committed such a dubious act. If he could do it after living with Jesus for three years, then who is immune? We too ask with the Twelve: "Is it I?" Judas's kiss rocks our core because we know our own past actions and words of duplicity. We are haunted by times when we played the traitor's role at the expense of our faith. No wonder it is on Wednesday that the church extinguishes the lights; one by one, the church snuffs the flickering candles. We all reflect together that we are the ones who say, "Aha, Aha!"[1] The words of verse 2, "May those who seek my life be put to shame and confusion; may all who desire my ruin be turned back in disgrace" (NIV), are being said about us. As Friday approaches, we must also reflect on our participation in the divine story.

Although not spoken by Jesus in the Upper Room or the garden below, Psalm 70 vividly echoes in the scene. Jesus tells Judas, "Go and do it quickly." Jesus prays to God, "May this cup pass." Prayerless, Peter stands to fight. Prayerless, the others run and hide. Judas has left the table to gather soldiers. The dark night of betrayal is not a path Jesus easily embraces. The kiss of betrayal pierces Jesus' side as surely as the spear. Jesus endures the hostility (Heb. 12:3) because he knew about a third path. Jesus knew "God is great!" (v. 4). Jesus embodies the role of a faithful sufferer who entrusts himself fully to God, who is able to deliver. Jesus could have easily penned the psalm.

TIMOTHY R. SENSING

---

1. Jerome F. D. Creach, "Psalm 70," *Interpretation* 60, no. 1 (Jan. 2006): 66. http://find.galegroup.com/itx/start.do?prodId=AONE.
2. Ibid.

1. Although the lectionary does not indicate a connection to Jesus' death on the cross, various commentaries connect the "Aha" of v. 3 to Mark 15:29 and the jeers of those who mocked him.

comes on the heels of the proclamation of God's greatness (v. 4b). By highlighting the profound difference between God's greatness and the psalmist's lowliness, the petitioner seeks to induce a sense of tension in the very heart of God. If God really is great—as the community proclaims again and again (v. 4)—then the lowliness of this faithful one becomes utterly incomprehensible. The psalmist is appealing to the community's testimony about God's nature in order to motivate God to act in accordance with it. That is, salvation for the psalmist is completely in order, given who God is and how God's salvation so delights the community of faithful (v. 4).

The psalm ends with a reiteration of the prayer that God would act quickly. The psalm opened with imperative verbs: "Be pleased. . . to deliver. . . . Make haste to help" (v. 1). The imperative mood returns in v. 5: "Hasten to me. . . . Do not delay!" However, the opening pleas and the concluding ones are not quite identical. Indeed, in the final verse of the psalm, the psalmist makes unique claims on YHWH's identity, calling God "my help and my deliverer" (v. 5). These bold proclamations signal an intensification of the psalmist's rhetoric from the beginning of the psalm to the end. We might understand this movement as an increase in faith that comes about through the act of praying itself. Somehow encouraged by his own prayer, the psalmist concludes by making overt claims about God's nature as one who embodies deliverance in a real, present, and personal way.

On the Wednesday of Holy Week, the psalmist's remarkable characterization of God as deliverance embodied (i.e., incarnate) moves us irresistibly to a consideration of the Gospel account of God's ultimate saving act. The particular urgency of this psalm resonates deeply with the Gospel reading, John 13:21–32, where Jesus is "troubled in spirit" at the thought of his friend's handing him over to those who seek his life (cf. Ps 70:2). In the pain, desperation, and shame of the psalmist's voice, we can hear Jesus praying these very words during his passion. Simultaneously, through the mystery of the Trinity, we can see Jesus—God's salvation—as the very answer to the psalmist's prayers.

JOEL MARCUS LEMON

innocent. Think of the assassination of Martin Luther King Jr. and others in the twentieth century. Assassins rarely target despots; they tend to go after liberators. The speaker of Psalm 70 self-identifies as one of the innocent. There may be some unintentional hypocrisy here—"Who, me?"—but it is probably safer to read this psalm in a plain and not ironic sense. People are out to get the speaker, who has done nothing wrong. This is an opportunity to speak both within the Jesus story and within the stories of one's audience. If only unconsciously, we all know ourselves to be both aggressor and victim. The events of Holy Week are a good time to let that knowledge up into the realm of our wide-awake minds and compare our passions with the passion of Jesus.

Though it begins in pain and confusion, Psalm 70 ends on a hopeful note, as does the week we are living through. The speaker tells God, "You are my help and my deliverer" (v. 5) and announces that those who seek God will "rejoice and be glad" in God (v. 4). Because of the hoped-for deliverance, those who love God's salvation will say evermore, "God is great!"

Remembering that Holy Week explores the mysteries of human sin and suffering, it is vital that we remember the overarching theme of this week: "God is great!" Preaching on this last day before the Triduum, the homilist has one final opportunity to remind the assembly that there is a divine if hidden logic to what is going on here. We do not celebrate Holy Week in order to wallow in our prurience for cruelty. We do not observe it as a way of setting ourselves up as either more or less guilty than anyone else. We observe Holy Week as our central Christian act of asserting that something in the equation between God and us requires Jesus to stand in the hard places he is called to be in this week, and he does so finally to help us proclaim, with the speaker of Psalm 70, "God is great!" That message is the most important thing one can say on Wednesday of Holy Week.

GARY R. HALL

Hebrews 12:1-3

¹Therefore, since we are surrounded by so great a cloud of witnesses, let us also lay aside every weight and the sin that clings so closely, and let us run with perseverance the race that is set before us, ²looking to Jesus the pioneer and perfecter of our faith, who for the sake of the joy that was set before him endured the cross, disregarding its shame, and has taken his seat at the right hand of the throne of God.

³Consider him who endured such hostility against himself from sinners, so that you may not grow weary or lose heart.

Theological Perspective

In various ways multiple metaphors invigorate the theological expressions about suffering in this brief passage. Some of the images retain their vibrancy for us even today: the cluster of witnesses is described as a cloud, the challenge of pursuing a disciplined life in faith is likened to running a race, and Jesus is referred to as a perfecting pioneer. Other figures of speech included in these verses have become more common expressions, yet still possess a disclosive power: for example, the obstacles of faith are compared to weights, and the challenge of enduring faith is not "to lose heart." Unpacking these images discloses the theological depth of the passage.

The linguistic focus of these various metaphors is a footrace, an athletic image introduced into the emerging churches' literature by Paul in his First Letter to the Corinthians (9:24–27). Here in Hebrews, as with Paul, the primary meaning of the contest image is the same: In the words of Eric Liddell, 1928 Olympic champion and missionary to China, the idea is "to see the race through to its end."[1] Beyond this common adjuration, a few nuanced differences emerge in the context of Hebrews, each of which suggests theological distinctions between Hebrews and the Pauline writings.

1. From *Chariots of Fire* (1981), screenplay by Colin Welland.

Pastoral Perspective

Some of the familiar phrases from the preacher in the book of Hebrews begin with "therefore": "Let us therefore approach the throne of grace with boldness" (4:16); "Therefore lift your drooping hands and strengthen your weak knees" (12:12). The preacher's "therefores" in the book of Hebrews send a signal to the listener's ear. Perhaps no example is stronger, no "therefore" more familiar, than this one for the Wednesday of Holy Week from the very beginning of the twelfth chapter. Regardless of how the word may function grammatically as the Hebrews preacher connects thoughts and communicates an argument, this profound "therefore" invites readers/listeners to take a deep breath and get ready for the word that is about to come. It is as if on the Wednesday of Holy Week, the gathered community of expectant and experienced listeners of the Word would be anticipating the long pause offered as the Scripture lesson is being read in their hearing: "Therefore . . ."

Most often the word serves as a bridge between two streams of thought. In the case of Hebrews 12, the connection to the litany of names that is chapter 11 is quite clear. In fact, outlines of the book of Hebrews often make a break after 12:2. In Hebrews 12:1–2, the reference to the "great cloud of witnesses" establishes the link to those who have gone before in faith and those who have gone before in the text; but in Holy

Exegetical Perspective

This stirring exhortation to look to Christ as the ultimate model of the life of faith that his followers are called to lead concludes a long list of examples of fidelity to God that occupies chapter 11. That chapter illustrates what "faith" means by evoking stories of the faithful from the Hebrew Scriptures. Some embodied faith as a belief (Enoch), some as a hope (Abraham, prophets, and martyrs), some as an act of obedience in the face of opposition (Moses). Faithfulness to God, in other words, has had a long history and a complex character, but that whole story is epitomized and concentrated in the story of Christ. The whole of the Epistle to the Hebrews attempts in many ways to make the point that is so dramatically scored here.

The passage opens with a memorable image, often cited in sermons, of the "great cloud of witnesses" (v. 1). Part of what the author evokes becomes clear later in the verse, where the image of a stadium and athletic contestants appears. The "witnesses" then are the fans in the bleachers, cheering their favorite athletes on, but they are no ordinary athletic fans. The fact that they are a "cloud" of witnesses suggests that they are the members of that lineage of faithful folk sketched in chapter 11: the patriarchs, prophets, and martyrs of the people of God from long ago. Describing them as a "cloud" evokes the heavenly

Homiletical Perspective

The scene is that of a stadium where a relay race is underway. Runners fill the lanes on the track, each in uniform carrying a baton. In the stands sits a throng. Looking closer, one can see that everyone in the stands is in uniform too, but each wears the uniform of another day and time. Some are decades old, some centuries, some even millennia. They are those who have gone before, the "cloud of witnesses." Hebrews 11 lists many of those who are now done with their part of the race, but are still waiting in anticipation for its completion: Abel, Abraham, Sarah, Isaac, Jacob, Moses, Gideon, Barak, Samson, Jephthah, David, Samuel, and the prophets—"of whom the world was not worthy."

Why are they here, and why are they so interested? Because the race is not over. Even more urgently, because the ultimate outcome for them rests on the subsequent runners. The Hebrews writer makes an uncomfortable claim: "Yet all these . . . did not receive what was promised, since God had provided something better so that they would not, apart from us, be made perfect" (11:39–40). The Hebrews writer believes that the motivation for current runners to run with diligence and perseverance and personal self-sacrifice is partly due to a recognition of those who have preceded us, those who have faithfully run their leg and passed the baton on to those who

Hebrews 12:1-3

Theological Perspective

In Paul's usage, the length of the race is not specified, although his expectation of an imminent return of Christ suggests that his idea of a race might not be long. Still, whether short dashes or distance runs, all races feature a *telos*, a goal or finish line. Simply, Paul focuses on the significance of the finish line, emphasizing the fruits of victory that come to the winner at the end of the race (cf. Phil. 3:12–16). Unlike Paul, however, the author of Hebrews implies that the race is an endurance run, like the long journey of faith, a pilgrimage. Consequently, Hebrews highlights the importance of the manner in which the race is run. Rather than featuring the crown of glory that the victor wears following the completion of the race, the author of Hebrews stresses the need for believers to exercise discipline, dedication, and durability so that they might persevere through the suffering generated by the race's running.

A second variance between Paul and Hebrews is that, for Paul, the purpose for running the race is to secure the single prize of victory. By contrast, Hebrews attests that Christ as "the pioneer"—or front-runner—"and perfecter of our faith" has already secured the victory for those who run with him, since already he "has taken his seat at the right hand of the throne of God" (v. 2). This exaltation comes from victory achieved through sacrificial suffering, for the author earlier had identified the "pioneer of salvation" with perfection "through suffering" (2:10), which was consummated in the crucifixion. Christ's suffering can be embraced, not because of the torture that was inflicted by humans, but because of his complete exercise of discipline in humbling himself and becoming "obedient to the point of death—even death on a cross" (Phil. 2:8).[2]

In Paul's epistle, the image of the race is also coupled with a boxing trope: Even as Paul asserts that he does not "run aimlessly," he declares that he does not "box as though beating the air" (1 Cor. 9:26). Although there are no explicit references to fisticuffs here in Hebrews, the identification of "the drooping hands" and "weak knees" (v. 12)—which are evidence of a boxer's fatigue—indicates that the readers of Hebrews are being enjoined to exercise strength in addition to perseverance.

The other images in the cluster of metaphors support the author's urging to persevere through suffering. Overseeing the earthbound footrace, the "cloud of witnesses" adds a transcendent element to the

Pastoral Perspective

Week, there is a broader connection to be made as the listener prepares to experience the Scripture.

The community gathers on Wednesday with the full anticipation of the journey that will play out in the days to come. Maundy Thursday will bring a Communion service, maybe a service of Tenebrae, even a foot washing. Good Friday will come with the clear focus on the passion narratives of the Gospels read and proclaimed. Yes, Easter Sunday's coming, but foremost in the listener's imagination are the trial and the suffering and the death of Jesus.

There may be a few in worship who have to leave town on business; others are preparing to turn a few days off from school into spring break instead of the end of Holy Week and the celebration of the Day of Resurrection. For the most part, however, everyone hearing a reading from the beginning of Hebrews 12 will be leaning forward and looking to Jesus, rather than looking back at the great cloud of witnesses. So, at least for this experience of a familiar "therefore," emphasis falls on Jesus the pioneer and perfecter of our faith, rather than on our race to run and our perseverance and the sin that clings so closely to us. After all, the days to come in the congregation's worship life ought to be more about him than they are about us.

With the cues coming from the days of the liturgical calendar that lie ahead, the focus falls upon Jesus and the joy of his obedience, the suffering he endured upon the cross, and the shame he set aside in willfully going to the cross. Obedience, suffering, endurance, and shame are so common to the human experience. The shame of the cross came in the taunts from those on the ground and from the public display of physical suffering and death raised up for all to see. Brutal punishment and death on the cross may be uncommon, but shame is a feeling so many can understand. Whether we are taunted by others, or our failures are put on display for all, or the feeble parts of our humanity are magnified for the world to see—shame is part of the human condition. There is an irony of comfort when the incarnation becomes real to us this Holy Week. Even as we look to the unique suffering that came in the form of Jesus' death, we also know that it is exactly that death that unites him to us. We will all die, just as we all know shame, we all live the human condition. When we allow the focus for a time to fall on Jesus and not on us, even then we see something of our humanity staring right back at us. We see Immanuel, God with us.

The text references both what Jesus endured on the cross and what he endured in the form of hostility

---

2. See Dorothee Soelle, "Suffering," in Donald W. Musser and Joseph L. Price, eds., *New and Enlarged Handbook of Christian Theology* (Nashville: Abingdon Press, 2003), 488.

status of the benches on which they view the athletic contest of believers.

More athletic imagery follows in verse 1. The addressees of this homily are told to cast off whatever hinders them so that they may run their race. The verse evokes very contemporary images of joggers carrying weights as they run, and exercising habits may have changed little in 2,000 years. The homilist interprets the running weights, or the cloak that one may wear to the track, as "sin" that "entangles" (NIV; NRSV "clings so closely") and trips up the runner. Sin must be put aside to run the race of life well. Theologians who emphasize the importance of God's gracious act of forgiveness in the remission of sin may wince at this formulation, but our homilist is convinced that the faithful have a role to play in the elimination of sin in their lives.

The suggestion that the race must be run "with perseverance" implies that at the metaphorical level the author envisions not a sprint but a marathon or contest of some distance. Applied to the situation of the addressees, the image suggests that the author wants them to think about their whole lives as a race that they must run. The image is reminiscent of the way in which "Paul" in 2 Timothy 4:7 describes his life, as a long-distance race the end of which approaches. The author of Hebrews appeals not only to this athletic metaphor, but also to the image of a boxing match (v. 4), to symbolize the short-term difficulties that his community has faced.

In the second verse of the passage, the author calls attention to the front-runner in this race of faith, Jesus, the "author and perfecter" (NIV; NRSV "pioneer and perfecter") of faith. The pair of epithets applied to Jesus involves a clever play on words and a large play on themes deployed in Hebrews. The Greek term translated as "author" (archēgos) appeared once before, in Hebrews 2:10, where, using a play on etymology, it depicted Christ as the one who "leads the way," to a heavenly destiny. If leading the way played on the arch- element of archēgos, the term "perfecter" evokes the theme of perfection that runs through the letter (2:10; 5:9; 10:1, 14). The point is that Christ, as the one who bore witness to God, provides the perfect example for those who would follow in his footsteps and thereby be "perfected" or qualified, like priests, to enter into the presence of God.

The image of Christ in view of the "joy that was set before him" choosing the cross seems a bit odd to some modern ears, influenced perhaps by an ethic inspired by Kant, in which one chooses what is right because it is one's duty. However, in the view of our

follow. There is, therefore, an ethical edge in the text. There is a mission, a responsibility, a motive that is based in community and continuity with those who have gone before.

No relay race is complete until the anchor leg completes the home stretch. If anyone drops the baton, runs out of the lane, or otherwise is disqualified, no one finishes. It does not seem fair, but the writer wants to drive home the organic interrelatedness of believers past, present, and future.

The text reminds us that we are called by God into a life of faith that, due to its strenuousness, resembles a relay race. We are part of a community that stretches back through time, and we are in some ways responsible, in the way we run that race in the present, for those who have gone before, just as they were when they were on the track. By extension, we will be dependent on those who come after us.

I may want to reduce the significance of faith and faith's traditioning process down to what it is that God effects and sustains, or to what I do apart from anyone else, but that is unwittingly to simplify a much more complex phenomenon, namely, the mystery of God's cooperative work in and through us, all of us in communion with one another, even through time. We are intimately connected not just with God and those in our lifetimes. We are connected with all who have been called and have been prompted to lives of faith and hope—those children of the promise, both past and future.

Preaching the gospel means naming God's work, as the text declares it and as the text helps us see God's ongoing work in our world. It is also an invitation for those who hear our preaching to embrace God's work and to become active agents of God's present work. This text names God's work and invites us to a concrete mission. This is the twelfth of thirteen chapters, of course, and much groundwork has been laid to this point to name God's work, thus establishing the foundation for the call to mission. In fact, that groundwork is partly rehearsed in the image of the focal point for the runners. Whereas a "perishable wreath" or "temporal crown of glory" may be the focus for many literal runners, or a tape stretched across the track for many familiar with contemporary track competitions, the Hebrews writer focuses the eyes of the readers on Jesus: "looking to Jesus the pioneer and perfecter of our faith." That focal point is to help those in the race look away from their present "agony" (agōn = race) and to the one who epitomizes endurance through agony. Not even the suffering of the cross could take Jesus' own

Hebrews 12:1-3

Theological Perspective

scenario, suggesting an angelic host of unseen encouragers. In the context of the entire epistle, however, the metaphor of the "cloud of witnesses" also connotes a gathering of saints who have preceded the faithful, including those who suffered "mocking and flogging, and even chains and imprisonment" for their fidelity to the first covenant (11:36). In this regard, the author also affirms the continuity between the covenant with Abraham and the new covenant in Christ (cf. 9:11–15).

While instructing the faithful to endure the drudgeries and difficulties afforded by the race's demands, the author also calls upon them to set aside impediments that might detract from their discipline. The "weight and sin" that threaten to beset believers who run the long race are not the deliberate acts that would disqualify competitors (cf. 10:26), but nagging anxieties and slothful sins, such as indifference, indolence, and intolerance. Whether runners are challenged by these burdens and distractions or by the painful experience of discipline, the author admonishes them to "not grow weary or lose heart" by staying focused on "him who endured such hostility against himself from sinners" (v. 3).

Although the passage mixes metaphors, their theological implications are unified in the author's consistent call for the faithful to subject themselves to divine discipline, to maintain strength, and to work through the pains of suffering, growing through it to enjoy "the peaceful fruit of righteousness" that comes "to those who have been trained by it" (v. 11). In effect, the faithful are called to transform their suffering into a sacramental act. The commendation of suffering in Hebrews is not the suffering of pestilence or warfare, of natural disaster or disease, of abject poverty or personal abuse. Instead, it is the suffering afforded by what Dietrich Bonhoeffer called "costly grace," which is "*costly* because it calls us to follow, and . . . grace because it calls us to follow Jesus Christ. It is costly because it costs a man his life, and it is grace because it gives a man the only true life." "Above all," Bonhoeffer adds, "it is *costly* because it cost God the life of his Son," who bought each of us "with a price" (cf. 1 Cor. 7:23).[3]

JOSEPH L. PRICE

Pastoral Perspective

from sinners, from the world. His endurance is on display for all to see. He endured death on the cross. From sinners, one could assume, he endured everything else the world had to offer: yes, the physical suffering at the hands of those tortured him, but also the suffering of the heart at the hands of those who betrayed and deserted him. Jesus endured everything that life and death had to throw at him. Fully human, Jesus endured all that this human condition could muster. Fully God, Jesus understands all that any human being would endure.

"Therefore . . ." After a period of silence, the congregation ponders the obedience, the suffering, the shame, and the endurance of Jesus. Any who are wearied by life are invited to find strength in his journey in the days to come. Any who are discouraged at the world's plight are invited to take heart and be comforted. Jesus has now "taken his seat at the right hand of the throne of God." His journey is finished. His sacrifice is complete. His work is done. His victory is won. As the reader learns in Hebrews 10, Jesus sits down because his work is finished and he "has perfected for all time those who are sanctified" (10:12–14).

It may be only Wednesday, but we have been here before. Yes, we know how the drama of the next few days ends, and we know where our life begins. Indeed, we are surrounded by so great a cloud of witnesses. Along with Jesus, the church is headed once again to Gethsemane and Golgotha and the empty tomb. Therefore, we are "looking to Jesus the pioneer and perfecter of our faith" (v. 2).

DAVID A. DAVIS

---

3. Dietrich Bonhoeffer, *The Cost of Discipleship,* trans. R. H. Fuller (New York: Macmillan, 1959), 37.

Exegetical Perspective

author, the example of Christ models Christian hope in a God who rewards and punishes according to what people have done (2:2–3; 6:6; 11:6; 12:29). Our author is not reticent to attribute to Christ a motivation for his behavior that takes consequences into account.

The assertion that Christ accepted suffering on the cross "scorning its shame" (NIV; NRSV "disregarding its shame") also models that kind of behavior that Christians are to embrace, accepting social marginalization, life "outside the city gate" (13:12–13) as a result of following Christ.

That Christ took his seat at the right hand of God (v. 2), an allusion to Psalm 110:1, recalls one of the recurrent motifs of the homily, that Christ has been exalted to the presence of God (1:13; 2:7–9; 8:1; 10:12), which the homilist proposes as a ground for the continued fidelity of the addressees. The final verse of this reading (v. 3) makes the appeal to the addressees explicit. In considering Christ who endured "hostility . . . from sinners," the addressees are invited to see themselves and to take heart. What they are experiencing in the persecutions that they have faced (10:32–34), Christ endured before them. That they might "grow weary or lose heart" seems to be the major concern of the homilist. He is concerned that some of the addressees of Hebrews may be disheartened because of external pressure or because of disappointment that eschatological promises have not yet been realized and are "neglecting to meet together" (10:25). The author of Hebrews wants to keep such people committed to God and reminds them that following in the footsteps of Jesus in the "race" of life is the means to do so. He will issue a similar admonition to them in the concluding chapter of the letter (13:12–13).

HAROLD W. ATTRIDGE

Homiletical Perspective

eyes off "the joy that was set before him." Thus he was able to endure. In the same way, we can endure by having both a primary focal point, Jesus, who pioneered and perfected our faith, and a secondary reference point, the cloud of witnesses for whom we are responsible and to whom we are accountable.

How does the text help us to see God's similar work and call to mission in our world? Jesus remains the one who pioneered and perfected the faith for all God has called. What is less clear is how faith for Christians in the Western world, especially in North America, is an agonizing endurance race. Our imagination can envision those first-century Christians wavering in their faith as the temple fell and Rome attempted a Jewish-Christian genocide. Endurance in the face of agony was a timely call to them, as was a dual reminder: Jesus' endurance of the cross and the placarding of those from the past who had endured "being sawed in two," among other unimaginable tortures. Our "torture" consists of deciding which kind of Christian worship to attend this week—traditional, contemporary, emergent, high liturgical, low liturgical, aliturgical, messianic—or should we just sleep in? Elie Weisel once famously asked, "Why does God weep?" only to answer acerbically, "Because He [sic] must listen to sermons."

The preacher's challenge in using this text for preaching today is to identify in the preacher's world just where the race, the agony to be endured, is for faith. The text helps orient us to the potential resources for endurance, the bifocal motivations of community and Jesus, but the preacher must name faith's endurance test for his or her hearers.

ANDRÉ RESNER

John 13:21-32

21After saying this Jesus was troubled in spirit, and declared, "Very truly, I tell you, one of you will betray me." 22The disciples looked at one another, uncertain of whom he was speaking. 23One of his disciples—the one whom Jesus loved—was reclining next to him; 24Simon Peter therefore motioned to him to ask Jesus of whom he was speaking. 25So while reclining next to Jesus, he asked him, "Lord, who is it?" 26Jesus answered, "It is the one to whom I give this piece of bread when I have dipped it in the dish." So when he had dipped the piece of bread, he gave it to Judas son of Simon Iscariot. 27After he received the piece of bread, Satan entered into him. Jesus said to him, "Do quickly what you are going to do." 28Now no one at the table knew why he said this to him. 29Some thought that, because Judas had the common purse, Jesus was telling him, "Buy what we need for the festival"; or, that he should give something to the poor. 30So, after receiving the piece of bread, he immediately went out. And it was night.

31When he had gone out, Jesus said, "Now the Son of Man has been glorified, and God has been glorified in him. 32If God has been glorified in him, God will also glorify him in himself and will glorify him at once."

Theological Perspective

In John's portrayal of the Last Supper, Jesus both washed the feet of the disciples and announced to them that he would be betrayed. In spite of the facts that the events leading toward the glorification of Jesus had begun, that the disciples had been commissioned to carry out the word, and that the powers of darkness had begun to be defeated, all was not well. Among the disciples, the nascent church's leadership were not altogether clear about where this was all leading. Ambiguity existed within and among them about what Jesus was doing. Peter objected to Jesus' self-humbling action. Did the foot washing represent a Levitical practice of ritual purification at the time of Passover, a kind of commissioning for a new mission, an exemplary act of service of master to followers, or a "sacramental" act? The question is still debated.

What is clear is that the disciples were not unified, faultless, or certain about what all Jesus' words or acts meant after being exposed to them. Doubts still were present in the most loyal disciples. Still, Jesus assured them that those who receive a witness to him through such followers, receive what they have to offer from the Lord (13:20). This assurance has been a comfort to missionaries, evangelists, clergy, and witnessing laity over the centuries.

There was also a deeper fissure among the movement's leadership that Jesus had chosen, although the

Pastoral Perspective

The stakes get higher and higher as we make our way with Jesus through Holy Week. The final stories of Jesus' last days before his crucifixion and death are intense. The passage for this Wednesday of Holy Week is a story of personal betrayal. The modern listener is quite likely to have experienced betrayal in one form or another. Whether one has been betrayed, or has in fact betrayed another, can influence how one responds to this text.

Jesus and his disciples are reclining around the table when Jesus becomes troubled in spirit. His thoughts move from the importance of humble acts of love, embodied in the washing of feet, to the sting of betrayal. "Very truly, I tell you, one of you will betray me"(v. 21). The disciples are stunned. One of us will betray Jesus? Surely not one of us! We are his disciples, the ones whom he has called, the ones who have said yes, the ones who have been with him day in and day out. If someone is going to betray Jesus, it is going to be one of them, not one of us. They look around the table, seeking a sign. Is someone smirking? Does someone have a guilty look upon his (or her) face? Who is averting her (or his) eyes?

The suspense is killing them. Jesus has not shared the identity of the betrayer. Finally, the "disciple whom Jesus loved" pries it out of him. Jesus tells them that the betrayer is the one who will eat the

Exegetical Perspective

John 13 presents the cosmic conflict between darkness and light in a narration of the Last Supper. Satan enters into Judas (v. 27). The story of Judas's betrayal is reshaped by the author of the Fourth Gospel to highlight the role of Satan and Jesus' ultimate control over the action. In the course of what seems to be an ordinary human meal, the decisive act in the cosmic conflict between God and evil is set in motion. The story ends in verse 30, "So, after receiving the piece of bread, he immediately went out. And it was night." Judas goes out into the night, aligned with the forces of darkness. This is not a reference to the time of day but an intimation of what is coming. Evil, in this case betrayal, takes place under cover of darkness, not in the light. The unit concludes with a Johannine saying about the glorification of the Son of Man.

For those who attend both Monday and Tuesday services, there may be a sense of déjà vu at the beginning of this passage, which seems to echo Monday's Gospel. This is a different day and a different place. The markers of changed time and space appear in the beginning of chapter 13, in the text reserved for Maundy Thursday later in the week. The ironic "Now my soul is troubled" of 12:27 bears only superficial likeness to the genuine distress Jesus expresses when declaring that one of the disciples will betray him. All of Jesus' words of suffering stand under the shadow

Homiletical Perspective

On Wednesday of Holy Week, the lights begin to dim and the shadow of death looms large. The festive cries of "Hosanna" are now a distant memory, and the furious cries of "Crucify him" will soon ring in the ear. We have yet to see the disciples at their worst, but we can smell the acrid aroma of betrayal, denial, and death in the air. The sanctuary has not yet been covered in black, but the dark day the church calls "good" is just two days away.

Preaching on Holy Wednesday will mean not only engaging the text, but engaging the desperate mood that many of the faithful experience before and after Holy Week. On this day, preachers have a prime opportunity to tie the emotional mood of the biblical text with the emotional mood of the people of God some centuries later. Whether it is war or the economy or disease or despair, on Holy Wednesday preachers will encounter many hearers who experientially understand this day long before the first biblical text is read.

Fortunately, the lectionary offers the preacher a portion of John 13 as the text for this emotionally complex day. In this text, we find a less-than-fully-clad Jesus hanging up the towel that he has just used to wash his disciples' feet. He is deeply troubled and shares the reason why amid this intimate company of friends. He may be deeply troubled by his sense that

John 13:21-32

Theological Perspective

references to parts of it seem to be stated very subtly. On one side was Judas, the symbol of all that would betray Christ and the movement. He accepted the material nourishment Jesus had offered him. Further, he may have lifted his foot to be washed, signaling a readiness to receive this blessing. Jesus' comment that he "lifted his heel" (v. 18) may imply that he had already turned his back on Jesus and was walking away. The two meanings of verse 18 may both be so, suggesting that he received but rejected the meaning of the gift, for he already had plans to leave the movement and to plot Jesus' death. He had also been suspiciously said to advocate giving money to the poor, while he really wanted it for himself or for some movement other than Jesus' that he was dedicated to (12:6). In this connection, he is said to be the son of Simon Iscariot for no apparent reason—unless 13:26 suggests that he was partial to the group of nationalist rebels, the "sicarii," who advocated violence as a way of "saving" Israel from Roman rule.

On the other side was the one "whom Jesus loved," who remains unnamed in the text. By tradition, of course, he is understood to be the one to whom Jesus gave the care of his mother at the foot of the cross, the one who founded the tradition that authored this Gospel and the other Johannine books, and the son of Zebedee. He is portrayed as the exemplary disciple, the model Christian, who often clarified Jesus' identity and intent to Peter and James, but who had the modesty not to name himself before the public. Peter tried to get him to find out from Jesus who the betrayer was, but he got no direct response. Still the inquiry was a signal that there was distrust in the group, and perhaps a self-doubt among the disciples. No wonder Jesus "was troubled in spirit" (v. 21).

In any case, our text says that when Judas received the morsel given by Jesus, a sign that identified the betrayer, even though the other disciples did not recognize it as one, Satan entered him. This has been taken by parts of the tradition as an indication that those who want to appear to be communing with Christ, but have intentions that are contrary to all that is implied in the Last Supper, are open to a diabolical spiritual resolve that is damning. That is "Satan"—the historic personalized word for an objective force that can subjectively distort reason, misguide the will, and misdirect the affections. It represents the shadow of unbelief to the point where it engenders the temptation, accusation, and the slandering of authentic belief, due to the placing of belief in a false center of loyalty. Thus a wrong way, an untruth, and a consequence of death—not "the way,

Pastoral Perspective

bread that he dips. Amazingly, Judas accepts the bread from Jesus and then immediately leaves to do the dirty work of betrayal. Also amazing is the fact that the other disciples still do not understand what Jesus has said and what is happening at that very hour. They hear Jesus' words. They see Judas accept the morsel and depart. They just cannot wrap their minds around the thought that Judas is off to betray Jesus. Surely he must be off handling administrative details related to the coming festival. If not that, then perhaps he is off helping the poor. This is the kind of behavior they expect from Judas. The disciples are living these events day by day. We, who live on the other side of the crucifixion and resurrection, have always known Judas Iscariot as the one who betrayed Jesus. The disciples, on the other hand, do not know this at the time.

Betrayal always comes as a shock. If you could see betrayal coming, you might be able to arm yourself or defend yourself. The very essence of betrayal comes with the surprise. The sting of betrayal hurts precisely because we cannot imagine this friend or family member or coworker treating us like that.

Modern readers of this story would be consoled a bit if all the disciples had known that Judas was the betrayer. "Of course it was Judas, remember the time when he . . ." "Obviously it is Judas. He never really fit in. He is not like the rest of us." "Judas was just a bad apple."

We like to believe that people who are capable of this kind of betrayal are such horrible human beings that everyone would know and be on guard. This is simply not the case. Only Jesus knew the heart and mind of Judas. Everyone else, apparently, thought he was just a regular guy. When a crime is committed today, folks who live near the perpetrator are often shocked by what they learn. When the reporters talk to the neighbors, you hear the same story over and over again. "He seemed like a real nice guy. I never would have thought he could do that. He lived right next door. Scary."

Many people in our congregations will know the sting of betrayal firsthand. It comes in the form of a gambling addiction or an extramarital affair. Maybe the betrayer says, "I never loved you in the first place." Perhaps it is the relative who pawns family heirlooms to buy drugs. Maybe it is the financial advisor who takes your retirement money and runs. Perhaps the betrayer shared with others what you had offered in confidence. The betrayer may be the company where you worked for years as a loyal employee, only to find yourself in the unemployment

Exegetical Perspective

of the cross, but this particular affliction occurs in the context of a meal, where fellowship is sacred and social bonds are reinforced. Betrayal takes place within the innermost circle. Judas is a friend who becomes a traitor. Nothing prepares us for betrayal by friends—especially not in the heart of our most sacred time, Passover for Jesus, Holy Week for us. Like the troubled passage of chapter 12, the betrayal provides another locus for the glorification of God and, this time, of the Son of Man.

John's account of the Last Supper features the unknown Beloved Disciple. Historically this has been thought to be a modest oblique reference to the author, assumed to be the apostle John. More recently, other identities have been proposed for this figure: John (author or not), Lazarus, and Mary Magdalene; but there is nothing in the text that points definitively to an identity. Perhaps the Beloved Disciple is a composite symbol whose actions and discipleship mirror ways for the Johannine community to follow Jesus.

As is common in John, the meal becomes an occasion for extended discourse. Here Jesus inaugurates a series of final talks he will give in John's Gospel. These Farewell Discourses are Jesus' last will and testament to disciples and listeners in the Gospel. Of this particular form there are many examples in the Bible: Moses (Deut. 33), Paul (Acts 20:17–38), Stephen (Acts 7:2–60). These discourses function in the life of the ongoing community just as the "I Have a Dream" speech of Dr. Martin Luther King Jr. has. We can see the process as it evolves, in the reception of "The Last Lecture" by Professor Randy Pausch, who at 48 was dying of cancer; this received eight million viewings on YouTube by the end of 2008.

John's Gospel shows Jesus preparing his community for the death that is about to happen, but John develops this distinctive material of Jesus' last speeches more to reinforce an understanding of that death for the Johannine community. Material for these discourses comes from sayings of Jesus spoken earlier in the Gospel. We have discussed the lifting up on the cross as exaltation. The Son of Man will be lifted up on the cross, but to the eyes of faith, he will be lifted, exalted into God's glory (12:32). The path through the darkness of what is to follow will lead to the divine presence. Without diminishing its pain, John transforms the hour into an hour of celebration and victory (12:31–33).

John 13:31–32 is a typically Johannine statement in which the strands of meaning are interwoven into a dense cord. After Judas departs, Jesus begins, "Now

Homiletical Perspective

death, his own death, is near, but this text focuses his troubled spirit elsewhere. Jesus is troubled because someone is going to betray him. Not just "someone"; he will be betrayed by a friend whose feet he has now washed and with whom he is sharing a meal.

In John, Jesus knows his betrayer, anticipates his foul deed, and still kneels at his feet and gives him bread to eat. The love that Jesus calls forth from disciples in this Gospel is modeled in John 13: love even for the one who betrays. It is that kind of rugged love that binds together a community even when the shadow of death grows, betrayal hovers, and division threatens the family. The Fourth Evangelist invites preachers to preach that kind of de-romanticized love as they proclaim God's love on Holy Wednesday.

It is worth preachers' time to pay close attention to how John understands the love commandment of Jesus. As Gail O'Day writes,

> To love one another as Jesus loves us does not automatically translate into one believer's death for another, nor does it mean to deny oneself for others. Jesus did not deny himself; he lived his identity and vocation fully. Rather, to love one another as Jesus loves us is to live a life thoroughly shaped by a love that knows no limits, by a love whose expression brings the believer closer into relationship with God, with Jesus, and with one another. It is to live a love that carries with it a whole new concept of the possibilities of community.[1]

Preaching this text will also demand that preachers deal with John's cosmic appreciation for evil. Judas does not simply make an error in judgment when he executes the betrayal of Jesus, nor is he simply an embedded thief in a community that trusts him. In John, Judas lives out the evil that always seeks to thwart God's love. Try mangling this text to preach a prosperity gospel. It just will not preach such pabulum. John wants every disciple to know that followers of Jesus are not immune to the evil that exists in the world and even within the church. At the same time, as he tells this story, even the possessed Judas follows the instruction of the one whom he will betray.

With three short words, "It was night," the evangelist does more than tell us the time of day of Jesus' betrayal. Throughout John's Gospel, Jesus is portrayed as the light bearer in a world consumed by darkness. In this text, preachers are reminded that betrayal is a dark act, but also that Jesus loves when "it was night." With these three words, the Gospel

---

1. Gail R. O'Day, "The Gospel of John," in *New Interpreter's Bible* (Nashville: Abingdon Press, 1995), 9:734.

John 13:21-32

Theological Perspective

and the truth, and the life" (14:6)—remain the ruling principles of this world. Objective evil remains in the world and can infect those who are thought to be close to the Lord.

Jesus instructed Judas to do what he was going to do quickly. Again the disciples did not understand what was going on or why Jesus had said this. They failed to realize the evil in their own midst. Instead, they attributed Judas's departure as he went out—significantly, into the darkness—as due to his alleged care for the poor or his buying more provisions for the festival. Jesus knew what Judas was up to, and recognized that this departure would set in motion the final chapter in his earthly life and the beginning of his heavenly reign. Thus Jesus issued the revealing meaning of it all: his glorification as the eschatological Son of Man was at hand, and in the process God was to be glorified. Further, if God was glorified in Christ, Jesus too would be glorified in God—all at the same time.

This ends our reading, but it may be helpful to note three points about the chapters that follow. First, the earthly sign of this glorification would be the manifestation of love. Jesus issues the commandment that his disciples must love one another and points out that the world will see this as the authenticating mark of fidelity. Second, the disciples still do not fully get the point that Jesus is united with God. Peter, Thomas, and Philip want to know where Jesus is going and what empirical evidence there is for this. Third, Jesus offers his longest discourse to the disciples—but that is another text.

MAX L. STACKHOUSE

Pastoral Perspective

line. Maybe the betrayer stole your childhood. Maybe the betrayer is the lover who sent you to the emergency room with a bloody face.

To be betrayed is to be vulnerable to a unique kind of pain. It can take many years to recover from the sting of betrayal. In our pews, there may be folks whose hearts are still raw and in need of healing and wholeness. The betrayal of Jesus may touch upon this pain and present opportunities for pastoral care. The other painful reality in proclaiming this text is the realization that if the disciples could not see betrayal coming from Judas, maybe those who betray are not the demons we imagine them to be. Those who would betray are a lot more like you and me. It is easy to look down our noses at Judas and imagine us among the other eleven disciples. As painful as it is, we must admit that we also are capable of betraying those we love, including our Lord.

In an era when prayers of confession are considered by some to be passé or depressing, we must hold fast to the Christian understanding of sin and acknowledge the pervasiveness of sin in our lives. "All have sinned and fall short of the glory of God," the apostle Paul proclaims in the book of Romans (3:23). The good news of the gospel is that by God's grace we are forgiven. The Good Friday cross is good news for all of us, who, like Judas, have betrayed both our friends and our God. The resurrection of Jesus is good news for those who seek wholeness and healing from the sting of betrayal.

NANCY A. MIKOSKI

the Son of Man has been glorified." This "now," referring to the complex of events that Judas's departure has initiated, is the same "now" as in 12:27. So it is best to take the "now" in 13:31 as also referring to the whole event that has arrived. In this event God will be glorified "in" the Son of Man, because Jesus will be bringing his mission to completion, and God and Jesus engage in acts of mutual glorification. Later Jesus will invoke this reciprocal glorification in 17:1, 4, citing the completion of the work God has given him. On the cross he will declare: 'It is finished' (19:30). The prayer in 17:5 sheds further light on what is being said here: the Father glorifies the Son "with himself" (NRSV "in your own presence"), that is, with the glory that is the divine presence.

Simply put, the Son will seem to enter darkness, but this is the pathway through which God will bring the Son home and surround him with glory. That glory is nothing other than God's own being. The lectionary ends the reading here, with an abrupt dissection of the discourse. The somewhat convoluted statement in verses 31–32 indicates that Jesus knows he has reached the end of the journey and will soon be rewarded with the divine presence. The reward is not things or places but the person of God. Oneness with God, not absorption into God, is the goal and the reward, as it has also been the characteristic of Jesus' whole life. That is why John can also say that already in his life we saw God's glory (1:14). Jesus' suffering *is* his glory.

The continuing discourse in verses 33–35, however, suggests an organic connection between Jesus' glorification of God and the disciples' exercise of love for one another. The lectionary notwithstanding, the glorification of God does not cease with the withdrawal of Jesus from the earth.

DEIRDRE J. GOOD

captures the mood of Holy Wednesday. Preachers would do well both to acknowledge the mood and to anticipate the impending betrayal, torture, and death of Jesus, but also to proclaim, as John does throughout this Gospel, "The light shines in the dark, and the darkness did not overcome it" (1:5).

This text ends on a word that readers have heard from John with some frequency, "glory." John refutes any notion that Jesus was an unsuspecting victim of a brutal betrayal by a misguided disciple or was the unwitting victim of the vagaries of fate. Jesus is no victim, and God's purpose for Jesus will not be deterred by a community thief, even one possessed by Satan. For John, Jesus will die victoriously and in so doing will fully reveal the glory of God. "Now the Son of Man has been glorified, and God has been glorified in him" (v. 31). "To glorify (vv. 31–33) is to make visible the presence of God. This teaching highlights the mutual glorification of God and Jesus that began when the Word became flesh (1:14) and so makes God visible to the world."[2]

Perhaps the greatest preaching clue given in John and highlighted in this text is for preachers to maintain the tension between dark and light, death and glory. Too often sermons either omit darkness/death and present trouble free "good news," as if any truly "good news" could be trouble free, or they omit light and glory, lest the congregation underestimate the rigors of discipleship. John talks about Judas *and* Mary. Readers are left to decide which will lead them through the darkness into the glorious light of God's glory.

GARY W. CHARLES

2. Gail R. O'Day and Susan E. Hylen, *John*, Westminster Bible Companion (Louisville, KY: Westminster John Knox Press, 2006), 141.

Exodus 12:1-4 (5-10), 11-14

¹The Lᴏʀᴅ said to Moses and Aaron in the land of Egypt: ²This month shall mark for you the beginning of months; it shall be the first month of the year for you. ³Tell the whole congregation of Israel that on the tenth of this month they are to take a lamb for each family, a lamb for each household. ⁴If a household is too small for a whole lamb, it shall join its closest neighbor in obtaining one; the lamb shall be divided in proportion to the number of people who eat of it. ⁵Your lamb shall be without blemish, a year-old male; you may take it from the sheep or from the goats. ⁶You shall keep it until the fourteenth day of this month; then the whole assembled congregation of Israel shall slaughter it at twilight. ⁷They shall take some of the blood and put it on the two doorposts and the lintel of the houses in which they eat it. ⁸They shall eat the lamb that same night; they shall eat it roasted over the fire with unleavened bread and bitter herbs. ⁹Do not eat any of it raw or boiled in water, but roasted over the

Theological Perspective

The Passover is the major feast in the Jewish religion. Its beginnings are linked to God's "passing over" (Heb. *pesach*) the households of Israel, in slavery in Egypt, that were marked with the blood of a lamb "without blemish" (v. 5) on the two doorposts and lintel of the houses (v. 7). Without this sign, "every firstborn in the land of Egypt, both human beings and animals" (v. 12) would be struck down by God. The blood on the doorposts assured safety. The Passover meal, celebrated that night, was prescribed by God, and what later became the Passover ritual became central to the Jewish faith to this day. Passover was a prelude to the exodus through which the people were led out of their servitude in Egypt and began their journey to the promised land of Canaan. God commanded the day of the Passover to be remembered and celebrated "as a festival to the Lᴏʀᴅ; throughout your generations you shall observe it as a perpetual ordinance" (v. 14).

Jesus was in Jerusalem to celebrate Passover with his disciples during the last week of his life (Mark 14:12–16). The last meal with his disciples was either a Passover meal or held on the eve of the Passover (the Synoptic Gospels and the Gospel of John appear to indicate the date differently). As Jewish faith was centered on a Passover meal, so Christian faith also became centered on a meal, the Lord's Supper. In the

Pastoral Perspective

It is unlikely that anyone will preach on this text on Holy Thursday, since the Gospel lection is the foot-washing scene in John, combined with Jesus' teaching about loving one another. Yet this text gives us the opportunity to emphasize the Jewish origins of Christian faith and the ongoing liturgical connection between Passover and the Lord's Supper or Eucharist.

Passover and Holy Communion are ritual meals, and the liturgy for these meals has been shaped not only by historical events, but also by the historical accounts themselves. In fact it is remarkable how closely the themes and facts of Passover and the Lord's Supper overlap.[1]

This is made more explicit by Paul's account of the Eucharist in 1 Corinthians 11 than in the Gospel accounts, all of which vary slightly in detail and perspective. However, whether in Paul or in the Gospels, the theme of the Last Supper is "blood deliverance" or deliverance by suffering, as the meal acknowledges in its celebration. "This cup is the new covenant in my blood," Jesus said as he offered one of the Passover cups to his disciples. "This is my body, broken for you. [Take and eat] in remembrance of me" (1 Cor. 11:24–25).

1. Terence E. Fretheim, *Exodus*, Interpretation series (Louisville, KY: John Knox Press, 1991), 133–39.

fire, with its head, legs, and inner organs. ¹⁰You shall let none of it remain until the morning; anything that remains until the morning you shall burn. ¹¹This is how you shall eat it: your loins girded, your sandals on your feet, and your staff in your hand; and you shall eat it hurriedly. It is the passover of the Lord. ¹²For I will pass through the land of Egypt that night, and I will strike down every firstborn in the land of Egypt, both human beings and animals; on all the gods of Egypt I will execute judgments: I am the Lord. ¹³The blood shall be a sign for you on the houses where you live: when I see the blood, I will pass over you, and no plague shall destroy you when I strike the land of Egypt.

¹⁴This day shall be a day of remembrance for you. You shall celebrate it as a festival to the Lord; throughout your generations you shall observe it as a perpetual ordinance.

Exegetical Perspective

Passover (*pesach* in Hebrew) begins the Jewish liturgical year, and we read of its inception in Exodus 12:1–14. That Easter nearly always occurs in the same week as Passover in Western Christianity is hardly surprising, since all four Gospels associate the last days of Jesus' life on earth with the Jewish holiday. While Passover and Easter have their unique religious significance, it is hard to deny that they are synchronous with older pagan celebrations of the rites of spring. Both modern holidays celebrate renewal, as do all celebrations of spring.

While these two religious commemorations are viewed against the more universal celebration of renewal each spring, the direct links between Passover and Easter are even more compelling. According to the three Synoptic Gospels, the Last Supper occurred on the first night of Passover and, as such, was a Passover Seder meal. The Synoptics portray Jesus' Last Supper as the new dispensation of an ancient Jewish practice that, in Christianity, becomes the Eucharist. For the Gospel writers, the Eucharist is the "new and improved" replacement for the Passover Seder.

The association of bread with wine, representing Jesus' blood, has clear precedent in Passover as it was celebrated in late Second Temple Judaism. Exodus 12 stipulates that Israel celebrate Passover with

Homiletical Perspective

The Passover provides an essential background for the New Testament presentation of the death of Jesus and for understanding the meal Jesus shared with his disciples on the night before he died. In the Synoptic Gospels, Jesus' Last Supper with his disciples is a Passover meal. In John, the Last Supper, together with Jesus' arrest, trial, and crucifixion, occurs on the Day of Preparation; Jesus dies as lambs for Passover are slaughtered. Jesus is the Passover lamb (cf. John 19:36), a sign for us of God's promise to pass over and not bring the plague of death upon us.

Exodus 12 is appointed precisely to provide this background for the events the church celebrates on Maundy Thursday and in the days to follow; but preachers must exercise care as they make this connection. It is inappropriate to reduce the Passover to prefiguring Jesus' death or even to imply that the Lord's Supper somehow renders the Passover feast meaningless or obsolete. The Passover remains the ritual event in which the Israelites remember and actualize their redemption and beginning as a people freed by God. Passover commemorates a mighty act of God worthy of reverence and respect.

Scholars suggest that the Passover festival is rooted in a nomadic rite of passage (see Exod. 3:18) in which fertility of the flocks and availability of suitable grazing land were of prime concern. This rite

Exodus 12:1-4 (5-10), 11-14

Theological Perspective

emergence of the Christian church from the New Testament onward, connections between the Jewish faith and the Christian faith have been strong; and the Passover has been a major feature of this connectedness.

In the Gospels, the death of Christ was set against the backdrop of the Passover. Paul wrote, "For our paschal lamb, Christ, has been sacrificed" (1 Cor. 5:7). Jesus Christ is the "Lamb of God who takes away the sin of the world" (John 1:29; cf. Heb. 10; 11:28). As the people of Israel were charged to "remember" and "celebrate" the Passover event, so Jesus commanded the same of his disciples (1 Cor. 11:23–26). Thus remembering the story of the first Passover from the book of Exodus has become an appropriate Christian scriptural reading on Holy Thursday, when the church celebrates the Lord's Supper and anticipates the coming death and resurrection of Jesus Christ in Good Friday and Easter.

The central convictions of the Christian church about who Jesus Christ is as the fulfillment of Old Testament prophecy and God's promised Messiah led to a different understanding of the place of the Passover in the church, compared to its position in Judaism. For the Jews, Passover is a clear summons to remember God's deliverance of Israel from its slavery in Egypt, a liberation into freedom to live as God's covenant people. The church remembered Israel's deliverance, but it also focused on Jesus Christ. He promised a new dimension. Redemption and liberation were now to be found in him. As Brevard Childs put it, "Both the New Testament and early church history testify to the struggle in coming to terms with a new understanding of the passover in the light of the gospel, which seemed both to confirm and to refute their Jewish heritage."[1]

Christian theological reflection on the account of the first Passover points to these issues. It also helps interpret the nature of God's redemptive activities in Jesus Christ.

God Saves the People. It is God who provided for the safety of the people of Israel through the blood on the doorposts in the midst of the death that occurred outside of that "sign of safety." God continued this saving work through liberating the people in the exodus from Egypt.

So also, in Jesus Christ, God saves people now. The Lord's Supper on Holy Thursday is another meal

Pastoral Perspective

In similar fashion, the observance of Passover involves remembering what happened: the slaughter of the lambs, the blood on the doorposts of Jewish homes, and the passing over Egypt of the angel of death—so that the firstborn of Israel were preserved while the firstborn of Egypt, both human and animal, all died.

The similarities between these rituals are important for both Jewish and Christian communities of faith, and stressing them will proclaim the indissoluble connection between Jews and Christians. However murky or bloody our history with each other from the earliest days, and however uncomfortable Christians are with what are now labeled the "anti-Semitisms" in the New Testament, the fact is that Jewish faith is the root and branches of the olive tree, and Christians remain those who are grafted on. Jews and Christians are connected in our history, in our identity, and in our current existence.

There is no better night in the church year to assert these connections and to celebrate them, as many Christian congregations now do with a Seder before Maundy Thursday Communion. Observing both of these rituals helps the church witness to itself that we are inextricably joined to the people of Israel: to the descendents of Abraham and Sarah; to Jacob and his wives, sons, and daughters; to Moses and the prophets; to the psalms; to Jewish people everywhere. We do not know how this relationship will be resolved until the last day, but with Paul we can claim that it will be resolved, because God does not reject those who are elected.

At the Lord's Table on Holy Thursday we are reminded to claim with joy our family heritage, remembering how the bread we break and the wine we share at this table were for Jesus and his disciples their last Passover meal together. Bread and wine now have an enlarged meaning for us. They signify the new covenant in Christ's blood. For those in the upper room it was a Passover supper, a celebration of God's victory over the power and arrogance of Pharaoh. Now this supper has become the Christian victory meal. "The powers of death have done their worst, but Christ their legions has dispersed" (from "The Strife is O'er, The Battle Done," anonymous, 1695), as God dispatched the army of Pharaoh in the Red Sea waters.

However, the use of this text also raises the issue of theodicy: How could God have been so cruel as to kill all the firstborn in Egypt, including little innocent children who had done no sin? Of course, not all firstborn were children; some would have grown to

---

1. Brevard S. Childs, *The Book of Exodus*, Old Testament Library (Philadelphia: Westminster Press, 1974), 212.

Exegetical Perspective

unleavened bread (*matzah*) and the blood of the sacrificial lamb. This pairing of *matzah* with blood is likely the result of combining two originally distinct holidays. Indeed, in Exodus 23:14–15 the text knows only of the spring celebration of the feast of Unleavened Bread (*hag hammatzot*) and contains no mention of the sacrifice of an animal.

It is clear that the Eucharist is the Christian analogue to the Jewish celebration of the Passover, but perhaps the most compelling associations between Exodus 12 and the passion of Jesus lie in John's account of the crucifixion. While the Synoptic Gospels agree that the Last Supper was a Seder, the Gospel of John differs, in recording Jesus' crucifixion as taking place the day before the evening Passover Seder.

In John, Jesus represents the Passover offering, or the paschal lamb, which was to be sacrificed during the day leading up to the Seder. John's association of Jesus with the paschal lamb had profound effects on Christianity and has deep roots in several traditions in the Hebrew Bible. Since John does not refer to any of these, we cannot be sure that he alludes to them, but the degree to which John's account resonates with sacrifice in the Hebrew biblical tradition is remarkable. A brief summary of the theological antecedents to the Christian understanding of Jesus as the lamb of God is in order.

The association of Jesus with the paschal lamb is relatively clear. In Exodus 12, the blood of the lamb, spread on the doorposts, allows for the firstborn Israelites to escape death and leads to the redemption of Israel from a life of bondage to a life of freedom. Jesus' death and subsequent resurrection accomplishes much the same thing. The constellation of features, including a lamb, blood, redemption, and firstborn or only child, resonates with other stories in the Hebrew Bible. A number of accounts of sacrifice in the Hebrew Bible share key ingredients with the Christian notion of Jesus as sacrificial lamb. In the following we consider a number of other texts that incorporate other elements shared by Exodus 12 and early Christian understanding of the passion.

In Genesis 22 we read of the binding of Isaac (*'Aqedah*), which is often inaccurately referred to as the sacrifice of Isaac. The account came to be understood as an adumbration of the passion in Christian tradition. In Genesis 22:2 Abraham is told, "Take your only son (*yehiydkha*) Isaac, whom you love(*'asher 'ahavta*)" and then told to offer him as a burnt offering. A last-minute reprieve allows Isaac to live when a ram is substituted for him. In the *'Aqedah*, we have many of the same ingredients that

Homiletical Perspective

was transformed by changing circumstances and a new context. With the exodus, the old ceremony was given a new set of meanings that symbolized Israel's new beginning. Israel incorporated an existing nomadic rite into the heart of the event of its liberation and presented that rite as commanded by God. Christians likewise confess that Jesus incorporated the Passover ritual into God's act of salvation in Christ and commanded the disciples to do this in remembrance of him.

As Christians respect and revere Passover, we need not apologize for continuing this process of reinterpretation by finding in our experience of Passover a way to understand and articulate both the meal given by Jesus and his suffering and death. In fact, the language and images of the Passover provide an effective way to help worshipers enter into washing feet, sharing the Lord's Supper, and stripping the altar on Maundy Thursday.

In Exodus, God's saving event and the ritual associated with it are so integrally interwoven that neither can be understood apart from the other. In fact, the Passover liturgy *precedes* the liberating event. God provides the details, order, and rubrics for the Passover ritual *before* executing judgment on the gods of Egypt by striking down all the firstborn and passing over the Israelites. The Passover rituals were so incorporated into the story of Israel's liberation that they influenced how that story is composed, remembered, and told.

In fact, the Passover liturgy stresses that worshipers in every celebration actually participate in God's saving activity. Through the Passover ritual, God works salvation both initially and continually in the lives of participants, "(re)constituting them as the redeemed exodus community."[1] The exodus redemption becomes real and effective for every generation of Israelites. Every generation confesses: God brought *us* out of Egypt. God delivered *us*. By keeping Passover as "a day of remembrance" (12:14), participants enter into the reality of God's saving event in such a way as to be reconstituted as the people of God.

Understanding Jesus' death and resurrection as Passover invites preachers to undertake more than analogies or scriptural connections between the Exodus and Gospel stories. As the Lord gave Moses and Aaron the Passover ritual before the Passover event, so Jesus gave foot washing and the Lord's Supper before being stripped as a servant and sacrificed on a

---

1. Terence E. Fretheim, *Exodus*, Interpretation series (Louisville, KY: John Knox Press, 1991), 139.

Exodus 12:1-4 (5-10), 11-14

Theological Perspective

where "memory" and "celebration" are joined in focusing on Jesus Christ, who died and was raised again for the salvation of believers. The common meal in Israel and the church attest to God as the initiator of a redemptive relationship that is eternal.

God Gives Grace. In the Passover, Israel remembers it was spared from death, purely by God's grace. As Israel went on to live as God's covenant people, receiving God's law and being the witness to God they were called to be, the Passover celebration was a yearly reminder of God's gracious choosing of this people to be "my nation" (Isa. 51:4).

The church affirms that God's grace is given in Jesus Christ and that in him, "every one of God's promises is a 'Yes'" (2 Cor. 1:20). By God's grace we have been "saved through faith" (Eph. 2:8). In the Lord's Supper, which points to Christ's death, God's grace is given to sinners (Rom. 5:8) so we might live in the relationship of love and trust that God intends, both with God and with others. This is solely by God's "amazing grace."

God Grants Future Hope. The hope of the Jewish faith is toward God's future and the establishment of righteousness and peace (Zech. 9–14; Isa. 24–27, 35, etc.). The Passover is an ongoing "festival to the Lord" that John Calvin said helped Israel "in the recollection of their past deliverance" and nourished in them "the hope of future redemption; and therefore the Passover not only reminded them of what God had already done for His people, but also of what they were hereafter to expect from Him."[2]

For Christians, the celebration of the Lord's Supper on Holy Thursday has this future dimension as well, since we "proclaim the Lord's death until he comes" (1 Cor. 11:26). In Jesus Christ, God's future "has come" and "will come" as we anticipate our "hope of sharing the glory of God" (Rom. 5:2) and the establishment of the "new heaven and a new earth" (Rev. 21:1) while all praise and worship is given to "the Lamb" (Rev. 5:12).

DONALD K. MCKIM

Pastoral Perspective

adulthood and therefore been at risk on Passover night. No matter; this behavior on God's part appears (especially to those who have lost children) both capricious and cruel. Did Jesus not say to love our enemies anyway?

Here are some possible responses. God killed the firstborn of Egypt, which was a just but far from equal retaliation for what Pharaoh did when he ordered, at the beginning of the exodus story, the death of all male Hebrew children.[2] Pharaoh was genocidal. He was attempting to eliminate the whole people of the Hebrews; and to the extent that God is in a contest with Pharaoh for the rule of the earth, God is not trying to obliterate the Egyptians, but merely, we might say, to bring them to heel. What, after all the plagues and the pleadings of Moses and Aaron, will get the Egyptian's attention?

Further, the Passover ritual includes no rejoicing over the death of the firstborn.[3] It is only after God has brought Israel safely through the Red Sea waters and their Egyptian pursuers are destroyed that shouts of victory and thanksgiving are raised up to heaven.

Finally, there is simply a reality about human life that bears recounting with honesty and humility: no human community exists without violence and bloodshed. This understanding frames human and holy history: Cain murdered his brother Abel and was the founder of cities, and Romulus killed his brother Remus (the two were orphans—orphans!) and founded Rome. We do well to remember this as we proclaim the gospel of God's grace, or else that grace is cheapened into positive feelings—and communities so constituted never abide.

Perhaps the reason for so much intractable conflict in the church is God's reminder that those on opposite sides of "holy church wars" may be humbled only by the cross. Jesus willingly gave up his life for the sake of the church.

O. BENJAMIN SPARKS

---

2. John Calvin, *Commentary on Exodus* 20:5.

2. Ibid.
3. Ibid.

Exegetical Perspective

appear in the account of the Passover. The sacrifice of the ram/lamb substitutes for and allows only for the firstborn to survive.

Clearly, in the 'Aqedah, the ram is a secondary choice, but it functions similarly to the lamb of Passover. Genesis 22 is fascinating for its resonance with the Passover and the passion, in particular, where the lamb, rather than substituting for the son, is the son, yet remains a substitute. Again, while the ingredients of these two precedents in the Hebrew Bible are consistent, the recipe that guides their function and sequence differs.

There is another compelling connection between Genesis 22 and the passion. Jesus, like Isaac, is the beloved and only son of his father. The reader in both stories is likely to understand the profound loss represented by the death of this only son. While the age of Isaac in Genesis 22 is unknown, the text seems to suggest that he is unaware of his fate and, therefore, an innocent victim. Rabbinic tradition, based on Sarah's age in the next chapter, suggested that Isaac was thirty-seven and fully aware of his fate. Jewish tradition's indecision about the innocence versus willingness with regard to Genesis 22 has its analogue in the Gospel accounts, where Mark's Jesus begs to avoid his fate while John's seems unperturbed by it.

One more account of sacrifice in the Hebrew Bible sheds light on the complex associations among its texts and how they inform the New Testament. Leviticus 16 details the rites pertaining to the Day of Atonement (Yom Kippur). While the rites are complex, note the role of two goats. The first is to be slaughtered, and its blood contributes to the purging of sin from the community. A second goat, on which Aaron is to lay hands and confess the sins of the Israelites, is then sent off into the wilderness as the original scapegoat. While not identical in form or function with the animal in the 'Aqedah or Passover, the role of the goat on the Day of Atonement should sound familiar.

The genius of reading Exodus 12:1–14 on Holy Thursday lies in its remarkable associations with other texts in the Hebrew Bible and how it, along with those texts, illumines the passion narratives of the New Testament.

LARRY L. LYKE

Homiletical Perspective

cross. As with Passover, liturgy is so incorporated into the Holy Week story of God's saving activity in Christ that we receive the saving power of Christ's death and resurrection because God continues actively to redeem us through participation in worship. As our feet are washed and we receive the meal, we are those disciples for whom Jesus is betrayed, denied, handed over, and crucified. As is true with the Passover, participants do more than recount or reenact historical facts. Participants do more than bring to mind a story from their past. When Israel celebrates the Passover and when Christians participate in the Lord's Supper, the ritual celebration is as much God's saving activity as was the original event.

In both the Passover and the Lord's Supper, this is possible because of God's word—God's promise associated with the sign, and not the signs themselves. In Exodus, God says that the blood on the houses will be "a sign *for you*" of God's promise to pass over, so that no plague will destroy you (12:13). Likewise, Jesus said, "This is my body that is *for you*" (1 Cor. 11:24). Neither the lambs' blood painted on Israel's doorposts nor the bread and wine of Jesus' Table possess properties in and of themselves that automatically provide protection or salvation. Both the blood on doorposts and the bread and wine of the Supper are signs "for you," that is, for God's people, of God's promise and commitment to save. When we participate in worship, we participate in God's promise.

Finally, the Passover reminds us that God has in mind to reconcile humanity to one another, as well as to God, and to create a unified people. The instructions that God gave through Moses are meant to unite all the households of Israel around a common destiny. The lambs are to be roasted whole, not cut up. "The whole congregation of Israel" is to participate, and they are to eat the lamb only together with others at the same time. The Passover is not a private meal. So Jesus instructed the disciples to wash one another's feet as he washed theirs, and gave the bread and wine for all to eat and drink.

CRAIG A. SATTERLEE

Psalm 116:1-2, 12-19

¹I love the LORD, because he has heard
  my voice and my supplications.
²Because he inclined his ear to me,
  therefore I will call on him as long as I live.
. . . .
¹²What shall I return to the LORD
  for all his bounty to me?
¹³I will lift up the cup of salvation
  and call on the name of the LORD,
¹⁴I will pay my vows to the LORD
  in the presence of all his people.

Theological Perspective

How do you pay back something that is beyond price? That is on the psalmist's mind in Psalm 116, and it is certainly on the mind of the church as it enters into the Triduum, the three days encompassing Good Friday, Holy Saturday, and Easter.

The psalm begins with the writer's reasons for loving God, "because he has heard my voice and my supplications" (v. 1). The psalmist has been in a bad spot, though the verses that describe the situation (vv. 3–11) are omitted in this reading. "The snares of death" and "the pangs of Sheol" (v. 3) have made themselves felt in his life. There have been moments of consternation and false accusation—"I said in my consternation, 'Everyone is a liar'" (v. 11).

Through every difficulty, the psalmist has kept faith with God and walked before God "in the land of the living." God, in turn, has also been faithful, has "delivered my soul from death, my eyes from tears, my feet from stumbling" (v. 8). Now the issue is, "What shall I return to the LORD for all his bounty to me?" (v. 12).

God's saving power has been demonstrated, and the psalmist understands that there is really only one way to repay the gift of God's faithfulness: worship. So he says, "I will lift up the cup of salvation" (v. 13), thus invoking the concept of the libation, or the

Pastoral Perspective

Psalm 116 is a psalm of thanksgiving. Liturgically, it is last of the Hallel Psalms (beginning with Ps. 113), intended to be read during Jewish festival times, especially during the first night of Passover.

The psalmist is thankful because she has been delivered—from what calamity we are uncertain. In later years, perhaps because of the lifting up the "cup of salvation" reference (v. 13), the psalm has come to recall the harried exodus from Egypt. Christians read it on Maundy Thursday, mindful that Jesus himself may have read these very words as part of his intimate meal with friends on that Passover celebration long ago.

At the center of the psalmist's gratitude is God's faithfulness. She called; God answered. What is described is not a personal SOS about a small matter but a fervent plea from the suffering depths. The psalmist is grateful that God not only heard but delivered. She knows her worthiness was not the reason God acted; it was God's graciousness, righteousness, and mercy (v. 5). No simple liturgical thank-you note will suffice.

She is changed, and her life will be tuned to a frequency of praise: she will lift cups, make vows, render service, and give thanks.

God had better get used to the psalmist's voice, because she pledges to call again, and again, forever.

¹⁵Precious in the sight of the Lord
   is the death of his faithful ones.
¹⁶O Lord, I am your servant;
   I am your servant, the child of your serving girl.
   You have loosed my bonds.
¹⁷I will offer to you a thanksgiving sacrifice
   and call on the name of the Lord.
¹⁸I will pay my vows to the Lord
   in the presence of all his people,
¹⁹in the courts of the house of the Lord,
   in your midst, O Jerusalem.
   Praise the Lord!

Exegetical Perspective

Psalm 116 begins with the simple declaration, "I love." The Hebrew text suspends any further delineation of an object at this point, and the Hebrew verb here translated love (*'ahav*) contains connotations of a committed and pledged bond. Hebrew has another word for delight and emotion-based love (*dod*), which tends to denote sensual and transient pleasure, for instance, in Song of Solomon 1:2: "Your love is better than wine."

The love that the worshiper initially proclaims in Psalm 116:1, then, is more literally rendered, "I am devoted." Now, in the midst of the second sentence within the Hebrew text, the psalmist reveals both to whom he or she is devoted, and why: "Because He will hear—YHWH—my voice when pleading favor" (my trans.). The verb "'to hear" as written within the Hebrew text conveys future realization, although it is interpreted as "he has heard" in the NRSV and other versions.

Verse 2 elaborates further the psalmist's beginning confession: "Since He extended His ear to me; Yea! In my days I shall call out!" (my trans.). The last phrase means not only to utter a sound, but also to make a proclamation; and the expression "my days" within ancient Hebrew usage has the ominous sense of days of trouble or testing. The worshiper is now making clear that not only is he or she abidingly committed

Homiletical Perspective

Holy Thursday is one of the biggest days of the church year, leading us into the highest holy days we have. Yet it is a day with more freedom to preach in it than Good Friday or Easter Sunday. It has less baggage—fewer expectations from the congregation—and feels, at least to this preacher, more flexible and open. To preach on the psalm assigned for the day means even more freedom, as familiar stories from either Gospel or Epistle readings are put aside and the preacher can contemplate the intimate world of the psalm.

Psalms tend to be, at first glance, abstract. You do not have a story to hang your sermon on. It may help to think of psalms as poems, for psalms—like poems—are bursts of words and images, with the raw emotion that engendered the work still present and available, even after all the careful crafting of words that went into the making of the psalm.

A human hand and human feeling mark the poem (or psalm) more than they mark other kinds of writing. A psalm is evidence that hundreds, even thousands, of years ago there existed a person who had thoughts and feelings and made of them a work that is still accessible to us. This is pretty amazing when you think about it, since the psalms date from at least the sixth century BCE (and that is just when they were written down). So, before even looking at the content of these psalms, take a moment to

Psalm 116:1-2, 12-19

Theological Perspective

drink offering. Further, he says he will "call on the name of the LORD (v. 13)," which is indicative of liturgical action. In making his act of worship, the psalmist will make good on his promise, possibly made during the time of adversity, and "pay my vows to the LORD" (v. 14).

Worship, then, is the appropriate response to the gracious action of God. The question in verse 12 is on the mind—or should be on the mind—of all who open themselves to the reality that God's goodness is greater than anything the human mind can fathom. As a result, there is nothing we can do to repay it. What is more, God does not expect us to repay it. The Creator understands full well the limitations and the frailties of the creature. All God asks is that humanity express our gratitude through worship.

This psalm becomes tied with the thanksgiving that the believer is to offer to God. As Israel has been brought through the exodus to offer worship, so the "new Israel," the church, offers worship in thanksgiving to God. For Christians, the thanksgiving par excellence is the Lord's Supper, appropriately called the Eucharist. The Eucharist accomplishes a dual purpose as the church thanks God for the saving action of its Lord and, in the process, tells the story, thus re-membering the body of Christ gathered around the sacramental table.

Whether it is called the liturgy, the visible gospel, or the seal of the covenant, the Eucharist accomplishes the same thing; it offers God appropriate worship and reminds the church why it exists. Michael Ramsey summarizes the essence of the Eucharist in *The Gospel and the Catholic Church* when he writes:

> The Gospel of God is here set forth, since the bread and the wine proclaim that God is creator, and the blessing and breaking declare that He has redeemed the world and that all things find their meaning and their unity only in the death and res- urrection of the Christ who made them. Here therefore Christian doctrine, with the scriptures and the creeds, finds its true context. *Lex orandi, lex credendi*. . . .
>
> And the meaning of all life is here set forth, since men exist to worship God for God's own sake. . . . For the liturgy is not an exercise of piety divorced from common life; it is rather the bringing of all common life into the sacrifice of Christ. The bread and the wine placed upon the altar are the gifts of the people betokening the food and work and toil and livelihood of men, brought to Christ to bless and to break to the end that all creation may be

Pastoral Perspective

One word describes this shift: *Hallelujah*. Used throughout the Hallel Psalms, it means "praise the Lord," and that is how the psalmist endeavors to live the rest of her days: with praise.

Our voice rightly picks up her faithful strain and joins with the harmony of faithful persons through the centuries who also know the relief of having called out in some dark night and been answered. So we make vows. We worship. We serve.

"What shall I return to the LORD for all his bounty to me?" (v. 12). For most of us, it is an absurd ques- tion. What will I give—to neighbor, to God? How will I repay the debt of gratitude I owe? The very absurdity of the question reminds us how vast the debt is and how paltry our efforts to pay it off are.

The psalmist might be confused by our modern sensibility that we can actually settle the bill, and even more appalled that some of us do not even think we owe one! Comparatively, Western Christians have deep pockets. We like the idea of tithing and other "percentage giving" schemes that allow us to put God on a reasonable dole. Fosdick was right to say we are "rich in things and poor in soul."[1] We lull ourselves into believing that our debt to God, like our home mortgages, will be paid off in a timely manner before we retire.

It is ludicrous, when we think about it.

God's delivering us is not an invitation to pay him back but an invitation to live sacrificially, with grati- tude. We do not simply open up our wallets; we open our hearts. Whatever we give, we give with love. "I love the LORD," the psalmist sings—not "I owe the Lord."

We are right to sing the words Isaac Watts (1674–1748) wrote for congregations of people who had been heard and delivered:

> I love the Lord who heard my cry
> and chased my grief away;
> O let my heart no more despair
> while I have breath to pray.

On the night of Jesus' arrest, the night the other Gospel writers report his sharing the Passover meal with his disciples, John underlines Jesus' "command" (the Latin word *mandatum*, "command," is the source of the odd term "Maundy") to "love one another as I have loved you" (John 15:12).

What Jesus did that night transcends anything that had come before. He hiked up his robe, got down on his tired knees, took his disciples' weathered

---

1. Harry Emerson Fosdick, "God of Grace and God of Glory," 1930.

Exegetical Perspective

to YHWH, but in a time of personal trial the psalmist will make himself or herself heard, not necessarily only to entreat the Lord's favor, but also to testify actively to allegiance.

Next, in verses 3–11, the psalmist recounts in gripping detail a deathly onslaught from which the Lord provided a passageway of escape once his name was invoked. YHWH is thus venerated in 116:5 as benevolent and compassionate—in verse 6 as "One guarding those who are vulnerable, and saving those who languish" (my trans.).

Then somewhat unexpectedly we overhear the psalmist in verse 7, after professing the Lord's past aid, commanding his or her soul to return to its "resting place," namely, God. The reasoning for this is given in the last phrase, where it is acknowledged further that "the LORD has dealt bountifully with you." In an evocative and personal elaboration of God's care, the worshiper now addresses YHWH directly, declaring, "For You plundered my soul—from death; my eyes—from wailing; my feet—from tripping" (v. 8, my trans.).

The psalmist now proclaims victoriously in verse 9 his or her blessed privilege of walking about "in the presence of YHWH; in lands of the living" (my trans.). In verse 10 the basis for such a lofty attainment is stated simply as "I believed" (my trans.). This last pronouncement appears within the Hebrew text as a causative rendering of the Hebrew verb meaning "to confirm or support" ('amen, pronounced a-MAIN), the most basic form of which provides our English assent "Amen."

The psalmist here announces that he or she "caused to confirm or support," implying not only an inner trust that was activated, but also an outer witness of confident action, which in turn influenced others to belief. As evidence of fidelity to the goodness of YHWH, and willingness to impact the public with it, the psalmist cites him or herself as having acknowledged openly when in trouble, "I, I am greatly bowed down" (v. 10, my trans.). Even while in a state of trepidation, he or she was willing to concede: "Every mortal is proven a liar" (my trans.)—hence confessing not only the psalmist's own inextricable state of sin but also his or her sheer dependence upon God's abiding concern and willingness to respond.

Verses 12–19 furnish an outburst of the worshiper's praise for God's beneficence. He or she begins by marveling as to how one might attempt to respond properly to the Lord's gracious intercessions, and then vows to "lift up the cup of salvation" (v. 13),

Homiletical Perspective

remember their antiquity, their authors, and the long history of our human desire to make images and convey strong feeling.

Then, head on to the sermon. Even though you do not have a story from which to preach, what you do have, in a psalm, is all this feeling and image and urgency. You have what Dr. Martin Luther King Jr. called "the fierce urgency of now."[1]

In Psalm 116 the author is not only describing and revealing his faith; he is also describing and revealing himself as if in the present, in the "now." There are more personal pronouns, more uses of "I" in the Psalms, than in any other part of the Bible.

> I love the LORD, because he has heard *my* voice and *my* supplications. (v. 1)
> Because he inclined his ear to *me*, therefore *I* will call on him as long as *I* live. (v. 2)
> *I* will offer to you a thanksgiving sacrifice, and call on the name of the LORD. (v. 17; emphases all mine)

As the poet Tomas Tranströmer wrote in his poem "Outpost," whatever place you are in—even when you are speaking from a pulpit—is "the place where creation is working itself out."[2] The author of Psalm 116 is telling us how "creation" worked itself out in him. He says he loves the Lord because he knows that God has heard his pleas. God has even leaned down to hear his individual voice. He is telling us about his experience of God and his personal and specific response to that encounter. Creation worked in him, he tells us, and the psalm is his way of telling us what that looked like.

Out of that experience, for this psalmist, has come a particular trust in God ("He hears my voice and my supplications and so I love him and will call upon him again"). This trust is not a sentimentalist's easy cliche, but a profound and hard-won wisdom. The author of psalm 116 knows what he is talking about. His trust comes out of his experience. This may be the kind of trust that carried Jesus through the awful days following his Last Supper with his friends.

The psalm offers the preacher the springboard to speak from the same dangerous and vulnerable place from which the psalmist speaks. How is creation working itself out in you? If your experience is like that of the psalmist—that is, if trust was born out of your encounter with God—what does your trust

---

1. From his speech "I Have a Dream," delivered August 1963 at the Lincoln Memorial, Washington, DC.
2. Tomas Tranströmer, "The Outpost," in *The Great Enigma: New Collected Poems* (New York: New Directions Publishing, 2006), 116.

Psalm 116:1-2, 12-19

Theological Perspective

summed up in His death and resurrection, to the glory of God, the Father.[1]

If God gives humanity *everything*—as one liturgical prayer says, "even our desire to thank you is, itself, your gift"—and if the Eucharist is the apex of thanksgiving, why is it not normative worship for every Christian? This is a huge and controversial question, which can perhaps best be answered by something Annie Dillard wrote:

> Why do we people in churches seem like cheerful, brainless tourists on a packaged tour of the Absolute? . . . On the whole, I do not find Christians, outside the catacombs, sufficiently sensible of conditions. Does anyone have the foggiest idea what sort of power we so blithely invoke? Or, as I suspect, does not one believe a word of it? The churches are children playing on the floor with their chemistry sets, mixing up a batch of TNT to kill a Sunday morning. It is madness to wear ladies' straw hats and velvet hats to church; we should all be wearing crash helmets. Ushers should issue life preservers and signal flares: they should lash us to our pews.[2]

The *maund* of Maundy Thursday is, "I give you a new commandment, that you love one another. Just as I have loved you, you also should love one another" (John 13:34).

We are to take loving one another as seriously as we take having been loved. A life lived in loving service is the liturgy that is, ultimately, most pleasing to God. To lift up the cup of salvation, to call on the name of the Lord, to fulfill our vows to the Lord, implies offering worship and leading lives that are consistent. There should be little distance between our worship and our work. If we are to be "sufficiently sensible of conditions," we will work to live as eucharistically—that is, as thankfully and unselfishly—as Christ did.

STEVEN A. PEAY

Pastoral Perspective

feet into his carpenter's hands, and washed them. When Peter tried to protest, Jesus told him that *this is what love looks like.* Such gratitude cannot be equaled by thoughtlessly cutting a weekly check for the operating fund or guiltily volunteering to serve in the church nursery (as infrequently as possible). Those gifts do not matter if they do not spring from love and are not part of a whole life of genuine service.

"I love the Lord, because he has heard my voice" (v. 1). I was made to be part of a family as numerous as stars. I was saved from the flood. I was delivered from hard labor under Pharaoh's whip. My wayward daughter made it through the shoals of adolescence. The cold days of a long marriage warmed. The waning passions for church service flared. The chemo has slowed that stubborn cancer. We do not know how God enriches and guides our steps, only that God does. God is active listening, healing, stirring the face of the waters, on his holy knees washing our dirty, stinking feet. God's name is Righteous, Merciful, Gracious.

The lyrics of Isaac Watts still shine, as do myriad modern ones of Jaroslav Vajda, John Bell, Brian Wren, and others. We are invited to treasure the life God has entrusted to our care, exploring ways to say thanks to our life's end. We are invited to get on our servant knees in the manner of Christ and to live into the kingdom that his life, death, and resurrection initiate. This will take more than a few dollars offered from our surplus reserves, and more than an efficient percentage of our time and energies.

We pray gratefully. Anne Lamott wrote, "Here are the two best prayers I know: 'Help me, help me, help me,' and 'Thank you, thank you, thank you.'"[2]

How do we pray at the grave? In the familiar words from *The Book of Common Prayer*, "All of us go down to the dust; yet even at the grave we make our song: Alleluia, alleluia, alleluia."[3]

This is a great way to pray—and to live.

WILLIAM P. "MATT" MATTHEWS JR.

1. Michael Ramsey, *The Gospel and the Catholic Church* (Eugene, OR: Wipf & Stock, 2008), 119.
2. Annie Dillard, *Teaching a Stone to Talk* (San Francisco: Harper & Row, 1982), 40.

2. Anne Lamott, *Traveling Mercies: Some Thoughts on Faith* (New York: Pantheon Books, 1999), 82.
3. *Book of Common Prayer* (New York: Seabury Press, 1979), 499.

Exegetical Perspective

honoring the name of YHWH before "all his people" (v. 14).

In ancient culture, such a gesture could signify a libation ritual that acknowledges one's cosmic benefactor. A cup, in such a case, would actually represent a cultic bowl common at religious festivals. Even more specifically, in verse 15 the psalmist rehearses the very words that will accompany this act of homage: "Precious in the eyes of YHWH is the death of His devoted ones" (my trans.).

An entirely unique form of the Hebrew word for death appears in the text at this point; hence, what it means precisely is unclear. Since the psalmist is here testifying to the Lord's rescue of him or her from snares and death (v. 8), one wonders whether the sense of the phrase is most prominently that YHWH is attentive to the deathly state of his committed ones.

The worshiper's next statement furthers this conjecture, since he or she states that "I am Your servant—the child of Your maidservant" (my trans.), and yet "you have loosed my bonds" (v. 16). Naming oneself as born of a maidservant (*'amah*) is an expression within Hebrew Scripture that conveys great humbleness; hence it affords the one being addressed utmost reverence and obligation (Ruth 3:9; 1 Sam. 1:11; Ps. 86:16).

What follows in verse 19 is a resounding invitation for all those within the courts of the house of YHWH and in the midst of Jerusalem to "praise the Lord," an imperative command of the Hebrew verb "to praise or boast" followed by its direct object (*yah*). This Hebrew word represents an abbreviated form of the unpronounceable name of Israel's God, YHWH. It is employed here and elsewhere within the well-known Hebrew phrase *Hallelu-Yah*, meaning literally, "Praise *Yah*!"

As its first words, "I love," demonstrate, Psalm 116 recounts a deep trust in the Lord that acknowledges not only the blessedness of the psalmist's abiding commitment to God, but a consequential outpouring of thanksgiving and praise over God's people and the very midst of his or her city.

JENNIFER PFENNIGER

Homiletical Perspective

look like? Is it the kind of trust that would carry you through torture and death? If not, why not?

These questions are not to make the preacher feel guilty for not matching the psalmist's or Jesus' trust, but instead to urge the preacher to think through what trust means in an individual life: what trust is, how it works in you, what it might mean to trust your own experience of God as much as the psalmist or Jesus does.

A word of caution: The "I" of (successful) poetry and literature is a creation of the author. It is not a fiction, but a "created" self that has distance and detachment from the material at hand.

For example, many of us have read memoirs we found embarrassing. The author told us things we really did not want to know. On the other hand, most of us have read memoirs that revealed all kinds of secrets that should have been embarrassing but were not. Instead, guided by a trustworthy narrator, we came to know something about the human condition. The difference between the first kind of memoir and the second is that the second author found the right narrating voice with which to tell the story. The "I" of the psalms is this kind of "I."

The authors of the Psalms found their narrating voices. The "I" in these pieces of writing is trustworthy. They are full of feeling and energy, but they are not confusing, boring, or embarrassing. The psalmists, in a word, trust in their own voices and experience.

With this freedom in mind, find a voice—an "I"— that can preach on this psalm with the urgency of a psalm and the detachment of a psalm's author. This psalm invites the preacher to respond with your own "I," to find the part of you that has a fierce urgency to speak into the now.

NORA GALLAGHER

1 Corinthians 11:23-26

23For I received from the Lord what I also handed on to you, that the Lord Jesus on the night when he was betrayed took a loaf of bread, 24and when he had given thanks, he broke it and said, "This is my body that is for you. Do this in remembrance of me." 25In the same way he took the cup also, after supper, saying, "This cup is the new covenant in my blood. Do this, as often as you drink it, in remembrance of me." 26For as often as you eat this bread and drink the cup, you proclaim the Lord's death until he comes.

Theological Perspective

Finding ourselves in familiar terrain, we often traverse it by the paths we know best. The familiarity of both the terrain and the path may make us inattentive to features to which we might beneficially pay heed. So it is with this lesson from 1 Corinthians. Every year brings us to Maundy Thursday; and every Maundy Thursday brings us to encounter these same lections. We further encounter the words of the epistle, or words like them, throughout the yearly rhythm of our gatherings. Communities whose worship includes the weekly celebration of Holy Communion do so every Sunday.

Thus we may traverse Paul's words on this day by one of two foot-worn paths. One path is to address the question of the nature of Christ's presence. Is Christ present physically, spiritually, or symbolically? The other path is to take seriously Jesus' command to remember, offering reflection that imaginatively recreates in some detail the various elements of, in the words of an old hymn, "that dark, that doleful night, When powers of earth and hell arose."[1] Though each path has its value, either may lead us away from more rewarding reflection. This brief text

1. Isaac Watts, untitled hymn, in *The Virginia Selection of Psalms, Hymns, and Spiritual Songs*, comp. Andrew Broaddus (Richmond: Smith, Drinker, & Morris, 1846), 62.

Pastoral Perspective

"This is my body that is for you. Do this in remembrance of me" (v. 24). We hear these words read frequently in our liturgy, but only once a year on Holy Thursday are they read for preaching. It would be a pity not to take this opportunity presented so rarely.

In 1 Corinthians 11:23–26 we encounter the merging of word and sacrament, for the very celebration of the Lord's Supper is itself an act of proclamation. As Paul tells us, "for as often as you eat this bread and drink the cup, you proclaim the Lord's death until he comes" (v. 26). Proclamation and Eucharist coalesce on Holy Thursday. The unity of the two acts of worship is accomplished.

This unity of Word and sacrament, proclamation and Eucharist, opens up for us an often-overlooked critical point: the foundational link of the Eucharist with social justice. Paul sets the stage in the verses immediately preceding and following verses 23–26. Here we find the context of Paul's passing on of the tradition of the Lord's Supper is the Corinthians' insult to the poor.

While the specific details are few, there is no question that Paul is quite exasperated with the Corinthians. The Lord's Supper occurred during the course of a larger gathering and common meal of the Corinthian community. It appears that the practice had gotten out of hand. The earlier guests were those

Exegetical Perspective

Although the Fourth Evangelist reflects on the eucharistic "bread from heaven" in chapter 6, this evening's text from John 13 makes Jesus' "last supper" with his disciples the context rather than the subject of the passage. The lectionary's pairing of 1 Corinthians 11 with John 13 is therefore something of a harmonizing of the Gospel accounts, using Paul's version of the Lord's Supper, rather than Matthew 26:26–30, Mark 14:22–25, or Luke 22:14–23.

The collection of verbs—take, bless [or give thanks], break, give—that describes Jesus' actions at Passover occurs also at Matthew 14:19, Mark 6:41, Luke 9:16, and Acts 27:35—stories that recall the church's sacramental experience and effectively turn all meals into reminders of Jesus' death and resurrection. At no time, though, are Christians more aware of those events and their consequences than during Holy Week, when the church reenacts the events that set in motion God's redemption of the world.

Memory and commemoration of Jesus' death and resurrection are at the heart of Paul's discussion in 1 Corinthians 11. The literary context concerns disruptions in worship (11:2–14:40)[1] that have been prompted by divisions within and among the house

1. Excepting 14:33b–36, which is surely an interpolation (Gordon Fee, *The First Epistle to the Corinthians*, New International Commentary on the New Testament [Grand Rapids: Eerdmans, 1987], 699–712).

Homiletical Perspective

The girl was five years old with very fair skin and very blond hair that kept escaping in curls from her braids. I was sitting behind her in church when I heard her say to her mother in a loud whisper, "I'm hungry and I'm thirsty!"

"I know, sweetie," her mother said. "Church will be over soon, and we'll have coffee hour and you can get a snack."

"No," the girl said, a little louder. People were beginning to look. "I'm hungry and I'm thirsty and I want to go!"

"I know, dear," her mother said. "Shhh! Here, let's sing the hymn together."

"I'm hungry and I'm thirsty," the girl said, "and I want to go to Communion!" With that she grabbed her mother's hand, stepped out into the church aisle, and led her mother to the Communion table.

On this night of all nights in the liturgical year, we are "hungry and thirsty" for Communion. We come to Holy Thursday with a longing to understand what happened around that Last Supper table. We hunger to understand what Jesus was trying to tell his friends as he improvised on the Passover meal. We thirst for the intimate experience of that fellowship as we enter the crucible of Holy Week. On this night the proclamation *is* the meal. How do we homiletically set the table for the richest Communion experience possible

Theological Perspective

carries us to the heart of identity, both Jesus' and our own, and does so by way of memory; but we need a richer understanding of memory.

Memory (*zakhor* in Hebrew, *mimnēskomai*, "remember," in Greek) is important in Scripture and in Christian theology. In today's lection Jesus instructs that his actions be reenacted ritually "in remembrance" of him. He utters these words on what is to be perpetually "a day of remembrance" (Exod. 12:14) for the people of Israel. Though we often treat it as such, this is not memory as we generally understand it, that is, as the mental recall of facts and experiences from the past. There is a static quality to memory so conceived. Memory is understood as analogous to a photograph, a recording, or a transcription. What is past remains past, but some record of it is brought into the present for some purpose. The gap between what is past and what is present only grows, so objects and accounts are employed as a memorial "bridge."

This is not memory as we see it in Scripture. To think about biblical memory, we must begin with the realization that while our accounts of events may have beginnings and endings, events themselves lack such definition. Consider the stories told at family gatherings. While narratives of the events involving family members past and present relate the happenings of limited periods of time, the events narrated are preceded and followed by precipitating and consequent events that continue even to the present time. In sharing the stories, tellers bring listeners to participate in the unfolding story of the family that includes the events narrated. In this way, the family identity is passed on.

Yet there is more. As indispensable as narrative is, a rich memorial context—and so identity—consists of more than narrative alone. Staying with the analogy of family gatherings, memory is also borne and conveyed by rituals and by physical things. There are traditional games, recipes, and activities; there are objects that have been passed down through the generations. Though in our families this sharing is always laden with some measure of ambiguity, that identity is never merely self-made. It is always something that in some degree is given and received through complex modes of memory.

In Scripture we find memory embedded in a rich nexus of narratives, rituals, and physical objects that function as memorials (*zikkaron*). For example, after passing dry-footed through the Jordan, Israel piles stones so the children of later generations will know their identity as part of a people delivered by God

Pastoral Perspective

of higher social status, who brought with them great quantities of food and drink and then proceeded to consume them with gluttony and drunkenness before the rest of the guests had arrived. Those who came later were the servants and those of lesser means, who often had very little to bring with them to contribute to the feast and who found little food and drink left by those who had come earlier. Paul is disgusted with the upper-class guests, choosing rather cutting remarks to describe their behavior.

The wealthier members of the community were acting selfishly, and their selfishness also flaunted their indifference to the needs and situation of the lesser members and the poor in general. Paul censured the Corinthians on their divisions in other passages of his letter, but the class struggles at the sacred Supper were of the worst sort. It was a sin against the body of Christ and a celebration unworthy of the tradition. The gluttony and drunkenness were bad enough, but the mistreatment of members of the community injured the church and violated the very body of Christ being remembered.

What does this mean for us today? It means first of all that we are nourished by the body and blood of Christ so that we will become more Christlike. We are fed so that we will have a greater capacity to help our neighbors in need and to break down the barriers of race, class, gender, and so forth that divide us in both church and society. The centripetal force that draws us into the heart of worship and the center of the community must be matched by an equally powerful centrifugal force that propels us out to serve. This will happen only if the words and actions of worship—in sermons, prayers, offering, and even church announcements—proclaim this inseparable link. Those in many Christian traditions are reminded at the end of worship, "Let us go in peace, to love and serve the Lord." Worship without service is incomplete.

The abuses of the Corinthians stand as vivid reminders of the danger of separating the body of Christ "that is for you" (v. 24) from the body of Christ that is the living community of faith where the hungry are fed, the sick visited, the lonely lifted up, and the poor provided for. Pope John Paul II in his encyclical *Sollicitudo Rei Socialis* (*On Social Concerns*) wrote,

> The Lord unites us with himself through the Eucharist—Sacrament and Sacrifice—and he unites us with himself and with one another by a bond stronger than any natural union; and thus united, he sends us into the whole world to bear

Exegetical Perspective

churches in Corinth. After discussing the veiling of women who lead worship (11:2–16),[2] he turns to the Lord's Supper: "Now in the following instructions I do not commend you, because when you come together it is not for the better but for the worse" (v. 17). While the distinctions among the Corinthian Christians are clearly religious and ethnic, they are also economic, because when they gather for their common meal, "each of you goes ahead with your own supper, and one goes hungry and another becomes drunk" (v. 21).

The pattern derives from conventional social behavior. Hosts of dinner parties typically seat their closest friends and social peers close to them on the raised platforms of their dining rooms (cf. Jas. 2:3: "Have a seat here, please," "Stand there," "Sit at my feet"). The favored guests are served the best food and wine, while those seated or standing around the edges of the room receive lesser fare. The purpose is to demonstrate to the watching world (the homes of wealthy urban men are deliberately open to the street) the host's wealth and honor, as well as his largesse to those beneath him in the complex pyramid of Greco-Roman society.

The Christian hosts of Corinthian congregations have apparently carried on their accustomed patterns of entertaining, and this infuriates the apostle, who says their practices amount to something other than the Eucharist: "it is not really to eat the Lord's supper" (v. 20). When those who come early (the wealthy peers of the host) eat and drink better than those who arrive late (the social inferiors), the congregation belies its unity and the common identity of the baptized. Those who are hungry are those who arrive after the food is gone; the drunk are those who began drinking when the party started. Intentionally getting your guests drunk is not simply a modern fraternity-house phenomenon. In Greco-Roman cities, it demonstrates the abundance and superiority of the host's wine cellar.

To correct the situation, Paul rehearses what he has already told the Christians in Corinth: "For I received from the Lord what I also handed on to you" (v. 23). The historical context is critical. It was "on the night when he was betrayed." The word "betrayed" of course suggests Judas's treachery, although it is the same verb as "I . . . handed on" and more frequently in Paul's letters refers to God's handing Jesus over to

Homiletical Perspective

on this night? How do we exegete the mystery of this meal, the memory of which is indelibly stamped on the heart of the church?

Paul does not deliver a nostalgic recitation of Jesus' words in this text. Instead, he proclaims his understanding of the meaning of the meal. The social context of the passage gives us some clues to that meaning. The members of the Corinthian church are following one of the socially acceptable practices of the day. The rich members of the community are eating their evening and ritual meals while separated from the poorer members—even though all are in the same house! What is more, the poorer members may not be able to afford an evening meal!

Paul speaks to the injustice of the passage. He wants the Corinthians to remember in order to re-member. The purpose of remembering Christ's words as they eat the meal together is to bring them together as Christ's community, collapsing the barriers among them (whether they are socially acceptable or not) and reuniting them in covenant with one another and with God. The liturgical action of remembering and the communal action of covenanting in a radical new kind of community create the vehicle for proclamation as far as Paul is concerned. The content of the proclamation is the good news of "the Lord's death."

Jesus' sacrificial death through crucifixion is the great and scandalous mystery of Christian faith. The word "sacrifice" has become synonymous with suffering and with the substitution of one life for another. Marcus Borg and John Dominic Crossan offer us a third way to experience the word, which literally comes from the Latin phrase *sacrum facere,* meaning "to make sacred."[1] Jesus' death made human life sacred in the face of the violence of human injustice. This is Jesus' proclamation at the Passover table that became his Last Supper with his disciples.

Following in the Passover tradition and the tradition of temple sacrifice of his time, Jesus proclaims that in an intentionally shared meal the presence of God's divine justice is imminent.[2] God is ultimately the one who sets the table of life, inviting us all as guests with equal status because we are made in God's image. When we eat this meal in a community that takes this to heart, we are invited to break open our lives for one another as we break the bread. We are invited to pour out our lives in covenant with one

---

2. This may be the most convoluted argument in the Pauline corpus. For a thoughtful discussion, see Jouette M. Bassler, "1 Corinthians," in *The Women's Bible Commentary,* ed. Carol Newsom and Sharon Ringe (Louisville, KY: Westminster John Knox Press, 1998), 411–19.

1. Marcus J. Borg and John Dominic Crossan, *The Last Week: What the Gospels Really Teach about Jesus's Final Days,* (San Francisco: HarperSanFrancisco, 2006), 37.
2. Ibid., 118.

1 Corinthians 11:23-26

Theological Perspective

(Josh. 3:1–4:7). The various feasts likewise preserve Israel's corporate identity (e.g., Lev. 23:34–43). Foremost in the memory of Israel was and is Passover, a complex weave of narrative, ritual, and memorial objects that continues to embrace each successive generation (see Deut. 6:20–23).

Likewise Paul was told, and now shares, Jesus' interpretation of his own identity in the evocative imagery associated with the seminal event of the Last Supper and its commemoration. His life was part of the ongoing story of God's deliverance of Israel, yet it was not just a part. Jesus recast the event for his followers in terms of his life.

In the complex of narrative, ritual, and physical objects, Christians join with and become part of the ongoing story of God's redemption, the center of which is Christ. This enables a different perspective on the question of Christ's presence in the Supper. The eucharistic controversies of the Middle Ages and the period of the Reformation brought about a reinterpretation of an earlier, threefold sense of the body of Christ. As the early theology of the Eucharist developed, a distinction was made between the *historical* body of Christ, now ascended, and the "*true* body" (*corpus verum*) of Christ gathered around the altar in memory of Jesus. The *sacramental* body on the altar connected these two, so the event of the historic body continues in the gathered body.

Several recent works in liturgical theology reference in this regard Augustine's declaration, "If, then, you are Christ's body and his members, it is your own mystery which you receive [in the sacrament]."[2] In time, with the argument over the nature of Christ's presence, the true and mystical body became conflated. The host became identified with Christ, at the expense of the church's identity; but the older emphasis is well worth heeding. Sharing in the memory of Christ's life by means of narrative and ritual acts utilizing the bread and wine, the people of God are made participants in the story and so the identity of Christ.

PHILIP E. THOMPSON

Pastoral Perspective

witness, through faith and works, to God's love, preparing the coming of his Kingdom and anticipating it. . . . All of us who take part in the Eucharist are called to discover, through this sacrament, the profound meaning of our actions in the world in favor of development and peace; and to receive from it the strength to commit ourselves ever more generously, following the example of Christ.[1]

The unity of Word and sacrament, Eucharist and social justice, can also prompt us to examine the commitments of our gathered worshiping community. Is it oriented primarily inwardly toward services to members, or is it outwardly focused on those outside church walls? Too often our congregations seem oriented almost exclusively inside, with a small outreach or benevolence budget and program filling in the leftover space. Here the irony is that the centrifugal force that sends us outward to build a more caring and just society produces an even more compelling centripetal force attracting new members and a greater depth of commitment by both new and existing members.

Working alongside others in Christian service to "the least of these" (Matt. 25:40) engages people and invites them to become more actively faithful at the center of the community as well. The orientation outward toward social justice produces greater inner strength in the life of the congregation. What better time than Holy Thursday, when we observe the Lord's Supper in its original setting, to remind our members of the crucial importance of our calling to look outward in service to the world?

This is, after all, Maundy Thursday, when Jesus introduced a "new" commandment (*mandatum*) to love one another (John 13:34) and expressed it in the extraordinary act of foot washing (John 13:3–11). Love has turned upside down the expected parts, as teacher becomes disciple and master becomes servant of all. Worldly standards of class and status are shattered, and we are called to follow the life of Christ.

GARY B. REIERSON

---

2. Augustine, "Sermon 272," in Mary Collins, *Worship: Renewal to Practice* (Washington, DC: Pastoral Press, 1987), 291.

1. John Paul II, *Sollicitudo Rei Socialis: On Social Concerns* (Vatican: The Holy See, December 30, 1987), no. 48, http://www.vatican.va/holy_father/john_paul_ii/encyclicals/ documents/hf_jp-ii_enc_30121987_sollicitudo-rei-socialis_en.html.

Exegetical Perspective

death (cf. Rom. 4:25; 8:32). Jesus' arrest, trial, and execution are not simply miscarriages of Roman justice. They are God's saving intention.

When the Lord Jesus takes bread, gives thanks for it, breaks it, and gives it to those at table with him, he not only follows the Passover Seder; he also radically reinterprets it as "my body that is for you" (v. 24). Although various early manuscripts try to harmonize Paul's version with the Gospels by adding "which is broken for you" or "which is given for you," neither is necessary. For Paul, Jesus' body is always the broken body of the crucified, and it is always for us.

So also, the language over the cup echoes the Seder and forces it beyond its normal meaning. The yearly remembrance of redemption in the exodus is transformed under the impact of Jesus' death into a weekly reminder of God's dawning cosmic victory over the forces of sin and death and a promise of the fulfillment to come. "This cup is the new covenant in my blood," he says (v. 25). The "new covenant" reminds biblically literate listeners of Jeremiah 31:31 (Luke 22:20; but cf. Matt. 26:28; Mark 14:24, where the covenant is not "new") and reinforces Paul's proclamation that, in Jesus' death and resurrection, God extends the covenant with Israel to Gentiles through Jesus' faithfulness.

Both bread and cup are "in remembrance" of Jesus. This is not merely cognitive memory; it is emphatically behavioral. It is akin to Israel's remembering God's law (Exod. 20:8; Judg. 8:34) and God's remembering the covenant (Gen. 9:15; Lev. 26:42; Ps. 137:7). For Israel, to remember is to obey God's command. For God, to remember is to rescue the covenant people. For Christians, to remember Jesus is to (re)appropriate the consequences of his death and resurrection, to know themselves as the body of Christ, to renounce their privilege for the sake of one another, to lay down their lives for the world as Christ did, to "wait for one another" at table (1 Cor. 11: 33), and to love one another as God loves them.[3]

E. ELIZABETH JOHNSON

Homiletical Perspective

another and with God as we pour out the wine and share the cup. As we eat this meal, we participate *with* Jesus in death and resurrection.

The preacher who leads the members of her community to the table on this night invites them to bring their whole lives to the feast. Through Paul's admonition to the Corinthians, she invites them to consider what is creating division in their hearts and the heart of their community. What is creating division in their own denomination? What is dividing the church universal? Her task is to name and acknowledge the divisions through the vulnerability of prayer and confession, so that transformation may occur.

The preacher can also consider what stories surround the central story of the evening. Stories illuminate one another as they are told in tandem. What other stories tell of God's justice in the face of human injustice? What other stories speak of God's actions in leading people from bondage into liberation? What other stories speak of the abundance of God that can feed the world with bread and love? Such stories may come from the salvation history of Scripture, from the lives of official and unofficial saints in history, and from the life of people from the gathered congregation. Their telling in worship may facilitate the sharing of lives, the sharing of the hopes and dreams of the community, as they seek to be faithful in covenant.

The hunger and thirst we bring to the Communion table on Holy Thursday is to remember our covenant with God and with one another. We long to have our hearts broken open, poured out, and transformed by this ritual meal. It is only when our hearts are broken and made vulnerable that they can be truly transformed through love. When Jesus offered his life to be broken and poured out for God's love and justice, his death was transformed to new life through the resurrection. This meal is the opportunity to empty ourselves as Jesus did on the cross, so that we too may be filled with the power of God's grace and love in resurrection.

JANE ANNE FERGUSON

---

3. For more on this, see Nils A. Dahl, "Anamnesis: Memory and Commemoration in Early Christianity," in *Jesus in the Memory of the Early Church* (Minneapolis: Augsburg, 1976), 11–29.

John 13:1-17, 31b-35

¹Now before the festival of the Passover, Jesus knew that his hour had come to depart from this world and go to the Father. Having loved his own who were in the world, he loved them to the end. ²The devil had already put it into the heart of Judas son of Simon Iscariot to betray him. And during supper ³Jesus, knowing that the Father had given all things into his hands, and that he had come from God and was going to God, ⁴got up from the table, took off his outer robe, and tied a towel around himself. ⁵Then he poured water into a basin and began to wash the disciples' feet and to wipe them with the towel that was tied around him. ⁶He came to Simon Peter, who said to him, "Lord, are you going to wash my feet?" ⁷Jesus answered, "You do not know now what I am doing, but later you will understand." ⁸Peter said to him, "You will never wash my feet." Jesus answered, "Unless I wash you, you have no share with me." ⁹Simon Peter said to him, "Lord, not my feet only but also my hands and my head!" ¹⁰Jesus said to him, "One who has bathed does not need to wash, except for the feet, but is entirely clean. And you are clean, though not all of you." ¹¹For he knew who was to betray him; for this reason he said, "Not all of you are clean."

Theological Perspective

This chapter marks the transition in John's Gospel from the activity of Jesus, which is done in light of the coming "hour," to the arrival of the hour itself, which is primarily understood as the hour of his crucifixion and death. All of the signs that Jesus does in the preceding chapters are meant to point to and be fulfilled in the coming of this hour. The arrival of the hour takes place just before the festival of the Passover, which leads us to think of the departure of Jesus to the Father in his death in light of the deliverance of Israel from Egypt.

Indeed, the death of Jesus will take place in John at the time that the Passover lamb is slain in the temple in Jerusalem. Just as the Israelites came from the promised land of Canaan and were departing from Egypt to return there, so Jesus knows that he has come from God and is departing to return home with God. Just as the deliverance of the Israelites from captivity in Egypt is the consummate expression of God's love for Israel, so John tells us that the return of Jesus to the Father in his death is the full and complete expression of his love for "his own."

By framing the coming of the hour in this way, John seems to invite the reader to think of the dramatically different ways the love of God is manifested in the exodus, compared to the way the love of God is said to be completely expressed in the death of Jesus.

Pastoral Perspective

Foot washing. Embarrassing, unusual, and, for most of the faithful, blessedly optional. Somehow, when Jesus says in the Synoptic Gospels, "Do this in remembrance of me," some liturgical traditions have decided it covers the whole evening and the Fourth Gospel. What exactly is it that we think we are doing when we wash feet? Lord knows we spend a lot of time worrying about how to do it. Heaven forbid we perform a liturgical act without thoroughly understanding why and how—but what are we doing?

The Gospel of John sends its usual mixed message, perplexing and challenging and wondrous at the same time. Ask Christians which is their "favorite" Gospel, and more than half will say, "John." To which I say, "Have you *read* it lately?" I know, I know, "God so loved the world" and all that; but read fully, and you may find yourself faced with more than you bargained for.

In the Fourth Gospel, Jesus is not baptized, institutes no Eucharist, and is entirely in control every moment, waiting until his hour has come, substituting a Farewell Discourse for agonizing prayer in Gethsemane, then marching forth to confront those who would betray and arrest him. At every moment in his trial, torture, and execution, Jesus remains ironically in charge, so much so that in the Fourth Gospel Jesus does not die, but declares that his work

¹²After he had washed their feet, had put on his robe, and had returned to the table, he said to them, "Do you know what I have done to you? ¹³You call me Teacher and Lord—and you are right, for that is what I am. ¹⁴So if I, your Lord and Teacher, have washed your feet, you also ought to wash one another's feet. ¹⁵For I have set you an example, that you also should do as I have done to you. ¹⁶Very truly, I tell you, servants are not greater than their master, nor are messengers greater than the one who sent them. ¹⁷If you know these things, you are blessed if you do them."...

³¹ᵇJesus said, "Now the Son of Man has been glorified, and God has been glorified in him. ³²If God has been glorified in him, God will also glorify him in himself and will glorify him at once. ³³Little children, I am with you only a little longer. You will look for me; and as I said to the Jews so now I say to you, 'Where I am going, you cannot come.' ³⁴I give you a new commandment, that you love one another. Just as I have loved you, you also should love one another. ³⁵By this everyone will know that you are my disciples, if you have love for one another."

Exegetical Perspective

On the night before the crucifixion, the disciples gathered with Jesus for supper. While the Synoptic Gospels remember this gathering as a celebration of Passover, John situates the meal "before the festival of the Passover" (v. 1). Both the Synoptics and John connect the meaning of Jesus' death with Passover, but John does so differently, by narrating the beginning of Passover at the moment Jesus is handed over to be crucified (19:14). For John, the focus of the Last Supper is not the meal, but the act of foot washing.

The opening verse declares the arrival of Jesus' "hour" (v. 1). By indicating that Jesus' hour has "not yet come" (2:4; 7:30; 8:20), John has led the reader to expect the arrival of Jesus' hour. In John, Jesus' hour is not only the moment of his crucifixion, but also includes the resurrection and ascension. The arrival of Jesus' hour in verse 1 links the foot-washing scene with the other events that form the culmination of Jesus' ministry.

The opening verse identifies the foot-washing scene as a paradigmatic example of Jesus' love. Jesus loves his own "to the end" (Gk.: *eis telos*). The Greek can also be translated "to the utmost." In each case, the phrase alludes to Jesus giving up his life in the crucifixion. However, it also introduces the foot-washing story and thus frames the foot washing as an

Homiletical Perspective

Preaching Holy Week is an invitation to trust the power of Scripture by staying within the narrative, because all the drama, tension, and resolution are already provided. Superlatives are not needed. Those who are coming to hear a sermon on Maundy Thursday, Good Friday, and Holy Saturday are coming to be engulfed in the mystery of our faith. Let the drama of this mystery unfold by sticking to a homiletic form that simply retells the story—uncorking a few key themes to let breathe when appropriate. In the story that follows, let us look at three themes that may be helpful to let breathe for those who have come to worship.

The first theme is *time* itself. The story opens with John suggesting that Jesus knew that his "hour" had come. This hour marks the end of Jesus' public ministry, and at the same time begins Jesus' private ministry to his disciples. From here on out, Jesus is preparing those he loves for his hour of glory. Take note that, in John's account, this hour begins not with the Passover feast, as it does in the Synoptic tradition, but in the ordinary meal at the end of the day before Passover. In other words, this hour begins with an ordinary meal, on an ordinary day in time.

When you prepare the sermon, consider that many of the people arriving to worship on Maundy Thursday may be coming in from "an hour" off for

John 13:1-17, 31b-35

Theological Perspective

The love of God is revealed to Israel by the way God sees the misery of God's people in Egypt, hears their cry in their afflictions, knows their sufferings, and comes down to deliver them, to bring them to the land of promise, where they are to dwell in peace (Exod. 3:7–10). In the process, God hands over to death the enemies of God's own people who oppress and afflict them (Exod. 15:21). Because the Israelites know that the love of God acts in this way, they can call on God in their own afflictions, confident that God will see their affliction, hear their cry, know their suffering, and come down to deliver them from death by handing those who oppress them over to death (Ps. 57:3). The faithful know that God loves them when they are freed from death and look in triumph on those who oppressed them (Ps. 59:10).

The works Jesus does leading up to the hour of his death seem to express the love of God according to the pattern of the exodus, culminating in the raising of Lazarus from the power of death, the last sign Jesus performs before entering into Jerusalem. The raising of Lazarus would be an understandable expression of God's love as it was known to the Jews from the exodus. It therefore comes as a complete and horrifying surprise, both to the disciples and to us, that Jesus in fact has a radically different understanding of love, one that does not deliver its own from the power of death, but rather one that freely, voluntarily, and completely offers itself to death, leaving his followers helpless in the face of their own inevitable death at the hands of those who hate them. "Indeed, an hour is coming when those who kill you will think that by doing so they are offering worship to God" (John 16:2).

The complete expression of God's love does not look like love at all, but rather looks like the experience of the Israelites under the wrath of God. Given this radically different idea of love, it is no wonder that the arrival of the hour has the effect of repelling the closest followers of Jesus away from him, seen in the predictions that Judas will betray Jesus and that Peter will deny him. Even when the disciples confess that Jesus has come from the Father and is returning to the Father, Jesus knows that they do not have any idea what this means, for when they see this return enacted in his death, they will all abandon him and leave him alone (John 16:31–32).

Just as Jesus has a radically different understanding of love, he also has a radically different understanding of power and authority. The reader is told that Jesus knows that "the Father had given all things into his hands" (v. 3). One would expect this to mean

Pastoral Perspective

is completed, bows his head, and gives up his spirit, a spirit no one can take from him, a spirit his Father will give to us all.

Only in John do we have the scene we read on this holy night. In the other Gospels Jesus serves—feeds, heals, and exorcises. In John Jesus strips, kneels, and washes—not himself but his followers—and tells them to do the same for each other. Here Jesus acts out the christological hymn we love in Philippians 2, taking the form of a servant. As Jeremy Taylor wrote of Jesus some 350 years ago:

> And he chose to wash their feet rather than their head, that he might have the opportunity of a more humble posture, and a more apt signification of his charity. Thus God lays everything aside, that he may serve his servants; heaven stoops to earth, and one abyss calls upon another, and the miseries of [humanity], which were next to infinite, are excelled by a mercy equal to the immensity of God.[1]

There is a second question on many minds this night, parallel to the question of what we think we are doing. It is Jesus' own question: Do you know what I have done for you? For once, the disciples have sense enough not to answer, learning along the way that Jesus asks tricky questions.

Do you know what I have done for you? If we cannot answer that question, or at least try to answer it, how can we know what we think we are doing, not only with basin and towel but with bread and wine? Jesus admonishes his followers to "do as I have done to you" (v. 15). Unless we understand what that is, how can we imitate it?

Do you know what I have done for you? That is a question for tonight, tomorrow, and Saturday. It is a question for every day. The "saving" work of Christ, what Jesus has done and does for us always, is not just about the cross. It is about the birth and the baptism, the teaching and the healing, the body and the blood, the basin and the towel, the life and the death.

So we ask again, do we know what Jesus has done for us? What exactly do we think we are doing? If our washing and eating and drinking mean anything, they respond to Jesus' question and to his command, not only to wash one another's feet, but to love one another as Jesus has loved us.

We get confused about what this loving service looks like and what it means, mistaking pious imitation for discipleship. The Fourth Gospel does help us here, as the author chooses a provocatively loaded

---

1. *The Whole Works of Jeremy Taylor* (London: Longman, Brown, 1856), 2:628–29.

act of Jesus' love. (By closing with the command to love in v. 34, the lectionary heightens this effect.)

The Greek word for love here is *agapaō*. It is a common mistake to characterize this love as being sharply different from *phileō*, the love of friendship. John uses the terms as synonyms. For example, both verbs are used to speak of God's love of Jesus (e.g., 3:35; 5:20). The lexical distinction is not important to John. Here it is the act of washing the disciples' feet that sheds light on the nature of Jesus' love.

Jesus' act of washing the disciples' feet is one that first-century people would have understood as an act of humility and service. The detailed description of Jesus' actions in verses 4–5 draws attention to the role of a slave that he assumes. The conversation with Peter has a similar effect (vv. 6–10). Peter seems to find Jesus' acts improper. He twice resists being washed (vv. 6, 8), until Jesus tells him he will have no "share" with Jesus unless he is washed (v. 8). The particular word "share" (Gk.: *meros*) is not used frequently in John. It resonates with Jesus' words later in the Farewell Discourse, that he goes to prepare a "place" for the disciples in his Father's house (14:2–3), as well as with the more frequent instruction to "abide" with Jesus (e.g., 15:4–7). Peter must receive Jesus' love and service in order to remain a disciple.

Jesus' act is further defined by the inclusion of Judas in the foot-washing scene. John points out from the beginning that Judas is included in this group (v. 2). Jesus' foreknowledge of Judas's betrayal is noted explicitly in v. 11. With full knowledge of coming events, and at the moment of his "hour," Jesus washes the feet of his betrayer. Jesus' love, as it is defined through the foot washing, includes one who poses a threat to his life.

The disciples are meant to follow Jesus' example. Jesus' words explicitly indicate that they ought to wash one another's feet (v. 15). He also qualifies the command to "love one another" with the words "just as I have loved you" (v. 34). Christian love emulates the love of Jesus, and in chapter 13 that love centers on the foot washing. Some interpreters have understood the command to "love one another" (vv. 34, 35) as parochial, being directed only toward other Christians. However, although Jesus' paradigmatic act of love is directed toward his own disciples, the inclusion of Judas suggests that love of "one another" cannot be limited only to an enclave of believers. In their context, versees 34–35 identify love as the defining characteristic of those who follow Jesus, but do not pose limitations on the recipients of that love.

lunch, or an hour after work, whenever the service happens to be. For many it will be a typical Thursday. Nothing at work, or in their culture, is altered or set aside. It is an ordinary day as far as their life goes; but people will come. They will come burdened with lists of things to do, pressures at work, distractions at home, but also with the hope that something prayed, or sung, or preached may charge their ordinary "hour" with an extraordinary event of revelation.

This is an opportunity to enter the pulpit with their same hope of expectation. For those gathered on Maundy Thursday, knowing or unknowing, all are walking into an hour in which Jesus shows all who love him the mission and strategy of the church's love for the world.

Thus, a second theme may be to explore this mission and strategy of Jesus as symbolized in his washing the disciples' feet. Jesus is preparing his disciples for his hour by showing them what glory looks like in the kingdom of God. The lesson and significance of Jesus, the Son of God, washing the feet of his disciples encapsulates the mission of all who will follow after him. At the same time, this act is meant to show the strategy of the mission: "If I, your Lord and Teacher, have washed your feet, you also ought to wash one another's feet" (v. 14).

In the foot washing, like the incarnation, the method is the message. In the washing of the disciples' feet Jesus chooses to empty himself rather than to promote himself. This act of humble service and submission is the church's model of mission into the world, the means by which God's "glory'" will be experienced by all who will follow after Jesus has gone to the Father. The genius of this strategy is that everyone can do it—whatever rank, title, gender, or race—all can serve another. If we did, this strategy would allow God's glory to shine into every life. Hence this foot washing is more than a humble act of deference; it is a sermon to the world about how to love. The significance of this silent sermon of Jesus is not lost on his disciples.

Thus, a third theme that may be worth exploring is in Peter's response of protest: "Jesus, you will never wash my feet" (v. 8). It may be important to remember that Peter is coming off the excitement of Jesus' triumphant entry into Jerusalem (John 12:12–19). This band of brothers have been firsthand witness to seven different signs signifying that Jesus is "the Messiah, the Son of God, the one coming into the world" (John 11:27). Their anticipation for Jesus to fulfill his identity by putting the world to rights and raising Israel from the ash heap is electric. As they enter

John 13:1-17, 31b-35

Theological Perspective

that Jesus would have "dominion and glory and king-ship, that all peoples, nations, and languages should serve him" (Dan. 7:14). However, Jesus completely contradicts this expectation, acting as the slave of his disciples by washing their feet as they recline at table. Peter refuses to accept this act of slavery on the part of Jesus—"You will never wash my feet" (v. 8)—echoing the way he rejects the prediction that Jesus is going to Jerusalem to suffer and die (Matt. 16:22). How can the one who is equal to God (John 5:18), who says of himself, "I AM" (John 13:19), be the one who acts as the slave of his closest followers?

Jesus knows that none of this can be understood by those who claim to be his followers; it can only be lived. Hence he does not tell us how power and authority can be so humble; rather, he commands us to wash one another's feet, so that we also might experience the power of voluntary humility and slavery (v. 15). He does not explain how the love of God can be completely expressed by the offer of his life unto death; rather, he commands us to love one another the way he loves us (v. 34). However, we will never understand how this is love, and will only come to believe it the more we, like Peter, are taken captive by those who hate us and led in solitude to our own death (John 21:18–19).

RANDALL C. ZACHMAN

Pastoral Perspective

term to describe Jesus' action as he and his disciples sat at table for a private farewell dinner, with no servant to wash their feet. It is not hard to imagine the disciples looking warily at each other and thinking, "One of you guys do it. I'm not doing it."

So Jesus "got up from the table," literally, "arose"—the same Greek term used by John in 5:8 to describe Jesus' command to the paralytic and in 2:20 proleptically to describe Jesus' own rising, the term that Luke uses in the passion predictions and Easter account (24:6) to describe Jesus' resurrection. This getting up from table, taking basin and towel, was not an act of weakness, but an act of powerful and empowering service, on the night of the betrayal, nothing less than a foretaste of the resurrection.

"As often as you eat this bread and drink the cup, you proclaim the Lord's death until he comes" (1 Cor. 11:26). As often as we stumble or shuffle our way to the basin and the towel, we claim the power of loving service, as sure a foretaste of what it means to love one another as the bread and wine are a taste of heaven.

Tonight powerful feelings are set loose in the church: sorrow, loss, regret, even fear, in all likelihood; but also the powerful feelings set loose by Jesus: commitment, conviction, and determination. God, as Jeremy Taylor reminds us, "lays everything aside" tonight. It might not be a bad idea for the gathered faithful to reflect on what they in turn might set aside, and what they might lift up.

WILLIAM F. BROSEND

Exegetical Perspective

The language of the passage suggests that following the example of Jesus' love is an act of service to God and to Jesus. The language of verse 16, "servants are not greater than their master," can also be translated "slaves are not greater than their Lord." The metaphor of slavery to God is a conventional one (e.g., Rom. 1:1). The "slave of God" is one who, being owned by God, is wholly devoted to the service of God. In following Jesus' act of foot washing, the disciples would also take on the role of a slave in relation to the one whose feet are being washed, but Jesus' words reframe the act as service to God.

In addition to being an act of love, the washing of feet relates to the "cleanness" of Jesus' disciples. Peter's third objection to having his feet washed changes tactics. He no longer refuses to be washed, but suggests that Jesus should wash all of him: hands and head as well as feet (v. 9). Jesus responds, "One who has bathed does not need to wash, but is entirely clean. And you are clean, though not all of you" (v. 10).

This saying has two potential meanings. On the level of the story, Peter would probably understand Jesus to be saying that Peter is clean, although not all parts of his body. Thus it makes sense for Jesus to wash only his feet. The narrator's aside (v. 11) indicates a second meaning to the statement, that the disciples are "clean" except for Judas. In either case, the point of the foot washing is not to render one clean. (If it were, it should have the same effect on Judas.) It points the reader back to the foot washing as an act of humble service and love, one that disciples of Jesus should both receive and perform.

SUSAN E. HYLEN

Homiletical Perspective

Jerusalem for Passover, they see that the masses have gathered with all the energy, hype, and exultation due a conquering hero. However, Jesus washing their feet is anything but kingly. This is not the glory modeled by Caesar or Herod, and certainly not the glory Peter has anticipated for the long-awaited Messiah!

Peter's response suggests he has his own vision or agenda of what Jesus should do and be—for Peter's fate is linked to that of Jesus. After three years of being taught, tested, and tried by Jesus, the rewards of glory are just in sight for him. The hour of Jesus' triumph is also the hour when Peter anticipates the rise of his own status. Peter's protest resembles ours, whenever we are confronted with a Jesus who does not serve our expectations or fulfill our desires. Peter's protest is the seed in the heart of betrayal. Thus Jesus says to him, "Unless I wash you, you have no share with me" (v. 8). It may be that Jesus' response to Peter is intended not only for him, but for all whose hearts are tempted to ignore the revelation of God that shines in the darkness.

The witness of Jesus is as counterintuitive as the instinct to power and privilege is subverted. This subversion, however, is the way of love and the mark of a true disciple: "I give you a new commandment, that you love one another. Just as I have loved you, you should love one another. By this everyone will know that you are my disciples, if you have love for one another" (John 13:34–35).

This is the choice faced by all who have gathered to follow Jesus in his hour.

TRYGVE DAVID JOHNSON

Isaiah 52:13-53:12

^{52:13}See, my servant shall prosper;
  he shall be exalted and lifted up,
  and shall be very high.
¹⁴Just as there were many who were astonished at him
  —so marred was his appearance, beyond human semblance,
  and his form beyond that of mortals—
¹⁵so he shall startle many nations;
  kings shall shut their mouths because of him;
 for that which had not been told them they shall see,
  and that which they had not heard they shall contemplate.
^{53:1}Who has believed what we have heard?
  And to whom has the arm of the LORD been revealed?
 ²For he grew up before him like a young plant,
  and like a root out of dry ground;
 he had no form or majesty that we should look at him,
  nothing in his appearance that we should desire him.
 ³He was despised and rejected by others;
  a man of suffering and acquainted with infirmity;
 and as one from whom others hide their faces
  he was despised, and we held him of no account.

 ⁴Surely he has borne our infirmities
  and carried our diseases;
 yet we accounted him stricken,
  struck down by God, and afflicted.
 ⁵But he was wounded for our transgressions,
  crushed for our iniquities;
 upon him was the punishment that made us whole,
  and by his bruises we are healed.

Theological Perspective

Isaiah 53 has been called "probably the most contested chapter in the Old Testament."[1] It is one of the four Servant Songs identified in Second Isaiah (42:1–4; 49:1–6; 50:4–9; 52:13–53:12) describing "my servant" (49:3) in both his humiliation and exaltation. Of the twenty occurrences of "servant" in Isaiah 40–55, thirteen most clearly identify the "servant of the LORD" with Israel. The seven remaining occurrences are in the Servant Songs, and the interpretive issue is who is meant in these passages.

The two interpretive poles have been a collective and an individual interpretation. Israel is called "my servant" (41:8–9; 49:3). So the figure could represent Israel, as a king embodies his people or as conceived in the concept of "corporate personality."

1. Brevard S. Childs, *Isaiah*, Old Testament Library (Louisville, KY: Westminster John Knox Press, 2001), 410.

Pastoral Perspective

While it is customary to preach from the Gospel reading on Good Friday (John 19 overflows with choice texts), one cannot find a better outline of the passion narratives than this fourth Servant Song of Isaiah. Through the use of this wrenchingly beautiful poem in Isaiah, we may begin to undermine those charges of anti-Judaism with which we have for many years been particularly besieged during Holy Week. Such has often been the pressure that one felt compelled to make a hundred disclaimers before publicly reading one of the Gospel narratives. Be careful, for the use of this text provides an implicit, not an explicit, benefit.

Here is a pastoral opportunity not to be overlooked. The stories of Jesus' crucifixion are embedded with descriptions of this Servant: "He was despised and rejected by others; a man of suffering. . . . He was oppressed, and he was afflicted,

⁶All we like sheep have gone astray;
   we have all turned to our own way,
   and the LORD has laid on him
   the iniquity of us all.

⁷He was oppressed, and he was afflicted,
   yet he did not open his mouth;
   like a lamb that is led to the slaughter,
   and like a sheep that before its shearers is silent,
   so he did not open his mouth.
⁸By a perversion of justice he was taken away.
   Who could have imagined his future?
   For he was cut off from the land of the living,
   stricken for the transgression of my people.
⁹They made his grave with the wicked
   and his tomb with the rich,
   although he had done no violence,
   and there was no deceit in his mouth.

¹⁰Yet it was the will of the LORD to crush him with pain.
   When you make his life an offering for sin,
   he shall see his offspring, and shall prolong his days;
   through him the will of the LORD shall prosper.
¹¹ Out of his anguish he shall see light;
   he shall find satisfaction through his knowledge.
   The righteous one, my servant, shall make many righteous,
   and he shall bear their iniquities.
¹²Therefore I will allot him a portion with the great,
   and he shall divide the spoil with the strong;
   because he poured out himself to death,
   and was numbered with the transgressors;
   yet he bore the sin of many,
   and made intercession for the transgressors.

Exegetical Perspective

These fifteen lines, known as the fourth Servant Song, are among the most compelling and controversial in the Hebrew Bible. Christians have long understood these verses to predict the coming of Jesus the Messiah and, as a result, the passage is read on Good Friday as a reference to Jesus' suffering and crucifixion. While this understanding of this passage makes sense in the context of the passion narratives, it is our purpose to gain the perspective of the author and culture from which the Isaiah passage comes. In so doing, we enrich our understanding of not only Isaiah 52:13–53:12 but also its relation to Good Friday.

We begin by noting that the Suffering Servant of our passage is associated with the appearance of the Servant ('ebed) in other parts of Second Isaiah. Scholars generally agree that the book of Isaiah can be divided into two, possibly three, distinct parts that represent different historical periods. First Isaiah

Homiletical Perspective

Isaiah's Suffering Servant, who on Good Friday can be no one other than Jesus, provides an important counterbalance to John's account of the crucifixion. Some who come to church on Good Friday find John's proclamation of Christ's crucifixion as victory—with no agony in the garden and an intentional downplaying of the indignities heaped upon Jesus by his enemies—difficult, even painful, to hear and embrace. This Jesus is too far removed from these worshipers' experience. Some years, this may be a corporate rather than an individual experience, as the circumstances that surround Good Friday worship—whether in the faith community or in the world—make all too true John's assertion that the world cannot see Christ's crucifixion as God's ultimate victory. Proclaiming victory comes across as hollow, empty, unauthentic, even inappropriate.

Isaiah 52:13–53:12

Theological Perspective

But since the Servant here has a mission to Israel, this personification could refer to a king or a prophet. Many biblical figures, such as Moses, a prophet, even King Cyrus of Persia, or the writer of Second Isaiah, have been suggested. If the Servant is an individual, is he historical or someone still to come? By heightening the individualization of the figure, is the writer looking for one who would come to embody more fully who the Lord's Servant should be? So questions throng about the identity of the Servant in this passage.

Traditionally, the church has seen the Servant of this passage as fulfilled in Jesus Christ. This is why the passage is particularly appropriate as a reading for Good Friday. Scholars have debated whether the Servant figure was in the "mind of Jesus" and whether this shaped his ministry. Images from the Isaiah Servant Songs are found at points in the New Testament (e.g., John 12:37–40) and the Suffering Servant concept is alluded to in the early New Testament church (1 Pet. 2:18–24). When the Ethiopian eunuch inquired of Philip about the identity of the Servant in Isaiah (53:7; Acts 8:26–40), Philip "began to speak, and starting with this scripture, he proclaimed to him the good news about Jesus" (8:35).

Theologically the early church and the church till now view Jesus Christ as the appropriate figure to be described by this Servant Song, regardless of what was in the mind of the Second Isaiah or what theories as to the Servant's identity, otherwise, are offered. There is a "fuller sense" to the poetics of Second Isaiah than the writer knew or than was carried out by whatever figure might have been originally intended or, if the intention was Israel, collectively. This has been the Christian church's appropriation of the passage, seeing in it a description of the life and ministry and work of Jesus of Nazareth as Jesus the Christ, whom the church confesses as the "suffering servant of God."

The uniqueness of this passage, among the other Servant Songs, is that the Servant carries or bears the "iniquity of us all" when all "like sheep have gone astray" (53:6). He was "wounded for our transgressions, crushed for our iniquities; upon him was the punishment that made us whole" (53:5). He "bore the sin of many, and made intercession for the transgressors" (53:12). As one scholar put it, the Servant "not only encountered and accepted suffering in the course of his work; in the final phase suffering became the means whereby he accomplished his work, and was effective in the salvation of others."[2]

2. *Interpreter's Dictionary of the Bible*, ed. George A. Buttrick (Nashville: Abingdon Press, 1962), 4:294.

Pastoral Perspective

yet he did not open his mouth. . . . They made his grave with the wicked and his tomb with the rich; although he had done no violence, and there was no deceit in his mouth." The references are pointed. Yes, we can argue that the Gospel writers had the Servant Songs beside them as they composed their narratives. What they had beside them were their Scriptures— their holy Scriptures that became our Scriptures also. After all, these were Jews, writing about the extraordinary life, death, and resurrection of a Jew. What could have been more natural—or faithful and inspired—than to use their own Scriptures to help them describe those awe-full, degrading, and miraculous events of Good Friday and Easter?

This Servant Song is redolent also with what we might call New Testament theology—or at least the theology and interpretation that undergird the New Testament understanding of Jesus' crucifixion and resurrection. The first verse of the text, before describing the suffering, the vicarious atonement, the death and burial of the Servant, says that this Servant will prosper and be lifted up, exalted. These words call to mind Paul's letter to the Philippian Christians when he ends his own "servant song" about the suffering and self-emptying of Jesus: "Therefore God also highly exalted him and gave him the name that is above every name" (Phil. 2:9).

Then there is Paul's letter to Corinth, with his meditation on wisdom and power. In that letter he declares that "God chose what is foolish in the world to shame the wise; God chose what is weak in the world to shame the strong; God chose what is low and despised in the world . . . to reduce to nothing things that are, so that no one might boast in the presence of God" (1 Cor. 1:27–29). The Servant in Isaiah "shall startle many nations; kings shall shut their mouths because of him" (Isa. 52:15).

Finally there is the pivot of the entire passage, which comes twice. It is the claim that keeps this Servant from simply being one more victim in a world of victims: "[for] we accounted him stricken, struck down by God and afflicted" (53:4), or again, "Yet it was the will of the LORD to crush him with pain" (53:10). This point is emphasized by Paul Hanson when he writes:

> The servant was not a pawn in the hands of an arbitrary god but one who committed himself freely to a deliberate course of action. Not a victim of circumstances, not a pathetic casualty in the ruthless atrocities that have always been part of human existence, but one who willingly and obediently followed the vision of God's order of righteousness in

Exegetical Perspective

(chaps. 1–39) is understood to come predominately from the original prophet and can be dated to the last half of the eighth century BCE.

Isaiah 40–66 constitutes Second Isaiah, which was likely produced in the late exilic and early postexilic period (ca. 550–500 BCE). Some scholars identify chaps. 56–66 as Third Isaiah. It is the context of the exile and early postexilic period that helps to explain the content and focus of our Good Friday passage. As literature formed in the crucible of exile and its attendant traumas and disappointments, Second Isaiah struggles to understand the tragedies in the recent past.

The period subsequent to the Babylonian invasion and destruction of Jerusalem and its temple (ca. 586 BCE) was the most traumatic period in Israelite history and a time of intense self-reflection, both personal and communal. In sorting out what had happened, many among the remnant of Judah immediately questioned why the catastrophe had occurred. Survivors had witnessed unspeakable horror, made worse because the events surrounding Jerusalem's destruction seemed to abrogate God's covenant with the Davidic dynasty and with God's own children. Among answers to the painful questions raised by Jerusalem's downfall, some blamed the lack of righteousness among her citizens. Others raised questions about God's faithfulness, while others, like our text, sought to see in the suffering of Jerusalem and her people some redeeming quality.

The identity of the Suffering Servant in our passage is unclear and irresoluble. In Jewish interpretation some take "him" (the noun *'ebed* is grammatically masculine) to represent all Jews, while others see in the Servant a righteous minority within Judah. In contrast, some in Jewish tradition have made the case that the Servant is an individual, who has been identified alternately as Jeremiah, Moses, and the Messiah. In reality, the text never identifies the Servant, and Christian tradition saw in him an adumbration of Jesus' own suffering.

In the initial speech, God emphasizes the Servant's reversal of fate. In 52:13 God announces the exultation of the Servant that will follow his humiliation. The announcement uses three distinct terms, exalted (*yarum*), lifted (*nissa'*), and high (*gavah*). The repetition reinforces the elevation of the Servant and highlights the utter change in his fortunes. Clearly, for Christian readers, the threefold exultation resonates with the doctrine of the Trinity, and the irony of the Servant's exultation coming on the heels of humiliation would be familiar. Jews in the exilic and postexilic period would have hoped for just such a reversal of their own fortunes. In verse 15 we are told that the

Homiletical Perspective

On those occasions, we do not need the Christ who controls every event, from the garden to the cross, asserts before Pilate his supremacy in the world, hands over his spirit, and declares his work accomplished. Instead, we need the Jesus who, in the words of Isaiah, "was despised and rejected by others; a man of suffering [sorrows] and acquainted with infirmity, . . . [who] has borne our infirmities and carried our diseases" (53:3–4). Though distinct from us in terms of his innocent life and total service to God, this Jesus is one with all people in suffering and sorrow.

Some would argue that the best way to proclaim the Jesus described in Isaiah's Servant Song is not with a sermon. Better to ensure that the passage is read well, so that the congregation experiences its extraordinary power of sound, balance, and contrast. The reading, then, becomes the sermon, as the Servant's participation in our suffering and sorrow becomes palpable, and allusions to Christ's passion reverberate through the room for those with ears to hear.

Alternatively, an effective Good Friday sermon might name ways that Christ bears our infirmities, carries our diseases, and heals us by his bruises. In other words, the sermon will move from a theological treatment of atonement to address Christ's sharing the people's specific suffering and acute sorrow. As a third approach, the Good Friday sermon might make allusions to Christ's passion explicit. Preparing this kind of sermon might involve less formal study and more prayerful and repeated reading of the passage, while remaining attentive to the details of Christ's life, particularly his passion, that can be teased out of one's biblical imagination. The form of such a sermon might be a meditative exposition, with descriptive vignettes from Jesus' passion providing explanations of verses of Isaiah's song.

For example, the references to the *young plant* and *root* (53:2) recall the promised shoot that will come out from the stump of Jesse, on whom the spirit of the Lord will rest (Isa. 11:1–2). This shoot will be weak and inconspicuous, like a baby lying in a manger, a criminal dying on a cross, and countless faithful who seek to do God's will in the world. Like many who hear this sermon, the Servant experiences the unendurable affliction of being rejected by one's own people, as Jesus was in his hometown and again when those he came to save railed, "Crucify him!" That the Servant "did not open his mouth" recalls both Synoptic accounts of Jesus before the high priest and countless victims of injustice who cannot claim their voices.

The comparison to a lamb that is led to the slaughter is Passover language (53:7). "By a perversion of

Isaiah 52:13–53:12

Theological Perspective

While this passage is rich in images about the work of the Servant, for Good Friday, three theological focuses stand out in describing the Servant as Jesus Christ.

Carries Our Pains. We are familiar with verse 4 in the King James Version: "Surely he hath borne our griefs and carried our sorrows." The Hebrew terms here convey a range of meanings: sickness, weakness, pain, suffering. These point to the fullness of the identification of the Servant with the people, with us. The grim realities of our lives are absorbed and carried by the Sufferer. This is the "miracle," the astounding assertion that reaches us at our deepest levels. All the things wrong with us are carried by the one who suffers for us and with us. Theologically, this is the incarnation, God becoming a human being in Jesus Christ. On this day, the identification of God and humans is so complete—and so personal—that all the griefs and sorrows and pains and sicknesses that are *ours*, are also *his*. He carries our pains so we do not bear them alone. The Servant takes what is ours and makes it his.

Wounded for Our Transgressions. The Servant is thus "wounded for our transgressions, crushed for our iniquities" (v. 5). Beyond our afflictions is our deepest problem, our sin. What separates us from God and all our ways of countering God in our lives—this wounds and crushes and bruises and pierces the Sufferer. In one translation: "But it was our sins that did that to him, that ripped and tore and crushed him— *our sins!*" (*The Message*). This is what the Servant does for us that we cannot do for ourselves. This is the way he saves us from our worst situation, our living contrary to the God who loves us. Israel heard prophetic voices calling for lives and a society in accord with God's will. We hear the same voices. Now we find that through the Sufferer, this way of life is possible. The Sufferer is wounded and crushed "for us."

Healed by His Bruises. By these wounds of the Sufferer, "we are healed." This is what we need for our lives now, the healing that can bring wholeness to the lives in which our sin is forgiven. The work of the Sufferer is ongoing. Our reconciliation with God is the "medicine" we need. Its effects are to bring "healing" or "salvation," the fullness of life God intends us to have, with God and with others. The Sufferer brings fullness by making us new persons, healed from the wound of our sin by his own wounds. By his "bruises" we can be made whole.

DONALD K. MCKIM

Pastoral Perspective

defiance of all worldly wisdom and human cowardice. Such was the Servant who chose to make his life an instrument God's healing.[1]

While it may have been the will of the Lord to bruise him (the old translation), it was the willingness of the Servant to pour himself out to death that makes this startling—to kings as well as to us. This makes Good Friday a day to startle the powers that be with the claims of reality that we find in this fourth Servant Song. This same reality became Jesus the Messiah, the one we say was born of a woman as is every child, and yet was born of God's spirit as is no other child.[2]

He is the one who grew to maturity and healed the sick, preached the kingdom of God through repentance and forgiveness, calmed the storm, and cast out demons as fierce as Legion. However, when the time came for him to be handed over, to be delivered up, Jesus did not raise the sword in his defense or call upon legions of angels. Rather, as he hung dying on the cross, he said with simplicity, "Father, forgive them; for they do not know what they are doing" (Luke 23:34). Bystanders cursed him, mocked him, and spat upon him. So God declared that at the name of Jesus, every knee should bow and every tongue "confess that Jesus is Lord [and Caesar is not], to the glory of God the Father" (Phil. 2:11).

Here is the good news of Good Friday. Here is God in the flesh. Here is the counternarrative to the world's tired old narrative that might makes right, and that those who live by the sword will really live. Not so, says the Lord of Hosts; not so, says YHWH; not so, says Jesus; but Jesus says it, not in prophetic word, but in prophetic deed. The mouths of kings have been shut in wonder (and often in rage) ever since.

O. BENJAMIN SPARKS

---

1. Paul D. Hanson, *Isaiah 40–66* (Louisville, KY: John Knox Press, 1995), 160.
2. *A Declaration of Faith* (Presbyterian Church in the United States, 1977), 6.

Servant's elevation will come as a shock to the rest of the world. Clearly, in the exilic and postexilic experience of ancient Jews, any such elevation would have been as surprising to them as to foreigners.

In 53:1–11a we read an amazed observer's reflections on the Servant. The observer declares unbelievable the events he has witnessed. In verse 3 he notes that the Servant was "despised, rejected" and "a man of suffering." The perspective articulated in verses 4–6 is perhaps the most remarkable part of our passage. The author suggests that the Servant's suffering serves a positive purpose. To the modern and Christian ear, this notion hardly seems unusual; but within the biblical idiom, it is new. The author makes this claim in several ways, but verse 5 is the most moving: "But he was wounded for our transgressions, crushed for our iniquities; upon him was the punishment that made us whole, and by his bruises we are healed."

Again, to the modern ear, verses 4–6 seem obviously to suggest the notion of vicarious suffering of the Servant and consequent restoration for a community. This notion would be entirely new to the Hebrew Bible, and we might be meant to understand that rather than suffering alone, the Servant innocently suffers along with his community. While the latter idea is more in keeping with ancient Israelite understanding of corporate guilt and punishment, clearly Christian tradition understands the Servant's suffering to be vicarious.

In verse 7, "like a lamb that is led to the slaughter" resonates closely with Jeremiah 11:19 and has encouraged some to identify the Servant with that prophet. More to the point, in verses 7–10 the text makes frequent and varied references to death. The Hebrew Bible often uses such references as hyperbolic ways of describing distress (e.g., Psalm 18:5–6; Jonah 2:2). Because the Servant is delivered from his fate at the end of the episode, the notion that he has actually died would be unique in the Hebrew Bible.

As the fourth Servant Song concludes, we learn that the Servant's merit lies in exposing himself to death, bearing the guilt of many, and making intercession for sinners. Clearly, to the degree that one understands this Servant Song in the context in which it was written, it provides a moving account of tragedy and redemption of a Servant, group, or community that was as good as dead. The continuing frustration of subjugation and oppression over the next five hundred years would make Jewish Christians turn anew to Isaiah 52:13–53:11 to understand a new and equally remarkable resurrection that was to be the final victory in a long history of death and catastrophe.

LARRY L. LYKE

justice he was taken away" (53:8) is a fitting description of Jesus' trial and what too frequently happens to people throughout the world. Some versions translate 53:5 as "he was pierced for our transgressions," bringing to mind that "one of the soldiers pierced his side with a spear, and at once blood and water came out" (John 19:34). That "the LORD has laid on him the iniquity of us all" (53:6) suggests the cross laid on Jesus and, in fact, is Christian kerygma for God handing over the Son to death (Matt. 17:22; John 18:30, 35). "They made his grave with the wicked" (53:9) suggests the place of crucifixion and the criminals crucified on either side of Jesus. That "his tomb [was] with the rich" (53:9) points to Joseph from Arimathea, a rich man who took the body of Jesus, wrapped it in a clean linen cloth, and laid it in his own new tomb (Matt. 27:57–60). The Jesus evoked by Isaiah's Suffering Servant joins humanity in suffering and sorrow, then and now.

The reason Isaiah's Servant Song is so powerful and moving may not be its allusions to Christ's passion or its proclamation of the Servant sharing our suffering and sorrow. Instead, this song may be so profound because Isaiah gives us words and a voice with which to respond to Jesus' crucifixion and death. While the opening verses (52:13–15) are spoken by God and announce the Servant's victory, which results from his obedience to God's wise plan of salvation, the speaker abruptly changes from God to express startled reaction to the Servant's fate (53:1).

Here Scripture gives voice to the shock, bewilderment, disbelief, shame, and hope that we often experience when we enter into a reading of Christ's passion and a ritual such as the adoration of the cross. Moreover, who can hear 53:4–6 without recalling disciples that flee, Peter who denies, and our own complicity in and guilt over Jesus' death? We confess that we are responsible for Jesus' suffering and sorrow. We also confess that Jesus endured our suffering and that his obedience gives us new life. Like the author, we cannot turn away from the cross and yet cannot face the tremendous suffering and sorrow of the Servant. Again and again we return to gaze at the cross and can only repeat Isaiah's words. Ultimately, we cling to Isaiah's final declaration, again spoken by God (53:10–11), who announces resurrection, worldwide renewal, and the Servant's sharing his goodness with us, God's suffering, sinful people.

CRAIG A. SATTERLEE

Psalm 22

¹My God, my God, why have you forsaken me?
　Why are you so far from helping me, from the words of my groaning?
²O my God, I cry by day, but you do not answer;
　and by night, but find no rest.

³Yet you are holy,
　enthroned on the praises of Israel.
⁴In you our ancestors trusted;
　they trusted, and you delivered them.
⁵To you they cried, and were saved;
　in you they trusted, and were not put to shame.

⁶But I am a worm, and not human;
　scorned by others, and despised by the people.
⁷All who see me mock at me;
　they make mouths at me, they shake their heads;
⁸"Commit your cause to the Lᴏʀᴅ; let him deliver—
　let him rescue the one in whom he delights!"

⁹Yet it was you who took me from the womb;
　you kept me safe on my mother's breast.
¹⁰On you I was cast from my birth,
　and since my mother bore me you have been my God.
¹¹Do not be far from me,
　for trouble is near
　and there is no one to help.

¹²Many bulls encircle me,
　strong bulls of Bashan surround me;
¹³they open wide their mouths at me,
　like a ravening and roaring lion.

¹⁴I am poured out like water,
　and all my bones are out of joint;
my heart is like wax;
　it is melted within my breast;
¹⁵my mouth is dried up like a potsherd,
　and my tongue sticks to my jaws;
　you lay me in the dust of death.

Theological Perspective

Early in its life the church heard the suffering Christ in the words of the psalmist—"My God, my God, why have you forsaken me?" It is clear that the evangelists Mark (15:34) and Matthew (27:46) interpreted and recorded the passion in the light of this psalm; even offering those words as Jesus' own. It is not

Pastoral Perspective

In the congregation I serve, it is our custom to read the passion from Mark's Gospel for our Good Friday evening worship. Every time, one by one, we extinguish candles affixed to a wooden cross. The sanctuary gradually darkens as the twilight outside wanes, until evening has shrouded our normally bright

¹⁶For dogs are all around me;
  a company of evildoers encircles me.
  My hands and feet have shriveled;
¹⁷I can count all my bones.
  They stare and gloat over me;
¹⁸they divide my clothes among themselves,
  and for my clothing they cast lots.

¹⁹But you, O Lord, do not be far away!
  O my help, come quickly to my aid!
²⁰Deliver my soul from the sword,
  my life from the power of the dog!
²¹Save me from the mouth of the lion!

From the horns of the wild oxen you have rescued me.
²²I will tell of your name to my brothers and sisters;
  in the midst of the congregation I will praise you:
²³You who fear the Lord, praise him!
  All you offspring of Jacob, glorify him;
  stand in awe of him, all you offspring of Israel!
²⁴For he did not despise or abhor
  the affliction of the afflicted;
  he did not hide his face from me,
  but heard when I cried to him.

²⁵From you comes my praise in the great congregation;
  my vows I will pay before those who fear him.
²⁶The poor shall eat and be satisfied;
  those who seek him shall praise the Lord.
  May your hearts live forever!

²⁷All the ends of the earth shall remember
  and turn to the Lord;
  and all the families of the nations
  shall worship before him.
²⁸For dominion belongs to the Lord,
  and he rules over the nations.

²⁹To him, indeed, shall all who sleep in the earth bow down;
  before him shall bow all who go down to the dust,
  and I shall live for him.
³⁰Posterity will serve him;
  future generations will be told about the Lord,
³¹and proclaim his deliverance to a people yet unborn,
  saying that he has done it.

Exegetical Perspective

The psalm's Hebrew title, "Concerning the Hind of the Dawn" (my trans.), is entirely unique within all five books of the psalms. Although the word "dawn" appears commonly within the Psalter, references to the hind (*'ayyalah*) are relatively rare. The hind's employment in Proverbs 5:19, where the wife of one's

Homiletical Perspective

Good Friday sets a trap for even the most mindful preacher. The story is at once overwhelming and too well known. If met head on, in its gruesome terror, the preacher may fear that people will run out of the church. So arises the ongoing habit of mentioning the resurrection in Good Friday

Psalm 22

Theological Perspective

surprising, then, that this psalm has long been a part of the church's celebration of Good Friday.

The suffering one is forsaken and unheard. It is as though God has turned a deaf ear and averted the all-seeing eye. Nevertheless, in that moment of seeming abandonment or absence, God's presence is most real—even in the feeling of isolation and aloneness accompanying suffering. Humiliated and brought low, the suffering one is indeed vulnerable, but also open and able to understand God's presence-in-absence.

One who had experienced suffering herself, Julian of Norwich sees the opportunity for being "*oned*" or united with God through it. In her *Showings* or *Revelations of Divine Love*, the suffering Christ is the means by which God identifies with all suffering, human or otherwise. She records:

> Here I saw a great unity [*oneing*] between Christ and us, as I understand it; for when he was in pain we were in pain, and all creatures able to suffer pain suffered with him. That is to say, all creatures which God has created for our service, the firmament and the earth, failed in their natural functions at the time of Christ's death, for it is their natural characteristic to recognize him as their Lord, in whom all their powers exist. And when he failed, their nature constrained them to fail with him, insofar as they could, because of the sorrow of his sufferings. And so those who were his friends suffered pain because of love, and all creation suffered in general; that is to say, those who did not recognize him suffered because the comfort of all creation failed them, except for God's powerful, secret preservation of them.[1]

As Kerrie Hide comments on this passage, "Furthermore, creation in Christ unites humanity to all creation. This bond is such a *great oneing* that as Christ experiences the pain of the Passion it reverberates over the entire cosmos." The psalmist's words in verse 27 echo: "All the ends of the earth shall remember and turn to the LORD; and all the families of the nations shall worship before him."

The fullness of remembering is found in that innocent one who undergoes suffering and in so doing transforms it from destruction to redemption. One who can do this demonstrates a freedom beyond human imagining. The innocent one's declaration, "I am poured out like water, and all my bones are out of joint; my heart is like wax; it is melted within my breast" (v. 14), evokes Paul's description of Christ's *kenōsis* in Philippians.

Hans Urs von Balthasar asserts that in assuming human nature and a human body, God in Christ has

Pastoral Perspective

proceedings like a pall. Every time we get to Mark 15:34, many of us stumble over the Aramaic transliteration of those Hebrew words: *Eloi, Eloi, lema sabachthani?*

My God, my God, why have you forsaken me? Christians are not supposed to say such things. We have been taught to give *pat answers* in the face of life's difficult questions, and that, certainly, is not one of them. But Jesus knew what he was saying. By uttering these words from Psalm 22:1, he is challenging, *daring,* us to consider things we would rather not, notions as sublime as the inseparability of suffering and glory, of incarnation, of eschatological hope from the ashen brink of death.

One problem with our culture is that we are increasingly unable to be around death, much less to learn from it. We are not accustomed to sitting with the dying; we pay people to do that for us. When the time of death comes and the body must be prepared and disposed of, we pay somebody to do that too.

We do not mind the empty tomb or, better yet, the resurrected Jesus on the beach cooking fish with his friends at breakfast (John 21). We are okay with that sweet resurrection morn and beyond—but not with crucifixion, not with the dying cry. We are not okay with Caravaggio's painting (*The Deposition,* 1604) of the sagging body—so pale, so dead—being awkwardly retrieved from that ugly cross.

We are not *okay* with Good Friday or its services, which is why most of us do not attend. Much to our loss, we cannot sit with suffering long enough to learn from it.

Our funeral traditions in the West bear this out. Thomas Lynch, Michigan poet and funeral director, suggests that our growing preference for memorial services without the body of our dearly deceased is a step in the wrong direction in terms of the way we grieve and heal from our losses. "A funeral without the dead body has the religious significance of the Book of Job without the sores and boils."[1]

If we have no exposure to the corpse because it is too painful, we run the risk of trying to slip around our grief instead of, more helpfully, working our way through it. Lynch adds: "The defining truth of our Christianity—an empty tomb—proceeds from the defining truth of our humanity: we fill tombs." While we rightly do not dwell on death, we best appreciate life from its shadow. Liturgically, we cannot have Easter without Good Friday.

---

1. Quoted in Kerrie Hide, *Gifted Origins to Graced Fulfillment: The Soteriology of Julian of Norwich* (Collegeville, MN: Liturgical Press, 2001), 100.

1. Thomas Lynch, "An Undertaker's Reflections: Good Grief," *Christian Century,* July 26, 2003.

youth is likened to "the loving hind" (KJV), could help direct its meaning, as might its appearance in Jeremiah 14:5: "Even the hind forsakes the one calved in the field, because there is no grass" (my trans.). Both of the accompanying references to this Hebrew word for hind convey this female animal's loving quality. The exact impact of the title of Psalm 22 will await a close reading of its content.

The psalm begins with the psalmist's confrontation of the Divine. He or she challenges: "My God, my God, why have you forsaken me?" God is addressed not, as one might expect, by God's personal and unpronounceable name, YHWH, but by a generic and very ancient name for any god (*el*), borrowed by the Israelites from preexisting Canaanite nations.

The speaker of the psalm presses this Being further with the claim: "Far from my salvation are the words of my roaring" (v. 1b, my trans.). The Hebrew word often rendered "groaning" (*she'agah*) means literally "roaring," hence its common usage within Hebrew Scripture to describe the commanding self-assertion of a lion (Judg. 14:5; Ps. 104:21; Amos 3:4, 8) or invading armies (Isa. 5:30; Ezek. 19:7). The need for the speaker's great outburst becomes clear in verse 2, where it is declared that his or her continual calling out through both day and night has received no apparent response.

In verses 3–5 the Hebrew text employs a conjunctive sign (*we*) that grants at least two options as to how the psalmist now proceeds from his or her initial charge of God's abandonment. This signal could represent "but," and hence would convey an assent to God's ultimate sovereignty, resulting in God's choosing to help whomever God wills—in this case, the speaker's forebears. The psalmist would then be releasing God of his or her current crisis simply because God is God.

More likely the psalmist here employs the reinforcement function of this Hebrew conjunction, giving a sense of "Yea!" or "Indeed!" in order to emphasize God's willingness to demonstrate salvation for the Israelites of the past. This proves incriminating, since the speaker is effectually strengthening rather than relinquishing his or her grievance against the Divine's apparent noninterest stance in regard to his or her own trials. The psalmist subsequently concludes his or her opening argument by confirming outrightly that "they," that is, "our ancestors" (v. 4) trusted in you "and were not put to shame" (v. 5).

In great contrast, the speaker of Psalm 22 has been put to shame. Rather than being "slipped away" (my trans.) from danger as were the forebears in verses 4–5, the psalmist finds himself or herself in a state of

sermons, as if the second life preceded the first one.

Preaching on Psalm 22 is a way out of the trap. It is less common to preach on the psalm prescribed for the day rather than the Gospel, and thus more likely to bring a fresh perspective both to the preacher and to those who hear her or him. The words of the psalm, while known, are not as well known as the stories from the Gospels. In addition, teaching about psalms may wake up your congregation: this psalm, written probably or possibly by King David, was meant to be sung in the temple, like a hymn.

Apart from that, the preacher has just to face into it. This is a sad, tragic, remorseless poem. David must have understood some terrible truth, undergone some awful event, to have written so beautifully about torture, pain, physical affliction, and, worst of all, abandonment.

There at least two major human themes presented to us on Good Friday: powerlessness and abandonment. Very few situations are worse to imagine than these. The task of the Good Friday preacher is to contemplate them both without climbing onto the safety of Easter. There are several identifiable risks to doing this.

First, the preacher can become mesmerized by the drama, going into great detail about the horror, the blood, the dragging of the cross. Lots of blood and horror only make us numb.

Second, the preacher can treat sacrifice as a generic doctrine, using tired language to repeat the well-worn news that we are sinners for whom Jesus died. Certainly, sacrifice is present both in the psalm and in the Good Friday story. It is also a deeply complex idea. Preachers who decide to take it on in the sermon for today will spend time finding a fresh perspective on it, or risk sending listeners out of church on Good Friday with the same mix of guilt and confusion that has been placed in the minds of too many congregants.

A third risk emerges for the preacher who decides to tell a story about a recent event in which someone died saving someone else. This has possibility, but must share the sweep and gravity of the Good Friday story. Otherwise the sermon can fade off into the retelling of an abstract news story or even slide into a political rant.

The final and perhaps most serious risk is to preach a sermon that blames the Jews for what happened to Jesus. We cannot speak of this enough: the Jewish authorities did not kill Jesus. Faithfulness to the text and to Christian witness demands a more nuanced telling of the Good Friday story.

The bottom line is that the pitfalls of preaching on this day are many, but the potential rewards are just as great.

Psalm 22

Theological Perspective

taken on not only creatureliness, but also the "concrete destiny" of humanity as well. "The Incarnation has accordingly no other ultimate purpose than the Cross: 'He descended into what was ours, that he might assume not only the substance, but also the condition of the sinful nature; and the Son of God had no other cause of his birth than that he might be able to be fastened to the Cross' (Leo the Great)."[2] From the moment of his birth, Christ took up the cross. Von Balthasar cites Bernard of Clairvaux's poignant preaching, "It is perhaps we ourselves who are Christ's Cross, to which he is fastened."

Thus the church can echo the psalmist: "You who fear the LORD, praise him! All you offspring of Jacob, glorify him; stand in awe of him, all you offspring of Israel! For he did not despise or abhor the affliction of the afflicted; he did not hide his face from me, but heard when I cried to him" (vv. 23–24).

The church, then, is the community God calls into being out of the suffering of the Christ. Its task, its call, is to remember what God has done. It is to tell the story and—in telling—to live it. Through their worship, God's people fulfill their calling as the "new Israel." The psalmist has said, "Yet you are holy, enthroned on the praises of Israel" (v. 3).

There was no image in the temple; it was enough that God's people offered praise for the Lord's saving acts. In the act of remembering—in the resultant worship—God's throne and God's presence became visible. Since God took flesh in Jesus Christ to reunite the image with the likeness in which we were made, the community itself becomes the icon and continues the incarnation through worship, service, and suffering, which is never in vain. As Paul tells the church at Colossae: "I am now rejoicing in my sufferings for your sake, and in my flesh I am completing what is lacking in Christ's afflictions for the sake of his body, that is, the church" (1:24).

All innocent suffering is taken up into the suffering of the Innocent One. In Christ, the Suffering Servant, the heart of God, opens to humanity by taking on our suffering.

Each Good Friday the church tells the story of the suffering God again, answering its call and praying for the fulfillment of the psalmist's words: "Posterity will serve him; future generations will be told about the Lord and proclaim his deliverance to a people yet unborn, saying that he has done it" (vv. 30–31).

STEVEN A. PEAY

Pastoral Perspective

Not everyone in the "funeral business" is as theologically astute as Lynch. A pastor friend reported in a sermon that when he was new to town, the local funeral director took him to lunch, preceded by a tour of the funeral home from which many of the parishioners in his new parish would be buried. In the casket showroom, my friend asked why he had never seen a black casket, to which the funeral director responded in all seriousness, "The color black is too suggestive of death."

We cover up death at a funeral for the same reason we stay away in droves from Good Friday's Tenebrae: we fear we will never find our way out of the shadows. The Solemn Reproaches of the Cross, rehearsing God's faithfulness and our penchant to deny, will speak too convincingly in that formidable darkness. If we dare go there, we may never be able to hear good news again, not on Easter Sunday, not ever.

The counsel of the psalmist suggests otherwise. In fact, we *can* bear suffering because God can be trusted to deliver us. What Ellen Davis calls the extravagant ebb and flow in the psalm between lament (v. 1, "Why?") and praise/trust (v. 24: "for he . . . heard when I cried to him") "explodes the limits" of our traditional understandings of God, of the world, of life, and of death.[2]

Yes, the psalmist laments that she feels that God has forsaken her, but to whom does she lament? She laments to the God who does not forsake us. When Jesus cried out on that cross, he was not speaking to existential nothingness, but to the God who hears and delivers the afflicted. His words did not express a lack of faith, but were a revolutionary credo of trust in the only one who could comfort him—and us.

Psalm 22 offers a terrific view of the abyss below from the safety of the bridge above. Yes, it is frightening to make the passage from one side of the chasm to the other, but the bridge is sound. The psalmist's movement from seeking God to finding God further portrays what God intends for all creation, affirming God's eternal sovereignty regardless of appearances. Jacob the Baker,[3] the amiable creation of writer Noah benShea, puts it helpfully when he says, "Know that you are a man with a lantern who goes in search of a light."

God illumines the most harrowing of passages—even the one we make on this ill-lit Friday night.

WILLIAM P. "MATT" MATTHEWS JR.

2. Hans Urs von Balthasar, *The Glory of the Lord: A Theological Aesthetics*, vol. 7: *Theology: The New Covenant*, trans. Brian McNeil (San Francisco: Ignatius Press, 1989), 212.

2. J. McCann, *The New Interpreter's Bible* (Nashville: Abingdon Press, 1996) 4:762.

3. Noah benShea, *Jacob the Baker* (New York: Ballantine Books, 1989), 51.

Exegetical Perspective

being "A grub! Yea! Not a man—an object of reproach to humankind, and scorned by a people" (v. 6, my trans.). Here, where the speaker grimly compares God's care for those before with his or her own near nonhuman existence, three realms of contempt and isolation are employed.

The psalmist, seemingly male, is stripped of gender; he is deprived of human likeness; now a gender-shared term for "humanity" (*'adamah*, lit. "groundling") appears to signify the widening degree of isolation from humankind that is being experienced. Finally, the speaker's declaration that "a people" despise him expresses the loss of fellowship with kin. Even the relational and communal facet of the speaker's life is passing away.

Verses 7–8 rally the speaker's case to a climax as he or she upholds for God the visual imagery of taunters mocking and "wagging their heads" (my trans.) in response to the psalmist's disfigurement—even to the point of insulting God. Here for the first time the address "YHWH" appears, and at the pronouncement the speaker's tone noticeably softens, even as the psalmist continues to plead his or her case in verses 9–11. In verse 10 YHWH is gently reminded: "On you I was cast from my birth, and since my mother bore me you have been my God." With utmost transparency the psalmist now approaches the Divine, acknowledging: "Be not far from me—for distress is near, and there is no one helping" (my trans.).

The last phrase of verse 21 records a marvelous happening. The psalmist pronounces astonishingly, "You have answered me!" (my trans.). For the rest of the psalm, the speaker's words resound with victory at rehearsing the thanksgiving that he or she will now inspire within the midst of the congregation. All offspring of Jacob will be commanded to praise and glorify YHWH who "did not despise or abhor the affliction of the afflicted" (v. 24).

The speaker exuberantly declares God's sovereignty over all nations, testifying boldly that "all the families of the nations" will remember and turn to YHWH (v. 27); indeed, all the proud will bow down before him (v. 29). The psalmist testifies triumphantly in 22:29–31 that "all those who go down into the dust"—that is, any mortal—"cannot even keep his own soul alive" (my trans.). However, offspring will serve the Lord and tell of YHWH's righteousness "to a people yet unborn" (v. 31). The speaker ends the psalm in awe, declaring: "For he"— and one might add, "The Loving One of the Dawn"—"has acted" (my trans.).

JENNIFER PFENNIGER

Homiletical Perspective

One tack that may help is to place the events of Good Friday in historical context, reminding listeners of the political realities that were involved. To describe the Roman Empire—what it did and did not tolerate, how it punished those who threatened its imposed order, and why this person Jesus might have posed a real problem—may perk up the ears of listeners in the pews. The psalm helps here because it is a lament about human evil.

Jesus lived in occupied territory. Israel was colonized by the great Roman Empire: builder of aqueducts, commander of the largest and most efficient army in the world, and inventor of that peculiar form of execution, the cross.

Theologian Walter Brueggemann writes, "Empires are never built nor are they maintained on the basis of compassion."[1] Roman rulers expected their citizens to remain silent in response to the human cost of war, to remain mute in the face of the human cost of greed. They kept their colonies in check by systemic terror. The price of prophetic witness was death.

Jesus speaks up. He acts. He heals the sick and recovers the sight of the blind. He eats with the poor and the abandoned. By and through his compassion, he takes the first step in revealing the abnormality, as Brueggemann says, that has become business as usual. This leads him finally and inexorably to the cross, to the place where power and vulnerability intersect or—more accurately—collide. A Good Friday sermon that takes this context into account may illumine the ways in which the choices he made show us how to make such choices ourselves.

Another sermon on this text might develop the theme of abandonment. Psalm 22 is about being left alone, helpless, to face an implacable power, until your heart melts into wax and falls into your gut. Worse, the author of the psalm feels abandoned by God. One way into this sermon is to remember the times you were abandoned yourself—not because you will tell such stories in the sermon, but because you need to remind yourself what abandonment actually feels like.

To be abandoned, you have to know what it was to be among friends and family, loved by them, and then left by them. Almost everyone except Jesus' mother (you could preach a whole sermon on her courage that day), faced with a Roman soldier carrying a sword, dropped him. He was alone, finally, and entirely, and that is the stark reality we contemplate.

NORA GALLAGHER

1. Walter Brueggemann, *The Prophetic Imagination* (Minneapolis: Augsburg Fortress Publishers, 1978), 85.

Hebrews 4:14-16; 5:7-9

^{4:14}Since, then, we have a great high priest who has passed through the heavens, Jesus, the Son of God, let us hold fast to our confession. ¹⁵For we do not have a high priest who is unable to sympathize with our weaknesses, but we have one who in every respect has been tested as we are, yet without sin. ¹⁶Let us therefore approach the throne of grace with boldness, so that we may receive mercy and find grace to help in time of need....

^{5:7}In the days of his flesh, Jesus offered up prayers and supplications, with loud cries and tears, to the one who was able to save him from death, and he was heard because of his reverent submission. ⁸Although he was a Son, he learned obedience through what he suffered; ⁹and having been made perfect, he became the source of eternal salvation for all who obey him.

Theological Perspective

In theology we use words, phrases, and ideas in order to illuminate Scripture's complex witness. This scriptural complexity arises from the presence of a variety of ways of speaking of God and God's ways in and with the world. Our theologies will produce narrative accounts of reality. Our theological responsibility is to produce accounts as faithful as possible to the broad witness of Scripture. Though a perfect faithfulness is no more possible in this than it is in other aspects of life, we must take care not to allow one facet to overwhelm all others. This danger exists perhaps preeminently when offering accounts in response to the perennial question of how the life and death of Jesus of Nazareth are bound up in God's work of salvation. Thus Good Friday is a day on which we must exercise great care. Pitfalls abound as we speak of the events of the day and how they are part of what took place "for us and for our salvation."

All of the lections assigned for today call us to mindfulness of Jesus' suffering. We can neither avoid nor minimize the facts that his was a most cruel and painful death, nor that he endured it in some sense for the sake of others. Scripture attests that it is so, and employs multiple models and metaphors to illuminate how these things are so. It does not, however, give priority to any. Neither has the church given dogmatic definition of salvation as it has of God in the Nicene

Pastoral Perspective

The concept of Jesus Christ as high priest is an alien one to twenty-first-century people. Because the concept is so unusual to our hearing, it is tempting on Good Friday to focus on the images we might associate with a high priest—sacrifice, death, and blood— or to engage in a psychological analysis of whether Jesus the high priest was truly tested "in every respect . . . as we are, yet without sin" (v. 15). To those who were born and educated in the wake of the Freudian revolution, that is simply a contradiction.

The central theme of the author of Hebrews is neither the sacrificial atonement of Jesus as high priest nor the psychological experience of Jesus. He could not conceive of Christ as having sin. It is a theological position being posited, not a historical analysis. Either of these paths diverts us from the meaning of this passage for our lives of faith. That is where the interests of the writer of Hebrews really lie and the subject of this pastoral perspective.

Our journey this church year began with the anticipation of the birth of "Emmanuel, which means, 'God is with us'" (Matt. 1:23). The story of that birth is brought to its fulfillment on the cross. Only here do we become aware of how fully God is with us. The focus of Hebrews on Jesus' full humanity brings to our attention the full reality of the incarnation. The Gospel readings since the beginning

Exegetical Perspective

Although the lectionary omits the central section of this paragraph (5:1–6), the preacher ought not do likewise. The logical relationship between Jesus' identity as high priest and his identity as God's Son is not self-evident, but relies on the author's exegesis of Psalm 2:7 ("You are my son, today I have begotten you") and Psalm 110:4 ("You are a priest forever according to the order of Melchizedek"). The exegetical connection, not exactly obvious to a modern interpreter, is the phrase "you are," which appears in both verses and invites the author of Hebrews to connect them. In the context of Good Friday, this passage serves to highlight the pastoral as well as the priestly functions of Jesus' death.

Hebrews 4:14 initiates a new section of the letter—it is really better described as a sermon—by reflecting further on Jesus' identity as the priest (he is already so named at 3:1) who offers his people access to God because he has "passed through the heavens" into God's presence. Of course, Jesus was already in God's presence from before creation (1:10), which means that 4:14 reinforces the picture of Jesus' descent into this world "for a little while" (2:7). This priest not only offers sacrifice for sin; he is himself the sacrifice (see also 7:26–28).

Hebrews 4, though, emphasizes Jesus' compassion for sinners because he is "one who in every respect

Homiletical Perspective

Why is this day called "Good" Friday? The name is counterintuitive to the story of the day. It is also unique to the English language. In other Western languages it is "Black" Friday, "Mourning" Friday, or "Holy" Friday, all of which seem more fitting. There is speculation that the name Good Friday is derived from an old English designation, God's Friday. So the name sticks. Today we discover God as the crucified One *and* the loving, grieving Creator *and* the Spirit of comfort and challenge binding the whole event together. It is the crucified One who takes center stage; the book of Hebrews gives us a mystical vision of this person of the Trinity in its image of Jesus as great high priest.

Jesus as great high priest is particularly poignant for the preacher on God's Friday. On this day, as on no other in the liturgical year, the preacher is called to be high priest for her people. Throughout the rest of the year she can pick and choose whether or not to deal with the more difficult texts in the canon, but not on this day. Once again the time has come to interpret the core story of Christianity, for without crucifixion, resurrection is shallow triumphalism.

As the preacher preaches, tells the story, and prays on this day, she is called to stand in the holy gap between God and the people. On God's Friday she is called to be a vessel—an offering plate—bringing to

Hebrews 4:14-16; 5:7-9

Theological Perspective

Trinitarian doctrine or Chalcedonian Christology. Not a few, however, embrace a particular account of how salvation has taken place, embracing it as though it were an unalterable dogmatic formulation.

Both the account and criticism of it have long pedigree. Broadly, the account maintains that Jesus' suffering was something God required as a condition for granting forgiveness, an idea known as "penal suffering." Persons who espouse this account emphasize human sin as being so offensive to God that things could be set right only by the full venting of divine wrath and the unleashing of divine punishment. Justice must be served before the relationship between God and humanity can be restored.

Further, the one upon whom this punishment falls must be without sin, because it is that one's role to bear the sins of others. Jesus was this sinless victim who bore punishment commensurate with the offense against the divine majesty to secure our pardon. It is not difficult to call to mind portions of Scripture that inform and give rise to this interpretation, and for this reason it is perhaps understandable that there would be so many who would embrace it. However, the narrative of penal suffering imposes limitations that obscure the larger scope of biblical witness; so the account is unsatisfactory for a number of reasons.

For one, it imposes a single, limited understanding of justice on God, rather than understanding justice in light of the character of the God Scripture tells us "is love" (1 John 4:8). Second, it insufficiently illuminates the ethical shape of redeemed human life. More germane to our purpose, though the language of substitution is present in the biblical witness to Jesus, this account reduces him to little more than a substitute; hence it is called the "penal substitution theory" of atonement. The effect is to make his life apart from his passion less important for our salvation. At best, his prophetic words and actions become primarily testimonies that authenticate the efficacy of his death. While the Gospels speak of his resolve to go to Jerusalem, sensing what awaited him there, in this account his purpose can be encapsulated in the phrase often heard in popular piety, "He came to die."

Our lection can help us by gesturing toward another narrative, one also possessing pedigree back to the second century of the Common Era. In this account our salvation is bound up thoroughly in Jesus' life as a whole. Though John Calvin's discussion of Christ as redeemer gives far greater prominence to penal substitution due to his understanding of the cross's centrality, Calvin began his discussion

Pastoral Perspective

of Advent have placed Jesus at the center, but they can be read and preached without gauging what his life means for the life of faith.

The author of Hebrews places that meaning of Jesus' life as the focus of his writing in this chapter: Jesus is our mediator precisely because he has experienced life as we do and understands and sympathizes with our struggles, and he is our model of a faithful life of obedience to God. This focus—Jesus as mediator and model—is readily accessible to contemporary hearers, and it opens up for us an avenue for appreciating the author's message for our day.

Jesus the mediator cares about our pain and struggles, has compassion for our striving for justice and our labors for peace. We can "approach the throne of grace with boldness" (4:16) in asking for God's help because in Jesus God sympathizes with our weakness and because Jesus has been tested too. The Jesus of Hebrews is truly exalted in glory just as in the Gospel of John, but in Hebrews (unlike John) Jesus also struggles against his weaknesses, is tested and tempted in every way that we are.

Our tests and temptations are not the martyrdom and desertion of our faith under threats of death (which is the context of this letter and what the author has in mind). Only rarely do any human beings today face a comparable level of testing, though torture, genocide, and terrorism still occupy our world. Our trials tend to be of a more garden-variety sort, nevertheless real.

Try reading the catalog in the pocket in front of the seat on an airline. Flipping through page after page, one wonders why on earth human beings require any of these gadgets. Why, indeed? The allurements of our world are quite real, greed and possessions among them. We are tested too, to "hold fast to our confession" (v. 14) of faith as we seek to stand faithfully with those who are oppressed, disenfranchised, unemployed, homeless, or simply poor. Offensive abuse comes from all quarters blaming such as these. Witness the scurrilous attacks on immigrants. Locker-room jokes and sidewalk taunts of physically or mentally handicapped people or of people of different races, ages, or religions are all around us. Can we hold fast to our faith and defend those who often cannot defend themselves?

Our sacrifices are mostly not of the type facing late-first-century Christians, but are we willing to make the sacrifices necessary, for example, to preserve and protect God's creation? How willingly will we stop using our cars so frequently, lower our thermostats in the winter and raise them in the summer,

Exegetical Perspective

has been tested as we are, yet without sin" (v. 15). Jesus' empathy for sinners should make us bold to approach God, despite our sinfulness, because we know we will find mercy and "grace to help in time of need," that is, in times of temptation (v. 16; the same Greek word can be rendered "test" or "tempt"). The priest who has shared people's lives in every respect—including their deaths—is "able to deal gently with the ignorant and wayward" (5:2), because he too was tempted. This recasts the image of judgment away from punishment or vengeance toward sympathetic truth telling—God's naming sin for what it is and redeeming it through Jesus' death.

Because Jesus does not need to offer sacrifice on his own behalf (since he is God's Son and since he obediently submits to the cross), he is the ideal priest—literally ideal, in the sense that all other priests are fashioned after him. He is also the perfect priest (5:8) in the sense that his work is completed, finished.[1] In his death, once for all, Jesus accomplishes what human priests must do repeatedly, both on their own behalf and for the sake of the people.

Psalm 110:1 was the first text of the author's sermon at 1:5, where it established Jesus' identity as God's Son. Now, in 5:5–6, the author turns to verse 4 of the same psalm to connect Jesus' identity as king—and therefore as God's son—to his identity as priest. Because one does not volunteer oneself for the priesthood, but is called by God (5:4), the author returns to Psalm 110 to show that God has also called Jesus to be priest, even as God called him Son. The adverb "forever" further identifies Jesus as an unprecedented sort of priest whose tenure lasts not only during his earthly life ("in the days of his flesh," 5:7), but also after his resurrection.

Psalm 110:4 appears again at Hebrews 7:1, where the author invokes the strange story from Genesis 14:17–24, in which Abram encounters King Melchizedek of Salem, "priest of God Most High" (14:18). The Canaanite king blesses Abram and Abram's God and then receives a tithe of the patriarch's wealth and entourage. These two passages in Hebrews are the only places outside Genesis and Psalm 110 where the figure of Melchizedek appears.

Because Melchizedek is both king (of what would become Jerusalem, no less) and priest, he is the proper sacerdotal ancestor of Jesus, who is executed as a messianic (that is, royal) pretender and vindicated by God by his resurrection from the dead.

1. Cf. the two uses of the same verb, "to complete," at Jesus' death: "All was now finished" (John 19:28) and "It is finished" (19:30).

Homiletical Perspective

God the sorrow and sufferings, the longings and hopes of her worshiping people. On God's Friday she is also called to be the channel and mouthpiece who proclaims the mysterious character, nature, and actions of God in their midst. Standing in the holy gap as high priest, the preacher can find herself in a daunting, lonely place.

Preachers sometimes need a pastoral word themselves in order to pastor and preach to their people. The first-century writer/preacher of Hebrews provides the twenty-first-century preacher with just such a word in this lectionary passage. She is not alone as she stands in the holy gap between God and the people. As the crucified One, Jesus stood first in this place and stands there still.

Hebrews reminds the preacher that prayerful reliance on the model of Jesus as high priest is the preacher's gateway into the preaching event of God's Friday. Hebrews 5:8 tells us that Jesus' tenacious obedience to God made him "perfect," that is, whole and complete. The Latin root word for obedience, *oedire*, means "to listen deeply." Jesus' deep listening to God made him whole, even in the midst of suffering and death, leading him to become high priest for all creation, "the source of eternal salvation" (v. 9).

This obedience or deep listening gives the preacher the model for a very intimate practice of prayer relationship with God. Jesus knew how to offer up prayer from the depths of his soul. A vivid expression comes to his lips at the very moment of his death: "My God, my God, why have you forsaken me?" Proclamation of God's Word changes when the preacher's process is driven by more than an intellectual exegesis of text and congregation. It comes passionately alive when the intellect finds expression in the heart-centered experience of the preacher's own prayer relationship with God.

This may seem too simple a precept to mention. Is prayer not always a part of the preaching process? One would hope. It is the experience of many pastor/preachers that the demands of ministry can leave little time for the preacher to participate personally in prayer, meditation, and study—all of which she encourages her congregation to do. Hebrews 4:14–16 invites the preacher to go deeper into the mystery of relationship with God. "Let us hold fast to our confession," the epistle writer says. Let us remember whose we are.

The text invites the preacher to return to the core of who she is—first as a baptized child of God given particular gifts and graces, and then as one called to be preacher/pastor/high priest. We confess we are in

Hebrews 4:14-16; 5:7-9

Theological Perspective

oriented more to this other account. First affirming the mission of Christ as an aspect of God's love, he declared that Christ abolished sin, reconciled persons to God, and acquired righteousness "by the whole course of his obedience."[1]

So it is in our lection. The lectionary omits the enigmatic connection of Jesus' priesthood to that of Melchizedek and juxtaposes a refrain of encouragement that resounds in Hebrews with the salvation Jesus has won through his "having been made perfect" (5:8), which perfection comes through his learning obedience through suffering. Even if the events of his passion are implicitly the supreme instances of this suffering (and they are liturgically, whether or not they are in authorial intent), the reference is broader.

Of great importance in our reading and in this alternative account of salvation, is a firm assertion of the humanity Jesus has shared fully with us. From this affirmation we may move to speak in another, better way of substitution, instead of Jesus being our substitute only as the recipient of divine wrath. Where humanity had from the beginning failed to live in faithful communion with God and all creation, Jesus was faithful even to death. This brings us to consider the wrath and suffering, which we cannot omit from our reflection. Throughout his ministry Jesus proclaimed God's righteous reign in contrast to earthly kingdoms, exemplified by Rome, with their politics of violence. It is in the collision of kingdoms that we locate discussion of wrath and suffering Jesus has shared and suffered—the tests common to all humanity—yet without sin (4:15). This saving victory was not because of his divinity. That would hold small consolation for us who are not divine. His victory was "in the days of his flesh" (5:7). It is a great mystery of salvation that by his whole life Jesus has taken humanity into the life of God; thus he may be called our high priest.

PHILIP E. THOMPSON

Pastoral Perspective

recycle, and otherwise reduce our carbon footprint so that future generations will have the same joy and delight in the created world without the higher risks of storms, floods, droughts, and disease?

Hebrews tells us that in Jesus we find both mercy and grace—mercy for our failures to meet the test of faith, and grace to empower us to fulfill our calling to do the good that God bids us do. Such is the paradox of the faith Hebrews portrays.

The British novelist and philosopher Iris Murdoch observed how immensely difficult, but nevertheless crucial, it is to be or do good in a world that seems to be increasingly mad. In *The Sovereignty of Good* she asks, "Are we not certain that . . . goodness really matters?"[1] Finally, from Murdoch's perspective, we desire to do good, not to seek eternal reward or to avoid eternal punishment, but because of the independent imperative that calls us to be moral and good. "The only genuine way to be good is to be good 'for nothing.'"[2]

Basil the Great put it similarly: "If we turn away from evil out of fear of punishment, we are in the position of slaves. If we pursue the enticement of wages, . . . we resemble mercenaries. Finally, if we obey for the sake of the good itself and out of love for him who commands . . . we are in the position of children."[3] As we "approach the throne of grace with boldness" (4:16), may we follow the example of Jesus Christ by being obedient as God's children, and may we find the grace to help us meet the test of faith and do the good God calls us to do.

GARY B. REIERSON

---

1. John Calvin, *Institutes of the Christian Religion*, ed. John T. McNeill, trans. Ford Lewis Battles, LCC (Philadelphia: Westminster Press, 1960), 2.16.5, p. 507.

1. Iris Murdoch, *The Sovereignty of Good* (London: Routledge & Kegan Paul, 1970), 60.
2. Ibid., 71.
3. Basil the Great, *Regulae fusius tractatae, prol.* 3: PG 31, 896 B, quoted in *Catechism of the Catholic Church*, 2nd ed. (Vatican City: Libreria Editrice Vaticana, 1997), 450, no. 1828.

Exegetical Perspective

Perhaps it is also the king's offering of "bread and wine" to Abram (Gen. 14:18), reminiscent as it is of the church's sacramental meal, that suggests to the writer of Hebrews that Melchizedek's order (rather than some other priest's order) is the appropriate one in which to locate Jesus' priestly lineage.

Psalm 110:1 was the single most favorite Bible verse in early Christianity, quoted more frequently than any other.[2] "The LORD says to my lord, 'Sit at my right hand until I make your enemies your footstool'" offered a picture to the first Christians of where Jesus was and what he was doing between his death and resurrection (then in the past), and his future coming in glory. In this picture, God gives the risen Jesus the greatest seat of honor in heaven during the period between Easter and the Parousia, while Jesus' enemies are being defeated and God's rule completed. Only the author of Hebrews reads beyond that first verse to include the second image of the king as priest.

During his earthly ministry, Jesus "offered up prayers and supplications, with loud cries and tears, to the one who was able to save him from death, and he was heard because of his reverent submission" (5:7). Perhaps the author of Hebrews has in mind Jesus' agony in the garden (Mark 14:32–42 and parallels), although the psalms of the righteous sufferer (Pss. 22:1–2; 116:8–11) provide the more likely source, particularly as they come from the voices of people who, like Jesus, steadfastly obey God in their suffering. Jesus thus becomes not only the priest who intercedes for his people, offers the perfect sacrifice for their sin, and understands their weakness. He also becomes the model for their lives.

E. ELIZABETH JOHNSON

Homiletical Perspective

relationship to God through the one who held fast to God's grace-filled, merciful power in the midst of the greatest test of suffering, weakness, and limitation "without compromising his humanity, without straying from his calling to be a human being."[1] In this way he became our great high priest. As such, Jesus brings to God in offering nothing less than the entirety of the human condition.[2]

Remembering her own God-given, God-filled nature through a prayerful relationship with God, the preacher is empowered in proclamation. Stepping fully into her humanity she steps into the holy gap as high priest on God's Friday to pour out her congregation's deepest needs in confession, offering them to God, just as Jesus poured out his life on the cross. She also represents to her congregation the whole character, nature, and actions of God on this day.

In the crucible of our paradoxical world—a world full of violence, oppression, and self-destruction, yet equally full of compassion, empowerment, and love—congregations are hungry for life-empowering experiences of the mysteries of God. On God's Friday, we not only meet the crucified one, our great high priest; we also meet God, the creator of the cosmos, whose great love holds the web of all life in tension. We encounter God the Spirit, who binds together in love the oppressed, the persecuted, and the annihilated, along with the oppressor, the persecutor, and the executor in hopes of oneness and reconciliation.

Jesus our "great high priest" makes it possible to approach all of God, to "approach the throne of grace with boldness, so that we may receive mercy and find grace" (4:16) in the midst of the human condition. The preacher/pastor who is listening deeply, offering the whole of her humanity in prayerful relationship to God, will stand boldly as high priest to proclaim the profound mysteries of God's Good Friday.

JANE ANNE FERGUSON

---

2. Matt. 22:44; 26:64; Mark 12:36; 14:62; Luke 20:42; 22:69; Acts 2:34–35; 5:31; 7:55–56 (where Jesus stands to honor Stephen's witness); Rom. 8:34; Eph. 1:20; Col. 3:1; Heb. 1:3, 13; 8:1; 10:12; 12:2; 1 Pet. 3:22. See David M. Hay, *Glory at the Right Hand: Psalm 110 in Early Christianity*, Society of Biblical Literature Monograph Series 18 (Nashville: Abingdon Press, 1973).

1. Thomas G. Long, *Hebrews*, Interpretation series (Louisville, KY: John Knox Press, 1997), 64.
2. Ibid., 65.

John 18:1-19:42

18:1After Jesus had spoken these words, he went out with his disciples across the Kidron valley to a place where there was a garden, which he and his disciples entered. 2Now Judas, who betrayed him, also knew the place, because Jesus often met there with his disciples. 3So Judas brought a detachment of soldiers together with police from the chief priests and the Pharisees, and they came there with lanterns and torches and weapons. 4Then Jesus, knowing all that was to happen to him, came forward and asked them, "Whom are you looking for?" 5They answered, "Jesus of Nazareth." Jesus replied, "I am he." Judas, who betrayed him, was standing with them. 6When Jesus said to them, "I am he," they stepped back and fell to the ground. 7Again he asked them, "Whom are you looking for?" And they said, "Jesus of Nazareth." 8Jesus answered, "I told you that I am he. So if you are looking for me, let these men go." 9This was to fulfill the word that he had spoken, "I did not lose a single one of those whom you gave me." 10Then Simon Peter, who had a sword, drew it, struck the high priest's slave, and cut off his right ear. The slave's name was Malchus. 11Jesus said to Peter, "Put your sword back into its sheath. Am I not to drink the cup that the Father has given me?"

12So the soldiers, their officer, and the Jewish police arrested Jesus and bound him. 13First they took him to Annas, who was the father-in-law of Caiaphas, the high priest that year. 14Caiaphas was the one who had advised the Jews that it was better to have one person die for the people.

15Simon Peter and another disciple followed Jesus. Since that disciple was known to the high priest, he went with Jesus into the courtyard of the high priest, 16but Peter was standing outside at the gate. So the other disciple, who was known to the high priest, went out, spoke to the woman who guarded the gate, and brought Peter in. 17The woman said to Peter, "You are not also one of this man's disciples, are you?" He said, "I am not." 18Now the slaves and the police had made a charcoal fire because it was cold, and they were standing around it and warming themselves. Peter also was standing with them and warming himself.

19Then the high priest questioned Jesus about his disciples and about his teaching. 20Jesus answered, "I have spoken openly to the world; I have always taught in synagogues and in the temple, where all the Jews come together. I have said nothing in secret. 21Why do you ask me? Ask those who heard what I said to them; they know what I said." 22When he had said this, one of the police standing nearby struck Jesus on the face, saying, "Is that how you answer the high priest?" 23Jesus answered, "If I have spoken wrongly, testify to the wrong. But if I have spoken rightly, why do you strike me?" 24Then Annas sent him bound to Caiaphas the high priest.

25Now Simon Peter was standing and warming himself. They asked him, "You are not also one of his disciples, are you?" He denied it and said, "I am not." 26One of the slaves of the high priest, a relative of the man whose ear Peter had cut off, asked, "Did I not see you in the garden with him?" 27Again Peter denied it, and at that moment the cock crowed.

28Then they took Jesus from Caiaphas to Pilate's headquarters. It was early in the morning. They themselves did not enter the headquarters, so as to avoid ritual defilement and to be able to eat the Passover. 29So Pilate went out to them and said, "What accusation do you bring against this man?" 30They answered, "If this man were not a criminal, we would not have handed him over to you." 31Pilate said to them, "Take him yourselves and judge him according to your law." The Jews replied, "We are not permitted to put anyone to death." 32(This was to fulfill what Jesus had said when he indicated the kind of death he was to die.)

³³Then Pilate entered the headquarters again, summoned Jesus, and asked him, "Are you the King of the Jews?" ³⁴Jesus answered, "Do you ask this on your own, or did others tell you about me?" ³⁵Pilate replied, "I am not a Jew, am I? Your own nation and the chief priests have handed you over to me. What have you done?" ³⁶Jesus answered, "My kingdom is not from this world. If my kingdom were from this world, my followers would be fighting to keep me from being handed over to the Jews. But as it is, my kingdom is not from here." ³⁷Pilate asked him, "So you are a king?" Jesus answered, "You say that I am a king. For this I was born, and for this I came into the world, to testify to the truth. Everyone who belongs to the truth listens to my voice." ³⁸Pilate asked him, "What is truth?"

After he had said this, he went out to the Jews again and told them, "I find no case against him. ³⁹But you have a custom that I release someone for you at the Passover. Do you want me to release for you the King of the Jews?" ⁴⁰They shouted in reply, "Not this man, but Barabbas!" Now Barabbas was a bandit.

¹⁹:¹Then Pilate took Jesus and had him flogged. ²And the soldiers wove a crown of thorns and put it on his head, and they dressed him in a purple robe. ³They kept coming up to him, saying, "Hail, King of the Jews!" and striking him on the face. ⁴Pilate went out again and said to them, "Look, I am bringing him out to you to let you know that I find no case against him." ⁵So Jesus came out, wearing the crown of thorns and the purple robe. Pilate said to them, "Here is the man!" ⁶When the chief priests and the police saw him, they shouted, "Crucify him! Crucify him!" Pilate said to them, "Take him yourselves and crucify him; I find no case against him." ⁷The Jews answered him, "We have a law, and according to that law he ought to die because he has claimed to be the Son of God."

⁸Now when Pilate heard this, he was more afraid than ever. ⁹He entered his headquarters again and asked Jesus, "Where are you from?" But Jesus gave him no answer. ¹⁰Pilate therefore said to him, "Do you refuse to speak to me? Do you not know that I have power to release you, and power to crucify you?" ¹¹Jesus answered him, "You would have no power over me unless it had been given you from above; therefore the one who handed me over to you is guilty of a greater sin." ¹²From then on Pilate tried to release him, but the Jews cried out, "If you release this man, you are no friend of the emperor. Everyone who claims to be a king sets himself against the emperor."

¹³When Pilate heard these words, he brought Jesus outside and sat on the judge's bench at a place called The Stone Pavement, or in Hebrew Gabbatha. ¹⁴Now it was the day of Preparation for the Passover; and it was about noon. He said to the Jews, "Here is your King!" ¹⁵They cried out, "Away with him! Away with him! Crucify him!" Pilate asked them, "Shall I crucify your King?" The chief priests answered, "We have no king but the emperor." ¹⁶Then he handed him over to them to be crucified.

So they took Jesus; ¹⁷and carrying the cross by himself, he went out to what is called The Place of the Skull, which in Hebrew is called Golgotha. ¹⁸There they crucified him, and with him two others, one on either side, with Jesus between them. ¹⁹Pilate also had an inscription written and put on the cross. It read, "Jesus of Nazareth, the King of the Jews." ²⁰Many of the Jews read this inscription, because the place where Jesus was crucified was near the city; and it was written in Hebrew, in Latin, and in Greek. ²¹Then the chief priests of the Jews said to Pilate, "Do not write, 'The King of the Jews,' but, 'This man said, I am King of the Jews.'" ²²Pilate answered, "What I have written I have written." ²³When the soldiers had crucified Jesus, they took his clothes and divided them into four parts, one for each soldier. They also took his tunic; now the tunic was seamless, woven in one piece from the top. [24]So they said to one another, "Let us not tear it, but cast lots for it to see who will get it." This was to fulfill what the scripture says,

"They divided my clothes among themselves,
and for my clothing they cast lots."

[25]And that is what the soldiers did.

Meanwhile, standing near the cross of Jesus were his mother, and his mother's sister, Mary the wife of Clopas, and Mary Magdalene. [26]When Jesus saw his mother and the disciple whom he loved standing beside her, he said to his mother, "Woman, here is your son." [27]Then he said to the disciple, "Here is your mother." And from that hour the disciple took her into his own home.

[28]After this, when Jesus knew that all was now finished, he said (in order to fulfill the scripture), "I am thirsty." [29]A jar full of sour wine was standing there. So they put a sponge full of the wine on a branch of hyssop and held it to his mouth. [30]When Jesus had received the wine, he said, "It is finished." Then he bowed his head and gave up his spirit.

[31]Since it was the day of Preparation, the Jews did not want the bodies left on the cross during the sabbath, especially because that sabbath was a day of great solemnity. So they asked Pilate to have the legs of the crucified men

Theological Perspective

The narration of the condemnation, execution, and burial of Jesus in the Gospel of John focuses on two claims made by Jesus about himself, the first having to do with his application of the divine Name to himself, and the second having to do with his identity as the Son of God, the King of the Jews. Both claims have been made prior to this climactic scene in the Gospel.

When the Jews ask Jesus how Abraham rejoiced that he would see his day, Jesus replies, "Before Abraham was, I AM" (John 8:58). When Jesus enters Jerusalem, a great crowd greets him, and shouts out, "Blessed is the one who comes in the name of the Lord—the King of Israel!" (John 12:13). The conclusion of the life of Jesus in chapters 18–19 supplies the reader with the shocking understanding Jesus has of both claims regarding himself, an understanding that seems directly to contradict what these titles have meant to Jews throughout their history.

The use of the divine Name, "I AM/YHWH" by a human being should be deeply shocking and offensive to the reader, as it was to the Jews in the Gospel. However, if—like the disciples—one came to accept this claim in faith, then one would of course associate Jesus with the God who revealed himself to Moses as the one who would deliver the Israelites from Egypt from their slavery and oppression under Pharaoh.

When God reveals the Name, God tells Moses, "Say to the Israelites, 'I AM YHWH, and I will free you

Pastoral Perspective

Everybody sings "O Come, All Ye Faithful." Only the faithful sing "O Sacred Head, Now Wounded." This week, for better and worse, we are pretty much on our own. That is the cultural difference between Christmas and Holy Week—but why do the faithful, and to be honest, the wondering and questing and not-really-sure-at-all, come to a Good Friday service?

If you have a great choir, it could be for the Bach. Those days are mostly gone for most of us—no *St. John Passion* on the calendar this Friday, even in churches that keep the *Messiah* and Lessons and Carols traditions going in Advent. No, it is not the music—not that the music is not wonderful and important. It is something else, something more elusive and indescribable. There is a distinct yearning on Good Friday like no other. If you can speak to what this is, you and they will be blessed.

John Dominic Crossan and Marcus Borg rightly pointed out that in many traditions "Palm Sunday" has become "Passion Sunday" for the simple reason that no one is coming to church during Holy Week.[1] So the only way the gathered people will hear the story of the passion before the story of the resurrection is if it supplants Palm Sunday. More the pity, as those familiar with Holy Week traditions realize—the

1. Marcus J. Borg and John Dominic Crossan, *The Last Week* (San Francisco: HarperSanFrancisco, 2007).

broken and the bodies removed. [32]Then the soldiers came and broke the legs of the first and of the other who had been crucified with him. [33]But when they came to Jesus and saw that he was already dead, they did not break his legs. [34]Instead, one of the soldiers pierced his side with a spear, and at once blood and water came out. [35](He who saw this has testified so that you also may believe. His testimony is true, and he knows that he tells the truth.) [36]These things occurred so that the scripture might be fulfilled, "None of his bones shall be broken." [37]And again another passage of scripture says, "They will look on the one whom they have pierced."

[38]After these things, Joseph of Arimathea, who was a disciple of Jesus, though a secret one because of his fear of the Jews, asked Pilate to let him take away the body of Jesus. Pilate gave him permission; so he came and removed his body. [39]Nicodemus, who had at first come to Jesus by night, also came, bringing a mixture of myrrh and aloes, weighing about a hundred pounds. [40]They took the body of Jesus and wrapped it with the spices in linen cloths, according to the burial custom of the Jews. [41]Now there was a garden in the place where he was crucified, and in the garden there was a new tomb in which no one had ever been laid. [42]And so, because it was the Jewish day of Preparation, and the tomb was nearby, they laid Jesus there.

Exegetical Perspective

John's trial and crucifixion scenes are crafted to high-light Jesus' divine power and his identity as judge, king, and Passover offering. The narrative is ironic in that those who reject Jesus nevertheless contribute to the reader's understanding of his identity.

Jesus' Divine Power. In the arrest scene (18:1–11), Jesus uses the Greek phrase *egō eimi*, which can be translated equally well as "it is I," or "I am." John has both meanings in view. In context, "It is I" identifies Jesus as the one for whom the soldiers are looking. The phrase also connotes God's name, "I AM" (cf. Exod 3:14). The soldiers respond as if they recognize the power at work in Jesus: they "stepped back and fell to the ground" (18:6), a conventional response to an appearance of God. Although they go on to arrest Jesus, the scene suggests that the soldiers are not in control of these events.

In the trial before Pilate, Pilate and the Jews are locked in a struggle for power. Pilate uses the opportunity to ridicule the Jews' desire for self-rule. The Jews' desire to see Jesus dead leads them to declare allegiance to Rome. In the midst of this, Jesus appears as the one in control. His words to Pilate, "You would have no power over me unless it had been given you from above" (19:11), underscore that, to the extent that Pilate does wield power, he does so in the service of God.

Homiletical Perspective

The reading for Good Friday is full, as the narrative includes Jesus' arrest, trial, beating, death, and burial. On this day, trust that 90 percent of the message is simply reading the story aloud. Everyone who gathers for a Good Friday service comes to be engulfed by the story of Jesus' final hours. The meaning of the sermon is grounded in the occasion for the sermon. Not much more needs to be added. Nevertheless, after the reading a homily is given. With so much material to work with, where do we focus attention for even a brief sermon?

One recommendation is to focus on one verse—or a single conversation or character—within the narrative. This gives the sermon a close relationship to the text and a controlling framework. It also allows the hearer to return to a single focus point after hearing such a long reading. In other words, savor the meaning of Good Friday by chewing on a small bite of Scripture.

One might zero in on Peter's denial (John 18:15–18; 25–27), Caiaphas's interrogation of Jesus (John 18:19–24), or Pilate's question to Jesus, "What is truth?" (John 18:38). Any of these might provide a small window to see into the expansive meaning of Good Friday. The key to this sermon style is to find a specific location in the story that allows one to look both forward and backward. A Good Friday sermon needs to enable listeners to feel the full horror of

Theological Perspective

from the burdens of the Egyptians and deliver you from slavery to them'" (Exod. 6:6). Both the Egyptians and the Israelites come to know the true identity of the God whose name is I AM by the way this God delivers the Israelites from slavery and certain death, while handing Pharaoh and his army over to death and destruction (Exod. 14:4). When Jesus first ascribes this Name to himself, he does so in the context of a discussion of true slavery and freedom, thereby reinforcing in the reader's mind this association with the exodus (John 8:31–59).

In today's passage, Jesus again uses the divine Name in relation to himself, now near the beginning of Passover, which celebrates the deliverance I AM/YHWH brought about in the exodus (John 18:4–8). The power of this Name is revealed by the fact that its mere utterance makes the soldiers and police who have come to arrest Jesus fall down. It is no wonder, then, that Peter takes out his sword to fight (John 18:10), for he believes that the God who delivered the Jews from all their enemies is personally present in Jesus.

Jesus enters Jerusalem with the shout of the crowd welcoming the coming of the King of Israel (John 12:13). Hence it is not surprising that his trial before Pilate should focus on this claim, for it would attract the immediate and lethal force of Rome to itself: "Are you the King of the Jews?" (John 18:33). The King of the Jews is associated with the same power to defeat the enemies of Israel as is the Name of God: God says of David, "I will crush his foes before him and strike down those who hate him" (Ps. 89:23). Psalm 118, quoted by the crowd when Jesus enters Jerusalem, celebrates this power of God to defend the King: "All nations surrounded me; in the name of the LORD I cut them off!" (Ps. 118:10). The King will be a Son to God, and God will be Father to the King (2 Sam. 7:14).

Jesus enhances the meaning of the relation of the King as Son to God as his Father by implying that he is equal to the Father, in the same way he ascribes the divine Name to himself. "The Father and I are one" (John 10:30). Thus Jesus claims he is not only the king like Solomon who will build a more glorious temple in which the Name of God will dwell (Hag. 2:9), but he claims to be the King who is himself the temple in which the Name dwells (John 1:14, 2:19). The presence of God in the temple gave Jerusalem the assurance of safety from all its foes (Ps. 46:5). As both the king and the temple, Jesus should be invincible against all his foes, for even the sight of Jerusalem caused its enemies to flee in panic (Ps. 48:4–8). This may explain the reason why Pilate was more afraid

Pastoral Perspective

abrupt shift from "Hosanna" to "Crucify him" fifteen minutes later is very hard to process and understand, even if most Passion Sunday sermons focus precisely on this difficulty. Perhaps we should give a pass to those who pledge to come on Friday, and let them wave their palm branches a little longer before folding and twisting them into crosses.

Maybe, just maybe, some will come at noon, and others at night, this Friday. Why? What are they coming for, and how does the preacher help them find it? By looking with them, not for them. They have two questions: Why did Jesus die/have to die? What does this death mean for my life? Not the easiest questions, but we are not needed for the easy ones. There are times when the role of the preacher is to get out of the way and let the texts and the occasion speak for themselves. Good Friday is not one of those times.

So, pastor, why *did* Jesus die/have to die? Help me understand how my emerging theology of God's love and grace meshes with the sacrificial atonement bloodiness inescapably lurking behind the texts for this day. Is this the best plan God could come up with? Is this the tradition's way of fitting what happened with what it hoped for? I understand the brutality of the Roman Empire, the fragility of life for those in the underclasses in ancient Mediterranean societies, and the collaborative instinct of the ruling religious elite in Judah in the first century. Could God not overwhelm this as God overwhelmed Pharaoh? If not, *why* not?

While you are at it, pastor, you might want to explain how I am supposed to make some sense of "the old rugged cross" for my present overwhelming circumstances. Even wearing a cross around my neck does not seem to help me understand its meaning. If Jesus "died for my sins" and I believe that "Jesus Christ is Lord," why do I still feel so trapped in my skin, so souled out every day? How does the work of the cross impact the reality of my increasingly lousy and desperate life?

Such are the real questions that those who are questioning enough to come to church on Good Friday bring with them. They are not the only questions, and all the questions do not feel so negative or so difficult to answer; but if you try to answer these two questions in your sermon—(1) why did Jesus die/have to die? and (2) what does his death mean for my life?—then you should not be surprised if folks with different questions are seriously interested in your answers to these two. Like most preachers, you have thought long and hard about your answers to these critical questions, which inevitably blend the

Exegetical Perspective

Even at the moment of his death, John portrays Jesus as exercising control. Jesus carries his own cross (19:17). He has knowledge of the completion of his work (19:28), and he himself declares, "It is finished" (19:30). The active verbs in verse 30, "he bowed his head and gave up his spirit," show Jesus' control over his death. The verb translated "gave up" is the same verb used of Judas's betrayal (18:2, 5), as well as the actions of the Jews (18:30, 35) and of Pilate (19:16) in "handing [Jesus] over" to be crucified. The use of the verb in 19:30 reminds the reader that, in the end, only Jesus can "hand over" his Spirit (cf. John 10:18).

Jesus as Judge. In a similar vein, Jesus is portrayed as judge at his own trial. Turning the tables on the usual process, Jesus asks questions of his accusers (18:23, 34), and Pilate appeals to Jesus as the arbiter of truth (18:38). In addition, 19:13 raises the question of who has authority in these proceedings: Pilate "brought Jesus outside and sat on the judge's bench." The Greek word, "sat" (*ekathisen*), can be translated two ways: *without* a direct object (Pilate sat) or with one (Pilate seated him—that is, Jesus). The language leaves the question open: who is seated on the judge's bench? While it is Pilate's prerogative, John paints a picture of Jesus as the one with authority to judge.

King Jesus. Pilate's question, "Are you the King of the Jews?" (18:33, 37), serves as a focal point for the trial. Pilate uses the claim of kingship as a way of ridiculing the people: this is what Rome will do to your king. The Jews insist that Jesus is not their king (19:14–15). By calling them "the Jews," John underscores the irony that Jesus is rejected by his own (cf. 1:11). "The Jews" seek to crucify the "King of the Jews."

For John, Jesus' kingship is revealed in his crucifixion. All four Gospels record the same inscription above the cross: "Jesus of Nazareth, King of the Jews" (John 19:19; Matt. 27:37; Mark 15:26; Luke 23:38). John draws attention to this detail (19:19–22). The three languages (Hebrew, Latin, and Greek, 19:20) make it seem an official proclamation. This is further supported by the solemnity of Pilate's words, "What I have written I have written" (19:22). Though Pilate intends the inscription as a further insult to the Jewish people, John shapes the story so that the reader may understand the crucifixion as Jesus' enthronement as king.

Jesus' burial also provides further opportunity to reflect on his identity as king. Nicodemus and Joseph of Arimathea give Jesus a burial fit for a king (see commentary for Holy Saturday, pp. 323–27).

Homiletical Perspective

what is happening, while at the same time allowing them to look ahead with hope to a glory yet to be revealed.

Another possibility would be to frame a sermon around Jesus' last words from the cross in John's Gospel: "It is finished" (John 19:30). Good Friday is a day when worshipers gather with Jesus' mother, her sister, Mary Magdalene, and the Beloved Disciple at the foot of the cross to hear the full weight of these last words. We gather to watch as Jesus gasps his final breath. Crafting a sermon that sheds light on Passover offers a backdrop for these last words.

Passover is the festival that echoes back to Israel's deliverance from Egypt, when the firstborn of the Jews were spared by the angel of death after they spread blood over the doorposts of their homes. The preacher who sets Jesus' last words within the larger covenantal story of Passover encourages Christian hearers to connect the hope of Israel's successful liberation with the bloody sacrifice of God's only Son on the cross.

It was by the blood of lambs that Israel escaped God's judgment and won their liberation from bondage in Egypt. On the cross, more blood is shed—this time by the Lamb of God—to the same end of protecting and liberating the people from the bondage of death. In this way, Jesus' last words resonate with hope in the face of despair. This tight homiletic focus allows the hearer to interpret Jesus' mock trial, beating, sentence, and execution on the cross through the eyes of John the Baptist, who much earlier said, "Here is the Lamb of God who takes away the sin of the world" (John 1:29).

Good Friday is the day Jesus fulfills John's prophetic cry with his cry. We are helpless as we watch the darkness seemingly overcome the light. Just before the light is snuffed, with his last breath and final strength, Jesus offers the world one last sermon, capturing the reality and force of the entire Gospel: "It is finished" (John 19:30).

This is the period at the end of the sentence—or is it a comma? Is Jesus looking backward at this point, or is he looking forward? Is this last word from him a word of defeat or the cry of victory, announcing a new era of good news?

For those who gather at the foot of the cross, "It is finished" suggests that this death is not an ending but a new beginning. The Greek for finished, *tetelestai*, from *teleō*, suggests that something is complete or has reached its end. Jesus' last words might be better translated, "It is accomplished!", meaning that Jesus' life has not only reached its earthly finish.

Theological Perspective

than ever when Jews told him that Jesus blasphemously claimed to be the Son of God (John 19:7–8).

If we can overcome the offense of a human being calling himself by the divine Name and claiming to be the Son of God who is equal to God (John 5:18), then we will be even more deeply offended by what this equality with God means to Jesus. This equality is not only the primary reason that leads the Jews to want to kill him (John 10:33); it is also the power by which Jesus allows himself to be killed (John 10:18). Jesus uses his power as I AM/YHWH, not to free his people from their oppressors, but to be arrested and bound by the soldiers and police. Jesus uses his power as the Son of God to give Pilate the power to condemn and crucify him (John 19:11).

Far from destroying his enemies, Jesus allows Pilate to ridicule and mock him, both before his soldiers and before the Jews. We should hardly be surprised that the disciples betray and deny Jesus when they realize that he intends to use his divine power to die, and we should be even less surprised that the Jews do not recognize as their King this powerless teacher who blasphemously claimed to be equal to God. How could this man who allowed himself to be arrested and bound be the God of the exodus? How could this man who willingly allowed himself to be ridiculed, flogged, condemned, and executed by the Roman authorities be the King of the Jews?

RANDALL C. ZACHMAN

Pastoral Perspective

biblical, theological, spiritual, and pastoral. In other words, you are prepared to address exactly the sort of topic set before you today.

Pastorally, the second question (what does Jesus' death mean for my life?) may be more important than the first, however interrelated they are. A sound pastoral approach, then, would be to start with the second question and let it lead you to the first (why did Jesus die/have to die?). Death, any death, often unconsciously brings anxiety about our own deaths into our feelings, thoughts, and questions. The closer to home a death is, the more concern and anxiety it will generate. By extension, the closer a person feels to Jesus, the more profoundly that person will experience Jesus' death, and want guidance in understanding what his death means for his or her life.

Continuing in this line of thought, is it not possible that the second question and the first question finally blend? Not just, why did Jesus die/have to die? but, why do I die/have to die? The virgule (/), then, is an illusion. "Die" and "have to die" are the same from the moment of birth, for all who are born, including Jesus. What is needed, pastorally and theologically, is a radically incarnational understanding of the cross, an understanding that relates the cross to the whole of Jesus' life from annunciation to crucifixion. In providing this, the preacher helps the congregation relate the whole of their lives to the whole of the life of Christ, so that the death of Christ is not just about their deaths, but profoundly also about their lives.

WILLIAM F. BROSEND

Exegetical Perspective

Their actions testify that Jesus' kingship extends beyond the cross.

Jesus the Passover Offering. John's language suggests that Jesus' death should be viewed as a Passover sacrifice. The narrative has been building toward the Passover festival (11:55; 12:1; 13:1; 18:28; 18:39). John's chronology is different from that of the Synoptics, for whom the Passover festival began on the day before Jesus' crucifixion (Matt. 26:17; Mark 14:12; Luke 22:7). In John, the beginning of the festival occurs at the moment of Jesus' condemnation (19:14). Noon was the time at which the slaughter of the Passover lambs began. Jesus' crucifixion is decided at the same moment (19:16).

The strange inclusion of hyssop (19:29) may also relate to John's understanding of Jesus in relation to the Passover. Hyssop is a spindly plant not well suited to the task of raising a wet sponge to Jesus' lips, but it is also the plant used by the Israelites to mark their doors with the blood of the Passover lamb (Exod. 12:22). If hyssop is meant to evoke the Passover, it may suggest that Jesus, having been "marked" as God's own by the hyssop, will ultimately be delivered from the plague of death. Those who share in the Passover offering of Jesus will likewise be delivered from the final plague.

More explicit is John's interpretation of the death of Jesus by quoting Exodus 12:46 (John 19:36). Breaking the legs of the crucified was a common act meant to hasten the death of the condemned. Jesus' legs are not broken (19:33), which John identifies as a fulfillment of the instruction not to break the legs of the Passover sacrifice.

John never spells out Jesus' relationship to Passover explicitly. The reader is left to draw conclusions from the way the story is narrated. It seems likely, based on what John says elsewhere, that he expects the reader to associate Jesus' death with the function of the Passover offering: that is, he is a life-giving meal (cf. 6:52–28) and the initiator of freedom from slavery to sin (8:34–36).

SUSAN E. HYLEN

Homiletical Perspective

Not only is his unimaginable suffering finished, not only is his obedience finished on the cross; "It is finished" is a declarative statement of finality! Something that was not a possibility before, has now been made a possibility.

Crafting a sermon around a single verse like this can offer hearers a small key to a larger announcement that something new has begun. What has begun is nothing less than a new world, where the means of reconciliation and salvation with God have been accomplished for all. On the day of preparation for Passover, Jesus, the only Son, is offered by God, as God's own lamb, without blemish or broken bone, in the perfection of obedience. There at The Place of the Skull, with the hyssop plant touching his bloody face, he offers the perfect sacrifice, offered on the cross for the sin of the whole world, crying out with a soul too deep for words, "It is finished."

As Jesus cries out, the knife falls on the innocent Lamb of God, and in that moment all the sacrifices of all the ages by all people, from then until eternity, are gathered up and rendered obsolete forever. Never again will there be another need for a sacrifice for sin. Never again will an innocent need to shed blood. Never again will a debt need to be paid for our salvation. God has accomplished it. *It is finished! Forever!*

By working one verse like this, a sermon can stay tight and focused, while at the same time allowing the preacher to retell the larger drama. This may not be the right verse for your sermon, but the point is to find a narrow focal point within the larger text to give your sermon a sharp focus. This allows the sermon to stay close to the story, while at the same time allowing the full drama to be experienced by the hearer.

TRYGVE DAVID JOHNSON

Lamentations 3:1-9, 19-24

¹I am one who has seen affliction
　　under the rod of God's wrath;
²he has driven and brought me
　　into darkness without any light;
³against me alone he turns his hand,
　　again and again, all day long.

⁴He has made my flesh and my skin waste away,
　　and broken my bones;
⁵he has besieged and enveloped me
　　with bitterness and tribulation;
⁶he has made me sit in darkness
　　like the dead of long ago.

⁷He has walled me about so that I cannot escape;
　　he has put heavy chains on me;

Theological Perspective

"Holy" or "silent" Saturday is one of the most somber days in the Christian year. It has to be. It follows Good Friday, the day on which Jesus Christ was crucified. In the biblical narrative, this devastating event could only leave the followers of Jesus completely hopeless and forlorn. The sense of God's presence experienced in the man Jesus now is a paralyzing "absence." The most wonderful life they have known has suffered and died. He cried out, "My God, my God, why have you forsaken me?" (Matt. 27:46). Now it seems this God has forsaken them as well. "Saturday" is the harshest possible postlude to Friday.

The church turns to Lamentations on this day. Here is the "lament" of a solitary figure who also felt the heaviness of God's "hand" (v. 3), feeling that God is a "bear lying in wait for me, a lion in hiding" (v. 10). The images are vivid and distressing. God is against him: "He has made my flesh and my skin waste away, and broken my bones" (v. 4). There is "bitterness" and "tribulation" (v. 5). God has "shot into my vitals the arrows of his quiver" (v. 13), so that the writer is a "laughingstock of all my people" (v. 14). God has "filled me with bitterness, he has sated me with wormwood" (v. 15), so that his "teeth grind on gravel" and he cowers in ashes (v. 16). All in all: "My soul is bereft of peace; I have forgotten what

Pastoral Perspective

Contemplation of this text called to mind lines from T. S. Eliot's "Choruses from 'The Rock'" where the speaker declares:

> It is hard for those who have never known
> 　　persecution,
> And who have never known a Christian,
> To believe these tales of Christian persecution. . . .
>
> It is hard for those who live near a Police Station
> To believe in the triumph of violence.[1]

Thus it is also hard for those who have never known the devastation of conquest and exile, the destruction of cities and neighborhoods, and the cruelty of conquerors to interpret within a historical context the poems of Lamentations.

The majority American experience is empty of such depredations, but there are minorities within America who could have sung along with the poet the sad, sad song: "I am one who has seen affliction under the rod of God's wrath" (v. 1). These include African Americans set upon by dogs, police, lynchings, and officially sanctioned oppression; Native Americans

---

1. T. S. Eliot, *The Complete Poems and Plays* (New York: Harcourt, Brace & World, 1952), 105.

^{8}though I call and cry for help,
    he shuts out my prayer;
^{9}he has blocked my ways with hewn stones,
    he has made my paths crooked.

. . . .

^{19}The thought of my affliction and my homelessness
    is wormwood and gall!
^{20}My soul continually thinks of it
    and is bowed down within me.
^{21}But this I call to mind,
    and therefore I have hope:

^{22}The steadfast love of the LORD never ceases,
    his mercies never come to an end;
^{23}they are new every morning;
    great is your faithfulness.
^{24}"The LORD is my portion," says my soul,
    "therefore I will hope in him."

Exegetical Perspective

The book of Lamentations was produced in the wake of the greatest tragedy of ancient Israel. It commemorates the destruction of the First Temple in 586 BCE by the Babylonians, which, in turn, led to the fifty-year Babylonian captivity. At history's darkest hour, the book unblinkingly recites an account of Jerusalem's utter destruction and the unbearable suffering of her people. It would be hard to find a cultural artifact that more clearly represents the nadir of a people and their hopes. Things really could not get any worse!

Of particular interest in this book is the realization that a primary promise of God seems to be abrogated. It was bad enough that God's chosen city and the temple, God's residence, had been leveled. On top of this spectacle was the realization that God had failed to keep the promise to David that his dynasty would be eternal (2 Sam. 7:14–16).

The commemoration of this historical moment in Israelite history has its analogue in Christian understanding of Jesus' entombment. For Lamentations, the fear is whether God will stand true to his promises and make things right again. In reading Lamentations 3:1–9, 19–24 on Holy Saturday, Christian tradition marks the similarly bleak outlook for the promises of God while simultaneously suggesting

Homiletical Perspective

On Holy Saturday (as opposed to the Easter Vigil), Jesus lies bound by death in the tomb's dark prison. In the words of Lamentations, we can almost hear Jesus say, "[God] has made me sit in darkness like the dead of long ago. [God] has walled me about so that I cannot escape" (vv. 6–7). Whereas the Gospel reading presents Jesus lovingly laid to rest by Joseph of Arimathea and 1 Peter portrays Jesus proclaiming the gospel to the dead, so that they might live in the spirit as God does (1 Pet. 3:19; 4:6), Lamentations offers a decidedly different, even shocking, perspective. The lectionary seems to put words of an unanswered individual lament into the mouth of Jesus. The speaker is not crying out on behalf of someone else. He offers a first-person description of his own horrendous suffering and a litany of God's deliberate destructive actions, specifically against this man himself. If we can imagine that the speaker is the Christ, this is a complaining Jesus. It is as though "My God, my God, why have you forsaken me?" (Matt. 27:46; Mark 15:34) were Jesus' first rather than final words.

If we can allow ourselves to hear Lamentations 3 as the words of Jesus, the lament becomes Christ's personal reflection on his passion. The intensity of the speaker's suffering is evident both in his

Lamentations 3:1-9, 19-24

Theological Perspective

happiness is; so I say, 'Gone is my glory and all that I had hoped for from the LORD'" (vv. 17–18). In the starkest language, this lamenter believes God has brought upon him, in Calvin's words, the "extremity of all evils."

The lamenter pours out his soul, expressing the harshness; but then things change. Even as the thought of his "affliction" and his "homelessness" come to mind, so also does another thought: "This I call to mind, and therefore I have hope" (v. 21). It is remembering an "alternative reality" to all the deadly oppressiveness that enables a new outlook and a new confidence.

This new remembrance is of the character of God. The God who has seemed to be the cause of all his troubles is now known, truly, as the source of new life for the future. Here (as in the book of Job), the assumption is that "knowledge of the true nature of God will bring comfort and hope to the sufferer."[1] The next three verses are deep in theological descriptions of the nature of the God to whom the sufferer had been pouring out his heart.

Steadfast Love (v. 22). One of the richest words in the Hebrew Bible is *hesed.* Here it is translated "steadfast love." The term has overtones of the covenant and can be rendered "covenant loyalty." Besides deep emotional dimensions, the word also means "a favor done from a sense of obligation or fidelity."[2] God will continue to exercise mercy and love, even when outward events and the darkness and distress of the situation makes it appear that God is working against the sufferer. When God's character as a loving and merciful God is remembered, assurances can arise. God's love and mercies will not "cease" or "come to an end," even in the midst of the most dire calamities of life. The covenant God will not let go of the covenant people and will always exercise the essential divine nature, even when events seem utterly to make one doubt this reality. This is the perspective of faith, to believe in the endless mercy and love of the covenant God who, contrary to outward or merely "human" perceptions, is still at work to embrace people in love.

The church remembers this on Holy Saturday, where all hope seems lost and the love found in Jesus of Nazareth appears to end. This day the church hears the ancient sufferer who, in calling to mind the God to whom his life in the community of his faith is dedicated, knows steadfast love and mercy are there

Pastoral Perspective

who endured the destruction of their culture and the "Trail of Tears"; and Southerners themselves, whose cities were burned and whose lives, fortunes, and sacred honor were given for a lost and questionable cause. All of these we can imagine echoing the lament: "[God] has driven and brought me into darkness without any light; against me alone [God] turns his hand, again and again, all day long" (vv. 2–3).

It is important at least to allude to such historical memories, lest we drain all the power of Lamentations by turning it into a cry into the darkness of personal suffering. The Scriptures have much to say of personal suffering, but not here, not in this little-noticed and little-used book of the Bible. It is little noticed and used because those who write commentaries such as these and publish them, myself included, can for the most part only be tourists in the Holocaust museums of the twentieth century, or voyeurs when we read the accounts of the violence and suffering of our ancestors.

One longs to hear a sermon preached on this text in a congregation in Atlanta after the city was burned, or in an African American congregation in Birmingham after the bombing of the 16th Street Baptist Church in which four little girls were killed. Then one might rightly cry aloud, weeping and wailing with sighs too deep for words and with tears that never stop flowing: "[God] has made my flesh and my skin waste away, and broken my bones; . . . he has made me sit in darkness like the dead of long ago" (vv. 4, 6).

The words in these laments are radically discontinuous with our experience in twenty-first-century mainline Christianity, and we dare not trivialize them or turn them into a therapeutic trajectory of handy ways to deal with suffering. At the same time, I do not mean to trivialize the suffering to which all our flesh is heir—but rather to distinguish it in kind from the personal suffering that is part of a generalized evil caused by marauding militias and the inexorable march of armies—and bombs flying in air. Think of the film *Hotel Rwanda* to understand the distinction I am making and to see an appropriate context for Lamentations.

We are using this text on Holy Saturday, and the particular choice of verses ends in the fragile hope of remembering God's steadfast love and mercy from morning to morning, from generation to generation (see the hymn "Great Is Thy Faithfulness"). In spite of the fact that the experience of human history has not changed at all since the Babylonian conquest (only the names have changed, of empires and

---

1. Adele Berlin, *Lamentations*, Old Testament Library (Louisville, KY: Westminster John Knox Press, 2002), 92.
2. Ibid., 93.

that, in Jesus, God will fulfill the ancient promises to David, albeit in revised and resurrected form.

Before reading our passage in detail, we need to consider Lamentations's place in the Jewish liturgical reading cycle. Jews read five books, known as the Megilloth or scrolls, over the course of every year on particular holidays. On Passover (April), Jews read Song of Solomon, which is understood to be a reference to the honeymoon of God with Israel after the exodus. Ruth, a celebration of harvest, fullness, and fertility, is read on Pentecost (May-June), which is an agricultural festival in the Hebrew Bible. On the ninth of Av (July-August), Jews read Lamentations. The ninth of Av is a commemoration of all great tragedies of Israelite and Jewish history. Ecclesiastes is read on Sukkot (September-October) and Esther on Purim (March). This liturgical reading cycle moves from celebration of the exodus and fullness (Ruth) to the catastrophe recorded in Lamentations and then to the final and improbable victory of the Jews over their enemies in Esther.

In other words, the cycle of reading the Megilloth follows a very typical pattern in the Hebrew Bible that sees history as a type of V. The past is understood to be rooted in triumph and glory (the left side of the V); the present is usually understood to represent the middle or lowest point in the V; and the future will probably replicate the past. Lamentations is, without doubt, the low point in Israelite and Jewish history, but understood as merely the interlude before things return to the heights of the glorious past. This represents a subtle historical analogue to the notion of resurrection.

For Jews, out of the ashes of Jerusalem will come a resurrected community worthy of Ezekiel's vision of dry bones (Ezek. 37). Clearly, reading Lamentations on Holy Saturday has in mind Jesus' coming glorification. As if to signal that, the Lamentations passage we are considering has the only positive formulations in the entire book. In addition, that our passage ends with those hopeful sentiments is hardly coincidental.

The first part of chapter 3, verses 1–9, is an individual lament written in the first person. In many ways this section resonates with Jeremiah's laments and Job's complaints. The author complains that God has driven him "into darkness without light" (*hoshek velo'-'or*). While this is likely not a direct reference to the first chapter of Genesis, the proximity of "light" and "darkness" in this verse resembles similarly proximal occurrences in Genesis 1:4–5. We may be meant to see in the current situation a reversal of the safety of created order, and clearly

"intimate, personal, and anguished voice"[1] and in the way the speaker piles up verbs to describe God's destructive action against him: driven, broken, besieged, enveloped, imprisoned, walled about, shut up, and blocked. His suffering includes physical distress, utter passivity and helplessness, and the sense of being violated from without. He knows what it is to be so isolated, abandoned, and encircled that there is no way out except through liberation. "Beseeching his jailer is the only avenue of relief open to the speaker."[2] This is certainly reminiscent of the torture, humiliation, crucifixion, and entombment that Jesus endured and provides an unsettling yet insightful way to ponder Jesus' prayer in Gethsemane (Matt. 26:39; Mark 14:36).

Most striking of all, the speaker indicts God as the cause of his suffering. All that he experiences is God's doing. The God revealed in Lamentations is not the God that we expect. This God brings darkness rather than light. This God turns the divine hand against rather than to save. This God wields the shepherd's rod—which we expect to comfort and lead us to the safety of green pastures and still waters—in anger, so that it brings us into imprisonment.

This God refuses to hear prayer. We find this God offensive, terrifying, and even unimaginable. Putting these words in Jesus' mouth compels us to struggle with and even rail against a bloodthirsty God who demands that Jesus suffer and die. Still, many in our churches know this God. They object so vociferously to this God precisely because they encounter and experience this God and want there to be a reason—something they can do, something they can change, so that God will stop being their adversary. They are afraid honestly to lament because the church does not speak honestly to their experience.

Nonetheless, without negating or denying his experience, and with an unexpected twist of irony, the speaker voices hope in this God. The speaker expects that the very hand that God used against him will save him from his enemies. The speaker dares to hope in this God, whose steadfast love never ceases, whose mercies never come to an end, whose faithfulness is great (vv. 22–23). The speaker's hope is not based on experience, but rests on God's promise. This is not an easy hope. It is a hope born out of pain that requires resolve. Recalling God's covenant love seems to make the speaker aware of its present reality

1. F. W. Dobbs-Allsopp, quoting Kathleen O'Connor, in *Lamentations*, Interpretation series (Louisville, KY: John Knox Press, 2002), 109.
2. Paul R. House, *Word Biblical Commentary*, vol. 23B (Nashville: Thomas Nelson Publishers, 2004), 411.

Lamentations 3:1-9, 19-24

Theological Perspective

and endure, even in the midst of the silent suffering of death.

Great Faithfulness (v. 23). This assurance is accompanied by the conviction that these realities emerge "new every morning," and this elicits praise: "Great is your faithfulness." God's covenant love is complemented by God's covenant faithfulness. The sufferer believes God is faithful to Israel. The backdrop of Lamentations is the exile, lamentations for the destruction of the temple and of Jerusalem. Both personal and corporate calamities are the lot of the sufferer, but the memory of God's fidelity to covenant promises, which are renewed "every morning," leads the sufferer to break into praise. God's mercies, compassions, and faithfulness have not failed, after all. They do not fail because they are the exact expressions of who God is. God is true to God's own character. God is faithful to the promises God has made to the people, to be their God as they are God's people (Exod. 19:1–9). Just as God provided manna daily for the wilderness people's needs, so now the covenant God remains faithful, providing steadfast love and mercy that are fresh every morning. Even on silent Saturday, when the "faithfulness of God" seems tested, it does not break.

Always Hope (v. 24). This covenant God brings hope, as the sufferer remembers that "the LORD is [his] portion." He shares in the covenant that God established and receives the benefits of the covenant relationship. This is his faith. He realizes "the only true foundation of patience and hope [is] to trust in God alone."[3] The sufferer's trust in the faithful God of love is the fountain of hope. There is no ultimate satisfaction aside from participation in the life of the covenant God, who remains faithful in loving mercy.

On Holy Saturday, the church waits. It waits in the deep darkness of that night. The word of hope will come. For the Lord is *our* portion; therefore we will trust in God!

DONALD K. MCKIM

Pastoral Perspective

populations), we do proclaim on this day when Jesus lay in the tomb, and the world was dark for those terrified disciples and even the women, that God is faithful and that God's promises are to be trusted—even when "[I am] walled about so that I cannot escape . . . [and] though I call and cry for help, [God] shuts out my prayer" (vv. 7, 8).

We do see in these verses from Lamentations 3 a trajectory of human suffering and God's faithfulness that prefigures the cross and resurrection, something again of Paul's words to the Philippian Christians that though Jesus emptied himself of glory and took on our human flesh—even the form of a slave—and was crucified, God raised him up in honor, because God's mercies never come to an end. Then we see rightly a hope that is not easily come to, but one born out of great pain and suffering.[2]

Is that not the reason that the Scriptures constantly renew our minds and transform the way we think of suffering at all, of suffering in any context—because of the realism of Scripture, which does not permit us to give into despair, or to embrace the cheap and costless assumption that our behaviors do not count, but says that we are held accountable for them by our Maker and Redeemer? The answer, of course, is yes. It matters ultimately, eternally, and personally whether we understand the events and experiences that make up our existence as underneath the everlasting arms—or as fate, the luck of the draw.

Here and now, even in the midst of the darkness of the tomb, or of the inexorable roll call of history that has within it no succor, no help for pain, no antidote to death and war, or to the ravages of time and circumstance—here and now God not only stands in the shadows keeping watch; God enters our plight, as accuser and redeemer, and rescues us—and not only us, but the world itself—from getting our own way.

That is good news, the good news of the gospel, even as Jesus remains in death, in the darkness of the tomb, on a day the church calls holy.

O. BENJAMIN SPARKS

---

3. John Calvin, *Commentary on Lamentations* 3:24.

2. F. W. Dobbs-Allsopp, *Lamentations,* Interpretation series (Louisville, KY: John Knox Press, 2002), 117.

Exegetical Perspective

this language could be understood as a reference to a tomb!

In verse 4 the text records that flesh (*basar*) and skin (*'or*) waste away and bones (*'etsem*) are broken. These same terms are used in Ezekiel 37 to describe the resurrection of Israel after its demise. This Lamentations passage is in the same idiom of loss and renewal that informs Ezekiel and is part of the background that informs Christian conceptions of Jesus' death and resurrection. Much of the rest of this first part of the passage reinforces the bleakness of the situation and the hopelessness of the author. In verse 8 we find a good example of his anxiety: "though I call and cry for help, he shuts out my prayer." This is a common refrain in laments from the Hebrew Bible, and its association with Jesus connotes his partaking in that venerable tradition.

With the second part of our passage, the tone changes. This is especially noteworthy in Lamentations, since it represents the only hopeful note in the book and is followed by continuing laments. By ending on its positive formulation, Christian tradition emphasizes Jesus' triumph over a long history of Jewish suffering, while simultaneously subtly dismissing it. The passage records that while the present situation is intolerable (vv. 19–20), the author calls to mind that "the steadfast love of the LORD never ceases, his mercies never come to an end" (v. 22). This section ends in verse 24 with the declaration of the author's hope in God's restorative power.

In the context of Lamentations and the aftermath of Jerusalem's destruction, this hope is as moving as it is courageous. So bold is this hope that the rest of Lamentations returns to the utter futility of the current situation. By reading this passage on Holy Saturday, Christian tradition partakes of the hopelessness of Lamentations, while equally asserting that in Jesus God has finally set things straight and fulfilled those ancient and eternal promises that are the focus of Lamentations.

LARRY L. LYKE

Homiletical Perspective

and to move the speaker from hopelessness to resolve to hope, even when there is no indication that God has acted or intervened to alleviate his suffering. This kind of hope empowered Jesus to pray, "Yet not what I want, but what you want" (Matt. 26:39; Mark 14:36; Luke 22:42), and brought Jesus willingly from garden to tomb.

A daring sermon would help the congregation to encounter this Jesus. He is not a Sleeping Beauty sort of Jesus, peacefully lying in the tomb and quietly counting down the hours until the angels arrive and it is time to get up; nor is this the unstoppable superhero Christ, who seizes descent to the dead as one more opportunity to proclaim the gospel and save.

This Jesus is trapped in a tomb, lamenting his fate and complaining to God. This Jesus "has seen affliction under the rod of God's wrath" (v. 1). More than witnessing suffering and sorrow, this Jesus knows and experiences them firsthand. This Jesus vividly and personally knows what it is to experience God as adversary, even tormentor. He reveals a God that we do not want to know, but that many people regularly encounter. This Jesus shares in what so many experience and describe as God's personal attack on them. This Jesus gives voice to and protests against situations more dire than physical death and cries out to God for help, release, and protection. This Jesus also remains hopeful that the dawn will come, that God will act, that there will be resurrection, because that is what God has promised.

In a sermon that joins this Jesus in the tomb on Holy Saturday, Jesus becomes one with anyone who has suffered greatly; Jesus becomes one with everyone who feels helplessness, hopelessness, pain, and despair because it seems that God is against them. In the tomb Jesus addresses our experiences honestly and frees us to lament. Then Jesus recalls God's promises, giving us resolve to hope. Since Jesus can become one with us in despair, Jesus can bring us with him through trouble to patient faith and resolute hope. For most of us, this is the resurrection we need.

CRAIG A. SATTERLEE

Psalm 31:1-4, 15-16

[1]In you, O Lord, I seek refuge;
    do not let me ever be put to shame;
    in your righteousness deliver me.
[2]Incline your ear to me;
    rescue me speedily.
  Be a rock of refuge for me,
    a strong fortress to save me.
[3]You are indeed my rock and my fortress;
    for your name's sake lead me and guide me,
[4]take me out of the net that is hidden for me,
    for you are my refuge.
. . . .
[15]My times are in your hand;
    deliver me from the hand of my enemies and persecutors.
[16]Let your face shine upon your servant;
    save me in your steadfast love.

Theological Perspective

On Holy Saturday, the triumphal entrance into Jerusalem on Palm Sunday is almost forgotten. The effects of the betrayal on "Spy Wednesday" have been felt. Holy Thursday's new mandate has been given in the upper room, then lived out in the Garden of Gethsemane and on Good Friday's cross. Holy Saturday, then, is about *sepultus est*—he was buried. This is the day of rest, "the 'Second Sabbath' after creation,"[1] for God is creating the world anew. God is reuniting the image to the likeness and bringing a new day, the eighth day, of creation.

Rarely do we linger on that statement in the creed, "was crucified, dead, and buried." Today that is the whole point. Holy Saturday is the day when Jesus experienced a taste of what Lazarus knew for four days. He was wrapped in cloths again, but not like a newborn; yet in some ways we can say that Jesus went into the depths of the earth to be born anew as the risen Lord. After all, is that not what he had preached when he said, "Very truly, I tell you, unless a grain of wheat falls into the earth and dies, it remains just a single grain; but if it dies, it bears much fruit" (John 12:24).

What Jesus preached and practiced, Paul looked to as the fulfillment of the Christian's life. "Just as we

1. Pius Parsch, *The Church's Year of Grace*, vol. 2 (Collegeville, MN: Liturgical Press, 1953), 337.

Pastoral Perspective

Holy Saturday is a long, mournful day. It is a wandering day for the church, for on that day there really is no church at all, not between crucifixion and resurrection, not yet. Jesus lies in that tomb all alone. From the clay we have come, to the clay we return. There are no church soup kitchens, no church pews peopled with folk eager to hear the gospel, no church building, no church bells, no church steeple.

Ash Wednesday ashes streak endlessly across a leaden sky, heated from that molten eruption of violence the day before. The world went raving mad, and we tried, weakly, to put on the brakes, but it was too late; though the madness convulsed to a stop and the brakes finally held, it was too late. There was the smell of metal against metal, and heat, and loss: too little, too late. What on earth could *we* have done, anyway? Our best efforts would have amounted to little more than spitting against the wind.

Now, of course, there is no wind. The midday storm howled and soaked us, but passed quickly into the nothingness from which it came. Today is airless, still, and unholy hot. It is Holy Saturday. We are bone-weary sad, and more than a little afraid that they can still get us, can still kill us in a second, just for knowing him, for loving him. We did love him, but our love proved useless, and God's love—well, God must have just looked the other way.

Exegetical Perspective

The psalm's superscription (not printed above) relates it specifically to David. The Hebrew preposition (*le*) accomplishes this purpose and presents three possibilities as to how specifically Psalm 31 became aligned with this particular king of Israel. It could signify, first, that the psalm was written "for" David; second, that it "belonged to" him, that is, was part of King David's collection; or third, that it has been deemed to convey something "about" or "concerning" the historical person David.

It is nearly impossible for a translator to know which function of the preposition to choose. However, such a choice is especially consequential when it affects an opening inscription that essentially frames the meaning of the following piece for the reader. It is important, then, to consider openly all three implications of the received Hebrew preposition. In this case, the psalm seems to support evidence that Psalm 31 ultimately relays something "about" King David.

The speaker begins the psalm with the confession that he or she has sought refuge in Israel's God, YHWH. As an opening statement, this declaration carries great influence as to how the rhetoric of the psalm will develop. Since the personal and experiential name for God is used, it is clear that the speaker belongs to God's chosen people, the Israelite nation.

Homiletical Perspective

On this day between Good Friday and Easter, nothing happens. Jesus is dead. All movement stops. The events have played themselves out. Holy Saturday has a quality of limbo, neither here nor there. This can be hard to endure.

David Richo, a former Jesuit priest and a therapist, once spoke in my hearing about our fragmented lives, our grief and depression, and the need simply to be held in that state. Richo said the day was like the *Pieta*, Mary holding the body of Jesus. He said that looking at the sculpture made him realize that as Mary held Jesus, she loved him, even in this broken and fragmented state, and this love prepared him for his resurrection.[1]

The preaching task today can take its cue from the idea of holding, being held, in a broken state, without immediate resolution. Psalm 31 is one of David's psalms. The excerpts chosen from it for this day are heartbreaking but have in them images of things that can hold us: a rock, a house, a fortress, the ear of God, God's face. The preacher for Holy Saturday will have to practice restraint in turning to these images, remembering that Easter has not yet come.

The central dilemma in this sermon is how to stay focused on holding and accepting fragmentation and

---

1. David Richo, "The Void," retreat at Trinity Episcopal Church, Santa Barbara, CA, May 10, 1997.

Psalm 31:1-4, 15-16

Theological Perspective

have borne the image of the man of dust, we will also bear the image of the man of heaven. . . . For this perishable body must put on imperishability, and this mortal body must put on immortality. When this perishable body puts on imperishability, and this mortal body puts on immortality, then the saying that is written will be fulfilled: 'Death has been swallowed up in victory'" (1 Cor. 15: 49, 53–54).

This is the time when Jesus "descended into hell" and "made a proclamation to the spirits in prison" (1 Pet. 3:19). It is beautifully described in the ancient homily used in the Roman *Liturgy of the Hours* "Office of Readings" on Holy Saturday:

> Something strange is happening—there is a great silence on earth today, a great silence and stillness. The whole earth keeps silence because the King is asleep. The earth trembled and is still because God has fallen asleep in the flesh and he has raised up all who have slept ever since the world began. God has died in the flesh and hell trembles with fear.
>
> He has gone to search for our first parent, as for a lost sheep. Greatly desiring to visit those who live in darkness and the shadow of death, he has gone to free from sorrow the captives Adam and Eve, he who is both God and the son of Eve. . . . Rise, let us leave this place. The enemy has led you out of the earthly paradise. I will not restore you to that paradise, but I will enthrone you in heaven. . . .The kingdom of heaven has been prepared for you from all eternity.[2]

Here, indeed, is the renewal of the original Sabbath. Here is the result for which the psalmist prays, "My times are in your hand; deliver me from the hand of my enemies and persecutors" (v. 15).

Psalm 31:5 is on Jesus' lips as his life ends on the cross, "Into your hand I commit my spirit." It seems appropriate to read the verses before that to show why the speaker can offer himself up with such confidence. The one offering the prayer *is* confident and knows that the Lord will hear. This confidence is expressed in the strong, vivid imagery used to describe the one to whom he turns in trust. For the psalmist the Lord is a "rock," "crag," "fortress," and "stronghold." These are places of refuge when one flees to them; one finds safety and security in the face of danger. This refuge is more than an airy hope ("pie in the sky when you die by and by"), but the assurance of one who knows and trusts the Refuge.

Pastoral Perspective

Forever is how long this day seems to last, forever and a day. We are stunned and hoarse, and have nothing left to cry. We pace, we pace.

Preaching on this day means dealing with the stuckness between crucifixion Friday and Easter. When Easter comes, only then does the dark Friday before deservedly get named "Good." Only because of Easter does the wait on Holy Saturday become bearable.

Rhetorically, the great preacher-poet George MacDonald would one day ask, "Did Christ not foil and slay evil by letting all the waves and billows of its horrid sea break upon him, go over him, and die without rebound: spend their rage, fall defeated, and cease?"[1]

On that first Holy Saturday, evil was not yet foiled or slain. Those first disciples and friends must have thought the battle was over. With Jesus lying in a tomb, nothing had been won, nothing. The dark, angry waves came and broke upon Jesus, but on that first Holy Saturday, that tidal surge was not yet spent.

So, too, on every Holy Saturday since: faith requires us to sit in this desolate place, dried tears upon our faces. How could Rome, the religious leaders of the day, people like you and me—indeed, *us*—how could we do what we did?

No wonder this day moves so slowly.

When someone asks the pastor, "Why do we have a prayer of confession in the first place? I am hardly ever guilty of the sins we pray about every week," all she needs to do is point to this day. Our sin leads us to do things like *this*. On Holy Saturday, our waiting *and our preaching* necessarily plumb this difficult truth.

On Holy Saturday the women weep and tremble. They will make their way to the tomb with the burial spices, laden with their incomprehensible grief. Tomorrow the women will trudge to the tomb, before the stench begins to rise. The rest of us will wait for our regular lives to begin again—life without Jesus. We will drop Mary back off at home, as small as a fist, defiant, unbelieving, dazed by it all, stoned from insults that cut us all to the quick. We will kiss her lightly good-bye and shuffle away through the dust.

For a while, what Jesus said sounded so in tune with what the psalmists had sung, and the ranting of the prophets, and God's age-old promise for the future. Our hopes were just beginning to rise with thoughts of justice, hope, freedom, and love. It all sounded so good.

---

2. "An Ancient Homily for Holy Saturday," in *The Liturgy of the Hours: According to the Roman Rite*, vol. 2, *Lent and Easter Season*, ICEL (New York: Catholic Book Publishing Co., 1976), 496–98.

1. George MacDonald, *Unspoken Sermons* (Charleston, SC: BilbeoBazaar, 2006), 359.

Exegetical Perspective

The Hebrew verb translated "refuge" in 31:1, *hasah*, means literally to seek protection or shade and often appears in OT passages describing the shelter of the Lord's wings (e.g., Pss. 36:7, 57:1, 91:4; Ruth 2:12). The speaker here grounds his or her demonstrated reliance upon God's security. Based on his or her declared loyalty to YHWH, the psalmist directs, "So let me never be put to shame" (v. 1, my trans.). Next, appealing even more forcefully to the Lord's righteous character, the speaker commands directly, "Rather, cause me to escape!" (my trans.).

It becomes evident in verse 2 that the psalmist is being threatened and in a vulnerable stance. YHWH is again commanded to extend his ear quickly, and respond with immediate rescue. The speaker here intensifies his or her stance of reliance on YHWH by putting forth an elaborate and compelling "word collage" of nearly every Hebrew configuration representing fortresses or bastions of security (vv. 2–4).

YHWH has come to encompass all imaginable structures of safety for the psalmist. Words representing natural defense stations like cliffs and crags are evidenced, alongside magnificently designed entrenchments and siegeworks. After extolling the mighty position the Lord's protection has come to occupy for the speaker, he or she bids forcefully that YHWH, for his own name's sake, *act* (v. 3).

The psalmist's integration of the Lord's name in his or her argument for being saved is a persuasive one. In ancient Semitic culture generally, one's name reveals one's character; for instance, the name "Jacob" (*ya'aqob*) means "striver" or "deceiver." Having already called attention to God's righteous quality in verse 1, the speaker now adds the significance the name or reputation YHWH engenders, that is, what YHWH is known for.

In verse 5 the speaker affirms, "You have ransomed me, O YHWH—O God of firmness" (my trans.). The uttering of the Hebrew word "ransom" (*padah*) hearkens back to God's cosmic act of salvation in the exodus narrative, offering a repeated reminder that "[I am] the Lord your God—who brought you out of the land of Egypt and ransomed you from the House of Slavery" (my trans., Deut. 13:5). By further granting God the attribute of firmness or reliability, the speaker is clearly petitioning another act of deliverance.

Next, to litigate even further his or her case for God's immediate attention and assistance, the psalmist supplies evidence of reviling those who worship idols (v. 6); and in verse 7 promises that once YHWH acknowledges the direness and poverty of his

Homiletical Perspective

brokenness without offering the pabulum of "everything is all right." Mary really does not think "everything is all right" as she holds Jesus at the foot of the cross. After someone has died, in those days that follow, we do not really think that everything will be all right. That is not the first thing that comes to mind.

What *can* happen is that we enter a deep reality, separate from our daily grinds, one that is slow and often full. We may feel as if we are living in what the Celts called "thin space," where heaven meets earth. The disciples and Jesus' family must have experienced some of this after the horrors of Good Friday. While certainly shocked and terrorized, they were also full of shared grief. If they could, they must have comforted and held each other, just as Mary comforted and held the body of Jesus.

The natural world offers solace to many in this state—rocks are old and patient. For others, the comfort will come from the image of a house—a beloved place with its mark of human things and memories. For others, the idea of a fortress is most appealing—a place that keeps out enemies and is walled and safe. Using any of these images requires caution, since people experience rocks, houses, and fortresses in different ways. The skillful preacher will allow listeners to choose an image without too much guidance about how they should feel about it.

If you are preaching in a church that celebrates the Easter Vigil, this sermon fits right in. The Vigil begins in the dark, an often comforting and quiet place to experience brokenness, fragmentation, and grief. From the back of the church, someone will light a dish of charcoal with a flint. From the fire a deacon will light the paschal candle as she or he sings, "The light of Christ."

Every life must be retold and remade. The Easter Vigil retells the history of Christianity from Genesis to the exodus to the moment when Magdalene, gone to the tomb, is greeted by an angel who says, "I know that you are looking for Jesus who was crucified. He is not here" (Matt. 28:5). This is history of another, other world, what Simone Weil called a "different order."[2] In the darkness, lit only by our own frail candles, we sit and listen to how the Spirit "brooded" over the face of the waters, how the dove returned to Noah with an olive leaf in its beak, how Abraham lifted his knife over his son, how Moses stretched his staff over the sea.

In almost every language except English the same word is used for the Jewish Passover and the

---

2. Simone Weil, "Spiritual Autobiography," *Waiting for God* (New York: Perennial Library, Harper & Row, 1951), 63.

Psalm 31:1-4, 15-16

Theological Perspective

To seek such a refuge, to know that "my times are in your hand" means that one has known God and has experienced God's goodly providence. While we read the psalm from the perspective of the Lord in the tomb today, these assurances are as much for those who are living. Our times are in God's hand, and God has demonstrated over the previous days how intentional God is in walking life—from beginning to end—with us.

As James Luther Mays comments, "Indeed, it is a question whether they can be said at the end in authenticity unless they have been our confession all along the way. In the mouth of Jesus the sentence is surely a profound interpretation of his entire life. Calvin said that unless a person practices such a reliance on the providence of God in the living of life, 'he is not yet learned aright what it is to live.' (Calvin, 1:503)."[3] To know that our times are in God's hand and to live accordingly is to live rightly and confidently.

Holy Saturday's purpose may be far more than the quiet interlude before the Vigil unfolds the story of our redemption for us and Easter joy spills over. This is the day where the crucified Lord goes looking for those destined to be with him for all eternity. This is the day when the new creation gestates and prepares to break forth. This is the day when one comes to know, truly, that our times are in God's hand as we wait for the fullness, the giddiness of the declaration: "This is the day the LORD has made; let us rejoice and be glad in it!" (Ps. 118:24).

As Lent is a "bright darkness," perhaps Holy Saturday is a working Sabbath?

STEVEN A. PEAY

Pastoral Perspective

At the end, when he was on the cross, Jesus quoted the fifth verse of Psalm 31 (omitted, ironically, from today's lection): "Into your hand I commit my spirit." It was a final and complete affirmation of the trust he had in a God who would not let him, ultimately, be put to shame. Jesus knew that his future, as uncertain as it may have seemed to him and as utterly bleak as it was to his disciples, could be trusted wholly to God's merciful care.

"My times are in your hand; deliver me from the hand of my enemies and persecutors. Let your face shine upon your servant; save me in your steadfast love" (vv. 15–16). Jesus trusted God with his life.

On Holy Saturday, we keep vigil. We lament because we are part of the sharp-edged chaos that wounds the world. We lament that shame, idolatry, wayward egos, and a host of other sins cripple our best efforts. We have every reason to be worn out and to bury our lined faces deep into our hands. We have ample reason to be glad, too. We have hope because we trust a God unfettered by mockery and grave-clothes.

"Jesus' words from the cross are not simply an interpretation of how Jesus died but also an interpretation of how Jesus lived his whole life—trusting God, proclaiming and embodying the reign of God in word and deed."[2]

Our calling is to live free from the hopelessness of Holy Saturday. Our consolation is that after the long vigil, he rose again sometime in the wee hours. We do not toast a dead hero. We serve a living Lord.

Easter Sunday dawns early and bright. On Holy Saturday we count the hours to that redemptive dawn.

WILLIAM P. "MATT" MATTHEWS JR.

---

3. Calvin, *Commentary on Psalm 31:5*, quoted in James Luther Mays, *Psalms*, Interpretation series (Louisville, KY: John Knox Press, 1994), 144.

2. J. McCann, *The New Interpreter's Bible* (Nashville: Abingdon Press, 1996), 4:802.

Exegetical Perspective

or her current condition by procuring release, he or she "will exult and rejoice in your steadfast love."

The Hebrew word rendered "steadfast love" (*hesed*) most literally means "proper act," "devotion," "loyalty," or "faithfulness." Since *hesed* almost exclusively appears in Hebrew Scripture to describe specifically the Lord's response to and relationship with his people, it is critical to acknowledge the obligatory dimension of God's acting that is integral to this noun. It conveys God's ultimate willingness to be faithful to God's own revealed character. In this way YHWH manifests proper devotion and loyalty to his people. The psalmist again showcases God's own character in making a claim for God's immediate and saving response to his or her predicament.

Psalm 31:10–12 presents another word collage, this time not delineating the safe enclosures of God's protection (vv. 2–4), but rather the debilitating effect upon spirit and body of an absence of God's intervention. The psalmist heaps up multiple words and images that convey languishment, sighing, and marginalization. He or she tells of being taunted, abhorred, moth-eaten, and abandoned. In verse 12 the psalmist declares defiantly, "I have been forgotten—like one who is dead. More than a heart, I have become an organ that is perishing" (my trans.).

In the vulnerable and near-death silence in which the speaker now subsists, he or she hears whisperings and plottings of the wicked all around (v. 13). The psalmist, perhaps with one final breath, entreats the Lord why he would allow this servant, who says, "I trust in you, O YHWH" (my trans., v. 14), to diminish, while condoning deceptive lips "that speak insolently against the righteous" (v. 18). The speaker suggests boldly, "Let them go dumbfounded to Sheol" (v. 17). Despite all circumstances, even to the very end, the psalmist resolves: "My times are in your hand" (v. 15).

Verses 21–24 present unexpectedly the psalmist's celebration of the Lord's abounding goodness to all who seek protection from him. YHWH has now "wondrously shown" his abiding concern (v. 21). In verse 22 the speaker joyfully proclaims, "Truly, you did hear the voice of my supplications when I cried out to you for help" (my trans.), and enjoins all hearers and readers in grateful confidence to "be strong, and let your heart take courage, all you who wait for the Lord" (v. 24).

JENNIFER PFENNIGER

Homiletical Perspective

Christian Easter: Pascha or Passover. This is the night that Jesus passes over from death into life; this is the night that people are traditionally baptized—drowned to the old life, to insensibility and unconsciousness—and raised to a new life of compassion, availability, and abundance.

In a sermon at Trinity Episcopal Church in Santa Barbara, the late Bishop George Barrett once said, "Tonight, we look over our shoulders at our history. We look over our shoulders at Jesus and at where we have been." Addressing a baptismal candidate, Bishop Barrett said, "Now your history is bound to the history of God."[3]

On Holy Saturday, we make the decision to bind ourselves to the history of Jesus and to the history of God. We experience the brokenness of a more-than-good man who bound himself to God. Christianity is not, on this day, glorious or triumphant. The day itself is a time of quietly following enormous suffering, when human compassion is one of the few gifts we can offer and one of the few we can take.

The task of the preacher is to be restrained, compassionate, and quiet as she or he finds words that spring from the images in Psalm 31 and does that psalm justice. The words need to come from the body, mind, and soul of the preacher. This is not a day to display fabulous oratory or clever language, but rather a day to reveal one's own true heart.

NORA GALLAGHER

---

3. Bishop George Barrett, Easter Virgil sermon, at Trinity Episcopal Church, Santa Barbara, CA, 1995.

1 Peter 4:1-8

¹Since therefore Christ suffered in the flesh, arm yourselves also with the same intention (for whoever has suffered in the flesh has finished with sin), ²so as to live for the rest of your earthly life no longer by human desires but by the will of God. ³You have already spent enough time in doing what the Gentiles like to do, living in licentiousness, passions, drunkenness, revels, carousing, and lawless idolatry. ⁴They are surprised that you no longer join them in the same excesses of dissipation, and so they blaspheme. ⁵But they will have to give an accounting to him who stands ready to judge the living and the dead. ⁶For this is the reason the gospel was proclaimed even to the dead, so that, though they had been judged in the flesh as everyone is judged, they might live in the spirit as God does.

⁷The end of all things is near; therefore be serious and discipline yourselves for the sake of your prayers. ⁸Above all, maintain constant love for one another, for love covers a multitude of sins.

Theological Perspective

Many churches do not formally observe a liturgy for this day, variously known as Holy Saturday and the Great Sabbath. Starkly distinct from the Great Vigil that begins at sundown, the daylight hours constitute a difficult day, one with which we may not know just quite what to do. The sorrowful events of the past two days are concluded. The resurrection lies yet ahead. A preacher of the early church proclaimed, "Today a great silence reigns on earth, a great silence and a great stillness."[1] Today we are waiting with Jesus' friends and companions.

There is, however, a significant difference that enables us to approach this difficult day in a way they could not. Those who were with Jesus during the last week of his life did not know what would happen next. They were numb with grief, feeling as though time itself had been suspended. Grief is like that. We know we are waiting in hope. That fact alone, however, makes us aware of the ambiguities of this day.

The day is indeed rife with ambiguities. *The Book of Common Prayer* directs that the Eucharist is not to be celebrated. Having for two days encountered largely sensible, observable realities in our epistles, with 1 Peter's words concerning the proclamation of

Pastoral Perspective

It is not popular these days to preach on "human desires" (v. 2) such as those named in verse 3, particularly on Holy Saturday, but preachers may on occasion find themselves in a setting where the commentary of 1 Peter 4:1–8 on such desires could be a very powerful and helpful one. Those in such circumstances often wrestle mightily with a whole host of addictions and excesses (alcohol, gambling, drugs, pornography, sex, etc.). The hope for Christians with such challenges, as presented by the writer of 1 Peter, lies in the reminder that opens this passage: Christ suffered too.

God in Christ suffers with us. God's love endures through all addictions. Jesus Christ is our companion in all distress. Fellowship with others is supportive in times of struggle. Love of others not only nurtures those in such situations, but "covers a multitude of sins" (v. 8). While the exact meaning of this phrase is not clear, one possible interpretation is that love causes "forgiveness and reconciliation to abound (both among members of the community and in the eye of God), and therefore God's judgment about other lesser failings is abated."[1]

---

1. "Ancient Homily for Holy Saturday," quoted in *Catechism of the Catholic Church: With Modifications from the Editio Typica* (New York: Doubleday, 1997), 181.

1. Donald P. Senior, CP, and Daniel J. Harrington, SJ, *1 Peter, Jude, and 2 Peter*, vol. 15, Sacra pagina (Collegeville, MN: Liturgical Press, 2003), 124.

Exegetical Perspective

Although the lectionary connects 1 Peter 4:7–8 with verses 1–6, the first paragraph speaks of the way Christians are to live in the midst of nonbelievers, while verse 7 initiates a second paragraph (vv. 7–11) that describes their life together in the church (v. 8, "Above all, maintain constant love for one another").[1] Despite the fact that the night before Easter is a notably in-house occasion, with fewer visitors than Easter morning will likely bring, we do well to bear in mind the world's response to the gospel as we mark Jesus' death and await his resurrection.

First Peter addresses Gentile Christians in Asia Minor who are members of non-Christian households and surrounded by non-Christian neighbors. The author notes that his listeners meet with continuing hostility from their families and neighbors because they "no longer" share in the common life of their culture (v. 4).

Paganism was particularly enthusiastic in Asia Minor; the New Testament offers several illustrations. The crowd stirred up by the silversmith Demetrius protests Paul's cutting into the idol business by his preaching by shouting in opposition, "Great is Artemis of the Ephesians!" (Acts 19:28). The apostle

---

1. See the discussion of the structure of chap. 4 in Paul J. Achtemeier, *1 Peter*, Hermeneia (Minneapolis: Fortress Press, 1996), 276.

Homiletical Perspective

Holy Saturday is a place to pause on the journey of Holy Week. After the intensity of Maundy Thursday and Good Friday, we need time for reflection, renewal, and celebration. On Holy Saturday the people of God consider the big picture. "How has God worked through all salvation history? What is the significance of this history in light of my faith community? In light of my faith?" As a part of the testimony of salvation history, 1 Peter 4:1–8 invites the preacher to imagine with her community their present and future embodiment of Christ in the world.

It is, however, a complex invitation for twenty-first-century sensibilities. The rhetoric of suffering for Christ and putting aside human desires is reminiscent of an asceticism that has been used to abuse and dominate throughout Christian history. Upon first reading for twenty-first-century Christians, there is a "holier than thou" sense to the passage. There is a resistance to the notion that God requires suffering and that the essence of God's action in Jesus' life, death, and resurrection is made valid because of his bodily suffering.

On Holy Saturday, when we pause to consider and feel into the immensity of the Christ story in light of salvation history, it is the preacher's right and task to push the congregation's envelope. Being a Christian is not about being a "good and nice person," an

1 Peter 4:1-8

Theological Perspective

the gospel to the dead we venture into an utterly inaccessible realm. The language is interpretive and evocative, not in any way the reporting of "fact" in even the broadest sense. If we know that Good Friday is not the final word, that we await the beginning of the new creation, then why pay attention to this interim? Still, it is good for us to slow down any tendency to rush from Good Friday to Easter Sunday, not simply to get through this day but to dwell with it. In spite of its difficulty and ambiguity, Holy Saturday brings important insight, illumined by this word from 1 Peter. In particular, our passage provides a word addressing issues of pastoral and moral theology.

The suspension experienced on Holy Saturday, the interval between the cross and the empty tomb, opens space for us to acknowledge that human life is marked by times of waiting. Often we think little of this. We wait between the planning and completion of a project. That waiting is not difficult. We are busy and can see ourselves moving toward a goal. However, there are other times of waiting that bring a sense of suspension: between the test and the diagnosis, between the rupture of relationship and the first contact afterward. Such times call us to awareness that the great reality of our lives is that of waiting. Our cycles of planning and completion fill time, and at their best sanctify it; yet the deep mystery of our life unfolds slowly. It is something on which we wait, and for which we lack proper words.

Liturgical theologian James Farwell has thus observed, "Holy Saturday is the truth of our lives, so close to where we are that it serves as the heart of the paschal liturgies but is itself, as the very nature of the divine-human encounter, a mystery beyond even the power of liturgy to encode."[2] Not only are we doing little; there is little we can do, for the mystery of existence is received, but not seized.

Theology and pastoral practice converge in the awareness that we do not merely wait with a vague sense of hope. No, God in Christ has entered the abyss and so taken every aspect of human existence and experience into God's inexhaustible life. Resurrection is not merely the happy resumption of the story interrupted by tragedy. Resurrection takes place in the midst of, not apart from, suffering and desolation—and so in the midst of all our forms of waiting.

The words of Gregory Nazianzen during the Apollonarian controversy over Jesus' full humanity apply here as well. "That which he has not assumed

2. James Farwell, *This Is the Night: Suffering, Salvation, and the Liturgies of Holy Week* (New York: T. & T. Clark, 2005), 69.

Pastoral Perspective

The foregoing discussion is not to suggest that others in the Christian community do not struggle with addictive desires. To the addictions named could be added the compulsive use of computer and video games, the Internet, and television, but Holy Saturday quite likely is not the occasion for such a focus. A more fruitful direction to turn would be to consider another theme of this lectionary text: that faith is best nurtured in community.

The writer of 1 Peter sees Christians as resident aliens. Elsewhere in this letter the terms "exiles" and "aliens" (1:1 and 2:11) are used explicitly, but the argument in 1 Peter 4:1–8 in this regard is still very clear. This passage sets up a contrast between living "by human desires" and living "by the will of God" (v. 2), and again later between being "judged in the flesh" and living "in the spirit" (v. 6). This contrast separates Christians from non-Christians. "Gentiles" (v. 3, meaning non-Christians or pagans, not non-Jews) live by human desires or passions that stem principally from their "lawless [i.e., unholy] idolatry" (v. 3). Therefore, Christians must necessarily live in, but not of, the world.

This stark contrast between Christians and non-Christians is not easily translated into contemporary life. Except for Christians living in parts of Africa and Asia where they are in the minority, particularly where they are isolated, ostracized, or under some threat, for most Christians the contrast is more subtle and nuanced and less directly hostile. European and North American Christians may instead see the contrast between those who participate regularly and actively in worshiping communities and those who, while not necessarily hostile to churchgoers, are dismissive of organized religion.

Such individuals may well describe themselves as religious, even Christian, but seek to live lives independent of the trappings of an organized faith. These are the ones who may see themselves as seekers or as more "spiritual" than "religious," and they may explore and use a variety of spiritual practices such as yoga and meditation, as well as focusing on personal health habits such as diet, exercise, appropriate sleep, and weight training. Many such practices have much to recommend them.

Others may prefer to live out their faith privately and individually, rather than attend to the messiness of institutional church life. They may well be devout people living their lives in faithfulness to Christ's example. They care for the poor, protect the environment, and work for peace and justice. They just do so

himself recalls that he "fought with wild animals [that is, magicians] at Ephesus" (1 Cor. 15:32). The Apocalypse is addressed to "the seven churches that are in Asia" (Rev. 1:4). Although Revelation speaks of a local religious official who enforces worship of the emperor (the second beast in 13:11–18), this is not so much planned imperial persecution of the church as it is endemic, sustained cultural hostility toward people who are seen to be different, antisocial, even atheistic. Christians (like Jews) were thought by pagans to jeopardize public welfare because they did not honor the ancestral gods or support the empire's promotion of *pietas* (roughly equivalent to "family values"), which required households to espouse the religious convictions of the head of the family.

The Christian women and slaves to whom 1 Peter is addressed come in for just such criticism and ostracism. The author of 1 Peter calls it suffering. Although popular Christian imagination today tends to think of suffering as martyrdom, what these Christians face is the daily, hourly scorn of relatives and neighbors and the contempt of their betters. In the long run, to live day after day with being shunned and made fun of may take more courage than to be thrown once to the lions.

What precedes this evening's passage is a discussion of baptism, which gives Christians access to God through the death and resurrection of Jesus, "who has gone into heaven and is at the right hand of God, with angels, authorities, and powers made subject to him" (3:22, another reference to Ps. 110, much as in the Epistle lesson for Good Friday, Heb. 4:14–16; 5:7–9). Christ's suffering on our behalf "in the flesh" means that we too suffer because "whoever has suffered in the flesh has finished with sin" (4:1). This reprises the themes struck in 2:18–25, where the author of 1 Peter reflects at length on Jesus as the servant of the Lord (Isa. 52:13–53:12) who suffers undeserved abuse and thereby redeems others who suffer because they follow in his footsteps (2:21).

Four imperatives bracket the passage: "arm yourselves" (v. 1), "be serious and discipline yourselves" (v. 7), and "maintain constant love" (v. 8). These exhortations highlight the contrast between the behavior of believers and that of "the Gentiles" (v. 3), who in the vocabulary of 1 Peter are non-Christians. Those Gentiles order their lives by "by human desires" rather than by God's will, "living in licentiousness, passions, drunkenness, revels, carousing, and lawless idolatry" (v. 2).

The adverb "no longer" in verse 4 reminds the addressees of the profound alteration of their lives

"upstanding member of society." Christ's message has a radical edge that leads one to strip away all that hinders one from following Christ's model of intimacy in relationship to God and so in relationship with the community, the body of Christ. This stripping process certainly may involve discontinuing the practices that you find in this text. More importantly what are the attitudes of the false self that fuel the listed behaviors? Can an understanding of the will of God in light of God's saving grace and love throughout salvation history help a congregation get past the list and into a deeper experience of the Divine? If an individual and/or a community is intentionally on an exilic pilgrimage away from culture's distractions, what will be shed so that sin or separation from God is finished? And so that the twenty-first century Body of Christ in all its manifestations can authentically and fully embody Christ in the world?

Perhaps a story from twenty-first-century salvation history can lead us into the vision of this text for the people of God. It began one recent Holy Saturday. As the people approached the old stone downtown church for the Easter Vigil service, they were greeted by the smell of burning pinion wood and the sound of an African drum. A small bonfire burned on the front steps, and the drummer was smiling a welcome to all who entered. Inside there was the busy chaos of creation. Preparations were underway for the enactment of salvation history stories. Finger puppets were passed around to be animals in the cardboard ark. PowerPoint presentations were set up for a high-tech experience of Ezekiel's dry bones. Incense was burning. The baptismal waters were poured into the old marble font and the Communion feast, complete with homemade Easter bread, was spread out on the table.

The pilgrimage of the Vigil began with praise and prayer and chanted psalms intermingled with playful but reverent renditions of the stories of faith. The paschal candle was lit from the bonfire on the steps, and joyously the light was sung back with ancient liturgy into the sanctuary. The people chanted the names of all their saints, the famous and the personal, sheltering their candles from the wind, as they walked up and down the inner-city block around the church. They shed tears of gratitude as a young man came up dripping from the waters of baptism and as they responded by confessing their faith through reading the centuries-old creed. Strangers and friends became community, the body of Christ, as they took Communion from the newly ordained pastor who wore jeans and a clerical collar under her vestments.

1 Peter 4:1-8

Theological Perspective

he has not healed."[3] Our lection attests that even the desolation of death is not removed from the divine life. Thus our times of suspension and waiting are not something that God stands apart from. Rather, they are the condition in which God is present, working resurrection even in an utterly hidden fashion.

Another, and different, insight we receive from this lection on this day has to do with moral theology. Christian life is to be different, because in Christ's descent to the dead we witness the drama of the end of the old age and the coming of a new age. Paul reflects this, referring to Christians as persons "on whom the ends of the ages have come" (1 Cor. 10:11). This perspective is implicit as well as 1 Peter addresses persons "given . . . a new birth into a living hope" (1 Pet. 1:3). It is this dramatic mystery, this mysterious drama of the inauguration of the age to come, that lies behind the New Testament's moral vision. There is an eschatological dimension that informs how life is to be lived in Christ. Christian morality reflects confidence that a new age has been inaugurated and hope that it will be consummated.

Both the old and new ages have distinctive politics. By "politics," we mean the ordering of human life in accordance with a vision of what life is to be if it is to be authentically human. The old age, still present, is ordered by actual and threatened force and violence. Its vision of the purpose of human life leads to destructive behaviors, missing the mark of God's intent. Christian life is to embody a different way, one ordered by love and forgiveness. It is to continue the life of Christ in the midst of the world. In this way love covers a multitude of sins.

PHILIP E. THOMPSON

Pastoral Perspective

as individuals and/or with like-minded friends. All this is admirable and exemplary.

The concern expressed in 1 Peter 4:1–8, however, is that faith is nurtured best in community. So the author ends the discussion of the challenges of living as Christians among those whose religion and lives are very different and threatening with the admonition to "above all, maintain constant love [*agapē*] for one another" (v. 8). In the verses that immediately follow (vv. 9–11), there is a strong stress on building up community life and a compelling vision for how the "constant love for one another" is to be expressed. Christians are "hospitable . . . without complaining" (v. 9), gifted by God in multiple and differing ways (v. 10), and "good stewards" (v. 10) of those God-given gifts, and they use the gifts to serve others (v. 10). This service is humble, unassuming, and Christlike, and it is given for the common good of the community.

Why does Christian faith need such community life? Among other things, it helps us see beyond our own individual perspectives. Individualistic spiritual practices are at risk of focusing too much on self. There is nothing like the challenge of a community member to lift us out of ourselves. We need one another to keep ourselves honest and open. There is also the important role of support that a community can bring, support in times of tragedy and loss, but also support in joining with others in tackling larger community, national, and global issues that are difficult and often overwhelming to address all by oneself.

Robert Putnam, in his seminal book *Bowling Alone*,[2] documents what he calls "the collapse of American community." He shows how we Americans have become increasingly disconnected from one another, and our social structures are disintegrating. Putnam believes we need to reinvent ourselves. What better place for such reinvention to take place than in religious communities. Why? Because "houses of worship build and sustain more social capital—and social capital of more varied forms—than any other type of institution in America."[3]

GARY B. REIERSON

---

2. Robert D. Putnam, *Bowling Alone: The Collapse and Revival of American Community* (New York: Simon & Schuster, 2000).
3. Saguaro Seminar, John F. Kennedy School of Government, Harvard University, *BetterTogether*, 2nd ed., 2001, 66; http://bettertogether.org/thereport.htm.

3. Gregory Nazianzen, "Epistle 101," in *Christology of the Later Fathers*, ed. Edward R. Hardy, Library of Christian Classics (Philadelphia: Westminster Press, 1954), 218.

Exegetical Perspective

that takes place at baptism. Their fundamentally changed loyalties issue in fundamentally changed lives. They no longer participate in the household and civic cults that shape life in Greco-Roman antiquity, and their ethical standards keep them from joining in much of the common life of their community. Paul J. Achtemeier observes:

> Christians are necessarily nonconformists, as followers of Christ, in an age that prized social unity and conformity as one of the highest virtues, and the sufferings imposed on Christians by their non-believing contemporaries are therefore as unavoidable and inevitable as the sufferings visited upon Christ himself.[2]

Historically, this text has earned a place in the Holy Saturday liturgy, not because of its exhortation to nonconformist Christian living in a pagan culture, but because of its claim that "the gospel was proclaimed even to the dead" (v. 6). Early Christian exegetes such as Clement of Alexandria and Augustine connected this odd sentence in chapter 4 with the equally strange one in 1 Peter 3:19 that says that, during the days of Noah, Jesus preached to the "spirits in prison." The presumption was that, between Good Friday and Easter, while he was dead, Jesus sojourned among the dead and announced to them the saving gospel they had no opportunity to hear before his incarnation.

Many problems attend this interpretation, notably the fact that the purpose of this proclamation is said to be that the dead are "judged in the flesh as everyone is judged, [so that] they might live in the spirit as God does" (v. 6). In the context of 1 Peter's promise of eschatological judgment (v. 5), this understanding of judgment "in the flesh" seems strange indeed. First Peter 4:6 betrays no indication that it is Jesus who evangelizes the dead. The verb *euēngelisthē* ("it was preached") is passive, and there is no mention of the agent who does the preaching. So also, the identity of "the dead" is not clear. Are they all the people who have ever died or all the Christians who die before the Lord's coming in glory? If the latter, then the image is designed to comfort those who care about Christians who suffered during their lifetimes for their adherence to the gospel and who also have died prior to the vindication promised them in Christ.[3]

E. ELIZABETH JOHNSON

Homiletical Perspective

As she lifted her arms in blessing, her sleeves fell back revealing beautifully tattooed arms, pictures of the saints of light permanently etched in flesh.

The community that hosted this Easter Vigil is part of the emergent church and calls itself the House for All Sinners and Saints. In some important ways they are a twenty-first-century echo of 1 Peter's first-century community. Twenty- and thirty-something professionals, university students, street people, inner-city working-class singles and couples, gay and straight and transgendered, they joined together on a Saturday night as exiles from their urban culture to catch a glimpse of living out the radical values of Christ-centered community. They came not to deny who they are as people of their time and their secular American culture, but intentionally to step into an experience of God in worship. They came to be fully human in all its varieties of embodiment, intellectually, emotionally, sexually and sensually, physically and spiritually. And they came to be fully Christian.

It is in its full embodiment that the community of the House for All Sinners and Saints lives out the essential message of the 1 Peter text. Shedding old behaviors to understand Christ's suffering is an empty act of piety unless one is constant in love—love of God, love of neighbor, and love of one's self made in God's image. They are a people who live, haltingly at times, yet mystically into 1 Peter's exhortation, "Above all, maintain constant love for one another, for love covers a multitude of sins" (v. 8). They are serious seekers who as a community can laugh at themselves, at their culture, and at the niceties of falsely Christian morality that inhibit the most essential messages of Christ. They are faith pilgrims seeking authentic, embodied lives of worship and prayer, study and service, laughter and play. Through the leadership of communities such as these, the twenty-first-century church and twenty-first-century preachers must ask themselves what is the essence of faith in light of salvation history? What must really be shed in our communities and in our proclamation, in order for God to be made manifest, to be embodied, in Christianity revelation in our times?

JANE ANNE FERGUSON

2. Ibid., 276.
3. David Bartlett, "1 Peter," in *The New Interpreter's Bible* (Nashville: Abingdon Press, 1998), 12:303.

John 19:38-42

³⁸After these things, Joseph of Arimathea, who was a disciple of Jesus, though a secret one because of his fear of the Jews, asked Pilate to let him take away the body of Jesus. Pilate gave him permission; so he came and removed his body. ³⁹Nicodemus, who had at first come to Jesus by night, also came, bringing a mixture of myrrh and aloes, weighing about a hundred pounds. ⁴⁰They took the body of Jesus and wrapped it with the spices in linen cloths, according to the burial custom of the Jews. ⁴¹Now there was a garden in the place where he was crucified, and in the garden there was a new tomb in which no one had ever been laid. ⁴²And so, because it was the Jewish day of Preparation, and the tomb was nearby, they laid Jesus there.

Theological Perspective

The Gospel of John orients the entirety of the life and ministry of Jesus to his death on the cross. This death is not a tragedy that befalls him, raising the question as to whether God has forsaken him, as in Mark and Matthew, but is rather the destiny that Jesus consistently and consciously chooses for himself, in obedience to the will of his Father who sent him. The divine power that Jesus claims for himself keeps anyone from taking his life from him, but this same power allows Jesus to lay his life down when he so wills. "No one takes it from me, but I lay it down of my own accord" (John 10:18).

Jesus never wavers in his obedience to this command of the Father, and does not ask the Father to take the cup from him, as in the other Gospels, but rather calmly says, "And what should I say—'Father, save me from this hour?' No, it is for this reason that I have come to this hour" (John 12:27). Jesus reminds Peter of this obedience when Peter tries to fight for him in the garden: "Am I not to drink the cup that the Father has given me?" (John 18:11). The willingness of Jesus to lay down his life on the cross therefore makes his death into the moment of his greatest glorification, and the focal point of his saving power. "And I, when I am lifted up from the earth, will draw all people to myself" (John 12:32).

Pastoral Perspective

The times when the four Gospels agree on tidbits of data are few, and the description of the burial of Jesus is one of them. The agreements are incomplete, however. The Synoptic Gospels agree that the tomb was "hewn from rock." Matthew, Luke, and John state that the tomb was "new," or "one in which no one had ever been laid." All the Gospels agree that the body was "wrapped" or "wound" in linen cloth, but use different verbs and nouns—just enough to keep the Shroud of Turin a slim possibility, but not nearly enough to support its historicity.

John adds that Nicodemus came also and anointed the corpse with one hundred pounds of spices (Mary Magdalene comes alone in John 20:1). The only real point of complete agreement is that Joseph of Arimathea (a village we know nothing about, historically or archaeologically, with any certainty) took responsibility for the burial. Joseph offered Jesus the tomb he had prepared for himself.

We know as little about Joseph as we do about the village he came from. We surmise he was wealthy, and Mark 15:43 tells us he was "a respected member of the council, who was also himself waiting expectantly for the kingdom of God," whose devotion to Jesus was such that he "went boldly" to Pilate asking for the body. Given Joseph's status in the community, asking for the corpse of an executed criminal was

Exegetical Perspective

John's version of the burial of Jesus differs significantly from the Synoptic accounts in its vocabulary and details. In all four narratives, Joseph of Arimathea asks Pilate for the body of Jesus and buries him. Only John identifies Joseph as a "secret" disciple (19:38). Matthew calls him a "disciple of Jesus" (Matt. 27:57), while Mark and Luke indicate simply that he was "waiting expectantly for the kingdom of God" (Mark 15:43; Luke 23:50–51). Luke and Mark also agree that Joseph is a "member of the council" (i.e., the Sanhedrin), while Matthew identifies him as a "rich man." John uses neither of these designations, although the connection to Nicodemus may associate him with the authorities (see the descriptions of Nicodemus in 3:1; 7:50).

The inclusion of Nicodemus in John's burial account is the most significant difference from the Synoptic versions. Nicodemus is a character who appears only in John's Gospel (3:1–10; 7:45–52). He joins Joseph in burying the body of Jesus and provides a large quantity of spices. By contrast, in Mark and Luke, the women come with spices on Sunday morning (Mark 16:1; Luke 23:56–24:1). It is not possible to harmonize the four Gospel accounts. More important is to notice how John tells the story of Jesus' burial in such a way that it forms a fitting conclusion to the trial and crucifixion narrative. The inclusion of Nicodemus

Homiletical Perspective

Holy Saturday (in Latin, *Sabbatum Sanctum*), the "day of the entombed Christ," is the Lord's day of rest, for on that day Christ's body lay in his tomb. This is a day where grief is given space to settle into the hearts of the disciples as they lay Jesus' bones to rest. Hence the tone of the sermon, like that of John's text, is one of reflective sadness and controlled grief. It is controlled because this is a day suspended between two worlds, between darkness and light, between death and resurrection. Thus this sermon that takes place between the hours of Good Friday and Easter Day gives voice to the finality of death, even as we wait for the inauguration of a new era made possible on the day of Christ's resurrection.

Because Holy Saturday provides its own theme and focus, let us look at a few things to avoid, before we look at some ideas to consider for the sermon.

First, avoid preaching hope. On this particular occasion, the church is given permission to mourn. There is a somberness that comes with waiting at the tomb. Ours is not a culture that grieves with ease. We resist death, trying to prevent it at all costs. When death does occur, we do not know what to do or how to respond, so that we may skip over it too quickly.

Do not let the sermon follow this reluctance. Christ is dead. John's text gives no hint of hope and does not try to hide from the reality of Jesus' death

John 19:38-42

Theological Perspective

Thus, when Jesus dies, he does not cry out with a loud voice, "My God, my God, why have you forsaken me?" and then give a loud cry and breathe his last (Mark 15:34, 37), but rather, knowing that his death completes the work the Father gave him to do, quietly says, "It is finished," bows his head, and gives up his spirit (John 19:30).

John also goes to greater lengths than do the other Gospels to show that Jesus is truly dead. The soldiers come to break his legs so that he will die before the Sabbath begins, but discover that he is already dead. To make sure, they pierce his side with a spear, and water and blood at once come out, showing if nothing else that Jesus is truly dead, adding the insistence that these things are witnessed firsthand (John 19:34–35). All of this seems to indicate that, for John, what is of significance for the world is not only the dying of Jesus, but also the being dead of Jesus, his complete and utter lifelessness, that is attested by the Jews, Roman soldiers, and the unnamed firsthand witness.

The paradoxical saving power of the one who is himself dead is attested in John by the appearance of Joseph of Arimathea and Nicodemus at the foot of the cross when they come to bury Jesus. Joseph is said to be a disciple of Jesus, "though a secret one because of his fear of the Jews" (John 19:38). Mark and Luke add that Joseph is also a member of the council that condemned Jesus, indicating that he is a powerful person in the Jewish community in Jerusalem, from which Jesus did not appear to win any followers.

Similarly, John describes Nicodemus as a Pharisee and a leader of the Jews in Jerusalem (John 3:1). Nicodemus first comes to Jesus at night, indicating that he also is a disciple, though a secret one because of his fear of his fellow Jews. The question then arises as to how these two men, who hide their allegiance to Jesus during his life out of fear of persecution, come to have the courage publicly to ally themselves with Jesus after he is condemned by the Jews and executed by the Romans. The answer that John seems to suggest is that the saving power of Jesus is even more effective after Jesus is dead than it was during his life—as Jesus told Nicodemus himself in their first meeting at night: "And just as Moses lifted up the serpent in the wilderness, so must the Son of Man be lifted up, that whoever believes in him may have eternal life" (John 3:14). Thus the death of Jesus shows its power by drawing unto him two prominent Jews who saw firsthand that both the Romans and their own people would seek to kill anyone who followed

Pastoral Perspective

indeed bold, but not so much in the face of Pilate as before the community as a whole. By honoring the body of Jesus, Joseph risked bringing dishonor upon himself. Courage, surely, was not the only motivating virtue or emotion. Grief, respect, and, if faint, hope, were all mixed in. Was Joseph much different from any who grieve the loss of one they love?

Joseph offered Jesus the tomb he had prepared for himself. Where is that tomb? If you come to Jerusalem, you have to pick between two tombs, the Church of the Holy Sepulchre, established in the early fourth century, and the "garden tomb" identified a century or so ago. They are less than a mile from each other, but could not be more different—Holy Sepulchre crowded and crumbling with competing communions, the garden tomb surrounded by a bus station on three sides and an ominous "Skull"-ish-looking rock formation on the fourth. I have no idea how pilgrims who visit both sites on the same day make any sense of the competing histories and ecclesial ideologies.

Does it matter which is the "real" tomb? No. The surprising thing to Holy Land pilgrims may be that there are only two to choose from. There is a larger distinction for the preacher to consider, between a "geography of spirituality" and a "geography of faith." Competing holy sites, like differing pieties, hymnody, and liturgy, are more about spirituality than faith. The Lutheran may sing a different tune or stand in a different posture from that of her Pentecostal sister, but they share the same Lord. We express, form, and grow the one true faith in a variety of modes. What matters is not that we know where the tomb is, but that we know there was a tomb. Today is about that knowing, as discomforting as it may be.

Joseph offered Jesus the tomb he had prepared for himself. For many gathered on Holy Saturday, the issue is profoundly similar: what do I need to bury so that I may be prepared for the new day promised me in Jesus' name? There is a powerful pastoral reality to Holy Saturday, the reality of absence, in the mystery and contradiction of the tomb. Few traditions have liturgies for Holy Saturday; even fewer have well-attended services. Easter egg hunts abound. Good liturgy not so much. In my own tradition the liturgy for Holy Saturday requires one page, and half of it is instructions. One instruction, the first one, jumps off the page. *There is no celebration of the Eucharist on this day.*[1] Holy Saturday is the only day on which the

---

1. *The Book of Common Prayer* (New York: The Church Hymnal Corp., 1986), 283.

Exegetical Perspective

suggests that the reader is meant to reflect back on this character's earlier interaction with Jesus and on the significance of his actions here.

The opening words of the passage, "after these things" (*meta tauta*, v. 38), link the burial story to the preceding narrative. Nicodemus brings a vast quantity of spices—"a mixture of myrrh and aloes, weighing about a hundred pounds" (v. 39, equivalent to about 75 pounds by our measuring system). While spices were commonly used in burial, the overabundance of spices points to Jesus' importance or social status (on the use of spices in burial, see, for example, 2 Chr. 16:14; Jer. 34:5; Josephus, *Ant.* 17.8.3).

John never specifies how the reader should interpret the actions of Nicodemus. Read as the conclusion to the trial and crucifixion narrative, however, the large quantity of spices corresponds to the theme of Jesus' kingship that John develops there. Jesus is "King of the Jews" (19:19); see the commentary under Good Friday, pp. 299–303), even in the events of his crucifixion and burial.

The words "after these things" also link the story to the passage that immediately precedes it. There, the Jews have also made a request of Pilate, "to have the legs of the crucified men broken and the bodies removed" (19:31). The request is not fulfilled, because in the course of their duties the soldiers discover that Jesus is already dead. John interprets the fact that Jesus' bones are not broken as a fulfillment of the instructions for keeping the Passover (19:36), reinforcing Jesus' identity as the Passover offering.

Like the request of the Jews, the request of Joseph of Arimathea and the burial that follows ultimately serve as a testimony to Jesus' identity—in the case of the burial, that Jesus is King of the Jews. John does not indicate whether the characters of the passage, Joseph of Arimathea and Nicodemus, participate knowingly in this testimony, or whether they are unwitting witnesses to the kingship of Jesus, as Pilate was in his inscription on the cross of Jesus (19:19–22).

Nothing in the narrative clarifies the intentions of the actors. John describes Joseph as a "disciple of Jesus, though a secret one because of his fear of the Jews" (v. 38). Secrecy has negative connotations in the Gospel. Elsewhere, John is critical of those who do not confess faith in Jesus because of fear (12:42–43). Such secrecy contrasts with Jesus' own openness in speaking about himself (18:20). However, in seeking to bury Jesus, Joseph engages in public acts: making a request of Pilate, as well as procuring the body of Jesus from the cross. These public acts are in tension with the notion of Joseph's

Homiletical Perspective

with a false sentimentality. The sermon needs to stay close to the tomb, just as John's witness does.

Second, avoid trying to solve the problem of death. If we follow the text from John, the disciples go about their work of preparing Jesus' body with a sad seriousness. The text does not luxuriate in asking why Jesus is dead. Holy Saturday is the silence between notes. Resist the temptation to find resolution in this hour between death and resurrection. This is not a day to find answers. It is a day to take seriously the reality of Christ's human mortality, without trying to answer the problem of his death.

Third, avoid saying too much in the sermon. Ideally, Holy Saturday should be the quietest service of the church year. Though the sermon is a time to speak, it is not a time to be chatty or garrulous. The occasion is sober, and the sermon needs to reflect and honor this mood. As when a friend dies, it is better to sit in silence than to say too much. The general rule for preaching on Holy Saturday is that less is more. Hence, the sermon for Holy Saturday may ruminate and embrace silence, giving the hearer permission to contemplate a world fallen under the spell of death's finality.

With these few suggestions about what to avoid in mind, let us consider a few ideas that may help a sermon take shape.

First, let the sermon give voice to the world's sadness. Preaching, like other forms of leadership, is about naming reality. This is a day to name the reality of death. This is not a time to hide from grief, but to gaze into its face. Take one of the characters, such as Joseph of Arimathea or Nicodemus (or even Pilate), and follow him, allowing the congregation to overhear as he moves through the story.

Everyone, at one point or another, will go to the tomb—and the feelings associated with it are as real as they are universal. Holy Saturday offers the preacher an opportunity to name a grief that touches all. Jesus is dead, and those who do the work of last rites do so in the belief that the story is finished. John's testimony to Jesus' burial is sharply factual, and does not give into emotional melodrama, yet there is a deep sadness behind these words that is felt. The same should be true of the sermon.

Second, it may be wise to reflect on the significance of the ritual of Jesus' burial. This will allow the congregation to contemplate their own customs. Many of us, even in churches, have lost any sense of proper rites for the dead. There is a methodical nature to John's description of the preparation of Jesus' body for the tomb. Joseph and Nicodemus give

John 19:38-42

Theological Perspective

Jesus, thinking in so doing that they were "offering worship to God" (John 16:2).

This narrative thus raises the question posed by Bultmann as to whether the resurrection narrative should even be considered as an original part of the Gospel of John. After all, the decision of Joseph and Nicodemus to make a public profession of their faith and discipleship takes place when Jesus is indisputably dead, not after he is attested to be raised from the dead. All that Joseph and Nicodemus can see is that Jesus is dead, and they already know that both their own people and the Romans will seek to kill anyone who professes faith in him. They do not wait until they can see that their venture of faith will be guaranteed to succeed in light of the resurrection of Jesus, but rather believe his message that the eternal life he came to offer is most powerfully effective when he is raised up on the cross, in spite of the fact that this guarantees that their own lives will likely be lost for the sake of his name.

After all, if Jesus is loved by God and shows the complete extent of his love for the world precisely when he lays down his life of his own accord, how could it be otherwise than that his followers would show their love for him and for one another by laying down their lives for the sake of his name?

RANDALL C. ZACHMAN

Pastoral Perspective

sacrament is specifically not offered, the "reserve sacrament" remaining from Maundy Thursday consumed on Good Friday.

On Saturday there is nothing left but death and tomb. Who comes to worship that? The faithful. They may be there only to complete all corners of the Triduum, the great three days of Holy Week; but however few, if you are preaching to them, your challenge is to find a way to bless them and their devotion. The temptation to be avoided above all others is the temptation to resolve the tension and gloss over the emptiness of this particular, peculiar day. On this Saturday there is nothing left but death and tomb. Do not roll away the stone. Today is not supposed to be easy, the story so hard to tell that John seems to give it backwards, mentioning the tomb as an afterthought: "Now there was a garden in the place where he was crucified, and in the garden there was a new tomb in which no one had ever been laid. And so, because it was the Jewish day of Preparation, and the tomb was nearby, they laid Jesus there" (vv. 41–42).

Joseph offered Jesus the tomb he had prepared for himself, and invites us to ask what we may need to bury on Holy Saturday. There is nothing easy about death and tomb and stone. There is nothing easy about this day. There is only waiting.

> O God, Creator of heaven and earth: Grant that, as the crucified body of your dear Son was laid in the tomb and rested on this holy Sabbath, so we may await with him the coming of the third day, and rise with him to newness of life; who lives and reigns with you and the Holy Spirit, one God, for ever and ever. Amen.[2]

WILLIAM F. BROSEND

2. Ibid.

Exegetical Perspective

secrecy, yet John never states explicitly whether Joseph's act should be understood as an open declaration of his belief in Jesus.

Nor does the Gospel writer clarify Nicodemus's understanding or intentions. Nicodemus appears three times in the Gospel (3:2; 7:50; 19:39), twice (3:2; 19:39) with the description that he "came to Jesus by night." The repetition of the phrase makes this designation seem significant, although it is unclear what the reader is meant to conclude about Nicodemus. On the one hand, "night" may associate Nicodemus with the darkness that stands in opposition to the light (1:5; 3:19–21; 12:46); yet Nicodemus also has "come" to Jesus, a metaphor John uses elsewhere to indicate belief in Jesus (e.g., 5:40; 6:35). The reader is left to decide what level of understanding or belief Nicodemus has attained. His actions may simply underscore the fact of Jesus' death, and imply that Nicodemus does not expect Jesus' resurrection. However, they might also suggest that Nicodemus understands what the reader also knows through the trial narrative, that Jesus is king. The actor's intentions and level of understanding remain ambiguous. Even so, they continue to point to Jesus' kingship in his death.

For the reader of the Gospel, the abundance of spices might also bring to mind Mary's previous anointing of Jesus in 12:1–8. She anointed Jesus' feet with "a pound of costly perfume made of pure nard" (12:3), enough to fill the whole house with its fragrance. Many interpreters understand her act as an outpouring of love for Jesus. Jesus' own interpretation identifies the anointing as being "for the day of [his] burial" (12:7). Now that Jesus' burial has arrived, the prodigious quantity of spices reflects a similar outpouring from an associate of Jesus. John never gives an explicit indication of what either Mary or Nicodemus believes about Jesus, yet in the context of the Gospel, the reader may see the acts of both characters as carrying out Jesus' instruction to "abide in my love" (15:9).

SUSAN E. HYLEN

Homiletical Perspective

Jesus an honorable burial, according to Jewish custom, and they seem to spare no expense. They bring for his embalming a vast quantity of spices that would befit a king (cf. 2 Chron. 16:14). This good work must be done before the Sabbath begins.

What are the rituals and customs of your congregation when someone dies? Is there a way to reflect on those who have died in the past year, reflecting on the preparation for grief you have done with your congregation? What might we learn about how to do this in our own churches from the way Jesus was buried?

Third, allow the form and language of the sermon to reflect the aesthetic mood of the service. Holy Saturday is intended to be one of the most contemplative services in the church cycle. The aesthetic of this service is typically marked by a stark and Spartan mood. There are no flowers, banners, or even musical instruments. The text is not hurried, and should be read slowly, with long pauses along the way.

The same mood should be reflected in the tone and tenor of the sermon. On this day, as on no other, we are invited into the profound silence of God, whose Son Jesus lies buried in a tomb. This is the reality we can perceive from this side of Easter.

TRYGVE DAVID JOHNSON

Exodus 14:10-31; 15:20-21

14:10As Pharaoh drew near, the Israelites looked back, and there were the Egyptians advancing on them. In great fear the Israelites cried out to the LORD. 11They said to Moses, "Was it because there were no graves in Egypt that you have taken us away to die in the wilderness? What have you done to us, bringing us out of Egypt? 12Is this not the very thing we told you in Egypt, 'Let us alone and let us serve the Egyptians'? For it would have been better for us to serve the Egyptians than to die in the wilderness." 13But Moses said to the people, "Do not be afraid, stand firm, and see the deliverance that the LORD will accomplish for you today; for the Egyptians whom you see today you shall never see again. 14The LORD will fight for you, and you have only to keep still."

15Then the LORD said to Moses, "Why do you cry out to me? Tell the Israelites to go forward. 16But you lift up your staff, and stretch out your hand over the sea and divide it, that the Israelites may go into the sea on dry ground. 17Then I will harden the hearts of the Egyptians so that they will go in after them; and so I will gain glory for myself over Pharaoh and all his army, his chariots, and his chariot drivers. 18And the Egyptians shall know that I am the LORD, when I have gained glory for myself over Pharaoh, his chariots, and his chariot drivers."

19The angel of God who was going before the Israelite army moved and went behind them; and the pillar of cloud moved from in front of them and took its place behind them. 20It came between the army of Egypt and the army of Israel. And so the cloud was there with the darkness, and it lit up the night; one did not come near the other all night.

21Then Moses stretched out his hand over the sea. The LORD drove the sea back by a strong east wind all night, and turned the sea into dry land; and the

Theological Perspective

"Who Is the LORD?" (Exod. 5:2). Pharaoh's question haunts not only the Egyptians and the Israelites, but all humanity. The Red Sea lies at the center of a "plague" designed to answer the question for the eleventh time in the saga. Again the Egyptians learn the hard way to recognize the Lord. Again the Israelites move from unbelief to relief. Led by Moses and Miriam, the rescued Hebrews sing praises that declare who the Lord is.

The Easter Vigil immerses believers in Israel's experiences of salvation, reminding us who God is, through what God has done and is still doing. Paul linked the Red Sea crossing to Christian baptism and entry into God's people (1 Cor. 10:2). Israel prefigured the journey of individuals into God's people and the resulting church itself. The Vigil liturgy takes the faithful through the baptismal waters—some literally, others in remembrance—after which they join in glorifying the Lord Jesus Christ revealed in death and resurrection.

Knowing the Lord involves more than mere acknowledgment of God's existence. Cognizant that Egypt and Israel still do not know him, the Lord reprises the pattern established in the plagues. The

Pastoral Perspective

A woman sets one place at a table that has been set for two for over forty years. Even after eight months of this altered ritual, her heart still aches. Will she ever feel joy again?

The envelope is opened with such hope; surely the director of admissions has good news to share. But this letter begins, "We regret to inform you . . ." What will the future hold now?

He took his marriage vows with every intention to be a faithful husband. Now that he has stepped beyond the bounds of fidelity, can he ever return to the circle of trust he and his wife once held sacred?

The formative stories of the Bible speak to our human need for deliverance . . . redemption . . . resurrection. As the Hebrew slaves in Egypt longed for freedom, so we long for deliverance from the challenges that threaten to enslave us to sorrow, fear, and resignation. God heard their cries and called them forth from slavery to freedom; God hears our cries, moving to deliver us from our bondage too. Like the Hebrews, we must choose to take steps that lead forward, not back to where we were.

waters were divided. [22]The Israelites went into the sea on dry ground, the waters forming a wall for them on their right and on their left. [23]The Egyptians pursued, and went into the sea after them, all of Pharaoh's horses, chariots, and chariot drivers. [24]At the morning watch the Lord in the pillar of fire and cloud looked down upon the Egyptian army, and threw the Egyptian army into panic. [25]He clogged their chariot wheels so that they turned with difficulty. The Egyptians said, "Let us flee from the Israelites, for the Lord is fighting for them against Egypt."

[26]Then the Lord said to Moses, "Stretch out your hand over the sea, so that the water may come back upon the Egyptians, upon their chariots and chariot drivers." [27]So Moses stretched out his hand over the sea, and at dawn the sea returned to its normal depth. As the Egyptians fled before it, the Lord tossed the Egyptians into the sea. [28]The waters returned and covered the chariots and the chariot drivers, the entire army of Pharaoh that had followed them into the sea; not one of them remained. [29]But the Israelites walked on dry ground through the sea, the waters forming a wall for them on their right and on their left.

[30]Thus the Lord saved Israel that day from the Egyptians; and Israel saw the Egyptians dead on the seashore. [31]Israel saw the great work that the Lord did against the Egyptians. So the people feared the Lord and believed in the Lord and in his servant Moses.

[15:20]Then the prophet Miriam, Aaron's sister, took a tambourine in her hand; and all the women went out after her with tambourines and with dancing. [21]And Miriam sang to them:

"Sing to the Lord, for he has triumphed gloriously;
horse and rider he has thrown into the sea."

Exegetical Perspective

This text contains the bedrock of Israel's faith: "the Lord saved Israel . . . from the Egyptians" (14:30). The story moves from fear to faith, from slavery to freedom, from death to life—an appropriate reading for the Great Vigil of Easter "at the morning watch" (v. 24; cf. 12:42), celebrated in the hymn "Come, You Faithful, Raise the Strain." Traditionally 15:1b–13, 17–18 are also included.

Exodus 14 combines several literary sources, producing numerous inconsistencies. In one scenario God makes the sea bed dry with a wind, moves in a cloud between the Israelites and the Egyptians, leads them to the other side, and then the sea returns, drowning the Egyptians, whose chariots had become mired in the sand. In another, the sea is divided, with walls of water making a corridor, through which Israel and the Egyptians pass, until the walls collapse on the troops. Not only is it impossible to know "what actually happened," but we should read the story as historical fiction—more an *interpretation* of an event than a report of the facts.

The movement from fear to faith is ironic. The Israelites panic when they see the Egyptian troops

Homiletical Perspective

At the Easter Vigil, a historic celebration of the whole of salvation history and Christ's saving work for the cosmos, we experience the passage from slavery to freedom, from sin to salvation, from death to life. A significant scriptural part of that great story is the narrative of Israel's salvation by the power of God at the Sea of Reeds. The tale is told in a very complex way in Exodus 14 and then celebrated by the poem of Exodus 15. As familiar as the story may be, it raises any number of problems for the modern congregation.

The most obvious difficulty is the brutality of the story. Israelite victory by the power of God is gained at the expense of dead Egyptians, floating facedown in the sea. The God who kills Egyptians in order to save the chosen ones has long been deeply problematic and is, for modern people, finally dangerous. It is troublesome theologically, because the God of the sea is the God who will soon be revealed to Moses as a God "slow to anger and abounding in steadfast love and faithfulness" (Exod. 34:6). How can the preacher reconcile this superb and inclusive image of God with the Egyptian murders of Exodus 14?

Exodus 14:10-31; 15:20-21

Theological Perspective

Egyptians refuse to respect the Lord (14:5), who in turn hardens them in that attitude (14:8, 17) so "the Egyptians shall know that I am the LORD" (14:4, 18). Israel and Egypt must acknowledge that the Lord alone accomplishes the victory.

Forced into inaction by the cloudy pillar, Egypt's forces share an unhampered view with Israel. Together they witness the Lord who is glorified in the salvation of the covenant people (14:17–18). At each stage, God takes the initiative in salvation; each wonder discloses more fully who the Lord is.

Crises at the Crossing. The crossing is a crisis in knowing the Lord, although Egypt does not realize this. Surrounded by Egyptians, the people and Moses cry out (14:10, 15), wondering what, if anything, God will do. They still have not learned that the Lord consistently responds to the cry of the vulnerable.

Ephrem the Syrian (fourth century) pondered God's outreach to the Egyptians.[1] By repositioning the cloudy pillar as a reminder of the plague of darkness, God hoped to frighten the Egyptians into turning back, literally repenting, and saving their lives. Furthermore, the all-powerful Lord divided the sea slowly, giving the Egyptians an entire night to repent. Sadly, once the Egyptians committed themselves to the chase, the Lord revealed his face through the pillar (14:24). At last the panicking Egyptians recognized both the Lord and their doom (14:25). Ephrem's reflections reveal two things. First, humanity has an amazing capacity to seek death in preference to submitting to God. Second, God persistently offers opportunities for repentance, even to enemies.

Crossing into the church generates its own crises. Converts occupy an uneasy position. Between the pursuing "forces" of a destructive yet familiar past and the prospects of certain death, catechumens reasonably cry out in fear. The old life seems preferable to the wrath of former masters or the death of the familiar self that attends new life in God.

Christian tradition explains that God accompanies the baptized to the promised land and equips them for the oft-arduous journey. However, the sobering truth is that the baptized employ these holy gifts unevenly. Gregory of Nyssa (fourth century) remarked that some drag the "Egyptians" through the saving waters. Unwilling to break ties, they remain enslaved to old, sinful habits and desires, while claiming God as their new master. Gregory

Pastoral Perspective

This Scripture from Exodus is among many appointed to be read during the Easter Vigil, a liturgical retelling of the story of God and God's people on the eve of Easter. Arlo Duba, who served as professor of worship at both Princeton and Dubuque Theological Seminaries, points out that the Vigil

> first of all, connects us with the old covenant. The Jewish people viewed "this night" as the night of deliverance from bondage and slavery and as the night in which the establishment of covenant deliverance was commemorated and reenacted (see Exodus 12). . . . This theme of deliverance is clearly carried over into the New Testament. While scholars may disagree about the actual chronology of the first Holy Week, they do not question that Jesus directly related his passion and the institution of the Lord's Supper to the Passover. The early Christians followed his example by making the exodus of the children of Israel and the exodus that Jesus accomplished in Jerusalem (Luke 9:31) the central focus of their Easter/Paschal celebrations.[1]

The story of the deliverance of the Hebrews from slavery in Egypt sets the pattern for God's interaction with his people. God seeks to set his people free: free from the sins that hold a person and a culture in bondage to the past, and free from the powers that oppress an individual and a society. This pattern is seen in God's work in priests and prophets, in the personal interactions of Jesus with men and women, and most powerfully in the redeeming work of Christ in crucifixion and resurrection. God's grace gives us the energy to keep our feet moving in the right direction.

Moses leads the Hebrews away from their Egyptian masters, with Pharaoh's soldiers in hot pursuit; yet before the refreshing breeze of freedom even has the chance to cool the sweat upon their brows, the people turn fearful. "We were better off before," they moan to Moses. Change is more frightening than the chance for a new life. Just as the substance abuser dares to begin to live clean, the temptation to return to familiar patterns, no matter how destructive, becomes even more compelling.

Moses answers the people with the words of prophets and angels: "Do not be afraid, stand firm, and see the deliverance that the LORD will accomplish for you today" (Exod. 14:13). God has not forgotten you! In fact, God is leading the way. "Keep moving," God says. "Do not look back. I will deliver you, but you need to take the steps that will lead you to the promised land."

---

1. Commentary on Exodus XIV.4–5, in *St. Ephrem the Syrian. Selected Prose Works*, trans. E. G. Matthews Jr. and J. P. Amar (Washington, DC: Catholic University of America, 1994), 221–65.

1. Arlo Duba, "Keeping Vigil" "*Reformed Worship*" 6 (Dec. 1987): 11.

Exegetical Perspective

pursuing them, complaining to Moses: "Was it because there were no graves in Egypt that you have taken us away to die in the wilderness?" (14:11). Previously Israel was "going out boldly" (v. 8), even "prepared for battle" (13:18, but cf. 13:17). Now courage has turned to cowardice—at the very *moment* of salvation! They would rather return to slavery than incur the risks of freedom: "It would have been better for us to serve the Egyptians than to die in the wilderness" (14:12). Fear of death has stifled their yearning for liberation (2:23). They are dragged, kicking and screaming, into God's saving grace. Then irony reverses with the Egyptians' fear (14:25). Jewish legend praises a boy, Nachshon ben Aminnadab, who first stepped between the walls of water.

"Let us serve the Egyptians" (14:12) points to the fundamental political dimension of the story. The spiritual movement proceeds from fear of death to fear *of the Lord* (i.e., reverence, the same Hebrew word); in the end, Israel "believed [Heb. "amen"] in the Lord and in his servant Moses" (14:31). In this story Israel is saved from Pharaoh, not saved from sin. The exodus story is the foundation of what we call "liberation theology." Israel is not "in bondage to sin"; Israel is in bondage to a ruthless political system that perpetuates the evil of oppression and genocide (1:16, prevented only by two brave women). Their request to "serve" Pharaoh would be something like Jews in 1940 saying they wanted Hitler as their leader.

"Service" connotes obedience and allegiance. Whom one serves is one's "lord," whatever the political title might be. The deepest dimension of Israelite faith—and the most politically subversive—is the claim that *God* is Israel's lord, and no other (Exod. 20:2, 5; Deut. 6:4). Israel's trust in God at the end is only one step in a trajectory that began with the summons to "serve God on this mountain" (3:12, my trans.). God then demanded that Pharaoh free Israel *so that* they may serve God (4:23 and passim). The movement leads to Sinai, where Israel formally accepts the status of covenanted servant to the God "who brought you out of the house of servitude" (20:1, my trans.).

The violence of the story makes us uncomfortable. The defeat of evil here is not achieved by peaceful diplomacy but through warfare. God is the warrior, and Israel an inactive beneficiary (14:14; cf. 15:3). God fights against a military power, expressed repeatedly by reference to "Pharaoh and all his army, his chariots, and his chariot drivers" (14:17, 18, 23, 26, 28—*five* times). In the end, the corpses of "the entire army of Pharaoh" (14:28) litter the seashore.

Homiletical Perspective

The story is also dangerous when modern ears imagine themselves as the chosen of God, free to call down the anathemas of God on those they deem their enemies. After the horrors of September 11, 2001, in New York and Washington, it became easy for many Americans to respond to the events with fury at the perpetrators, labeling them "evil," fully worthy of destruction by any means possible. Even the loud celebrations of Miriam and the choirs of Israel in Exodus 15 ring hollow in the face of the bodies floating nearby.

It is instructive to know that these problems were seen very early in the ongoing theological life of Judaism, and we modern preachers may learn valuable lessons by reading some of this literature. Listen to one Talmudic commentary on Deuteronomy 28:

> Now does the Holy One, blessed be He, rejoice in the downfall of the wicked? Is it not written, as they went out before the army, and say, *Give thanks unto the Lord, for His mercy endureth forever* (2 Chron. 20:21), and R(abbi) Johanan further said, Why are the words "for he is good" omitted from this thanksgiving? Because the Holy One, blessed be He, does not rejoice in the downfall of the wicked? (an allusion to Ez. 18:23, 32) And R. Johanan further said, What is the meaning of the verse, *And one came not near the other all the night* (Ex. 14:20)— The ministering angels wanted to chant their hymns, but the Holy One, blessed be He, said, The work of my hands is being drowned in the sea, and shall you chant hymns? (*b. Megillah* 10b)

The rabbis struggled as we do with this portrait of a God of war, but rather than passing over the picture in silence, or merely celebrating along with Miriam unquestioningly, they raise in delightful and challenging imagination an alternative image of their God, demanding that the angels, ever eager to chant God's praises, keep silence in the face of God's dying children. This approach to the text does not "solve" the theological problem of the God of war, but it wonderfully offers the paradox of God's multiple presentations in the tradition, and remains dissatisfied with simple consistency. It has been well said that we Christians often have far too low a tolerance for ambiguity.

As we proclaim this story at the Easter Vigil, we will of course connect it to the freedom Christ's victory over sin and death has brought to us in his resurrection. The early church long connected Israel's victory at the sea to the Christian's victory over sin and death. Early Christians also added to the rich allegorical meanings presented by the exodus narrative that of baptism: just as Israel went into the sea

Theological Perspective

suggested, "If someone should still serve [the 'Egyptians'], even if he should happen to have passed through the water, according to my way of thinking, he has not at all touched the mystical water whose function is to destroy tyrants."

Similarly, Paul warned Christians not to take baptism for granted. The Israelites' "baptism" at the Red Sea did not guarantee their relationship with God: "God was not pleased with most of them, and they were struck down" (1 Cor. 10:5). John Chrysostom (late fourth century) explained that believers could lose all benefit from baptism "except they go on and show forth a life worthy of this grace."[2]

Worshiping God. The Easter Vigil, like the Red Sea crossing, moves from darkness to light, from death to life. Dawn reveals God's victory over death. Just as "Israel saw the Egyptians dead on the seashore" (14:30) at daybreak, so the first witnesses of the resurrection observed guards fallen "like dead men" at the empty tomb (Matt. 28:4). Miriam led the Hebrew women in a victory song (15:20–21), and the women at the tomb proclaimed the first shaky good news. The good news summarily answers the question, "Who is the Lord?" (Exod. 5:2). The Lord is the one who "triumphed gloriously."

Jacob of Sarug (d. 521) praised his native Syrian tradition, which linked Miriam and the Hebrew women to Mary and Christian women (Miriam=Mary). Baptism creates a single people where Eve's daughters regain their role in proclaiming God. Syrians regularly witnessed this gendered aspect of salvation in public worship through male and female choirs of vowed Sons and Daughters of the Covenant.[3] Since Syrian hymnody functioned as sung homilies, Jacob rejoiced that women could rightly be called "teachers." Together with Mary, who gave birth to the conquering Lord, holy women join in battle against Satan and false teaching through their musical proclamation of the good news.

So at Easter, all Christians "sing to the Lord," for Jesus "has triumphed gloriously" (15:21). The Lord is risen, the waters are crossed, and the pilgrim people of God carry the victory with them through the wilderness and toward the kingdom.

LISA D. MAUGANS DRIVER

Pastoral Perspective

The "strong east wind" (14:21) forms a wall of water on the left and the right for the people. How often does God form a wall on either side and enable us to journey forward in a threatening time?

A widow invites a friend to dinner, not as a way of replacing her husband's memory, but as a way of reclaiming the goodness of life that is still hers to live. A student denied a place in the university of her dreams discovers that there is more than one place where she can follow her heart. The unfaithful spouse chooses to put his energy back into his marriage, and the wronged spouse chooses forgiveness as "the only way to heal the wounds of a past we cannot change."[2] Here is the exodus message, and the underlying theme in Scripture: God delivers people. God opens doors. There is hope for something new: nothing less than the new life that only God can give.

The Hebrews wade out of the muddy edges of the Red Sea before the walls of water come tumbling down. Their former captors are swept away, and ahead of them the vista of a new beginning edges into view. Moses breaks into song, and Miriam leads the women in a delighted dance. The long vigil ends, and the unstoppable joy of resurrection erupts with the dawn. God intends for us to live again!

On election night 2008, Barack Obama was elected the first African American president of the United States of America. John Lewis, a black congressman and veteran of the struggle for civil rights, responded with this acclamation:

> When I heard last evening that Pennsylvania had gone for Barack Obama, I think I had an out-of-body experience. I jumped, and I shouted for joy. And my feet left the floor, and I just kept jumping. Something lifted me up, and I shed some tears. And I tell you, I have cried so much during the past few hours, I don't think I have any tears left.[3]

When we discover that we have survived defeat, divorce, disappointment, even death, our hearts sing for joy, our spirits dance. The dance belongs to everyone who has been set free by God. It is the dance that leads us out of slavery, away from the empty tomb, and into new life.

KATHLEEN LONG BOSTROM

2. Gregory of Nyssa, *The Life of Moses*, trans. A. J. Malherbe and E. Ferguson (New York: Paulist Press, 1978), 129; John Chrysostom, *Homily 23 on 1 Corinthians*, in *Nicene and Post-Nicene Fathers*, Series 1 (New York: The Christian Literature Co., 1889), 12:133.
3. Susan Ashbrook Harvey, "Revisiting the Daughters of the Covenant: Women's Choirs and Sacred Song in Ancient Syriac Christianity," *Hugoye: Journal of Syriac Studies* [http://syrcom.cua.edu/syrcom/Hugoye] vol. 8, no. 2 (July 2005).

2. Lewis Smedes, *The Art of Forgiveness* (New York: Ballantine Books, 1996), 176.
3. John Lewis, on "Voice of America," www.voanews.com, November 5, 2008.

Exegetical Perspective

Obviously this picture of God as warrior raises deep theological questions. Jewish legend is aware of that. When the angels start rejoicing, God silences them and says, "How can you sing when my children lie dead in the sea?" The story reveals the tragedy of history involving the defeat of tyrannical régimes. The motif of Pharaoh's hardened heart emphasizes the ruthlessness of evil. Pharaoh's "heart" (KJV; NIV, RSV, NRSV "mind") changes (14:5), but to the author Pharaoh's resistance ultimately is part of God's doing, in order to manifest God's glory (14:4). Again, the language is political: Pharaoh's prior refusal to "know" God means to *acknowledge* God's sovereignty (5:2). God's victory vindicates that sovereignty and reveals God's identity (cf. 20:2; the title "Lord" stands for the personal name YHWH).

Christians often ignore the political liberation in this story, as well as in the Easter story (e.g., the lectionary omission of 15:14–16), but in both stories God has conquered the power of an evil empire. We may struggle with the picture of a warrior God, but we should not spiritualize the liberation of the oppressed.

Finally, the motif of the divided sea reflects mythic traditions in which a deity defeats the sea, a monster representing the powers of chaos, dividing its body and bringing order to the cosmos. The story is prominent in Mesopotamian and Canaanite mythology and numerous biblical references (e.g., Pss. 74:12–17; 77:16–20). Also, 15:1–18 alludes to this myth (vv. 5, 8, 10), concluding with a declaration of God's sovereignty (v. 18). Similarly, in creation God divides "the waters" so that "dry land" will appear (Gen. 1:6–9; cf. Exod. 14:21–22). Thus the cosmic language of divine victory *over* sea describes God's victory *at* the sea. God divides the sea, only to use it as a weapon against the empire of Egypt, in *creating* the *people* of Israel (15:16). Israel's redeemer is the world's creator, vanquishing all other gods (12:12; 15:11). "Exodus" becomes a mythic paradigm for *every* time (from Isa. 51:9–11 to the spiritual "Go Down, Moses").

The lection ends with Miriam's company of women rejoicing with tambourines, singing and dancing, the deepest expression of Israel's faith and of Easter joy (see commentary on Jer. 31:4, pp. 353–57).

THOMAS W. MANN

Homiletical Perspective

and emerged free and the people of God, so those baptized went into the water and emerged free from sin and new people of God. The Easter Vigil was seen as the perfect time for the baptism of the newest Christians in the community. A sermon at the Vigil could readily follow the order of a baptismal service that recalls the salvation history of God's actions for the cosmos, lingering on the tale of the sea as a summary of God's continual work for God's creation.

Another critical observation arising from the story in Exodus is that it is God's actions alone that bring safety and freedom. We are never the authors of our own salvation, nor are we chosen for God's gifts because of any greatness in ourselves. It was God who saved Israel at the sea, just as it was God who raised Jesus from the grave. In modern United States congregations, this is often the most difficult news for us to hear. We, both lay folk and clergy, have been taught from our earliest days that we can be anything we wish to be. If we just apply ourselves, work hard, go to the right schools, choose the right mates, all will turn out greatly to our advantage. Moses's words (Exod. 14:14) stop us in our tracks: "The Lord will fight for you, and you have only to keep still." Such a demand flies in the face of much that we have been taught to be and do.

Thus, along with the theological problems thrown up by this text, we can add a very human problem. Whatever victories we may experience in our lives are finally not a result of our work at all, but are gifts from the God who desires our freedom; we have only to stand still and celebrate the power of that God's work for us. However, we must always remember as well that God's will for good is for *all* of God's children, not just for us. This Exodus text is riddled with important ideas, any one of which can challenge and surprise a congregation as it prepares to celebrate the beauty and glory of Easter.

JOHN C. HOLBERT

Psalm 114

¹When Israel went out from Egypt,
  the house of Jacob from a people of strange language,
²Judah became God's sanctuary,
  Israel his dominion.

³The sea looked and fled;
  Jordan turned back.
⁴The mountains skipped like rams,
  the hills like lambs.

⁵Why is it, O sea, that you flee?
  O Jordan, that you turn back?
⁶O mountains, that you skip like rams?
  O hills, like lambs?

⁷Tremble, O earth, at the presence of the LORD,
  at the presence of the God of Jacob,
⁸who turns the rock into a pool of water,
  the flint into a spring of water.

Theological Perspective

In a few short verses this psalm captures in lively language and striking imagery the central events of the whole exodus-conquest tradition of ancient Israel's religion. In verses 1–2 the names "Israel" and "house of Jacob" evoke the narration of Israel's election by God, followed by the trial of slavery in Egypt and eventual escape through the sea to freedom. The story culminates in the entrance into the promised land and the establishment of this land as God's domain, who rules from Judah's sanctuary.

The power and awesome nature of these historical events, which were accomplished under divine guidance, is suggested in the rhetorical references to the sea, both the Red Sea and the Jordan, and the mountains in verses 3–6. The sea is questioned why it fled—or parted—under Moses and later under Joshua, letting the people cross dry-shod. The mountains are asked the reason for their tremors—skipping "like rams," verse 6—in an allusion to the theophany of God on Sinai when he gave the Law to Moses. The psalm climaxes with a response to these questions, indicating the silent force that disturbed both sea and mountain, and proclaiming the ultimate source for all these events: the powerful, mysterious, and continuous presence of God with his people.

This is the ultimate truth at the heart of the psalm. The divine presence is witnessed by the

Pastoral Perspective

Congregations embracing the tradition of Easter Vigil discover that it is a unique service of Word and sacrament. Many readings and both sacraments rehearse the drama of salvation in what *The Book of Common Worship* calls "a panoramic view of what God has done for humanity."[1] As light fills the church that has been left dark and silent since Good Friday, readings from the Scriptures illumine the sacred story from creation to the new creation.

The Great Vigil of Easter is full and lengthy. Worshipers accustomed to a one-hour service may balk at the prospect of eleven readings; however, those who have made the Vigil part of their Holy Week journey attest to the significance of hearing the whole story, well read, accompanied by reflective silence. It is not worship as usual on this extraordinary night!

In the order of service, the singing of a psalm follows each reading. There are nine psalms in the Service of Readings for this night, the same in each lectionary cycle. They express thanksgiving, trust, and praise; they are prayers for hope, deliverance, and victory. Psalm 114 is a hymn of praise that concludes the set, echoing some of the previous themes, summarizing the redemptive power of God. If the

1. *The Book of Common Worship* (Louisville, KY: Westminster/John Knox Press, 1993), 294.

Exegetical Perspective

Before the exile in Babylon, the Israelites gathered every autumn for the celebration of the new year. This was a time of remembrance, during which the stories of God's saving actions were told and hymns of praise were sung for all that God had done in the history of the people. After the occupation of the Babylonians and the exile, the New Year moved to the spring, to conform to the Babylonian calendar, but the autumn festival remained a time of pilgrimage and renewal for Israel.

Psalm 114 was one of the psalms sung at this festival, serving the dual function of a remembrance psalm and a hymn of praise. The sense of unity expressed in it is almost defiant in light of later history. The people who sang it had seen their land divided north from south. Later still, a stronger power divided them one from another, taking their best and brightest away into Babylon.

Israel was fractured, for reasons they would come to understand as stemming from their own disobedience and faithlessness. Nevertheless, at their autumn festival, whether it was the new year or the autumn pilgrimage, they sang out loud the story of who they really were: not a splintered, defeated people, but a people whose unity was in God and God's action in their historical life.

Homiletical Perspective

Psalm 114 is an unlikely sermon text, given the context of the Easter Vigil, yet its place in the order of readings gives insight into the proclamation that takes place on this night. The Easter Vigil is a night of darkness and light, fire and water, mystery and revelation. Here, at the apex of the Christian year, we tell the whole story of God and God's people, in order to understand the amazing proclamation of Jesus' resurrection. From the opening words of Genesis through the accounts of the exodus and the promises of prophets, we hear how again and again God has brought forth life from death. The Psalms figure prominently in the progression of readings, as worshipers sing the ancient words of Israel in praise of this God of life.

This is a brief psalm, just eight verses, that celebrates God's presence with the people. When the Hebrew people fled Egypt and escaped into the wilderness, God became their home, sings the psalmist. This God is of such power that the sea pulled back and the mountains leapt away! The same God is filled with such mercy that water gushes forth from the rocks when the people thirst in the wilderness.

In a few short lines we see one of the deepest mysteries of the Divine: the God before whom mountains shrink and waters recede is the one who shelters Israel, causing water to spring forth in the desert,

Psalm 114

Theological Perspective

various epiphanies of God in Israel's history, as suggested in the psalm: the calling of Israel's ancestors, the exodus, the giving of the Law, the conquest, the temple, all the deeds and miracles of God. Then, as if to seal faith in this God who established Israel and continues to uphold them, the psalm finally recalls how God brought forth life-giving power from lifeless stone in the wilderness miracle of the water gushing from the rock.

The terse, compact, and imaginative language of the psalm creates a dynamic sense of immediacy between the events described and those who pray the psalm. The events are brought forward, so to speak, into the present. To put it another way, those who pray this psalm are themselves placed in the presence of these events. What is our reaction? The psalm asks for answers: "Why is it, O sea, that you flee? O Jordan . . . O mountains . . . ?" (vv. 5–6).

The questions placed before the seas and the mountains become questions addressed to us. Can *we* bear witness by whom all this was accomplished? Do *we* have that reverential awe and fear of the Holy One displayed by the sea that fled at his approach? The emphasis of the psalm here is important. The epiphany of God was revealed in those ancient events and is present again in the cultic and prayerful retelling of those events. Those events, though they took place in the past, touch the lives of each succeeding generation of believers. Each generation must affirm its own belief in God, who continues to save by those events. By faith the divine actions of the past can change *our* lives.

All the historical events alluded to in the psalm—events originally separated, carried out under different leaders—are presented almost as one unified complex that now signal the presence and plan of God's saving power. Originally independent and distinct historical events are juxtaposed in a kind of "cultic immediacy" in their retelling, because faith, looking back over Israel's history and under the inspiration of God, makes this new perspective possible.

It is the power of memory, under divine grace, that looks back at past events—seemingly insignificant at the time—and is able to understand their relationship to each other and their profound importance for the life of the people. So those events, recalled and celebrated regularly in cult and festival, enable faith to grow and deepen in knowledge and understanding. Therefore, this psalm is also about the importance of memory, of recollection, of celebration of the great events that give life to and nourish faith.

Pastoral Perspective

readings and psalms are reduced or changed by worship planners, Psalm 114 should be retained, sung or read after the Epistle, Romans 6:3–11. Its images of the sea and pools and springs of water reflect Paul's description of dying and rising with Christ in baptism and turn us to the Service of Baptism, which follows the Service of Readings. Its exultant tone is a prelude to the reading of the Easter Gospel.

In the years that Jewish and Christian liturgical calendars converge, Holy Week and Easter observances will coincide with Passover. Psalm 114 is one of the Hallel Psalms (Pss. 113–118), central to the celebration of Passover and thus an affirmation of God's power in the world shared by both traditions. The worship leader may choose to lift up Passover imagery in the liturgical texts of the Vigil ("This is our Passover feast," "Christ, the true Lamb"), with sensitivity to anti-Jewish interpretations of the passion.

In the context of the Easter Vigil, Psalm 114 recalls the exodus and freedom from slavery and points to Jesus' freedom "from the prison of the tomb. . . . The one who was dead now lives . . . the Lamb upon the throne."[2] The Passover lambs are alive and rejoicing at the transformation worked by God (114:4, 6), and the image of the lamb echoes the ancient Christian practice of singing the Agnus Dei at the breaking of the bread. "Lamb of God, who takes away the sin of the world, have mercy on us." The Lamb of God shares his life to heal the brokenness of the world in mercy and peace. The Lamb rejoices in resurrection life, and the lambs who feed at the table rejoice in its forgiveness.

The Easter Vigil is a liturgical embodiment of a pastoral reality, one given powerful and poignant expression in psalms that trace the journey from despair to hope, lament to joy, injury to recovery, tragedy to healing. Exodus experiences of spiritual wilderness, social rejection, communal loss of direction, conflicted purpose, and violated trust mark the journeys of those keeping this Vigil. Psalm 114 affirms that although we sheep of God's pasture may limp and fall rather than "skip," resurrection promises that all creation will tremble with God's life-giving presence, not God's absence.

Many congregations are familiar with the choral music of John Rutter, a prolific contemporary British composer and conductor of the acclaimed Clare Chapel Choir at Cambridge. Rutter's oldest son, Christopher, sang in the choir. One early spring night, after choir practice, Christopher was struck by

---

2. Great Thanksgiving, in ibid., 319.

Exegetical Perspective

They sang praise rather than lamenting. There are lamentation psalms that express the people's dismay and grief at being divided and overcome, but Psalm 114 takes a different approach.

The psalm begins with the story of God's saving and uniting action on Israel's behalf in verses 1–2. God called them "out from Egypt . . . from a people of strange language." The poet not only proclaims the deliverance from Egypt, but also announces that God has chosen the Israelites for his own people and his own dwelling place: "Judah became God's sanctuary, Israel his dominion." "Dominion" implies that in Israel, at least, God reigns supreme.

The next verses continue the story with an account of the miracles that accompanied the deliverance from Egypt and the triumphal entry into the promised land. The sea and the Jordan River are both anthropomorphized as the poet remembers how "The sea looked and fled; Jordan turned back" (v. 3).

This refers, of course, to the parting of the Red Sea, which seems to have fled at Moses's command, only to return with a vengeance and consume the pursuing enemy. The Jordan too was parted at the command of Joshua as he led the Hebrews into Canaan, a fitting reminder of the power of God for the children of Israel to take into their new home with them.

Verse 4 also recalls incidents that took place after the deliverance from Egypt. After the Israelites had escaped and been led by Moses into the wilderness to worship at Mount Sinai (Exod. 3:12; this is the sign that God had promised Moses when he first called him), the Lord commanded Moses to have the people consecrate themselves for three days, because the Lord was going to reveal himself to the people. On the morning of the third day, there were noises so loud—including an earthquake, a heavenly trumpet blast, and peals of thunder (Exod. 19:16–20)—that not only did the mountain quake, but so did the people, at the approach of the Lord.

This event is artfully recounted in Psalm 114:4, where the poet recalls that the mountains skipped like rams and the hills like lambs. By choosing "skipping" instead of "quaking," "trembling," or "thundering," the poet evokes the joy and celebration of the occasion at hand, when the Israelites gather to sing this psalm.

The playful mood set by the image of skipping rams and lambs continues in verses 5 and 6, where the poet seems to jeer at the elements that have retreated from the Lord's presence.

Homiletical Perspective

even dwelling within and among the people. "Tremble, O earth, at the presence of the LORD," the psalmist exhorts (v. 7). Such greatness fills the psalmist—and us—with awe, as he wonders aloud at the impossibilities God makes possible, the manifestations of God's presence and power.

In recalling the exodus story and the parting of the sea, this psalm reminds us of how the power and mercy of God are reflected in the reality of water. The waters of the sea pulled back to allow safe passage for God's people, then brought death to the enemy. Water has the power to kill and destroy; yet it is necessary for life. As Jean Danielou once said, "water is, on the one hand, the principle of destruction, the instrument of judgment destroying the sinful world; and on the other hand, it is the principle of creation, the life-giving element in which a new creature is born."[1]

During the Easter Vigil, Psalm 114 is sung or read after the congregation has heard Romans 6:3–11, where the apostle Paul compares Christian baptism to dying and rising with Christ. We are baptized into Christ's death, he says, so that we may also be raised with him. So we sing about the greatness of this God, who saved the people through the waters of the Red Sea and delivered them from slavery to freedom.

This is the same God who drew us from the saving waters of baptism, delivering us from death to life. Here again we are reminded of the saving and killing powers of water. We remember that just as we were born in a burst of water from our mothers' wombs, we are born anew in the waters of the font. (Some ancient baptismal founts were constructed in a circular shape to symbolize a womb.) The preacher who hears the swell of this song will sing out the good news in tones that reflect the awe, the wonder, and the joy of this night.

Psalm 114, then, holds an interpretive key for preaching during the Vigil. Baptism (or a reaffirmation of baptismal vows or thanksgiving for baptism) is central to the Easter Vigil, and water winds through the stories of creation, the exodus, Romans 6, and Psalm 114. This psalm is followed by the Gospel reading in which resurrection is proclaimed, and so the congregation hears a crescendo of praise. We have heard the stories of God's delivery of God's people, we have sung songs of praise, and now we hear the proclamation of life that is born from death. "He is not here; for he has been raised," the angel declares (Matt. 28:6). Just as God destroyed tyranny

---

1. Jean Danielou, SJ, *The Bible and the Liturgy* (Notre Dame, IN: University of Notre Dame Press, 1956), 71.

Psalm 114

Theological Perspective

Lastly, the psalm vividly portrays how the forces of nature—indeed all the powers opposed to God and God's plan—are under the divine power. The most solid structures of creation, the mountains, are jostled from their place at the command of God. Dumb hard rock becomes a source of life-giving water. The waters of the sea and the Jordan, symbolizing the most powerful natural forces, recoil at the epiphany of God. The waters also evoke the story of creation. There the watery chaos is subdued, controlled, and organized by the creative action of God, and life begins. All the forces opposed to life and goodness are rendered impotent. The psalm recalls this theme in terms of Israel's own history, acknowledging how God continually brings forth life in the face of every kind of difficulty and opposition.

Why this psalm for Easter? This psalm celebrates the saving presence of God in human history. How fitting, then, that it should now celebrate the definitive epiphany of God in Jesus Christ and the most manifest sign of God's power over death and all that is opposed to his divine plan for our welfare! The resurrection indicates that God is with us through all trials until the end of time. God became one of us that he might be with us always. Even death is powerless before God—and even before us in union with him.

However, the resurrection is not simply an event of the past. The power of the resurrected Jesus transcends time and space and touches the lives of all in any age and any place. Our celebration of this event makes Jesus' resurrection present for us. We must come forward and renew our faith in the living Jesus, so that we may share in his life. Our celebration, year by year, will deepen our faith and our awareness of his continued saving presence in our lives.

THOMAS P. MCCREESH

Pastoral Perspective

a car and killed. One week later his funeral was held at Clare Chapel, where he sang as a child and a teenager and where he had been baptized.

Two years later John Rutter's *Mass of the Children* premiered at Carnegie Hall. It was the first thing he was able to write after his son's death, part tribute to Christopher, part catharsis for himself. In liturgical terms, it is a *missa brevis*, "a brief mass," which means it does not include the creed. Perhaps, for the composer and bereft father, his brief mass made a statement about brief life. Even without a creed, the work makes a statement of faith: Just as God's presence turns the rock into a pool of water (v. 8), so God's presence turns the hard places of suffering into healing places where life and faith are embraced.

"The sadness, of course, never goes," John Rutter said in an interview. "Anybody who's experienced what our family has knows that it draws you closer together, and perhaps from that closeness comes a sense of inspiration."[3] Composers use the word "inspiration" to express a spark to the imagination, the birth of a new artistic creation; but inspiration is also the rekindling of the human spirit, as we breathe in and feel life infusing us again. "A sense of inspiration" invites skipping on the hills, even when we have walked in the valley of the shadow of death. It is in the deep darkness and hopelessness and pain of the world that God inspires us with the resurrection of Jesus Christ. The Lamb of God brings light and hope and life.

Rutter's *Mass of the Children* begins with an old English morning hymn and ends with an old English evening hymn, creating the framework of a complete day. A child's voice thanks God for the day's blessings and asks to be kept safe during the night. "Keep me, O keep me, King of kings, Beneath thy own almighty wings." In the Easter Vigil our adult faith voices trust in the God who works in the night. Jesus Christ is born in the night, and Jesus Christ is resurrected in the night, not as a coincidence of the story, but as the intention of God to meet us there. "Tremble," says the psalmist. God is here.

DEBORAH A. BLOCK

---

3. Interview by Vicki Mabrey, CBS News, December 17, 2003.

Exegetical Perspective

Why is it, O sea, that you flee,
  O Jordan, that you turn back?
O mountains, that you skip like rams?
  O little hills, like lambs?

The text has changed from past tense to present tense, as though the poet were standing at the foot of Sinai or on the shore of the Red Sea with his people.

Of course, this is true; religious festivals such as the Jewish New Year celebration are about more than just remembering something that happened a long time ago. They are about authentically participating in those events, through the ritual reenactment of them. The psalmist is part of the same joyful, delivered people, and as such is justified in making comments on the events as though they were happening at that moment.

After finishing the steps of retelling the stories and participating in their reenactment, the poet then turns to the people assembled in his own time. He seems to be addressing the earth itself, exhorting it to an appropriate response in the presence of a God who can do the things just described; yet there is more to the exhortation than simply a call to the earth to tremble (again) "at the presence of the God of Jacob" (v. 7).

The psalmist also presents the people with a fresh opportunity to give praise to the God whose story they are telling. Using the common formula, "Give praise to God, who . . . ," the poet calls the earth to tremble at the presence of the God of Jacob, who continues to save them, by giving them water in the desert (v. 8).

Finally the psalm serves as an admonishment to the people of Israel, who trembled at the Red Sea and again at the foot of Zion. Though joy and celebration are the main themes of this psalm, it is still appropriate to tremble before the Lord.

KATHERINE C. CALORE

Homiletical Perspective

through the waters of the sea, God destroys death through the waters of baptism. By sharing in the baptism of Jesus Christ, we share in his death and resurrection. On this night, we celebrate God's new creation.

Even the Gospel story appointed for this night sends us to the water: "Do not be afraid," says the risen Jesus, "go and tell my brothers to go to Galilee; there they will see me" (Matt. 28:10). Galilee, of course, is where it all happened—where Jesus was baptized in the Jordan, where he walked on water and calmed the stormy sea, where he taught by the lakeshore, pointed the disciples to the greatest catch of fish they had ever seen, and cooked them breakfast on the beach. Christ's life took place in, on, and around water; we who are called Christians are born by water and spirit and our lives are defined by the waters of baptism.

At the end of the second century, Tertullian wrote that "we, little fishes, after the example of our Ichthus [great fish] Jesus Christ, are born in water, nor have we safety in any other way than by permanently abiding in the water."[2] In other words, it is only by living out our baptismal vocations, abiding with Christ in waters that defeat death and give life, that we really live—not only for our own sakes, but for the sake of a world that needs clean water to drink, access to water for cultivating, and that living water who is Jesus Christ, who brings justice and mercy to all.

KIMBERLY BRACKEN LONG

---

2. Tertullian, *De baptismo*, c. 1, as quoted in Maxwell E. Johnson, *The Rites of Christian Initiation: Their Evolution and Interpretation*, rev. and expanded ed. (Collegeville, MN: Liturgical Press, 2007), 84.

Romans 6:3-11

³Do you not know that all of us who have been baptized into Christ Jesus were baptized into his death? ⁴Therefore we have been buried with him by baptism into death, so that, just as Christ was raised from the dead by the glory of the Father, so we too might walk in newness of life.

⁵For if we have been united with him in a death like his, we will certainly be united with him in a resurrection like his. ⁶We know that our old self was crucified with him so that the body of sin might be destroyed, and we might no longer be enslaved to sin. ⁷For whoever has died is freed from sin. ⁸But if we have died with Christ, we believe that we will also live with him. ⁹We know that Christ, being raised from the dead, will never die again; death no longer has dominion over him. ¹⁰The death he died, he died to sin, once for all; but the life he lives, he lives to God. ¹¹So you also must consider yourselves dead to sin and alive to God in Christ Jesus.

Theological Perspective

In this passage, Paul interprets baptism as an event that joins Christians to Jesus' death and resurrection. This understanding of baptism as paschal mystery has dominated in Western churches since the fourth century. Theodore of Mopsuestia, for instance, said in a baptismal homily in the late fourth century, "When I am baptized and put my head under the water, I wish to receive the death and burial of Christ our Lord, and I solemnly profess my faith in his resurrection; when I come up out of the water, this is a sign that I believe I am already risen." Scholars have suggested several reasons for the emergence of Romans 6 as the primary lens for interpreting baptism in the West:

—The end of martyrdom in the early fourth century meant that imagery of sharing Christ's death and resurrection could now be expanded from the martyrs specifically to all Christians generally.

—The rise of interest in holy places associated with Christ's passion and death fostered interest in reproducing liturgically the path of the historical Jesus, especially his suffering and death.

—While many Eastern churches had interpreted baptism primarily as participation in Jesus' own baptism in the Jordan, this focus had prompted in some places a more adoptionist Christology. By contrast, the Pauline emphasis on baptism as

Pastoral Perspective

When Christians gather for a funeral service, there is always some expectation that the preacher will have known the deceased well enough to share some words of comfort that will prove deeply meaningful. Maybe the one conducting the service will be able to stir the assembly in such a way as to help everyone make fresh sense of life and death. This is the anticipation as worshipers look up and stare forward, awaiting the start of the service.

Then, in language that many liturgical traditions share, the voice of the apostle Paul abruptly breaks the silence. The opening words comprise what is arguably the most potent statement on baptism written in the entire New Testament: "All of us who have been baptized into Christ Jesus were baptized into his death. Therefore we have been buried with him by baptism into death, so that, just as Christ was raised from the dead by the glory of the Father, so we too might walk in newness of life" (Rom. 6:3–4).

The echo of Paul's voice careening off the sanctuary walls signals that the service has begun, not with a whimper but a bang. There is nothing soft or mushy about Romans 6. Funeralgoers who have tried to live the Christian life for the bulk of their years suddenly find themselves straightening up and thinking, "Oh my! I guess my baptism was more than I thought it was. I knew we had a lot of friends show

Exegetical Perspective

It is hard to understand why the lectionary omits the first two and the last three verses of this part of Romans; the preacher should not do so, since Paul's argument does not make sense without them. The questions he raises at verse 1, "What then are we to say? Should we continue in sin in order that grace may abound?" arise directly from the argument in 5:12–21. There Paul says that the law "snuck in on the side" (5:20, my trans.) to make sin more deadly by holding it accountable as transgression. As a result, grace abounded even more than sin had, because God's grace in Jesus Christ addressed both the guilt of sin and its power to enslave.

If the causal relationship between sin and grace were merely hypothetical, rather than real, one might perhaps reason that we ought indeed to sin more, in order to experience more grace. The human predicament is quite real, though. We are not only mortally wounded by the power of sin and its ally death; we are guilty for our own wounds, because the law holds us responsible for our actions, even though we are powerless to avoid them. We are in need of both a hospital and a prison, and Jesus' death and resurrection address both needs. That is why Paul answers his own question: "By no means! How can we who died to sin go on living in it?" (v. 2).

Homiletical Perspective

Preachers more than occasionally have trouble finding solid homiletical footing in Paul. The (authentic or attributed) epistles of Paul are full of *theology*, after all, and in recent generations many pulpiteers have abandoned theological preaching altogether. Jaded themselves, perhaps, the preachers are likewise convinced that their listeners are unaccustomed to and uninterested in "doctrine." Others, meanwhile, have become sermonic Pharisees—laying "heavy burdens" of exegesis and conceptual analysis on the shoulders of the gathered.

In either case preachers do not seem to trust the text itself—which is to say they do not work to let the Scripture do its own work. Those who dissect the text forget that its parts are not greater than the whole, that while chloroform and scalpels can aid one kind of understanding, greater truths can be learned only from living specimens. Similarly, those who disdain the theological heart of a text in the hopes, say, of fostering "encounter" through anecdote, moralizing, or other rhetorical means, forget that theology documents the divine-human encounter, and that the church has already given us means to reiterate and reappropriate that encounter: the sacraments.

"Sacrament" may be (and in fact historically has been) defined in a multitude of ways. These multifarious denotations aim, however, at a single

Romans 6:3-11

Theological Perspective

participation in Christ's death and resurrection is not as susceptible to such "unorthodox" Christologies.[1]

Whatever the reason, the rise of Romans 6 as the primary meaning of baptism went hand in hand with the emphasis in the fourth century on Easter as the most appropriate day to celebrate baptism, an emphasis that has been retrieved in recent liturgical renewal. Celebrating baptism at Easter Vigil clearly connects this central Christian symbol with the events of Christ's death and resurrection.

Contemporary preachers wrestling with this text, at Easter or any other time of the Christian year, have a rich opportunity to deepen a congregation's understanding of baptism and its connection with the whole Christian life. Three questions provide possible launching points for this reflection: what does it mean to be buried with Christ? What does it mean to be raised with Christ? How exactly does baptism accomplish this dying and rising?

"Buried with Him by Baptism into Death." With this striking claim, Paul insists that in baptism, something really dies. Christian life means the end of something. What is that something? Luther describes this in typically passionate fashion: "Your baptism is nothing less than grace clutching you by the throat: a grace-full throttling, by which your sin is submerged in order that ye may remain under grace. Come thus to thy baptism. Give thyself up to be drowned in baptism and killed by the mercy of thy dear God, saying, 'Drown me and throttle me, dear Lord, for henceforth I will gladly die to sin with Thy Son.'"[2] Luther understood baptism as the act that decisively demonstrates the good news of justification by grace through faith: baptism as death to sin means that we are no longer captive to sin, but we are set free by the utter grace of God in Christ. For this reason, Luther cried out in moments of crisis: "I am baptized!" Nothing now could separate him from God's mercies.

"So We Too Might Walk in Newness of Life." Not only does something die in baptism, but new life emerges. Significantly, Paul talks about this new life in both future and present tenses: *"we will certainly be* united with him in a resurrection like his" (v. 5b); *"so you also must consider yourselves* dead to sin and alive

1. Theodore of Mopsuestia, "Baptismal Homily III," in *The Awe-Inspiring Rites of Initiation,* ed. Edward Yarnold, 2nd ed. (Collegeville, MN: Liturgical Press, 1994), 183.

2. Martin Luther, quoted by Karl Barth in *The Epistle to the Romans,* trans. from 6th ed. by Edwyn C. Hoskyns (Oxford: Oxford University Press, 1968), 194.

Pastoral Perspective

up that day. I remember seeing all the church photos. The party afterwards looked terrific. I understand the cake was lovely; but I guess what really happened that day is that I died. I died? Yep, I died."

Baptismal language gives definition to the bookends of the Christian life. It marks both the beginning *and* end of one's journey of faith. There is something else that helps the start and finish cohere; it is a sacred furnishing inside many churches. The paschal candle that once burned bright for a person's baptism glows again for the funeral service of the same individual. It burns, in part, to underscore the sense of unity belonging to those conjoined twins we call "life" and "death."

In liturgical traditions that observe Easter Vigil worship, it is customary at one point in the liturgy for an assigned worshiper to press five wax nails into small nail holes embedded in the paschal candle. This is always a deeply reflective moment. The nails are pressed hard into the outline of the cross that adorns the side of the candle. As this happens, worshipers sit quietly in the dark, contemplating the privilege of Easter. They recall the five wounds of Christ with these five red nails that have now become a permanent feature of the paschal candle.

"Do you not know that . . . " says Paul as he begins this section on dying and rising. There is an air of obviousness to his words, a suggestion of self-evident truth spoken as if everyone else in the world might be catching on to what you are not grasping. By Paul's way of thinking, baptism is inextricably linked to death. He summarily sweeps away all illusions among those who want to confine baptism to a bubbly ritual of religious happiness. He insists there is no such thing as baptism worth anything in the Christian life unless one takes death into account at the same time. It is dying and rising always held together—inseparable sides of the same life—that constitute a faithful way to make sense of one's bond with Christ.

Think of the act of burial. Some of the best graveside services in cemeteries happen when there is a mix of ages present. Elderly relatives and friends hobble over the uneven ground to move from their cars to the rickety chairs beneath the green tent. Young adults hide together behind sunglasses, embarrassed by their emotions over death and their discomfort with a committal service. Toddlers run around under the big sky, playing tag among the surrounding tombstones. Graveside services with all of these players can make for an especially memorable day. As carefree kids scurry about, and young adults stare into an earthen hole, and elderly persons wonder,

Exegetical Perspective

We have died to sin because Christ died to sin, and in our baptism we die with Christ. Paul asks at verse 3, "Do you not know [and when he asks, do you not know? you may be certain he assumes that we do indeed know] that all of us who have been baptized into Christ Jesus were baptized into his death?" The metaphor of slavery casts the cosmic power of sin in the role of the master and human beings in the roles of slaves. Sin is not simply human misbehavior—that is what Paul calls "trespass" or "transgression"—it is the force in the universe that holds us hostage and uses us for its own ends.

Beverly Gaventa describes sin as "not a lower-case transgression, not even a human disposition or flaw in human nature, but an upper-case Power that enslaves humankind and stands over against God."[1] For Paul, "sin" is almost always in the singular, and its opponent is not forgiveness but the grace of God in Jesus Christ. God uses Jesus' death to defeat the powers of sin and death, and we become the beneficiaries of God's victory in baptism. The death of the slave ends the master's power, so we who die to sin are freed from it.

Sometimes prepositions are the most important words in a Pauline sentence. Here, the prepositions "with" and "in" are critical to following the apostle's logic. We die "with" Christ in baptism, and we will be raised "with" Christ at his coming in glory. Between now and then, however, we walk "in" newness of life (v. 4). This is roughly synonymous with his more common phrases, "in Christ" and "in the Spirit" (e.g., 3:24; 6:11, 23; 8:1–2, 9; 9:1). It is the location of the Christian life under the sovereignty of God, embraced by the love of Jesus, in the realm of the Spirit. Although this life is certainly not yet the resurrection life (note the future-tense verbs "we will . . . be united" and "we will . . . live" in vv. 5, 8), it is *new* life, life made possible by the death and resurrection of Christ and empowered by God's Spirit.

Paul is not naive about the lingering reality of sin in human experience. Even the baptized are all too familiar with the presence of evil, of sin and death, of weakness and mortality in our lives. Even—or particularly—at the Easter Vigil we are keenly aware of what is not yet true of the world in which we live. Christ is risen indeed, we will say at midnight or tomorrow morning, although we know full well that we are not. We still struggle with the forces of evil that continue to torment God's world. We still face the

1. Beverly Roberts Gaventa, "The Cosmic Power of Sin in Paul's Letter to the Romans: Toward a Widescreen Edition," *Interpretation* 58 (2004): 231.

Homiletical Perspective

connotation: the "more," the "surplus of meaning," which suffuses the particular gestures and rituals we recognize *as* sacraments. Granted, disparate traditions enumerate and even identify the sacraments differently. Still, these gestures are both acts of obedience to Jesus' command (hence, the term "ordinance") and prayers of deep trust, that these sacred moments both flow from and are taken up into the life and ongoing work of God. Human agency notwithstanding, the faithful believe these temporal observances are divine activities, each particular obedience rooted in God's universalizing grace.

Accordingly, sacraments are gestures of both memory and hope, empowered by anamnesis—"summons." The prayers of the people summon both the witness of history and the presence of God into a particular moment and whatever elements are at hand. Participation in the sacraments grafts believers into God's covenantal purposes, sustains them in their faith and call, and reconstitutes the community as a locus of testimony.

These sacramental and theological observations have homiletical importance for the Easter Vigil in at least two ways. The first is cautionary: unwise preachers turn too quickly from symbol to exposition, overlook the power of the sacraments to proclaim the heart of Christian theology—especially at Easter. If sacraments indeed convey what we can only attempt to exposit, there is theological content and experiential quality in the rituals themselves that cannot be exhausted or explained by words alone. It is not too much to say that the entire life of faith, the entire content of theology, the history of the church are indeed gathered up into these sacred gestures, these acts of ritualized memory: the always and everywhere, delivered *now* by means of *this*.

This leads to the second important observation: Paul himself, in our lesson for tonight, uses the specific sign of actual baptismal practice to convey the heart of his theology. Paul is content to let the water do the talking, as it were, and perhaps we should follow his lead and let the water, the light, the Scriptures themselves, the gathered community testify to the deep truth of what is sometimes lost in translation.

The Easter Vigil is cued by the long-ago and ever-new story of Jesus' followers, one or a few of the women (and the men only later, and then reluctantly) making their way to the tomb-garden while it was yet dark. Long centuries have not diminished the near-comedy of the ritual. If skeptics of the nascent faith were bewildered by the annual midnight ritual—Christians making their way to cemeteries to

Romans 6:3-11

to God in Christ Jesus" (v. 11, emphasis added). How shall we understand the relationship between future resurrection and present regeneration? The life we live now draws strength from Christ's accomplished resurrection. Like a twig that is grafted onto a tree, we receive new life from our union with the risen Christ. The present life also draws strength from the future, from the knowledge that we will be united with Christ in his resurrection. Our true lives are already bound to the risen Christ; this is the new life that we are empowered to live even now.

"By Baptism"? How does baptism itself work to unite us with Christ's death and resurrection? This has puzzled and divided theologians for centuries. On one side are those who stress sacramental acts as real means of grace (so baptism unites us substantially with the crucified and risen Christ). On the other are those who emphasize the freedom of God's activity, which is not bound by signs (so baptism symbolizes Christ's dying and rising, but does not really join us to Christ). In his early commentary on Romans, Karl Barth suggests one way beyond this divide. Baptism is a sign that really declares the Word of God, a human act that is "enclosed" by the action of God. To those with faith, baptism "speaks of death," particularly the death of Christ, and of the new life that comes beyond death.[3]

Though Barth does not say it in quite this way, he portrays baptism as a living Word that communicates both God's judgment on human life and the freedom that emerges with the resurrection. Baptism thus unites us with Christ's death and resurrection in the same way that every proclaimed word can do: not magically through its own innate powers, but by the grace of God as received by receptive faith.

MARTHA MOORE-KEISH

"Am I next?" one cannot help but think of the rhythm of life. Dying and rising come together in plain view when a two-year-old goes up and pats a casket before it is lowered into the ground.

In towns where cemeteries charge an additional fee for families who wish to stay and see the casket and vault lowered into the excavated hole, most people are willing to pay. There is something powerfully definitive about a seeing a body go into the ground. So too with holy baptism down at the riverbank. When a baptized individual steps in and goes underwater with some clothing on, it is the appearance of drowning that leaves a lasting impression on those gathered. Dying to sin (v. 2) and being "baptized into . . . death" (v. 3) no longer remain abstract words of Scripture on such occasions.

Paul is clear that the way to make sense of dying and rising is always to link our lives with Christ. We do not die alone, and we do not rise alone. Baptism into death and life means baptism into the death and life of Christ.

It would make for a constructive reading project to boldface or highlight the preposition "with" in this Romans 6 passage. We could even afford to give special accent to this word during a public reading in worship. Six separate times, Paul speaks of our lives being all tied up *with* Christ. Everything Christ enjoys or suffers, we too should expect to enjoy and suffer.

This conviction of being bound up *with* Christ gives Paul the extraconfident measure of faith to which all believers aspire. "We know that our old self was crucified," he writes (v. 6). Only three verses later he returns to the same "we know" confidence: "We know that Christ, being raised from the dead, will never die again" (v. 9). This confidence of faith should remind every preacher and congregation never to let a notice or mention of death occur without some renewed commitment by all to walk in newness of life.

PETER W. MARTY

---

3. See Barth, *The Epistle to the Romans*, 192–94.

Exegetical Perspective

certainty of our own deaths. What has changed at our baptisms—because it happened at the cross and resurrection of Christ—is not the existence of sin and death but their inevitability, their deadly hold on us.

Sin is no longer lord, because Jesus is Lord. God has transferred us from one slavery—slavery to sin—to slavery to righteousness (6:15–23). In a very real sense, then, we are not who we once were: "We know that our old self [our old "humanity" or "human nature"] was crucified with [Christ] so that the body of sin might be destroyed, and we might no longer be enslaved to sin" (v. 6).

Paul will flesh out in greater detail the nature of this transfer of sovereignty and its consequences for Christian ethics in his next paragraph. Here it is enough to say the change has taken place. Because Christ's death to sin is "once for all" (v. 10) and we share his death through baptism, we now can cease "living in sin," that is, in its deadly power. This is why Paul urges us to "consider [ourselves] dead to sin and alive to God in Christ Jesus" (v. 11). This change of sovereignty—we have been freed from one master and claimed by another—has concrete manifestations in Christian experience.

The metaphor shifts from slavery to kingship in 6:12. "Do not let sin reign as king," he says (v. 12, my trans.), because God is the only true king. "Do not present your members [that is, your bodies] to sin as weapons of wickedness . . . but to God as weapons of justice" (v. 13, my trans.). Because we "have been brought from death to life" (v. 13), sin is no longer king; God is. We who were once under the power of the law are now under the power of grace and empowered to live lives of justice (v. 14).

E. ELIZABETH JOHNSON

Homiletical Perspective

light candles, sing, and pray—even believers in these later days may find themselves wondering what we are doing out here at this hour of the night/morning.

I see us gathering in a large graveyard, about a stone's throw from the small aluminum-sided sanctuary, a few chilly souls, bundled, sleepy, and shivering. The dead far outnumber the quick, while the darkness takes scant notice of the lone candle around which we cluster. An early spring breeze glides through the still-bare branches of trees warding the sacred acre, makes the candle flame dance, or teeter. What little light there is flickers and more than once all but goes out. Soon we will make our pilgrim way along the long concrete walkway from cemetery to sanctuary—from the darkness into light, from the memory of death into hope for new life.

The assembled few represent the absent many, and all of us simultaneously shackled to yesterday and straining toward tomorrow. "Night" describes not only the time of day but the condition of our souls (John 13:30). We stand here half from habit and half in hungering hope, the latter often unrecognized and certainly unconfessed. Yes, we believe what we are about to proclaim; but Lord, help our unbelief. What we say again we have said so many times before: "Alleluia! Christ is risen! The Lord is risen indeed!" We want to believe everything has been changed by this proclamation; soon, however, we will leave this service and go back into the darkness, all the deeper now than when we gathered—it is later, after all—where nothing seems at all different.

Resurrection alone can answer the darkness of death. It is God's final word and the gospel's first word: life. The proclamation of Easter—and even this text, assigned as part of the Easter Vigil—grapples with both death and life, both darkness and light. Neither can be denied, though various attempts are made.

As baptism is a symbol of both death and resurrection, so is the Easter Vigil—and all resurrection proclamation. Whether stammered out in the cold of a cemetery or jubilated with accompaniment by Handel, Easter acknowledges the reality of death but announces the greater reality of life. There is more to this moment than what we see and do, far more than we could say or explain.

That is the truth of the sacraments. That is the theology of sacramental encounter. That is the hope and nerve of Easter's first service, the Vigil.

THOMAS R. STEAGALD

Matthew 28:1-10

[1]After the sabbath, as the first day of the week was dawning, Mary Magdalene and the other Mary went to see the tomb. [2]And suddenly there was a great earthquake; for an angel of the Lord, descending from heaven, came and rolled back the stone and sat on it. [3]His appearance was like lightning, and his clothing white as snow. [4]For fear of him the guards shook and became like dead men. [5]But the angel said to the women, "Do not be afraid; I know that you are looking for Jesus who was crucified. [6]He is not here; for he has been raised, as he said. Come, see the place where he lay. [7]Then go quickly and tell his disciples, 'He has been raised from the dead, and indeed he is going ahead of you to Galilee; there you will see him.' This is my message for you." [8]So they left the tomb quickly with fear and great joy, and ran to tell his disciples. [9]Suddenly Jesus met them and said, "Greetings!" And they came to him, took hold of his feet, and worshiped him. [10]Then Jesus said to them, "Do not be afraid; go and tell my brothers to go to Galilee; there they will see me."

Theological Perspective

Matthew's Gospel has a distinctive deployment of agents and portents when heaven and earth intersect. Karl Barth has observed that angels return to the story at this point of empty tomb and resurrection, having been absent since the birth and temptation narratives.[1] Barth is mainly correct. There is also an intermediate appearance of heavenly figures in Matthew's Gospel at chapter 17, when Elijah and Moses converse with Jesus on the mount of transfiguration. Thus for Matthew, at the decisive points of God's special presence in the world: the incarnation, the transfiguration, and the resurrection, the story necessarily involves actors and actions that are extraordinary.

This text is no exception. As those two Marys approach the sealed tomb, all heaven appears to break loose. An earthquake occurs, not as the means of opening the tomb but as a result of the angel of the Lord breaking in on the scene, rolling back the stone that seemed to separate Jesus utterly from the life that he had lived, and sitting down upon it in an obvious sign of divine triumph. This angel's appearance is described in allusions to Daniel 10:5–6 and Revelation 1:14, dressed in garments whiter than

1. Karl Barth, *Church Dogmatics*, III/2, *The Doctrine of Creation* (Edinburgh: T. & T. Clark, 1960), 453.

Pastoral Perspective

Luke's account of Jesus' birth and Matthew's account of Jesus' resurrection provide identical words of reassurance, which, when read together, seem to wrap the entire gospel narrative in those words: "Do not be afraid." According to Luke, those are among the first words the angel Gabriel utters when he approaches Mary with the news that she has found favor with God and will bear a son named Jesus (Luke 1:30). Later, when Mary's son is born, they are the first words offered to the shepherds in the field: "Do not be afraid" (Luke 2:10).

Then, according to Matthew, when Mary Magdalene and the other Mary find the tomb of Jesus empty and the earth shakes, presumably shuddering under the awesomeness of what has just happened, an angel uses the same words to reassure them: "Do not be afraid" (v. 5).

When the women leave to tell the disciples what had happened, Jesus himself appears before them and, after a brief salutation ("Greetings!"), his next words are the same: "Do not be afraid" (vv. 9, 10).

When was the last time anyone said something like that to you, and did so with authority? That is, when was the last time someone said something like that to you and you believed it?

When I was a child, if I were in the grip of fear, and my mother or my father held me close, blotted

Exegetical Perspective

It is difficult for us to put ourselves in the place of the women who come to Jesus' tomb early in the morning on the first day of the week—Easter morning! It is not that we do not know about Easter. Rather, we know too much about Easter; and the women know nothing at all. Still, it is possible to see the story from their point of view, for Matthew tells us not only what they say and do, but how they feel. He tells the story from their perspective.

This story begins quietly as the day is dawning on the first day of the week. Mary Magdalene and the other Mary are going to *see* the tomb. We do not know who this "other Mary" is. It would be an odd way to refer to Jesus' mother. Mark has "Mary the mother of James." In any case, we shall discover that *seeing* is an important theme in the story.

The two Marys go to see the tomb (v. 2). The guards faint for fear when they see the angel (v. 4). The angel, however, invites the women to see where Jesus lay (v. 6), adding that they will see Jesus himself in Galilee (v. 7). Actually, they will see him sooner than that.

"Behold" (v. 9, RSV—see also the discussion below), he meets them.

If the story begins quietly, it soon becomes noisy in a way that is both difficult to explain and frightening. There is a great earthquake. Even small quakes

Homiletical Perspective

The Easter Vigil is a grand celebration, even though it is ignored by large segments of the Christian church. Augustine called it the Mother of All Vigils. Celebrating it today involves incorporating numerous readings (usually seven, as many as twelve in some traditions), each followed by a psalm. The service moves from darkness to light and recounts in the readings the entire biblical salvation history.

Matthew's version of the resurrection story fits perfectly as the final reading for this celebration. Matthew's is the Gospel most closely linked to the Old Testament history and the developing story of God's grace. It also parallels in narrative the darkness-to-light theme of the Vigil. Just as the people gather to celebrate the Vigil in darkness and move toward the light, the story has "Mary Magdalene and the other Mary" (v. 1) coming in the darkness of first dawn and moving toward an understanding of the resurrection as the sun breaks.

Sermons on this version of the Easter story can take advantage of the fulsomeness of Matthew's version. Mark's account (Mark 16:1–8) is spare and ends abruptly. Luke's version (Luke 24:1–12) fills in some detail, with the angels tying the resurrection to things Jesus had predicted. Still, it leaves the reader with many questions about what must have happened. John's resurrection story (John 20:1–18) takes its

Matthew 28:1-10

Theological Perspective

snow and with an appearance of lightning. By this use of angelic actors and signs and portents, Matthew asserts that God is irrupting into the world in a new and decisive manner. Indeed, God's renewed reign is heralded by this symbolic vocabulary and imagery. Consequently, the soldiers stationed to guard the tomb are shocked into a helpless, deathlike state.

Matthew's core theological point is that there is no merely naturalistic way of speaking of the resurrection. This is not about human capacities or possibilities. It is wholly about God's capacity and determination. If goodness and mercy are to withstand the onslaught of religiously based self-righteousness and control, it is not because good people just keep trying hard. If death as a final conclusion to even the most finely lived human life is to be transcended, it is not because such goodness just naturally lives on. It is, rather, because God acts at that boundary of life we call death and does something altogether new. Angels and earthquakes are the inevitable elements of the resurrection narrative, because that is the only way Matthew can make clear that we are confronted with God's possibilities and not our own.

Having dispensed with the guards through overwhelming fear, the angel speaks reassuringly to the women, "Do not be afraid" (v. 5). The angel quickly couples to these reassuring words an acknowledgment of the women's purpose, "I know that you are looking for Jesus who was crucified." They were looking for their fallen leader. The reason they need not fear at the angel's dramatic and mighty presence is that their fallen leader "is not here; for he has been raised, as he said" (v. 6). To drive the point home, the angel says—almost offhandedly—"Come, see the place where he lay" (v. 6). Past tense! Where he had lain, but where he lay no longer. Come see the empty space, the empty tomb.

The empty tomb is not a dispensable theological point for Matthew. It is not the main point, but it is important. Without the empty tomb, resurrection theology reduces to a generalized capacity for goodness somehow to outlast and overcome evil. Such a resurrection hope is only as powerful as the latest experience one may have had with goodness hanging on against such evil. In the grand sweep of human history, there is too much evidence to the contrary to nurture hope in most of us.

That the tomb was empty is a different kind of assertion. It says that—notwithstanding all the evidence in the sad story of humanity that manifests hurt and harm holding sway over healing and

Pastoral Perspective

my tears, stroked my hair, and said, "You do not need to be afraid. There is nothing to be afraid of," I would believe it. It came as a great comfort—but that seems like a very long time ago.

For adults, the fears can be more complex and words of reassurance harder to come by. As we get older, we cannot escape the realization that, in Ernest Hemingway's phrase, "life breaks everyone" at some time or another or, at the very least, wears one down relentlessly. As adults, we live with an increasing sense that death is greedy, eventually claiming everyone we love. When grown-up fears are stirred by such enormous realities, it can seem as if words of reassurance are nowhere to be found.

In fact, we know enough about the way the world works that, if someone tells us not to be afraid, we can be suspicious: "Ladies and gentlemen, you will have noticed that we are experiencing an unusual amount of turbulence in our flight today, but let us assure you that there is no reason for concern." One's reaction to that kind of attempt at reassurance can be, "Hmm. I was not particularly worried before. I wonder why he felt the need to tell us that?"

As a pastor, I spend a portion of my time in close proximity to illness and death. In such regions, shadowed by fear and loss, I so much want to reach for words that are reassuring. In the end, I do not have such words to offer, at least none of my own. I am not alone in this, of course. Neither do the doctors. In the end, ultimately, doctors do not have the authority to say, "Do not be afraid." Doctors do not know the future. They do not have the antidote to uncertainty. They cannot accompany a patient down every road. None of us can.

Nevertheless, that is what the angels come to say—in Scripture and, occasionally, in our lives: "Do not be afraid." It is an angel's calling card. It is how you know that you are being visited by an angel. Who else can say, "Do not be afraid," and do so with authority? Well, come to think of it, Jesus can and does. Quite a number of times in the Gospels Jesus says, "Fear not." It is another visitation.

When the angel says, "Do not be afraid," or when Jesus says, "Fear not," it is not assurance that nothing can go wrong, because often things do go wrong. It is not assurance that everything turns out for the best, because, if we are honest about it, it seldom does. Rather, it is assurance that, whatever may happen to us, whatever a day may hold, God has the power to strengthen us and uphold us; that whatever we must face, we do not face it alone; that nothing we encounter is stronger than God's love; that ultimately

Exegetical Perspective

are alarming. The dishes in the cabinet rattle, and the silver in the kitchen drawer clicks; the house feels as if it may move off its foundation. In a great quake, the dishes may well fly out of the cabinets, and the silver may jump out of the drawers; the foundation of the house may splinter and the house may fall—thus the experts' advice to run outside.

The quiet of the dawn is interrupted by the earth's quaking *and* by the appearance of an angel that requires contradictory images to describe. He is riding the earth's quaking, flashing like lightning, and dressed in snow! He is powerful enough to roll away the stone in front of the tomb and then, calmly, to sit on it. It is no wonder that the guards shake and fall over as if dead, when they see him. Actually, the guards *quake*, as with fear. The Greek translated "shook" in the NRSV (v. 4) is directly related to the Greek word for "earthquake" (v. 2). The guards shiver and shake; they quake and pass out from fear.

The angel, though, turns to the women and says, "Do not fear." He reassures them, though we are not certain how reassured they are. Is it reassuring to find out that not only has the earth been shaking; it has been so shaken that the dead have been stirred back to life? Mark's Gospel ends when the women, who have seen the angel and the empty tomb, flee with "terror and amazement" from both.

In Matthew's story, the women also run away from the angel and the tomb, but they are running toward the disciples, according to the angel's instructions, "Then go quickly and tell his disciples." *Go quickly*. It is important not to focus so much on the story's excitement—earthquakes and angels, rolling stones and empty graves—that its urgency is overlooked. In verse 2 the NRSV translates *idou* as "suddenly," capturing the urgency of the word but not its visual aspect. A better translation might be, "Look here!" Also note the repetition of "quickly" in verses 7 and 8, as the women leave the tomb to run and tell Jesus' disciples what they have seen. Then again— *suddenly* (*idou*)—Jesus meets them.

This first Easter is exploding with excitement and urgent energy. It is like being five years old and running down a grassy hill full speed, not caring whether you might fall, not even thinking you might fall, though if you did, you would be rolling up to see how quickly you could get back to full speed. The women *run* to take the message of the angel to the disciples that Jesus is going ahead of them to Galilee, and they will *see* him there.

They run with both fear and great joy (v. 8). Again the evangelist must call on contradiction to describe

Homiletical Perspective

own course, with Jesus appearing to Mary Magdalene alone and mysteriously telling her not to touch him. It has intimacy, but not much detail.

Matthew, on the other hand, gives plenty of information. He tells of the guard placed at the tomb and the rationale for sealing it with a large stone (27:62–66). Matthew tells of two early-morning visitors to the tomb. He has them experience an earthquake and witness the angel moving the stone away from the tomb. They also see the incapacitation of the military guard who "shook and became like dead men" (v. 4). Matthew's angel invites the women in to see the empty tomb and offers an explanation of his absence: "He is not here, for he has been raised, as he said" (v. 6).

In Mark, there is only fear and silence. In Matthew, there is understanding and joy mixed with fear among the women. Finally, Jesus appears to them and speaks. They fall at his feet and worship him as Lord. Matthew, then, tells even of the reaction of the chief priests, who hear of the resurrection from the returning guards. He indicates how they seek to tidy up the story with a lie designed to deflect any influence the Messiah might have: "You must say, 'His disciples came by night and stole him away while we were asleep'" (v. 13). Sermons on this text can revel in the details of the story.

Matthew is a masterful storyteller. He knows to put in vivid imagery that inspires the imagination of readers and listeners. He offers rationale for the Easter event and explains the motives of various characters. Such information is an aid to the inquiring minds of those who are unfamiliar with the story. For those who know it well, the details make the event come alive anew in the imagination.

Sermons on this text will do well to follow Matthew's lead, telling the story again with all the color and movement of a Renaissance painting. Subtlety and implication can be saved for sermons on Mark's version of the story. Matthew gives warrant for preachers to reach into the poet's tool bag. They can develop the account with strong imagery, character development, dialogue, and unambivalent emotion.

Beyond retelling the story with all its attendant energy and magnificence, sermons on this text can use its vivid imagery as a key to tap into the wonder, uncertainty, and joy of present-day listeners. When we hear of the earthquake, we resonate with the fear of women and the guards. When we see the brilliant angel descending from heaven and effortlessly rolling the sealed stone away, we are caught up in wonder at what the hand of God can do. When we hear the

Matthew 28:1-10

Theological Perspective

wholeness—in this case God has acted to overcome the hurt and harm to Jesus. This case serves as a promise that in the divine reign fully realized, the same will be true for all of us. It is indispensable to say, "*He* is not here." Therefore, there is deep hope for the world.

The even more important thing Matthew wants to say beyond this, is that Jesus is going ahead of his disciples to Galilee, and that he will meet them there. This is a fulfillment of the promise he made to his disciples in 26:32, a promise that, though the sheep would be scattered, he would gather them together again in Galilee.

His crucifixion had sent them scurrying for safe haven and had evoked explicit denials of association from Peter. They never had been able to come to terms with the vision Jesus kept sharing of a suffering Messiah who called disciples to a similar servanthood, complete with its own share of pain and loss. When Jesus died fully into this vision, they were indeed scattered. Now the angel's full-blown message of the resurrection is heard: he (this very crucified one) has been raised, and he is going ahead of you to Galilee, where he will gather you around him in forgiveness and for a renewed sense of mission.

Galilee is not only the place where Jesus had promised to gather his scattered sheep again. It is also the place where his ministry, which embodied the dawning reign of God, had been lived out—where he called disciples, taught the crowds, healed the sick, appointed the Twelve, showed compassion on the suffering, offered the weary rest, spoke in parables, fed the multitudes, blessed the children, challenged a rich man, and taught about a Messiah who would suffer. The theological point of telling the disciples to meet him in Galilee is thus straightforward: the risen Jesus is to be expected in the places of his once and future ministry, in all those places of grace-full endeavor, where healing, feeding, teaching, and even suffering are undertaken in his company.

The encounter with the risen Jesus is not a self-contained, solitary spiritual experience. It is promised in the midst of the mission he pursues even now, and invites us to join.

D. CAMERON MURCHISON

Pastoral Perspective

God gets the last word; that in the end—and sometimes even before the end—God's love is triumphant. Only God can offer such assurance, and that is why, in the end, only God, or one of God's messengers, can say, "Do not be afraid," and say it with authority.

It is not the words that are said that matter. Rather, what matters is the source. Søren Kierkegaard illustrated the difference by observing that when a theological student says, "There is eternal life," and God's own Son says, "There is eternal life," the words may be the same and equally true, but there is a critical difference: only one assurance is said with authority.

The words, "Do not be afraid," take strong root in the hearts of the characters of this Gospel story, because they accept that these words come from the only one who has the authority to give such assurance. There is only one who can offer such words in the face of life's uncertainties and before the certainty of death, and do so with authority. So, if we as pastors are to offer words of strength, of comfort, of assurance, we must offer them as messengers from another source.

It is striking, however, that, in this old story, those who let such words of assurance steep in their souls, end up singing praises and offering blessings. In such lives there are deep, resonant echoes of the ancient benediction, as a promise fulfilled: "May you fear God so much, that you fear nothing else at all."

MARTIN B. COPENHAVER

Easter Vigil

Exegetical Perspective

the women's wonder. They are altogether too full: they are afraid for joy. It is the kind of feeling we have when we fall in love, when we witness the birth of a child, when we lean over the rim of the Grand Canyon, joyous and fearful at the same time. The women are running, afraid for joy, to tell the disciples, when they run into Jesus. "Greetings," he says. It is true that the word the evangelist puts into Jesus' mouth here, *chairete*, is a standard Greek greeting, but it means more than "Greetings"; it also carries the sense of "Rejoice."

So the women do. They come to Jesus, take hold of his feet, and bow down to him. Then echoing the words of the angel, he tells them not to be afraid. Then "Go and tell my brothers," he says (v. 10).

Note finally how the story focuses on a series of messages. The angel tells the women to tell the disciples, and they run to tell them. They run into Jesus, who tells them again: "Tell my brothers"; then they run off again with their news. The story also focuses on the messengers, on what the women see—the angel and the empty tomb and Jesus himself—and on how the women feel. Again, at the angel's behest they run to tell the disciples, "quickly with fear and great joy" (v. 8). Then they run into Jesus, who tells them a second time, "Do not be afraid," for he is going before them into Galilee. If the women hear and heed him, what is left? What is left when their fears are gone? Great joy!

RICHARD S. DIETRICH

Homiletical Perspective

announcement of the angel, it sparks the hope in us that the inconceivable is somehow possible and plausible. Imagining the suddenness of Jesus' appearance and hearing his words of encouragement inspire the joy that accompanies fulfilled hope.

There is another thread to be followed in this tapestry of bright images. The Easter Vigil is the traditional time for celebrating and/or remembering baptism. In the earliest traditions, new converts were catechized during Lent and brought for baptism during the night of Holy Saturday. (This practice continues in many churches, especially Roman Catholic churches following the Rites of Christian Initiation for Adults.)

Historically, there has been awareness of the symbolism of Jesus descending to the tomb and rising in the light of Easter morning. This symbolism is paralleled in the Easter Vigil when neophytes are brought in in the shadow of the night service to be baptized as darkness turns to daybreak. Sermons for such baptismal services can also benefit from Matthew's use of imagery. How better to frame baptism, already rich with multivalent meaning, than with the hope-laden imagery of the Easter story?

Death is overcome. Descent into the watery tomb is followed by ascent into the reign of God. The people who have lived in darkness arise to see a great light. Whatever might be lost and washed away by baptismal water is supplanted by the greeting of Christ in the morning of new life. Finally, it is his promise that he may precede us, but we will see him.

The preacher at such a baptismal vigil might also collect one image from the lectionary Epistle typically paired with Matthew's Easter story, Colossians 3:1–4. The baptized are those who are raised with Christ. His resurrection is our resurrection, and his glory is our glory. Matthew's (and Paul's) penchant for vivid imagery offers the preacher an abundance of material with which to craft a resounding and resonating message of hope.

CLAYTON J. SCHMIT

Jeremiah 31:1-6

¹At that time, says the Lord, I will be the God of all the families of Israel, and they shall be my people.

²Thus says the Lord;
  The people who survived the sword
    found grace in the wilderness;
  when Israel sought for rest,
³ the Lord appeared to him from far away.
  I have loved you with an everlasting love;
    therefore I have continued my faithfulness to you.
⁴Again I will build you, and you shall be built,
    O virgin Israel!

Theological Perspective

"The people who survived the sword found grace in the wilderness" (v. 2b), the prophet says. For the first hearers of the psalm, the "wilderness" in this verse is both figurative and literal. In the figurative sense, the wilderness is where God called the people to be God's people after rescuing them from the sword of the Egyptians; even after their sin at Sinai and their subsequent sin in the wilderness of Paran at Kadesh, God graciously persisted in calling them to be a holy people unto God.

In the literal sense, the wilderness is where the people are living in exile, having survived the Babylonian sword. Again they find grace in the wilderness as God calls them forth, promising them that not only shall they again build, but they shall also be built (v. 4).

God loves with an everlasting love (v. 3), a love that exists before our existence and beyond our existence. This love is not predicated upon ourselves, but exists within the nature of God. This love moves beyond the love of a thousand generations in Deuteronomy 7:9, to a love that "bridges the generations and makes restoration possible."[1] This love is both the cause of Israel's and our existence and

Pastoral Perspective

There is something to be said for second chances.

A bride and groom stand in front of the church and pledge their vows to one another. Each promises to be a loving and faithful spouse in joy and in sorrow, in plenty and in want, in sickness and in health, throughout all their days.

Making such promises always brings with it a risk, but one made even clearer when the bride and groom are not exchanging vows for the first time, when they have made these promises before. For one member of the couple, or for both, a previous marriage has ended. This new marriage is an opportunity to love and to be loved, when that possibility had previously seemed too far out of reach to imagine ever possible.

There is something to be said for second chances.

The bride and groom know that there is a possibility that this marriage too might fail, although that is certainly not their plan. This is not a fatalistic stance as much as it is a realistic one. People begin with good intentions, but that is not always enough to sustain a marriage through all the foreseen and mostly unforeseen stresses that lie ahead. Sometimes a "marriage dies at the heart."[1] There are literal deaths, when husband or wife must take on the unwelcome moniker of

---

1. Gerald L. Keown, Pamela J. Scalise, Thomas G. Smothers, *Jeremiah 26–52*, Word Biblical Commentary 27 (Dallas: Word Books, 1995), 108.

1. The Westminster Confession of Faith, in *The Book of Confessions* (Louisville, KY: Presbyterian Church (USA), Office of the General Assembly, 1999), 6.137.5, p. 151.

Again you shall take your tambourines,
  and go forth in the dance of the merrymakers.
⁵Again you shall plant vineyards
  on the mountains of Samaria;
the planters shall plant,
  and shall enjoy the fruit.
⁶For there shall be a day when sentinels will call
  in the hill country of Ephraim:
"Come, let us go up to Zion,
  to the LORD our God."

Exegetical Perspective

Jeremiah 31:1–6 is near the beginning of the Book of Consolation (see 30:1–3, its introduction), the collection of Jeremiah's work that proclaims hope for Israel's future (chaps. 30–31), most likely from the exilic period. The text describes the coming restoration of Israel to their homeland, rooted in God's eternal love for God's covenant people.

"At that time" frequently refers to a future event (e.g., 3:17; 4:11; 33:15), often with eschatological dimensions. The rest of verse 1 is the standard covenant formulary that defines Israel's relationship to God (7:23; 11:4; 24:7; 30:22; cf. Gen. 17:7–8; Exod. 6:7; Deut. 26:17). In effect, the formulary foreshadows the renewal of God's covenant in 31:31–34, and here extends to all of the "families" or "clans." Perhaps the inclusiveness looks toward the reconciliation and reunification of the northern and southern realms in verses 5–6 (or, more broadly, of Diaspora Jews).

The initial oracle now leads into the prophetic messenger formula (v. 2a) and a reference to Israel's wilderness traditions (vv. 2b–3a). The "sword" apparently concerns Israel's escape from Egypt (cf. Exod. 18:4) or from an attack on the way from Egypt to Canaan (possibly by Amalek and his army, cf. Exod. 17:8–16). Jeremiah could have referred to God's provision of water, bread, and meat in the wilderness here, but probably chose surviving the sword because it

Homiletical Perspective

Why in the world would a Christian preacher give any attention to a passage from the seventh-century-BCE prophet Jeremiah on the holiest day of the Christian calendar? The congregation has not come to hear from a 2,700-year-old curmudgeon, but has shown up in their best duds to celebrate the resurrection of the Lord and Savior of the cosmos. Bring on the trumpets and banners, topped off with the "Hallelujah Chorus" from you know who.

Still, the prophet, who was called by God as a very young man and was reluctant to take up that call, spent nearly his whole life attempting to relay the challenging and hopeful words of YHWH to a people who were undergoing the greatest crisis of their nation's history: the decline, destruction, and exile of Israel. Jeremiah witnessed all of that in his forty years of active ministry, watching the temple collapse under the merciless onslaughts of the Babylonians, observing the murder of King Zedekiah's sons and the blinding of their grieving father. How could one live through those events and retain the hope of a future with God? How can you and I live in a time of terror, riven with deep uncertainties, shot through with economic, social, and political upheavals, and still come to celebrate and find hope in the risen Christ? Perhaps Jeremiah has something to teach us modern preachers after all.

Jeremiah 31:1-6

Theological Perspective

sustains our existence. God's everlasting love is the foundation of all that exists.

There is a tension here that cannot be resolved. The tension is between God's everlasting love and God's wrath/punishment for sin. The profession of everlasting love comes out of a situation of wrath and abandonment. Israel's sin brought God's wrath and abandonment to the Babylonian sword; nevertheless, God still loves God's people and calls them out of the wilderness. This tension cannot be resolved, because both love and wrath are present to YHWH.[2]

God's love, while everlasting and the ground of existence, is often unrequited when poured out on humanity. God's love is unconditional, but human love is predicated upon conditions. God's love is spontaneous and unmotivated, but human love is acquisitive. God's love is indifferent to value, but human love is based upon value.[3] Because God's love is dissimilar and far removed from human love, we are incapable of responding adequately to God's love, if at all; so God's love is often unrequited, without reciprocation. God created us in love, and God's love continually reaches out to us—calling to us, invoking and inviting us into fellowship and relationship—but often we reject God's love.

Sometimes, however, it may not be rejection but, rather, our inability to recognize and receive true love. Love almost always comes with strings attached. Rarely does someone love us for being ourselves and ourselves alone; more often, they love us for things we can do or bring to the relationship. When we finally experience a love that seeks nothing in return, we may reject it rather than risk being hurt again.

This happened at Sinai. While God was establishing the parameters of the relationship, the people were forming a golden calf. It happened at Kadish. When God sent the people into the land of promise, they refused, saying they were not able to take the land. It happened at Ramah. When God sought to be the only ruler of the people, they instead implored Samuel to give them a king. It happened to Solomon when he chose many wives over God, and it led to the division of the kingdom. It happened in both the northern and southern kingdoms when the people failed to keep God's commandments and worshiped Baal instead of God. It happened over and over. God extended God's love, and Israel rejected it.

Pastoral Perspective

"widowed," left to deal alone with the length of days and years that stretch into the future.

Knowing all this, it is especially wonderful when the bride and groom are willing to take the risk once more to love and trust and give themselves—body, mind, and spirit—to another human being.

It is rare, but not impossible, for people to remarry the spouse from whom they have been divorced, as they seek to move forward and carve out a whole new marriage. There is simply too much baggage, too many hurts, too forceful a flow of "water over the dam." Remarriage happens, and when it does, when it is not only possible but the right thing to do, our hearts dance with joy.

This is what the prophet Jeremiah promises to the people of Israel, as they mourn in lonely exile in Babylon, an exile Jeremiah tried to warn the people to avoid at all costs. Jeremiah speaks of the chance for the people to renew their vows with God.

The people have broken the covenant God made with them many generations before. Not only have the people ignored Jeremiah's warnings to get their faith back in line; they have engaged in idolatry, the worship of false gods. This unacceptable behavior, a breaking of one of the Ten Commandments, is likened to an act of adultery. God has been betrayed by those in whom God has placed unwavering trust.

God offers the chance to wipe the slate clean, to start over, to have a fresh, new start. Despite the fact that the nation has been caught in adultery and broken God's covenant beyond repair, God does not abandon them forever. Instead, God carves out a new covenant with the same people. God loves them! God will not give up.

For God, it is not a matter of sucking it up and pretending nothing wrong has happened. God is not sweeping all the sins of the people under some celestial rug, but shaking that rug out in the fresh, open air, and laying it down smooth and clean.

God—in God's untimely wisdom—knows the people will fall off the wagon again, but that does not stop God from renewing the promise.

Verse 1 is later echoed in Revelation 21:3:

See, the home of God is among mortals.
He will dwell with them;
they will be his peoples,
and God himself will be with them.

God's promise to renew the covenant is made through Jeremiah and the other prophets. The promise comes to full realization in Jesus Christ. At the

---

2. See Walter Brueggemann, *A Commentary on Jeremiah: Exile and Homecoming* (Grand Rapids: Eerdmans, 1998), 283.
3. Anders Nygren, *Agape and Eros,* trans. Philip S. Watson (Chicago: University of Chicago Press, 1982).

Exegetical Perspective

evokes painful memories of the military assault of the Babylonians who destroyed Judah and Jerusalem in 587 BCE (the Assyrians conquered Northern Israel in 721 BCE). Literally verse 2 reads: "he found grace in the wilderness, a people, sword survivors, going to find his rest, Israel." Grammatically and theologically, grace takes precedence over the sword in this passage. The "appearance" of God—that is, a theophany—also punctuates the wilderness traditions (Exod. 16:10; Num. 14:10; 16:19; cf. Exod. 24:15–18, etc.).

The gracious, saving presence of God in Israel's past exemplifies God's eternal love, which is the foundation for the continuance of God's faithfulness to Israel in the future (v. 3b; cf. the natural metaphor in 31:35–37). God's covenant is rooted in that unconditional, unmerited love, but it is "tough love," that is, it is love that punishes Israel's unfaithfulness. Jeremiah would approve of Flannery O'Connor's judgment: "Before [grace] heals, it cuts with the sword Christ said he came to bring."[1] That is the message of 30:12–17.

Of course, blaming the enormous suffering of warfare on human sin presents deep theological questions, but that is not a subject for today's lection. God continues to love Israel despite Israel's taking other "lovers" (either political allies or gods; 30:14; 3:1–2). Now, beyond defeat and exile, God's love will lead into actions marked by the word "again." God loves again, and again, and again (cf. Deut. 7:8; 10:15; Isa. 41:8 ["friend" is "my love"]; 43:4).

Two promises reflecting Israel's covenant tradition frame a promise of celebration: "again I will build you" (v. 4) and "again you shall plant" (v. 5). In effect, each promise reverses a covenant curse: "You shall build a house, but not live in it. You shall plant a vineyard, but not enjoy its fruit" (Deut. 28:30; cf vv. 39, 42). Indeed, one could summarize Jeremiah's prophecy in terms of the movement from tearing down to building up, from uprooting to replanting (1:10; 24:6; 29:5, 28; 42:10). Israel will again enjoy two of the blessings of well-being—shelter and food. (The word for "enjoy" literally means "treat as if profane," suggesting that what seemed extraordinary is now ordinary, that what was scarce is now common.)

Inside the frame of building and planting there is celebration, and surely this would be the focus for an Easter Sunday sermon: "Again you shall flaunt your tambourines and twirl merrily" (31:4, my trans.). Here is another reversal: God will turn mourning into dancing (cf. v. 13; Ps. 30:11). The word for "take"

1. *The Habit of Being: Letters of Flannery O'Connor*, ed. Sally Fitzgerald (New York: Vintage, 1979), 411.

Homiletical Perspective

What is usually read from Jeremiah 31 is the famous new covenant passage later in the chapter (vv. 31–34), but the chapter's beginning demonstrates its importance and relevance for a proper appropriation of Easter Day. Easter is about the absurd announcement that there is no death so dead that God cannot find life in it. Easter is not about a magic act; Jesus does not pop out of God's top hat as the awesome climax of a divine show. Easter is about the sort of God we worship, a God who will always have the last laugh, even in the face of that old dog, death.

This is not a truth that Easter demonstrates for the first time. God has long been in the business of breathing life into God's deathly creatures, and Jeremiah 31 is a clear witness to that. In the face of Israel's exile, while the leaders of the community are force-marched to Babylon, leaving a shattered nation behind, seemingly forever, Jeremiah preaches nonsense. The prophet announces that God "will be the God of all the families of Israel at that time" (v. 1). At what time? The temple is destroyed, the king stumbles blindly toward his doom, the priests' sacrificial fires are banked, the land promised to the descendants of Abraham is no more. Only a fool would speak now of the God of all Israel. Only a fool would proclaim, in the face of the death of all expectations, all hopes and dreams, that "we shall be God's people." Only a fool would proclaim the resurrection of the Christ in a world where 2 billion live on $2 a day, where militarism and war sap the men and women of countless nations, where money spent on killing is drained from so many who yearn for living.

What can Jeremiah possibly see in the hopeless experience of Israelite exile and death? How dare we modern preachers shout hallelujah to the risen Lamb while countless brothers and sisters die of AIDS and hunger and preventable disease? Is there not something finally obscene in such celebration? No! We must celebrate the foolishness of God, most especially when celebration seems so wrong.

This is so because, as Jeremiah says, we are the people who survived the sword in the wilderness long ago in the escape from Egypt, who experienced victory over the Egyptians and then found "grace in the wilderness" (v. 2). It is in our wildernesses that we most clearly find the grace of God. Why? Because the Easter God announces to us, "I have loved you with an everlasting love; therefore I have continued my faithfulness to you" (v. 3). Easter is not about the resuscitation of a corpse; it is about the God who has loved us with an everlasting love all of our days.

Jeremiah 31:1-6

Theological Perspective

It happens in individual lives as well. God calls us into a life of love, fellowship, and relationship. Initially we accept; then we wander off, seeking our own desires, our own ambitions, our own fulfillment. We may return for a while, but the lure of our desires is too strong to resist, and we reject God again. This rejection is rarely intentional and is often filled with sorrow and regret; yet, in spite of all our remorse, we reject God.

Rejection is a painful thing; no one wants to be rejected. To be rejected over and over again must be unbearable. I cannot begin either to contemplate or imagine how devastating it must be continually to face rejection of your affections—to extend yourself and your love to someone, only to have both you and your love rejected; to be spurned for the love of someone or something else.

Normally we would not let that happen to us more than twice. The first time we may be caught totally off guard and unaware. The second time we are more cautious, guarded, and reserved. We protect ourselves as best we can, slow and pensive to extend ourselves; and when we do, we are crushed. It is no wonder that many give up on love and relationships altogether. Never would we put ourselves in a position to be rejected over and over again. We would rather be alone and without relationship than to experience such pain.

This is exactly what God experiences with us. It is no wonder that we cannot fathom the love of God. God continually extends God's self in love, and we continually reject God. Over and over God extends God's self, calling us into relationship, and we reject the relationship that is offered. Often this rejection carries the consequences that disobedience brings. Disobedience brings punishment for sin, but punishment for sin itself is an act of love (Heb. 12:5–6). God's punishment may cause us to wander in our own wilderness experience, but this punishment is designed to bring us back into a loving relationship and prevent us from leaving again. In the midst of our wilderness, God finds us, calls us, and extends the offer of love and relationship again. This tension is never resolved.

REGINALD D. BROADNAX

Pastoral Perspective

end of time, when Christ returns in glory, eternity with God is sealed.

God is the faithful one. God is the one taking all the risks. God does not quit us, although we may deserve it. God welcomes us into the fold, even when "we like sheep have gone astray" (Isa. 53:6). God does not love us grudgingly or with hesitation; God is eager, indeed, God is yearning for a renewed relationship with God's people. As Jeremiah says,

> I will cleanse them from all the guilt of their sin against me, and I will forgive all the guilt of their sin and rebellion against me. . . . There shall once more be heard the voice of mirth and the voice of gladness, the voice of the bridegroom and the voice of the bride, the voices of those who sing, as they bring thank offerings to the house of the LORD:

> "Give thanks to the LORD of hosts,
>   for the LORD is good,
>   for his steadfast love endures forever!"
>   (Jer. 33:8, 10, 11)

We are invited to the wedding. We are not invited as guests, to stand at a distance as God's covenant is renewed. As the church, as the family of believers, we are the bride, standing before God and the whole eternity of witnesses, having our vows with God renewed for all time and beyond. The vows we take are these: that "neither death, nor life, nor angels, nor rulers, nor things present, nor things to come, nor powers, nor height, nor depth, nor anything else in all creation, will be able to separate us from the love of God in Christ Jesus our Lord" (Rom. 8:38–39).

To be loved with such a mighty love is truly beyond our understanding. We can be thankful that such love does not rest on our understanding. It rests on the saving grace we receive through our Savior, Jesus Christ. That is the message of Easter. That is the truth that sets us free.

Yes, there is something to be said for second chances. Let us shout "Hallelujah!" Let us rejoice, and give thanks.

KATHLEEN LONG BOSTROM

Exegetical Perspective

means "deck oneself" or "flaunt." Two allusions compound the reversal. The celebratory tambourines now replace the garish jewelry with which Israel had flaunted herself to her lovers (4:30). Moreover, Israel's dance flaunts God's victory over Israel's oppressors (v. 16), much as Miriam's tambourine dance taunted the Egyptians (Exod. 15:20). Now, as implied in verse 2, there will be a new exodus to celebrate (cf. Isa. 40:3; 43:14–20, etc). Israel will come rejoicing, singing the "Lord of the Dance" (a most appropriate Easter hymn, and what better time for liturgical dance?). A more fitting lection from the Psalter would be Psalm 150 (see v. 4; 149:3).

The new vineyards will be "on the mountains of Samaria" (v. 5), the capital of the former northern realm of Israel, otherwise named Ephraim. The oracle moves to the image of sentinels who pronounce a call to worship: "Come, let us go up to Zion, to the LORD our God" (v. 6; cf. Isa. 52:8). Here is the greatest reversal of all. North and South (Israel/Ephraim and Judah) will be one people again. The ruined city of Jerusalem will be rebuilt (cf. 31:38–40). Above all, the movement of God's grace in renewing the covenant will prompt the renewal of the people's allegiance to YHWH. God's designating them again as "my people" will lead to Israel's renewed affirmation that YHWH is "our God." Exile is not the end of Israel's story, in other words; homecoming is the end, with a pilgrimage that will take Israel from Babylon to Jerusalem (cf. Isa. 2:3; 35:10; 51:11; Ps. 126).

The liturgical year begins in Advent with the church singing "O come, O come, Emmanuel, and ransom captive Israel that mourns in lonely exile here."[2] The year turns on Easter Sunday, when the church sings, "God has brought all Israel into joy from sadness."[3] It is a time to break out the tambourines and dance a jig, a reel, or a tarantella.

THOMAS W. MANN

Homiletical Perspective

When Jeremiah witnessed the end of Israel, when his disciples dragged him to safety in Egypt against his will, despair was not the outcome of these horrific sights. As he watched the temple fall, he proclaimed, speaking in God's own voice, "Again I will build you, and you shall be built, O virgin Israel!" (v. 4a). As he witnessed the abuse of his king and his sons, he shouted, "Again you shall take your tambourines and go forth in the dance of the merrymakers" (v. 4b). Again, he said, there will be vineyards and fruit on Samaria's hills and people to enjoy them (v. 5). Again, he said, the people will be called to worship on the hill of Zion (v. 6).

What the modern preacher can learn from old Jeremiah is the reality of the context of Easter's brouhaha. We sing our hallelujahs despite a world that is hardly inclined to sing and finds very little to sing about. We sing because we know that there is another way to run a world, a world where death is not the final word, where despair is not the winner, where human power and hierarchies are not thought to be inevitable and unchangeable. Like Jeremiah, we need to look squarely in the face of the world's ugliness and horror and hopelessness and shout, "Christ is risen!" because the God who raised Jesus from the dead loves us with an everlasting love and will always, always continue divine faithfulness to us. Perhaps a look at Jeremiah on Easter Day is not so irrelevant for a Christian, after all.

JOHN C. HOLBERT

---

2. Anonymous ancient antiphons, "O Come, O Come, Emmanuel."
3. John of Damascus, ca. 696–754, "Come, You Faithful, Raise the Strain."

Psalm 118:1-2, 14-24

¹O give thanks to the LORD, for he is good;
  his steadfast love endures forever!

²Let Israel say,
  "His steadfast love endures forever."
. . . .
¹⁴The LORD is my strength and my might;
  he has become my salvation.

¹⁵There are glad songs of victory in the tents of the righteous:
  "The right hand of the LORD does valiantly;
¹⁶ the right hand of the LORD is exalted;
  the right hand of the LORD does valiantly."
¹⁷I shall not die, but I shall live,
  and recount the deeds of the LORD.
¹⁸The LORD has punished me severely,
  but he did not give me over to death.

Theological Perspective

This Psalm response is composed of thirteen verses from Psalm 118 that highlight the thanksgiving perspective of the psalm. The opening refrain in the first verse signals the theme: "O give thanks to the LORD!" The joyous mood continues throughout, finally acknowledging that the celebration is due to "the LORD's doing" (v. 23). The central verses (17–18) hint at what the Lord has done that calls forth such joy: "I shall not die, but I shall live." Though the psalmist was punished and suffering, the Lord did not allow him to succumb. It is clear how fitting these verses are for the celebration of the resurrection of the Lord, who was punished—but for the sins of others—and then rose from death. The NT specifically applies verse 22 ("The stone that the builders rejected . . .") to the death and resurrection of Jesus.

The opening verses are a summons to worship God, to thank God, and to acknowledge that God's love is steadfast. The believer is reminded of the continuous obligation to thank the Lord for his goodness. In an interesting use of words, the psalmist indicates not merely that the Lord has given help and rescue, but that the Lord *is* such. The Lord *is* my strength, my might, my salvation (v. 14). Salvation from God signifies not only divine action but also a strong, personal, and intimate relationship with God. This comes to full realization most of all in the resurrection, which

Pastoral Perspective

"This is the day that the LORD has made; let us rejoice and be glad in it." Psalm 118 not only resounds through every Easter morning but reprises the Liturgy of the Palms the week before. The one who has entered through the gates of righteousness to shouts of "Hosanna!" (118:25) now sings of victory over death and thanksgiving for salvation. Psalm 118 is for singing! Isaac Watts thought so and paraphrased it for singing on Easter Day. "This is the day the Lord hath made: The hours are all God's own; Let heaven rejoice, let earth be glad, And praise surround the throne." This *is* the day that the Lord has made—and it is amazing!

The Easter morning congregation is a challenge to preach to. The infrequent worshiper and the peripheral Christian may hear the psalmist and the evangelist as more amusing than amazing, more mundane than "marvelous." The Easter morning congregation lives in a culture where this day celebrates the cycle of seasonal renewal rather than the inbreaking newness of resurrection, where the day is a nod to tradition rather than an experience of transformation. Worship leaders stretch for words in a culture where "awesome" and "amazing" comment on the trivial. Music choices will help to give expression to the profound good news of this day.

Psalm 118 finds a contemporary echo in a poem by e.e. cummings that has been given several choral

¹⁹Open to me the gates of righteousness,
  that I may enter through them
  and give thanks to the LORD.

²⁰This is the gate of the LORD;
  the righteous shall enter through it.

²¹I thank you that you have answered me
  and have become my salvation.
²²The stone that the builders rejected
  has become the chief cornerstone.
²³This is the LORD's doing;
  it is marvelous in our eyes.
²⁴This is the day that the LORD has made;
  let us rejoice and be glad in it.

Exegetical Perspective

Psalm 118 is a complex psalm, in that it recounts a liturgy with several different roles. It is also beautifully simple, in that it tells a straightforward story of victory for Israel achieved by the power of God. This psalm showed up a week ago on Passion/Palm Sunday, because it tells the story of a ritual procession, but it is equally appropriate for Easter Day, because it proclaims the king's victory over suffering and death.

Psalm 118 is a victory psalm, sung as a ritual reenactment of a king's emerging victorious from battle. Once a king of Israel led his armies to victory, he then led them into Jerusalem, where they would immediately enter the temple along with the priests and people to give praise and thanks to God. It is particularly appropriate for Easter because the victorious king does not forget that he suffered on his path to victory, nor does he lose sight of the fact that it was God who allowed the suffering in order to bring about the victory.

The liturgy based around Psalm 118 is a dialogue of sorts between *priests*, *king*, and *people*. The parts of the liturgy break down in this way:
—The *priests* speak verses 1–4, inviting the people of Israel to give thanks to the Lord and to proclaim that "His steadfast love endures forever" (vv. 1b, 2b, 3b, 4b).

Homiletical Perspective

It is not surprising that scholars believe Psalm 118 was originally used in liturgical processions of some kind. One can hear the first four verses sung or proclaimed in call-and-response fashion: "O give thanks to the LORD, for he is good"; the leader proclaims, "his steadfast love endures forever!" Then the leader bids Israel, the house of Aaron, indeed all the people, to declare God's goodness, and they pick up the cry, "His steadfast love endures forever!" in a dialogue of praise.

Several directions for preaching present themselves with this psalm. Scholars have identified Psalms 113 through 118 as a group of songs used at Passover.[1] Since this was the occasion when Israel recalled the exodus from Egypt, it follows that this psalm is appointed for both Palm/Passion Sunday and Easter. In the Christian tradition, Pascha has come to refer not only to Passover, but to the Easter event as well. Taken as a whole, the psalm celebrates God's past triumph of delivering the Hebrew slaves, acknowledges some present threat, and expresses hope for future deliverance.

Although the pericope for the day includes only verses 1–2 and 14–24, a preacher might draw on this

---

1. J. Clinton McCann, Jr., "Psalms," in *The New Interpreter's Bible* (Nashville: Abingdon Press, 1996), 4:1153.

Psalm 118:1-2, 14-24

Theological Perspective

proclaims both our definitive salvation by Jesus and our union with him in his new life.

The psalmist and his community give thanks in "songs of victory" (v. 15), but the praise belongs to "the right hand of the LORD" (vv. 15b, 16). The "right hand" (also "the hand" or "strong hand") is an ancient symbol of the Lord's power being wielded on behalf of the righteous (e.g., Ps. 139:10; Exod. 13:9; Deut. 7:8; Ps. 78:42, lit. "his hand"). In using this metaphor the psalm suggests that the Lord's deeds on behalf of his people are constant and sure and therefore are dependable for the future. This psalm also acknowledges that the Lord was present in the suffering and then brought it to an end (v. 18). The saving deed is both suffering and deliverance. This "divine dimension" of suffering is at the heart of Jesus' own experience. Our participation in the resurrection of Jesus, therefore, is an experience, first of all, of the Lord's presence in our own suffering, as a prelude and promise of our experience of him in resurrected life.

The psalm shifts between an individual who gives praise for being saved from danger and the community that seconds this with its own words of thanks. This has an important significance for the proper setting of such prayer. The individual's prayer, though it presumably responds to a particular situation of deliverance, finds its proper place within the community liturgy.

In other words, God's graciousness toward us is not expressed in individualized, separate, and independent actions that have no relationship to each other. Individuals are saved and justified as part of a community. It is only appropriate, therefore, that thanksgiving, even if only from an individual, should still be voiced from the midst of the community. The individual deliverance and thanksgiving are part of and evidence pointing toward God's whole plan of salvation for all.

This theme helps us understand another important aspect of the resurrection. Jesus' victory over death is not just his own, personal triumph. He died and rose for all. Therefore, his victory is ours as well. By faith and union with Jesus, we are assured of realizing victory over death in our own bodies and of sharing in his divine life for eternity. This is the most outstanding example of how our own thanks are also the song of the whole faith community. Jesus has united us all to himself in his victory; so our own celebration of that victory has to be in the community. Our own song makes no sense outside of that community.

The individual at the center of this psalm, and the accompanying suffering, are examples. The

Pastoral Perspective

settings. The singing of a new and fresh anthem in the context of Easter morning worship may help to put the "amazing" back in Easter. The poem "i thank You God for most this amazing day" reflects a personal story of transformation, and to the Christian eye and ear awakens the good news of Jesus' resurrection. Composer Elliott Levine suggests an Easter context; a solo male voice sings, "I who have died am alive again today."

> i thank You God for most this amazing
> day: for the leaping greenly spirits of trees
> and a blue true dream of sky; and for everything
> which is natural which is infinite which is yes
>
> (i who have died am alive again today,
> and this is the sun's birthday; this is the birth
> day of life and of love and wings: and of the gay
> great happening illimitably earth)
>
> how should tasting touching hearing seeing
> breathing any—lifted from the no
> of all nothing—human merely being
> doubt unimaginable You?
>
> (now the ears of my ears awake and
> now the eyes of my eyes are opened)[1]

Edward Estlin Cummings served as an ambulance driver in World War I. He was suspected of treason and sent to a French prison camp for three months. When he was released in early 1918, this was among the poems he wrote. The context was the dark night of war, death, and deprivation. The words reflect a captive's gratitude for the simple blessings of green trees and blue skies, a yes to life that comes with release from death and a coming peace. The poem addresses doubt, and dismisses it. This amazing day—how could anyone doubt this life, this love, this "yes," this You that is the God who has lifted from "no," raised from death? Amazing!

Psalm 118 sounds the notes of God's saving work: "The stone that the builders rejected has become the chief cornerstone. This is the LORD's doing; it is marvelous in our eyes" (vv. 22–23). It is amazing! Trace the word "amazing" through the Gospels, and you can get a pretty good idea of what God was up to in the life of Jesus. Follow the reaction and response of "amazed" and see when God has been here: When Jesus calmed the storm, after they got over being

---

1. e. e. cummings, "I thank You God for most this amazing day," in *Complete Poems: 1904–1962*, ed. George J. Firmage (New York: Liveright Publishing Corp., 1992).

Exegetical Perspective

—The *king* takes up the call in verses 5–19. He tells his story in terms of the steadfast love that has just been proclaimed to all the people, reminding them that those who have the Lord on their side need not fear. He continues his tale with an account of his sufferings and tribulations, then brings the narrative back to the victory that the Lord brought out of all the suffering, and the Lord's faithfulness in doing so. Then he requests entry into the temple.

—The *priests* respond to his request in verse 20.

—The *king* thanks God for making him worthy to enter in verse 21–22.

—The *people* respond with a loud affirmation in verses 23–24.

—Verse 25 is a short prayer asking God for continued salvation, which may have been said by the *priests* alone or by the whole *people*, followed by a blessing pronounced on the king in verses 26–27.

—The *king* returns his attention to the Lord in verse 28, again giving thanks.

—The *priests* exhort those present to give thanks as well, repeating the refrain from the first four verses, "for his steadfast love endures forever."

As outlined above, verses 1–2 call the whole community to join with the king and the priests in giving thanks to the Lord for the victory that Israel's king and army have achieved. The invitation includes the house of Israel (which means all the faithful people of the community), the house of Aaron (which means all the priests and professional religious), and all those who fear the Lord (which may mean not only members of the community, but also believing Gentiles, foreign slaves, and proselytes).

The psalmist recounts the king's difficulties in battle, but then starts praising God for the victory and salvation he has given even through the suffering the king has endured (v. 14). When this psalm is read on Easter, it emphasizes God's saving work of deliverance out of the hands of death, and victory in the face of defeat.

In verses 15–16, the king tells of how the armies praised God when he first delivered them from defeat, and how all of the "righteous," that is, all the children of Israel, proclaim together what the "right hand of the LORD" has done. The right hand of the Lord symbolizes God's strength and power; the right hand is the sword hand, and the Lord is being praised as the mightiest of warriors, against whom no enemy can stand.

Verses 17–18 show the king proclaiming that he is still alive because of the Lord's intervention. Yes, he

Homiletical Perspective

past-present-future perspective to proclaim the incredible good news of the resurrection. We celebrate what God has done in the Christ event, give thanks for the new life given in the here and now, and express our confidence in what God will do when Christ comes again. The psalm points us toward celebration—not only for the personal benefits we receive through the resurrection, but for the redemption and restoration of the whole community. God raised up this Jesus so that we might all revel in new life. Whatever threats, challenges, or trials we face today, from the most trivial to the most tragic, we know we have already been taken up into the glory of redeemed and resurrected life. Even more, we inherit the promise of life everlasting.

Psalm 118 suggests a second preaching trajectory. The perceptive preacher will note that words from this psalm are often used as opening sentences in worship: "This is the day that the LORD has made; let us rejoice and be glad in it!" (v. 24). These words are the climactic point in the psalm, and the preceding verses (vv. 13–23) lead the congregation through a crescendo of causes for praise. Certainly these words are most fitting on the central day of the Christian year, the day that defines who God is in Christ and who we are as Christians.

However, we do not save them for this singular day in the calendar. We use these words many times through the year, on ordinary Sundays, and recall that each Sunday is a celebration of the risen Christ, and that we walk in resurrection light. On other days as well, at occasional services or in daily prayer, we proclaim, "Let us rejoice and be glad in it," for in fact each and every day is "the day the LORD has made." We live each day of our lives as resurrection people.

A third preaching possibility also arises from this psalm. Of all the wonders of Jesus' ministry, including the events of his own birth, the reality of his resurrection is the most miraculous of all. Whether a congregation hears the account from Matthew's Gospel, or that of John, it is clear that this is a mysterious event, one that cannot be explained. Reason does not serve us well when proclaiming the message of Easter, but Psalm 118 reminds us that this is not entirely unbelievable. In singing a song of Israel in which we remember the exodus, and hearing Israel's confidence that God will deliver the people again, we realize that we *know* this God. The God who raised Jesus is the God who delivered the people from death and oppression so long ago. This is a saving God who rescues the people when they are in danger. In the resurrection of Jesus Christ, this saving God has

Psalm 118:1-2, 14-24

Theological Perspective

deliverance experienced by this individual is a symbol of the Lord's power to transform tragedy into victory. Jesus' own passage from death to life is the supreme example of just such an experience. However, the saving experience is more; it needs to be announced. The point of such deliverance, in the context of this psalm, is to proclaim and witness the saving deeds of the Lord. The Lord acts so that we may come to know his saving love for us and proclaim it to others. What the Lord does for us impels us to praise and thank him.

The psalmist, then, asks to be admitted through "the gates of righteousness" (v. 19) of the temple to give fitting thanks for his deliverance. The term "righteousness" signifies more than mere fulfillment of the law; it indicates those who have personally experienced the Lord's salvation and proclaim it. In the context of the resurrection, the gates through which Jesus passes are his death and resurrection. Jesus is *the* "righteous one" who accepted the discipline of his Father's will, including his suffering and death. Thus, he has entered the true and heavenly temple—and we have entered with him. We must proclaim it!

Like a refrain, the psalm repeats the theme that the Lord has "become my salvation" (vv. 14b, 21b). The point is clear. The Lord has not just *done* something, he has *become* something for his people. The resurrected Jesus has not only accomplished our salvation; he *is* our salvation. A new community, a new family is being formed that will share life in him forever. Jesus is that cornerstone, rejected on earth, which has become the foundation for that new family. The psalm concludes that only the Lord could do this. This is the new day of a new creation he is forming for us. We must rejoice!

THOMAS P. MCCREESH

Pastoral Perspective

afraid, the disciples were *amazed*: "What sort of man is this?" (Matt. 8:27). When Jesus forgave sins, "they were all *amazed*" (Mark 2:12; Luke 5:26, emphasis added). When Jesus drove the demonic spirit out of a man, "the crowds were *amazed* and said, 'Never before has anything like this been seen'" (Matt. 9:33, emphasis added).

When Jesus cured someone blind and mute, "all the crowds were *amazed* and said, 'Can this be the Son of David?'" (Matt. 12:23, emphasis added). When "the lame, the maimed, the blind, the mute, and many others" were put at his feet and cured, "the crowd was *amazed* when they saw the mute speaking, the maimed whole, the lame walking, and the blind seeing. And they praised the God of Israel" (Matt. 15:31, emphasis added). When Jesus quoted Psalm 118 to the chief priests and the Pharisees, asking them, "Have you never read in the scriptures: 'The stone that the builders rejected has become the cornerstone; this was the Lord's doing, and it is amazing in our eyes'?" they were *not amazed* (Matt. 21:42, emphasis added). When Jesus refused to answer the charges against him, Pilate, it is written, "was *greatly amazed*" (Matt. 27:14, emphasis added). When Peter saw the empty graveclothes in Jesus' tomb, he was "*amazed* at what had happened" (Luke 24:12, emphasis added).

"This is the LORD's doing; it is amazing[2] in our eyes." The first word in the Easter morning lexicon may be "Alleluia!" but the best word to summarize and describe this day is "amazing." Hebrew exegesis yields its riches; but here a pastoral word is evoked by the Norwegian and Swedish origins of "amazing." It means not asleep, eyes open. The psalmist's joyful wake-up call to the immediacy of God's saving work (this "doing," this day) joins the evangelist's confident, comforting word to those looking for Jesus, "Come, see . . . he has been raised . . . you will see him . . . they will see me" (Matt. 28:6–10).

A preacher looking out on her Easter morning congregation knows the stories of long nights and dead hopes and confused searches for meaning. She has witnessed faith asleep to newness and eyes closed to God; she has had her own eyes opened to the marvelous "doing" of God in the ordinary and the difficult. Giving voice to the psalmist gives depth and authenticity to the amazing, life-giving news of *this* day for all our days.

DEBORAH A. BLOCK

2. The NRSV uses "marvelous" here; the REB and the NAB use "wonderful."

Exegetical Perspective

has suffered—"the Lord has punished me severely"—but even so, "he did not give me over to death." Though these verses were written for an earthly king and are probably not considered messianic prophecies, they call to mind Jesus' own suffering, which was severe punishment indeed, but from which he was also restored.

In verse 19, the king now calls to the priests to let him in through the temple gates so that he may give thanks to the Lord. In verse 20, the priests respond that only the righteous may enter into the temple, so the king comes back with the act of a righteous man—a prayer of thanksgiving to the Lord for being his salvation (vv. 21–22).

He proclaims that he himself was the rejected stone—presumably implying that he was in danger of losing the battle he had embarked on—but that now he is their chief cornerstone, the victorious ruler who will form the foundation of a stronger kingdom. For Christians, of course, the rejected stone is often applied to Jesus, who is the foundational stone of the Christian community.

The passage ends with an exclamation of praise, naming this victorious day the creation of the Lord, and inviting all others to rejoice in it. This day of victory made possible by the action of the Lord is as relevant to God's children today as it was to God's children then.

KATHERINE C. CALORE

Homiletical Perspective

rescued God's people from the ultimate enemy, death itself, saving them once and for all. The future deliverance that Israel anticipated has come in Jesus Christ and will be brought to completion on the day he returns to lead us all to glory.

The paintings known as Jesus Mafa illustrate the events of the life of Christ in an African vernacular. The images are simple and clear and express the grace and joy of African Christian spirituality. In a painting titled "Easter," one sees Mary falling on her knees, arms out, to greet the risen Christ, who, as it turns out, is not the gardener.[2] She has dropped the jar of spices she brought along—she does not need it now. Her hands are outstretched in what can only be a gesture of praise; her face is radiant with joy as she recognizes the man before her. She wears pink—the color of joy—and a diaphanous head scarf trails behind her, so that, even while kneeling, she looks as if she is dancing. In this moment she is not fearful or wondering; she is marveling and rejoicing.

Later, when she tells the story, she will not be able to explain it, but she may well echo the words of the psalmist, "This is the day the LORD has made!" Who but the God of deliverance, the God of rescue, the God of salvation could do such a thing? Then she will exhort her fellow disciples to join her in the song: "Let us rejoice and be glad in it!" Indeed, the words of this psalm enable us all to marvel in joy while gazing in awe at mystery.

KIMBERLY BRACKEN LONG

2. The painting may be viewed online at http://www.jesusmafa.com/anglais/pagetprod2.htm.

Colossians 3:1-4

¹So if you have been raised with Christ, seek the things that are above, where Christ is, seated at the right hand of God. ²Set your minds on things that are above, not on things that are on earth, ³for you have died, and your life is hidden with Christ in God. ⁴When Christ who is your life is revealed, then you also will be revealed with him in glory.

Theological Perspective

In this passage, the writer of Colossians counters certain misunderstandings about how Christians are supposed to live. As part of this, he reminds his audience that they have died and been raised with Christ. This baptismal language uses geographic imagery, raising perplexing questions for contemporary readers. Where is Jesus? Where are we? How then shall we live?

Where Is Jesus? The writer urges readers to "seek the things that are above, where Christ is, seated at the right hand of God." The church echoes this image when we recite the Apostles' Creed ("[he] ascended into heaven and is seated at the right hand of God the Father Almighty"). Though Luke distinguishes resurrection and ascension, the writer of Colossians makes no such division. Jesus Christ is simply "raised" above us. What does it mean to say that Christ has ascended and is seated at God's right hand?

This odd geographic claim affirms two basic christological points. First, the image of Christ "seated at the right hand of God" shows that he is united with God, whom he called "Father." The language comes from Psalm 110:1, which New Testament writers and early church theologians often used in describing Jesus' identity. Jesus Christ is the one of whom the psalmist said, "The Lord says to my lord, 'Sit at my right hand until I make your enemies your

Pastoral Perspective

Alan Tibbels is a resident of Sandtown, a low-income neighborhood on Baltimore's west side. Sandtown is a seventy-two-square-block area known most for its open drug traffic, high crime rate, and (until recent years) derelict housing. In 1987 Tibbels and his all-white family moved into this African American community. His purpose was to begin the long journey of becoming a permanent neighbor to people in need and to begin the serious project of community development. This would mean rebuilding rundown housing stock, creating safe day-care programs, and offering basic health care to local residents.

What has made Tibbels's remarkable string of community development successes in Sandtown unique is the fact that he is quadriplegic, the result of a basketball accident from his young adult years. When asked in an interview how he sustains his purpose and drive in life, especially given the constraints of his disability, Tibbels turned immediately to his favorite verse and word in the New Testament. At the end of 1 Corinthians 15, right after the apostle Paul has made his case for the veracity of the resurrection, he writes: "Therefore, my beloved, be steadfast, immovable, always excelling in the work of the Lord, because you know that in the Lord your labor is not in vain" (1 Cor. 15:58).

Exegetical Perspective

The Epistle lesson for Easter is a sliver taken from a larger section (2:20–3:17). The argument employs a common early Christian understanding of baptism to combat the teachings of religious terrorists who threaten the Colossian church.[1] In many ways, it reflects the baptismal tradition in Romans 6:1–14 (the Epistle lesson for the Easter Vigil) about dying and rising with Christ: believers go under the waters of baptism and are buried with Christ (Rom. 6:4; Col. 2:20). The corollary is that, as Colossians says, Christians come up from the water as those who "have been raised with Christ" (3:1). Although Paul insists Christians will be raised in the future (Rom. 6:5), Colossians describes resurrection as part of our present experience.

How are we to understand the difference between the two? Is the Easter Vigil about the "not yet" of Christians' resurrections, and Easter morning about the "already"? Does the author of Colossians embrace the same realized eschatology that Paul scolds the Corinthians for holding (1 Cor. 15)? Might the letter to the Colossians instead address a markedly different situation with the same basic understanding of baptism?

In 2:6–19, the author tells us something of what these other teachers who have invaded the Colossian

1. E. Elizabeth Johnson, "Colossians," in *HarperCollins Bible Commentary*, rev. ed., ed. James L. Mays (San Francisco: HarperSanFrancisco, 2000), 1126–30.

Homiletical Perspective

The Fountains Abbey in Yorkshire was a Cistercian monastery founded in 1132. Inactive since 1539, it remains a popular tourist attraction. The official guide for the Abbey's Chapter House reads, "Here the monks gathered every Sunday to hear a sermon from the Abbot, except on Trinity Sunday, owing to the difficulty of the subject."[1]

We might wonder what the good abbot did on Easter Day, for certainly the subject at hand—resurrection—is no less difficult in its own way than the Trinity. In fact, it may be even more difficult, at least for us. If the abbot's Trinity proclamations were irredeemably hindered by the relative *unfamiliarity* of the topic and its relevance, even among the praying faithful, our predicament is the reverse, and therefore the more dire: our Easter proclamation is often irredeemably hampered by the relative *familiarity* of the subject at hand, even among the unpraying and unfaithful. Nominal believers, biannual visitors, even outright skeptics pretty much know what to expect of the preacher's Easter morning sermon: "Christ is risen! The Lord is risen indeed!"

Yeah, well, we heard that same sermon last year. "There is no lack of information in the land," as

1. Lesslie Newbigin, "The Trinity as Public Truth," in *The Trinity in a Pluralistic Age: Theological Essays on Culture and Religion* (Grand Rapids: Eerdmans, 1997), 2.

Colossians 3:1-4

footstool.'" Being seated at God's right hand, Christ is joined to the love, purpose, and power of God.

Second, the image of Christ raised and seated with God proclaims that Christ is no longer subject to death. To be "above" means to have moved beyond the realm of "things that perish" (Col. 2:22). To avoid the spatial confusion of "above" and "below" for congregations who no longer think in terms of a three-story universe, it may be helpful to use language like "beyond," to convey the point that Christ lives on the other side of death.

So although the writer of Colossians appears to be making an antique geographic claim about *where* Jesus is, he is actually affirming *who* Jesus is: one with God, beyond the threat of death that pervades this world.

Where Are We? The writer also uses spatial metaphors to describe where we are. By saying "you have been raised with Christ" (3:1) and that our lives are "hidden with Christ in God" (3:3), "Paul" destabilizes our secure street address. We no longer live flat-footedly in the realm of "things that perish"; we are bound to Christ at God's right hand. This claim that we are raised and hidden with Christ can give rise to two problems: some may dismiss the up/down geography as outdated, while others may read into it a dualism that shuns the material world as not only perishable but inherently evil.

To address the first misunderstanding, it may be helpful again to translate the language of "raised" and "above." The point is not that we are located at a particular altitude, but that our identities are no longer defined by the world in which things and people die. We who rest our faith in Christ's resurrection know that death does not have the last word. We place our faith beyond this realm, and so we in a real sense draw our lives, our identities, from Christ on the other side of death.

To answer the second misunderstanding (dualism of "earthly things" and "things that are above"), notice that it says "set your minds on things that are above" (v. 2), not "scorn everything here on earth." This passage was likely addressed to a community that was drawn to dualism, including rejection of the body and worship of angels (see 2:18). This passage actually rejects such stark dualism. The writer teaches, not that earthly things are nothing, but that they are perishable and therefore not worthy of ultimate loyalty. A little later, 3:12–13 clearly shows a concern for practical life in community—hardly the mark of someone who regards the present world as

Paul's "therefore" is Alan Tibbels's favorite word in the New Testament. Why? It signals a new power or condition that is available to us, thanks to the resurrection of Christ. In Tibbels's case, this "therefore" inspires him to pursue all sorts of challenging goals in spite of true physical adversity. If, in fact, Christ has been raised from the dead, *therefore* new expectations are placed upon us. *Therefore,* new possibilities become accessible to us. *Therefore,* new capabilities are given to us.

The same understanding of "therefore" opens the third chapter of Colossians. Whether Paul or, more likely, a close disciple of Paul penned this letter, the meaning and significance of this "therefore" in Colossians is essentially the same as the one at the end of 1 Corinthians 15. "Therefore, if you have been raised with Christ, seek the things that are above, where Christ is." The assumption here in Colossians is not only that Christ has been raised from the dead, but that we too have been raised with him—already!—by virtue of our baptism. It is our baptism into Christ's resurrection that evokes special ethical expectations. Baptism into Christ means being empowered to live a life that is informed by the resurrection.

The Colossians passage here does not make specific mention of baptism, but all of the allusions surrounding it have to do with sharing in Christ's resurrected power through the gift of baptism. Thus, the middle section of this same chapter of Colossians speaks of "clothing" ourselves with particular virtues, and "putting on" the garments of Christ (3:8–14)—clear references to the act of baptism.

For many congregations, the highlight of Easter Day is the practice of hosting baptisms. Pastors will often tell their parishioners there is no more glorious day to be baptized than Easter. They are quite right about this. Historically, the church has utilized the focus of Christ's new life to give birth to new Christian lives, born through the sacrament of baptism. What better way to acknowledge new life in a person than for that one to experience baptism?

Imagine this: You have agreed to be baptized on Easter Day. You stumble into the church you know well, or not so well, mostly awake, wearing your Easter best, and suddenly question that "Yes" you earlier gave to being baptized in front of an overflow crowd. Nevertheless, you submit. You go ahead with your baptism as planned. Moments later, when the liturgy of baptism has concluded and you are back in your seat, you hear these high-flying words of Colossians read to the assembly.

Exegetical Perspective

church say. Their "philosophy and empty deceit" (2:8) likely refer to religious teachings and practices influenced by Jewish mysticism. They apparently insist not only on circumcision (2:11), Sabbath and other calendrical observance (2:16), and ascetic practices (2:16–19), but also on obedience to the demands of "principalities and powers" (1:16; 2:8, 10, 15, 18), including visions and worship according to angelic practices ("worship of angels" in 2:18 is perhaps better rendered "worship with angels"). The picture is of a hostile universe, populated by harsh beings who stand between people and God (perhaps they think Christ is one of these exalted beings) and who allow access only as people pay the guardians of divinity proper homage along the way.

The author seeks to reassure the church that all this is "human tradition" and has nothing to do with authentic Christian faith. Christ is not simply one of the principalities and powers; he embodies "the whole fullness of deity" (2:9). He has already defeated the powers on the cross ("triumphing over them [the powers] in it [the cross]," 2:15), and he now sits in glory at God's right hand (3:1).

Believers share Christ's status because they died with Christ in baptism and the powers no longer have any authority over them. Just as Christ sits at God's right hand (a reference to Ps. 110:1, the single favorite Bible verse in the early church[2]), so also Christians' lives are "hidden with Christ in God" (3:3). This is why they should not allow anyone to "condemn" or "disqualify" them (2:16, 18). They are literally in the presence of the risen Christ, and no one can change that, no matter how threatening their theological teaching.

The status of baptized believers has more than doctrinal consequences. As with virtually every reference to baptism in the New Testament, this text points also to the ethical ramifications of dying and rising with Christ. The entire passage is structured by two parallel if/then arguments: "If with Christ you died" (2:20) and "So if you have been raised with Christ" (3:1). Each "if" is followed by a "then" that describes the Christian life. If you died with Christ, then "why do you live as if you still belonged to the world? Why do you submit to regulations?" (2:20). If you were raised with Christ, then "seek the things that are above, where Christ is" (3:1). A lengthy string of imperatives follows : "Set your minds on things that are above" (3:2); "put to death . . . fornication,

2. David M. Hay, *Glory at the Right Hand: Psalm 110 in Early Christianity*, Society of Biblical Literature Monograph Series 18 (Nashville: Abingdon Press, 1973).

Homiletical Perspective

Kierkegaard said. Even if it can be effectively argued that the culture is increasingly unaware of Christianity's comprehensive testimony, on Easter Sunday morning at least, almost everyone enters the sanctuary with at least a rudimentary sense of the subject at hand—not least because that same sermon may be the only proclamation some of the assembled have ever heard.

On Trinity Sunday, the abbot let silence do his preaching. That is not a bad idea, sometimes. That said, silence will not carry the freight on Easter morning, although, truth be told, believers as well as skeptics may be as dubious as to Easter's relevance as the monks were regarding the Trinity. While the doctrine of God's inner life may always seem conceptually abstruse and therefore far removed from the gritty concerns of daily life, Easter proclamation is supposed to *mean* something. Sadly, even preachers are not always clear as to what that is. Our Easter preaching can come off sounding fanciful and irrelevant—a fairy tale, a somewhat unsurprising denouement, a word of hope and encouragement—pleasant to hear but without teeth.

Faced with familiarity, skepticism, bewilderment, or simple apathy, preachers can make three crucial errors in their proclamation. First, and perhaps most commonly, preachers try to make resurrection a "general truth"—something that can be discerned from nature or discovered in the human spirit. Second, preachers try to explain the resurrection, defend the Gospels' veracity one way or the other, by one canon or the other—the *possibility* of resurrection (even some *scientists* say it is conceivable!)—and therefore suggest the probability that Jesus' experience, and the disciples' experience of Jesus, was real.

These strategies never work. Resurrection is not sentimental, after all, or seasonal. Moreover, as Augustine reminds us, true mystery is something that cannot be discovered, only revealed; and even after revelation, what has been revealed cannot be explained to others. Even if you could demonstrate the physics of resurrection, the question of relevance would still be in play: so what?

Sadly, and ironically, the gospel truth of the resurrection rarely makes for scintillating preaching, rarely sets preachers or anyone else free for genuine praise or authentic testimony. We are called to say *something*, however. Still, if sentimentality and apology are our only options—those or mere *discursus*, which is the third error: just reiterating the day's narrative, documenting the story, without much else in the way of either conviction or connection (my homiletics

Colossians 3:1-4

Theological Perspective

entirely worthless. "Seek[ing] the things that are above," then, does not mean world-denying asceticism, but freedom to live in the world without fear of death or ultimate regard for things that perish.

The opening of each classical Great Prayer of Thanksgiving joins the congregation in the response "Lift up your hearts." / "We lift them to the Lord." In similar fashion here, the writer urges readers to lift up their hearts, not to abandon the present world, but to regard the present world in proper perspective, from the point of view of Christ in glory.

How Then Shall We Live? Since Christ is "above," and since we have been raised with and hidden in Christ, we are freed for new life. In the previous chapter, the writer urged readers not to get caught up in worldly regulations of what to handle, taste, or touch (2:20–23). Apparently there was at work in the community a philosophy that encouraged ascetic rigor to ascend to heaven. These verses insist that any "ascent" for Christians comes not from our efforts but from Christ's already accomplished resurrection. We do not raise ourselves, but we *are raised* by being united with Christ. Our own seeking then depends on the statement that our true selves reside in Christ's embrace.

Rudolf Bultmann underscores this point: if you have been raised with Christ (indicative) then seek the things which are above (imperative). As he says, in Colossians "the present is conceived as a time of salvation brought about by God's deed in Christ. . . . By appropriating this occurrence through baptism, believers are emancipated from domination by the powers. . . . Believers have died with Christ, been buried and raised with him, made alive. Upon this indicative the imperative is founded."[1]

This is liberating news! Death is behind us, and our life is not defined by the powers that rule the world, or even our own efforts to achieve greatness. Instead, our life is safe, protected, hidden in the risen Christ who is beyond the powers that kill.

MARTHA MOORE-KEISH

Pastoral Perspective

The water is not even dry on your head, or your body, and you find yourself trying to absorb soaring words from a biblical writer who is determined to command attention with the word "therefore." "Therefore, if you have been raised with Christ, seek the things that are above. . . . Set your mind on things that are above . . . hidden with Christ." Talk about exhortation! Here is ethical guidance clearer than your mother ever gave you. For anyone who has invested their hope in the risen Lord, it turns out that certain expectations go with that bond. There is a proper way to conduct oneself in light of the resurrection event.

If you have taken the step to be baptized with Christ, so you also must be serious about living the resurrected life with him. This means you are to organize your days with a certain conduct in mind, just as you are to fashion the decisions of your days around the moral identity of Christ Jesus. In essence, you are to orient your existence around the very things that matter to Christ. Petty legalistic rituals having to do with touching, handling, and tasting (2:20) find no place in the life of one who takes the word "therefore" to heart. They are now out of bounds. The same holds true for earthly temptations like "fornication, impurity, passion, evil desire, and greed" and vices such as "anger, wrath, malice, slander, and abusive language" (3:5, 8). These deserve no home in one who has been "raised with Christ."

As you reflect further on the day's reading from Colossians, you realize that your repetition of that word "renounce" in the liturgy of your own baptism had more ethical implications than you first understood. "I renounce the devil and all the forces that defy God. I renounce the ways of sin that draw me away from God." The logic of resurrection behavior has baptized people all over the world verbally stomping on every form of life that is not patterned after Christ.

The preacher's task on this day is to help hearers know how to yearn for this better way. The minute we say (negatively), "I renounce," how then shall we seek (positively) the features of life that matter most to Christ?

PETER W. MARTY

---

1. Rudolf Bultmann, *Theology of the New Testament* (New York: Charles Scribner's Sons, 1955), 2:176.

impurity, passion, evil desire, and greed" (3:5); "get rid of . . . anger, wrath, malice, slander, and abusive language" (3:8); "do not lie to one another" (3:9). Further reference to baptism comes in the verbs "strip off" and "clothe yourselves" in 3:9–10, alluding to the early Christian practice of being baptized in the nude and receiving new clothing afterwards.

Just as believers remove the old clothing of their pre-Christian lives and receive the new garments of life in Christ, so they are called to put away the behaviors of the old life and replace them with lives marked by unity (v. 11, "no longer Greek and Jew, circumcised and uncircumcised, barbarian, Scythian, slave and free"), "compassion, kindness, humility, meekness, patience," and forgiveness (vv. 12–13). "Clothe yourselves with love. . . . let the peace of Christ rule in your hearts. . . . be thankful. . . . teach and admonish one another . . . sing psalms, hymns, and spiritual songs to God" (3:14–16). The motivation for all these practices is summed up in the final exhortation: "Whatever you do, in word or deed, do everything in the name of the Lord Jesus" (3:17).

These two uses of baptismal traditions in Romans 6 and Colossians 3, lessons for the Easter Vigil and Easter Day, are thus very similar and quite different. Both Paul and the author of Colossians, writing in his name, point to believers' deaths and resurrections with Christ to exhort Christians to live as new people. Paul says they "walk in newness of life" (Rom. 6:4); Colossians says they have put on a "new self" (3:10). Both point to right ethical behavior as the consequence of this newness. Paul asks, "How can we who died to sin go on living in it?" (Rom. 6:2); Colossians urges its readers to lives of love and self-giving.

On the other hand, the two authors' construals of Christians' resurrections address very different contexts. Paul reserves the reality of Christians' resurrections to the eschatological future, as a way to take seriously the perdurance of sin and the necessity of ethical vigilance ("Do not offer your members to sin as weapons of injustice, but . . . to God as weapons of justice," Rom. 6:13, my trans.). Colossians, however, speaks to Christians who are terrified that they are not qualified to share Christ's resurrection and assures them that God's power in Jesus' death and resurrection has already accomplished that for them.

E. ELIZABETH JOHNSON

professor said that starting in the Bible and staying in the Bible renders a sermon unbiblical!)—better to emulate the abbot and remain silent.

Stanley Hauerwas has said that, as regards Christian life and ministry, the right image is crucial for transformation,[2] for how we might "consider ourselves" (Rom. 6:11). The same is true for authentic preaching, perhaps most especially at Easter. In this passage, as in the Romans text set for the Easter Vigil, Paul chooses the image of baptism, of dying and rising with Christ, which is both death and birth. Baptism is the watermark of our initiation into the community and begins our knowing participation in the divine life.

As is well known, the Greek construction in verse 1 has the force of "since you have been raised with Christ." Paul's indicative suggests the corresponding imperative: "seek the things that are above." Either the command to "seek the things that are above" or obedience to that command can be trivialized as escapist. However, the cascade of ordinances that follow in verses 5 through 17 (outside our assigned lection) confirm that this life is not for naïfs. Indeed, only those whose lives are somehow "hidden in Christ," for whom Christ is "(their) life" (v. 4a) are able fully to obey the primary command and its corollaries. Those who seek the Christ who is "above" will inevitably be led into back into earthy circumstance and situations—much as Peter, James, and John were led by Jesus back down from the mountain of transfiguration into a context of controversy and disease.

Easter proclamation, then, must attend to both death and life—not one without the other. Paul uses baptismal imagery of "dying and rising" as a theological assessment of Christian life made possible by the resurrection and ascension of Christ.

Many have argued that the church's failure to incarnate its own gospel—our desire to be right more than godly, our inclination to let the gospel promise narcotize us to its ethical imperative—is at the heart of evangelism's failure. Easter inescapably calls us to see ourselves in Christ, and Christ among us, so to make us live as Christ in relation to others.

THOMAS R. STEAGALD

2. Stanley Hauerwas, *Vision and Virtue* (Notre Dame, IN: University of Notre Dame, 1981), 2, cited in Eugene Peterson, *Under the Unpredictable Plant: An Exploration in Vocational Holiness* (Grand Rapids: Eerdmans, 1992), 6.

John 20:1-18

¹Early on the first day of the week, while it was still dark, Mary Magdalene came to the tomb and saw that the stone had been removed from the tomb. ²So she ran and went to Simon Peter and the other disciple, the one whom Jesus loved, and said to them, "They have taken the Lord out of the tomb, and we do not know where they have laid him." ³Then Peter and the other disciple set out and went toward the tomb. ⁴The two were running together, but the other disciple outran Peter and reached the tomb first. ⁵He bent down to look in and saw the linen wrappings lying there, but he did not go in. ⁶Then Simon Peter came, following him, and went into the tomb. He saw the linen wrappings lying there, ⁷and the cloth that had been on Jesus' head, not lying with the linen wrappings but rolled up in a place by itself. ⁸Then the other disciple, who reached the tomb first, also went in, and he saw and believed; ⁹for as yet they did not understand the scripture, that he must rise from the dead. ¹⁰Then the disciples returned to their homes.

Theological Perspective

John's account of Easter morning stands in significant relief to the Synoptic Gospel accounts. The theme of ascension takes a chronological and substantive priority over the theme of resurrection in John's witness to what happened "early on the first day of the week, while it was still dark" (v. 1). After the well-known footrace of Peter and the "other disciple" to the tomb upon hearing Mary Magdalene report that the body had been stolen from the tomb, John tells us what each experienced upon entering the tomb.

Peter is described as having observed the linen graveclothes lying in one place and the "cloth that had been on Jesus' head, not lying with the linen wrappings but rolled up in a place by itself" (vv. 6–7). In contrast, we are told not only that the other disciple went in and saw (presumably what Peter had also seen), but that this other disciple "believed" (v. 8).

Both elements of this report carry their own puzzlement. It is intriguing to ponder what is to be made of Peter's viewing the linen wrappings in one place and the cloth that had been on Jesus' head "in a place by itself." The overarching force of mentioning the graveclothes is to emphasize that they were cast aside because Jesus did not and would not need them anymore. This contrasts with Lazarus (11:44) who comes out of his tomb still wearing his graveclothes,

Pastoral Perspective

John's Easter account begins with a lot of running. When Mary Magdalene finds the tomb empty, she runs to tell Simon Peter and the Beloved Disciple. Her words, like the shot of the gun that begins a race, send the two disciples running to check it out for themselves.

When you look out at the congregation on Easter morning, not many will be breathless. Perhaps no one ran to get there—although some may race to get a seat because the church will be fuller than usual. Why did they all come? Did they come to hear something new, or to hear the old, old story once again? Is anything more than the force of habit at work?

Swiss theological giant Karl Barth said that what brings people to worship—not just on Easter, but any day—is an unspoken question clinging to their hearts and minds, and that question is simply this: "Is it true?" Is it true that God lives and gives us life? Is it true that God not only established a routine, what we call the laws of nature, but that one day God broke the routine and somehow raised Jesus from the dead? Is it true that something so extraordinary happened on that morning that we can only rebuild our lives on its foundation? Is it true?

These are such powerful questions—and they are unavoidable on a day such as this. Sometimes I am tempted to conclude that Easter is not a day for

¹¹But Mary stood weeping outside the tomb. As she wept, she bent over to look into the tomb; ¹²and she saw two angels in white, sitting where the body of Jesus had been lying, one at the head and the other at the feet. ¹³They said to her, "Woman, why are you weeping?" She said to them, "They have taken away my Lord, and I do not know where they have laid him." ¹⁴When she had said this, she turned around and saw Jesus standing there, but she did not know that it was Jesus. ¹⁵Jesus said to her, "Woman, why are you weeping? Whom are you looking for?" Supposing him to be the gardener, she said to him, "Sir, if you have carried him away, tell me where you have laid him, and I will take him away." ¹⁶Jesus said to her, "Mary!" She turned and said to him in Hebrew, "Rabbouni!" (which means Teacher). ¹⁷Jesus said to her, "Do not hold on to me, because I have not yet ascended to the Father. But go to my brothers and say to them, 'I am ascending to my Father and your Father, to my God and your God.'" ¹⁸Mary Magdalene went and announced to the disciples, "I have seen the Lord"; and she told them that he had said these things to her.

Exegetical Perspective

At its simplest level, any story is about its characters and its plot—what the characters do and the order in which they do it (though that may not be the order in which it is presented). In this passage the characters include Mary Magdalene, Peter, and the other disciple—the one Jesus loves—two angels, and, finally, Jesus himself, who comes in only at the story's end. Here is what these characters do: they come and go and run to see; they bend down and go in, then they see. They also have expectations, they become confused, and they weep; then again, they see.

This story, in both its characters and plot, has many of the elements of classic comedy. The main characters are common people: a woman no better than she ought to be, a fisherman, another one whose name we do not even know. The angels are another matter; they are enablers of the plot—characters whose role as confidant is a means of providing the reader with information while avoiding direct address from the narrator. The plot is the very stuff of comedy—missing bodies, running onto and off the stage, mistaken identity. It requires divine intervention in order to be resolved, and its resolution does not end the story; instead, the story opens outward toward what will happen next.

Almost every comedy has a "hero," the character the audience is to identify with. Here it is Mary

Homiletical Perspective

There is no more homiletically rich material in Scripture than the Easter story. It has been proclaimed from the first day (Mary Magdalene went and announced to the disciples, 20:18) and ever since by a believing church. John's version holds promise for preachers in many ways. It is, in fact, inexhaustible as a resource for preaching. Here are a number of preaching perspectives that might be explored.

"Mary Magdalene Came to the Tomb and Saw That the Stone Had Been Removed" (20:1). "Come and see" is one of the abiding themes of John's Gospel (1:39; 1:46; 4:29, 11:34). "Come and see" is a strong Easter theme as well. It links Easter to Christmas (the shepherds went and saw). Mary Magdalene came and saw that things were not as expected. The resurrection upsets all expectations, and the only way to apprehend it is to come and see that things are different. Things are always different than expected with Jesus. Might it also be that things could be different with his followers? How wonderful it would be if people said: "These followers of Jesus are not like other people; come and see how they love the world."

"They Have Taken the Lord" (v. 2). What do we do when faced with the incomprehensible? We try to make some sense of it. They must have taken him

John 20:1-18

Theological Perspective

needing to be unbound by others at Jesus' command. The implication is that in Lazarus's case the graveclothes could be removed for now by others, but that Jesus' graveclothes have been removed fully and cast aside as irrelevant before he ever appears to anyone.

Why the special attention to the head cloth? Most likely it is a narrative way of depicting that like Moses, Jesus needed no veil on his face when he was in the presence of God (Exod. 34:33–35). Just as Moses would take the veil off as he went into the direct presence of God, so Jesus has laid aside the head covering because he has now entered the direct presence of God. It is this feature of the story that provides a link between the account of what Peter saw and the report of what the other disciple experienced.

By itself, the report about the other disciple leaves us scratching our heads. On the one hand, he observes the same scene and is reported to have "believed." The easy assumption, that he "believes" that Jesus is risen from the dead, is snatched away by the sentence that follows in 20:9: "for as yet they did not understand the scripture, that he must rise from the dead." If this disciple (along with Peter) has not yet understood about the resurrection, what then does he "believe"? His single set of clues was the graveclothes, and especially the head cloth. Frances Taylor Gench has cited Sandra Schneider's suggestion that these led him to the belief that, far from annihilating Jesus' life, the cross was in fact Jesus' glorification—his return to God, where he needs no veil over his face.[1]

Thus the first, bold element of John's Easter proclamation is not that Jesus is raised, but that he is ascended—or at least that he is in the process of ascending, living into and out of the very life of God. Indeed, this becomes even plainer in the next scene (vv. 11–18), as Mary stands weeping outside the tomb. She responds in turn to the angels and to Jesus himself as they sequentially inquire about why she is weeping. To all she implores that they tell her where Jesus' body has been taken, so that she may render it proper care. As Jesus speaks her name, "Mary," the sheep hears the shepherd's voice and responds to him, "Rabbouni!" Then Jesus explicitly declares his new reality to her: "Do not hold on to me, because I have not yet ascended to the Father. But go to my brothers and say to them, 'I am ascending to my Father and your Father, to my God and your God'" (v. 17).

The Easter message that Jesus is ascended has a power that is well embodied in the phrase, "ascended

1. Frances Taylor Gench, *Encounters with Jesus: Studies in the Gospel of John* (Louisville, KY: Westminster John Knox Press, 2007), 130.

Pastoral Perspective

beginners. Rather, it can seem as if Easter is the advanced course for Christians, to be undertaken only after completing the introductory courses that deal with Jesus' life and teachings. Begin with the Sermon on the Mount. Marvel at Jesus' wisdom. Learn from him. Become fascinated by his life, fixed on his person. If one begins there, perhaps then one will be better prepared to hear this mysterious tale about Jesus rising from the dead.

It can seem quite odd that people would flock to worship on Easter, of all days, a day on which we proclaim the very things that may be hardest to believe. However, it is clear from those who knew Jesus, from the apostles of the early church and from the authors of Scripture, that Easter is not the dramatic conclusion to the story for those who are able to follow it that far. Rather, Easter is the beginning.

Read the first sermons that were ever preached in the early church as recorded in Acts. With what do they begin? They make no reference to Jesus' teachings. His earthly life receives scant attention. It is almost as if the story of his life is of interest only if we see it from the vantage point of Easter. Even Jesus' teachings are not seen as important in their own right, because there is little that is original in them. Rather, they take on meaning only when we take into full account who the teacher is, that is, God's chosen one who is to die and be raised again.

This is why the Gospels have been called Easter accounts with extended prologues. For the early followers of Jesus, the beginning point of Christian proclamation was the Easter event. Over and over the disciples started with proclamations about Easter, as if it were the only place to begin. Through the centuries Christians have begun their journey of faith by running to the empty tomb. As modern people, who like to think of ourselves as sophisticated, we sometimes forget that the idea that God could raise someone from the dead would be as difficult for these ancient people to believe as it is for us. These ancient people were not stupid. They had seen many people die and never once had they seen anyone come to life again.

Yes, there was something in the story to doubt. There is also another way to put it: there was something in the story that reached the deepest regions of their hearts and minds, where both doubt and faith are found. That is, in the resurrection God gave us such a miracle of love and forgiveness that it is worthy of faith, and thus open to doubt. The very doubts we may hold attest to the scale and power of what we proclaim. So the place to begin in the life of faith is not necessarily with those things we never doubt.

Magdalene, who also holds the story together. The plot begins with her coming to the tomb through the dark of the first day of the week; it ends with her going from there to tell the disciples, "I have seen the Lord" (v. 18). Hers is the movement that gets the story going; she has its last word. As in the best of comedies, there is much that happens in between.

When Mary comes to the tomb, she finds the stone has been removed—"rolled back" or "away," according to the Synoptics (Matt. 28:2; Mark 16:4; Luke 24:2). So, Mary . . . runs away. She runs to Peter and the other disciple, the one without a name, and tells them that Jesus' body has gone missing—though we are not sure how she knows that. She has not yet looked into the tomb to see.

The disciples set off immediately, running. It becomes a race: The other disciple outruns Peter, and he looks in and sees the cloths in which the body had been wrapped. Peter *goes* in to see what is going on—or is not! Then the other disciple goes in as well, where he can better see, and—having seen—he believes, though what he believes is not clear. The tomb is empty, but who, at this point, can say why? None of the characters knows yet that Jesus has risen from the dead.

Mary must have run with or right behind the disciples, for she is there at the tomb when they leave to return home. She remains, weeping. Then she (finally) bends down to look into the tomb herself; but, in the kind of surprise that comedy relies on, the tomb is no longer empty. Rather, "where the body of Jesus had been lying" (v. 12)—but then was not—sit two angels. (The plot must be about to be resolved.)

The angels want to know why Mary is weeping. Because, she says, they have taken Jesus' body away, and she does not know where. Then, she turns around and sees—where *nothing* was before—a man standing behind her. Oh! The man—he must be the gardener—asks her also why she is weeping. She has been peering into an empty tomb. What is she looking for?

Again, in typical comedic—and human—fashion, the characters talk past one another. The gardener asks Mary whom she is looking for. Mary says, in effect, that it does not matter; but if the gardener has taken him away, just tell her where, so she can get him back.

Comedy thrives on surprise and disguise. We, the audience, see through Jesus' disguise, if that is what it is. Again, in typical comedic fashion, we have recognized him all along, from the moment Mary saw him standing there; but he is in disguise to Mary until he lets on that he knows her, calling her by name. Then

away. He cannot be alive. He must have been merely wounded, never really dead. He must have been God only and not human, for humans cannot do such things (Gnosticism). There must have been a conspiracy to hide him by his followers, in order to concoct a cult to dupe the world for millennia. He was never really there. He was only a rabbi or an avatar, but not the Messiah. Fill in the blank. Any explanation but the one he gave: "I am the resurrection and the life" (11:25). The truth was soon to be known. He was not taken away, but raised from the dead. He appeared to Mary and then to the others. In the face of every other, more plausible explanation, Easter gives us the truth. It is as simple as Mary said: "I have seen the Lord" (20:18).

"But He Did Not Go In" (v. 5). The evidence was there, but the one Jesus loved did not go in. It took the boldness of Peter, the blundering one, to approach and comprehend the truth. Peter went on to proclaim the good news because he was a witness. The only approach to Jesus today is still a bold one. Preachers cannot be timid. They are witnesses, and the Word creates witnesses anew when they proclaim the resurrection.

"He Saw and Believed; for as Yet They Did Not Understand" (vv. 8–9). Faith precedes understanding. It is a gift. The mystagogical catechesis (the historical teaching about the mysteries of the faith to new converts) follows baptism. Faith comes first as a gift. Sorting it out comes later. It is like love for a child, which precedes knowing who she will be.

"And She Saw Two Angels in White" (v. 12). Such messengers are rare (the Greek *angelos* means "messenger"). God seems to use them only when there is no other way to make things plain: the annunciation, Joseph's reassurance, Zechariah's notification, the announcement to the shepherds. We might want for more angelic announcements, but they are reserved for God's greatest messages. Greatest of all: he was not there; he is not dead, he is alive. Remember the old joke? The pastor knocks on a door and hears a woman inside call out, "Is that you, angel?" The pastor replies, "No, but I am from the same department." We are all from the message department. Ours is to proclaim the same news: Christ is risen. He is risen indeed.

"She Did Not Know That It Was Jesus" (v. 14). How could she know? He was not where he was supposed

John 20:1-18

Theological Perspective

to my Father and your Father, to my God and your God." Here we find the fulfillment of the assertion in the opening chapter of John's Gospel, that "the Word became flesh" (1:14) that those who receive him and believe in his name will be given "power to become children of God" (1:12). By living into and out of the life of God, the ascended Jesus extends the relationship of children of God for all who are united in him as sisters and brothers.

Of course in the largest sense, ascension and resurrection always make a continuous theological point. They both claim that death has not ended an otherwise grand and noble project undertaken by Jesus—that the mercy and grace of God in Christ triumphs over all that would undo it. Moreover, ascension is typically intended as a claim that extends the promise of resurrection. It does so by asserting that the new life manifest in resurrection is enduringly located in the heart of God. It is not new life that lives only to die another day. Instead it is new life that abides in God, and thus abides forever.

What is distinctive about John in this regard is that he inverts the conventional order. He speaks first about the abiding location of that new life in the endlessly creative life of God. He wants the disciples to know first and foremost that Jesus now lives in the very life of God. While he will want them to know that Jesus also lives with and for them, John echoes at the Easter climax of his Gospel what he declared at its beginning: "the Word was with God" (1:1). Now he proclaims, the Word *is* with God, and the Word's disciples thus have power to become children of God.

D. CAMERON MURCHISON

Pastoral Perspective

Realities about which we hold no doubt may not be large enough to reveal God to us. So we say without apology or hesitation: what we proclaim at Easter is too mighty to be encompassed by certainty, too wonderful to be found only within the borders of our imaginations.

Easter may be just the place for beginners, after all. The place to begin in the life of faith is not necessarily with those things that are beyond the reach of our doubt. Rather, perhaps we need to begin where the early church began, with the larger realities and deeper mysteries that are open to doubt, but are also large enough and deep enough to reveal something of God to us. That is the promise held out to us this day, the promise of Easter, which has throughout history been the occasion of the greatest doubt and also the source of the most profound faith. Perhaps we will find that the early church was right to begin just here, where the stakes are highest, risking doubt in order to claim a larger faith. Could it be that one of the reasons churches are filled on a day such as this is that we long to swim in the depths of realities that are large enough to reveal God to us, where both the risk and the promise are that much greater?

As pastors, we may hope that when our parishioners leave worship on this day, they will have exchanged their question marks for exclamation points—but a question mark is a good and fitting place to begin.

MARTIN B. COPENHAVER

she knows him. She speaks to him: "Teacher" (v. 16), and reaches out to take hold of him, before he somehow gets away again, goes missing (or puts on another disguise), so she cannot find him.

He tells her, however, not to hold on: he *is* going away, again. Tell my brothers, he says to Mary, that "I am ascending to my Father and your Father, to my God and your God" (v. 17). The plot of the comedy is resolved when, after the angels come, the missing body is found—alive! The story, however, is not yet at its end. Again, this is typical of classic comedy, which ends in marriage; so, as the curtain falls, a new story is beginning (see Rev. 21:2).

Jesus' words—"my Father and your Father, my God and your God"—recall other words, from Jesus' last conversation with his disciples. (See, for only two examples, 14:10 and 14:20.) In that conversation too, Jesus promised that even as he went away, he would remain with his disciples in the Spirit (e.g., 14:16–17, 26; 15:26).

Thus, the action of the play may be coming to an end, but the story will continue. Jesus will also give his disciples the Spirit, breathing it into them, in the story that follows this one (20:19–23). This Spirit not only blows where it wills (3:8), but it will blow the followers of Jesus where it wills. An Easter faith cannot hang on.

So Mary lets go. She goes, as Jesus tells her, to carry the news to the disciples, *her* news. You may have seen the empty tomb, Mary says, but "*I* have seen the Lord." So she has. Will we also *see*, and believe? That is a central theme in the next passage, John 20:19–31.

RICHARD S. DIETRICH

to be. When we see acquaintances in the wrong context, we often do not recognize them. Mary beheld a living man, but the Teacher should have been dead. How could she have known it was he? Consider how often we do not recognize him: in the face of a needful stranger, in the Word of the sermon, the bread and the wine. How can we ever really know it is he? He tells us, and we believe.

"I Will Take Him Away" (v. 15). We are good at tidying up a mess. Something is wrong, we will fix it. Jesus is taken from his tomb? He needs to be laid to rest in a safer place. This is untidy business, and God will not allow us to fix it. The world is turned on its ear with this news, and nothing will return it to its preresurrection state. All things are new, nothing will ever be the same, and no one can tidy it up. There is only one thing to do: proclaim the new world, and be a part of its cataclysmic action in the world.

"Go to My Brothers and [Tell] Them" (v. 17). Listen, you who come to Easter services, who see the stone rolled away, who hear the trumpets and the report of the angels: go to the people and tell them. This is how the word spreads. It depends on us, as it depended on Mary.

"Mary Magdalene Went and Announced . . . 'I Have Seen the Lord'" (v. 18). This is the first sermon. It is delivered by a woman. She saw and believed and announced. She did not require ordination or an accredited preaching course. She required only a word from Jesus. Then she went and told. Here is the message for us: Christ is risen—go tell someone.

Each of these themes—and more—is worth homiletical exploration. The preacher will determine which perspective to follow, based on her or his preaching setting. Ultimately, each sermon today will simply be a way of telling the central truth: Christ is risen. He is risen indeed.

CLAYTON J. SCHMIT

Acts 2:14a, 22-32

¹⁴But Peter, standing with the eleven, raised his voice and addressed them, . . . ²²"You that are Israelites, listen to what I have to say: Jesus of Nazareth, a man attested to you by God with deeds of power, wonders, and signs that God did through him among you, as you yourselves know—²³this man, handed over to you according to the definite plan and foreknowledge of God, you crucified and killed by the hands of those outside the law. ²⁴But God raised him up, having freed him from death, because it was impossible for him to be held in its power. ²⁵For David says concerning him,

'I saw the Lord always before me,
   for he is at my right hand so that I will not be shaken;
²⁶therefore my heart was glad, and my tongue rejoiced;
   moreover my flesh will live in hope.

Theological Perspective

The resurrection of Jesus is the foundation of Christian faith. Paul says that without the resurrection, both his preaching and our faith are in vain (1 Cor. 15:14). For the early Christian community, everything depended on the resurrection, for it was the foundation of their proclamation of Jesus as the Messiah, the Christ. So, as Paul says, if he was not raised from the dead, then our faith is in vain.

A distinction must be made here between resuscitation and resurrection. Lazarus was resuscitated; his body was reanimated for a period of time, only to die again. However, Jesus was resurrected and still lives! Jesus was raised from the dead; and his resurrection becomes for Christians the opportunity for a new and transformed life in God, and life in the age to come.

The Gospels tell us that there were some questions as to what really happened to the body of Jesus; some even suggested that it was stolen (see Matt. 28:11–15). The shorter ending of Mark leaves the whole story in question, not only because do we not know what happened after the resurrection, but also because those who were at the tomb fled in fear and terror.

Peter asserts that it was God who raised Jesus from the dead (v. 24). This assertion by Peter becomes the proclamation of the community and foundation of Christian faith. Jesus was handed over to those who were outside of the law (the Romans)

Pastoral Perspective

"When did God become more than a name to you?" This is one of the "Quaker Questions" often used as an icebreaker in church groups. A corollary question would be, "When did Jesus become more than just a name to you?" The name may be one you grew up hearing as part of your daily life, or perhaps it was only mentioned in the midst of all the secular festivities of Christmas and Easter. Whether by gradual understanding or a lightning-bolt moment, somewhere along the way your spirit awakened to the truth that Jesus is more than the name of someone who lived a couple thousand years ago.

It is one thing to hear the names bandied about in conversation, but quite another to understand that God and Jesus are far more than just names. Indeed, when Moses asked God to provide a name, God was hesitant. God did not wish to be condensed into one small word. In truth, God *cannot* be defined merely by a few consonants and vowels. At some point in our lives, God becomes personal.

In the second half of Acts 2, Peter speaks to a crowd of people gathered in the holy city of Jerusalem. It is the day of Pentecost, when the Holy Spirit that Jesus had promised before his death arrives full-force in tongues of fire and in the tongues of all the languages represented by the multitude of folks in earshot and beyond.

27For you will not abandon my soul to Hades,
or let your Holy One experience corruption.
28You have made known to me the ways of life;
you will make me full of gladness with your presence.'

29"Fellow Israelites, I may say to you confidently of our ancestor David that he both died and was buried, and his tomb is with us to this day. 30Since he was a prophet, he knew that God had sworn with an oath to him that he would put one of his descendants on his throne. 31Foreseeing this, David spoke of the resurrection of the Messiah, saying,

'He was not abandoned to Hades,
nor did his flesh experience corruption.'

32This Jesus God raised up, and of that all of us are witnesses."

Exegetical Perspective

The lection (along with vv. 14–21 and 33–36, 38–39) is typical of Lukan speeches, illustrating how the NT writers used their Scripture to interpret what had happened in the life, death, and resurrection of Jesus. As in rabbinic circles, Luke presents a midrash on the quoted text, providing a proof text for his christological claims.

The lection ignores the context of the Pentecost story and how Jesus' resurrection is connected to the question "'What does this mean?'" in verse 12. In fact, the lection leaves out the "therefore" of verse 36, the very point of the previous verses—that Jesus' resurrection proves he is both "Lord and Messiah [Christ]." From his exalted status "at the right hand" of God, Jesus sends the Holy Spirit, which ties in again with the Pentecost story. The Pentecost phenomena happen because of what has happened to Jesus: God has resurrected and exalted him, and he has sent the Spirit.

Verse 22 signals a shift in audience from Jews "from every nation under heaven" (v. 5) to Israelites, and the opening lines end with an indictment of those responsible for Jesus' death. First, Peter emphasizes how appalling the rejection of Jesus was, by reminding his audience of the "deeds of power, wonders, and signs that God did through him." The performance of "wonders and signs" is a favorite motif

Homiletical Perspective

This choice of texts from the longer account of Peter's speech at Pentecost focuses on his announcement that Jesus, God's prophet whom Peter's audience crucified, even though they had the deed itself performed by "those outside the law" (namely, Roman officials, v. 23), had been resurrected to life by the power of God. In this Second Sunday of Easter, the congregation is still in the celebratory mood of the wonder of Jesus' resurrection. Five Sundays hence, at Pentecost, we may all worry about the mysterious actions of tongues-speaking, although it seems rather clear that these spoken tongues are perfectly and astonishingly understandable by anyone and everyone who happens on the scene, no matter what language each one speaks. There is no need of any interpreter here, unlike the need Paul will refer to in 1 Corinthians 14.

The larger problem here for the modern preacher has to do with the accusations of murder leveled at the Judeans who are listening to Peter, himself a Judean. Peter addresses his compatriots and accuses them of "crucifying and killing" Jesus, who has turned out to be God's Messiah, direct descendant of David, the very one all of them had long expected. This incipient anti-Jewishness has caused no end of horror in the subsequent growth of the Christian tradition, culminating in the monstrous Holocaust of

Acts 2:14a, 22-32

Theological Perspective

and crucified, "But God raised him up, having freed him from death, because it was impossible for him to be held in its power" (v. 24).

That God raised Jesus from the dead is essential to the community's proclamation because it stresses a continuity of events. The Jesus who was from Nazareth, who lived and taught in the region of Galilee, and who was crucified and buried in Jerusalem, is the same Jesus who was resurrected and appeared to the community. It was important for the community to show that there was continuity between the pre-Easter Jesus of Galilee and the post-Easter Jesus, because there were those who charged otherwise. Both the docetists and the gnostics argued that Jesus did not have a physical body and could not have actually died, that his death was merely an appearance, a kind of first-century bodily illusion.

However, the Gospels are clear that Jesus was a physical human being; in fact, it was precisely his humanness that brought contention among the Pharisees. Consistently in Luke the Pharisees charged that Jesus ate and drank with sinners. Beyond this, John makes a point of having the resurrected Jesus not just appear to the community, but eat and break bread with them. This is to show that the Jesus who was physically with the community pre-Easter is the same Jesus who is with the community post-Easter. This continuity is essential to the community's proclamation, because it shows that it was God who raised Jesus from the dead.

Because God raised Jesus from the dead, Jesus' resurrection becomes the confirmation of his earthly life. In Jesus' resurrection from the dead, God confirmed Jesus' earthly ministry: his works and deeds, his teaching and authority. In raising Jesus from the dead, God confirmed that Jesus was sent by God to perform miracles—to heal the sick, give sight to the blind, raise the dead—and to teach with authority.

This confirmation would also extend to the ministry of the disciples, as exhibited by Peter and John in Acts 4. Not only did God confirm Jesus' ministry; God also vindicated Jesus' innocence of the charges against him. The Pharisees said that Jesus cast out demons by the ruler of demons (Matt. 9:34). Jesus was charged at trial with blasphemy and was executed by the Romans as a state criminal. By raising Jesus from the dead, God proved that these and other charges were false. God also proved that Jesus was not just a prophet (a good man, a kind of noble teacher) but was indeed the Christ, the anointed of God.

In this confirmation by God we begin to see the early development of the church's Christology.

Pastoral Perspective

Pentecost was one of the pilgrimage festivals, so Jews from many nations had gathered from as far away as 1,000 miles. Thus many of the Jews to whom Peter spoke had not been eyewitnesses to Jesus' life and death. They may never have even heard of Jesus of Nazareth. Others had been in Jerusalem at the time of Christ's crucifixion, death, and resurrection, but they struggled with the consequences of these life-altering events. To them, Jesus was a name, but so far, no more than that.

"All of you listen up!" Peter says. "This Jesus, whom you crucified, is more than just a name. He is more than a prophet and a good man. He is the Messiah, the Holy One proclaimed by David and our other prophets. This is the Savior for whom we have been waiting for generations. Every single one of you is a witness to this truth. Whether you saw Jesus with your own eyes or are now hearing the good news for the very first time, you are a witness to what I am telling you today."

Let Jesus be more than just a name to you, Peter says. Let Christ be your Savior. Hear with your heart as well as with your ears. Then you can proclaim Jesus as Lord and know the joy of Christ's amazing, saving grace.

For multitudes gathered in that Pentecost crowd, it was like seeing a sunrise for the very first time— not just *seeing* the sun rise but *feeling* the sun's warm, glorious beams break through the chill darkness of the night.

The people were stirred to the depths of their souls. The Bible says that "Peter's words pierced their hearts" (Acts 2:37 ESV). The good news broke through the barriers of language and culture and religion and social stature and pierced the people to their very hearts, just as the good news is meant to do.

Three thousand people were baptized that day. We do not know the exact count of the crowd, but the percentage of folks whose lives were changed forever was enormous. The number of new believers was more than enough to slow the flow of the Jordan River and make everyone around stop and take notice.

Peter's impromptu sermon is the first of nearly thirty such speeches found in the book of Acts. It kicks off the church like a bottle of fine champagne cracking the stern of a ship on its inaugural launch. Full steam ahead! There is no going back now, at least not without this good news to share. The Jews from Egypt and Mesopotamia and Crete and Arabia and Rome and many other far-off places took the message of Christ with them when they left Jerusalem to return to their homes.

employed by Luke to demonstrate the authority of his protagonists (v. 43; 4:30; 5:12, etc.; cf. Luke 24:19).

Second, Peter emphasizes the shame of killing Israel's Messiah, a title that emerges in the midrash on the psalm of David. Jesus was the long-awaited descendant of David whom God had promised to enthrone (v. 31; 2 Sam. 7:12). Readers should avoid the stigmatization of Jews in general as "Christ killers" latent in verse 23. Luke spreads the responsibility to include the Jews in Jerusalem at the time of Jesus' death, the Roman authorities (the actual executioners), and, for that matter, God, in that Jesus' crucifixion is part of God's plan. How one construes human freedom along with divine "foreknowledge," of course, presents a classic theological conundrum (as does God's sending Jesus to be tortured and killed), but the trajectory of the passage is toward Jesus' resurrection and exaltation.

Peter proclaims that "God raised him up" (v. 24) and then employs a midrash of Psalm 16:8–11 to show that Jesus' resurrection is prefigured in Scripture and that Jesus' body did not undergo the normal physical decomposition. Luke reads the psalm as David's prediction of Jesus' words praising God for being at his "right hand" and not "abandoning" him to Hades or letting him "experience corruption" (v. 27). Peter argues that David could not be speaking of himself in the psalm, since everyone knows that he is long dead and buried (v. 29). To put it more crudely, his body rotted. Not so with the resurrected Jesus (more explicitly in 13:35–37, again citing Ps. 16:10). The word "corruption" comes from the Greek text of the OT (for "Pit," misunderstanding the Hebrew root) and refers to the disintegration of the physical body after death. Luke quotes the last verse again in verse 31, changing it to the third person and replacing "your Holy One" with "his flesh," thereby emphasizing physicality even more.

The claim in verse 31 raises some thorny problems. The Hebrew text has the word Sheol (LXX "Hades"). As recent studies suggest, Sheol was not the destination of everyone when they die; instead, it was "almost always the destination of those who die violently, unjustly, in punishment, or with a broken heart." Thus the psalmist is not claiming that he will never die; rather, "he is expressing his faith that, 'You [God] will not let your faithful servant die *an untimely, evil death.*'"[1] However, that is precisely the kind of death that Jesus suffered—untimely, evil,

the 6,000,000 at the hands of the Nazis during the Second World War. What are we to do with this difficulty, rooted deeply in the founding of our tradition?

At the very least, we cannot avoid it, pretending that the rise of Christianity was not accompanied by widespread notorious calumnies and overt violence against the Jews. We must never forget that it was not until the Second Vatican Council of 1965 that the phrase "Christ-killers" with reference to the Jews was expunged from official Roman Catholic doctrine. Nor have many of our Bible translations been helpful for us, continuing to offer readings that portray all Jews as enemies of an emerging Christianity. For example, chapter 4 of Acts presents "priests, the captain of the temple, the Sadducees" (4:1) and later in the account "their rulers, elders, and scribes," led by "Annas the high priest, Caiaphas, John, and Alexander" (4:5–6), a phalanx of religious authorities who harshly question Peter and John, presenting implacable antagonism toward these two Judeans who are convinced that Jesus is the resurrected Messiah of Israel. The authorities attempt to silence the pair and then threaten them with severe punishment (4:21) before letting them go. However, Peter and John go right on to proclaim what they had earlier said, that "Herod and Pontius Pilate, with the Gentiles and the peoples of Israel, gathered together against [God's] holy servant Jesus" (4:27) and had him murdered.

This near-universal claim that "the Jews" (see especially many places in the Gospel of John) were the killers of Christ is a terrible problem. Preachers who would use these texts need to work hard to clarify just who is being portrayed in these narratives. Not all Jews conspired to kill Jesus. After all, the earliest followers of Jesus were nearly all Jews, as of course Jesus himself was. The struggle in the emergent church was an intra-Jewish struggle, not a struggle between Jews and "Christians." It can safely be said that there were no "Christians" in the very earliest communities of the followers of Jesus; there were only Messianist Jews, convinced that Jesus was the risen Messiah of Israel. Such clarification can help a congregation move beyond an anti-Jewish bias and toward a repudiation of the idea of modern Judaism as a kind of "almost-Christian" heresy. Modern Judaism is a whole religion, still expecting the Messiah of Israel, while modern Christians believe that their Messiah has come.

That belief in Jesus as the Messiah is what Peter determines to convince his brothers and sisters of in this speech at Pentecost. The kind of proof he offers of this belief raises another problem for a modern congregation. His use of Psalms 15 and 109, both

1. Jon D. Levenson, *Resurrection and the Restoration of Israel* (New Haven, CT: Yale University Press, 2006), 73–74, quoting Ruth Rosenberg, my emphasis.

Acts 2:14a, 22-32

Theological Perspective

Because God raised Jesus from the dead, we begin to see the movement from the pre-Easter Jesus of Nazareth to the post-Easter Christ. Prior to the event of the crucifixion, Jesus was a Galilean who preached, taught, and performed miracles. After the resurrection, he is referred to in the Acts and the Epistles as the Christ. The early community saw in Jesus the fulfillment of the promises of the Old Testament and the fulfillment of Israel's calling by God to be a holy people wherein God would establish God's reign forever. Thus the proclamation of Jesus as the Christ is the church's own assertion that Jesus is the promised of God, the one in whom these promises are fulfilled, and the one in whom resides the promise of a new age to come.

In this sermon of Peter we can also see the early formulations of what would become the church's early creedal statements. Peter says in verse 25 that David had spoken of Jesus and in verse 30 that Jesus is the fulfillment of the promise that the Messiah would be a descendent of David and sit upon his throne. Thus Jesus' death and resurrection fulfilled the Scriptures.

C. H. Dodd shows this with reference to the preaching of Paul. Dodd outlines what he calls the Pauline kerygma: that Jesus was the seed of David, died and resurrected according to the Scriptures, and exalted at the right hand of God.[1] This kerygma can also be seen in the early affirmations of Ignatius of Antioch and Justin Martyr,[2] and it carries forward into the later more familiar Apostles' and Nicene creeds. While these are the creedal affirmations more familiar to modern Christians, these affirmations have their origins in the sermon of Peter and the early proclamations of the community.

REGINALD D. BROADNAX

Pastoral Perspective

So the church began, not confined to one city but spreading far and wide with a message that startled everyone who heard it. Who knows how many lives were changed along the way and how many more once the word got out?

One of the greatest gifts children give us is the ability to see the world through fresh eyes. Everyday wonders we have long since taken for granted become fresh and new again. A dandelion is no longer a weed; it is a cluster of fairies we can send dancing on a breeze with one quick puff. A crack in the sidewalk is not a nuisance plotting to trip us: it is a whole world waiting to be discovered. The gentle lick of a puppy's tongue on our cheek is not disgusting; it is cause for giggles of delight. The wonder and joy of every experience is not diminished by repetition, as many parents are reminded when their child utters the words "read it again" for the hundredth time.

Unfortunately, as we grow up, we lose that sense of wonder and awe. Even our faith is at risk of becoming ho-hum. Perhaps Peter's pronouncement in Acts is not only a "listen up" call to the people in that crowd, but a "wake up" call to those of us hearing the good news for the first, tenth, one-thousandth time. Every time we hear and receive the good news of Jesus Christ, it is Pentecost, all over again. We are set on fire with the thrill of it, just as the disciples were lit up by the flame of the Holy Spirit on that very first Pentecost celebration.

The question to ask, therefore, is not simply, "When did God become more than just a name to you?" but rather, "How is God more than just a name to you now, in this moment, at this time in your life?" It is a timeless question that bears asking time and time again.

KATHLEEN LONG BOSTROM

---

1. See C. H. Dodd, *Apostolic Preaching and Its Development* (London: Hodder & Stoughton, 1936).
2. See John H. Leith, ed., *Creeds of the Churches*, 3rd ed. (Louisville, KY: John Knox Press, 1982).

Exegetical Perspective

violent, and with a broken heart. Perhaps Luke's claim here reflects *his* version of the crucifixion, where Jesus' cry of dereliction is replaced by the trusting words "'Father, into your hands I commend my spirit'" (Luke 23:46). Moreover, on the cross Jesus trusts that "today" he will be "in Paradise" (not Sheol!).

Luke's reading of Psalm 16 thus seems to insist that Jesus was *not* abandoned by God and to emphasize the physical integrity of his resurrected body (Luke 24:39–43). For Luke, Jesus died and was buried, but he did *not* "descend into hell," to cite the later creed. Thus Luke's position here goes against the basic Reformed view that Jesus' agony and abandonment by God on the cross *was* a descent into hell.

The point of using Psalm 16 is to ground Luke's claim that Jesus is "both Lord and Messiah" (v. 36). It is puzzling why the lectionary omits the very conclusion to which Luke's midrash moves. Again, the Pentecost context disappears, even though the conclusion of Peter's speech provides the answer to the question raised in verse 12: the risen and exalted Christ is the agent who "pours out" the "Holy Spirit," the manifestation of which the people "see and hear" (v. 33).

Peter's accusation against those who crucified Jesus leads to an agonized sense of guilt and a desperate plea—"What shall we do?" (v. 37; cf. Luke 3:10)—and then to Peter's call for repentance and baptism. In fact, the speech moves from judgment to the promise by which the people may be forgiven of their sins and receive the Holy Spirit (v. 38), thus connecting the two parts of the speech. The result is a mass conversion that would make any revival pastor proud (v. 41). An inchoate Trinity lurks in verse 36 (cf. vv. 33 and 17), but doctrine is not Luke's purpose. Rather, it is to demonstrate once again that movement of the Spirit that drives his narrative, both his Gospel and Acts—and, in his view, all of history.

THOMAS W. MANN

Homiletical Perspective

from the Greek translation, the Septuagint, assumes four first-century shared presuppositions: (1) the Psalms were written by David, the second king of Israel; (2) David was God's "anointed" (Ps. 2); (3) God had promised to David an eternal dynasty through his descendants (2 Sam. 7); (4) things spoken of in the Psalms would therefore refer either to David himself or to his descendant, the Messiah. Peter argues from these presuppositions that since David is clearly dead, his tomb available for visitation at any time (2:29), then references such as "God's Holy One never seeing corruption" (Ps. 16:10) and "not being abandoned to Hades" are in fact references to the "resurrection of the Messiah," whom Peter believes to be Jesus, David's descendant.

All four of these 2,000-year-old literary presuppositions have been seriously disputed by modern biblical criticism. This is not to say that no one any longer finds such arguments persuasive, but it is to say that many moderns may have difficulties with them. Nevertheless, the result of Peter's speech about the resurrection of Jesus is that "they were cut to the heart" and implored Peter to tell them what now they were to do, in the light of this new information about Jesus (v. 37). He calls for their repentance and baptism, and 3,000 responded. Peter's sermon was a successful one, using the materials of his day to make his claims, proclaiming the power of the resurrection in the face of great skepticism.

Might that not be the lesson for the modern preacher? We need to use the tools of our day to announce the power and wonder of Jesus' resurrected life that has changed everything about us. In our world of death-dealing violence, of haves and have-nots, of those in and those out, the pretty people and the nobodies, we need to announce the fact that death holds no sway over us anymore. That means that hierarchies have no meaning, those who would dominate others have lost their power; in Jesus all things are truly made new.

JOHN C. HOLBERT

Psalm 16

¹Protect me, O God, for in you I take refuge.
²I say to the LORD, "You are my Lord;
  I have no good apart from you."

³As for the holy ones in the land, they are the noble,
  in whom is all my delight.

⁴Those who choose another god multiply their sorrows;
  their drink offerings of blood I will not pour out
  or take their names upon my lips.

⁵The LORD is my chosen portion and my cup;
  you hold my lot.
⁶The boundary lines have fallen for me in pleasant places;
  I have a goodly heritage.

Theological Perspective

The first reading for the Second Sunday of Easter is from Acts 2:14a, 22–32, in which this psalm is quoted (according to the Septuagint) in Peter's speech. The Greek translator of the Hebrew psalm took some liberties, transforming parts of the Hebrew text from an earthly perspective to the prospect of personal immortality with God. Nonetheless, the original Hebrew text's emphasis on the fact that earthly life is surrounded by the presence of God and that true life is to live in God's presence opens this psalm to just such a transformation. For those who read this text with faith founded on the resurrection, that transformation has reached its complete fulfillment. Psalm 16 helps us to prepare for the mystery of life we celebrate at Easter.

Despite the difficult text for verses 3–4, the psalmist's theme of trust in God is clear. From the opening prayer for protection (vv. 1–2) through the remaining verses, the psalm uses different images to assert that the Lord is the only good and certain happiness (vv. 2, 9), a true inheritance (vv. 5–6), the only wise counselor (v. 7), a sure protection from mortal dangers (vv. 1, 8, and 10), and the guide to life (v. 11).

The opening petition is grounded in the confessions of trust that follow. For good reason this psalm has been called a "prayer song," for the psalmist confesses throughout the psalm why grave personal needs should be placed before the Lord. This is the

Pastoral Perspective

Alleluia? In too many churches the Sunday after Easter belies the profound good news of Jesus' resurrection. The worship service preaches, "Jesus Christ Was Risen Last Sunday." The alleluias have faded, the lilies have wilted, the congregation has dwindled, the pastor has gone on vacation. "Our triumphant holy day" is now "Low Sunday," a sanctioned *holi*day from even the usual order of service. We are "churched out" and enervated, as if we had preached and prayed and sung Jesus out of the tomb by our own efforts.

Worship planners need to take seriously the message that is perhaps inadvertently preached by a diminished service today. The Second Sunday of Easter is not intended to be second rate, but a second round. All those Easter morning sermons about death not being the end, about life after death, about beginnings and not endings—where is the integrity of our Easter preaching, if the next Sunday is dead? Faithful to the Gospel of this day in every lectionary cycle, Jesus is alive and among his own, imparting his life-giving peace and forgiveness (John 20:19–31). Christ is risen, indeed! Alleluia! It is not over!

Can Psalm 16 resurrect the Second Sunday of Easter?

Do not skip the psalm today. Not only does it sound the notes played in the other readings; it is the

^{7}I bless the Lord who gives me counsel;
  in the night also my heart instructs me.
^{8}I keep the Lord always before me;
  because he is at my right hand, I shall not be moved.

^{9}Therefore my heart is glad, and my soul rejoices;
  my body also rests secure.
^{10}For you do not give me up to Sheol,
  or let your faithful one see the Pit.

^{11}You show me the path of life.
  In your presence there is fullness of joy;
  in your right hand are pleasures forevermore.

Exegetical Perspective

Psalm 16 is a psalm of confidence, which means that even in the midst of trials and suffering, the psalmist finds reasons to express confidence that God will save his people. Psalms of confidence often take a lamenting tone, at least in part, as the psalmist takes time to list the things that are wrong in his world and the things that he alone, or the people alone, are helpless to defeat. Only after making sure that the reader or listener is aware of the depths of the darkness does the psalmist allow the light of God to shine on the experience.

Once this light is brought to the psalm, it is affirmed in loud, clear language and strong images. There is no equivocation on the part of the psalmist when he declares his confidence in the Lord's saving power. As with other psalms assigned to the Easter celebrations of the Christian community, this psalm acknowledges both the reality of suffering and the ever-present help of the Lord.

Psalm 16 follows the pattern of other confidence psalms in that it acknowledges suffering and allows the psalmist a moment to be distressed about it. Phrases such as "Protect me, O God," "I take refuge," and "I shall not be moved" (vv. 1, 8) suggest conflict and opposition in the psalmist's life, but also express a firm, even fierce, confidence in the Lord's presence. It goes on to assert that those who do not

Homiletical Perspective

Resurrection proclamation continues unabated on the Second Sunday of Easter. Having heard the good news of Jesus' rising on Easter Day, the church gathers to witness anew to the wonders God has done. Psalm 16 gives voice to that proclamation with its rejection of death and its confidence in the unfailing care of God for God's people. Peter's inclusion of it in his sermon to the people of Judea (Acts 2:25–27) points today's preachers to the psalm as well.

Here at the beginning of the Easter season, we are still marveling at the miracle of resurrection life; yet we also remember what came before. Just as the psalmist remembers times of need and disorientation, so the church remembers the fear, violence, death, and despair of the three days before the resurrection. It seemed that death had triumphed, that evil had done its worst; yet God did not abandon Christ, who might well sing with the psalmist, "You do not give me up to Sheol, or let your faithful one see the Pit" (v. 10). Neither does God abandon us. Indeed, the God who lived and died as one of us has saved us from death as well, joining us to Christ in his death and resurrection.

One of the Eastern Church's best-known iconographic images is that of the risen Christ reaching down into the grave to rescue Adam and Eve. Standing on the broken gates of hell, he raises them to

Psalm 16

Theological Perspective

essence of prayer: not that we are informing God of something unknown, but that we are reminding ourselves of divine love and protection as a basis for growing in our faith.

The initial petition (vv. 1–2), which speaks of protection and "refuge," would seem to indicate a situation in which physical security or asylum was sought from the Lord. This would be supported by the references to death ("Sheol" and the "Pit") in verse 10. The next verse also broadens the plea into a more universal sentiment. The immediate need is expressed in language that recalls God's continued, universal covenant loyalty and protection for the whole people. The awesome words of verse 2, "no good apart from you," express the universal domain and exclusive loyalty belonging to God that is found in the second commandment. So the petitioner of this psalm appropriately acknowledges the power and dominion of the Lord, appealing to the Lord's own covenant loyalty and fidelity as the basis for trust in divine aid.

The following four verses (vv. 3–6) appear to contrast this confession by those who trust in the Lord, the "holy ones," with those who depend on other gods and offer cultic worship to them. This is more than just an oblique confession of the Lord's supremacy. The psalm is acknowledging the appeal that other, seemingly more proximate and practical, sources of help can have, especially in serious situations.

In the psalmist's wider culture there are many different gods to call upon. They are rejected. This is not necessarily an easy choice. Nor is dependence on God any easier for us. Human ingenuity, technological advances, and accumulated epochs of learning are our "idols," which can finally appear to have erased the need for otherworldly realities. The story of human achievements has made the memory of God's saving deeds vague and mysterious. Resurrection can become a modern symbol for the next human advance. Real faith, as exemplified by the psalmist, stretches the person beyond human capability and earthly realities.

The unusual images in verses 5–6 build upon the confession found in verse 2. The images "portion," "lot," "boundary lines," and "heritage" reflect covenant language for the distribution of the land after the conquest. The psalmist is not boasting of land he has received; rather he boasts that the Lord is his inheritance. Like the Levitical priests of old, the psalmist receives his sustenance from the Lord. The "inheritance" is not material possessions, as with the Levite, but the experience of the Lord's closeness, protection,

Pastoral Perspective

only reading on this day from the Old Testament. The psalm might be included in the order of service as an opening prayer, read responsively or in unison. Its expression of confidence and trust rightly grounds the worship experience in God's presence any week of the year. Do not skip this psalm on this particular day. Its gratitude and rejoicing lifts the worshiper's whole self ("heart," "soul," "body" in v. 9) to see "the path of life" (v. 11) beyond death. On the Second Sunday of Easter, it gives voice to the experience of being held in God's hand, secure in God's goodness in every circumstance of life driving our need for protection and refuge.

Psalm 16 may be sung by the congregation. The hymn "When in the Night I Meditate" is a paraphrase from the 1912 Psalter. Some congregations will recognize the tune from Lenten worship services. "Lord, Who throughout These Forty Days" is also sung to the tune St. Flavian and may provide a musical and liturgical continuity when its last line is brought forward into this day: "Abide with us, that so, this life/Of suffering overpast, An Easter of unending joy/We may attain at last!" In its reading, praying, and/or its singing, Psalm 16 offers themes and images to the readings from Acts 2 and John 20.

This psalm makes a formal appearance in the life of the church when cited by Peter in his Pentecost sermon. First- and twenty-first-century believers alike hear compelling good news. Jesus was "crucified and killed. . . . But God raised him up . . . it was impossible for him to be held in [death's] power" (Acts 2:23–24). Luke was sure that the words of Psalm 16 were on the tip of Peter's tongue, a ready interpretive framework for any and all who would doubt that God raised Jesus from death, neither abandoning his soul to Hades nor allowing his flesh to experience corruption (Ps. 16:10 and Acts 2:27). In the next breath of that sermon, there is witness to life, joy, and gladness; again the psalmist's words offer a script to the heretofore ineloquent Peter (Ps. 16:11 and Acts 2:28). "You show me the path of life. In your presence there is fullness of joy; in your right hand are pleasures forevermore" (Ps. 16:11). What language shall we borrow?

Hearing the words of the psalmist in the sermon of Peter was compelling to first converts. It may be comforting for latter-day believers, new and long-time, who struggle for words to express their faith. "You are my Lord. . . . You do not give me up. . . . You show me the path of life" (vv. 2, 10, 11). The intent of Peter's sermon is christological; the intent of the

demonstrate such confidence in the Lord will be left out of the rewards of knowing him.

Even with the acknowledgment of suffering and the inclusion of those who do not put their trust in the Lord, the tone of this psalm is strongly joyful, using moving and vivid words such as gladness, rejoicing, security, joy, and pleasure to express his experience of the God in which he has so much confidence.

Verses 1–2 set the tone for the psalm: confident, but with an acknowledgment of danger. The psalmist cries out for God's protection, confident that he will be protected when "in you I take refuge" (v. 1). He assures God that he is faithful, that he has no other recourse to blessing, and that God is sovereign in his life.

Verses 3–4 are somewhat problematic because of translation difficulties; scholars are not entirely sure what the phrase usually translated "multiply their sorrows" is intended to mean. However, it is clear that these verses address the case of those who worship other gods. Because the psalmist is confident in the Lord alone, he rejects the acts of those who turn to other gods instead. No good can come of that (an idea continued from "I have no good apart from you" in v. 2); they will only multiply their sorrows. The psalmist will not be tempted to offer sacrifice to these other entities ("drink offerings of blood"), nor will he use their names in incantations and prayers ("take their names upon my lips"), because again, his confidence is in the Lord alone.

In verses 5–6, the psalmist emphasizes that he has chosen to place his confidence in the Lord, "my chosen portion and my cup." "Cup" here is a metaphor for destiny, the path one's life will follow. The psalmist has chosen a destiny linked to the Lord's, and he is well satisfied with it. He is content with his allotment in life, and confident that the Lord will sustain him in it.

In some sense he may see this as a reward for his confidence. It is typical for the psalms to assert a worldview in which faith is rewarded and guilt punished, and we have already seen this in the preceding verses, which indicate that those who do not place their confidence in the Lord have their sorrows multiplied. For the psalmist, however, the rewards are tangible—a heritage and a share in the land given to Israel.

Verses 7–8 suggest that there are also less tangible rewards given to those who trust in the Lord. The psalmist receives counsel—that is, wisdom and prudence—as he seeks the Lord in his heart through prayer. He gains steadfastness, a quality much admired by the Hebrews and often attributed to God himself. The psalmist asserts, "Because he is at my

new life with him. The message is clear: death has been defeated once and for all through Christ who saves us. Because of the good news of resurrection, those who preach with Psalm 16 in mind will lift up the unswerving faithfulness of God in every circumstance. It has been said that in baptism we have already died with Christ—we have seen the worst. Since we have also been raised with him, we can live in confidence that God has already saved us from all that might destroy us. Throughout all of the many deaths and fears and trials we face in the course of our lifetimes, God remains our constant refuge.

Preaching from the psalm might also focus on the nature of the Christian life. "The LORD is my chosen portion and my cup," says the psalmist (v. 5); as followers of Jesus, we choose him again and again. Here on this Second Sunday of Easter, we can still proclaim resurrection joy and confidence in the Divine, but as the sound of the trumpets fades and we journey on through our lives, we forget that joyful confidence, and doubt creeps in. If we live as the psalmist lives, however, we continually choose Christ, reaffirming our trust in him. As the church we remind one another of God's faithfulness, even in the face of the Pit, upholding one another as we seek to live faithfully.

In the other readings for the day we hear the voices of Peter, Paul, and John, each of them bearing witness to what he has seen and heard. Although, like Thomas, we have not seen the risen Christ with our own eyes, the church also bears witness because we have received the testimonies of so many who have gone before us. To preach from the psalm in the context of all the readings, then, is to affirm that we know the faithfulness of God, not only through our own experiences as individuals or communities, but through the experiences of so many faithful ones in every time and place. To stand with so many witnesses is to rejoice in all things and at all times, for the steadfast, saving love of God is sure.

After my father's funeral, my mother shared all sorts of memorabilia with the family: the seersucker sport coat and the white bucks that fit my older son perfectly; the collection of Orioles caps; the photographs of my father as a young boy, riding a scooter with his constant companion, Skippy, a Boston bull terrier. There were letters and notes and sermons. Then my mother showed me a few typewritten pages that took my breath away and made the tears flow. On those pages were the words my father said at the grave of my stillborn sisters. My mother had carried the twins full term before it was clear that something had gone wrong. What had been a growing wave of joy in

Psalm 16

Theological Perspective

and mercy. The true inheritance of the believer is to live in the presence of the Lord (v. 2). A dramatic fulfillment of this is Paul's affirmation that now "Christ lives in me" (Gal. 2:20). The psalm hints at such a union, but Paul celebrates this union with the resurrected Lord. Through Christ, it is the Lord who has made us his inheritance.

The consequences of this divine union are drawn in the next verses (vv. 7–11). Divine counsel and guidance are present day and night. The Lord is guide and protective companion during the journey through life. Therefore, body and soul are made joyful, secure. Moreover, in the face of physical death, the psalmist is certain that the Lord will sustain his life. The Lord leads only on a path to life and joy.

The assertion that the Lord will surround us with divine presence is a challenge. This ancient psalm understands the Lord's mercy and love so well that it affirms faith in the Lord as the giver of life, even against all odds. The Lord is the one who leads to life, and the psalmist rests in the security of this belief. Christians transform this faith to a belief that the Lord sustains life even after death. Nor should we doubt, since we have been given the resurrection of the Lord to sustain this faith. Is our faith in eternal life with God still as powerful, as steadfast, and as sure as that of the ancient psalmist, who did not have the knowledge we have been given?

In summary, the psalm is a hymn celebrating faith in the Lord's saving presence among us. The psalmist witnesses to the steadfast trust and praise that such a faith should inspire. The real meaning of life is to belong to the Lord, to remain in the divine presence. The gift of that presence is realized and celebrated in the resurrection.

THOMAS P. MCCREESH

Pastoral Perspective

psalmist's prayer is more personal. Faith begins here, in the simple language of relationship and address.

Psalm 16 is generous with personal pronouns, especially "I" and "you," and they are used interpersonally: "In you I take refuge. I say to the LORD, 'You are my Lord; I have no good apart from you" (vv. 1–2). In this song of trust the word "trust" is never used. Trust is spoken in the language of relationship. Belonging sustains and nurtures believing. As pastors have heard from those distanced from the church or doubting its beliefs, saying creeds and confessions in church can be confusing, meaningless, even disingenuous.

Nevertheless, this pastor has heard from those who affirm that saying, "In life and in death we belong to God," opens a whole new experience and perspective for them. New and longtime members express that the Brief Statement of Faith of the Presbyterian Church (U.S.A.) is "welcoming," "assuring," "grounding," "good news." It affirms that faith is relational, not ideational. The ensuing convictions of trust in Jesus Christ, God, and the Holy Spirit—not in a list of "I believe's"—both reflects and evokes deep personal confidence in God and commitment to life in "holy and joyful" community.

Worshipers will also hear the language of Psalm 16 in the reading of the Gospel. The psalmist begins his or her prayer with an unequivocal "You are my Lord." John ends this resurrection account with Thomas's climactic confession, "My Lord and my God!" Do some of us start with strong faith and then move through the unpleasant places and dark nights unmoved and unalone? Do some of us start with doubt and work and wait toward believing? Great is the mystery of faith! For the preacher opening the homiletical door to Thomas's doubt and our own, the psalmist's "You are my Lord. . . . You show me the path of life" sets us on our post-Easter journey. What we are given to see is the life-transforming presence of God and "the fullness of joy."

Can Psalm 16 resurrect the Second Sunday of Easter?

DEBORAH A. BLOCK

Exegetical Perspective

right hand, I shall not be moved." This could also have a military interpretation. The "right hand" often refers to the sword hand, and the psalmist could be saying that his confidence in the Lord makes him courageous and steadfast in battle. It could, however, also be applied to the metaphorical battles of life, in which steadfastness is just as necessary. Steadfastness is much easier for anyone who can confess: "the LORD [is] always before me."

Because the Lord gives counsel, instruction, and steadfastness, the psalmist is glad. In verse 9, he rejoices in his spirit, and even his body rests secure under the protection of the Lord that he sought at the beginning of the psalm. Verse 10 seems to indicate that the psalmist had once been near death, either through sickness or in battle, and that he was rescued from this fate because of his faithfulness to the Lord.

One interpretation of this rescue is that it is the source of the psalmist's confidence, and he can be assured that his confidence is merited because God has already proven through this rescue that he can be trusted to save. However, the rescue can also be seen as a reward for the confidence in the Lord that the psalmist has already displayed, adding it to the list of the numerous benefits that those faithful to the Lord receive.

The psalm ends with a proclamation of the Lord's continuing consent to provide guidance by showing the psalmist the path of life. This may reference the rescue above, but it also may have more spiritual connotations. This interpretation is enforced by the next lines, which speak of the Lord's presence in vivid emotional terms—fullness of joy and pleasures forevermore. This psalm declares not only confidence but joy and pleasure in the ongoing presence of the Lord.

KATHERINE C. CALORE

Homiletical Perspective

our family came crashing down when the girls were lost to us even before they were born. It was different in those days; there was no funeral or even a time of prayer with the family. My parents refused to allow the hospital to dispose of the bodies, however, and my father took the girls to be buried in the family plot. Only one dear friend accompanied him. Though it was only the two of them, there were things that needed to be said. For all of the pain in my father's heart, all he could do was give thanks for the goodness of God—the God who welcomed my sisters home, the God who held our lives in divine hands, the God whose faithfulness is beyond measure.

For all of the jubilation of Easter, Psalm 16 expresses a sort of quiet joy. This is the kind of joy that comes from having seen the worst and lived through it—joy that is tempered with the knowledge of what the world, and life, can do. It is a song of confidence and trust in the one who does not abandon God's people to death. One might even say that it is something of a love song, sung not because the psalmist has led a perfect existence, but because God has been faithful, even through the worst of life. It is God who has been steadfast; the Lord who has given guidance and security. "You show me the path of life," the psalmist sings, "In your presence there is fullness of joy" (v. 11).

KIMBERLY BRACKEN LONG

1 Peter 1:3-9

³Blessed be the God and Father of our Lord Jesus Christ! By his great mercy he has given us a new birth into a living hope through the resurrection of Jesus Christ from the dead, ⁴and into an inheritance that is imperishable, undefiled, and unfading, kept in heaven for you, ⁵who are being protected by the power of God through faith for a salvation ready to be revealed in the last time. ⁶In this you rejoice, even if now for a little while you have had to suffer various trials, ⁷so that the genuineness of your faith—being more precious than gold that, though perishable, is tested by fire—may be found to result in praise and glory and honor when Jesus Christ is revealed. ⁸Although you have not seen him, you love him; and even though you do not see him now, you believe in him and rejoice with an indescribable and glorious joy, ⁹for you are receiving the outcome of your faith, the salvation of your souls.

Theological Perspective

This reading continues the Easter proclamation: by great mercy, God "has given us a new birth into a living hope through the resurrection of Jesus Christ from the dead" (v. 3b). The grammar of the opening sentences underscores Easter's declaration about the relationship between God and humanity. The first sentence is an exclamation of praise in which the human community is represented by a modifier ("our"). In the second sentence, the human community ("us") is an indirect object, the recipient of new birth. Finally, in the third sentence, humanity ("you") becomes a subject. This is the gospel in miniature: (1) the first word is praise, because (2) God acts toward us in mercy, and thus (3) we are enabled to act in joy.

Beyond its suggestive grammatical movement, this passage presents several theological themes for exploration. What is the "faith" that the writer mentions three times in seven verses? How should the Christian community interpret suffering? What is actually meant by "salvation"?

Faith. While Christians with roots in the Protestant Reformation have long proclaimed "faith alone" as the way we are saved, there has been great debate over what faith means. In the sixteenth century, Calvin and early Reformed confessions emphasized

Pastoral Perspective

Inheritance is more than a modern idea spawned by an exponential growth of global wealth in the last few centuries. Since earliest times, people have talked and argued about inheritance. They have both protected it and squandered it. Virtually every society has known the anticipation of receiving property from someone who has died. To be an heir is to be the recipient, or the someday recipient, of something considered precious.

Pastors do not have to dig too deeply to notice all of the families in a congregation that skirmish over inheritance-related matters. Festering wounds in certain clans, of promises anticipated, argued, and broken, are just below the surface. Sometimes a family fight over inheritance will be manifest in the resistance, or claimed inability, to make a generous offering or pledge commitment. Occasionally it works the other way around, and a church's mission may be blessed by someone sharing a substantial gift inherited.

The Bible makes more than 250 references to inheritance, a clear sign that everyday conversations about legacy took place in ancient life as well. Some of the references are found in well-known stories: "But when the tenants saw the son, they said to themselves, 'This is the heir; come, let us kill him and get his inheritance'" (Matt. 21:38). "Someone in the

Exegetical Perspective

First Peter addresses communities in Asia Minor (1 Pet. 1:1) whose members appear to be Gentile (1:14, 18; 4:3–4) Christian (1:2) slaves (2:18–25) and women (3:1–6) owned by or married to non-Christian men.[1] These people are at the very bottom of the social pyramid they inhabit. As slaves and women, they have low status to begin with. Because they violate the prime virtue of espousing the religious practices of the heads of their households, though, their friends, neighbors, and family members also consider them to be antisocial, rebellious, even "atheistic," since they refuse to honor their families' gods. They defy traditional family values by refusing to obey the head of household, and they jeopardize community welfare by insulting civic religion.

Greco-Roman pagans can tolerate anything except intolerance, and Christians (and Jews too, it might be added) are seen as supremely intolerant. Their confessions of Christian faith place them at odds with everyone around them, and they receive constant scorn and contempt simply for believing in Jesus. The author of 1 Peter assures them in 4:12–19 that this treatment is only to be expected, since Christ

Homiletical Perspective

One of the more resonant sentences in Scripture is found in verse 8 of the Epistle text for today: "Although you have not seen him, you love him." Paul tells us that only about 500 persons *ever* saw the risen Christ (1 Cor. 15:5–8), while Matthew records that not all, even of his disciples, were fully convinced after they did (28:17). Doubt and love are almost always mutually exclusive, which may be why Luke recounts that those gathered in the upper room before Pentecost numbered around 120.

If only a very few were blessed with both faith and sight, subsequent converts have been persuaded by the praise, proclamation, and communal life of believers. Doxology, genuine praise, helps us experience and express Christian faith.

In *Blue Like Jazz*, Donald Miller writes, "I never liked jazz music because jazz music doesn't resolve. But I was outside the Bagdad Theater in Portland one night when I saw a man playing the saxophone. I stood there for fifteen minutes and he never opened his eyes. After that I liked jazz music. Sometimes you have to watch somebody love something before you can love it yourself. It is as if they are showing you the way."[1]

---

1. The author once addresses some Christian husbands (3:7) who may also be slaves.

1. Donald Miller, *Blue Like Jazz: Non-Religious Thoughts on Christian Spirituality* (Nashville: Thomas Nelson, 2003), ix.

1 Peter 1:3-9

Theological Perspective

that faith consists of both knowledge and deep trust in God's benevolence. The Heidelberg Catechism (1563) provides a good example: true faith "is not only a certain *knowledge* by which I accept as true all that God has revealed . . . , but also a wholehearted *trust* which the Holy Spirit creates in me through the gospel, that, not only to others, but to me also God has given the forgiveness of sins, everlasting righteousness and salvation, out of sheer grace solely for the sake of Christ's saving work."[1] This definition intended to counter any notion that faith was simply assent to what the church taught, without personal reliance on God's grace.

In the twentieth century, Swiss theologian Karl Barth began a discussion of faith by emphasizing the particular *object* of faith, the triune God. He acknowledged that the subjective side of faith cannot be ignored, but insisted that personal trust is not the primary aspect of faith. When we explore what it means to say "I believe," we do not start with "I" but with the object in which we believe. The subjective dimension relies on the object of faith.

This passage includes both of these dimensions. The "genuineness of your faith" (v. 7) suggests an authentic personal quality to that faith. The object of faith is clearly identified as Jesus (v. 8) and, more specifically, "the resurrection of Jesus Christ from the dead" (v. 3). Faith in that specific object—or better, faith in that specific *person*—evokes joy and praise.

The "outcome of . . . faith" (v. 9), according to 1 Peter, is salvation, but in the short term, faith leads to suffering. How shall we hold these together?

Suffering. "Now for a little while you have had to suffer various trials" (v. 6). The writer acknowledges that the Christian churches to whom he is writing have endured suffering, just as gold is tested by fire. Christian theological history is filled with debates about human suffering: how could a God who is good and powerful permit suffering? This has produced many responses over the centuries (e.g., suffering is punishment for sin, suffering is God's way of teaching patience and trust, suffering is an incomprehensible mystery).

This passage is not describing suffering in general. Instead, the writer addresses a particular situation: the suffering of persecuted Christian communities. This he interprets as "testing" to prove the genuineness of their faith. Such teaching can be dangerous. If

1. Heidelberg Catechism, question 21, in *Book of Confessions: Study Edition* (Louisville, KY: Geneva Press, 1999), 4.021.

Pastoral Perspective

crowd said to him, 'Teacher, tell my brother to divide the family inheritance with me'" (Luke 12:13).

Who can know all the motivations for the excitement we attach to the prospect of receiving an inheritance? Is it the monetary value that gives an heir the sudden sense of abundance, wealth, and leisure? Is it an emotional or sentimental tie to the prior generation(s) that feels so good? Is it some romantic hope that a new possession will open the door to the "privileged life"? Who can say? Every experience of inheriting property or contemplating as much is different.

Inheritance is hardly the exclusive domain of the wealthy. We can bequeath all kinds of items to another person, even if we do not dwell in the land of riches. Take one poignant example from Boston's Holocaust Monument, a walk-through sculpture that bears this inscription of a concentration camp survivor:

> Ilse, a childhood friend of mine, once found a raspberry in the camp and carried it in her pocket all day to present that night to me on a leaf. Imagine a world in which your entire possession is one raspberry and you give it to your friend. (Gerda Weissman Klein)

Imagine giving a single raspberry to your best friend as your last act of kindness in life, before being shuffled off to the gas chamber. *That* is generosity!

Consider a different extreme—gifts to others that can only be called bizarre. When the controversial hotel magnate Leona Helmsley died a few years ago, she made news by leaving her Maltese dog $12 million in her will. The dog may still be sorting through what do with the inheritance.

To all the properties ever passed along to successor generations, to all earthly inheritances, one thing is common. They all lack permanence. Regardless of whether an inheritance has a high or low estimated value, it will always wither and fade, like the grass and flowers of which the prophet Isaiah once spoke. Even a precious raspberry given with the generosity of a whole life behind it is temporal.

When the writer in 1 Peter speaks of believers being gifted with an inheritance that is "imperishable, undefiled, and unfading" (v. 4), a reader naturally perks up. What could possibly be given to us that would not decay? Even land given by the Lord as a possession (Deut. 15:4)—a prized inheritance for the ancient Hebrews—can come up short through erosion, drought, infestation, and takeover.

The writer of 1 Peter says one inheritance will put the insignificance of all others into perspective. This

Exegetical Perspective

suffered before them and they share his suffering by associating with him.

The author uses a remarkable number of Old Testament ideas to describe these Gentile Christians. They are "exiles of the Dispersion" (1:1; cf. Jer. 24:5; 29:1, 4), "chosen and destined by God" (1 Pet. 1:2; cf. Jer. 15:2), "protected by the power of God" (1 Pet. 1:5; cf. Josh. 24:17), God's "holy priesthood" (1 Pet 2:5), holy as God is holy (1 Pet. 1:16; cf. Lev. 19:2), "a chosen race, a royal priesthood, a holy nation, God's own people" (1 Pet. 2:9; cf. Exod. 19:6; Isa. 43:20–21; Hos. 1:9; 2:23). This abundance of biblical language for Israel, applied to Gentile Christian women and slaves, is what Steven R. Bechtler calls a "revalorization of shame," 1 Peter's transformation of the scorned status of Christians in Asia Minor into the exalted status of the people of God.[2] This is thus a letter of comfort, intended to assure Christians that, no matter how their neighbors criticize them, God says they are right to hold fast their confessions of faith, and may look forward to the same kind of vindication God gave Jesus by raising him from the dead.

The letter begins with a benediction, blessing God for the mercy Christians have received through Christ's resurrection (v. 3). This mercy is further defined as believers' inheritance, the inheritance of God's own name and their identity as God's people. Although they are hounded by hostile family members and friends and surrounded by enthusiastic pagan religious practices, their patrimony in heaven is "imperishable, undefiled, and unfading" (v. 4) and will be revealed to all when Christ returns in glory. Despite their current humiliation, they will be exalted "in the last time" (v. 5).

As with most other New Testament letters, the first paragraph sets the tone for much that follows. The description of the addressees as "sanctified by the Spirit to be obedient to Jesus Christ and to be sprinkled with his blood" (v. 2) reminds them of their baptism, a theme that runs throughout chapter 1, concluding with the description of Christians as those who have been reborn (v. 23).

First Peter then explains why these Christians suffer the contempt of their friends and families. It is "so that the genuineness of your faith . . . may be found to result in praise and glory and honor when Jesus Christ is revealed" (v. 7). Their faithfulness to Christ under difficult circumstances is kerygmatic; it preaches the

2. Stephen R. Bechtler, *Following in His Steps: Suffering, Community, and Christology in 1 Peter*, Society of Biblical Literature Dissertation Series 162 (Atlanta: Scholars Press, 1998).

Homiletical Perspective

The early church shows us the way by means of its praise, but for our part we can find doxology particularly difficult, and not merely on this "Low Sunday."

It is an interesting term, Low Sunday. The first point of reference, of course, is attendance. The crowds are gone, whatever the reasons for their advent seven days ago. Moreover, many among the faithful also vacate today, preachers and people alike, some of them simply overtired from the Lenten fasts and Easter Vigils, the sunrise services and special music. Just as the First Sunday after Christmas evidences a kind of "postpartum depression" in congregations, so Low Sunday has its own discreet melancholy—another connotation for this day's nomenclature.

Whatever challenges we might face in terms of temporary burnout and low attendance (in the choir loft as well as the nave), the lectionary texts compound them. Setting aside textual matters in 1 Peter, issues of composition and audience, the preacher is yet faced with a cluster of other issues; most notable among them the fact that the lesson is framed with doxology. Praise is the first word and last word, and a mirror, it would seem (at least in the apostle's mind), of authentic human response to the gospel.

Faith characterized by praise and doxology is near the heart of the gospel's transmission and reception. "Singing the faith" is part and parcel of both the early church's testimony to the truth of the resurrection and its invitation for the unaware to come and be a part of the resurrection choir. In sum, the praise of the first believers is a love song to God, while the church's song echoes God's love for all creation. Doxology bears witness to the good news.

These days, however, we might conclude that the good news is not really "news" at all, given how often we have heard and preached it. We might also note that, Peter's encouragement notwithstanding, folk "like us" are not much given to singing anymore. Doxology is difficult for the overly analytical; it is really hard to sing with your fingers crossed. Even a mild case of skepticism affects the vocal cords, pinches the nerve of praise, makes it hard to stand and sing.

We find it *safer* to reflect on the experiences of others, *easier* to interpret biblical praise in its context, more *satisfying* to explore the historical and sociopolitical aspects of Israel's worship and developing convictions regarding the Christ. This hermeneutic of doubt, whether formal or informal, grants us to *understand* how the first Christian believers, much as Miriam at the Reed Sea or Israel at Sinai, sang praise

1 Peter 1:3-9

Theological Perspective

all suffering of Christian communities is interpreted as God's will to "purify" the faithful, then powerful Christians can justify the suffering of the powerless as God's testing, while the powerless can passively accept their suffering, rather than recognizing and resisting instances of genuine oppression.

It matters that these words come from someone who does not stand outside the community, but speaks out of profound knowledge of that suffering. From the inside, 1 Peter's analysis carries christological overtones: the suffering of the Christian community connects that community to the cross. Barth insists, "We do not believe if we do not live in the neighborhood of Golgotha. And we cannot live in the neighborhood of Golgotha without being affected by the shadow of divine judgment, without allowing this shadow to fall on us." Golgotha alone represents God's judgment, but Christians live in the shadow of that judgment. He links this point directly to 1 Peter 1:3: "We would not have to suffer if it were not that we are 'begotten again unto a lively hope by the resurrection of Jesus Christ from the dead.'"[2] Suffering of the Christian community "tests" our faith in this sense: it points us to the lasting shadow of the cross that extends over earth's landscape.

Salvation. Faith may lead to suffering in the short term, but 1 Peter affirms that its ultimate goal is salvation: "You are receiving the outcome of your faith, the salvation of your souls" (v. 9). Some have understood salvation as a future reward given to those who remain faithful throughout their lives. Others have interpreted salvation as a quality of present life, wholeness of being here and now. Paul Tillich suggests a balance: "Salvation is derived from *salvus*, 'healthy', or 'whole', and it can be applied to every act of healing: to the healing of sickness, of demonic possession, and of servitude to sin and to the ultimate power of death."[3]

In this passage, salvation has both future and present dimensions: "a salvation ready to be revealed in the last time" (v. 5) and "you are [already] receiving . . . the salvation of your souls" (v. 9). This dialectical view of salvation offers clear-eyed joy in the present and living hope for the future, on the far side of death and judgment, when Christ will be revealed in glory.

MARTHA MOORE-KEISH

Pastoral Perspective

one is given by divine mercy, made possible by the resurrection of Jesus Christ, and secured in heaven. It will be best received as a gift and best known through the life of genuine faith. What constitutes such genuine faith is where a preacher can anchor a quality sermon on this memorable passage.

Genuine faith will always possess the impetus to rejoice, regardless of circumstance. This may be one of the toughest realities for Christians to adopt. We may profess joy with our lips, but when the chips of life are down, will we rejoice from the center of our being? Can we find a way to elicit praise even in life's darkest moments? True joy is not a piece of, or an addendum to, the Christian life; it weaves itself into every facet of the Christian life.

The author of the Peter letter speaks several times of joy. He connects "an indescribable and glorious joy" (v. 8) with the suffering of "various trials" (v. 6). Joy and suffering go together in a genuine faith. Most of the time in Scripture, joy actually springs from sorrow or suffering. It can even be a consequence of defeat. It need not arise from the neatness of life, when all is running smoothly. Paul is emblematic of those who know that joy and sorrow are comingled—never separated entities in the eyes of God. In fact, he wrote his most remarkable treatise on joy from a prison cell.

A pastoral approach to preaching on this 1 Peter text will find a way to help listeners wade through their hardships so as still to be moved to praise. Worshipers can be reminded that they were made for joy. If only we could eliminate all hurts in the world—all of the pain, grief, and disappointment. However, no one ever promised as much, and Christians who seek to live a genuine faith often discover that joy is sown in tears.

Jesus left us an inheritance that is "imperishable, undefiled, and unfading." The preacher should turn to the contents of this inheritance. Remember, Jesus bequeathed two things to his disciples before departing: peace and joy. The first he breathed; the second he lived. "I have said these things to you so that my joy may be in you, and that your joy may be complete" (John 15:11).

PETER W. MARTY

2. Karl Barth, *Church Dogmatics*, II/1 (Edinburgh: T. & T. Clark, 1957), 406.
3. Paul Tillich, *Systematic Theology,* vol. 1 (Chicago: University of Chicago Press, 1973), 146.

Exegetical Perspective

gospel. When it is confirmed at Christ's Parousia, the whole world will see it and give praise to God.

A second, related reason for Christians' experience of exclusion and hostility is a somewhat more conventional view of suffering as testing or training for virtue.[3] First-century Jews and pagans alike reflect on human suffering in terms of its educational value. To suffer righteously, not because of one's wickedness or error, is an opportunity to be made stronger. First Peter says Christian faith is more costly than gold, a precious metal "that, though perishable, is tested by fire" (v. 7). So also, Christian faith is purified by suffering.

These words sometimes sound masochistic to modern believers, particularly in the West, where our faith is not only seldom tested, but is rarely even noticed by outsiders. We tend to think of ourselves as surrounded by a culture that is at the least benign and at the best supportive of our confessions. We think, therefore, that we must look to Christians in non-Christian contexts to see the kind of suffering to which 1 Peter speaks. We point to Korean pastors in prison or Iraqi Christians driven from their homes or underground Chinese congregations. Of course those communities are better able than we to hear the comfort 1 Peter offers. It is not necessary to look only so far from home, however, for analogies.

Western Christians too sometimes find ourselves at odds with our culture and our neighbors and families. The marginalization of the so-called mainline churches means we now stand outside the circles of power we only recently inhabited. Some Christians' convictions about the death penalty, about fair housing, about a living wage for the poor, about immigration reform, or about foreign policy make them opponents of popular social and political trends. Christians' varied experiences of the faith move some also to embrace movements for justice within the church that are decidedly unpopular with other groups of Christians. These too might be seen as contexts within which 1 Peter's assurance can be a comfort: "Although you have not seen [Christ], you love him; and even though you do not see him now, you believe in him and rejoice with an indescribable and glorious joy, for you are receiving the outcome of your faith, the salvation of your souls" (vv. 8–9).

E. ELIZABETH JOHNSON

Homiletical Perspective

to God for their liberation (from sin and death) and constitution (as a people). It makes sense to us how the *early* church sang praise for their birth to a living hope, to an "imperishable, undefiled, and unfading" hope (v. 4). In point of fact, however, our own praise is fading—whether old songs, new songs, or any songs that have God for their subject, God's work for their object.

Yes, we *get it*, what Peter is saying; but that only means we will not be *gotten*. It is *interesting*, to one degree or another, perhaps even worthy of more thought and due consideration—but singing about it feels kitschy.

No wonder preachers find preaching on this day so hard to do. We are called to proclaim praise, to enable praise, to give reason and voice to jubilation! Many of us demur, content in ourselves that such self-forgetful praise is a vestige of a precritical zeitgeist.

We may be squeamish about this kind of material, but Peter maintains that genuine faith generates genuine praise. He harbors no illusions about this life, one way or the other. Contra prosperity theology, Peter maintains that there will be suffering to accompany the faithful precisely because of their faithfulness. Then, contra those whose faith is only cruciform, there is the assertion that the suffering is not the last word at all, and in fact is not even the first word—just a weak middling word between the great words of creation and re-creation.

What does the resurrection mean for us as a people? It means there is a "not yet" to the fullness of the salvation, but a "now" to the anticipation and joy of that fullness. That alone is reason enough to sing. Accordingly, one of the more poignant sentences in all of Scripture also occurs in verse 8: "though you do not see him now, you believe in him and rejoice with an indescribable and glorious joy." Believe in him? Sure. Rejoice with unutterable and exalted joy? That is another challenge entirely, one that the preacher will do well to take up this Low Sunday.

THOMAS R. STEAGALD

---

3. Charles H. Talbert, *Learning through Suffering: The Educational Value of Suffering in the New Testament and in Its Milieu,* Zacchaeus Studies (Collegeville, MN: Liturgical Press, 1991).

John 20:19-31

¹⁹When it was evening on that day, the first day of the week, and the doors of the house where the disciples had met were locked for fear of the Jews, Jesus came and stood among them and said, "Peace be with you." ²⁰After he said this, he showed them his hands and his side. Then the disciples rejoiced when they saw the Lord. ²¹Jesus said to them again, "Peace be with you. As the Father has sent me, so I send you." ²²When he had said this, he breathed on them and said to them, "Receive the Holy Spirit. ²³If you forgive the sins of any, they are forgiven them; if you retain the sins of any, they are retained."

²⁴But Thomas (who was called the Twin), one of the twelve, was not with them when Jesus came. ²⁵So the other disciples told him, "We have seen the Lord." But he said to them, "Unless I see the mark of the nails in his hands, and put my finger in the mark of the nails and my hand in his side, I will not believe."

Theological Perspective

Whereas John celebrates Easter morning as a witness to Jesus' ascension and return to God, Easter evening and the following week are narrated in terms of resurrection appearances in which Jesus returns to and commissions his disciples. Among the theological themes that arise in these verses are the peace that comes in the presence of the resurrected one, the mission entailed in resurrection, and the importance of continuity between the crucified one and risen one.

Notwithstanding the strong message that Mary Magdalene announced to the disciples earlier in the day, the curtain rises on the scene of this passage with them fearfully meeting behind locked doors. Now John shifts the focus from the empty tomb as testimony to Jesus' abiding presence in the life of God, to a resurrection appearance of Jesus to these frightened disciples. Without explanation, Jesus is among them, speaking directly to their fear: "Peace be with you." Not once but twice Jesus gives the greeting (vv. 19, 21), inevitably recalling the words of comfort that he had spoken at the Last Supper: "Peace I leave with you; my peace I give to you. I do not give to you as the world gives. Do not let your hearts be troubled, and do not let them be afraid" (14:27).

The difference between the words of peace in chapter 14 and chapter 20 is that the latter come not from the faithful threatened one, but rather from the

Pastoral Perspective

In some parts of the Christian church this Sunday after Easter is officially dubbed Low Sunday. For worship leaders and worshipers of any tradition, that can seem like a very apt description, indeed. Although this Sunday is also called the Second Sunday of Easter and is meant to be the joyous continuation of the Easter celebration, in many churches it can feel like Low Sunday. The Easter lilies have been taken away, the fanfares are but an echo of what bounced joyously around the room the week before. There are fewer people and less hoopla. Perhaps the pastor is taking the Sunday off. To be in worship on such a day can feel a bit like showing up at a party after most of the guests have left and those who remain report on what a grand time you missed by coming too late.

It may be helpful on such a Sunday to remind our parishioners—and ourselves—that we missed Easter also, by a mere two thousand years. We have never lived at any time other than the time after Easter. For most of us, every Sunday is more like the Sunday after Easter. We can hear the accounts, but we were not really there. We did not see and touch and experience it for ourselves.

It is common to focus on Thomas and his doubts. He is even given the nonscriptural moniker "doubting Thomas," as if he is the designated doubter. So it can be helpful to be reminded that Mary Magdalene

²⁶A week later his disciples were again in the house, and Thomas was with them. Although the doors were shut, Jesus came and stood among them and said, "Peace be with you." ²⁷Then he said to Thomas, "Put your finger here and see my hands. Reach out your hand and put it in my side. Do not doubt but believe." ²⁸Thomas answered him, "My Lord and my God!" ²⁹Jesus said to him, "Have you believed because you have seen me? Blessed are those who have not seen and yet have come to believe."

³⁰Now Jesus did many other signs in the presence of his disciples, which are not written in this book. ³¹But these are written so that you may come to believe that Jesus is the Messiah, the Son of God, and that through believing you may have life in his name.

Exegetical Perspective

An interesting aspect of John's Gospel is the number of recurring characters in it—not just Simon Peter and the brothers James and John, all secondary characters of the Synoptics. In John's Gospel, Philip and Nathanael are more important than John and James, who are not named at all. Philip calls Nathanael (1:43–51), answers Jesus' question about how they are to feed the multitude (6:6–7), and wants to see his Father (14:8–11).

Philip also intercedes for some Greeks who wish to see Jesus (12:20–26), and with Andrew, who comes from the same town he does, Bethsaida. Andrew follows John before he follows Jesus, but he precedes his brother, Simon Peter, whom he invites to come to see the Messiah he has found (1:40–41). We do not know who calls Thomas, or why Thomas is called "the Twin," but he is another character who plays more than one part in John's story of Jesus and his followers.

In connection with this story in chapter 20, we have tended to think of him as "doubting Thomas," but he is hardly only that. At the beginning of chapter 11, he may be "courageous Thomas" (or even "foolish Thomas") when he says to his fellow disciples, who are reluctant to follow Jesus to Bethany, "Let us . . . go, that we may die with him" (11:16). Did not someone just try to stone Jesus there?

Homiletical Perspective

The human mind searches for order: to make sense of things, to understand the world, to organize all the data that comes to our awareness. This is the impulse that pushes us toward scientific discovery. It is at the core of legal argumentation and forensic debate. It is the reason that we love mystery stories. We possess the keen desire to follow the evidence until a mystery is solved.

Faith is a mystery of the heart that the mind wants to solve. To admit that we take certain things on faith is to say that we are willing, in limited circumstances, for things not to make perfect sense. Still, we want faith to be shored up by certain evidences, so that the leap of faith is a manageable one. In Easter season we celebrate the biggest mystery of faith: that Jesus was slain for the sins of the world and that he rose from the grave. This fact of faith, compared to all the other fantastic stories about Jesus (healing miracles, walking on water, knowing people he has never met), is the hardest one for the human mind to apprehend. Nothing in life is more certain than death. It is easy to determine, as inevitable as taxes, and, above all, permanent. For Jesus to be raised from the dead belies every instinct of the mind. It cannot happen. Period.

The Gospel of John is the story of Jesus written for the courtroom. It not only tells what he did in life; it also gives the motives behind the facts. John

Theological Perspective

faithful resurrected one. The peace that is not offered by the world is the peace that comes from the knowledge that, in spite of all the hurt and harm the world can and does inflict, God's compassion and care embodied in Jesus stands again in their midst, the crucifixion notwithstanding. While Christians have for millennia made the promise of peace from John 14 a staple of funeral liturgies, its reiteration to the frightened disciples makes plain that it supplies courage at points other than the inevitable end of life. It applies at every point where we fear that God's goodwill for the world's well-being is a pious dream, out of touch with the chaos and hatred of everyday life. For the one who offers the words of peace is the very one who has endured the brunt of that chaos and hatred, yet now stands in their midst—risen, indeed!

No sooner is the word of peace offered than the sending of the disciples in mission is enjoined: "As the Father has sent me, so I send you" (v. 21). As Jesus breathes on the disciples and tells them to receive the Holy Spirit, John has succeeded in recalling to his readers' minds the promises of the Spirit or Advocate who would sustain them (14:26; 15:26–27; 16:7b–11, 12–15).

Moreover, Jesus' act of breathing on the disciples also recalls the creative breath of God bringing life into being in Genesis 2:7 and new life to the valley of dry bones in Ezekiel 37:9.[1] Thus mission is made possible by the power of the Spirit, who simultaneously represents the continuing presence of the risen Christ with his disciples and the creative power of God always at work to enliven creation itself.

Thus empowered, the mission entrusted to disciples then and now involves retaining and forgiving sins, not in any grandly pontifical sense, but by continuing the work of making God and God's ways known in the world. In the church's so doing, the world is brought to judgment and decision through its response to Jesus.[2] To the extent that the world responds to Christ in faith and receives grace to turn away from the narcissism of pride and sloth, sins are forgiven. To the extent that the opposite happens, the world continues in the pride and sloth that are its own destruction. The unequivocal purpose of this Spirit-breathed mission is to offer the new and renewed life that the risen one promises.

A final important theological theme of this text manifests itself in the unfortunate portrait of "doubting Thomas." Typically Thomas is interpreted

1. Gail O'Day and Susan Hylen, *John*, Westminster Bible Companion (Louisville, KY: Westminster John Knox Press, 2006), 195.
2. Ibid.

Pastoral Perspective

saw the empty tomb, but she did not believe until the risen Christ appeared and spoke to her directly, personally. Then, when she told the disciples about her encounter ("I have seen the Lord"), they dismissed her words, because they had not seen for themselves, and locked themselves in a room to hide. When, on Easter evening, Jesus did appear in the dark corner to which they had retreated, he showed them his hands and his side, and it was only then that the disciples rejoiced.

So Thomas was not the only one to have doubts when merely hearing about the resurrection appearances. Like other characters in the story, he wanted to see for himself: "Unless I see the mark of the nails in his hands, and put my finger in the mark of the nails and my hand in his side, I will not believe" (v. 25).

Notice that when Jesus a week later appeared to disciples, this time including Thomas, Jesus did not express impatience with his disciple's skepticism and his need for something more. Instead, Jesus told Thomas, "Put your finger here and see my hands. Reach out your hand and put it in my side. Do not doubt but believe" (v. 27). In other words, "You need something more than a secondhand encounter with me? You want to see for yourself? I do not condemn you. Touch. See. Believe."

We are not told if Thomas took Jesus up on his offer of tangible demonstration of his existence. What we do know is that Thomas's response to that offer—"My Lord and my God!"—is one of the strongest declarations of faith recorded in all of the New Testament. Perhaps it was enough for Thomas just to know that Jesus cared enough to give him what he needed, that Jesus did not despise his doubt. Perhaps that was enough for Thomas to see the risen Christ for who he is and to address him with reverence and awe.

To be sure, Jesus did go on to say, "Blessed are those who have not seen and yet have come to believe" (v. 29). It seems like a particularly fitting blessing for those who show up in worship a week late for the Easter celebration. That also describes the blessing that is offered the previous week as well. Those who gather for worship on Easter morning did not go to the empty tomb and see the risen Christ for themselves, and yet many of them believed. Blessings on you, says Jesus.

It is awfully good news that Jesus blessed Thomas as well. We can be thankful that Jesus did not set up obstacles by expecting his followers to perform acts of credulity that seem beyond us. He was, and is, in the business of meeting people where they are. He is

Exegetical Perspective

Not that Thomas knows what *dying* with Jesus will mean. In the fourteenth chapter, he may be "confused Thomas" with regard to that matter. When Jesus tells his disciples that there are many dwelling places in his Father's house, that he is going to prepare a place for them, and that they know the way there, Thomas interrupts: "Lord, we do not know where you are going. How can we know the way?" (14:5).

In short, as John depicts him, Thomas is much more than simply doubting. Moreover, if we look at the stories in the passage before us—there are two of them, closely related (20:19–23 and 20:26–29) with an interlude (20:24–25)—we shall discover that Thomas expects no more "proof" than the other disciples have already seen, though it is true that he doubts their testimony.

The parallels between the two stories are very close. In the first (20:19–23), Jesus comes to the disciples (without Thomas); in the second (20:26–28), he comes to the disciples *and* Thomas. The two stories have the same setting; Jesus comes among the disciples in the same way, greets them in the same way, and demonstrates his identity in the same way.

In the first story, the disciples are in the house with the doors locked when Jesus comes and stands among them. He says, "Peace be with you." Afterward, he shows them his hands and his side. After that, he repeats, "Peace be with you," and breathes the Holy Spirit into them.

In the second story, the disciples (including Thomas) are in the house with the doors locked, when Jesus comes and stands among them. Again, he says, "Peace be with you." Then he shows Thomas his hands and his side, though inviting him also to reach out and *see*.

It is difficult to overestimate the importance of *seeing* in John's Gospel, where the incarnation comes as light into darkness, where miracles are signs (so that "Seeing Is Believing," as Robert Kysar has it),[1] and where a form of the word "see" is used more than twenty times with the same range of meaning it has in English, from physical seeing to comprehending.

So in these stories Jesus shows his hands and his side to his disciples that they may see them, and they rejoice when they do see him (seeing that it is "him"). Seeing is believing is rejoicing. Thomas's point in the intervening conversation is that he has not seen what they have. "We have seen the Lord," the other disciples tell him. (Are they simply reporting the facts, or

---

1. Title of chapter 3 in Robert Kysar, *John, the Maverick Gospel* (Atlanta: John Knox Press, 1976), 65–83.

Homiletical Perspective

writes in clear, unambiguous terms. He provides simple metaphors to help us understand who Jesus is and how he relates to us (Jesus is the Bread of Life, the Vine, the Good Shepherd, Living Water, etc.). John is not like Mark, who revels in mystery. Mark's Jesus performs miracles and then orders people "to tell no one about what they had seen" (Mark 9:9). Mark does not explain things, but confounds them: "Everything comes in parables, so that . . . they may indeed listen, but not understand" (Mark 4:12).

John, on the other hand, provides a clear message that helps us see the truth. He gives evidence so that people will know with certainty: "these are written so that you may come to believe that Jesus is the Messiah, the Son of God, and that through believing you may have life in his name" (John 20:31).

The story of skeptical Thomas is quintessential John. Jesus is risen and has appeared to his followers. When Thomas hears of this extraordinary event, he is unconvinced. He is like us. If something sounds too good to be true, it is almost certainly untrue. Such things are hard to believe. They demand evidence. The mind cannot make the leap of faith based merely on the testimony of friends. What makes greater sense is that they, in their emotional upheaval, are speaking of things they imagine, things they wish could be true. Such testimony is highly impeachable. Only one thing will prove the case: evidence.

When Jesus appears eight days later, Thomas is with them. He demands proof. His mind searches for clarity. Jesus proves an effective witness. He knows that belief depends upon some evidence. He lets Thomas probe his fresh wounds. Thomas's finger comes away with blood on its tip. This is real. This is proof. This is the truth. Jesus *was* killed—and he *is* risen. He is risen indeed! Perhaps it was Thomas himself who coined that Easter cry that we still use with astonishment today. John knows that we need such stories: unambiguous, detailed, evidentiary witness.

The Second Sunday of Easter is part of what has been known as the Great Fifty Days, the period between Easter and Pentecost. The historical practice of preachers was to use this season to explain the mysteries of the faith to those recently added to the faithful by baptism at the Easter Vigil. Their preaching (known as the mystagogical catechesis) taught things the mind has difficulty comprehending. It is no surprise that the writings of John have become associated with this period.

John's intention is to explain the mysteries to believers. He is still doing this today, and the story of Thomas rings as helpfully as ever. The further

John 20:19-31

Theological Perspective

negatively as a disciple who cannot take the other disciples' testimony as adequate, but instead has to see Jesus for himself before he will believe. However, a careful review of the passage reveals that all the disciples have essentially the same evidence offered to them as Thomas.[3] Jesus "showed them his hands and his side" (v. 20), even as he pronounced his first blessing of peace. Thomas wants the same assurance of hands and side, even if he is more graphic in stating his need to put his finger on the nail marks of Jesus' hands and to put his hand in Jesus' side. Either all the disciples are doubters, or there is something else that needs attention.

What Thomas and all of the disciples need in their encounter with the risen Jesus is assurance—that the one from whom they hear the word of peace and by whom they are commissioned to represent God in the world is the very one who was crucified, dead, and buried. Only that one heralded the reign of God at hand and embodied the reality of that dawning reign in his teaching, healing, and presence. The risen one must have the nail prints and the wounded side to manifest the triumph of God's grace in the face of deepest tragedy.

Thus it is not that Thomas doubts anything. He merely, along with the other disciples, needs to know that the one in their midst *now* is the one who has called them together *then*. Though we latter-day disciples may be blessed for believing though not having actually seen those telltale signs ourselves, we are disciples capable of greater faith and courage because we trust that Thomas and the others saw them on our behalf. Thereby we are assured that the risen one is indeed the crucified one. Thus hope endures.

D. CAMERON MURCHISON

Pastoral Perspective

like a good doctor, in that he does not give the same prescription to everyone. Instead, he approaches his followers in different ways because, after all, our experiences are different and our approaches to life are different. He finds a way to bless us.

According to John, that is the way Jesus handles doubt. He gives us what we need. John concludes this passage by commenting, "Now Jesus did many other signs in the presence of his disciples, which are not written in this book. But these are written so that you [us!] may come to believe that Jesus is the Messiah, the Son of God, and that through him you may have life in his name" (vv. 30–31).

That is the way most of us have come to believe. We did not see or touch. We were not there. We heard. Someone told us the story in a way that invited us to say yes. We heard someone say something, perhaps a small something, that spoke to us, as if calling our name, from depth to depth. There was a sermon, a passage, a prayer. We heard.

If those in our congregations need something else, something beyond the verbal, beyond the simple telling of the story, something that looks and feels more like life, then that is OK also, John seems to say. Jesus can still give them—each of us—what we need. So, for instance, we are invited to come to the Lord's Table, to open our empty hands, to touch and taste for ourselves. On this Sunday—whether we experience it as Low Sunday or approach it as the Second Sunday of Easter—Jesus still has the power to give us what we need.

MARTIN B. COPENHAVER

---

3. Cf. Frances Taylor Gench, *Encounters with Jesus: Studies in the Gospel of John* (Louisville, KY: Westminster John Knox Press, 2007), 137.

Exegetical Perspective

do they say it mockingly? We do not know.) Thomas replies, "Unless *I* see him, too, I will not believe." Then he does see. Again, that is what Jesus invites him to do, to put out his finger and *see*. Then, having seen—there is no evidence in the passage that Thomas also touches, though there is also no evidence that he does not—Thomas confesses his belief: "My Lord and my God!"

Seeing and believing are hardly the only themes in the passage, though they unite the stories both with the interlude and with their conclusion, which is, most scholars are convinced, the original conclusion of the Gospel. Another theme concerns the fearfully locked doors, which nevertheless cannot keep out God's grace. Indeed, neither the doors nor fear can prevent the risen Christ's coming to his disciples. They may be able to lock others out, but they cannot lock him out. His "Peace be with you" may be another way of saying what the angel says (and Jesus also says) to Mary in Matthew's account: "Do not be afraid" (Matt. 28:5, 10).

Seeing and believing are not the only themes in these stories. Moreover, as the second story concludes, it is possible to believe without seeing. Jesus says to Thomas, "Have you believed because you have *seen* me? Blessed are those who have *not seen* and yet have come to believe" (20:29). So it is also possible to believe without having seen. What is written in the book (that the reader must be able to see to read—and read to comprehend) are Jesus' signs, legible manifestations of his presence, visible testimony to who he is—the light that has come into the darkness, "the true light that enlightens everyone coming into the world" (1:9 NRSV note), so that we also "have *seen* his glory" (1:14).

RICHARD S. DIETRICH

Homiletical Perspective

removed we are from the events of the passion and resurrection, the more urgently we need trustworthy witnesses to provide credence for this inconceivable good news. Does the witness of Thomas hold up today? Can his cry "My Lord and my God!" speak to our faith in this century? It can and it does, provided it is preached boldly by preachers whose own lives have been convicted by this astounding evidence.

It is not, however, the witness of Thomas alone that is convincing. The word of Thomas, spoken through the voice of John, comes to us interpreted by Thomas's legal counsel. Jesus promised in John (15:26) to send an advocate, a counselor, to aid us in our understanding of mysterious things of faith. Preachers rely on the witness of Thomas and John, but we are convicted by the power of the Holy Spirit to bring in the verdict. The human mind wants evidence. The heart needs deeper assurance. John knew that ultimately evidence was not enough. The Spirit is needed to provide closing argument for skeptical minds. In the last analysis, to own the mystery of resurrection is a gift of grace. The evidence merely shores up the conviction given to the heart as faith.

What shall preachers make of this story today? Let it serve, as John intends, as a great witness. Our jury is made up of Thomas's peers, people very much like him both in skepticism and in hope. We hear this evidence and face the choice. Either Jesus is risen, or he is not. On the face of it, it is a simple choice. The One who has hardwired our brains to seek understanding also holds the key to the heart. When preachers proclaim the good news, the persuasive power of the Spirit sweeps through the jury box and wins a verdict that evidence cannot prove. He is risen indeed!

CLAYTON J. SCHMIT

Acts 2:14a, 36-41

¹⁴But Peter, standing with the eleven, raised his voice and addressed them, . . . ³⁶"Therefore let the entire house of Israel know with certainty that God has made him both Lord and Messiah, this Jesus whom you crucified." ³⁷Now when they heard this, they were cut to the heart and said to Peter and to the other apostles, "Brothers, what should we do?" ³⁸Peter said to them, "Repent, and be baptized every one of you in the name of Jesus Christ so that your sins may be forgiven; and you will receive the gift of the Holy Spirit. ³⁹For the promise is for you, for your children, and for all who are far away, everyone whom the Lord our God calls to him." ⁴⁰And he testified with many other arguments and exhorted them, saying, "Save yourselves from this corrupt generation." ⁴¹So those who welcomed his message were baptized, and that day about three thousand persons were added.

Theological Perspective

Repentance, baptism, and the Holy Spirit are here, all packaged up as a bundle of theological topics, all ready for controversy. Even apart from these themes, this passage vividly portrays the longing of the human heart for the life offered in the gospel: Even though Peter's first sermon ended in accusation rather than invitation, three thousand sought to enter the new community of faith.

Peter had three thousand inquirers asking what to do. He started with the least seeker-sensitive theme: repentance—"Repent, and be baptized" (v. 38), to be more precise, a pairing analogous to that of faith and baptism found elsewhere (e.g., Mark 16:16). This supports the idea that baptism is primarily a call to new life or an act of established discipleship, as in traditions that practice believer's baptism. Baptism certainly contains this call. Descent into the waters portrays death to old ways, and rising up signifies new birth in Christ, the actions embodying the call for repentance, a changed mind (cf. Rom. 6:3–14). We are not merely born to better ethical and moral behavior. We are born to life in Christ, joined to Christ's body the church. We need a transformed mind to begin to see through Christ's eyes, and to guide our transformed lives participating in his mission of reconciliation and justice. The intensity of this call to discipleship presented in baptism is seen

Pastoral Perspective

This passage from Acts begins on the day of Pentecost, after a diverse crowd of amazed spectators has gathered around the apostles. The apostles themselves have experienced something like a violent rush of wind, and a phenomenon that Luke describes as something like "divided tongues" (2:3), or tongues of fire, that has appeared to them and rested upon them. This Holy Spirit of God then suddenly and urgently grants the apostles the ability to speak and be understood in languages other than their own. It is this final spectacle that gathers a crowd. The text gives no sense that people in the crowd even feel the rushing wind or see the tongues of fire, but they do hear themselves addressed by the apostles in their own native languages, and even this impresses them deeply. They hear these Galilean Christians testifying to God's power in words they can understand, and they are amazed.

Acts 2:14a, 36–41 depends upon this joyful Pentecostal context, but has been separated from it. The passage has also been separated from all but the end of Peter's response to the curious crowd. The lectionary passage begins as Peter stands to respond, but is quickly truncated at verse 14a, before he has spoken one word. It picks up again at verse 36, without any reference to the force of Peter's apologetic in verses 14b–35. Thus separated twice from its

Exegetical Perspective

According to Luke, this event occurs on the day of Pentecost (2:1), a Jewish harvest festival period historically commemorating the giving of the Law on Mount Sinai, fifty days (Gk. *pentēcostē*, "fifty") after the exodus from Egypt. This initial sermon of Peter, as Luke depicts it, sets the stage for the developing Christian community as a people whose primary task is to "witness" to the events they have seen and heard. For Luke, the headquarters for the mission is "Jerusalem" (1:12; Luke 24:47–49; *not* Galilee, as in Mark 16:7–8).

With Jesus' departure, the group replaces Judas and organizes the mission for the community (Acts 1). In this idealized portrayal, the message is clear: Jesus' followers immediately engage in the process for continuing the mission that Jesus has set for them to become "witnesses" to the "ends of the earth" (1:8; cf. 1:22).

On the day of Pentecost, Jesus' followers are "filled with the Holy Spirit" (Acts 2:4), a promise Jesus gave the disciples at the end of the Gospel of Luke (Luke 24:49). The immediate result of this empowerment is that they speak in the various languages represented in the audience on that day (2:4–11a), which—in turn—fulfills (literally) the mission offered in Acts 1:8. Peter's speech addresses questions this phenomenon raises: How are we hearing these Galileans speak in our native languages? What does this mean? Are they drunk?

Homiletical Perspective

The conclusion of Peter's Pentecost sermon has, unfortunately and incorrectly, served as a springboard for those who preach with an anti-Jewish agenda. Peter is undeniably preaching to Israelites and unabashedly pointing out their guilt as he tells the story of Christ's victory over the cross: "Therefore let the entire house of Israel know with certainty that God has made him both Lord and Messiah, this Jesus whom you crucified." Verse 36 is the second time he has pointed to their responsibility (see also v. 23).

Nonetheless, it is necessary to recognize Peter's position as a Jew among Jews. "Fellow Israelites," he addresses them in verse 29. Implied here is not simply a religious and cultural kinship, but also a likeness in guilt. We recall Peter's own denials of Jesus following Christ's arrest. Though Peter had vowed in Luke 22:33, "Lord, I am ready to go with you to prison and to death!" Jesus predicted that Peter would deny him three times. Peter, having fulfilled that prediction, knows the conviction of guilt more deeply than most. However, for this very reason he also knows so profoundly just how good the good news is. His understanding of God's will in Christ to overcome human betrayal and rejection is, of course, rooted in his experience of being forgiven for his own betrayal. His persistence in pointing to the responsibility of his fellow Israelites in the death of

Theological Perspective

in the next passage, where the new believers are led to radical changes of lifestyle, including economic redistribution and new spiritual disciplines.

Though baptism contains a call, there is also an emphasis here on baptism as promise. To Lutheran and Reformed theologians of the sixteenth century, this emphasis made infant baptism tenable. First, there is the statement of baptism's purpose: it is for forgiveness of sins (v. 38). The Reformers saw the promise of forgiveness in Christ as the heart of the gospel, described in Paul's terms as justification by faith. The action of baptism communicates this most directly: as water washes bodies, the sacrament proclaims the promise that God graciously washes away sin.

Second, Peter emphasizes baptism as a gracious gift, rather than a disciple's response, when he extends the call for "every one of you" to be baptized by saying that the promise is also "for your children" (v. 39). John Calvin took this phrase as quite sufficient to silence any opposition to infant baptism, taking the act as God's seal, or signature on the promise.[1] A little child cannot repent or believe in any way adults can discern, nor can an infant commit any particular sins. On the other hand, one can certainly pronounce God's promises over a baby, saying truly that through Christ we belong to God, are part of Christ's body the church, and that in him we have forgiveness. God's love comes before the speaking of the promise, so the process does not begin with baptism. But in baptism the promise is proclaimed, and cannot be revoked. The sign of this promise is given to the world, as well as to the child, who will be reminded of it later. The child will need to grow up, hear the gospel, and respond with faith and repentance—but telling the good news begins now.

There is also a third aspect of promise in Peter's directions to the new converts: "you will receive the gift of the Holy Spirit" (v. 38). There is a tantalizing ambiguity here. Is Peter saying that the gift they will receive is the very presence of the Holy Spirit, God dwelling within and working to make us new people in Christ (see Gal. 5:16–25)? Is he saying they will receive the particular dramatic gift of tongues, through which they heard of God's mighty acts in their own languages that very morning (Acts 2:5–13)? Is he saying that they will receive the kinds of gifts for service Paul writes about in his letters, or even faith itself (see 1 Cor. 12:4–12, 27–31; cf. Eph. 2:8)? The ambiguity continues elsewhere in Acts, since the

1. John Calvin, *The Acts of the Apostles 1–13*, trans. John W. Fraser and W. J. G. McDonald, *Calvin's New Testament Commentaries*, vol. 6 (Grand Rapids: Eerdmans, 1965), 79–83.

Pastoral Perspective

rhetorical power, the resulting pericope could easily mislead a naive reader and lead one to conclude that the conversion of members of the crowd occurred independent of what they heard and independent of Peter's full apologetic.

The passage presents us with the last words in an exhortation by Peter proclaiming the divinity of Jesus, followed by his concluding assertion that Jesus' execution occurred at the hands of Peter's listeners: "God has made him both Lord and Messiah, this Jesus whom you crucified" (v. 36). In this abridged version of the story, Luke goes on to tell us that his hearers are stricken when they hear this, and that some three thousand persons "welcomed his message [and] were baptized" (v. 41). On its own, taken out of context, this passage presents modern Christians with a very serious interfaith dilemma. Lifted out of Acts, the astonishing beauty and mystery of the gift of the Spirit to the apostles is superseded by the bold declaration of Jesus' authority and power, and the very evidence of the Spirit's power to unite people is supplanted by a bond forged in indictment and guilt. It becomes disarmingly easy to read this passage out of context in a dangerously anti-Semitic way.

It is paramount, therefore, to take care with the presentation of this passage, which presumes not only familiarity with the larger story but sophisticated understanding of its argument. The conversion of some three thousand people, based seemingly on the testimony of Peter that the very Jews themselves to whom he is speaking (in v. 36, "you") crucified Christ, is a major stumbling block to any interfaith sensitivity or dialogue. The preacher will not want to interpret the text in ways that could lead the congregation to conclude that it is the Jewish people who are guilty of the crucifixion of Jesus.

The passage does describe the overwhelming response of people from the crowd—many of whom are baptized that very day—and this seems to be the major point of the lectionary reading. Whatever else Peter has said, here he asserts the messianic identity of Jesus and his innocent death at the hand of his detractors, and people respond. They are converted, even to the point of baptism in Christ's name. If we are not to presume that they submitted to baptism out of a personal sense of guilt for complicity in Jesus' death, what does transpire in the story, and how might one understand its meaning today?

Popularly, we might see the repentance of Peter's listeners as the proper pious and contrite response to an accusation. Peter points out to the assembled Jews

Exegetical Perspective

Peter's speech is a type of "sermon," or, at least, Luke's idealized summary of Peter's sermon. Peter must have said more, but Luke emphasizes a few key elements (see below). Peter's brief story of Israel points to the story of Jesus. Jesus' coming is the central element of God's story with Israel. His coming initiated the activity of the Spirit that is realized in their midst. The rhetorical nature of this speech is midrashic in orientation, that is, an explanation (midrash) follows a citation from Scripture. Our lectionary reading offers the concluding note on this sermon and the reaction to Peter's argument, in which the Israelites react favorably and join the growing number of Jesus' followers.

What is missing from the lectionary reading is the core of the sermon, a speech that includes the following themes: (1) Luke's Peter draws on Joel to explain the pouring out of the Spirit upon sons, daughters, and slaves as one of the signs of God's final redemption (2:16–21); (2) he charges the Israelites with the death of Jesus "by the hands of those outside the law" (2:22–23); (3) he draws on the psalms of David, through whom the Spirit speaks (David is called a "prophet" by Luke only, 2:30; cf. 1:16) to highlight God's resurrection of Jesus, a descendant of David (2:24–35).

The central feature of Peter's speech is defining the kind of Messiah Jesus was. In ancient Judaism, most people expected the messianic figure to be a political figure with access to military power. He would arrive on the scene to throw off the political overlords of the day. He would reestablish the empire of David in the world and inaugurate God's empire. Peter's emphasis is different.

The idea of "repentance" is a key motif in the book of Acts. It is central to Peter's message to Israelites (2:38; 3:19; 8:22) and Paul's message to Gentiles (17:30; 26:20). The term is associated with seeking forgiveness for thinking incorrectly (cf. 2:38; 3:19) and acting inappropriately (8:22). In our present lectionary passage, the idea of repentance is directly associated with the "gift of the Holy Spirit" for the Israelites (2:38). Later, in Acts, there is an analogous scene for Gentiles, in which "speaking in tongues" occurs again (10:44–48; cf. 11:15–18).

In the nineteenth century there was a "revival" of interest in experiences associated with these first-century developments, especially those associated with "speaking in tongues." In some of these charismatic circles, there was a direct connection to the idea that such "tongues" were directly associated with speaking actual "languages" in the contemporary

Homiletical Perspective

Christ is not about assigning blame to one distinct group of people and exonerating others; rather, it is about inviting sinful people to know a grace that is far stronger than even the greatest of sins.

As preachers work to apply the message of grace to modern minds with current concerns, Rowan Williams's words in a 2009 speech on "Ethics, Economics, and Global Justice" prove insightful:

> What religious belief has to say in the context of our present crisis is, first, a call to lament the brokenness of the world and invite that change of heart which is so pivotal throughout the Jewish and Christian scriptures; and, second, to declare without ambiguity or qualification that human value rests on God's creative love and not on possession or achievement. It is not for believers to join in the search for scapegoats, because there will always be, for the religious self, an awareness of complicity in social evil.[1]

Preachers might take on the task of lifting up our human complicity in the sinfulness of *any* context, not for the sake of berating the guilty, but, rather, for the purpose of encouraging Pentecost-like transformation and an awareness of human value rooted, first and foremost, in the grace and love of God. The power in a preacher's reminder for people to find worth in the outpouring of God's very self in love (as opposed to finding worth and a lack thereof in one's accomplishments and failures) cannot be overestimated.

The thrust of this pericope has to do with the crowd's very admirable response to the bold message that Peter has proclaimed. The people do not act defensively; rather, they are "cut to the heart" and they ask the disciples, "What should we do?" (v. 37). Perhaps Acts idealizes those early days just a bit. Even so, imagine how receptive we might be to the Spirit's movement if we could listen like the crowd without the need to defend!

Peter responds: repent, be baptized for the forgiveness of your sins, and receive the Holy Spirit (v. 38). The debate about Peter's intention and the conditionality of forgiveness remains alive and well. Are sinners forgiven only after repenting and being baptized? Is the Spirit's arrival dependent upon these prerequisites? These are interesting questions, but Acts seems not too concerned with them. Only eight chapters later Peter baptizes the Gentile Cornelius and his household *following* the Spirit's descent upon them. Acts is more interested in conveying the compelling force of the Spirit's movement. The resurrection of

1. http://www.archbishopofcanterbury.org/2323

Acts 2:14a, 36–41   403

Acts 2:14a, 36-41

Theological Perspective

Spirit can come before baptism (Acts 10:44–48) or long after (Acts 19:1–6). Again, different traditions place the emphasis differently. After a century in which Pentecostal Christianity swept the globe, it is hard to read this passage without assuming Peter's promise is the gift of tongues, but for nearly two millennia Christians had no such expectation.

No matter what one thinks about these issues, both the call and the promise remain powerful in this passage. The call is to those who are there hearing the gospel: "Save yourselves from this corrupt generation," he says (v. 40), dangling the promise before them at the same time. Neither call nor promise is merely personal. When he says, "The promise is for you, for your children, and for all who are far away" (v. 39), he calls them to bring that promise to others.

The unfolding story will show that God's gracious intention is to draw in many who are not there in Jerusalem, including Saul, who was so opposed to the way of Christ that he took a job as persecutor (Acts 22:4–5). God's intention in Acts is to reach out even beyond the bounds of the nation and religion, as Peter and then Paul take the gospel to the Gentiles (Acts 10:9–43; 13:45–47). This is, of course, the very plan of Luke's Gospel and Acts, where the disciples are witnesses to Jesus "in Jerusalem, in all Judea and Samaria, and to the ends of the earth" (Acts 1:8). To belong to Christ through repentance and baptism is to receive a call. We are to participate in Christ's mission, taking the promise of forgiveness in Jesus and new life through the Spirit to our neighbors and communities, our nations and the world.

GARY NEAL HANSEN

Pastoral Perspective

their complicity in Jesus' death, and the people, stricken by his words, repent and are baptized. However, looking at the chapter as a whole, it makes more sense to say that the people do not respond primarily to some assertion of their own complicity in Jesus' death. They respond because Peter's apologetic for God's saving activity includes this very audience— their lives, their Scriptures, and their concerns. The entire passage is predicated upon a new and amazing unity of language, so that the fact that these diverse peoples all heard their own experiences reflected in these strangers must have been very moving.

As Peter stands and addresses the people, rather than imagining the force of his indictment of his listeners, one might become equally or even more convinced of the power of their inclusion. When we read the entire chapter, we see that it is a story not of condemnation but of invitation. The book of Acts describes an interstitial period for Judaism and Christianity, when the two world religions, which share a common history and tradition, have not yet separated into two distinct strands. Because we are so accustomed to the institution of the church and even the Christian nation, it is impossible for modern Christians to imagine the apostles as representatives not of an institution but of a nascent movement, people of "the Way."

This is the story Luke is led to reveal, the story of Christianity's unique message growing up in the midst of both real spiritual quest and great diversity. Peter's apologetic begins with the common ground, with shared Scripture and tradition. It is in the form of a narrative, an appeal, rather than an exaction of blame. In preaching even just his closing remarks, something of the unity that was experienced that day, something of the intrigue and invitation, must be expressed along with the fact of Jesus' death, especially since Jesus lives again and the Spirit that he promised has appeared. Even this pericope makes room for that.

SUSAN B. W. JOHNSON

Exegetical Perspective

world. In other circles, the "tongues" were defined as "heavenly languages," that is, "unknown" and unrelated to any known human language.

According to Acts, Peter has become the de facto leader of the Jesus movement after Jesus' departure. This development is not clearly indicated in the first part of the two-part series (i.e., the Gospel of Luke). The third Gospel is the only one of the Synoptic Gospels that chooses not to include Peter's confession of Jesus as Messiah. Matthew's account adds Jesus' extremely positive assessment of Peter's confession—"flesh and blood has not revealed this to you" (Matt. 16:17)—along with an acknowledgment of Peter's future leadership role (Matt 16:18–19). Luke's Gospel is much more ambiguous about Peter's potential as a leader.

Crucial to this account is the "global" audience who speak in a variety of languages (e.g., "Parthians, Medes, Elamites, and residents of Mesopotamia, Judea and Cappadocia, Pontus and Asia, Phrygia and Pamphylia, Egypt and the parts of Libya belonging to Cyrene, and visitors from Rome, both Jews and proselytes, Cretans and Arabs," 2:9–11). A word of caution is in order. In Peter's context, putting the blame on the Jewish leadership (2:36) rather than on Rome (3:13–15) makes sense in a context in which the Way is viewed as a sect of Judaism. Peter's critique provides an "in-house" critique. In our contemporary world, the internal analysis can still be pertinent as long as the characters in the story are relabeled. To contemporize a straightforward literal interpretation runs the danger of anti-Semitism. Christianity, unfortunately, is no longer as closely related to its sister religion, Judaism.

Luke may view the outpouring of the Spirit as a new giving of the Law, since this event occurs on the day of Pentecost. Just as God gave the Law to Moses and Israel on Mount Sinai to initiate the shaping of the identity of a people, so for Luke, the *Messiah* is responsible for the giving of the Spirit to shape the (new) identity of this new people. For these early Spirit-inspired followers of Jesus, the Messiah himself is a charismatic, Spirit-granting agent of God. So, what are the new ways in which God's Spirit inspires and shapes the identity of the Christian community today?

EMERSON B. POWERY

Homiletical Perspective

the crucified Jesus has given birth to the outpouring of the Spirit and the fulfillment of prophecy (2:17–21, 29–35). Christ lives and his ministry is revealed through the witness and proclamation of his followers, who are empowered by the Spirit. The thrust here is that the movement is building with impressive force. The day began with 120 believers and ended with 3,000!

Regardless of the order, people are repenting, being baptized, finding forgiveness, and experiencing the Holy Spirit. The church is emerging as a community wherein lives are connecting with and being transformed by a boundless God who was incarnate in Jesus and in the witness of those who welcomed the Spirit. This passage offers us, as preachers and leaders of congregations, the wonderful and important opportunity to reframe congregational activities in the context of the church's original experience with the Spirit. When a congregation shares this experience, all the administrative work, the meetings, the efforts to remain financially stable, all that energy is tied to a purpose that empowers it. On the other hand, when that vision of the church's primary experience is forgotten and not shared, a congregation finds itself tired and shrinking. Today's pericope offers the opportunity for preachers to lift up that early vision so that congregations may reclaim their existence as the church of Christ.

A pastor once asked a group of vacation Bible school children what forgiveness felt like. The class of six-year-olds looked up at him blankly. Suddenly, an expression came over one child's face. It was clear that an idea had struck. He smiled knowingly and raised his hand. "I know what forgiveness feels like," said the child. "It feels like it's your birthday. It feels like you get to start again new."

In his Pentecost sermon Peter is inviting fellow sinners to start again new. The Holy Spirit is guiding the people of God into new life, and a sacred community called the church is being born. This Third Sunday of Easter is a time for congregations to surrender their defenses and rejoin the movement.

TIMOTHY B. HARE

Psalm 116:1-4, 12-19

¹I love the LORD, because he has heard
  my voice and my supplications.
²Because he inclined his ear to me,
  therefore I will call on him as long as I live.
³The snares of death encompassed me;
  the pangs of Sheol laid hold on me;
  I suffered distress and anguish.
⁴Then I called on the name of the LORD:
  "O LORD, I pray, save my life!"
. . . .
¹²What shall I return to the LORD
  for all his bounty to me?
¹³I will lift up the cup of salvation
  and call on the name of the LORD,

Theological Perspective

As we seek to gather our wits on the Third Sunday of Easter, we could be forgiven at this point for finding it difficult to maintain a meditation upon the risen Christ in the thick of days that occasionally feel distinctly un-Eastery. How might we sustain a sense of resurrection while keeping a grip on *this-worldly* existence, the realm of life *before* death, the space where our metaphysical musings will have to take hold if they are to take hold at all? This lection invites us to bring our imaginations to bear upon concrete moments of recognition concerning the goodness of God, a sense of resurrection to be accessed and attested to in the details of the hours between Sundays. Might *that* have something to do with *this*? Might we cultivate a sense of connection between the wonder-working power that raised Jesus from the dead (Eph. 1:19–22) and the revitalizing presence of the God we call upon from week to week? Are we to believe that the same power is somehow at work in us? If so, how?

As we take up the testimony of the psalmist, we note that the words of exultation are neither speculative nor somehow dutifully optimistic. It is precisely for having been decisively heard and specifically saved that the psalmist feels compelled to announce, "I love the LORD." The witness does not entertain a God who, in some vague or strained sense, might yet

Pastoral Perspective

If we were to give this psalm a simple title, it might be "Why I Love God, and How I Demonstrate That Love with My Life." The psalmist says, "I love the LORD, because he has heard my voice and my supplications. Because he inclined his ear to me, therefore I will call on him as long as I live" (vv. 1–2). We are presented with the remarkable image of God, Lord of the universe, bending down and turning an ear to listen when the psalmist cries. So much for the notion of God as distant and unavailable! Our God is not too occupied with running the universe to take time to listen when one of God's children cries for help.

What is the psalmist crying about anyway? He describes the pressures of sickness and impending death. The psalmist's depiction of his predicament in the Hebrew text is exquisite and all too familiar to us in the twenty-first century. Verse 3 may be translated, "The cords of death surrounded me; the constrictions of Sheol squeezed me. I found trouble and sorrow." It is as though, while wandering through a dimly lit forest, the psalmist has been grabbed by a huge python that is inexorably squeezing the life out of him. There is no escape. There is no hope.

Our congregants know how he feels. Many of them recall times in their lives when they, or their loved ones, have literally faced death. A solemn-faced doctor has delivered the grim prognosis as

¹⁴I will pay my vows to the L<small>ORD</small>
    in the presence of all his people.
¹⁵Precious in the sight of the L<small>ORD</small>
    is the death of his faithful ones.
¹⁶O L<small>ORD</small>, I am your servant;
    I am your servant, the child of your serving girl.
    You have loosed my bonds.
¹⁷I will offer to you a thanksgiving sacrifice
    and call on the name of the L<small>ORD</small>.
¹⁸I will pay my vows to the L<small>ORD</small>
    in the presence of all his people,
¹⁹in the courts of the house of the L<small>ORD</small>,
    in your midst, O Jerusalem.
    Praise the L<small>ORD</small>!

Exegetical Perspective

While scholars might discuss whether the psalms were used in communal worship or personal prayer, a liturgical underpinning manifests itself in almost every psalm. Psalm 116 is no exception. Traditionally understood as an individual hymn of thanksgiving, the psalm continues to be used in multiple contexts. The psalm, part of the Hallel (the Talmudic name for Psalms 113–118), is recited verbatim as a prayer in public performance as part of some traditional Jewish celebrations. Perhaps written for the celebration of the feast of Hanukkah, the Hallel has long been recited during the pilgrim festivals, Passover (Pesach), the festival of Booths (Sukkot), and the celebration of the Giving of the Torah (Shavuot). In some traditions, the Hallel is also read at the Beginning of the New Month (Rosh Chodesh), at the feast of Unleavened Bread, and at the festival of Pentecost. Appropriated in contemporary contexts as well, one example appears in Richard Smallwood's *I Love the Lord*, sung by Whitney Houston in the movie *The Preacher's Wife*, where the first verse of the psalm coincides with the opening and title of the song.

The framework of the psalm as a whole provides rhetorical interest. Shifting in voice and tone at least seven times, the psalm sets a dialogical tone—perhaps providing a leader:people responsive reading in liturgy. The psalmist balances personal experiences

Homiletical Perspective

A Prayer of Thanksgiving. When is the proper time to give thanksgiving (praise and adoration) to God? Do we give thanks to God merely because something incredibly good has happened to us, or because it is a regular part of our spiritual discipline? Sports fans have seen many an athlete give a sign of adoration to the sky when a home run is hit to win the game, when a new world record has been set, or when a touchdown pass has been caught to win the Super Bowl. Folks are quick to praise God when a family member has recovered from an ailment that was thought to have been incurable. However, what if a person happens to be on the losing side of an athletic contest? What is the proper response when a loved one does not respond to surgery, medication, and rest as expected? Does this mean that our God is not as caring or loving toward us when things do not work out according to our hopes and dreams? Does this mean that our God has not actually heard our prayers? Of course not. A proper understanding of thanksgiving acknowledges that thanksgiving is a faithful and proper response to all the vicissitudes of life.

The psalmist begins on a note of complete adoration to a God who has already answered his prayer, "I love the L<small>ORD</small>, because he has heard my voice and my supplications." The reader is faced with the question, would the author be filled with as much love and

Psalm 116:1-4, 12-19

Theological Perspective

come through. On the contrary, this God has been called upon by a beleaguered party, one for whom all hope was lost, and this God has heard and responded to the call. A life overcome by death and disorder has been redeemed and reordered. The testimony recollects the specific experience of pain and abandonment and thereby deepens this claim of absolute assurance of having been heard and lifted out of darkness, a claim that explains and undergirds the psalmist's startling profession of love.

In this sense, this lectionary prayer in which we are invited to enlist our own voices expresses a sensibility of believing realism. Out of the particulars of abandonment, a verifiable sense of disenfranchisement, the faithfulness of God has been, from time to time, visibly realized. In view of this faithfulness we claim and by which we feel claimed, a reorientation is called for. Against the popular presumption that it is owing to our own excellent efforts and exemplary decision making that we have somehow wrestled from the chaos a space of personal flourishing, safety, and peace of mind, we assume a posture of loving receptivity and gratitude to the Lord who has inclined an ear to hear our cries. As we credit God with the sustaining powers our thriving depends upon, we are made to undertake a reinvigorated consideration of our material circumstances, entering into an awareness that the power of God is alive and signaling, even within the minute particulars, a redeeming concern that charges and illumines our every nook and cranny. We note and rehearse again this God-givenness to our existence, a sense of contingency that occasions both mindfulness and worship. An opening has occurred, and within it, the faithful will locate themselves, calling on the Lord with candor, thankfulness, and expectation as long as they live.

The commitment to do so, to cry out aloud in this way and bank everything on the faithfulness of God, is expressed in the opening line of the psalm ("I love the LORD"). Indeed we can see this affirmation as a response to the question the psalmist poses in the last verse: "What shall I return to the LORD for all his bounty to me?" (v. 12). If we allow the lection to double back in this way with the psalm's end contained in its beginning, the idea that the speaker loves the Lord *because of* blessings bestowed might strike us as less self-serving. More in keeping with the doctrine of justification *by grace* through faith, the psalm presumes as a given that there is no giving back to the Lord in some material sense, no giving back save a witness to God's saving work. Lifting up the cup of salvation (v. 13) as one who was uprooted and now is rooted

Pastoral Perspective

one of them has sat in stunned silence before asking, "How much time left?" Other church members have struggled not so much with physical death but with emotional or spiritual death: a loveless marriage pressing the joy out of life, financial woes strangling the ability to live with any sort of freedom, a high-pressure and unrewarding job that crushes gladness and fulfillment from the soul. Our congregants know about the cords of death and the constrictions of Sheol.

Then the psalmist announces a divine reprieve from this seemingly inescapable death sentence: "Then I called on the name of the LORD: 'O LORD, I pray, save my life!'" (v. 4). By God's unimaginable mercy, the sentence is commuted; the psalmist is saved from physical, as well as spiritual death (vv. 8–9). The remaining verses of the psalm are primarily a description of the psalmist's response to God's amazing power and love.

How will the psalmist respond? "I will lift up the cup of salvation and call on the name of the LORD, I will pay my vows to the LORD in the presence of all his people. . . . I will offer to you a thanksgiving sacrifice and call on the name of the LORD" (vv. 13–14, 17). The psalmist responds with *public* thanksgiving to God and with *public* fulfillment of responsibilities to God offered within the gathered faith community. What a marvelous and *challenging* vision of the faithful life!

Unfortunately, we live in a time of shallow, privatized, and individualized faith characterized by statements such as the following: "What I believe is between God and me"; "I am spiritual, but I do not practice *organized* religion"; "I am Christian, but I practice my faith by myself by being a good person." For too many church members, faith has become little more than mouthing the words "I believe in God and in Jesus" as some sort of magic formula. There is not a public and communal dimension of thanksgiving and responsibility. Perhaps the preacher can even recall instances when persons have prayed for healing in the face of terrible illness, devastating emotional trauma, or almost certain death. When healing did come, there was little thanksgiving offered to God, or the thanksgiving was short-lived—a couple of perfunctory appearances at worship before relegating thanksgiving and worship to the dustbin. How sad.

The psalmist will have none of this. God has granted him healing and saved him from death. So his entire life is transformed. He will be thankful to God *publicly*. He will be responsible to God *publicly*. He will love God in return *publicly*.

Exegetical Perspective

with a recounting of both the transcendent and immanent characteristics of the Divine. Taken as a whole, the psalm provides a chiastic structure (as defined by a reversal in order of two otherwise parallel words or phrases, as in A B C C B A) as follows:

1	A	The Lord hears my voice
2	B	I call on the Lord
3	C	Cords of death compassed me
4–5	D	I call on the name of the Lord
6	E	He [*sic*] saved me
7	F	The Lord dealt bountifully
8	G	You saved me from death
9–11	G	You let me live
12	F	All God's bounty
13a	E	The cup of salvation
13b–14	D	I call on the name of the Lord
15–16	C	You saved me from the bonds of death
17	B	I call on the name of the Lord
18–19	A	I pay my vows to the Lord[1]

Grammar and morphology (the shape of the word in Hebrew) have long presented challenges for translators of the psalms, and Psalm 116 is no exception. For example, a typical translation (KJV, NRSV, NASB, ESV) of verse 1 begins with "I love the Lord," but presenting such a translation requires the addition of a direct object after the subject and verb, "I love," where there is none in the Hebrew. A more literal translation of this verse would be "I love, for the Lord heard my cry for mercy."

Translation again proves interesting in verse(s) 4 (and 8) with the Hebrew word *nephesh*, often translated "soul." In the Shema in Deuteronomy 6:4–6 (translated in the RSV as "Hear, O Israel: The Lord our God is one Lord; and you shall love the Lord your God with all your heart, and with all your soul, and with all your might. And these words which I command you this day shall be upon your heart"), *nephesh*, translated "soul," is set as one of three human attributes, along with "heart" and "strength." While "soul" may have served as an adequate translation at some points in history and tradition, the connotation of *nephesh* often becomes trapped in a body-soul dichotomy. The Hebrew word carries a fuller, more comprehensive meaning, something along the lines of "the whole self," representing the totality of one's being. Thus verse 5 of the Shema would be translated, "You shall love the Lord your

1. Identified by scholar Robert Alden in "Chiastic Psalms (III): A Study in the Mechanics of Semitic Poetry in Psalms 101–150," *Journal of the Evangelical Theological Society* 21, no. 3 (Summer 1978): 199–210.

Homiletical Perspective

thanksgiving if things had not gone as well? However, to be obsessed with thoughts such as this overlooks the force of the message that is before us.

Psalm 116 is essentially a prayer of thanksgiving. We are not given the specifics of the event that occasion its writing. However, it is quite clear that the psalmist considered himself/herself to have been close to death.

> The snares of death encompassed me;
> the pangs of Sheol laid hold of me;
> I suffered distress and anguish. (v. 3)

Approaching "Death." Something important can happen to people when they are at the brink of death. They can either succumb to that which they consider to be inevitable, or they can surrender to the Divine. Succumbing to the inevitable can leave a person literally gasping for each breath, thinking that it represents a finite end. For them it is impossible to realize that there is something beyond what we can touch, see, feel, or hear—a wind or *pneuma* (spirit or wind) beyond what we can breathe. Surrendering to the Divine leaves people on their knees with the understanding that they must submit themselves to the will of the one who alone has the authority to heal both body and soul.

There is a certain finality to physical death, but that does not mean that other types of death cannot be just as debilitating. Spiritual death, when one feels separated from God, displays a void that leaves a person without life. Emotional death, when a person has been emptied of all love and feeling toward others, can be equally painful. (Divorce can leave one in this state.) There is hope present in this psalm that delivers the promise of salvation to all who may feel as though they are on the precipice of a death. This is expressed in verse 4, as the psalmist beseeches, "O Lord . . . save my life."

A Thanksgiving Sacrifice. The first four verses of this particular psalm give thanks and praise to the Lord for salvation. Verses 12–19 focus the attention of the reader on an authentic way for the faithful actually to give thanks.

The wording of verse 12, "What shall I return to the Lord for all his bounty to me?" is reminiscent of the language of Micah 6:6,

> With what shall I come before the Lord,
> and bow myself before God on high?

The contexts of the writings are very dissimilar. Micah addresses the need to ask forgiveness for sins

Psalm 116:1-4, 12-19

Theological Perspective

anew, was lost and is now found, might be properly viewed as a feat of attentiveness on the part of the place-bound psalmist, a commitment to mindfulness and truthful speech open to public scrutiny, the public that is the presence of God's people (vv. 14, 18).

All of this is in keeping with a profound understanding of God's gifts. The lives that we live and the breath we use to speak of that life are all gift, all the time. Prayer, in this account, is speech that knows (or means to know) what it is doing. Here is how Eugene Peterson expresses the matter: "Prayer is speech at its most alive. The breath that is breathed into us by God is breathed back by us to God. When we pray we are using language closest to the source of language.... We habituate ourselves to the language native to the country of salvation, the land of the living."[1]

How do we go about enacting—or living out—a response to the saving, healing, redeeming love of God? For starters, the context of such living is—can only be—the sweet old world we are already in, "the country of salvation." The response we bring, the sacrifice of praise we offer, is, perhaps paradoxically, a *thanksgiving* sacrifice (v. 17). The energy we bring to our attempted obedience originates with the God we call the giver of all good things, the God whose purposes toward us, we are assured, do not end in entropy, corruption, or decay (Ps. 16:10). In the meantime, this redeeming power, the power signaled both in the biblical accounts and in our experience of the risen Christ, is to be realized primarily in the ebb and flow of our life together, our lives that partake of and participate within the body of Christ. Resurrection, in this sense, has nowhere to happen but here.

J. DAVID DARK

Pastoral Perspective

I remember visiting with a family whose three-year-old son had been diagnosed with a large brain tumor that would require surgery. A few days before the surgery, they asked me to come to their home to pray with them, which I did. Then the morning of the operation arrived. About a dozen family members, friends, and I sat in the waiting room of one of the world's great hospitals as a team of surgeons performed the most intricate surgery imaginable. Time crawled as we chatted and tried to think and talk about subjects other than what was actually happening in the operating room. Gradually, the waiting room emptied as work was completed on the other patients, and their families left. Behind our smiles, the tension building among us was almost unbearable.

Finally, after almost six hours, the receptionist called the mother and father of the boy over to her, and she told them that their son had come through the surgery successfully. The couple collapsed into each other's arms, and, of course, the rest of us burst into tears of relief and joy as we hugged anybody in the vicinity. The receptionist herself began to cry and said, "Now you people cannot do this to me. I still have several hours left on my shift." A nurse also joined the celebration as she hugged us and proclaimed again and again, "Yes, he is able! He is able! He is able!" At last, the family asked me to pray with them. We stood and held hands in a circle, and I could barely choke out the words, "Loving God, we are so grateful . . ."

A character in one of Walker Percy's novels asks, "Suppose you ask God for a miracle and God says yes, very well. How do you live the rest of your life?"[1] The psalmist has made his answer clear. How do you live, indeed?

JEFF PASCHAL

1. Eugene Peterson, "Land of the Living," *Ex auditu* 18.1 (2002): 176.

1. Walker Percy, *Love in the Ruins: The Adventures of a Bad Catholic at a Time Near the End of the World* (New York: Ivy Books, 1971), 320.

Exegetical Perspective

God with all your heart, with your whole self, and with all your might." Verse 4 of Psalm 116, which the NRSV translates as "Then I called on the name of the LORD: O LORD, I pray, save my life," would be rendered, "Then I called to the name of God: Please— God—please deliver my whole being."

Verse 15 presents a long-standing exegetical challenge for translators. A literal rendering of the Hebrew yields: "Precious/esteemed/valued in the eyes of YHWH [is] the death to/of/upon his pious/kind/ devoted." The word translated "the death" is a *hapax legomenon*, a word that appears only once in the available texts, here in Psalm 116. While scholars have presented various interpretations to explain why God would find the death of God's devoted ones precious, others have seen fit to emend the text. The addition of a single letter in the middle of the Hebrew word would change the meaning of the word from "the death" to "the trust," so that the verse would be translated: "Precious in the eyes of God is the trust of God's devoted ones," a translation remaining in keeping with the rest of the psalm's emphasis on trust. Such an emendation could be justified in consideration of how a manuscript copyist could easily and accidentally leave out a letter (a letter that looks quite like a single line) when making a copy of the psalm.

The lectionary reading (vv. 1–4, 12–19) omits a crucial aspect of the psalm in verse 7, which provides the psalmist a point of self-reflection in the form of a command. Spoken in the imperative, the verse says, "Turn, my whole self, to my resting place/condition of rest." Omitting the commas, an alternative translation would read, "Turn my whole being to my resting place." In other words, I can, I must, turn to my point of rest in God, because God has delivered me.

ALICE W. HUNT

Homiletical Perspective

(both individual and corporate), while Psalm 116 presents an image of thanksgiving from one who has been delivered from a near-tragic situation. However, both challenge the contemporary reader to embrace only those forms of worship that are truly genuine— from the heart.

Who is truly at the center of our acts of thanksgiving? In nations such as the United States that actually set aside a national holiday for "thanksgiving," it is quite apparent that much of the attention has become focused on the self. We have our special meals to prepare and to consume. We think about where we are to go, whom we are to be with, which football game we are to watch. Mention of the need to thank the one who constantly provides us with all that we need is normally an afterthought in the form of a prayer hastily thrown together or during a sparsely attended community ecumenical worship service. Unfortunately we are too consumed by thoughts of the self even to realize what we need to be doing. It does not need to be that way. The words of the psalmist present a beautiful image of service,

> I will offer to you a thanksgiving sacrifice
> and call on the name of the LORD.
> I will pay my vows to the LORD
> in the presence of all his people.
> (vv. 17, 18)

Atlanta (like many other cities) provides multiple venues for people to give thanks in authentic ways. On holidays such as Thanksgiving, Christmas, and Easter, there are opportunities to volunteer in soup kitchens, visit the homebound, and assist the homeless. These opportunities are, of course, available throughout the entire year. When we give of ourselves, these are authentic activities through which we give thanks to our God.

JOHN E. WHITE

1 Peter 1:17-23

¹⁷If you invoke as Father the one who judges all people impartially according to their deeds, live in reverent fear during the time of your exile. ¹⁸You know that you were ransomed from the futile ways inherited from your ancestors, not with perishable things like silver or gold, ¹⁹but with the precious blood of Christ, like that of a lamb without defect or blemish. ²⁰He was destined before the foundation of the world, but was revealed at the end of the ages for your sake. ²¹Through him you have come to trust in God, who raised him from the dead and gave him glory, so that your faith and hope are set on God.

²²Now that you have purified your souls by your obedience to the truth so that you have genuine mutual love, love one another deeply from the heart. ²³You have been born anew, not of perishable but of imperishable seed, through the living and enduring word of God.

Theological Perspective

One of the most complexly rich intersections in theology is that between Christology and soteriology. Scripture's witness to Christ's work and its effects is manifold, providing theologians a diverse array of images, ideas, and experiences to mine. At the same time, the churches have not pronounced dogmatically in this area, aside from Chalcedon's decisions on Christ's person, so that we are free and even encouraged to explore a diversity of interconnections in order to flesh out the full depth and breadth of Christ's work to save and our experience of God's love in that work. Calvin, for example, uses the rubrics of Christ's threefold office and our justification and sanctification to play out an eclectic vision of the impact of Christ's work and history on our lives.[1]

This passage from 1 Peter explores one path through this garden. Peter's exposition centers on soteriology—the fruit that Christ's work bears in our lives—but only as that soteriology is grounded in a christological vision. The end to which this passage is driving concerns our sanctification—our shaping into persons who bear an obedient love for one another—but it is a christological argument that gets us to this place. In Peter's understanding, Christ's

1. See Stephen Edmondson, *Calvin's Christology* (New York: Cambridge University Press, 2005), for one description of Calvin's work in this area.

Pastoral Perspective

In the world of gardening, there are seeds that are perishable, and there are seeds that are imperishable. Anyone who has ever shaken the morning glory seeds off the dried-up plant in the fall knows this wonderful fact. The seeds fall like rain into the dirt below, and the next magnificent season of "morning glory" is almost surely guaranteed. Not so with the six-packs of hothouse hybrids, planted one spring and gone forever at the first freeze.

Writing to a community of people who were keenly aware of the transient nature of their faith, the author of 1 Peter attempts to lay some groundwork for Christian longevity and future generations. Whether this community was being harassed openly for their belief, or just marginalized and made to feel self-conscious, the author coaxes confidence from new believers: "You were ransomed from the futile ways inherited from your ancestors, not with perishable things like silver or gold, but with the precious blood of Christ" (v. 18). Though silver and gold in any context are rarely seen as perishable, still the tone is set: Jesus' death and resurrection will have lasting power like nothing else you know. Later the wordplay will be used again. This time the reference will explain how being born anew is irrevocably attached to the "imperishable seed" that is actually the "living and enduring word of God" (v. 23).

Exegetical Perspective

Verse 17 begins the third in a series of four imperatives sketched in chapter 1 by the author. First, on account of the mercy of God (vv. 3–12), believers are *to set their hope* completely on the coming grace (1:13). Second, on account of the holiness of God, believers are *to become holy in every aspect of life* (vv. 14–16). Third, on account of God's impartial justice and the liberation effected by Christ's death, believers are *to live in reverent fear* (vv. 17–21). Fourth, on account of their consecration of themselves and their new birth, believers are *to love one another deeply* (vv. 22–23). These last two commands stand in parallel insofar as both are cast in familial terms. Already known for calling upon God as "Father" (v. 17), believers have experienced a "new birth" (vv. 3, 23) and are now recognized as sisters and brothers, a kin group. In the context of trying times, the author counsels a fresh way of understanding past, present, and future, as well as a rejection of ancestral and contemporary conventions for behavior—a response of resistance made possible by a liberation that reverberates with echoes of the story of Israel's exodus from Egypt.

The author has at least two important reasons for portraying things past. Consider, first, a slogan from the world of 1 Peter: "the old is better." If the author dismisses the former lives of his readers as "futile ways inherited from your ancestors" (v. 18), he must

Homiletical Perspective

On this Sunday, preachers will be drawn to the Emmaus road, and it will be difficult to take a detour into 1 Peter. Chances are good that last Sunday's sermon skipped this letter too, focusing on Thomas's encounter with Jesus rather than the opening lines of this letter to "the exiles of the Dispersion." It is, however, not too late to consider preaching a series of sermons on 1 Peter over the following Sundays. Preaching on the epistles is most effective when preacher and congregation can dig deeply into the letter over time rather than dipping in for only a moment. What is the setting of this letter? What do we know about the community? What issues are at stake? Why does the author address these people as "exiles"? The exegetical material, starting with last Sunday, will be especially helpful to give historical background and set the context for this letter. (Such insights will be especially important when people hear troubling words next Sunday about being beaten.)

Think of 1 Peter as an Easter letter, not only written to people living centuries ago, but passed down to your particular community in these days after Easter. As your congregation hears this letter over the next few weeks, the preacher can help people make the connections between struggles faced by those exiles in Asia Minor and people who feel in exile now. This exile may be spatial. How many

Theological Perspective

Pastoral Perspective

ransom of our souls opens within us a trust of God, an obedience to the truth, and a love for one another. This dynamic of soteriology flowing out of Christology reflects the deeply christocentric view of the world found in the first chapter. There Peter moves from our birth into hope through Christ's resurrection, to the love for Christ that we find in this new birth, to the holiness that this hope and love should form within us. The consistent movement here is from Christ's work to our sanctification.

At the heart of our passage, then, is a robust understanding of what Christ has done for us that marries what we might call an objective understanding of that work with a subjective understanding, yielding an unusual result. The letter offers us first the metaphor of Christ's ransoming us from our bondage by the price of his blood. The metaphor of ransom is a powerful one in Christian theology, collecting into one a strong sense of our bondage in sin, the price of Christ's blood, and the freedom that we find in Christ. However, the metaphor is problematic as well, as various theologians have pointed out, most notably Anselm.[2] Vladimir Lossky summarizes Gregory of Nazienzen's earlier objection to this metaphor, asking from whom Christ ransomed us.[3] Satan has no true claim on us, as a liar and a thief, and surely God need not ransom us from himself.

Peter's use of this image, however, offers us a third way to understand it. He testifies to Christ's ransoming us from our own futile ways, and argues over the course of this passage that his ransom turns us in trust to God, in obedience to the truth, and in love to our neighbor. It seems, for Peter, that Christ ransoms us from ourselves—from our captivity to our own broken wills. Christ pays the concrete price of the gift of himself to free us from our bondage, but he buys for this price a reformation of our wills, a change of our hearts. Christ's objective work here is fundamentally relational.

If we turn from the christological foundation of this passage to the soteriological dynamic that it imagines, 1 Peter depicts a clear progression in our spiritual reformation. The center point of this progression is our holiness. In the verses immediately preceding this passage, the letter reminds us of God's command in Leviticus that we are to be holy as God is holy (Lev. 11:44–45). So a clear goal in our passage is our obedience to the truth, a clear marker of our holiness. Coupled with this command in the earlier

While we cannot possibly know what it might be like to live out our faith in a climate of constant persecution, North Americans are certainly familiar with the perishable. Even with a growing awareness of all things green, the "throwaway" nature of life is, well, natural. When computers fail, they are thrown out, not fixed. When cell phones die, they are replaced with the newer model. When the toaster breaks, China will provide us with another in the time it takes to walk out to the alley and deposit it in the trash bin. Extended to the arena of health, the human body has "throwaway" parts as well. New eyes, new hips, new hearts can be expected when the first fail. The thought that one might die with all original body parts intact is a fleeting one. North Americans understand perishable.

"Imperishable" may be as foreign to a postmodern as it was to an ancient. For the new Christian living in exile in the first century, to take on belief in Christ would mean shaking off some real fears about isolation. Would faith in Jesus enhance an already-tentative existence in the world? Would it just open the way for more heartache and despair? What would it mean to be at the start of such a movement? Cradle Christians can hardly picture the way without the patriarch or matriarch of the church family out front taking the first set of blows for the cause.

A cleaner connection between old and new may be made with the newest members of our church communities, that population of young adults left adrift by boomer parents who wanted their children to "make up their own mind about faith." They come to faith communities all on their own, with no background, no family allegiance, no collection of Sunday school attendance pins. They have no baptismal certificate and seem hungry for knowledge about why one would even consider the sacraments. "What is Christmas really all about?" is not an unusual question. Never satisfied with a simplistic faith, new members soak up information like a child first learning to read. What might it mean to overcome the fears of affiliating with an "institution," something no postmodern should be caught dead doing? What might it mean to anchor one's life in the imperishable and enduring word of God, when all around them the perishable runs the show? It is happening. The teaching bears up under the test of time for a new generation of first-time believers.

Across all of time, God's people search for meaning and purpose in life, and the author of this epistle works at shedding some light on that quest. The life of faith that leads one to God is the key. Christ

---

2. Anselm of Canterbury, *Cur Deus homo?*
3. Vladimir Lossky, *The Mystical Theology of the Eastern Church* (Crestwood, NY: St. Vladimir's Seminary Press, 2002), 152.

provide them with a heritage of at least equal antiquity; this he does, with reference to "the foundation of the world" (v. 20). Second, in a way both reminiscent of Greco-Roman historians and at home with Israel's own historical interests, the author urges that, beneath the surface of day-to-day events, divine guidance is at work. This is true even of Christ's sacrificial death, an act of horrendous suffering that gains significance when understood within the whole narrative of God's eternal purpose. This is important because the audience of 1 Peter is marked by experiences of suffering as a result of their following Christ rather than their own ancestral traditions. Roman culture valued what was handed down from generation to generation, and to break from one's ancestral religion was to invite disaster in the form of recriminations from the gods thus scorned. Accordingly, those who set aside ancestral traditions invited contempt for undermining the fabric of society by engaging in nonconformist behavior.

The author conflates three images in order to articulate his atonement theology: (1) "liberation" or "ransom"—derived from God's liberating Israel from enslavement in Egypt (e.g., Exod. 6:6; 15:13; Deut. 7:8; Isa. 43:1); (2) the image of the "lamb" borrowed from the Passover sacrifice (Exod. 12)—celebrated annually, Passover both memorialized and reappropriated for generations of God's people God's election and great act of deliverance; (3) the combination of "blood" and "a lamb without defect or blemish," recalling Israel's system of sacrifice. In a pivotal text, Leviticus 17:11–14, the shedding of blood—regarded as the substance of life and therefore sacred to God—signifies the offering of the lives of those for whom the sacrifice is made. Here, the life of an unblemished animal substitutes for blemished human life, thus restoring right relations with God. In 1 Peter 1:18–19, "the futile ways inherited from your ancestors," rather than sin and its consequences, is the focus of redemption. This suggests the potency of the desires of that former life, as though an "inherited way of life" and its "desires" might serve as forces against which God has undertaken battle.

With regard to the future, in this section of the letter the author refers only to the nature of future judgment—and he does so above all to speak of the character of God. Today, the reference to God's impartiality in judgment (v. 17) might suggest notions of God's neutrality or objectivity in matters of justice. To the contrary, even if the pages of Israel's Scriptures include references to divine impartiality (e.g., 2 Chr. 19:4–7), the scales of divine justice are

members were born in this city or town? Who moved here from another place? Raise your hand if you have moved more than three times in the last five years. Some people have never left the town where they were born, yet the world seems to be changing around them. *I do not know any of these new hymns. Who are these new people? Why do they not they speak English?* Exile is far more than a matter of geography.

You might find ways to connect Cleopas and the unnamed disciple with those who received this letter. We last see the two disciples as they bring news of Jesus' appearance to the others in Jerusalem. They were so excited when they recognized Jesus in Emmaus that they ran back to Jerusalem in the dark—not a time to be on the road! They could not wait to share the news, so they ran in the dark, filled with bread and resurrection. Perhaps they stayed in Jerusalem with other disciples, waiting in the city for the gift of the Holy Spirit. Who knows where they went from there?

Let us imagine that they traveled north out of Jerusalem into those places named at the beginning of this letter: "To the exiles of the Dispersion in Pontus, Galatia, Cappadocia, Asia, and Bithynia." Unroll a large map or project a map on a screen so people can see we have arrived in Turkey—that is, a real place, then and now. Even if Cleopas and his friend never made it that far, they passed the word along to others, who passed it on to others. By the time this letter was written, news of Jesus who had been raised from death had traveled far beyond Jerusalem. The bright light of Easter was shining far beyond the tomb. Can we help people see that spreading light?

When I was growing up in Iowa, it was illegal to sell margarine. Well, not exactly. Stores could sell margarine, as long as it did not look like butter. My father was pleased about this, because we sold Grade B milk for making butter, and we surely did not want competition from something that pretended to be butter! Do you remember how margarine was sold? It came in a plastic bag and looked like a lump of white lard—except for one thing: there was a bright red-orange pellet of color in the middle of the bag. Even though my dad refused to have oleo in the house, my grandma dared to buy a package now and then. Sometimes, when I was staying with her, she let me squeeze the bag. I pressed my fingers into that bright red-orange dot until it broke open inside the bag. Then, I kept squeezing and squeezing until that bright spot of color had turned the whole lump into beautiful, yellow almost-butter.

1 Peter 1:17–23

1 Peter 1:17-23

Theological Perspective

verses that we strive toward holiness is the clear perception that our holiness flows from the grace that we find in Jesus. Hence, in our passage the trust of God engendered in us by Christ's offer of love serves as the foundation of our obedience. Christ's sacrifice works in us the fundamental conversion from the ways that we inherited, to the new inheritance that is ours in Christ as we learn to trust the ways of God. The holiness born in us from this trust in God then opens our hearts to a true love of our neighbor. As in Luther, true love is not a work that turns God to us, but a fruit of our turning to God in trust, in response to God's love in Jesus.

Revelation—which is a clear soteriological mover in this letter—interlaces the discussion. On the one hand, revelation in 1 Peter bears christological weight, insofar as Christ's revelation to us in Scripture is the primary mode of his presence to Peter's audience. Earlier the letter notes that "although you have not seen [Jesus], you love him" (1:8), and in our passage the letter clarifies that we have come to this love "through the living and enduring word of God" (v. 23). Indeed, it is God's word that brings new life in Christ to birth within us. Revelation in this case serves as the vehicle of Christ's presence to us. It serves, in a broader context, as the vehicle through which God's love presents itself to the world. Inasmuch as the gospel reveals Jesus to us, Jesus reveals God's eternal love. Indeed, it seems for 1 Peter that the eternity of God's love (insofar as Jesus was predestined from eternity) is one basis for our trust in God. First Peter's use of the idea of revelation helps us to see again the intertwining of Christology and soteriology. Through revelation the eternal love of God is manifest in Christ, who is manifest through God's word, and this twofold revelation leads us to trust, obedience, and love.

STEPHEN EDMONDSON

Pastoral Perspective

facilitates a life of hope in God that is reliable, trustworthy, and worth the risks. This life enables one to love from the heart, another radical thought for most Christian newbies. Love might come from eHarmony—maybe. Love might be fostered over the Internet, where backing out is always an option and anonymity reigns supreme. Love might be briefly found, with no real expectation of a lifelong commitment. Love might be expressed in the Boys and Girls Club, but only as a résumé item. Love from the heart? Love that would be imperishable? What a foreign concept!

The implications for literacy around our holy texts are obvious. To understand the word of God as living and enduring, exposure has to be more than surface deep. Multiple tools of interpretation need to be readily available, offered in classes, preaching, and conversation, so that access to this rich resource for life can be offered to the newest and the oldest in our midst.

First Peter stands as gospel news for new Christians who are caught in their own web of risk and reward thinking. To find purpose in a life based on the imperishable is as countercultural a claim as one might make today. To love from the heart with no guarantees and no escape clause is a prophetic statement by any standard or life condition. To find meaning in ancient texts that have been broken open for review, providing palatable food for life, is a responsibility to take seriously. To bear the imperishable seeds (*the very "living and enduring word of God*," v. 23) and shake them off for new birth in the next season is a step toward the church of the future.

There are perishable seeds and imperishable seeds. The hothouse hybrids will not last through the winter. First Peter would have us sow imperishable seeds and be prepared for all the morning glory we can handle.

JOY DOUGLAS STROME

Exegetical Perspective

hardly blind. After all, the God who liberated Israel from Egypt is the God who directs people to show regard for the oppressed and marginal. The idiom the author employs is "to acknowledge someone's face" or "to show favor," particularly with regard to rank or status. The point, then, is that God is not swayed by the measures of prestige prevalent in the world of 1 Peter (e.g., gender, age, ancestry, landed wealth, the status of one's circle of friends), considering instead how one's deepest allegiances and character are displayed through one's practices.

With these perspectives on past and future in hand, we come finally to the real focus of the author's attention, the present, with regard to which the author is now in a position to outline the character of faithful living in the midst of difficult circumstances. He positions his audience as exiles (see 1:1–2; 2:11). For persons thus branded as "not at home," familiar with day-to-day slander and calamity, the temptation is especially to embrace the values and behaviors at home in the wider world. This is the threat of assimilation and defection. As an antidote, 1 Peter counsels "reverent fear" (v. 17) and heartfelt love (v. 22). The latter is framed as familial love, qualified further in a way that allows no room for playacting. Note the structure of the argument in verses 22–23: because you have consecrated yourselves for the purpose of familial love (v. 22a) *and* because God has given you new birth (v. 23), *therefore* you must love one another (v. 22b).

One possible distortion of the author's message in verse 17 is that we might imagine that God's judgment is itself motivation for fearful living. This is countered by reference to God as Father, connoting images from Scripture of God's faithful beneficence rather than God's threatening judgment; by the author's reference to impartial judgment in order to counter concerns with social standing in his world; and by our understanding that "fear" (cf. 1:17; 2:17; 3:2, 14, 16, NRSV sometimes "reverence") in 1 Peter has to do, not with intimidation, anxious dread, or terror, but with the fundamental orientation of one's life toward God, with according the highest value to one's relationship with God, so that it determines all else.

JOEL B. GREEN

Homiletical Perspective

Could Easter be like that? The bright light of resurrection did not stay at the tomb. Resurrection could not be contained in that place, any more than the stone could contain Jesus' body. The two disciples sitting at Emmaus felt the power of that light: "Were not our hearts burning within us while [Jesus] was talking to us on the road, while he was opening the scriptures to us?" (Luke 24:32). That life-giving light did not stay in one place, but spread to Mary Magdalene and Thomas, to Cleopas and—well, we could put our own name in the blank Luke left unfilled. Fifty days later, the red-orange light of resurrection swept down like tongues of fire on women and men waiting in Jerusalem. The good news of resurrection spread like wildfire from Jerusalem to Judea and Samaria and to the very ends of the earth.

Wherever the news traveled, communities began to gather around the story. This news was not private, but plural. Those who heard and believed the good news about Jesus were changed in profound ways. Whatever they had been before, they are now so different that the letter writer says they have been "born anew" (v. 23). Indeed, they are still so new that they have not quite learned how to walk. They are toddlers in the faith. Like Jesus on the road to Emmaus, the writer of this letter opens the Scripture to them. No doubt, those new to the faith had lots of questions. How should we live now? What does it mean to be ransomed? Some of them must have been slaves, a reality that becomes clear as the writer speaks directly to slaves later in this letter. As this portion of the letter builds to a close, we come to the most important question of all: how can we have "genuine mutual love" (v. 22) for one another? The next several Sundays can help preacher and listeners struggle to discern answers to these questions.

BARBARA K. LUNDBLAD

Luke 24:13-35

¹³Now on that same day two of them were going to a village called Emmaus, about seven miles from Jerusalem, ¹⁴and talking with each other about all these things that had happened. ¹⁵While they were talking and discussing, Jesus himself came near and went with them, ¹⁶but their eyes were kept from recognizing him. ¹⁷And he said to them, "What are you discussing with each other while you walk along?" They stood still, looking sad. ¹⁸Then one of them, whose name was Cleopas, answered him, "Are you the only stranger in Jerusalem who does not know the things that have taken place there in these days?" ¹⁹He asked them, "What things?" They replied, "The things about Jesus of Nazareth, who was a prophet mighty in deed and word before God and all the people, ²⁰and how our chief priests and leaders handed him over to be condemned to death and crucified him. ²¹But we had hoped that he was the one to redeem Israel. Yes, and besides all this, it is now the third day since these things took place. ²²Moreover, some women of our group astounded us. They were at the tomb early this morning, ²³and when they did not find his body there, they came back and told us that they had indeed seen a vision of angels who said that he was alive. ²⁴Some of those who were with us went to the tomb and found it just as the

Theological Perspective

The narratives following the crucifixion of Jesus are freighted with *sensus plenior*, a surplus of meaning. Far more than strict chronology, they are laden with theological depth that continues to inspire interpreters of these rich texts. Luke 24 is part of the forty days between resurrection and ascension—that time when Jesus "opens their minds to understand the scriptures" (v. 45). The theological chronology of Luke–Acts provides an interpretive framework for understanding the relationship of Christ and Spirit, which is reciprocal. It also describes the movement from the "discipleship of equals" gathered around Jesus to the larger church, and how witness is sustained by baptism and Eucharist.

This particular text provides far more than a simple recounting of the journey of grieving followers of the man from Galilee, cruelly executed by the Romans with collusion by temple authorities. Throughout the history of the church the story of the encounter of Jesus with bewildered and disconsolate pilgrims has illumined the theology of resurrection, the nature of faith sustained by the Holy Spirit, the promise of Eucharist through hospitality, and the necessity of communal practice.

The resurrected Jesus eludes easy identification. Throughout the Gospels, Luke included, there is both a sense of continuity and discontinuity when

Pastoral Perspective

Three weeks into the church's great fifty-day celebration of Easter, we are reminded that Easter's dawn is a *kairos* moment, not simply a variable date after a full moon. It is easy to get stuck at Good Friday as a custodian of the crucifixion or on Holy Saturday with decimated hopes sealed in a sarcophagus. Everything does have its own season; not everything can come to fruition in a Triduum, a sacred three days of expectation and prayer. Cleopas and the unnamed other have left Jerusalem for Emmaus, a seven-mile jaunt, and are "talking and discussing" (v. 15). Their words and their hearts are heavier than any supplies they carry home from the annual Passover pilgrimage to their holy city, now a city of horrors. They may be headed home after their Seder meal, but the angel of death has not spared their infant hopes for the dawn of a messianic age. They have heard that it is "Easter" from the women at the tomb, but as of yet they do not know it in the marrow of their soul.

On this road of broken dreams, the incognito Jesus joins their journey. The embodiment of their expectations for liberation walks beside them! The raconteur recounts that "their eyes were kept from recognizing him" (v. 16), but does not indicate the source of their blindness. As often happens in a well-told story, the obscured details allow the text to serve as a mirror of the reader. As an act of sanctioned

women had said; but they did not see him." [25]Then he said to them, "Oh, how foolish you are, and how slow of heart to believe all that the prophets have declared! [26]Was it not necessary that the Messiah should suffer these things and then enter into his glory?" [27]Then beginning with Moses and all the prophets, he interpreted to them the things about himself in all the scriptures.

[28]As they came near the village to which they were going, he walked ahead as if he were going on. [29]But they urged him strongly, saying, "Stay with us, because it is almost evening and the day is now nearly over." So he went in to stay with them. [30]When he was at the table with them, he took bread, blessed and broke it, and gave it to them. [31]Then their eyes were opened, and they recognized him; and he vanished from their sight. [32]They said to each other, "Were not our hearts burning within us while he was talking to us on the road, while he was opening the scriptures to us?" [33]That same hour they got up and returned to Jerusalem; and they found the eleven and their companions gathered together. [34]They were saying, "The Lord has risen indeed, and he has appeared to Simon!" [35]Then they told what had happened on the road, and how he had been made known to them in the breaking of the bread.

Exegetical Perspective

The appearance on the road to Emmaus is one of the most enticing stories of the Gospel literature. The story is unique to Luke and characteristic of his style and perspective (a faint echo is found in Mark 16:12–13).

The passage follows Luke's account of the discovery of the empty tomb (vv. 1–12); the women report their discovery to the "eleven" (v. 9) but are met with disbelief. Peter, however, runs to the tomb, finds it as they had reported and goes home amazed. The Emmaus story serves as a transition between this ambiguous reaction to the empty tomb and the ultimate appearance of Jesus to all of the disciples (vv. 36–53).

The account begins poignantly, with two of the disciples who have heard the women's "idle tale" (v. 11) leaving the community and making their way to Emmaus, a village "seven miles" from Jerusalem. They converse about the dramatic events that have taken place. As the story unfolds, they will, in effect, give a summary of Jesus' mission and the story of his passion, but without full understanding. This latter point is one of the fundamental purposes of the Emmaus story—the risen Christ reveals to the disciples the true meaning of his death and resurrection.

The setting of this story in the context of a journey is also typical of Luke, who places Jesus' entire mission in the context of a journey that moves from Galilee to Jerusalem (see, for example, 9:51–53) and

Homiletical Perspective

The morning begins at midday on the road with two sorry disciples who have bet their lives on the wrong savior. Where are they headed? They are headed back to fishing nets, tax offices, missed appointments, and merciful routine. They are on the road that will return them to what T. S. Eliot simply called the human condition, "The condition to which some who have gone as far . . ./Have succeeded in returning. They may remember/The vision they have had, but they cease to regret it,/Maintain themselves by the common routine,/Learn to avoid excessive expectation."[1] What preacher has not asked after the haplessness of the human condition that persists long after the alleluias have subsided? What difference has the claim of a risen savior made, we wonder, if death still appears to have dominion?

Another question insinuates itself into this conversation along the way, a question from a time and place these two could not yet imagine. After Peter rehearsed salvation history for the gathered crowd on Pentecost, joining their lives to the plot already in progress, they asked, "What should we do?" (Acts 2:37). Peter's answer led three thousand to repent and be baptized. The two on the road to Emmaus

1. T. S. Eliot, *The Cocktail Party* (New York: Harcourt, Brace & World, 1950), 139.

Luke 24:13-35

Theological Perspective

followers encounter the one resurrected from the dead. Part of the challenge is that his disciples did not expect a proleptic inbreaking of the end time, but a resurrection at the "last day." When disciples see the risen Christ, there is familiarity and mystery, recognition and confusion. They sense that he is the one with whom they have shared at table; they recognize that he continues to teach and encourage them even in their vanquished hope. While Luke does not articulate a fully developed resurrection theology, the reader can conclude that the stranger these folk encounter on the road to Emmaus can be none other than the crucified one now in their midst. The theology of resurrection affirms that we "will know as we are also known." Relationships of depth, grounded in forgiveness and hope, will endure.

The narrative of Jesus' encounter with Cleopas and fellow traveler also provides insight into the nature of faith. Faith does not require visible proof, although memory can prompt hope. Perhaps they remembered other meals; perhaps they knew the tradition of the Passover meal with his inner circle. Luke's enigmatic phrase, "but their eyes were kept from recognizing him" (v. 16), suggests that a deeper knowing will ensue. The travelers, after imploring Jesus to stay with them, experience a Christophany. They recognize him in the breaking of the bread. The cherished formula: he *took*, *blessed*, *broke*, and *gave* stirs their awareness of his presence, yet they now know him as the risen Lord, whose own body has been given for them. In time, the early martyrs of the church would understand that they too were given over as sacraments of grace; they had become the emblems of sacrifice.

Luke provides a key bridge for understanding divine presence as seeming "absence." Christ "vanished out of their sight" as an indication that visible apprehension could not sustain enduring faith; holy presence would remain, but not in the form they had known. From the beginning of this Gospel, the role of the Holy Spirit has been proclaimed. The one conceived by the Spirit would baptize in the Spirit, as John the Baptist professed (3:16). The hope of Pentecost was that the Holy Spirit would come upon them, and in the Spirit they would recognize the holy presence—although Jesus was no longer physically present. The ascension theology of Luke–Acts offers a tension: that Jesus has been taken up implies that the Spirit has been poured out. The risen Christ offers gifts from his position of exaltation; the Spirit ensures that the teaching of Jesus is vindicated. The presence of the Spirit makes bearable the absence of Jesus.

Pastoral Perspective

voyeurism, readers are allowed, or even invited, to project their own hermeneutic onto the text; the gaps in a detailed narrative help us to locate our reflection and, therefore, our place on the road of heartbreak. Did God restrain their vision? Who among us have not felt blindsided in times of distress and wondered if even God can see what is around the bend? Did their minds, through their narrative interpretation, prevent them from recognizing their role in the drama? Did they miss their entrance in the passion play that now yields to a final act of resurrection? Is their eyesight made myopic by their misery? Do their wounded hearts blind them? Undoubtedly, we can see our reflection in any of these narrative mirrors. The text bids us to look deeply at ourselves; the road leading away from the holy city is ours. The soles of our shoes know the brokenhearted steps of a road away from an unrecognized resurrection.

In an affective coagulate of confusion, sadness, dismay, betrayal, and anger—to sift just a few emotional elements from the quagmire—Cleopas responds to Jesus' insensitive and invasive interrogative concerning their discussion with a long litany. The narrator inserts a creed of an early Christian community, but the writer still has some tenderness in the recitation. There are emotions in the new dogma: "but we had hoped that he was the one to redeem" (v. 21); "moreover, some women of our group astounded us" (v. 22); "but [we] did not see him" (v. 24). It is a creed of a vulnerable head and heart; scavenger angels sweep over the road searching for signs of spiritual life among the fragments. Can faith be found in the rubbish of shattered dogma? The heart knows more than the head.

At first blush, Jesus' response seems to be pedantic in its erudition. It is as if Jesus whips out his pocket Torah scrolls, complete with the Prophets, and gives a multipointed lecture on messianic completion; his PowerPoint is affectively vapid. This exchange reads more like a heady sermon from the Gospel of Matthew than the usual tenderhearted, relational stories from Luke. However, a well-told story also serves as a window from which we can look back into history and draw strength to imagine and move into the future. Jesus shows his connection to the faith tradition of their past. The two travelers on the road, the disciples left in Jerusalem, and other readers to come—they and we are connected not only to a tradition, but also to a hope that yearns for fruition. It is a history of *kairos*, not clocks and calendars. Every blossom blooms in its own season; some come when snow is still on the ground, and others flourish in the

ultimately, through the ascension, to the right hand of God. Luke casts the unfolding history of the early community as a journey, beginning in Jerusalem and reaching "to the ends of the earth" (Acts 1:8). The community itself would be named the "people of the journey" (Acts 9:2; 22:4; 24:14, 22). For Luke the journey of Jesus and of the church itself expresses the unfolding history of salvation that finds its origin in Israel and through the Spirit extends salvation to the "ends of the earth."

The key moment comes when the risen Jesus joins the two disciples and walks with them. They fail to recognize him (preparing for the revelatory moment in v. 31), but one of them, Cleopas, responds to Jesus' leading question about the events they are pondering. Filled with melancholy the two disciples recount the events that have so changed their world. Their way of describing Jesus and his mission as a "prophet mighty in deed and word before God and all the people" (v. 19) fits well into Luke's perspective, beginning with the inaugural scene in Jesus' hometown synagogue of Nazareth where he announces his prophetic mission (4:16–30) and in subsequent scenes where Jesus is acclaimed as a prophet (e.g., 7:16) and expresses his own fierce commitment to healing and exorcism as God's prophet (13:31–35). In Acts too, both Peter (3:22) and Stephen (7:37) refer to Jesus as a prophet sent by God.

The Emmaus disciples "had hoped that he was the one to redeem Israel" (v. 21), but the death of Jesus had shattered those hopes. The reader is reminded of the longing for redemption that broke out in the opening of the Gospel story: Zechariah gives thanks to God that the longed-for salvation will be fulfilled (1:68), and the temple prophets Simeon and Anna have been awaiting the moment of Israel's redemption (2:30, 38). To compound the disciples' despair, some of the women in the community have brought back the preposterous news that the tomb was empty and claimed they had a vision of angels announcing that Jesus was alive (vv. 22–24).

Luke has set the stage for Jesus' own interpretation of his sufferings. The suffering and death of Jesus were to be understood not as an ultimate defeat of God's purpose, but as the necessary pathway to new life. The risen Jesus illumines this for his disciples by appealing to the teaching of "Moses and all the prophets," indeed by drawing on the lesson of "all the scriptures" (v. 27). It is futile to attempt to identify specific passages. The pattern of life emerging from death is, in fact, a fundamental pattern of the entire biblical saga. From the original chaos God creates

likely ask the same question of themselves, as though there were no plot. What are the conversations we have on the way to nowhere in particular when the horizon stretches only as far as the petty pace of tomorrow and tomorrow and tomorrow permits? What should we do when we have reached our wit's end, when what we once thought was worth our lives has left us washed up emotionally, financially, physically, spiritually?

The road to Emmaus is a seven-mile journey, affording the preacher a good deal of time to dwell with the hopelessness and helplessness that Christ's disciples then and now know all too well. Three brief weeks after Easter, the emptied-out pews remind us of the disappeared who are headed toward Emmaus with no clue about where they are going or what they ought to do. Neither will they recognize the one who has assumed their condition and accompanies them. The same may be said of the faithful who remain. Present or absent, they talk along the way about all these things that have happened as though nothing more than death has happened. They wonder about what to make of the troubles they have seen. They speak as if fate rather than destiny were their lot.[2] How shall the time be filled by them who sorrow as those who have no hope other than a wish-dream cobbled together with the help of the culture? Where do the "oughts" of human existence originate when they come to us from without and at enmity with our being? Though Luke spends only a sentence on the conversation between the disciples before a stranger joins them, we know that this conversation can last a lifetime.

Then, as the shadows lengthen and the evening comes and the busy world is hushed, another character falls into step with them and asks what they were discussing with each other while they walked along. This question stops them in their tracks. "They stood still," Luke says (v. 17), suggesting that when God enters a conversation we think we are having with one another—when our horizontal perspective on the human condition is assumed from above and crossed by the vertical perspective of God's word— we cannot but find our lost selves standing still. We have surely come to a crossroad. At issue are not the miles before us but the moment at hand and the eternity that has just invaded time.

Preachers also must stand still at the crossroad where the risen Christ asks us to reflect on the meaning of the things that have taken place. When has

---

2. See Glenn Tinder, *Against Fate: An Essay in Personal Dignity* (South Bend, IN: University of Notre Dame, 1981).

Luke 24:13-35

Theological Perspective

Surely Luke 24 offers an emerging eucharistic theology. The promise of this text is that Jesus will meet his beloved "in the breaking of the bread." The hospitality of the traveling companions becomes the doorway to grace. The willingness of the stranger to enter their space suggests trust and hope—and Jesus more than repays their convivial overture. Hospitality expresses deep vulnerability; welcoming a stranger is always risky, and the tables might be turned—for good or ill. It is not readily apparent who the guest really might be. Jesus becomes the host at this meal, which becomes an expression of thanksgiving and deepened faith. Eucharistic hospitality should emulate the expansive welcome portrayed in this text.

It has been suggested that hospitality is the key to evangelism in our day, so this text offers a window to spiritual practice in postmodernity. Actions more than words, welcome more than self-protection provides the space where others might fearlessly enter and find themselves at home. Sharing the common meal transgresses boundaries and allows communion with Christ, who meets us whenever we gather at the Lord's Table—or at the tables that provide self-giving welcome.

It should not surprise us that this story moves from isolation to community. Christ joins himself to those on the way, who then make space for him in the village. God always creates space for the "other" in order that true community might be formed. After Jesus is no longer in view, the disciples begin to talk with one another with transparent self-revelation: "Were not our hearts burning within us while he was talking to us on the road, while he was opening the scriptures to us?" (v. 32). Scripture is best understood in community, because we need others to interrogate our insular readings; indeed, we need others' interpretations to challenge a narrowness of heart.

What they had experienced must be shared. The return to Jerusalem denotes the outward spiral of the gospel. News this good must be shared. News this transforming creates new community. Those illuminated by the grace of the Lord Jesus Christ must offer witness to others that they too might come to know him in the breaking of the bread.

MOLLY T. MARSHALL

Pastoral Perspective

heat of the summer. Easter does not always come in three days. Stones are rolled away, but sometimes we stay in the tomb.

The text implies that Jesus feigns his departure. Perhaps the travelers' hearts hunger for more; maybe they are living out the mandates of hospitality. Either way, still unaware that the Christ accompanies them, they invite him to linger. Then, in a scene that would be comical, save that it is so touching in its revelation, they share a eucharistic meal. Jesus takes the bread that is on hand, and, in the blessing and in the breaking, new life and new eyes are offered. The masquerade is over, the sacred memory of the heart is rekindled, the wellspring of hope bubbles and gurgles again, and the incognito is revealed. If we have kept the text at a distance, we will join the disciples in asking how they could have been so dull. If we have been vulnerable enough to allow our name to be inserted in the place of Cleopas's unnamed traveling companion, we too will experience the wonder-full amazement. The stones sealing the tombs of our hearts will be rolled back too.

In a moment of tangible love that embraces the brokenness of betrayal and cross, the rays of Easter's sunrise have illumined the crypt of their entombed hopes. Broken bread nurses our broken faith and can nourish the courage we need to leave our grave-clothes behind and vacate the vault of our defeated dreams. The weary travelers feel alive; their hearts are renewed. The witness of the women at the empty tomb is now their testimony too. In the breaking of bread, the beams of resurrection's dawn have reached about seven miles from Jerusalem. Their burning hearts illumine their blind eyes and quicken their weary souls for a seven-mile nighttime run in the moonlight of Easter. Their sacred city is made holy again, and their pilgrimage of faith has just begun.

SHANNON MICHAEL PATER

Exegetical Perspective

life. From the slavery of Egypt come freedom and a homeland. From the destruction of exile comes a renewed people. Jesus' interpretation of the Scriptures for the disciples gives them true understanding of the meaning of Jesus' death and resurrection; now their hearts "burn" within them (v. 32). Here is a key point of Luke's account: the risen Christ present within the community enables them gradually to understand the full meaning of the paschal mystery.

The story reaches its climax with a meal shared with Jesus and the disciples. As evening approaches and Jesus appears to go on his way, the disciples implore him to stay with them. Meals are a hallmark of Luke's narrative, and he concludes this account in the same way. These meals evoke the longed-for gathering of Israel (Isa. 25:6–9) and express the inclusive spirit of Jesus' own mission (Luke 14:7–14, 15–24; 15:25–32; 16:19–31; 19:1–10). Full revelation of who Jesus is and what his death and resurrection mean comes at the meal (vv. 31, 35). Jesus' words and gestures are the same as at the feeding of the multitudes (9:16) and reminiscent of the final Passover meal (22:19). Without doubt Luke also intends the reader to make a connection with the celebrations of the "breaking of the bread" described in Acts (2:42, 46; 20:7, 11; 27:35).

At the conclusion of the story, the risen Jesus vanishes from their sight, and the two disciples leave immediately to return to the community in Jerusalem. There, they learn that the risen Jesus has already appeared to Simon (an appearance Luke does not narrate), and they too give their testimony about their encounter on the road and at the meal. Luke has driven home several of his characteristic themes: that Jesus' death and resurrection are in accord with God's plan of salvation; the dawning understanding of the community's experience based on their reflection on the Scriptures and the inspiration of the Spirit of the risen Jesus; the breaking of the bread as a rich symbol of the community's life and mission; the importance of not leaving the community but persevering with it.

DONALD SENIOR

Homiletical Perspective

God's Word interrupted the church's idle conversations and effectively called a halt to our frantic forward momentum? Where were we going when the question of a stranger prompted us to confess that we had lost our way? What was it about the one who listened that turned the details of despair into beseeching?

Then, without being asked, the stranger tells them a story, tracing God's saving purposes over the events of the last days. Luke gives us no indication that their hearts were burning, only that the hour was late. Drawing near to their destination, Jesus leaves them free to continue on without him. The preacher might mention this as well. His love is such that we are always free to turn our backs upon him, close the door of our hearts against him, bolt our minds shut in fear of what inviting him in might involve. Here he makes no ethereal entrance as in John. An invitation must be issued.

The preacher can only suggest that the congregation urge Christ to join them at the table, especially if the table has already been set. Even so, the invitation is finally his, and Luke's words are often a part of the invitation we proffer in his name: "When he was at table with them, he took bread, blessed and broke it, and gave it to them. Then their eyes were opened, and they recognized him" (vv. 30–31). To wit: "Revelation is the clue that enables one to put together the disparate experiences of life into a meaningful, coherent whole, to see a pattern and purpose in human history," writes John Leith, "to overcome the incongruities between what life is and what life ought to be."[3]

By word and sacrament, Christ opens the eyes of them who rejoice that they have reached their destination in him. Christ's church has been making diligent use of his given means of grace since the evening of the first day of the week, in hopes that, on the way home, perhaps two in the crowd might even say, one to the other, "Did not our hearts burn this morning as the scriptures were opened to us!"

CYNTHIA A. JARVIS

---

3. John H. Leith, *Basic Christian Doctrine* (Louisville, KY: Westminster/John Knox Press, 1993), 30.

Acts 2:42-47

⁴²They devoted themselves to the apostles' teaching and fellowship, to the breaking of bread and the prayers.

⁴³Awe came upon everyone, because many wonders and signs were being done by the apostles. ⁴⁴All who believed were together and had all things in common; ⁴⁵they would sell their possessions and goods and distribute the proceeds to all, as any had need. ⁴⁶Day by day, as they spent much time together in the temple, they broke bread at home and ate their food with glad and generous hearts, ⁴⁷praising God and having the goodwill of all the people. And day by day the Lord added to their number those who were being saved.

belonging

Theological Perspective

As the portrait of the church's first blossoming, this text captures immediate interest. There is the sheer abundance of new converts: in v. 41, the community jumped from apostolic band to megachurch of 3,000 after one sermon; now in v. 47 numbers grow daily, filling a mainline pastor with envy. There are "wonders and signs," not least of which is a radical economic transformation: new Christians embrace communal life, the rich gladly sell property and share with the needy. As justice rolls down we too are filled with wonder—and then we look back to our congregations with despair. The standard is beyond the reach of our leadership or even our imagination. We are tempted to nostalgia for those biblical days. From there it is a short step to nostalgia for our own church's better days, when pews were full, programs were exciting, and we had an impact on the larger community.

We idealize this economic transformation, despite the fact that having "all things in common" (v. 44) was not the final model for the church, even in Acts. There is only one further description of Christians living without individual ownership in Acts, including Barnabas's sale of property (Acts 4:32–37) and the cautionary tale of Ananias and Sapphira (Acts 5:1–11). Giving generously as an expression of Christian unity and love did remain an important priority, as seen in Paul's call to help the Jerusalem church

Pastoral Perspective

How does one convey the promise and momentum of a movement? Countless books and films have attempted to express not only the fight for colonial self-determination during the American Revolution, but the depth of unity, collaboration, and camaraderie of the colonists. Again, books, movies, poetry, and song could not express the reverence, solidarity, and resolve that were experienced by participants in the civil rights movement in the United States, nor could these media adequately portray the struggle. The American Revolution and the civil rights movement are just two examples of historical social movements with both spiritual and political underpinnings and goals that authors, poets, historians, composers, painters, sculptors, photographers, filmmakers, and others have attempted to convey. Participants in each of these shifting times experienced profound internal wrestling, wide-ranging and conflicting styles of leadership, and intense periods of hardship and oppression, and yet emerged from those experiences with a deeply exhilarating sense of renewed human community, a kind of transformation that it is difficult to describe to someone who was not there.

Luke is neither a historian nor a journalist in the modern sense, but the book of the Acts is our most comprehensive history of the spiritual and political movement that gave birth to the early Christian

Exegetical Perspective

This is a story about the growth of the early Christian movement. In Luke's account, there is an immediate jump from 120 (1:15) to 3,000 (2:41), which leads to a period of intense discipleship (2:42–47). Crucial in the spiritual development of these new believers (see 2:42) was a concrete sense of joining a new community, even to the point of financial commitments: giving proceeds from sold possessions to "any [who] had need" (v. 45). In this idealized portrayal, Luke is not reluctant to record instances in which there were serious difficulties with this type of commitment, as in the case of Ananias and Sapphira (5:1–11). Although it is not indicated explicitly, the tradition of sharing with those less fortunate was a central feature in Jesus' teaching as well. Luke's Gospel moves beyond the other Gospels in this regard, including accounts such as Jesus' story about a "rich man and Lazarus" (Luke 16:19–31) and his conversation with Zacchaeus, the toll collector (Luke 19:1–10). So the activity here in Acts 2 provides continuity with the early mission.

The other important historical feature of this account is how this portrayal, at least initially, presents the developing movement as one in continuity with Judaism as they continue to spend "time together in the temple" (2:46). Despite the tensions between Jews and Jewish Christians later in the

Homiletical Perspective

When we preach from the Gospels, we often liken the people in the pews to the disciples. In contrast, when we preach from Acts, the inclination is to identify parishioners with the group of receptive believers who compose the burgeoning church.

One possibility for preachers of today's text is to interpret it with a Gospel-like approach. In other words, if worshipers *expect* to see themselves as the gathering of awe-struck converts, the preacher's decision to align parishioners with the disciples might very effectively challenge church members into a greater sense of their calling to be spiritual leaders themselves. As parishioners identify with Peter and the other disciples, they may begin to see how they too are empowered by the Spirit to inspire radical and hopeful change in the lives of others.

Church bulletins often feature a noticeable text box wherein worshipers are reminded that though the pastor is but one person the "ministers" of the church are all its members. Today's scripture supports this confession and reminds churchgoers that, like the disciples, their Spirit-filled leadership will make a difference in and beyond the life of the church.

Acts offers a wonderful vision of a community committed to mutual support—a group gathered in one heart and one soul in which no one claimed private ownership of any possessions. Everything was

Acts 2:42-47

Theological Perspective

(2 Cor. 8:1–15). It has been embodied in the lives of countless Christians who distributed their earthly wealth to live out Jesus' call to "perfect" life (Matt. 19:21) in monastic communities. Though Scripture does not make it a standard, this picture of sacrificial giving for communal needs is appealing. It is a challenge to Christians in an affluent society, especially one where personal autonomy and acquisition of wealth are ideals.

Numerical growth and sacrificial sharing, though, are the effects, not the cause. They grow out of the rich faith of these early Christians. Before telling our churches to put these effects into practice, we would be wise to look for what built the faith of the early Christians. Verse 42 suggests that a particular set of practices, four habits or priorities, nurtured their lives as Christians and as church: "They devoted themselves to the apostles' teaching and fellowship, to the breaking of bread and the prayers"—all before discussing their sharing of property. This is the earliest listing of what came to be called "marks" or "notes" of the church—characteristics beyond the confession of Jesus as Lord that identified the church as the church.

Three centuries later the Nicene Creed would affirm the church as "one holy catholic and apostolic." In the Reformation of the sixteenth century, Protestants would tend to identify the true church by the faithful preaching of the biblical message, the administration of the sacraments according to Jesus' institution, and sometimes also proper discipline. The question of how to identify an authentic church is a good one, especially in a culture where people actively "shop" among denominations. Our text gives these four things as a viable set of categories, whether we are Christians hoping to nurture our own faith, ministers seeking to encourage vitality in a congregation, or people in a new town trying to figure out what to look for in a church.

First of all they devoted themselves to "the apostles' teaching." A mark of authenticity and health in a church is what it does with the writings of those early Christian leaders. We are called to explore the texts that come down to us in their names. Specific theological perspectives and hermeneutical approaches are not specified, but active effort is. We all are called to dwell in Scripture. However, as in most of Christian history, many people encounter Scripture primarily when it is read aloud and preached on Sunday morning. Much of the responsibility for nurturing this priority, then, lies with preachers, whose sermons must help members hear and understand the Scriptures.

Pastoral Perspective

church. Beginning with the resurrection of Jesus Christ, Acts chronicles the deliberations and actions of the church at Jerusalem and the spread of Christianity across Greece and Asia Minor, culminating in the apostle Paul's very public Christian presence in Rome.

As we move through Acts, what we think of as the Christian church is everything from an offshoot of its parent faith tradition to radical sect. It is a tentative movement and a street festival, a subversive activity and a public forum, a new current within Judaism and its own distinct and separate religion. This did not happen all at once or through a tidy progression, but through the grace of God, the faith of individuals, and the sometimes very messy expressions of human resolve. Even this description does not do justice to the common experience of faithful people in renewed spiritual communion with one another through their efforts by grace. How does one express the momentum of a spiritual movement? The short pericope of Acts 2:42–47, written by Luke, has become the emblem of early Christian community.

The ensconced reality of the contemporary Christian church, however, and its many equally ensconced denominations, sects, and factions, have removed the modern reader far from the reality described in the book of the Acts of the Apostles. Though it is tempting to see in these early verses from Acts the existence of a new and separate tradition, distinct from its Jewish heritage and crystallized in its new direction, there is little doubt that this passage from Acts is an enthusiastic depiction of that transitional time when Jewish practice and new beliefs were still coalescing into a new way of life. The mere mention of the time these believers spent together in the temple is an indication that they still felt at home in Jewish practice.

In Acts the fledgling Christian community is referred to as men and women "of the Way" (9:2; 19:9, 23; 24:14, 22). Still, it remains unclear whether Luke himself gave the movement this name, he was recording how these new believers referred to themselves, or this was how outsiders referred to them. It is at least suggested in Acts 9:2 that the name had some wider currency at that time, since Saul is reported to have asked for letters to the synagogues at Damascus in his pursuit as a kind of spiritual enforcer of people "who belonged to the Way."

There is no doubt that the early Christian church emerged from Jewish practice as it was reinterpreted, modified, and augmented by Christian experience. Luke's description of the early church, however, attempts to convey not simply new understandings, but enormous shifts in faith and practice. There is

Exegetical Perspective

history of Christianity, this depiction expresses a close relationship between the two groups.

This is one of Luke's summary sections. Such summaries are important for understanding the narrator's perception of events. It is easier to see what the narrator/author is up to in these summaries than to determine the author's ideological slant from the depiction of the events themselves or the dialogue and speeches within the events. Some of this material, though certainly not all, may go back to an earlier tradition. The summaries, on the other hand, provide insight into the author's own theological perspective in a more direct manner.

The summaries also move the entire narrative from one situation to another. They function as transitions in the overall narrative. Acts 2:42–47 serves as a transition from Peter's first sermon (2:14–36, 38–40) to his second (3:12–26). The first sermon explains the coming of the Messiah as David's Lord and the pouring out of the Spirit upon Jesus' followers. (The lectionary omits this lengthy sermon!) The second sermon examines Jesus' messianic role again (3:12–16) and then highlights how God's prophets earlier foretold this day (3:18–26). Acts 2:42–47 provides a summary of the *positive* reaction to Peter's first sermon, in anticipation that this will occur again in the near future, but this is not always so! Peter's second sermon results in a mixed reaction. On the one hand, there is another increase in followers numbering "about five thousand" (4:4). Luke's depiction, if taken literally (as it should not be), has led to an emphasis on numerical growth as the primary evidence for testing the spiritual state of Christian community. On the other hand, Peter's sermon disturbs temple leaders, who place Peter and John in prison (4:1–4).

The "apostles' teaching" (2:42) is not fully explored here, nor is the phrase used elsewhere in Acts. We may assume that, in literary terms, Peter's "sermons" (e.g., 2:14–40; 3:12–26) provide the specific content for what some of that teaching may look like. An anonymous late first- or early second-century writing known as the *Didache* (Gk. "teaching") may have been composed to fill in the gap for this "apostles' teaching." Its longer title was *The Teaching of the Twelve Apostles*, but it is not associated directly with the apostles. In short, it provides the first written catechism for the early church.

The "breaking of bread" (2:42) may be a double entendre. It may refer both to common meals and the Eucharist. The early chapters of Acts frequently recall themes from the end of Luke. In Luke 24, two of Jesus' followers were on their way to a village,

Homiletical Perspective

held in common. Another homiletical move is to determine the degree to which the modern church should imitate the early church. It is not much of a stretch to imagine parishioners listening to this text and wondering if perhaps their congregation is radically off the mark. Certainly, very few mainstream churches practice the kind of pooling of resources and communal living that is pictured here.

Early hearers of the text would likely have been familiar with the utopian vision that was widespread in Hellenistic literature, wherein the sharing of personal possessions was a primary characteristic. If it seems that Acts' depiction of the church is idealized, it is likely that, rather than having a misleading effect, the depiction will registered in the minds of worshipers as a vision of what could be: a vision of the newborn church as a place where the deepest human longings for God, community, and basic provision were being met in abundance for all.

Acts' primary agenda at this point is to make clear the connection between the birth of the church and the divine work of the Spirit. The response of the people, noted throughout these chapters, is awe and amazement. Their response is evidence that these recent events are God-driven and not rooted in basic human ambition. The God of Israel is showing once again God's covenant faithfulness, and with the pouring out of the Spirit, God is fulfilling the promises of prophecy. The embodiment of church that we find here in Acts represents the people's discernment in response to the Spirit.

Our churches today are called equally to this task of discernment. Because we so easily forget this calling, preachers might see here an opportunity to reclaim the congregation's identity as a Spirit-led community and to explore with worshipers ways in which the Spirit is calling them to embody Christ's church in the present.

Certainly stewardship, the use of our resources, is an important point of examination. If we are not called to sell off all of our possessions, how exactly are we called to use our resources and, in particular, our money? Preachers might offer some questions to guide our discernment. Consider the causes to which we give:

Do they heal?
Do they bring hope?
Do they remake a part of the world so that people can rebuild their lives?
Do they invite us to participate in God's work of transformation?

Acts 2:42-47

Theological Perspective

Second, they devoted themselves to "fellowship." A mark of authenticity and vitality in a congregation is the quality of peoples' relationships and their efforts to include others in those relationships. There are churches that view themselves as friendly and welcoming, but within which a visitor will not be drawn into conversation—where even members can suffer silently, unknown and unloved. Devotion to fellowship means nurturing the habits of hospitality—and it takes work: It takes courage to notice a newcomer, helping him or her find the coatrack or a classroom. It takes initiative to invite someone to lunch or a cup of coffee after worship—those early Christians did enjoy breaking bread in their homes. It takes creativity to start a regular gathering where a small group can begin to know and care for each other. With devotion to fellowship, people are made to feel at home, growing close enough for genuine rejoicing, encouragement, and support.

Third, they devoted themselves to "the breaking of bread." Authenticity and health in a congregation are surely seen in the way they eat together, but this is more than fellowship. This "breaking of bread" seems to allude to the Lord's Supper, faith and community fed by the sacrament. Many miss the life in the Eucharist, whether it is offered every Sunday or four times a year. Only if pastors make concerted efforts will people find the richness offered in Christ's broken body and shed blood. The promise of the gospel, portrayed there in more than words, is available to all our senses—but we will miss it if we are not devoted to it.

Fourth, they devoted themselves to "the prayers." A mark of authenticity and vitality in a congregation will be their involvement in prayer. More than a part of worship, prayer is for each of us the opportunity for communion with God. It is clear by the plural that the earliest Christians were learning some kind of set prayers—the Lord's Prayer, the Psalms, or other forms. There are now many ways to pray, but to be "devoted" to it, individuals and communities must pursue prayer intentionally and with energy.

God's grace causes growth, but these are ways of nourishing the plant.

GARY NEAL HANSEN

Pastoral Perspective

still considerable debate over whether these shifts are all part of one new coherent practice, or whether they are listed as the many ways that a new interpretation of spiritual life is emerging. Whether or not they represent a truly cohesive communal practice, the picture is nevertheless one of a maturing community in the process of developing its own ethic, economy, and culture.

First and foremost, it is fascinating to recognize how broad and encompassing these shifts are. In six verses Luke tells us that Christian faith has changed where people live, how they understand property ownership, their sense of communal obligation in response to personal crisis. Further, it has changed how they understand something as basic as a meal, its purpose, and its implications. Eating together, not simply the ritual of the Lord's Supper, has become a spiritual activity, and it is accompanied by depths of gratitude and spiritual awareness that Luke wants us to understand as explicit and real. In his mention of temple worship and particularly his mention twice of the regularity of these new practices ("day by day," vv. 46, 47), Luke depicts new spiritual disciplines that set these people apart. They are, he wants us to see, people of a new "way."

Our struggle in the contemporary church has focused on how to decide what to make of this new Christian ethic, economy, and culture. Our first efforts have in some ways been focused on its believability. What does it mean that they were "all together" and that they "had all things in common"? Did people truly pool their resources or share them as needed? If so, what does this mean to us today? Was Luke reporting on actual practices, or was he in some sense exaggerating in his attempt to express the movement? These may be the wrong questions. The real question for the contemporary church may be to understand what momentum, what new spiritual and political movement, is at work today, refreshing our ensconced and institutional religious tradition.

SUSAN B. W. JOHNSON

Exegetical Perspective

Emmaus, several miles from Jerusalem; the resurrected Jesus confronted them and explained to them what the prophets had said. It was not until Jesus had "broken bread" with them that "their eyes were opened, and they recognized him" (Luke 24:31, 35). In Acts, this action recalls the significance of centering these meals on Jesus in some meaningful way, whether that is a formal eucharistic meal or not.

In this passage, there are no chief characters. Earlier, Peter plays the lead role, as spokesperson on behalf of the others. Here, Luke presents the "apostles" as a collective group "teaching" (2:42), performing "wonder and signs" (2:43), and contributing to a strategy for assisting the less fortunate (2:44–45). We have an (idealized?) picture of a developing community of persons in perfect harmony with one another. This will not last, as Luke himself will show.

The four elements crucial to the developing Christian community, in Luke's portrayal, still have contemporary relevance: apostles' teaching, fellowship, breaking bread, and prayers. The "teaching" and "fellowship" may take on new expressions, but the centrality of Jesus Christ in each of these components should remain. Equally important, contemporary communities should not overlook seeking how to continue to live out the sense of responsibility each one has for the other. Was the distribution of goods only for the early foundation of the movement? Is there a crucial Christian message in this distinctive activity, in which followers of Jesus should continue to "sell possessions" in order to care for others in an organized, structured manner? Are we still called to ensure that those with less may benefit without our calling attention to the less fortunate in a direct way? Throughout the history of Christianity, many believers have attempted to grapple with the distribution of goods "to any [who] had need." In Luke's story world, this action became an effective means of "evangelism" for the early church as God "added to their number" daily (2:47).

EMERSON B. POWERY

Homiletical Perspective

Of course, these questions are not simply limited to an examination of our use of money. They might also be used to focus the congregation's priorities and ministries and more deliberately to align them with God's will.

Verse 43 tells us that "awe came upon everyone, because many wonders and signs were being done by the apostles." While our reflections often focus on the *actions* of the early church, preachers might also choose to highlight Acts' attention to these *emotional responses*. The Christian life is about adjusting ourselves to the existence of a gracious God. Acts describes for us what this adjustment looks like. The awe and wonder that characterize the early church remind modern believers that authentic fellowship with God includes a humbling awareness of God's divinity in the midst of human mortality and of God's wondrous deeds interrupting our ordinary lives. The appropriate emotional response to the Spirit is amazed appreciation.

What a gift it would be if, on Sunday morning, preachers were to renew for parishioners their sense of awe and wonder at the Eternal in their midst! Personal accounts of awe-inspiring experiences paired with theological reflection might encourage the kind of emotional response to God that is in keeping with Acts. I recall a parishioner's experience of first visiting the Grand Canyon. Its age, beauty, and vast expanse turned her literally speechless and brought her to tears. She became intensely aware of the awe and wonder that she felt toward a God of such infinite wisdom and power. She also marveled at the generous grace of a God who chose to include her in the great gift of creation.

I am reminded of a man who gathered in a crowded field with thousands of others to watch the launching of the space shuttle. As he described the craft's disappearance into the beyond, he noted how a sensation of awe permeated the people. Suddenly the mass of hot and impatient spectators had become a community of courteous and smiling people who felt newly united by the wonder that they had just witnessed.[1]

The awe and wonder that we feel point us to God, because they point us beyond our common awareness to the beauty and mystery that always surround us. Sermons that open our eyes to this beauty and mystery unite us with the experience of the early church and lead us into Spirit-filled discipleship.

TIMOTHY B. HARE

---

1. Rusty Freeman, "Night of Wonder," *Journal for Preachers*, Advent 2000, 11.

Psalm 23

¹The LORD is my shepherd, I shall not want.
² He makes me lie down in green pastures;
  he leads me beside still waters;
³ he restores my soul.
  He leads me in right paths
    for his name's sake.

⁴Even though I walk through the darkest valley,
  I fear no evil;
  for you are with me;
    your rod and your staff—
    they comfort me.

Theological Perspective

On the Fourth Sunday of Easter, our reflection upon the victory of God made manifest in Jesus' resurrection meets that popularly representative text of the biblical canon: the Twenty-third Psalm. One immediate way of making this particular prayer our own, in such a way as to push beyond familiar associations with greeting cards and cross-stitch patterns, is to note (or confess) the ways in which the opening profession ("The LORD is my shepherd, I shall not want") will likely feel demonstrably false. The economy of the psalms, we realize, runs completely counter to the prevailing economies playing upon our felt needs with all manner of false covenant, promising a wholeness and a satisfaction that is ours for the taking by way of one more impulse to buy. The Twenty-third Psalm is a live and signal counter environment to such bad theology, placing before our senses an imagery that is integrative rather than distorting, and attesting to a confidence in a God whose purposes of restoration and redemption are somehow so comprehensive that in virtue of God's abiding presence we would lack no good thing.

These are the same good purposes in which Jesus trusted in his short life of faithful witness and obedience even unto death. We do well to note that the pastoral imagery the psalm places before our senses may have struck the beleaguered second-class

Pastoral Perspective

The Twenty-third Psalm is daunting for the preacher, not only because it is so pastorally rich but also because it is so familiar, read at innumerable bedsides of the dying and at countless funerals. How does one begin to reflect on the *Mona Lisa* of the Psalms and help the congregation to see this beloved scripture with fresh eyes? Perhaps the preacher feels some stress about the whole undertaking, and apparently stress is what the psalmist feels too. In response to this stress, he reminds us who the Lord is, what the Lord does, and who *we* actually are.

What pressures does the psalmist face here? We do not know for certain, but we are given some clues. He writes, "The LORD is my shepherd, I shall not want" (v. 1). Maybe the psalmist faces the pressure of lacking enough—enough to eat and drink, enough safety and shelter to live, enough money to pay for what is necessary.

Then he also writes, "Even though I walk through the darkest valley . . ." (v. 4). The Hebrew is ambiguous. It may refer to deep distress, extreme danger, or even the world of the dead. The exact meaning is unclear, but the inference is clear enough—the pressure of distress and danger that could turn deadly.

Finally, the psalmist says, "You prepare a table before me in the presence of my enemies" (v. 5). The word for enemies here carries the sense of someone

⁵You prepare a table before me
  in the presence of my enemies;
 you anoint my head with oil;
  my cup overflows.
⁶Surely goodness and mercy shall follow me
  all the days of my life,
 and I shall dwell in the house of the LORD
  my whole life long.

Exegetical Perspective

Ingrained in our cultural consciousness, Psalm 23 socializes us and is socialized culturally, liturgically, and spiritually. The psalm, particularly in the King James Version, functions a cultural assumption. Nevertheless, homileticians may find new paths to explore in the nuances of exegesis.

On a general note, the Psalms provide a relatively straightforward opportunity to consider the ways form criticism enhances interpretation. Certainly the Psalms may be viewed as liturgical songs or prayers, but to view the collection in the vein of a *Book of Common Prayer* anachronistically imposes contemporary structures on the ancient material. Form analysis provides but one of the many approaches to reading the psalm. Noted for his seminal work in form criticism, Hermann Gunkel[1] searched for structural patterns in the psalmic collection and identified the following types of psalms:

A. Hymns: General Hymns, Songs of Zion, Enthronement Songs;
B. Songs of Lament: Communal Laments, Individual Laments;

---

1. Hermann Gunkel, "The Psalms: A Form Critical Introduction," in *Die Religion in Geschichte und Gegenwart*, Handwörterbuch in gemeinverständlicher Darstellung, redigiert von Gunkel, Heitmüller, [u.a.] unter Mitwirkung von Hermann Gunkel und Otto Scheel, herausgegeben von Friedrich Michael Schiele (Tübingen: Mohr, 1909–13).

Homiletical Perspective

The Ever-Flowing Cup. There is no doubt that Psalm 23 is *the* most familiar psalm, and perhaps *the* most popular passage in all of the Scriptures. This psalm is often read and heard in the midst of death and dying, as it can offer comfort to a grieving family as well as hope for all who listen, but to limit this psalm exclusively to this usage limits the power and scope of its message. Of course it presents the thought that the faithful will be strengthened during the times of deepest need, and in this regard I prefer the phrasing of the King James Version for verse 4: "Yea, though I walk through the valley of the shadow of death, I will fear no evil, for thou art with me." However, we also find an overarching message (even in this fourth verse) that a powerful and comforting God, a Shepherd, will always be present for those who are faithful. The image of a shepherd is meaningful in that a shepherd would be vigilant, tough enough to thwart predators, and extremely reliable.

Thus this particular psalm is not merely for moments of death. It needs to be read, heard, and understood more importantly as a psalm about living, for it puts daily activities, such as eating, drinking, and seeking security, in a radically God-centered perspective that challenges our usual way of thinking. Furthermore, it calls us not to think alone of our individual comfort, but to take our place with others in the household of God.

Psalm 23

citizenry of first-century Palestine as every bit as idealistic and out of sync with certain lived realities as it does within our distracted and harried attention spans. As was doubtless the case for Jewish peasants attempting lives of peace, abundance, and faithfulness to God's law under Roman occupation, the psalm constitutes a powerfully countercultural summons to our imaginations, even as it invigorates them with a poetic witness that insists that, in spite of all evidence to the contrary, the peace of God is nevertheless objectively with us.

Against the rhythms dictated by the mechanisms of a merely mercantile world, we are invited to locate our life and livelihood in an agrarian scene of mutual interdependence sustained and shepherded by the God whose concern interpenetrates the details of our lives. In light of this confession—these facts on the ground—the psalmist "will fear no evil" and will consistently experience restoration of soul as consciousness of God's righteous ordering of the world, as that restorative experience again takes hold, the animating faith that would put everything in its right place (vv. 3–4). Those other, distorting rhythms, we understand, will have to be engaged repeatedly by the psalmist's testimony, challenging again that other, differently animating faith of anxiety without end, what Marcia Y. Riggs describes as the "commercially driven imagination that produces images of ourselves that hinder our ability to recognize one another and the wholeness (the integrity) of our global reality."[1]

With or without our recognition, this is the God-given cosmic integrity that funds and sustains our lives. Within it, as the apostle Paul maintained, we live and move and have our being (Acts 17:28). According to this subversive anthropology that we can discern within the psalm, life itself is most wisely understood as a gift rather than an acquisition. In keeping with the sense of abundant life always on offer and always renewed ("My cup overflows"), the gift is understood as always more permanently enduring than the self-consciously acquired (v. 5). Against delusions of personal autonomy and self-sufficiency, we are met by a posture of attentive receptivity. The psalmist prays out of and in anticipation of a peace and a flourishing that, counter to prevailing voices, will not come to us exclusively through acts of will but primarily through an acceptance of God's acceptance: "You are with me" (v. 4). With an eye also upon those experiences that can be characterized only

1. Marcia Y. Riggs, "The Globalization of Nothing and *Creatio ex Nihilo*," in *Theology that Matters: Ecology, Economy, and God*, ed. Darby Kathleen Ray (Minneapolis: Fortress Press, 2006), 150.

who is a foe, someone who vexes or harasses. So the psalmist may be facing stress from several sources.

Stress from multiple sources is what our congregants face. They encounter stress as they sit in traffic gridlock, as they work ever-increasing hours in a sputtering economy, as they contend with the challenges of school, as they struggle with relationships, as they worry about having enough money, as they interact with angry and hurting people, as they search to find meaning in their lives, as they live in retirement, and as they face death itself. Stress is ever-present, wielding its insidious power. In fact, most visits to the physician's office have a stress-related component. We are practically drowning in stress.

In the heat of this pressure cooker the psalmist offers cool, refreshing peace found in knowing and celebrating who God is and who we are. "The LORD is my shepherd, I shall not want. He makes me lie down in green pastures; he leads me beside still waters; he restores my soul." In our culture, which clings to the myth of "rugged individualism" and "self-made" people, the psalmist instead proclaims the truth—none of us is "self-made." None of us is strong and independent. We are God-made, utterly dependent upon God, as sheep are dependent upon the shepherd. Yes, we work, save, study, and plan, but God is ultimately the one who meets our needs. God is the one who makes us rest. God is the one who slows us down and restores our very being.

The psalmist continues, "He leads me in right paths for his name's sake" (v. 3). In other words, despite simplistic imaginings about our own goodness, *God* is the one who enables us to be good and to do any good at all. Any right paths we take in this life are the result not of any particular wisdom on our part but of the wise direction of God.

"Even though I walk through the darkest valley, I fear no evil; for you are with me; your rod and your staff—they comfort me" (v. 4). Though God is a vulnerable God, a crucified God, the psalmist reminds us that God is also a powerful protector. Yes, God suffers with us in our pain, sorrow, and loss, but like a shepherd with a rod and staff, God also guides us and fights off predators that would harm us. In fact, God's protective power is so great that the psalmist has the audacity to proclaim, "You prepare a table before me in the presence of my enemies; you anoint my head with oil; my cup overflows" (v. 5). We are invited to imagine entering a room filled with our enemies. God says to us, "Right this way. I have prepared a banquet table for you. Please be seated." So we take a seat and begin to eat the feast God has

Exegetical Perspective

C. Royal Psalms;
D. Thanksgiving Psalms: Individual Thanksgiving, Communal Thanksgiving;
E. Wisdom Psalms;
F. Other Psalms: Pilgrimage Songs, Legends, Liturgies, Mixtures, and Miscellaneous.

Psalm 23 fits neatly into none of these categories and has been regarded by most scholars, including Gunkel, as a Song of Confidence, because of its over-arching motif of trust. Often called a psalm of individual thanksgiving, the psalm may have played a role in ritual at a festival, perhaps sung or recited on the journey to a festival. Scholar Mark S. Smith sees Psalm 23 as a pilgrim song.[2] Because of the iconic nature of this psalm, reliance on the beautiful King James Version translation may introduce some questionable readings to the interpretation of the text.

A verse-by-verse analysis may prove helpful. Psalm 23 is one of only eight biblical psalms marked only with "psalm of David" in the inscription. (The others are Psalms 15, 24, 29, 101, 110, 141, and 143.) Verse 1 portrays God as a shepherd. A common metaphor in both the Bible and the ancient Near East, the Hebrew Bible references using this metaphor include Genesis 48:15; 49:24; Psalm 28:9; 80:1; Isaiah 40:11; 44:28 (reference to Cyrus); Jeremiah 31:10; and Ezekiel 34:11, 12, 15. In the larger ancient Near East, Assyria's Tiglath-pileser is characterized as the shepherd of humanity; the Sumerian deity Enlil is the faithful shepherd, the master of all nations; and Babylon's Markuk is also portrayed as shepherd.

The King James Version says the shepherd leads the sheep, or God leads the psalmist, "beside" the still waters. While the translation might be viewed as poetic, the Hebrew preposition most often means "to" or "upon" as opposed to "beside." "God leads me to the waters of rest"; "God causes me to be refreshed upon the waters of rest": either translation emphasizes the practical work of a shepherd.

Verse 2 raises a crucial translation issue seen throughout the Hebrew Bible. The traditional translation, "He restoreth my soul" somehow is perhaps misleading. The word in question is the Hebrew word *naphshi* from the noun *nephesh*. In the Shema in Deuteronomy 6:4–6 (translated in the RSV as "Hear, O Israel: The LORD our God is one LORD; and you shall love the LORD your God with all your heart, and with all your soul, and with all your might. And these words

Homiletical Perspective

In a consumer-oriented society, it is extremely difficult to hear the simple but radical message of Psalm 23: that God is the only necessity of life! The psalm begins, "The LORD is my shepherd, I shall not want." These are words that are particularly appropriate in a culture that teaches people to want everything. Driven by greed rather than need, we can hardly imagine having only the necessities of life: food, drink, shelter, protection. Clever advertisers have succeeded in convincing us that what former generations considered incredible luxuries are now basic necessities. To say in our prosperous context that God is the *only* necessity of life sounds hopelessly quaint and naive. Then again, the words of Jesus may also strike us as naive: "Therefore I tell you, do not worry about your life, what you will eat or what you will drink, or about your body, what you will wear. Is not life more than food [and drink], and the body more than clothing? . . . But strive first for the kingdom of God and his righteousness, and all these things will be given to you as well" (Matt. 6:25, 33).

In other words, to live by the message of Psalm 23 or the words of Jesus means that we will not worry about our lives (or our deaths). God will provide, and God's provision is grounded in the reality of God's reign. The proper response to the simple good news of Psalm 23 and Jesus Christ is simply to trust God.

Some think that adherence to the words of the psalmist means that we are sentenced to "settle" with just enough to "scrape by," or that we should be satisfied with the bare minimum, while those around us find their coffers filled twofold, threefold, and perhaps even tenfold, when compared to that which we have. Nothing could be farther from the truth. The shepherd not only provides for our physical needs; the shepherd, more importantly, tends to our spiritual needs. These are just the beginning! Still they permeate each and every area of our beings.

Walter Brueggemann, in his book *The Message of the Psalms: A Theological Commentary,* writes,

> It is God's companionship that transforms every situation. It does not mean (that) there are no deathly valleys, no enemies. But they are not capable of hurt, and so the powerful loyalty and solidarity of Yahweh comfort, precisely in the situations of threat.[1]

In verses 1–3 God is portrayed as the good shepherd, one who takes care of the faithful by providing us with food (green pastures), drink (still waters), life

2. "Setting and Rhetoric in Psalm 23," *Journal for the Study of the Old Testament* 41 (June 1988): 61–66.

1. Walter Brueggemann, *The Message of the Psalms: A Theological Commentary* (Minneapolis: Augsburg Publishing House, 1984), 156.

Psalm 23

Theological Perspective

as "darkest valleys," we can take up the psalm all the more as our own, rendering it, in some sense, a series of realizations concerning the good life that has been and is being bestowed upon us. We rehearse the prayer, reciting it against and in spite of the life-diminishing voices that would tell us who and what we are, voices with which Jesus, we will recall, was deeply familiar.

In sync with, in fulfillment of, and yet in a fashion that was also a scandalous innovation upon the law and the prophets, the life and ministry of Jesus recasts and revisions the righteous purposes of God. He posits on behalf of the one he called Father what he and the witnessing community that followed him took to be, in Mark Heim's words, "an unalterably saving will toward all creation."[2] When the psalm speaks of a "goodness and mercy" that will somehow ineluctably accompany and saturate every moment of the psalmist's life, we can turn our minds to Jesus' experience of his own vocation of reconciliation and consider the theological challenge of bringing a doctrine of reconciliation to a largely desacralized (and all the more deeply impoverished) world. As he is in this sweet, old world, so are we, and his charge is ours (1 John 4:17). While the absolute fulfillment and realization of God's unalterably saving and redeeming will awaits the eschaton, in the glorious meantime we have poetic signposts like the Twenty-third Psalm. Its imagery of flourishing, stewarding, and attentiveness feeds our contemplation of the vindication of God's love we affirm when we proclaim the risen Christ— the divine love that is both our community's vocation and its regulative ideal.

J. DAVID DARK

Pastoral Perspective

prepared—and we eat *right in front of our enemies*. If that is not enough, then God anoints our head with oil and fills our cup until it overflows. Christians facing physical and spiritual enemies may call this image to mind and rejoice.

Then the psalm ends. "Surely goodness and mercy shall follow me all the days of my life, and I shall dwell in the house of the LORD my whole life long" (v. 6). The Hebrew here may be translated, "Surely goodness and kindness shall dog me all my life." Imagine that. Every moment of life God is pursuing us, *hounding* us with goodness and kindness. What kind of God is this? The psalmist says this God is our shepherd, who grants our needs, causes us to rest and be restored, leads us in the right way of living, protects us from evil, honors and blesses us, and never stops pursuing us with goodness and kindness. What kind of creatures are we? Well, not exactly self-sufficient super-stars—more like needy, dependent sheep.

This psalm offers a wealth of liturgical possibilities. Rather than the frenetic pace that characterizes so much contemporary worship, the psalmist beckons us to allow the Shepherd to slow us down. The first two verses could be used as a call to contemplative worship. While serving Holy Communion, the preacher might walk into the congregation and speak the psalm from memory as the elements are served to elders or to the congregation as a whole. The psalm could be used in a service of healing and wholeness as the participants come forward to be anointed with oil. A sermon could be delivered with the preacher (possibly seated for a moment) using a portion of the sermon time to teach the congregation "centering prayer," "breath prayer," or other ancient forms of prayer echoing the peace this cherished psalm invokes for a people who crave its blessed promise.

JEFF PASCHAL

2. S. Mark Heim, *The Depth of the Riches: A Trinitarian Theology of Religious Ends* (Grand Rapids: Eerdmans, 2001), 76.

which I command you this day shall be upon your heart"), *nephesh* is translated as "soul." While "soul" may have served as an adequate translation for *nephesh* at some points in history and tradition, the meaning often becomes trapped in a body-soul dichotomy. *Naphshi* carries a fuller, more comprehensive meaning—"my whole self," representing the totality of one's being. Thus verse 5 of the Shema would be translated, "You shall love the LORD your God with all your heart, with your whole self, and with all your might." The first portion of verse 2 of Psalm 23, instead of reading, "He restoreth my soul," would read, "God restored/ repaired my whole being," giving an indication of God's complete care. Regarding the final portion of the verse, translated in the King James Version as "he leadeth me in the paths of righteousness for his name's sake," a slight nuance is in order. The Hebrew word translated here as "leads me" carries a weightier meaning, along the lines of "God leads me as a helpless one," so that the notions of trust and reliance carry a more substantial signification of total reliance.

A brief note about the Hebrew word in verse 4 translated as "the valley of the shadow of death": the word carries multiple meanings and is perhaps more accurately translated as "valley of deepest darkness/ despair." Also worthy of note in verse 5 is the reference to eating in the presence of enemies. A sheep almost always eats in the presence of enemies, and does so safely only when accompanied by a trustworthy shepherd. The weight here then rests on the presence and preparation of the shepherd, again creating a space for absolute trust.

Various versions of verse 6 yield different translations with regard to a single word. The King James Version translates the verse as "Surely goodness and mercy shall follow me all the days of my life: and *I will dwell* in the house of the LORD for ever." The word in question, traditionally translated as "I shall dwell," can also, if the exegete follows certain Hebrew manuscripts, be read as "I will turn back/return to the house of God." An English translation of the word as "return" or "turn back" would follow the Masoretic Text, as opposed to "dwell," which follows the Septuagint. Perhaps Mitchell Dahood's translation, "sitting still," is the most accurate, rendering the verse, "I will sit still in the house of God for the length of my days."

The themes of trust and a complete yielding to God are not named explicitly in this psalm but permeate both the imagery and the text.

ALICE W. HUNT

(restores our souls), and protects us from danger (by leading us in the right paths), all for his name's sake. In the pivotal verse 4 we are presented with the comfort that is so necessary successfully to negotiate the challenging moments that we all face. In verses 5 and 6 we have the metaphor of the gracious host who does for the guest exactly what the shepherd does for the sheep—provides food (a table prepared) and drink (the cup that is overflowing).

This hardly sounds like a picture of the bare minimum—especially the image of the overflowing cup. I have tried to imagine exactly how that would appear. Maybe it would be like a spring that bubbles forth from the earth, but instead would bubble forth from inside the cup. Perhaps a better illustration, one more consistent with the text, is the image of a host beside you who would have an ever-present pitcher to fill your cup once it becomes empty, or even when it is still half full. In this connection we are reminded of the words of Jesus, who said to the Samaritan woman at the well, "Everyone who drinks of this water [from the well] will thirst again, but those who drink of the water that I will give them will never be thirsty. The water that I will give them will become in them a spring of water gushing up to eternal life" (John 4:13, 14).

Yes, our Lord is the shepherd; God is also our host. Throughout the entirety of our lives, we should never lose sight that we dwell in the house of the Lord. We rejoice in the constant presence and vigilance of a God who has cared for us, and will always care for us, both as individuals and as a community of the faithful.

JOHN E. WHITE

1 Peter 2:19-25

¹⁹For it is a credit to you if, being aware of God, you endure pain while suffering unjustly. ²⁰If you endure when you are beaten for doing wrong, what credit is that? But if you endure when you do right and suffer for it, you have God's approval. ²¹For to this you have been called, because Christ also suffered for you, leaving you an example, so that you should follow in his steps.

²²"He committed no sin,
 and no deceit was found in his mouth."

²³When he was abused, he did not return abuse; when he suffered, he did not threaten; but he entrusted himself to the one who judges justly. ²⁴He himself bore our sins in his body on the cross, so that, free from sins, we might live for righteousness; by his wounds you have been healed. ²⁵For you were going astray like sheep, but now you have returned to the shepherd and guardian of your souls.

Theological Perspective

This passage is a tricky one. The omitted demand that slaves be submissive to their masters, which introduces our passage, offers simple evidence of this fact. The creators of the lectionary concluded that this plea for submission would distract us from the overriding thought of this passage, but the dangerous dynamic manifest in that plea remains embedded in the passage as a whole. First Peter here seemingly valorizes suffering, such that the passage can be used to justify the oppression of the powerless, while also encouraging the overzealous to seek suffering for its own sake. The reality of this danger has been borne out throughout the history of the church.

Nevertheless, this passage cannot be simply dismissed, given the profound fruits that it has nurtured within the life of the church. The Franciscan movement, in its early days, could be seen as a reflection on this passage, and when the passage and the movement of Francis and Clare are understood together, they open up for us a new vista on the Christian life. The Franciscan life was an embrace of poverty and all that poverty entailed in thirteenth-century Europe. For Francis and Clare, this was a life walking in Christ's footsteps (see v. 21). (They were quite fond of 1 Peter's metaphor.) For them, holy poverty, revealed in the incarnation of God in a manger, goes to the heart of the gospel. Through his voluntary poverty,

Pastoral Perspective

It would not take too much to leap off the 1 Peter train at verse 18. Perhaps this is why the lectionary omits this verse—to keep the riders on the train and on track. However, without it, we are missing an important detail. New Christians who happened to be slaves in pagan households were being harassed for their beliefs. Living in a world where jumping to the master's every whim was considered acceptable behavior, these fledgling Christians had to add insults about their own belief to the list of ways that life was difficult.

First Peter attempts a pastoral word to these folk. Making the distinction between suffering for a just cause and suffering for an unjust cause, the text teases a qualified sanction for suffering under certain circumstances. Nowhere does it suggest that suffering is a legitimate condition for those who are abused, coerced, or oppressed. Nowhere does it suggest a stoic tolerance for violence against anyone. Nowhere does it suggest that God's name be invoked as the hand strikes or the belt comes out or the vestments come off.

What is suggested is preference for an alternative ethic, an alternative to the pagan culture of which these fledging Christians are a part and an alternative in their own tradition. The radical choice to hold fire when under attack is almost more than mere mortals can imagine, yet Christ modeled this. Abuse did not produce more abuse. Suffering did not produce more

Exegetical Perspective

In the context of Peter's household code (2:13–3:12), Peter transitions from general instruction to his Christian audience (2:13–17) to address household slaves (2:18–20). A parallel focus on wives (and husbands) will appear in 3:1–7. However, three observations show that Peter's audience here is actually all believers and not household slaves per se. First, household codes generally provide instruction in pairs, so that we would expect obligations outlined for both masters and slaves. Peter speaks of masters (2:18), but does not address them at all. Peter probably envisions Christian slaves in the households of non-Christian masters, and this is a microcosm of the wider situation that Peter addresses in this letter—with Christians a marginal group within the wider world. Second, the author has already addressed his audience as "free persons" and as "slaves of God" (2:16), clearing the way for us to read his instructions to slaves here as including all who comprise the "household of God." Third, the christological material in verses 21–25 gives no hint that the example of Jesus applies to slaves alone. Indeed, the proverbial character of verses 19–20 points already to the more general reach of Peter's instruction. In this way, "household slaves" refers to all of Peter's addressees, rejecting typical concerns with status within the household of God and addressing the

Homiletical Perspective

Some Bible verses should never be read aloud in public. At least that is what the lectionary committee must have decided, because this reading leaves out the thesis sentence that begins this section of the letter: "Slaves, accept the authority of your masters with all deference, not only those who are kind and gentle but also those who are harsh" (1 Pet. 2:18). Awful as those words are, this verse gives preachers permission to talk about the need for biblical interpretation. What shall we do with texts that have been used to harm people? How will abused women hear words about enduring pain and beatings? This is a text that cries out for a sermon, even when the preacher might prefer to preach on the other readings—sharing goods in Acts 2 or the good shepherd in John 10. Indeed, some people will not move on to hear the Gospel if this text is left hanging in the sanctuary air.

There are good reasons why this sentence was left out. After all, the *public* reading of Scripture is a communal event, not a private reading; but we miss the chance to struggle with this verse if we do not hear it. We also miss the chance to help people in the congregation understand the ongoing need for interpretation of texts. It was one thing to read these verses from 1 Peter in Pontus or Bithynia near the end of the first century, but what did these words mean at the height of the slave trade in the United

1 Peter 2:19-25

Theological Perspective

Jesus embodied for his followers the freedom and joy of living in utter dependence on God. For Francis and Clare, humans were made for such poverty—Adam and Eve owned nothing in Eden, they would argue—so that our craving for ownership is the fruit of our fall. Early Franciscans joined Christ in a discipline of poverty, both as a testimony to the essential joy of this trusting life and as a testimony against the rise of mercantile capitalism, which drove so many to an involuntary poverty that destroyed life and spirit.

Clare, in her fourth letter to Agnes of Prague, offers a rich metaphor for what it means to follow in Christ's footsteps.[1] She takes up the metaphor of the mirror (popular in this period) and asks Agnes to prepare herself by gazing into the mirror of Christ. As she sees herself in Christ's humility and suffering, and adorns herself with the virtues therein revealed, she too can serve as a mirror of Christ's love and faith to the world. Clare's letter is useful for understanding our passage in its insistence that the meaning of the passage turns on its christological component—that we understand our suffering only in the light of Christ's suffering, and that we grasp the sense of this suffering only as we realize its redemptive purpose. Clare understands 1 Peter's testimony that Christ did not embrace poverty and the suffering that it entails for their own sake, but out of trust in God (v. 23) and love for humanity (v. 24). Through this suffering poverty, Christ mirrors for us the fruitfulness of a faith-filled life.

An enigmatic story centered on Francis testifies to the truth of 1 Peter's vision for the early Franciscan movement:

> The same [Brother Leonard] related in the same place that one day at Saint Mary's, blessed Francis called Brother Leo and said: "Brother Leo, write." He responded: "Look, I'm ready!" "Write," he said, "what true joy is."
>
> "A messenger arrives and says that all the Masters of Paris have entered the Order. Write: this isn't true joy! Or, that all the prelates, archbishops and bishops beyond the mountains, as well as the King of France and the King of England [have entered the Order]. Write: this isn't true joy! Again, that my brothers have gone to the non-believers and converted all of them to the faith; again, that I have so much grace from God that I heal the sick and perform many miracles. I tell you true joy doesn't consist in any of these things."
>
> "Then what is true joy?"

1. *Francis and Clare: The Complete Works,* trans. Regis J. Armstrong, O.F.M. Cap., and Ignatius Brady, O.F.M., Classics of Western Spirituality (New York: Paulist Press, 1982), 203–6.

Pastoral Perspective

suffering. Hurt was not the knee-jerk response to being hurt. To trust God in the midst of suffering was considered the high calling to which these new believers should aspire. A hard lesson under any condition, for slaves it must have been brutal.

Though slavery still sadly exists in parts of the world, this may not be the best place to start a conversation with folks in the pews. Preachers/pastors may find traction, even urgency, around the notion of an alternative ethic. Consider that most of the world we know is measured in bytes and binary compounds. Choose 1 or 0. Choose 1 or 0 over and over again in countless combinations. This is the basic premise of our digital world. The one-zero choice rules our airwaves, computer screens, cell phones, almost every decision. Embedded even in our smallest moves, this theory drives our days without our giving it much thought. It informs at a deep level what we think is possible and what we think is not. Limited choices lead us to fall back impulsively to right-wrong, either-or, yes-no, fight-flight actions.

We see evidence of binary thinking across the spectrum of life. On the streets, one gang member's slight becomes another's death warrant. In the boardroom, one failed contract becomes the automatic justification for downsizing. In the schoolroom, one quirky learner quickly becomes labeled as a problem. In the family, one disappointment in a relationship becomes the foundation for divorce. In the church, one year of decline means the church is dead. By and large, we work under the constraint of this mind-set all of the time.

Embedded in our 1 Peter text, however, is the subtle message that there are always more than two choices. One can be abused and not become a serial abuser. One can suffer ridicule or physical harm and not fall into a cycle of never-ending violent behavior. Jesus' experience on the cross teaches us that God always has options—life-giving options, options that expand possibilities and trigger in us instincts that only God can touch.

Our author suggests to struggling Christians that their world may not be as restricted and contained as they think. To suffer ridicule or abuse from their master does not ultimately determine their own self-worth. God will judge justly, both master and slave (v. 23). As an antidote to all the ways life is frightening and dangerous, God offers a way. It is an expansive way.

In solidarity with our first brothers and sisters in the faith, we understand something of what it means to be boxed in or even enslaved. While we are not in

vulnerability and alienation of all believers vis-à-vis the wider world.

As in 2:13, "to subordinate" (v. 18 NRSV "accept the authority"; NIV "submit yourselves"; RSV "be submissive") is the negative of "to withdraw" rather than an alternative to the exercise of power or defiance. Finding and occupying responsibly one's place in society—not passive or unreflective subjection—is the point. The unusual phrase "because of one's consciousness of God" (v. 19 NRSV, "being aware of God") identifies the motivation and muscle behind the courageous steadfastness Peter counsels. The author thus refers to that communal understanding of God and his will that allows and encourages behavior patterning of life around the will of God (see 2:15; 3:17; 4:2, 19).

"Suffering for doing good" is thematic in 1 Peter (e.g., 3:17; 4:16; 5:10), but this does not mean that the author urges his audience to look for opportunities to suffer. He is not supporting the equation: the more suffering, the more commendation from God. Obedience to God and the gospel is the issue. Instead, Peter urges that rejection by humans is not a barometer of God's perspective (see 2:7), and such suffering will be undeserved. Peter adds a third perspective in 2:21–25: innocent suffering is a following in the footsteps of Christ.

The structure of 2:13–3:12 identifies 2:21–25 as its pivot point, with this christological argument supporting courageous steadfastness in the face of unjust suffering among all Christians. The elegance of Peter's reflections on Christ may blind us to the primary concerns of this text. He is really not about christological reflection here, but deploys Christology in the service of his instruction concerning faithful life and witness in the world. His argument is that believers have been called to lives patterned on the obedience of Christ (v. 21) and have been transformed through the work of Christ from a past life of sin so that they may live today as Christ lived (vv. 24c–25). The four relative clauses comprising verses 21–24b ("who," "who," "who," "by whom," clearest in KJV) provide the warrant for Peter's instructions on discipleship, rooting them in the character and significance of Jesus' suffering.

Peter's vision of response in the midst of adversity is assisted by three affirmations. (1) Suffering is not an aberration in the lives of Christians but grows out of the transformation of their lives stemming from new birth. Suffering in this setting is the result of living for, not against, God. (2) The term for "example" is found only here in the NT. Elsewhere the term is

States? As Walter Wink has noted, "One hundred and fifty years ago, when the debate over slavery was raging, the Bible seemed to be clearly on the slaveholders' side. Abolitionists were hard-pressed to justify their opposition to slavery on biblical grounds."[1] Those opposed to slavery had to find other sources of authority. Part of that authority came from the slaves themselves, both their experience of slavery and how that shaped their interpretation of Scripture. New Testament scholar Vincent Wimbush asks a perplexing question: "How does a people enslaved by a people of a Book come to accept that Book as authoritative and legitimate?" Then he answers his own question:

> The most defensible explanation lies in a meeting of "worlds" . . . between African Americans and the "worlds" of the Bible. With its arresting stories of underdogs surviving and conquering and of a Savior figure who is mistreated but who ultimately triumphs, it is little wonder that the Bible came to be embraced by African Americans. . . . Again and again the real situations of the heroes and heroines of the Bible appeared to be similar to those of the historical experience of most African Americans.[2]

For African slaves the Bible itself became a witness against oppressive texts. If—as Jesus said—all the law is summed up in the commandment to love God and neighbor, then texts that demean and diminish our neighbor are called into question.

Avoiding verse 18 also means that we will miss something important: slaves were part of this community of faith. Those who received this letter included people who were at the bottom of the heap in the larger culture. How could slaves live as followers of Jesus within the oppressive reality of slavery? Could they see their own lives reflected in Jesus, who also suffered, but ultimately triumphed?

Howard Thurman knew what it meant to redefine himself and his children in the face of racism, the residue of slavery in America. In his autobiography, he recalls the day he took his little daughters to Daytona Beach, where he had grown up:

> We sauntered down the long street from the church to the riverfront. This had been the path of the procession to the baptismal ceremony in the Halifax River. . . . At length we passed the playground of one of the white public schools. As soon as Olive and Anne saw the swings, they jumped for

1. Walter Wink, ed., *Homosexuality and Christian Faith: Questions of Conscience for the Churches* (Minneapolis: Fortress Press, 1999), 47.
2. Vincent Wimbush, "Reading Texts through Worlds, Worlds through Texts," *Semeia* 62 (Atlanta: Scholars Press, 1993), 138.

1 Peter 2:19-25

Theological Perspective

"I return from Perugia and arrive here in the dead of night. It's winter time, muddy, and so cold that icicles have formed on the edges of my habit and keep striking my legs and blood flows from such wounds. Freezing, covered with mud and ice, I come to the gate and, after I've knocked and called for some time, a brother comes and asks: 'Who are you?' 'Brother Francis,' I answer. 'Go away!' he says. 'This is not a decent hour to be wandering about! You may not come in!' When I insist, he replies: 'Go away! You are simple and stupid! Don't come back to us again! There are men of us here like you—we don't need you!' I stand again at the door and say: 'For the love of God, take me in tonight!' And he replies: 'I will not! Go to the Crosier's place and ask there!'

"I tell you this: If I had patience and did not become upset, true joy, as well as true virtue and the salvation of my soul, would consist in this."[2]

For Francis, joy is found not in anything that he accomplishes in the world, for these accomplishments are mere possessions that possess us more than we them. Such success only breeds a concern that we continue the success, leading us to rest our souls in the successes that we so precariously possess. We find joy, rather, when we have the humility to claim nothing as our right, when we "own" no prerogative, not even to find housing among our own, but simply offer ourselves to God in trust, accepting what the world offers us, secure in God. For Francis this freedom and joy we find in Christ—"by his wounds we are healed"—and insofar as we walk in Christ's footsteps, we offer this same freedom and joy to those whose lives we touch.

STEPHEN EDMONDSON

Pastoral Perspective

the situation of first-century slaves, we have plenty that makes us feel less than free. Our enslavement today may be to a mind-set that is strangled by binary thinking. Fears and dangers in our own world enslave and limit our creativity for solutions. Anxieties about health and work and the next paycheck can enslave our instincts for hope in the future. How do we learn from these early believers about trust in the midst of our own suffering?

Today's faithful Christians find themselves up against the wall in a culture that could not care less about an alternative ethic or about trusting God. The prevailing ethic is self-centered at its root and considers "the other" only as an item on the tax return. Trust is defined as the safest place to store money. Hemmed in on all sides, we are spiritually claustrophobic and caught in the limits we have set for ourselves. The antidote we need will burst open the tombs that hold us captive and liberate us for the expansive way that God offers. We walk out of that tomb unfettered for a life that might actually mean something one day.

The text ties to the other lections for the day as it closes in shepherd imagery. In the arms of the shepherd, our soul is being guarded. The shepherd knows our name and leads us through this age and the next. With our soul guarded by the good shepherd, the freedom to act alternatively in the world starts to look like a possibility.

I overheard a conversation between my young nephew and his friend, who was a much bigger boy. "I could beat you up," the friend said, to which my nephew replied, "Yes, but why would you want to?" The conversation ended. God always offers a life-giving option. We are called to find that option and live with it!

JOY DOUGLAS STROME

---

2. See *Francis of Assisi: The Saint: Early Documents*, vol. 1, ed. Regis J. Armstrong, William J. Short, and J. A. Wayne Hellman (New York: New York City Press, 2002), 166.

Exegetical Perspective

used for the pattern drawn for children learning to imitate or of the letters of the alphabet set out for children to copy.[1] To this, he adds the image, "follow in his footsteps" (cf., e.g., Mark 8:34). These word pictures direct believers to put into play in one's own life the dispositions on display in the obedience of Christ. (3) Finally, in verse 25, Peter underscores the contrast between the past and current lives of believers—life without a proper sense of direction versus life with Christ as shepherd and guardian (see Ezek. 34).

Peter interprets the suffering of Jesus as exemplary (to be modeled in the lives of believers) and as atoning (unique in providing the basis for faithful life). Central to his argument is his appropriation of material related to the Servant of YHWH in Isaiah 53, and his weaving the details concerning Christ's suffering into the fabric of the letter:
—The audience's suffering (2:19, 20, 21, 23; 3:14, 17, 18; 4:1 [2x], 15, 19; 5:10) is like Christ's.
—Christ's nonretaliation in the face of suffering is a model for his followers (e.g., 2:19–20, 22–23).
—Earlier, Peter described God as the "Father" who judges impartially (1:17). Now he observes that Jesus entrusted himself to the just Judge, and he will go on to urge his audience to entrust themselves to a faithful Creator (2:23; 4:19)—in spite of unjust suffering (2:19, 22–23).
—Peter refers to Jesus' having been executed "on the tree" (v. 24, NRSV "on the cross"), drawing attention to the presumed ignominy of Jesus' death (see Deut. 21:22–23). Rather than deny the shame of Jesus' execution, Peter seems actually to embrace it, since the cross is the signature of the God whose purpose is realized through the atoning death of Christ.
—Just as Peter directs his audience to "do good" rather than "sin" (e.g., 2:15, 20), so he notes that Jesus was without sin (2:22). Moreover, because he "bore our sins in his body on the tree," believers, having died to sins, can live to righteousness (2:24; see 4:1).

Thus we see how fully Peter's christological remarks are embedded in his instructions to Christians—not so that they can share his christological perspective (though this is not ruled out), but so that his christological perspective will shape them. The story of Christians experiencing adversity is nothing less than their participation in the story of Jesus, itself deeply rooted in Scripture.

JOEL B. GREEN

Homiletical Perspective

joy. "Look, Daddy, let's go over and swing!" This was the inescapable moment of truth that every black parent in America must face soon or late. What do you say to your child at the critical moment of primary encounter?
"You can't swing in those swings."
"Why, Daddy?"
"When we get home and have some cold lemonade I will tell you." When we had had our lemonade, Anne pressed for the answer, "We're home now, Daddy. Tell us."
I said, "It is against the law for us to use those swings, even though it is a public school. Only white children can play there. But it takes the state legislature, the courts, the sheriffs and policemen, the white churches, the mayors, the banks and businesses, and the majority of white people in the state of Florida—it takes all these to keep two little black girls from swinging in those swings. That is how important you are! Never forget, the estimate of your own importance and self-worth can be judged by how much power people are willing to use to keep you in the place they have assigned to you. You are two very important little girls."[3]

Thurman refused to let the unjust laws of state and nation define him or his daughters. For him this was not only a secular notion but the strong assurance that he was a child of God. No matter what the world said, he had been ransomed and set free. He had heard the voice of Jesus the shepherd, saying not only, "I know my own and my own know me," but also, "I have other sheep that do not belong to this fold. I must bring them also" (John 10:14, 16). Faced with the realities of racism and exclusion, Thurman could say to his daughters, "You are two very important little girls."

BARBARA K. LUNDBLAD

---

1. See Plato, *Prot.* 326d, and Clement, *Strom.* 5.8.49.

3. Howard Thurman, *With Head and Heart: The Autobiography of Howard Thurman* (New York: Harcourt, Brace & Co., 1979), 97.

John 10:1-10

¹"Very truly, I tell you, anyone who does not enter the sheepfold by the gate but climbs in by another way is a thief and a bandit. ²The one who enters by the gate is the shepherd of the sheep. ³The gatekeeper opens the gate for him, and the sheep hear his voice. He calls his own sheep by name and leads them out. ⁴When he has brought out all his own, he goes ahead of them, and the sheep follow him because they know his voice. ⁵They will not follow a stranger, but they will run from him because they do not know the voice of strangers." ⁶Jesus used this figure of speech with them, but they did not understand what he was saying to them.

⁷So again Jesus said to them, "Very truly, I tell you, I am the gate for the sheep. ⁸All who came before me are thieves and bandits; but the sheep did not listen to them. ⁹I am the gate. Whoever enters by me will be saved, and will come in and go out and find pasture. ¹⁰The thief comes only to steal and kill and destroy. I came that they may have life, and have it abundantly."

[handwritten margin note: life abundant]

Theological Perspective

One of the beloved images of Jesus in the Fourth Gospel is that of the attentive shepherd. Visual and musical presentations of the shepherding savior have long captured artistic imagination. Throughout this Gospel, John accumulates Old Testament metaphors for God and ascribes them to the Incarnate One through the "I AM" declarations. In John 10, Jesus fulfills the hopes of Israel for a good shepherd. Deep in the tradition is this iconic understanding that God will intimately shepherd the people. Whether through the shepherd king, David, or the promised Messiah, who would "gather the lambs with his arm," and "gently lead those that are with young" (Isa. 40:11 KJV), God would provide protection and identity for God's own.

Several key theological issues are present in this text, and the interpreter must read it canonically as well as within the tableau of this Gospel. The varied figures of speech used by Jesus (he is both shepherd and gate) not only baffle his hearers, but make contemporary interpretation a challenge, as well. At stake in this passage is the christological and soteriological understanding of the shepherd who gives his life. Both the identity of the shepherd and the idea of redemptive sacrifice pose interpretive hurdles as we query: "What is the nature of this salvation?" "Is the work of this shepherd exclusive?" Thus the

Pastoral Perspective

Proclaiming the good news, telling the gospel story, takes many forms; in John 9–10, it is presented as a three-act play. The dramatic action of act 1 (9:1–12) features the miraculous healing by Jesus of one who was born blind. The introduction by the disciples (9:2) of "sin" as the source of the blindness is an immediate reminder that sightedness is a metaphor. Blindness or sight in the Gospel of John is not a biological ability or limitation, but rather a spiritual orientation and openness to the revelation of God in Jesus. In John, sight indicates an embrace of the Jesus' vision. Act 2, complete with separate scenes with and without Jesus, presents a religious controversy prompted by the miracle. The play concludes in act 3, with Jesus acting as a narrator while giving the Good Shepherd discourse (John 10:1–21).

The pattern in this particular Gospel is to present a miracle story, followed by a dialogue or controversy, and to conclude the triptych with an interpretive discourse. As often happens in the narrative of our own lives, the chapter notations are just marking points, but the story is a whole. Central to any pastoral exchange is an understanding of the milieu of those to whom we give care; said another way, a text does not have substance without a context. Stories shape us as much as we shape them; we are informed by a story through our interpretation and incarnation of its

Exegetical Perspective

Although identification of Jesus as the Good Shepherd will continue through verse 18, this passage covers only the first ten verses. The confrontation with the Pharisees in chapter 9 draws a sharp contrast between healing action of Jesus on behalf of the man born blind and that of the religious leaders who reject the blind man's testimony about Jesus, label him a born sinner, and ultimately "drive him out" (9:34). The man whose sight is restored ends up worshiping Jesus as "Lord" (9:38), while the Pharisees themselves are judged to be "blind" (9:40–41). This contrast between Jesus and the faithless religious leaders continues in 10:1–10, but in a different mode.

The image of the shepherd as a symbol of leadership has strong roots in the Bible and was also a familiar metaphor in Greco-Roman literature. God is depicted as the shepherd of Israel in a number of Old Testament passages, perhaps most memorably in Psalm 23, where there is the note of intimacy and protection also found in John 10 ("The Lord is my shepherd, I shall not want"). David is also celebrated as the ideal shepherd king (see 1 Sam. 16:6–13). However, no passage is more important than Ezekiel 34:1–31, which undoubtedly influences John 10. Ezekiel 34 invokes the notion of God as shepherd of Israel, portrays the people as "sheep" to be led and protected, sharply critiques the leaders as false

Homiletical Perspective

Packed into this parable's first three verses are a number of images. The *gate* is put forward as the proper entrance to the sheepfold. The *shepherd* enters by the gate where the sheep already are. At the gate is a *gatekeeper* who opens the gate for the shepherd. Then the shepherd who has entered the gate is drawn in detail. His voice is known. He calls each sheep by name. He leads them out of the fold. He goes ahead of them. Which image does Jesus mean to place up against himself to effect the metaphor: the gate? the gatekeeper? the shepherd? The lectionary expects us to guess the latter.

However, in response to the Pharisees' lack of understanding, Jesus at first claims what seems to us the least likely image for himself, saying, "I am the gate." Gate brings to mind something that separates those on the inside from those on the outside, for purposes of protection or privilege. For two thousand years, the church's proclamation of Jesus as the gate has served both purposes. Certainly the words of Jesus to the disciples in John's fourteenth chapter have become the theological content of this metaphor for many: "I am the way, and the truth, and the life. No one comes to the Father except through me." For John's community, those who entered by the gate that was Christ necessarily had to close the gate on the flock that remained in the

John 10:1-10

Theological Perspective

interpreter is pressed to consider how one is to regard other shepherds. In addition, a distinctive Johannine ecclesiological accent, the significance of life-giving community, resides in this passage.

The Christology of the Fourth Gospel has been the matter of much discussion in the history of interpretation. Scholars agree that it is a distinctive perspective, with the identity of the Word, the Son, fully imbedded in the life of God prior to incarnation. In a sense, the whole Gospel is a narration of what it means for the Word to be made flesh. The arc of the Gospel is the growing recognition that the One "from above," sent by God, is the very embodiment of Logos.

Whereas in the Synoptic tradition Jesus is proclaimed as the Christ at the end of his ministry (Mark 15:39), more of an inductive approach, John's Gospel assumes his divine origin. From the soaring prologue, which echoes the creation story of Genesis, to the end of the Gospel, where Thomas ascribes the divine name to the risen Christ, "my Lord and my God" (20:28), the writer(s) of the Fourth Gospel underscores Christ's divinity.

The soteriological vision of this text follows from the awareness of who Jesus is. He is the one whom the sheep should follow because of his tender knowledge of each of them, calling them by name. He is the one whose sole purpose is to ensure the safety of the flock. He is the one willing to lay down his life that abundant life might be possible for his flock. Not only is he the shepherd; he is also the gate through whom persons enter, becoming members of God's own people. A certain salvific exclusivity echoes here; he is the way by which persons receive salvation, and no one should attempt to bypass this point of entry.

In the history of interpretation, the issue of supersessionism has been regnant, and this text has sometimes been used to proclaim that "all who came before" Jesus (v. 8) were less than worthy. Tensions between Jesus and the synagogue leaders are noted in chapter 9; this should not be ignored, but some interpreters have sustained a polarizing hermeneutic throughout the Gospel. A better reading simply accents that it is perilous to follow the wrong shepherd. Some interpreters have suggested that Jesus is warning against "messianic pretenders" that preyed upon the flock of God. First-century Palestine had its share of revolutionaries, according to Josephus.

The role of the shepherd is to lead the sheep, providing protection, freedom from fear, and sustenance. Jesus assures his followers, "Whoever enters by me will be saved, and will come in and go out and find pasture" (v. 9). Unlike those who steal, kill, and

Pastoral Perspective

"truth." How we make sense of one event of our lives shapes the focus of the next.

The pericope for the Fourth Sunday of Easter, halfway to Pentecost, is the theological interpretation of a man healed by the tender spittle of Jesus and the Pharisees, who remain blind to the graceful vision of the emerging realm of God. The third act of this Johannine play is not a soliloquy; Jesus speaks to "them" (v. 6), that is, to the Pharisees. The contextual audience and the reader are meant to be listening in. This portion of the Good Shepherd discourse is the continuation of the efforts to grant sight to those who want to see and is an attempt to provide illumination to those who are still in the dark. To the religious scholars and leaders, Jesus presents a "figure of speech" (v. 6), a riddle. For many, Jesus is the riddle, and by the end of this lesson, we might all wonder if we are blind. Do we understand the vision Jesus has for the world? It might be a confusing congruence for the Pharisees to challenge one who has been blind and not be able to "see" what Jesus is saying. Jesus' healing ministry has been a tangible proof of his message; his actions have spoken louder than words, but now his words seem a bit muddled. Is Jesus trying to say that he is a shepherd or a gate? What do the conglomerated metaphors mean? Are we blind to his message?

Jesus' riddles are consistent with the wisdom methods of the blind seers of ancient Greek playwrights and Shakespeare's wise fools. *Oedipus* and *King Lear* are cautionary tales that remind us that we dismiss the foolish or blind wisdom herald at our own expense. Did Jesus study with a Zen master the art of the koan? What is the sound of one hand clapping? The challenge of a koan is not just to get the answer "right," but to live into its delicacy. As with a good napoleon torte, the richness is between the layers. The befuddlement is meant to draw us away from the distracters and into the subtlety that is so obvious that it could be dismissed as too simple. The hermeneutic key to unlocking Jesus' Johannine puzzle is in verse 10: "I have come that they may have life, and have it abundantly." To be distracted by the definitions of the roles in the pastoral play, who is the gatekeeper or who is the shepherd, is to miss the image of the abundant life in the emerging realm of God. The abundant life is the vision Jesus has for all.

To begin pastorally approaching the metaphors of the Good Shepherd discourse, it might be helpful to remember a notion from the Jesuit paleontologist Teilhard de Chardin, who submits that we are primarily spiritual beings having a human experience, not human beings having a spiritual experience. The

shepherds who harm the sheep, and praises David as the true shepherd who will care for God's sheep.

This traditional imagery inspires John's portrayal of Jesus as the "good shepherd" (v. 11) who, in contrast to leaders who are "thieves and bandits" (v. 1), brings them protection, guidance, and abundant life.

There are two distinct segments of the passage: verses 1–6 contrast the true shepherd with the "thieves" and "bandits" who harm the sheep; in verses 7–10 the dominant metaphor is that of Jesus as the "gate." In both instances, the discourse is addressed immediately to Jesus' opponents, presumably the Pharisees of chapter 9, although the whole is obviously intended as instruction for the audience of the Gospel.

The passage begins with an "amen" saying that is a further reflection on the "blindness" of the Pharisees demonstrated in chapter 9, but now the contrast is between the shepherd who enters the sheepfold by the gate and the "thief" and "bandit" (v. 1) who climb in another way. In traditional agrarian societies, then and now, an enclosure for the sheep would be constructed of a stone wall adjacent to the house, perhaps topped by branches of thorns to discourage climbing. There would be one gate or entrance, usually able to be locked shut to prevent anyone coming in to steal the sheep. Thievery was common and caused a devastating loss, since sheep were a source of food (meat and milk) and clothing and a major source of barter for other necessary goods.

The situation imagined here is that there is also a "gatekeeper" (v. 3) who guards the entrance, particularly at night. This implies that the sheepfold was sufficiently large to justify a hired hand as a gatekeeper, perhaps a place where several families kept their herds. The gatekeeper recognizes the true shepherd and allows him in. The sheep too recognize their shepherd by knowing his voice. Here again, the passage reflects actual circumstances. Ancient and current experience in traditional societies confirms that the shepherd often knows each sheep by name, and they in turn recognize his distinctive call. In contrast to Western practice, where the shepherd follows the herd, in the Middle East one can still see shepherds walking out in front of their herd, repeatedly calling to them to keep them together. In John's scene the true shepherd leads his flock out of the sheepfold to pasture.

This segment closes by noting that Jesus' opponents (the presumed audience) "did not understand" the "figure of speech" Jesus used (v. 6). John uses the Greek term *paroimian*, which in this context is similar to the term "parable" or an extended metaphor or

synagogue. On both sides, questions of exclusion and inclusion raged: who was in and who was out theologically, morally, ethnically? According to John, water and not blood marked the sheep that entered through the gate that was Christ. Since John's time, a multitude of theological demarcations—often decreed by what turned out to be the voice of a stranger rather than the voice of the shepherd—have herded the faithful into separate folds.

Though this may seem far removed from the pastoral scene evoked by the pericope before us, a morning spent on Jesus as a gate to our theological wanderings might be helpful, particularly in a time when the voice of the stranger is often lurking in the spirituality du jour. Unfold before the congregation the *filioque* controversy, and consider the present-day implications of the scandalous particularity of the Son as the one gate through which God is fully known. Inhabit another image Jesus uses, and test the voice of a stranger by the voice of the Son. Reflect on the truth claims of present-day thieves and bandits that steal the lives of the flock at the end of the day. How are we to discern the voice of a stranger, when the stranger promises to show us the way, the truth, and the life for the price of a seminar or a book or a DVD? Does the church do the same for the price of a pledge? What do the disciplines of worship, Bible study, and fellowship have to do with recognizing the voice of the shepherd or knowing him who is the gate to abundant life?

The gate can also swing another way, and has, throughout the centuries for those deemed to have fallen too far from grace morally. Step away from the current controversies concerning sexual orientation to the sixteenth-century practice of fencing the Table. Surely the gate must have a fence to hang upon! Here Jesus is the gate and the church the moral gatekeeper. Even if the congregation is far removed from the theological tradition of Calvin, the words in the Genevan liturgy for the Lord's Supper will make most in the pews pause before they dare to approach the gate and join the fold at the Table, lest they partake unworthily. In the sixteenth century, the Libertines were at issue; in the twentieth century some in the Confessing Church fenced Nazi officers from both the Table and the font. Reflecting critically on this practice, Michael Welker observes,

> This has repeatedly been the spot at which a diffuse moral and religious sensibility has been propagated among the laity, and a more or less rigid readiness to exercise moral and religious control has been propagated among priests, pastors, presbyters, and

John 10:1-10

Theological Perspective

destroy, this trustworthy shepherd offers abundant life. A contemporary theological understanding of abundant life might include a purposeful vocation that serves the common good, participation in a generative ecclesial community, delight in sustaining relationships, and a sense of security in Christ no matter what comes.

The role of the community is focal in John, and the Gospel offers several unique portrayals. Jesus is the life giver who restores Lazarus to community (11:38–44); community with Jesus is portrayed by the organic image of the vine and branches (15:1–11); finally, the nautical image of the untorn net in which all the kinds of fish can be contained (21:11) speaks of Jesus' capacity to form community from disparate entities. In this passage, the shepherd seeks to keep the sheep together—as one community. This is a clue to Johannine ecclesiology. Forming a flock and protecting it from scattering portrays Jesus' intention for an indestructible relationship between sheep and shepherd. Likewise, the church must be known by its relationship to Jesus. When christological awareness ebbs in congregational life, that is, when the story of Jesus is neglected, the church becomes unmoored and rudderless. Christology teaches us that God is not willing to remain at a distance from us; rather, in God's humility the Trinitarian history of God includes creation. The Word becomes flesh as God is made "after our likeness," as the prologue of John narrates.

The church would be helped if it could recover the theological meaning of the shepherding imagery. In the iconography of the church, by the fourth century Jesus as shepherd was gradually replaced by Jesus as Pantocrator, the elevated ruler over all, as Constantine united the church with the secular state. As the church became an expression of imperial power, the shepherd's staff was replaced with a gilded crozier; a crown of thorns was displaced by the triple tiara of the pope. Recovering shepherding imagery could call the church to simplicity, sacrifice, and solidarity—needed in a time when many have lost their way.

MOLLY T. MARSHALL

Pastoral Perspective

subtle, but significant, flip of the interpretive lens is consistent with the maverick, mystery-embracing author of this Gospel, the same author who has Jesus tell Nicodemus, a religious scholar, that he must be "born again" to see the realm of God (3:3).

Throughout the Gospel, Jesus claims to provide the critical elements of abundant life: water (4:14), bread of life (6:35), light of the world (9:5), and here, shelter in the form of a sheepfold. Nicodemus, who wondered how to reenter his mother's womb, might now be considering the measurements of the sheep pen or calculating the costs of caring for the flock. If he does so, his head will blind his heart to the bucolic imagery of Psalm 23: the Lord is my shepherd, I shall not want. There are good, green grass and still waters, but it is the presence of the shepherd that makes the field safe and nourishing.

Part of the mystery of faith and the riddle of the discourse is the presence of danger, even while in the sheepfold and the fields of good, green grass. There are strangers, thieves, and bandits; the flock will even cross through the "valley of the shadow of death" (Ps. 23:4 KJV). Moreover, with the disciples of act 1, we may ask who sinned (9:2). It sometimes is easier to find reason in blame than comfort in presence. The sheep know to whom they belong; they respond to the call of their name. They are comforted by the voice and presence of the shepherd, even when there is danger and confusion.

As the blossoms of the Easter lilies fade, we are invited to continue to embrace the riddle of faith: by dying, the shepherd provided abundant life. Sometimes it is hard to see and understand; but the single hand still claps.

SHANNON MICHAEL PATER

"figure of speech," as the NRSV translates it. Jesus' interlocutors often fail to fully understand the meaning of Jesus' words in John's Gospel (see, for example, the confusion of Nicodemus and Pilate). For those open to Jesus' word, however, the meaning is clear. Jesus is a true shepherd, not only in the spirit of David, but reflective of God's own providential love. Jesus' relationship with his disciples is one of intimacy and trust. They listen to his voice and recognize him. He brings them no harm but protects them. They willingly follow him, and he brings them to the source of life (see also v. 10).

The final segment (vv. 7–10) moves in a somewhat different direction. Another emphatic "amen" saying identifies Jesus as "the gate for the sheep" (v. 7). This is underscored in the "I AM" saying of verse 9: "I am the gate." Throughout the Gospel the Johannine Jesus makes such revelatory declarations that fuse the divine name (*egō eimi*, "I am") with particular qualities expressing human longing or sustenance: bread (6:35), life (11:25), light (9:5), truth (14:6), the way (14:6). Reflective of John's Christology, Jesus reveals the divine presence (1:18) and thereby brings God's redemptive love into vital contact with human yearning (3:16–17).

The image of the "gate" by which the sheep can go to "find pasture" is used to express Jesus' role of bringing God's saving love to the world (3:17). While the thief comes to "steal and kill and destroy," Jesus comes "that they may have life, and have it abundantly" (10:10). The concept of *zōē*, "life," is fundamental to John's Gospel. At the outset of the Gospel "life" is proclaimed as the very essence of God that is brought to the world through the Word (1:3), and in the climactic discourse of Jesus on the brink of the passion, the bestowal of life is declared to be the very purpose of Jesus' mission (17:2, 3). Jesus himself embodies God's "life" for the world (11:25; 14:6). "Life" in Johannine terms, therefore, is to be understood not only as the vital force that animates the human person, but as "eternal life" (*zōē aiōnios*), a share in the very being of God through faith in Jesus (20:31).

DONALD SENIOR

ecclesiastical hierarchs. . . . Subjected to moral and religious observation, the Supper could no longer be understood as a feast of reconciliation. . . . Instead it came across to many persons as an anxiety-producing means of moral gate-keeping.[1]

Is the church the gatekeeper and Jesus the gate to protect the morally weak and vulnerable within the fold or to privilege a community of the ethically pure? Is the church a hospital for sinners, as Augustine believed, or a society of the morally perfectible, as Pelagius thought? Does Christ as the gate keep the flock from corruption by the world, or did God so love the world that the gate swings open for the lost sheep in particular? Is Jesus alone the gate, so that, in the end, every disparate flock will be made one in him (John 17:20–21)?

Finally, these ten verses in John's tenth chapter cannot be understood in isolation from the verses that follow (not to mention the story that precedes them). However, the division of verses imposed by the lectionary can also act as a magnifying lens placed over one of Jesus' "I AM" statements that is forgotten in the pastoral rush to proclaim him the Good Shepherd on what is, for those who observe such designations, Good Shepherd Sunday. If we are not alert to the complexity of images used by John at the beginning of this chapter, the congregation likely will echo the words of the Pharisees as they say to us at the door, "We did not understand what you were saying to us." Likewise, had the lectionary committee been alert to Jesus' own exegesis of the first five verses, the better psalm for the day and the year might have been Psalm 118:19–20: "Open to me the gates of righteousness, that I may enter through them and give thanks to the LORD. This is the gate of the LORD; the righteous shall enter through it."

CYNTHIA A. JARVIS

---

1. Michael Welker, *What Happens in Holy Communion?* (Grand Rapids: Eerdmans, 2000), 70.

Acts 7:55-60

⁵⁵But filled with the Holy Spirit, [Stephen] gazed into heaven and saw the glory of God and Jesus standing at the right hand of God. ⁵⁶"Look," he said, "I see the heavens opened and the Son of Man standing at the right hand of God!" ⁵⁷But they covered their ears, and with a loud shout all rushed together against him. ⁵⁸Then they dragged him out of the city and began to stone him; and the witnesses laid their coats at the feet of a young man named Saul. ⁵⁹While they were stoning Stephen, he prayed, "Lord Jesus, receive my spirit." ⁶⁰Then he knelt down and cried out in a loud voice, "Lord, do not hold this sin against them." When he had said this, he died.

Theological Perspective

If chapter 2 of Acts portrays the best response ever given to someone's first sermon, here Stephen receives the worst response imaginable to what was definitively his last. Perhaps all unsuccessful preachers should take some comfort here. If their congregations merely complain or fire them, at least they do not stone them. Stephen's hearers include more than those who were present. He is remembered as the first "martyr." That word is a transliteration of a Greek word meaning "witness," so etymologically, to be a martyr is to bear witness. The risen Christ told the disciples that they would be his witnesses to those nearby and far away (Acts 1:8), and this passage teaches us of the nature of Christian witness—done poorly and done well.

In courtrooms "expert witnesses" may be asked to speak of what they know from study, but most of us are asked to say what we have seen or experienced. The same is true in Jesus' call to be his witnesses. Rather than presenting arguments, we are to tell what we have seen and experienced of Jesus. This is what the martyrs of the first three centuries generally did. Officials pleaded with Polycarp, the aged and kindly bishop of Smyrna, asking him to renounce Jesus, to burn incense, and to proclaim that Caesar was Lord, so that they could release him. Polycarp gave no lecture. He stuck to telling what he knew: "Eighty-six

Pastoral Perspective

The stoning of Stephen, though told as a fairly crisp and straightforward narrative, is rich and complex in its themes. Immediately one hears in it parallels to Luke's narration of Jesus' crucifixion. Immediately one senses the growing tension and hostility toward the Christian community. Immediately one sees, in the shadows of persecution of the church, the prime mover of the future church. In a few compact verses, Luke records everything from the death of the first Christian martyr and a distinctly Christian way to die to the beginning of persecution against the Christian community and the signs that the community will flourish regardless.

Luke writes of the last moments of Stephen in striking parallel to those of Jesus. Three times Stephen speaks, and each time his speech echoes the words of Christ. When he is arrested, Jesus is brought before the chief priests and scribes, where he is taunted in the hope that he will commit blasphemy. Instead of declaring himself the Christ, which he says they will not believe, Jesus tells them, "From now on the Son of Man will be seated at the right hand of the power of God" (Luke 22:69). In a similar way, Stephen's persecutors bring forward false witnesses against him and attempt to get him to blaspheme God, but instead, the lectionary passage tells us, Stephen sees just this vision and testifies to it in verse

Exegetical Perspective

Stephen's audience reacts negatively to his words (v. 54) and to his vision of Jesus as the "Son of Man" figure on God's right side (v. 56). To see the "glory of God" places Stephen in very good company (e.g., Abraham, in 7:2; Moses, in Exod. 33:18–22; Ezekiel, in Ezek. 1:28; cf. John 1:14), but it is this vision—placing the crucified Jesus in close relation to God—that has angered the people beyond the point of return.

In the book of Acts, Stephen's life and mission, among other things, serves as a transitional figure in the development of Luke's history of the early church. With Stephen's death, Luke also introduces readers to the beginning of the leading missionary to the Gentiles, Saul/Paul. Luke's audience learns that Saul is one of the leading persecutors of the developing Christian community (7:58; 8:1, 3). This will soon change, and Paul will become the great missionary to the Gentiles. Although it is Peter's vision to take the gospel to the Gentiles (in Acts 10), and his last spoken words in the narrative of Acts include this commission (15:7), from chapter 13 on in Luke's account, most of this task will fall to Paul. In Paul's own writings, he does not quite see the initiation of the gospel message to the Gentiles in the same way as Luke (Gal. 1–2).

As is common in Luke's account, many of the major figures are "filled with/full of the Holy Spirit": the 120 (2:4); Peter (4:8); Barnabas (11:24); Paul

Homiletical Perspective

On this Fifth Sunday of Easter the lectionary jumps from Acts 2 to Acts 7. This leap suggests that preachers would do well to review the context of our pericope as well as its boundaries. Though much happens between last week's text and this week's text, we might make special notice of a theme that emerges in these chapters: the growth of the church and the spreading of the gospel is propelled, despite opposition, by the force of a God whose divine will cannot be stopped.

Stephen's martyrdom is best understood in this context. In the face of an angry crowd Stephen delivers a message that accuses the people of rejecting the prophets and opposing the Holy Spirit. In the midst of his stoning, Stephen remains undeterred and prays for his persecutors. Stephen's confidence reinforces Acts' image of a Spirit-filled church that is emerging with holy determination. In reading just beyond our passage, we see how Stephen's murder spawns a greater persecution and results in the scattering of Christians throughout the countryside of Judea and Samaria. Even here, the Spirit continues to work. The scattering only serves to spread the word of the gospel and to introduce the mission of the church to the Gentiles.

Preachers might see here an opportunity to explore the relentless nature of God's love. We are

Acts 7:55-60

Theological Perspective

years I have served him, and he never did me any wrong. How can I blaspheme my King who saved me?"[1] Other early martyrs simply affirmed "I am a Christian."[2] They paid with their blood for telling the truth about what they personally knew of Jesus.

In the passages prior to this, Stephen was called to bear witness before the Sanhedrin, and in some ways it looks as if he did a poor job (Acts 6:12–7:53). This might seem like the ideal opportunity to bring the good news to his people's leaders, using his famous wisdom and grace (Acts 6:3, 8). Rather than a sermon, though, Stephen gave a summary lecture on biblical history to the learned assembly, ending it with insults and rebukes. He never named Jesus, but he accused them of his murder. It was no surprise that they were infuriated rather than converted. It was at best a prophetic speech, a fulfillment of Jesus' promise to provide words for those called before the authorities (Luke 12:11–12); but one must admit there are problems in his rhetorical strategy.

In our text, Stephen turns the tables and bears witness well. However, the crowd was already against him, and it cost him dearly. After his speech, still in front of the angry Sanhedrin, he had a vision of Christ in glory. At that point he simply told what he saw: "I see the heavens opened and the Son of Man standing at the right hand of God!" (Acts 7:56). In this he truly bore witness with his words. As they took up stones to kill him, he bore witness with his actions too. He prayed, as Jesus had prayed from the cross (Luke 23:34, at least in late manuscripts), that his killers would be forgiven—showing a life changed to reflect Jesus' love. As Jesus had prayed for his Father to receive his spirit (Luke 23:46), Stephen asked Jesus to receive his—showing a life changed to reflect Jesus' trusting faith. Telling what he knew of Jesus, and showing what he was because of Jesus, he bore witness with power and grace.

This theme of bearing witness to Jesus is also present in the other texts assigned for this day: Peter affirms that our calling is to "proclaim the mighty acts of him who called [us] out of darkness into his marvelous light" (1 Pet. 2:9), and Jesus declares that if we believe in him we will do works like his—and more (John 14:12). However, if bearing witness is telling what we see of Jesus' work, we need to look with care to see his work within and around us. If we

1. "The Martyrdom of St. Polycarp," 9.3, in *Early Christian Fathers*, trans. and ed. Cyril C. Richardson, Library of Christian Classics, vol. 1 (Philadelphia: Westminster Press, 1953), 152.
2. "Letter of the Churches of Vienne and Lyons," 20, in *Some Authentic Acts of the Early Martyrs*, trans. E. C. E. Owen (London: Society for Promoting Christian Knowledge, 1933), 60.

Pastoral Perspective

56: "I see the heavens opened and the Son of Man standing at the right hand of God!" Just as Jesus in Luke's Gospel cries out from the cross, "Father, into your hands I commend my spirit" (Luke 23:46), so Stephen cries, "Lord Jesus, receive my spirit" (Acts 7:59). Then, just before Stephen dies, he kneels and cries out in verse 60, "Lord, do not hold this sin against them." Jesus cries out from the cross, "Father, forgive them; for they do not know what they are doing" (Luke 23:34).

So it is that Stephen, first recorded martyr of this new Christian faith, bears witness to Christ in the very way that he dies. Jesus' death becomes the model for our own suffering, our own persecution, our own death. The apostle Paul wrote in the early 60s that one should not let the sun go down on one's anger, but here the admonition reaches an eternal proportion, as the believer is admonished by Christ's example not to "sleep" in death before offering forgiveness to those who have harmed you. Stephen, who has been marked for service from the beginning (Acts 6:5, 8, 15), remains faithful to the end and presumably is welcomed by Christ himself into eternal peace, the words of forgiveness the last thing to cross his lips.

Other themes, however, also emerge. Stephen's death parallels Jesus' death because Stephen's response to death imitates his Lord's. Stephen—like Jesus—is not tolerated as a prophet among his own people. The spiritual change they usher in arouses fear in their detractors, and their executions stem from that fear. In Stephen's case, however, something new also occurred. The semblance of order, even an occupier's order, is gone. Unlike Jesus, Stephen is not brought before any magistrate; there are no negotiations that result in his death. Stephen is dragged by an angry mob of religious leaders, and stoned immediately.

The text tells us that as Stephen testifies to the vision he sees—the Son of Man at the right hand of God—the members of the council cover their ears. Is his vision so offensive, or do they stop their ears because they cannot continue to listen to him while they do what they are determined to do? In the commission of inhumane acts, one must forcibly shut out the humanity of the person who is subjected to it, in order to carry out the act. Their violence against him begins with stopping their own ears and shouting over his voice, obliterating his testimony. Rushing toward him and shouting, dragging him out of the city and stoning him to death, they represent a new tension, a rising intolerance, in the face of a growing and increasingly separate Christian community.

Exegetical Perspective

(13:9); and the disciples (13:52). In most of these descriptions, this "filling" relates directly to the power to speak, whether it is in various languages (2:4) or to offer verbal challenges to rulers or opponents (4:8; 13:9). Such is the case in Acts 7.

According to Luke, the Spirit gives Stephen, in addition to the authority to speak, his ability to witness the heavenly vision. The "opening" of the heavens recalls two other visions in the Luke–Acts collection. In Luke 3:21–22, the heavens open and the Spirit descends upon Jesus "as a dove." In addition, God acknowledges Jesus as "my beloved Son." In Acts 10:11, Peter sees the heavens opening and a vision of a giant sheet with "unclean foods" on it. In Peter's vision, God speaks to him as well, providing the meaning to the vision, "What God has made clean, you must not call profane" (10:15). Stephen's vision is explicit; however, there is no voice from heaven speaking to him. The lack of a voice, or any indicator, has left commentators speculating on the meaning of Jesus' "standing" at the right side of God. The repetition of this act—offered first by the narrator, then spoken by Stephen (7:55–56)—implies its significance.

Normally, Jesus is "seated" on God's right side (2:33–34; 5:31). This is also true in the wider New Testament (Matt. 19:28; Mark 14:62 par.; Heb. 8:1; 10:12; 12:2). Some scholars suggest the act of standing indicates a readiness to speak on behalf of someone (i.e., Stephen?); others think it may refer to Jesus' posture as he prepares to welcome the soon-to-die martyr. It may also indicate Jesus' first step to prepare for the coming future judgment. It is difficult to know with certainty the meaning of this expression in light of the context in Acts 7. Whatever else it might signify, Jesus' stance is a position of influence, authority, and power that Stephen envisions for him. On the other hand, the vision terribly disturbs the audience and they react accordingly.

The lectionary reading leaves out Stephen's speech, which is a "lengthy" (relative to other passages in the NT) retelling of Israel's history, highlighting particularly the stories of Abraham, Jacob, Joseph, and Moses. Stephen then connects Israel's rejections of their leaders, especially Moses, with his audience's rejection of Jesus as the Messiah: "You stiff-necked people, uncircumcised in heart and ears, you are forever opposing the Holy Spirit, just as your ancestors used to do" (7:51). This type of use of Scripture is distinctive of the book of Acts in the NT (7:2–53; 13:17–25). It is also one of the primary ways that one shapes and revises the identity of a community. Tell the story! In Stephen's retelling, the

Homiletical Perspective

given, once again, the chance to claim God's Easter victory over the cross. God's love cannot be destroyed. It is poured out with unhindered generosity, much the way God's gift of the church in Acts will not be prevented. Bishop Jeremiah Park of the United Methodist Church is fond of reminding confirmands, "God loves you, and there is nothing you can do about it!" There is great emotional power to such a simple confession, because it acknowledges the truth of God's victory and at the same time leads us to accept it for ourselves.

An equally important lesson in the scattering of the church that follows Stephen's death is the understanding that God uses a negative situation as an opportunity to bring about a positive change. Although the scattering is caused by an unjust persecution of the faithful, God uses it to introduce Christianity to non-Jewish areas for the first time. Often our times of greatest growth occur during or in response to our greatest struggles. A worthy effort for preachers might be to connect this sense of growth to the redeeming and relentless love that God has for all God's people. Perhaps Stephen, with his confidence in the face of darkness, may serve as a reminder of God's faithfulness for those who are in the midst of their own struggles.

Stephen's death shares a number of parallels with Christ's. The two most obvious are Stephen's final words in verses 59 and 60. The difference is that when Stephen addresses the Lord, he is speaking to the post-Easter Jesus, the one whom he sees standing in victory "at the right hand of God." The message for the early church is loud and clear: the Christian movement is tied to God's ultimate victory in Jesus. Believers are sustained, even in oppressive circumstances, by the knowledge of that victory. Their assurance of the future empowers their living in the present.

Preachers might seek to encourage a similar perspective in today's believers. Unfortunately, Christianity has a reputation for being a religion that concerns itself primarily with the question, "What happens when I die?" The impression for many people is that Christianity is less interested in the life that we have here and now than it is in the afterlife. A helpful sermon might highlight the message of victory in a way that encourages parishioners to embrace the freedom and hope that can color life in the present. Christians are free to follow God's priorities and to embody God's love in redemptive ways, regardless of clashing interests in the society around us, because we have the assurance that God's ways are ultimate.

Acts 7:55-60

Theological Perspective

think of Christian faith primarily as doctrine or behavior, we may not be looking for the traces of God's providence guiding us, or for the work of the Holy Spirit in reshaping our lives. If we expect the risen Christ to be at work in our character and circumstances, and beyond us in society and the world, we just might see signs of grace—or judgment, or healing, or justice. Telling others what we experience and see of Jesus' work, we bear witness; and as we live in faith and faithfulness, our actions will testify to him as well.

Whether it was his words about Christ in glory, or his action in forgiving his own murderers, Stephen's testimony was powerful enough for the church to remember him as the prototype of the faithful witness. Death by stoning seems a waste. What good could come from such faithfulness? Stephen's testimony may not have converted the Sanhedrin, but at least one who heard and saw eventually came to Christian faith: We first see Saul right here, as he watches and approves of Stephen's death. It would take another, more startling intervention by God to transform the persecutor into Paul the apostle, but this scene played a part. Perhaps Stephen's testimony should get some credit for the way Paul eventually bore witness to Christ in his life, in his writings, and, at least according to legend, in his martyrdom under Nero. Our own gentle and true words, our own loving and just actions, may also matter for the reign of God in ways we cannot foresee.

GARY NEAL HANSEN

Pastoral Perspective

Finally, the coats laid at Saul's feet also signal something of that new tension as well. Saul will later refer to his qualifications for religious leadership, calling himself "a Hebrew born of Hebrews; as to the Law, a Pharisee; as to zeal, a persecutor of the church; as to righteousness under the law, blameless" (Phil. 3:5–6). Much has been made of Luke's mention that the witnesses lay their coats down. It is not the accused who is stripped in the story, as Jesus was stripped of his garments; nor is it the chief priests, who might themselves strip for the physical labor of the lapidation. When the witnesses strip, it is as though they are readying themselves in the effort, a second eager crowd forming around the first angry gathering. How true of human behavior this is, and what an ominous portrait it paints! They are would-be persecutors, and witnesses to Stephen's martyrdom. And yet, their very coats also testify that Saul is there. They are portentous witnesses to a change that is moving forward even in the face of Stephen's death.

As modern Christians who live in a country where religious practice is not only tolerated and free, but in significant ways supported (e.g., tax-exempt housing allowance for clergy, exemption from real-estate taxes for houses of worship), we may find it troubling to incorporate sacrificial death and martyrdom into our spirituality. Especially since September 11, 2001, we may respond to the news of violent clashes between various religious and ethnic groups around the world with fear and retribution. The death of Stephen, however, encourages us to reflect not only upon our own immediate emotions, but upon our deepest convictions about justice and peace. Stephen's divinely inspired imitation of Christ breaks free of the victim mentality that otherwise perpetuates cycles of violence, and illuminates a new way.

SUSAN B.W. JOHNSON

Exegetical Perspective

emphasis falls on the rejection of God's servants *and* on the unnecessary nature of the temple for guaranteeing the presence of God among the people of God. On the latter point, Stephen emphasizes how God was with Israel throughout the wilderness period *before* the construction of the temple, when they were "resident aliens" (7:6, 29).

The lectionary reading also leaves out Saul's explicit role in this persecution. In our reading, Saul passively sits by, apparently guarding the clothes of the stoners, but he is more directly involved than that. He approves of Stephen's stoning (8:1), and he "ravages" the church (8:3). This persecution forces believers to flee Jerusalem, which, in turn, aids the spreading of the gospel. The latter was not part of Saul's plan, but it is a primary message of Luke's: persecution leads to a broadening of the base.

Much has already been said about the main character in this account. In Luke's depiction, Stephen is also a type of "Jesus" figure, since Luke portrays his death and the final prayer in a fashion similar to Jesus' own death (Luke 23:34–49). Both die unjustly as martyrs and yet ask forgiveness for those responsible (Acts 7:60; Luke 23:34). Stephen provides a model, in the spirit of Jesus, for how believers should pray on behalf of their enemies. Whatever else was Luke's intent with this story, a model for death for a worthy cause must be one of them. As Martin Luther King Jr. often reminded his children, a person who "had nothing that was worth dying for . . . was not fit to live." So Stephen is willing to die for the sake of the coming Messiah, and Luke portrays him dying in the manner of his Savior.

EMERSON B. POWERY

Homiletical Perspective

This confession is helpful when considering the act of forgiveness. As the angry crowd throws stones, Stephen prays, "Lord, do not hold this sin against them." Though most of us would struggle to adopt Stephen's attitude under such circumstances, we are helped by the knowledge that forgiveness is rooted not so much in the strength of human will but, rather, in the vision of "the glory of God and Jesus standing at the right hand of God" (v. 55). The challenge to forgive is a universal challenge. Every parishioner is able to identify with it. Preachers may be of unique help to their people if they are able to frame the effort to forgive within the image of God's victorious love. For example, parishioners may be encouraged to look upon their enemies through the loving eyes of God. Then, finding themselves more deeply aligned with God's heart, parishioners may pray to discern the next step in the forgiveness process. Forgiveness is not an act of individual heroism. It is, rather, an act of God.

Finally, the issue of martyrdom may feel irrelevant to many parishioners. Though Christians still die for their faith all around the world, many parishioners will never encounter such a threat. Nonetheless, even for these people Stephen's story remains worthy of a listen. In addition to the points made above, Stephen's story may prove helpful in guiding Christians to consider the ways in which faithfulness to God may clash with the common assumptions and practices of modern culture.

For example, what does Christian faith have to say about rampant consumerism and our complicity in it? What does Christianity have to say about our nationalistic impulses and the self-interest that guides the foreign policies of many nations? What does our faith have to say about environmental stewardship and our current patterns of living? Though many of us may never be asked to die for our faith, our faith still calls us to measure our priorities, to take a stand, and to express our beliefs through action. For those of us in this position, Stephen's story is still very much a relevant model of faithfulness and obedience.

TIMOTHY B. HARE

Psalm 31:1-5, 15-16

[1]In you, O Lord, I seek refuge;
 do not let me ever be put to shame;
 in your righteousness deliver me.
[2]Incline your ear to me;
 rescue me speedily.
 Be a rock of refuge for me,
 a strong fortress to save me.

[3]You are indeed my rock and my fortress;
 for your name's sake lead me and guide me,
[4]take me out of the net that is hidden for me,
 for you are my refuge.
[5]Into your hand I commit my spirit;
 you have redeemed me, O Lord, faithful God.
. . . .
[15]My times are in your hand;
 deliver me from the hand of my enemies and persecutors.
[16]Let your face shine upon your servant;
 save me in your steadfast love.

Theological Perspective

While an articulation of hope, trust, and confidence in the everlasting righteousness of God is on display throughout the Psalms, this lection gives rise to questions concerning how the psalmic imagination might have functioned within Jesus' vocational self-understanding culminating in his death on a cross. Did the animating concerns of the Psalms shape his understanding of the shape of things to come in his own life? If so, how might we take up these prayers as he did, allowing them to interpenetrate our understanding as we follow after him? "In your righteousness deliver me," the psalmist petitions in the thick of lamentation (v. 1). The demand that the Lord might yet be "a rock of refuge," "a strong fortress" (v. 2), and a resource of speedy rescue is kept in dramatic tension with the affirmation that, in some sense, the Lord is already somehow manifest in these ways.

On the Fifth Sunday of Easter, we remain within this tension, even as we proclaim the risen Christ. By holding our own concerns within the psalmist's sensibility instead of declaring them somehow definitively resolved, we expand the space within our liturgy for both renewed anticipation and confessional candor. The sense of God's faithfulness as, in any sense, a mission accomplished, must give way to what we also discern (and feel) to be a "not yet."

Pastoral Perspective

Mark Twain said, "Man is the only creature that blushes, or needs to." The psalmist could relate to that statement. As he faces enemies he prays, "In you, O Lord, I seek refuge; do not let me ever be put to shame; in your righteousness deliver me" (v. 1). We do not know who these enemies are, but we know the psalmist is concerned that they could cause him to be "put to shame." In fact, he uses the word "shame" three times in this psalm—twice asking God not to let him "be put to shame," and once asking God to "let the wicked be put to shame." It is doubtful that the psalmist considered shame itself to be his enemy here, but for modern readers it may indeed be our enemy.

What do we mean by "shame"? One person writes, "Psychologists and anthropologists . . . see guilt as feeling bad for what you have *done or not done*, while shame is feeling bad for who you *are*, measured against some standard of perfection or acceptability."[1] Churches are full of persons who struggle not merely with guilt but with shame. On Sunday mornings assembled in the pews before us we may see the following people: a small child who has somehow gotten the idea that she is "bad"; a teenager whose sexual explorations have made him believe

1. Harold S. Kushner, *How Good Do We Have to Be? A New Understanding of Guilt and Forgiveness* (Boston: Back Bay Books, 1997), 35.

Exegetical Essay

Pope John Paul II opened his remarks at Yad Vashem, the Holocaust memorial in Jerusalem, in 2000 with words from this song of personal lament: "The words of the ancient psalm, rise from our hearts: 'I have become like a broken vessel. I hear the whispering of many—terror on every side—as they scheme together against me, as they plot to take my life. But I trust in you, O Lord: I say, "you are my God."'" These poignant words from verses 12–14 resonate with ancient pain into the modern world's brokenness. The song cries to God for help (vv. 1–10), describes in detail the nature of the psalmist's despair (vv. 11–13), and gives thanks to God for deliverance (vv. 19–24). This lectionary selection (vv. 1–5, 15–16) focuses on the cry for help and guidance and the recognition of deliverance.

Scholar Artur Weiser finds that the psalm offers glimpses into the psychological aspects of human prayer, moving between petition and praise.[1] Weiser notes, as other scholars have agreed, that the psalm violates most of the typical patterns that psalms usually employ. This psalm does not conform to standard petition or to the usual shapes of praise. Elusively avoiding form-critical psalmic patterns, the

Homiletical Perspective

Save Me, and Save Me Now! A reading of Psalm 31 leads one to ask the question, "Where have I heard these words before?" and for good reason. Some of its words are repeated in Martin Luther's ageless hymn of the Reformation, "A Mighty Fortress Is Our God." However, there are differences. While Luther affirms the ever-abiding presence and power of God,

> A mighty fortress is our God,
> a bulwark never failing (stanza 1),[1]

Psalm 31 expresses the heartfelt prayer of one who is in need of the salvation still to come,

> Be a rock of refuge for me,
> a strong fortress to save me. (v. 2)

This is not to say that the author of this psalm was any less faithful than the great Reformer; rather, it is to acknowledge that the psalm was written during a time of great and personal need.

One way to understand fully this psalm is to look through the lens of oppression. The words of the psalm suggest that its author was under siege, as in a time of war. The imagery of an actual fortress could

---

1. Artur Weiser, *The Psalms: A Commentary,* trans. Herbert Harwell, Old Testament Library (Philadelphia: Westminster Press, 1962), 275–76.

1. Martin Luther, "A Mighty Fortress Is Our God," *The Presbyterian Hymnal* (Louisville, KY: Westminster/John Knox Press, 1990), #259.

Psalm 31:1-5, 15-16

Theological Perspective

By speaking, listening, and remaining within this tension and the space it conjures, we are better equipped to aspire toward and dwell within the way of the Lord, the way we count as most powerfully present in the life, the ministry, and the sufferings of Jesus. Perhaps the challenges Jesus faced in trying consistently and persistently to stake his own hopes within the faithfulness of God are not entirely dissimilar to our own. The feats of attentiveness and trust required of anyone who means to live a life of obedient anticipation concerning the promises of God will be undertaken along the continuum of courage we discern in Jesus and the prophets, the lives lived "by faith" that generated (and generate still) the life of our own believing and witnessing communities (Heb. 11).

In a life made up of difficult decisions and various crises not so radically different from the ones we face, Jesus sought first the kingdom of God and chose the paths that most embodied a faithful imitation of what he understood to be Godlike love: emptying himself, humbling himself, and embracing obedience to the point of death (Phil. 2:7–8). "You are my refuge," the psalmist affirms (v. 4). Like the psalmist, Jesus ventures his entire life and work, the very possibility of meaning, on such an affirmation being objectively true, on the faithfulness of God being somehow faithful to the end. According to this calculus, love is the only relation, and it is love alone that signifies. As Harold Oliver puts the matter: "Love is not one relationship among other relationships, but rather the supreme paradigm of the fundamentality of relatedness. . . . Love is not something *we* do; it is rather what *defines* who we are."[1]

"Into your hand I commit my spirit; you have redeemed me, O Lᴏʀᴅ, faithful God" (v. 5). Jesus himself takes up the first part of these words according to Luke's Gospel (23:46), but the second part, the assurance of having been redeemed, will call for some degree of imaginative speculation "by faith" concerning the meaning of Jesus' resurrection. We need to maintain the dramatic tension between the psalmist's hope and the sometimes dingy reality of the world, in order to be faithful to the whole of the biblical witness. Nevertheless, we can affirm that the resurrection is, for starters, a vindication of Jesus' proclamation that God's kingdom is near and that God cares for us, meets us in our needs, and will somehow sustain our existence in such a way as to

Pastoral Perspective

that he may be damned; a businesswoman who has made an unethical work decision and is unable to feel or accept God's forgiveness in spite of her repentance. What these people, and others like them, have in common goes beyond merely accepting responsibility for sins they may have committed.

Instead, what they feel is shame about their very personhood, shame about who they are. A fictional character thinks to herself,

> It was her life itself; that was the sin she wanted hidden from her father and the houses and sleeping people they passed; and she wanted to forgive herself but could not because there was no single act or even pattern she could isolate and redeem. There was something about her heart . . . she felt that her every action and simplest moments were soiled by an evil she could not name.[2]

There is something about *our* heart. The psalmist has an answer for the enemies he faces—the same response we have as we face the enemy of shame. The solution is not what we might expect in twenty-first-century culture, which alternately prizes self-sufficiency on the one hand and victimhood on the other. The psalmist does not promise to work harder. He does not swear to be more careful or brave. He does not scheme or complain that God is unfair. Instead, the psalmist turns and asks God for help: "Incline your ear to me; rescue me speedily. Be a rock of refuge for me, a strong fortress to save me" (v. 2). In other words, "God, listen to me! Hurry up and help me! Be a rock refuge for me." Notice *how* the psalmist appeals for God's intercession: "For your name's sake lead me and guide me, take me out of the net that is hidden for me" (vv. 3–4). The psalmist asks God to intercede, not because the psalmist himself is such a nice person, but *in order to protect God's name*. What blessed audacity.

How can the psalmist make such a brazen plea to the creator of heaven and earth? He can plead because he has faith in the nature of God. As he says, "You are indeed my rock and my fortress . . . you are my refuge. . . . you have redeemed me, O Lᴏʀᴅ, faithful God" (vv. 3–5). The psalmist believes God is ultimately *for* him, not against him (cf. Rom. 8:31). God is faithful. So the psalmist proclaims, "My times are in your hand" (v. 15). This is not a claim that God causes or controls every single event in life, but the psalmist *does* trust that in every moment of life, from disappointment to success, from sorrow to joy, from

---

1. Harold H. Oliver, *Relatedness: Essays in Metaphysics and Theology* (Macon, GA: Mercer University Press, 1984), 17.

2. Andre Dubus, "The Pretty Girl," in *The Times Are Never So Bad* (Boston: David R. Godine, Publisher, 1986), 39.

psalm's structural bouncing between pleas for deliverance and declarations of thanksgiving for the approach of transcendent emancipation rings familiar with what some today might understand as a portrait of a person suffering from bipolar disorder or deep depression. Although we cannot know the personality or experiences of the writer, this psalm sets forth clearly the depths of severe personal pain and may well echo with persons today who are suffering. Such suffering rends the heart and mind, shattering perceptions of reality and forcing extremes of thought and behavior. This psalm points to a traumatic experience, the horror of which is beyond words and beyond mere comprehension.

The phrases and themes of the psalm, evoking a visceral response upon each reading, converge on the notion of utter dependence on God. No other rescue would be relevant in the face of such suffering; survival will henceforth be impossible unless God intervenes. Although the lectionary reading does not include verse 12, "I have passed out of mind like one who is dead; I have become like a broken vessel," this central verse expresses the depth of despair of one stripped bare and completely vulnerable, only able to turn to God.

In particular, the lectionary seems to have also chosen this psalm for Holy Week, because of verse 5: "Into your hand I commit my spirit; you have redeemed me, O LORD, faithful God." Luke's account of Jesus's crucifixion echoes the first half of this line from Psalm 31, when Jesus cries out his last words and breathes his last breath (23:46), although none of the other Gospels indicate this. The Gospel uses the psalm to portray Jesus as one in the midst of despair, facing death, and fully dependent upon God, but the quotation from Psalm 31 leaves out the assurance of the verse's second half, as well as later parts of the entire psalm. Did Luke intend for us to supply the rest of the psalm, at least in its meaning, or merely to give the reader this one clarion note of despair?

The lectionary joins the lament of verses 1–5 to a cry for salvation and rescue in verses 15–16. In the larger context of the psalm, these latter verses are part of a call for help, combined with a request that God punish the wicked by putting them to shame and rejecting them for their lies (vv. 17–18). As a whole, the psalm asks God to step into the psalmist's life to bring justice for the good, as well as justice for the evil people in the world. God has been absent, or at least slow to act. God has not rewarded the righteous or punished the wicked, despite the psalmist's assurance that God will eventually repay everyone for

give the feeling of comfort and protection. However, not many of us living in the northern half of the Western Hemisphere in the twenty-first century have experienced the horrors of modern warfare. Women and men who have returned from the battlefields of the world are often unable to speak about the atrocities they have experienced. We should never forget the millions of innocent victims of war: the citizens who are refugees, sometimes in their own land, as well as those who are forced to flee—running hundreds of miles to find the basics of life: food, water, shelter. Darfur is an image that we cannot escape.

We do not want to minimize the pains that have been witnessed in these extreme situations, but it can also be said that others have experienced their own "battles." They have confronted their own enemies and have legitimate claims on the validity of this Psalm 31 for them. A single mother struggling to raise her two children is experiencing an ominous enemy. A person facing a layoff from work in a time of double-digit unemployment is forced to confront a daunting opponent. A young child whose parents have just been claimed by an automobile accident is about to enter a battlefield loaded with land mines. Victims of racism have fought enemies working overtime to hold them back.

The classic and tragic mistake often made in the midst of war is entering into battle thinking that we are totally capable of defending ourselves. A recurrent theme in this psalm is that we must humble ourselves and put our trust in God. First, we must realize that we are in a selfish web (or net) from which we cannot escape on our own accord. Often the net is well camouflaged to entrap us, and before we know what has happened, we have been snared. This trap can come in many forms: a career that has delivered comfort to both us and our families; an investment portfolio that promises security for a lifetime; the "need" for a second home when most of the world would be thankful for a simple shelter to protect them from the elements. The image that comes to mind is our Lord telling the story of the folly of a rich man desiring to build even more barns to store his crops (essentially his wealth), thinking that his possessions are the sum total of his life (Luke 12:16–21).

Once we have assumed our proper posture of humility, realizing that we simply do not have any strength or will of our own, then we must give ourselves over to our God. In verse 5 we find the words that were utilized by Jesus himself as he hung upon the cross, "Into your hand I commit my spirit." In Luke's telling of the passion narrative, these were

Psalm 31:1-5, 15-16

Theological Perspective

make the hope of everlasting life warrantable. Drawing upon the psalmist's assurance concerning God's redemptive actions (what was and is and is to come), the witness of the New Testament contends, by way of innovation upon innovation, that the relatedness—the love—that defines us will know no end.

We are still compelled toward petitionary prayer: "Save me in your steadfast love" (v. 16). The doctrines of prayer without the practice of prayer will not feelingly persuade. As Dietrich Bonhoeffer reminds us, the psalms teach us to pray "with heart, mouth, and hands."[2]

The lectionary passage instructs us in both affirming more than we feel and praying our way toward hope without lying. While the witness of the Psalms alone does not generate a doctrine of resurrection, we do find, taken together with the New Testament's celebration of the risen Christ, an anticipation of unprecedented saving acts to come in view of the reign of God's steadfast love. Jürgen Moltmann's language is especially apt here:

> What was impossible before will then become possible. Energies will awaken which before were constricted. A future will be opened which was hitherto closed and inaccessible. Over against the reality of the visible world awaken the possibilities of change for that world, and its transformation into the kingdom of God.[3]

As we commit our spirits to the not-yet-seen ends of the never-not-redeeming God, we strain and exult, complain and hope, worry and celebrate through and within the prayers Jesus learned and repeated, tension included. These are the dramas of divine relation in which we discover ourselves, the context of our life and worship. It is the space where redeeming love functions. There is no other.

J. DAVID DARK

Pastoral Perspective

birth to death, God mysteriously, powerfully, and finally holds his life and times. So the psalmist has confidence to pray for deliverance from enemies and even to ask, "Let your face shine upon your servant; save me in your steadfast love" (v. 16)—a request for God to look upon him with joy and love.

As we struggle with the great enemy of shame, the psalmist's strategy is an invitation for us to come before the all-knowing one with audacious trust that God is for us, not against us. God holds our times in God's hands, and as we live in faith, God will be a refuge and rescue for us as we confront various enemies, especially the enemy of shame.

Several years ago, Frank Warren began an unusual art project. He invited people anonymously to mail him personally decorated postcards with their secrets written on them. Over time, Warren has compiled thousands of those secrets in several books and on a popular Web site. An anonymous writer from Mississippi epitomized the significance of this modern-day confessional, "Every single person has at least one secret that would break your heart. If we could just remember this, I think there would be more compassion and tolerance in the world."[3]

Our compassionate Lord was crucified on a cross. Not only was this the most excruciatingly painful death known at the time, it was also considered to be the most shameful. According to Luke, Jesus' last words from the cross were spoken to God—a quote from this psalm: "Into your hand I commit my spirit" (v. 5). As we live and die in faith, we too commit our spirit to the one who holds our times in his hand and saves us from our enemies, even from the enemy of shame.

JEFF PASCHAL

---

2. Dietrich Bonhoeffer, *Psalms: The Prayer Book of the Bible*, trans. James H. Burtness (Minneapolis: Augsburg Press, 1974), 42.
3. Jürgen Moltmann, *God in Creation: A New Theology of Creation and the Spirit of God*, trans. Margaret Kohl (San Francisco: Harper & Row, 1985), 172.

3. Frank Warren, *The Secret Lives of Men and Women* (New York: HarperCollins, 2007), 49.

Exegetical Perspective

their deeds (v. 23). The expectation of eventual justice provides the psalm's ground for hope and courage, as well as motivation for human patience and service to God (vv. 23–24). We are to love God because of the salvation and recompense that God will surely bring (vv. 7, 17).

Thus the psalmist speaks to radical human dependence upon God, while in the depths of experiencing God's absence in the present moment. The portions of the psalm that the lectionary omits speak all the more strongly to God's distance from the world. Consider verses 9–10:

Be gracious to me, O LORD, for I am in distress;
     my eye wastes away from grief,
     my soul and body also.
For my life is spent with sorrow,
     and my years with sighing;
my strength fails because of my misery,
     and my bones waste away.

In such words of lament, we can hear the psalmist's reality that God has not intervened over a long period of time. This stands in stark contrast to the frequent Christian expectations of Good Friday and Holy Saturday, when even the strongest sense of grief resides next to an assurance of God's impending action in Easter. Christians envision God hovering nearby the cross, ready to help but waiting just a bit longer, a few days more until Easter arrives. The psalmist, on the other hand, sees only foes at hand and does not feel God's presence, while the suffering of life endures for years and no respite is in sight. Pope John Paul II's recitation of this psalm at the Yad Vashem memorial to the Holocaust recognizes the lingering, persistent suffering that endures all the way to death and threatens to wipe away all human meaning with it. When the psalm speaks its certainty that God's goodness is abundant (v. 19), God's faithful rescue seems very far away indeed.

ALICE W. HUNT

Homiletical Perspective

actually the last of the words painfully, yet audibly spoken by the Christ (Luke 23:46). Some have wrongly assumed that these words were a sign of weakness as Jesus was about to die. Nothing could be further from the truth. Within the context of the psalm we are made aware of the connection between total submission and redemption. It is as if we must first die to self, before we can be opened up to the possibilities of grace and life available within God. In other words, it is God's faithfulness, not our acts of faith, that reign supreme: "You have redeemed me, O LORD, faithful God" (v. 5b).

"Let go, let God" is a common phrase that has almost been overutilized, but its sentiment rings true. When we truly let go of those selfish motives and concerns that can hold us back, the wonders of God can be experienced and allow us to flourish.

In the face of all the enemies that can cause us to cower in despair, all that remains is hope in the one who has been our refuge through all of our trials—through the good times and the bad. "My times are in your hand," writes the psalmist. "Deliver me from the hand of my enemies and persecutors" (v. 15). One clearly must be among the oppressed fully to understand this psalm. The truth rings out, "We have all been oppressed." Some have been oppressed in our want, others in our abundance. Know that we are all in need of the redemption that only our God can provide.

JOHN E. WHITE

1 Peter 2:2-10

[2]Like newborn infants, long for the pure, spiritual milk, so that by it you may grow into salvation— [3]if indeed you have tasted that the Lord is good.

[4]Come to him, a living stone, though rejected by mortals yet chosen and precious in God's sight, and [5]like living stones, let yourselves be built into a spiritual house, to be a holy priesthood, to offer spiritual sacrifices acceptable to God through Jesus Christ. [6]For it stands in scripture:

"See, I am laying in Zion a stone,
  a cornerstone chosen and precious;
and whoever believes in him will not be put to shame."

[7]To you then who believe, he is precious; but for those who do not believe,

"The stone that the builders rejected
  has become the very head of the corner,"

Theological Perspective

In this passage, a mixture of Old Testament and mystical imagery intersects with the Christocentrism that we have observed in surrounding passages. The passage illustrates the capacity of Scripture to inspire a variety of rich theological reflection through its juxtaposition of ideas, images, and scriptural motifs. We will follow one thread through this passage, pursuing its vision of the eucharistic community's spiritual reality.

Our passage is deeply rooted in the literature of Hebrew Scriptures, especially in the Psalms and the Prophets. The experiential language of tasting God's goodness (v. 3) is native to the liturgical environment of the psalmist, as is the call for God's people to remember God's chosen cornerstone (v. 6). The proclamation that God has made a people of no people fulfills the ancient promise of Hosea's prophecy (v. 10). This rootedness in Hebrew Scriptures accounts for the evocative language of the passage, and this is not without theological significance. It reminds us of Peter's earlier claim for the capacity of God's living word to serve as a medium for communicating God's transforming presence (1:23).

The scriptural roots of this passage also lend the text a fundamentally communal focus. God's lively and enlivening presence is here depicted as transformative of God's people, precisely as a people. It is the

Pastoral Perspective

Four Sundays after Easter, and the last bloom from the lily has dropped. Alleluia has been tucked away for next year, and we are precious close to Pentecost and Ordinary Time. What better day to call for a refresher course about the impact of Easter Sunday? Though every Sunday is supposed to be a little Easter, we all know that the march through Ordinary Time can feel long and drawn out. All the Easter gladness we can collect must carry us across that long trek and sustain us, fully convicted by the power of the resurrection.

It is a pep talk of sorts that 1 Peter attempts in chapter 2. Pulling out all the Hebrew Scripture stops, the technical connections between past and present are presented. "O taste and see that the LORD is good" (Ps. 34:8) becomes the condition for salvation: "if indeed you have tasted that the Lord is good" (v. 3). The living stones of Isaiah 28 predict the cornerstone that the new Christians believe has become Christ. Finally, the pitiful rejection of Hosea's children becomes the reversal of fortune for those who follow Christ (v. 10)! While these connections are historically compelling, the pastoral connection is much more practical. If you are throwing your lot in with these Christians, then do so with full disclosure. Connections to the past are obvious and the launchpad for all that comes next.

^{8}and

> "A stone that makes them stumble,
>   and a rock that makes them fall."

They stumble because they disobey the word, as they were destined to do.

^{9}But you are a chosen race, a royal priesthood, a holy nation, God's own people, in order that you may proclaim the mighty acts of him who called you out of darkness into his marvelous light.

^{10}Once you were not a people,
>   but now you are God's people;
> once you had not received mercy,
>   but now you have received mercy.

Exegetical Perspective

Peter's reference to "beloved" in 2:11 marks a new section within his letter. This means that 2:4–10 is the climax of the first section, focused on the identity and vocation of Peter's audience. The preceding verses, 2:1–3, pave the way for identifying believers as God's "spiritual house" (v. 5).

The logic of verses 1–3 is straightforward. Those who have set aside past, toxic behaviors (v. 1) and who have tasted the Lord's kindness (v. 3) must grow into salvation (v. 2). With his reference in verse 2 to the "pure milk of the word" (NRSV: "pure, spiritual milk"), the author gives no hint that he is thinking of the worldly or immature (cf. 1 Cor. 3:1–3; Heb. 5:11–14); instead, the author emphasizes the intensity of their desire for the word—like a newborn's craving for milk.

In 2:4–10, Peter reads the situation of his audience from the perspective of the career of Jesus Christ, and the career of Jesus Christ from the perspective of Israel's Scriptures. With regard to structure, verses 4–5 set the theme for this unit, on which Peter then expands in verses 6–10. Thus, verses 4–5 borrow the vocabulary of the biblical texts cited and appropriated in verses 6–8 (Isa. 28:16; Ps. 118:22; Isa. 8:14), building on a series of basic polarities: honor/shame, choose/reject, belief/disbelief. Believers, introduced as "living stones" in verse 5, then become the special focus of verses 9–10, which also draw on biblical texts (Isa.

Homiletical Perspective

This portion of 1 Peter is probably the most familiar to people in the congregation, with its wonderful image of living stones and strong affirmation of people who have felt abandoned. These words would have been especially reassuring to these resident aliens dispersed from their homelands. "Now you are God's people" (v. 10) would have meant the world to people who were seen as nothing in the larger culture. All of this was possible because of Jesus Christ, the living stone who was rejected by many—even as many who received this letter knew rejection in their own lives.

"Come to him, a living stone . . . and like living stones, let yourselves be built into a spiritual house" (vv. 4–5). The preacher might consider some of the stones scattered throughout the Bible: the stone Jacob used for a pillow on his journey away from home; the stones carried from the Jordan River when the homeless former slaves finally reached the promised land; the stone called to be a reminder of the people's promise before God in Joshua 24: "See, this stone shall be a witness against us; for it has heard all the words of the LORD that he spoke to us" (Josh. 24:27). Was that stone somehow alive? John the Baptist declared that stones *could* come to life when he preached at the Jordan: "I tell you, God is able from these stones to raise up children to Abraham" (Matt. 3:9b).

1 Peter 2:2-10

Theological Perspective

worshiping community that is called to taste and see that the Lord is good, even as the worshiping community forms the audience for the psalmist's proclamation of God's cornerstone. Likewise, God's call and election are declared to a race, a people, a collegium of priests (v. 9). By rooting itself in scriptural language, our passage cannot conceive of God's action in the world apart from God's relationship with the whole of God's people.

At the same time, this passage moves us past a soteriology based on remembrance to one based on presence, on experience. "Be fed by pure spiritual milk," we are told. Taste and see that the Lord is good. Our passage calls us to a mystical experience of God's goodness made present in Christ. It roots the Christian life and Christian thinking where so much Orthodox theology begins—with the concrete tasting of God's goodness and God's mystery in the mystical experience of prayer. How is this impacted by the Old Testament vision of God's communally directed activity? How does the clear Christocentrism of this passage form our understanding of the mystical experience of God to which it calls us?

Vladimir Lossky offers an Orthodox articulation of the deep connection of Christian life and thought to relationship with God realized in prayer.[1] For Lossky, any true knowledge of God is rooted in our transformation through our encounter with God in the depths of our soul. This encounter both empties us and opens us to be conformed to the God whom we meet, allowing us the possibility of true life with God and knowledge of God.[2] This conforming capacity of our encounter with God fits nicely with our passage's desire that we become living stones to be built into a spiritual house. However, the insistence that our transformation be grounded in our relationship with the chief cornerstone, Jesus, calls us to hear Lossky's theme in a variation.

Alexander Schmemann offers us a divergent Orthodox approach to a mystically rooted vision of Christian life with his emphasis on the role of the eucharistic community in our encounter with God. For Schmemann, we are constituted as church, as recipients of new life in Jesus, through our participation in the Eucharist. The Eucharist is "the eternal actualization of the Church as the body of Christ."[3]

1. Vladimir Lossky, *The Mystical Theology of the Eastern Church* (Crestwood, NY: St. Vladimir's Seminary Press, 2002), 7–43.
2. Ibid., 39–42.
3. Alexander Schmemann, *For the Life of the World* (Crestwood, NY: St. Vladimir's Seminary Press, 1973) and *Introduction to Liturgical Theology* (Crestwood, NY: St. Vladimir's Seminary Press, 1966). The quotation is from *Introduction*, 24.

Pastoral Perspective

For most contemporary audiences, these references lie flat on the page. Even if our congregations are well versed in the scriptural connections, what happened in the past is past. What concerns most Christians is carving out a meaningful role for Christian identity today. Not entirely unlike the predicament of 1 Peter's readers, Christianity today has become an increasingly alienating pursuit. Can one claim to be Christian, but not one of *those* Christians? Can one claim to be a follower of Christ, without conjuring up the online jokes and stereotypes plaguing anyone remotely associated with organized religion? What kinds of resources are given to believers today so that they can withstand the onslaught of cultural disdain for Christianity? How can longing for spiritual milk, living stones, and the designation of royal priesthoods be any help?

There is always some trial and error when a new mother learns to breastfeed her newborn. A mom has to be relaxed enough for the milk to flow. A mom has to be attentive enough to help the baby latch on. A mom has to have taken care of herself with food and drink enough to produce the milk. On the baby's side, some learning has to happen as well. The baby has a natural inclination to search for the breast. Babies still need help to find the right place, suck hard enough for the milk to let down, and not wear themselves out in the effort. In the first week of life, mother and child have to work together to find a rhythm that will make this work. The miracle is that both mother and child "know" at some deep level how to do this. Their DNA has been hardwired for sustaining life.

Likewise, a new Christian "knows" at some deep level that "spiritual milk" is what will nurture their life of faith. The analogy is a good one, as we compare the give-and-take that happens between believer and God before a new Christian grabs on to the miracle of the life of faith and begins to grow. To be sustained for the risks and challenges of a long life of faith, we start as a newborn starts, with raw material of Jesus' teachings, the good milk that is especially designed to meet our most basic needs.

Basic needs give way to building blocks, living stones that lay a foundation for the challenges sure to follow. A solid foundation gives way to an identity that will not shrivel up at the first sign of trouble. An identity that includes beautiful descriptors like *a chosen race, a royal priesthood, a holy nation, God's own people* (v. 9).

God's own people live in the real world. The real world is in real peril. Included in our identity as

Exegetical Perspective

43:20–21; Exod. 19:5–6; Hos. 2:23). On the basis of this complex interaction of texts and motifs, Peter seeks theologically to shape the identity of his audience.

First, he articulates the basis for judgments concerning honor and shame. Peter dismisses typical, human evaluations (e.g., genealogy, gender, congenital defect) in favor of divine ones, with God's evaluation regarded as decisive and ultimate (e.g., vv. 4, 5, 9, 10). What matters is God's choice, God's grace.

Additionally, there is the question whether one adopts God's valuation of people and things, understood in terms of belief or disbelief in the gospel (vv. 6–7). In other words, status is rooted in how one responds to Christ, whether with faith or rejection. God's purpose is at work with respect to both believers and disbelievers. The former are chosen as God's elect (v. 9), while the fate of the latter, "stumbling," has been predetermined by God (v. 8). The result of refusing the gospel is that its subject, Jesus Christ, is experienced as an obstacle. Faith, then, allows one to see what could otherwise not be seen. From a point of view illumined by conventional wisdom, Jesus and his followers are humiliated, rejected; but from a perspective illuminated by Christ's suffering, they are God's elect, honored. This means that faith and unfaith are matters of human volition, but the consequences of faith and unfaith have been predetermined.

Second, drawing on Isaiah 28:16, verse 6 sets out a stark contrast. A "cornerstone" is not only the stone set at the corner of two intersecting walls (as the name implies), but is one prepared and chosen for its exact 90° angle; as such, it is the basis for the construction of the whole building. Choosing the right corner is basic not only to the aesthetics of the building but also to its stability and longevity. Obviously, as they set out to build, God and those who reject Jesus have radically different bases for appraisal.

Third, Peter develops the identity of his audience in terms of the imitation of Christ. The parallel between Jesus and Peter's Christian audience is significant:

Jesus
A living stone
Rejected by humans
In God's perspective, elect
In God's perspective, honored

Peter's Audience
Living stones
(Implicit: rejected by humans)
In God's perspective, elect
In God's perspective, honored

Homiletical Perspective

Now the stones have indeed come to life in Asia Minor. People trodden underfoot like stones are now honored as a royal priesthood. Without a temple, they will become a temple of living stones. This is not their own doing, nor is it our own doing. "Let yourselves be built into a spiritual house": this is far different from saying, "Build a spiritual house." If we were to build a spiritual house, we might think about capital campaigns and a new education wing, enlarging the church campus or renovating the worship space. This building, however, is not something we do: "let yourselves be built" is the essential word. This is something Jesus Christ is doing and is not dependent on what the church building looks like. Nor can it be measured by the saying, "We worship about 1,500 on Sundays." (We hope that Jesus is somewhere among the 1,500!)

When we let ourselves be built into a spiritual house by the presence of the living Christ, the results may not be very impressive. Some of these living stones are very well educated, others have not finished high school. There is a woman who sits in the balcony because she does not think her clothes are good enough for the nave. Two people saying, "Peace be with you," to each other have not spoken since the contentious church council meeting. A baby keeps crying during the quietest parts of your sermon, and you can hear several people saying, "Pastor, this is why we need a policy: no children under five in worship." Seven teenagers are in the side section slightly hidden behind a pillar. You know they are texting their friends who are sitting at the end of the row. "At least they are here," you say to yourself. You would text them yourself from the chancel, if you knew how.

All these living stones are assured that they are now God's people. They have become a holy priesthood. The text closes with a wondrous antiphonal liturgy. We can hear one side of the congregation responding to the other:

Once you were not a people,
    but now you are God's people;
once you had not received mercy,
    but now you have received mercy. (1 Pet. 2:10)

A few years ago a worship service was held at Union Seminary, planned and led by homeless people. One of the seminary students had worked with a group called Picture the Homeless as part of her senior thesis project. For months she met with people who were accustomed to living on the streets. The focus of the service was to remember the hundreds of people who had been buried on Hart Island, New

1 Peter 2:2-10

Theological Perspective

The Eucharist is the place where we "taste and see" that the Lord is good. Schmemann speaks of human persons as fundamentally "hungry" beings, insofar as we are hungry for God. In the Eucharist this hunger is satisfied, especially as it allows us to see that God has given us a world, not to satisfy our hunger, but so that we will turn from the world in thanks to God and there be satisfied. We are fed, then, through our connection to the eucharistic community, and in this feeding we are at the same time constituted as the church—as the community fed by God.

In Schmemann, we find an understanding of encounter that is christological. We not only meet and come to know God chiefly as God has been revealed to us in Jesus, but we also are transformed through this encounter into Christ's body, manifesting Christ's ministry in the world. In the Eucharist we come to Christ, the living stone, so that, like living stones, we are "built into a spiritual house, to be a holy priesthood, to offer spiritual sacrifices acceptable to God through Jesus Christ" (v. 5). This eucharistic conception of our mystical encounter with God captures as well the scriptural emphasis of the communal foundation and fruit of this encounter. Schmemann's vision, then, offers an apt framework for living into 1 Peter's understanding of our encounter with God in Christ.

We fully grasp the dynamics of this passage, however, only when we emphasize the scriptural context in which its eucharistic vision has been articulated. However much this passage plays on the distinction between those who have rejected Christ the cornerstone and those who have accepted him, it clearly makes the scriptural narrative of God's people, Israel, the norm for understanding the Christian life. If the overall trajectory of the passage is guided by a eucharistic vision, it outlines this vision with images of the temple (into which we are built) and the priesthood (with which we are empowered to serve). It defines the status of those previously outside God's covenant as "not a people" (v. 10), who are given identity through God's merciful incorporation of them into God's people, Israel. In this sense, the theology of 1 Peter reflects closely Paul's theology in Romans 9–11, though it articulates this theology with brevity, through its evocative use of scriptural imagery.

STEPHEN EDMONDSON

Pastoral Perspective

Christians is the call to proclaim something of what we know about God to the world. That is no small call. To counter the stereotype of small Christian living takes the weight of a person who has, according to 1 Peter, been warmly nurtured in the faith, who has the strength of one whose spiritual house rests on the cornerstone of Jesus Christ, and whose identity is strong and secure in the arms of a God who serves up spiritual milk like no other.

Five Sundays into Easter, the power of the resurrection is palpable. The genius of God's actions on Easter Sunday is that there is death to counter every day, not just at Easter. There are oppressive structures to overturn every day, not just at Easter. There is life to be celebrated every day, not just at Easter. First Peter insists that the Christian life particularly equips believers with all they will need to proclaim the mighty acts of the one who calls us out of darkness into the light. For today, our role is clear and we are compelled to act. God's own people are empowered through Christ to sing, protest, dance, pray, and march. No stereotype can define us, because we have been claimed by God. No ridicule can undo us, because we have been named by God. No shallow expression of faith can represent us. We make our way into Ordinary Time with the most *extra*ordinary claim: Christ is risen! Risen indeed. It is enough to sustain us. It is enough to support us. It is enough to empower us for the days ahead. Alleluia! Amen.

JOY DOUGLAS STROME

Exegetical Perspective

This is a message of hope, since it demonstrates that their suffering does not signal their rejection by God. After all, Jesus was rejected by humans but chosen by God.

Fourth, appropriating for his audience a number of historic designations associated with Israel, Peter gives them their identity (vv. 5, 9):

—Spiritual house: Rebirth entails incorporation into a new community—the new temple that was to accompany the restoration of Israel.

—Holy priesthood: The purpose of this priesthood is to offer "spiritual sacrifices," a likely reference to holiness of life (1:15) and mutual love (1:22). Peter emphasizes the priestly identity and role of the community of believers in the world at large.

—Elect clan: The phrase derives from Isaiah 43:20, which identifies Israel as God's chosen people in relation to exodus and restoration from exile.

—Royal priesthood and holy nation: Alluding to the narrative of God's mighty deliverance of his people from bondage, Peter borrows language from Exodus 19:6. God hears the cries of his people in distress, acts to rescue them, and enters into covenant with them.

—A people for God's possession: Peter's language reminds us of Exodus 19:5 and Isaiah 43:21, and so with the twin notions of God's care for the distressed and the formation of God's people in exodus and restoration.

This community is to "proclaim the mighty acts of him who called you out of darkness into his marvelous light" (v. 9; see Isa. 43:20–21). In Peter, "praise" includes both worship and proclamation, and has as its content God's mighty deeds—especially the saving death of Christ and God's having raised him from the dead (1:3, 18–19, 23). The move from darkness to light is a typical metaphor for conversion (e.g., Acts 26:18; Eph. 5:8; 1 Thess. 5:5) with roots in representations of exodus and return from exile (e.g., Pss. 107:13–14; 118:27; Isa. 42:16; 58:10).

The result is the creation of a people that previously did not exist (v. 10). In naming his children Lo-ruhamah ("shown no mercy," Hos. 1:6) and Lo-ammi ("not my people," Hos. 1:9), Hosea had pronounced judgment on Israel, but also anticipated a reversal, when his children would be renamed Ruhamah ("shown mercy," 2:1, 23) and Ammi ("my people," 2:1, 23). Borrowing these categories, Peter celebrates the saving mercy of God and gives his audience their identity as God's people.

JOEL B. GREEN

Homiletical Perspective

York City's potter's field. Most of them had been buried without names, never honored with religious services. The goal of Picture the Homeless was to move city officials to allow religious observances on the island, even if names were never known. Some of those planning the service could not read, so they memorized their parts. Everyone worked very hard to get things right.

When the day came to lead worship, they led the service with power and grace. Dawn led the opening litany; Robert read the story of Lazarus and the rich man—then preached an impromptu sermon that was not part of the planning. Others told their own stories of living on the streets. At the close of the service, each person in the congregation was invited to write the name of a homeless person on a purple Post-it. A large sheet had been stretched between two tall candle stands at the front of the chapel. Scattered at random all over the sheet were anonymous names: John Doe, Jane Doe, Baby Doe. People were encouraged to place their purple squares over those anonymous names. One by one people went forward. It was obvious that the leaders from Picture the Homeless knew far more names than the rest of us.

However, the names kept falling off the sheet. It is not easy to stick a Post-it to a sheet suspended between candle stands! Dawn was undeterred. She went back again and again to pick up the fallen names. Finally, a student held his hands behind the sheet to give her something to push against. She did not sit down until every name was in place. It was then that we discovered that the anonymous names had not been printed at random. The purple Post-its spelled out words: WE ARE HERE. We are here, even though we were buried without names. We are here, even though you may not meet our eyes on the street. Once we were not a people, but now we are God's people. What does this promise look like where you are?

BARBARA K. LUNDBLAD

John 14:1-14

"Do not let your hearts be troubled. Believe in God, believe also in me. ²In my Father's house there are many dwelling places. If it were not so, would I have told you that I go to prepare a place for you? ³And if I go and prepare a place for you, I will come again and will take you to myself, so that where I am, there you may be also. ⁴And you know the way to the place where I am going." ⁵Thomas said to him, "Lord, we do not know where you are going. How can we know the way?" ⁶Jesus said to him, "I am the way, and the truth, and the life. No one comes to the Father except through me. ⁷If you know me, you will know my Father also. From now on you do know him and have seen him."

⁸Philip said to him, "Lord, show us the Father, and we will be satisfied." ⁹Jesus said to him, "Have I been with you all this time, Philip, and you still do not know me? Whoever has seen me has seen the Father. How can you say, 'Show us the Father'? ¹⁰Do you not believe that I am in the Father and the Father is in me? The words that I say to you I do not speak on my own; but the Father who dwells in me does his works. ¹¹Believe me that I am in the Father and the Father is in me; but if you do not, then believe me because of the works themselves. ¹²Very truly, I tell you, the one who believes in me will also do the works that I do and, in fact, will do greater works than these, because I am going to the Father. ¹³I will do whatever you ask in my name, so that the Father may be glorified in the Son. ¹⁴If in my name you ask me for anything, I will do it."

Theological Perspective

The lectionary readings for the Sundays after Easter are replete with instructions for the disciples about how to live as Jesus taught without his physical presence in their midst. This week's reading is a part of the Johannine Farewell Discourse of Jesus, preparing believers to consider not only his journey through death to life, but their own. Many rich theological themes surface in this passage, including the believer's union with Christ; hope for life after death; Jesus as Savior; the relationship between Jesus and "Abba," the Sending One; and a theology of prayer.

Following the betrayal by Judas, Jesus informs the disciples that he will be with them only a little longer, which prompts Peter to ask where he is going. Chapter 14 provides assurance that they will have an ongoing relationship with Jesus not severed by death, even though they cannot follow him now. Jesus exhorts them to believe in God and in him—which is an assertion by the writer that Jesus participates fully in divinity and is the proper object of worship. Because they have already witnessed his power as "the resurrection and the life" in the raising of Lazarus, they can trust that though he might go ahead of them into a future they cannot see, they will be empowered to follow. He will be able to secure their identities beyond death.

Pastoral Perspective

This opening pericope of the Johannine Farewell Discourse (John 14–16) was the text of my first venture in preaching. I was fourteen, and the occasion was a "youth service" celebrating the eleventh anniversary of the congregation's call to our pastor. My family started attending the church the same Sunday he assumed his pulpit duties. I still remember my angst-riddled and audacious adolescent sermon title: "A Cure for Heart Dis-ease." As a teen, I was excited because I thought that my word study on "troubled" had cleverly revealed the distress of the disciples: it was the anxiety of their hearts on that night that kept them from hearing Jesus give final instructions. My title was, in fact, a confession of my own nervousness at nascent preaching. At fourteen, what did I know about preaching, let alone about the workings of the heart?

The disciples who gather with Jesus for the farewell meal almost certainly have a measure of heartburn. Their hearts are torn and disquieted as they hear Jesus say a long good-bye. They have been following Jesus since he began his public ministry, but they are, at best, adolescent in their understanding of his message, vision, and mission. They are not able to comprehend that their lived theology is about to radically change. They have been looking for a Messiah and believe that they have found him. They believe the

Exegetical Perspective

This passage takes the form of a Farewell Discourse. Examples of a great leader bidding a poignant farewell can be found in Greco-Roman literature—such as Plato's account of Socrates' farewell to his disciples. Perhaps a more influential example for John's Gospel is the farewell of Moses to the people in Deuteronomy. Other New Testament examples are Jesus' words at the Last Supper (especially in Luke 22:14–38 with briefer parallels in Mark 14:17–31 and Matt. 26:20–35) and Paul's farewell to the elders of the church at Ephesus (Acts 20:17–38). The function of this passage is similar to that of many of these scenes; Jesus announces his imminent departure, consoles his followers, gives them directions for the future, and promises to be with them again.

The so-called apocalyptic discourse found in Mark 13 (with parallels in Matt. 24:1–44 and Luke 21:5–38) also has an important parallel to John 14:1–14. Gathered with his disciples on the eve of his passion, Jesus speaks both of the impact of his absence on the community and the promise of his final triumphant return.

14:1–7. In the preceding exchange Peter asked one of the Gospel's intriguing open-ended questions: "Lord, where are you going?" (13:36).When Jesus told Peter that he could not follow where Jesus was going, Peter's

Homiletical Perspective

Jesus' words at the beginning of John's fourteenth chapter are words we have spoken countless times to a congregation gathered at the edge of a freshly dug grave. At the edge of his own grave, Jesus means to reassure his disciples that his death is not the end but the beginning of the "way," whose destination is the room he is making for them in God. The disciples are incredulous. So are most in the pews.

On any given Sunday, our congregations are full of hearts troubled by the fact that the gift of mortal life does not last. Begin, therefore, where Jesus begins. Begin with the troubled heart he assumed and so redeemed in his own grief at the news of Lazarus's death (John 11:33). Begin with the question that anticipates Jesus' answer: What would free the human heart from being troubled? The world has a multitude of answers. Jesus has only one: *Believe in God, believe also in me* (v. 1). John speaks of believing almost exclusively not as something to which one assents inwardly, but as an outward and active commitment to a person, the person being Jesus. The words of Luther in The Large Catechism come immediately to mind. In response to the First Commandment, Luther asks what it means to have a God and answers that God is what you hang your heart upon.[1] The heart that is

1. See Paul Lehmann's discussion in *The Decalogue and a Human Future* (Grand Rapids: Eerdmans, 1995).

John 14:1–14   467

John 14:1-14

Theological Perspective

The eschatological perspective of the text is laden with hope for life after death and the promise that they will be with him. The theology of resurrection (which is not the explicit concern of this chapter) has moved beyond the conflicted perceptions of the Sadducees and Pharisees in the Synoptic Gospels. The Fourth Gospel's perspective does not address some of the unresolved tensions found in Paul's theology of resurrection. During the time of the Maccabean revolt (180–161 BCE), the theology of resurrection developed as a response to the question, what will God do for those who die for a righteous cause? The hope of resurrection was articulated by one of the martyred brothers: "You dismiss us from this present life, but the King of the universe will raise us up to an everlasting renewal of life, because we have died for his laws" (2 Macc. 7:9). At the end of the first century, the writer of the Fourth Gospel reflects a much more sophisticated doctrine, that is, that persons will die and rise in Christ (John 12:23–25).

Fascination with unknowable detail inexorably accompanies attempts to distill theological insight about *where* Jesus is going, *what* he will be doing as preparation, and *how* he may return for the faithful. Thomas voices the insistent question: "Lord, we do not know where you are going. How can we know the way?" (v. 5). The place of the dead remains a mystery for those yet living; it is an impenetrable realm where God abides, yet a place that has room for all who believe in Jesus' identity with God. It is the perichoretic essence of the triune God to make space for others, and the Johannine assurance is that Jesus accompanies the believer home.

Not only will Jesus go ahead of his beloved followers, traversing the chasm between the temporal and the eternal; he will prepare a place for them to be with him, granting their lives enduring significance because he calls them his own. The persistent question lingers for those who engage the world of the Johannine text: Is belief in Jesus necessary for hope beyond death? John 14:6 has often been coupled with Acts 4:12 to construct an exclusive doctrine of salvation. Many today would hear these words as descriptive of the Christian hope, without arguing that no other salvific trajectories suffice. Triumphalism has never been an attractive part of Christianity, and the interpreter must remember that John uses "insider language" for the faithful.

Central to this passage is the relationship between Jesus and God. In the fourth century Arius contended that Jesus did not share the same substance as God, and this passage in John helped the counterargument

Pastoral Perspective

Messiah to be immortal, but he is about to be executed. They have a vision of a messianic strongman who will liberate the people from occupation, but he is about to be seemingly defeated by oppression. They believe that the Messiah will usher in an eternal kingdom of peace, but they are about to experience horror beyond their most terrified imaginations.

How does the heart feast at the banquet table of disappointment and defeat? This pericope is oft used as a passage of comfort and support to families and mourners at funeral and memorial services, but the disciples of the text find no balm in the words. They do not know it yet, but it is not just Jesus who is saying farewell; his crucifixion will mean the death of how they understand the messianic message and mission. All that they have hoped for throughout their lives, which they have believed has come to fruition in Jesus, will soon be nailed to a cross. It will be a long time before they realize that the messianic message is eternal, even if the Messiah is not immortal. Death will have neither the last nor the lasting word.

With post-Easter eyes, it might be easy to skip to the end of the last canonized Gospel and bypass the ethereal words in red. However, the disciples are unwittingly about to be simultaneously dispatched as both hospice chaplain and maternity midwife. The red-lettered words that follow are their primer. When their hopeful visions for a just and peaceful messianic kingdom melt in the crucible of crucifixion, the hearts of the disciples will be diseased—and their anxiety will be blinding. More than Jesus' body will perish; a hospice chaplain is needed in the upper room as the disciples' understanding of the mission of Jesus, and of themselves, passes away.

The settings of a maternity midwife and a hospice chaplain are startlingly similar. As the new is birthed, something dies and that which is eternal can find its full nativity only in death. In both the maternity wing and the hospice room, the family is changed—all things *are* being made new. Birth and death are but the bookends of a shelf full of stories of transformation; birth and death are repeating cycles in the narrative of our lives. Visions of who *we* are and are becoming give us life, even as a previous sense of our self dies. However, in these moments, even as Christ is leading us, we often echo Thomas in asking how we can know the way if we do not know where God is going; with Philip we claim that we will be satisfied if we can just see. The role of the midwife and the hospice chaplain is to be fully present, even as they cannot see and do not know what comes next in the narrative of life.

response was plaintive: "Lord, why can I not follow you now?" (13:37). Jesus now consoles his followers, urging them not to "let their hearts be troubled"; as they believe in God, they should also believe in Jesus. The intimate relationship between Jesus and God is a strong motif of this entire discourse (see 14:8–11).

Jesus begins to speak more directly of his departure and its purpose (vv. 2–3), a reference both to his impending death and to his glorification. Evoking the image of a magnificent villa or cluster of dwellings, Jesus will prepare a place where his followers will be with him in the world beyond death. The promise of eternal life is a fundamental note of John's Gospel (e.g., 10:10). Despite the separation that death will cause, the bond of love and fidelity between Jesus and those who believe in him cannot be broken. Here the Gospel anticipates the motif of the vine and the branches in 15:1–17, the breathtaking promises of Jesus' final prayer in chapter 17, and the reassuring appearances of the risen Christ to his disciples (chaps. 20–21).

Jesus' reference to "the way to the place that I am going" moves the discourse forward (v. 4). As happens several times in John's Gospel, an uncomprehending question enables Jesus to elaborate further. Thomas (14:5; see also 11:16 and esp. 20:24–29) asks where they are going and what is the "way." This in turn leads to one of the Johannine "I AM" statements, which both declare the divine name ("I AM") and fuse it on to human longing. This statement includes three key metaphors. The notion of the "way" (hodos) has deep roots in the biblical saga, including the journey of Israel to the promised land. In the Synoptics, it describes the journey of Jesus from Galilee to Jerusalem, which the disciples must also walk (see, e.g., Luke 9:51–62). In Acts, Luke notes that the Christian movement was entitled "the Way" (see 9:2; 19:9, 23; 22:4; 24:14, 22), following in the "way" of Jesus and carrying the gospel to the ends of the earth (Acts 1:8).

In John, Jesus himself embodies the way to God and therefore the "way" of discipleship. Jesus is also the "truth," evoking the revelatory nature of Jesus' mission as first indicated in the prologue (1:14, 17), affirmed in Jesus' dispute with the religious leaders in chapter 8 (8:21–47), and brought to full realization by the gift of the "Spirit of truth" (15:26–27; 14:17). The entire purpose of Jesus' mission was to bring "life" to the world (see 1:4 and esp. 10:10). The "life" promised by Jesus to his disciples is "eternal life" (zōē aionios), that is, participation in the very being of God (10:28; 17:2–3).

troubled is a heart not hung upon God but hung rather on all the things the world peddles to soothe a troubled heart. Jesus tells the disciples in their time of deep uncertainty, Hang your hearts on God; hang your hearts on me.

The next tack Jesus takes deals directly with the gift of another kind of life: eternal life. He tells the disciples that the God on whom they may hang their hearts "has room for them." Robert Jenson writes about God's roominess in relation, not to the space, but to the time God has for us. "'What is time?' My answer is created time is room in God's own life. If creation is God's making room in himself, then God must be roomy. . . . this roominess of God should be thought of as his 'time,' that God's eternity is not immunity to time but his having all the time he needs."[2] The metaphor of God's roominess as God's eternity is also worth the Sunday morning.

What has troubled the disciples' hearts is the very real sense that their time with Jesus has come to an end. We have the same relationship to time: its brevity robs us of those we love. Consider the *metanoia* that is God's grace to one who hangs her heart on the God who has all the time God needs for her and for those she loves. The place Jesus is preparing in God's own life is *eternal life*, which, as Robert Jenson often says, is simply another name for God. As in the beginning of this Gospel God has come to dwell with us in Jesus Christ, explore the content of the Christian hope contained in the promise that we will dwell through him in God.

At this point, the congregation may resonate with Thomas who is, quite literally, lost. Philip is not far behind. Both of their questions reveal how little we (like the darkness) comprehend the God who has come to us in Jesus Christ. Frankly, we prefer the darkness. Jesus' response to Thomas has been heard and used by religion as a gauntlet thrown down before those who do not believe God was in Christ and so, according to religion, dwell in darkness. Apparently the disciples, who had spent three years with him, did not believe this either . . . or as Jesus says to Philip (emphasizing the Johannine understanding of belief as active commitment to a person), "Have I been with you all this time, Philip, and you still do not know me?" (v. 9). Who among us does know him? Does knowing him coincide with inward assent to the church's dogma or doctrine? Is every human apprehension of God's glory that coincides

---

2. Robert Jenson, "Aspects of a Doctrine of Creation," in Colin Gunton, ed., *The Doctrine of Creation* (London: T.&T. Clark, 1997), 24.

Theological Perspective

that the Son was not a "created being." Jesus was fully revelatory of the Sending One; one who encountered Jesus encountered God. They were witnesses to Word made flesh, dwelling among them, full of grace and truth. Through him, they are able to see and know God as never before.

The passage then picks up Philip's query: "Show us the Father" (v. 8). Utter identification of Father and Son is expressed through language of mutual indwelling, yet this is difficult for his hearers. The God of Israel was the unseen, transcendent presence whose name they approached through circumlocution. The statement "whoever has seen me has seen the Father" is one of the highest christological claims placed on the lips of Jesus in the Gospel. Not only does Jesus not speak on his own; he does not perform works on his own, either. It is solely because he is fully indwelt by God that both words and works are revelatory of life from above, to use John's spatial construction. While the great teaching on mutual abiding occurs in the next chapter, readers understand that the relationship between Jesus and God will be paradigmatic for their own fruit bearing.

The final theological theme in this thick text is a brief notation on prayer. The brevity of the words belies the depth and breadth of Jesus' teaching. Those who believe in him are promised that they will do greater works because (1) Jesus will be with God, a place of advocacy and intercession, and (2) these works will bring glory to God through the Son. Works that glorify God issue from prayer that is in accordance with Jesus' own mission. The disciples are instructed to "ask in [his] name" (v. 13), and he assures them he will grant what is asked.

A superficial interpretation of the privilege of praying "in Jesus' name" is that if the formula is used, this is tantamount to effectual prayer. To pray "in the name of Jesus" is to align one's spiritual longing with that of one's Lord. When one believes in Jesus, one begins to believe in God with the same depth of trust and hope, out of which mature prayer flows.

MOLLY T. MARSHALL

Pastoral Perspective

The disciples want to cling to the perceived safety of location—they want to know where Jesus is going and how to go there with him. Throughout the Gospel of John, however, location is used as a metaphor for the intimacy of a close relationship. The sheep are kept close to the shepherd; Jesus is proximal to the heart of God. As they are sitting in the room sharing the feast of loss, John's Jesus attempts to assure them that there will be a place with plenty of rooms for them; the relationship is going to continue, even as it changes. They will not be forgotten.

The opening imperative of the Farewell Discourse is not just an affective command. "Do not let your hearts be troubled," is a direction to the disciples' will. It is a command to stand firm, even when their hearts abandon them. Their theology of a messianic military strongman will be replaced with the revolution that only engaged compassion can bring. Birth and death are fraught with pangs and the potential for transformation.

Tumultuous teens, in fact, know this space of faith in their very body and soul. No longer in the relative safety of childhood, but not yet in the supposed self-sufficiency of adulthood, adolescence is a space of liminality, that is, an in-between space. Doorframes are liminal places: a space between rooms, a portal from the outside to the inside. Teens need a companion who can be both midwife and chaplain, someone who will help them navigate the loss of infancy and facilitate a safe crossing to the terrain of adulthood. For the adolescent disciples, that will soon be the Holy Spirit. The Comforter will come to cure their diseased hearts and help them stand firm in the coming transformation. Perhaps an adolescent preacher does know something about the heart disease of the text, even if he does not know it yet.

SHANNON MICHAEL PATER

Exegetical Perspective

14:8–14. Another question moves the discourse forward. Philip asks, "Lord, show us the Father, and we will be satisfied." Philip was among the first drawn to Jesus (see 1:43; 6:7; 12:21), but fails to grasp the Gospel's fundamental Christology. John portrays Jesus as the true revealer of God, not only in what he says or does, but in his very "flesh" embodying the divine presence (1:14–18). Jesus speaks the true words of God (8:26; 17:8); his healing touch reveals the compassion of God (4:46–54; 9:4; 11:1–44); above all, his death, as an act of friendship love, reveals God's redemptive love for the world (3:16–17; 15:13; 13:1–2). Jesus' words to Philip boldly express this perspective: "Whoever has seen me has seen the Father" (14:9).

The high stakes of Johannine Christology underwrite its exclusive claim, as in 14:6: "No one comes to the Father except through me." For the Fourth Gospel, Jesus eclipses all other ways to God, even that of the Old Testament prophets such as Moses (see 1:17–18; 6:32) or Abraham (8:53–59). The purpose of John's Gospel is to proclaim as forcefully as possible the profound meaning of Jesus for Christian faith and for the destiny of the world, but the Gospel should not be construed as a definitive comment on whether there is any validity to other ways to God beyond Christianity.

The segment closes by turning to the future. Because Jesus is going to the Father, the disciples will do even "greater works" than Jesus himself (v. 12). This anticipates the missionary impulses of 17:18 and 20:21. As Jesus has been "sent" by the Father to proclaim God's love to the world, so too will the disciples be sent. The meaning of "greater works" is debated, referring perhaps to the widening circle of the church's mission to the Gentiles or, since it is linked to Jesus' going to the Father, the disciples' empowerment through the Spirit brought to the world though the death and resurrection of Jesus (see 20:22). In the meantime, the disciples are to pray with confidence that they will be heard, an assurance that has echoes in Jesus' exhortations in the Synoptic Gospels (see Mark 11:24; Matt. 7:7–11; 21:22; Luke 11:9–10).

DONALD SENIOR

Homiletical Perspective

with the signs or the works Jesus performed (from the wedding at Cana to the raising of Lazarus) what he meant when he said to the disciples, "If you do not [believe that I am in the Father and the Father is in me], believe me because of the works themselves" (v. 11)? Are there others on the Way whose lives bear witness to his works but whose lips have yet to confess his name—others for whom Jesus is preparing a place, even if religion will not?

Instead of hearing the exclusivity of the Christian claim in John 14, consider the pains Jesus takes to assure us that we come to God by *God's initiative* in Christ. We are not the actors here. As Jenson puts the matter, "God . . . is not known by us because he is amenable to the exercise of our cognitive powers. He is known to us in that he grants us what we could never reach or even know we could or should reach: he takes us into his own knowledge of himself."[3] What is this knowledge? In a Word made flesh, God's self-knowledge is disclosed in the self-giving, self-emptying love that is God's Son. "No one has ever seen God," wrote John in his prologue. "It is God the only Son, who is close to the Father's heart, who has made him known" (1:18). What we know of God in Jesus Christ is that God has chosen not to be God without us. In this is love (1 John 4:10), the love that is God. This is a Word worth a Sunday morning.

Finally, and contrary to the covenant we make with one another ("until death do us part"), God's promise to love us, to make room for us, to know and be known by us, never ends (1 Cor. 13:8). Therefore our hearts need never be troubled.

CYNTHIA A. JARVIS

---

3. Robert Jenson, *Systematic Theology: The Triune God* (New York: Oxford University Press, 1997), 227.

Acts 17:22-31

²²Then Paul stood in front of the Areopagus and said, "Athenians, I see how extremely religious you are in every way. ²³For as I went through the city and looked carefully at the objects of your worship, I found among them an altar with the inscription, 'To an unknown god.' What therefore you worship as unknown, this I proclaim to you. ²⁴The God who made the world and everything in it, he who is Lord of heaven and earth, does not live in shrines made by human hands, ²⁵nor is he served by human hands, as though he needed anything, since he himself gives to all mortals life and breath and all things. ²⁶From one ancestor he made all nations to inhabit the whole earth, and he allotted the times of their existence and the boundaries of the places where they would live, ²⁷so that they would search for God and perhaps grope for him and find him—though indeed he is not far from each one of us. ²⁸For 'In him we live and move and have our being'; as even some of your own poets have said, 'For we too are his offspring.'

²⁹Since we are God's offspring, we ought not to think that the deity is like gold, or silver, or stone, an image formed by the art and imagination of mortals. ³⁰While God has overlooked the times of human ignorance, now he commands all people everywhere to repent, ³¹because he has fixed a day on which he will have the world judged in righteousness by a man whom he has appointed, and of this he has given assurance to all by raising him from the dead."

Theological Perspective

Eternally grateful for a theological education, I realize such endeavors are the opportunity of a privileged few. I remember well the arduous hours of reclining on the sofa, reading masterpieces of brilliant minds long laid to rest. I recall laboring over term papers, comprehensive exams, and dissertation proposals. Before dawn, I awoke to coffee and the computer while my wife drove to the local hospital to care for the sick and hurting. By the end of the day, I had hardly moved, cemented to the chair from which I began. Though the labors were intense, the venture remained an exercise in leisure. For the journey itself demanded time, time free from other obligations to ask questions of eternal significance.

Living in a center of intellectual pursuits, the Athenians understood the leisure of such pursuits, in which everyone "would spend their time in nothing but telling or hearing something new" (Acts 17:21). They loved learning, and this insatiable desire drove their waking hours. Especially in religion, they hungered for more and determined to leave no stone unturned. Upon entering the city, Paul noted the expanse of their religiosity, an expanse indicative of a much deeper existential restlessness. He saw a city replete with idols, and he described her residents as "religious in every way" (17:16, 22). They even erected an altar "to an unknown god" (v. 23),

Pastoral Perspective

Perhaps the Athenians were superstitious people—people who covered all their bases by erecting a shrine "to an unknown god," just in case they had missed a god in the creation of their pantheon of deities. Perhaps they were sophisticated enough to know that there were gods or dimensions of deity that would always extend beyond the human capacity to know. At any rate, the writer of Acts indicates that Paul was unhappy to find such a proliferation of gods throughout the city of Athens. However, he did not vent his anger with the Athenians over their polytheism, as he would later do with the Romans (Rom. 1:18–23.).

He may have felt some anxiety, having just been run out of both Thessalonica and Beroea. Athens was new territory for him, a university town, a great seat of learning, sophisticated philosophizing, and religious curiosity. He was not reticent to challenge Athenian philosophies or pagan practices, but he did so with his own sophisticated sensitivity to the audience.

As we have been often reminded, Paul was not a systematic theologian. Though surely a mind of great wit and intelligence, of wisdom and understanding, his primary calling was as an evangelist. His task was to spread the good news, and he was comfortable adapting the message to his audience. Above all he was concerned to be heard and understood. How often have we self-righteously hung on to a favored

Exegetical Perspective

Luke puts Paul on trial, but there is no court in session. Scholars do not agree on the historicity of this scene from the Acts of the Apostles. Some see Paul appearing here before the "Council of the Areopagus," while others dispute any sort of legal procedure whatsoever. What Luke does here is invoke the trial of Socrates, without even calling his name! The incident on Mars Hill is a literary re-presentation of what happened to the famous Athenian philosopher. Paul speaks in the marketplace to everyone—like Socrates (Acts 17:17). The people think he is introducing new gods—like Socrates (17:18). In this scene, Paul stands before some sort of court—like Socrates. Socrates' appearance before an Athenian court brought about a sentence of death. Thus the encounter—at least at a literary level—suggests a high-stakes interaction between the apostle and the intelligentsia of this famous city.

"So they took him and brought him to the Areopagus and asked him, 'May we know what this new teaching is that you are presenting?' It sounds rather strange to us, so we would like to know what it means'" (17:19–20). The polite question after Paul's teaching renders even an informal legal investigation unlikely, and the emphasis in the passage on the curiosity of the Athenians as a dominant feature almost completely precludes any sort of court scene.

Homiletical Perspective

Paul's speech in front of the Aeropagus in Athens is very suggestive of sermon possibilities. Our culture, like that of Athens, is a culture of many idols: consumer goods, military power, sex, and technology, to name just a few. Before setting forth themes for preaching that focus on witness in the midst of such idolatry, however, the preacher may want to take a moment simply to celebrate Paul: a brilliant and dedicated follower of Christ who worked long and hard to communicate the gospel in all kinds of difficult circumstances. Here is Paul, alone in Athens, after being driven out of Philippi, Thessalonica, and Beroea, a solitary witness, once again trying to be faithful in yet another strange and complex situation.

Determined, Adaptive Witness. How can we help our listeners identify with this kind of determined, adaptive witness? What will it take for us, like Paul, to adapt quickly and decisively to the culture and subcultures around us in order faithfully to communicate the good news? Rather than encouraging listeners to run from the dominant culture or accommodate to that culture, we might invite our congregations to consider what it means to witness in such a situation. If we take our cue from Paul, we will first learn to listen carefully to the culture, hearing deep within it aspects of the ways people are seeking and

Acts 17:22-31

Theological Perspective

respectfully recognizing any erroneously overlooked deity. A source of pride for those who considered themselves religious, the Athenian pantheon pointed toward a cavernous abyss left in the wake of heartfelt spiritual pursuit. For though they were religious, they remained uncertain and failed to find the rest for which they longed.

Pascal described an "infinite abyss" within the soul of every person reserved for God alone, and centuries earlier Augustine confessed, "You have made us for yourself, and our heart is restless until it rests in you."[1] Before the Areopagus, Paul acknowledged the wellspring out of which the panoply of worship poured. Rather than dismantling the religions of the Athenians, he affirmed their quest for the ground of being. Despite their highly structured way with the gods, they intuited more. Creating space for "the unknown god," maybe they simply placated the Divine, as if to ask forgiveness for their omission. Maybe their spiritual sensibilities drove them beyond the identified deities toward that which could truly satisfy, and yet remained just beyond reach. Without hesitation, Paul declared, I know this God, and this God created and sustains heaven and earth (vv. 23, 25). Guardian over the space and time of your earthly pilgrimage, this God set your life in motion to assure that your sojourn would be a journey home. Groping and searching, you will remain restless until you find your rest in him (vv. 24–27).

For Paul, personal experience was one reliable source of revelation, and he urged the Athenians to listen to their own poets, who intuited the nearness of this one yet named. "In him we live and move and have our being," Paul said, and in him we discover our own divine heritage (v. 28). Beginning with Jesus and the resurrection (v. 18), Paul stirred their curiosities, and the strangeness of his message elicited a request for clarification. For the first time, the unnamable had been named, but in no sense, as Anne Graham Lotz declared, could Jesus simply be lined up alongside the other gods as if he were just one of the boys. For in him we live and move and have our being! So long as the allegiances of the Athenians could be divided and compartmentalized among the various deities responsible for their well-being, a spiritual pantheon would suffice, but with the identification of their ground of being, Paul introduced a radical exclusivity.

Pastoral Perspective

way of speaking our truth only to see it sail over the heads of our listeners? How often have we insisted on having it our way when an effort to enter the worldview of the other would have served communication so much better? William Willimon suggests that "the church, rather than standing back from pagan religiosity, pointing our fingers in righteous indignation, should, like Paul in Athens, minister to their searching."[1]

While it was true that Paul claimed to be "all things to all people" (1 Cor. 9:22) as the occasion demanded, it must also have been true that a personality as strong as his did not have chameleon-like adaptability. However he shaped his arguments to his audience—using his Jewish rabbinical training and deep-seated commitment to the one true God; his belief in Jesus as the Christ; his own dramatic conversion experience; and/or his passion for persuasion—his faith must have come through invariably whenever he appeared on the scene and opened his mouth. Clearly some were drawn to his message; some were mildly irritated by his certitude, though impressed by what he had to say; and some were angry and alienated from his insistent arrogance in "explaining it all to them." In this text, he was dragged before the court of religious opinion in Athens to account for himself before the authorities.

He was cunning in his courting of their attention and favor, "Athenians, I see how extremely religious you are in every way" (v. 22). He played a card something like Augustine's famous "Thou hast made us for thyself, O Lord, and our hearts are restless until they rest in thee." "God has made [humans] so that instinctively [they long] for God. There is that in [humans] which makes [them] grope in the darkness after God because [humans are children] of God and kin to God."[2]

It is interesting that this passage contains words that have become familiar favorites to many who seek to center their lives in the holy. Following the thought of Seneca and Epimenides, Paul refers to God as the one in whom we "live and move and have our being" (v. 28). Though this phrase, ironically, comes from Greek thought rather than Judeo-Christian tradition, it has still become a key concept in contemporary Christian thought. This reference has inspired thinking such as Paul Tillich's notion of God as the ground of all being and Marcus Borg's

---

1. Blaise Pascal, *Pensees* #425, http://www.ccel.org/ccel/pascal/pensees .viii.html.; Augustine, *Confessions*, trans. Henry Chadwick (Oxford: Oxford University Press, 1998), 3.

1. William H. Willimon, *Acts*, Interpretation series (Atlanta: John Knox Press, 1988), 143.
2. William Barclay, *The Acts of the Apostles*, Daily Study Bible Series (Philadelphia: Westminster Press, 1955), 143.

Exegetical Perspective

On the other hand, "took him and brought him" (*epilabomenoi*, v. 19) sounds almost like an arrest (as in 16:19). That the philosophers wanted to avoid the noise and bustle of the city is obvious to the reader, but at the time Athens was a rather quiet provincial town. So, instead of trying to historicize this encounter between Paul and the philosophers, we should recognize that Luke is using a different narrative technique. The German New Testament biblical scholar Ernst Haenchen says it best:

> Luke actually utilizes a motif technique. The narrative framework is composed of a number of motifs which at the time every half-educated person recognized as specifically Athenian: the many temples and images, the special religiosity of the Athenians, their philosophical schools, the Areopagus (hill and court!), the Socratic dialogues in the marketplace, the introduction of new gods, the Athenian curiosity. Luke has let these motifs follow one another so closely that the impression of Athenian life and spirit grips the reader.[1]

Today's passage begins with Paul's speech before the Areopagus, but the scene begins some six verses earlier. Unless one takes into account what it is Paul is reacting to—"he was deeply distressed to see that the city was full of idols" (v. 16)—it is difficult to understand the nature of Paul's speech before the council. In some ways, this incident is meant to impress upon the reader the danger of Paul's adventures. We cannot breathe easy until we are told, "At that point Paul left them" (v. 33). Luke does not involve Paul here in a legal process before an Athenian court with the possibility of endangering the good name and life of the apostle, who is clearly the hero of the second part of Acts.

What is important is the speech itself. What the speech attacks, using the very arguments of Greek philosophy, is popular Greek religious practice—the worship of idols—and not the religious theorizing of the philosophers. Then why direct his speech at these philosophers? It may be because they represent the highest of Greek culture. Nevertheless, something is still odd about this passage. One does not get the impression that Luke is thinking of such a specialized audience, cultured elites who occupy their time with intellectual matters. Paul speaks, in a sense, to the whole of Athens, and through Athens to the entirety of Greek culture and religiosity. Thus Luke's use of various motifs is meant to construct an "ideal setting"

Homiletical Perspective

searching for the one true God. What does this listening entail? For one thing, we can learn to *pay attention* to details. Paul looked around him and saw not only idols, but what was *inscribed* on them. He learned how to read carefully the signs of theological problems and possibilities within the dominant culture. Beyond paying attention, however, Paul *looked for openings* into the hearts of the people he sought to reach with the message of Christ's resurrection. Note that he did not weigh in immediately with critique, but embodied intellectual and spiritual *hospitality*. There is a spirit of welcome in the way Paul communicated his message. He acknowledged whom he was talking with, granted them their own creative powers of thought and invention, and invited them to go further in their thinking with him. Finally, Paul was *bold*. Proclaiming foreign divinities in this manner could have gotten Paul into a lot of trouble, as it did Socrates and others before him. The assertion that Christ, crucified and resurrected, is in fact God's final answer to all forms of human longing was a dangerous, and some would say reckless, strategy. Nonetheless, such boldness is at the heart of what it means to be a Christian witness. Paul did not water down his message, becoming lukewarm in his commitment to Christ. He asserted boldly what he believed, no matter the consequences.

Thoughtful Witness. This is one of the great pictures of sharp, articulate, intellectually tuned witness in the New Testament. Although these verses are clearly part of a longer speech that Paul would have delivered, it is clear from the outset that Paul has taken the time to think through his circumstances and to apply that thinking where he finds himself. This suggests that we too might sharpen our abilities to think through our own idols and their evangelical and theological possibilities. It is one thing simply to lambaste all idolatry, and another to think carefully about what a particular form of idolatry represents in terms of human aspiration, and to identify theological and evangelical possibilities within this aspiration. For instance, the idolatry of consumerism, considered carefully, could indicate a deep desire for future fulfillment: consumers are always pursuing the "next best thing." In order to think about God within this framework, one would need to place God within the context of the human desire for future fulfillment. In what sense does God in Jesus Christ meet our deepest desires for human fulfillment and wholeness? On the other hand, an idolatry such as military power suggests another theological and evangelistic

1. Ernst Haenchen, *The Acts of the Apostles: A Commentary*, trans. R. McL. Wilson (Philadelphia: Westminster Press, 1971), 527.

Acts 17:22-31

Theological Perspective

No longer did he merely affirm the Athenians in their spiritual quest. Suddenly, the polite nod to the unknown god was answered with the demand for repentance. In his commentary on Acts, Gerhard Krodel insists, "There comes a point when the Christian witness must speak of Christ's resurrection and its consequences and take the risk of being switched off by the partner in dialogue."[2] Rather than merely adding Jesus to the myriad of gods and goddesses, Paul introduced him as the one before whom the entire world must give account. By virtue of the resurrection from the dead, Jesus determines the standards of righteousness and will judge the world accordingly (vv. 30, 31). It is no surprise that many laughed, while others suspected he might be right (17:32–34).

Two millennia later, our pluralistic context resembles the Athenian pantheon. Apart from the ornamental worship around golden altars, our loyalties are equally divided, and among the gods crowding our lives, Jesus' claims are equally disruptive. In a world where tolerance is hailed as the cardinal virtue and spirituality is defined as self-fulfillment, religion takes its place alongside other leisure activities. So long as time allows, we will pursue the higher life. Even some Christians have nearly surrendered belief in the eternal significance of allegiance to Christ in favor of a casual faith deeming all religions equally true. However, as we confess in the Apostles' Creed, "we believe in Jesus Christ, God's only Son . . . who ascended into heaven and is seated at the right hand of the Father, from whence he shall come to judge the living and the dead." In our own restlessness, we have retrieved "the unknown god" and entrusted those who consider themselves religious to name this deity as they will. Reminiscent of the ancient philosophers, Ravi Zacharias writes, Jesus "told us that the only way we could understand who we are is to cast our gaze . . . on the relationship toward which we move in the sum total of our being," the relationship with Christ and Christ alone.[3]

SEAN A. WHITE

Pastoral Perspective

panentheism. "This concept imagines God as *the encompassing Spirit* in whom everything that is, is. The universe is not separate from God but *in* God."[3]

Here is evidence of what a syncretistic religion Christianity is. Christianity has often been willing to use other religious traditions in order to make the gospel intelligible to non-Christian cultures. Paul shows us how to handle cultural relativism. He used Athenian openness to other religions at the same time he challenged that openness with his faith in the one true God. We live in a time when it is easy to say there is one God but there are many paths to God, that it does not matter what path you take as long as you take one. Clearly Paul did not believe this; he was no universalist. What he did do with Athenian religious practice was to use it to point to the way, the truth, and the life as he understood it. His witness was respectful of the view of others, demonstrating insight into and understanding of other faiths; at the same time, he insisted on sharing the truth as he had come to know it through his own experience. Not only is this a model for witnessing to non-Christians; it is also a model for witnessing to those of no religious persuasion.

The challenge is to say to those around us, "We see your spiritual hunger. Might we offer sustenance from our rich store of spiritual resource?" The challenge is to find the imagery and language that allow us to enter another's world in order to speak our truth honestly, respectfully, and effectively. What does it mean to be so fully rooted and grounded in God, so centered in our own experience of the Christian story, that we cannot keep from sharing it? In the words of the old hymn, when we feel our faith in our very bones, "how can we keep from singing?"

RANDLE R. (RICK) MIXON

---

2. Gerhard Krodel, *Acts* (Philadelphia: Fortress Press, 1981), 53, quoted in James L. Blevins, "Acts 13–19: The Tale of Three Cities," *Review and Expositor* 87 (1990): 445.

3. Ravi Zacharias, *Jesus among Other Gods: The Absolute Claims of the Christian Message* (Nashville: W Publishing Group, 2000), 34.

3. Marcus Borg, *The Heart of Christianity: Rediscovering a Life of Faith* (San Francisco: HarperSanFrancisco, 2003), 66.

Exegetical Perspective

for the apostle's proclamation of the gospel, one that baffles any and every attempt to translate it into historical reality. With the problem of the scene's historical connectedness resolved, we can now move on to the speech itself, which is really the important part.

"What therefore you worship as unknown, this I proclaim to you" (v. 23). Scholars have been particularly interested in the question whether the Paul who speaks here is the Paul of the letters. Clearly this passage has some connection to what the apostle says in Romans 1. At the beginning of his letter to the church in Rome, Paul reveals his conviction that idolatry has denied God the glory due to God, and that God has punished idolaters by giving them over to moral depravity (Rom. 1:18–32). Such an understanding is at odds with the talk in Acts of an overlooking of "the times of human ignorance," mentioned in 17:30. This doctrine of the religious status of non-Jews is peculiar to the Paul presented in Acts. Luke intentionally steers for the theme of the "unknown God" (*agnōstos theos*) and keeps to it faithfully. That the Greeks honor the unknown God demonstrates the complicated relationship in which all non-Jews stand with respect to the true God: They do not know this God, but they honor God nevertheless. This simultaneous yes and no to God makes it possible for the apostle to proclaim the Christian God to a religious population unfortunately mired in ignorance. In short, this speech represents one of the ways the early Christian missionaries Christianized Greco-Roman culture.

In Athens, Paul is portrayed as not only the first Christian philosopher but also as a proponent of human universalism. As New Testament scholar Marla Selvidge concludes, "[Paul's] greatest achievement was his ability to step out of his sectarian past to shake hands with others throughout the Roman Empire. Paul's egalitarianism touched the lives of women from different classes, slaves, uncircumcised Jews, politicians, artisans, tent makers, followers of John the Baptist, sailors, Jewish-Christians, and even procurators and kings."[2]

MICHAEL JOSEPH BROWN

Homiletical Perspective

framework: if one thinks carefully about this idolatry, the goal is not fulfillment but *security*, achieved through the use of power and violence. Placing the God of Jesus Christ at the center of this human aspiration leads the witness to think more clearly about how God in Jesus Christ provides our true security in this world. This kind of on-the-ground theological thinking is the cornerstone of thoughtful witness and is one of the most helpful insights in this story.

Trusting God's Spirit in All Things. This story affords the opportunity for the preacher to remind congregations that it is God who makes the first move toward us, creating us and giving us all of our own creative powers. Although the products of our labor present us with multiple opportunities to make potentially idolatrous choices, they nonetheless come from God *and* can become an opportunity to seek the God who wants to be known as their Creator. Not all the things of this world have to be idols; some can be good gifts from God, pointing us toward God. Although creation surely falls short of revealing everything about God, it does nonetheless carry God's imprint. Much of the art and creative productivity in this world, at its deepest level, is expressive of the *Spiritus Creator*, God's ever-creating Spirit present within all creative process. Rather than shunning this creative potential, Paul recognizes it all around him and celebrates it as something that could potentially open us to the God who wants to be known in Jesus Christ. We as preachers can encourage congregations toward this same kind of "doxological living," in which we are thankful for all of the gifts around us, no matter how ambiguous, and are always looking for and finding in all human endeavors the unknown God and the desire to know more about that God.

JOHN S. MCCLURE

---

2. Marla Selvidge, *Exploring the New Testament* (Upper Saddle River, NJ: Prentice-Hall, 2003), 169.

Psalm 66:8-20

⁸Bless our God, O peoples,
  let the sound of his praise be heard,
⁹who has kept us among the living,
  and has not let our feet slip.
¹⁰For you, O God, have tested us;
  you have tried us as silver is tried.
¹¹You brought us into the net;
  you laid burdens on our backs;
¹²you let people ride over our heads;
  we went through fire and through water;
  yet you have brought us out to a spacious place.

¹³I will come into your house with burnt offerings;
  I will pay you my vows,
¹⁴those that my lips uttered
  and my mouth promised when I was in trouble.

Theological Perspective

The psalmist worries about how we may mature in
our relationship with God. Are the people growing
closer to God, as evidenced by their sound of praise,
or are they slipping further away from God? "For
you, O God, have tested us; you have tried us as silver
is tried" (v. 10). This question of measuring spiritual
maturity is a crucial question of Christian spirituality, because life in a violent world is such that we can
easily form habits by which our apparent love for
God is merely our own love for ourselves.

How do we measure our spiritual growth? The
psalmist answers that our growth is measured by the
ways in which we embody prayer. How we pray indicates our maturity level. If prayer constitutes a mono-
logue in which individual desires seek ultimate
attention, then such prayer is infantile. When we pray,
we should focus our attention upon our ultimate need
for God. We are immature in the spiritual life anytime
we become inattentive to God and instead become
ultimately attentive to our own desire. Simone Weil
states, "Something in our souls has a far more violent
repugnance for true attention than the flesh has for
bodily fatigue. . . . Every time we really concentrate our
attention, we destroy the evil in ourselves."[1] So the

---
1. Simone Weil, "Reflections on the Right Use of School Studies with a View to the Love of God," in *Simone Weil Reader*, ed. George A. Panichas (New York: McKay, 1977), 49.

Pastoral Perspective

Psalm 66 brings the reader to worship where the
faithfulness of God is remembered, offerings are
made, and one worshiper offers testimony to all who
will listen.

The first seven verses of Psalm 66, omitted from
the lection, echo the exodus. In verses 11–12, the
psalmist speaks of a time of testing and trial, using
language that echoes the prophets' descriptions of
the exile. In the face of trial, God has proved to be
faithful. Such recitation of God's mighty deeds constitutes a song of God's faithfulness.

In the midst of this congregational praise, a solo
voice rises up to declare, "I will come into your house
with burnt offerings" (v. 13). Gratitude for God's
faithfulness results in offerings, but attention to the
entire psalm reveals that the offerings include more
than gifts which are laid upon the altar. God's faithfulness revealed in the old stories of God's people
provides the lens through which the solo singer
interprets his or her own life. Just as God has previously responded to the needs of God's people, now
God "has given heed to the words of my prayer"
(v. 19). God has listened. Because God has listened, in
addition to gifts laid on the altar, the psalmist must
offer testimony: I will tell what God has done for me.

One student of the text writes that this witness to
God's faithfulness speaks in "the simple formulaic

15I will offer to you burnt offerings of fatlings,
    with the smoke of the sacrifice of rams;
    I will make an offering of bulls and goats.   *Selah*

16Come and hear, all you who fear God,
    and I will tell what he has done for me.
17I cried aloud to him,
    and he was extolled with my tongue.
18If I had cherished iniquity in my heart,
    the Lord would not have listened.
19But truly God has listened;
    he has given heed to the words of my prayer.

20Blessed be God,
    because he has not rejected my prayer
    or removed his steadfast love from me.

Exegetical Perspective

This psalm belongs to the second major collection within the Psalter (Pss. 42–72), the so-called Elohistic Psalter, because of the preference for addressing God simply as Elohim, "God." The four literary units that comprise this reading contain elements typical of individual psalms of thanksgiving. The first (vv. 8–12) includes the initial two typical elements: an introductory statement of thanksgiving or praise (v. 8), and a description of the conditions of distress and God's deliverance (vv. 9–12). The second (vv. 13–15) offers a sacrifice of thanksgiving. The third unit (vv. 16–19) confesses God as deliverer. The fourth (v. 20) concludes in traditional fashion with the elements of a hymn. Though the form is mixed, it is reminiscent of a communal psalm of thanksgiving, seen in the regular use of "us" and "our" in verses 8–12.

The use of plurals in verses 8–12 is suggestive of a cultic setting, in which assembled singers and musicians participate in the rites. The reasons for calling for praise are given in verses 9–12. The reference "kept among the living" (v. 9) reveals the serious nature of the distress, expressed in the language of verses 10–12. The demanding nature of the experience is made manifest in terms of being "tested" and "tried." Such language invokes the imagery of metallurgy, commonly used to express dimensions of religious experience. The heart is tested (Pss. 7:9; 17:3;

Homiletical Perspective

The Christian contemplative Thomas Merton urges us to read the Psalms as a map of inner experience. "There is no aspect of the interior life, no kind of religious experience, no spiritual need of [human beings] that is not depicted and lived out in the Psalms."[1]

Having walked on the desert of the earth and through the wilderness of the spirit, the children of Israel have taken an outer and inner spiritual journey: "For you, O God, have tested us; you have tried us as silver is tried. . . . We went through fire and through water; yet you have brought us out to a spacious place" (vv. 10, 12).

On the other side of tribulation, after their insides were turned out—after giving up, giving in, and giving out—the children of Israel finally reach the borders of the promised land.

We are conditioned to think of the promised land as a piece of real estate. What if this land of milk and honey is something deeper than a geographical destination? What if the promised land is not only a physical location but also an interior awareness? What if the promised land is also understood as an inner spacious place where one experiences safety, security, and peace?

1. Thomas Merton, *Praying The Psalms* (Collegeville, MN: Liturgical Press, 1956), 44.

Psalm 66:8-20

Theological Perspective

psalmist prays, "If I had cherished iniquity in my heart, the Lord would not have listened" (v. 18). After all, what is the benefit of being tested if there is no reference point in one's attention span for God's love? The answer to this question is found less in words and explanations than in action and experience.

It is said that a desert father once observed, "I would rather you would walk with me to the top of the mountain and experience the sunrise than to embark upon glowing accounts of what the sunrise does to you when you gaze at it from the top of the mountain." The same is true for maturing in love for God. In God we experience a divine socialization process that transforms us into someone not of our choosing. In short, we are given an identity that is constituted by our relation to God and to one another. We are brought into community. The psalmist offers access to how communal spirituality facilitates personal maturity. In my own vocation as an Episcopal priest I seek to regain the communal sense of our Christian faith, so as to provide better understanding between love of God and mature behavior in this world. So what do I mean by communal spirituality, and how does it help individuals mature in the spiritual life?

Analogous to mysticism, communal spirituality is the infusion into us of the direct presence of God, culminating in union with God, which no one can bring about through effort or merit. There is a long tradition within communal spirituality in which individuals are called to deepen their love for God. Praying the Psalter is one of the crucial exercises in such maturity. Such explicit attention toward maturity is called ascetical theology, which is concerned with acquired prayer and virtue as it deals with volitional response to the love of God by training, effort, and discipline. For many of us who are associated with the Protestant tradition, ascetical theology is difficult to reconcile with the concept of grace. Still, the psalmist prays, "You brought us into the net; you laid burdens on our backs" (v. 11). Assumed here is not the heresy of Pelagianism (our works earn God's favor), but prevenient grace, that is, God's grace in our good actions from the beginning. The burdens on our backs entice us to pray and to create community. These burdens are as essential to our spiritual growth as physical exercise is to our physical well-being.

So the psalmist both invites us into spiritual maturity and presents the difficult notion that we have to work at prayer. Like daily exercise, the rewards of daily prayer are tremendous, as the Psalmist explains, "Truly God has listened; he has

Pastoral Perspective

story of answered prayer from the ritual of thanksgiving: I cried to him—he heard my prayer."[1] "Formulaic" perhaps, but it is a testimony that breaks forth and cannot be contained. "Come and hear, all you who fear God, and I will tell you what he has done for me" (v. 16).

Regarding testimony, some might say, "I don't like to talk about my faith. I let the deeds of my life speak for me." It is faithful for the gospel to be lived and our faith to show up in our daily deeds; but trusting the pattern of our life to testify, like a story told without a narrator, may show overconfidence in the clarity of our deeds. This psalmist must speak: "Come and hear, all you who fear God."

Why must the psalmist testify? Already burnt offerings, the sacrifice of rams, and offerings of bulls and goats have been made to the living God. Why is testimony important? Testimony reveals that "God has given heed to the words of my prayer" for a larger purpose. What God has done "for me" is not for me alone. The grace and faithfulness of God to me reveals God's orientation of grace and faithfulness to all. God has "kept us among the living," not for our sake solely, but because God's love is for the world. As Terence Fretheim comments regarding the exodus, "The deliverance of Israel is ultimately for the sake of all creation. . . .The issue for God is finally not that God's name be made known in Israel, but that it be declared to the entire earth. God's purpose in these events is creation-wide.[2]

Just as God's faithfulness to Israel reveals a redemption that is creation-wide in purpose, so God's faithfulness to the psalmist results not only in offerings of fatlings, but also in testimony that is creation-wide in purpose. The psalm reminds the worshiping community that the purpose of worship cannot be limited to the "internal" experience of the worshiper, but the worshiping community is called to look through the sanctuary stained glass to "all who fear God," for they too are the object of God's love.

Before we lift our voices in testimony to a world that may not have noticed us, we should allow our testimony to be shaped by God's choice to listen. There is an irony in the psalm; the psalmist speaks because "God has listened" (v. 19). The psalmist calls all who will hear to listen, as "I will tell" (v. 16). Everyone is listening to this psalmist. It is the psalmist who speaks. Of course, testimony is speech,

---

1. James L. Mays, *Psalms*, Interpretation series (Louisville, KY: Westminster John Knox Press, 1994), 223.
2. Terence Fretheim, *Exodus*, Interpretation series (Louisville, KY: Westminster/John Knox Press, 1991), 13.

Exegetical Perspective

Prov. 17:3; Jer. 12:3) while YHWH's gaze *"examines*
humankind. The Lord tests the righteous and the
wicked" (Ps. 11:4–5).

The essential image is a removal of impurities and
a refining, a reduction to that which is otherwise
bound to and hidden within the form. Zechariah
13:9 describes a catastrophe in which two-thirds of
the people and their leader fall to the sword. YHWH
refines the surviving one-third "as one refines silver"
and tests them "as gold is tested." This use of the verb
ṣrp connotes the idea of trial or temptation as a
means of obtaining knowledge or understanding.[1] As
a result, the people recognize and declare, "The Lord
is our God," while YHWH declares, "They are my
people." Perhaps in these cases, it further suggests a
removal of the superficial material trappings of existence, which loom so large in daily life.

Commentators have variously accounted for the
reference to fire and water (v. 12). It too plays on the
imagery of metallurgy. It may further reflect an allusion to a well-known motif in an older narrative tradition now lost to us. It may allude to the practice of
the ritual ordeal. It might more simply be a grammatical synecdoche in which two parts (here "fire"
and "water") suggest a more comprehensive whole—
here the whole range of daunting tests. Although lack
of evidence precludes precise determination of the
reference, what seems to be clear is an emphasis on
the extreme nature of the experience.

The "spacious place" (v. 12) to which the people
were brought may allude to Canaan (i.e., as a land of
liberation and freedom of movement), particularly if
read in conjunction with the allusions to the exodus
and crossing of the Jordan in verse 6 (the Hebrew
suggests [*a place of*] *saturation*, while other ancient
versions read "to fullness" or "to freedom"). The KJV
similarly rendered "into a wealthy place" reading it as
a reference to the land (cf. Deut. 26:5–9). If these
verses draw on the wilderness traditions, such a reference, in the context of the cult, is not simply com-
memorative of a past event. Indeed, verse 6 combines
"they" and "we" references, bringing about a coales-
cence of past and present, so that it is emblematic of
a reality perpetually made evident. In this psalm,
what brings the worshiper to the sanctuary and what
moves the congregation to praise is present experience, effectively expressed in terms of the past.

The worshiper's proclamation of sacrifice (vv.
13–20) is an official cultic announcement of vow

1. G. Botterweck and H. Ringgren, eds., *Theological Dictionary of the Old Testament* (Grand Rapids: Eerdmans, 1977), 2:70.

Homiletical Perspective

What if the wilderness is that inner experience
where life is experienced as arid, alone, and conflicted? In the wilderness of experience it is sometimes hard to breathe.

What if the wilderness and promised land are
states of consciousness within us?

Life is difficult. As the late Martha Graham, the
grande dame of modern dance, put it, "Every person
is an athlete of God." Sooner or later, life requires
every human being to be a spiritual athlete. There are
hurdles to jump over, oceans to swim, and mountains to climb. Sometimes we do not think we can
make it. Sometimes it seems that we just do not have
it in us. Spiritual athletics requires us to reach down
inside of ourselves to discover resources we never
knew we had.

Properly understood, feeling lost in the wilderness
is a preparation for entering the promised land.
When we are lost, we are open to the possibility of
being found. Life in the wilderness requires us to
reach down inside ourselves to discover innate
resources we never knew we had.

Sometimes, when life seems hard and impossible,
we make promises to God: O God, if you will get me
out of what I am in, I promise to do what you want
me to do, to be who you want me to be. O God, if
you will get me out of this, I will make it up to you. I
will repay you with plump offerings. I will offer generous sacrifices.

This is an ancient human propensity—in the heat
of the moment, when things go wrong, to strike a
bargain with God to get us out of what we are in. On
our way to the basement of life, we beg and
beseech—we try to bargain with God. Then, once the
storm passes, after the memory fades, we forget the
vow we made.

"I will come into your house with burnt offerings; I will pay to you my vows, those that my lips
uttered and my mouth promised when I was in trouble" (vv. 13–14). The psalmist has not forgotten
what it was like when life seemed hard and impossible. The psalmist knows nothing of this amnesia. "I
cried aloud to [God] and [YHWH] was extolled
with my tongue. If I had cherished iniquity in my
heart, the Lord would not have listened. But truly
God has listened" (vv. 17–18).

The prayers of the psalmist spring not from the
tongue or lips but from the heart. Wholehearted
prayers, heartfelt supplications offer no guarantee
that we will be delivered from whatever difficulty we
find ourselves in. "You brought us into the net; you
laid burdens on our backs; you let people ride over

Psalm 66:8-20

Theological Perspective

given heed to the words of my prayer" (v. 9). In the tradition of ascetical theology, Christians matured in prayer through three stages: purgation, illumination, union. The goal was to be perfect, even as our heavenly Father is perfect. Purgation meant to free the body from sin by penance and mortification. The psalmist gives an illustration of this first stage—purgation—in the prayer "You let people ride over our heads; we went through fire and through water" (v. 12). The second stage, illumination, advances awareness of the love of God to form inner virtues by prayer and the imitation of Christ. The psalmist prays, "You have brought us out to a spacious place" (v. 12c), a sign of awareness and freedom in which we have the sight and capacity to move closer to the love of God. The last stage is union, the habitual recognition of the presence of God. In this stage our human faithfulness cooperates with God's own action. The psalmist prays, "Blessed be God, because he has not rejected my prayer or removed his steadfast love from me."

In this last stage we discover mystical theology, in which there can be reflection on the ecstasy of living in God. Works by authors such as Pseudo Dionysius and John of the Cross are good to read for mystical theology. According to such Christian mystics, there are the privileged few to whom God unites God's self ineffably by flooding them with light and love. No one can effect these mystical phenomena through self merit; it is the goodness of God that shapes the body and soul of the ascetic into a dwelling place for the divine presence. In other words, the Christian disciple becomes available to receive the miracle of God's union. To put it another way, you have to mature enough to appreciate and move toward the gift of God's love, yet even the maturing and the moving are the gifts of God.

MICHAEL BATTLE

Pastoral Perspective

but the psalmist speaks because he or she has been heard by God. God's choice to listen reveals humility. It is this humility that should inform the pattern of our testimony with others.

Testimony is not limited to speech about what God has done. Testimony is speech shaped by what God has done. Testimony is language that seeks with honesty and humility to allow another to hear, perhaps even experience, what we have experienced or known in God. In the case of this psalmist, such testimony would necessarily be speech that is accompanied by a listening ear.

Growing attention is being given to the role and practice of testimony in Christian worship and ethic. Tom Long asserts that the practice of telling our story is the means by which we come to understand our own faith. Testimony is not simply telling what we have already come to believe, but testimony is a means by which we come to believe.[3] True enough, but there is more revealed in Psalm 66. Testimony is the means by which we are reminded that God's faithfulness to us is not limited to us. God's love is not limited to those in the sanctuary. The object of God's redemptive love is creation-wide.

This is why it is essential for people of faith to speak faithfully, to offer our testimony. Our testimony should express the humility witnessed in God's gracious choice to listen to us. Therefore we should spend as much time listening as we do speaking. A practice of testimony in this fashion would be far more than simply showing respect for our neighbor; it would reveal our trust in God's love for our neighbor. If our testimony does not demonstrate a holy love that is creation-wide in scope, it will not be a faithful testimony to the God who truly has listened.

THOMAS L. ARE JR.

---

3. Thomas G. Long, *Testimony* (San Francisco: Jossey-Bass, 2004), 6.

fulfillment and is marked by a shift to the first person singular. Whether this would have been spoken by a king or cult leader or by the private individual offering the sacrifice is unknown. That the sacrifice was "promised when I was in trouble" (v. 14; cf. v. 17) reflects the fairly common human experience whereby vows are uttered in the face of dire circumstances (Pss. 22:19–22, 25; 61:8; Jonah 2:2, 9). That the psalm celebrates the idea of deliverance from extreme hardship is seen also in the type of sacrifice offered—a burnt offering, whereby the entire sacrifice is given over to God and none is reserved for consumption by the worshiper.

The statement noting that God would not have listened to the petition had the worshiper "cherished iniquity" is similar to expressions found in lament psalms in which the petitioner proclaims innocence (Pss. 7:4–6; 17:3–5; 18:21; cf. Job 31). It also appears to be best understood in the light of penitential psalms such as Psalm 32 (esp. vv. 6–7). The innocence of the worshiper is wrought in part by the severity of the trial, which in itself reorients the values of the individual and is consonant with the imagery of refining.

The psalm is a celebration of deliverance, which is understood and expressed in terms of God. In the broader literary context of the reading, verses 1–7, which form part of the introductory statement, make reference to the exodus event and to the crossing of the Jordan into Canaan. The tone of verses 1–7 pits the community of the psalmist against the "enemies" of God (v. 3) and the "rebellious" among the nations (v. 7). The universalism of verses 1–4 reveals interest in the human condition most broadly construed, not simply the welfare of Israel.

The combination of communal and individual dimensions reflects how worship in ancient Israel was strongly rooted in both the experience of the individual and the experience of the community. The community provides a store of tradition and a forum for sharpening what the individual perceives. The psalm celebrates the miracle of preservation against seemingly insurmountable odds and captures emotions that give rise to a story that must be shared.

DEXTER E. CALLENDER JR.

our heads; we went through fire and through water" (vv. 11–12).

The holy Presence does not promise to keep suffering at a distance. Rather, the Holy One is a ubiquitous Presence that forever reveals to us the spirit that is resilient within us by testing us in ways that make us stretch. This is not a coercive Presence that changes our external situation. God is rather the persuasive Presence that holds us so that, no matter what happens to us, we know we are not alone. Uttering words with our mouths is not a true act of prayer, but even in the toughest of times, if we pray for Presence, if we yearn to be held in the everlasting arms, we know in our hearts that "truly God has listened."

For practitioners of pastoral ministry it is not uncommon to sit with people who are seeking to find their way through the painful and challenging times of some personal wilderness. People come to clergy in search of answers. The psalmist reminds us that when we cannot get out of it, we have to go through it—carrying the burdens on our backs—we have to go through the water and the fire.

Through it all, God listens to us, not from a distance, but from within. Always, there is this inner listening Presence that knows us even better than we know ourselves. As we awaken to this Presence, we get that spacious feeling, and from this inner spaciousness we see that our lives are always lived in the presence of the One who "listens," the One who is eternally paying attention—this inimitable Presence liberates us because it accepts us as we are.

Perhaps this is why the psalmist concludes with a blessing: "Blessed be God, because YHWH has not rejected my prayer or removed from me, the love that is divine" (my wording).

Seen in this light, Psalm 66 provides not only a prayer of gratitude for the liberation of the Israelites from captivity. This psalm is an enduring reminder that whatever our experience, God is the patient and listening Presence, the power to transport us from the wilderness to the promised land within.

ROBERT V. THOMPSON

1 Peter 3:13-22

¹³Now who will harm you if you are eager to do what is good? ¹⁴But even if you do suffer for doing what is right, you are blessed. Do not fear what they fear, and do not be intimidated, ¹⁵but in your hearts sanctify Christ as Lord. Always be ready to make your defense to anyone who demands from you an accounting for the hope that is in you; ¹⁶yet do it with gentleness and reverence. Keep your conscience clear, so that, when you are maligned, those who abuse you for your good conduct in Christ may be put to shame. ¹⁷For it is better to suffer for doing good, if suffering should be God's will, than to suffer for doing evil. ¹⁸For Christ also suffered for sins once for all, the righteous for the unrighteous, in order to bring you to God. He was put to death in the flesh, but made alive in the spirit, ¹⁹in which also he went and made a proclamation to the spirits in prison, ²⁰who in former times did not obey, when God waited patiently in the days of Noah, during the building of the ark, in which a few, that is, eight persons, were saved through water. ²¹And baptism, which this prefigured, now saves you—not as a removal of dirt from the body, but as an appeal to God for a good conscience, through the resurrection of Jesus Christ, ²²who has gone into heaven and is at the right hand of God, with angels, authorities, and powers made subject to him.

Theological Perspective

The author of 1 Peter is writing to a people who are facing, or will soon be facing, persecution. If indeed the apostle Peter wrote the letter, with the assistance of Silvanus (5:12; hence explaining the letter's refined Greek), it must have been written prior to the Neronian persecutions, which started in 64 CE. This might explain why Peter counseled loyalty to the emperor (2:13–17) as a possible means of avoiding the persecution to come. If, instead, the letter was written toward the end of the first century by an author familiar with Peter's thoughts, as some scholars suggest, then the recipients of the letter may have already experienced empirewide persecution or, more likely, spontaneous localized persecutions. Regardless of who wrote the letter and when the letter was penned, this section of the letter expresses the author's aim to exhort believers to stand firm in their faith in the face of their present sufferings and the persecution they are experiencing or will experience. Those oppressed by the empire are encouraged to respond to their persecution by imitating Christ. For the author, a theology of identity in the midst of trials and tribulations is constructed.

Christians are called to live just lives that are above reproach. How they live becomes their best defense against those desiring their ruin; but even when living justly fails to prevent persecution, such a

Pastoral Perspective

At first read, this text seems to be calling us to an unrealistic standard. "Do not be afraid of those who want to harm you." Really? "Do not get upset"? Intellectually, we can understand this standard, but when push comes to shove, is this really livable? Of course, for Jesus it was, but the point of this text is not to put distance between Jesus and the reader, but to do just the opposite, that is, to grow closer to being able to live like Jesus in our own lives. Of course, we may not want actually to live the life that Jesus led, as his was filled with scorn, mockery, violence, and misunderstanding. However, we who believe Jesus to be the most complete revelation of the nature of God's love, and who seek to make that love real in our own lives, can look to none other than Jesus for the model. The question is how? How does this text allow us to grow closer to living a life like Jesus, when it so easily can be perceived as setting an unreachable standard that only Jesus met?

To begin, we need to look first to the end of the text, where we find a discussion about baptism. The process of growing closer to living a life like Jesus begins with a recognition of the meaning of our baptism. As the theology goes, our baptism represents the notion that before anything else, God loved us. What came first in each of our lives was a love from God, which is unaffected by whether or not we choose to

Exegetical Perspective

First Peter 3:8–12 sets the themes for today's lesson. The epistle, addressing the issue of unmerited suffering, reminds those who receive the letter not to repay evil for evil (v. 9). We do not know how immediate the threat of persecution was for the Christians of Asia Minor who are the recipients of this letter. The repeated emphasis on their status as outsiders suggests that they were subject to social sanctions and perhaps even to physical violence.

Suffering for Doing Good (vv. 13–17). The section begins with a hopeful rhetorical question: "Who will harm you if you are eager to do what is good?" The author's own response is less hopeful: "Well, maybe somebody will. But even if this happens you are blessed." The blessing is both a promise for the final days (see v. 9) and an assurance for the difficult present (see v. 12).

Verses 14b–16 tell the readers how to live out the blessedness of suffering. The most difficult injunction to interpret is verse 14b: "Do not fear what they fear." This is a quotation from the Septuagint, Isaiah 8:12–13. In that passage God calls on Isaiah to separate himself from the attitudes and behavior of the people around him. First Peter suggests that Christians, unlike the timorous community around them, should fear God alone. First Peter interprets that godly fear

Homiletical Perspective

Two themes in this text may attract our attention: the descent into hell and the suffering Christians experience in their life of faith.

Verses 19–20 are the biblical locus classicus for the claim in the Apostles' Creed that Jesus descended into hell, or what is sometimes called "the harrowing of hell." Here Jesus is envisioned "in the spirit" (v. 18) proclaiming the gospel among the dead. Today preachers who seek to emphasize this theme in a sermon may need to find ways to subvert the sense of unreality some in every congregation will find almost unavoidable.

While the mental picture of a ghostly Jesus walking around preaching and teaching in a place like Dante's hell is unlikely to find many friends today, the reality that the hope we have in Christ is more powerful than death remains vivid. One way to make this clear is to accept the lectionary's invitation to preach this passage alongside one or more of the others for the day.

In this way, a preacher can show that death is one of the many circumstances the gospel addresses. Like the Athenians whom Paul addresses, like the Gentiles and God-fearers of Psalm 66, and even like the anxious, barely believing disciples of Jesus in John 14, so also the "spirits in prison" (v. 19) are among the recipients of the gospel of grace in Jesus Christ. If the

1 Peter 3:13-22

Theological Perspective

life should still be lived for the sake of justice. Let such a life shame those who malign one's lifestyle; if questioned as to why one remains a Christian, answer courteously. Let the believers look to Christ as their example. Innocent of malice or wrongdoing, he suffered upon the cross, an act that brought humanity back to God, even for those in prison (hell? v. 19) who refused to hear the warnings of Noah prior to the coming flood.

To understand a theology that stresses the identification of Christ with the faithful, we need to indicate who today continues to suffer and be persecuted by the empire. To obey and follow Christ who was persecuted on the cross is to share in his suffering. This is a message radically different from what is usually preached about the consequences of being a follower of Christ. For many, to be a Christian is not a life of suffering, but one of worldly rewards. Prosperity theology, the assumption that Christians are blessed with material rewards and good health, contradicts what the author of 1 Peter sets out to be the norm for Christians—that suffering and persecution are inevitable for the one who believes. Prosperity theology becomes the religious justification for a lifestyle that defines riches produced by global structures of oppression as God's blessings upon one group.

Some who adhere to prosperity theology interpret negative public reaction to a Christian lifestyle that arrogantly attempts to impose a particular faith on others as "suffering" or "persecution." Communal disapproval for strong-arm evangelical tactics is not what this passage attempts to describe. The author realizes that for the recipients of 1 Peter to obey Christ is to live apart from the empire of their time. Likewise, for us today, to obey and follow Christ is to live apart from the empire of our present era. Many Christians question and refuse to submit to a neoliberal globalization that creates poverty throughout the third world so that a small group of Western industrialized nations (mainly Eurocentric and self-professing Christians) can use and abuse the vast majority of the world resources. This invites the hostility of the dominant culture, and attempting to radically change these structures to reflect the liberating message of the gospel is to ensure persecution.

Ironically, many of those today who claim Christianity as their faith are oppressing the vast majority of the world's non-Europeans as the means by which they sustain and preserve their wealth, privilege, and power. Merging Christianity with empire, a process whose roots date to Constantine (313 CE), has aligned those in the developed world who profess

Pastoral Perspective

respond to or recognize that love. God loves us—period. We may not feel it. Some may not want it. Others may choose to ignore it. Regardless of our response, God's love endures. Of equal importance in this equation is an understanding that the purpose of baptism is not conversion: "Because God loved you first, you need to love God back." Baptism is really about perception. It is an invitation to perceive our lives through a new lens, from a perspective that is broader than our own limited assessment of self.

The lens I am speaking of is God, whose assessment of our intrinsic and eternal value is positive, so positive that Jesus was willing to die for us. To begin to perceive our lives, our value, our worth through this lens, is to begin to free ourselves from the tyranny of self-pity and doubt, which are all too often the byproducts of suffering. Suffering endured without connection to a greater purpose—suffering that we experience while void of any sense of a larger identity not defined or bound by the suffering—produces only self-pity, fear, and doubt. To begin to perceive ourselves as first and foremost loved by God, whether we think we have earned that distinction or not, is to begin to widen our spiritual, emotional, and intellectual horizons, to see beyond that which oppresses in the here and now. Rather than being consumed by the suffering, we are rejuvenated by the recognition of a larger purpose, a connection to a power greater than that which oppresses.

In this way we enable ourselves to grow closer to an ability to live as Jesus did—to turn the other cheek, to love our enemies, to love those who torment us, to lift up in prayer those who seek to tear us down. In this way, and perhaps more effectively than in any other, we "defend our confidence in God." For the greatest defense comes not from words, but from actions. To engage the world and those who would oppress us in this way, is most fully to defend or reveal our confidence in God. The more able we are to reveal our confidence in God through behavior choices, the more closely we grow to living like Jesus, whose entire life was a picture of living confidently in God.

This brings us to the last point of this commentary, which focuses on the text's reference to "those who disobeyed." The author is referring to those in Noah's day who angered God to the point of flooding the earth. Of course, the broader implication is for all of us, not just those in Noah's time, to avoid disobeying God. Obeying God is an interesting and important concept. The call to obey has existed for many, many years; it goes all the way back to Adam and Eve, who did not obey God. Today, however, the word

Exegetical Perspective

christologically. The way to show fear of the Lord is "in your hearts to sanctify Christ as Lord" (v. 15).

The phrases that the NRSV translates as imperatives ("be ready," "keep your conscience clear") are actually subordinate clauses and show the hearers what it looks like to "sanctify Christ as Lord." They sanctify Christ "by being ready" and "by keeping their conscience clear."

The NRSV translates verses 15b–16a, "Always be ready to make your defense to anyone who demands from you an accounting for the hope that is in you; yet do it with gentleness and reverence." The faithful are called to suffer only for doing good, not for doing evil. Now, more than that, they are to respond to the suffering by doing even more good

The letter may encourage a brave defense before the authorities. It certainly encourages defense before those nonbelievers who slander and demean the faithful. What believers defend is their hope. "Hope" is a term that reminds us that this community lives under the promise of God's coming judgment and redemption.

The NRSV translates 3:16b, "Keep your conscience clear, so that, when you are maligned, those who abuse you . . . may be put to shame." "Shame" for 1 Peter does not mean that the opponents will feel bad. It means that they will lose standing and social power because they have been outflanked by kindness. "Shame" probably also refers to the final, eschatological shaming that the opponents can expect on the day of judgment (see 2:12; 4:5) The reference to a clear conscience brings us back to the claim that believers should suffer only for doing good, not for doing evil (3:13; see also 4:17).

Christ's Suffering (vv. 18–22). Our passage closes when 1 Peter spells out what it means to suffer according to God's will. The narrative about Christ that follows is the grounding and reason for the admonitions that precede verse 18. Note what the affirmation means.

> You believers are not the first to suffer; Christ also suffered.
> You are not the first to suffer for the unrighteous; Christ did that.
> Apart from Christ's sufferings, you would not be counted among the righteous at all.
> You suffer from time to time and faithfully; Christ suffered once and for all (for all time; for all people) and redemptively.
> Our suffering may shame our opponents; his suffering brought the faithful to God's righteousness.

Homiletical Perspective

gospel can come even to the dead, is there any situation, any culture, any life Jesus cannot claim and make his own?

A second way to bring this tradition to life, showing Christ's power over death at the heart of it, is to recall relatively recent depictions of it in the movies *The Lion, the Witch, and the Wardrobe* and *The Return of the King,* and in the books by C. S. Lewis and J. R. R. Tolkien that stand behind them.[1]

At the climax of *The Lion, the Witch, and the Wardrobe,* Aslan, the lion who represents Jesus in the story, after his death and resurrection enters the hellish castle of the evil White Witch and by his breath restores life to the many Narnians she has turned to stone and placed in a kind of limbo in her domain. They are free to return joyfully to the life of the land of Narnia, which at that moment means throwing themselves into the struggle against the White Witch's army, a struggle that had been going badly but turns in favor of the Narnians with the new strength of those who have been set free.

Similarly, in *The Return of the King,* the third installment in the *Lord of the Rings* series, the battle against the forces of Mordor has become all but hopeless when Aragorn, the king of the title, arrives at the head of an ancient army of dead soldiers who had failed in antiquity to fulfill an obligation. They have lingered in a ghostly existence for ages. Aragorn, one of the several characters with Christlike dimensions in *Lord of the Rings,* enters their domain and offers them an opportunity to help in his cause and so fulfill their promise and be set free. In the book they are liberated from their limbo when they move a fleet of ships, freeing Aragorn to fight for the good, while in the movie they actually engage in the battle at Gondor, buying crucial time for the forces of good in the battle that marks the end of the age.

Such stories may not sound any less mythological in the telling than a more descriptive exposition of the harrowing of hell (if such is possible), but they do provide contemporary visual images of the hope it represents: death is not the last word on life. Indeed, death is apparently not even a barrier to hearing and responding to the gospel, contrary to much American revival preaching. Other literary explorations of this idea include Charles Williams's novel *All Hallows Eve,* which follows two women as

---

1. *The Lion, the Witch, and the Wardrobe,* movie, directed by Andrew Adamson (Burbank, CA, 2005), based on C. S. Lewis, *The Lion, the Witch, and the Wardrobe* (New York: HarperCollins, 1994). *The Lord of the Rings: The Return of the King,* movie, directed by Peter Jackson (New York: New Line Cinemas, 2003), based on J. R. R. Tolkien, *The Return of the King* (London: George Allen & Unwin, 1955).

1 Peter 3:13‑22

Theological Perspective

obedience to Christ with the persecutors of the early church more than with the church to whom 1 Peter was addressed. The paradox created by this reversal of roles is that those who do not profess allegiance to Christ are at times more "Christian" than those who call themselves believers.

An example can be provided in the events that occurred during the missionary conquest of the "savage pagans" of the Americas. Although they were not Christians, the original inhabitants of the Caribbean islands suffered cruelly at the hands of the Christian conquerors. One of the caciques (a chieftain) of these people named Hatuey created a loose confederation of Indians to resist the invading Christian colonizers. For three months he carried out a style of guerrilla warfare against the Spaniards. By 1511, an expedition to capture the renegade chieftain and pacify the island was carried out. Once apprehended, Hatuey was condemned to death as an example for others. As Hatuey was about to be burned at the stake, a Franciscan friar attempted to convert him to the Christian faith with the promise of heaven and the threat of hell. Hatuey is reported to have asked if Christians went to heaven. The friar answered in the affirmative, to which the condemned Hatuey retorted that he did not want to go to heaven where he would see such cruel people.

The Christian conquistadors and missionaries were the true savage pagans. Hatuey and all other non-Christians who resist empire, then and now, are the real "Christians." They may never have read 1 Peter, but they have suffered persecution for living righteous lives. And when they have been questioned about their beliefs, they have shamed those bent on their destruction. A theology of identity forces those who claim Christianity as their faith to examine their lives to see if they have more in common with the empire the author of 1 Peter writes about, or with the victims of empire—be they the early Christian church or the Hatueys of today.

MIGUEL A. DE LA TORRE

Pastoral Perspective

"obey" gets a bad rap. I have been told it is oppressive and insensitive.

The word "obey" in Hebrew means to listen closely, to listen acutely. So, for example, when God tells Adam and Eve to obey, God is not saying, "Do what I tell you, or else." No, God is saying, "Listen closely to me." Indeed, the Greek word for obedience carries the same meaning: to listen closely. What made Jesus so great was that he listened so closely to God, which led him to serve and to love humanity in radical, selfless ways. In introducing the notion of obedience into this text, the author's point is not to threaten. Rather, it is to awaken in us the desire to listen closely to God, to listen to God in a way that reveals our confidence in God. As we do so, we will avoid the paths set by those of Noah's day, who did not rely on God. Their confidence in God was weak at best and nonexistent at worst. Instead, ours will be a story of close listening. Ours will be a story of trust, of confidence in God, revealed most clearly in our actions toward others. To live this way is to grow closer to living as Jesus did.

GORDON MCCLELLAN

Exegetical Perspective

Now comes the hard part. What does it mean to say that Christ was put to death in the flesh but made alive in the spirit? In 1:24 the author quotes Isaiah 40 with the reminder that flesh is like grass—perishable. It may therefore be that the author here suggests that what was perishable in Christ—his flesh—died, while that which was imperishable—his spirit? God's Spirit?—was raised to triumph. It may also mean that Christ was put to death by the powers of the flesh—all his opponents—and triumphed by the power of the Spirit (see Rom. 1:4–5).

Among the many interpretations offered for the claim that Christ preached to the spirits in prison, I find it most likely that our text claims that on his way to the highest heaven the risen Christ stopped off at one of the lower heavens where the souls of the Nephilim of Genesis 6:1–4 were imprisoned. They preceded Noah, and their misdeeds were sometimes thought to account for the antediluvian wickedness that made Noah's story possible and necessary.[1]

Whatever the meaning of these puzzling verses, they bring the author to his liturgically grounded conclusion. The spirits are related to Noah; Noah is related to the flood; the flood prefigures baptism. The typology seems a little lame. Noah was saved *from* the water, those who believe in Christ are saved *through* the water, though both immersions represent both death and life.

According to 1 Peter, baptism provides the "appeal . . . for a good conscience" (v. 21). The term for conscience, also used in 2:19 (NRSV "being aware of God") and 3:16, refers to the orientation of the whole person toward God. Baptism is the sign of that reorientation. Of course it is not baptism that saves; it is the resurrection of Christ into whom the faithful are baptized. His suffering has validated their suffering, and his resurrection confirms their hope.

What makes possible a conscious relationship to God, a conscientious relationship to other people, and faithfulness in suffering is the resurrection of the one who was subject to suffering but who now, at God's right hand, holds all the world subject to himself.

DAVID L. BARTLETT

Homiletical Perspective

they continue to develop, one toward blessedness and the other toward final misery, after dying together in a plane crash.[2]

Some preachers will think it less than obvious that the harrowing of hell is the central idea at the heart of this passage. After all, it is tucked away in a prepositional phrase, offered almost parenthetically in a sentence about something else. Thus preachers may look for strategies for conveying the passage's more central message, on the problem of suffering as a result of faith in Christ.

The text does not suggest a sermon on the problem of "bad things" happening to "good people." First Peter is very clear what it means by goodness: it is "righteousness" (v. 14; NRSV "what is right") and "good conduct in Christ" (v. 16). In addition, it is clear that what it means by suffering is not "bad things" that cause pain in a life that is, on the whole, honorably lived and therefore somehow undeserving of suffering. Rather, the text is about suffering that comes precisely as a consequence of being faithful "in Christ."

A sermon that takes up this dimension of the passage might begin where the lectionary passage begins, with the common-sense assumption that no one will hurt you "if you are eager to do what is good." This assumption, like much that passes for common sense, often does not work out in the Christian life. Indeed, Jesus acknowledged as much, in Matthew 10:16–23, for example, a passage the preacher could well pair with this one in for a sermon on this theme.

Seen from this angle, the passage offers wisdom to guide persecuted Christians' behavior, identifies the believer's suffering with the passion of Christ, and finally proposes baptism as the suffering Christian's "appeal to God for a good conscience" (v. 21).

MICHAEL D. BUSH

---

1. I borrow this largely from W. J. Dalton. See the discussion of the exegesis of these verses in David Bartlett, "The First Letter of Peter," in Leander Keck, ed., *The New Interpreter's Bible* (Nashville: Abingdon Press, 1998), 12:292–96.

2. Charles Williams, *All Hallows Eve* (New York: Pelligrine & Cudahy, 1948).

John 14:15-21

15"If you love me, you will keep my commandments. 16And I will ask the Father, and he will give you another Advocate, to be with you forever. 17This is the Spirit of truth, whom the world cannot receive, because it neither sees him nor knows him. You know him, because he abides with you, and he will be in you.

18"I will not leave you orphaned; I am coming to you. 19In a little while the world will no longer see me, but you will see me; because I live, you also will live. 20On that day you will know that I am in my Father, and you in me, and I in you. 21They who have my commandments and keep them are those who love me; and those who love me will be loved by my Father, and I will love them and reveal myself to them."

Theological Perspective

"If you love me, you will keep my commandments."

In ethics, it is dubious to conflate "is" with "ought," the indicative mood with the imperative. The indicative is how we imagine things *are*; the imperative is how we imagine what we *should* do or how we should live. Anthropologist Clifford Geertz associates the former with a culture's *worldview*, the latter with its *ethos*. Ordinarily, to confuse these matters is, well, confusing. To say, "There is no point in going against the way things are," may involve moral complacency—especially when "the way things are" is really a rationalization of vested interests. If one said, "You need not lock your doors in our little town, because we are all God's children and God is love," that would be naive. Deriving "is" from "ought," or "ought" from "is," is often fallacious.

However, Geertz thinks that, among its several functions, a religious symbol or ritual does work to (1) "synthesize" a culture's ethos and worldview, each side grounded in the authority of the other; (2) "clothe" communal identities in this synthesis of "is" and "ought"; and (3) give the synthesis an "aura of factuality."[1] This aura means that while those within the religious community cannot see the world

1. Clifford Geertz, *The Interpretation of Cultures* (New York: Basic Books, 1973), 89–90.

Pastoral Perspective

Our passage opens with the poignant moment of Jesus trying to make something plain to his followers: all he asks of them is their embrace of the love he has lived among them as the goal for their own lives. Coming quickly to the close of his earthly ministry, he can only speak of love and the assurance that the God he knows so intimately as Father will continue to accompany them through the Paraclete, who will also be their advocate in recognizing that God's love is what is most true.

John's Gospel was written in an age of empire, for people surrounded by agents of the emperor, images of imposed dominion, and the weapons to enforce the imperial power. We find in John's Gospel this strikingly different claim about the power and order that love brings to life and relationships. It is difficult to imagine a sharper contrast to the imperial understanding of the way the world is or the definition of power. Jesus relies principally on himself as the object lesson to disclose this linkage of love and truth. It is not surprising that Jesus assures his followers they will not be alone in their efforts to live a life shaped by love. He is acknowledging that choosing to see reality through the lens of love in the midst of empire is very difficult.

This difficulty is not unique to the Johannine community. Many of us know that challenge,

Exegetical Perspective

Though the Last Supper is often pictured as a serene meal among friends, the Fourth Evangelist presents Jesus as consoling the chaos, confusion, and concern among the disciples. The scene begins with the narrator's announcement that "Jesus knew that his hour had come for him to pass on from this world" and had "loved them to the end" (13:1, all quotations my trans.), and the scene grows more ominous as Jesus informs the disciples of his impending departure (13:33), sends Judas out to betray him (13:21–30), and predicts Peter's denial (13:36–38). The disciples' panic is clear in their constant questioning of Jesus (13:36; 14:5, 8). The Farewell Discourse (John 13–17) announces the coming departure of Jesus but consoles those who remain on earth to continue God's work.

John 14:15–21 is one such comforting text. Jesus has just emphasized that he is the way to the Father (14:6–7), and in verses 15–21 he addresses how those who remain on earth continue to access this way. This passage presents parallel statements (vv. 15–17 and vv. 19–21) surrounding the central message: "I will not leave you as orphans; I am coming to you" (v. 18). Jesus emphasizes continued access to the Father, even after his departure from earth. In the surrounding verses, Jesus describes how his followers will continue to access the Father (vv. 16–17, 19–20), so long as they love him by keeping his commands (vv. 15, 21).

Homiletical Perspective

"In" is a tiny word. It seems as if it should not matter all that much. Nevertheless, here is Jesus, promising to be "in" the people who keep his commandments, his earliest disciples, and promising too that those disciples will be "in" him. So here are we, who may think of ourselves as the heirs to those disciples, and maybe we are wondering about that "in" too. Is Jesus actually "in" us? How would we know?

The key may be that Advocate, that Paraclete, the Spirit of truth, who Jesus has promised will be with them—who will be with us—forever. It is easy for us to hear "Spirit" and immediately think of warm, personal feelings—feelings of security, of connection with God. Many of our hymns seem to focus on an experience of the Spirit that is personal like that. This understanding offers many of us comfort, especially when the world around us seems to be spinning out of control.

Think for a moment, though, about what else the word "advocate" might conjure up. "Advocate," Greek "paraclete," means "one who has been called to our side" to stand up for us, to explain us to the court. Think of lawyer shows on television. Think of detectives and mystery and action. The Paraclete, the Advocate, is a force on the move.

Jesus calls the Spirit *another* Advocate. The earlier Advocate is Jesus himself (1 John 2:1 states this

John 14:15-21

Theological Perspective

otherwise, those outside that community will probably think its convictions quite bizarre. To many, science and historical-cultural experience do not support the idea that divine love creates the universe. Nietzsche, an outsider to the aura of Christian symbols, considered the double love of God and neighbor to be a weak, insipid ethic and obviously counterfactual. Yet those of us whose identities are clothed by symbols of divine love can hardly view the world otherwise, and are commanded to synthesize the "is" and the "ought." Created by love, we believe we should imitate the Creator's love.

This brings us to the Paraclete.

Paraklētos—John's term for "the Spirit of truth" or "Holy Spirit" (14:26)—is variously paraphrased: advocate, counselor, comforter, helper, mediator, even "broker."[2] By any definition, it is a religious symbol, and so we might interpret it as a gift that unites the ethical and worldview sides of Christian belief. The ethical *imperative to love* is synthesized with *divine love as indicative of reality*. John, moreover, identifies the Paraclete with "the Spirit of truth"—thereby asserting that *this* fusion of ethos and worldview is not arbitrary and relative, as the anthropologist in "the world" might see it, but is inscribed in the very grain of reality. However, this interpretation may seem rather pat. Almost any religious idea or practice in any tradition could receive the same Geertz-inspired treatment. John's discourse must be more interesting than that if it is to challenge how we imagine reality and live our lives. So let us look again.

The Paraclete appears in discourses where Jesus asserts strong, if not strict equivalences. The Father is one with the Son; to obey is to love; our knowing God goes with God's abiding in us; Christ's life adjoins with the disciples' life; and above all, the Father's love is one with the Son's love, which is one with the disciples' love. Do these near-equivalences amount to quid pro quo: "if you do for me, I will do for you" or "if we love the Son, the Son will send another Paraclete"? Such conditionality would be surpassed by the "logic of love"[3] animating Johannine literature. With 1 John 4:8—"God is love"—we begin to see that when love is the condition of all things, and when love is both infinite and practical ("I will not leave you orphaned," Jesus says with poignant insight into the disciples' limitations), then love overrides quid pro quo.

2. Jerome H. Neyrey, *The Gospel of John,* New Cambridge Bible Commentary (New York: Cambridge University Press, 2007), 21–25, 149.
3. On the "logic of charity" (*agapē*), see Jean-Luc Marion, *God without Being* (Chicago: University of Chicago Press, 1991), 183–86.

Pastoral Perspective

although our challenge lies in being shaped not by an occupying empire but by the nations of the West. Surely this promise, that the Spirit who continues Jesus' ministry of pointing to the truth of God's love now dwells in us, is as important now as it was in the first century.

The love Jesus wants his hearers to embrace is not an abstract philosophical concept but the lived reality revealed in the life, relationships, and actions of a simple Nazarene who looks and talks like them and lives simply among them. He feeds the hungry, touches lepers, heals the sick, and speaks and acts toward women with care and regard. Love is seen in his life as service and compassion. It is also seen in his fierce protests against those who abuse this vision of the value of each person and the importance of an ethic of mutual regard and care. Instead of power as domination, Jesus invites those who meet him to imagine power that has as its goal the well-being of all persons regardless of social status.

It is not hard to imagine how parched the souls and hopes of those among whom Jesus lived must have been. Poor and cast aside in the apparent main narrative of world history, with the added insult of imperial rule, the people Jesus called by name were likely hoping to be invisible to those in power, so that they and their families would be safe. Then, through Jesus' presence the contagion of genuine love takes hold. Gradually a community of hope is born. Imaginations are quickened so that persons dare to wonder if the power of love that Jesus embodies is more real—more truthful—than the subjugation and humiliations of Roman rule. Then comes his remarkable assurance that the love he offers them is in fact God's love. He and God are one. Promises of redemption and liberation that they must have thought God had set aside once again seem trustworthy, available, and true.

Sometimes understanding a foreign idea requires a truly transforming experience. Jesus chose the Passover meal to drive home his point about love and the truth of the relational power it creates, as he took up a basin and towel and washed the feet of those who called him Teacher and Lord. The love to which God calls us does not intend hierarchy. The reality that love creates discloses to us the truth that God calls us to be neighbors—to recognize in the "other" one whom God also loves and calls us to love.

Jesus not only claims that God's love is true; he also claims that God's love is the source of life. This love is both the source of our lives and the goal of our lives. Alan Paton, in his novel *Ah, But Your Land*

Exegetical Perspective

In verses 16–17, Jesus promises the Paraclete to sustain the community after his departure. Though this Johannine term for the Spirit (see 14:26; 15:26; 16:7; 1 John 2:1) literally refers to a legal advocate or assistant, most important here is the similarity of the Gospel's language about the Paraclete and Jesus. Readers should not overlook Jesus' promise of "another Paraclete"; Jesus describes the Paraclete as his continued presence. Both Jesus and the Paraclete are sent from God (14:16; cf. 3:17, 34; 14:26; 15:26), are rejected by the world (14:17; cf. 1:10; 7:7; 15:18), are known by Jesus' followers (14:17; cf. 10:14), and represent "the truth" (14:17; cf. 1:14, 17; 8:45; 14:6). In chapter 16, Jesus acknowledges that the Paraclete, like himself, speaks God's word instead of its own (16:13; cf. 3:34; 7:16; 12:49). The Paraclete also bears witness to Christ (15:26; 16:14). It is Jesus who is the first "Paraclete to the Father" (1 John 2:1). However, while Jesus is departing soon, the Paraclete will "be with you forever" (14:16).

In verse 15 Jesus shows that the coming of the Paraclete depends upon the disciples' loving Jesus, and love is demonstrated by keeping his commands. Jesus does not simply offer moral exhortation. The Fourth Gospel describes the appropriate human response to Christ in a number of ways, including believing, loving, abiding, and keeping the commands. In all of these ways Jesus demands that believers share with him a full identity with the Father (see 8:31–59). This total devotion is made clear in his identification of keeping his commands as an act of love, demonstrated by Jesus in washing the disciples' feet (13:1–20). Later in the discourse he teaches that "no one has greater love than this: that someone would lay down his life on behalf of his friends" (15:13). Jesus commands the disciples to love, and he demonstrates this total love in his self-sacrifice for them. Jesus commands an active love, as he tells Peter at the end of the Gospel (see 21:15–17).

On the other side of verse 18, Jesus ties the promise of his continued presence to the anxious situation the disciples face. In verse 19 he acknowledges that he will soon depart from them but reassures them that they will continue to see him, though the world will not. Jesus does not give them hope of a distant future in which he will return, but an immediate hope of continuing to know him, even though he is not physically present on earth. This ability to see when the world does not comes from the life that is made available in Christ (cf. 1:4; 10:10). The final phrase of verse 19 indicates how it is that they see and yet the world does not: "And you will see me because I am living and you

Homiletical Perspective

explicitly), and Jesus was most certainly a force on the move. Think of the meals with outcasts and sinners. Think of the money changers in the temple. Think of the healings and the preaching, the travels between Galilee and Jerusalem. The story of Jesus is a story not of private feelings and comfort, but of action.

This Paraclete, this Advocate, Jesus promises, will be "with you . . . in you." Jesus himself will be "in" the disciples, as he is "in" the Father, and as the disciples will be "in" him. Is it enough to imagine some kind of mystical union? Is the indwelling of Christ or the Spirit of truth like a sense of warmth or a feeling of confidence? Is it an abstract notion or a state of grace?

Remember that scene of Jesus standing before Pontius Pilate in Pilate's headquarters? Pilate asks, "What is truth?" Jesus stands there in silence. Why does he not answer?

The answer is right there. You are looking at it, Pilate. The truth is standing in front of you. Watch him, and you will find out what truth is.

We cannot see Spirit, but we can see Jesus. We can see him healing, and teaching, and dying in his faithfulness. Draw an outline around that moving picture of Jesus, and you have a framework for recognizing the truth Pilate was asking about. You have a framework too for recognizing the Spirit of truth, the Advocate, Jesus himself dwelling in us and among us.

In the Gospel record, we see Jesus operating in community, with his disciples and with the other people he serves. The story of Jesus is not about Jesus and a single disciple, like some stories of prophets or holy men from other traditions. Jesus is present and active with groups of people—real people who sometimes struggle just to get along and other times enjoy sharing their successes, their hopes, and their questions. So when Jesus promises to be "in" his disciples, and promises that they will be in him, it seems clear now that he cannot be promising only mystical union with individuals. Everything we know about him suggests someone operating as an active presence in a communal context.

Indeed, the Greek words usually translated "in you" can also legitimately be translated "among you (plural)." How might it affect our ability to receive Jesus' promise if we put less emphasis on our individualized, mystical interpretation and more on that communal idea? Might it reduce our anxiety about whether we are really "right with God"? Might it, in fact, lead us to dwell less on our own, individual worthiness and focus our energy rather on an active life of faithful service?

John 14:15-21

Theological Perspective

Consider the first sentence again. If the command is to love God, and if God is love, then to love God implicitly means *loving Love lovingly* and *practically*, leaving none orphaned. The object of the command (God, Love, neighbor) and the subject (those who love) begin to blur into the command's reality (love). Consider this sentence: "You know him [Paraclete, Spirit of truth, divine love], because he abides with you, and he will be in you" (v. 17b). The subject ("you") and the object (divine love, truth, etc.) blur into the predicate (knowing, abiding). This blurring is not trivial, because the relations that love encompasses are ever expanding. Love enlarges to encompass knowing, abiding, comforting, feeding, giving, discovering, touching, healing, naming, praising, justifying, and so forth. Because such love expands, it is fitting that Jesus addresses the present in terms of the future. He abides in the disciples now and, with the coming of the Paraclete, will abide more.

However, there is a tragic sense of exclusion in these near-equivalences: "This is the Spirit of truth, whom the world cannot receive, because it neither sees him nor knows him" (v. 17a); "Judas (not Iscariot) said to him, 'Lord, how is it that you will reveal yourself to us, and not to the world?'" (v. 22, after the lection). What are we to make of the sense of exclusion?

It might be that because any fusion of ethos and worldview is hard to comprehend apart from the language of particular communities, theological universalism can get short shrift. One insight could be that while we cannot impose ultimate inclusivity as a necessity for God, we may nonetheless witness to God's will that none be lost. Another insight could be that in verse 22, the disciples may not yet grasp the logic of love. In any case, we should acknowledge that it is *love* that the Paraclete discloses. The gift that overcomes the world's exclusions—the horrible disjunctions between *life as we imagine it realistically* and *life as it might be*—is the *loving that God is*, abiding in us and crossing our limits, the infinite love for the world that we are commanded to enact.

LARRY D. BOUCHARD

Pastoral Perspective

Is Beautiful, pictures a scene that may illustrate this life-giving power of love and the assurance that God's love discloses what is most true.[1] Paton describes a situation in South Africa during apartheid, when laws prevented black South Africans from mixing with whites. At the death of a white South African official who had worked within the system to humanize life for the oppressed, the blacks were turned away from his funeral, despite the wishes of the family. It was a terrible insult. Isaiah Buti, a black pastor, visited the white chief justice, whom he had reason to imagine as a friend to his oppressed people. He asked the judge to participate in the Good Friday service where the congregation would observe Jesus' practice of washing the disciples' feet. He asked the chief justice to wash the feet of a congregant who had been a servant in the judge's home and had cared for his children. The chief justice readily agreed, though he asked to participate in the service without any prior announcement.

When the time came for the judge to wash Martha Fortuin's feet, the judge came forward and washed and dried her feet. Before he rose to return to his seat, he took her feet and gently kissed them both. It was a gesture that set healing in motion, because in that simple extra expression of care, he disclosed the truthfulness and the life-giving power of God's love. Of course the act became known and the judge's career was affected, but he had no regrets, because he too experienced the life-giving power of love that helps us recognize each other as neighbors.

NANCY J. RAMSAY

---

1. Alan Paton, *Ah, But Your Land Is Beautiful* (New York: Scribners, 1981), 229–35.

Exegetical Perspective

will be living." True life, made available through Christ, allows the community to continue to see Jesus even after he has gone. Seeing Jesus is equated with knowledge that just as Jesus abides in the Father, so his followers abide in him and he in them.

Jesus closes verses 15–21 by essentially repeating what he said in verse 15: finding continuity between the time of Jesus' earthly presence and the time of his absence depends upon loving him, demonstrated through keeping his commands. In verse 21, though, Jesus repeats this emphasis on love in the third person singular: "The one who has my commands and keeps them, this one is the one who loves me." In this rephrasing, the narrative audience of the Last Supper fades into the background, and the reader of the Gospel is addressed by the speaker. Anxiety in the face of life without Jesus on earth does not belong only to the disciples in the room, and appropriately Jesus' response addresses not only the disciples, but the reader as well.

The parallel structure of this passage continues even after the lectionary text. In verse 22 Jesus once again emphasizes loving him through keeping his word as the way to be separate from the world. Repetition in verses 15, 21, and 23–24 suggests that loving Jesus by keeping his word is the essential calm for those anxious about a life without Jesus on earth.

The Fourth Gospel likely took its final shape at the end of the first century CE, in a community where most of the members never knew Jesus on earth. This community saw itself in the telling of the story of the anxiety of the disciples facing life without their teacher. The community addressed its own anxiety by repeating the calming words of Jesus, reminding them that access to the Father continues in the community's adherence to his commands and the promised Paraclete. Regardless of time or place, Jesus' message stands: "I will not leave you as orphans; I am coming to you."

RICHARD MANLY ADAMS JR.

Homiletical Perspective

Mother Teresa of Calcutta famously left her record of a lifetime of struggle—struggle with the darkness that plagued her because, for more than half her life, she did not feel the presence of Christ.[1] Nonetheless, among Christians she has been generally accepted as a modern saint. Some consider her an even greater saint because in spite of the dark she continued to be faithful. Even though she had not been gifted with spiritual certainty, she steadfastly pursued the mission to which she believed she had been called, and the Christian community recognized and affirmed that mission.

Jesus clearly promises his presence and the presence of the Spirit to those who keep his commandments to love and serve one another. The love Jesus commands is not a feeling—not even a feeling of certainty about union with Christ. The love Jesus commands is about a master washing the feet of his disciples, and a king dying the death of a criminal. We have that outline around the moving picture of Jesus, an outline that can define the Spirit of truth as it appears in our own lives and our own actions.

What if we were to understand Jesus' words this way? What if we were to recognize that Christ is truly present *among us* when we keep his commandments to love and serve one another? Look around you in your community—your church community as well as the greater community in which you live and serve—and see where you can discern that outline around the picture of Jesus on the move. See where, in the familiar life of this group of people, you can discern the presence of the Spirit of truth.

LINDA LEE CLADER

---

1. Mother Teresa, *Mother Teresa: Come Be My Light: The Private Writings of the Saint of Calcutta* (New York: Doubleday, 2007).

Acts 1:1-11

¹In the first book, Theophilus, I wrote about all that Jesus did and taught from the beginning ²until the day when he was taken up to heaven, after giving instructions through the Holy Spirit to the apostles whom he had chosen. ³After his suffering he presented himself alive to them by many convincing proofs, appearing to them during forty days and speaking about the kingdom of God. ⁴While staying with them, he ordered them not to leave Jerusalem, but to wait there for the promise of the Father. "This," he said, "is what you have heard from me; ⁵for John baptized with water, but you will be baptized with the Holy Spirit not many days from now."

⁶So when they had come together, they asked him, "Lord, is this the time when you will restore the kingdom to Israel?" ⁷He replied, "It is not for you to know the times or periods that the Father has set by his own authority. ⁸But you will receive power when the Holy Spirit has come upon you; and you will be my witnesses in Jerusalem, in all Judea and Samaria, and to the ends of the earth." ⁹When he had said this, as they were watching, he was lifted up, and a cloud took him out of their sight. ¹⁰While he was going and they were gazing up toward heaven, suddenly two men in white robes stood by them. ¹¹They said, "Men of Galilee, why do you stand looking up toward heaven? This Jesus, who has been taken up from you into heaven, will come in the same way as you saw him go into heaven."

Theological Perspective

I suspect no other festival in the Christian year is more important and less emphasized than the ascension of the Lord. At the heart of our confession stand the crucifixion and resurrection, and a close second is the founding of the church at Pentecost. Doubtless, our communal life depends upon the certainty of these seminal events, but the transformation of that timid band of believers, fearfully hovering in silence, remains inexplicable apart from the ascension of the Lord. Likewise, the theological shift from proclaiming the kingdom of God to announcing Jesus as Lord also germinates in the disciples' experience of Jesus' departure.

Apart from Mark's longer ending (Mark 16:19), Luke is the only evangelist to report the ascension. In both Matthew and John, the writers omit this event and leave the reader with a sense of the risen Lord's perpetual presence. In Matthew, Jesus promises, "I am with you always, to the end of the age" (Matt. 28:20), and in John, Jesus' conversation with Peter abruptly ends with the assurance that there is more—so much more that the telling would fill the world's books and forever occupy our attention (John 21:25). With such open-endedness, the evangelists rightly create space for the continuation of God's story unfolding in Jesus. By contrast, the postresurrection experience in Mark 16:8 leaves the

Pastoral Perspective

"Well, dear Theophilus, God-lovers all, the story continues . . . " Jesus lives on in the church through the Holy Spirit, the Comforter, the one who fills us with courage and strength. The text tells us that life in the Holy Spirit is not only promised to the disciples in the days to come; the Spirit is actually the one through whom the disciples have received instructions from Jesus. So the Spirit has already been active in their lives indirectly; now the promise for them is direct experience of that same Spirit.

Much of Christian tradition has made a claim for the resurrection as the culmination of Jesus' life and ministry, but a case can be made for the ascension. Although the resurrection is surely a most spectacular event in the story of Jesus, life goes on, as the writer of Acts shows us. The good news for those left standing on that Judean hillside is that Jesus not only comes from God, he returns to God. This is the true scope of movement for followers of the Way—we come from God, we return to God. The challenge in the meantime is to keep our lives centered on God, rooted and grounded in God, allowing God to be the one in whom we "live and move and have our being" (Acts 17:28), here and now, on this earth.

In contrast to the end of the Gospel of Luke, the ascension story comes in Acts only after Jesus has had an extra forty days with the disciples, "speaking

Exegetical Perspective

If I were going to place a title upon today's passage, it would be something like this: "Looking Back. Looking Forward. Looking Up." These are the three movements found in today's scripture. Thus, I would like to address each part separately, although they are certainly interrelated.

Looking Back. Acts begins like any other ancient historical work, with a renewed dedication to its patron (Theophilus) and a backward glance to the first book, the Gospel according to Luke. The author says, "I wrote about all that Jesus did and taught from the beginning until the day when he was taken up to heaven" (vv. 1–2). By doing this, the writer demonstrates two things. First, Christianity is adopting literary forms. The movement is at the point of leaving the realm of ordinary people (that is, oral tradition) and entering the world of literature. This is one of the few explicit indications in the New Testament that at least some Christians wanted to move beyond the confines of a largely Palestinian Jewish—largely oral—world into the expansive environment of the Greco-Roman world. Second, Luke's determination to present the entirety of the Christian tradition signals the intent at this point in the life of the church to fix the form of the Jesus tradition for all time. We are moving then from the realm of anecdote

Homiletical Perspective

Most of us know very little about the ascension of Jesus Christ. Some have seen paintings of the scene, or an "ascension window" beautifying some dark corner in a cathedral. These depictions usually show Jesus drifting upward into the clouds in flowing white robes while awe-filled disciples gaze upward in amazement or confusion. The ascension of Jesus Christ was so important to our ancient forebears in the faith that they made it a part of the earliest Christian creeds. The Apostles' Creed says, "On the third day he arose again from the dead; he ascended into heaven, and sitteth on the right hand of God the Father Almighty."

Within Christian theology the ascension marks the end of Jesus' earthly experience and the beginning of the role of Jesus as advocate and intercessor at God's side. Calvin imagines Christ acting as a kind of holy distraction for God, his perfect presence averting God's eyes from our sins. He encourages us to see Christ persuading God to look with favor on us, paving the way for us into the heavenly reign of God. Looking closely at the text itself, there are several key themes for preaching.

Living in the In-between Times. For the early followers of Jesus, the ascension marked the end of their earthly experience of Jesus and the beginning of the

Acts 1:1-11

Theological Perspective

women fleeing in terror—trembling, bewildered, and silent. In John, the apostles huddle in an unknown location, bound by fear, isolated, and locked out of the world (John 20). Even Peter, having seen the resurrected Lord, returns to the water. "I am going fishing," he says. "We will go with you," the others respond (John 21:3). Resurrection? What does it all mean? Maybe Jesus is right after all. Maybe his leaving really is for the best (John 16:7).

Witnessing to the glorification of Christ, the resurrection and ascension are inseparable, but the convergence of the two into a singular whole mistakenly requires the resurrection to bear the weight of glory alone. Jesus may have risen, but fear captivates the hearts of would-be witnesses. Though the resurrected Lord moves elusively in and out of the disciples' lives, their loyalty drifts back to the world they knew before the rabbi appeared. As for the Lukan account in Acts, the sociopolitical lens shaping messianic hopes remains firm. "Lord," they ask, "is this the time when you will restore the kingdom to Israel?" (v. 6). Thus the resurrection alone fails to captivate the believing community with the expansive vision characteristic of their later witness.

Jesus' postresurrection appearances leave the disciples conflicted, and only in the time during Jesus' departure do they glimpse the glory that eternally shapes the Christian proclamation and sets them on a course that changes world history. In Luke–Acts, the ascending Christ extends a "blessing" to those watching him disappear. "He led them out as far as Bethany, and, lifting up his hands, he blessed them. While he was blessing them, he withdrew from them and was carried up into heaven" (Luke 24:50–51). With this conveyance of divine favor, Jesus becomes something for the disciples that he had never been before. Returning to Jerusalem, they joyfully worship him and uninhibited they remain at the temple praising God (Luke 24:52–53). No more fishing, no more fear of the authorities, and no more hiding.

Karl Barth argues, "There is . . . a relatively thin line in the New Testament, which speaks of Christ's ascent into heaven," but in these moments an ultimately unrivaled "historical turning-point" occurs.[1] In *The Rediscovery of Eschatology in the Message of Jesus and Its Impact on Theology in the Twentieth Century*, Terry Dohm contends that the turning point for the disciples was the resurrection. "Because Jesus of Nazareth had been raised," he asserts, "the

---

1. Karl Barth, *Dogmatics in Outline*, trans. G. T. Thomson (1949; repr., London: SCM Press, 1957), 124, 126.

Pastoral Perspective

about the kingdom of God" (v. 3). You may imagine that these followers, who have already demonstrated difficulty in understanding Jesus' purpose among them, can use all the help they can get if their movement is to have any future at all. You may also imagine that the turmoil in Jerusalem, along with the turmoil in their own lives from the events of Passover week, has not entirely subsided. Though they are elated to have Jesus with them, they are still cautiously hiding out in locked rooms, bags packed for the return trip to the relative quiet and safety of Galilee. They want to go home, but they also do not want to let go of Jesus.

The challenges of the Way continue for them. Jesus instructs them to remain in Jerusalem, even though he is planning to leave them physically. He has promised them the gift of the Spirit, if they can just hold on a little longer. Their innate curiosity kicks in, though their question shows how much more they have to learn: "Is this the time when you will restore the kingdom to Israel?" (v. 6). They continue to show shortsightedness; they cannot yet envision the big picture. "Your vision is too small. You are not ready for, nor do you need to know, the details of how God is operating here. You need to get yourselves ready for the coming of the Spirit that will be the next leg of your journey on the Way. It is enough for now. It is all you can handle."

They are to be Christ's witnesses, beginning where they are, spreading the good news to the "ends of the earth" (v. 8). Before they can ask a follow-up question, before their very eyes, he ascends into the clouds and disappears from sight. Again, we can imagine that they are dumbfounded, left standing on that hillside, their necks craning to see beyond the clouds, their mouths hanging open. More miracles—angelic voices bring them back to reality: "Why do you stand looking up toward heaven? This Jesus . . . will come in the same way you saw him go" (v. 11).

From God, to God, yes; but in this coming and going the membrane between heaven and earth is eternally altered. There is now the promise of coming and going in new and exciting movement along the Way. The beginnings of a thoroughfare have been outlined, and Jesus has been the first to travel it. The promise is that many more will travel it in the days ahead, because these same awkward, gaping disciples, empowered by the Holy Spirit, will show the Way.

Among other things, this text underlines how God works through the simplest of folk—peasants and outcasts, thick-skulled and fearful folk—to change the world. These disciples are given responsibility for

and oral exchange into one of doctrine and emerging theology.

Looking Forward. Beginning with verse 3, the author shifts his focus from one of looking back to one of looking forward. The most striking thing about this transition is that it goes back to the final point of reference in the Gospel, the ascension (Luke 24:51). Now we are told of the "many convincing proofs" of the resurrection. Acts tells us that during the forty days following the resurrection, Jesus was repeatedly in the disciples' company and spoke to them of the "kingdom of God." In verses 4–5 we are also reminded of Jesus' command to the disciples to stay in Jerusalem until they receive the Holy Spirit (see Luke 24:49). This description provides a context for the coming question regarding restoration of the kingdom to Israel (v. 6).

"Lord, is this the time when you will restore the kingdom to Israel?" This question is not meant to imply that the disciples are ignorant. Rather it serves to clarify a problem of the highest order, one that is theological as well as historical. The earliest believers regarded the outpouring of the Holy Spirit as a sign that the end of the world was near. In other words, they wondered, does the coming of the Spirit signal the beginning of Israel's restoration? This also signals an underlying concern for Acts: Is the kingdom restricted to Israel? Jesus' response in 1:7 draws upon a statement found in the other Synoptics (Mark 13:32; Matt. 24:36). Here in Acts, which edits out the phrase "not even the Son of Man knows that day and hour," the declaration forbids the asking of any questions about the timing of the second coming. From this statement we see the author of Acts looking forward as the spokesperson of a new age, one where the focus moves from the end to the mission. As Ernst Haenchen, whose commentary on Acts has been influential in modern scholarship, argues, "[Luke] has decisively renounced all expectation of an imminent end."[1] Thus today's text refocuses us as readers, from asking, "When will the end come?" to "What are we called to do while we are waiting for the end to come?"

As a missionary enterprise, the church in Acts answers the second question that underlies the first and explicit one: the mission of the church is not confined to Israel alone. In laying down the course of the Christian mission from Jerusalem to the "ends of the earth," the author concisely highlights the content of Acts: the progress of the gospel from Jerusalem to

1. Ernst Haenchen, *The Acts of the Apostles: A Commentary*, trans. R. McL. Wilson (Philadelphia: Westminster Press, 1971), 143.

"in-between times" leading up to Jesus' second coming. This is a time of between-ness that we still experience today. In the words of one of R.E.M.'s most popular songs, we live at "The End of the World as We Know It" (but without their added acclamation, "And I feel fine!"). In-between-ness, for most of us, is no fun. Everything seems up for grabs in this postmodern, posteverything generation. After the gas-powered automobile, then what? After the polar ice caps are gone, then what? After global terrorism, then what? After churches and denominations, then what? Many today, like the disciples, wonder, "Is this the time when God will restore the kingdom to Israel?" What better time for God to come in glory and make the world whole again? We all know, at the very depths of our being, what it is like to live the in-between times, socially and personally, times in which our lives feel like a difficult passage from one world into the next.

From Frustration to Spiritual Purpose. A second theme quickly appears in this story. Jesus responds to his disciples' question: "It is not for you to know the times or periods that the Father has set by his own authority" (v. 7). This was probably frustrating news to the disciples, and it certainly is for us. As if we were not already fully aware of the passage of centuries, all the while hoping for God's restoration of peace and justice on earth. As if we were not already living with the constant sense of insecurity and incompletion, with no end in sight. Thank goodness the biblical story does not stop here!

The next thing that happens is that we are given a purpose—a mission: "But you will receive power when the Holy Spirit has come upon you; and you will be my witnesses in Jerusalem, in all Judea and Samaria, and to the ends of the earth" (v. 8). We are reminded that we are not left in an in-between world without spiritual power and purpose. There are very important things to do during these times as we work toward God's new day: visiting the sick, being advocates for justice, renewing the church, feeding the hungry, housing the homeless, praying, studying the Bible, worshiping together. The in-between time is a time to turn from ourselves toward others, living and ministering beyond ourselves in the power of the Holy Spirit. The ascension looks directly toward Pentecost and the spiritual witness of the church in the world, right up to our own uncertain day.

Leaving Home, Taken to the Heart of God. Mission, however, is not enough to sustain us during this

Acts 1:1-11

Theological Perspective

apocalyptic new aeon or Eschaton that they had been anticipating, had begun. . . . The focal point [had] become that Jesus was raised and was alive, and that in his death the salvation of the world was accomplished."[2] Granted, Dohm's emphasis is the glorification of Christ, of which the ascension remains an integral part, but the ascension stands as a distinct article of faith and must not be conflated with the resurrection into a singular event. "I believe in . . . Jesus Christ, God's only Son, our Lord . . . who suffered under Pontius Pilate, was crucified, dead, and buried. On the third day, he rose again from the dead and ascended into heaven." In the Lukan account, the ascension is the revelatory moment beyond which the disciples are never the same.

To our twenty-first-century minds, it may be tempting to dismiss the record of one ascending into the abyss of space, as if God somehow dwells "out there" beyond the vast astronomical expanse. However, lest we forget, even the earliest disciples were trapped in their own understanding of time, space, and the kingdom of God. In Acts 1:3, Jesus spends forty days teaching them about the reign of God, yet they still misunderstand. Only after the ascension and their peculiar experience with the absent and yet ever-present Lord are their conceptions of time and space transformed. Certainly, the "restoration of Israel" remains a viable hope, but the center of Jesus' rule shifts from Jerusalem to the heavenly realms where he takes his place at the right hand of the Father. From such transcendence Jesus reigns (Eph. 4:10), and God's kingdom expands beyond the limitations of all earthly kings and kingdoms, revealing the man from Nazareth as the Lord, the Lord who is one.[3] Out of their experience with the risen *and* ascended Christ, the substance of the Christian kerygma takes shape.

SEAN A. WHITE

Pastoral Perspective

Jesus' radically revolutionary movement to turn the world right side up. On the surface, they may seem an unlikely group, caught up in conventional concern for the restoration of the literal Davidic kingdom in Israel, not able to see beyond their concrete desires for their own welfare. Nonetheless, Jesus stays with them long enough to be able to pass them off to the Spirit, who will continue the work he has begun in and among them. They are about to find voices that will indeed speak truth to power and spread good news to the very ends of the earth.

The challenge for us modern disciples is to do likewise. When and where do we find ourselves standing, "looking up toward heaven," hoping that Jesus or someone will do it for us? How are we hamstrung by our inability to see beyond the conventional into the miraculous promises that are still given to us today as followers of the Way? What would it take for us, as individuals and as communities of faith, to travel this thoroughfare that leads from God to God?

Those first disciples must have shared with one another their anxieties and fears, their hopes and dreams, their wonder and anticipation as they retraced their steps to Jerusalem that first Ascension Day. Jesus gathered them as a community, taught them as a community, and left from the midst of their little community. The Spirit was promised to them in community. Of course, individuals can and do have experiences of the Spirit, but Jesus makes it clear that it is the Spirit, working in the community, that will spread the good news around the world and bring in the reign of God. That reality has not changed in two millennia. It still takes a community of faith, Spirit-filled, to spread the good news and bring in the reign of God. That is our challenge and our commission as the body of Christ, followers of the Way.

RANDLE R. (RICK) MIXON

---

2. Terry C. Dohm, *The Rediscovery of Eschatology in the Message of Jesus and Its Impact on Theology in the Twentieth Century* (Regensburg, Germany: S. Roderer Verlag, 2003), 30.
3. See Martin Luther, "About the Story and Fruit of Ascension," in *The Complete Sermons of Martin Luther*, vol. 6, ed. Eugene F. A. Klug, trans. Eugene F. A. Klug et al. (Grand Rapids: Baker Books, 2000), 117–18; Theodore P. Ferris, "The Acts of the Apostles," in *The Interpreter's Bible* (Nashville: Abingdon Press, 1954), 9:25, 29.

Exegetical Perspective

Rome (v. 8). In other words, the outpouring of the Holy Spirit will equip the disciples to move beyond their narrow confines and narrow vision—Jerusalem and the restoration of the kingdom to Israel—into a larger, diverse world telling them "God's deeds of power" (2:11).

In his resolve to look back as a basis for looking forward, Luke does create a problem for his readers in 1:9. The Gospel of Luke ends with Jesus' ascension (Luke 24:51). Some might question this narrative inconsistency, but to the author of Acts it is most important that the story of the church should begin "not with the disciples left to their own devices, but with the Lord, who visits and instructs them for forty days more."[2] The implication may be that we banish the idea that the apostles were self-sufficient, fully prepared human beings. This time of instruction, the outpouring of the Spirit, and the other acts of divine intervention throughout the book imply that the apostles were in need of divine assistance. The Christian mission is not merely a human enterprise. As Jesus' final words to his followers indicate, it is a divinely ordained and guided one.

Looking Up. The description of the ascension—the point at which the narrative begins to look up—is terse and seamless. Directly after Jesus commands them to "be my witnesses" (v. 8), he is lifted up before his disciples (v. 9). They are the eyewitnesses to this event, similar to what we hear in 1 Corinthians 15:7. With the cloud taking "him out of their sight," the report cannot describe Jesus' entry into heaven itself. In this way, Luke's account differs from others found in Judaism and the Greco-Roman world (e.g., *1 Enoch* 39; Livy, *Ab urbe cond.*), as well as the more detailed description outlined by John in Revelation (Rev. 4:1–2). Just as in Luke 24:5–6, human beings are rebuked for their reaction to the event (vv. 10–11). In this way, the ascension in Acts differs markedly from other descriptions of the event (e.g., the *Gospel of Peter*), in that it avoids sentiment, even rebuking it, for the sake of austerity. The focus remains on the mission. The ascension is simply that event that inaugurates it.

MICHAEL JOSEPH BROWN

Homiletical Perspective

in-between day. In fact, most of us would simply feel worn out and weary, were it not for what happens next in Luke's story. According to Luke, Jesus was "lifted up, and a cloud took him out of their sight," leaving them "gazing up toward heaven" (vv. 9–10). Our first thought might be that this is an awful thing, a picture of God abandoning us, only to send a phantom spirit later. This is because we tend to focus our attention on the divinity of Jesus, to see Jesus as God loaned to us for a while, coming down from on high, and then leaving us to go back to be with God in glory. We see the ascension as Jesus going home to be with God after a long, tough visit with us here on earth. Luke's language hints at another perspective. Luke says that Jesus was "taken up," he was "lifted up," a cloud "took him." The language sounds more as if Jesus is leaving home here on earth, rather than going home to God in majesty. The text goes on to say that he will come back or return "in the same way" (v. 11), that his homecoming will be a return to the world. Pandipeddi Chenchiah, an Indian theologian, says that this stresses the "ongoingness, the permanence of the humanity of Jesus."[1]

Luke, the physician, is showing us a picture of the humanity of Jesus taken into the heart of God, and in that picture we see all of humanity taken up into God's heart, perhaps more deeply than ever before. This is profound good news for us in the in-between times. As the world changes, we confront new forms of insecurity. We experience oppression and sometimes violence. We confront suffering and death. We long for healing and wholeness. We work for justice. *Through it all* we carry with us this vision of our real value to God, of the Human One, who made himself at *home* with our humanity, for a time taken up into God, sustained, valued, and held, before returning home to restore the world.

JOHN S. MCCLURE

---

1. Pandipeddi Chenchiah, quoted in George Hunsberger, "'The day when he was taken up . . .'—A Meditation from Acts 2:1–9," *International Review of Mission* 86, no. 343 (Oct. 1997): 391.

2. Ibid., 146.

Psalm 93

¹The LORD is king, he is robed in majesty;
   the LORD is robed, he is girded with strength.
 He has established the world; it shall never be moved;
²your throne is established from of old;
   you are from everlasting.

³The floods have lifted up, O LORD,
   the floods have lifted up their voice;
   the floods lift up their roaring.
⁴More majestic than the thunders of mighty waters,
   more majestic than the waves of the sea,
   majestic on high is the LORD!

⁵Your decrees are very sure;
   holiness befits your house,
   O LORD, forevermore.

Theological Perspective

Developing language about God should not exclude or marginalize others; rather, God talk should invite deeper conversations about God's communal nature. "The LORD is king, he is robed in majesty; the LORD is robed, he is girded with strength. He has established the world; it shall never be moved" (v. 1). God as a king—such language should not call for exclusivist rhetoric of patriarchal dynasties; rather, in its best intentions, kingly language is a proclamation to the individual hearer that God is inextricably bound to God's kingdom. God is unintelligible apart from community. In the same way, earthly existence is unintelligible apart from God.

To be fair, the argument against patriarchal God talk occurs due to the erroneous ways in which the church has used such talk to justify the marginalization of women in society. When we are trapped in patriarchy, there is little incentive to transcend competitive schemes for male domination and control. These historical difficulties that arise when we talk about God should not, however, prevent our speech about God. For example, noise can become a symphony orchestra in which each particular part knows its uniqueness in relationship to other parts. The psalmist prays, "O LORD, the floods have lifted up their voice; the floods lift up their roaring. More majestic than the thunders of mighty waters, more

Pastoral Perspective

Psalm 93 is a psalm the people of God will want to sing on the day of the ascension of the Lord. It is this day that the church gathers to remember and proclaim that it is Jesus Christ who sits at the right hand of God. Through this psalm the voices of the congregation rise up in praise: "The LORD is king." This liturgical affirmation is voiced even in the face of roaring floods. The raging floods may erode the basis for this bold claim of faith among many; yet such affirmations are common as God's people gather for worship. Not only on the day of ascension, but also the liturgy of weekly worship overflows with such affirmations:

"This is the day the Lord has made."
"As far as the east is from the west, so far has God removed our transgressions from us."
"The word of the Lord."
"This is the cup of the new covenant poured out for you."
"Go in peace."

These liturgical statements of faith rest in the belief that the Lord is sovereign, but confidence in God's reign is not uttered from the mountaintop, so to speak. This psalm of royal praise is sung in the face of rising waters. Even the casual reader of Scripture

Exegetical Perspective

Psalm 93 belongs to the fourth section or book of the Psalter. It is typically understood as an enthronement psalm (along with Pss. 47; 96–100), thought to have been used in ceremonies in the temple that proclaimed and celebrated the kingship of God over all. It has been suggested and is widely accepted among scholars that such hymns hail from a fall festival recognizing the New Year. As such, the enthronement of YHWH reflected the renewal of creation in the defeat of chaos in the primordium.[1]

Sigmund Mowinckel considered the elements of the enthronement psalms to suggest reflection on the actual present. More than mere poetic metaphor that is otherwise disconnected from immediate life, they directly engage the objective and experience of contemporary worshipers. The image of the Lord ascending to his throne, having accomplished great deeds, represents an allusion to a common and no doubt easily recognized mythic motif, known throughout the ancient Near East and expressed in various forms. Kingship was common language for conceptualizing the sacred. The idea of becoming king in a given moment might be explained in a

1. See B. C. Ollenburger, *Zion the City of the Great King* (Sheffield: Journal for the Study of the Old Testament Press, 1987), 25–33. For further discussion and references, see M. Tate, *Psalms 51–100* (Dallas: Word Books, 1990), 477.

Homiletical Perspective

As we celebrate the ascension of our Lord, here is the picture: God sits as a king on the throne while Jesus rises to take his rightful place. For many Christians, a literal interpretation is a source of comfort. Many others will prefer to explore the mystery of the metaphor of the throne from which God reigns.

Where is this throne? The conventional tone of the word "throne" implies that God rules with power from a distant place. From this throne, God moves things around in the world.

Several days after Hurricane Katrina struck the Gulf Coast of the United States, a story was published in *USA Today* about Edward and Bettina Larsen and their three children, who had sailed their boat to the Florida Keys. As hurricane warnings were posted, the Larsens' friends became concerned that they had not returned to home port and notified the Coast Guard. The Coast Guard started a search, but high winds and rough seas forced them to call it off.

A day after the storm had passed, the Coast Guard resumed the search and miraculously spotted the family of five, stranded near their beached boat on a mangrove island sixteen miles out to sea. One by one, the family members were hoisted into a Coast Guard helicopter and then taken safely home.

Commenting on the rescue, a family friend said, "Sometimes there is a thing called divine intervention."

Psalm 93

Theological Perspective

majestic than the waves of the sea, majestic on high is the Lord!" (vv. 3–4). Just as a symphony orchestra first needs to make noise in order for the players to tune their instruments before a concert, human beings are maturing in their conversation about God.

When the psalmist prays to God as king, we see a crucial use of apophatic theology—a way of unknowing in order to know the idol from reality. What we call God is really not God. Apophatic theology helps us with the problem of naming God. When we name the ineffable, we constantly discover contradiction. For example, it is an unnecessary contradiction to juxtapose conservative and liberal Christianity. Each group learns from the other. As conservative Christians teach us, we all need to become aware that there is direct intervention by heaven in this world. I learn from my conservative friends that heaven really exists. Liberal Christians teach us that heaven is transforming earth to become a place capable of possessing the unusual nature of God's community. In other words, heaven must always be transforming our perceptions of where heaven exists; after all, in a new heaven and earth there will be no need of a sun or moon (Rev. 21:1). Apophatic theology provides the confession that, because of the poverty of our words, Christians can describe only very imperfectly how God is revealed on earth.

Until we can see more clearly in our mirror dimly, apophatic theology is one of the best methodological ways of understanding heaven on earth. Although some "conservative" Christians have difficulty thinking about what God is not, such a theological task is important, because it protects our God talk from the inherent dangers of an individualistic cosmology, often represented by those happy to call God king over private realms only. The difficulty here is that personal salvation is not the ultimate goal of a Christian; God is. Apophatic theology reminds us that God's gifts transcend our anxiety for our own personal salvation. The ultimate goal of redemption is always God, who is both subject and object.

The danger for the "liberal" Christian also resides in individualism—striving for a privatism in which tolerance somehow becomes a sufficient virtue. God revealed in Christ, however, is not about tolerance. Jesus reveals shalom, which is a way of flourishing together in peace, not simply a way of being tolerant of one another. With flashing neon-light persistence, the Word of God shows liberals and conservatives alike that we must be saved together; otherwise, none of us arrives in heaven. Returning to where we began in this commentary, the use of the title "King" for

Pastoral Perspective

will recognize the "flood" as an ancient metaphor for the chaos that intrudes upon God's children in a fashion that is anything but metaphorical. Worship may take place in a sanctuary, but worship does not create sanctuary from the chaos and brokenness of life. Those faithful to God's decrees are not insulated from the harsh and injurious ways of life. The faithful know what it is to be engulfed by grief. The faithful know what it is to wade through disappointment or to be swallowed by the crushing burden of oppression or poverty or disease. Still, even up to their necks in the rising floods, the congregation sings of God's faithful reign: "The Lord is sovereign."

The psalmist speaks honestly of the chaos of life. Three times the psalmist faces the chaos:

> The floods have lifted up;
> The floods have lifted up their voice;
> The floods lift up their roaring. (v. 3)

The raging floods mean that God's voice must be heard amidst the roar of other voices. We know these voices of chaos. These voices speak of greed rather than generosity. They speak of violence rather than peace. They speak of selfishness rather than compassion. Their unremitting theme is fear. Such voices are constantly lifted up in the long journey of the human story. The psalmist is not blind to the power of their fury. The psalm is not sung from a place of sanctuary far removed from the brokenness of life. The psalmist holds no naiveté about the world in which we live. Quite to the contrary, faith in God is voiced while looking the chaos and evil squarely in the face. In every circumstance, including in the face of the flood, it is God's decrees that can be trusted. It is the Lord who is robed in majesty. It is the Lord's voice that is reliable: "Your decrees are very sure" (v. 5). The Lord's decrees provide a power of life that is claimed in the midst of torrential floods. This power of life can be trusted because the Lord who is "from everlasting" is our sovereign!

The voices of the flood declare that the day belongs to us; but when God is our sovereign, "this is the day that the Lord has made" (Ps. 118:24). The voices of chaos proclaim that we are captured by the evil of our past, but the holy decrees promise, "as far as the east is from the west, so far [God] removes our transgressions from us" (Ps. 103:12). The currents of the world assert, "My life is my own," but the promise of our baptism shouts, "Jesus Christ is my Lord and Savior." The believer always lives in a world of violence, but into this world the promise and calling is to "go in peace." When the voices of selfishness rush against us,

number of ways, such as in the selection or "salvation" of Israel. The nature of the saving acts is not simply historical, but cosmic or mythical, as suggested in the language of creation, which the congregation in some sense witnesses. Future salvation is similarly described in Second Isaiah, most likely influenced by the same cultural materials as the enthronement psalms.[2]

In its present literary context, Psalm 93 is set between two thanksgiving psalms, and some have suggested that Psalms 92–94 form a larger unit, to be read together. There are a number of links between Psalm 92 and 94: the appearance of "dull" in both (92:6, 94:8); the image of YHWH as rock (92:15; 94:22); "evildoers" (92:7, 9; 94:4,16). Psalms 92 and 93 share use of "on high" (92:8; 93:4). The superscription to Psalm 92 refers to it as a "Song for the Sabbath Day." The Mishnah (*Tamid* 7:4) notes that Psalm 92 was sung on the Sabbath and Psalm 93 was read in the temple on Friday, which Rabbi Aqiva (b. *Rosh Hash.* 31a) explained by linking the reference in 93:1, "the world is firmly established," to the completion of creation on the sixth day.[3] A reading of Psalm 93 suggests three primary units: (a) an exaltation in verses 1–2; (b) an allusion to primordial watery chaos, vanquished by YHWH, in verses 3–4; and (c) a statement in verse 5 validating the authority of YHWH as evidenced in his decrees.

The psalm employs common imagery that features the divine king in his role as warrior, "girded" for battle (cf. David who is girded with strength for battle in 2 Sam. 22:40 [=Psalm 18:39]) and fighting to protect and deliver the people from threatening forces. The domain controlled by YHWH is the world itself (v. 1). The psalm ascribes the establishment of the world to YHWH and associates it with the establishment of the divine throne by placing it in the primordial period ("from of old" [*me'az*]) and declaring YHWH "from everlasting" [*me'olam*]). Placing the events in the primordium is not simply a reference to creation in the temporal past, but also understands the events as underlying the present cosmic reality.

The context of the imagery is that of creation— the imposition of order upon chaos. In the thought world of the ancient Near East, water provided an image suggestive of chaos. Chaos was the state that obtained prior to the establishment of order, and order was derived from the very elements of chaos.

---

2. S. Mowinckel, *The Psalms in Israel's Worship* (Sheffield: Journal for the Study of the Old Testament Press, 1992), 110–11.
3. See Tate, *Psalms 50–100*, 475–76.

More often than not, the reign of YHWH is equated with a God who intervenes on behalf of the faithful. Is this how God rules?

Many believe the God who reigns is a deity who takes sides. The psalmist says, "The LORD is robed, God is girded with strength" (v. 1). The literalist hermeneutic will point to concrete events in the world as evidence of the God who rules from a distance.

Where is the throne of God? Where do we see God's strength? The psalmist proclaims: "The world stands firm and cannot be moved, your throne stands firm from ages past, from eternity you exist. The seas are shouting YHWH—the seas raise their voices, the seas shout with pounding waves. Stronger than the thunder, mightier than the breakers of the sea, mightiest is YHWH" (vv. 1b–4, my trans.).

The thoughtful preacher is confronted with two questions in this text: Where is this throne of God, and what does it mean to say this throne is everlasting?

The external world gets our attention.

I am familiar with the argument that if it happens in the world, it is the will of God; but the psalmist makes a deeper claim.

The strength of God is "mightier than the breakers of the sea." What could be mightier than the power of the external world than the power that animates the external world? What if God rules, not by manipulating external events, but as the very power of life that gives life? What could be mightier than the power of the external world than the power that gives life?

Here is where the Christian mystical tradition helps us. Along with other Christian mystics, the sixteenth-century Teresa of Avila does not see the throne of God as some remote place where God rules. Like Meister Eckhart, she says that God rules from the very soul of life. The soul is an interior castle, and God sits on the throne. The mystics speak from personal experience rather than dogmatic certainty. Unanimously, they say the real throne, the real strength, the real ruling power of God is located not in the external world but in the very heart of life.

What if the throne on which "God sits" is the throne of the heart? What if God is not met in temples, churches, or synagogues? What if God is not really encountered in anything external? What if God is only and always met in the interior castle? What if this God "robed in majesty" lives in the innermost heart of every human being?

Emily Dickinson wrote this verse:

Psalm 93

Theological Perspective

God reminds us that all speaking of God is imperfect, because our words cannot capture God's ineffable perfection.

Seeking first the kingdom of heaven frees us from the limitations of our God talk, because we are no longer bound to names for God that we know are immature ways of seeing God. We know God is ineffable and cannot be fully named. As Christians we know this mystery due to the incarnation of Christ. Jesus taught the world new God talk, and it was not from the kingly perspective of power and prestige. In fact, people mocked Jesus by calling him a king. So, if you are certain in your ideology and theology, be careful lest your names for God prevent you from recognizing the living God.

Through apophatic theology we avoid the misconceptions surrounding the Christian message—especially those misinterpretations that condone perpetual violence, war, famine, sickness, slavery, and the poor always being with us. Most of these descriptions abandon us in the rhetoric of kingdoms (that require kings), heavens detached from earth, or our biding of time until things get better. As our biblical teachers will show us, we must learn to interpret Scripture from its deeper sense, looking beyond the misconceptions that some use to marginalize and oppress others.

The psalmist gives us a larger way of seeing God: "More majestic than the thunders of mighty waters, more majestic than the waves of the sea, majestic on high is the LORD!" (v. 4). Such a perspective frees us from the world of false gods that we are all inclined to make. The psalmist's intention is not to decode the mystery of God; instead, we need to become humble witnesses who experience the mystery of God in heaven. We do not witness God primarily in the sphere of theoretical thought, and the domicile of God is not found fifty billion light years away. Rather, it is in this earthly existence. Heaven is not a place where God is an individual satisfied within "himself," but a place where God communally acts and communally *is* with us—here and now. We must all become concerned about each other's "personal" journey to God—that God's whereabouts need not be privately remote.

MICHAEL BATTLE

Pastoral Perspective

and the currents of greed threaten to wash us away; when fear seeks to erode our footing, the psalmist proclaims life, because the Lord is our sovereign.

> More majestic than the thunders of mighty waters,
> more majestic than the waves of the sea,
> majestic on high is the LORD! (v. 4)

Such is the language of worship. It is never naive; but in the face of the forces that would destroy life, it is always defiant, boldly proclaiming the sovereignty of God, even when the waters of brokenness and evil are rising.

The faithful singer of Psalm 93 does not sing of a truth that is proclaimed because of the circumstances, but sings a truth that is spoken in defiant tone into the face of the circumstances. In a world where constant division seems to be true, the church proclaims that, in truth, people will come from north, south, east, and west and sit at table together. In a world defined by violence, the church asserts that the day will come when swords will be beaten into plowshares and spears into pruning hooks. The same word of defiance is witnessed as the people of God walk from the sanctuary into a world defined by brokenness and enslaved to fear with the marching orders to "go in peace."

The language of liturgy sees beyond the present circumstance and speaks that which is known only in holy imagination but is also known as that which is eternally true. The flood waters are real, but they are not ultimate. Never have the powers of evil and chaos been able to drown out the praise of God's people who in humble yet bold defiance sing what is true yesterday, today, and in every tomorrow: the Lord is sovereign. The ascension of the Lord celebrates on *one* day that which is true *every* day.

THOMAS L. ARE JR.

Ascension of the Lord

Exegetical Perspective

The image of a sea that rages in one moment, is calm in the next, and then rages again captures the idea of a creation within which lies an inherent chaos—a disorder that threatens to erupt. In verse 3, "floods" renders Hebrew *neharot*, "rivers," found in other cosmogonic contexts. Psalm 24:2 similarly considers the world (*tebel*) the domain of YHWH, and finds it established on the rivers. Similarly, Psalm 74:13–15 makes reference to cosmogonic struggle against waters (v. 15 "you dried up ever-flowing *streams*" [*naharot*]). In the *Baal Cycle* of Canaanite literature, the hero Baal "Lord" defeats Yamm "Sea," supplanting Yamm's dominion. Yamm also bears the title River. In the Babylonian epic *Enuma Elish*, the god Marduk slays Tiamat, whose image is that of salt waters representing primordial chaos. This common motif of cosmogonic struggle is expressed in Psalm 93 in terms of the frightful din of the waters and floods, which display the threat of their power in lifting up their voice and roaring (v. 3).

That this imagery is not simply a reference to past events seems evident in similar language found in Isaiah 17:12; 51:9–15; Jeremiah 6:23, where the roar of threatening nations is explicitly compared to the roar of the waters. Mythic imagery in this psalm is thus likely employed to describe political and social threats to the community and to the individual. Rather than a simple espousal of the virtues of bellicosity, the psalm engages the idea of the quelling of destructive forces and the subsequent renewal or continuance of life. Accordingly, divine salvation is absolute in coming from the very source of cosmic order. The proclamation of YHWH as king is the recognition of a fundamental reality of existence, namely, that deliverance comes from beyond the boundaries of the created order. The affirmation of YHWH as the source of the created order and the one by whom the world itself is established is the central idea. To invoke the one responsible for the conditions of existence is to reflect upon and attempt to transcend the chaotic forces which often rise up and appear to threaten it.

DEXTER E. CALLENDER JR.

Homiletical Perspective

Tell the truth but tell it slant
Success in Circuit lies
Too bright for our infirm Delight
The Truth's superb surprise
As Lightning to the Children eased
With explanations kind
The truth must dazzle gradually
Or every(one) be blind.[1]

When it comes to where to find the throne of God and how God rules, the hermeneutic of poets and mystics is profoundly persuasive. We are awakened to the divine Presence everywhere when we see that the life that lives in us is the same life that lives in every other living being. This truth is such a profound mystery, one to which we can only point with metaphor and other figures of speech.

Questions are more provocative than answers. Perhaps Psalm 93 is not a prescriptive answer but a provocative question. Is the throne of God somewhere else? If so, it will inevitably divide the world into "us" and "them." But if the divine throne lives in the very heart of life, it is not something that separates but the very power that connects all of life.

What if, while we live our many lives, there is but one life living through us? What if life is the throne of God, and how we relate to this ruling presence is what finally makes the rule of God real and present in the world?

On the surface, Psalm 93 appears to point to a God who "reigns and is robed in majesty." The deeper questions may well be, from whence does God rule, and what is the nature of this divine power?

Is God some distant power that coerces us, or is this persuasive power of the heart? Is God met in some external fortress, or within the interior castle of the soul? If God sits in the throne of every heart, what does this change about the way we see ourselves and relate to the world?

Psalm 93 may raise more questions than it answers.

ROBERT V. THOMPSON

---

1. Thomas J. Johnson, ed., *The Complete Poems of Emily Dickinson* (Boston: Little, Brown & Co., 1960), 506.

Ephesians 1:15-23

15I have heard of your faith in the Lord Jesus and your love toward all the saints, and for this reason 16I do not cease to give thanks for you as I remember you in my prayers. 17I pray that the God of our Lord Jesus Christ, the Father of glory, may give you a spirit of wisdom and revelation as you come to know him, 18so that, with the eyes of your heart enlightened, you may know what is the hope to which he has called you, what are the riches of his glorious inheritance among the saints, 19and what is the immeasurable greatness of his power for us who believe, according to the working of his great power. 20God put this power to work in Christ when he raised him from the dead and seated him at his right hand in the heavenly places, 21far above all rule and authority and power and dominion, and above every name that is named, not only in this age but also in the age to come. 22And he has put all things under his feet and has made him the head over all things for the church, 23which is his body, the fullness of him who fills all in all.

Theological Perspective

Crucifixion is a scandal. The cross signifies failure, powerlessness. The powerful are not hung (lynched) from a tree. Only those who are disenfranchised, those who are marginalized, can be abused, persecuted, and oppressed. Society does not reject its citizens. Only the outcasts face this Roman form of execution, reserved for those who refuse to acknowledge the Caesars of history. There is nothing glorious or wonderful about an instrument of death, especially when presented as some old wooden cross. For God in flesh to be lynched becomes a scandal because it questions God's omnipotence, it questions all Christ claimed. For the one we claim is above all that is, all that was, and all that will be, there is the finite act of bloody crucifixion, there is shame. There is nakedness, loss of control over bodily functions, and excruciating pain. What the cross truly signals is the failure of Christ's ministry.

Yet many Euro-Americans rush to look upon the cross as a sign of hope, as a salvific symbol, not pausing long enough to dwell on the tragic, on the hopelessness, on the failure, on the powerlessness of the moment. For them, there is redemption in Jesus' sufferings, there is atonement. The cross becomes a necessity for their salvation and a life of bliss in the hereafter. However, for most marginalized communities still seeking a life in the here and now, there is

Pastoral Perspective

The most intriguing part of this text for me is this notion that the church completes Jesus. When I read this, I think about the many ungodly decisions that have been made by "the church" throughout the ages. From the Crusades, to forcing conversions of Native Americans, to supporting slavery, the church has been the perpetrator of a number of terribly hurtful and misguided policies. How does this complete Jesus? What is it about an institution—run by imperfect human beings and with history to prove it—that makes it the vehicle to complete Jesus Christ?

I think the answer is to be found in verse 17. There, we hear of the goal to come to "know [Christ] better" (NIV). This, it seems to me, is the true purpose of the church—not always to get it right, or to have a pristine history of always being on the right side of every issue. Rather, the purpose of the church is to be a vehicle that works continually to know and reveal Christ better. In this sense, there is no other vehicle, no other institution like it on earth. This is what allows the church the opportunity to "complete Jesus." By presenting to the world a model of what it looks like continually to strive to know Christ better, the church has the unique opportunity to complete the mission and ministry of Jesus Christ.

This work can take many forms. Clergy must be defined by humility, recognizing that our role is not

Exegetical Perspective

Ephesians is the New Testament's strongest affirmation of unity—the unity of God the Father and Christ the Son, the unity of heaven and earth, the unity of believers with Christ, and the unity of the church—so it is fitting to read this text on the day when we celebrate Jesus' ascension to unite with the Father.

The style of Ephesians 1 models the unity the apostle advocates. Instead of writing his letter in separate sentences, the author writes two long sentences that subsume a whole host of subordinate clauses into a complicated whole. Our passage for today, like the passage that precedes it, is one long sentence. Our translations seek to make it more accessible by turning the long string of dependent clauses into a series of independent sentences, but the author wrote Ephesians 1:15–23 without even pausing for breath.

The Apostle's Prayer (vv. 15–19). Whether or not Ephesians was written by the apostle Paul, it follows the typical order of Pauline letters and of other letters of the time. It begins with a salutation and greeting in verses 1–2. The author expands the greeting by the addition of the lengthy doxology in verses 3–14. Then, as Paul almost always does, the author writes a word of thanksgiving (vv. 15–23). It is by now an established claim of New Testament interpretation

Homiletical Perspective

The author of Ephesians (whom we call Paul, just as we call Homer the author of the *Odyssey*) writes in an elevated prose style, perhaps borrowing liturgical and familiar theological language to give a hint of familiarity to the argument. Adjectives and adverbs carry much of the weight, lifting abstract and spiritual-sounding concepts higher and higher, until the reader is unsure precisely what has been said but feels certain it is significant. English translations, including the NRSV, break up this single sentence into more readable pieces, but seem to want to preserve the feeling of building toward a climax in "the fullness of him who fills all in all" (v. 23). The celebratory rhetoric of the passage is at least as striking as its conceptual content, and preachers can make creative use of this fact.

By specifying this passage for the festival of ascension, the lectionary focuses attention on the second half of the reading. A sermon that is primarily working from one of the ascension narratives (from Acts 1 and Luke 24) could benefit by borrowing language from Ephesians. The events Luke narrates in his straightforward way can begin to shine with theological and cosmological significance. Paul affirms with ringing rhetoric that the ascension of the Lord was an event of importance not only for the disciples who witnessed it and later testified to it. He identifies

Ephesians 1:15-23

Theological Perspective

nothing redemptive about suffering. We are not saved exclusively because of Jesus' death on the cross. We find salvation in Jesus' birth, Jesus' life, Jesus' teachings, Jesus' praxis, Jesus' resurrection, Jesus' spirit, and yes, Jesus' death. The importance of Jesus' crucifixion is not atonement; it is solidarity. Although his death is no more redemptive than any other aspect of his life, it is an action he undertook so that Divinity could learn, through solidarity with the oppressed, what it means to be among the wretched of the world.

The theology of substitionary atonement was elaborated by Anselm of Canterbury (ca. 1033–1109), who reasoned that the cross was necessary to satisfy God's anger. Sinful humans could not redeem themselves before an angry God who required satisfaction. Only a sinless God-as-human-being could complete the process, make restitution, and restore creation. In other words, in order to satisfy God's vanity, God's only begotten Son must be humiliated, tortured, and brutally killed, rather than the true object of God's wrath. Is filicide what placates God? The problem with Anselm's theology of atonement is that it casts God as the ultimate abuser, the ultimate oppressor, who finds satisfaction through the domination, humiliation, and pain of God's child. This makes the theology of atonement difficult to reconcile with the concept of a loving Father.

For many marginalized communities, the importance of the cross is that it is the location where Christ chose solidarity with the world's marginalized. Christ becomes one with the crucified people of his time, as well as with all who are crucified today on the crosses of racism, sexism, classism, and heterosexism. These crosses are places of violence, littered with broken lives and bodies. Jesus' solidarity with the world's failures and the world's powerlessness points to the God of the oppressed. Here is the importance of the cross. God is not the God of those who crucify, only of those who are crucified. The paradox of the cross is that, in spite of what it symbolizes, there is resurrection.

This wisdom held by the marginalized is considered nonsense by the world. How can the shameful act of being crucified be God's road to solidarity with the oppressed? In the real world, those with power can avoid crosses. Others are crucified so that they can enjoy their protected space within society. Others die so that they may have an abundant life. Who will comfort the oppressed as they hang from trees to secure the privilege of the few? Who will provide the crucified hope?

Pastoral Perspective

to be "the authority" but rather to be "the model" for what it looks like continually to grow in Christ. Worship can become less formulaic and more of a living example of what it looks like to search our faith continually and to engage Jesus in new and deeper ways. Mission can become less about bringing something to someone and more about truly learning the needs of those around us and changing our lives accordingly. Membership can become less about a name on a roster and more about a changed purpose. These are some of the ways that the church can lead to what the text calls "deeper insight" (v. 18),[1] which I understand to be the purpose for our labors as a church.

If we seek to be a social club, we will lose to the country club. If we seek to be the local hangout, we will lose to the coffee shop. However, if we seek to provide an atmosphere where we can think, grow, and feel in ways that gain deeper insight into ourselves, our world, and the God who works within it, we will tap into that "glorious wealth" (v. 18)[2] to which the text refers. That is, we will realize our potential as the church, which is meant to complete Jesus Christ by serving as a vehicle for his work, not only in our own lives, but in the lives of others and for the world we all share.

Another point to be taken from this text has to do with the reference to bringing Jesus back to life.

While I was a seminary student, I took an impromptu survey of five other people I was having lunch with one day, to see how many believed in the resurrection. Out of the six divinity students eating around that table, only three believed in the resurrection of Jesus Christ. I asked those who did not believe to tell me why. All three had essentially the same answer: it is not rational to believe that someone can be resurrected from the dead. From a purely rational perspective, I would agree, but since when is God limited to what is rational? When we pray, we ask God to work beyond what is rational. We ask God to act in ways that we cannot understand. We ask God to do what reason would say is impossible. We would never limit our prayers to the rational. That defeats the purpose of a prayer.

If we count on God to exist and work outside of the rational when we pray, we must also be willing to accept when God reveals God's power to us in ways that are "irrational." This requires allowing our faith to exist beyond the limits of our reason—a crucial

---

1. God's Word to the Nations, *God's Word* Translation (Holiday, FL: Green Key Books, 1995), 1035.
2. Ibid.

Exegetical Perspective

that the thanksgiving portions of Paul's letters give a major clue to the themes that the letter will present.[1]

This is true for Ephesians 1:15–23. The prayer for the illumination of the readers in verses 17–18 foreshadows another prayer for enlightenment in 4:14–19. The prayer for hope in verses 18b–19 points ahead to the promise of new life in 2:1–10. The prayerful affirmation that the church is Christ's body will be developed in the material on church unity in 2:11–22 and 4:1–16.

God's Strength (vv. 20–23). The NRSV somewhat misleadingly makes it look as though the author here begins a new sentence: "God put this power to work . . ." In the Greek the verse is yet another subordinate clause, so that syntactically there is no break between verse 19 and verse 20. A more accurate reading of the bridge between verse 19 and verse 20 would say: ". . . according to the working of his great power, which he put to work in Christ when he raised him from the dead."

Ephesians presents a view of the resurrection that combines resurrection intimately with ascension. Jesus does not rise, then appear on earth, then ascend, as in Luke's Gospel. He is raised and then (immediately?) ascends. This close association, almost identification, between resurrection and ascension distinguishes Ephesians from Paul in 1 Corinthians 15 and from our four Gospels. There may be a hint of such a doctrine of resurrection in Acts 2:32–33; 5:30–31 (differently, Acts 10:40–42; 13:30–31).

In these verses we do not get a description of Christ's ascension. We do not get a picture of Jesus going up into the clouds, leaving his amazed disciples to stare after him, as in Acts 1:6–11. These verses are concerned with the effect of the ascension on the cosmos. They are concerned not so much with how Jesus ascends as with where he ends up: at God's right hand. The effect of the ascension is described by a series of words that emphasize God's omnipotence: "the powerful exercise of the strength of God's might which he exercises—strongly" (vv. 19–20, my trans.). By Christ's ascension God claims the whole creation for God's own, with Christ as God's representative and coruler.

God exercises might by giving Christ authority over every kind of power, heavenly and earthly, benign and malevolent. Christ has this authority in

1. The classic work that persuaded scholars of the relationship between the thanksgiving and the rest of a Pauline letter is Paul Schubert, *The Form and Function of Pauline Thanksgivings*, Beihefte zur Zeitschrift für neutestamentliche Wissenschaft 20 (Berlin: Topelmann, 1939).

Homiletical Perspective

Jesus as the Lord who reigns above every competing power, both now (Paul's "now" and ours as well) and in the eschatological future. Ephesians 4:7–10 also includes language about the ascension of Jesus, identifying "the one who ascended" with "the one who descended," using Psalm 68 to connect the ascended Lord with the church.

A preacher focusing primarily on the Ephesians passage may find here a challenge for many congregations: it seems unlikely that many congregations experience life together in the terms Ephesians uses to describe the community's theological importance. Christians who think of their congregations as "friendly" may nevertheless doubt that many outsiders have heard of their love for each other and "all the saints." Not all Christians experience "wisdom and revelation" (v. 17) as a matter of course, or find themselves caught up in "the immeasurable greatness of his power for us who believe" (v. 19) at the monthly potluck supper. The church officer who finishes a term of service on a congregation's governing board disillusioned with the church and its ministry is almost a proverb. For many Christians, perhaps for most of us, life in the church, even at its best, is far more ordinary than it sounds in Ephesians.

It may be that Ephesians was written in part to emphasize that it is precisely within the ordinary and even deeply disappointing vagaries of life in this world—a world into which Christ has come and in which he is filling all things—that we receive a perfectly adequate spiritual wisdom. "The God and Father of our Lord Jesus Christ" (1:3) will by his Spirit bypass every limitation and will give us knowledge of himself. If it helps to call that gift grand names, such as wisdom or enlightenment, that is fine. In fact, the wisdom that comes from God in Christ is worth such names. The "immeasurable greatness of his power" is not a special experience reserved for a select few: it is at work in "us who believe" (v. 19), who are united to Christ already, in the ordinary mess.

An excellent sermon on this text might avoid cynicism about the church while nevertheless focusing on the contrast between many people's experience of the ordinariness of the church and Ephesians' exalted vision of theological and spiritual unity. After creating a sense of tension between the biblical ideal and the experienced reality, the preacher might use well chosen and focused stories to show that God is unexpectedly at work in ordinary moments, so that Ephesians' superlatives turn out to be surprisingly appropriate.

Ephesians 1:15-23

Theological Perspective

The writer of the Epistle to the Ephesians understood this paradox. The author, whether it is Paul or not, self-identifies as "a prisoner of Jesus Christ" (3:1 note), writing as "a prisoner in the Lord" (4:1), who is "an ambassador in chains" (6:20). The writer of Ephesians is probably awaiting execution, soon to be counted among the crucified (loosely understood as execution). As the author awaits what is most feared, death—the supposed end of existence—she or he finds reassurance in a God who walks in solidarity toward the gallows. Because there is resurrection, there is hope for the crucified. Hence the author's prayer is that the epistle's readers be given "the Spirit of wisdom, the Spirit which brings a new revelation" (v. 17, translations mine). Only through the "eyes of [their] hearts" can they be enlightened so that they can know the hope of God's calling, the riches of glory which is their inheritance—an inheritance that surpasses the greatness that exists in his power (vv. 18–19). What power is this? It is "the power wrought in Christ to raise him from among the dead, and to set him at God's own right hand in the heavenly places, above all principality and power and lordship, above every name which is held in honor, not only in this age, but also in the age to come" (vv. 20–21).

Here lies the great paradox. The tragedy known as cross, the symbol of failure and shame within our reality, is transformed to glory and power through Christ's solidarity with all who are crucified and continue to be crucified. This transformation is not brought about because of anything salvific in the instrument of violence and death. It is brought about because Christ went to the cross to hang with the oppressed. Through this act of solidarity, the church of the oppressed was born. Death is resurrected as one body—composed of the crucified, with Christ as its head (vv. 22–23).

MIGUEL A. DE LA TORRE

Pastoral Perspective

point for those who want to go from delivering lectures to giving sermons. It is vitally important for pastors to instill in others an understanding that God's reality is beyond what we can comprehend, because it is there that hope can be found. To lead people to the unlimited reservoirs of hope is to lead them to the ability to come to "know Christ better."

This text is leading us to recognize that part of "completing Christ" is learning to engage the world beyond the limits of our own reason. To be willing to live in the mystery of what we cannot always comprehend, is to open ourselves to the possibilities of what we cannot imagine. This is what the author of Hebrews was getting at when he described faith as being "sure of what we hope for and certain of what we do not see" (Heb. 11:1 NIV). To live this way is to refuse to abandon hope. To live this way is to insist upon believing in that which we cannot yet see. Ultimately, to live this way is to "complete Christ," by committing to live in the promise of what is yet to come. In this way we imperfect human beings, and the imperfect church we lead, can truly fulfill our mission as described by Paul in this first chapter of his Letter to the Ephesians.

GORDON MCCLELLAN

Exegetical Perspective

the present age and will continue to have this power in the age to come; his sovereignty is not for these days only but for all eternity.[2]

Thus God exercises might both by making Christ head over the whole church and by making him head over the whole creation. Moreover, Christ is head over the whole creation precisely for the sake of the church. In these verses, the stress on Christ as "head" is on his authority over the body more than on the joining of head and body. He is "head" over the body because he has the authority to put all things under his feet. He is head of the world and church as the sovereign is head of the nation.

The last sentence of our passage is perhaps deliberately ambiguous. The church is Christ's body, "the fullness of him who fills all in all." Does Christ fill up the church, or does the church fill up Christ? From the words themselves there is no way of knowing. What we do know is that Christ is the fullness not of church alone but also of all the world.

Christ is entirely present, fully present in the church. Christ is fully present in the world. The claim seems at best paradoxical and at worst self-contradictory, but it is a way of affirming two great claims that Ephesians makes. Christ gave his entire self for the church. Christ gave his entire self for the world. Put it another way: Christ fills both church and world, but both church and world contain him whole.

Of course the apostle did not know that the editors would end a chapter with this verse. He wants the Ephesians to know that Christ's resurrection and ascension both prefigure and make possible their own resurrections and ascensions. Through him, they who were dead in their trespasses, have also now been raised up to the heavenly places, where they receive the benefits of God's astonishingly mighty power. Christ's ascended unity with the Father is manifested in his unity with the church and with the whole creation.

DAVID L. BARTLETT

Homiletical Perspective

The four novels that comprise Frederick Buechner's *Book of Bebb* provide a literary picture of flawed faithfulness that at times, in spite of everything, reflects the spiritual reality of the church toward which Ephesians points. The vicissitudes of evangelist Leo Bebb's ministry reflect both sides of this tension.[1] Bebb himself is a complicated and not particularly saintly person through whom the Spirit of God nonetheless works God's glory time and again.

If the preacher believes, as some scholars do, that Ephesians was written against the background of an early proto-Gnosticism, a sermon on this text could reassure struggling congregations and Christians, while challenging the risk of spiritual pride in others. Much of the passage's conceptual language may be drawn from the spiritual jargon of some in the church who felt themselves and their theology superior to the ordinariness of the church. In our situation, just as in ancient Asia Minor, there are always some Christians who believe they know who are God's favorites and who are not. They have certain theological passwords that others either do not know or cannot utter with integrity.

Ephesians says there is no password. "The God and Father of our Lord Jesus Christ" has already "blessed us . . . with every spiritual blessing in the heavenly places" (1:3). Those who are in Christ do not need any other special knowledge. There is no special vocabulary. Ephesians shows this language is not so hard to use by picking up the jargon and using it to talk straightforwardly about the grace and mercy of the God we know in Jesus Christ. A preacher interpreting this passage in a sermon might well do the same, integrating theological concepts and religious passwords that are too often used among Christians to show that "we" are not like "them." This approach may help everyone in the congregation realize that what binds them together is "one Lord, one faith, one baptism, one God and Father of all" (Eph. 4:5–6)

MICHAEL D. BUSH

---

2. This seems to contrast with 1 Cor. 15:28 and 1 Cor. 3:23.

1. Frederick Buechner, *Book of Bebb* (San Francisco: HarperCollins, 2001).

Luke 24:44-53

⁴⁴Then he said to them, "These are my words that I spoke to you while I was still with you—that everything written about me in the law of Moses, the prophets, and the psalms must be fulfilled." ⁴⁵Then he opened their minds to understand the scriptures, ⁴⁶and he said to them, "Thus it is written, that the Messiah is to suffer and to rise from the dead on the third day, ⁴⁷and that repentance and forgiveness of sins is to be proclaimed in his name to all nations, beginning from Jerusalem. ⁴⁸You are witnesses of these things. ⁴⁹And see, I am sending upon you what my Father promised; so stay here in the city until you have been clothed with power from on high."

⁵⁰Then he led them out as far as Bethany, and, lifting up his hands, he blessed them. ⁵¹While he was blessing them, he withdrew from them and was carried up into heaven. ⁵²And they worshiped him, and returned to Jerusalem with great joy; ⁵³and they were continually in the temple blessing God.

Theological Perspective

The ascension of Jesus astonishes. Though it happens at a particular place, near Bethany, it surpasses ordinary perception. Jesus blesses the disciples and is "carried up into heaven," in but four Greek words. No mode of ascension is reported, no deus ex machina. In Acts 1:9–11 a "cloud" takes and obscures him, and two angel-like figures ask sardonically, "Why do you stand looking up toward heaven?" Indeed, Luke leaves room for our imaginations to enter. He hints that the astonishment[1] of the witnesses—who become prostrate (*proskunesantes*, v. 2, same MSS) when Jesus departs—is more significant than the divine aerodynamics.

Implied Ascension. I grew up in a tradition where the ascension received little notice, and I recall no sermons about it. Later, when first attending an Ascension Day service, what came to mind were sci-fi special effects! My first serious encounter with the ascension was a short book by Norman Perrin, who proposed that the empty tomb and appearance narratives—including the explicit ascensions in Luke–Acts and Mark 16:19—developed from an earlier, implied view of *resurrection as ascension.* Jesus

1. On astonishment, see William Desmond, *Being and the Between* (Albany: State University of New York Press, 1995), 8–11.

Pastoral Perspective

In this brief summary about the appearance of the risen Christ to his disciples and his ascension, Luke is intent on providing a clear and empowering narrative for those of us who step into this story looking back through the life of the church, which began with Jesus' blessing on those surrounding him as he ascended to join God. At the close of his ministry on earth, Jesus is focused on helping believers understand his life and ministry, death and resurrection, and the scope of God's saving love. He rehearses the key points of the witness we are called and empowered to make, and finally he blesses us.

For us who read this passage with the benefit of two millennia in the life of the church, it may be difficult to remember that the significance of the resurrection was not immediately clear, nor would Jesus' disciples and those who were with them that evening readily grasp the larger context that best framed this amazing event. We too know well the experience of suddenly recognizing connections among disparate ideas that yield a whole new way of thinking. Truth be told, perhaps we are more honest to acknowledge that, even with the benefit of time and experience, we too need to be reminded that this man Jesus incarnates the love and vision of God in continuity with the much larger witness of the Law, the Prophets, and even the Psalms.

Exegetical Perspective

Luke's Gospel ends not with a summary of Jesus' ministry, but with a transition to the church's ministry; Luke 24:44–53 foreshadows the growth of the church in the Acts of the Apostles. Though the lectionary text begins in the middle of the narrative of Jesus' appearance to the disciples, verse 44 marks a change in focus. In his first appearance on the road to Emmaus (vv. 13–35) and in his initial interaction with his disciples (vv. 36–43), Jesus explains his death in terms of Scripture, addressing confusion resulting from his death. The lectionary's selection instead focuses on the church's continuing his mission. The resurrection appearance (vv. 44–49), the ascension (vv. 50–51), and the disciples' response (vv. 52–53) are united in transitioning the story from the ministry of Jesus to the ministry of the church.

In the appearance with the disciples, Luke focuses the reader's attention on the character Jesus; no other character has a speaking role, and Jesus is the subject of all active verbs. In verse 44, Jesus emphasizes the continuity of his message with what he preached before his death, namely, that his life and ministry are a fulfillment of Scripture. Jesus' mission is indeed framed as a fulfillment of Scripture throughout Luke, most recently on the road to Emmaus (v. 27) and notably at the beginning of his ministry in his announcing after reading the Isaiah scroll, "Today

Homiletical Perspective

There is a tradition in painting and sculpture that shows the disciples gathered on a hilltop, straining their faces upward. Above them is a cloud with a pair of feet just showing beneath it. Of course, the painting or bas-relief is of the ascension of the Lord. Most of us today chuckle at the awkwardness of trying to paint a mystery, but this tradition points at one of the challenges preachers must face in treating this story.

We may try to puzzle about what "really happened"—what Luke might have been trying to describe when he said Jesus "withdrew from them and was carried up." Shall we struggle with the reality that today, with the wonderful technology of the Hubble telescope, we have all seen beyond the blue dome Jesus' contemporaries might have identified with heaven? Where did he really go? What did the disciples actually witness?

A more fruitful approach will be to explore how the elements of this story affect us today. What are the realities of our own lives, and of our faith, that this story touches or expands for us? What are its challenges, its assurances, its revelations to us here and now?

One challenge to us from today's pericope is to take seriously the emphasis on Jerusalem and the temple. The mission of the disciples will originate in

Theological Perspective

moved immediately from death to "heaven," and *from* this divine realm appeared to people in or near Jerusalem, or in Galilee, or to Paul.

Perrin also regarded the appearance narratives as prolepses or anticipations of the Parousia.[2] If so, then resurrection-as-ascension would be a presupposition of the whole logic of the story: Jesus must ascend before he can appear. This is essential in an even more prosaic way. Jesus not only leaves behind an empty tomb and eats fish among doubtful disciples (Luke 24:39–43), but his tomb *stays* empty. The risen Lazarus eventually died and was buried, but no body of Jesus is found. The ascension then is crucial to early witnesses to the resurrection.

What is witnessed? What are we to *make* of the words "carried up into heaven"? Perhaps nothing. Could that be the point: there is nothing to make of it? The ascension is framed by two scenes that initially seem less than astonishing. The first scene is hermeneutical: Jesus interprets scriptures wherein his suffering and resurrection are figured; then he tells the disciples to wait for what God has promised, "power from on high," identified in Acts as the Holy Spirit. In the last scene, the disciples are back in Jerusalem, in the temple, blessing God and waiting. What may we make of these scenes?

Framing the Ascension. The first frame is almost bookish. Yet on closer look, Jesus "opened their minds to understand the scriptures" (v. 45), which may suggest a mysterious, expansive uniting of mind and identity with God's past and future. It may echo how Paul introduces the *kenōsis* hymn (Phil. 2:5): "Let the same mind be in you that was in Christ Jesus." Luke suggests a series of equivalences. Christ's understanding is *at one* with Scriptures; the Scriptures enter the disciples' minds; their understanding is opened to Christ and the Scriptures *by* Christ and the Scriptures. The Law, Prophets, and Psalms *and* the mind of Christ *and* the minds of the disciples are *emptying into each other* in a mutual *kenōsis* that involves the future—because repentance (change of mind and heart, *metanoia*) will pour out from Jerusalem into the world, and the disciples will witness this motion.

Thus, the anticipation of what God has promised—to "clothe" the disciples "with power from on high" (v. 49)—is another statement of this expansive motion. To be "clothed" is not just a promise of new

Pastoral Perspective

Jesus' ministry is not a cipher in time, an accident of history. No, Jesus insists, his life and ministry is continuous with God's presence with humankind from the beginning. He embodies God's deepest longing for us and all creation. His ministry is a fulfillment of God's covenant with us made long before. God's Word does not return empty. Jesus' rising is not simply like that of others he raised from the dead. No, this moment is to open our eyes to see the power of God's love that takes the worst world can do and transforms it into a witness to God's redemptive love and power.

As he did with the followers that he accompanied to Emmaus, Jesus puts the pieces of the narrative together in a compelling way so that their eyes are opened and they recognize him, not only as the risen manifestation of the teacher they have followed, but as the risen Lord, the son of the living God. Of course, to recognize Jesus as the incarnation of God not only changes their previously partial understanding of Jesus and their imagination about God, but also requires a complete revision of their view of themselves and everything around them. It is as if a veil has dropped. Now they see more fully that God is actively at work redeeming all of creation. Now they come to understand they too have a role in this redemptive work.

Jesus gives them their marching orders and the sermon outline: The Messiah has suffered and died and risen from the dead, and all nations are called to repentance and forgiveness of sins in his name. Right away the challenge of their ministry is clear. The idea that God's Messiah had to suffer and die is not going to "market" well. It does not fit with any prevailing notion of God or God's redemptive power. Neither will their audiences hear readily that this message is for the entire world. However, both themes are woven through the narrative of the Hebrew Bible just as Jesus claimed. We know this latter point about the breadth of God's love and the wideness of God's grace was a stumbling block in the early church until Peter's experience with Cornelius, and we know that matters of privilege in interpreting tradition and determining inclusion continue to plague the life of the church even now.

Luke's Jesus assures his followers that they and we are not left to our own devices in this challenging work of witness. The Spirit that they and we receive at Pentecost will give us the power we need to be effective witnesses as preachers and teachers. Consider Jesus' description of the power we will receive from the Spirit. The Spirit will help us be effective in

---

2. Norman Perrin, *The Resurrection according to Matthew, Mark, and Luke* (Philadelphia: Fortress Press, 1977), 3, 25, 33, 72–74.

this text stands fulfilled in your hearing" (4:21; all quotations are my own trans.). That this resurrection scene is not mere repetition of Jesus' earthly teaching, though, is clear in Luke's description that he "opened their mind to understand the Scriptures" (v. 45). Throughout the Gospel, it is the lack of understanding that characterizes the disciples (18:34; cf. 2:50; 8:10). Here, however, the resurrected Jesus gives true understanding to the disciples (note the singular "mind" in v. 45).

Whereas the Gospel has shown that Jesus' suffering and resurrection were foretold in Scripture, in verse 47 Jesus adds that Scripture also foretells, "Repentance leading to forgiveness of sins is to be proclaimed in his name to all the nations, beginning from Jerusalem." This saying might well serve as a summary of the entire Acts narrative, where repentance and forgiveness in the name of Christ become staples of the apostles' preaching, which begins in Jerusalem, reaches all nations (Acts 2:38; 13:38; 22:16), and is described as a fulfillment of Scripture (Acts 2:14–21; 15:15–21). In verse 48, Jesus specifically ties the disciples to this continued proclamation, labeling them as "witnesses of these things," a title not found elsewhere in the Gospel, yet a common designation for the apostles in Acts (Acts 1:8, 22; 2:32; 13:31). God's story, told in all of Scripture, continues through Jesus, and continues yet again in the work of the disciples.

In verse 49 the resurrected Jesus also looks forward to the church when he recalls his Father's promise. The Gospel makes reference to a Spirit from God, often associated with Jesus (see 4:1), that is promised to Jesus' followers (11:13; 12:12). That promise is fulfilled in the coming of the Spirit at Pentecost (Acts 2:1–13) and the growth of the church, as the Spirit becomes the driving force behind the spreading of the gospel. Jesus' promised "power" (*dynamis*) is associated with God, Jesus, and the Spirit in the Gospel (see 1:35; 5:17; 6:19; 22:69), but in the book of Acts it is the apostles who now act with that "power" (Acts 4:7–10 [Peter]; 4:33 [the apostles]; 6:8 [Stephen]; 8:6 [Philip]; 19:11 [Paul]).

Luke's ascension scene (vv. 50–51) also transitions from the ministry of Jesus to the ministry of the church. Luke uses geography to shift the narrative, noting that Jesus "led them out as far as Bethany." Bethany is the place from which Jesus begins his triumphal entry into Jerusalem (19:29–40). In the Gospel, Jerusalem is the destination of Jesus' ministry; most of the Gospel is recounted as Jesus' walking toward Jerusalem (see 9:51). By taking his disciples to

Jerusalem, where the final verse of the Gospel finds them "continually in the temple blessing God." The story has circled back to its beginning in the temple, with its portrait of Zechariah, the priest and father of John the Baptist (1:5–23). Here and throughout Luke's Gospel, Jerusalem is the beginning point of God's activity, tying Jesus' mission and the mission of the church to the story of Israel that precedes them.

In the resurrection appearance immediately preceding today's reading (vv. 36–43), Luke fairly shouts at us that Jesus is present in his real, physical being. Similarly, here he seems to be shouting at us to remember that Jesus and all his disciples were devout Jews. This temple is not a metaphor for Jesus' body or for our modern worship in neighborhood churches. This is the temple of the Lord's presence, the center of the Jewish cult. If anyone is inclined to imagine that the story of Jesus replaces or supersedes the record of the Hebrew Bible, Luke's emphatic setting of the temple for the beginning and ending of his story should be enough to remind us otherwise.

Luke has also taken pains to fill his story of Jesus with echoes from great moments in the overarching story of God's steadfast love and saving action. Mary's song, as well as Zechariah's prophecy in chapter 1 (Luke 1:46–55; 68–79) make clear connections between this new story and Israel's past. Now, at the close of the Gospel, Jesus "open[s] their minds to understand the scriptures" (v. 45), rehearsing how the Law of Moses, the Prophets, and the Psalms have all been fulfilled in his suffering, death, and resurrection. Luke's story culminates in an emphatic statement that the great story is all one.

That one story, of God's faithfulness and justice and mercy, is now being entrusted to the disciples to proclaim to the world. Here lies another challenge for us. Jesus directs the disciples, soon to be empowered by the promised Holy Spirit, to go forth and proclaim repentance and forgiveness of sins in his name. He does not explicitly direct them to tell his story or proclaim his messiahship. He does not send them out to convert the world to believe in him alone. He does not direct them to promise resurrection. The message they are to take abroad is the good news of God's mercy.

Indeed, the ancient story of God's mercy has been embodied and realized in the life, ministry, death, and resurrection of Jesus, now clearly identified as the promised Messiah. So the story has been personified. When Jesus raises his wounded hands to bless his friends, he is blessing them with the fullness of God's mercy, the mercy they are being commissioned to proclaim.

Luke 24:44-53

Theological Perspective

identity and cultural perception; it transforms the very meaning of identity. The disciples are moving beyond Jew or Greek, male or female (or, today, culturally secular or culturally "Christian"), insofar as they are "in" Christ's body, mind, and motion. The bookish scene, then, *is* astonishing. Ordinary perceptions are surpassed by a beyond that is also within.

In the last framing scene, they "returned to Jerusalem with great joy; and they were continually in the temple blessing God" (vv. 52–53). Again, at first this seems not extraordinary, but simply a way to close the curtain on act one of Luke–Acts. Nevertheless, consider how the act of "blessing God" participates in Christ's own activity of blessing. Once again there is an extraordinary mystic implication in the "ordinary" activities of praising, praying, and waiting.

There is also *location*. Most scholars date the Gospel of Luke after the destruction of the temple in 70 CE, when Jews and early Christians were undergoing religious and social transformation. Moreover, the movement in Acts from Jerusalem into the world is anticipated here. Once more the disciples are in a particular place. Their joyous oneness of mind and heart, as they anticipate being in the infinity of God, remains particular, concrete, embodied. The temple is a finite locus of God's infinite space and time. For a few days, dwelling in the temple, they enjoy knowing they are *already where they will be*, in the space-time of God.

So far, however, we have "made nothing" of the ascension itself.

Within the Ascension. Is the problem that, being beyond ordinary space and time, there is literally nothing to see? Is it because Acts directs us away from "looking up"? Might the oneness of our minds and perceptions with Christ, and the continual anticipation of the Spirit, open our imaginations to another possibility? The framing scenes invite us to shift perspectives, from being observers to being participants.

If we make this shift—if the ascension is now understood as a *motion that includes* the minds, bodies, and locations of the disciples—then, as it occurs, there is really nothing to make of it, *precisely because we are within its space and time*. We are *within the ascension*, not looking upon it, but looking outward from within it. What would we then "see"? Nothing of the ascension—but something else. From within it, we would see the people and creatures of the universe, discerned lovingly in the loving of God.

LARRY D. BOUCHARD

Pastoral Perspective

sharing these two challenging ideas as the mission of the church in the world.

Our work is not easy, because the sort of loving God we proclaim upends the ordinary understanding of power. This God allows the triumph of love to become clear through the life and ministry of a human being who finally is tortured and killed because of the way he loves and whom he loves. However, death does not have the last word; it simply makes very plain how powerful God's love is. Then and now such notions of power seem foolish. They do not translate easily into the world in which we live, where the integrative power of love is often rejected for more hierarchical models that include the marginalization and objectification of others to maintain the privilege of a few.

This God to whom we bear witness intends to offer salvation to all the nations, and that is no easier to swallow now than then. The Spirit that clothes us at Pentecost is necessary for the witness to which we are called.

It is important to realize that as Jesus ascends to God so that this urgent work of the church may begin, he blesses us. Jesus begins his final conversation with the disciples and those who are with them with words of peace. Blessing conveys to those who receive it the goodness and favor of God. Many of us know the power of such ritual moments at confirmations, weddings, and other acts of commitment to fulfill God's best hopes for us. The efficacy of this blessing is disclosed in the words that follow in this passage. Those with Jesus worship him and return to Jerusalem, not to weep, but to live with great joy and confidence in anticipation of the promise of power for their ministry of witness.

NANCY J. RAMSAY

Ascension of the Lord

Exegetical Perspective

the place of his own triumphal entry and commanding them to return to Jerusalem, Jesus sends the disciples on their own mission, one in which Jerusalem is the origin rather than the destination.

The transition to the disciples' ministry is also marked by Luke's depiction of Jesus, using imagery reminiscent of Moses and Elijah, who appeared with Jesus at the transfiguration and "were speaking of his departure, which he was about to accomplish at Jerusalem" (9:31). Jesus' raising his hands and offering blessings recalls Moses (see Exod. 17:11; 39:43), and the description of his being taken up into heaven recalls Elijah's ascension (see 2 Kgs. 2:1–14). Common to both OT figures is their transfer of leadership to the next generation at the end of their ministry, Moses to Joshua (Deut. 34:9) and Elijah to Elisha (2 Kgs. 2:9–14). In using this imagery, Luke points to the transition of Jesus' prophetic mantle to his disciples. Like Elisha, they will receive a share of the master's spirit.

Luke closes the Gospel by focusing on the disciples after Jesus' departure, noting they "worshiped him." For Luke, only God is worthy of worship; Jesus emphatically denies Satan's request for worship, quoting Deuteronomy 6:13: "Worship the Lord your God, and serve him alone" (4:8), and Peter rejects Cornelius's attempts to worship him (Acts 10:26). Luke closes the Gospel with the disciples' recognizing Jesus as no mere mortal, but rather as God, worthy of worship. Luke then shows the reader that Jesus' prophecy regarding the church will come true. The disciples fulfill Jesus' command to return to the city (v. 49) and await the coming power. Even without the canonical second act, Luke's reader understands that the mission of Jesus will continue in the work of his disciples.

The NT tells the story of Jesus and the story of the church. Luke, more than any NT writer, combines these two stories: the church continues God's action on earth that began in Christ. In 24:44–53, Luke focuses the reader's attention directly on the importance of the church as the instrument of God's continued action on earth. The end of the Gospel of Luke is not the end of the story of Jesus but, rather, the beginning of the story of the church, begun by the resurrected Jesus and continued by his followers.

RICHARD MANLY ADAMS JR.

Homiletical Perspective

The final stage in the disciples' firsthand experience of Jesus is his withdrawal and ascent to the Father. The earthbound man with whom they have walked for these months has now been taken up into the Godhead. We may even be able to see this as a sign of the ascent of all humankind—not only the glorification of Jesus the Christ, but a recognition of God's acceptance of us all.

To what extent are we to take this story of a commissioning, two thousand years ago, and apply it to our own mission as disciples and apostles of Christ? To what, exactly, have we ourselves been witnesses? Upon what do we stand when we undertake to proclaim a gospel of God's forgiveness and mercy? How do we acknowledge and share the blessing we have received?

The story of the ascension of the Lord can offer us a set of images and ideas to grapple with these questions. When we try to describe our own experience of Christ in our lives, we often choose to tell stories of God's grace in human encounters. We may tell about instances we have witnessed of sacrificial love, of devotion to the truth, of someone's willingness to forgive an outrageous sin. We may recount personal recognitions of God's mercy in our own lives. Often we find ourselves at a loss to explain what we think has happened beyond a feeling, an awareness, or simply a faith that such incidents are inklings of God's presence.

The picture Luke paints of Jesus' departure creates a channel for those inklings. Now we can say that Jesus' ascent means the communication between human and divine is a highway with clear markers. We do not have to depend on saying our experience is reminiscent of things Jesus did in his earthly ministry. We can recognize and identify the grace of God in our small, personal affairs, because it truly *is* the grace that the Father bestowed upon Jesus. In his resurrection and ascension, we may even say that Jesus has carried our humanity into God's eternal presence, along with his own.

LINDA LEE CLADER

Acts 1:6-14

⁶So when they had come together, they asked him, "Lord, is this the time when you will restore the kingdom to Israel?" ⁷He replied, "It is not for you to know the times or periods that the Father has set by his own authority. ⁸But you will receive power when the Holy Spirit has come upon you; and you will be my witnesses in Jerusalem, in all Judea and Samaria, and to the ends of the earth." ⁹When he had said this, as they were watching, he was lifted up, and a cloud took him out of their sight. ¹⁰While he was going and they were gazing up toward heaven, suddenly two men in white robes stood by them. ¹¹They said, "Men of Galilee, why do you stand looking up toward heaven? This Jesus, who has been taken up from you into heaven, will come in the same way as you saw him go into heaven."

¹²Then they returned to Jerusalem from the mount called Olivet, which is near Jerusalem, a sabbath day's journey away. ¹³When they had entered the city, they went to the room upstairs where they were staying, Peter, and John, and James, and Andrew, Philip and Thomas, Bartholomew and Matthew, James son of Alphaeus, and Simon the Zealot, and Judas son of James. ¹⁴All these were constantly devoting themselves to prayer, together with certain women, including Mary the mother of Jesus, as well as his brothers.

Theological Perspective

"Christian faith is expectant faith. It eagerly awaits the completion of the creative and redemptive activity of God."[1] Daniel Migliore captures well the essence of biblical faith. From the call of Abraham to the revelation of John, God's people have always been "on their way," fervently anticipating the fulfillment of the promise. Sandwiched between the celebration of the ascension and the sacred bedlam of Pentecost, the Seventh Sunday of Easter beckons us beyond the anxiety of not knowing what is next into the divinely established purpose of life in the meantime.

For forty days, Jesus has expounded upon the kingdom of God, and his instruction culminates with a promise. He orders them to remain in Jerusalem and wait for "the promise of the Father. . . . 'You will be baptized with the Holy Spirit not many days from now'" (Acts 1:4–5). Deaf to the word of the Lord, the disciples remain committed to their original vision, and they ask, "Lord, is this the time when you will restore the kingdom to Israel?" (v. 6). Interestingly, we have not advanced very far in our understanding since that question was first asked.

Our confusion manifests itself in a variety of ways.

Pastoral Perspective

Eleven men and maybe a few fellow travelers stood on a Palestinian hillside and watched in amazement as their teacher, their mentor, their leader disappeared into the clouds. One would think that by now they might have grown beyond amazement at the course their life had taken since they had met Jesus in Galilee. Perhaps it is true that wonders never cease. Two men in white robes chided them for standing there, "looking up toward heaven," so they returned to Jerusalem to wait as they had been instructed, to see what amazing thing would happen next.

There are two notable things they did while they waited: they stayed together, and they prayed. Both of these activities are instructive for the church today. William Willimon reminds us, "Waiting, an onerous burden for us computerized and technically impatient moderns who live in an age of instant everything, is one of the tough tasks of the church. Our waiting implies that the things which need doing are beyond our ability to accomplish solely by our own effort, our programs and crusades. Some other empowerment is needed, therefore the church waits and prays."[1]

This group, gathered on the hillside and then in the upper room, were real human beings, with names,

---

1. Daniel L. Migliore, *Faith Seeking Understanding: An Introduction to Christian Theology* (1991; repr., Grand Rapids: Eerdmans, 1997), 231.

1. William H. Willimon, *Acts*, Interpretation series (Atlanta: John Knox Press, 1988), 21.

Exegetical Perspective

Today's text may seem anticlimactic, given that last Sunday's reading covered many of the same verses. Nevertheless, today's account provides us with an opportunity to explore two additional emphases found at the beginning of Acts: (1) a programmatic statement regarding the reception of the Holy Spirit and (2) the formation of the first congregation in Jerusalem. Although connected to the account of the ascension, these important aspects of the text should not be lost.

Luke, the author of Acts, summarizes for Theophilus the events that took place at the end of the Gospel of Luke, including the commissioning of the apostles and the promise of the Holy Spirit. Important in this summary is the programmatic statement of verse 8: "But you will receive power when the Holy Spirit has come upon you; and you will be my witnesses in Jerusalem, in all Judea and Samaria, and to the ends of the earth." Through the proclamation of the gospel of Jesus Christ, God inaugurates a new world order, one that began with the ministry of Jesus and continues through the apostles by the power of the Holy Spirit. The apostles are God's initial agents in the transformation of the world. Acts 1:8 demonstrates that Luke is quite aware of the potential political and religious nature of Jesus' message regarding the inbreaking of the kingdom of God.

Homiletical Perspective

We have focused on Acts 1:1–11 in the lesson for Ascension Day. The story of the ascension is relevant for this Sunday, especially if there has been no special celebration of the ascension. The focus of this homiletical perspective shifts to verses 12–14, in which the disciples retire to the upper room in Jerusalem. After such an amazing event as the ascension, it is of interest to see what the narrator tells us the disciples do next.

Places of the Heart. With Jesus now gone, and the possibility of an imminent return looming, the disciples return to the upper room in Jerusalem, perhaps the very room in which they celebrated the Last Supper. In many respects, this is the beginning of the church, and anticipates the explosion of the church at Pentecost. Here the disciples and several women, including Mary, devote themselves to prayer. In times of deepest insecurity, this practice of returning to a familiar, centering space is typical. After 9/11, sanctuaries were filled with people seeking to attach themselves to familiar, meaningful patterns and rituals, seeking places that represented their deepest emotional and spiritual home. Only these places of the heart can provide some sense of stability and mooring in a sea of chaos.

It is fascinating along these lines to observe how many in our postmodern, postdenominational

Acts 1:6-14

Theological Perspective

Given the recent success of end-time novels, interpretations of the Middle Eastern crisis, and conferences on biblical prophecy—all said to be based on the Bible—many disciples are still determined to understand the kingdom in sociopolitical terms. In North America, the "restoration of the kingdom" often remains bound to the return of the United States to the pristine ideal of a Christian nation. As if God's creative and redemptive purposes depend upon the re-Christianization of this great country, our hopes are as misplaced as those of the original eleven disciples. Jesus simply says that there are certain things we are not meant to know. By implication, there are certain hopes that make the Christian promise far too parochial and small. Returning to the promise, Jesus assures them, "You will be baptized with the Holy Spirit" (1:5), and you will share the power of the kingdom—a power that makes enemies friends and propels you beyond the myopic vision of national sovereignty over against other international powers.

In Jerusalem, Judea, Samaria, and the ends of the earth, you will be my witnesses, Jesus explains. Far from establishing a kingdom wielding the world's power, he promises a community empowered to bear witness. John Calvin argues that Jesus "banish[es] from the disciples' minds a false impression regarding the earthly kingdom," for Christ reigns by "subdu[ing] the world to Himself by the preaching of the Gospel."[2] As the creed declares, Jesus "ascended into heaven, and sitteth on the right hand of God the Father Almighty," and from there he reigns and purports to rule over the hearts of all people.

Without reducing the kingdom to a spirituality devoid of material implications, Luke testifies to a definite shift that revolutionizes the apostolic witness. No one nation is allowed preeminence, but the *ecclesia*, or those called out from among the world, bear the testimony to the redemptive plan. "You will be my witnesses," Jesus declares, and within the relational matrix of your life together, the Father's purpose will be made known. Karl Barth posits the church as the embodiment of divine reconciliation, or the witness to the new ontological reality achieved in Christ. No warring serves God's kingdom, no zealous uprising, not even the expulsion of occupying forces, but simply the communal witness and their preaching of the gospel, a preaching aimed at

Pastoral Perspective

identities, histories, and hopes. They followed Jesus as far as they could; then they waited for the coming of the Spirit. It is they who made up the first church. Though the times have changed radically, it is still real human beings, men and women with names, identities, histories, and hopes, who gather to wait for the coming of the Spirit. It is we who make up today's church as we gather to pray for the coming of the Spirit in our own lives and in the life of our congregations. Even now, we wait for Pentecostal power.

Willimon, again, says, "Our waiting and praying . . . indicate that the gift of the Spirit is never an assured possession of the church. It is a gift, a gift which must be constantly sought anew in prayer. . . . Until those who know the facts also experience the power, they do well to wait in Jerusalem and pray."[2] They—and we— pray for understanding, wisdom, guidance, strength to go on. They—and we—pray in hope and fear, in faith and doubt, in obedience and wonder.

What lay ahead for them? They had anticipated the kingdom of Israel restored in all its ancient power and glory, but Jesus kept talking about the kingdom of God. Apparently they were not the same thing. The realm of God is here and yet it is still coming. Jesus spent his postresurrection time with them reinforcing all he had tried to teach them about the reign of God. No, it would not be like the return of the glorious old Davidic kingdom for which they longed. Jesus would not fulfill their rapidly disappearing hope of driving out the Romans, doing in the religious authorities, overthrowing the rich and powerful, and putting them in those places instead. The reign of God would, however, come riding on their shoulders, through the work of their hands, following the journeys of their feet.

What is this realm of God? Is it just spiritual? Is it also social and political? What will it look like, feel like, sound like, taste like? How will it work? Who will be in charge, and what will be their (or our) roles in such a realm? When will it come? William Barclay offers the perspective that "by the Kingdom Jesus meant a society upon earth where God's will would be as perfectly done as it is in heaven. Because of that very fact it would be a Kingdom founded on love and not on power."[3] So this coming reign of God will be characterized by love and its cousins, compassion and justice, not by power and privilege, wealth or might.

2. John Calvin, *The Acts of the Apostles: 1–13*, trans. John W. Fraser and W. J. G. McDonald, ed. David W. Torrance and Thomas F. Torrance (1965; repr., Grand Rapids: Eerdmans, 1982), 32.

2. Ibid., 21.
3. William Barclay, *The Acts of the Apostles*, Daily Study Bible Series (Philadelphia: Westminster Press, 1955), 4.

Exegetical Perspective

One way to understand this message is as a far-reaching critique of all political claims of earthly rulers, including those of the Roman Empire. Although the concern of the apostles is for the restoration of the kingdom of Israel (vv. 6–7), an idea that is not entirely dismissed in the text, the real plan of God reaches well beyond Israel to include those who were previously disenfranchised from Israel's commonwealth, the Gentiles. Hence, the kingdom of God for Luke also challenges the claims of Israel regarding its perceived exclusive rights and position within God's plan. This is why the inclusion of the Gentiles in the "new" people of God is an overarching concern in the book of Acts.

After it has been made clear to the apostles what they must renounce—any idea of the exclusive rights of the kingdom of Israel—they learn what they are to be given: the disciples receive the Holy Spirit in order to serve as Jesus' witnesses to the ends of the earth. This statement is a command and a promise at the same time. It defines for the church the terms of its commission, one that is global and not merely local. (Interestingly, the apostles in Acts serve as the church's representatives, which may explain why they—with the exception of Peter—stay quietly in Jerusalem and allow Paul to carry out the main mission.) As presented in Acts, the church is a missionary enterprise, a world undertaking not restricted solely to the salvation of Israel.

The words of Jesus, however, have yet one more implication. In laying down the course of the Christian mission from Jerusalem to "the ends of the earth," these words also prescribe the content of the book: the movement of the gospel from Jerusalem to Rome. Any ordinary statement of the book's contents (e.g., as the earliest history of the church) is presented to the reader by the Lord himself as a God-willed sequence of events. It is the Lord himself who points the way forward for the church. To put it another way, the story of the church is the history of divine salvation.

After the ascension, the disciples' new situation is sketched in a couple of concise strokes: "they returned to Jerusalem," and "they went to the room upstairs where they were staying" (vv. 12–13). It is interesting to note that this upper room has not been previously mentioned but serves as a narrative link to the earlier Gospel. According to Ernst Haenchen, "Upper rooms of this kind . . . used to 'serve the learned as place[s] of assembly, study and prayer,' but

Homiletical Perspective

generation, having felt something missing in shallow "church-lite" experiences, are migrating toward older traditions of worship and ritual practice. The Eastern Orthodox Church is one of the fastest-growing churches today, primarily due to the need of many for an anchor amid a sea of change. Within the "emerging church" or "emerging conversation," there is a movement once again toward simple, well-known patterns of table fellowship, prayer, and conversation similar to early house-church or "upper room" church experience, and toward the consultation of ancient traditions of worship for future ways of being the church.

Anticipation. In verse 8, Jesus tells the disciples, "You will receive power when the Holy Spirit has come upon you; and you will be my witnesses in Jerusalem, in all Judea, and in Samaria." The disciples seem to have taken Jesus at his word: that the Spirit will come, and that Jerusalem is at least one key place where they are to bear witness. Evidently, before Jesus comes again, "in the same way as you saw him go into heaven" (v. 11), there is to be a powerful pouring out of the Holy Spirit. The disciples gather in the upper room to await this experience. Here, at the very beginning of the church, we see a fundamental posture of *anticipation* that (a) God will do something, and (b) the church will be empowered for witness when God acts. On the Seventh Sunday of Easter, with Pentecost on the horizon, the church can take its cue from this text. Are we in charge of our own destiny as the church, or are we anticipating God's Spirit to show us the way? Do we really expect God's Spirit to come into our midst? Are we offering prayers together that God's Spirit might come upon us in power? Do we *want* this spiritual power? Do we even want to be witnesses to this generation? The preacher might raise these questions, not in a spirit designed to shame a congregation, but in a way that genuinely questions our identity as the people of God, challenging us actually to anticipate the work of God's Spirit in our midst.

The Witness of the Whole Church. There are women gathered in the upper room with the disciples, including Mary the mother of Jesus. Although many are quick to restrict the role of witness to a closed circle of the Twelve (in this case, the eleven), it is clear that many others were actively anticipating the pouring out of God's Sprit upon *them*, and thus anticipating their own lives as witnesses. Gail O'Day argues that the presence of Mary "establishes

Acts 1:6-14

Theological Perspective

winning converts to the lordship of Christ and his reign within their own communities.

In the ascension, Jesus reasserts his *basileia* vision, and he dispels any hint of establishing an earthly kingdom. He begins a "rule . . . with a more immediate power," a power now "diffused and spread beyond the bounds of heaven and earth."[3] Through the Holy Spirit, the apostles experience Jesus' absence and yet know as intimately as ever his abiding presence. Nonetheless, if the two men in white (v. 11) can be trusted, Jesus' embodied presence does not simply transmute into a spiritual reality. For "this Jesus," they assert, "will come in the same way you saw him go into heaven." As a "meantime" community, the ecclesia embodies Jesus' life-giving presence, but the expectant longing for his physical return remains firm.

Given the delay of the Parousia, many have surrendered hope in Jesus' bodily return. At the same time, others have waged theological war over his 1,000-year reign. While faithful scholars present divergent eschatological views, one of the most difficult to square with Scripture and life experience is realized eschatology. Given the depth of brokenness and pain lurking beneath the surface of even Christian people, it is hard to imagine that the kingdom can be reduced to present reality. If Christ's promised return was fulfilled at Pentecost and extends through God's continual indwelling of people of faith, an entire testament of witness proves problematic. Certainly Jesus' presence is known through the Spirit, but the presence of the Spirit does not diminish the New Testament's hope for Christ's visible and physical return. Even after Pentecost, the church looks for Jesus' return. If the creative and redemptive activity of God corresponds to life's deepest existential groanings, we do well to hear again, "He is coming back," and to long expectantly for the completion of all that God has begun.

SEAN A. WHITE

Pastoral Perspective

If this is so, it is a challenge for us, as it must have been for the people in our text. Is God's kingdom indeed a realm for here and reign for now? What sort of kingdom is founded on love and not power? What ruler/subject, leader/follower on earth forgoes power and privilege in order to provide charity and compassion? It is difficult enough to take care of oneself, while trying to follow society's rules and culture's expectations, without getting hung up on God's will. Nevertheless, doing God's will is what Jesus called them to do; that is precisely what they signed on for. They must do the work of the one who called them and sent them; they must center themselves in God and God's will; they must listen for the voice of love and wrap themselves in its empowering cloak. Are our life stories to be any different?

At least by implication, this passage recognizes the central place of community in the life of the church. It is not enough to go it alone. They met, traveled, and worked together. We too must meet, travel, and work together in Christ's name. We need each other's witness and support, challenge and care, in order to live into the possibilities and expectations of God's realm.

As Christians, we are clearly admonished to live in the present and not be overly concerned about things that are in God's hands, things such as the final fulfillment of the kingdom. There is plenty to be done here and now in building the kingdom; its end is God's business. We are also challenged to spread the word, following the gospel's movement from Jerusalem, as an essentially Jewish sect, outward to the ends of the earth, incorporating Gentiles into God's desire that all nations and peoples come back into communion with the Creator, the great God of the universe. This text calls Christians to be both Great Commandment people—loving God with our whole being and our neighbors as ourselves; and Great Commission people—carrying the good news of God's love in Christ to ends of the earth.

RANDLE R. (RICK) MIXON

---

3. John Calvin, *Institutes of the Christian Religion*, ed. John T. McNeill, trans. Ford Lewis Battles, LCC (Philadelphia: Westminster Press, 1960), 523.

were sometimes also [rented] out as dwellings."[1] The life of the circle of disciples and others during this period is characterized as one devoted to assembly, prayer, and contemplation. In other words, it is a time of preparation for the expected revelation of the Holy Spirit, even if this was not the expressed or only purpose of the apostles' prayers.

We also learn that the eleven, according to Luke, do not form the whole of the core of the early church; in solidarity with them, leading a life steadfastly devoted to prayer, there are also "the women," who are probably the witnesses to the empty grave, as well as the mother of Jesus and his brothers. As Haenchen also highlights, "Thus at least eight other persons, forming two distinct groups, must be added to the Eleven: 'the women' are well-to-do followers of Jesus, some of high position; Jesus' relatives comprise not one but several families, since you must picture his brothers as married (nothing is known of their trades or professions)."[2] The first congregation has been formed.

Luke is trying to illustrate the history of the very earliest congregation. He begins by naming the eleven. Initially, they appear to have been the sole witnesses of Jesus' ascension and to have gathered afterward in the upper room in Jerusalem. Now, however, Luke adds women to their number. Since he has shown no interest in the wives of the apostles or of Jesus' brothers, but some interest in the women who supported Jesus, it is to them that he refers here. "With their generosity and loyalty they are in Luke's eyes shining examples as well as being the highly important witnesses for the empty tomb."[3] Finally, he mentions Jesus' mother and brothers. Although other Gospel accounts claim that the members of Jesus' family did not believe in him, 1 Corinthians 15:7 says that one of the postresurrection appearances was to James. Thus, we can infer that the apostles were not the only witnesses to Jesus' ascension. As a result, James and Jesus' mother and other brothers decided to join this first community of followers.

MICHAEL JOSEPH BROWN

continuity between the birth of Jesus and the birth of the church."[1] In other words, just as there could be no birth of Jesus without Mary, there could be no birth of the church, the body of Christ on earth, without the leading role of women. Here, as throughout Jesus' life and ministry, we see the broad, hospitable nature of discipleship, and eventually of the church's leadership in witness. All are welcome at the table of fellowship. All are welcome to pray in anticipation of the Spirit's power. All are welcome into the full ministry of Christian witness.

From the Mountaintop to the Valley. Many scholars associate the ascension with the transfiguration as one of the most powerful theophanies in the New Testament. The ascension truly was a "mountaintop experience." Just as the disciples come off the mount of the transfiguration and enter the valley of ministry, so here, after the ascension, the disciples move directly into a holding pattern in anticipation of a new form of ministry. Following the transfiguration, ministry focuses on healing. In this situation the focus turns to broader forms of witness, including verbal proclamation of the gospel of Christ's resurrection. We might give some thought, as preachers and liturgists, to how the liturgy for this Sunday after Ascension Day might incorporate this mountaintop-to-valley rhythm.

Many in the Protestant traditions do not have special services on Ascension Day itself. If this is the case, the initial portion of the Sunday worship service could incorporate the telling of the ascension story, perhaps in dramatic fashion. Then, as the service develops through preaching and intercessory prayer, the liturgy might capture this same movement into anticipation of new forms of ministry within a general atmosphere of prayer and eucharistic fellowship. In this way, the overarching rhythms of the ascension story might be incorporated into the entire service of worship.

JOHN S. MCCLURE

1. Ernst Haenchen, *The Acts of the Apostles: A Commentary*, trans. R. McL. Wilson (Philadelphia: Westminster Press, 1971), 153.
2. Ibid., 154.
3. Ibid., 155.

1. Carol A. Newson and Sharon H. Ringe, eds. *The Women's Bible Commentary* (Louisville, KY: Westminster/John Knox Press, 1992), 307.

Psalm 68:1-10, 32-35

[1]Let God rise up, let his enemies be scattered;
   let those who hate him flee before him.
[2]As smoke is driven away, so drive them away;
   as wax melts before the fire,
   let the wicked perish before God.
[3]But let the righteous be joyful;
   let them exult before God;
   let them be jubilant with joy.

[4]Sing to God, sing praises to his name;
   lift up a song to him who rides upon the clouds—
   his name is the LORD—
   be exultant before him.

[5]Father of orphans and protector of widows
   is God in his holy habitation.
[6]God gives the desolate a home to live in;
   he leads out the prisoners to prosperity,
   but the rebellious live in a parched land.

Theological Perspective

A chaplain at the central prison in Raleigh, North Carolina, told me that Christians in the United States really do not believe in God's reconciliation, because most people believe in their own versions of retributive justice and capital punishment. The psalmist, however, states that God "leads out the prisoners to prosperity" (v. 6b). Although many Christians hear in churches Scripture about God having reconciled the world, in reality many Christians in the United States still hold on to static concepts of justice that deny that God can transform sinners. In other words, capital punishment contradicts God's ability to redeem a person's life and contradicts the wisdom of the psalmist that God "gives the desolate a home to live in" (v. 6a). If Christians in the United States really believed that God creates *ex nihilo* and is able to inhabit hell (according to Ps. 139:8), they would know that God's love constantly invites reconciliation without limit.

Gregory of Nyssa (380 CE) proclaimed that God's reconciliation is constantly made available to us, even to the most vile sinner in prison. Such a love was so constant for Gregory that he believed in a universal redemption in Christ for all creatures within the universe. He believed this because God's constant love will never give up until we are all in heaven. Quoting Philippians 2:10, where Paul said every knee would

Pastoral Perspective

The enemies of God flee and melt and perish, while the righteous are "jubilant with joy." Joy results as the God who rides the clouds displays power to protect the widows, to be a parent to the orphan, and to provide not simply shelter but home to the homeless. The psalmist draws distinction as if etched in neon between the righteous and those who hate God. For those who are righteous, "it's all good," as they say. The gracious protection of God falls like rain on the righteous.

This psalm of praise rests easily in the Easter season, because it speaks a truth that we have yet to know in all its fullness. The protection for widows is spoken because there is a noticeable lack of protection for widows. Orphans need belonging, and the homeless need place. As James L. Mays says, "This song belongs to the lowly."[1] The people of God gather for worship and sing of the full protection of and blessing of God's power. At Easter we sing, "The strife is o'er, the battle done"; however, there is still a "not yet" at Easter, as the praise of the faithful rises up from those who know the reality of death.

In relation to these competing powers, the psalmist speaks of a clear division between the righteous and

---

1. James L. Mays, *Psalms*, Interpretation series (Louisville, KY: Westminster John Knox, 1994), 229.

⁷O God, when you went out before your people,
    when you marched through the wilderness,   *Selah*
⁸the earth quaked, the heavens poured down rain
    at the presence of God, the God of Sinai,
    at the presence of God, the God of Israel.
⁹Rain in abundance, O God, you showered abroad;
    you restored your heritage when it languished;
¹⁰your flock found a dwelling in it;
    in your goodness, O God, you provided for the needy.
. . . .
³²Sing to God, O kingdoms of the earth;
    sing praises to the Lord,   *Selah*
³³O rider in the heavens, the ancient heavens;
    listen, he sends out his voice, his mighty voice.
³⁴Ascribe power to God,
    whose majesty is over Israel;
    and whose power is in the skies.
³⁵Awesome is God in his sanctuary,
    the God of Israel;
he gives power and strength to his people.

Blessed be God!

Exegetical Perspective

A sense of the tangible presence of God effectively working on behalf of the community lies at the heart of this reading. Psalm 68 is known for the difficulties it presents in terms of formal structure and content, leading some commentators to consider it a pastiche of various fragments. Albright considers it "a Catalogue of Early Lyric Poems," while others see in the edited whole a song of victory.[1] In this reading, verses 1–3 call for the manifestation of God's presence; verses 4–6 offer praise to the God of heaven, the deliverer of the helpless; verses 7–10 rehearse the saving acts of the God of Israel (vv. 7–8 in the wilderness, vv. 9–10 in the cultivated land); verses 32–35 praise God of heaven and ruler of Israel.

The imagery of verses 1–3 invokes the ark tradition, specifically the battle cry of Moses in Numbers 10:35: "Arise, O LORD, let your enemies be scattered, and your foes flee before you." The ark of the covenant is thought by many scholars to have functioned as a war palladium, manifesting the presence of the Deity, which guaranteed the protection of the community (see 1 Sam. 4–6). The ark also functioned as a fixed symbol of divine presence in the temple. God's tangible and effective presence, further

1. For references and further discussion, see H. J. Kraus, *Psalms 60–150* (Minneapolis: Fortress Press, 1993), 49.

Homiletical Perspective

There are some texts that do not ring a preacher's chimes. The Sixty-eighth Psalm may be such a text, and the reading of it may also leave some congregants cold.

In this psalm, the predominant metaphor is God as a sky rider. In our culture a sky-rider God sounds more like an archetype of a superhero than the ubiquitous Presence that sustains us in the moments and minutes of our lives.

Those who engage this are likely to be aware of not only what is said but what is not said. The reading excludes verses 11–31, where it is promised that "God will shatter the heads of his enemies" so that "you may bathe your feet in blood" (vv. 21, 23).

Many preachers have heard congregants in moments of raw honesty confess that they are not sure whether they actually believe in God. In my experience these people are questioning not so much the reality of God but rather what kind of God they can believe in.

God is of course just a word—a symbol—a feeble representation of a Truth that defies our definitions and comprehension. For many Christians, God is a pie-in-the-sky Überperson who takes sides. This God-who-is-separate is a creator who remains at a distance. For many, God is a Supreme Being with a supreme ego who is easily angered by misbehaving

Psalm 68:1-10, 32-35

Theological Perspective

one day bow and every tongue confess the lordship of Christ to the glory of God, Gregory commented, "In this passage is signified, that when *evil has been obliterated* in the long circuits of the ages, nothing shall be left outside the limits of good; but even from them [all creatures made by God] shall be unanimously uttered the confession of the Lordship of Christ."[1]

Through God's reconciliation, all evil will ultimately be removed. The psalmist states, "O God, when you went out before your people, when you marched through the wilderness, the earth quaked, the heavens poured down rain at the presence of God, the God of Sinai, at the presence of God, the God of Israel" (vv. 7–8). Although the psalmist distinguishes between the "wicked" and the "righteous," salvation is brought near to us by God who "marched through the wilderness." As Christians read the Psalms, they interpret such power as God's doing the impossible by reconciling sinners to God's self and to one another. Paul says, "Having been reconciled, . . . we [will] be saved by [Christ's] life" (Rom. 5:10). Therefore, Paul says that such enemies are to be reconciled to God, in whom death no longer has authority. "Death will be destroyed" (1 Cor. 15:54), a clear statement that the power of evil will be utterly removed. The psalmist states, "Let God rise up, let his enemies be scattered; let those who hate him flee before him" (v. 1).

When all enemies become subject to God, they will recognize a trace of divinity in themselves. For Gregory, once death has been destroyed, then not even death will exist. We will be subjected to the reign of God's life, but this subjection does not mean we are slaves in any way. Our subjection consists of a blessedness living in us.[2] Gregory provides the example of how endless torment was for many early Christians incompatible with the gospel. Another important early Christian voice is Jerome (400 CE), who was a translator of the Hebrew and Greek testaments of the Bible into the common Latin of the time. He was fully aware of all the controversies involving a so-called eternal damnation, which some translators today render as endless and unrelenting torments, but Jerome taught the redemption of all, even the devil and demons! Jerome states:

> In the restitution of all things, when the true physician, Jesus Christ, shall have come to heal the body

1. *St. Gregory of Nyssa: The Soul and the Resurrection*, trans. Catharine P. Roth (Crestwood, NY: St. Vladimir's Seminary Press, 2000), 63–64.
2. *The Church's Bible: 1 Corinthians Interpreted by Early Christian Commentators*, trans. and ed. Judith Kovacs (Grand Rapids: Eerdmans, 2005), 256.

Pastoral Perspective

the unrighteous. We know from our experience that in flesh and blood these lines are never drawn so neatly. Such unambiguous divisions are reserved for old-time western movies in which the bad guys wore black hats and the heroes wore white hats. In the drama of our living we never leave a trail of faithfulness with such clarity. The human heart is the garden for both weed and wheat. Therefore, a God known for protecting and parenting some and scattering and melting others will be heard as good news by few who are finding their way to a Seventh Sunday of Easter pew.

However, for those who know the world to have crushed them, for those who live on the bottom, this language of certainty is the only prayer that rings authentic. Sometimes the only prayer we can pray from the pit is that the enemies would perish. From the bottom, we pray for God to make things right, to set things straight, to destroy death and all the tools of death. This song belongs to the lowly. It may not offer a literal description of God's way in this world, but it does provide a picture of the only prayers we sometimes know from the bottom.

There is a second pastoral learning we can receive from the psalmist. More and more, our understanding of God is defined by what some would call our "experience" of God. We sing of God as protector and home because we have experienced God as the same, but this is not the case for the psalmist. The confession of God's protection is rooted not in the soil of the psalmist's own experience, but rather in the shared memory of the faith community. These holy memories empower the psalmist to engage in a work of holy imagination that is born not of the present experience of the faithful, but from the testimony of previous faith communities.

The psalmist remembers the journey Israel has had with God. The lection recalls the wilderness wandering, the gift of the law at Sinai, and the blessing of God showered upon God's people in the land. Reciting this journey, this story of God's faithfulness, empowers the psalmist to praise. Because of God's faithfulness in leading Israel through the wilderness and showing the way at Sinai and granting Israel a home, we trust that God will protect the weak and needy.

The psalm parallels the confession Christian people make. We gather to remember the work of God, not simply in our own experience, but in the journey of the church. Because God raised Jesus Christ from the dead, we have a narrative of hope to proclaim, even if we find ourselves among the weak and lowly. We remember what God has done and therefore profess with joy what God will do.

signaled in the comparisons to the effect of the wind driving away smoke and fire melting wax, neutralizes threats to the community.

Verses 4–6 call for praises to be sung to God, the one "who rides upon the clouds" (*rokeb ba'arabot*), invoking an epithet used of the storm deity, Baal, found in Canaanite literature (*rkb 'rpt*). Appeal to the imagery of the storm to describe God was common in Israel (e.g., Deut. 33:26; Pss. 18:9; 29:1–9; 68:33; Isa. 19:1). The violent storm theophany is also associated with war imagery, but the war imagery is in the service of God's fierce protection for his loyal subjects. Not so much God's belligerence as God's steadfastness is in view here. The reasons for the praise of God are given in standard language found elsewhere in the Bible and in the ancient Near East, casting the Deity as protector of the disenfranchised: widows, orphans, the desolate, and prisoners (*'asirim*). The "rebellious" (*sorerim*), on the other hand, receive no protection from God. Instead of enjoying basic family or clan protection, security, shelter, and prosperity, the space they inhabit is described as "a parched land" (v. 6).

God "in his holy habitation" (v. 5, *ma'on*) refers to both the "heavenly" dwelling (cf. Deut. 26:15; 2 Chron. 30:27; Jer 25:30; Zech 2:13) and its earthly counterpart, the temple. Throughout the ancient Near East, the temple was considered the interface between human and divine realms (e.g., the Esagila temple of Marduk in Babylon, called the "bond of heaven and earth"). This reference to God's "holy habitation" may suggest that the psalm was used in a temple (see vv. 24–27, which allude to cultic processions into the sanctuary). The Jerusalem temple may be the locus for such a procession, given that it is mentioned in verse 29 (and perhaps in verse 16).

Storm and war imagery combine again in verses 7–10, here recounting the traditional language of the exodus, the march through the wilderness, and the Sinai theophany (see Exod. 19:16–18; 20:18). God as divine warrior marches forth before the people. Such allusions in the psalm re-present in cult the reality captured in narrative terms in Israel's constitutive salvation history. The notation *selah*—generally considered to be a musical marker and perhaps related to the verb *sll* "lift up the voice" (as in v. 4, "lift up a song" [*solelu*])[2]—may here be indicative of an instruction to intone a particular selection from the traditional narrative.[3] More than simply reciting past

human beings. The Father in heaven easily slips into the role of the disapproving dad. Understood as an anthropomorphic deity, God is one who takes sides.

Suffice it to say that the word "God" carries a lot of baggage. Those of us who employ the word "God" in sermons and in pastoral care may intend to invoke this word to mean one thing, but the meaning of the word depends on the conditioning of the one who hears and uses it.

Although most believers agree that God is Spirit, a subtle conditioning pervades. Try substituting the word "Goddess" for "God" in a sermon. When "God" is replaced by "Goddess," it becomes immediately apparent that the word "God" is not as inclusive as we might think.

This continuing quandary has compelled us to expand our vocabulary for the Divine—and rightly so. One solution is to revert to the sacred word in the Hebrew Bible, YHWH, but this answer raises other questions.

YHWH is a warrior god: "Let God rise up, let God's enemies be scattered; let those who hate God flee before God" (v. 1). Sometimes YHWH even becomes an avenging god: "As smoke is driven away, so drive them away; as wax melts before the fire, let the wicked perish before God" (v. 2).

The sky god YHWH in the Hebrew Bible is a complicated deity. YHWH is a god that takes sides. In general the Bible, and in particular this psalm, argues that you are either for YHWH or against YHWH.

There is no ambiguity, no middle ground. When preaching on texts like Psalm 68, the preacher has at least two alternatives.

The first is to let YHWH remain in the sky. The sky god is a metaphor for the God who remains at a distance. Looking down on the world, this "sky rider" sees human folly and injustice. Looking down on the world, this Rider of the skies is the trumpeted champion of the oppressed, the fiery pillar and, if necessary, the ultimate avenger. However, in many texts, even in Psalm 68, alternative metaphors abound. When the God of the heavens comes down to earth—when the God of distance becomes the God of presence—the world is not punished but transformed: "God creates families for those who are alone, and leads captives to freedom, but the rebellious dwell in a parched land" (v. 6, my trans.).

God creates families for those who are alone? This God lives not at a distance but up close. The rebellious, those who insist upon living alone, are destined to live a shriveled existence. It is not that God is a distant judger but, rather, that we judge ourselves (that

---

2. See M. D. Goulder, *The Psalms of the Sons of Korah* (Sheffield: Journal for the Study of the Old Testament Press, 1982), 102–4.

3. See M. Tate, *Psalms 51–100* (Dallas: Word Books, 1990), 177.

Psalm 68:1-10, 32-35

Theological Perspective

of the Church, every one shall receive his proper place. What I mean is, the fallen angel will begin to be that [of an original state] which he was created, and humanity (who was expelled from Paradise) will be once more restored to the tilling of Paradise. These things then will take place universally.[3]

What if we believed that God's love is as relentless as Gregory and Jerome described it? What if we believed that there is nothing in God's creation that is beyond the reach of God's redeeming grace, that there are no orphans and widows, but also no sinners and no murderers, who do not finally have a home in God's holy habitation (vv. 5–6)? Would we not have to reconsider how we solve our problems on earth? Especially, would we not have to rethink capital punishment and the atheism that it implies? I think the answer has to be yes.

How did we become so nearsighted as Christians that we cannot see the unbounded reach of God's reconciling grace? Perhaps our nearsightedness is our sinful assumption that, as long as we are in heaven, the suffering of others does not matter. The psalmist reminds us that God's reconciling grace is not just for the individual but for the community. God provides a home for those who have no home. It is not the mighty but the desolate, the prisoners, and the needy who have reservations in God's "holy habitation" (v. 5). Those who trust in their own strength and do not seek reconciliation flee before God and live in a parched land (vv. 1, 6). There is, after all, no difference between those who are executed and their executioners. Both are needy—sinners in need of God's reconciling grace. The executioners, no less than their prisoners, are among the desolate and needy and may also have a place in God's home.

MICHAEL BATTLE

Pastoral Perspective

Faith will lack power to carry us through the valley of the shadow if it is not claimed personally. Faith is rooted in the experience of the believing one, but God cannot be limited to my experience alone, because God is bigger than my experience of God. Particularly when God's people lift prayers and praise from the pit, particularly when we cry out to God burdened by the cross we are called to carry, we must lean into the full story of God's faithfulness. It can place into our own mouths the language of praise.

Christ is risen, but the boundary between life and death is not drawn in neon. Death is defeated, but still fights. So we are left to journey through our own wilderness in the presence of life's enemies. There has never been a day in the history of the church that there were not those who bore the title of "widow" or "orphan" or "homeless" or "lowly and needy." The powers of life and death struggle in a blurry battle. Nonetheless, like those who sing ahead of schedule, we remember the story of God's faithfulness: grace raining down in the wilderness; a way of life given at Sinai; home, at last, after the journey; and life slipping from the grip of death to live anew and forever.

Let God rise up. Ascribe power to God, the rider in the heavens. Blessed be God. This is the language of praise, uttered by those who know the powers that erode and seek to destroy life, and yet have come to know God as one who calls the walking dead to breathe. As James Mays says, "This song belongs to the lowly, who in the midst of the powers of this world remember and hope for the victory of God."[2]

THOMAS L. ARE JR.

---

3. Quoted by Elizabeth A. Clark in "The Place of Jerome's Commentary on Ephesians in the Origenist Controversy: The Apokatastasis and Ascetic Ideals," *Vigiliae Christianae* 41, no. 2 (June 1987): 154.

2. Ibid.

events, the references, particularly in the context of the cult, invoke the idea that deliverance is at hand for those who count themselves among God's people (cf. Judg. 5:4–5; see also Mic. 1:3–4; Nah. 1:3–5; Hab. 3:3–12).

The references to the God of Israel (v. 8) set Israel over against other nations, but more importantly designate a community in danger. What is paramount in the image is God's preservation of the community in the face of threats to its existence. God's presence (*mippeney 'elohim*, lit. "from the face of God," v. 8) causes the earth to quake and the heavens to rain. The languishing "heritage" that is restored by God (v. 9) is a specific reference to the deity's hereditary land. The storm theophany brings fructifying rains that result in habitable grazing land for God's "flock"—those who understand themselves as dependent upon the Deity.

The concluding hymn in verses 32–35 presents God in universalist terms, as Israel invites the nations into its particular experience of the sacred, the God who resides at the Jerusalem temple (v. 35, cf. v. 29). The imagery of the "rider in the heavens" (v. 33) brings the psalm full circle, back to the imagery presented at the outset (v. 4). Here, God rides the "ancient heavens," again underscoring the divine locus as not equivalent in simple terms to the normal time-space continuum of human existence. The presence of God is manifested both in cosmic terms (vv. 33–34) and in cultic terms "in his sanctuary" v. 35; cf. Ps. 29:7–9). The sanctuary of God is a microcosm of the universe and expresses the intimate relationship of the creator to the creation. Ultimately, both in the world and in its microcosmic model, the sanctuary, the deity empowers the community, "his people" (v. 35).

DEXTER E. CALLENDER JR.

is, live in a parched land), by choosing not to see ourselves one and all as members of the family of God. "You gave rain in abundance, O God. You restored the land—our inheritance—when it languished; your tribe found a dwelling in it, in your goodness, O God, you provided for the needy" (vv. 9–10, my trans.). When the sky god comes to earth, it is like a rain that showers us with abundance, and our thirst is quenched, our hungers are satisfied. Psalm 68 reminds us that our tradition contains many metaphors for God. Many take solace in the metaphor of YHWH as the sky God who condemns our enemies and confirms us as being on God's side.

But when the Rider of the sky comes to earth, something extraordinary happens. God gets humanized. God is no longer the distant Father but the ubiquitous Abba. Jesus reminds us that the most meaningful and challenging of metaphors is God in the flesh.

In today's Gospel lesson, Jesus says, "All mine are yours, and yours are mine; and I have been glorified in them. And now I am no longer in the world, but they are in the world, and I am coming to you. Holy [One], protect them in your name that you have given me, so that they may be one, as we are one" (John 17:10–11). "Let God arise," says the psalmist; "so that they may be one, as we are one," says Jesus.

Thus the psalmist's Rider in the sky becomes in Jesus the intimate divine Parent who reminds us that all human beings—regardless of culture, ethnicity, religious tradition, gender, or gender orientation—are members of one family.

ROBERT V. THOMPSON

1 Peter 4:12-14; 5:6-11

⁴:¹²Beloved, do not be surprised at the fiery ordeal that is taking place among you to test you, as though something strange were happening to you. ¹³But rejoice insofar as you are sharing Christ's sufferings, so that you may also be glad and shout for joy when his glory is revealed. ¹⁴If you are reviled for the name of Christ, you are blessed, because the spirit of glory, which is the Spirit of God, is resting on you. . . .

⁵:⁶Humble yourselves therefore under the mighty hand of God, so that he may exalt you in due time. ⁷Cast all your anxiety on him, because he cares for you. ⁸Discipline yourselves, keep alert. Like a roaring lion your adversary the devil prowls around, looking for someone to devour. ⁹Resist him, steadfast in your faith, for you know that your brothers and sisters in all the world are undergoing the same kinds of suffering. ¹⁰And after you have suffered for a little while, the God of all grace, who has called you to his eternal glory in Christ, will himself restore, support, strengthen, and establish you. ¹¹To him be the power forever and ever. Amen.

Theological Perspective

First Peter reminds his readers that Christ suffered; therefore, they should not be surprised when Christians also suffer. Christians should not suffer for wrongdoings; they suffer for doing what is right, resting in the assurance that God's glory will be revealed. In a strange twist, to be reviled by this world for the sake of Christ is to be considered a blessing. Christians are to remain humble and let God exalt them. They are not to be anxious, for God cares. They are to be watchful of the satanic (the Empire) that is responsible for their persecution. They are to resist the satanic, lest they become complicit with the powers and principalities of this world (Eph. 6:12).

First Peter attempts to provide comfort and reassurance for those who face, or will be facing, persecution due to their commitment in following Jesus. Euro-Americans, who usually place an emphasis on orthodoxy, have assumed that the cause of the hostility toward the early church was what they believed. However, Empire seldom cares what the masses believe, as long as allegiances to the ruling elites are not compromised. The early churches were persecuted not for what they *believed*, but for what they *did*. They preached a message of liberation. To preach good news to the poor, freedom to the imprisoned, sight for those blinded, and liberation to the oppressed (Luke 4:18–19) is to reject conformity

Pastoral Perspective

For the most part, the people reading this commentary will never have suffered, truly suffered, because of our faith in Jesus Christ. Except for rare and isolated examples, those in the United States are allowed to practice religion without oppression. This freedom is written into the very document around which the country was founded and from which it still governs itself. This is not the case for people in every country around the world, however. My friend Benyamin Yusuf experienced brutal persecution for his choice of religion. He was raised in Africa by a strict Muslim family. When he decided to become Christian, his father disowned him and banished him from their home. Benyamin decided to leave his native land for a more tolerant society. His feet being his only means of transportation, he began walking to the border. Along the way, he was captured and put in prison. The prison guards spent every night for several months trying to beat a renunciation out of him. Benyamin never renounced his faith. Instead, he would forgive the guards at the conclusion of every beating.

One of the jailers became intrigued by Benyamin, who offered such love in the face of such cruelty. One night, after a particularly vicious beating, the jailer came to the cell to ask Benyamin why he forgave him and the other guards after every beating. Benyamin

Exegetical Perspective

Of course we are immediately suspicious when the lectionary leaves out a chunk of the biblical text—here 1 Peter 4:15–5:5. The missing passage includes two main themes. In the midst of a discussion about suffering, there is a parenthetical reminder that if Christians are going to suffer, they had better suffer for doing good and not evil (4:15–19; see also 2:20–21). In the midst of a general exhortation to the believers in Asia Minor, there is a reminder to church leaders of the special responsibilities that they bear in caring for their flock (5:1–5).

As in the first three chapters of this epistle, the author acknowledges that the Christians who read or hear his letter will be subject to suffering for their faith. What is not clear is whether some new and more dangerous crisis has arisen that inspires the apostle to write this chapter. In 1 Peter 1:6–7 and 3:14–15 the author expects that the faithful will suffer for the sake of their faith, but the suffering consists largely of rejection and slander. In 1 Peter 4:12 the language of threat seems to escalate: "Do not be surprised at the fiery ordeal that is taking place among you to test you."

It may be that, between the time that he wrote the first chapters of the epistle and the time that he writes chapters 4 and 5, the apostle has heard of some outbreak of physical persecution, no longer an

Homiletical Perspective

To hear what 1 Peter has to say about persecution and humility many congregations will have to overcome some commonsense assumptions. How can a preacher or congregation be asked to take seriously the idea of suffering as a "test" from God? Who in our congregations today is prepared to accept persecution as unsurprising and even a normal prelude or prerequisite to sharing the glory of Christ? Even in an increasingly secular society, very few congregations in the developed world have experienced "sharing Christ's sufferings" (4:13) in any ways comparable to what Peter describes.

Many Christians in the developed world may read the text as a biblical or theological puzzle that may or may not have a satisfying solution. Perhaps preachers would be wise not to rush past this possibility too quickly. A doctrinal sermon that takes up one or more of the issues that being "reviled for the name of Christ" (4:14) raises and then goes on to challenge hearers with 1 Peter's God-centered eschatological perspective, could provide an occasion for theological reflection and growth. At least a portion of the homiletical agenda here might be to challenge developed-world congregations to see how realistic 1 Peter's perspective seems to Christians living in other parts of the world. It is important to note that though the end of the reading is full of hope and

1 Peter 4:12-14; 5:6-11

Theological Perspective

with the prevailing power structures. Thus 1 Peter reminds readers: "Beloved, do not be surprised at the fiery ordeal that is taking place among you" (4:12). To live the gospel is threatening. Liberation for the oppressed is a direct assault on the forms of subjugation society has legitimized.

The hostility provoked by the early church, or any other church that radically lives the gospel, should not be surprising. Those whom society benefits employ whatever means necessary to protect and expand their power and privilege. The threat to the Empire was not that this group of Christians believed Jesus was the Son of God or that he rose from the dead. The threat was that Jesus, not Caesar, was Lord. If this claim is true, the question facing the churches of today is why Christians do *not* experience hostility. Could it be that today's church has become irrelevant because it has traded the gospel message of liberation for conformity and complicity with empire? If today's churches were to place less emphasis on orthodoxy (correct doctrine) and more on orthopraxis (correct action), would their efforts to bring about justice provoke persecution?

In the midst of anxiety over suffering and persecution, 1 Peter provides comfort, misnamed by future Eurocentric theologians as a "theology of hope." Such a theology finds hope or redemption in suffering, but few who have constructed such theologies of hope actually experienced the suffering or persecution they write about. If they did, they too would discover that there is nothing redemptive about suffering. Maybe we would be more correct in naming the comfort offered by 1 Peter as a theology of hopelessness.

Why a theology of hopelessness instead of hope? Because, according to 1 Peter, the Christians' adversary "like a roaring lion" is looking to devour them (5:8). When Jesus sends us like lambs before the wolves (Matt. 10:16), the sure bet is on the wolves. The gospel message of liberation is hopeless in the face of power structures designed to prevent justice. The disenfranchised must stand before the vastness of neoliberalism, and the empire it benefits. The fact that there is little hope for radical change leaves us with few ethical alternatives. Regardless of good intentions or optimistic praxis, the devastating consequences of empire will worsen as the few get wealthier and the many sink deeper into poverty. Suffering is the norm for the vast majority of the world's population. For theologians from societies that benefit from the present global economic order to offer the persecuted a theology of hope, can be perceived as somewhat disingenuous.

Pastoral Perspective

told the guard about Jesus and the lessons of selfless love and forgiveness he taught. The guard left in disbelief, but returned much later that night with the surprise announcement that he had come to help Benyamin escape. Escape he did, eventually making his way to the United States, where he earned a PhD in religious studies before returning to Africa to plant churches.

This story reminds us that people suffer for their faith, even in our modern world. So we must ask whether this text is pertinent to the majority of us who have not suffered for our faith. Is this text speaking only to those who have been oppressed, beaten, or expelled for their faith? If the answer to this question is yes, then we would have little need to study the text further. However, I think the answer is no. This text is not addressed only to those who have literally suffered for their faith. This text is speaking to all Christians.

It is 5:9 that leads to this conclusion. Whether referring to persecution or to the more common distresses and frustrations we all feel every day, the point is that as Christians we are not flying solo. In other words, the Christian faith is not individualistic. It is not solely about my personal relationship with Jesus Christ. This is important, for sure, but at its core, Christianity invites people to become part of one body of Christ, which is larger than the troubles, successes, or frustrations of any one person. Too often, Christianity is reduced to the singular. Too often, faith is focused on one's personal relationship with Jesus and little else. This text, and 5:9 in particular, reminds us that as Christians we are a part of the whole. Others through the ages have pressed the importance of this lesson. John Donne wrote in his "Meditation XVII" that "no man is an island entire of itself; every man is a piece of the continent, a part of the main." Martin Luther King quoted Donne in his sermon at the Temple Israel in Hollywood on February 26, 1965, to underscore this point that we do not exist merely for our own needs.

Such an awareness is essential to our ability to relate to others and the needs they have or particular troubles they face. The ability to empathize, to achieve solidarity, and to find common ground ultimately stems from an understanding of one's self as part of a larger whole. The further removed we are from this understanding, the less able we are to engage the world in Christlike love, the very essence of which is to love our neighbor as we love ourselves. This can be successful only if we understand our own

Exegetical Perspective

annoyance but an ordeal. It may be that, as he moves toward the conclusion of his letter, he stretches the rhetoric, making the same point in more colorful language. It may be that he is now deliberately placing the situation of his readers within an apocalyptic framework. The slights and rejections that the Christians suffer are not only annoyances; they are signs that "the end of all things is near" (4:7).

As in 3:18–22, the apostle provides comfort to his audience by suggesting that the suffering that Christians undergo finds its archetype and its fulfillment in the sufferings of Christ. As in 3:18–22, the comfort that 1 Peter provides depends on the claim that Christians live out the pattern of Christ's suffering death and of his resurrection. Those who share in his sufferings will share in his glory. The word that the NRSV translates as "share" is the verb *koinōneō*, the root of the familiar noun *koinōnia*. It means not only to share but to participate in something, to be in communion. Christians not only suffer as Christ does; they participate in his suffering. They are in communion with him. Therefore they will also participate in his resurrection and ascension "so that you may also . . . shout for joy when his glory is revealed" (4:13).

As with so much of the New Testament, the comfort that 1 Peter pronounces is both comfort for the present and comfort for the future: God's promised mercy is both already present and yet to come. Believers wait for the moment, not yet come, when they will shout for joy at the glory of the Lord. Believers take comfort in the present because—however strange it seems to us—in being reviled they are also blessed. This is because their persecution shows clearly that they live under God's Spirit, and God's Spirit, even in the midst of distress, is itself God's blessing. The Spirit of God is also "the spirit of glory" (4:14). Through the Holy Spirit, the glory for which the faithful wait is already made present—as blessedness.

First Peter 5 spells out the practical implications of the life lived in the presence of blessing and in the hope for glory.

In 1 Peter 5:1–5a the author addresses his instructions first to the elders and then to "the younger" (5:5a). Most likely this is not simply a demographic designation but distinguishes church leaders (the elders) from the larger community (those who are young), leaders from followers.

In what follows in 5:5b–11, 1 Peter addresses leaders and followers alike. All alike are to humble themselves before God. At the beginning and end of this section, the author revisits the contrast between present suffering and future glory. Though

Homiletical Perspective

promise (Christ will "restore, support, strengthen, and establish you," 5:13), this need not be read as a promise that suffering will cease while we live.

A preacher might well accept at face value the lectionary's suggestion that the preacher read only three verses from chapter 4 before skipping 4:15 through 5:5. The reading resumes with the admonition to "humble yourselves" (5:6) and "resist [the devil]" (5:9) as an apt response to persecution. This approach may be especially useful when this passage is paired with the Gospel for the day. The verses omitted might have a tendency to draw the hearer's mind in a direction unrelated to the prayer of Jesus in the Gospel reading.

A sermon that works with the passage in this way might turn on the example of Jesus in the Gospel reading. He prays that, having been humbled for the sake of his people, he will now be glorified. First Peter may be read to suggest that we, his people, are to be willing likewise to humble ourselves in relation to God and the world, for the sake of future glory together with Christ. In this sense, our passage looks forward to a time in the eschatological future when those who belong to Christ will share in the glory of his ascension. This points to a theme introduced earlier in this epistle. The sufferings of Christians mirror and participate in the suffering of Christ (2:21–23; what makes this text problematic is that the sufferers who are being comforted in this passage are slaves suffering at the hands of their masters). In the homiletical effort to speak to suffering in the light of eschatological hope, preachers may find it useful to reflect upon the vivid, dramatic vision Jonathan Edwards describes in the last two sermons in his series *A History of the Work of Redemption*.[1]

Alternatively, a sermon on these selected verses might explore 1 Peter's expectation that suffering is a normal aspect of the Christian life, shared with "brothers and sisters in all the world" (5:9). Moreover, persecution can be expected to continue "a little while" (5:10). Indeed, there are brothers and sisters elsewhere in the world who are able to show concretely what can be involved in sharing Christ's sufferings, both its challenges and rewards. Such organizations as Voice of the Martyrs (www.persecution.com) can provide preachers with stories and other resources to bring the reality of persecution home for congregations. In some locations, preachers may be able to find individual Christians

---

1. John Wilson, ed., *Works of Jonathan Edwards*, vol. 9, *A History of the Work of Redemption* (New Haven, CT: Yale University Press, 1989), 502–28.

1 Peter 4:12‑14; 5:6‑11

Theological Perspective

The dominant culture, including progressive theologians, may be willing to offer charity, but few are willing to take a role in dismantling the very global structures designed to privilege them at the expense of others. Few are willing to experience the wrath of the very power structures designed to privilege them, if they attempt actually to dismantle those structures for the sake of Christ and justice. The virtue of hope becomes a class privilege experienced by those protected from the reality of disenfranchisement or an opiate used by the poor to numb them to that same reality. Regardless of the optimism professed, they, their children, and their children's children will more than likely continue to live in the suffering of an ever-expanding poverty, caused to benefit the empire's center.

The theology of hopelessness here advocated is not disabling; rather, it is a methodology that propels Christians toward praxis. All too often, hope gets in the way of listening and learning from the oppressed. The semblance of hope becomes an obstacle when it serves a mechanism that maintains rather than challenges the prevailing social structures. The hopelessness in vanquishing the empire's neoliberalism is never an excuse to do nothing. The disenfranchised have no options but to continue their struggle for justice. Such a theology, which upsets the prevailing social order designed to maintain empire, is a theology that arises from the margins of society.

While Euro-American theologians and ethicists insist on social order, marginalized communities call for social disorder. Perhaps such disorder might lead some within the dominant culture to share in the hopelessness of overcoming the global forces of neoliberalism. If so, it will be the only way that progress is made. A theology of hopelessness can be frightening to those who are accustomed to their power and privilege, because hopelessness signals a lack of control. Because those who benefit from the present social structures insist on control, sharing the plight of being vulnerable to forces beyond control, like the original readers of 1 Peter, will demonstrate how hope falls short. Perhaps this is the sad paradox: hope is found in the hopelessness described in Paul's admonition to imitate father Abraham, who, "against all hope . . . in hope believed" (Rom. 4:18 NIV).

MIGUEL A. DE LA TORRE

Pastoral Perspective

existence to be intricately tied to and part of the existence of our neighbor.

The text also refers to the devil, who "like a roaring lion . . . prowls around, looking for someone to devour" (v. 8). I suppose there are many ways to interpret this line, and indeed there are many ways to interpret what Scripture means by "the devil." With regard to this particular text, it helps to note that perhaps the greatest form of violence the devil can render is to separate people from one another—that is, for people to forget or abandon this notion of our connectionality, of being united with all Christians around the world in our struggles, triumphs, joys, and fears. So to forget would be to sever the most important tie that binds people of faith together in the commitment to love one another as Christ loved.

Indeed, these ties are being tested today, as we argue with our brothers and sisters from every side of the Christian faith over ordination issues, sexuality questions, and more. Whether that is the work of the devil, or simply what comes with differing opinions on emotionally charged issues, is for each of us to decide on our own. For sure, it is imperative that the differences that exist between Christians not be allowed to sever the connectionality that we have and that this text urges us never to abandon.

GORDON MCCLELLAN

Exegetical Perspective

the christological pattern of crucifixion/resurrection that 1 Peter uses in chapters 3 and 4 is no longer explicit, the implicit story behind these exhortations is still the story of suffering, death, and resurrection/ascension.

Humble yourself therefore under the mighty hand of God,
so that he may exalt you. (5:6)
After you have suffered for a little while,
the God of all grace . . . will . . . restore, support, strengthen, and establish you. (5:10)

Between these assurances 1 Peter further defines the time in which its readers live. This is not only the time of suffering and of opposition from annoying opponents. This is the time when the devil is on the prowl, and the opponents, knowingly or not, serve the prince of evil. It is not just that unrepentant neighbors harass you, says 1 Peter; through them, Satan himself seeks to destroy you.

In the face of this pervasive danger, the faithful are to cling in hope to God's promised good. They are to do this in three ways. First, they act humbly, acknowledging the power and providence of God. Second, they act watchfully, disciplined enough not to doze off in the face of impending danger. Third, they act faithfully, by resisting the evil one and those who follow in his entourage.

The primary comfort that the epistle provides for those who suffer is the comfort of God's present grace and eventual triumph. There is, however, also a secondary comfort. The *koinōnia* that these believers share with Christ is echoed in the *koinōnia* they share with their fellow Christians, who also suffer. First Peter calls upon the faithful to "resist," in part by reminding them that they are part of a resistance movement that extends far beyond their own communities and reaches all the world (5:9).

Appropriately the promise of God's triumph over the forces of evil moves from description to doxology: "To him be the power forever and ever. Amen" (5:11).

DAVID L. BARTLETT

Homiletical Perspective

who have experienced persecution firsthand. Preachers might well invite such people into the worship service, and perhaps into participation in the sermon.

Another approach is to focus attention on the four imperative verb phrases by which 1 Peter relates suffering and glory. First Peter proposes that Christians make four responses: humble yourselves, cast your anxiety on God, discipline yourselves and keep alert, and resist the power of evil (5:6–9). In such a sermon Viktor Frankl's insight in a Nazi death camp, that the meaning of suffering is found in the response of the sufferer, may provide a point of entry.[2]

On the other hand, some preachers have found over time that, when the lectionary skips verses, the most interesting and difficult challenges for themselves and the congregations they serve—and perhaps the most sanctifying ones—will sometimes be in those verses. Whether or not that is the case here, it is clear that including these verses opens other homiletical options.

For example, 4:15–19 provides resources with which the preacher can fill out a sermon on the problem of persecution, as already suggested. Whereas in our world some businesses advertise their owners' Christian faith in the telephone directory, in 1 Peter's environment, "Christian" was a term of abuse (4:16). In such a situation, to be "reviled for the name of Christ" (4:14) is one thing, while giving occasion for one's own suffering through criminal activity or meddling in other people's business (4:15) is quite another. In a sermon on persecution, this could be a crucial point. In contrast to the naive expectation that relatively good people can expect a life more or less free of tragedy and pain, these verses make it clear that some suffering is "in accordance with God's will," and the appropriate though painfully difficult response is to trust "a faithful Creator . . . while continuing to do good" (4:19).

MICHAEL D. BUSH

---

2. Viktor Frankl, *Man's Search for Meaning* (New York: Simon & Schuster, 1970).

John 17:1-11

¹After Jesus had spoken these words, he looked up to heaven and said, "Father, the hour has come; glorify your Son so that the Son may glorify you, ²since you have given him authority over all people, to give eternal life to all whom you have given him. ³And this is eternal life, that they may know you, the only true God, and Jesus Christ whom you have sent. ⁴I glorified you on earth by finishing the work that you gave me to do. ⁵So now, Father, glorify me in your own presence with the glory that I had in your presence before the world existed.

⁶"I have made your name known to those whom you gave me from the world. They were yours, and you gave them to me, and they have kept your word. ⁷Now they know that everything you have given me is from you; ⁸for the words that you gave to me I have given to them, and they have received them and know in truth that I came from you; and they have believed that you sent me. ⁹I am asking on their behalf; I am not asking on behalf of the world, but on behalf of those whom you gave me, because they are yours. ¹⁰All mine are yours, and yours are mine; and I have been glorified in them. ¹¹And now I am no longer in the world, but they are in the world, and I am coming to you. Holy Father, protect them in your name that you have given me, so that they may be one, as we are one."

Theological Perspective

What is "glory"?

Imagine a candidate on election night, standing before a sea of supporters. Candidate and crowd are visibly exhausted from a victorious campaign, yet are momentarily beside themselves in joy, radiance, and delirious peace. Then, as carefully chosen words ring out, speaker and audience are lifted into an even greater state of ecstasy. The sentences, already well crafted, now mean more. New horizons of possibility can be seen, which heretofore seemed too distant to contemplate. All are momentarily perceiving and acknowledging more than they could before. Tingles go up the spine, tears flow. However, what we are imagining is a fairly ordinary example of glory.

Ordinary, because familiar—we have known such moments, but my own imagination stalls when trying to grasp the theological senses of "glory" in Scripture or liturgy. I am at a loss until triangulating the scriptural and theological with the word's range of ordinary meanings.[1]

Glory (Heb. *kabod*, Gr. *doxa*) can mean weight, repute, fame—and fame can *shine*. So glory can be

Pastoral Perspective

These verses bespeak Jesus' most urgent hopes for his disciples. While shaped here as his prayer, Jesus meant for his disciples—and arguably for us two millennia later—to overhear his petitions. Hours from the crucifixion, Jesus focuses precisely on what matters most from his entire ministry. This desire to communicate one last time what is at the center of one's life and hopes is an enduring human experience. A colleague in ministry tells the story of a young mother dying of cancer in a hospital who finds purpose and energy from the opportunity to construct a videotaped message for her preschool daughters, so that when they are older they can listen to what she most hopes will guide their lives. It is very important to her to make sure her daughters receive her motherly care and love, even though she will not be alive to speak to them in person. While this mother can only hope that the videotape will help keep her memory accessible to her children, Jesus speaks knowing that the Spirit who abides in us is able to keep his message alive in our hearts.

What is central among Jesus' concerns? For him the culmination of his work is that we know God through his life and ministry. His final hopes are not a celebration of himself, but the recognition that his life and ministry are windows into God's love and saving purposes. So Jesus prays that people will come

1. See Anthony J. Kelly and Francis J. Maloney, *Experiencing God in the Gospel of John* (New York: Paulist Press, 2003), 11–14; Hans Urs von Balthasar, *The Glory of the Lord: Theological Aesthetics*, 7 vols., trans. Erasmo Leiva-Merikakis and Brian MacNeil (San Francisco: Ignatius Press, 1983–91), 6:32–37; 7:239–44.

Exegetical Perspective

John 17:1–11 begins what scholars often refer to as the high-priestly prayer, a designation suggesting that here Christ acts as a high priest, making intercession to God on humanity's behalf. While the image is not exact, the title highlights Jesus' offering to God the concerns of a community faced with remaining in the world after his departure. John 17 continues and completes many of the themes found elsewhere in the Gospel and recalls much of Jesus' language elsewhere in the Farewell Discourse (chaps. 13–17, esp. 13:31–35). Chapter 17 recasts Jesus' teaching as a prayer between the Son and the Father. This new rhetorical form changes the narrative scene of the Farewell Discourse, as the disciples fade into the background, and the reader is invited to overhear Jesus' intimate conversation with his Father.

Jesus' comment that he has "conquered the world" (16:33), while turning his eyes toward heaven, marks a transition in the narrative from ministry to passion. This transition is also signaled by Jesus' announcement that "the hour," much anticipated throughout the Gospel (see 2:4; 4:21; 5:28; 7:30; 8:20), has arrived (17:1). The entire Farewell Discourse is set at the hour's arrival (13:1), though here Jesus' announcement of the hour's arrival, the final such reference in the Gospel, sets in motion its concomitant actions. The passion narrative begins immediately after Jesus' prayer.

Homiletical Perspective

On this last Sunday of the Easter season, we look both backward and forward. We have heard about Jesus' appearances to his disciples; we have gloried in his ascension; we have received hints of the coming of the promised Paraclete. Next week, we will celebrate the birth of the new church, exploding into mission with the gifts of the Spirit. Today, we pause for a moment to hear again the prayer Jesus prayed for his disciples, a prayer we claim as his prayer for us.

There is assurance and certainty in Jesus' prayer. Jesus has made his Father's name known to the disciples. He has given them knowledge of the truth. Now he prays for their protection. Later he will elaborate on the need for the Father's protection: the disciples have been hated by the world, and they are endangered by evil or the evil one (vv. 14–15). Here he asks protection for them for a particular purpose, "so that they may be one, as we are one" (v. 11).

Because it is part of Jesus' prayer, that prayer for unity can also offer us assurance and certainty, but for many of us, it may also raise questions. Can we see any evidence that Jesus' prayer was answered? What does Jesus mean anyway, when he says, "one, as we are one"?

Think about the way John's Gospel starts: "In the beginning was the Word, and the Word was *with* God, and the Word *was* God." From the very first

Theological Perspective

seen. Epic heroes desire to be remembered—Homer sings of the "fames of men"—and at great moments they shine. In society, glory is created by perception and acknowledgment. The crowd and candidate together contribute to a glory long in the making; antecedent impressions are newly enlarged. The moment is like praise chants in some African communities, where a leader's power is built up by the performance of "praise singers." The leader is thereby enabled to confront the challenges at hand.

Glory, then, can be transactional. People and leader make the phenomenon and are caught up in it; they discern glory—a heightened unity and mutual empowerment—that encompasses and enters them, affecting them in ways that can be recorded (postures, countenances, or speech rhythms). Yes, glory can be signified conventionally in ceremonies, vestments, and formulaic utterances, but these recapitulate what sociologist Émile Durkheim understood as great moments of social effervescence.

The glory, about which Jesus prays, can both illuminate this social dynamic and transform it. The continuity is felt in the transactional, expansive, and participatory nature of glory. Jesus prays: "Glorify [*doxason*] your Son so that the Son may glorify you" (v. 1); "I have made your name known to those whom you gave me from the world" (v. 6); "all mine are yours, and yours are mine; and I have been glorified in them" (v. 10). The discontinuity is in how Jesus, *on behalf of the disciples,* turns away from the dynamic of glory for one's own sake: "I am asking . . . on behalf of those whom you gave me" (v. 9). Did not our earlier description of glory seem worrisome? Vainglory, false pride, and empty vanity are all vices bearing on fame. Moreover, ordinary glory specifies no content. Our candidate might be anyone with any cause; the crowd might be a mob cheering a demagogue. Jesus rejects the vanity and relativity of glory, insofar as John associates the glory of the Father and Son with the cross and with the coming of another Advocate or Paraclete, the "Spirit of truth" (14:17; 15:26), the truth of divine love, encompassing the world and transcending it.

Glory, then, must be understood within the cruciform logic of "God is love" (1 John 4:8). All relations, actions, and meditations find their norm and full extent in love, an implication of verses 2–3: "authority" connects with "to give eternal life to all whom you have given him." What is "eternal life"? It is to "know" God and Christ. What sort of knowing is this? Again, knowing God must entail continuity and discontinuity with ordinary forms of knowing; but in

Pastoral Perspective

to *know* God through him. "Knowing" describes a powerful, active, confessional, and intimately relational claim on our lives. Knowing God is an experience that draws believers into a new reality in which the new order that will be shaped eternally by God's vision for love and justice and service can also be realized in relationships and communities now. Knowing God will be evident in our obedience to love, the singular commandment of this Gospel. In other words, eternal life has deeply ethical implications for the present.

The Johannine community also realized that this reference to eternal life provides a dramatic contrast to Rome's claim to be the eternal city.[1] This polemical edge in John's Gospel contrasting God's vision for humankind and the claims of the Empire sadly has a continuing resonance for contemporary Christians. Jesus claims a different authority from that of Empire. It is God who authorizes him over all people to offer eternal life, which is so starkly different from the pretense of the claims of Rome. God discloses a very different vision of what is true and worthy of the trust of those who live by it.

How, though, are we to deal with the exclusive language in this prayer that implies God's eternal life is not available to all? The dualism of the Johannine community poses a challenge for us. For this community, the term "world" most often refers to a dangerous and hostile place that opposes God's hopes for justice and love and mercy. In this passage Jesus prays not for the whole world but for those whom he has taught and guided into knowledge and love of God. He prays confidently for their (and our) protection in a hostile world. While such dualism is not unique to this community of believers, the wideness of God's mercy in many other passages in Scripture and the recognition that we believers also often oppose God's will mean that we do well to interpret this text more generously. We all need God's protection from our own worst impulses as well as from others whom God also loves. What we can rely upon, as Jesus did, is the assurance of God's grace and providential care.

In a time when great divisions threaten the unity of so many Christian communions, the poignancy of Jesus' prayer that we believers may be one is striking. He prays from the context of the profound intimacy he enjoys with God, an intimacy that elsewhere in John Jesus also ascribes to his relationship to the Spirit or Paraclete. Jesus, the Father, and the Paraclete

---

1. Warren Carter, *John: Storyteller, Interpreter, Evangelist* (Peabody, MA: Hendrickson Publishers, 2006).

Exegetical Perspective

The passage divides into three sections. In the first (vv. 1–5), Jesus declares to the Father that his work is complete and requests to return to his place alongside the Father. In the second section (vv. 6–8), Jesus offers the disciples' response as proof that he indeed has completed the task given him. In the third section (vv. 9–11), Jesus asks God to protect those whom he leaves behind. This concern for the community dominates the rest of the high-priestly prayer.

In the first section Jesus requests glorification due to his completed mission. The repetition within verses 1–5 suggests a chiastic structure, where the central definition of eternal life (v. 3) is surrounded by a summary of Jesus' accomplishment (vv. 2, 4) and the repeated request for glorification (vv. 1, 5). Jesus speaks of his accomplishment with a diversity of images, all found elsewhere in the Gospel, but the center of the chiasm suggests Jesus' primary role is to reveal the Father. In verse 3 Jesus defines eternal life: the knowledge of the one true God. Unlike in the Synoptics, where eternal life is rarely mentioned but stands as a future hope (see Matt. 19:16–30 and par.), in John, eternal life is a present reality, available immediately to those who believe in Jesus and the one who sent him (3:15–16, 36; 5:24; 6:47). Jesus summarizes his work on this earth as creating the opportunity for people to know God.

In verses 1 and 5, since he has completed God's work, Jesus repeats his request for a return to glory, his precreation position with the Father (see 1:1–5). The translation "glory" for the Greek *doxa* misses the nuance of the noun, which in Greek literature can indicate opinion, reputation, or appearance. In the NT the meaning ranges from brightness (Acts 22:11) to greatness (Matt. 6:29) to honor (1 Thess. 2:20). In the Septuagint, *doxa* is frequently used to translate the *kabôd YHWH*, often meaning the presence of the Lord (Num. 14:10). The diverse use of the term in the Gospel resists a single definition. True *doxa* is something that comes only from the Father (5:41–44) and was given to Jesus (8:54), and the revelation of God's *doxa* is an essential part of Jesus' action on earth (1:14; 2:11). The glorification of the Son leads to the glorification of the Father, which most concerns Jesus (see 11:4; 15:8; 21:19).

In verses 6–8 Jesus offers his disciples' response to his revelation as proof of his completion of God's work and the foundation of his request for glory. In verse 2 Jesus emphasizes the universality of his mission, recognizing his "authority over all flesh." However, in verse 6 he distinguishes his followers from

Homiletical Perspective

verse, John struggles to express the mystery of Jesus—that he *was* God and *distinct from* God at the same time. We look at Jesus and say, "That is what God looks like."

When Jesus prays that his followers may be one as he and the Father are one, he is praying all of us into this mystery too. Not just that we should each become one with God, or one with Christ, but that we should become one with each other in the way Jesus and the Father are one.

In some ways, the first part of that mystery is the easy part. We all have our ways to grow in our oneness with God. We may ground our own growth in corporate worship. We may follow a spiritual discipline of private prayer, study, and service in God's name. We may dedicate ourselves to a particular ministry in a cause of justice, or healing, or pastoral presence. No matter which path we follow toward oneness with God, the Holy Spirit can act in our lives to draw us closer, and to reveal to us the presence of God that is already nearer to us than our own heartbeats. We have only to open our eyes and our ears, and remain willing to receive and respond.

Jesus is also praying that his followers may be one with one another. There, of course, is where the pain lies for us today.

It would appear that *disunity* is the defining notion in this church of ours, in this church of Jesus Christ. We have our denominations and our subdenominations. We argue over who can be ordained and what words we can use when we pray. We argue over our alliances with this or that group around the world, or within our parish community. We argue over how our churches participate in secular life, or how religion interacts with the state. It causes enormous pain. Perhaps it is helpful to remember that it is also nothing new.

When there were still people walking the streets who had known Jesus face to face, the Christian community was arguing. They argued over who could share a meal. They argued over whose party represented the "real" church. They argued over whether you were really a Christian if you did not exhibit certain spiritual gifts. So we may wonder whether all this contention, in the past and in the present, means that Jesus' prayer has never been answered.

That option does not seem satisfactory. Does John's portrayal of Jesus seem truthful in some fundamental way? Have we found it encouraging to hear once again how Jesus prayed for his disciples and for us? Do we trust that God does hear prayers and does answer them? Do we also trust that God heard Jesus'

John 17:1-11

Theological Perspective

any case, it must be a knowing and also living that ultimately seeks its form in forms of loving. To know and love the Father and the Son is also to know and love the truth, which is the truth of God as loving. Likewise with *seeing*: to behold the Mother's and the Daughter's glory is to see love via love: love sees love lovingly. This love is not only an abstract ideal but loving action. Jesus prays that God "protect" the disciples in God's "name," which is Lov(ing) (v. 11).

The glory of the Lord—and its relation to truth, love, and sight—is also linked with beauty and continues to inspire work in theological aesthetics.[2] But beauty is nearly as puzzling as glory. Beauty ordinarily connotes a perceptible sensuousness and a fulsome ideal, yet these meanings can be eclipsed both by the invisibility of infinite loving and by historical extremes of suffering and oppression. The logic of love implies that to discern transcendent beauty or to glorify another ultimately means to regard self and other in the selfless emptying of divine love.

Thus, within the logic of love, when we say "beauty" and "glory" we also name the despised, diseased, ugly, Godforsaken, crucified, exiled, imprisoned, the guilty . . . along with the idiotic, psychotic, asinine, homicidal, bully, tyrant, rapist, pedophile . . . *as well as* the dancing parent, touching cop, economic artist, shining actor, curious politician . . . and the hopeful oxymoron, gay soldier, lesbian diva, delightful health maintenance organizer, inquisitive mailwoman, guy selling bagels . . . and who else? On whose list is the exception in verse 12, after our lection, the one "destined to be lost" (or "son of destruction")? Is it Judas? Pilate? Osama bin Laden? Who is *not* held in the beauty of divine glory? The moment we answer that question, by naming some one or some category of persons—whom Jesus refrains from naming—do we not then revert to the world's dynamic of glory? Are we not, for that moment, lost?

LARRY D. BOUCHARD

Pastoral Perspective

enjoy a positive interdependence that allows for difference. Perhaps this early Trinitarian theme is suggestive for how we may imagine our oneness in Christ. Surely it does not mean we must be identical in thought and practice, any more than the persons of the Trinity are in their dynamic interdependence.

Just as Christians around the world grow more able to be in good communication and learn with and from one another, so we also find ourselves sorely tested by such things as radically different interpretations of the wideness of God's love and the boundaries of the church; the full inclusion of all God's people; and deep and historically shaped emotions about the way God's vision for economic justice has implicated Christians in dominant and developing countries differently. Oneness will necessarily require that we seek ways to honor the particular gifts, experiences, and insights of each community of believers and also that we support one another through accountability to the Gospel that we hold in common. History has taught Christians that the Johannine community's confidence that danger was only outside the church is misplaced.

Our oneness in Christ also faces new challenges as we recognize the urgency of interfaith opportunities to repair and build relationships among the Abrahamic religious traditions and beyond. Especially in the context of increasing religious fundamentalism across Christianity, Judaism, and Islam, we do well to remember how Hebrew prophets came to understand that God's love transcends a particular people and place, to create one human community linked by a covenant of mutual responsibility. As Rabbi Jonathan Sacks suggests in his book *The Dignity of Difference*, we need a theology of religions to help us recognize the image of God in the face of those who are not in our own image.[2] To find God in the faces of all humankind surely is a goal of the eternal life into which Jesus invites us to live our commitments now. The God of Abraham intends that all the families of the earth be blessed.

NANCY J. RAMSAY

2. See Frank Burch Brown, *Good Taste, Bad Taste, Christian Taste: Aesthetics in Religious Life* (Oxford: Oxford University Press, 2000), 95–127.

2. Jonathan Sacks, *The Dignity of Difference*, rev. with new preface (New York: Continuum, 2003).

the world, pointing to the disciples' recognition that Jesus comes from God, described variously as acceptance, knowledge, and belief, terms used synonymously throughout the Gospel to characterize the proper response to Jesus' message. Jesus characterizes his primary accomplishment in verses 1–5 as revealing knowledge of God, and in verses 6–8 he claims as his disciples those who have accepted his revelation.

In verses 9–11, Jesus' prayer turns into supplication, asking the Father to keep those whom he leaves, who remain in the world, though they are not part of it. In Jesus' request that the Father "keep them," he hands "those whom you gave me" back into the custody of the Father. Jesus speaks of his "guarding" them while he was on the earth (v. 12), and now that he comes to the Father, he asks for their continued protection, echoing his earlier promise to ask the Father to send the Paraclete (see 14:16–19; 15:26–27; 16:7–11). Even in Jesus' absence, the community will maintain its access to the Father. This concern for the community after Jesus' departure is the dominant theme of the Farewell Discourse, and it becomes the focus of the remainder of the prayer.

Some may find harsh Jesus' explicit denial that he asks on the world's behalf. This disregard for the world should be read within the dualistic view, throughout the Gospel and within the Gospel's historical context, of an early Christian group attempting to carve out identity within a world that rejects its message. John describes the world (*ho kosmos*) as God's creation worthy of saving (3:16–17), though it has fallen under the control of another (12:31; 14:30) and rejects Jesus (1:9–10; 3:19). Here Jesus focuses on those who have achieved eternal life; later (vv. 18–23) he prays for unity between the disciples and those who have believed through their word, a unity modeled on that of the Father and the Son. Jesus prays that this unity stand as the basis upon which his disciples take his word into the world and the world comes to believe that God sent the Son (17:21).

RICHARD MANLY ADAMS JR.

prayer that we all might be one? If we do, then our problem may be with our own assumptions of what unity is. We may need to think differently somehow, when we think about Christians "being one."

Jesus prayed "that they may be one, *as we are one*" (17:11). "The Word was *with* God, and the Word *was God*" (1:1). Some ancient theologians who studied these very verses talked about Jesus' oneness with the Father in terms that suggest *movement*—a kind of interweaving or even a dance among the Father, the Son, and the Holy Spirit. What if the answer to Jesus' prayer for unity was not about solidifying into a monolithic block but, rather, was about joyful interplay, glorious dancing? If we tried that idea on for awhile, could it affect how we view our own disagreements with our brothers and sisters? Perhaps the vision toward which we strive is not one of total agreement but of the ability to join, in our disparate ways, in the common dance of faith.

It is just possible that this *is* what Christian unity looks like—a body, as Paul said, with many parts, a dance with many dancers, a song with many voices. The challenge to us, in response to all this variety, is to say yes. Yes, those *other* people really are Christians too. Yes, there is pain in all this diversity, but there is also possibility. Yes, there is struggle, but there is also glory.

Do we find all this movement, all this action, disorienting? Does our anxiety about conflict lure us into wishing for something less dramatic? This Christian community of ours can be wild and frustrating and crazy, but we place our trust in that prayer of Jesus. The disciples Jesus loved, and the community he loves now, lived and still live—enveloped by that prayer.

LINDA LEE CLADER

Contributors

Richard Manly Adams Jr., PhD Student, Emory University, Atlanta, Georgia

Katherine E. Amos, Resident Professor of Spirituality and the Arts, Wake Forest University School of Divinity, Winston-Salem, North Carolina

Maryetta Anschutz, Founding Head, The Episcopal School of Los Angeles, California

Thomas L. Are Jr., Pastor, Village Presbyterian Church, Prairie Village, Kansas

Harold W. Attridge, Dean and Lillian Claus Professor of New Testament, Yale Divinity School, New Haven, Connecticut

David L. Bartlett, Professor of New Testament, Columbia Theological Seminary, Decatur, Georgia

Michael Battle, Rector, Church of Our Savior, San Gabriel, California

Angela Bauer-Levesque, Academic Dean and Harvey H. Guthrie Jr. Professor of Bible, Culture, and Interpretation, Episcopal Divinity School, Cambridge, Massachusetts

Christopher A. Beeley, Walter H. Gray Associate Professor of Anglican Studies and Patristics, Yale Divinity School, New Haven, Connecticut

Jon L. Berquist, Executive Editor for Biblical Studies, Westminster John Knox Press, Louisville, Kentucky

Deborah A. Block, Pastor, Immanuel Presbyterian Church, Milwaukee, Wisconsin

Kathleen Long Bostrom, Co-pastor, Wildwood Presbyterian Church, Grayslake, Illinois

Larry D. Bouchard, Associate Professor, Department of Religious Studies, University of Virginia, Charlottesville, Virginia

Reginald D. Broadnax, Dean of Academic Affairs, Hood Theological Seminary, Salisbury, North Carolina

William F. Brosend, Associate Professor of Homiletics, School of Theology, Sewanee, the University of the South, Sewanee, Tennessee

Michael Joseph Brown, Associate Professor of New Testament and Christian Origins, Candler School of Theology, Emory University, Atlanta, Georgia

Robert A. Bryant, Associate Professor of Religion, Presbyterian College, Clinton, South Carolina

David M. Burns, Executive Pastor/Acting Pastor, Trinity Presbyterian Church, Atlanta, Georgia

Michael D. Bush, Vice President for Seminary Development and External Relations, Erskine Theological Seminary, Due West, South Carolina

Gay L. Byron, Baptist Missionary Training School Professor of New Testament and Christian Origins, Colgate Rochester Crozer Divinity School, Rochester, New York

Dexter E. Callender Jr., Associate Professor of Religious Studies, Department of Religious Studies, University of Miami, Coral Gables, Florida

Katherine C. Calore, Pastor, St. Stephen's Episcopal Church, Monett, Missouri

Gary W. Charles, Pastor, Central Presbyterian Church, Atlanta, Georgia

Linda Lee Clader, Dean of Academic Affairs and Professor of Homiletics, Church Divinity School of the Pacific, Berkeley, California

Kenneth I. Clarke Sr., Director, Cornell United Religious Work, Ithaca, New York

John B. Cobb Jr., Professor Emeritus, Claremont School of Theology, Claremont, California

Kelton Cobb, Professor of Theology and Ethics, Hartford Seminary, Hartford, Connecticut

Martin B. Copenhaver, Pastor, Wellesley Congregational Church, United Church of Christ, Wellesley, Massachusetts

Barbara Cawthorne Crafton, The Geranium Farm, Metuchen, New Jersey

William Joseph Danaher Jr., Dean, Faculty of Theology, Huron University College, London, Ontario, Canada

J. David Dark, Adjunct Faculty, David Lipscomb University, Nashville, Tennessee

David A. Davis, Pastor, Nassau Presbyterian Church, Princeton, New Jersey

Miguel A. De La Torre, Associate Professor, Iliff School of Theology, Denver, Colorado

Richard S. Dietrich, Minister, First Presbyterian Church, Staunton, Virginia

Lisa D. Maugans Driver, Associate Professor of Theology, Valparaiso University, Valparaiso, Indiana

James O. Duke, Professor of History of Christianity and History of Christian Thought, Brite Divinity School, Fort Worth, Texas

Stephen Edmondson, Rector, St. Thomas Episcopal Church, McLean, Virginia

James H. Evans Jr., Robert K. Davies Professor of Systematic Theology, Colgate Rochester Crozer Divinity School, Rochester, New York

Ward B. Ewing, Dean and President, The General Theological Seminary, New York, New York

Stephen Farris, Dean, St. Andrew's Hall, and Professor of Homiletics, Vancouver School of Theology, Vancouver, British Columbia, Canada

Judy Fentress-Williams, Associate Professor of Old Testament, Virginia Theological Seminary, Alexandria, Virginia

Jane Anne Ferguson, Associate Minister, First Plymouth Congregational Church, United Church of Christ, Englewood, Colorado

Robert W. Fisher, Associate Rector, All Saints-by-the-Sea Episcopal Church, Santa Barbara, California

Anna Carter Florence, Peter Marshall Associate Professor of Preaching, Columbia Theological Seminary, Decatur, Georgia

Nora Gallagher, Writer, Preacher-in-Residence, Trinity Episcopal Church, Santa Barbara, California

Susan R. Garrett, Professor of New Testament, Louisville Presbyterian Theological Seminary, Louisville, Kentucky

Deirdre J. Good, Professor of New Testament, The General Theological Seminary, New York, New York

Joel B. Green, Professor of New Testament Interpretation and Associate Dean for the Center for Advanced Theological Studies, Fuller Theological Seminary, Pasadena, California

Christopher Grundy, Assistant Professor of Preaching and Worship, Eden Theological Seminary, St. Louis, Missouri

Douglas John Hall, Professor Emeritus of Christian Theology, McGill University, Montreal, Quebec, Canada

Gary R. Hall, Dean and President, Seabury-Western Theological Seminary, Evanston, Illinois

Gary Neal Hansen, Assistant Professor of Church History, University of Dubuque Theological Seminary, Dubuque, Iowa

Timothy B. Hare, Pastor, Huntington United Methodist Church, Shelton, Connecticut

John C. Holbert, Lois Craddock Perkins Professor of Homiletics, Perkins School of Theology, Southern Methodist University, Dallas, Texas

Alice W. Hunt, President, Chicago Theological Seminary, Chicago, Illinois

Susan E. Hylen, Assistant Professor of New Testament, Vanderbilt Divinity School, Nashville, Tennessee.

Cynthia A. Jarvis, Minister and Head of Staff, The Presbyterian Church of Chestnut Hill, Philadelphia, Pennsylvania

E. Elizabeth Johnson, J. Davison Philips Professor of New Testament, Columbia Theological Seminary, Decatur, Georgia

Nicole L. Johnson, Assistant Professor in Religious Studies, Mount Union College, Alliance, Ohio

Susan B. W. Johnson, Minister, Hyde Park Union Church, Chicago, Illinois

Trygve David Johnson, Hinga-Boersma Dean of the Chapel, Hope College, Holland, Michigan

Deborah J. Kapp, Edward F. and Phyllis K. Campbell Associate Professor of Urban Ministry, McCormick Theological Seminary, Chicago, Illinois

Joel Marcus LeMon, Assistant Professor of Old Testament, Candler School of Theology, Emory University, Atlanta, Georgia

Karoline M. Lewis, Assistant Professor of Biblical Preaching, Luther Seminary, St. Paul, Minnesota

Michael Lodahl, Professor of Theology, Point Loma Nazarene University, San Diego, California

Kimberly Bracken Long, Assistant Professor of Worship, Columbia Theological Seminary, Decatur, Georgia

Barbara K. Lundblad, Joe R. Engle Professor of Preaching, Union Theological Seminary, New York, New York

Dwight M. Lundgren, Director of Reconciliation Ministries, American Baptist Churches USA, Valley Forge, Pennsylvania

Larry L. Lyke, Visiting Assistant Professor, Department of Religion, Mount Holyoke College, South Hadley, Massachusetts

Thomas W. Mann, Retired Professor of Hebrew Bible and United Church of Christ Parish Minister, Winston-Salem, North Carolina

Molly T. Marshall, President and Professor of Theology and Spiritual Formation, Central Baptist Theological Seminary, Shawnee, Kansas

Martin E. Marty, Fairfax M. Cone Distinguished Service Professor Emeritus, University of Chicago, Illinois

Peter W. Marty, Pastor, St. Paul Lutheran Church, Davenport, Iowa

William P. "Matt" Matthews Jr., Pastor, St. Giles Presbyterian Church, Greenville, South Carolina

Tyler Mayfield, Adjunct Faculty, Claremont School of Theology, Claremont, California

J. Clinton McCann Jr., Evangelical Professor of Biblical Interpretation, Eden Theological Seminary, St. Louis, Missouri

Gordon McClellan, Pastor, First Presbyterian Church, Corvallis, Oregon

John S. McClure, Charles G. Finney Professor of Homiletics and Chair of Graduate Department of Religion, Vanderbilt Divinity School, Nashville, Tennessee

Thomas P. McCreesh, Associate Professor, Theology Department, Providence College, Providence, Rhode Island

Thomas Edward McGrath, Pastor, Hope Presbyterian Church, Winter Haven, Florida

Donald K. McKim, Executive Editor for Theology and Reference, Westminster John Knox Press, Germantown, Tennessee

Allen C. McSween Jr., Pastor, Fourth Presbyterian Church, Greenville, South Carolina

James McTyre, Pastor, Lake Hills Presbyterian Church, Knoxville, Tennessee

Nancy A. Mikoski, Pastor, Pennington Presbyterian Church, Pennington, New Jersey

Veronice Miles, Ruby Pardue and Shelmer D. Blackburn Assistant Professor of Homiletics and Christian Education, Wake Forest University School of Divinity, Winston-Salem, North Carolina

Randle R. (Rick) Mixon, Pastor, First Baptist Church, Palo Alto, California

Martha Moore-Keish, Assistant Professor of Theology, Columbia Theological Seminary, Decatur, Georgia

D. Cameron Murchison, Dean of Faculty, Columbia Theological Seminary, Decatur, Georgia

Carol A. Newsom, Charles Howard Candler Professor of Old Testament, Candler School of Theology, Emory University, Atlanta, Georgia

Frederick Niedner, Professor of Theology, Department of Theology, Valparaiso University, Valparaiso, Indiana

Donald P. Olsen, Minister, Plymouth Congregational Church, Wichita, Kansas

Jeff Paschal, Pastor, First Presbyterian Church, Wooster, Ohio

Shannon Michael Pater, Minister, Central Congregational United Church of Christ, Atlanta, Georgia

Amy Plantinga Pauw, Henry P. Mobley Professor of Doctrinal Theology, Louisville Presbyterian Theological Seminary, Louisville, Kentucky

Steven A. Peay, Senior Minister, The First Congregational Church of Wauwatosa, Wisconsin (NACCC), and Adjunct Professor of Church History, Nashotah House Theological Seminary, Nashotah, Wisconsin

Pheme Perkins, Professor of New Testament, Theology Department, Boston College, Chestnut Hill, Massachusetts

Jennifer Pfenniger, Instructor of Biblical Hebrew, Emmanuel College, University of Toronto, Toronto, Ontario, Canada

Emerson B. Powery, Professor of Biblical Studies, Messiah College, Grantham, Pennsylvania

Joseph L. Price, Genevieve S. Connick Professor of Religious Studies, Whittier College, Whittier, California

Nancy J. Ramsay, Executive Vice President and Dean, Brite Divinity School, Texas Christian University, Fort Worth, Texas

Stephen Breck Reid, Professor of Christian Scriptures, George W. Truett Seminary, Baylor University, Waco, Texas

Gary B. Reierson, President, Greater Minneapolis Council of Churches, Minneapolis, Minnesota, and Adjunct Professor, School of Theology·Seminary, St. John's University, Collegeville, Minnesota

André Resner, Professor of Homiletics and Church Worship, Hood Theological Seminary, Salisbury, North Carolina

John D. Rohrs, Associate Rector, Christ Episcopal Church, Raleigh, North Carolina

John Rollefson, Pastor, Lutheran Church of the Master, Los Angeles, California

Craig A. Satterlee, Professor of Homiletics, Lutheran School of Theology at Chicago, Illinois

Clayton J. Schmit, Arthur DeKruyter/Christ Church Oak Brook Professor of Preaching and Academic Director of the Brehm Center for Worship, Theology, and the Arts, Fuller Theological Seminary, Pasadena, California

Donald Senior, President, Catholic Theological Union, Chicago, Illinois

Timothy R. Sensing, Associate Professor of Ministry, Abilene Christian University, Abilene, Texas

G. Malcolm Sinclair, Preaching Minister, Metropolitan United Church, Toronto, Ontario, Canada

O. Benjamin Sparks, Presbyterian Church (U.S.A.) Pastor, Retired, Nashville, Tennessee

Max L. Stackhouse, Rimmer and Ruth de Vries Professor of Reformed Theology and Public Life Emeritus, Princeton Theological Seminary, Princeton, New Jersey

Thomas R. Steagald, Pastor, Lafayette Street United Methodist Church, Shelby, North Carolina

Brent A. Strawn, Associate Professor of Old Testament, Candler School of Theology, Emory University, Atlanta, Georgia

Joy Douglas Strome, Pastor, Lake View Presbyterian Church, Chicago, Illinois

George W. Stroup, J. B. Green Professor of Theology, Columbia Theological Seminary, Decatur, Georgia

Laird J. Stuart, Interim President, San Francisco Theological Seminary, San Francisco, California

Philip E. Thompson, Professor of Systematic Theology and Christian Heritage, Sioux Falls Seminary, Sioux Falls, South Dakota

Robert V. Thompson, Minister, Lake Street Church, Evanston, Illinois

Douglas Travis, Dean and President, Episcopal Theological Seminary of the Southwest, Austin, Texas

James A. Wallace, Professor, Department of Word and Worship, Washington Theological Union, Washington, D.C.

Neal H. Walls, Associate Professor of Old Testament Interpretation, Wake Forest University School of Divinity, Winston-Salem, North Carolina

Don Wardlaw, James G. K. McClure Professor Emeritus of Preaching and Worship, McCormick Theological Seminary, Chicago, Illinois

Audrey West, Adjunct Professor of New Testament, Lutheran School of Theology at Chicago, Illinois

John E. White, Dean of Students, Columbia Theological Seminary, Decatur, Georgia

Sean A. White, Pastor, Eastminster Presbyterian Church, Knoxville, Tennessee

Andrea Wigodsky, Chaplain, St. Mary's School, Raleigh, North Carolina

Patrick J. Willson, Pastor, Williamsburg Presbyterian Church, Williamsburg, Virginia

Randall C. Zachman, Professor of Reformation Studies, University of Notre Dame, Notre Dame, Indiana

Scripture Index

Author Index

Katherine C. Calore	Easter Vigil PS EP, Easter Day PS EP, Easter 2 PS EP	James H. Evans Jr.	Lent 2 PS TP, Lent 3 PS TP, Lent 4 PS TP
Gary W. Charles	Mon. of Holy Wk. G HP, Tue. of Holy Wk. G HP, Wed. of Holy Wk. G HP	Ward B. Ewing	Lent 2 E TP, Lent 3 E TP, Lent 4 E TP
Linda Lee Clader	Easter 6 G HP, Ascension G HP, Easter 7 G HP	Stephen Farris	Lent 5 PS HP, Liturgy of Palms PS HP, Liturgy of Passion PS HP
Kenneth I. Clarke Sr.	Lent 5 E PP, Liturgy of Passion E PP	Judy Fentress-Williams	Lent 1 OT EP
John B. Cobb Jr.	Mon. of Holy Wk. OT TP, Tue. of Holy Wk. OT TP, Wed. of Holy Wk. OT TP	Jane Anne Ferguson	Holy Thursday E HP, Good Friday E HP, Holy Saturday E HP
Kelton Cobb	Lent 5 OT TP, Liturgy of Passion OT TP	Robert W. Fisher	Lent 2 PS PP, Lent 3 PS PP, Lent 4 PS PP
Martin B. Copenhaver	Easter Vigil G PP, Easter Day G PP, Easter 2 G PP	Anna Carter Florence	Lent 2 G HP, Lent 3 G HP, Lent 4 G HP
Barbara Cawthorne Crafton	Mon. of Holy Wk. OT PP, Tue. of Holy Wk. OT PP, Wed. of Holy Wk. OT PP	Nora Gallagher	Holy Thursday PS HP, Good Friday PS HP, Holy Saturday PS HP
William Joseph Danaher Jr.	Ash Wednesday OT TP, Lent 1 OT TP	Susan R. Garrett	Lent 5 E EP, Liturgy of Passion E EP
J. David Dark	Easter 3 PS TP, Easter 4 PS TP, Easter 5 PS TP	Deirdre J. Good	Mon. of Holy Wk. G EP, Tue. of Holy Wk. G EP, Wed. of Holy Wk. G EP
David A. Davis	Mon. of Holy Wk. E PP, Tue. of Holy Wk. E PP, Wed. of Holy Wk. E PP	Joel B. Green	Easter 3 E EP, Easter 4 E EP, Easter 5 E EP
Miguel A. De La Torre	Easter 6 E TP, Ascension E TP, Easter 7 E TP	Christopher Grundy	Ash Wednesday E HP, Lent 1 E HP
Richard S. Dietrich	Easter Vigil G EP, Easter Day G EP, Easter 2 G EP	Douglas John Hall	Ash Wednesday G TP, Lent 1 G TP
Lisa D. Maugans Driver	Easter Vigil OT TP	Gary R. Hall	Mon. of Holy Wk. PS HP, Tue. of Holy Wk. PS HP, Wed. of Holy Wk. PS HP
James O. Duke	Lent 5 G TP, Liturgy of Palms G TP, Liturgy of Passion G TP	Gary Neal Hansen	Easter 3 NT TP, Easter 4 NT TP, Easter 5 NT TP
Stephen Edmondson	Easter 3 E TP, Easter 4 E TP, Easter 5 E TP	Timothy B. Hare	Easter 3 NT HP, Easter 4 NT HP, Easter 5 NT HP

John C. Holbert	Easter Vigil OT HP, Easter Day OT HP, Easter 2 NT HP	Larry L. Lyke	Holy Thursday OT EP, Good Friday OT EP, Holy Saturday OT EP
Alice W. Hunt	Easter 3 PS EP, Easter 4 PS EP, Easter 5 PS EP	Thomas W. Mann	Easter Vigil OT EP, Easter Day OT EP, Easter 2 NT EP
Susan E. Hylen	Holy Thursday G EP, Good Friday G EP, Holy Saturday G EP	Molly T. Marshall	Easter 3 G TP, Easter 4 G TP, Easter 5 G TP
Cynthia A. Jarvis	Easter 3 G HP, Easter 4 G HP, Easter 5 G HP	Martin E. Marty	Lent 5 PS TP, Liturgy of Palms PS TP, Liturgy of Passion PS TP
E. Elizabeth Johnson	Holy Thursday E EP, Good Friday E EP, Holy Saturday E EP, Easter Vigil E EP, Easter Day E EP, Easter 2 E EP	Peter W. Marty	Easter Vigil E PP, Easter Day E PP, Easter 2 E PP
		William P. "Matt" Matthews Jr.	Holy Thursday PS PP, Good Friday PS PP, Holy Saturday PS PP
Nicole L. Johnson	Mon. of Holy Wk. PS TP, Tue. of Holy Wk. PS TP, Wed. of Holy Wk. PS TP	Tyler Mayfield	Ash Wednesday OT EP
		J. Clinton McCann Jr.	Lent 2 PS EP, Lent 3 PS EP, Lent 4 PS EP
Susan B. W. Johnson	Easter 3 NT PP, Easter 4 NT PP, Easter 5 NT PP	Gordon McClellan	Easter 6 E PP, Ascension E PP, Easter 7 E PP
Trygve David Johnson	Holy Thursday G HP, Good Friday G HP, Holy Saturday G HP	John S. McClure	Easter 6 NT HP, Ascension NT HP, Easter 7 NT HP
Deborah J. Kapp	Lent 2 G PP, Lent 3 G PP, Lent 4 G PP	Thomas P. McCreesh	Easter Vigil PS TP, Easter Day PS TP, Easter 2 PS TP
Joel Marcus LeMon	Mon. of Holy Wk. PS EP, Tue. of Holy Wk. PS EP, Wed. of Holy Wk. PS EP	Thomas Edward McGrath	Lent 5 PS PP, Liturgy of Palms PS PP, Liturgy of Passion PS PP
Karoline M. Lewis	Lent 2 G EP, Lent 3 G EP, Lent 4 G EP	Donald K. McKim	Holy Thursday OT TP, Good Friday OT TP, Holy Saturday OT TP
Michael Lodahl	Ash Wednesday PS TP, Lent 1 PS TP	Allen C. McSween Jr.	Ash Wednesday OT PP, Lent 1 OT PP
Kimberly Bracken Long	Easter Vigil PS HP, Easter Day PS HP, Easter 2 PS HP	James McTyre	Lent 2 OT HP, Lent 3 OT HP, Lent 4 OT HP
Barbara K. Lundblad	Easter 3 E HP, Easter 4 E HP, Easter 5 E HP	Nancy A. Mikoski	Mon. of Holy Wk. G PP, Tue. of Holy Wk. G PP, Wed. of Holy Wk. G PP
Dwight M. Lundgren	Ash Wednesday E PP, Lent 1 E PP		

Joy Douglas Strome	Easter 3 E PP, Easter 4 E PP, Easter 5 E PP	Don Wardlaw	Lent 2 E HP, Lent 3 E HP, Lent 4 E HP
George W. Stroup	Lent 2 G TP, Lent 3 G TP, Lent 4 G TP	Audrey West	Lent 5 G EP, Liturgy of Palms G EP, Liturgy of Passion G EP
Laird J. Stuart	Lent 2 E PP, Lent 3 E PP, Lent 4 E PP	John E. White	Easter 3 PS HP, Easter 4 PS HP, Easter 5 PS HP
Philip E. Thompson	Holy Thursday E TP, Good Friday E TP, Holy Saturday E TP	Sean A. White	Easter 6 NT TP, Ascension NT TP, Easter 7 NT TP
Robert V. Thompson	Easter 6 PS HP, Ascension PS HP, Easter 7 PS HP	Andrea Wigodsky	Ash Wednesday PS PP, Lent 1 PS PP
Douglas Travis	Lent 5 E HP, Liturgy of Passion E HP	Patrick J. Willson	Ash Wednesday G HP, Lent 1 G HP
James A. Wallace	Lent 5 OT HP, Liturgy of Passion OT HP	Randall C. Zachman	Holy Thursday G TP, Good Friday G TP, Holy Saturday G TP
Neal H. Walls	Ash Wednesday PS EP, Lent 1 PS EP		

green press
INITIATIVE

Westminster John Knox Press is committed to preserving ancient forests and natural resources. We elected to print this title on 30% post consumer recycled paper, processed chlorine free. As a result, for this printing, we have saved:

46 Trees (40' tall and 6-8" diameter)
15 Million BTUs of Total Energy
4,362 Pounds of Greenhouse Gases
21,009 Gallons of Wastewater
1,276 Pounds of Solid Waste

Westminster John Knox Press made this paper choice because our printer, Thomson-Shore, Inc., is a member of Green Press Initiative, a nonprofit program dedicated to supporting authors, publishers, and suppliers in their efforts to reduce their use of fiber obtained from endangered forests.

For more information, visit www.greenpressinitiative.org

Environmental impact estimates were made using the Environmental Defense Paper Calculator. For more information visit: www.edf.org/papercalculator